PREFACE TO TENTH EDITION

Author thanks to readers for overwhelming response of the book. New information have been added at many places and Acronyms have been updated to make the text more useful.

Author hope that readers will be benefitted with this new edition and find it more useful. Any suggestions for improvement from readers are welcome.

Dated : 25-10-2013 Mahendra Pal

PREFACE TO EIGHTH EDITION

Author thanks to readers for overwhelming response to the book.

In this revised and updated edition all most all chapters are thoroughly revised and updated. A new section on Environmental Science have been added to enhance the value of the text. At many places new information has been incorporated.

Author hope that readers will be benefitted with this new edition and find it more useful. Any suggestions for improvement from readers are welcome.

Dated : 15-1-2010 Mahendra Pal

PREFACE TO FIFTH EDITION

Examination/test has become an extensively accepted and a routine mode and method of selection both for jobs and admissions to colleges/universities/professional courses now-a-days, The questions in these competitive examinations besides being large in number are mostly objective (say pointed) type to be solved within a strictly observable time schedule. It may be added that framing as well as answering of the volley of highly varying (in nature) questions within a time frame is no child's play. Sterling performance in these competitive examinations essentially calls for having a thorough knowledge at finger tips to answer the questions in these hurricane like tests. The success of a competitor does not only need to secure a predetermined percentage of marks to pass through, but to obtain a percentage enough to find a place in the final merit list.

Agriculture like other sciences is witnessing the generation of newer and newer knowledge to add to the already existing large ocean of knowledge. The modern agricultural science denotes an amalgamation of knowledge of more than 24/25 disciplines. Thus, a would-be successful competitor must earn, embody and keep at finger tips these subjects plus the recent advances therein. It is no easy job and hence all would-be successful aspirants look for a comprehensive compilation containing the subject matter on as many subjects as could be possible under one cover. This necessitated a crop of question banks, but most of them without the answers to the questions. One has to make a herculean effort to find out the correct answers and in the process has to scan through the huge volumes of books which, in effect, requires a great deal of time and effort.

However, there could be no single publication to embody all the information under one cover. A question bank with the answers may be immensely helpful in equipping and arming an aspirant competitor only partially to take a competitive test. It is a matter of satisfaction both to the author and the publisher that three earlier editions of the Agriculture Question Bank has been accepted well and has been of utility to the readers. Second and third edition have been suitably revised and enlarged. The Fourth and Fifth has also enlarged. The following subject matter has been incorporated:

* El Nino .... Nature's Vicious Circle
* Mexican Poppy (*Argemon mexicana* L.) with colour photos of plant, fruit and seed
* A few useful formulae
* Legume seeds and Rhizobia
* Solved Question Papers..... SRF, JRF, NET, RAS etc.
* Sowing seasons in India, Rainfall distribution etc.
* Area under foodgrain—cultivated and Irrigated
* Water Resources of India
* Substantial additions under glossary
* Plant stress

Inspite of these enlargements, it cannot be claimed that the fourth edition embodies all that needed for success in an examination/test in agriculture. That is, it comprises merely a handy aid-cumguide and a drop of answers in an ocean of questions. The readers are requested to feel free to make useful suggestion to augment its comprehensibility in the next edition. Though all sincere and careful efforts have been made to check, correct and prevent continuance of typographical or other types of mistakes, it is neither claimed nor can be claimed that there are no deficiencies. Therefore, the readers are requested to bear with and let us know for suitable corrections thereof wherever essential. Finally, it is fervently hoped that the enlarged edition would find a still better and positive response of the readers.

July, 2001 Mahendra Pal

AGRICULTURE QUESTION BANK WITH ANSWERS

Dr. Mahendra Pal
M.Sc. (Agron.), Ph.D (IARI), FISA
FUWAI
Retired Head (Div. of Agronomy)

Indian Agricultural Research Institute
New Delhi-110012 (India)

10th REVISED AND ENLARGED EDITION

2014

JAIN BROTHERS (New Delhi)
16/873, East Park Road, Near Dr. N. C. Joshi Hospital,
Karol Bagh, New Delhi -110 005
Phones : 011- 23618426, 45097398
E-mail : jain_bros@hotmail.com
Website : www.thejainbrothers.com

Published by :

Shri Sunil Kumar Jain
for
Jain Brothers (New Delhi)
16/873, East Park Road, Karol Bagh, New Delhi-110 005
Phones : 011-23618426, 45097398

Branch Office at :

1. **M/s Sunil Book Service**
   Fatima Nagar, Opp. Andhra Bank,
   KAZIPET-506004 (A.P.)
   Ph. : 0870-2459617, Mob. : 9390115435
   E-mail : kpkulshrestha@yahoo.com
2. **M/s Jain Brothers**
   Vidya Vihar, Pilani (Rajasthan)
   Phone : 01596-242144

First edition	:	1994
Second edition	:	1996
Third edition	:	1999
Fourth edition	:	2000
Fifth edition	:	2001
Sixth edition	:	2003
Reprint	:	2006
Seventh edition	:	2008
Eighth revised edition	:	2010
Ninth edition	:	2012
Tenth edition	:	2013

Price : ₹ 325.00

ISBN : 978-81-8360-132-0

Laser Typesetting by :

Niyati *Graphics*
754/23, Khajoor Road,
Karol Bagh, New Delhi

Printed at :

Reliance Industries (P) Ltd.
Mayapuri Phase-I, New Delhi

Dedicated to
the memory of

Late Sh. MADAN LAL JAIN

(1928 - 1995)

Founder of M/S JAIN BROTHERS (New Delhi)

CONTENTS

SECTION 1

(A) SOIL, PLANT AND ENVIRONMENT

I. Fill up the blanks :

1. _______ (1840) reported that crop yields were increased by adding "minerals" or inorganic elements to the soil.
2. "The level of plant production can be no longer greater than that allowed by the most limiting of the essential plant growth factors" is called the _______.
3. V.V. Dakuchaev and associates investigated unique _______ in soil that were associated with different combinations of climate, vegetation and underlying soil material.
4. _______ refers to the study of the origin of the soils in their natural environment, its classification and description.
5. _______ is the study of the soil properties in relation to plant (higher) production.
6. _______ refers to the upper biochemically weathered portion of the regolith.
7. When soil is ploughed and cultivated the natural state of the upper 12-18 cm is modified and this manipulated portion is referred to as _______.
8. The arrangement of sand, silt and clay particles within the soil is termed as _______, while their relative amounts as texture.
9. The _______ is the negative logarithm of the concentration (activity) of H^+ ions in the soil solution.
10. Each unit change in pH makes a _______ change in the activity of H^+ and OH^- ions.
11. Clay and humus have a large surface area per unit weight due to their extremely _______ particle size.
12. "The differential heating and cooling causes lateral stress which, in turn, peels surface layer away from the parent material" this has been termed as _______.
13. Freezing of water develops a force equivalent to about _______.
14. _______ of the fragments of rock detached from heights above and carried down the slope mostly by gravity.
15. A _______ often is a continuation of a floodplain (its front) and it is clayey in nature and likely to be swampy as well.
16. _______ refers to all material of glacial origin, whether deposited by the ice or associated waters.
17. _______ means the materials deposited directly by the ice, these are heterogeneous mixtures of debris of the diversity of the magnitude varying from rocks to clay.
18. An _______ plain is formed by streams that are heavily charged with glacial sediment flowing from the ice.
19. _______ were found when ice-front came to a standstill where there was no ready escape for water.
20. The wind blown materials consisting primarily of silt with some fine sand and clay are called _______.

21. Eolian deposits other than loess exist, such as volcanic ash and _______.
22. Vegetative cover reduces the natural soil _______ thereby slowing down the rate of mineral soil removal.
23. The organic matter content of the grassland soils is generally higher than that of _______ areas, especially in the surface horizons.
24. _______ does not only modify the effects of climate and vegetation, but also has direct effect on soil formation and on the type of soil that forms.
25. Soil genesis is caused by weathering and breakdown of organic matter, _______ and accumulation.
26. As minerals are translocated from one soil zone to another, soil _______ are formed.
27. A vertical exposure of horizon sequence is known as _______.
28. A natural body called a soil, characterized by three dimensions unit (*pedon*), the related groups of which are termed as _______.
29. The terms *viz.*, sandy or clayey as well as limestone soils and lake-laid soil have a _______ connotation.
30. The comprehensive soil classification system, called _______ (Soil Survey Staff, 1975) maintains the natural body concept.
31. Alfisol soils are mostly _______ in respect of their fertility and are used either as cropland or forest or rangeland
32. _______ are typically formed in a water-saturated environment such as that found in a peat bog.
33. Video image analysis comprises a new technique of examining _______ to distinguish 256 shades of grey compared to only 32 for the human eye.
34. _______ is used to improve the quality and to reduce the cost of soil surveys.
35. Land capability classification is based on the assumption that each piece of land is used commensurating with its _______.
36. The soil texture is not changed by _______ management.
37. _______ of aggregation are commonly influenced by practical methods of soil management
38. _______ of structure of a soil is often inherited from the parent materials, especially those laid down by water or ice.
39. The _______ subtypes aggregate-fragment size varies from 1 to 10 cm
40. The density of most of the mineral soils varies from _______ to _______ mg/m^3
41. The organic compounds orient the clays in a common plan, and then from bridge between the individual soil particles, thereby binding them together in _______
42. Adsorbed Ca^{2+}, Mg^{2+}, or Al^{3+} may encourage soil aggregate formation starting with a process called _______.
43. The films of clay _______ often surround the soil peds, and help provide stability.
44. Tilling of wet clay soils results in break down of aggregates, individual particles tend to act independently and disappearance of macropores, such a soil is said to be _______.
45. _______ refers to physical condition of the soil in relation to plant growth, while the tillage involves mechanical manipulation to promote it.
46. Matric potentials are always _______.
47. Unlike matric potential, the _______ has little effect on the mass movement of water in soils.
48. The most common means of expressing soil water content is the _______ of water associated with their specified quantity of soil solids.

49. Indirect methods of measuring soil water content consist of resistance method and _______.
50. Three recognized types of soil water movement are saturated flow, unsaturated flow and _______.
51. When the water movement after rain or irrigation becomes negligible after 48-72 hours the soil is said to be at _______.
52. The soil moisture content at which the plants remain wilted day and night (or in a humid chamber), that moisture content is called _______.
53. At _______ water is so tightly held by soil particles (– 31 bars) that it is considered non-liquid and can move only in vapour phase.
54. In physical classification of water, the terms gravitation, capillary and _______ waters are used.
55. The soil moisture retained in the soil between field capacity and wilting coefficient is known as _______.
56. Though the total soil air pressure and that of the atmosphere may be the same, a higher concentration of _______ results in its net movement into the soil.
57. The best measurement of the aeration status of a soil is _______.
58. _______ provides a measure of the tendency of a system to reduce or oxidize chemicals, it is usually measured in volts or millivolts.
59. Most of the plants are likely to suffer if the soil volume occupied by air is less than _______ per cent.
60. "During summers (temperature > 35°C) covering of ground with transparent plastic sheet raises the temperature of upper few centimeters of soil to about 50°C resulting in control of wilt causing fungus and adversely effects the seeds of weeds and soil borne insects." This is called _______.
61. Freezing and thawing of upper layers of soil can also result in _______ of perennial forage crops.
62. The bare soils warm up more _______ and cool off more rapidly than those covered with vegetation or with plastic mulches.
63. Frost penetration during the winter is considerably greater in _______ land.
64. The specific heat of pure water is 1.00 cal/g as against _______ cal/g that of a dry soil.
65. The low variation is sub-soil temperatures is an advantage not only from the standpoint of _______ but also for other sectors.
66. _______ keep surface soils cooler than where no cover is used during periods of hot weather.
67. _______ tillage leaves much if not all the crop residues at or near the soil surface.
68. The _______ are the seat of most of the chemical, physical and biological properties of soils.
69. The colloidal surface area in the upper 15 cm of a hectare of a clay soil could be as high as ----
70. Colloidal particles referred to as _______ attract hundreds of thousands of cations (positively charged ions) giving rise to an ionic double layer.
71. The colloidal matter of amorphous or crystalline structure not sufficiently ordered for detection of X-rays due to lack of three dimensional crystalline structure are sometimes referred to as _______.
72. Micelle _______ $+ 2H^+ \rightarrow$ Micelle $H^+ + Ca^{2+}$
73. Tetrahedral and _______ sheets are the fundamental structural units of silicate clays.
74. Aluminium can fit in the centre of the tetrahedron in place of the silicon without changing the basic structure" the process is known as _______ substitution.
75. There is ordinarily no expansion of kaolinite on wetting as its structure is fixed due to _______ bonding.
76. Water molecules, along with magnesium and other ions, are strongly adsorbed in an inter layer space of _______.

77. The changes that occur as muscovite mica is altered to fine-grained mica represent a good example of _______.

78. The illustration below assumes that two silicon atoms are associated with four oxygen atoms _______

Tetrahedral sheet (no substitution)	Tetrahedral sheet (_______)
Si_2O_4	Si Al O_4
No change	One excessive –ve change

79. In trioctahedral sheet, three Mg ions are surrounded by oxygen and hydroxy groups, and the sheet has no charge, but if an Al^{3+} ion substitutes for one of Mg^{2+} ion then, a net _______ charge results.
80. On addition of acid forming chemicals to an alkaline soil in dryland area, the H^+-ions would replace _______ on soil colloids, and the pH would decrease.
81. On application of limestone to an acid soil, calcium replaces hydrogen and other cations H^+ is neutralized by _______ ions and the soil pH increases.
82. The sum total of the exchangeable cations that a soil can adsorb is known as _______
83. Cation exchange capacity is expressed in centimoles of _______ per kilogram of soil (C = mol/kg).
84. Sandy soils have lower CEC than _______ soils because the coarse textured soils are commonly lower in both humus and clay content.
85. The proportion of any soil of the CEC satisfied by a given cation is termed as _______ for that cation.
86. Potassium uptake by plants is limited by high levels of _______ in some soils due to antagonistic effect
87. _______ together with cation exchange largely determines the ability of soils to provide nutrients to plants promptly.
88. Most of the swelling of soils results due to water attracted to colloids and adsorbed ions and from tiny _______ entrapped as the water moves into extremely small soil pores.
89. Highly hydrated monovalent cations like _______ are not tightly held by the micelles, enhance soil dispersion.
90. _______ hydroxy ions are partly responsible for the " pH-dependent" charge of soil colloids.
91. There are three kinds of soil acidities *viz.*, active acidity, easily exchangeable acidity and _______.
92. The percentage of the CEC that is satisfied by the base forming cations is known as _______.
93. Resistance to a change in pH in soil solution is termed as _______.
94. The higher the exchange capacity of a soil, the greater is its _______.
95. Variation in pH may result from local _______ due to uneven distribution of organic residues in the soil
96. _______ is also effective in the control of potato scab because the actinomycetes responsible are discouraged by acidity.
97. Fill in the blank below:

$$\_\_\_\_\_\_ = \frac{\text{Exchangeable sodium (C mol / kg)}}{\text{Cation exchange capacity (C mol/ kg)}}$$

98. Fill in the blank below:

$$\text{Sodium Absorpion Ratio (SAR)} = \frac{[Na^+]}{\_\_\_\_\_\_}$$

99. Soil organisms are classified on the basis of their source of _______ as either autotrophic or heterotrophic.

100. The earth worm casts (material passing through their bodies) are definitely higher in bacteria _______ and available nutrients than the soil.

101. Termites have a complex social life in honeycombed mounds which essentially serve as their _______, made by transporting soil from lower layers to and above the surface soil level.

102. The effect of termites on soil productivity is generally less beneficial than that of _______.

103. Nematodes, commonly called _______ are found almost in all soils.

104. Soil _______ include amoeba, ciliates and flagellates.

105. Some protozoa are _______ on soil bacteria and other microflora especially in rhizosphere.

106. The activities of _______ are mainly confined to peat bogs and wet areas of mineral soils.

107. The compounds called _______ are organic in nature, are released or sloughed off from plant roots and they surround young roots.

108. The mucigel layer may facilitate contact with the surrounding soil especially during periods of soil _______.

109. Soil algae are divided into the groups *viz.,* blue, green, yellow green and _______.

110. _______ growing within the leaves of aquatic fern A*zoll*a are also able to fix nitrogen in quantities significant for rice production.

111. The low pH tolerance of _______ is especially important in decomposing the organic residues in acid forest soils.

112. Although mushrooms are not as widely distributed as moulds, these fungi are of significance locally especially in the break down of _______.

113. Moulds are more important than _______ in humus formation and aggregate stabilization in soil.

114. _______ are single cell organisms, one of the simplest and smallest (seldom exceeding 4 - 5 mm or 0.004 - 0.005 mm) forms of life known.

115. Different _______ bacteria have the ability to oxidize (or reduce) selected chemical elements in soil.

116. "_______ a biochemical combination of atmospheric nitrogen with hydrogen to form ammonia which then incorporated into organic nitrogen compounds usable by higher plants" is largely dependent on bacteria.

117. _______ disease of cabbage may be controlled by raising the pH to 7.0 and above.

118. Monoculture cropping systems, which generally reduce species number and _______, and may actually increase the organism count of certain species.

119. The application of 20 Mt (metric tones) of farm manure containing 5,000 kg of dry matter embodies _______ of latent energy.

120. The transformation of carbon is known as _______ which in reality is a "biocycle" or "cycle of life"

121. Among all the carbon products, _______, is by far the most abundant and in terms of human welfare, by far the most important.

122. The humic substances are characterized by aromatic, ring type structures that include _______ and polyquinones.

123. Humic substances have been classified into three groups *viz.,* fulvic acid, _______ and humin.

124. _______ is a complex and rather resistant mixture of brown or dark brown amorphous and colloidal substances that result from microbial decomposition and synthesis, and has chemical as well as physical properties of great significance to soils and plants.

125. The water holding capacity of humus on mass basis is 4-5 times that of the _______ clays.

126. Some amino acids such as _______ can be directly absorbed by plants.
127. Mature residues, whether legume or nonlegume generally have a higher C/N ratio than do younger _______ materials.
128. A soil's organic matter content cannot be increased without simultaneously increasing its _______ content.
129. _______ embody the maximum organic matter content (per cent) as against that the minimum embodied by Aridisols.
130. The nature of the grassland residues and their mode of decomposition encourages _______ and thus a higher organic matter status is found under forests.
131. The soils high in clay are able to protect protein, nitrogen and, in turn, the organic matter from degradation through the _______ complexes.
132. The peat deposits are grouped in three general types *viz.*, fibrous, woody and _______.
133. Fibre pots made of compressed peat are used to start plants, which are later transplanted without being removed from _______.
134. Both phosphorus and potassium contents of _______ are lower than those of a mineral soil.
135. The management of plants in containers is much different than the management of _______ plants.
136. The interaction among the various forms of nitrogen in soils, plants and animals and nitrogen in atmosphere constitute the _______.
137. The process of tying up nitrogen in organic forms is called immobilization; whereas its slow release, specifically from organic to inorganic is termed as _______.
138. Ammonium ions are subject to interlayer fixation (binding) by _______ and, to a certain extent, by fine-grained micas and organic matter.
139. The rates of nitrification decline at temperature above _______ °C and essentially cease at 50°C.
140. Nitrifying organisms are highly _______ to pesticides.
141. Reduction of nitrates to nitrogen oxide compounds and to elemental nitrogen is known as _______.
142. Nitrous oxide can also be formed in small quantities by certain _______ bacteria during ammonia oxidation in aerobic soils.
143. Loss of nitrous oxide (N_2O) from the soil into the atmosphere constitutes an environmental _______.
144. The pH of the sulphur rich _______ may be 4 or even lower compared to about 5.6 for natural precipitation.
145. The phosphorus content of soils ranges from 200 to 2000 kg per HFS (hectare furrow slice) with an average of about _______ kg per HFS.
146. H_2PO_4 ions is some what relatively _______ available to plants than is the HPO_4^{2-} ion.
147. The availability of phosphorus in alkaline soils is largely determined by the solubility of the _______ compounds in which it is found.
148. Potassium is essential for _______, protein synthesis, starch formation and the translocation of sugars.
149. _______ has been found partially to take place of potassium in the nutrition of certain plants.
150. Amounts of potassium in soils as great as _______ are not at all uncommon.
151. Crop removal of _______-with the possible exception of nitrogen, generally exceeds that of the other essential elements.
152. Copper, iron and molybdenum are capable acting as" _______ " in enzyme systems that bring about oxidation-reduction reactions in plants:

153. The term _______ is applied to the compounds in which certain metallic ions are complexed or bound to an organic molecule or anion.
154. The excessive growth of algal and other aquatic species takes place in waters overly enriched with nitrogen, phosphorus and other nutrients through the process known as _______.
155. _______ depletes water of its oxygen, with disastrous effects on fish and other aquatic animals.
156. Surface runoff waters from heavily fertilized lands may contain levels of _______ toxic to livestock.
157. A _______ system can be created by pulling through the soil at the desired depth a pointed cylindrical plug about 7-10 cm in diameter.
158. _______ and especially running water facilitate carrying away of loosened soil.
159. The erosion that exceeds 0.2-0.5 mg/ha per annum becomes unusually destructive and is referred to as _______ erosion.
160. Freezing and _______ flowing water and rain drop impact comprise major soil detaching agencies.
161. Sheet, rill and _______ are three recognized types of water erosion.
162. Of the two phases of rainfall, amount of total rainfall and its _______ the latter is usually more important.
163. Doubling of the flow velocity enables water to move particles 64 times larger. allows it to carry 32 times more material in _______ with four times greater erosive power.
164. Maize and potato crops have lower soil _______ ability than wheat and oats in respect of soil erosion.
165. Inclusion of a close-growing forage crop in rotation with row crops helps to control both _______ and runoff.
166. Strip cropping *per se* and _______ help in the control of soil erosion.
167. _______ are used where rather complete control of the water runoff must be achieved as in rice-paddies.
168. Reduced tillage practices are collectively called conservation tillage in contrast to _______ tillage.
169. The movement of soil by a short series of bounces along the surface of the ground is toned as _______.
170. Application of clay to sandy soil is known as _______.
171. The movement of dust particles of a fine sand size and small, parallel to the ground surface and upward is called _______.
172. Susceptibility to wind erosion is related to the _______ content of soil.
173. Wind erosion is influenced by _______ soil surface conditions, soil characteristics and nature and orientation of vegetation.
174. The tillage that provides a cloddy surface condition should be at _______ to the preventing winds to control erosion.
175. A _______ is the maximum combined water and wind erosion that can take place on a given soil without degrading the soil's long term productivity.
176. The farmers in _______ for years have received cost-sharing assistance in the establishment and use of conservation practices.
177. Chemical revolution in agriculture truly began after the discovery of insecticidal properties of DDT in 1939 along with the _______ of 2, 4-D in 1941.
178. Some 600 chemicals in about _______ formulations are used extensively world wide to control pests.
179. Chlorinated hydrocarbons are less biodegradable insecticides than _______.
180. The fungicides containing mercury, arsenic and copper have been largely replaced due to their _______ to humans and animals.
181. The fungicides currently in use are _______ such as dithiocarbamates and organophosphates.

182. Herbicides are generally biodegradable, and most of them are relatively low in _______ toxicity.
183. Some of the carbamates used as nematicides are quite soluble in water, are not _______ by soil and hence leach down into the ground water.
184. Some soil fumigants like methyl bromide are selected because of their very high _______ which permits them to penetrate soil pores to contact the target organism.
185. The conditions that encourage adsorption will discourage
186. DDT, diaquat, and triazines are subject to slow _______ activated by solar radiation.
187. Triazines (*e.g.*, atrazine) degrade _______, primarily by chemical reaction.
188. DDT and other _______ may persist in soil from 3 to 15 years.
189. The pesticides that resist degradation embody the potential to damage the _______.
190. Fumigants have a more drastic effect on both the soil _______ than do other pesticides.
191. Many pesticides have only mildly depressing effects on the number of _______.
192. Lead, nickel and boron are _______ that are released into the atmosphere and carried to the soil through rain and snow.
193. _______ and limestone usually contain small quantities of cadmium, copper, manganese, nickel and zinc.
194. Once the toxic elements become a part of the life cycle of soil, they may accumulate in _______ body tissue to toxic levels.
195. _______ commonly carry significant quantities of inorganic and organic chemicals that can have harmful environmental effects.
196. It is essential to assure that the levels of inorganic chemicals in sludge are not sufficiently high to be _______ or to humans and other animals who consume the plants.
197. The soil-applied _______ are not readily absorbed by plants and they are not easily leached from soils as well.
198. _______ contamination of soils primarily occurs from the air borne source of it from automobile exhausts.
199. Flourine and _______ toxicities are generally localized problems.
200. Methyl mercury is quite _______ and available for plant and animal absorption.
201. Heavy phosphate application reduces the availability of _______, but has opposite effect on arsenic which is found in the anionic form.
202. _______ ions are subject to leaching into the ground water, which may later be used for drinking purposes.
203. "Sanitary landfills" are sometimes not so _______.
204. Leaching and runoff from sanitary _______ sites can contaminate both surface and ground water.
205. Contamination of soils with salts is one form of _______ primarily agricultural in origin.
206. Acid rain (acid precipitation) water contains nitric and _______ acids.
207. Fruits and seeds generally contain less radionucleotides than leaves hence they have a higher potential to contaminate _______.
208. The soil is the primary source of _______ gas that can cause lung cancer.
209. Radon gas is formed from the radioactive decay of _______, a breakdown product of uranium found in minute quantities in most of the soils.
210. CFCs are used as aerosal propellants, _______ and solvents.

211. The soil is a source of several gases involved in greenhouse phenomenon including carbondioxide, nitrous oxide and _______.

212. If the entire ozone is brought down to the soil surface, it will make only _______ thick layer yet it is very important.

213. The conversion of oxygen to ozone call for the presence of oxygen in _______ form, the reaction gets energy from shortwaves.

214. The world population by 2,000 A.D. has been estimated to be between 6 and 7 billion, that is, _______ per cent higher than it is at present.

215. Out of more than 13 billion hectares of global acreage, only _______ per cent has the physical potential for cultivation.

216. Shifting cultivation is primarily a system of nutrient conservation, _______ and recycling.

217. Planting of a desired crop among the native trees (plants) without their complete removal has been termed as _______ system.

218. _______ is an agroforestry system that involves growing of food crops in alleys, the borders of which are formed by fast growing trees or shrubs.

II. Tick mark (✓) the correct answer:

219. Soil strength for engineering purposes is determined by the characteristics *viz.*,
(*a*) Compressibility (*b*) Compactibility
(*c*) Bearing resistance (*d*) All of these

220. Type of water vapour movement which occurs in soils is _______.
(*a*) Internal (*b*) External
(*c*) Both of these (*d*) None of these

221. Capillary movement of water is complemented by _______.
(*a*) Stem elongation (*b*) Root extension
(*c*) Leaf orientation (*d*) None of these

222. When a plant is under soil moisture stress, the roots _______.
(*a*) Shrink in size (*b*) Expand in size
(*c*) Remain unaffected (*d*) Both a + *b*

223. The positive and high value of redox potential indicates _______.
(*a*) Reducing conditions (*b*) Strong oxidizing conditions
(*c*) Equally reducing and oxidizing conditions (*d*) None of these

224. The concept of soil as a natural body was first developed by _______.
(*a*) C.F. Marbut (*b*) K.D. Glinka
(*c*) V.V. Dakuchaev (*d*) E.W. Hillgard

225. In a waterlogged soil the concentration of _______ is high.
(*a*) Ethane (*b*) Methane
(*c*) Carbon dioxide (*d*) Carbon monoxide

226. A. soil absorbs about _______ of incoming solar radiation.
(*a*) 5% (*b*) 10%
(*c*) 15% (*d*) 20%

227. The global average of solar radiation reaching the earth is _______.
(a) 20% (b) 30%
(c) 40% (d) 50%

228. Humus colloids are composed basically of _______.
(a) Carbon (b) Nitrogen
(c) Helium (d) Ozone

229. The most important silicate clays are known as _______.
(a) Photosilicates (b) Phyllosilicates
(c) Auto silicates (d) Simply silicates

230. Non-humic substances are less complex and are _______ to microbial attack than those belonging to humic group.
(a) More resistant (b) Less resistant
(c) More susceptible (d) Less susceptible

231. Humus enhances the mineral breakdown and increases the availability of some _______.
(a) Anions (b) Cations
(c) Neutral ions (d) None of these

232. Which of the following is harmful to the higher plants _______.
(a) Phenol carboxylic acid (b) Vanillic acid
(c) Dihydroxystearic acid (d) All of these

233. Soil organic matter has many remarkable effects and one of them is given below, identify the same.
(a) Encouraged granulation (b) Increased plasticity
(c) Enhanced cohesion (d) Low cation exchange

234. The C/N ratio in the organic matter of the furrow slice (upper 15 cm) of arable soils commonly ranges from
(a) 3.1 to 4:1 (b) 6:1 to 7:1
(c) 18:1 to 19:1 (d) 8:1 to 15:1

235. Which of the following rotations is likely to leave soil richer in organic matter.
(a) Continuous sorghum (b) Continuous maize
(c) Continuous oats (d) Maize-Oats-Clovers

236. Ammonium and potassium ions are apparently just the right size to fit into the cavities between the crystal units of _______.
(a) Kaolinite (b) Montmorillonite
(c) Vermiculite (d) None of these

237. Ammonia present in the soil can be lost in significant quantities from _______.
(a) Acid soils (b) Alkaline soils
(c) Both of these (d) None of these

238. Etridiazol and nitrapyrin oxidation of ammonia to nitrates
(a) Accelerates (b) Maintains
(c) Inhibits (d) No effect

239. In soils where the negative charge is pH dependent, liming increases CEC which results in an increased potassium by the soil colloids and _______ in solution.
(a) Increases (b) Decreases
(c) Little effect (d) None of these

240. The soils of _______ zones can supply adequate potassium for many years even under irrigations.

(*a*) Temperate
(*b*) Humid
(*c*) Arid
(*d*) Sub-tropical

241. The tropical soils high in hydrous oxides of iron and aluminium embody________ to torrential rains.

(*a*) Susceptibility
(*b*) Resistance
(*c*) None of these
(*d*) Both of these

242. The prime objective of conservation tillage is _______.

(*a*) Removal of plant residues.
(*b*) Complete retention of plant residues.
(*c*) Partial retention of plant residues.
(*d*) None of these

243. In no-tillage systems,. the surface soil layers have_______.

(*a*) Higher bulk density
(*b*) Lower bulk density
(*c*) Higher total pore space
(*d*) Lower water infiltration

244. Conservation tillage tends to encourage _______.

(*a*) Higher microbial population
(*b*) Lower number of earthworms
(*c*) Reduced soil fauna
(*d*) None of these

245. Wind laden with soil particles embodies the abrasive action which is_______.

(*a*) Greatly increased
(*b*) Greatly decreased
(*c*) Absolutely unaffected
(*d*) None of these

246. The diameter of most erodible soil particles is _______.

(*a*) 0.2 mm
(*b*) 0.4 mm
(*c*) 0.3 mm
(*d*) 0.1 mm

247. Cost-sharing assistance for soil conservation has been in practice for years in_______.

(*a*) India
(*b*) England
(*c*) U.S.A.
(*d*) China

248. The size of pesticide molecule, if all other conditions are constant, greatly influences it's_______.

(*a*) Absorption
(*b*) Solubilization
(*c*) Adsorption
(*d*) Volatilization

249. Some pesticides with positively charged groups are also absorbed by_______.

(*a*) Illite clays
(*b*) Kaolinite clays
(*c*) Montmorillonite clays
(*d*) Silicate clays

250. In general, herbicides are _______ than either fungicides or insecticides.

(*a*) More mobile
(*b*) Less mobile
(*c*) Equally mobile
(*d*) More immobile

251. Some degradation products of pesticides are even _______ than the original pesticides.

(*a*) Less toxic
(*b*) More toxic
(*c*) Non-toxic
(*d*) Equally toxic

252. The total number of bacteria frequently _______ after fumigation.

(*a*) Increases
(*b*) Decreases
(*c*) Remains constant
(*d*) None of these

253. The process of ammonification is often _______ by the use of pesticides.

(*a*) harmed (*b*) benefited

(*c*) Not affected (*d*) None of these

254. The estimates postulate that the carbon dioxide content of atmosphere has increesed from 280 parts per million to _______ during last three decades.

(*a*) 300 ppm (*b*) 350 ppm

(*c*) 400 ppm (*d*) None of these

255. Nitrate levels in drinking water above about _______ mg per litre are considered a human health hazard.

(*a*) 5 (*b*) 10

(*c*) 15 (*d*) 20

256. The discovery of oxygen was done by_______ which proved the keystone of other discoveries that went far toward unlocking the mystery of plant life.

(*a*) John Mayow (*b*) John Woodward

(*c*) Benjamin Franklin (*d*) Priestly

257. There was not only one "principle of vegetation" as reflected by agricultural writings during 17th and 18th centuries, it was observed by _______.

(*a*) Willian Michael (*b*) Guy Baird

(*c*) Francis Home (*d*) Jone Cummings

III. Match the following:

258. Match the quantities of the following essential elements found in the soil solution in arid regions _______.

(*a*) N (*i*) 15-40 kg/ha

(*b*) P (*ii*) 0.1-0.2 kg/ha

(*c*) K (*iii*) 140-280 kg/ha

(*d*) Ca (*iv*) 5-20 kg / ha

259. Match the commonly dominant minerals in different types of sedimentary rocks _______.

(*a*) Limestone (*i*) Clays

(*b*) Sandstone (*ii*) $CaCO_3$ (Calcite)

(*c*) Shale (*iii*) SiO_2 (Quartz)

(*d*) Congomerate (*iv*) Variable

260. Match the chemical formula with the primary mineral given below:

(*a*) Muscovit (*i*) $KAlSi_3O_8$

(*b*) Biotite (*ii*) $CaAl_2Si_2O_8$

(*c*) Orthoclase (*iii*) $KAl(Mg, Fe)_3Si_3O_{10}(OH)_2$

(*d*) Anorthite (*iv*) $KAl_3Si_3O_{10}(OH)_2$

261. Match the loss of a mineral constituent in the weathering of limestone to clay.

(*a*) MgO (*i*) 24.9 per cent

(*b*) K_2O (*ii*) 99.4 per cent

(*c*) Fe_2O_3 (*iii*) 0.0 per cent

(*d*) Al_2O_3 (*iv*) 57.5 per cent

262. Match the flood-plain given below with the country where it is located.

(*a*) The Nile River valley	(*i*) Brazil
(*b*) Mississippi River Flood plain	(*ii*) U.S.A.
(*c*) Amazon Basin	(*iii*) China
(*d*) Hwang Ho River Valleys	(*iv*) Egypt

263. Match the horizon of a soil with the striking characteristics.

(*a*) A-horizon	(*i*) Eluviation of clay, iron and aluminium oxide
(*b*) E-horizon	(*ii*) Illuviation of minerals
(*c*) B-horizon	(*iii*) Unconsolidated material underlying the solum
(*d*) C-horizon	(*iv*) Strong mixture of humified organic matter

264. Match the nomenclature in relation to different categories employed in the soil classification system.

(*a*) Mollisols	(*i*) Great group
(*b*) Aquolls	(*ii*) Subgroup
(*c*) Argiaquolls	(*iii*) Order
(*d*) Typic Argiaquolls	(*iv*) Suborder

265. Match the following soil mineral with the chemical composition.

(*a*) Gibbsite	(*i*) Iron and aluminium silicates
(*b*) Feldspar	(*ii*) Hydrous iron oxides
(*c*) Micas	(*iii*) Hydrous oxide of aluminium
(*d*) Geothite	(*iv*) Aluminosilicates

266. Match the height of soil water column expressed in cm with the soil water potential in megapascals (MPa).

(*a*) 10.2	(*i*) – 15
(*b*) 102	(*ii*) – 0.01
(*c*) 15,300	(*iii*) – 10.0
(*d*) 102,000	(*iv*) – 0.001

267. Match the optimum temperature range with the growth stage of the crop given below.

(*a*) Maize seedlings	(*i*) 16-21°C
(*b*) Maize root growth	(*ii*) 24°C
(*c*) Potato-tuber development	(*iii*) 7-10°C
(*d*) Best wheat growth	(*iv*) 25°C

268. Match the ionic radius with the silicate clay.

(*a*) Si^{4+}	(*i*) 0.074 nm
(*b*) Zn^{2+}	(*ii*) 0.099 nm
(*c*) Ca^{2+}	(*iii*) 0.155 nm
(*d*) OH^-	(*iv*) 0.042 nm

269. Match cation exchange capacity with soil types.

(*a*) Sand	(*i*) 18
(*b*) Sandy loams	(*ii*) 25
(*c*) Loams and silt loams	(*iii*) 5
(*d*) Silty clay loams	(*iv*) 12

270. Match the biomass of soil flora and fauna based on the following estimates.

(*a*) Actinomycetes	(*i*) 1120-11,200 kg HFS
(*b*) Fungi	(*ii*) 11-110 kg HFS
(*c*) Nematodes	(*iii*) 110-1100 kg HFS
(*d*) Earth worms	(*iv*) 450-4500 kg HFS

271. Match the C/N ratios given below with the source.

(*a*) Legumes	(*i*) 4:1 to 9:1
(*b*) Strawy residues	(*ii*) 400:1
(*c*) Sawdust	(*iii*) 100:1
(*d*) Microbe-bodies	(*iv*) 20:1 to 30:1

272. Match the representative maximum CEC Cmol/kg of the following colloids.

(*a*) Organic humus	(*i*) 120
(*b*) Vermiculite	(*ii*) 3
(*c*) Kaolinite	(*iii*) 300
(*d*) Hydrous oxide	(*iv*) 5

273. Match the cross-inoculation groups of legumes and the associated *Rhizobia.*

(*a*) R. *japonicum*	(*i*) Alfalfa
(*b*) R. *phaseoli*	(*ii*) Soybeans
(*c*) R. *leguminosarum*	(*iii*) Lentil
(*d*) R. *Meliloti*	(*iv*) Runner bean

274. Match the genus with family of the following Actinomycete-nodulated nonlegume Angiosperms.

(*a*) Casuarina	(*i*) *Rhamnaceae*
(*b*) Ceanothus	(*ii*) *Betulaceae*
(*c*) Alnus	(*iii*) *Myricaceae*
(*d*) Myrica	(*iv*) *Casu rinaceae*

275. Match the following antagonistic relationships between various essential elements.

(*a*) Excess of Cu or SO_4	(*i*) Mn-uptake adversely affected
(*b*) Excess of Zn, Mn, Cu, Mo	(*ii*) Reduced B-uptake
(*c*) Excess of Na or K.	(*iii*) Adverse effect on Mo
(*d*) Excess of lime	(*iv*) Fe-deficiency

276. Match the river with the country(ies) of its location.

(*a*) Yellow river	(*i*) Mynamar
(*b*) Irrawady	(*ii*) India, Nepal
(*c*) Mississippi	(*iii*) China
(*d*) Kosi	(*iv*) U.S.A.

277. *Match the total (net) cropped land (million hectares) as estimated in various countries.

(*a*) Soviet Union (undivided)	(*i*) 99
(*b*) U.S.A.	(*ii*) 140
(*c*) India	(*iii*) 251
(*d*) China	(*iv*) 167

*Brown and Wolf (1984)

278. The humans, animals and plants have been experiencing the injurious effects of pests, match their number causing injury.

(*a*) Insect species	(*i*) > 1500
(*b*) Weed species	(*ii*) > 1300
(*c*) Plant diseases	*iii*) > 10,000
(*d*) Nematodes	(*iv*) > 600

279. Match the pesticide-class with the target

(*a*) Insecticides	(*i*) Weeds
(*b*) Fungicides	(*ii*) Diseases (fungal)
(*c*) Herbicides	(*iii*) Insects
(*d*) Nematicides	(*iv*) Nematodes

280. Match the following herbicides with the trade name.

(*a*) Dalapon	(*i*) Karmex
(*b*) Chloramben	(*ii*) Lasso
(*c*) Alachlor	(*iii*) Dowpon
(*d*) Diuron	(*iv*) Amiben

281. Match the common designations of the following herbicides with the common name

(*a*) Propachlor	(*i*) Treflan
(*b*) Trifluralin	(*ii*) Dacthal
(*c*) DCPA	(*iii*) Eptam
(*d*) EPTC	(*iv*) Ramrod

282. Match the most imposing limitations of soils for agriculture in major geographic areas of the world.

(*a*) Soil moisture deficit	(*i*) S-E Asia, S.America
(*b*) Mineral deficiencies	(*ii*) North, Central, S.Asia
(*c*) Soil shallowness	(*iii*) S-E Asia
(*d*) Excess water	(*iv*) Australia, Africa, S.Asia

283. Match the cultural stage and globally available land area per person for sustaining the global human population.

(*a*) Neolithic (10,000 years ago)	(*i*) 1.5 hectares
(*b*) 500-1450 AD	(*ii*) 0.3 hectare
(*c*) Late 1700s	(*iii*) 40.0 hectares
(*d*) Twentieth century	(*iv*) 0.7 hectares

284. Match the following observations with the observer.

(*a*) Water is a principal nourishment of plants.	(*i*) Jethro Tull (1674-1740)
(*b*) Plants embody salts, spirits, earth and oil, formed from water	(*ii*) Robert Boyle (1627-1691)
(*c*) Saltpeter (KNO_3) and not water was the principle of vegetation	(*iii*) Francis Bacon (1561-1624)
(*d*) Soil pulverization provides *proper pabulum* for the growing plants	(*iv*) J.R. Glauber (1604-1668)

285. Match the conversion factor with the form to convert from one to other one

(*a*) Ca to CaO	(*i*) 2.50
(*b*) Ca to $Ca(OH)_2$	(*ii*) 1.40
(*c*) Ca to $CaCO_3$	(*iii*) 1.67
(*d*) Mg to MgO	(*iv*) 1.85

286.

Form	**Factor**
(*a*) Mg to $Mg(OH)_2$	(*i*) 3.50
(*b*) Mg to MgO_3	(*ii*) 1.67
(*c*) Mg to Ca	(*iii*) 4.17
(*d*) Mg to $CaCO_3$	(*iv*) 2.42.

287.

Form	**Factor**
(*a*) MgO to $CaCO_3$	(*i*) 1.19
(*b*) $MgCO_3$ to $CaCO_3$	(*ii*) 3.50
(*c*) Ca to CaO	(*iii*) 2.50
(*d*) Mg to $MgCO_3$	(*iv*) 1.85

288. Match the following with the formula.

(*a*) Hydrated magnetite	(*i*) $Fe_3PO_4 \cdot 8H_2O$
(*b*) Black hydroilite	(*ii*) $Fe_3O_4 \cdot n\,H_2O$
(*c*) White siderite	(*iii*) $FeS \cdot n\,H_2O$
(*d*) Blue vivianite	(*iv*) $Fe\,CO_3$

289. Match the following terms used to designate the status of essential nutrient elements in plants.

(*a*) Deficient.	(*i*) Level lower than needed for growth, an imbalance with another nutrient, deficiency symptoms seldom seen,
(*b*) Insufficient	(*ii*) Level sufficiently high to cause shortage in corresponding nutrient
(*c*) Toxic	(*iii*) Low concentration severely limiting yield, show more or less distinct deficiency symptoms; may lead to death
(*d*) Excessive	(*iv*) Concentration sufficiently high to reduce growth severely, may lead to plant death

290. Match the following zinc deficiency diseases as observed in various crops given below.

(*a*) White bud	(*i*) Rice-paddies
(*b*) Little leaf	(*ii*) Citrus crops
(*c*) Mottle leaf (frenching)	(*iii*) Maize and sorghum
(*d*) *Khaira*	(*iv*) Cotton

291. Chloride containing fertilizers have been found to reduce the incidence of some diseases in certain crops, match them suitably with the crop.

(*a*) Take-all root-rot	(*i*) Maize
(*b*) *Fusarium* dryland rot	(*ii*) spring barley
(*c*) Stalk rot	(*iii*) Wheat heads
(*d*) *Septoria*, leaf. disease	(*iv*) Winter wheat

292. Match the generally observed cation exchange values (expressed in meq per 100 g) with the clay mineral

(*a*) Mineral colloids 1:1 (*i*) 20-40
(*b*) Mineral colloids 2:1 (*ii*) 100-300
(*c*) Chlorites 2:1:1 (*iii*) 1-10
(*d*) Organic colloids (*iv*) 80-150

293. Match the phosphate compound with the mineral name.

(*a*) $Al_5(NH_4)_3H_6(PO_4)_8 \cdot 18H_2O$ (*i*) Leucophosphite
(*b*) $Al_5K_3H_6(PO_4)_8 \cdot 18H_2O$ (*ii*) K-leucophosphite
(*c*) $Al_2K(PO_4)_2OH \cdot 2H_2O$ (*iii*) K-taranakite
(*d*) $Fe_2K(PO_4)_2OH \cdot 2H_2O$ (*iv*) NH_4 taranakite

294. Match the following phosphate compound with the mineral name.

(*a*) $Ca_8H_2(PO_4)_6 \cdot 5H_2O$ (*i*) Flurapatite
(*b*) $Ca_{10}(PO_4)_6(OH)_2$ (*ii*) Octocalcium phosphate
(*c*) $Ca_{10}(PO_4)_6F_2$ (*iii*) Vivianite
(*d*) $Fe_3(PO_4)_2 \cdot 8H_2O$ (*iv*) Hydroxyapatite

295. Match the formula of the following orthophosphate fertilizer (water soluble).

(*a*) Dicalcium phosphate dihydrate (*i*) $Ca_4HPO_4 \cdot 3H_2O$
(*b*) Anhydrous dicalcium phosphate (*ii*) $CaHPO_4 \cdot 2H_2O$
(*c*) Octocalcium phosphate (*iii*) $CaHPO_4$
(*d*) Calcium ferric phosphate (*iv*) $CaFe_2(HPO_4)_4 \cdot 5H_2O$

296. Match the following formula with the phosphate compound.

(*a*) $KFe_3H_8(PO_4)_6 \cdot 6H_2O$ (*i*) Basic potassium aluminium phosphate
(*b*) $(NH_4)Fe_3H_8(PO_4)_6 \cdot 6H_2O$ (*ii*) Acid ammonium ferric phosphate
(*c*) $KAl_2(PO_4)_2 \cdot OH\,2H_2O$ (*iii*) Basic potassium ferric phosphate
(*d*) $KFe_2(PO_4)_2 \cdot OH\,2H_2O$ (*iv*) Acid potassium ferric phosphate

297. Match the following:

(*a*) Total (*i*) Balance (remains) after water and citrate extraction
(*b*) Available (*ii*) Souble in water and soluble in citrate
(*c*) Citrate insoluble (*iii*) Available + citrate insoluble
(*d*) Water soluble and citrate soluble (*iv*) Water soluble + citrate soluble

298. Match the following P_2O_5 species with the formula.

(*a*) Ortho (*i*) $H_4P_2O_7$
(*b*) Pyro (*ii*) $H_6P_4O_{13}$
(*c*) Tetra (*iii*) H_3PO_4
(*d*) Penta (*iv*) $H_7P_5O_{16}$

299. Match the mineral with the formula.

(*a*) Microdine (*i*) $[K(Mg, Fe)_3AlSi_3O_{10}(OH)_2]$
(*b*) Muscovite (*ii*) $KAlSi_3O_8$
(*c*) Biotite (*iii*) $[KMg_2Al_2Si_3O_{10}(OH)_2]$
(*d*) Phlogopite (*iv*) $[KAl_3Si_3O_{10}(OH)_2]$

300. Match the following potassium .fertilizer with the per cent K_2O content.

(*a*) Potassium sulphate — (*i*) 60-62

*(*b*)Potassium chloride — (*ii*) 25-26

(*c*) Potassium orthophsophates — (*iii*) 50-52

(*d*) Potassim calcium pyrophosphate — (*iv*) 30-50

* Also known as muriate of potash (MOP)

301. Match the per cent P_2O_5 with the fertilizer.

(*a*) Potassium orthophosphates — (*i*) 39-54

(*b*) Potassium polyphosphates — (*ii*) 30-60

(*c*) Potassium metaphosphate — (*iii*) 40-60

(*d*) Potassium calcium pyrophosphate — (*iv*) 55-57

302. Match the following four forms of the approximately estimated potassium fractions varying in their availability to plants in a soil system.

(*a*) Structura/mineral — (*i*) 1-10 ppm

(*b*) Non-exchangeablel/fixed — (*ii*) 50-750 ppm

(*c*) Exchangeable — (*iii*) 5,000 - 25,000 ppm

(*d*) Solution — (*iv*) 40 - 600 ppm

303. Match the following sulphur bearing mineral found in rocks with the formula.

(*a*) Gypsum — (*i*) $MgSO_4 \cdot 7H_2O$

(*b*) Epsomite — (*ii*) $Na_2SO_4 \cdot 10H_2O$

(*c*) Mirabilite — (*iii*) $FeS_2 \cdot FeAS_2$

(*d*) Arsenopyrite — (*iv*) $CaSO_4 \cdot 2H_2O$

304. Match the following sulphur containing fertilizer material with the formula.

(*a*) Ammonium thiosulphate — (*i*) $Fe(NH_4)_2 \cdot (SO_4)_2$

(*b*) Ferrous ammonium sulphate — (*ii*) $CaSO_4 \cdot 4CO(NH_2)_2$

(*c*) Hydrated gypsum — (*iii*) $(NH_4)_2S_2O_3$

(*d*) Urea gypsum — (*iv*) $CaSO_4 \cdot 2H_2O$

305. Match the formula given below with the material.

(*a*) $MgSO_4 \cdot 7H_2O$ — (*i*) Ammonium bisulphate

(*b*) $NaHSO_4$ — (*ii*) Langbeinite (Sulphate of potash magnesia)

(*c*) $K_2SO_4 \cdot 2MgSO_4$ — (*iii*) Nitre cake (Sodium bisulphate)

(*d*) NH_4HSO_3 — (*iv*) Epsom salt (Magnesium sulphate)

306. Match the magnesium content (Mg) with the material given below.

(*a*) 55% — (*i*) Synthetic chelates

(*b*) 16% — (*ii*) Magnesium silicate serpentine

(*c*) 26% — (*iii*) Magnesia (MgO)

(*d*) 2-4% — (*iv*) Magnesium nitrate [Mg $(NO_3)_2$]

307. Match the boron fertilizer with the formula.

(*a*) Colemanite (Portabor)	(*i*) $Na_2B_{10}O_{16} \cdot 10H_2O$
(*b*) Sodium pentaborate	(*ii*) $Na_2B_4O_7 \cdot 5H_2O + Na_2B_{10}O_{16}\ 10H_2O$
*(*c*) Fertilizer borate-48	(*iii*) $Ca_2B_6O_{11} \cdot 5H_2O$
**(*d*) Solubor	(*iv*) $Na_2B_4O_7 \cdot 5H_2O$

*Sodium tetraborate, also called *agribor* or *tronabor*

**Fertilizer porate-68

308. Match the iron mineral with the formula from among the following.

(*a*) Olivene	(*i*) $[FeO(OH) \cdot nH_2O + Fe_2O_3 \cdot nH_2O]$
(*b*) Limonite	(*ii*) Fe_2O_3
(*c*) Hematite	(*iii*) $FeOOH$
(*d*) Geothite	(*iv*) $[(Mg, Fe)_2SiO_4]$

309. Match the iron fertilizer with its formula as given below.

(*a*) Ferrous sulphate	(*i*) $(NH_4)_2SO_4 \cdot FeSO_4 \cdot 6H_20$
(*b*) Ferrous ammonium phosphate	(*ii*) $Fe(NH_4)PO_4 \cdot H_2O$
(*c*) Ferrous ammonium sulphate	(*iii*) $Fe(NH_4)HP_2O_7$
(*d*) Iron ammonium polyphosphate	(*iv*) $FeSO_4 \cdot 7H_2O$

310. Match the iron chelate given below with the approximate content of Fe expressed in percentage.

(*a*) NaFe EDTA	(*i*) 5-9
(*b*) NaFe HEDTA	(*ii*) 10
(*c*) NaFe EDDHA	(*iii*) 5 - 14
(*d*) NaFe DTPA	(*iv*) 6

311. Match the manganese mineral with the formula as given below.

(*a*) Pyrolusite	(*i*) $MnSiO_3$
(*b*) Hausmannite	(*ii*) $MnCO_3$
(*c*) Rhodochrosite	(*iii*) MnO_2
(*d*) Rhodonite	(*iv*) Mn_3O_3

312. Match the following molybdenum fertilizer with the respective *Mo* content expressed in percentage.

(*a*) Ammonium molybdate	(*i*) 39
(*b*) Sodium molybdate	(*ii*) 1-30
(*c*) Molybdenum trioxide	(*iii*) 54
(*d*) Molybdenum frits	(*iv*) 66

Note: $(NH_4)_6Mo_7O_{24}.2H_2O$, $Na_2MoO_4.2H_20$ and MoO_3 are the formulae respectively of (*a*), (*b*) and (*c*)

313. Match the source with the formula of zinc fertilizer.

(*a*) Zinc sulphate monohydrate	(*i*) $ZnSO_4 \cdot 7H_2O$
(*b*) Zinc sulphate heptahydrate	(*ii*) $ZnSO_4 \cdot H_2O$
(*c*) Basic zinc sulphate	(*iii*) $Zn_3(PO_4)_2$
(*d*) Zinc phosphate	(*iv*) $ZnSO_4 \cdot 4Zn(OH)_2$

Note: (*a*), (*b*), (*c*) and (*d*) contain 35, 23, 55 and 51% of zinc, respectively.

314. Match the following sodic soil with the Exchangeable Sodium Percentage (ESP).

(*a*) Slightly Sodic	(*i*) 15-20
(*b*) Moderately Sodic	(*ii*) 20-30
(*c*) Very Sodic	(*iii*) >30
(*d*) Extremely Sodic	(*iv*) 7-15

315. Match the crop with the sodium uptake.

(*a*) Sugar beet	(*i*) Medium
(*b*) Potato	(*ii*) Very low
(*c*) Barley	(*iii*) High
(*d*) Maize	(*iv*) Low

316. Match the sodium uptake by the crop given below.

(*a*) High	(*i*) Buckwheat
(*b*) Medium	(*ii*) Millet
(*c*) Low	(*iii*) Cabbage
(*d*) Very low	(*iv*) Spinach

317. Match the per cent chlorine (Cl^- content with the fertilizer source as given below.

(*a*) 66	(*i*) Potassium chloride
(*b*) 74	(*ii*) Ammonium chloride.
(*c*) 47	(*iii*) Calcium chloride
(*d*) 65	(*iv*) Magnesium chloride

318. Match the potassium mineral with the formula.

(*a*) Carnallite	(*i*) $(K,Na)_2SO_4$
(*b*) Polyhalite	(*ii*) $K_2SO_4 \cdot MgSO_4 \cdot 2CaSO_4 . 2H_2O$
(*c*) Schoenite	(*iii*) $KCl_2 \cdot MgCl_2 \cdot 6H_2O$
(*d*) Aphthitalete	(*iv*) $K_2SO_4 \cdot MgSO_4 \cdot 6H_2O$

319. Match the neutralizing value (CCE) of the pure forms of some commonly used liming materials.

(*a*) $Ca(OH)_2$	(*i*) 109
(*b*) $CaMg(CO_3)_2$	(*ii*) 100
(*c*) $CaCO_3$	(*iii*) 86
(*d*) $CaSiO_3$	(*iv*) 136

320. Match the plant part found representative for testing nitrate concentration in tissue testing technique.

(*a*) Maize (under 37.5 cm)	(*i*) Petiole basal leaf
(*b*) Cotton (to early bloom)	(*ii*) Base of stalk
(*c*) Maize (ear to early dent)	(*iii*) Lower stem
(*d*) Small grains (shoot to milk stage)	(*iv*) Mid-rib, basal leaf

321. Match the soil test rating with fertility index.

(*a*) Very low	(*i*) 25-50
(*b*) Low	(*ii*) 50-100
(*c*) Medium	(*iii*) 0-10
(*d*) High	(*iv*) 10-25

322. Match the fertilizers with the salt index given below.

(*a*) Ammonium sulphate	(*i*) 2.990
(*b*) Diammonium phosphate	(*ii*) 3.253
(*c*) Ammonium nitrate	(*iii*) 6.060
(*d*) Sodium nitrate	(*iv*) 1.614

323. Match the salt index with the fertilizer as given below.

(*a*) 1.618	(*i*) Potassium sulphate
(*b*) 0.390	(*ii*) Potassium chloride
(*c*) 0.853	(*iii*) Urea
(*d*) 2.189	(*iv*) Single superphosphate

IV. Numericals :

324. One cubic metre of a clay soil weighs 1.4 mg, its bulk density will be_______.

325. Height of capillary rise in a tube is determined as, height = 0.15/_______of the tube.

326. The height of capillary rise in a tube of 0.001 mm radius will be_______.

327. Flow of water through unsaturated soils through a pore of 1 mm radius is equivalent to_______ pores with a radius of 0.1 mm.

328. (*a*) Water content of a soil is 30 kg/100 kg of dry soil, the calories required to raise the temperature of 0.3 kg of water by 1°C will be _______.

(*b*) The corresponding figure for one kg of soil solid is _______.

(*c*) Thus, total _______ calories will be required to raise the temperature of 1.3 kg of moist soil by. 1°C.

(*d*) Since the specific heat represents the number of calories required to raise the temperature of one kg of wet soil by 1°C in this case will be _______.

329. Calcium (Ca) equivalent of $CaCO_3$ is_______ ($Ca/CaCO_3$)

330. CaO equivalent of $CaCO_3$ is _______ ($CaO/CaCO_3$)

331. CaO equivalent of $MgCO_3$ is _______ ($CaO/CaCO_3$)

332. $CaCO_3$ equivalent of $MgCO_3$ is _______($CaCO_3/MgCO_3$)

333. The burned lime has neutralizing ability equal to _______ of CaO.

334. CaO weighing 980 kg is equal to_______of pure $CaCO_3$ and limestone needed is 1944 kg.*

*1750/0.90

Do You Know That

1. Total geographical area of India is 328.7 million hectares.
2. Nature takes 300 years to form 2.5 cm (1 inch) of soil.
3. About 52 per cent of area in India is under agriculture as against world average of 11 per cent.
4. The oceans hold 13,800 geogrammes of water.
5. The global rate of evaporation has been estimated at 3.8 Gg of water per annum.
6. The annual evaporation from oceans amounts to 83,700 cubic miles.
7. Prevailing wind patterns mean that the acids often fall many hundred kilometres from where the original pollutants were discharged.

9. Mixing of gases at sea level and at a height up to 80 km is identical.
10. Entry of water into soil-through the soil surface in vertical or lateral direction is called *infiltration*.
11. In stratosphere (20-25 km of height in atmosphere) formation and breakdown of ozone (O_3) continues naturally.
12. Excess of ozone near the land surface is highly detrimental to the animals, but it's presence of 20-25 km above the land surface is highly useful.
13. If entire ozone is brought down to the earth surface, it will make only 3 mm thick layer yet it is very important.
14. Stratosphere, beyond lower atmosphere extends into space wherein the temperature is relatively constant between – 45 and –75°C. Its lower edge is quiet but the upper one is turbulent.
15. One hectare furrow slice of a typical surface soil weighs about 2.2 million kilogramms (to a depth of 15 cm) or 2 million pounds per acre furrow-slice.
16. Potassium plays a very important part as an antagonist to nitrogen and calcium.
17. Magnesium is an essential plant nutrient because it is a constituent of the chlorophyll, protochlorophyll, pectin and phytin.

KEY

(1) Justus von Liebig (a German scientist) (2) Law of the minimum
(3) Horizontal layers (4) Pedology (Greek word *pedon* = soil or earth)
(5) Edaphology (Greek word *edaphos* = soil or ground) (6) Soil
(7) Surface soil or top soil furrow slice (where turned and sliced)
(8) Soil structure (9) pH (10) Ten fold
(11) small (12) Exfoliation
(13) 1465 metric tonnes/m^2 or 150 onnes/ft^2 (14) Colluvial debris
(15) Delta (16) Draft (17) Glacial till
(18) Outwash (19) Glacial lake (Lacustrine) (20) Loess (Pronounced "lius")
(21) Sand-dunes (22) Erosion rates (23) Forest
(24) Topography (25) Translocation (26) Horizon
(27) Soil profile (28) Soil series (29) Geological
(30) Soil taxonomy (31) High (32) Histosols (organic soils)
(33) Aerial photographs (34) Ground penetrating radar (35) Capability and limitations
(36) Cultural (37) Granular and crumb sub-types (38) Platy type
(39) Blocky and subangular blocky (40) 2.60 to 2.75 (41) Water-stable aggregates
(42) Flocculation (43) Clay-skin (44) Puddled
(45) Tilth (46) Negative (47) Osmotic potential
(48) Mass or volume (49) Neutron scattering (50) Vapour movement
(51) Field capacity (metric potential ranges from-0.1 to – 0.3 bar)
(52) Wilting co-efficient, or permanent wilting point. (soil water potential shows a value of –15 bars for most of the crops)
(53) Hygroscopic coefficient (54) Hygroscopic (55) Available water
(56) Oxygen (57) Oxygen diffusion rate
(58) Oxidation-reduction potential or redox potential (59) 10-12
(60) Soil solarization (61) Heaving (62) Quickly
(63) Bare non-insulated (64) 0.2 (65) Agriculture

(66) Mulches
(67) Conservation
(68) Colloidal particles (clays and humus)
(69) 700,000 km^2
(70) Miscelles (microcells)
(71) Short-range order minerals
(72) Micelle, Micelle, Ca^{2+}
(73) Octahedral
(74) Isomorphous
(75) Hydrogen
(76) Vermiculite
(77) Alteration
(78) Al^{3+} substituted for Si^{4+}
(79) Positive
(80) Metal cations
(81) OH^- or CO_3^{2}
(82) Cation exchange capacity or CEC
(83) Positive charge
(84) Clay
(85) Percentage saturation
(86) Calcium
(87) Anion exchange
(88) Air bubbles
(89) Sodium
(90) Aluminium (and iron)
(91) Residual acidity
(92) Percentage base saturation
(93) Buffering
(94) Buffer capacity
(95) Microbial action
(96) Sulphur
(97) Exchangeable Sodium Percentage or ESP
(98) $\sqrt{1/2\left\{\left[Ca^{2+}\right]+\left[Mg^{2}\right]\right\}}$
(99) Energy and carbon
(100) Organic matter
(101) "Cities"
(102) Earthworms
(103) Thread worms or ulworms
(104) Protozoa
(105) Predators
(106) Rotifers
(107) Mucilages
(108) Moisture stress
(109) Diatoms
(110) Blue Green Algae
(111) Molds
(112) Woody tissue
(113) Bacteria
(114) Bacteria
(115) Autotrophic
(116) Nitrogen fixation
(117) Clubfoot
(118) Diversity
(119) 105 million kilo joule (kJ) = 25 million kilo calories (KCl)
(120) Carbon cycle
(121) Carbon dioxide
(122) Polyphenols
(123) Humic acid
(124) Humus
(125) Silicate
(126) Alanine and glycine
(127) Succulent
(128) Organic nitrogen
(129) Histosols
(130) Rate of decay
(131) Organo-mineral
(132) Sedimentary
(133) The pot
(134) Peat
(135) In-field
(136) Nitrogen cycle
(137) Mineralisation
(138) Vermiculite
(139) 35
(140) Sensitive
(141) Denitrification
(142) Nitrosomonas
(143) Pollutant
(144) Acid rain
(145) 1000
(146) More
(147) Calcium
(148) Photosynthesis
(149) Sodium
(150) 35,000 - 50,000 kg of per HFS
(151) Potassium
(152) Electron carriers
(153) Chelate (A Greek word meaning "claw")
(154) Eutrophication
(155) Eutrophication
(156) Nitrates
(157) Mole-drainage
(158) Raindrop splash
(159) Accelerated
(160) Thawing
(161) Gully
(162) Intensity
(163) Suspension
(164) Protective
(165) Erosion
(166) Strip cropping
(167) Bench terraces
(168) Conventional
(169) Saltation
(170) Marling
(171) Suspension
(172) Moisture
(173) Wind velocity and turbulence
(174) Right angles
(175) Tolerable soil loss
(176) U.S.A.
(177) Herbicidal effect
(178) 50,000

(179) Carbonates (180) Toxicities (181) Organic materials
(182) Mammal (183) Absorbed (184) Vapour pressure
(185) Leaching (186) Photo-decomposition (187) Slowly
(188) Chlorinated hydrocarbons (189) Environment (190) Fauna and flora
(191) Earthworms (192) Gasoline additives (193) Superphosphate
(194) Animal and human (195) Sewage sludges (196) Tonic to plants
(197) Heavy metals (198) Lead (199) Boron
(200) Soluble (201) Toxic cations (202) Nitrate
(203) Sanitary (204) Landfills (205) Soil pollution
(206) Sulphuric (207) Forage crops (208) Radon
(209) Radium (210) Refrigerant (211) Methane
(212) 3 mm (213) atomic (214) 25
(215) 25 (216) Accumulation (217) Mixed-tree crop
(218) Alley-cropping
(219) (*d*) (220) (*c*) (221) (*b*)
(222) (*a*) (223) (*b*) (224) (*c*)
(225) (*b*) (226) (*b*) (227) (*d*)
(228) (*a*) (229) (*b*) (230) (*b*)
(231) (*b*) (232) (*c*) (233) (*a*)
(234) (*d*) (235) (*d*) (236) (*c*)
(237) (*b*) (238) (*c*) (239) (*b*)
(240) (*c*) (241) (*b*) (242) (*c*)
(243) (*a*) (244) (*a*) (245) (*a*)
(246) (*d*) (247) (*c*) (248) (*c*)
(249) (*d*) (250) (*a*) (251) (*b*)
(252) (*a*) (253) (*b*) (254) (*b*)
(255) (*b*) (256) (*d*) (257) (*c*)
(258) (*a*)-(*iv*) (*b*)-(*ii*) (*c*)-(*i*) (*d*)-(*iii*)
(259) (*a*)-(*ii*) (*b*)-(*iii*) (*c*)-(*i*) (*d*)-(*iv*)
(260) (*a*)-(*iv*) (*b*)-(*iii*) (*c*)-(*i*) (*d*)-(*ii*)
(261) (*a*)-(*ii*) (*b*)-(*iv*) (*e*)-(*i*) (*d*)-(*iii*)
(262) (*a*)-(*iv*) (*b*)-(*ii*) (*c*) (*i*) (*d*)-(*iii*)
(263) (*a*)-(*iv*) (*b*)-(*i*) (*c*)-(*ii*) (*d*)-(*iii*)
(264) (*a*)-(*iii*) (b)-(*iv*) (*c*)-(*i*) (*d*)-(*ii*)
(265) (*a*)-(*iii*) (*b*)-(*iv*) (*c*)-(*i*) (*d*)-(*ii*)
(266) (*a*)-(*iv*) (*b*)-(*ii*) (*c*)-(*i*) (*d*)-(*iii*)
(267) (*a*)-(*iii*) (*b*)-(*iv*) (*c*)-(*i*) (*d*)-(*ii*)
(268) (*a*)-(*iv*) (*b*)-(*i*) (*c*)-(ii) (*d*)-(*iii*)
(269) (*a*)-(*iii*) (*b*)-(*iv*) (*c*)-(*i*) (*d*)-(*ii*)
(270) (*a*)-(*iv*) (*b*)-(*i*) (*c*)-(*ii*) (*d*)-(*iii*)
(271) (*a*)-(*iv*) (*b*)-(*iii*) (*c*)-(*ii*) (*d*)-(*i*)
(272) (*a*)-(*iii*) (b)-(*i*) (*c*)-(*iv*) (*d*)-(*ii*)
(273) (*a*)-(*ii*) (b)-(*iv*) (*c*)-(*iii*) (*d*)-(*i*)

(274) (a)-(iv) (b)-(i) (c)-(ii) (d)-(iii)
(275) (a)-(iii) (b)-(iv) (c)-(i) (d)-(ii)
(276) (a)-(iii) (b)-(i) (c)-(iv) (d)-(ii)
(277) (a)-(iii) (b)-(iv) (c)-(ii) (d)-(i)
(278) (a)-(iii) (b)-(iv) (c)-(i) (d)-(ii)
(279) (a)-(iii) (b)-(ii) (c)-(i) (d)-(iv)
(280) (a)-(iii) (b)-(iv) (c)-(ii) (d)-(i)
(281) (a)-(iv) (b)-(i) (c)-(ii) (d)-(iii)
(282) (a)-(iv) (b)-(i) (c)-(ii) (d)-(iii)
(283) (a)-(iii) (b)-(i) (c)-(iv) (d)-(ii)
(284) (a)-(iii) (b)-(ii) (c)-(iv) (d)-(i)
(285) (a)-(ii) (b)-(iv) (c)-(i) (d)-(iii)
(286) (a)-(iv) (b)-(i) (c)-(ii) (d)-(iii)
(287) (a)-(iii) (b)-(i) (c)-(iv) (d)-(ii)
(288) (a)-(ii) (b)-(iii) (c)-(iv) (d)-(i)
(289) (a)-(iii) (b)-(i) (c)-(iv) (d)-(ii)
(290) (a)-(iii) (b)-(iv) (c)-(ii) (d)-(i)
(291) (a)-(iv) (b)-(ii) (c)-(i) (d)-(iii)
(292) (a)-(iii) (b)-(iv) (c)-(i) (d)-(ii)
(293) (a)-(iv) (b)-(iii) (c)-(i) (d)-(ii)
(294) (a)-(ii) (b)-(iv) (c)-(i) (d)-(iii)
(295) (a)-(ii) (b)-(iii) (c)-(i) (d)-(iv)
(296) (a)-(iv) (b)-(ii) (c)-(i) (d)-(iii)
(297) (a)-(iii) (b)-(iv) (c)-(i) (d)-(ii)
(298) (a)-(iii) (b)-(i) (c)-(ii) (d)-(iv)
(299) (a)-(ii) (b)-(iv) (c)-(i) (d)-(iv)
(300) (a)-(iii) (b)-(i) (c)-(iv) (d)-(ii)
(301) (a)-(ii) (b)-(iii) (c)-(iv) (d)-(i)
(302) (a)-(iii) (b)-(ii) (c)-(iv) (d)-(i)
(303) (a)-(iv) (b)-(i) (c)-(ii) (d)-(iii)
(304) (a)-(iii) (b)-(i) (c)-(iv) (d)-(ii)
(305) (a)-(iv) (b)-(iii) (c)-(ii) (d)-(i)
(306) (a)-(iii) (b)-(iv) (c)-(ii) (d)-(i)
(307) (a)-(iii) (b)-(i) (c)-(iv) (d)-(ii)
(308) (a)-(iv) (b)-(i) (c)-(ii) (d)-(iii)
(309) (a)-(iv) (b)-(ii) (c)-(i) (d)-(iii)
(310) (a)-(iii) (b)-(i) (c)-(iv) (d)-(ii)
(311) (a)-(iii) (b)-(iv) (c)-(ii) (d)-(i)
(312) (a)-(iii) (b)-(i) (c)-(iv) (d)-(ii)
(313) (a)-(ii) (b)-(i) (c)-(iv) (d)-(iii)
(314) (a)-(iv) (b)-(i) (c)-(ii) (d)-(iii)
(315) (a)-(iii) (b)-(i) (c)-(iv) (d)-(ii)
(316) (a)-(iv) (b)-(iii) (c)-(ii) (d)-(i)

(317) (*a*)-(*ii*)	(*b*)-(*iv*)	(*c*)-(*i*)	(*d*)-(*iii*)
(318) (*a*)-(*iii*)	(*b*)-(*ii*)	(*c*)-(*iv*)	(*d*)-(*i*)
(319) (*a*)-(*iv*)	(*b*)-(*i*)	(*c*)-(*ii*)	(*d*)-(*iii*)
(320) (*a*)-(*iv*)	(*b*)-(*i*)	(*c*)-(*ii*)	(*d*)-(*iii*)
(321) (*a*)-(*iii*)	(*b*)-(*iv*)	(*c*)-(*i*)	(*d*)-(*ii*)
(322) (*a*)-(*ii*)	(*b*)-(*iv*)	(*c*)-(*i*)	(*d*)-(*iii*)
(323) (*a*)-(*iii*)	(*b*)-(*iv*)	(*c*)-(*i*)	(*d*)-(*ii*)
(324) 1.4	(325) Radius	(326) 15 mm	(327) 10,000
(328) (*a*)-(300)	(*b*)-(200)	(*c*)-(500)	(*d*) 385
(329) 0.40	(330) 0.56	(331) 0.67	(332) 1.19
(333) 980 kg	(334) 1750 kg		

SECTION 1

(B) SALINE AND ALKALI SOILS

I. Fill up the blanks:

1. The average estimated chlorine and sulphur content of the earth's crust is________, respectively.
2. On an average sodium, calcium and magnesium each occur in earth's crust to the extent of ________.
3. ________ions form as a result of the solution of atmospheric or biologically evolved carbon dioxide in water.
4. ________ occur for the most part in regions of arid or semi-arid climate.
5. Restricted drainage either owing to high ground water-table or to low soil permeability usually contributes to ________.
6. ________ of the soil causes poor drainage by impeding the downward movement of water.
7. The salinity problem of principal ________ arises when irrigation makes previously non-saline soils saline.
8. Ca and Mg cation in the soil solution are more strongly adsorbed by the exchange complex than ________.
9. The word saline refers to the soils for which the conductivity of saturation extract is ________, exchangeable sodium percentage less than 15 and ordinarily pH is less than 8.5.
10. In case of saline-alkali soils the conductivity of the saturation extract is greater than 4 mmhos/cm at 25°C and the percentage of exchangeable ________.
11. Saline-alkali soils are formed as a result of the combined processes of ________ and alkalization.
12. With the lowering of concentration of salt in soil solution, some of the exchangeable sodium ________ to form sodium hydroxide.
13. Sodium formed through hydrolysis in a soil solution may change to________upon reaction with carbon dioxide absorbed from the atmosphere.
14. In a strongly alkaline soil (pH > 8.5), the particles ________ and soil becomes unfavourable for entry and movement of water and for tillage.
15. Non-saline-alkali soils show exchangeable-sodium percentage more than 15 and conductivity of the saturation extract ________, and pH usually ranges between 8.5 and 10.
16. Large quantities of exchangeable and________ may occur in non-saline-alkali soils.
17. Non-saline-alkali soils in some areas of Western U.S.A. have exchangeable-sodium percentage considerably above 15 and yet the pH especially in the surface soil may be as low as 6, De Sigmond (1938) named such soils as ________.
18. The relative concentrations of various cations in soil water extracts also give information on the composition of the________ in the soil.
19. High levels of boron in soils can usually be reduced by________.
20. Boron concentrations below ________ ppm are safe for sensitive plants, 0.7 to 1.5 ppm is marginal limit and more than 1.5 ppm boron is unsafe.
21. Saline and alkali soils commonly contain ________carbonates and a relatively high concentration of soluble salts.
22. Neutral normal ammonium is the salt solution most commonly used for the saturation of the ________ in determination of cation exchange capacity.

23. The presence of fine alkaline-earth carbonate particles is thought to improve the________of soils.
24. ________ upon application of acid can be used to detect as little as 0.5 per cent of alkaline earth carbonates in soils.
25. It often happens that________is sufficiently restricted to cause the infiltration rate to decrease considerably with time.
26. The infiltration rate lower than 0.25 cm/hr (0.1"/hr) involves special________ problems.
27. ________ of soil, in qualitative sense, refers to readiness with which the soil conducts or transmits fluids.
28. In quantitative sense, involving numerical values, the term ________ is mostly used and refers to length-squared measurement.
29. It is expected that if the hydraulic conductivity of surface soil is as low as 0.1 cm/hr (0.04"/hr)________ may present serious difficulties.
30. ________ additions, while slower to give results, have long been used in agriculture.
31. The aggregating can be an effective research tool for investigational work with________ soils.
32. The soils of low structure-stability disperse and slake on wetting by rain or irrigation water, may develop ________ as the soil surface dries.
33. Sodium-Adsorption-Ratio (SAR) and ________ are employed for discussing the equilibrium relationship between soluble and exchangeable cations.
34. The pH of gypiferous soil at saturation percentage is seldom in excess of 8.2 regardless of________.
35. A pH reading at saturation percentage in excess of 8.5 almost invariably indicates an________.
36. A high gypsum-value indicates that only leaching is required while low gypsum value indicates the need for ________ in an alkali soil.
37. Plant growth is a function of total soil moisture stress, that is, the sum of soil moisture tension and ________ of the soil solution.
38. Water flows, in both saturated and unsaturated soil in accordance with________.
39. Soils that are flocculated and permeable when saline may become________ when leached.
40. ________ methods of irrigation should be favoured if salinity constitutes a serious problem.
41. Furrow irrigation is well adapted to________ and is suitable where topography is too rough or steep for other methods.
42. Drip or trickle method of irrigation is the most ________ of all the methods, but it is costly.
43. ________ is the ratio of the equivalent depth of water to the depth of irrigation water expressed either as a fraction or per cent.
44. Drainage in ________ is the process of removal of excess water from soil.
45. The ratio of the water flow velocity to the hydraulic gradient is called ________.
46. Lime sulphur is an acid or acid-former type of chemical amendment applied in ________.
47. Though boron toxicity is not limited only to saline/alkali soils, excess is common in________.
48. In non-saline soils, there is usually a relatively abrupt transition from low to high ________ and wilting of plants indicates the need for irrigation.
49. Sugar beets are very salt tolerant during later growth stages, but are extremely sensitive during ________.

II. Tick mark (✓) True or False :

50. Cation adsorption occurs as a consequence of the electrical charges at the surface of the soil particles.
51. Cation adsorption, a surface phenomenon, is identified mainly with the fine silt, clay and organic matter fraction of soils.
52. Ca and Mg are the principal cations found in the soil solution and on the exchange comp'ex of normal soils in humid regions.

53. Saline soils correspond to Hilgard's (1906) "White alkali" soils and to the "Solonchaks" of the Russian soil scientists.
54. Saline soils are often recognized by the presence of black crust of salts on the surface.
55. Saline soils due to the absence of significant amounts of exchangeable sodium ate generally deflocculated.
56. The management of saline-alkali soils continues to be a problem till the excess salts and exchangeable sodium are removed from the root zone and physical conditions restored.
57. Sometimes saline-alkali soils contain gypsum, when such soils are leached, calcium dissolves and replaces the exchangeable sodium concurrently with the removal of excess salts.
58. If allowed sufficient time, non-saline-alkali soils develop characteristic morphological features.
59. The anions in a non-saline-alkali soil mostly consist of chloride, sulphate and bicarbonate, small amounts of carbonates also often occur.
60. Measurements on soils indicate that over a considerable textural range the saturation percentage is nearly equal to four times the 15 atmospheric percentage.
61. The conductivity of the saturation-extract method is not applicable for the measurement of salinity in peat soils.
62. An increase in pH reading of 1.0 or more, as the moisture content is changed from a low to high value, has been found useful in some areas for detecting saline-alkali soils.
63. Toxic concentrations of boron have not been found in the saturation extract of a number of saline soils.
64. Neutral normal ammonium salt solution is most commonly used for extraction of exchangeable cations.
65. The alkaline earth-carbonates that occur in significant amounts in soils consist of calcite, dolomite, and possibly magnesite.
66. Water-movement rates attainable in soil under field conditions does not directly relate to irrigation, leaching, and drainage of saline and alkali soils.
67. The infiltration rate is measured under field conditions.
68. In a quantitative sense, when permeability is expressed with numbers, it seems desirable that it be defined as a property of the porous medium alone, that is, independent, of the fluid used in its measurement.
69. When bulk density of medium to fine textured sub-soils exceeds about 1.7 g/cm^3, hydraulic conductivity values will be so high that drainage may pose problem.
70. The soil aggregating chemicals may provide a rapid method for appraising the structural improvement potentially attainable from organic matter additions.
71. SAR and PAR are defined as $Na^+ / \sqrt{Ca^{++} + Mg^{++} / 2}$ and $K^+ / \sqrt{Ca^{++} + Mg^{++} / 2}$, respectively.
72. The pH of a calcareous soil at saturation percentage is invariably in excess of 7.0 and generally in excess of 7.5.
73. Leaching, in agriculture, is the process of dissolving and transporting soluble salts by the downward movement of water through soil.
74. In semi-arid and arid regions soil salinity is usually not an ever-present hazard.
75. In areas where water is neither cheap nor large volumes are used, irrigation practices are often inefficient.
76. The selection of an irrigation method for applying water to the soil is not related to salinity.
77. The basin method of irrigation is often used for orchards and various other crops in areas where water can be impounded in a rectangular basin.
78. The sprinkler method of irrigation allows a close control of the depth of water applied.
79. Sub-irrigation is the least common of the various methods of irrigation, but is suitable for use where salinity is a problem.
80. The water-table is the elevation in the profile at which the soil water is at atmospheric pressure.
81. The hydraulic head of ground water at each point in the soil is the elevation at which water stands in a riser connected to the point in question.

82. Physical improvement of an alkali soil involves rearrangement and aggregation of soil particles and replacement of exchangeable potassium.
83. Mesquite (*Prosophis juliflora*) and desert salt bush (*Atriplex ploycarpa*) are indicator plants for soil salinity.
84. On a weight or equivalent basis, chloride salts are more inhibitory to plant growth than sulphate salts.
85. Many plant species are no more sensitive to chloride salts than they are to iso-osmotic concentrations of sulphate salts.
86. Tomato, cabbage, lettuce, onion and cucumber show medium salt tolerance.
87. Radish and green bean are highly salt tolerant.
88. Barley, wheat, maize, and potato have been classified as semi-tolerant to boron.
89. Onion, cabbage and carrot have been found tolerant to boron.
90. Orange, lemon, apple and peach are sensitive to boron.

III. Tick mark (✓) the correct answer:

91. The following factors other than gypsum solution may effect the extraction of calcium and sulphate from a gypsiferous soil.
    (*a*) Calcium solution of gypsum
    (*b*) Exchange reactions wherein calcium replaces no cations
    (*c*) Sulphate solution from a source other than gypsum
    (*d*) None of these
92. The organic matter of soils is ordinarily obtained by multiplying the organic carbon content by
    (*a*) 1.52 (*b*) 1.62
    (*c*) 1.72 (*d*) 1.82
93. Gypsum, an amendment applied to alkali soils belongs to________ type.
    (*a*) Acid former (*b*) Low solubility
    (*c*) Soluble Ca-salt (*d*) None of these
94. The choice of a chemical amendment may be influenced by the________ required for reaction in the soil.
    (*a*) Time (*b*) Cost
    (*c*) Quantity (*d*) Quality
95. Calcium chloride is probably the most readily available source of soluble calcium, but seldom used due to
    (*a*) Non-availability (*b*) High cost
    (*c*) Application problem (*d*) None of these
96. The values above ________ ppm are associated with boron toxicity.
    (*a*) 150 (*b*) 200
    (*c*) 250 (*d*) 300
97. Among the fruits, lemon, apple, plum have been placed in the ________ salt tolerance group.
    (*a*) High (*b*) Low
    (*c*) Medium (*d*) None of these
98. Barley, rape and cotton are salt tolerant.
    (*a*) High (*b*) Low
    (*c*) Medium (*d*) None of these .

99. In general, waters with conductivity values below________ mmhos/cm are satisfactory for irrigation in so far as salt content is concerned.

(*a*) 1250 (*b*) 1150
(*c*) 950 (*d*) 750

IV. Match the following:

100. Match the following units of electrical conductivity when EC = 0.000694 mho/cm has been recorded for a soil saturation extract at 25°C.

(*a*) EC	(*i*) 69.4 (= k × 10^5)
(*b*) EC × × 10^3	(*ii*) 694 micromhos/cm
(*c*) EC × 10^5	(*iii*) 0.000694 mho/cm
(*d*) EC × 10^6	(*iv*) 0.694 millimho/cm

101. Match the ratio of SP (saturation percentage) to FAP (15-atmosphere percentage) in different soil textural groups.

(*a*) Coarse (2.0-6.5)	(*i*) 0.48
(*b*) Medium (6.6-15.0)	(*ii*) 0.60
(*c*) Fine (> 15.1)	(*iii*) 0.75
(*d*) Organic	(*iv*) 1.15

102. Match the pH value of $CaCO_3$ saturated solution with its solubility (meq/litre).

(*a*) 6.21 pH	(*i*) 1.1
(*b*) 7.12 pH	(*ii*) 0.82
(*c*) 8.60 pH	(*iii*) 19.3
(*d*) 9.20 pH	(*iv*) 7.1

103. Match the amendments (in tonnes) equivalent. to one tonne of sulphur.

(*a*) Gypsum	(*i*) 8.69
(*b*) Limestone	(*ii*) 5.38
(*c*) Iron sulphate	(*iii*) 3.06
(*d*) Sulphuric acid	(*iv*) 3.13

104. Match the leaching requirement with EC (mmhos/cm) of irrigation water if the EC (mmhos/cm) of the drainage water at the bottom of the root zone is 4 mmhos/cm.

(*a*) 2.5	(*i*) 250
(*b*) 6.2	(*ii*) 750
(*c*) 18.8	(*iii*) 2250
(*d*) 56.2	(*iv*) 100

Do You Know That

1. Approximately 10 per cent of the world's 33 billion acres of land is arable.
2. The first use of sound for weed control was patented in 1895.
3. In 1906, carbon bisulphide was introduced as a soil fumigant for the control of Canada thistle and field bindweed.
4. Potato scab disease favours the alkaline soils.
5. The crops Barley and sugar beet are highly salt tolerant.
6. Leaching closely relates with irrigation and helps in removal excess salts from plant root zone.

KEY

1. 0.05 and 0.06 per cent
2. 2 or 3 per cent
3. Bicarbonate
4. Saline soils
5. Soil-salinization
6. Low permeability
7. Economic importance
8. Sodium
9. More than 4 mmhos/cm at 25°C
10. Sodium is more than 15%
11. Salinization
12. Hydrolyzes
13. Sodium carbonate
14. Disperse
15. Less than 4 mmhos/cm at 25°C
16. Soluble potassium
17. Degraded alkali soils
18. Exchangeable cations
19. Leaching
20. 0.7
21. Alkaline-earth
22. Exchange complex
23. Physical condition
24. Effervescence
25. Subsurface drainage
26. Water-management
27. Permeability
28. Intrinsic permeability
29. Leaching and irrigation
30. Organic matter
31. Saline and alkali
32. Hard crust
33. Potassium Adsorption Ratio (PAR)
34. ESP
35. ESP of 15 or more
36. Amendments
37. Osmotic pressure
38. Darcy's law
39. Deflocculated
40. Flooding
41. Row crops
42. Efficient
43. LR (Leaching Requirement)
44. Agriculture
45. Hydraulic conductivity
46. Alkali
47. Saline soils
48. Moisture stress
49. Germination
50. True
51. True
52. False
53. True
54. False
55. False
56. True
57. True
58. True
59. True
60. True
61. False
62. True
63. False
64. True
65. True
66. False
67. True
68. True
69. False
70. True
71. True
72. True
73. True
74. False
75. False
76. False
77. True
78. True
79. False
80. True
81. True
82. False
83. True
84. True
85. True
86. True
87. False
88. True
89. True
90. True
91. (*c*)
92. (*c*)
93. (*c*)
94. (*a*)
95. (*b*)
96. (*c*)
97. (*b*)
98. (*a*)
99. (*d*)
100. (*a*)-(*iii*) (*b*)-(*iv*) (*c*)-(*i*) (*d*)-(*ii*)
101. (*a*)-(*iv*) (*b*)-(*i*) (*c*)-(*ii*) (*d*)-(*iii*)

Note: FAP ranges are arbitratarily selected to designate the textutal groups.

102. (*a*)-(*iii*) (*b*)-(*iv*) (*c*)-(*i*) (*d*)-(*ii*)
103. (*a*)-(*ii*) (*b*)-(*iv*) (*c*)-(*i*) (*d*)-(*iii*)
104. (*a*)-(*iv*) (*b*)-(*i*) (*c*)-(*ii*) (*d*)-(*iii*)

SECTION 2

AGRICULTURAL GEOGRAPHY, ADAPTATION, DISTRIBUTION AND ECOLOGY

I. Fill up the blanks :

1. Agriculture is different from________ which is the practice of breeding and rearing of certain herbivorous animals.
2. The study of relationship between economic activities *viz.*, primary (agriculture and mining), secondary (industry) and the tertiary (services) and their environment was given a special title of the science of________.
3. Scientific methods in agricultural geography are the procedures by which________ are formulated, tested and confirmed.
4. A simple three-stage breakdown of aids has been suggested *viz.*, iconic (portrait), analogue (likeness) and________.
5. Both agricultural geography and________ had their genesis about the same period.
6. Agricultural economics is influenced more by socio-economic environment; whereas agricultural geography is dominated by the combination of both________ factors.
7. ________ has always dominated the cultural landscape and has claimed most of man's working hours over a period of several thousand years.
8. The________ in investigating farming systems is far more important than the statistical one.
9. ________ determinism decidedly turned the focus on man and imparted a scientific tenor to the study of agricultural geography.
10. Agriculture is now being studied from the view-point of human________.
11. The stress on human determinism (possibilism) was responsible for transforming man's environment, which, in turn brought about________.
12. Man cannot altogether ignore the environment, can at the best modify, but never________it.
13. The agricultural sector in India has undergone significant changes in________ and in agricultural productivity since 1966, while physical features remain unchanged.
14. An ecosystem approach (from agri-geographic view-point) refers to the study of conditions of life at a level of individual organism (a crop) and________of organisms (crops in combination) in relation to immediate environment.
15. ________is not merely growing crops, but it is more a form of applied ecology.
16. In a well settled area, the physical and non-physical environment cannot be________.
17. Details of terrain are well encompassed by the elements of relative relief, average slope and________.
18. The direct effect of ________ operates particularly through elevation, rugged relief and slope.
19. At a height of 3500 m and above the decreased atmospheric pressure causes nausea and________ activities cannot be carried out despite the domestication of numerous plants.

20. In tropics, the altitude is of special significance for utilization of land for________.
21. The temperature decreases with altitude due to the________having low carbon dioxide content, moisture and other particles.
22. The restrictive result of altitude through temperature modification is most prominent in India as wheat crop is raised in Punjab-Haryana plains in winter but, in________ in Ladakh.
23. The rainfall on________ is usually heavier than that on leeward side.
24. The orientation of mountains not only blocks winds, but also steers them into a________.
25. In interior parts of Himachal Pradesh (India), the winds which move down from adjacent cold mountain-tops provide sufficient chilling atmosphere needed for successful________ at lower elevations.
26. The soils in mountainous region do not get properly________.
27. The variation in texture, drainage and nutrient status of soils with altitude cause________of agricultural land use.
28. Well drained volcanic soils are ________ than other types of soils.
29. Rugged relief of an area determines the value of terrain for________.
30. The most obvious direct effect of slope is in the form of restraint on________ and accessibility.
31. Both runoff and________ vary according to the steepness of slope.
32. ________ would prove more beneficial on sloping fields to recharge the soil moisture without any erosion.
33. Excessive water erosion areas coincide approximately with the areas of________of many tributaries or the areas of joints and cracks.
34. The climatic variations on the earth have primarily resulted from its________, unequal distribution of land and water, and unevenness of its surface.
35. The potential crop-producing capability of a given area is mainly dependent on________ and soil conditions.
36. The climatic conditions constitute the primary influents controlling the distribution of________.
37. Temperature conditions express the________ in the environment available for conversion of minerals and moisture into plant tissue.
38. ________ refers to the point at which a stimulus begins to bring a response.
39. Wind velocities increase with height, lower leaves escape drying and thus the plants maintain________.
40. The 'fohn and the Chinook' are mountain winds descending from the________ respectively.
41. "________" cause heavy loss to growers of olives, citrus and other fruits in the Mediterranean low lands.
42. Snow cover is advantageous to agriculture as it retards penetration of frost action, hastens soil availability for cultivation on thawing________ hence can be grown.
43. The snow-covered peaks of mountains provide cool climatic environment to orchards and________facilities at low elevation on melting of snow.
44. ________ is an active factor in the precipitation that an area is likely to receive.
45. The ideal condition for dew formation are calm weather,________during the day, low temperature at night and greater amount of water vapour in the atmosphere.
46. In some coastal, arid regions and on dry mountain slopes fog comprises an important factor in the determination of distribution of________.
47. Rainfalls________ is usually expressed as the actual total rainfall minus the total possible evaporation.

48. The average intensity of rainfall is equal to the________ over a given period divided by the total number of hours/rainy days.
49. Rainfall is most important climatic variable exerting________ over the use of agricultural land.
50. Moisture Index $= \frac{100s - x}{y}$, where $x =$________, $y =$________, $s =$________.
51. An________, if needed at all must be defined in terms of agricultural elements *viz.*, by crops, livestock, or enterprise data or by measurement of farming processes or farming organizations.
52. The map of agricultural regions represents a reflection of interactions between________environment.
53. Classification into the agricultural regions (units) is done to make regional comparisons in difference in patterns and for________of agriculture.
54. The concentration of a specific________ of agriculture usually postulates the concentration of a recognizable degree of that element in an area.
55. ________ comprises a useful alternative to measure the extent of diversification in cropping pattern in an area.
56. Agricultural typology is considered to be of primary importance in ________.
57. Agricultural types should be identified on the basis of ________ attributes of agriculture.
58. The great arid belt of the old world, from Atlantic shores of Sahara to the steppe of Mongolia, has been occupied by________ and pastoral nomads for at least 3,000 years.
59. Unlike commercial grain farming or grazing ________ is an ancient activity, that may also be called an aboriginal form of livestock raising.
60. Nomadic herding is. confined to a harsh natural environment unsuited for________.
61. Nomadic herders are constantly or intermittently on the move in search of regions embodied with________.
62. ________chiefly subsist on their herds almost for all their needs namely food, clothing, shelter and various artifacts.
63. It is widely believed that nomadic herding evolved in the continents of________where most of the domestic animals were first put to man's use.
64. The driest parts of the world still have characteristic________.
65. ________is said to be as old as the history of agriculture itself and could be traced back to about 7,000-8,000 B.C.
66. Shifting cultivation has long been recognized as the most widespread________ of the tropics encountered in Amazonia, the Congo Basin and South East Asia.
67. The cropping patterns most commonly adopted by *jhumias* is ________.
68. Tillage methods among ________farmers are relatively more intensive than those of shifting cultivators.
69. Most of the subsistence farming areas are located in the monsoon regions of________ and adjacent island.
70. Intensive subsistence farming systems are a form of________ nature.
71. Rice is the most distinctive and important staple food of the intensive________ areas.
72. ________agriculture is an ancient system representing a more stable collaboration between the man and the land.
73. The livestock ranching system embodies a number of characteristics in common with the________ agricultural system.

74. Commercial__________ is of recent origin and is both extensive and mechanized in respect of production technology.

75. __________ may have stemmed from the medieval agriculture of North-West Europe, which was essentially subsistence in character.

76. __________ is one of the largest mixed farming areas in the world despite small land area, vast alluvial and flood plains and engagement of less than 30 per cent of. working force in farming.

77. More than 80 per cent, nine-tenth, four-fifth and virtually entire world's production of__________, butter, cheese, and condensed/dried milk is produced in Europe, Russia, North America and Australia, respectively.

78. Among the__________ agricultural systems of the middle latitude, horticulture is practised only in the Mediterranean region.

79. Certain aspects of__________ are similar to those of plantation farming of the tropics.

80. The__________ system was devised and applied in the erstwhile Soviet Union during the period following the Bolshevik Revolution of 1917 (October Revolution).

81. __________ plantation farming is perhaps the most rational system which is totally different from peasant agriculture.

82. Commercial plantation farming system was introduced by Europeans into the__________ lands.

83. Commercial plantation system refers to the__________, capitalized and often highly centralized cultivation in the plantation of crops for export and exemplifies an export-oriented system.

84. The basic agricultural system means a regional unit of the surface of the earth which embodies throughout its extent identical agricultural __________.

85. A land use map is a__________, two dimensional graphic representation of the image of the land surface.

86. Topographic survey was the earliest form of a__________ survey which can accurately mark the location of various objects on the surface of the earth.

87. An__________ survey comprises survey of a comprehensive character conducted colloboratively by scientifically or operationally interrelated disciplines.

88. The mostly universally used remote sensing technique to prepare land-use maps is the__________ survey.

89. The__________ of the land-use survey is the interpretation of the aerial photographs.

90. Field surveys supply information on the location of land-use, while air-photo interpretations supply information on the__________ at a given time.

91. A land use survey, shows the static distribution of constantly__________ patterns.

92. Land capability classification comprises a scientific appraisal of the physical characteristics of land, __________ soil qualities, and the farm management practices.

93. Land capability maps divide soils into groups according to their potentialities and __________.

94. Actual__________ has been defined as the initial capability of the soils to produce a certain amount of crops per hectare per annum.

95. Adoption (introduction) of the most difficult and costly innovations in the farm management practices on a piece of land are done to harness__________ soil productivity.

96. The study of relationships between crop plants and their environment is referred to as *crop ecology*, but when the social factors are brought into picture, the entire area of study is then known as__________.

97. It has been said that no known form of life has been observed to multiply__________ without bumping against the limitations imposed by the space it occupies.

98. At__________a human population is in a state of balance between the forces of procreation and those of destruction.

99. Wheat is the crop which has been planted extensively outside of its__________limits.

100. The__________of plants has resulted from both natural causes and activities of man.

101. All the plants in the world today have come from__________.

102. The earth, according to geological time scale has existed through five era's namely, archeozoic, proterozoic,__________, mesozoic and cenozoic.

103. The__________are believed to have appeared for the first time during the lower cretaceous period of the Mesozoic era.

104. In the post-glacial period, it is known that there was a considerable shift in __________ toward continentality.

105. The tolerance of a species is a specific character subject to the laws and processes of__________in the same way as its morphological characters, but the two are not necessarily linked.

106. The range of tolerance of any larger taxonomic unit is the total of the ranges of tolerances of its__________species.

107. The tropical plants namely, rubber (*Hevea braziliensis*) cacao (*Theobroma cacao*) and banana (*Musa sapientum*) will not withstand__________temperature.

108. Adaptation implies an adequacy to cope with the conditions of natural environment, and to so utilize its resources as to maintain an __________.

109. A__________refers to the heredity received by an organism, which is relatively constant throughout life.

110. __________implies purposive adaptation, a need to be fulfilled by changing form or structure as is necessary.

111. __________involves giving of human traits to non-human organisms like avoidance and storage of food in roots.

112. The reproductive powers of animals are much __________ then is required to maintain their numbers.

113. In a random cross-breeding population at equilibrium, the relative frequencies of each gene allele tend to remain__________from generation to generation, unless their carriers survive or reproduce at different rates.

114. The presence of hydrocyanic acid in white clover has been established for many years; it is due to the presence of__________and a hydrolyzing enzyme.

115. An ecotype refers to a group of__________especially adapted to specific environmental niche.

116. It has been concluded by numerous studies that the present races of *Potentilla grandulosa* are the products of long time__________and have attained an equilibrium with their environment.

117. Darwin (1859) suggested that the primitive men have been forced to try to eat 'almost__________that he could chew and swallow'.

118. Mendel (1865) believed that studies of variation in cultivated plants could tell us what we need to know about the nature of__________in wild plants.

119. Vavilov concluded that the species represents a definite heterogeneous and variable morphological-physiological system, the origin of which is associated with a particular __________ and area.

120. Within a centre of origin, there would seem to be smaller centres, which Vavilov spoke of as__________groups.

121. The places, where interbreeding population are located have been named as __________ by Jack Harlan.

122. The objective in__________is to arrange in some convenient system all of the morphological and physiological characteristics to establish relationships.

123. Whole families of plants in general are characterized by definite cycle of__________ accuring through all genera and species making up the family.

124. The__________ is of special interest in any consideration of domestication of food plants.

125. One of the three great cultural-historical events which occurred in Near East constituted profound importance to the development of man of was,__________tradition about 40,000 years ago.

126. The appearance of __________ in Mesopotamia occurred some 5,500 years ago.

127. It has been emphasized that the locus of domestication of wild plants must necessarily be its area of natural __________.

128. The wild species of *Hordeum Spontaneum,* the probable progenitor of__________, is distributed widely from Turkestan to Morocco.

129. Wheat for domestication had to be moved from its __________ on mountain slopes between 2,000' and 4,300' above sea level, to more levelled areas at lower altitudes.

130. One of the oldest evidences of cultivation in Middle America is that of the__________ phase, dating from 7,000 to 5,000 B.C.

131. Initially, two places of maize origin have been suggested, the__________ and the Peru-Bolvia- Ecuador region.

132. One of the many species of grain amaranths, that originated in New World is *Amaranthus leucocarpus,* a desirable __________.

133. The ecology of populations and communities is often spoken as __________, in contrast to *autecology* which deals with the relationship between the individual, or species, and its environment.

134. The dynamic whole, formed by the, habitat and the associated living organisms that occupy it, is known as__________.

135. The factors of environment act singly, together, and, above all, in a __________ manner upon plants and animals.

136. It is conceivable that profound change by man in an ecosystem could result either in glorious future or__________.

137. In the__________ there is little overall change in available nitrogen in large ecosystem or in the biosphere as a whole.

138. __________ has been exceedingly useful in its quantitative exchange-rate measurement in different components of an ecosystem.

139. The cycling of radioactive strontium, iodine, cesium, __________, and other elements may become a grave concern for the ecologists of the atomic age.

140. __________can be transformed from one to another type, but can never be created nor destroyed is first law of thermodynamics.

141. The energy transformation will not occur__________in a process unless there is degradation of the energy from a concentrated form into a dispersed form.

142. The food chain has been defined as the transfer of__________ from the source in green plants through a series of organisms, with repeated eating and being. eaten.

143. In principle, the__________ the food chain, the greater the available energy which can be converted into the living weight (biomass) and/or dissipated by respiration.

144. In *ecology,* total assimilation of a tropic level is known as__________ through that level.

145. The tropic level of an organism is one of________ and not necessarily of species.
146. Plant communities may be considered to have a definite________ because of the interaction of food chain phenomena and size-metabolism relationships.
147. In ecological ________, the producer level forms the base and successive levels the tiers to make up the apex.
148. ________ is the amount of water vapour present in unit volume of air.
149. Relative humidity expresses the amount of water vapour in the atmosphere as a percentage of that which could be held at saturation at a particular temperature and ________.
150. The difference between the actual water vapour pressure and that needed to saturate the air at the same temperature is referred to as________.
151. Atmospheric moisture is measured with the psychrometer and the________.
152. In a clear weather, with little or no wind, cooling of the surface layers of atmosphere at night may result in the formation of________.
153. ________ may form, when air masses of high moisture content close to the surface are cooled.
154. The________ consists of evaporation, transportation, condensation and precipitation of water vapours.
155. The amount of average annual rainfall, measured in various parts of the world varies form 0.5 cm in________ to more than 2250 cm in Cherrapunji (India).
156. One of the early methods proposed by Transeau (1905) to measure precipitation effectiveness, was the ratio of total________ to total evaporation.
157. The amount of solar radiation reflected back into the atmosphere is known as________.
158. A________, obtained by comparing the water need at a given place with moisture surplus and deficit is essential for a satisfactory classification of climate.
159. Humidity index is equal to 100 times the water surplus divided by water________.
160. ________ is equal to 100 times the water deficit divided by water need.
161. ________ is equal to 100 times the surplus minus 60, times the water deficit divided by water need.
162. An ecological classification of plants on the basis of their water relations distinguishes them as hydrophytes, mesophytes and________.
163. Water requirement of wheat has been found to increase from 30 to 100 per cent due to________ infection.
164. The accepted principle of water movement in plants is that water moves along the gradient of decreasing ________.
165. The difference between the free energy of pure water and that of water in solution (in the soil or plant cell sap) is called________.
166. Diffusion-Pressure Deficit (DPD) is equal to Osmotic Pressure (OP) minus Wall Pressure (WP) and WP is equal to________.
167. Internal water________ occur in plant, when water loss through transpiration continues to be more than absorption of water through roots.
168. The total soil moisture stress is equivalent to the combined effects of soil moisture________ the osmotic pressure of the soil solution.
169. It has been observed that plant growth is________ before the permanent wilting percentage is reached.
170. Elongation of plant organs and increase in fresh or dry weight are ________ to soil moisture stress whereas; photosynthesis and respiration are relatively insensitive.

171. Maize is especially________ to soil moisture stress at the time of anthesis and shortly thereafter.
172. The watermelon responds little to irrigation even when a rather high soil moisture________is apparent.
173. The soil factors which affect________ may influence the response of plnts to decreasing moisture supply.
174. Soil temperature is also an important factor in determining the growth rate and________ of roots.
175. The term "________ "refers to a deficiency of soil moisture which produces water deficits in the plant sufficient to cause a reduction in growth.
176. The injurious results of atmospheric drought are most likely to occur in areas near the________ of production.
177. The capacity to endure desiccation constitutes the most important basis of true drought________.
178. ________ are plants characterized by a proliferation of parenchyma cells, enlargement of vacuoles, and reduction in the size of intercellular spaces.
179. Most of the succulents are ________ of water, in contrast with some xerophytes.
180. Creosote·bush (*Larrea tridentata*) shows great tolerance to desiccation and can tolerate________ to 50 per cent of its dry weight.
181. The alternate drying and remoistening bring on mechanical stresses strong enough to cause________ of the plant cells.
182. ________, is the primary source of light and heat energy for living organisms.
183. Insolation at the________ varies only slightly from month to month because the angle of the sun's rays does not deviate from vertical.
184. The sun is at zenith at noon twice a year, at the vernal equinox, March 21 and ________ equinox, September 21.
185. At the time of ________, the circle illumination reaches the North and South Poles simultaneously, days and nights are of equal length and are the same at all latitudes.
186. ________ change more slowly in a wet soil than in a dry soil.
187. ________ is often accentuated in mountanous area and temperature inversion are usually well developed.
188. Temperature ________ is such a common phenomenon on the Pacific Coast and in other mountainous areas that it is of great economic importance.
189. The northern limits of cultivation of many crops are determined almost entirely by________.
190. A positive summation of temperatures in excess of a certain "zero point of vital activity" is used as a measure of________.
191. An accumulation of positive temperatures is the basis for a number of "________" widespread use today.
192. "A biotic event in North America will, in general, show a lag of four days for each degree of latitude, 50 of longitude, and 400 feet of altitude, northward, eastward, and upward, in spring and________"
193. The number of heat units for one day is obtained by subtracting the base temperature from the actual________ for that day.
194. At the canning stage, a________ reading is used to determine the date of harvest, in order to insure a quality product.
195. High phosphorus (in soils)________ crop maturity.
196. Coverage of winter cereals and forages either with ice-sheet or with densely packed/encrusted snows for long periods causes________.

197. ________ damage in plants is caused by the formation of ice crystals within the plant issues.
198. High________is a limiting factor in the production of crops in many semi-arid and arid climates.
199. Heat ________ appears to depend on specific protoplasmic properties.
200. The response of plants to rhythmic fluctuation in temperature is known as________.
201. It has been observed that tomatoes, maize, peppers, and potatoes grow primarily during the________.
202. The theoretical basis for________ was found in Lysenko's phasic development theory.
203. Information on vernalization has helped to develop a clear picture of the difference between________.
204. Small quantities of light are measured in joules or ergs, one gramme calorie is equal to 4.18 joules or________ million ergs.
205. The actual values of solar radiation at the surface of the earth have ranged from about 1.75 g/cal/cm^2/hr on high mountain tops (12,000 foot-candles to 1.5 g/cal/cm^2/hr) (10,000 foot-candles) at________.
206. The amount of light received by the plants is determined by the________ of light and its duration.
207. About 10 per cent of the light that strikes the surface of a body of________ is reflected back into the atmosphere.
208. The amount of light required for photosynthesis to equal the respiratory compounds is termed as the________
209. Shade-tolerant and sun-loving species are known as sciophytes and________ .
210. In the seedling stages low light intensity may determine the failure of________ or grasses established with companion crops.
211. The growth orientation caused by light is known as________.
212. Forage crops are favoured by cloudy climate, while________ crops by intense light.
213. ________content is usually lower in full sunlight and tends to develop greater resistance to temperature injury.
214. The length of the dark period is critical in________ plants, because of its inhibiting effect.
215. After the ripe-to-flower condition (induction) has been achieved, the visual transition from vegetative to reproductive phase is marked by the differentiation of________.
216. The form of the blue pigment which________ depends on the colour of light to which the plant was last exposed.
217. In addition to the reversible photoreaction on flowering response, red light in the range of 640 to 670 mμ promotes ________ of lettuce, and promotes red colouring in apples.
218. The portion of the lower atmosphere, which is subjected to differential heating causing convection currents and turbulence, is known as________.
219. The atmospheric layers above 96 or 112 km, extending from 64 or 80 km outward for great distances, are collectively called________.
220. Above 64 km the action of ultraviolet and X-radiation from the sun causes the formation of innumerable ion and dissociation of________
221. The ionosphere characterized by being electrified, mainly through________ radiation from the sun.
222. The concentration of electrons in the ________ may reach a maximum somewhere 320 and 800 km from the earth.
223. The upper atmospheric zones carry energies from 20,000 electron volts to several million electron volts, with a maximum________ of the inner zone at 3200 km and of the outer zone at 16,000 km.
224. Disasters like Bhopal gas tragedy of 1984 in India, London________, and Belgium's Meuse Valley *etc.*, are some of the examples of air pollution.

225. Large-sized particles of soot and dust are rather easily removed from smoke, but very fine dust of 0.5 to 1.0 micron in size and the still smaller________ present a much greater problem of pollution.
226. Sulfur dioxide (SO_2) was considered for many years to be one of the most injurious________.
227. Acute sulfur dioxide injury to plants was characterized by collapsed marginal leaf areas, dull________ spots which bleached to an ivory or brownish appearance.
228. A unique type of air pollution is, that is known as________
229. Smog has come to mean________ concentrations of air-pollutants causing eye-irritation, plant damage and reduced visibility.
230. Air pollutants include carbon monoxide, sulfur dioxide, oxides of nitrogen,________, aldehydes, and organic acids.
231. Oats, spinach and table beets have been rated as________ to smog injury.
232. The typical smog damage is characterized by chlorotic leaf markings, banding, silvering and________ of leaves.
233. High________ has been found to favour greater damage to plants from than its lower level.
234. Both ozone and________ exposure drastically reduced the chlorophyll content within 24 hours.
235. A factor which tends to keep up the concentration of carbon dioxide in the atmosphere is its large quantity liberated from the________.
236. The rate of photosynthesis under________ intensity may be controlled by light.
237. The ratio of oxygen to carbon dioxide is also influenced by pore space and the________.
238. The equatorial regions receive________ than the regions farther south and north.
239. In general, the movement of air occurs from the poles toward________ where the air rises and returns toward the poles.
240. The general pattern of air movement is modified by the action of earth's rotation and the________ - differences caused by comparative sizes and positions of water and land masses.
241. Equatorward from subtropical high-pressure ridges, pressure declines until the equatorial________ trough is reached coinciding with the region of highest annual temperature.
242. From a subtropical high, pressure decreases toward the poles, reaching a rather low pressure at the latitude of the________ circles.
243. In the Northern Hemisphere the prevailing wind direction is.________ whereas; in the southern Hemisphere it is northwest.
244. From the subtropical high, located at 30° N and S, surface winds flow toward low-pressure areas, being turned into easterly winds by the________ force.
245. In general, there is predominance of________ in the tropics, and prevalence of westerly winds in the middle latitude.
246. Winds tend to correct the imbalance of________ and thus a cumulative excess of energy in the tropics and a deficit poleward.
247. Wind speed is measured by________.
248. Most winds are not uniform and steady air current, but rather a succession of________.
249. Trees may suffer more from drying effects of wind than do the________ plants.
250. If soil moisture available to plants is abundant, winds of moderate speed may not effect________.
251. Dwarfing and deformation of trees are common expressions of wind effects often found on sea coasts, exposed ridges and at________.

252. One of the most striking examples of importance to crop production is the spread of ________ by means of windborne spores.

253. Physiographic factors are those introduced by the ________ and behaviour of the earth's surface.

254. Near the Arctic Ocean, where it is always cold, a sticky compact, structureless and blue grey layer called *'glei'* develops at the bottom of the solum, this process is known as ________.

255. In ecological terms, the inherent ability of an organism to multiply may be considered the ________.

256. The biotic potential depends on mode of ________ and fecundity.

257. The forces which tend to limit the population of an organism are collectively known as environmental ________.

258. If an individual, a race or a species is able to cope with environmental resistance, it is said to have the quality of ________ in a given area.

259. ________ is the one of the key factors in ecological succession.

260. ________ often occurs from less complex plant communities to more complex ones dominated by plants of higher life form, or at least with greater competition potential.

261. The whole series of plant communities which develop in a given situation is known as *sere,* and the mature, relatively stable community is known as ________.

262. The broad tendency of succession is from simplicity to complexity, from dominance of lower to dominance of ________ which make exact demand on the habitat.

263. According to ________ idea any region has only one climax toward which all plant communities are developing.

264. Climax has been considered as steady state of ________ productivity, structure and populations, with the dynamic balance of its populations determined in relation to its site.

265. The climax vegetation is a pattern of populations which corresponds to the pattern ________ of gradients.

266. A common example of ________ competition is the use of companion crops to establish small-seeded legumes and grasses.

267. In plant breeding, the relative competitive ________ of individual varieties, strains or genotypes is highly important.

268. According to Gause's Principle, "the species having the ________ requirement comment live together in exactly the same niche because of completion".

269. A plant parasite is dependent on its host for its existence, it is therefore an environment factor in the ________.

270. The non-leguminous plants found to fix ________ include silver berry (*Elaeagnus* spp.), alder (*Alnus glutinosa*), sweet gale (*Myrica gale*) and *Casuarina* species.

271. The basic difference between the macro climate and microclimate lies in the ________ of the earth's surface.

272. From ecological view point, a number of organisms occupying the same general habitat may actually be living in a markedly ________ environment.

273. The bulk of the export type of cacao belongs to ________ type.

274. Banana and plantains are believed to have originated in ________.

275. Of the world's production of sugar, approximately 60 per cent comes from ________ and 40 perc ent from sugarbeet.

276. Sugarcane, a tropical perennial has high sucrose content and it was cultivated as a crop in ________ before the dawn of history.

277. ________ has been the world's leading producer of canesugar.

278. Of the many species of coffee (*Coffea*), indigenous to Africa, only three *viz.*, C. *arabica*, C. ________ and C. *liberica* have been found useful for coffee production.

279. A rice plant can transport________ from the leaves to the roots and thus live normally in aquatic environment.

280. Bolls in cotton seem to occupy a favoured________ position.

281. The successful use of cotton in________ depends on qualities like length, strength, and fineness of lint.

282. The strength of cotton fibre is determined by means of a device known as________ or a newer device called the stelometer.

283. The scientific name of sweet corn (Maize) is *Zea mays*________.

284. ________ soils are among the most favourable for maize because of their high native fertility.

285. ________, Brazil and Argentina are the highest maize producers.

286. ________ is planted in September and October and is harvested the following year in early summer.

287. Spring wheat is planted in early spring and requires________ days or more to reach maturity.

288. It has been estimated that the world is using only________ of the land physically adapted to wheat production.

289. Probably no crop illustrates to better advantage than the________ tree, the importance of adaptation to climatic conditions over a wide continental area.

290. In most of orchard fruits, the term variety may be more accurately described as________.

291. Apple (*Malus sylvestris*) has been cultivated for more than 2,000 years in Europe, and was introduced into________ by the early settlers.

292. The northern limits of latitude for deciduous fruits are determined by killing________ or long cold periods that kill the root.

293. The________ for commercial deciduous fruit production is determined by the amount of winter chilling required to break the rest period.

294. The________ of deciduous trees is that period during dormancy when the above-ground portion will not grow even under favourable environmental conditions.

295. Abundant sunshine favours ________ of apple fruits, occasioned in part at least by the effect of ultraviolet rays.

296. ________ is probably not as critical for deciduous fruit trees as it is for most of the field crops.

297. The apple tree is able to absorb nitrogen in form of ________ at low temperatures, 32° or 33°F to convert the same into organic nitrogen.

298. The________ refers to (in thermic or pulviometric terms) as the degree of temperature or millimetres of precipitation which distinguish normal from abnormal conditions.

299. The term________ refers to the largest ecological, system which includes all the organisms of the earth and the total environment.

300. The study of the plant community structure has been termed as________.

301. ________ deals with the application of ecological principles for a proper management of resources for high and sustained yield of useful biological materials for human welfare.

302. ________ and production ecology refer to the mechanism and quantum of energy conversions and its flow through organisms, production processes, rate of increase in biomass of organisms in relation to space and time both by green plants and animals.

303. The________ means the considerations of all the components simultaneously instead of the factor-wise conventional approach.

304. The terms ecosystem, biocoenosis, microcosm, holocoen and________ are equivalent terms.

305. There is self-regulatory mechanism in ecosystems of checks and balances and it is known as________.

306. The green plants called________ and the heterotrophic organisms as the secondary producers.

307. The close biotic interrelationships among the biotic components of the ecosystem are termed as commensalism, ________ and symbiosis.

308. ________ means the association of two different types of organisms (animals) to derive benefit from the other without a favourable or unfavourable effect on the benefactor.

309. ________ unlike the pyramids of number, biomass is always upright because the time factor is always taken into account.

310. The rate of conversion of trapped energy by green plants into organic materials from simple inorganic substances or increase in organic biomass is referred to as________

311. The total production due to photo or chemi-synthesis is gross productivity and deduction of respiratory losses from it equals________.

312. If the information on transfers between compartments are set in a tabular arrangement, it is known as transfer ________.

313. In the ecosystem, the control (cybernetics; kibernetes = pilot/governor) is diffused at all levels within the system and provides resistance as well as________.

314. The ratio of rate of reaction at a difference of 10°C is called________.

315. Most of the land plants thrive in wide range of temperatures (freezing to about 55°C) and are called________ as against stenothermic plants that thrive in a narrow range of temperatures.

316. The ice caps on the mountain tops and at the North and South poles have as much as 167 geogram in the form of ice and only about________ moves as vapour and clouds.

317. Out of the total estimated global rainfall of 857 mm, land and oceans receive________ per cent respectively.

318. Simmons (1974) estimated that the oceans receive the highest quantity of water in October when its level rises by 1-2 cm due to addition of about 7.5×10^{18} cm^3 water, whereas on land it is the highest in ________.

319. In India the rainfall is mostly of a special pattern of moist air movement called________.

320. The air masses in India move from the Arabian sea to the________ and from the Bay Bengal to the Eastern parts.

321. ________ has the aerial, under water or mud covered plant portions having aerechymatous tissues in gaseous continuations.

322. Roots of ________ growing in partially submerged conditions, show dimorphism.

323. Succulence in stems is common in the members of the plant families *Cactaceae* and________, while leaf-succulence in *Agavaceae*.

324. *Prospis juliflora* and *Acacia arabica* are the non-succulent shrubs which suffer from________ both in their internal and external environment.

325. The roots of some shrubs and small trees like *Prosopis cineria* (= P. *specigera*) may have ________ reaching more than 15 metres of depth.

326. ________ has been regarded as an effective way of conserving moisture due to reduced transpiring surface.

327. It has been estimated that on an average calcium storage is 365 and 203 kg/ha respectively in soil and________ pools.

328. In plant ecology, symbiotic associations include disjunctive and________ symbiosis wherein plants are not in constant contact and are in contact, respectively.

329. In lichens, the alga-fungus association is also present into their reproductive bodies called________.

330. ________ is exemplified by manufacture of food by algae, used by fungal component which protects the algae from drying up and thus to colonize dry rocks and tree barks.

331. In ________ the seeds germinate near the host plant and soon get attached to the root of the host.

332. The________ stem twines around a large variety of hosts and at contact points pierces their haustoria into the host tissue.

333. The host root of mustard grows much longer to establish contact with the root of *Orobanche* and such a mustard plant embodies more________ remains unexplained.

334. Roots of epiphytes often store water in special tissues called ________.

335. *Dischidia* has a remarkable adaptation to meet water requirement, its leaves fold and form a________ with a narrow mouth where water accumulates.

336. The woody stem of *Bauhinia vahlii* (a liana) is attached to the supporting tree, but not involved with it in a________

337. In________, found in humid forests of Assam (India) leaf lamina is folded and modified into a________ like structure, hence it is a plant known by that name.

338. In a pitcher plant the lid regulates entry and checks the exit of________ which are digested by some proteolytic enzymes.

339. In *Utricularia*, an aquatic insectivorous plant commonly found in India, is covered with________ wherein planktonic animals floating in water current enter and are ultimately digested.

340. If a species produces harmful substances for the life of another organism, it is called________.

341. When the individuals of the same species exert interference on one another, it is termed as________ competition unlike interspecific competition wherein two different species are involved.

342. The roots of certain plants produce certain chemicals, that inhibit the germination or growth of other species and this chemo-harming the population of other species is called ________.

343. The chemical secretions from one kind of organism into the inorganic medium (soil, water or air) and reaching and influencing other kind of organisms is termed as________.

344. ________ a fungus found in soil produces antibiotic substances that check the growth of number of variety of bacteria.

345. In allelochemic interactions, the chemical exudates or their decomposition products harm or depress one set of organisms, but the other set remains stable, is termed as ________

346. *Clerodendrum viscosum* has allelopathic effect on weeds *viz., Abutilon indicum, Cassia tora* and ________ *etc.*

347. Ecotypes are________ of the same species differentiated due to interplay of certain environmental conditions.

348. Plants always produce seeds in much larger number than the habitat could sustain if. all of them successfully ________

349. The seeds of coriander (*Coriandrum sativum*) are ________ .before sowing to ensure a higher percentage of germination.

350. The two seeds in each fruit of *Xanthium* often germinate in different seasons due to dormancy of one due to its ________ requirement.

351. ________ and their derivatives successfully inhibit the germination of a wide range of seeds.

352. ________ dormant seeds contain coumarins.

353. ________ are the plants of the same species which differ in appearance like size, erect or prostrate nature, reproductive vigour *etc.*

354. The plants ________ in disturbed conditions grow prostate but erect in undisturbed conditions.

355. ________ represents the ability of any population to increase through birth rate.

356. The ecological study of group attributes or population characteristics with respect to rates of birth, death, reproduction *etc.*, is called ________.

357. The range of environment that the *taxa* can tolerate is called ________.

358. Ecological ________ refers to the plant community character that is dynamic and changes in form and composition in the course of time.

359. A series of community changes ultimately result in the development of relatively stable community that retains its shape and composition indefinitely and virtually gets control over the area is called ________.

360. Large units representing an area of similar vegetation are often referred to ________.

361. ________ refers to zone of vegetation separating two different types of communities.

362. Zonal ________ organization of plants embodies a well defined area of physical habitat and has boundaries around it.

363. In a well defined zone, the plant communities as a whole exhibit group characteristics of its organization, growth and maturity, hence it is also known as ________.

364. The arrangement of plant communities in a series of environmental gradients wherein these communities are arranged in an order is called ________.

365. The place occupied by an organism is its habitat, and its habitat and functions performed thereby the organism is known as ________.

366. ________ niche represents the hyper volume that a population can fill in when there is no competition from any other plant population.

367. R.B. Root first proposed a term ________ which is now used for groups or clusters of plant species with an identical role in a community.

368. During the course of autogenic progression (succession), as observed, 'species diversity' decreases, but the 'pattern diversity, ________.

369. The plant species which have a strong control over energy flow and the environment in a given habitat are known as ecological ________.

370. In the origin and development of plant communities on a piece of bare land area starts with nudation followed by the arrival of diaspores, germination and ecesis, finally the process of ________.

371. ________ refers to an orderly sequence of plant or animal communities which occurs over a period of time at the same place.

372. The colonization of an area by organisms for the first time is known as ________.

373. The clearance of a colonized area regardless of the clearing agency, of the previous plants has been termed as ________.

374. Crop lands and other managed ecosystems wherefrom the primary production exceeds plant community respiration develop into ________ communities.

375. The climax serves as an indicator of climate which, in turn, indicates the ________ climax community of an area.

376. The quantity of solar energy goes on decreasing with increase in ________, both in Northern and Southern hemispheres.

377. About 20 per cent of the energy primarily fixed by green plants is lost as heat of________ and the rest goes to net production.

378. The range of change of energy content of a ________ is equal to the rate at which it absorbs the energy minus the rate of loss of energy from it.

379. CO_2 is taken up in green plants by RDP (a 5-carbon compound) and then broken in two molecules of ________ compound PGA, this pathway is called Calvin-Benson cycle (C-3 cycle).

380. If CO_2 first gets bound to PEP by its enzyme carboxylase (PEP-carboxylase) and a ________ compound OAA is formed. this pathway is known as Hatch-Slack or Hatch-Slack-Kortschak: cycle (C-4 cycle).

381. Maize and sugarcane are________ plants.

382. From PEP, OAA is formed which, in turn, gets converted into malic acid and gets stored in________ in succulent plants of Crassulaceae family.

383. In leaves of CAM plants, there exist very large vacuoles which serve as storage tank for ________ during night.

384. In C-4 plants ________ is limited to bundle sheath cells, whereas in C-3 plants all chloroplast containing cells carry on this process.

385. Leaf Area Index is the total area of the leaf (of one surface only) per unit area ________.

386. Use of radioisotopes especially C^{14} in the form of sodium bicarbonate ($NaHC^{14}O_3$) has been used to. measure the rate of primary production in ________.

387. The increase in production value either ceases or declines depending upon the type of plant species and prevailing conditions generally beyond ________.

388. Actual leaf are can be directly computed from length (L) and breadth (B) as $L \times B \times K$ where K is usually 0.9 and________ for narrow and broad leaves respectively.

389. Cultivated lands (worlds) occupy 14.0×10^6 km^2 and their approximate total annual production is ________.

390. Conservation ecology deals with practices and customs through which continuous yield of useful biological material is attempted and the ________ resources saved from degradation.

391. ________ means direct or indirect changes (usually but not always brought about by man) in one or more components of the ecosystem which are harmful to the system or at least undesirable to persons (organisms).

392. There are natural mechanisms of ________ through which the ecosystem self regulates and maintains, the ecological balance. .

393. When the forces of change are to severe, the________balance is upset leading to large scale ecological imbalances affecting the organisms and the man.

394. The present day oxygen' rich atmosphere has formed through an ________ brought about by the evolution of photosynthetic mechanism.

395. Atmosphere is responsible for maintain a narrow difference in the day and night ________, and provides a medium of sound transmission.

396. The chief pollutants are carbon monoxide, sulfur dioxide, certain ________ and particulate matter.

397. ________ accounts for more than fifty per cent of total weight of pollutants added to the atmosphere.

398. Carbon monoxide when inhaled combines with the ________ nearly 210 times faster than the oxygen does and results in oxygen deficiency.

amazon.in

Tax Invoice/Bill of Supply/Cash Memo
(Triplicate for Supplier)

Sold By :
Kulshrestha Suman
*

1-1-853, Siddharth Nagar, Kazipet-506004
WARANGAL, TELANGANA, 506004
IN

PAN No: DMBPK8592K
GST Registration No: NotApplicable

Billing Address :
BW ECOMMERCE PRIVATE LIMITED
Prop. No.4242, Ward No.11, Plot No.13, Gali No.
2, Ansari Ro, Central Delhi
NEW DELHI, DL, 110002
IN
GST Registration No: 07AAJCB8356L1Z4
State/UT Code: 07

Shipping Address :
BW ECOMMERCE PRIVATE LIMITED
Mohit Soni C/o Bw Ecommerce Pvt Ltd
2/19 Ansari Road,, Daryaganj
NEW DELHI, DELHI, 110002
IN
State/UT Code: 07
GST Registration No: 07AAJCB8356L1Z4
Place of supply: DL
Place of delivery: DELHI

Order Number: 405-8178900-7537118
Order Date: 20.07.2026

Invoice Number : IN-407
Invoice Details : TG-833090333-2627
Invoice Date : 20.07.2026

Sl. No	Description	Unit Price	Qty	Net Amount	Tax Rate	Tax Type	Tax Amount	Total Amount
1	Agriculture Question Bank with Answers (PB) | 8183601324 (3Q-B2DA-17JH)	₹250.00	1	₹250.00	0%	IGST	₹0.00	₹250.00
					0%	IGST	₹0.00	
					0%	None	₹0.00	
	Shipping Charges	₹110.00		₹110.00	0%	IGST	₹0.00	₹110.00
					0%	IGST	₹0.00	
					0%	None	₹0.00	
AL:							₹0.00	₹360.00

unt in Words:
Hundred Sixty only

For Kulshrestha Suman:

Authorized Signatory

ayable under reverse charge - No

Whether tax is p

399. The ________ second most common pollutant is harmful and causes diseases of eye, throat and lungs.

400. Sulfur dioxide enters the plant leaves through stomata, combines with water to form ________ in the intercellular species.

401. The sulfurous acid formed in plant leaves damages the membrane activity and converts chlorophyll 'a' into ________.

402. Lichens and some ________ have been found extremely sensitive to sulfur dioxide.

403. ________ allows solar radiation to pass through and strike earth's surface, but on its reradiation in the form of heat of infrared waves, it absorbs them and causes warming up.

404. The coal burning factories discharge________ gas.

405. It has been found that fluoride pollution reduces chlorophyll content biomass and leaf size of a forest tree, *Diospyros melanoxylon* in Mirzapur district of________ .

406. The leaves of fluoride affected *Diospyros melanoxylon* are used as________ in the manufacture of *biri* and thus reaches human lungs.

407. ________ are emitted in huge quantity by burning of petrol in the automobiles.

408. The combining of hydrocarbons with nitrous oxide produces________ smog.

409. ________ toxic effects on human beings and especially causes respiratory diseases.

410. ________ occurring in concenations higher than 15-20 ppm causes pollution.

411. ________, mixed in petrol as an antiknock agent comes out from the automobiles and is highly detrimental to human health.

412. PAN, a by product of ________ exhausts has been reported to suppress photosynthesis in plants.

413. The particles smaller than one micron are referred to as________, while those larger than one micron as dust (solids) or mist (liquids).

414. Particulates ________ reflect too much of light and reduce the visibility.

415. Cement dust falling on the leaf surface forms a hard crust after hydration and________.

416. Hard crust formed by cement dust on plant leaves disrupts the light absorption by chlorophyll and lowers the ________ .

417. The biological materials in the air namely bacteria, fungal spores, pollen grains *etc.*, often cause allergy and ________ troubles.

418. It has been estimated that the pollution load entering the air of calcutta and ________ (city of India) is as much as 1299 tonnes/day.

419. In a poorly oxygenated condition, with increased ________, fish, other animals and plants die and the clean river is turned into a stinking drain.

420. Among the pesticides________ used to control mosquitoes and agri-pests has become the most serious pollutant of soil and water.

421. ________ hydrocarbons are universal poisons, that is, are not very selective.

422. The________ of DDT and other identical pollutants means that the concentration of these harmful chemicals goes on increasing in successive trophic levels.

423. The pesticides gradually reach the ________ tissues of higher organisms including man and on breakdown of fats during respiration are released in the blood stream and cause toxic effects.

424. ________ are generally responsible for the spread of diseases like typhoid, dysentery and cholera.

425. An aquatic system depleted of oxygen suffers from the processes like anaerobiosis (fermentation of sugars and putrefication of proteins) which give rise to secondary________ .

426. The quantity of an' organic matter pollutant can be determined by________ of the volume of water in a water course or a body.

427. ________ also leads to pollution because the mat of algal blooms becomes quite thick.

428. ________ namely *Eichhornia Crassipes* and *Salvinia molesta* are also regarded as pollutants.

429. Ionising rediation cause muations, abnormality and________ in many organisms including man.

430. ________ the commonly used radioactive material in nuclear bombs has the half life of 24,360 years.

431. Fisson by products (both of nuclear detonation and water cooled atomic power reactors) consttute more of a potential hazard than direct ionizing radiation as they follow ________pathways.

432. If________ is present in sufficient quantity in the soil, radioactive strontium 90 is not taken up by the plants, but in its absence, strontium is absorbed.

433. The measurement of loudness on a logarithmic scale with reference of ten is called________.

434. *Decibel* or db refers to a ratio of ________ with reference to the softest audible sound.

435. The sound waves left behind by motor boats on water surface are known as________.

436. Sonic boom is expressed in________ unit and its number 1 equals the boom created by an object moving with the same speed as sound.

437. ________ refers to the botanical composition of a place, that is, the name of species.

438. Vegetation means the totality of forms in which the emphasis is not on names of________, but their life forms, number arid coverage *etc.*

439. The estimates postulate that there are approximately________ of flowering plants and 600 species of *Pteridophytes* in India.

440. The Indian flora is dominated by the families (of plants) Orchidaceae, Poaceae and ________.

441. If the life of earth so far is condensed to one year than the first man (*Homo sapiens*) the most recent creation of nature was born on ________ December at 10 p.m.

442. Molecule of water has a bent shape, ________ occupies centre with a negative charge and bent arms or two bonds with an atom of hydrogen on each with positive charge.

443. The bonded force in a water molecule is responsible for a high________ at normal pressure.

444. The average time usually required for one complete recycling of a water body is called________.

445. The turnover time for oceans is about 3,000 years and that of________ is 5,000 years.

446. Only about________ per cent of the toal incoming solar radiation is used in primary production.

447. Among the herbs, C_4 plants transpire ________ C_3 plants for each gramme of dry matter produced.

448. The________ may be sometimes as deep as 7-10 km or even more.

449. ________represent an ocotone or transification of mixing region of fresh and marine water.

450. The main sources of ________ pollution is by oil.

451. The problem of mercury pollutants has reached grave proportions in some ________ and Japanese sea water.

452. Carbonate content of hard water rivers has been estimated at 100 ppm or more as against less than 25 ppm of________ rivers.

453. Naturally occurring fresh and clean water appears colourless in shallow situations, but assumes________ tinge in deep or very deep conditions due to selective absorption of wave length of penetrating light.

454. ________ of a water sample is measured in terms of its relative strength, that is, upto which dilution level the smells remain detectable by human nose.

455. Threshold ______ and taste numbers (known as TTN and TON) are the measures to purify water by dilution with pure water.

456. The phenomenon of thermal pollution in water bodies is also known as ______.

457. Oxygen bubbles out of warming water and at times leads to trapping of fish that die of" ______ "

458. ______ of drinking water supposedly free of dissolved substances may be in the range of about 100-1000 μmhos/cm.

459. Hard water does not form lather with soap as the dissolved calcium and magnesium ______ present in it precipitate the soap.

460. When a dye ______ or calgamite is added to water (at pH 10) containing Ca and Mg, the water turns wine red.

461. There are two kinds of alkalinity in water *viz.*, caustic or ______ and total alkalinity.

462. ______ is an important property of warer which causes corrosiveness.

463. As the pH from 7 decreases to 6, 5, 4 and 3, the hydrogen ion concentration increases by 10, 100, 1000 and. respectively.

464. Dissolved oxygen in water is usually a critical factor and at times it may cause ______ and death of aquatic organisms.

465. The saturation level of dissolved oxygen is ______ ppm at 0°C in fresh, clean water and decreases with the rise in temperature reaching zero at 100°C.

466. More BOD means more microorganisms means the presence of more ______ pollution.

467. Carbon dioxide in free form evolved in water or as bicarbonate is usually abundant in ______ fresh and marine waters.

468. The importance of mercury as a pollutant was realized first in Japan in 1953 when ______ disease spread a causing 46 deaths.

469. Mercury consistently shows biological ______ in aquatic ecosystem.

470. Persons receive lead (Pb) through ______ and aquatic food chains and directly from air through inhalation.

471. Alga *Cladophora glomerata* and aquatic moss ______ are used as indicators of lead due to their. sensitivity.

472. Cadmium as a pollutant reaches the atmosphere through ______ ocean sprays, forest fires and weathering of rocks.

473. Cadmium reaches human bodies principally through food from ______ raised on cadmium enriched soil or irrigated by effected effluents.

474. People living in areas contaminated by cadmium, as in parts of Japan, long term consumption of rice grown on affected fields have caused a number of renal diseases *viz.*, ______, nephnitis and nephrosis.

475. It has been observed that Municipal sewage irrigated crops had twice or more ______ concentration than those irrigated by tube-well water.

476. Cadmium is associated with ______ in nature and enters into aquatic ecosystems from waste waters of eletroplating and chemical industries *etc.*

477. The toxic effects of ______ on plant life is on high concentrations only, while in traces it is stimulatory for a good growth.

478. Chromium (Cr) in ______ form is the most common contaminant of drinking water, while its trivalent form is not so common.

479. The maximum limit of chromium in________ as recommended by WHO is 0.05 mg/litre.
480. Chromium fumes in human beings may cause________ cancer.
481. Copper in small quantities is ________ essantial element both for plants and animals and an adult human about 2 mg or equivalent per day.
482. Copper sulphate with calcium carbonate is one of the commonest fungicides known as________.
483. Zinc is absorbed and accumulated in the body of ________ wherein its concentration in muscles has been estimated to be 863 times more than that in fresh water.
484. ________ is not a serious pollutant because in most of the waters its concentration is low ranging from 0.005 to 1.000 mg/litre of water.
485. ________ concentration exceeding 1mg/litre may cause a characteristic bitter sweet taste to drinking water.
486. High potassium content in drinking water may act as________.
487. Calcium richness of water is mostly dependent upon the ecology of________ and other belts through which water inflows into rivers or lakes.
488. The acceptable level of total________ in water is 0.03 to 0.40 mg/litre.
489. The organophosphates are________, that is, they do not kill only the target insects, but also effect other life forms and disrupt normal functioning of an ecosystem.
490. The continued________ leads to rapid upwelling of the water body.
491. ________ is the term to refer to chloride concentration and is usually expressed in grammes per kilogramme of water.
492. One litre of sea water is________ than one litre of fresh water.
493. In cities, the drinking water supply is________ to kill or deactivate water-borne disease causing bacteria and other microorganisms.
494. Sulphur is present in many characteristic________ plants like mustard, onion and garlic *etc.*
495. ________ is the important constituent of hard waters to form its salts with calcium and magnesium which reduce the quality of water.
496. ________ is among the most dominant air pollutant of the present day industrialized world.
497.________ is common in hot springs which are also known by its elemental name and putrefying the sewage wastes on decomposition.
498. ________ is rare form of sulphur in polluted water.
499. Agricultural runoff and infiltration are increasing the load of________ in surface and subsurface waters which may reach hazardous levels.
500. Though dissolved nitrates reach deep subsurface and ground waters in several years, the time when '________'will show its effect is not far away.
501. ________ water should not contain more than 10 mg/litre of nitrate nitrogen.
502. Many pesticides derived from tobacco and *Chrysanthemum* are non-persistent and________.
503. The biocides are basically meant to kill a very narrow range of undesirable organisms yet they can harm other________ organisms in the treated ecosystem.
504. The organic phosphate insecticides effect the nerve junction of insects by preventing the formation of________ between adjoining nerve cells.
505. Chlorinated hydrocarbon (insecticides like DDT) effects the central________ through which muscular tremors and convulsions occur.

506. Dead robin birds feeding on earthworm containing 80 ppm of DDT showed 120-750 ppm of DDT in their________, brain and liver.

507. ________ a metabolic derivative of DDT is found to affect fecundity, fertility and hatching success in birds.

508. There are scientists who say that DDT is not going to cause any human health problem as it may stabilize at ________ level in human fat (found upto 20 ppm in Israelis).

509. During 1976-78, the DDT residue in river Jamuna at Delhi was 0.249 ppm________ and 0.558 ppm in the downstream off Wazirabad.

510. Herbicidal sprays in rice fields profoundly effect the photosynthesis, respiration and nitrogen assimilating systems of________.

511. Organophosphates and carbamates directly attack on the enzyme________ of the nervous system of the animals.

512. Among the carbamates, methyl isocyanate [MIC (CH_3NCO)], as an environmental pollutant drew world-wide attention due to leakage from ________ factory Bhopal (M.P., India) on December 3, 1985.

513. ________ synthesis requires the use of phosgene ($COCl_2$), an extremely poisonous chemical.

514. Phenols, the organic pollutants are removed from the drinking water by treating with ozone or ammonia________.

515. A new group of pollutants of aquatic ecosystems are the synthetic________.

516. In recent years, there has been a switch over to a linear chain detergent known as linear alkylate sulphonate (LAS) which is easily________.

517. ________ is an ionic surfactant which produces a blue salt with methylene blue.

518. The phytoplankton smaller than 60 μm diameter are called________.

519. There are some animals which live at the water-air interface and are called________.

520. The aquatic animals which swim freely are known as________.

521. A ratio between faecal coliform and faecal streptococcus having a value less than 0.7 suggests that the pollution is from________ source.

522. The organic load of dead organic matter or sewage discharges on water bodies lead to explosive growth of many pathogenic microbes and outbreak of________.

523. Viruses from ________ sources also found to pollute water bodies.

524. Fungi are capable of breaking down a large variety of organic substances due to their wide ranging________ capability.

525. The fungus *Exophiala mansonii* causes ________ while *Trichosporium heteromonphum* causes pulmonary diseases.

526. The *Candida albicans* is found in the body of a large segment of human population without causing any disease.

527. Besides bacteria, viruses and fungi, a large variety of________ are also found in polluted waters and cause diseases in man and several animals.

528. Methane or ammonia are of comparable sizes as of________.

529. ________ a bacterium is responsible for cholera characterized by intense diarrhoea leading to dehydration and death.

530. In parts of Africa and parts of Asia one hundred million persons are affected by________ a disease caused by worms.

531. _______ from drinking water are removed with the help of *Nitrococcus denitrificans* and *Thiobacillus denitrificans* which dentrify and release nitrogen and water.

532. _______ is an 'ecosystem disease' and man is a part of ecosystem and not apart or outside it.

533. Plants get nitrogen in the form of nitrates and ammonium ions on its conversion by biological and _______ fixation.

534. Photochemical nitrogen fixation accounts for only about 35 mg/m^2/annum as against 14–700 mg/m^2/annum (even upto 20,000 mg/m^2/annum) through _______ fixation.

535. The quantity of carbon fixed by _______ annually on global basis ranges between 4–9 × 10^{13} kg.

536. Pollutants reach plants, animals and man, buildings, metalworks and paints *etc.*, and adversely effect the _______.

537. The air quality or pollution of any place is referred to as _______ or ambient pollution.

538. The species sensitive to a particular pollutant can be used an _______ of that pollutant.

539. The MIK in German, MAC in English refer to _______ in the air layer near the ground upto which it is harmless to man for short immission periods.

540. PSI is an index obtained by combining several pollution parameters *viz.*, total suspended particles, SO_2, CO_2, O_3 and NO_2 measured in μgm^3 on hourly/daily _______.

541. _______ is regarded as a natural sink for carbon monoxide pollution.

542. Several gases naturally present in earth's atmosphere absorb radiating out infra-red heat waves and reflect them back to the earth's surface causing its (air) warming known as _______.

543. Greenhouse effect at _______ is very essential for life to exist on this earth.

544. The estimates reveal that CO_2 content in atmosphere was approximately 270 ppm before 1850 which rose to _______ in 1985.

545. Chloroflurocarbons (CFCs) represent the chemicals _______ by man for use in several industries including refrigeration and they find their way into the atmosphere.

546. CFC 11 or _______ and CFI_2 (trade name Freon 12 or F_{12}) are the commonest of the CFCs.

547. The _______ form of CFC is suspected to damage the stratospheric ozone layer.

548. Even if CFC release rate in the atmosphere is not allowed to rise and maintained at a moderate rate, its concentration in air rises because it does not _______.

549. It has been estimated that if the CFC emission is totally stopped now, it will take about _______ to stop its migration from troposphere to stratosphere.

550. The rise in stratospheric water vapour is really a more important source of greenhouse effect than the direct effect of _______.

551. The temperature of 1.5-4.5°C due to green house effect will cause wheat and maize to suffer from _______ due to increased evaportranspiration.

552. _______ is a phytotoxic air pollutant gas of significant importance.

533. _______ of ozone in the atmosphere has been made possible by the use of ozone sensitive and ozone resistant pollen of tomato, *Petunia* and tobacco.

554. Plants recover a few weeks after the ozone exposure is _______.

555. In agricultural systems clover population is reported to decrease and _______ increase under 0.03-0.09 ppm ozone exposure for eight hours per day for over six weeks period.

556. A thick mantle/umbrella of ozone gas in the troposphere and lower atmosphere from about 16 to 40 km height at different latitudes shields against harmful effects of _______ coming from the sun.

557. Ultra-violet radiation of 280 to 320 nm wavelength called________ is most dangerous to plants, animals and man.

558. One________ atom can destroy several thousand ozone molecules before its conversion into hydrochloric acid and coming down as acid rain.

559. ________ like chlorine catalyzes the breakdown of ozone into oxygen.

560. N_2O produced by biological denitrification reaches the stratosphere, gets oxidized to NO which, in turn, catalyzes the________ of ozone.

561. It has been estimated that depletion of________ layer will lie about 2 per cent on global average and 8 per cent at 60°N latitude in the year 2030.

562. DNA and photosynthetic chemicals readily absorb UV-β rays and DNA disorders lead to mutation,________ and cancer development.

563. Depletion of thickness of________ is positively going to expose plants, animals and men to UV-β and adversely effect their yield, health and genetics.

564. ________ present in the atmosphere destroys chlorine monoxide and thereby checks ozone depletion.

565. ________ is a machine to produce ozone and it is solar powered, and can be taken up by balloons to plug the ozone hole.

566. The primary pathway of SO_2 entry in the plant body is throuth the________.

567. In plants SO_2 caused epidermal injury is of glazing and silvering of leaf surfaces; when these are not uniform, but spotted is called________.

568. SO_2 in combination with NO_2 even at low levels adversely affect growth, biomass and________ in oats, tobacco, tomato and radish.

569. SO_2 as such had no effect on________

570. SO_2 in combination with________ has been found to have synergistic effect on a number of plants.

571. It has been observed that SO_2 with HF act synergistically on maize and barley and causes bifacial________.

572. Usually for each tonne of coal burnt, there is 5-10 kg of________ emission.

573. It has been estimated that diesel and petroleum driven transports emit 25-30 kg of NO_2 per________ of fuel.

574. Higher concentration of NO_x embodies serious pollution property on extensive forest ecosystems as it is a precurssor of________ and ozone which are highly toxic to plants.

575. ________ is a gaseous hydrocarbon that has phytotoxic effects on plants.

576. Adverse effects on plants are seen when exposed to 30-50 ppm concentration of________.

577. *Gladiolus* is sensitive to________ air pollution and the photosynthesis is reduced.

578. The threshold limit value for MIC for man is________ and TD_{50} is 2 ppm in air.

579. Hydroxylamine or NH_2OH counteracts________ poisoning as it readily reacts and converts it into a safer compound.

580. Ormord (1984) has referred,________ to include solids, liquids or solid-liquid particles from 0.0005 to 500 μm diametre.

581. The fine and fibrous dust of asbestos enters the human nose and is reported to cause________ of the lungs.

582. The commonest pollutant gases in the indoor pollution are________.

583. In U.S.A. even________ is listed as an important indoor air pollutant.

584. It is necessary to prohibit________ inside the house or closed public halls or buses or trains or aeroplanes to reduce indoor pollution.

585. DDT reaches ________ *via* soil and air.

586. In India agricultural wastes are not ________ but, utilized in one or the other way unlike in U.S.A. where it is a major solid waste pollutor (about 2 billion tonnes per annum).

587. In________ the heterogeneous waste is reduced to simpler and more homogeneous mass on one hand and fuel gas on the other.

588. Nuclear energy is essentially done by taking 3 per cent of ^{235}U and 97 per cent of ^{230}U, ^{238}U, initiates neutron branch chain and ^{238}U captures, and produces________ and two electrons, this is technically called breeding.

589. ________is expressed in Curie [(Ci) (3.7×10^{10} atoms disintegrating/second or 2.2×10^{12}/minute)].

590. For________ purposes, radioactivity is expressed in terms of small units like millicurie (MCi) or 10^{-3} Ci) or________ or nanocurie (nCi or 10^{-9} Ci) or picocurie (PCi or 10^{-12} Ci).

591. Radiation unit is________ which is a dose of 100 ergs of energy absorbed/gramme of tissue and in biological studies millirad (mR 10^{-3}R) is used.

592. The radiation doses around________ rads kill the organism by damaging the tissues of heart and brain *etc.*

593. The first major legislation is the Environment Protection Act of ________ which empowers the Central Government to take necessary steps to protect and improve environment.

594. There are several enactments about the protection of environment in India, the most important being the Factories Act,________ and the Air Act of 1987 and Water Act of 1988 to enforce prevention of air and water pollution by factories.

595. Effluent and________ standards for 47 specific industries have been specified in India.

596. Special Act Plans (SAP) have been drawn up for the control of air and water pollution by________ in India.

II. Tick mark (✓) the correct answer:

597. ________ is the most important grain crop in the world.
(*a*) Maize (*b*) Sorghum
(*c*) Barley (*d*) Wheat

598. The great popularity of wheat is on account of________.
(*a*) Well balanced carbohydrates and proteins (*b*) Inability for complete mechanized production
(*c*) Short storage period of grain and flour storage (*d*) Limited to narrow range of climate

599. According to Vavilov (1951), the common bread wheats originated in
(*a*) The Caucasus-Turkey-Iraq area (*b*) Temperate zone of America
(*c*) Naturally fertile regions of France (*d*) Cool areas of China

600. Nitrogen fertilization in apples favours growth, but its excess________.
(*a*) Hastens maturity (*b*) Delays maturity
(*c*) Improves colour (*d*) Improves quality

601. More than________ per cent of earth's surface is covered by water in the form of seas, lakes and rivers.
(*a*) 40 (*b*) 50
(*c*) 60 (*d*) 70

602. Depending upon the temperature factor, the upper warmer region of lakes is called________.
(*a*) Epilimnion (*b*) Hypolimnion
(*c*) Thermocline (*d*) None of these

603. On the basis of productivity and fertility, the fertile and productive lakes have been classified as________

(*a*) Eutrotrophic (*b*) Oligotrophic
(*c*) Dystrophic (*d*) None of these

604. The marginal shallow region of a lake, where abundant light is avilable for plant growth is called ________.

(*a*) Limnetic zone (*b*) Profundal zone
(*c*) Littoral zone (*d*) None of these

605. The upper illuminated zone of lake is known as________.

(*a*) Compensation depth (*b*) Trophogenic
(*c*) Tropholytic (*d*) None of these

606. *Acacia Senegal* and *Alhagi camelorum* are the xerophytes belonging to________.

(*a*) Psammophytes (*b*) Psychrophytes
(*c*) Lithophytes (*d*) Halophytes

607. *Ceiba Parviflora* is a xerophyte that has the succulent________.

(*a*) Stems (*b*) Leaves
(*c*) Roots (*d*) Fruits

608. "The dominant species with maximum canopy coverage of two or more species" represents a community character known as________.

(*a*) Society (*b*) Location
(*c*) Consociation (*d*) Association

609. In________ the buds (life-forms) are invariably buried in the soil or the substratum as the bulbs and rhizomes.

(*a*) Chamaephytes (*b*) Crypto/geophytes
(*c*) Hemicryptophytes (*d*) Thermophytes

610. Secondary consequences of increasing elevation, both agronomically and economically significant are________.

(*a*) Decreased temperature (*b*) Decreased precipitation
(*c*) Decreased wind velocity (*d*) Increased soil fertility

611. "Diversion of water from mountain streams by diversion dams to canals of different length and breadth and ditches of varying size; and finally directed to individual fields" is an important practice in________.

(*a*) China (*b*) Egypt
(*c*) Philippines (*d*) Japan

612. The success or failure of the cropping season is determined by the intensity of________.

(*a*) Climatic factors (*b*) Political factors
(*c*) Social factors (*d*) None of these

613. The ideal conditions of temperature for crop production are between________.

(*a*) 12-18°C (*b*) 18-24°C
(*c*) 24-30°C (*d*) 30-36°C

614. The direct effect of strong winds on plants is of________ nature.

(*a*) Chemical (*b*) Biological
(*c*) Mechanical (*d*) None of these

615. Collective farming system has originated from________.
(a) Bulgaria
(b) Poland
(c) Soviet Union
(d) France

616. Commercial plantation farming comprises an________.
(a) Import-oriented system
(b) Export-oriented system
(c) Indigenous use-oriented system
(d) None of these

617. Agricultural growth is very soon likely to be hampered by scarcity of________.
(a) Natural resources
(b) Man-made resouces
(c) International cooperation
(d) Local coordination

618. The idea of a map showing the use of land was mooted in 1919 by________.
(a) Robert S. Plat
(b) A.J. Hunt
(c) Charles K. Paul
(d) Carl O. Sauer

619. A set of shared, similar characteristics (as applied to logically deduced and symbolically expressed models and observations) may be called as________.
(a) Negative isomorphism
(b) Positive isomorphism
(c) Neutral isomorphism
(d) None of these

620. At present, human population of the world is increasing approximately at the of________ persons per thousand per year.
(a) 10
(b) 15
(c) 20
(d) 25

621. Rubber has probably the________ range of tolerance for temperature.
(a) Narrowest
(b) Widest
(c) Medium
(d) None of these

622. The requirement and tolerances of a species may be considered as________.
(a) Supplementary
(b) Complementary
(c) Antagonistic
(d) None of these

623. Altitude, because of its________ effects, induces a zonation of vegetation similar to that found through a wide range of latitude.
(a) Humidity
(b) Radiation
(c) Temperature
(d) None of these

624. Rice, maize and sugarcane are replaced by temperate zone species at elevations of possibly________.
(a) 1000-3000'
(b) 4000-6000'
(c) 7000-9000'
(d) None of these

625. The principle that in modern times "the distribution of plant species on the the earth is not uniform" was established by________.
(a) Charles Darwin
(b) De Candolle
(c) Nikolai Vavilov
(d) Carl Von Linnaeus

626. Vavilov recognised primary centres of probable origin of cultivated plants numbering________.
(a) 4
(b) 5
(c) 8
(d) 10

627. Species and subdivisions in plants were designated respectively as Linneons and Jordanons by________.
(a) W.F. Libby
(b) L.P. Lotsy
(c) R.E. Reeves
(d) M.Y. Nuttonson

628. The settled village community farming based on small grain and animal domestication occurred in Near East about________ years ago.
(*a*) 5,000 (*b*) 7,500
(*c*) 10,000 (*d*) 10,500

629. Biogeochemical nutrient cycles have led to recognise that________ is very important.
(*a*) Balanced fertilization (*b*) Over fertilization
(*c*) Under fertilization (*d*) None of these

630. ________ nonessential elements in the ecosystem may accumulate at undesirable levels________..
(*a*) Normally (*b*) Occasionally
(*c*) Mostly (*d*) Invariably

631. At 0°C water is in equilibrium with a water vapour pressure of________ mm of mercury.
(*a*) 2.58 (*b*) 3.58
(*c*) 4.58 (*d*) 5.58

632. The atmosphere over one square foot of earth's surface at the Equator will contain approximately________ pounds of water vapour.
(*a*) 20 (*b*) 30
(*c*) 40 (*d*) 50

633. It has been found that peas will remain in good harvest condition twice as long at________ °F than at 80°F.
(*a*) 32 (*b*) 42
(*c*) 52 (*d*) 62

634. The changes that accompany hardening of plants include________.
(*a*) Increased sugar concentration (*b*) Decreased soluble proteins
(*c*) Decreased osmotic pressure (*a*) Decreased bound water

635. Cacao, a tropical plant has been found to produce the maximum growth in approximately________ of full sunlight.
(*a*) 5% (*b*) 10%
(*c*) 15% (*d*) 25%

636. When white light is passed through a prism, it is dispersed into different wavelengths of various colours and the orange colour appears at________.
(*a*) 435-490 mm (*b*) 574-595 mm
(*c*) 400-435 mm (*d*) 595-626 mm

637. It has been demonstrated that the________ light present in the white light prevents maximal growth rate.
(*a*) Blue (*b*) Red
(*c*) Green (*d*) Violet

638. Wavelengths longer than________ m/μ are not visible to the eye, and are called infrared.
(*a*) 450 (*b*) 550
(*c*) 650 (*d*) 750

639. It has been observed that in a number of outbreeding populations of rye grass, *Lolium perenne* could be brought about at low temperature (0-3°C) or________.

(*a*) Long day (*b*) Short day
(*c*) Intermediate day (*d*) None of these

640. In________long days promote bulb formation whereas, short days promote flowering and seed production.

(*a*) Sweet Potato (*b*) Artichoke
(*c*) Cassava (*d*) Onion

641. The________ variety Maryland Mammoth in the latitude of Maryland (U.S.A.) produces only leaves and needs shorter days for seed production.

(*a*) Tomato (*b*) Carrots
(*c*) Radish (*d*) Tabacco

642. Beyond the lower atmosphere, extending out into space, is the stratosphere, in which temperature remains relatively constant from________.

(*a*) – 15 to – 25 (*b*) – 45 to – 75
(*c*) – 80 to – 95 (*d*) – 5 to – 10

643. One of the characteristics of the stratosphere is the occurrence of a well-marked layer having an increased concentration of ________ at about 20 miles (32 kms) above sea level.

(*a*) Carbon dioxide (*b*) Carbon monoxide
(*c*) Ozone (*d*) Hydrogen

644. In the ozone layer, the ozone content does not exceed________ppm at 20 miles (32 kms) above sea level (stratosphere).

(*a*) 5 (*b*) 10
(*c*) 15 (*d*) 20

645. The gaseous mixing in the atmosphere is, in general, similar at sea level and at heights upto________km.

(*a*) 20 (*b*) 40
(*c*) 60 (*d*) 80

646. Ozonated hexane led to disruption of________in plants.

(*a*) Membrane permeability (*b*) Protein synthesis
(*c*) Lipid synthesis (*d*) Stem elongation

647. The spray drift of 2,4-D (ester form) can cause considerable damage in________.

(*a*) Maize (*b*) Rice
(*c*) Sorghum (*d*) Cotton

648. Animals and nongreen plants continually use oxygen and liberate________ into the air.

(*a*) Sulfur dioxide (*b*) Carbon monoxide
(*c*) Carbon dioxide (*d*) Nitrous oxide

649. The rate of photosynthesis under the condition of high light intensity may be controlled by________.

(*a*) Light (*b*) Carbon dioxide
(*c*) Water (*d*) None of these

650. North of the equator, surface winds are known as________.

(*a*) Northeast trade winds (*b*) Southeast winds

(*c*) Westerlies (*d*) Easterlies

651. In the humid tropics and subtropics the process of weathing (soil formation) is known as_________..

(*a*) Podzolization (b) Glezation

(*c*) Latosolization (*d*) None of these

652. The soils without a well developed soil profile characteristics are known as azonal soil and include ________.

(*a*) Planosols (*b*) Latosols

(*c*) Lithosols (*d*) None of these

653. Geological distribution of clay minerals is of considerable importance, southern clays (U.S.A.) are predominantly.

(*a*) Illite (*b*) Kaolinite

(*c*) Montmorillonite (*d*) None of these

654. Greasewood (vegetation) is found on desert soils where _________ problem prevails.

(*a*) Salinity (*b*) Acidity

(*c*) Alkalinity (*d*) Neutrality

655. The cactus from North America and the jack rabbit from Europe were introduced into________.

(*a*) Holland (*b*) Poland

(*c*) Austria (*d*) Australia

656. When competition effect is small for both the plant species so that the interspecific effects are_________ the intraspecific effects, both species may be able to live together.

(*a*) More than (*b*) Equal to

(*c*) Less than (*d*) None of these

657. The self-crowding effects represent the________ competition.

(*a*) Interspecific (*b*) Intraspecific

(*c*) Intergeneric (*d*) Intrageneric

658. The interplant competition drastically affects the________ of the plant.

(*a*) Size and shape (*b*) Number and size

(*c*) Number and shape (*d*) None of these

659. The nodules in_________ plants tend to be large, pinkish, fleshy, singly or in clusters about the tap roots or the first formed lateral roots.

(*a*) Biennials (*b*) Perennials

(*c*) Annuals (*d*) All of these

660. The identification of haemoglobin in legume root nodules has been made by Kubo (1931) through its characteristic_________ band maxima of 575 mμ and 540 mμ and by comparing with haemoglobin of the horse.

(*a*) Reflection (*b*) Deflection

(*c*) Absorption (*d*) Adsorption

661. Nodule haemoglobin appeared to have the typical haemoprotein characteristic of taking up and giving off________.

(*a*) Carbon dioxide (*b*) Hydrogen

(*c*) Nitrogen (gas) (*d*) Oxygen

662. The malecular nitrogen in a root nodule is reduced to_______ , from which it changes rapidly to amino acids.
(*a*) Ammonium.
(*b*) Ammonia
(*c*) Nitrate
(*d*) Nitrite

663. _______ of Austria first in 1918 published the climatic classification based an annual and monthly means of temperature.
(*a*) Wladimir Koppen-Geiger
(*b*) Rudolf Geiger
(*c*) Trewartha Geiger
(*d*) Geiger Hellman

664. Banana (*Musa Sapientum*) plant is an herbaceous_______ which may grow to a height of about 30 feet.
(*a*) Annual
(*b*) Biennial
(*c*) Perennial
(*d*) None of these

665. _______ has been the world's leading producer of cane suger.
(*a*) India
(*b*) Indonesia
(*c*) Hawaii
(*d*) Cuba

666. The range of coffee production is limited approximately by the _______ °F of isotherms for the coldest month.
(*a*) 25
(*b*) 35
(*c*) 45
(*d*) 55

667. Cotton has been grown in India as a crop of fibre for perhaps_______ years and was known in Peru as early as 1000 B.C.
(*a*) 3,000
(*b*) 4,000
(*c*) 5,000
(*d*) 6,000

668. The diversity pertaining to a plant composition in several plant communities in one range of environment is known as_______.
(*a*) Alpha index of diversity
(*b*) Beta index of diversity
(*c*) Gamma index of diversity
(*d*) None of these

669. Among the types of natural succession, the one which begins in water is known as_______.
(*a*) Xerarch (xerosere)
(*b*) Halosere
(*c*) Hydrarch (hydrosere)
(*d*) Psammosere

670. When one batch seral species react with the environment to. facilitate the entry of a new set of species, such a model is known as_______.
(*a*) Inhibition model
(*b*) Tolerance model
(*c*) Facilitation model
(*d*) Elucidation model

671. In the earth's atmosphere at _______ cal/cm^2/annum of solar energy is received.
(*a*) 15×10^6
(*b*) 15×10^8
(*c*) 15×10^{10}
(*d*) 15×10^{12}

672. Which of the following crops utilizes even upto 10-12 per cent of the total solar energy.
(*a*) Sorghum
(*b*) Rice
(*c*) Maize
(*d*) Sugarcane

673. Fixation of each gramme of carbon from carbon dioxide to organic compounds during photo synthesis traps_______ of solar energy.
(*a*) 124 kcal
(*b*) 134 kcal
(*c*) 144 kcal
(*d*) 154 kcal

674. C-3 plants show a light saturation upto 40,000 to 50,000 lux, while C-4 plants upto full sun in trapics upto________.

(a) 60,000-70,000 (b) 70,000-80,000

(c) 90,000-100,000 (d) 115,000-120,000

675. ________ pollutants are very harmful for human health and therefore such polluted waters should essentially be purified before their supply for drinking purposes.

(a) Biological (b) Physical

(c) Mechanical (d) Metallic

676. Ionising ________ are very important and harmful pollutants.

(a) Reflections (b) Deflections

(c) Radiations (d) Absorptions

677. The sounds beyond ________ dB are regarded as pollutant as it harms hearing ability.

(a) 60 (b) 80

(c) 100 (d) 120

678. If all the moisture present in the air at any one time is converted into precipitation, it would be equal to 2.5 cm or about ________ of water supply by precipitation (average residence time).

(a) 5 days (b) 10 days

(c) 15 days (d) 20 days

679. About 2.5 cm rainfall may be sufficient to produce over 10 tonnes of stream flow water on a watershed area of about________ m^2.

(a) 3,000 (b) 4,000

(c) 5,000 (d) 6,000

680. Fresh water bodies like rivers and streams are known as________.

(a) Palustrine (b) Lotic or riverine

(c) Lentic or lacustrice (d) None of these

681. On of the basis of temperature variation in the vertical column of water, or thermal stratification, lake ecosystems have been. divided into the following zones wherein________ comes in direct contact of sun and wind.

(a) Thermocline (b) Hypolimnion

(c) Epilimnion (d) None of these

682. Mercury level of ________μg Hg/g of fresh weight of fish is considered unsafe for human consumption.

(a) 0.5-1.0 (b) 1.6-2.0

(c) 2.1-2.5 (d) 2.6-3.0

683. Fish absorbs and may accumulate zinc in muscles amounting approximately upto________ times more than that in sea water.

(a) 3,700 (b) 4,700

(c) 5,700 (d) 6,700

684. Permissible limit of iron in drinking water is________.

(a) 1 ppm (b) 1.5 ppm

(c) 2.0 ppm (d) 2.5 ppm

685. Potassium in natural waters never assume toxic proportions and remains less than_____ mg/litre.

(a) 10 (b) 15
(c) 20 (d) 25

686. When with chloride ion in drinking water, the dominant cation is potassium or magnesium, the salty taste is not felt even upto_____ mg/litre.

(a) 500 (b) 750
(c) 1,000 (d) 1,250

687. The characteristic pungent odorous taste of onion is due to_____.

(a) Magnesium (b) Calcium
(c) Potassium (d) Sulphur

688. Many factory waters contain_____ mg/litre of nitrate nitrogen.

(a) 20 (b) 30
(c) 40 (d) 50

689. Chlorine added to drinking water supply when encountered with_____ gets neutralized and chloroamines are formed.

(a) Nitrous oxide (b) Carbon dioxide
(c) Methane (d) Ammonia

690. The nitrate content say in the range of 30 to 40 mg/litre lead to poor oxynation of blood haemoglobin and blood turns_____.

(a) Blackish (b) Whitish
(c) Bluish (d) Yellowish

691. In a study in U.S.A., the earthworms inhabiting a foliarly fed DDT-tree, contained upto 80 ppm of DDT even after_____ months.

(a) 5 (b) 7.5
(c) 10 (d) 10.5

693. The coliform bacteria count in drinking water is regarded safe if it is_____.

(a) 5 or less (b) 10 or less
(c) 15 or less (d) 20 or less

694. The PSI value range_____ has been classified as hazardous (air) causing premature on set of certain diseases and aggravation of symptoms.

(a) 200-299 (b) 300-399
(c) 100-199 (d) 50-100

695. Methane gas once released in the atmosphere stays for_____ years.

(a) 3-4 (b) 4-5
(c) 5-7 (d) 8-10

696. The earth during the last one century has warmed up by_____ °C as estimated.

(a) 0.3-0.7 (b) 0.8-1.0
(c) 1.2-1.3 (d) 1.4-1.5

697. The earth temperature during the past 20,000 years has risen by_____ °C.

(a) 2-3 (b) 4-5
(c) 6-7 (d) 8-9

698. Ultraviolet radiations are of smaller wavelengths than of visible light and those ranging from 320-400 nm are called ________.

(*a*) UV-C (*b*) UV-B

(*c*) UV-A (*d*) UV-D

699. CFCs, methane and nitrogen oxide gases have the capacity to react with ozone to convert into ________.

(*a*) Nitrogen (*b*) Hydrogen

(*c*) Oxygen (*d*) None of these

700. The estimates reveal that the maximum NO_2 emission in European countries is in________ in the range of 2Tg/annum (Teragramme = 10^{12} grammes).

(*a*) France (*b*) Germany

(*c*) England (*d*) None of tnese

701. The threshold concentration upto which no visible injury symptoms appear on plants due to NO_2 is 1 mg/m^3 on ________.

(*a*) Daily average (24 Hrs) (*b*) Weekly average

(*c*) Monthly average (*d*) Annual average

702. The suggested threshold level of fluoride pollution in atmosphere is ________ ppm.

(*a*) 10-40 (*b*) 50-80

(*c*) 90-100 (*d*) 110-115

703. Uranium contributes the radioactivity of about________ pci/litre of ocean water.

(*a*) 2 (*b*) 3

(*c*) 4 (*d*) 5

704. The Department of Environment in Independent India was formed in________ November.

(*a*) 1960 (*b*) 1970

(*c*) 1980 (*d*) 1990

705. Serious efforts on environmental protection in India began with the establishment of NCEPC by the Department of Science and Technology in February________.

(*a*) 1952 (*b*) 1962

(*c*) 1972 (*d*) 1982

706. Environmental Protection Act of 1986 came into force in India on ________, 1986.

(*a*) October 19 (*b*) November 19

(*c*) September 19 (*d*) August 19

707. In December, 1989 standards were laid for the noise limits in day and night time in various area and silence zones upto________ around educational institutions, hospitals and courts in India.

(*a*) 50 m (*b*) 100 m

(*c*) 150 m (*d*) 1200 m

707. (*a*) Beaufort scale is used for measuring ________.

(*a*) Water content (*b*) Wind pressure/strength

(*c*) texture (*d*) Radiation

707. (*b*) National Diversity Board is situated at ________.

(*a*) Chennai (*b*) Kolkata

(*c*) New Delhi (*d*) Mumbai

III. Match the following:

708. Match the wheat species with the with common name.

(*a*) T. monococcum	(*i*) Emmer
(*b*) T. decoccum	(*ii*) Club wheat
(*c*) T. turgidum	(*iii*) Einkorn
(*d*) T. compactum	(*iv*) Rivet wheat

709. Match the maize (corn) types with the botanical name.

(*a*) Pod corn	(*i*) Zea mays amylacea
(*b*) Flour corn	(*ii*) Zea mays everta
(*c*) Pop corn	(*iii*) Zea mays indurata
(*d*) Flint corn	(*iv*) Zea mays tunicata

710. Match the white light passed through a prism with dispersion into wavelengths of different colours.

(*a*) Violet	(*i*) 574-595 millimicrons
(*b*) Blue	(*ii*) 490-574 millimicrons
(*c*) Green	(*iii*) 435-490 millimicrons
(*d*) Yellow	(*iv*) 400-435 millimicrons

711. The seeds of many plants are sensitive to light for germination, match as per their light requirement.

(*a*) Lettuce	(*i*) Need darkness
(*b*) Carrot	(*ii*) Slight stimulation
(*c*) Vanilla fragrance	(*iii*) Stimulated
(*d*) Tobacco	(*iv*) Favoured

712. Match the following plants with their response to photoperiod.

(*a*) Potato	(*i*) Short day
(*b*) Chrysanthemum	(*ii*) Day neutral
(*c*) Sweet potato	(*iii*) Intermediate day length
(*d*) Sugarcane	(*iv*) Long day

713. Match the Beaufort descriptive terms with the wind velocity expressed in miles per hour.

(*a*) Gentle breeze	(*i*) 25-31
(*b*) Strong breeze	(*ii*) >75
(*c*) Strong gale	(*iii*) 8-12
(*d*) Hurricane	(*iv*) 47-54

714. Match the subprovinces set up by Thornthwaite (1931) with summer concentration of temperature, which varies with latitude from 25 per cent at the equator to 100 per cent in the permanent frost climate.

(*a*) 'a'	(*i*) 50-69
(*b*) 'b'	(*ii*) 70-99
(*c*) 'c'	(*iii*) 25-34
(*d*) 'd'	(*iv*) 35-49

715. Match the thermal efficiency with the climatic types according to the classification of temperature efficiency done by Thornthwaite.

(*a*) 5.1" TEI (PET in inches) (*i*)	(*i*) Microthermal
(*b*) 111.22" TEI (PET in inches)	(*ii*) Tundra
(*c*) 16.83" TEI (PET in inches)	(*iii*) Megathermal
(*d*) 44.88" TEI (PET in inches)	(*iv*) Frost

716. Match the crops with their optimum temperature (°F) for germination.

(*a*) Wheat	(*i*) 89-95
(*b*) Maize	(*ii*) 86
(*c*) Peas	(*iii*) 86-90
(*d*) Rice	(*iv*) 77

717. Match the albeds values (%) with the type of earth's surface.

(*a*) 0.260	(*i*) Oak woodland
(*b*) 0.175	(*ii*) Bare moist sand
(*c*) 0.140	(*iii*) Grass surface
(*d*) 0.0.90	(*iv*) Pine forest

718. Match the gradient of diffusion pressure gradient from soil to plant to air.

(*a*) Soil near field capacity	(*i*) 5.0-6.0
(*b*) Roots at zero turgor	(*ii*) 140.5
(*c*) Leaves at zero turgor	(*iii*) 0.1
(*d*) Air at 90% relative humidity	(*iv*) 10.0-30.0

719. Match climate classes of tropical Latin America "as classified by Sapper and James (1959) on the basis of altitude and agricultural crops", with the condition of the land.

(*a*) Jierra caliente	(*i*) Hot
(*b*) Jierra templada	(*ii*) Frost
(*c*) Jierra fria	(*iii*) Cool
(*d*) Jierra helada	(*iv*) Temperature

720. Match the crops with climatic zones (classes).

(*a*) Caliente	(*i*) Rice and maize
(*b*) Templada	(*ii*) Alpine pastures
(*c*) Fria	(*iii*) Rubber and coffee
(*d*) Helada	(*iv*) Wheat and barley

721. Match the height above sea-level of perpetual snow cover with the region where these are found.

(*a*) 4880-6100 m	(*i*) Alps and Pyrenees
(*b*) 4575 m	(*ii*) Himalayas
(*c*) 2440-3050 m	(*iii*) Near the squator
(*d*) 1220 m	(*iv*) N. Scandinavia

722. Match names of shifting cultivation commonly used in various countries.

(*a*) Ladang	(*i*) Central America and Mexico
(*b*) Caingin	(*ii*) Brazil
(*c*) Roca	(*iii*) Philippines
(*d*) Milpa	(*iv*) Indonesia

723. Match the Indian provinces with the name(s) of the shifting cultivation being used therein.

(*a*) Jhum or Jum	(*i*) Western Ghats
(*b*) Kumari	(*ii*) Northeast India
(*c*) Watra	(*iii*) Madhya Pradesh
(*d*) Penda, Bewar, Dahia or Deppa	(*iv*) Southeast Rajasthan

724. Match the basic Indian agricultural systems with the areas of their practice.

(*a*) Rice region	(*i*) Kashmir and Himachal Pradesh
(*b*) Wheat region	(*ii*) Deccan plateau, Peninsula arid Rajasthan, Haryana
(*c*) Millet region	(*iii*) Large part of northeastern and southeastern India
(*d*) Temperate Himalayan region	(*iv*) North-West India

725. Match the agricultural systems given below with the spatial spread.:

(*a*) Coconut, horticulture fine food olericulture	(*i*) U.P., Himalayas, W.E. Plains of U.P., uplands of U.P.
(*b*) Fine and coarse grain forming	(*ii*) Karnataka High Plateau
(*c*) Millet dominance, wheat forming in summer	(*iii*) North Kashmir Himalayas
(*d*) Ragi dominance, dry forming	(*iv*) Southern plains of kerala, South Kerala Hills

726. Match the categories of soil productivity and potentiality rating done by nine factor method.

(*a*) Excellent	(*i*) 8-19
(*b*) Good	(*ii*) 35-64
(*c*) Average	(*vi*) 65-100
(*d*) Below the average	(*iv*) 20-34

727. Match the following crops with their centres of origin.

(*a*) Maize	(*i*) New World
(*b*) Rubber	(*ii*) Africa
(*c*) Coffee	(*iii*) South America
(*d*) Grain amaranths	(*iv*) Middle America (Mexico-Guatemala)

728. Match the following four elements of an ecosystem with their components.

(*a*) Abiotic substances	(*i*) Green plants (autotrophic organisms)
(*b*) Producers	(*ii*) Animals (heterotrophic organisms)
(*c*) Consumers	(*iii*) Bacteria and fungi (heterotrophic organisms)
(*d*) Decomposers	(*iv*) Basic inorganic and inorganic substances

729. Match the relative humidity (%) and the vapour pressure (mm of mercury) recorded at 20°C.

(*a*) 10%	(*i*) 5.26
(*b*) 20%	(*ii*) 1.75
(*c*) 30%	(*iii*) 7.02
(*d*) 40%	(*iv*) 3.51

730. Match the vapour pressure deficit (mm of mercury) with the relative humidity (%) recorded at 20°C.

(*a*) 11.88	(*i*) 60
(*b*) 14.26	(*ii*) 80
(*c*) 16.63	(*iii*) 50
(*d*) 19.01	(*iv*) 70

731. Match the percentage of total land area in the world with the climatic classes.

(*a*) 55	(*i*) Sub-humid
(*b*) 20	(*ii*) Wet
(*c*) 11	(*iii*) Arid and semi-arid
(*d*) 14	(*iv*) Humid

732. Match the climate-classes with the average annual rainfall (range) received by them.

(*a*) Semi-arid and arid	(*i*) 500-1000 cm
(*b*) Sub-humid	(*ii*) 1000-3000 cm
(*c*) Humid	(*iii*) >3000 cm
(*d*) Wet	(*iv*) <500 cm

733. Match the following common names of wheat with the species.

(*a*) Shot wheat	(*i*) *T. Durum*
(*b*) Common wheat	(*ii*) *T. Sphaerococcum*
(*c*) Durum wheat	(*iii*) *T. Polonicum*
(*d*) Polish wheat	(*iv*) *T. Vulgare*

734. Match the primary productivity of the following field crops based on world average of cultivated and natural ecosystems, expressed in grammes per square metre per annum.

(*a*) Wheat	(*i*) 359
(*b*) Oats	(*ii*) 497
(*c*) Maize	(*iii*) 344
(*d*) Rice	(*iv*) 412

735. Match the primary productivity (range of values found in major environments of the world) expressed in grammes per square metre per day.

(*a*) Less than 0.5	(*i*) Open oceans (Probably deep lakes too)
(*b*) Less than 1.5	(*ii*) Continental shelf ocean wheats
(*c*) 0.5-5.0	(*iii*) Intensive agriculture
(*d*) 5.0-20.0	(*iv*) Deserts and semi-arid gross lands

736. Match the following plants with their climate/elevation of adaptation and growth.

(*a*) *Shorea robusta*	(*i*) Above 4000 m
(*b*) *Pinus roxburghii*	(*ii*) Around 3000 m
(*c*) *Cedrus deodara*	(*iii*) Warm and humid Himalayas
(*d*) *Rhododendrons*	(*iv*) Above 1500 m

737. Match the moving water in the form of hydrologic cycle in terms of geograms (One geogram = 10^{20} grammes).

(*a*) 11,300	(*i*) Runoff from land to sea
(*b*) 3.4	(*ii*) Evaporates
(*c*) 3.8	(*iii*) In the oceans
(*d*) Rest	(*iv*) Returns as rain

738. Match the global water availability of about 817 million cubic miles or one quadrillium acre feet, and loss through various processes.

(*a*) 83,700 cubic miles	(*i*) Moves with wind currents
(*b*) 9900 cubic miles	(*ii*) Recharges soil
(*c*) 900 cubic miles	(*iii*) Evaporates
(*d*) 2,100 cubic miles	(*iv*) Runs to oceans & underground flons

739. Match the following sub-divisions with the plants classified as macrophytes belonging to hydrophytes.

(*a*) Cyperus spp.	(*i*) Rooted hydrophytes, floating leaves
(*b*) Hydrilla	(*ii*) Marginal emergent hydrophytes
(*c*) Victoria amagonica	(*iii*) Submerged rooted hydrophytes
(*d*) Echhornia crassipes	(*iv*) Free-floating hydrophytes

740. Match the following soils with their agency of transportation.

(*a*) Alluvial	(*i*) Gravity
(*b*) Colluvial	(*ii*) Wind
(*c*) Glacial	(*iii*) River or running water
(*d*) Eolianor less	(*iv*) Ice or glaciers

741. Match the fate of calcium (on annual basis) with the agencies working on it.

(*a*) 50 kg/ha	(*i*) Replenished by weathering
(*b*) 8 kg/ha	(*ii*) Replenished by rain
(*c*) 5 kg/ha	(*iii*) Lost by stream out-flow
(*d*) 3 kg/ha	(*iv*) Exchanged between soil and biotic pools

742. Match the viability of the seeds of different plants as has been estimated by various sources.

(*a*) Shorea robust	(*i*) One thousand years
(*b*) Mimosa glomerata	(*ii*) A few weeks only
(*c*) Lens esculenta	(*iii*) More than 100 years
(*d*) Nelumbo nuicifera (Indian loturs)	(*iv*) Upto 50 years

743. Match the forest class with the altitude (Metres) in a tropical belt between 0 to 20° latitude.

(*a*) Tropical	(*i*) 1000-2000 m
(*b*) Sub-tropical	(*ii*) 4000-6000m
(*c*) Temperate	(*iii*) Upto 1000 m
(*d*) Arctic/Alpine	(*iv*) 2000-4000 m

744. Match the following phanerophytes with the height attained by the matured plant (tree/shrub/ climber).

(*a*) Megaphanerophytes	(*i*) 2-8 m
(*b*) Mesophanerophytes	(*ii*) <2 m
(*c*) Microphanerophytes	(*iii*) >30 m
(*d*) Nanophanerophytes	(*iv*) 8-30 m

745. Match the leaf size with its class as per the plant classification done by C. Raunkiaer (1934). Leaf size of each class is nine times larger than the preceding class.

(*a*) Leptophyll	(*i*) 2025 mm^2
(*b*) Nanophyll	(*ii*) 20 mm^2
(*c*) Microphyll	(*iii*) 225 mm^2
(*d*) Mesophyll	(*iv*) 18,225 mm^2

746. Match the natural succession with the substrata where it begins.

(*a*) Lithosere	(*i*) Saline area
(*b*) Halosere	(*ii*) Sand
(*c*) Psammosere	(*iii*) Water
(*d*) Hydrosere	(*iv*) Rock

747. Match the area and biomass productivity of ocean and terrestrial vegetation.

(*a*) Oceans	(*i*) 155 $g/m^2/yr$
(*b*) Biomass production (oceans)	(*ii*) 361×10^6 km^2
(*c*) Terrestrial vegetation	(*iii*) 730 $g/m^2/yr$
(*d*) Biomass production (Terrestrial vegetation)	(*iv*) 149×10^6 km^2

748. It has been estimated by the National Engineering Research Institute, Nagpur that the gaseous pollutants entering Kolkata and Howrah (900 + 405 = 1305 tonnes/day), of which ________ tonnes are ________ and 70 tonnes are oxides of nitrogen/day.

(*a*) Suspended particles	(*i*) 450
(*b*) Carbon monoxide	(*ii*) 123
(*c*) Sulfur dioxide	(*iii*) 102
(*d*) Hydrocarbons	(*iv*) 560

749. Match the dust loads as estimated by Datta (1984) for various metropolitan cities in kg/ m^3

(*a*) Kolkata	(*i*) 280
(*b*) Delhi	(*ii*) 221
(*c*) Chicago	(*iii*) 527
(*d*) London	(*iv*) 700

750. Match the level of sound expressed in dB with the source of its creation.

(*a*) 30	(*i*) Moderate conversation
(*b*) 60	(*ii*) Scooter, trucks and buses
(*c*) 90	(*iii*) Taking off plane
(*d*) 150	(*iv*) Calm and quiet places

751. Match the following common tree species with their Indian Botanical Regions.

(*a*) Acacia catechu (Khair)	(*i*) Gangetic Plains
(*b*) Prosopis guliflora (Khejri)	(*ii*) Easteren Himalayas
(*c*) Mangifera Indi a mango	(*iii*) Malabar
(*d*) Bambusa arundinacea (Bamboo)	(*iv*) W. Indian Desert

752. Match the Indian Botanical Regions with the tree species commonly found therein.

(*a*) The Deccan	(*i*) Rhizophera
(*b*) Central India	(*ii*) Shorea robusta (Sal)
(*c*) Andamans	(*iii*) Santalum album (Sandal wood)
(*d*) Assam	(*iv*) Terminalia tomentosa

753. Serruya and Pollingher (1983) has divided fresh water stock of 2838×10^3 km^3 into different sources as given below, match the volume with the source.

(*a*) 4000×10^3 km^3	(*i*) Atmosphere
(*b*) 24000×10^3 km^3	(*ii*) Fresh water
(*c*) 280×10^3 Km^3	(*iii*) Glaciers
(*d*) 14×10^3 km^3	(*iv*) Active ground water

754. Match the following mains lakes/reservoir with their country of location.

(*a*) Jiticaca	(*i*) Africa
(*b*) Kariba	(*ii*) India
(*c*) Great lake	(*iii*) South America
(*d*) Bhakhra	(*iv*) Kampuchea

755. Match the percentage of total runoff with the countinents wherein it occurs.

(*a*) 31	(*i*) Europe
(*b*) 25	(*ii*) Asia
(*c*) 10	(*iii*) South America
(*d*) 7	(*iv*) Africa

756. The concentration of DDT in sprayed water from a low level of 10^{-5} ppm biomagnifies in various organisms as shown below, match it suitably with the orgnism.

(*a*) Above 10^{-2} ppm (*i*) Minnow lating fishes
(*b*) 10^{-1} ppm (*ii*) Fish eating birds
(*c*) 1 ppm (*iii*) Zooplankton
(*d*) 10 ppm (*iv*) Minnows feeding the zooplalnkton.

757. Match the average consumption of pesticides (g/ha) as estimated in 1986 with the countries these are used.

(*a*) 336 (*i*) Mexico
(*b*) 750 (*ii*) U.S.A.
(*c*) 3,000 (*iii*) Japan
(*d*) 11,800 (*iv*) India

758. Match the permissible limits of pesticides (Ng/litre) in drinking water as estimated by Nicholson (1969) with the erisecticides given below:

(*a*) 50 (*i*) Organic phosphates plus carbamates
(*b*) 17 (*ii*) DDT
(*c*) 18 (*iii*) Heptachlor and heptachlor epoxide
(*d*) 100 (*iv*) Aldrin/Dieldrin

759. Match the following constituent gases with their percentage in the dry air.

(*a*) Nitrogen (*i*) 20.9467
(*b*) Oxygen (*ii*) 0.0314
(*c*) Argon (*iii*) 78.084
(*d*) Carbon dioxide (*iv*) 0.934

760. Match the percentage with the constituent gases in the air.

(*a*) 0.0018 (*i*) Methane
(*b*) 0.0005 (*ii*) Neon
(*c*) 0.0002 (*iii*) Krypton
(*d*) 0.0001 (*iv*) Helium

761. Match the pollutant Standard Index values with the quality of environment.

(*a*) 0-49 (*i*) Very unhealthy
(*b*) 50-100 (*ii*) Moderate quality
(*c*) 100-199 (*iii*) Good air quality
(*d*) 200-299 (*iv*) Unhealthy

762. In log (A – *y*) = log A – C (*x*) equation, if A is the maximum yield and considered to be 100%, then the equation reduces to log (100 – *y*) = log 100 – 0.301 (*x*). Assuming that none of the growth factor is available, that is, *x* = 0, then *y* = 0; but suppose that 1 unit of *x* is available, then

$$\log\ (100 - y) = \log 100 - 0.301\ (1)$$
$$\log\ (100 - y) = \_\_\_\_\_\_\_\_ - 0.301$$
$$\log\ (100 - y) = 1.699$$
$$100 - y = 50$$
$$y = \_\_\_\_\_\_\_\_$$

763. In question 19, if 2 instead 1 unit of growth factor wer present, then

$$\log\ (100 - y) = \log 100 = 0.301(2)$$
$$\log\ (100 - y) = 2.000 - 0.602$$
$$\log\ (100 - y) = \_\_\_\_\_\_\_\_$$
$$100 - y = \_\_\_\_\_\_\_\_$$
$$y = 75$$

764. The milli equivalent weights of Ca, Mg, Na and K are respectively 0.02, 0.012, 0.023 and 0.039, the milliequivalents of each of these ions will be 1.0, 1.5, 0.5 and 0.5, repsectively (because quantity in g divided by their respective milliequivalent, their quantities in 20 g of soil were 0.02, 0.006, 0.0115 and 0.0195 g found in ammonium acetate extract from the leaching of this soil)

Total bases = ________ per 20 g of soil or ________ meq/100 g soil

Total CEC = 15 meq/l00 g

So, percentage base saturation = 12.5/15 × 100 = ________

765. Determine the activity index (AI) [as used by the Association of official Agricultural Chemists] to evaluate the suitability (of urea-formaldehyde compounds) of a typical urea form containing 30 per cent of its nitrogen in forms soluble in cold water (25°C) called % CW/N and remaining 70 per cent soluble in hot boiling water (98 –100°C) abbreviated as ________.

766. (*a*) What will be % P in Ca HPO_4,

$$\%\,P = 31/x = 23\%$$

(*b*) Convert $\%\,P$ to $\%\,P_2O_5$

$$\%\,P_2O_5 = y \times 2.29$$

(*c*) Convert % P_2O_5 into % P

$$\%\,P = 5 \times 0.43$$
$$\_\_\_\_\_\_\_\_ = 53 \times 0.43$$

766. (*a*) What will be % P in $CaHPO_4$,

$$\%\,P = 31/X = 23\%$$

(*b*) Convert % P to % P_2O_5

$$\%\,P_2O_5 = y \times 2.29$$

(*c*) Convert % P_2O_5 into % P

$$\%\,P = 53 \times 0.43$$
$$Z = 53 \times 0.43$$

767. The potassi fertilizer *viz.*, potassium sulphate contains 44 percent K, determine its K_2O content

$$\%\,K_2O = \%\,K \times 1.2$$
$$= 44 \times 1.2$$

768. Potassium nitrate contains 44 percent of K_2O determine it's K-content

$$\%\,K = \%\,K_2O \times 0.83$$
$$= 44 \times 0.83$$

769. How much more effective is 100g of magnesium carbonate than the same quantity of calcium carbonate in neutralizing an acid.

Note: Molecular weight of calcium carbonate = 100

Molecular weight of magnesium carbonate = 84

$MgCO_3$ on weight basis will neutralize 1.19 times more acid as the same weigtht of $CaCO_3$.
Therefore, its neutralizing value (CCE) in relation to $CaCO_3$ = 100 is 1.19/1 × 100 = 119 per cent

770. If a limestone contains the guarantee 35 % CaO
15 % MgO

To express in CCE

As known 56g of CaO ≡ 100g of $CaCO_3$

(*a*) So multiply % CaO by 100/56
and CCE in (35 % CaO) is 35 % × 1.785 = ________

(*b*) Molecular weight of MgO = 40
Molecular weight of $CaCO_3$ = 100
Now multiply % MgO by 100/40 = 2.5
Hence CCE in 15% MgO = 2.5 × 15 = ________

(*c*) Total CCE for this limestone = a + b = 62.5 + 37.5 = ________

771. Work out the EEC of Solid Agricultural Lime (SAL).

If,	% $CaCO_3$ equivalent	= 90
Sieve analysis	% of 8 mesh sieve	= 2 (SAL)
	% on 60 mesh sieve	= 21 SAL
	% passing 60 mesh sieve	= 77 SAL

Now, calculate fineness factor

(*i*) %. on 8-mesh × 0 % fineness, 2 × 0 = 0
(*ii*) % on 60-mesh × 50 % fineness, 21 × 50 % = ________
(*iii*) % through 60-mesh × 100 % fineness, 77 × 100 % = 77

The fineness factor (%) = ________

Per cent ECC = Purity × fineness factor
= 90 × 88.5 = ________

772. Determine the ECC suspendable lime (SL)

Given,	% $CaCO_3$ equivalent	= 98
Sieve analysis	% of 8-mesh sieve	= 0
	% on 60-mesh sieve	= 2
	% passing 60-mesh sieve	= 98

Now, determine the fineness factor

% on 8 mesh × 0% effectiveness = 0 × 0 = 0
% on 60 mesh × 50 % effectivenes = 2 × 50% = 1
% through 60 mesh × 100 % = 98 × 100 % = 98
Fineness factor (%) = 1 + 98 = 99

Per cent ECC = Purity × fineness factor
= 98 × 99 %

% ECC = ________

773. Determine the storic index if the estimated soil factors namely texture, depth and drainage are 80, 90 and 10 respectively.

Storic Index = multiply the estimated percentages of soil factors

$$= \frac{80}{100} \times \frac{90}{100} \times \frac{10}{100} \quad = \frac{72,000}{1000000} \quad = \frac{72}{1000} \times 100 = ...$$

774. Work out the productivity rating if the

E_{ya} = expected yield of crop 'a' per unit area = 50 q/ha

S_{ya} = Standard yield of crop 'a' per unit area = 20 q/ha

$$\text{Productivity Rating or Index} = \frac{Eya}{Sya} \times 100$$

$$= \frac{50}{20} \times 100 \quad = \frac{5,000}{20} \quad = ...$$

775. Complete the effective right temperature (nycto-temperature) tnycto if

Maximum temperature (t_{max}) = 40°C

Minimum temperature (t_{min}) = 28°C

$$t_{nycto} = t_{min} + 1/4\ (t_{max} = - t_{min})$$

$$= 28 + 1/4\,(40 - 28) \quad = 28 + 1/4\,(12)$$

$$= 28 + 3 \quad = \_\_\_\_\_\_\_$$

776. Determine day light temperature (photo-temperature or tphoto) if

Maximum temperature (t_{max}) = 40°C

Minimum temperature (t_{min}) = 28°C

$$= 40 - 1/4\,(40 - 28) \quad = 40 - 1/4\,(12)$$

$$= 40 - 3 = \_\_\_\_\_\_\_$$

777. Compute water content of a soil if

Weight of wet soil = 100 g

Weight oven dry soil = 80 g

Water content = 100 – 80

= 20 g

Dry soil weighing 100 g with contain

$$= \frac{20}{80} \times 100 \quad = ...$$

778. Work out the per cent porosity of a soil if.

Soil particle density = 2.65

Soil bulk density = 1.5

$$\text{Per cent porosity} = \left[\frac{\text{Bulk density}}{\text{Particle density}}\right] \times 100$$

$$= 100 - \left[\frac{1.6}{2.65}\right] \times 100 \quad = 100 - 60.37 \ = 100 - 60.4 \ = ...$$

779. Compute the frequency of occurrence (per cent) in an aera surveyed and the following data were obtained

Quadrants studied = 50

Quadrants no. in which the species occurred = 40

$$\text{Frequency of occurrence (F)} = \frac{\text{No. of quadrants in which occurs} \times 100}{\text{Total no. of a quardrants studied}}$$

780. Work out the relative frequency of occurrence of species in a region based on the following reported data:

No. of occurrence of species = 25

No. of occurrence of all species = 50

$$\text{Relative Frequency (RF)} = \frac{\text{No. of occurrence of a species} \times 100}{\text{No. of occurence of all species}}$$

$$RF = \frac{25}{50} \times 100 = \_\_\_\_$$

781. Determine the abundance of bermunda grass in a grassland community if

Total no. of individuals of a species in quadrants = 43

Total. quadrats in which species occurred = 10

$$\text{Since abundant} = \frac{\text{Total no. of individuals of species in quadrants}}{\text{Total no. of quadrants in which species occurred}}$$

Here species represented by bermunda (individual)

Therefore, Abundance = 40/10 = ____

782. Calculate the density of *Euphorbia hirta* in numbers per square metre if

The total no. of individuals of this in all quadrants = 33

The total no. of 1 quadrats sampled = 10

$$\text{Since} \quad \text{density (D)} = \frac{\text{The total no. of individuals of species in all quadrants}}{\text{Total number quadrants sampled}}$$

D = 33/10 = 3.3

This is per quadrat of 30 × 50 cm = 0.25 m^2

Therefore, 3.3/0.25 = 330/25 = ____

783. Work out the relative density (RD) of Indigofera spp. if,

No. of individuals of species in all quadrants = 50

No. of individuals of all species in all quadrants = 250

$$\text{Since, relative density} = \frac{\text{No. of individuals of the species in all quadrats}}{\text{No. of individuals of all species in all quadrats}}$$

$$\text{Therefore,} \quad RD = \frac{50}{250} \times 100 =$$

Note : Relative dominance can be computed by replacing the number of species with area occupied by them both in numerator and denominator.

784. Determine the similarity index (s). if there are 10 species on site A and 10 on site B, and 7 species are common for the stands. (C),

As, $s = 2C/(A+B) =$ ——————

Note: Dissimilarity index (D) is, D = 1 – s and calculate D for above case

785. Determine the level of sound in terms of dB for a barely audible sound.

Since loundness is measured in the log scale in reference to a barely audible sound formula for dB of a sound is

$$dB = 10 \times \log 10 \frac{\text{(Power of given sound in watts)}}{\text{(Power of barely audible sound)}}$$

Thus, the dB for a barely audible sound will be $10 \times \log_1$ and $\log_1 = 0$

Therefore dB will be 0 (zero)

Do You Know That

1. Brutland Report (our common future) was prepared by world commission on Environment and Development in the year 1987.
2. Term Ecology was coined by German Biologist Ernest Hackle in the year 1866.
3. Carbon cycle is based on CO_2 gas which makes up 0·036% of the volume of troposphere and is dissolved in water.
4. Concept of ecological pyramid was developed by Charles Elton in the year 1927.
5. Ecological succession is the phenomena of transition from one biotic community to another.
6. In grass land ecosystem producers are of large size.
7. Phototrophs are the plants which produce food themselves through photosynthesis.
8. The sequence of living organism to transfer food energy from one organism into another is called food chain.
9. Agriculture in which several plant species are grown simultaneously to reduce insect Infestation is called heteroculture.
10. Gases responsible for ozone layer depletion are CFC, CO_2, SO_2 and methane.

KEY

(1) Pastoral farming	(2) Geonomics/geonoms	(3) Theories
(4) Symbolic	(5) Agricultural economics	(6) Physical socio-economic
(7) Agriculture	(8) Ecological technique	(9) Anthropocentric
(10) Determinism	(11) Agricultural transformation	(12) Metamorphose
(13) Cropping patterns	(14) Communities	(15) Agriculture
(16) Compartmentalized	(17) Dissection index	(18) Terrain
(19) Agricultural	(20) Agriculture	(21) Rarefied air
(22) Summer	(23) Windward slope	(24) Definite direction
(25) Apple growth	(26) Matured	(27) Regionalization
(28) More fertile	(29) Arable farming	(30) Cultivation
(31) Soil erosion	(32) Sprinkler irrigation	(33) Confluence
(34) Rotation and revolution	(35) Climatic	(36) Agricultural patterns

(37) Amount of energy
(38) Threshold temperature
(39) Prostrate habit
(40) Alps and Rockies
(41) Mistral
(42) Spring crops
(43) Irrigation
(44) Humidity
(45) Warm temperature
(46) Agricultural crops
(47) Effectiveness
(48) Total rainfall
(49) Volitional command
(50) $X = 60D$ and $y = PE$. S = surplus, D = Deficit, PE = Potential evapotranspiration
(51) Agricultural region
(52) Abiotic and biotic
(53) Planning
(54) Element
(55) Index of diversification
(56) Agricultural planning
(57) Endogenous/internal/inherent
(58) Osasis farmers
(59) Nomadic herding
(60) Commercial exploitation
(61) Forage and water
(62) Pastoral nomads
(63) Afro-Euracia
(64) Nomadism
(65) Shifting cultivation
(66) Agricultural system
(67) Mixed cropping or intertillage
(68) Sedentary
(69) South and East Asia
(70) Predatory agriculture
(71) Subsistence tillage
(72) Mediterranean
(73) Plantation
(74) Grain farming
(75) Mixed farming
(76) Western Europe
(77) Milk
(78) Occidental
(79) Industrial crops
(80) Collective farming
(81) Commercial
(82) Tropical and sub-tropical
(83) Large scale
(84) Characteristics
(85) Reduced
(86) Proximate
(87) Integrated
(88) Aerial photography
(89) Second stage
(90) Spatial coverage
(91) Changing
(92) Inherent
(93) Limitations
(94) Soil productivity
(95) Potential
(96) Ecological crop geography
(97) Indefinitely
(98) Equilibrium
(99) Tolerance
(100) Distribution
(101) Earlier forms
(102) Paleozoic
(103) Angiosperms (flower and seed bearing plants)
(104) Climate
(105) Organic evolution
(106) Constituent
(107) Freezing
(108) Ecological position
(109) Genotype
(110) Teleology
(111) Anthropomorphism
(112) Greater
(113) Constant
(114) Cynogenetic glucosides
(115) Biotypes
(116) Natural selection
(117) Anything
(118) Variability
(119) Environment
(120) Agro-ecological
(121) Gene microcentres
(122) Systematics
(123) Variability
(124) Near-east
(125) Blade-tool
(126) Urban civilisation
(127) Distribution
(128) Cultivated barley
(129) Natural habitat
(130) Infiermillo
(131) Mexico-Guatemala region
(132) Food crop
(133) Synecology
(134) Ecosystem
(135) Holocoenotic
(136) Complete destruction
(137) Nitrogen cycle
(138) Radioactive phosphorus
(139) Ruthenium
(140) Energy
(141) Spontaneouly
(142) Food-energy
(143) Shorter
(144) Energy flow
(145) Function
(146) Tropic structure
(147) Pyramids
(148) Absolute humidity
(149) Pressure
(150) Vapour-pressure deficit
(151) Hygrometer
(152) Dew/white frost
(153) Fog
(154) Precipitation cycle
(155) Arica (Chile)
(156) Precipitation
(157) Albedo
(158) Moisture index
(159) Need
(160) Aridity index
(161) Moisture index
(162) Xerophytes
(163) Leaf-rust
(164) Free-energy
(165) Diffusion pressure deficit
(166) Turgor pressure
(167) Deficits
(168) Tension
(169) Retarded

(170) Sensitive
(171) Sensitive
(172) Stress
(173) Root-density
(174) Distribution
(175) Drought
(176) Physiological limits
(177) Resistance
(178) Succulents
(179) Conservative users
(180) Dehydration
(181) Death
(182) Solar radiation/insolation
(183) Equator
(184) Autumnal
(185) Equinoxes
(186) Temperatures
(187) Air drainage
(188) Inversion
(189) Temperature
(190) Thermal efficiency
(191) Heat unit systems
(192) Early summer
(193) Mean temperature
(194) Tenderometer
(195) Hastens
(196) Suffocation
(197) Freezing
(198) Temperature
(199) Resistance
(200) Thermoperiodism
(201) Night hours
(202) Vernalisation
(203) Winter and spring
(204) 41.8
(205) Sea level
(206) Intensity
(207) Water
(208) Compensation
(209) Heliophytes
(210) Legumes
(211) Phototropism
(212) Food grain/seed
(213) Chlorophyll
(214) Long day
(215) Floral primordia
(216) Predominates
(217) Germination
(218) Troposphere
(219) Ionosphere
(220) Oxygen
(221) Electromagnetic
(222) Upper atmosphere
(223) Intensity
(224) Black fog period
(225) Gas molecules
(226) Air pollutants
(227) Water soaked
(228) Smog (smoke + fog)
(229) Obnoxious
(230) Hydrocarbons
(231) Most senstive
(232) Bronzing
(233) Soil moisture or Nitrogen fertilization
(234) Ozonated hexane
(235) Soil
(236) Low light
(237) Size of pores
(238) More heat
(239) Equator
(240) Temperature
(241) Low pressure
(242) Arctic and antarctic
(243) South-West
(244) Coriolis
(245) Easterly surface winds
(246) Solar energy
(247) Anemometer
(248) Gusts and lulls
(249) Herbaceous
(250) Growth rate
(251) Timberlines
(252) Cereal rusts
(253) Structure
(254) Gleization
(255) Breeding potential/biotic potential
(256) Reproduction
(257) Resistance
(258) Persistence
(259) Competition
(260) Succession
(261) Climax
(262) Higher life-forms
(263) Monoclimax
(264) Community
(265) Environmental
(266) Interspecified
(267) Ability
(268) Same environmental
(269) Biotic community
(270) Nitrogen symbiotically
(271) Proximity
(272) Different
(273) Forastero
(274) South-eastern Asia
(275) Sugarcane
(276) India and Indonesia
(277) Cuba
(278) Robusta
(279) Oxygen
(280) Nutritional
(281) Spinning
(282) Pressley breaker
(283) Saccharata
(284) Prairie
(285) South America
(286) Winter wheat
(287) 90 to 100
(288) One eighth (1/8)
(289) Deciduous orchard
(290) Clone
(291) America
(292) Winter nights
(293) Lowest latitude
(294) Rest period
(295) Good colouring
(296) Soil fertility
(297) Both nitrate and ammonia
(298) Meteorological equivalent
(299) Biosphere/ecosphere
(300) Plant sociology/phytosociology
(301) Conservation ecology
(302) Ecological energetics
(303) Holistic approach
(304) Biosphere

(305) Homeostasis (306) Primary producers (307) Mutualism
(308) Commensalism (309) Pyramid of energy (310) Primary productivity
(311) Net productivity (312) Matrix model (313) Resilience
(314) Temperature coefficient/Q_{10} (315) Eurythemic (316) 0.13 geogram
(317) 23 and 77 (318) March-April (319) Monsoon
(320) West coast (321) *Cyperus rotundus* (nutsedge) (322) *Xanthium strumarium*
(323) Euphorbiaceae (324) Water scarcity (325) Roots
(326) Microphyllyine (327) Biotic (328) Conjunctive
(329) Soredia (330) Mutualism (331) *Orobanche*
(332) *Cuscuta* (333) Robust growth (334) Velamen
(335) Jug like structure (336) Nutritional relationship (337) Pitcher plant
(338) Small insects (339) Bladders (340) Antibiosis
(341) Intraspecific (342) Allelopathy (*allelon* = each other and *pathy* = suffering)
(343) Ectocrine/exocrines/Environmental hormones (344) Penicillium
(345) Amensalism (346) *Amaranthus spinosus* (347) Genetical races
(348) Germinate and establish (349) Mechanically pounded (350) Higher oxygen
(351) Coumarins (352) *Trigonella arabica* (353) Ecads
(354) *Euphorbia hirta* (355) Natality
(356) Population ecology or democology (357) Ecological amptitude
(358) Succession (359) Climax community
(360) Biomes/provinces/biochores/formations (361) Ecotone/tension zone
(362) Community (363) Organismic (364) Ordination
(365) Ecological niche (366) Fundamental (367) Gild
(368) Increases (369) Dominants (370) Colonization
(371) Ecological succession (372) Primary succession (373) Secondary succession
(374) Self-sustaining (375) Type of (376) Latitude
(377) Respiration (378) Standing corp (379) 3-carbon
(380) 4-carbon (381) C-4 (382) Vacuole
(383) Malic acid (384) Photorespiration (385) Of ground
(386) Aquatic autotrophs (387) 4-5 LAI value (388) 0.6
(389) 1×10^6 tonnes (390) Non-renewable (391) Pollution
(392) Homeostasis (393) Ecological (394) Oxygen Revolution
(395) Temperatures (396) Hydrocarbons (397) Carbon monoxide
(398) Blood haemoglobin (399) Sulphur dioxide (400) Sulfurous acid (H_2SO_3)
(401) Phaeophytin 'a' (402) Bryophytes (403) Carbon dioxide
(404) Fluorine, generally in the form of HF (405) Uttar Pradesh
(406) Tobacco wrapper (407) Hydrocarbons (408) Photochemical
(409) Nitrous oxide (410) Ozone (O_3) (411) Lead
(412) Automobile (413) Aerosol (414) Pollutants
(415) Crystallization (416) Starch synthesis (417) Bronchial (asthma)
(418) Howrah (419) Carbon dioxide (420) DDT
(421) Chlorinated (422) Biological magnifica tion (423) Adipose
(424) Polluted waters (425) Pollutants
(426) Biochemical or biological oxygen demand (427) Eutrophication
(428) Aquatic weeds (429) Lethality (430) Plutonium
(431) Biogeochemical (432) Calcium

(433) Decibel (*deci* = 10 and *bel* after the name of Ghraham Bell) (434) Loudness
(435) Sonic booms (436) Mach (437) Flora
(438) Different plants (439) 1500'species (440) Leguminosae
(441) 31st (442) Oxygeb atom (443) Boiling point of 100°C
(444) Turn-over time (445) Deep ground water (446) 1.0
(447) Less than - (448) Oceans (449) Esluaries
(450) Sea water (451) European (452) Soft water or chloride
(453) Greenish (454) Odour (455) Odour
(456) Colefaction (457) Gas bubble disease (458) Conductivity
(459) Carbonates and bicarbonates (460) Eriochrome Black T (461) Phenophthalein
(462) Acidity (463) 10.000 times (464) Anoxia (oxygen deficieny)
(465) 14-15 (466) Organic matter or sewage (467) Standing and flowing
(468) Minamata Bay (469) Magnification (470) Terrestrial
(471) Fontinalis (472) Volcanic erruptions (473) Crops
(474) Itai-itai diseases (475) Cd (476) Zinc
(477) Arsenic (478) Hexavalent (479) Drinking water
(480) Bronchial (481) 2 mg (482) Bordeaux mixture
(483) Fish (484) Manganese (485) Iron
(486) Laxative (487) Watershed (488) Inorganic phosphate
(489) Non-selective (490) Eutrophication (491) Chlorinity
(492) Heavier (493) Chlorination (494) Pungent
(495) Sulphate (496) Sulphur dioxide (497) Sulphide
(498) Sulphite (499) Nitrate (500) Nitrate bomb
(501) Drinking (502) Biogradable (503) Non-target
(504) Cholinestrease (505) Nervous system
(506) Heart (507) DDE (508) 10 ppm
(509) Upstream (510) Blue-green algae (511) Cholinestrase
(512) Union Carbide (513) MIC (514) Superchlorination
(515) Detergents (516) Biogradable (517) Linear alkylate sulphonate
(518) Nanoplankton (519) Neuston (520) Nekton
(521) Non-human (522) Epidemics (523) Faecal and urine
(524) Enzymatic (525) Chromonycosis (526) Yeast
(527) Nematodes (528) Water (529) Vidbrio choleral
(530) Schistosomiasis (531) Nitrates (532) Air pollution
(533) Electrochemical (534) Biological (535) Green plants
(536) Acceptors (537) Ambient quality (538) Indicator
(539) Maximum allowable emmision concentration (540) Time scale
(541) Vegetation (542) Greenhouse effect (543) Natural level
(544) 345 ppm (545) Synthesised (546) $CFCl_3$
(547) Aerosol (548) Degrade (549) 100 years
(550) Methane gas (551) Soil Moisture stress (552) Ozone
(553) Bioassay (554) Withdrawn (555) Ryegrass
(556) Ultra-violet radiation (557) UV-B (558) Chlorine
(559) Bromine (560) Dissociation (561) Ozone
(562) Genetic defects (563) Ozone layer (564) Nitrous oxide
(565) Ozonator (566) Stomata (567) Flecking or strippling

(568) Reproductive processes (569) Nitrite reductase (570) Ozone
(571) Elliptical lesions (572) NO_2 (573) Tonne
(574) Peroxyactyl nitrate (PAN) (575) Ethylene (576) HF
(577) Fluoride (578) 0.02ppm (00.5 mg/l^3) (579) Isocyanate
(580) Aerosol (581) Asbestosis cancer
(582) Carbon monoxide and carbon dioxode (583) Formaldehyde
(584) Tobacco smoking (585) Human system (586) Wastes
(587) Pyrolytic methods (588) ^{239}plutonium (589) Radio activity
(590) Microcurie (mCi 10^{-6} Ci) (591) Rad (originally known rontgen) or R
(592) 10.000 (593) 1986 (594) Insecticide Act.
(595) Emission (596) Cement factories (597) (*d*)
(598) (*a*) (599) (*a*) (600) (*b*)
(601) (*d*) (602) (*a*) (603) (*a*)
(604) (*c*) (605) (*b*) (606) (*a*)
(607) (*c*) (608) (*d*) (609) (*b*)
(610) (*a*) (611) (*c*) (612) (*a*)
(613) (*b*) (614) (*c*) (615) (*c*)
(616) (*b*) (617) (*a*) (618) (*d*)
(619) (*b*) (620) (*b*) (621) (*a*)
(622) (*b*) (623) (*c*) (624) (*b*)
(625) (*c*) (626) (*c*) (627) (*b*)
(628) (*c*) (629) (*a*) (630) (*a*)
(631) (*c*) (632) (*d*) (633) (*d*)
(634) (*a*) (635) (*d*) (636) (*d*)
(637) (*c*) (638) (*d*) (639) (*b*)
(640) (*d*) (641) (*d*) (642) (*b*)
(643) (*c*) (644) (*b*) (645) (*d*)
(646) (*a*) (647) (*d*) (648) (*c*)
(649) (*b*) (650) (*a*) (651) (*c*)
(652) (*c*) (653) (*b*) (654) (*c*)
(655) (*d*) (656) (*c*) (657) (*b*)
(658) (*a*) (659) (*c*) (660) (*c*)
(661) (*d*) (662) (*b*) (663) (*a*)
(664) (*c*) (665) (*d*) (666) (*d*)
(667) (*b*) (668) (*b*) (669) (*c*)
(670) (*c*) (671) (*b*) (672) (*d*)
(673) (*c*) (674) (*c*) (675) (*d*)
(676) (*c*) (677) (*b*) (678) (*b*)
(679) (*b*) (680) (*b*) (681) (*c*)
(682) (*a*) (683) (*d*) (684) (*a*)
(685) (*a*) (686) (*c*) (687) (*d*)
(688) (*b*) (689) (*d*) (690) (*c*)
(691) (*c*) (692) (*c*) (693) (*b*)
(694) (*b*) (695) (*d*) (696) (*b*)
(697) (*b*) (698) (*c*) (699) (*c*)
(700) (*b*) (701) (*d*) (702) (*b*)

(703) (*b*)	(704) (*c*)	(705) (*c*)	(706) (*b*).
(707) (c)	(707) (***a***)-(*b*)	(707) (***b***)-(*c*)	
(708) (*a*)-(*iii*)	(*b*)-(*i*)	(*c*)-(*iv*)	(*d*)-(*ii*)
(709) (*a*)-(*iv*)	(*b*)-(*i*)	(*c*)-(*ii*)	(*d*)-(*iii*)
(710) (*a*)-(*iv*)	(*b*)-(*iii*)	(*c*)-(*ii*)	(*d*)-(*i*)
(711) (*a*)-(*iii*)	(*b*)-(*iv*)	(*c*)-(*i*)	(*d*)-(*ii*)
(712) (*a*)-(*iv*)	(*b*)-(*i*)	(*c*)-(*ii*)	(*d*)-(*iii*)
(713) (*a*)-(*iii*)	(*b*)-(*i*)	(*c*)-(*iv*)	(*d*)-(*ii*)
(714) (*a*)-(*iii*)	(*b*)-(*iv*)	(*c*)-(*i*)	(*d*)-(*ii*)
(715) (*a*)-(*iv*)	(*b*)-(*ii*)	(*c*)-(*i*)	(*d*)-(*iii*)

TEI = Thermal Efficiency Index

(716) (*a*)-(*iv*)	(*b*)-(*i*)	(*c*)-(*ii*)	(*d*)-(*iii*)
(717) (*a*)-(*iii*)	(*b*)-(*i*)	(*c*)-(*iv*)	(*d*)-(*ii*)
(718) (*a*)-(*iii*)	(*b*)-(*i*)	(*c*)-(*iv*)	(*d*)-(*ii*)
(719) (*a*)-(*i*)	(*b*)-(*iv*)	(*c*)-(*iii*)	(*d*)-(*ii*)
(720) (*a*)-(*iii*)	(*b*)-(*i*)	(*c*)-(*iv*)	(*d*)-(*ii*)
(721) (*a*)-(*iii*)	(*b*)-(*ii*)	(*c*)-(*i*)	(*d*)-(*iv*)
(722) (*a*)-(*iv*)	(*b*)-(*iii*)	(*c*)-(*ii*)	(*d*)-(*i*)
(723) (*a*)-(*ii*)	(*b*)-(*i*)	(*c*)-(*iv*)	(*d*)-(*iii*)
(724) (*a*)-(*iii*)	(*b*)-(*iv*)	(*c*)-(*ii*)	(*d*)-(*i*)
(725) (*a*)-(*iv*)	(*b*)-(*i*)	(*c*)-(*iii*)	(*d*)-(*ii*)
(726) (*a*)-(*iii*)	(*b*)-(*ii*)	(*c*)-(*iv*)	(*d*)-(*i*)
(727) (*a*)-(*iv*)	(*b*)-(*iii*)	(*c*)-(*ii*)	(*d*)-(*i*)
(728) (*a*)-(*iv*)	(*b*)-(*i*)	(*c*)-(*ii*)	(*d*)-(*iii*)
(729) (*a*)-(*ii*)	(*b*)-(*iv*)	(*c*)-(*i*)	(*d*)-(*iii*)
(730) (*a*)-(*iii*)	(*b*)-(*i*)	(*c*)-(*iv*)	(*d*)-(*ii*)
(731) (*a*)-(*iii*)	(*b*)-(*i*)	(*c*)-(*iv*)	(*d*)-(*ii*)
(732) (*a*)-(*iv*)	(*b*)-(*i*)	(*c*)-(*ii*)	(*d*)-(*iii*)
(733) (*a*)-(*ii*)	(*b*)-(*iv*)	(*c*)-(*i*)	(*d*)-(*iii*)
(734) (*a*)-(*iii*)	(*b*)-(*i*)	(*c*)-(*iv*)	(*d*)-(*ii*)
(735) (*a*)-(*iv*)	(*b*)-(*i*)	(*c*)-(*ii*)	(*d*)-(*iii*)
(736) (*a*)-(*iii*)	(*b*)-(*iv*)	(*c*)-(*ii*)	(*d*)-(*i*)
(737) (*a*)-(*iii*)	(*b*)-(*iv*)	(*c*)-(*ii*)	(*d*)-(*i*)
(738) (*a*)-(*iii*)	(*b*)-(*i*)	(*c*)-(*iv*)	(*d*)-(*ii*)
(739) (*a*)-(*ii*)	(*b*)-(*iii*)	(*c*)-(*i*)	(*d*)-(*iv*)
(740) (*a*)-(*iii*)	(*b*)-(*i*)	(*c*)-(*iv*)	(*d*)-(*ii*)
(741) (*a*)-(*iv*)	(*b*)-(*iii*)	(*c*)-(*i*)	(*d*)-(*ii*)
(742) (*a*)-(*ii*)	(*b*)-(*iii*)	(*c*)-(*iv*)	(*d*)-(*i*)
(743) (*a*)-(*iii*)	(*b*)-(*i*)	(*c*)-(*iv*)	(*d*)-(*ii*)
(744) (*a*)-(*iii*)	(*b*)-(*iv*)	(*c*)-(*i*)	(*d*)-(*ii*)
(745) (*a*)-(*ii*)	(*b*)-(*iii*)	(*c*)-(*i*)	(*d*)-(*iv*)

Note: Leaf size of each class is nine times larger than the preceding class.

(746) (*a*)-(*iv*)	(*b*)-(*i*)	(*c*)-(*ii*)	(*d*)-(*iii*)
(747) (*a*)-(*ii*)	(*b*)-(*i*)	(*c*)-(*iv*)	(*d*)-(*iii*)
(748) (*a*)-(*iv*)	(*b*)-(*i*)	(*c*)-(*ii*)	(*d*)-(*iii*)
(749) (*a*)-(*iii*)	(*b*)-(*iv*)	(*c*)-(*i*)	(*d*)-(*ii*)

(750) (*a*)-(*iv*)	(*b*)-(*i*)	(*c*)-(*ii*)	(*d*)-(*iii*)
(751) (*a*)-(*ii*)	(*b*)-(*iv*)	(*c*)-(*i*)	(*d*)-(*iii*)
(752) (*a*)-(*iii*)	(*b*)-(*iv*)	(*c*)-(*i*)	(*d*)-(*ii*)
(753) (*a*)-(*iv*)	(*b*)-(*iii*)	(*c*)-(*ii*)	(*d*)-(*i*)

Note: River contains 1.2×10^3 km^3.

(754) (*a*)-(*iii*)	(*b*)-(*i*)	(*c*)-(*iv*)	(*d*)-(*ii*)
(755) (*a*)-(*ii*)	(*b*)-(*iii*)	(*c*)-(*iv*)	(*d*)-(*i*)
(756) (*a*)-(*iii*)	(*b*)-(*iv*)	(*c*)-(*i*)	(*d*)-(*ii*)
(757) (*a*)-(*iv*)	(*b*)-(*i*)	(*c*)-(*ii*)	(*d*)-(*iii*)
(758) (*a*)-(*ii*)	(*b*)-(*iv*)	(*c*)-(*iii*)	(*d*)-(*i*)
(759) (*a*)-(*iii*)	(*b*)-(*i*)	(*c*)-(*iv*)	(*d*)-(*ii*)
(760) (*a*)-(*ii*)	(*b*)-(*iv*)	(*c*)-(*i*)	(*d*)-(*iii*)
(761) (*a*)-(*iii*)	(*b*)-(*ii*)	(*c*)-(*iv*)	(*d*)-(*i*)

(762) $z = 2$ and N = 50 (763) $z = 1.398$ and N = 25 (764) $x = 2.5$ meq, $y = 12.5$ meq, $z = 83.3$

(765) Per cent as HW/N

(766) $x = 136$, $y = 23$ and $z = 22.79$

Note: $\% P = \% P_2O_5 \times 0.43$

$\% P_2O_5 = \% P \times 2.29$

(767) $\% K_2O = \% K \times 1.2 = 44 \times 1.2$

$K_2O = 52.8 = 53\%$

(768) % K = 35.62%

(769) $\dfrac{84}{100} = \dfrac{100}{x}$

$x = 119$

Note: Molecular weight of calcium carbonate = 100

Molecular weight of magnesium carbonate = 84

$MgCO_3$ on weight basis will neutralize 1.19 times more acid as the same weight of $CaCO_3$. Therefore, its neutralizing value (CCE) in relation to $CaCO_3$ = 100 is 1.19/1 × 100 = 119 per cent

(770) (*a*) = 62.5 % (*b*) = 37.5 % (*c*) = 100 %

(771) $x = 11.5$, $y = 88.5$ and $z = 79.6$ (772) 97 %

(773) 7.2 (also called ratio or rating) (774) 205

(775) 31°C (776) 37°C (777) 25 g of water

(778) 39.6 % (779) 80% (780) 50 %

(781) 4.3 (782) 13.2 plants/m^2 (783) 20%*

***Note :** Relative dominance can be computed by replacing the number of species with area occupied by them both in numerator and denominator.

(784) 0.7 **Note:** Dissimilarity index (D) is = $1 - s$

and if D = 1.0,

then D = 1.0–0.7

D = 0.3

(785) 0 (zero)

SECTION 3
PLANT BREEDING AND BIOTECHNOLOGY

I. Fill up the blanks:

1. The earliest physical evidence of the antiquity of cultivation of plants goes back to ________ years.
2. The cultivation of plants is confirmed by their remains left by the lake dwellers of________.
3. The ruins of ancient ________ and Egyptian cities and from the barrows of British Isles corroborate the antiquity of cultivation of plants.
4. Both ________ are Asian in origin.
5. Tomatoes and barley originated from (as speculated) ________ and Asia Minor.
6. The Mendelian diversity arises basically from ________.
7. Sometimes a single mutation with drastic or ________ effects may considerably augment the usefulness of a plant species.
8. The development of ________ exemplifies a pattern of transformation characteristic of cultivated species of plants.
9. Barley, rice, maize, flax, tomatoes and common beans have developed in their unique way, but the general pattern for each is, that of ________.
10. The original ________ are still recognizable because the divergence in cultivated plants has not continued long enough despite conspicuous morphological differences in some of them.
11. ________ hybridization is succeeded by recrossing with parental species in a way that some features of one transferred to the other without impairing taxonomic integrity.
12. ________ refers to the variation arising through reduplication of chromosome sets.
13. The smooth functioning of the ________ mechanism requires the simultaneous presence of two chromosomes of each kind.
14. Commercial tobacco (*Nicotiana tabacum*) does not occur as a ________ species.
15. The domestication of ________ has been most dramatic for the production of antibiotics.
16. In modern plant breeding, ________ between deliberately chosen parents has become increasingly important.
17. In general, efficient inbreeding schemes are less difficult to secure than ________ outbreeding schemes.
18. In wheat, another burst before ________ so that the empty anthers hanging out are only a mockery.
19. In tomato, ________ follows opening of the flowers, but stamens form a cone enclosing the stigma almost to insure self-pollination.
20. Inbreeders arise constantly from ________.

21. In protandry and ________, the anthers and stigma of a flower mature at different times.
22. Self-incompatibility in higher plants is far more important than ________.
23. In ________, the incompatibility depends upon the genotype of the gametophyte.
24. In sporophytic or in diplo-diplo schemes, the ________ is impressed upon by the gametophyte by its sporophytic parent.
25. ________ reproduction leads to perpetuation of the same genotype with great precision.
26. In ________ reproduction seeds are produced, but through processes other than normal meiosis and fertilization.
27. The main effect of apomixis is an increase in the proportion of maternal individuals through prohibition, or modification of ________ and recombination.
28. Pure-line selection has been widely used to select ________ from the old "land" varieties.
29. ________ is different than pure-line selection as a number of plants rather than one are selected to make up a new variety.
30. The pedigree method of breeding derives its name from the records that are kept of ancestry of pedigree of each of the ________.
31. ________ is suited to transfer specific genes to a good variety deficient in one or a few characteristics.
32. The final product of back-crossing needs no agricultural evaluation as the ________ will be the same except for improved characteristics.
33. ________ varieties depend for their superiority pon heterosis that characterizes the Fl hybrids between certain genotypes.
34. ________ is a device to produce large quantities of seed of hybrid varieties.
35. ________ selection involves selection of desirable genotypes, their self-progeny and intercrossing in all combinations to produce population for reselection.
36. A ________ variety is the one that has been evolved from all possible intercrosses among a number of selected genotypes to develop a population to increase by open-pollination.
37. The species vary in the amount of ________ tolerable to them in the process of hybridization.
38. The 'Vilmorin Method' of 'Vilmorin Isolation Principle' was conceived by Louis de Vilmorin of ________.
39. The best organised and most widespread use of Vilmorin Method was done by ________ Seed Association established in Svalof in 1886.
40. ________ represents the progeny of a single self-fertilized homozygous individuals.
41. Self-pollination, excluding special genetic circumstances, rapidly reduces any population to the ________ condition.
42. ________ are the building blocks from which new varieties are fashioned.
43. The qualitative genes of classical genetics postulate more than a ________ manifestation.
44. The white eye mutant of ________ affects pigmentation of eye, testicular membrane, spermateca shape, length of life and general viability.
45. It has been observed that yield, and bushel weight in wheat are influenced by the gene pair governing ________ lemmas.
46. ________ lines can also be obtained by recurrent selection.
47. Linkage can be regarded as a conservative influence, tending to hold together existing ________ of genes.
48. G.V. Yule (1906) suggested that there is needed no conflict between particulate and continuous inheritances if many genes having ________ effects were postulated.

49. The size of tobacco ________ remains relatively constant under a range of environmental conditions.
50. Homozygosity within families increase with the continued ________.
51. The ________ cannot cause a character to develop unless they have proper environment.
52. In ________ breeding, the new variety is made up of the progeny of a single pure-line.
53. In ________ the progeny of many pure lines are composed to form the new variety.
54. Land-varieties in agriculturally less advanced countries (similar to that of Europe and N. America) still exist, therefore, pure-line selection method is important to delay the day predicted by ________.
55. Turkey wheat is quite ________ for gross plant type.
56. The ________ consists of a series of notes which give the relationships among the families that have been grown.
57. Competition among homozygous genotypes indicate that ________ are highly competitive against unadapted types ________.
58. The study of the survival of alternative alleles of a particular gene does not represent the effect of ________.
59. ________ handling often provides opportunity to make use of artificial aids to selection.
60. Backcrosses can also serve a useful purpose in ________ breeding programmes.
61. Occurrence of rust races in wheat especially in U.S.A. gave an impetus to the ________ method.
62. In random mating, individuals are mated together at random or ________.
63. The criteria of likeness or unlikeness are either ________ or appearance (phenotypic resemblance or distinction).
64. In genetic ________ mating, individuals which are less closely related than they would be under random mating.
65. The ________ devised by Wright is based primarily on the number and closeness of ancestral connections between male and female parents.
66. Disassortative mating best holds the ________ together.
67. Random mating has its place in plant breeding for example, in ________.
68. ________ monoecious and cross-pollinating, some of their lines lose little vigour on inbreeding.
69. Sunflower, a cross-pollinated species is fairly ________ to inbreeding.
70. ________ can be regarded as converse of the deterioration that accompanies inbreeding hybrid.
71. The beneficial effects of crossing are more widely recognised than ________ as these are observable in nearly all F1 hybrids.
72. ________ is regarded as an accidental condition with different genetic antecedents and implications from true heterosis.
73. Inbreeding depression as observed is not a process of degeneration, but a consequence of ________.
74. The populations suffering from inbreeding depression embody large number of ________ sheltered ,in heterozygotes.
75. The mating systems of some crop species encourage, but do not enforce ________ pollination.
76. ________ is not very common in plant species in general and occurs in only a few cultivated species.
77. In gametophytic ________ system, pollen tube growth is usually very slow in a style that contains the same allele of sand plants that are heterozygous at this locus.
78. Male sterility unlike incompatibility is not a regular mechanism for controlling ________ in natural populations.

79. Male sterile condition is ordinarily ________.
80. Plants carrying particular types of ________ are male sterile, but produce seed if pollinators are present.
81. ________ frequency also effects the efficiency of selection.
82. ________ recurrent selection is useful in simultaneous selection for both general and specific combining ability.
83. ________ designates a variety maintained from open pollinated seed succeeding its synthesis by hybridization in all combinations among a number of selected genotypes.
84. In many fungi, mating type is governed by a ________ with two alleles, mt^+ and mt^-.
85. Eriksson in 1894 demonstrated that microorganisms can include strains differing in pathogenicity, even though ________ undifferentiated.
86. Hansen and Smith in 1932 demonstrated first that unlike nuclei occur together in the same ________ of *Botrytis cinerea,* an imperfect fungus.
87. Heterocaryosis can lead to changes in ________ in a plant-disease organism.
88. ________ fungi can adjust themselves to circumstances as they develop.
89. Some fungi can be synthesized that carry ________ rather than haploid nuclei in their cells.
90. Crossing over and ________ in fungi are not two parts of a single process, following in that order, as they do in meiosis.
91. ________ cycle is helpful in breeding improved strains of asexual fungi used in industry.
92. ________ refers to the situations in which the issue is number of repetitions of entire chromosome sets.
93. ________ are usually less vigorous than their diploid progenitors.
94. ________ is equally or even more unpredictable than autoploidy in morphological and physiological effects on the phenotype.
95. Euploidy seems to arise most commonly through misadventures in ________.
96. Perhaps the most successful case of induced polyploidy among crop plants is ________ rye with n = 14 instead of n = 7.
97. Red fruited tomato belongs to sub-genus ________.
98. Out of about 30,000 plant species occurring on earth, only around 40 crop species provide the majority of calories and protein to human beings with 50 per cent being contributed by ________ species of cereals.
99. ________ refers to the development of embryo from egg-cell without fertilization.
100. Apogamy means the embryo-development from any one of the synergid or antipodal cells with the ________ without fertilization.
101. ________ denotes the development of embryo neither from egg-cell nor from synergids or antipodals, but from the gametes in or outside of embryo sac.
102. It has been estimated that a normal maize tassel produces 25 million ________.
103. ________ refers to the capacity of a genotype to adjust to a specific environmental condition to attain a certain level of phenotypic expression.
104. ________ refers to the capacity of a genotype to master macro-environmental factors in its favour to manifest a consistent performance over time and space.
105. Genetic assimilation is an ________ mechanism of an organism in all natural selections.
106. Heterozygotes show less variation than do homozygotes in an ________ population.
107. Outbreeding species carry a substantial ________ load.

108. The five phases of occurrence in host-parasite relationship are contact, preparation, penetration ________ and development.

109. Disease ________ means the disease control by natural rather than by physical or chemical means and indicates hereditary struggle against some causal agents.

110. ________ disease resistance means resistance to some races more than to others.

111. When the resistance is evenly spread against all the races. of a pathogen in a variety is known as ________ resistance.

112. The essence of ________ is the disease cycle which has neither beginning nor end.

113. ________ is associated with the rapid spread of a disease.

114. ________ refers to collective heritable characters tending to reduce the probability of a plant to act as the host to a pest/insect.

115. A '*Spontaneum* Expedition Scheme' was initiated in 1947 at the ________ Coimbatore (Tamil Nadu), India.

116. The introduction of ________ chestnut in U.S.A. carried a pathogen that wiped out local chestnut.

117. Biotechnology consists of a cluster of techniques of ________ of living organisms at the cellular and the molecular level.

118. ________ are developed by directly transferring regenes or genes guiding photo-respiration to plant cells through somatic fusion/hybridization.

119. Clonal propagation of ________ plants can be promoted by tissue culture of juvenile cells of apical meristem.

120. Where there is embryonic degeneration especially after distant hybridization ________ might help in recurrecting viable hybrids.

121. Different levels of polyploids can be developed by ________ obtained from anther-culture derived from plants.

122. The regeneration of a mixed population of plants of various poloidy introduces further ________ in plants.

123. Sooner than expected plant breeding at ________ level will be common place.

124. Hunaan ________, the first commodity product of biogenetic techniques was released for sale in September, 1982.

125. The enormous advantages of ________ of plant cells could successfully be translated into standardization of bioculture techniques.

126. It is possible now to regenerate a mature plant or even a tree from an isolated ________.

127. Tissue regeneration in its culture is ________ controlled.

128. Rapid multiplication of medicinal plants and ________ which cannot be bred by conventional methods.

129. The cell tissue culture technique generates numerous progenies useful in ________ breeding.

130. The isolated chloroplasts from cells belonging to a genotype carry the same, ________.

131. The protoplasts of diverse karyotypes fuse together to produce heterokaryon in the process of ________.

132. It has been possible to introduce N-fixing genes (nif-genes) into the bare protoplast during ________ digestion of the cell-wall.

133. *Rhizobia* can also function ________ with non-legume plant cells such as tobacco, wheat, carrot and rice *etc.*

134. It has been observed that there exists a kind of association between tropical grasses ________ bacteria.

135. The major bottleneck of the bioculture techniques is the development of suitable method(s) of regeneration of plants especially in ________.

136. ________ is circumscribed by a non-sexual transfer of genetic information coded on the DNA, from one to the other.

137. The chloroplast DNA (ct DNA) in plants codes for conversion of ammonia to________.

138. A partial or complete fixation of ________ in rice can be achieved without much difficulty.

139. Minor millets are rich source of protein and ________.

II. Tick mark(✓) True or False

140. Wheat and barley in Europe and Egypt are represented by a paucity of types.

141. According to Harlans Egyptians and Europeans obtained cultivated plants of barley and wheat from earlier plant breeders.

142. Lima beans found in the ruins in Peru embody seeds nearly 100 times smaller than those of their wild forms.

143. Gene mutations are the building blocks of plant species' evolution.

144. Reduplication of identical genomes is referred to as allopolyploidy.

145. Reduplication of dissimilar genomes is known as autopolyploidy.

146. Autoploids have not been important in natural evolution due to aberrant chromosome behaviour and high degree of sterility.

147. *Nicotiana tabacum* (tobacco) arose as a hybrid polyploid between *N. sylvestris* and *N. tomentosa*.

148. The earliest organised expedition for plant collection to procure incense trees from East Africa in 1500 was sent by Queen Hatshepsut of Egypt.

149. In Japan, there is a *Taji Mamori,* who went to China on imperial orders to bring citrus fruits back to Japan.

150. Alfalfa, besides an elaborate emtophalous pollinating mechanism, has some sort of compatibility system.

151. In monoecism, protandry and protogyny all individuals of the population are genetically alike in respect of out-breeding mechanism.

152. The cleistogamy provides an evidence of cross-pollination.

153. A synthetic variety is made up of genotypes tested for their ability to produce superior progeny when crossed in all combinations.

154. Outbreeding occurs when matings are made between closely related parents.

155. The interallelic interaction refers to nonaddivity of alleles.

156. In self-pollinated species epistasis is much less important than dominance.

157. Modifying genes are primarily quantitative, but cannot be measured.

158. Penetrance refers to the ability of gene to be expressed in individuals which carry it.

159. Gene penetrance and expressivity represent phenomena exerting clear-cut effects on gene character relationship.

160. Albino plants tend to occur in patches.

161. Plural segregating genes with similar effects explain the inheritance of the qualitative characters.

162. If the heritability is 100 per cent, the phenotype provides a perfect measure of genotypic value.

163. The substitution of one allele for another produces a plus or minus shift on the scale of measurement; the shift is the same regardless of the presence of other genes.

164. In the description of genetic variability, the significant hereditary parameters are defined precisely in terms of genetic models.
165. The progress in plant breeding depends on the nature, magnitude, and interrelations of genetic and non-heritable variation in agriculturally significant plant characteristics.
166. A breeder bases the hopes of improvement on evidence of genetic variations.
167. Selection in cross-pollinated crops is an ancient method of breeding, but more recently the understanding thereof bas developed.
168. Recombination even occasionally does not lead to the production of desirable features not found in either parent.
169. Natural epiphytotics adequate to distinguish between disease resistant and susceptible plants may not occur regularly.
170. Tbe diastatic power of malting barley cannot be decided visually accurately.
171. Tbe appearance, yield and adaptation of the parents is always a good indicator of superior combining ability.
172. In backcross breeding, a series of backcrosses are made to the variety to be improved and the desirable character(s) are maintained by selection.
173. Backcross improvement programme for cross-pollinated species fundamentally differs from that of self-pollinated species.
174. Backcross method can be carried out in any environment suitable for the development of the character being transferred.
175. The primary effect of genetic assortative mating is to decrease the probability that offspring will inherit the same genes from both of their parents.
176. The effect of inbreeding, with or without selection, is to decrease the genetic correlation between close relatives.
177. The coefficient of inbreeding has a value of zero in random-mating populations and increases toward one as the probable proportion of heterozygosity goes toward zero.
178. The genetic effect of mating like to like on the basis of phenotypic characteristics depends on gene number and heritability.
179. If the assortative mating is based on only two extreme phenotypes, fixation is achieved in one generation.
180. For economically important characters, gene numbers are likely to be small and heritability low.
181. Phenotypic disassortative mating is probably most useful in plant breeding to maintain closeness in populations.
182. Consanguineous matings were favoured by ancient Egyptians, Hebrews, Greeks and Nordic tribes to maintain superior bloodliness and/or property within families.
183. Although free crossing is a danger on one side, while too close inbreeding is a hidden danger on the other.
184. Onion is normally cross-pollinated species that is quite intolerant to inbreeding.
185. In date palm as male plants produce no fruits yet these are essential for the production of pollen.
186. In hops the commercial product is dried pistillate inflorescence.
187. The incompatibility process cannot operate at any stage between pollination and fertilization.
188. In homomorphic systems, the differences in floral morphology accompany the incompatibility.

189. Hybrid varieties (F1) can be obtained by crossing clones, open pollinated varieties, inbred lines or other populations that are genetically dissimilar.
190. The double cross, suggested 'by D.F. Jone in 1918 made hybrid maize economically feasible.
191. The discovery of physiological races in fungi provided no clue necessary for developing a method more permanent control.
192. The stability of disease resistant varieties has been short lived.
193. The term aneuploidy describes the organisms where chromosome number is not a whole number multiple of the basic number of the group.
194. Hybrids of *L. esculentum* and *L. hirsutum* are highly sterile.
195. High protein is associated with low yields in most of the cereals.
196. "Evolution under domestication is a close counterpart of evolution in nature".
197. "Genetic diversity is not necessary for significant heterosis, but sufficient not to guarantee, it".
198. "Multiple allelism cannot give the same result even in the absence of linkage and epistasis".
199. Larger the specific combining ability (SCA), smaller is the heterotic effect in the cross.
200. "It is futile, indeed harmful, to expect that yields can continue to be raised simply by breeding superior new varieties".
201. Pathogens manifest inherent variability.
202. Antibiosis relates to production of chemical factors injurious to pests by host plants.
203. The tolerance/endurance fails to enable the host plant to produce yield regardless of pest-attack.
204. In cross-resistance, some factors cause resistance in a host plant to one pest, but not to others.
205. The two major areas of biotechnology are genetic engineering (gene splicing/recombinant DNA technology) and bioculture (tissue culture).
206. Somaclonal variation in biocultures is not helpful for selection at the cellular level.
207. The compound meristematic tissues fail to produce complex chimeras on mutagenesis.
208. Haploid plants can be produced by anther culture, pollen culture makes it easier.
209. A great deal of natural variability exists in plant tissues.
210. In vegetatively propagated plants, new varieties cannot be maintained in a disease-free condition during multiplication before release.
211. Modifying genes mean the genes that effect the expression of a nonallelic gene/genes.
212. Meiosis refers to double mitosis occurring in sexual reproduction which results in production of gametes with haploid (n) chromosome number.
213. Embryos which normally rail to survive cannot be successfully cultured to maturity on suitable media specific for each crop.
214. In embryo culture/rescue fertilized egg cells are usually excised one/two weeks after fertilization and are cultured on suitable media.
215. Embryo culture does not facilitate wide crossing.
216. Embryo breakdown after hybridization cannot be offset by embryo culture.
217. Mutants for genes affecting photorespiration in plants can be induced within a cell.
218. The pollen culture does not afford any segregation potential.
219. Anther culture entails natural loss of inbred line.
220. Protoplasts regardless of their origin, tend to fuse when brought into intimate contact with each other.

221. Leaves are eminently suitable for protoplast isolation.

222. Ordinarily, both isolation and recombination of DNA are not very difficult feats to be achieved.

223. DNA are the pre-requisite for transformation.

224. The specificity of legumes to establish a symbiotic relationship with *Rhizobium* species is due to their capacity to produce lectin proteins directing bacterial invasion to root tissues.

III. Tick mark (✓) the correct answer

225. The main patterns concerning origin and domestication of cultivated plant species are ________.
(*a*) Mendelian variation (*b*) Interspecific hybridization
(*c*) Polyploidy (*d*) All of these

226. Cauliflower, cabbage, broccoli, kohlrabi and brussels sprouts have been derived from wild cabbage that still grows in coastal regions of ________.
(*a*) Latin America (*b*) Mesopotamia
(*c*) Europe and N. Africa (*d*) South Asia and South Africa

227. Seeds of lime beans found in Peruvian tombs prove that the modern types were cultivated as long ago as ________ year.
(*a*) 1200 (*b*) 1600
(*c*) 2600 (*d*) 3600

228. Commercial bananas have ________ instead of 22 chromosomes of ordinary diploid varieties.
(*a*) 13 (*b*) 23
(*c*) 33 (*d*) 43

229. Tetraploid potato has 48 chromosomes, whereas ordinary diploid species have ________ chromosomes.
(*a*) 34 (*b*) 24
(*c*) 14 (*d*) 10

230. The usefulness of cortisome for medicinal purposes led to the identification of ________ a potentially rich source of it.
(*a*) *Discorea* (b) *Colocasia*
(*a*) *Lantana* (*b*) *Canabis*

231. ________ are examples of protandrous species.
(*a*) Avocados (*b*) Walnuts
(*a*) Carrots (b) None of these

232. A plant breeder is interested to control pollination to ________.
(*a*) Prevent cross pollination (*b*) Control pollination
(*c*) None of these (*d*) Both of these

233. The chromosomal aberrations include ________.
(*a*) Duplication or deficiency (*b*) Translocation or inversions
(*c*) Multiplication or polyploidy (*d*) All of these

234. The term epistasis was originally used by ________ in 1909 to describe genes whose effects mark or cover the effects of other genes.
(*a*) Wagner (*b*) Bateson
(*c*) Hayman (*d*) Atwood

235. ________ in Ladino clover is governed by two dominant alleles, one produces cyanogenic glucoside, while the other releases the enzyme to catalyze its release from glucoside.
(*a*) Oxalic acid (*b*) IAA
(*c*) HCN (*d*) NAA

236. The genes that intensify or diminish the effect of major genes are known as ________ factors.
(*a*) Modifying (*b*) Nullifying
(*c*) Flsifying (*d*) None of these

237. In wheat and oat there are ________ genes for red versus white kernels.
(*a*) Two (*b*) Three
(*c*) Four (*d*) Five

238. Rose clover was introduced in ________ from Turkey in 1944.
(*a*) U.S.A. (*b*) U.K.
(*c*) France (*d*) Germany

239. Nilsson-Ehle of ________ was apparently the first to use the bulk popultion method to breed superior crop varieties.
(*a*) Sweden (*b*) Mexico
(*c*) France (*d*) Germany

240. Bulk population breeding is suitable for ________.
(*a*) Fruit crops (*b*) Vegetable crops
(*c*) Small grains (*d*) Flower crops

241. Development of a successful variety by backcross breeding calls for ________.
(*a*) Satisfactory recurrent parent (*b*) Retention of intensity of desired trait
(*c*) Sufficient backcrosses to reconstitute recurrent parent
(*d*) All of these

242. If parents differ in ten gene pairs, no selection is done; six backcrosses will produce a population having ________ per cent homozygous and identical individuals to recurrent parent at all ten *loci.*
(*a*) 65 (*b*) 75
(*c*) 85 (*d*) 95

243. Modern population genetics is found on a proposition deduced independently by Hardy in England in 1908 and ________ in Germany in 1909.
(*a*) Weinberg (*b*) Pugsley
(*c*) Briggs (*d*) Weibe

244. "If a gene is represented in an infinitely large random-mating population by adaptively neutral alleles, A and a, in the ratio of $qA:(1-q)\,a$, the genotypic proportions: $q^2AA + 2q\,(1-q)\,Aa + (1-q)^2\,aa = 1$" is known as ________.
(*a*) Stanford-Suneson law (*b*) Weibe- Thomas law
(*c*) Briggs-Harlan law (*d*) Hardy-Weinberg law

245. The first inbreeding experiments with maize were those reported by ________.
(*a*) Sprengel in 1866 (*b*) Darwin in 1876
(*c*) Sprague in 1886 (*d*) Baird 1896

246. Despite conspicuous deterioration of maize upon continuous selfing, it is more tolerant to inbreeding than ________.

(*a*) Lima beans (*b*) Barley
(*c*) Alfalfa (*d*) Buckwheat

247. ________ deteriorates drastically upon inbreeding.

(*a*) Carrot (*b*) Okra
(*c*) Brinjal (*d*) Broccoli

248. In ________ the first studies on artificial hybridization for which yields were reported were those of Beal during the period between 1877 and 1882.

(*a*) Sorghum (*b*) Pearlmillet
(*c*) Maize (*d*) Rye

249. The staminate ________ plants outyield pistillate plants by about 25 per cent.

(*a*) Asparagus (*b*) Lettuce
(*c*) Spinach (*d*) Hemp

250. ________ estimated that incompatibility occurs in more than 3,000 species among 20 families of the flowering plants.

(*a*) D. de Winton (*b*) M.B. Hughes
(*c*) W.H. Gabelman (*d*) E.M. East

251. Pseudofertility may also occur late in the season as in ________.

(*a*) Tomato (*b*) Tobacco
(*c*) Tapioca (d) Tea

252. In ________ pollen dispersal is poor and seed set is likely to be low on male sterile plants.

(*a*) Tomato (*b*) Cauliflower
(*c*) Broccoli (*d*) Carrot

253. ________ provides the best documented example of long time effects of selection.

(*a*) Sugarcane (*b*) Sweet sorghum
(*c*) Sugarbeet (*d*) Sugar maple

254. Vilmorin Principle progeny testing stimulated ________ to devise Ear-to-Row Method of maize breeding in 1886.

(*a*) H.L. Westover (*b*) C.G. Hopkins
(*c*) W.L. Brown (*d*) F.D. Richey

255. Thomas Andrew Knight first noted differences among wheat varieties in their resistance to ________

(*a*) Smut (*b*) Bunt
(*c*) Rust (*d*) Wilt

256. Chauncey Goodrich was the first ________ to publish a paper dealing with the resistance of potatoes to the blight disease.

(*a*) Britisher (*b*) German
(*c*) Dutch (*d*) American

257. Biffin in 1905 announced that resistance to yellow rust of wheat is governed by ________ gene in crosses.

(*a*) Single dominant (*b*) Single recessive
(*c*) Double dominant (*d*) Double recessive

258. It has been estimated that a maize tassel produces at least __________ pollen grains for each kernel

(a) 5,000 (b) 15,000

(c) 25,000 (d) 35,000

259. Paramutation in __________ is perhaps the one and only example of blending of alleles.

(a) Sorghum (b) Maize

(c) Pearlmillet (d) Foxtailmillet

260. Disease reaction, is by and large, a __________ process.

(a) Physical (b) Chemical

(c) Mechanical (d) Manual

261. Nutritional improvement for the tryptophan content has been achieved in a __________ cell-line.

(a) Tomato (b) Cucurbits

(c) Coffee (d) Tobacco

262. Tissue culture in eucalyptus gave __________ seedling per annum.

(a) 4,000 (b) 7,000

(c) 10,000 (d) 13,000

263. Tissue culture in teak produced __________ seedling per year.

(a) 500 (b) 1000

(c) 1500 (d) 2000

264. The embroid (formed by vegetative cell) develops into a plant which, in fact, grows out of anther as in __________.

(a) Tobacco (b) Wheat

(c) Barley (d) Sorghum

III. Match the following

265. Match the place of origin with the crops given below:

(a) Tropical America (i) Cotton

(b) Tropical N. America (ii) Soyabeans

(c) Asia Minor (iii) Wheat

(d) China (iv) Maize (corn)

266. Match the crops with their place of origin:

(a) Tobacco (i) Asia Minor or N. Africa

(b) Oats (ii) Africa

(c) Potatoes (iii) Tropical America

(d) Sorghum (iv) S outh America

267. Match the number of allelic pairs with king of gametes possible inf F1:

(a) 2 (i) 8

(b) 3 (ii) 1024

(c) 4 (iii) 4

(d) 10 (iv) 16

268. Match the names of the aneuploids with the formula:

(*a*) Nullisomic (*i*) $2x-1$
(*b*) Monosomic (*ii*) $2x+1$
(*c*) Trisomic (*iii*) $2x+2$
(*d*) Tetrasomic (*iv*) $2x-2$

269. Match the crop with the chromosome number:

(*a*) *Avena sativa* (Oats) (*i*) 26
(*b*) *Gossypium arborium* (Cotton) (*ii*) 21
(*c*) *Gossypium barbadense* (Cotton) (*iii*) 7
(*d*) *Hordeum vulgare.* (Barley) (*iv*) 13

270. Match the chromosome numbers with the crop

(*a*) 16 (*i*) *Nicotiana sylvestris* (Wild tobacco)
(*b*) 12 (*ii*) *Trifolium alexandrinum* (Egyptian clover)
(*c*) 24 (*iii*) *Medicago sativa* (Common alfalfa)
(*d*) 8 (*iv*) *Nicotiana tabacum* (Cultivated tobacco)

271. Match the crop with chromosome numbers:

(*a*) *Sorghum versicolor* (*i*) 8
(*b*) *Bromus carinatus* (mountain bromegrass) (*ii*) 5
(*c*) *Lotus corniculatus* (birdsfoot trefoil) (*iii*) 12
(*d*) *Trifolium hybridum* (alsike clover) (*iv*) 28

272. Match the gene/cytoplasm with the crop:

(*a*) Norin gene and timophevi cytoplasm (*i*) Rice
(*b*) Opaque-2 and T-cytoplasm (*ii*) Pearlmillet
(*c*) Dee-Gee-Woo-Gen (*iii*) Wheat
(*d*) Tifton 23A (*iv*) Maize

273. Match the following parts with the common term used:

(*a*) Ovary (*i*) Seed
(*b*) Ovule (*ii*) Peri sperm
(*c*) Definitive nucleus (*iii*) Fruit
(*d*) Nucleus (*iv*) Endospenrm

274. Match the following plants with the type of apomixis:

(*a*) Apple (*i*) Adventive embryony
(*b*) Maize (*ii*) Non-recurrent
(*c*) Citrus (*iii*) Vegetative apomixis
(*d*) Grass species (*iv*) Recurrent

275. Match the manifestation of heterosis with the process it is associated with :

(*a*) Molecular level (*i*) Metabolic regulation and morphogenesis
(*b*) Metabolic path level (*ii*) Growth and differentiation
(*c*) Cellular level (*iii*) DNA duplication, transcription and translation
(*d*) Organism level (*iv*) Increased mitosis

276. Match the following point mutation with acquired functions of the alleles:

(*a*) Hypomorphs	(*i*) Impeding/antagonising the function of normal allele
(*b*) Hypermorphs	(*ii*) Allele that has aquired a new function
(*c*) Neomorphs	(*iii*) Normal funstioning less efficiently
(*d*) Antimorphs	(*iv*) Allele functioning more efficiently than normal allele

277. Match the symptoms with the disease which they are commonly associated with :

(*a*) Necrosis	(*i*) Damping off
(*b*) Transformation	(*ii*) Foliage infection
(*c*) Hypertrophy and malformation	(*iii*) Green-ear disease
(*d*) Wilting	(*iv*) Ergot

278. Match the following some of the most importnt events in plant breeding with the Scientist(s) responsible for them:

(*a*) Diverse germplasm as a source of variability	(*i*) G.F. Sprague and L.A.Tatum (1942)
(*b*) Conversion improvement and multiple convergent	(*ii*) M.T. Jenkins (1940)
(*c*) General and specific combining ability	(*iii*) S.K Wu (1939)
(*d*) Simple recurrent selection techniques	(*iv*) F.D. Richey and G.F. Sprague (1931)

279. Match the following crop varieties with their source of development/introduction in India:

(*a*) Jaya and Padma (Rice)	(*i*) CO_1 × Bonganhilo
(*b*) CO_2 (Sorghum)	(*ii*) From Afric (introduced)
(*c*) Striga resistant sorghum	(*iii*) Sonora-64, isolated after irradiation
(*d*) Sharbati Sonora (wheat)	(*iv*) From a cross with TN-1 (from Taiwan)

280. Match the centres of diversity with the number of species of crops believed to have originated from:

(*a*) China	(*i*) 42 spp., 15 crops
(*b*) India	(*ii*) 136 spp., 11 crops
(*c*) Middle East	(*iii*) 83 spp., 20 crops
(*d*) Near East	(*iv*) 117 spp., 15 crops

281. Match the estimated plant species (spp.) and crops with their centres of diversity :

(*a*) 84 spp., 6 crops	(*i*) Ethiopia
(*b*) 38 spp., 15 crops	(*ii*) Mexico, Central America
(*c*) 49 spp., 9 crops	(*iii*) South America
(*d*) 45 spp., 7 crops	(*iv*) Mediterranean

282. Match the following mutants (variety) with the crop.

(*a*) Sharbati Sonora	(*i*) French bean
(*b*) TG-I	(*ii*) Wheat
(*c*) S-12	(*iii*) Peanut
(*d*) Pusa Parvathi	(*iv*) Tomato

283. Match the following crops with their mutant varieties :

(*a*) Rice	(*i*) Aruna
(*b*) Cotton	(*ii*) RDB-1
(*c*) Castor	(*iii*) MCU-7
(*d*) Wheat	(*iv*) IIT-60

284. Match the range of concentration recommended of mutagens to treat cereal seeds

(*a*) 0.05-0.3 M	(*i*) ENH and MNH
(*b*) 0.015-0.02 M	(*ii*) EMS
(*c*) 0.85-9.00 mM	(*iii*) dES
(*d*) 1.2-14.0 mM	(*iv*) EI

285. Match the spontaneous beneficial mutants with the crops wherein they occurred and later used in breeding:

(*a*) GEB-24	(*i*) Sorghum
(*b*) CO_2 and CO_{19}	(*ii*) Potato
(*c*) EC593 and 3735	(*iii*) Konamani Rice
(*d*) Red Triumph	(*iv*) Fingermillet

286. Match the stages of shoot differentiation in tissue culture of the following cereal crops

(*a*) Root	(*i*) Maize
(*b*) Shoot just. below first internode	(*ii*) Pearlmillet
(*c*) Mature/immature embryo	(*iii*) Sorghum
(*d*) Mesocotyl	(*iv*) Rice plants

287. Match the year of evolution of commercial hybrid with the field crops given below

(*a*) Maize (field corn)	(*i*) 1969
(*b*) Grain sorghum	(*ii*) 1965
(*c*) Pearlmillet	(*iii*) 1921
(*d*) Wheat	(*iv*) 1955

288. Match the crops with the commercial hybrid's year of release:

(*a*) 1972	(*i*) Rice
(*b*) 1968	(*ii*) Potato
(*c*) 1975	(*iii*) Barley
(*d*) 1980	(*iv*) Oats

289. Match the crop with the year of development of first commercial hybrid thereof:

(*a*) Soybean	(i) 1975
(*b*) Cotton	(*ii*) 1972
(*c*) Sunflower	(iii) 1933
(*d*) Sweet corn	(*iv*) 1980

290. Match the following vegetable crops with the year of development of first commercial hybrid

(*a*) Egg-plant	(*i*) 1943
(*b*) Tomato	(*ii*) 1939
(*c*) Onion	(*iii*) 1948
(*d*) Winter squash	(*iv*) 1950

291. Match the following crops with the year of release of its first commercial hybrid:

(*a*) Cabbage — (*i*) 1961
(*b*) Broccoli — (*ii*) 1964
(*c*) Carrot — (*iii*) 1966
(*d*) Cauliflower — (*iv*) 1954

292. Match the crop grains with their lysine content (mg/g N) as given below

(*a*) Rice — (*i*) 174
(*b*) Wheat — (*ii*) 224
(*c*) Maize — (*iii*) 237
(*d*) Pearlmillet — (*iv*) 167

293. Match the crops with the tryptophan content (mg/g N)

(*a*) Rice, — (*i*) 65
(*b*) Wheat — (*ii*) 78
(*c*) Pearlmiliet — (*iii*) 68
(*d*) Sorghum — (*iv*) 122

294. Match the net protein utilization (NPU %) with the different sources:

(*a*) 93.5 — (*i*) Milk casein
(*b*) 79.6 — (*ii*) Rice
(*c*) 76.7 — (*iii*) Hen's egg
(*d*) 70.2 — (*iv*) Beef

295. A plant population originally heterozygous for three gene pairs and selfed for four generations or $n = 3$ and $m = 4$, translate it into genetic terms. Find the value of x.

Since, $[1 + (2^m - 1)]^n$

Therefore, $[1 + (2^4 - 1)^3] = [1 + 15]^3$

$= 1^3 + 3(1)^2(15) + 3(1)(15)^3 + [15]^3$

In genetic terms:-

1 plant with 0 homozygous and 3 heterozygous *loci*

45 plants with 1 homozygous and 2 heterozygous *loci*

675 plants with 2 homozygous and 1 heterozygous *loci*

(x) plants with 3 homozygous and 0 heterozygous *loci*

———

4096

296. Fill up degrees of freedom (df) for error, families (F) × years (Y) × locations, R represents replications.

Source of variance	d.f.
Families	$F - 1$
Families × years	$(F - 1)(Y - 1)$
Families × locations	$(F - 1)(L - 1)$
$F \times Y \times L$	________
Error	________

297. When a variety that carries two dominant genes, each individually capable of producing a resistant phenotype, is crossed with a susceptible variety, the ratio expected in F2 generation is________.

298. Stability factor (SF) of Lewis (1954) employing only the mean is_______.

$$SF = \frac{\overline{x}HE}{\overline{x}LE}$$

where, $\overline{x}HE$ = High yielding environment

$\overline{x}LE$ = Low yielding environment

Maxilnum phenotypic stability is reflected by SF =

Do You Know That

1. Eugenics is the science of selective breeding to get a pre-determined set of genetic characteristics.
2. India is pioneer for hybrid research on pearl millet.
3. Puja Jai Kisan the first soma clone variety (commereial) of crop mustard was released by IDRI.
4. First cottom hybrid was developed by C.T. Patel in 1970.
5. The father of sugarcane is Sh. T.S. Venkatraman
6. Concept of disruptive selection was given by Mather in the year 1953.
7. Pusa Giant is a popular variety of Berseem.
8. In India, the maximum sugarcane productivity level is in the state of Tamil Nadu.
9. India is pioneer in the world for development and commerical cultivation of cotton hybrids.
10. Term mutation was coined by deVaries in the year 1900.
11. Highest adaptability is seen in multiple cross.
12. In India gamma garden is located at IARI, New Delhi.
13. Nobel prize was awarded to Muller in the year 1946 for experimental inductions of mutations by X-ray.
14. First pearlmillet and sorghum hybrids were released for commercial cultivation in 1964 and 1965, respectively.
15. High yielding varieties programme was launched in India in 1966.

KEY

1. 5,000-6,000	2. Switzerland	3. Mesopotamia
4. Barley and wheat	5. Tropical America	6. Gene mutations
7. Multiple	8. Lima bean	9. Mendelian variation
10. Taxonomic species	11. Introgressive	12. Polyploidy
13. Reproductive	14. Natural	15. Microorganisms
16. Hybridization	17. Equally effficient	18. Extrusion

19. Pollination
20. Outbreeders
21. Protogyny
22. Dioecy
23. Gametophytic or haplo-diplo scheme
24. Incompatibility
25. Asexual
26. Apomictic
27. Genetic segregation
28. New varieties
29. Mass-selection
30. Progenies
31. Back-cross
32. Recurrent parent
33. Hybrid
34. Male sterility
35. Recurrent
36. Synthetic
37. Mutilation
38. France in 1843
39. Swedish
40. Pure-line
41. Homozygous
42. Genes
43. Phenotypic
44. *Drosophila melanogaster*
45. Awned versus awnless
46. Isogenic
47. Combination
48. Small and similar
49. Flower
50. Self-fertilization
51. Genes
52. Pure-line
53. Mass-selection
54. Malthus
55. Homogeneous
56. Pedigree record
57. Adapted varieties
58. Gene alone
59. Bulk-population
60. Pedigree
61. Back-cross
62. By chance
63. Relationship (ancestry)
64. Disassortative
65. Coefficient of inbreeding
66. Population
67. Progeny testing
68. Cucurbits
69. Tolerant
70. Vigour/heterosis
71. Inbreeding depression
72. Luxuriance
73. Mendelian segregation
74. Recessive genes
75. Cross
76. Dioecy
77. Incompatibility
78. Hybridity
79. Recessive
80. Cytoplasm
81. Gene
82. Reciprocal
83. Synthetic variety
84. Single locus
85. Morphologically
86. Hypha
87. Pathogenicity
88. Heterocaryotic
89. Diploid
90. Haploidization
91. Parasexual
92. Euploidy
93. Aneuploids
94. Allopolyploidy
95. Meiosis
96. Autotetraploid
97. Eulycopersicon
98. Nine
99. Parthenogenesis
100. Embryo sac
101. Androgamy
102. Pollen grains
103. Adaptation
104. Adaptabulity
105. Adaptive
106. Interbreeding
107. Genetic
108. Establishment
109. Resistance
110. Vertical/perpendicular
111. Horizontal
112. Epidemiology
113. Aggressiveness
114. Pest-resistance
115. Sugarcane Breeding Institute (SBI)
116. Japanese
117. Genetic manipulation
118. Super hybrids/parasexual hybrids
119. Heterozygous
120. Embryo culture
121. Haploid anther
122. Genetic variations
123. Molecular
124. Insulin
125. Totipotency
126. Single cell/Callus
127. Genetically
128. Trees
129. Mutation
130. Karyotype
131. Somatic hybridization
132. Enzymatic
133. Symbiotically
134. N-fixing
135. Cereals and legumes
136. Genetic engineering
137. Glutamine

138. Hybrid vigour
139. Lysine
140. True
141. True
142. False
143. True
144. False
145. False
146. True
147. True
148. True
149. True
150. False
151. True
152. False
153. True
154. False
155. True
156. False
157. False
158. True
159. False
160. True
161. False
162. True
163. True
164. True
165. True
166. True
167. False
168. False
169. True
170. True
171. False
172. True
173. False
174. True
175. False
176. False
177. True
178. True
179. True
180. False
181. False
182. True
183. True
184. False
185. True
186. True
187. False
188. False
189. True
190. True
191. False
192. True
193. True
194. False
195. True
196. True
197. False
198. False
199. False
200. True
201. True
202. True
203. False
204. False
205. True
206. False
207. False
208. True
209. True
210. False
211. True
212. True
213. False
214. True
215. False
216. False
217. True
218. False
219. False
220. True
221. True
222. False
223. True
224. True
225. (*d*)
226. (*c*)
227. (*c*)
228. (*c*)
229. (*b*)
230. (*a*)
231. (*c*)
232. (*d*)
233. (*d*)
234. (*b*)
235. (*c*)
236. (*a*)
237. (*b*)
238. (*a*)
239. (*a*)
240. (*c*)
241. (*d*)
242. (*c*)
243. (*a*)
244. (*d*)
245. (*b*)
246. (*c*)
247. (*a*)
248. (*c*)
249. (*a*)
250. (*d*)
251. (*b*)
252. (*a*)
253. (*c*)
254. (*b*)
255. (*c*)
256. (*d*)
257. (*b*)
258. (*c*)
259. (*b*)
260. (*b*)
261. (*d*)
262. (*b*)

263. (*c*)	264. (*a*)		
265. (*a*)-(*iv*)	(*b*)-(*i*)	(*c*)-(*iii*)	(*d*)-(*ii*)
266. (*a*)-(*iii*)	(*b*)-(*i*)	(*c*)-(*iv*)	(*d*)-(*ii*)
267. (*a*)-(*iii*)	(*b*)-(*i*)	(*c*)-(*iv*)	(*d*)-(*ii*)
268. (*a*)-(*iv*)	(*b*)-(*i*)	(*c*)-(*ii*)	(*d*)-(*iii*)
269. (*a*)-(*ii*)	(*b*)-(*iv*)	(*c*)-(*i*)	(*d*)-(*iii*)
270. (*a*)-(*iii*)	(*b*)-(*i*)	(*c*)-(*iv*)	(*d*)-(*ii*)
271. (*a*)-(*ii*)	(*b*)-(*iv*)	(*c*)-(*iii*)	(*d*)-(*i*)
272. (*a*)-(*iii*)	(*b*)-(*iv*)	(*c*)-(*i*)	(*d*)-(*ii*)
273. (*a*)-(*iii*)	(*b*)-(*i*)	(*c*)-(*iv*)	(*d*)-(*ii*)
274. (*a*)-(*iv*)	(*b*)-(*ii*)	(*c*)-(*i*)	(*d*)-(*iii*)
275. (*a*)-(*iii*)	(*b*)-(*i*)	(*c*)-(*iv*)	(*d*)-(*ii*)
276. (*a*)-(*iii*)	(*b*)-(*iv*)	(*c*)-(*ii*)	(*d*)-(*i*)
277. (*a*)-(*ii*)	(*b*)-(*iv*)	(*c*)-(*iii*)	(*d*)-(*i*)
278. (*a*)-(*iii*)	(*b*)-(*iv*)	(*c*)-(*i*)	(*d*)-(*ii*)
279. (*a*)-(*iv*)	(*b*)-(*i*)	(*c*)-(*ii*)	(*d*)-(*iii*)
280. (*a*)-(*ii*)	(*b*)-(*iv*)	(*c*)-(*i*)	(*d*)-(*iii*)
281. (*a*)-(*iv*)	(*b*)-(*i*)	(*c*)-(*ii*)	(*d*)-(*iii*)
282. (*a*)-(*ii*)	(*b*)-(*iii*)	(*c*)-(*iv*)	(*d*)-(*i*)
283. (*a*)-(*iv*)	(*b*)-(*iii*)	(*c*)-(*i*)	(*d*)-(*ii*)
284. (*a*)-(*ii*)	(*b*)-(*iii*)	(*c*)-(*iv*)	(*d*)-(*i*)
285. (*a*)-(*iv*)	(*b*)-(*i*)	(*c*)-(*iv*)	(*d*)-(*ii*)
286. (*a*)-(*iv*)	(*b*)-(*iii*)	(*c*)-(*i*)	(*d*)-(*ii*)
287. (*a*)-(*iii*)	(*b*)-(*iv*)	(*c*)-(*ii*)	(*d*)-(*i*)
288. (*a*)-(*i*)	(*b*)-(*iii*)	(*c*)-(*iv*)	(*d*)-(*ii*)
289. (*a*)-(*iv*)	(*b*)-(*i*)	(*c*)-(*ii*)	(*d*)-(*iii*)
290. (*a*)-(*ii*)	(*b*)-(*i*)	(*c*)-(*iii*)	(*d*)-(*iv*)
291. (*a*)-(*iv*)	(*b*)-(*i*)	(*c*)-(*ii*)	(*d*)-(*iii*)
292. (*a*)-(*iii*)	(*b*)-(*i*)	(*c*)-(*iv*)	(*d*)-(*ii*)
293. (*a*)-(*ii*)	(*b*)-(*iii*)	(*c*)-(*iv*)	(*d*)-(*i*)
294. (*a*)-(*iii*)	(*b*)-(*i*)	(*c*)-(*iv*)	(*d*)-(*ii*)

295. $x = 3375$

296. For F × Y × L

(F– l) (Y– l) (L – l)

For Error (R – l) (FYL – l)

297. 15 resistant to 1 susceptible

298. 1

SECTION 4
PLANT PHYSIOLOGY

I. Fill up the blanks:

1. _______ cells contain no membrane-bound organelles.
2. Living organisms are _______ structures.
3. In living organisms, as in other machines _______ and function are intimately wedded.
4. _______ are smaller solid structures (5-7 nm in diameter) that act alone or in coordination with microtubules to produce cellular movement.
5. At least in many cells endoplasmic _______ is less like a collapsed sack than it is like an assemblage of thousands of tiny tubes called tubules.
6. Ribosomes forming a chain like, a string of beads are called _______.
7. Chlorophyll containing plastids are known as _______.
8. The plastids that contain the red pigments of tomato skin have been termed as _______.
9. _______ are spherical organelles bound by a single membrane.
10. _______ are special structures occurring in plants and some protistants, bound by a double- membrane system.
11. The _______ is the control centre of eukaryotic cell, and often is its most conspicuous organelles.
12. The nucleus contains one or more roughly spherical bodies called _______ each having a diameter of about 3-5μm (upto 10 μm).
13. Golgi bodies have been named after the name of an Italian _______ who discovered them in 1898.
14. The stacks of flattened hollow discs with convoluted margins surrounded by spherical bodies are called _______.
15. Two parallel surface membranes surrounding the nucleus are together termed as _______.
16. Most of the unique properties of water can be assigned to line segments connecting the centre of the _______ atom forming an angle of about 105° closer to the right angle than to straight line.
17. In water molecule, the hydrogen atoms approximate _______ on the surface of the oxygen atom.
18. In a water molecule, the protons distributed 105° apart on the surface of the oxygen atom provide a slight positive charge balanced by an equal _______ charge on the side, renders it neutral.
19. A molecule having equal positive and negative charges on opposite side is called a _______ molecule.
20. The positive side of one water molecule is attracted to the negative side of another forming a bond known as _______.
21. Hydrogen bonds are _______ than ionic and covalent bonds.
22. _______ attractive forces are even weaker than hydrogen bonds.

23. Water has a molecular weight of only 18, is a liquid at room temperature because hydrogen bonds provide a disproportionately high attractive forces among its molecules, inhibiting their ______ and escape as vapour.
24. For practical purposes liquid water is ______.
25. ______ calories are required to convert one gramme of water to one gramme water vapour at 20°C.
26. Unusually high latent heat of vaporization can be assigned to the tenacity of the ______.
27. Tetrahedrons are so arranged that the ice crystal is basically ______ demonstrated in the pattern of snowflakes.
28. The total volume of water ______ during melting.
29. The density of ice is ______ than the density of water.
30. The number of bonds per oxygen atom are ______ in ice than in water molecules.
31. Viscosity of water ______ markedly with increasing temperature.
32. The attraction between unlike molecules is called ______.
33. A falling water drop becomes spherical due to ______.
34. ______ pure water (extremely difficult to obtain) is a poor conductor of electricity.
35. Near room temperature $K = 10^{-14}$ $[H^+]$ $[OH^-]$ = [K], so in pure water $[OH^-]$ and $[H^+]$ = ______ molar (M).
36. The flow occurring in response to difference in pressure and involving groups of atoms or molecules together is termed as ______.
37. The net movement from one point to another due to random kinetic activities of ions and molecules is called ______.
38. Diffusion often occurs in response to differences in the ______ of substances between one point and another.
39. ______ states that the elementary particles (atoms, ions and molecules) are in constant motion at temperatures above absolute zero.
40. The average ______ molecule, near room temperature moves at 6,433 km per hour.
41. ______ occupies no space and has no mass, but can transform or act on matter.
42. Region of space or quantity of matter on which attention is focussed is called ______.
43. Everything not in the system is known as ______ and is separated by the boundary.
44. "You cannot get something for nothing" is the first law of ______.
45. "No real process can be 100 per cent efficient" is the ______ law of thermodynamics.
46. Photosynthesis will never be 100 per cent efficient because some of ______ driving the process will be converted into heat energy.
47. In a classroom 10 students can be arranged on 10 chairs in ______ ways.
48. ______ is a measure of the maximum energy available for conversion to work (at constant temperature and pressure).
49. If the pulling or pushing across the boundary is highly organized, it is called ______.
50. If the pushing, pulling or striking at the interaction boundary is random, chaotic and on the scale of atoms and molecules, it is termed as ______.
51. ______ in 1870 developed thermodynamic measure of energy passing across the boundary between a system and its surroundings available for work interaction.
52. Chemical bond energy in gasoline is ______ energy.

53. The basic equation for the Gibb's free-energy has an enthalpy factor and ______ factor.
54. The enthalpy factor of a system consists of the internal energy plus the absolute ______ multiplied by volume.
55. The entropy factor (entropy) multiplied by absolute temperature, is substrated from enthalpy to determine ______.
56. The free-energy per unit quantity of substance, specifically per gramme molecular weight (the free-energy mol^{-1}) is called ______.
57. Chemical potential like solute concentration and temperature is ______ of the quantity of the substance.
58. ______ for solute particles is the most common and important factor to establish chemical potential gradients that drive diffusion.
59. Particles diffuse from points of high to points of ______ activity.
60. Liquid water or water vapour often diffuses from deep into the soil to the surface when it is ______ at night.
61. The cooler gas diffuses into the ______ gas.
62. An increase in the pressure increases ______ and hence chemical potential for a system.
63. Mole fraction of a solvent is equal to ______ divided by moles of solute plus moles of solvent.
64. A material with surfaces that bind water is called ______.
65. The concentration of water molecules in vapour (gas) phase is expressed as ______.
66. The relative humidity above a solution (at equilibrium) is equal to the ______ of solvent expressed as per cent.
67. The rate of diffusion is given by a simple, but highly significant equation called ______ formulated in 1855.
68. Permeability is simply ______ of the resistance.
69. The factor by which a reaction rate increases with a 10°C increase in temperature is called ______.
70. Q_{10} for diffusion of many gases is about ______ times faster when temperature is raised by 10°C.
71. The solutes in water have Q_{10} values of ______ for diffusion.
72. A device that measures osmosis is termed as ______.
73. The cell wall and the cell ______ are two different structures.
74. Animal cells do not have ______ and hence they often burst when pressure(s) is (are) built.
75. Turgid ______ provide much of the rigidity to non-woody plant parts, while many animals are supported by a skeleton.
76. A cell never comprises a ______ osmotic system.
77. Equilibrium is achieved when water ______ are equal both side (the water potential difference between the two sides of the membrane is zero).
78. As equilibrium ______ will be equal in all parts of the system.
79. Osmotic potential has also been termed as ______ caused by the presence of solute particles.
80. Pressure is usually positive in living cells, but is often ______ in dead xylem elements.
81. In an osmometer, an ideal 1.0 molar sugar (say, glucose) solution at 28°C has an osmotic potential of ______.
82. The osmotic potential of a 1.0 molar glucose solution (or water potential of the same solution at atmospheric pressure) can be expressed in pressure terms as ______ MPa.

83. In the SI system kJ kg^{-1} have the numerical value as ________.
84. In 1887, ________ discovered an empirical relationship to determine an approximate osmotic potential from the molal concentration of a solution.
85. The most meaningful property that can be measured in soil-plant-air is the ________.
86. In 1948, V.S. Chardakov who devised a simple and efficient method of determining the test solution in which no change in concentration occurs was ________.
87. The amount of water vapour in air at a particular temperature compared with the amount of water vapour that the air could hold at that temperature is known as.
88. The saturation vapour density approximately doubles for each ________ increase in temperature.
89. A thermocouple operates on the principal of the ________.
90. The ________ is the opposite of the thermoelectric effect.
91. In 1877, Wilhelm F.P. Pfeffer made nearly perfect, rigid and semi-permeable membranes to measure ________.
92. ________ method applies equally well to the measurement of osmotic potential of a free liquid.
93. The properties of solutions that are functions of the mole fraction are called ________ properties.
94. Measuring freezing points to work out osmotic potential is known as ________.
95. It has been assumed that ________ occurs in tissues in which about half the cells are just beginning to plasmolyze.
96. Osmotic potentials of about – 0.1 MPa in aquatic plants and –20 MPa in ________ have been observed.
97. The adsorption of water by hydrophillic surface is called ________.
98. The ________ is a measure at atmospheric pressure of the tendency for a matrix to adsorb additional water molecules.
99. Larger particle when suspended in water, sometimes form a glue and hence they have been termed as ________.
100. When colloidal particles are observed in a light microscope, they appear as points of light due to ________.
101. ________ was discovered by the Scotish botanist Robert Brown in 1827.
102. Brownian Movement is the spectacular confirmation of ________.
103. A single solid cube 0.1 cm on each of its edges, when cut to parts each measuring 10 nm long on its edges, will have total surface of ________.
104. The ________ is the basis of the phenomenon of capillarity.
105. At equilibrium, the matric potentials of all the ________ surfaces in a system are equal.
106. It has been estimated that ________ of water were transpired to produce one kg of dried plant material.
107. When soil moisture becomes limiting, transpiration and carbon dioxide uptake are inhibited because ________ close.
108. If the leaf is warmed above air temperature by sunlight, wind lowers its temperature causing a decrease in ________.
109. Water molecules diffuse 1.56 times as fast as ________ because of their lower molecular weight.
110. The atmosphere at 35°C normally contains 0.3-1.4 mol m^{-3} of water and ________ of carbon-dioxide.
111. The amount of water used in plant growth is less than one per cent of the final ________ of the plant.
112. Lysimeter method was used to measure water loss through transpiration by ________ about 200 years ago.

113. _______ provide the most reliable field method to study evapotranspiration.

114. Cuvettes and _______ are appropriate in laboratory, where purposes to study transpiration are special.

115. Stomatal openings on leaf make up only _______ of surface area.

116. Greater the distance of diffusion through atmosphere, higher is the _______.

117. Plants are ideally adapted for carbon-dioxide from the atmosphere, but also for loss of _______ by transpiration.

118. Technically, the term stomate (stoma is singular, while stomata is plural) refers only to the openings between the _______.

119. One or two other modified epidermal cells adjacent to each guard cell are known as _______ cells.

120. Water evaporates inside the leaf from the palisade and spongy parenchyma cell walls to _______ spaces which is continuous with outside air when stomates are open.

121. Carbon-dioxide follows the _______ path into the leaf.

122. Palisade and spongy parenchyma cells are collectively called_______ cells.

123. _______ are apparently an adaptation to reduce transpiration.

124. Typical stomates of dicots consist of two _______ guard cells whereas; in grass, guard cells tend to be more elongated (dumbbell shaped).

125. The guard cells of some species as noticed in 1856 were slightly _______ along the concave wall adjacent to the stomatal opening.

126. Radial micellation is as important in grass as in _______ guard cells.

127. Some succulent plants native to hot and dry conditions open their stomates _______ and fix carbon-dioxide into organic acids in the dark and close their stomates during the day.

128. Opening of stomates generally need about an hour and ,closing occurs gradually throughout the _______.

129. Removal of carbon-dioxide by _______ cells during photosynthesis comprises the main reason that stomates of most species open in light.

130. The stomates close with the decrease in _______.

131. Potassium ions (K^+) move from the surrounding cells in the _______ cells when stomates open.

132. Stomates also close in response to the application of _______ as it causes loss of potassium from guard cells.

133. A leaf, at a temperature different from that of the surrounding air exchanges heat directly first by conduction and then by _______.

134. Leaves at night often radiate more _______ than they absorb.

135. Much of the _______ is reflected and transmitted, that is why leaves appear green.

136. Most of the ultraviolet radiation is absorbed by _______ in the upper atmosphere.

137. The velocity of all forms of radiant energy in vacuum is the same and it is equal to _______.

138. Green light has a frequency of about (vibrations or waves) _______.

139. A quantum of the electromagnetic field is known as _______.

140. The energy of a photon or quantum is directly proportion to the frequency of _______.

141. A universal constant of nature relating the energy of a photon to the frequency of the oscillator that is emitted is known as _______.

142. _______ yield refers to an expression when the absorption of a photon by a molecule results in photo-chemical reaction.

143. The wavelengths _______ to _______ nm are most active in photosynthesis.
144. _______ refers to any substance that absorbs light.
145. A surface that absorbs all the radiation falling upon it is a _______.
146. The difference between the radiation absorbed by an object and that emitted is the _______.
147. "The amount of a current flowing through a wire is proportional to the driving force and inversely proportional to the resistance encountered by the current in the wire" is the _______.
148. The _______ layer is thinnest and offers the least resistance to convective heat transfer for small leaves and high wind velocities.
149. The driving force for _______ is the difference in water vapour density within the leaf and in the atmosphere beyond the boundary layer.
150. Even if the leaf is exactly at the same temperature as the atmosphere beyond the boundary layer, there is under most conditions a vapour density _______ with higher values inside the leaf.
151. Temperature can greatly _______ the vapour density gradient.
152. Many desert plants, perhaps most have _______, providing thin boundary layers with consequent efficient convective heat transfer.
153. A suction pump can lift water only to the _______, which is the height that is supported by atmospheric pressure (1.0 atm.) from below.
154. According to the Guinnes Book of World Records (1983), the tallest tree in the world is the _______ a *Sequoia sempervirens* in Redwood Creek Grove, Redwood National Park, California (U.S.A.).
155. At zero pressure, water will normally _______ even at 0°C (actually it boils at 0.610 kP), its vapour pressure at 0°C.
156. Droplets of water exuded from openings in the tips or edges of grass or strawberry leaves is due to _______.
157. Root pressures are not found in _______ trees.
158. "The interaction between contacting surfaces of a solid and a liquid that distorts the liquid surface from a planar shape" refers to _______.
159. The cohesion theory for the ascent of sap consists of three basic elements namely, driving, force, hydration in the pathway, and the _______.
160. Special cells called _______ grow into vapour locked tracheids and vessels in some plant species act as seals against water loss and pathogen invasion.
161. The plants with roots grown in aqueous nutrient solution are known as _______.
162. The absorption of ammonium (NH_4^+) and other cations occurs simultaneously with transfer of hydrogen (H^+) from the _______ to the surrounding solution.
163. When sheep and cattle eat grasses abundant in _______ it is largely excreted in the urine, but sometimes it forms kidney stones.
164. _______ is required for nitrogen fixation by bacteria in root nodules on legumes.
165. Perennial range grasses conserve minerals by translocation to _______ and to lower stem tissues making up the crown in late summer.
166. Significant amounts of N, P, K and Mg move out of tree leaves into _______ before leaf fall.
167. A chelate is the soluble product formed when certain atoms in an organic molecule called chelating agent or ligand donate _______ to the metal cation.

168. _______ form extremely stable chelates with iron (Fe^{3+}) and are transported into microbial cells where Fe^{3+} is reduced to Fe^{2+} and released.

169. Plants respond to an inadequate supply of an essential element by forming characteristic _______.

170. One abundant and stable form of iron in leaves is stored in chloroplasts as an iron-protein complex called _______.

171. Inadequate supply of _______ causes several disorders related to disintegration of internal tissues like "heart rot" of beet, "stem crack" of celery, "water core" of turnip and "drought spot" of apples.

172. _______ deficiency causes disorders namely, "little leaf" and "rosette" of apples, peaches and pecans; *"khaira"* of rice and "white bud" of maize.

173. Citrus orchards are occasionally deficient in copper, in which case the dying young leaves led to the name _______ disease.

174. "Whip tail" disease of cauliflower and broccoli is caused by deficiency of _______.

175. In _______ soils addition of lime augments the availability of molybdenum.

176. A well documented function of molybdenum in plants is as a part of the enzyme _______.

177. In soybean and tomato, it is difficult to differentiate _______ and branch roots.

178. Plants adapted to dry regions are not necessarily _______ as shallow roots take better advantage of brief rains.

179. R.F. Sutton (1980) reported that a 100-year old-scot pine (*Pinus-sylvestris*) tree had _______ million root tips, and a mature red oak (*Quercus rubrum*) had _______ million live tips.

180. Cylindrical and _______ form of roots prove unexpectedly important for absorption of water and solutes from soils.

181. Exploration of large soil volume is important for roots to contact _______.

182. Two main groups of mycorrhizae are ectomycorrhizae and _______.

183. In ectomycorrhizae, there is no intercellular penetration into epidermal or cortical cells, but an extensive network called _______ is formed between these cells.

184. VAM fungi seem to penetrate directly into the _______ of cortical cells (to form vesiscles and arbuscules), that part of the fungus is surrounded by an invaginated plasma-membrane of the cortex cell.

185. Plants grown in shade are deficient in _______ and hence have poor mycorrhizal development.

186. The most well documented advantage of mycorrhizae to plants is increased _______ absorption.

187. The surfaces of clay minerals become negatively charged because some atoms of Si^{4+} are replaced by Al^{3+}, and some atoms of Al^{3+} are replaced by _______.

188. The availability of negative sites on surfaces of clay minerals results in attraction and adsorption of dissolved cations namely $H^+ >$ _______ $> Mg^{2+} > K^+ = NH_4^+ > Na^+$

189. The organic matter fraction of soils has an excess of negative charges due to ionized _______ and also ionized OH groups of phenolic compounds.

190. H^+ ions can replace any _______ adsorbed to a soil colloid and make it available to the roots.

191. Nitrate (NO_3^-), sulphate SO_4^{2-}) and chloride (Cl^-) are soluble, are repelled by negatively charged colloids and consequently are _______ with water.

192. Most of the crops (except legumes) require relatively large amounts of nitrogen fertilizers because of high nitrogen need and loss of _______ by leaching.

193. Most soils contain little ammonium (NH_4^+) as it is rapidly oxidized to nitrate (NO_3^-) form by _______.

194. The anions and cations most readily available to roots are those freely _______ in the soilsolution.

195. The symplastic and the _______ pathways contribute substantially to the transport of mostions.

196. Calcium (Ca^{2+}) is mainly transported by _______ pathway in plants.
197. The ions absorbed into root cell _______ usually move out slowly.
198. Both plant and animal cells keep concentration of calcium (Ca^{2+}) in their _______ at low concentrations partly because it precipitates both inorganic and organic phosphate compounds.
199. In the central region of plasmodesmata lies a tubular structure called _______.
200. The loss of epidermis and cortex in herbaceous dicots and grasses in the older region leaves _______ as the outermost layer of cells.
201. Electron micrographs show that most biological _______ are similar regardless of their location.
202. The principal lipids of most plant membranes are _______, glycolipids and sterols.
203. Plant membranes largely consist of _______ and lipids.
204. Proteins, in composition of plant membranes represent _______ of the membrane dry weight.
205. Fatty acids are hydrophobic whereas; glycerol is more _______.
206. Integral proteins are bound tightly within the plant membrane but _______ proteins are loosely bound to one or the other side of the membrane surface.
207. In some plasma-membranes of animal cells, some peripheral proteins called glycoproteins contain short _______ attached at the outer membrane surface.
208. If plant cells are not alive and metabolizing, their membranes become much more _______ to solutes.
209. Water molecules and dissolved gases (N_2, O_2, CO_2) penetrate all _______ rapidly.
210. _______ solutes penetrate at rates positively related to their lipid solubility.
211. Leaves absorb 2,4-D more effectively at pH _______ than at pH 8.
212. Hydrophillic molecules and ions with similar lipid solubility penetrate at rates inversely related to their _______.
213. The ion size relevant to penetration is that attained after _______ is attached.
214. The extent to which the concentration of essential solutes becomes greater within the cell than that in external solution is known as _______.
215. Transportation of accumulated sucrose and other carbohydrates (in high concentration) is generally essential for _______ leaf cells.
216. The diffusion to roots is a limiting factor in most plants in nature for the nutrients (nitrate, ammonium, phosphate and potassium) used in relatively _______.
217. Absorption of ions largely through channels in _______ has been termed as facilitated diffusion.
218. Each ionophore is especially selective for a certain cation, consistent with selective properties of _______.
219. If the actual ratio measured experimentally is more than the predicted ratio between outside and inside the membrane concentrations of ions at equilibrium the cell uses energy to absorb the ion, and this has been defined as _______ originally by H.H. Ussing (1949).
220. If the actual ratio is either equal or less, between ion concentration inside and outside the membrane, the ion absorption is known as _______.
221. Water with its dissolved minerals moves primarily upward in the plant through _______ tissues.
222. Plant assimilates more from _______ to sink.
223. Plant cells in some species with wall ingrowths and expanded membrane surfaces are called _______.
224. PCMBS does not penetrate the _______ of the cells and thus does not enter the symplast.
225. Increase in agricultural yields is associated with the increase in _______.

226. The phloem sap changes significantly in its composition, while underway from ______ to sink such as developing fruits or tubers.
227. The formation of large molecules from small molecules is called anabolism (from Greek *ana,* upwards) while the breakdown of large molecules to small molecules is termed as______.
228. Anabolism requires energy whereas, catabolism ______.
229. Enzymes generally speed up reaction by factors between ______.
230. Proteins consist of ______ of tens to thousands of amino acids.
231. The $-NH_2$ is the amino group and the $-COOH$ is the ______.
232. Electrophoresis is essentially the separation of dissolved proteins or other charged molecules in an ______.
233. Glycolation refers to the attachment of one or more sugars to the ______.
234. Phosphorylation means esterification of phosphate to the ______ of one or more serine or threonine.
235. The alteration in enzyme structure caused by numerous factors is known as enzyme ______.
236. Opaque-2 and Fluory-2 cultivars of maize are relatively richer in both lysine and ______ amino acids.
237. Water was implicated by ______ when in 1804, he made the first quantitative measurements of photosynthesis.
238. Synthesis of ATP in isolated chloroplasts only during light is known as ______ photosynthetic.
239. The thylakoid membranes in plants consist of two kinds of green ______.
240. In most of the plants including green algae, ______ are the most abundant carotenoids in thylakoids.
241. One mole (6.02×10^{23}) of photons has been called an ______.
242. According to ______ Law any molecules can absorb only one photon at a time and this photon causes the exitation of only one electron.
243. ______ refers to light production accompanying rapid decay of excited electrons.
244. In ______ and dinoflagellates xanthophylls called fucoxanthin and periodinin are highly effective in transfer of energy.
245. The enhacement in photosynthesis by supplying shorter wavelengths and longer red wavelengths at the same time is known as ______.
246. Green bands separate from chloroplast by electrophoresis contain chlorophylls a and b, xanthophyll, carotenoid but, little of β-carotene, all bound to proteins, are known as ______.
247. During last 15 years, many weed species have become resistant to triazines because a ______ has caused them to form a modified thylakoid protein.
248. Peter Mitchell in England in 1961 first proposed that pH gradients could provide energy for ATP formation in chloroplast, mitochondria and bacteria, it was later known as ______.
249. The Calvin Cycle occurs in the stomata of chloroplasts and mainly consists of carboxylation, reduction and ______.
250. Calvin Cycle is synonymous to C-3 photosynthetic pathway (as first product 3PGA contains three carbon atoms) and ______.
251. The species that produce 4-carbon acids as the primary initial CO_2-fixation products are commonly referred to as ______, those fixing CO_2 initially in 3-PGA are called C-3 species.
252. Most of the C-4 species are ______, especially grasses and sedges.
253. All *gynosperms, pteridophytes, bryophytes,* and algae that have been studied are ______ plants.
254. C-4 plant species under high light and warm temperatures can photosynthesize more rapidly and produce substantially more ______ than can C-3 plants.

255. The formation of aspartate from malate occurring in cytosol requires another amino acid such as alanine as a source of amino acid group is known as _______.
256. It has been recorded in 1920 that photosynthesis in algae is inhibited by O_2 and this inhibition occurs in all C-3 species studied, this effect is termed as Warberg effect often the name _______ a famous German biochemist.
257. The most striking feature of _______ plants is the formation of malic acid at night and its disappearance during day light.
258. World-wide increases in atmospheric carbon dioxide comprise a cause of concern because they could lead to _______ of the earth's surface.
259. The wavelengths between 400 and 700 nm are called _______.
260. The irradiance at which photosynthesis just balances respiration, that is, net CO_2 exchange is zero, is known as _______.
261. The more rapid photosynthesis of C-4 species under high irradiance results in lower _______ per gramme of dry matter produced, where CAM plants have much lower than either C-4 or C-3 species.
262. _______ refers to the ratio of leaf area of a crop to the ground area upon which that crop grows.
263. Oxidized forms of nitrogen in the atmosphere are important ecologically because when converted to NO_3^- they contribute to _______.
264. The process by which N_2 is reduced to NH_4^+ is known as _______.
265. Important non-legumes that fix N_2 are primarily _______.
266. Conversion of carbohydrates to fats requires production of fatty acids of glycerol backbone to which the fatty acids become _______.
267. The entire shoot system of a herbaceous plant is covered by _______ that shows water loss from its parts.
268. Most of the cuticle is composed of a heterogeneous mixture of compounds collectively called _______.
269. _______ is special case of allelochemy involving a negative chemical interaction between different plant species.
270. All _______ interpenoids are built from six isoprene units.
271. Milkweeds (*Aesclepias* spp.) produce a number of bitter-tasting _______ that protect them against herbivory by most insects and even cattle.
272. _______ cause foaming in the intestinal tract leading to bloat in cattle that eat young alfalfa plants.
273. _______ is the most abundant carotenoid found in higher plants and is the compound imparting the orange colour to carrot root.
274. Rubber, an isoprenoid compound contains some 3,000-6,000 isoprene units linked together in very long, _______ chains.
275. _______ represent a complex mixture of terpenes containing 10-30 carbon atoms.
276. Phenylalamine, tyrosine, and tryptophane are _______ amino acids.
277. _______ is a strengthening material that occurs with cellulose and other polysaccharides in the cell walls of all higher plants.
278. Most fruits and many flowers own their colour to _______.
279. The red pigment of beets is a _______, a betalain pigment coloured, but different from anthocyanins.
280. Aromatic nitrogenous compounds are called _______.
281. Those interested in crop productivity measure the plant growth by increase in _______ of a plant or a part thereof.

282. _______ structure grows to a certain size and then stops, eventually undergoing senescence and death.

283. In a great majority of species, seed germination begins with _______ rather than epicotyl (shoot) protrusion through the seed coat.

284. _______ is the opening of flowers with parts available for pollination, is sometimes a spectacular phenomenon, usually associated with full development of colour and scent.

285. Normal production of fruits lacking seeds is called_______.

286. The term auxin was first used by Frits Went, who as a graduate student in Holland in 1926, discovered that some unidentified compound probably caused curvature of oats _______.

287. The substances, not synthesized by plants but by chemists, nor they are hormones, have been classified as _______.

288. Bioassays take advantage of the extreme _______ and specificity of certain plant parts to a particular hormone.

289. In stems of most of the plant species, the apical bud exerts an inhibitory influence (apical dominance) upon the lateral (axillary buds) preventing or slowing their _______.

290. _______ hypothesis states that auxins cause receptive cells to secrete H^+ into their surrounding primary walls, H^+ lowers pH and growth occurs.

291. In the 1930s, T. Yabuta and T. Hayashi isolated an active compound from the fungus (*Gibberella fujikuroi*), which they named as _______.

292. _______ stimulates ripening of fruits, causes senescence and abscission of leaves.

293. The highest known rate of ethylene release is from fading flowers of Vanda orchids; 3.4 µl per g of _______ per hour.

294. In many fruits, little ethylene is produced until just before respiratory _______ signalling the onset of ripening.

295. _______ fruits synthesize little ethylene and are not induced to ripening by it.

296. ABA (dormin), a bud dormancy hormone if applied directly to _______ caused dormancy.

297. _______ are compounds in yam plants (*Disco rea batatus*) that seem to cause dormancy in bulbils arising from swelling of aerial lateral buds.

298. An upward bending of a leaf (or any organ) is called hyponasty; whereas downward bending is _______.

299. Nastic movement of leaves occurs due to water movement in and out of _______ at the base of the petiole blade or leaflet.

300. _______ movements in plants are rhythmic processes controlled by biological clock.

301. At night, water moves out of subepidermal cortical cells in the upper (ventral) side of the _______ and into cortical cells on the lower (dorsal) side.

302. Nastic movement results from touch (*thigmonasty*, Greek *thigma* = touch) in plants belonging to subfamily _______ in the Fabaceae (Leguminosae).

303. A number of plants are capable of _______ in which the flat blade of the leaf remains at right angles to the sun throughout the day maximising the light-harvest by the leaf.

304. "A stem appears to trace a more or less regular ellipse as the stem grows" Darwin (1881) called this phenomenon as _______.

305. Many plant cells are _______, that is, a nonembryonic cell has the potential to differentiate into an embryonic cell and then into a new plant under a suitable environment.

306. Seeds that require light for germination are said to be _______.

307. _______ provides seeds with a clue whether they are covered by a canopy of other plants or exist in an open area.

308. _______ refers to temperature induced movement of the tepals caused by growth.

309. _______ means exposure of plants to low temperatures for a few weeks to induce flowering on their return to normal temperatures.

310. _______ in seeds is due to external factors, while dormancy is due to its internal conditions.

311. Some plants grow better when the environment fluctuates on a 24-hour cycle, presumably to coincide with the phases of their _______.

312. _______ responses of organisms better the understanding of natural ecosystems, but out of about 300,000 plant species, only a few hundred have been grown with different artificial photoperiods.

313. Sex expression in many plant species is often strongly influenced by _______.

314. The night interruption by light inhibited flowering in short day plants and promoted flowering in short day plants and promoted flowering in long day plants, this phenomenon has been termed as _______.

315. The _______ of a plant represents the complex of climatic, edaphic and biotic factors.

316. The rate of cooling is an expression of the _______ for dry air in the atmosphere.

317. _______ are annual plants that escape the drought by existing only as dormant seeds during the dry season.

II. Tick mark (✓) the correct answer:

318. The total volume of water on melting _______.

(*a*) Increases (*b*) Remains constant
(*c*) Decreases (*d*) None of these

319. The attraction of like molecules for each other (because of hydrogen bonds) is called _______.

(*a*) Tension (*b*) Adhesion
(*c*) Cohesion (*d*) None of these

320. At equilibrium, the vapour density or pressure above pure water in a closed container is _______.

(*a*) 85% (*b*) 98%
(*c*) 95% (*d*) 100%

321. Water potential concept was formulated by _______.

(*a*) Peter Ray, 1960 (*b*) M.H. Mathew, 1954
(*c*) Otto Renner, 1915 (*d*) W.C. Hoffer, 1920

322. Probably the most useful measurable property in the soil-plant-air system is _______.

(*a*) Matric potential (*b*) Water potential
(*c*) Osmotic potential (*d*) Redox potential

323. In 1948, V.S. Chardakov who devised a simple and efficient method to determine the test solution in which no change in concentration occurs was _______.

(*a*) Austrian Scientist (*b*) American Scientist
(*c*) Bulgarian Scientist (*d*) Russian Scientist

324. Mitochondria were seen first in _______.

(*a*) 1850 (*b*) 1900
(*c*) 1940 (*d*) 1975

325. In water molecule, line-segments connecting the centres of the two hydrogen atoms with the centre of oxygen atoms form an angle of about _______.

(*a*) 85° (*b*) 95°

(*c*) 105° (*d*) 115°

326. The normal form of a plant is maintained by the presence of _______.

(*a*) Water (*b*) Gases

(*c*) Solids (*d*) None of these

327. A final component of thylakoid necessary for photophosphorylation is a complex protein called_________.

(*a*) ATPase/coupling factor (*b*) Detaching factor

(*c*) Reductase factor (*d*) None of these

328. Light harvesting complexes surrounded by both photosystem (I and II) and _________light energy to them.

(*a*) Draw (*b*) Accumulate

(*c*) Transfer (*d*) None of these

329. H^+- ions in thyroid channels arise from oxidation of H_2O and PQH_2 cause H^+-ions concentration in channels become, about _________ times as great as in the stroma when photosynthesis occurs.

(*a*) 500 (*b*) 750

(*c*) 1000 (*d*) 1250

330. The pH gradient across the cell membrane provides a powerful form of_________potential energy largely responsible for driving phosphorylation.

(*a*) Chemical (*b*) Physical

(*c*) Electrical (*d*) Biological

331. The atmosphere has less carbon than other reservoirs but, it still contains about 700 billion tonnes and roughly _________ per cent is annually used in photosynthesis.

(*a*) 5.0 (*b*) 7.5

(*c*) 10.0 (*d*) 12.5

332. The amount of carbon dioxide has increased slowly since about 1850 from 28 μl / l to slightly more than_________ μl / l in 1962.

(*a*) 310 (*b*) 320

(*c*) 330 (*d*) 340

333. A maize plant to produce one kg of grain (dry) transpires _________ kg of water.

(*a*) 900 (*b*) 800

(*c*) 700 (*d*) 600

334. Each gramme of water transpired absorbs _________ kJ of latent heat from the leaf and its environment.

(*a*) 2.0-2.1 (*b*) 2.2-2.3

(*c*) 3.4-3.5 (*d*) 2.7-2.8

335. Soil water that is available to plants seldom has a water potential more negative than _________

(*a*) 3.0 MPa (*b*) –1.5 MPa

(*c*) –2.0 MPa (*d*) –2.5 MPa

336. The solute transport into the cells is strongly dependent on _______ and ability of cells to respire aerobically and to produce it.
(*a*) ADP (*b*) ATP
(*c*) RNA (*d*) DNA

337. The efforts to enhance the partition of assimilates to storage organs of interest to farmers have quite successful due to _______.
(*a*) Improved component technology (*b*) Improved control of insects
(*c*) Better disease control (*d*) Better breeding techniques

338. The provision of light of shorter wavelength at the same time as longer red wavelengths _______ photosynthesis.
(*a*) Maintains (*b*) Enhances
(*c*) Reduces (*d*) No effect

339. Considering the supplies of total PAR to land area on growing crops, overall biomass product in efficiencies are always much below _______ per cent.
(*a*) 30 (*b*) 25
(*c*) 18 (*d*) 22

340. Rice plants exposed to temperatures below _______ °C at the time of pollen-mother cell division will not produce a crop.
(*a*) 22 (*b*) 20
(*c*) 18 (*d*) 16

341. It has been estimated that carbon dioxide content within the maize plant-canopies was 260 μl / l or less during day, whereas it rose to _______ μl / l during darkness.
(*a*) 400 (*b*) 500
(*c*) 600 (*d*) 700

342. Direct sunlight at noon in late June in the northern hemisphere corresponds to _______ footcandles.
(*a*) 5,000 (*b*) 7,500
(*c*) 10,000 (*d*) 12,500

343. Most of the _______ flowers contain carotenoid especially xanthophyll type and it is believed that they benefit certain plants by attracting pollinating insects.
(*a*) White (*b*) Red
(*c*) Pink (*d*) Yellow

344. One of the alkaloids listed below is found in cocoabeans.
(*a*) Theobromina (*b*) Caffeine
(*c*) Quinine (*d*) Colchicine

345. The removal of apical buds and young leaves _______ branching.
(*a*) Decreases (*b*) Increases
(*c*) Maintains (*d*) No effect

346. Gibberellins were first discovered in _______ in studies with diseased rice plants that grew excessively tall.
(*a*) Philippines (*b*) Thailand
(*c*) China (*d*) Japan

347. Gibberellins are now commercially used in_______ to increase sugarcane growth and sugar yield.
(a) India (b) Hawaii
(c) Japan (d) Korea

348. Cytokinins were first discovered in 1913 by Gottlieb Haberlandt in _______.
(a) Germany (b) Holland
(c) Poland (d) Austria

349. Zeatin has been isolated and identified from the milky endosperrm of _______.
(a) Wheat (b) Sorghum
(c) Maize (d) Barley

350. Ethylene especially in tomato plants has the following effects.
(a) Enhances stem elongation (b) Reduces radial expansion
(c) Retards formation of adventitious roots (d) Causes leaf senescence

351. Ethrel (trade name) of ethephone (common name) is used in various aspects of _______.
(a) Olericulture (b) Aquaculture
(c) Horticulture (d) Apiculture

352. The action of ethylene is effectively inhibited by _______ ion.
(a) Boron (b) Manganese
(c) Zinc (d) Silver

353. Foliar application of colloidal suspensions of triacontanol (30-carbon saturated primary alcohol isolated first from alfalfa shoots) enhanced the growth of seedlings of _______.
(a) Rice and maize (b) Soybean
(c) Castorbean (d) Clusterbean

354. *Brassins,* recently discovered steroid growth-promoters were first isolated from pollen grains of rope plants, but now known to be present in _______ also.
(a) Tea (b) Bean
(c) Rice (d) All mosses

355. ABA (abscic acid) appears to be universal among_______.
(a) Algae (b) Liveworts
(c) Vascular plants (d) In all of these

356. ABA has the following effects depending upon the tissue involved.
(a) On plasma membrane of roots (b) Inhibition of RNA-synthesis (transcription)
(c) Inhibition of protein synthesis (translocation) (d) All of these

357. _______ is obviously useful to a plant as the excitation by an insect of one or more sensory hairs of the venus's-flytrap (*Dionea muscipula*).
(a) Chemical potential (b) Action potential
(c) Physical potential (d) Biological potential

III. Match the following:

358. The coefficient of viscosity (centipoises) at 20°C is_______.

(a) Water	(i) 1.60
(b) Ethyl alcohol	(ii) 830.0
(c) Mercury	(iii) 1.002
(d) Glycerine	(iv) 1.200

359. Empirically determined osmotic potentials of leaves of the following plants were.

(*a*) Sunflower	(*i*) −8.9
(*b*) Chickweed	(*ii*) −4.8
(*c*) Pickleweed	(*iii*) −1.9
(*d*) Mandarin orange	(*iv*) −0.74

360. Stomates are variously arranged in various plants.

(*a*) Waterlily	(*i*) None at all
(*b*) Submerged plants	(*ii*) On both sides equally
(*c*) Grasses	(*iii*) On top
(*d*) Pine	(*iv*) Sub-stomatal crypt

361. Quantity and units (with symbols) are given below, correspond to each other (match them).

(*a*) Frequency	(*i*) Pascal (Pa)
(*b*) Pressure	(*ii*) Newton (N)
(*c*) Energy/work/heat	(*iii*) Joules (J)
(*d*) Force	(*iv*) Hertz (Hz)

362. At 20°C, match the atmospheric water potential with relative humidity (RH) per cent as given below.

(*a*) 98% of RH	(*i*) −14.2 MPa
(*b*) 90% of RH	(*ii*) −311 MPa
(*c*) 50% of RH	(*iii*) −2.72 MPa
(*d*) 10% of RH	(*iv*) −93.5 MPa

363. Match the texture class with the diameter range as specified in World System of Soil Classification.

(*a*) Coarse sand	(*i*) 0.02-0.002 mm
(*b*) Fine sand	(*ii*) 0.002 mm and less
(*c*) Silt	(*iii*) 2.0-0.2 mm
(*d*) Clay	(*iv*) 0.2-0.02 mm

364. Match the salts and their molarity as in Hoagland's solution.

(*a*) KNO_3	(*i*) 0.003
(*b*) $Ca(NO_3)_2$	(*ii*) 0.230
(*c*) $NH_4H_2PO_4$	(*iii*) 0.490
(*d*) $Mg{\cdot}SO_4{\cdot}7H_2O$	(*iv*) 0.010

365. The following are the concentrations of some essential elements considered adequate for most of the higher plants (in dry tissues), match them suitably.

(*a*) Molybdenum	(*i*) 20 ppm
(*b*) Copper	(*ii*) 0.10 ppm
(*c*) Zinc	(*iii*) 100 ppm
(*d*) Iron	(*iv*) 6.0 ppm

366. Match the following elements with their available form.

(*a*) Copper	(*i*) $MoO_4^{=}$
(*b*) Molybdenum	(*ii*) Cu^+, Cu^{2+}
(*c*) Zinc	(*iii*) H_3BO_3
(*d*) Boron	(*iv*) Zn^{2+}

367. Match the following concentrations with the essential elements (considered adequate on dry tissue basis for most of the plants).

(*a*) Sulphur (*i*) 5,000 ppm
(*b*) Magnesium (*ii*) 2,000 ppm
(*c*) Calcium (*iii*) 1,000 ppm
(*d*) Potassium (*iv*) 10,000 ppm

368. *Nutrient* *Concentration*

(*a*) Phosphorus (*i*) 50 ppm
(*b*) Nitrogen (*ii*) 2,000 ppm
(*c*) Chlorine (*iii*) 15,000 ppm
(*d*) Manganese (*iv*) 100 ppm

369. Nutrient Concentration

(*a*) Hydrogen (*i*) 450,000 ppm
(*b*) Carbon (*ii*) 50 ppm
(*c*) Boron (*iii*) 60,000 ppm
(*d*) Manganese (*iv*) 20 ppm

370. The forms of essential nutrients available to plants and the nutrients are as follows, match them.

(*a*) Nitrogen (*i*) Fe^{3+}, Fe^{2+}
(*b*) Iron (*ii*) $H_2PO_4^-$, HPO_4=
(*c*) Phosphorus (*iii*) SO_4 =
(*d*) Sulphur (*iv*) NO_3^-, NH_4^+

371. Enzymes are not uniformly mixed throughout cells, but are located at different sites to catalase different processes in plants as________.

(*a*) For photosynthesis (*i*) Nuclei
(*b*) For aerobic respiration (*ii*) In mitochondria
(*c*) For respiration (*iii*) In chloroplasts
(*d*) For mitosis/synthesis of DNA/RNA (*iv*) In cytosol

372. Match the following enzymes with their general reaction.

(*a*) Proteinases (*i*) Transfers phosphate group especially from ATP
(*b*) Transferases (*ii*) Hydrolyzes lipids (esters)
(*c*) Lyases (*iii*) From double bonds by elimination of chemical group
(*d*) Lipases (*iv*) Hydrolyze proteins

373. Match the enzyme with their general reactions.

(*a*) Ribonucleases (*i*) Rearrange atom/molecule to lower from
(*b*) Deoxyribonucleases (*ii*) Hydrolyze RNA
(*c*) Isomerases (*iii*) Breakdown chemical bonds
(*d*) Hydrolases (*iv*) Hydrolyse DNA

374. Match the carbohydrate content of the following seeds.

(*a*) Maize (*i*) 2 per cent
(*b*) Wheat (*ii*) 14 per cent
(*c*) Soybean (*iii*) 51-74 per cent
(*d*) Sunflower (*iv*) 60-75 per cent

375. Match the plants with the temperature at which they can photosynthesize.
(*a*) Bacteria, BGA (*i*) –60°C
(*b*) Conifers (extremely slowly) (*ii*) 35°C
(*c*) Exposed to bright sunshine (*iii*) – 18°C
(*d*) Antarctic lichens (*iv*) 70°C

376. Match the following plants with their maximum photosynthetic rate under natural conditions in mmol CO_2 per square meter per second.
(*a*) Maize (C-4 pathway) (*i*) 0.6-2.4
(*b*) Soybean (C-3 pathway) (*ii*) 3-12
(*c*) Century plant (CAM) (*iii*) 20-40
(*d*) European beech (*iv*) 10-20

377. Match the scientists with the observation which they made.
(*a*) Stephen Hales, 1927 (*i*) Implicated oxygen (dephlogisticated air)
(*b*) Joseph Priestley, 1771 (*ii*) Light, necessary for air purification
(*c*) Jan Ingenhousz (*iii*) Noxious. gas CO_2 stimulated O_2 production by plants
(*d*) Jean Senebier, 1782 (*iv*) Partial nourishment from atmosphere and light, participation

378. Match the following sterols.
(*a*) Sitosterol (*i*) Widespread in trace amounts in plants
(*b*) Cholestrol (*ii*) Sex attraction in aquatic fungus *Achlya bisexualis*
(*c*) Ergosterol (*iii*) Most abundant in green algae and higher plants
(*d*) Antheridiol (*iv*) Rare in plants, common in some fungi

379. Match the phytoalexins (Greek, *phyton*, plants; alexin, a warding off substance) with their plant parts wherein they occur.
(*a*) Pisatin (*i*) Carrot roots
(*b*) Phaseolin (*ii*) Bean pods
(*c*) Isocoumarin (*iii*) Red clover roots
(*d*) Trifolirhizin (*iv*) Pea pods

380. Match the alkaloids with the plants, they are associated with.
(*a*) Morphine (*i*) Flowering heads of cactus *Lophophora williamsii*
(*b*) Nicotine (*ii*) Cultivated tobacco varieties
(*c*) Atropine (*iii*) Opium poppy
(*d*) Meascaline (*iv*) Poisonous black night shade

381. Match the following plants responses to the environment.
(*a*) Gravitropism (*i*) Growth towards light
(*b*) Phototropism (*ii*) Nastic movement due to touch
(*c*) Thigmotropism (*iii*) Growth of several organs on intermediate angles
(*d*) Plagiotropism (*iv*) Response to gravity

382. Match the longevity of the seeds of the plants given below
(*a*) Cocklebur (*Xanthium strumarium*) (*i*) 221years
(*b*) Canada thistle (*Circium arvense*) (*ii*) 21 years
(*c*) Kentucky blue grass (*Poa pratensis*) (*iii*) 16 years
(*d*) Sensitive plant (*Mimosa glomerata*) (*iv*) 30 years

383. Match the following.

(*a*) Short day plant	(*i*) Kidney bean (*Phaseolus vulgaris*)
(*b*) Long day plant	(*ii*) Sugarbeet (*Beta saccharifera*)
(*c*) Intermediate day plant	(*iii*) Soybean (*Glycine max*)
(*d*) Day neutral plant	(*iv*) Tarweed (*Madia elegans*)

384. Match the organisms with compatible solute and increase in their cells during osmotic adjustment.

(*a*) Bacteria	(*i*) Sucrose
(*b*) Fungi	(*ii*) Sodium chloride
(*c*) Microalgal	(*iii*) Proline
(*d*) Angiosperms	(*iv*) Arabitol

III. Fill up the blanks:

385. The gramme molecular weight (1 mol) of sucrose is 342.3 grammes which is dissolved in 1000 grammes (55.508 mol) of water, its mole fraction will be ________.

386. At 20°C, vapour density equals 17.31 gm^{-3}, so by Raoult's law of vapour density above 1.00 molal solution of sucrose equals $17.31 \times 0.9823 =$ ________.

387. Fick's law is written in the following integrated form ________.

$$J = y_1 - y_2/r$$

where, $J =$ ________

y_1 = water potential as its highest point

y_2 = water potential at its lowest point

r = resistance to diffusion

388. Q_{10} values can be computed at any two temperatures when the rates of reaction are known.

$$\log Q_{10} = (10/T_2 - T_1) \text{ ________.}$$

where, T_1 = Lower temperature

T_2 = Higher temperature

k_1 = Rate at lower temperature

k_2 = Rate at higher temperature

389. Beer-Lambert law is written as ________

$$A = log\frac{10}{I} = El$$

where, A = Absorbance (optical density)

I_0 = ________

I = Irradiance of transmitted radiant energy

C = Pigment solute concentration

l = Length of the path of light (cm)

E = Extinction coefficient

390. The molecular weight of a small enzyme is 12,500, it consists of 100 amino acids with average molecular weight of 125, with usual 20 different amino acids, the number of possible arrangements would be nearly ________.

391. Respiratory quotient for the oleic acid in the following equation will be

$$C_{18}H_{34}O_2 + 25.5O_2 \quad 18CO_2 + 17H_2O$$

392. Solid particle density $= \frac{1.33}{\text{---}} = 2.66\ \text{Mg/m}^3$

393. Per cent pore space $= 100 - \left(\frac{Db}{Dp} \times 100\right)$

If *Dp* and *Db* values of a soil are 2.65 and 1.30, respectively, the pore space per cent will be ________.

Do You Know That

1. Sulphur occurs in the plant as sulphate esters (in Agar Agar obtained from the red algae) as structural component of amino acids (cystin, methionin), and as reactive sulphur containing substances, as well as in some secondary products like oil of garlic and mustard oil.
2. Magnesium is an essential plant nutrient because it is a constituent of the chlorophyll, protochlorophyll, pectin and phytin.
3. Potassium plays a very important part as an antagonist to nitrogen and calcium.
4. Manganese participates in protein synthesis and in the formation of ascorbic acid (vitamin C) besides the formation of chlrophyll, reduction of nitrates, respiration and as a catalyst in many metabolic processes. Potassium promotes its absorption.
5. Boron is found at the growing points, flowers, and conducting tissues, is necessary for cell division, germination of pollen, formation of flowers, fruits and roots, transportation of substances within the plant and, absorption of cations, Its deficiency injures cambium and phloem critical zone).
6. Copper appears to promote the formation of vitamin A and plants need it for oxidation and reduction.
7. Cobalt is a component of vitamin B_{12}.
8. Man and animals need Iodine and Fluorine for the formation of hormones and the development of teeth.
9. Although carbon dioxide is at a low concentration (0.034 per cent or 340 ppm). 85-92 per cent of a plant dry weight is derived from CO_2 uptake in photosynthesis. Crop yields could be considerably enhanced in an atmosphere enriched with CO_2 up to 1500 ppm. The increase in its (CO_2) concentration over past 100 years from about 290 to 340 ppm has increased crop yields and influenced crop maturation.
10. Energy content of a molecule of glucose is about 686 kcal.

KEY

1. Prokaryotic	2. Self-generating	3. Structure
4. Microfilaments	5. Recticulum	6. Polyribosomes/Polysomes
7. Chloroplasts	8. Chromoplasts	9. Microbodies
10. Plastid	11. Nucleus	12. Nucleoli (singular), nuclelus
13. Camillo Golgi	14. Golgi bodies	15. Nuclear envelope
16. Oxygen	17. Naked protons	18. Negative
19. Polar	20. Hydrogen bond	21. Weaker
22. Van der Waals	23. Separation	24. Incompressible
25. 586 or some 2452 Joules	26. Hydrogen-bond	27. Hexagonal

28. Decreases 29. Lower 30. Fewer
31. Decreases 32. Adhesion 33. Surface tension
34. Absolutely 35. 10^{-7}. ($10^{-7} \times 10^{-7} = 10^{-14}$) 36. Bulk flow 37. Diffusion
38. Concentration 39. Kinetic theory 40. Hydrogen
41. Energy 42. System 43. Surroundings (environment)
44. Thermodynamics 45. Second 46. Light energy
47. 3.628.800 (= $10 \times 9 \times 8 \times 7 \times 6 \times 5 \times 4 \times 3 \times 2 \times 1$) 48. Gibb's free energy
49. Work interaction 50. Heat interaction 51. J. Williard Gibbs
52. Potential 53. Entropy 54. Pressure
55. Gibb's free energy 56. Chemical potential 57. Independent
58. Activity (effective) concentration 59. Low
60. Cooled 61. Warmer 62. Free-energy
63. Moles of solvent 64. Matrix 65. gm^{-3} or grammes/cubic metre
66. Mole fraction 67. Fick's First Law 68. Inverse
69. Q_{10} 70. 1.03 71. 1.2–1.4
72. Osmometer 73. Membrane 74. Walls
75. Cells 76. Perfect 77. Potentials
78. Water potential 79. Solute potential 80. Negative
81. –2.5 kJ kg^{-1} or – 10.75 Cal.mol^{-1} or 25×10^{7} ergs g^{-1} 82. –2.5
83. Mega pascals 84. J.H. Von't Hoff 85. Water potential
86. Russian scientist 87. Relative Humidity (the saturation vapour pressure or density)
88. 10°C or 20°F 89. Thermoelectric effect 90. Peltier effect
91. Osmotic potential 92. Vapour pressure 93. Colligative
94. Freezing point or cryoscopic method 95. Incipient plasmolysis
96. Halophytes 97. Hydration or imbibition 98. Matric potential
99. Colloids = Kolla (Greek word) or glue 100. Tyndall effect
101. Brownian Movement 102. Kinetic theory 103. 600 m^2 or 6,000,00 cm^2
104. Meniscus (plural menisci) 105. Hydrophillic 106. 225 kg 107. Stomates
108. Transpiration 109. Carbon-dioxide 110. 0.0156 mol m^{-3}
111. Dry weight 112. Stephen Hales 113. Lysimeters
114. Photometers 115. One per cent 116. Resistance
117. Water 118. Guard cells 119. Accessory or subsidiary
120. Intercellular 121. Reverse diffusional 122. Mesophyll
123. Sunken stomates 124. Kidney shaped 125. Thickened 126. Dicot
127. At night 128. Afternoon 129. Mesophyll
130. Water potential 131. Guard 132. Abscisic acid
133. Convection 134. Energy 135. Green wavelength
136. Ozone 137. 3×10^{10} cms^{-1} or 300,000 kms^{-1} or 186,000 miles S^{-1}
138. 6×10^{14} pulsations S^{-1} 139. Photon or quantum 140. Radiation

141. Planck's constant
142. Quantum
143. 400 to 700
144. Pigment
145. Black body
146. Net radiation
147. Ohm's law
148. Boundary/unstirred
149. Transpiration
150. Gradient
151. Accentuate
152. Small leaves
153. Barometric height
154. "Tallest Tree"
155. Vacuum boil
156. Guttation
157. Conifer
158. Capillarity
159. Cohesion of water
160. Tyloses
161. Hydroponics
162. Root
163. Silica
164. Cobalt
165. Roots
166. Twigs and branches
167. Electrons
168. Siderophores
169. Deficiency symptoms
170. Phytoferritin
171. Boron
172. Zinc
173. "Die back"
174. Molybdenum
175. Acid
176. Nitrate reductase
177. Tap root
178. Deep rooted
179. 500 root tips and line tips. respectively
180. Filamentous-long and narrow
181. Water and ions
182. Endomycorrhyzae
183. Harting net
184. Cytosole
185. Sugars
186. Phosphate
187. Mg^{2+} or Fe^{2+}
188. Ca^{2+}
189. Carboxyl groups (–COOH ® COO + H^+)
190. Cation
191. Leached
192. Nitrate or NO_3^-
193. Bacteria
194. Dissolved
195. Apoplastic
196. Apoplastic
197. Vacuoles
198. Cytosoles
199. Desmotubule
200. Endodermis or periycle
201. Membranes
202. Phospholipids
203. Proteins
204. One-half to two-thirds
205. Hydrophillic
206. Peripheral
207. Polysaccharides
208. Permeable
209. Membranes
210. Hydrophobic
211. 5
212. Size
213. Hydration
214. Accumulation ratio
215. Photosynthetic
216. Larger amounts
217. Protein
218. Membranes
219. Active absorption
220. Passive absorption
221. Xylem
222. Source
223. Transfer cells
224. Plasmalema
225. Harvest index
226. Leaf
227. Catabolism (from Greek *kata*, downwards)
228. Release energy
229. 10^8 and 10^{20}
230. Polypeptide chains
231. Carboxyl group
232. Electric field
233. Enzyme
234. Hydroxyl group
235. Denaturation
236. Tryptophane
237. N.T. de Saussure
238. Phosphorylation or photophosphorylation
239. Chlorophyll a and chlorophyll b
240. b-carotein and lutein
241. Einstein
242. Stark Einstein
243. Fluorescence
244. Brown algae
245. Emersion Enhancement Effect
246. Light-harvesting complexes
247. Chloroplast mutation
248. Chemiosmotic theory
249. Regeneration
250. Photosynthetic carbon reduction cycle
251. C-4 species

252. Monocots 253. C-3 254. Biomass
255. Transamination 256. Otto Warburg
257. CAM (crassulacean acid metabolism) 258. Warming
259. Photosynthetically Active Radiation (PAR) 260. Light compensation point
261. Water requirement 262. Leaf Area Index (LAI) 263. Acidic rainfall of "acid rain"
264. Nitrogen fixation 265. Trees and shrubs 266. Esterified
267. Cuticle 268. Cutin
269. Allelopathy (Greek, *allelon*, of one other: *pathos*, disease) 270. Sterols (steroid alcohols)
271. Cardiac glycosides 272. Saponins (sterols attached to a short chain of one or more sugar)
273. b-carotein 274. Unbranched 275. Resins
276. Aromatic 277. Lignin
278. Anthocyanin (Greek, *anthos*, a flower: *kyanos*, dark blue)
279. b-cyanin, from red beet root 280. Alkaloids
281. Dry weight (freshly harvested plant material dried for 24-48 hours at 70-80°C)
282. Determinate 283. Radical (embryonic root) 284. Anthesis
285. Parthenocarpic fruit development 286. Coleoptyle
287. Growth regulators 288. Sensitivity 289. Development
290. Acid growth 291. Gibberellin 292. Ethylene
293. Fresh weight 294. Climacteric 295. Non-climacteric
296. Non-dormant buds 297. Batasins 298. Epinasty
299. Motor cells 300. Nyclinastic 301. Pulvinus
302. Mimosoideae 303. Solar tracking 304. Circumnutation
305. Totipotent 306. Photodormant 307. Phytochrome
308. Thermonasty 309. Vernalisation 310. Quiescence
311. Circadian clock 312. Photoperiodic response/photoperiodism
313. Photoperiod 314. Night interruption phenomenon
315. Operational environment 316. Adiabatic gradient or adiabatic lapse rate
317. Desert ephemerals 318. (*c*) 319. (*d*)
320. (*d*) 321. (*c*) 322. (*b*)
323. (*d*) 324. (*b*) 325. (*c*)
326. (*a*) 327. (*a*) 328. (*c*)
329. (*c*) 330. (*a*) 331. (*c*)
332. (*d*) 333. (*d*) 334. (*c*)
335. (*b*) 336. (*b*) 337. (*d*)
338. (*b*) 339. (*c*) 340. (*d*)
341. (*d*) 342. (*c*) 343. (*d*)
344. (*a*) 345. (*b*) 346. (*d*)
347. (*b*) 348. (*d*) 349. (*c*)
350. (*d*) 351. (*c*) 352. (*d*)

353. (*a*) & also maize 354. (*d*) 355. (*c*)
356. (*d*) 357. (*a*)
358. (*a*)–(*iii*) (*b*)–(*iv*) (*c*)–(*i*) (*d*)–(*ii*)
359. (*a*)–(*iii*) (*b*)–(*iv*) (*c*)–(*i*) (*d*)–(*ii*)
360. (*a*)–(*iii*) (*b*)–(*i*) (*c*)–(*ii*) (*d*)–(*iv*)
361. (*a*)–(*iv*) (*b*)–(*i*) (*c*)–(*iii*) (*d*)–(*ii*)
362. (*a*)–(*iii*) (*b*)–(*i*) (*c*)–(*iv*) (*d*)–(*ii*)
363. (*a*)–(*iii*) (*b*)–(*iv*) (*c*)–(*i*) (*d*)–(*ii*)
364. (*a*)–(*iv*) (*b*)–(*i*) (*c*)–(*ii*) (*d*)–(*iii*)
365. (*a*)–(*ii*) (*b*)–(*iv*) (*c*)–(*i*) (*d*)–(*iii*)
366. (*a*)–(*ii*) (*b*)–(*i*) (*c*)–(*iv*) (*d*)–(*iii*)
367. (*a*)–(*iii*) (*b*)–(*ii*) (*c*)–(*i*) (*d*)–(*iv*)
368. (*a*)–(*ii*) (*b*)–(*iii*) (*c*)–(*iv*) (*d*)–(*i*)
369. (*a*)–(*iii*) (*b*)–(*i*) (*c*)–(*iv*) (*d*)–(*ii*)
370. (*a*)–(*iv*) (*b*)–(*i*) (*c*)–(*ii*) (*d*)–(*iii*)
371. (*a*)–(*iii*) (*b*)–(*ii*) (*c*)–(*iv*) (*d*)–(*i*)
372. (*a*)–(*iv*) (*b*)–(*i*) (*c*)–(*iii*) (*d*)–(*ii*)
373. (*a*)–(*ii*) (*b*)–(*iv*) (*c*)–(*i*) (*d*)–(*iii*)
374. (*a*)–(*iii*) (*b*)–(*iv*) (*c*)–(*ii*) (*d*)–(*i*)
375. (*a*)–(*iv*) (*b*)–(*i*) (*c*)–(*ii*) (*d*)–(*iii*)
376. (*a*)-(*iii*) (*b*)–(*iv*) (*c*)–(*i*) (*d*)–(*ii*)
377. (*a*)-(*iv*) (*b*)–(*i*) (*c*)–(*ii*) (*d*)–(*iii*)
378. (*a*)-(*iii*) (*b*)–(*i*) (*c*)–(*iv*) (*d*)–(*ii*)
379. (*a*)-(*iv*) (*b*)–(*ii*) (*c*)–(*i*) (*d*)–(*iii*)
380. (*a*)-(*iii*) (*b*)–(*ii*) (*c*)–(*iv*) (*d*)–(*i*)
381. (*a*)-(*iv*) (*b*)–(*i*) (*c*)–(*ii*) (*d*)–(*iii*)
382. (*a*)-(*iii*) (*b*)–(*ii*) (*c*)–(*iv*) (*d*)–(*i*)
383. (*a*)-(*iii*) (*b*)–(*ii*) (*c*)–(*iv*) (*d*)–(*i*)
384. (*a*)-(*ii*) (*b*)–(*iv*) (*c*)–(*i*) (*d*)–(*iii*)
385. 0.9823 (98.23%)
386. 17.00 g/m^3
387. Water-flux density in $g/m^2/s^1$
388. Log k_2/k_1 389. Irradiance of incident radiant energy
390. 20^{100} or 10^{130} 391. 0.71 (18/25.5) as RQ is CO_2 to O_2 ratio
392. 0.5 393. 51

SECTION 5

EXCESS WATER (FLOODED CONDITIONS)

I. Fill up the blanks:

1. Approximately ———— per cent of earth's surface is covered by submerged soils or sediments.
2. The most disastrous Yellow River (of China) flood occurred in ———— when more than 900,000 people were drowned.
3. In northern India damage by flooding is counteracted by increased soil fertility as a result of ————.
4. In eastern Mexico, the gulf coast of Texas, and some parts of United States of America flooding is often associated with ————.
5. The term ———— refers to land adjacent to streams that has been flooded naturally in historic times.
6. The terms river bottom, bottomland, ———— and flood plain forests are often used synonymously.
7. Swamps at some distance from bottomland are classed as ————.
8. A disadvantage of reservoirs for flood control is that they accumulate the ———— carried by streams.
9. Impoundment by reservoirs often creates adverse sites for ———— plants.
10. In a flooded soil, ———— between the soil and air is drastically reduced.
11. Reduced water absorption and ———— of stomata lower the rate of photosynthesis indicating the earliest plant response to flooding.
12. Estimates have brought out that one-half to one-third of the world's hectarage of ———— embodies the drainage problem.
13. Irrigation from mountain streams by use of diversion canals was practised in ———— even before 600 B.C.
14. Irrigation was introduced in Egypt more than ———— year ago.
15. In China construction of the 700 miles long ———— in 700 A.D. provided irrigation for vast areas of crop producing land.
16. Erosion is critical on irrigated lands with slopes in ————
17. The gaseous diffusion virtually ceases when the gaseous pore space drops to about ———— perc ent.
18. The *albedo* values for dry clay is 0.23, for wet clay 0.16 and for water ————.
19. ———— swell more than calcareous/acid soils due to flooding.
20. The clay minerals namely, smectic and beidellite swell more than kaolinite and ———— when a dry soil is flooded.
21. Loss of cohesion decreases ———— rendering the use of heavy machinery on flooded soils impractical.

22. Alternate flooding and drying of a soil help in ————.
23. Subjecting flooded soil to compression or shearing forces ———— that follows the flooding of dry soil.
24. Drying and reoxidation of flooded soils help in partial restoration of structure through cracking and cementing by ————.
25. In porous, non-swelling soils flooding increases ———— due to greater head of water and increased hydraulic conductivity.
26. A percolation rate of ———— is necessary to meet the oxygen demands of roots in a flooded soil.
27. The percolation rate exceeding ———— improves rice yield.
28. The percolation at 2-3 cm/day does not oxygenate more than ———— of surface layer of a flooded soil.
29. The biomass production in the standing water of fallow tropical rice fields. may be as high as ———— of fresh matter per hectare.
30. Depletion of carbon dioxide by algal and macrophytes in the standing water may increase the pH to ————.
31. *Cyanobacteria* (BGA) in the standing water may fix as much as ————.
32. Formation of manganic oxide deposits below the plough sole of flooded rice fields has been attributed to the presence of ————.
33. Soil metabolism that causes denitrification, reduction of manganese, iron and sulphate as well as nitrogen fixation and methane formation is the work of ———— in oxygen-free zone of a flooded soil.
34. Redox potential falls rapidly after flooding, reaches the minimum within a few days, rises rapidly to a maximum and then decreases ———— with time.
35. The redox potential is high in ———— and in the first few millimeters of the surface soil.
36. Redox potentials of interstitial waters of flooded soils are meaningful as they have been used to explain the changes in concentration of ———— important ions in soil solution.
37. When an acid soil is flooded its pH increases, whereas the opposite happens in ————.
38. The pH value of most flooded mineral soils ranges between 6.7 and 7.2 and those of their interstitial solutions between ————.
39. The pH of a flooded soil having low reducible iron content does not rise above ———— even after months of submergence.
40. If the organic matter content of a high pH submerged soil is low, the pH may not decrease below ————.
41. When pH in a submerged ferruginous soil enhances the concentration of water soluble iron from ———— to ————, it causes iron toxicity.
42. Flooding increases the concentration of NH_4^+ and HCO_3^- and converts Mn^{2+} and Fe^{2+} to more soluble form which adds to the ————.
43. Ion exchange is the replacement by ions in the soil solution of cations and anions held by ———— on colloids.
44. Cations are held on soil colloids by permanent negative charges residing on the particles and by pH-dependent ————.
45. The permanent negative charge on a mineral colloid is ———— in the pH range of 2.5-10.0.
46. The Fe^{2+}, Mn^{2+} and NH_4^+ concentrations in the solutions of flooded soils may be as high as 10, 2 and 8 mM, respectively and these ions displace ———— into the soil solution.

47. NO_3^- and Cl^- are held by simple electrostatic attraction and are said to be ——— adesorbed.
48. The increase in water-soluble phosphate and silica concentration and desorption of sulphate due to flooding of soils may lead to decrease in ——— and increase in bicarbonate concentration.
49. Sorption is due to ——— or ——— exchange.
50. The Freundlich and ——— isotherms are used to describe sorption.
51. Changes in pH due to flooding may increase sorption or desorption as conditioned by ——— of the sorbent.
52. ——— play an important role in controlling the availability of nutrients and pollution by toxic metals and organic pesticides.
53. Upto ——— of carbon dioxide per hectare may accumulate in the ploughed layer of a flooded soil.
54. Organic matter decomposes more slowly in flooded soil than in ——— as depicted by accumulation of OM in waterlogged marshes and peats.
55. High C : N ratio of substrate, soil acidity, and low temperature retard ——— decomposition.
56. Reducing conditions ——— of insecticides, herbicides, and fungicides.
57. Decomposition of soil organic matter is a process in which microorganisms use the substrate to derive energy and carbon for ———.
58. Aerobic and anaerobic respiration follow a common pathway to the formation of ———.
59. In aerobic respiration pyruvic acid is oxidized to carbon dioxide through ——— cycle.
60. If the electron acceptors are inorganic, the process is termed as ——— respiration.
61. When the electron acceptors are organic substances the process is known as ———.
62. The mean pathways of pesticide degradation in flooded soils are reductive dechlorination, dehydrochlorination, ——— and reduction.
63. Conversion of organic nitrogen to inorganic forms in flooded soils stops at the ——— due to lack of oxygen.
64. A dry soil that is flooded releases more ammonium than does a ———.
65. Nitrate an intermediate product of both aerobic nitrification and anaerobic denitrification is unstable in both ——— media.
66. Relatively ——— is immobilized in flooded soils.
67. Flooding ——— a soil's capacity to fix nitrogen biologically.
68. A pH above 7, the presence of available phosphate and iron, and adequate amount of carbon dioxide in the flood water favour the growth of ———.
69. Abundant phosphorus, calcium, iron and molybdenum promote nitrogen fixation by ———.
70. Acid soils rich in manganese and organic matter build up water soluble Mn^{2+} concentrations as high as 90 mg / litre at ——— within 1-2 weeks after flooding.
71. The most conspicuous chemical change that takes place when soil is flooded is reduction of ———
72. The increase in ——— caused by flooding decreases the activity coefficient of ions in soil solution.
73. The increase in concentration of ——— phosphate and silica caused by flooding is due partly to desorption.
74. Flooding increases the availability of ——— but decreases that of zinc and copper.
75. Aquatic soils owe some distinguishing character to ———.

76. Cations displaced from a paddy-soil colloid by iron and manganese migrate out of root zone and are lost by ———.
77. The pH of acid sulphate soils is ———.
78. ——— is a yellow mineral characteristic of acid sulphate soils.
79. Sodic soils are found in arid areas in depression that undergo temporary ———.
80. Saline soils contain sufficient salts in the ——— to interfere with plant growth.
81. Continuous waterlogging/flooding provides conditions conducive to ——— formation.
82. The physiological adjustment and readjustment by a plant to stress conditions is called ——— response.
83. Plant roots and microorganisms consume 5-24 g of oxygen per day/m^2 of land surface through aerobic ——— under the temperate conditions during growing season.
84. Excess water around plant roots as an early response mainly increase ——— content.
85. Excess water around plant roots brings about modest depression in the concentration of oxygen termed as ———.
86. A rice plant grows well in flooded soils due to slow rate of ——— ethylene production in the roots.
87. Upland plants when submerged produce ——— at a faster rate leading to its larger accumulation to inhibitory level of gas.
88. Flooding can change markedly the ——— of root growth except in anoxia conditions.
89. Submergence induced hypoxia and ethylene accumulation stimulate formation of ——— within roots.
90. In anaerobic conditions leaching and ——— may deplete the soil nitrogen.
91. Root ——— may have a greater resistance to anoxia than do the apices of roots extending at the onset of the anaerobic treatment.
92. High water-tables cause plants of wet as well as non-wetland habitat to root more ———.
93. The severity of the effect of transient flooding on root system may depend on the ——— of the plant.
94. Paddy rice soils typically have a surface layer of water that is kept well ——— by algae.
95. In waterlogged, oxygen deficient conditions, the bacteroid and root cells of nodules generate considerable amount of ——— to damage the further nodulation.
96. Any ethylene formed and trapped within nodules is detrimental to nodulation and ———.
97. As little as ——— ethylene is sufficient to diminish nodulation by 90 per cent.
98. Carbon dioxide at ——— depresses the process of nodulation in legumes.
99. VAM in some agricultural crops improve the nutrient status of the plant for ——— and possibly other soil immobile nutrients.
100. Members of the Cyperaceae family frequently found in flooded environments are usually ———.
101. The anaerobic metabolism is unable to provide energy for initiation of ——— or mitosis in the root meristem.
102. Root-extension rates depend on the rates of cell ——— and elongation.
103. Aerenchyma formation regardless of its source of formation can be blocked by low concentration of ———.
104. Ethylene precursor ACC (1-aminocyclopropane-1-carboxylic acid) is produced in the hypoxic root tip and possibly converted to ethylene in the ——— zone in presence of oxygen diffusing from aerial tissue.

105. The loss of cortex renders ——— vulnerable to radial hydrostatic pressure on submergence.
106. Mitochondria of the excised growing roots of non-wet plants subjected to anaerobic conditions show abnormal ——— followed by generalized degeneration usually within 24-48 hours.
107. In excised roots, ———, and leaves of rice mitochondrial is complete in 1-2 days of anoxia.
108. Mitochondrial and cell survival of anoxia depend on an adequate supply of respirable substrates to maintain rapid ——— and sufficient energy for maintenance.
109. The membrane structure and functions in plants cells would be expected to be sensitive to oxygen supply which is essential for the synthesis of ——— fatty acids.
110. Provision of higher concentration of ions in the outer solution can partially offset the ——— inhibition of transport to the shoot.
111. Ion uptake by intact roots of wetland species is almost independent of ——— concentration of the solution.
112. In maize, gas-filled lacunae can occupy some 80 per cent of the ——— in aerenchymatous roots without effecting the transport of potassium.
113. The concentration of ——— in shoots of cereal species can increase during flooding.
114. Mostly the root growth and function are dependent on ——— respiration.
115. Generally, critical oxygen pressure is defined with respect to outer solution, but it fails to provide an accurate concentration within ——— cells.
116. Increased gas-space formation in rice roots is associated with radial leakage of ——— in the tip region.
117. Abundant precipitation of iron around epidermis and in the root cortex is indicative of appreciable movement of oxygen through the ———.
118. In fully aerobic conditions, the oxidation of 1 mol of glucose (sugar) to CO_2 and water yields ——— of ATP.
119. In the production of pyruvate by glycolysis, synthesis of 4 mol of ATP occurs through substrate linked phosphorylation of ADP.
120. Plant-cells under anaerobic conditions commonly produce ———.
121. Ethanol accumulation in flood-intolerant species is more rapid than in ——— species.
122. The energy status of cells cannot be reliably measured by ——— level alone.
123. Plant and animals under adverse environmental conditions synthesize increased amount of specific ———.
124. Under anaerobic conditions the behaviour of maize and wheat roots contrasts markedly with that of ———.
125. Flooding effects on the shoot arise from modifications to the internal flow of substances between shoot and ———.
126. Leaf growth is extremely sensitive to flooding and root ———.
127. Inhibition of ——— extension is almost always observable when soil is waterlogged.
128. Flood-induced adventitious roots from the stem base is best considered as ———.
129. In flooded maize, severe reductions in transpiration and ——— are relieved on emergence of adventitious roots.
130. In most instances ——— rooting occurs at or just below water level.

131. In flooded conditions, maize differs from sunflower by having ———— root primordia at stem nodes.
132. In most of the flooding situations original ———— are incapacitated by anoxia.
133. ———— of leaf petioles in tomato is probably the best known responses of shoot to soil waterlogging.
134. Flooding induces ———— in potato, tomato and sunflower.
135. The plants of strawberry clover (*Trifolium fragiferum*) grow prostrate in well drained conditions but when covered with water they grow ————.
136. In general, flooding accelerates ———— in plants namely barely, wheat, maize etc.
137. The ———— of living things is matched by the variety of deaths that await them.
138. Sometimes the senescence ———— in flooded plants may be induced by anaerobically generated toxins.
139. One day after flooding, anoxia in wheat disrupts cell structure and production of chemical energy needed to transport nitrate and ammonium from ———— and across roots to the stele.
140. Bioassays of hormones in xylem sap during the first three days of flooding show a marked decline in ———— and gibberellin-like substances.
141. A deficiency in root-sourced gibberellins and cytokinins may accelerate leaf ———— in some plants.
142. Stomatal closure may form a gradient between leaf senescence and reduction in ———— from roots to shoots.
143. Abrupt increase in phosphorus concentration in leaves of flooded peas offers an explanation for ———— to leaves.
144. In soils flooded for long periods, ———— soil microorganisms may produce toxins.
145. In the chemically reduced soils of paddy fields, overcast weather favours formation and penetration of hydrogen sulphide into rice plants, this may reach the shoots and causes ————.
146. The principal mode of action of hydrogen sulphide (H_2S) is to inhibit the action of ————.
147. In cotton, flooding destroys pollen viability leading to ovary abortion, senescence and ————.
148. Rapid wilting has been attributed to higher resistance to mass flow of water through roots of ———— plants.
149. About 75 per cent of world's coastline between 25°N and 25°S support twenty ———— of mangrove.
150. Most of the angiosperms are more flood tolerant than ————.
151. *Eucalyptus camaldulensis* seedlings adapt better to flooding than those of ————.
152. Decreasing order of sensitivity of citrus rootstock to waterlogging is rough lemon, ———— and sweet lime.
153. Trees are injured much more by ———— water than by flowing water.
154. Flood-induced stem roots in woody plants often emerge through hypertrophied ————.
155. Both formation of roots and loss of root polarity have been attributed to accelerate ———— production by flooded plants.
156. Flooding tolerance of *Eucalyptus grandis* is related to its capacity to form ———— roots.
157. Many species of trees respond to flooding by producing ———— lenticels.
158. Lenticel hypertrophy is induced by ———— that forms in response to flooding.
159. A number of tree species when subjected to flooding produce ————.
160. Pneumatophores often bear ———— that serve as aerating channels for submerged roots.

161. The arched still roots embody lenticels that function as ——— organs.
162. Usually trees often eventually killed by flooding, grow very rapidly for some time when they are first ———.
163. Flooding caused ——— closure in leaves that were fully expanded by the time the plants were first flooded.
164. Flooding did not induce stomatal closure of leaves that ——— during the flooding period.
165. The response of adaxial and abaxial stomata to flooding greatly varies ——— species.
166. Flooding induces rapid increases in ——— content of leaves.
167. Exogenous application of ABA to leaves results in ——— of stomata.
168. Water absorption by flooded plants is due to lowered ——— of roots.
169. ——— of tomato leaves after downpour of rain has been assigned to temporary ——— in permeability of roots.
170. High temperature in *Triticum aestivum* induces deficiency of———.
171. Flooding of soil ——— rate of transpiration.
172. *Helianthus annus* (sunflower) has an inbuilt ability to develop ——— roots rapidly on flooding.
173. Flooding causes depression and translocation of photosynthates from sources to sinks besides reducing the rate of ———.
174. Plant sodium content generally ——— under anaerobiosis.
175. In submerged soils the availability of iron and manganese increases due to their ———.
176. In calcareous soils, long term flooding tend to enhance availability of copper and molybdenum, but reduces that of ———.
177. Molybdenum concentration in ——— tissues increased in flooded maize.
178. High concentrations of substrate iron can induce ——— deficiency symptoms in rice plants.
179. Rice plants interact with a bacterium called ——— to carry out the reduction of sulphide in a flooded paddy soil.
180. Healthy rice roots are capable of ——— proximal sulphide to minimize direct injury from sulphide.
181. Sulphide oxidation may consume so many oxidizing equivalents from healthy rice roots that ——— oxidation is inhibited resulting in its toxicity.
182. Rice plants embodying low vigour suffer from ——— damage due to lack of sufficient oxygen transporting capacity.
183. Ethylene has ——— water solubility that limits its escape from plant tissues.
184. The diffusion coefficient of ethylene in water is ——— fold less than that in air.
185. Ethylene emanation from the shoots of ——— plants well in response to flooding.
186. ——— is the biological precursor of ethylene.
187. ——— is an intermediate between methionine and ethylene.
188. The signals from flooded roots might indirectly interfere with the biosynthesis in soils of the hormones ——— and ———.
189. One of the earliest symptoms of flooding stress in a number of herbaceous plants is ——— growth of petioles.
190. Epinasty is caused by more rapid elongation of the cells on the ——— of the petiole relative to those of the lower side.

191. ————, even at extremely low concentrations (0.1 ml/litre) will promote epinasty in sensitive species.
192. Exogenous GA and CKs effect ———— formation.
193. Root-growth is usually slowed by ————.
194. Anaerobiosis blocks ———— respiration resulting in root-starvation of energy for growth.
195. Waterlogging of roots in general brings about a reduction of ———— elongation.
196. Hypertrophy occurs in flooded conditions owing to ———— water rather than anoxia.
197. Mean annual carbon-dioxide concentration in the atmosphere currently is slightly above ———— per cent.
198. Oxygen in the atmosphere is nearly constant at ———— per cent.
199. About 78 per cent (by volume) of ambient atmosphere is nearly constantly composed of ————.
200. Gases produced in the soil are exhausted primarily by ———— to the ambient atmosphere along the concentration gradient.
201. Oxygen diffuses ———— times more slowly through water than through air.
202. Ready water adsorption on soil particle surfaces is owing ———— of water and predominant negative charge of clay minerals.
203. The phenomenon of ———— comprises the foundation on which much of the physics of soil flooding is based.
204. Soil water potential (chemical potential of soil water) expresses the ———— of water in soil relative to pure free water in the same position.
205. Soil water has capacity to do work than ———— at the same position.
206. The less water is in soil, more tightly the remaining water is held and therefore the ———— its potential.
207. On inundation of soil profile from surface flooding, the hierarchy of water entry (with respect to pore size) into the profile is the reverse of ————.
208. Gravel is often in the bottom of pots or planting beds for ————.
209. The frequency and ———— of flooding have a marked impact on soil properties and plant response.
210. The pore geometry of the ———— soils varies immensely with matric potential.
211. In persistently flooded soils, the physicochemical characteristics developed in insitu are basically those associated with ———— reducing environment.
212. Pathogen-dominant fungi are unspecialized pathogens that attack plants having little or no ———— disease.
213. ———— diseases involve pathogen-host association in which the host has greater influence than the pathogen on the course of disease.
214. Root ———— are essential for host-dominant diseases.
215. Soil water requirements for the formation of ———— in soil by *Phytophthora* are rather precise.
216. The transition of soil from a drained to a saturated state stimulates ———— release by *Sporangia*.
217. ———— and zoospores are believed to be the primary survival propagules.
218. Reproduction of a variety of ———— nematodes is severely reduced in continuously microaerobic environments.

219. Shunting back and forth between oxidative and fermentative metabolism prevents nematodes from developing an adequate capacity for continuous ———.

220. Zoospore of *Phytophthora* spp. swim in a ——— pattern.

221. Zoospore movement requires continuous ——— channels with a minimum of tortuosity.

222. Bacterial movement is restricted in soil dry than ———.

223. The ——— refers to the chemical/physical influence of living roots on microbial activity.

224. In flooded fields, zoospores comprise the initial inoculant as they are carried by moving water to plants in ——— areas.

225. Root pathogens may damage the host primarily by decreasing effective root ——— and ———.

226. A single rotation with paddy-rice controlled ——— wilt in cotton for 2-3 years.

227. The plants that adapt to tolerate anoxia metabolically are termed as ———.

228. The tolerance of paddy-rice to flooding is as strongly related to its capacity to transport ——— to the rhizosphere.

229. Stem hypertrophy coupled with knees and exposed roots facilitate internal ——— of the roots of same swamp tree species.

230. In sunflower and most herbaceous species stem hypetrophy is associated with the enlargement of ——— layer.

231. Flooding associated stem hypertrophy is more or less controlled by ———.

232. Flooding causes accumulation of ——— in flooded tissues of sunflower.

233. Knees are the result of ——— growth on the arched upper (adaxial) side of the tree roots.

234. Sweetgum (*Liquidambar styraciflua*), in response to flooding produce relatively more succulent roots known as ———.

235. Flooding of most agronomic plants causes the ——— all or most of the root system.

236. ——— of gases occur in floating water lily (*Nupher luteum* spp *macrophylla* and *N: luteum* spp. *variegatum*).

237. The coleoptile of ——— serves as the entry for oxygen to its germinating seed whether it germinates under water or in air.

238. Lenticels are primary entry points for oxygen diffusion to the ——— of several woody species.

239. The survival of wetland plants depends on their capacity to transform soil-borne ——— to less harmful products.

240. Rhizosphere oxidation occurs only when internal respiration demands are exceeded and root tissues are permeable to ——— of oxygen.

241. Permeability of roots of wetland species to oxygen decreases rapidly with increasing distance from the ———.

242. The air could be pulled through the xylem elements of species non-tolerant of waterlogging at ——— than through the lenticels.

243. Amino acid composition of roots and plant sap are significantly altered by ——— in the roots.

244. Rice under highly reduced conditions shows susceptibility to diseases associated with ——— toxins.

245. Lack of response to phosphorus is attributed to release of oxygen by rice roots which oxidizes ferrous iron to ———.

246. Lowland rice generally does not response to ——— under flooded conditions.

247. ——— can complete their life cycles in saline environment unlike glycophytes.

II. Tick mark (✓) the correct answer:

248. A decrease in redox potential below 0.2 V.
   (*a*) Destroys nitrates
   (*b*) Destroys NH_4 and N-fixation
   (*c*) Decreases phosphorus, silicon, iron and manganese availability
   (*d*) Increases sulphur, zinc and copper availability

249. A pH of 6.5-7.0 in soil solution regardless of pH before flooding.
   (*a*) Decreases phosphorus availability (*b*) Checks organic matter mineralization
   (*c*) Favours nutrient absorption (*d*) No effect on nutrient absorption

250. The main steps in pyrite formation in acid sulphate soil are ———.
   (*a*) Oxidation of sulphate (*b*) Dissolution of iron monosulphide
   (*c*) Reduction of hydrogen sulphide (*d*) None of these

251. Sodic soils contain sufficient of ——— to interfere with plant growth.
   (*a*) Exchangeable calcium (*b*) Exchangeable sodium
   (*c*) Exchangeable magnesium (*d*) Exchangeable potassium

252. The roots of tomato and sunflower when in contrast of water-table become ———.
   (*a*) Diageotropic/negative geotropic (*b*) Positively geotropic
   (*c*) Positive geotropic (*d*) Remain unaffected

253. In an anaerobic soil perfused with nitrogen gas kills apices in three hours of ———.
   (*a*) Cotton (*b*) Soybean
   (*c*) Mungbean (*d*) Cowpea

254. In degraded acid soils root extension into anaerobic and highly reduced layer is restricted due to injurious concentrations of ———.
   (*a*) Iron (*b*) Nitrogen
   (*c*) Phosphorus (*d*) None of these

255. The bacteroid *Rhizobium* is ———.
   (*a*) Macroaerobic (*b*) Microaerobic
   (*c*) Anaerobic (*d*) None of these

256. Additional wall structures presumably lignin/suberin in the aerenchymatous roots, in a water logged soil are formed in non-wetland plants namely ———.
   (*a*) Soybean (*b*) Mungbean
   (*c*) Groundnut (*d*) Maize/sorghum/wheat/barley

257. The changes in plant cells membrane, lipid composition can modify ———.
   (*a*) Fluidity (*b*) Alter permeability
   (*c*) Only one of these (*d*) Both of these

258. Flooding of soil grown plants show ————.

(*a*) Depression in N and K in shoots (*b*) Enhancement in phosphorus in shoots

(*c*) Promotes ion accumulation by shoots (*d*) None of these

259. In maize, gas filled lacunae can occupy upto 80 per cent of mid-cortex in aerenchymatous roots without an effect on transport to stele of ————.

(*a*) Boron (*b*) Zinc

(*c*) Manganese (*d*) Potassium

260. Rates of root fresh-weight increase close to maximal have been recorded at oxygen partial pressure of 0.015-0.05 atm. with ————.

(*a*) Wheat (*b*) Tomato/tobacco/soybean

(*c*) Sorghum (*d*) Safflower

261. The diffusion of $^{15}O_2$ from shoots to a point 15 cm along with a root has been readily detectable in ————.

(*a*) Aerenchymatous rice roots (*b*) Non-aerenchymatous barley roots

(*c*) In one of these (*d*) In both of these

262. Flooding in a wide range of plant species brings about ————.

(*a*) Rapid transpiration (*b*) Rapid wilting

(*c*) Rapid respiration (*d*) Rapid nutrient absorption

263. The decreased root permeability in flooded plants is on account of ———— concentration,.

(*a*) Low carbon dioxide (*b*) Low oxygen

(*c*) Low hydrogen (*d*) Low nitrogen

264. Zinc deficiency during early growth is caused by its immobilization in roots by carbonate ions soon after the submergence of ———— soils.

(*a*) Acid (*b*) Saline

(*c*) Saline-alkali (*d*) Alkaline

265. Iron toxicity can be ameliorated by ————.

(*a*) Continuous soil submergence (*b*) Application of lime and compos

(*c*) Application of P and N as urea (*d*) All of these

266. Rice plants show no manganese induced toxicity symptoms upto its tissue level of ———— ppm.

(*a*) 6000 (*b*) 5000

(*c*) 4000 (*d*) 3000

267. The diffusion coefficient of ethylene in water is less by ———— folds than it is in the air.

(*a*) 20,000 (*b*) 15,000

(*c*) 10,000 (*d*) 5,000

268. Biological precursor of ethylene is ————.

(*a*) Leucine (*b*) Lysine

(*c*) Arginine (*d*) Methionine

269. One of the most commonly observed morphological phenomena associated with waterlogging is the production of ————.

(a) Seminal roots
(b) Crown roots
(c) Tap roots
(d) Adventitious roots

270. The status of soil oxygen may be characterized as a ————.

(a) Quality factor
(b) Quantity factor
(c) Intensity factor
(d) None of these

271. Mean annual carbon dioxide concentration in the atmosphere currently is ————

(a) 0.02 per cent
(b) 0.03 per cent
(c) 0.04 per cent
(d) 0.05 per cent

272. Oxygen in the atmosphere is nearly constant at ————.

(a) 11 per cent
(b) 21 per cent
(c) 31 per cent
(d) 41 per cent

273. Nitrogen in the ambient atmosphere is nearly constant at ———— (by volume)

(a) 48 per cent
(b) 58 per cent
(c) 68 per cent
(d) 78 per cent

274. The zoospores of *Phytophthora cinnamomi* were attracted to ————.

(a) Histidine
(b) Methionine
(c) Glutamic acid
(d) Glycine

275. ———— show poor germination under water.

(a) Maize
(b) Celery
(c) Lettuce
(d) Bermuda grass

276. Good germination under water occurs in ————.

(a) Tomato
(b) Rice
(c) Buckwheat
(d) Lettuce

277. Stem hypertrophy associated with flooding is caused by ————.

(a) Interaction of ethylene and auxins
(b) Interaction of zinc and manganese
(c) Sulphur dioxide and oxygen
(d) Carbon dioxide and nitrogen

278. Flooding bring about the accumulation of ———— in flooded tissues of sunflower

(a) Indole acetic acid
(b) Naphthalene acetic acid
(c) Butyric acid
(d) Oxalic acid

279. Adventitious water roots have been observed to occur in ————.

(a) Tomato
(b) Cucumber
(c) Okra
(d) Gourds

280. The coleoptile of ———— serves an entry for oxygen to the germinating seed under water or in air.

(a) Sunflower
(b) Maize
(c) Rice
(d) Sorghum

281. Oxygen diffusion primarily in a number of woody species occurs through lenticels ————.

(*a*) Atmosphere (*b*) Rhizosphere

(*c*) Ionosphere (*d*) Stratosphere

282. It has been assumed that the development of intercellular space in the cortex of roots provides pathway for oxygen diffusion in ————.

(*a*) Wheat (*b*) Oats

(*c*) Buckwheat (*d*) Barley

283. Root anaerobiosis in tomato resulted in:

(*a*) Increase in glutamine (*b*) Increase in glutamic acid

(*c*) Decrease in alanine (*d*) Decrease in alpha-aminobutyric acid

284. Very salt-tolerant halophytes namely ———— can survive and grow in salinities in excess of 500 mol m^3 sodium chloride.

(*a*) *Vitis vinifera* (*b*) *Persea americana*

(*c*) *Suaeda maritima* (*d*) *Glycine max*

III. Match the following:

285. The duration of survival of roots of various plants in oxygen-free conditions in the laboratory has been observed as :

(*a*) Cotton (*i*) 7-9 hrs.

(*b*) Soybean (*ii*) 0.5-5 hrs.

(*c*) Field pea (*iii*) 3-days

(*d*) Tomato (*iv*) 0.5-3 hrs.

286. The following cultivated tree species have been placed in the flood tolerant categories:

(*a*) Very high mortality (*i*) *Rhododendron* spp.

(*b*) Lower mortality (*ii*) *Rubus procerus*

(*c*) Low mortality (*iii*) *Malus* spp.

(*d*) No mortality (*iv*) *Prunus laurocerasus*

Do You Know That

1. Ribulose bisphosphate-carboxylase is the most abundant enzyme on the earth.
2. Percolation is the movement of water under pressure through the soil profile under nearly saturated conditions.
3. Water held by forces of surface tension in capillary spaces of soil particle is called capillary water.
4. Solute potential due to solute present in soil system is osmotic potential.
5. Free movement of water in response to gravity that drains out of soil is gravitational water.
6. Saturated flow decrease as pore size of soil decreases. Flow in sand > loam > clay.
7. Seepage is the downward or lateral movement of water into soil from a water supply source.

KEY

1. 72 | 2. 1887 | 3. Deposition of silt

4. Hurricanes | 5. Flood plain | 6. Hardwood bottom

7. Inland/nonalluvial swamps | 8. Sediment | 9. Upland

10. Gas exchange | 11. Closure | 12. Irrigated land

13. Japan | 14. 5000 | 15. Imperial canal

16. In excess of 1 per cent | 17. 10 per cent | 18. 0.03-0.10

19. Sodic soils | 20. Halloysite | 21. Soil strength

22. Aggregate formation | 23. Aggravates the structure impairment

24. Hydrate iron oxides | 25. Percolation | 26. 15 m/day

27. 10 mm/day | 28. 1 cm | 29. 12 tonnes

30. 10 | 31. 500 g N/ha/day | 32. Manganese oxidising bacteria

33. Anaerobic bacteria | 34. Asymptomatically | 35. Flood water

36. Ecologically | 37. Alkaline soils | 38. 6.5 and 7.0

39. 5 | 40. 8 | 41. 35 to 350 mg/litre

42. Ionic strength | 43. Electrostatic attraction | 44. Negative charges

45. Constant | 46. Na^+, K^+, Ca^{2+} and Mg^{2+} | 47. Non-specifically

48. Anion exchange capacity (AEC)

49. Cation or anion.

Covalent bonding, action of van der Waals forces or isomorphous substitution

50. Langmuir | 51. Point of zero charge | 52. Sorption and desorption

53. 3 tonnes | 54. Well drained soil | 55. Organic matter

56. Accelerate the degradation | 57. Cell synthesis

58. Pyruvic acid | 59. Tricarboxylic acid (TCA) | 60. Anaerobic

61. Fermentation | 62. Hydrolysis | 63. Ammonium stage

64. Wet soil | 65. Aerobic and anaerobic | 66. Less nitrogen

67. Increases | 68. Blue green algae (Cyanobacteria)

69. Azolla | 70. 25-35°C | 71. Iron

72. Ionic strength | 73. Water soluble | 74. Phosphorus

75. Flooding/waterlogging | 76. Ferrolysis | 77. pH < 3.5

78. Garosite | 79. Flooding or waterlogging | 80. Root-zone

81. Peat | 82. Acclimatic | 83. Respiration

84. Ethylene | 85. Hypoxia | 86. Endogenous

87. Ethylene | 88. Direction | 89. Aerenchyma

90. Denitrification | 91. Primordia | 92. Superficially

93. Growth stage | 94. Oxygenated | 95. Ethanol

96. Nitrogen fixation | 97. 0.4 μl /litre of water | 98. 3 per cent (v/v)

99. Phosphate | 100. Non-mycorrhizal | 101. DNA-synthesis phase

102. Division 103. Ag^+ 104. Sub-apical
105. Aerenchymatous roots 106. Ultra-structure 107. Coleoptile
108. Glycolysis 109. Unsaturated 110. Anoxia-induced
111. Oxygen 112. Mid-cortex 113. Sodium
114. Aerobic 115. Root 116. Oxygen
117. Roots 118. 38 mol 119. 2 mol
120. Ethanol 121. Flood-tolerant 122. ATP
123. Polypeptides 124. Rice 125. Root
126. Anoxia 127. Stem 128. Regenerative
129. Leaf water potential 130. Flood-induced 131. Preformed
132. Roots 133. Epinastic curvature 134. Epinasty
135. Erect 136. Senescence 137. Diversity
138. Syndrome 139. Roots 140. Cytokinin
141. Senescence 142. Cytokinin-flux 143. Flooding-injury
144. Anaerobic 145. Browning diseases 146. Metalloenzyme
147. Abscission 148. Flooded 149. Woody species
150. *Gymnosperms* 151. *E. globules* 152. Coleoptra/mandarin/sweet orange
153. Standing 154. Lenticels 155. Ethylene
156. Adventitious 157. Hypertrophied 158. Ethylene
159. Knee roots/pneumatophores 160. Lenticels 161. Aerating
162. Flooded 163. Stomatal 164. Expanded
165. Amphistomatous 166. ABA 167. Closure
168. Permeability 169. Decrease 170. Oxygen
171. Decreases 172. Adventitious 173. Photosynthesis
174. Increases 175. Reduction 176. Zinc
177. Ear-leaf 178. Phosphorus 179. *Beggiotoa* spp.
180. Oxidising 181. Iron 182. Sulphide
183. Low 184. 10,000 185. Steam-girdled
186. Methionine 187. S-adenosylmethionine/SAM
188. GA and CK 189. Epinastic 190. Upper side
191. Ethylene 192. Root 193. Anaerobiosis
194. Aerobic 195. Stem 196. Excess
197. 0.03 198. 21 per cent 199. Nitrogen
200. Diffusion 201. 104 202. Dipolar nature
203. Capillarity 204. Energy-status 205. Free-water
206. Lower (more negative) 207. Desorption 208. Drainage
209. Duration 210. Shrink-swell 211. Steady-state
212. Resistance 213. Host-dominant 214. Exudates

215. Sporangia
216. Zoospore
217. Chlamydospores
218. Soil-inhabiting
219. Anabolism
220. Helical
221. Water-filled
222. Field-capacity
223. Rhizosphere-effect
224. Non-infested
225. Density and distribution
226. Verticillium
227. Truly anoxia tolerant
228. Oxygen to avoid anoxia
229. Aeration
230. Cortical
231. Water-effect
232. Indole acetic acid (IAA)
233. Meristematic
234. Altered roots
235. Death
236. Mass flow
237. Rice
238. Rhizosphere
239. Toxins
240. Radial diffusion
241. Root-apex
242. Lower tension
243. Anaerobiosis
244. Inorganic and organic
245. Ferric oxide
246. Phosphorus
247. Halophytes
248. (*a*)
249. (*c*)
250. (*d*)
251. (*b*)
252. (*a*)
253. (*a*)
254. (*a*)
255. (*b*)
256. (*d*)
257. (*d*)
258. (*a*)
259. (*d*)
260. (*b*)
261. (*c*)
262. (*b*)
263. (*b*)
264. (*d*)
265. (*d*)
266. (*d*)
267. (*c*)
268. (*d*)
269. (*d*)
270. (*c*)
271. (*b*)
272. (*b*)
273. (*d*)
274. (*c*)
275. (*a*)
276. (*b*)
277. (*a*)
278. (*a*)
279. (*a*)
280. (*c*)
281. (*b*)
282. (*d*)
283. (*b*)
284. (*c*)
285. (*a*)-(*iv*) (*b*)-(*ii*) (*c*)-(*i*) (*d*)-(*iii*)
286. (*a*)-(*iv*) (*b*)-(*ii*) (*c*)-(*i*) (*d*)-(*iii*)

SECTION 6

SOIL FERTILITY AND FERTILIZERS

I. Fill up the blanks :

1. Improved technology has led to the production of _______ forms of fertilizers.
2. Theophrastus (327-287 B.C.) noted that the bean crop (*vicia faba*) was ploughed under by the farmers of Thessaly and _______ to enrich the soil.
3. Virgil (70-19 B.C.) advocated the application of _______ to boost the yield of yellow wheat.
4. Early dwellers of Aegina recognised the value of _______ and hence dug it up to apply to their land.
5. Pliny (A.D. 62-113) stated that lime should be spread thinly on the ground and the treatment will be "_______ for many years, though not 50".
6. Columella suggested a _______ to measure the degree of acidity and alkalinity of soils.
7. Pietro de Crescenzi (1230-1307) who published "*Opus Ruralium Commodorum*" (a collection of local agricultural practices) is referred to by some as the founder of _______.
8. Around 1762, _______, a Tull-adherent established an experimental farm for public exhibition of experiments in agriculture.
9. Arthur Young (1741-1820) published, "_______" in 46 volumes which was highly regarded and made a considerable impact on English agriculture.
10. _______ was able to demonstrate that the plants absorbed oxygen and liberated carbon dioxide, the central theme of respiration.
11. _______ is called by some, the father of the field-pot method of experimentation.
12. The "*law of minimum*" stated by _______ in 1862 is a simple, but logical guide for predicting crop response to fertilization.
13. The famous agricultural research station was established at Rothamsted England in _______.
14. In 1878, Theodore Schloessing and Alfred Muntz, French bacteriologists concluded that nitrification was the result of _______.
15. Robert Warrington demonstrated that nitrification was a two-step phenomenon, the _______ first being conversion into nitrites and the nitrites subsequently to nitrates.
16. Two Germans, Hellrugel and Wilfarth (1886) gave the first specific information regarding _______ by legumes.
17. Nitrogen fixing organism was first isolated by _______ who called the organism *Bacillus radicicola*.
18. _______ is defined as progressive development of an organism.
19. It has been said that growers have the capability of controlling upto _______ of the identified 52 factors that affect plant growth.
20. _______ is defined as the aggregate of all the external conditions and influences affecting the life of an organism.

21. Physicists consider that the temperature of our universe ranges from a low of _______ to a high of several million degrees near the centre of the sun.
22. The temperature range of growth for most of the _______ is usually much lower, perhaps between 15 and 40°C, below and above these limits growth decreases rapidly.
23. When the activity of the micropopulation is great, there will be higher _______ of carbon dioxide of the soil atmosphere as the oxygen content decreases.
24. Variations in soil water deficits are mainly responsible for year-to-year _______ in crop yields.
25. Higher percentages of protein are generally associated with _______ of extractable soil moisture.
26. The tendency of plant nutrients to be taken up more readily as supplies of extractable moisture increase has a favourable effect on _______ .
27. _______ represents the amount of dry matter that can be produced from a given quantity of water and it is also described as weight of dry matter derived from a hectare centimeter of water.
28. Most plants are generally able to make good growth at light intensities of _______ full daylight.
29. According to _______ of the minimum, "even if all but one of the essential elements be present, the absence of that one will render the crop barren.
30. Mitscherlich's law of _______ states that yield can be increased by each single growth factor even when it is not present in the minimum as long as it is not present in the optimum.
31. Mitscherlich's Growth law states, "the increase in yield of a crop as a result of increasing a single growth factor is _______ to the decrement from the maximum yield obtainable by increasing the particular growth factor".
32. The plants require different absolute amounts of nitrogen, phosphorus and potassium, but the amounts in pounds of each required to produce a yield, that is, 50 per cent of the maximum is termed as _______.
33. The values of baule units in pounds per acre of N, P_2O_5 and K_2O are 223, _______ respectively as determined from the results of Mitscherlich's work.
34. O.W. Wilcox employed the Mitscherlich equation to extend a branch of science, termed by him as _______ .
35. According to _______ concept crop yields obey the percentage sufficiency concept of Mitscherlich for such elements as phosphorus and potassium which are relatively immobile in the soil.
36. The inclusion of an element in the list of essential elements based on its functioning in plant metabolism, whether or not its action is specific has been termed as "_______" by D.J. Nicholas.
37. Plants normally contain between 1 and 5 per cent _______ by weight.
38. A complex group of proteins known as _______ is involved in the control of developmental and hereditary processes.
39. Excessive nitrogen fertilization _______ the sugar content of sugarbeets.
40. _______ and phytin are taken in by plants from sterile sand or solution culture.
41. Phosphate compounds act as "_______" within plants.
42. Application of phosphorus especially on phosphorus deficient soils considerably reduces the risk of _______ .
43. Potassium can affect the rate of transpiration and water uptake by regulation of _______ opening.
44. The amount of carbon dioxide that is assimilated into sugars during photosynthesis drops off sharply with insufficient _______.

45. The _______ of sugar from leaves of sugarcane is greatly reduced in potassium-deficient plants.
46. The accumulation of _______ has been found in the leaves of potassium deficient barley plants.
47. Sulphur is a vital part of ferredoxin that participates in _______ process by transferring electrons.
48. Magnesium with _______ brings about significant increases in oil content of a number of oilseed crops.
49. Glutathione is a reducing agent which plays a very important role in the _______ of some metabolites injurious to plant cells.
50. N to S ratio between 9:1 and 12:1 is needed for effective use of recycled nitrogen by _______ microorganisms.
51. Boron alters the _______ activity with an accumulation of auxin in plants deficient in this nutrient.
52. Iron will form stable _______ with molecules containing oxygen, sulphur or nitrogen.
53. Ferredoxin (stable Fe-S proteins) is the first stable redox compound of the electron transport chain.
54. Manganese can substitute for _______ in many of the phosphorylating and group transfer reactions.
55. Crinkle leaf of cotton is caused by the toxicity of _______ on highly acid soils.
56. The normal concentration range is 25-150 ppm zinc in the dry matter of plants, but when the leaf level exceeds _______, toxicities will occur.
57. Molybdenum is an essential component of the major enzyme _______ in plants.
58. Molybdenum is also a structural component of _______, the enzyme actively involved in nitrogen fixation by root nodule bacteria of leguminous crops.
59. A useful function of _______ is the counterion during rapid potassium fluxes, thus contributing to turgor of leaves and other plant parts.
60. Chloride containing fertilizers greatly depress _______ root-rot infection in winter wheat.
61. Coconut and oil palms are especially responsive to _______.
62. Cobalt has been found to participate in leghaemoglobin metabolism and _______ reductase in *Rhizobium*.
63. There is no decisive evidence as yet that _______ is essential for higher plants, it is definitely considered essential for green algae *Scenedesmus*.
64. Many plants that embody the C-4 dicarboxylic photosynthetic pathway require _______ as an essential nutrient element.
65. Sodium in _______ influences water relations and enhances its resistance to drought.
66. Soluble silica mainly exists as _______ and plants are believed to absorb it in this form from soil solution.
67. _______ primarily impregnates the walls of epidermal and vascular tissues, where it appears to strengthen the tissue, reduce water loss and retard fungal infection.
68. The quantity of nitrogen fixed by properly nodulated legumes averages about _______ per cent of the nitrogen used in the growth of the plant.
69. _______ and peas are inefficient nitrogen fixer in comparison to faba beans.
70. Nitrogen fixation by a legume is at the maximum only when the level of available soil nitrogen is at the _______.
71. _______ of H^+ from OH^- groups at the broken edges of clay particles is the prime source of negative charge in the 1:1 clay minerals.
72. The growth of _______ throughout the soil mass and perhaps mycorrhizal infection enhances the significance of root absorption and contact exchange mechanisms of ion absorption.

73. _______ is the influence of one adsorbed ion on the release of the another from the surface of a colloid.
74. Fertilization helps to offset soil conditions that _______ the movement of nutrient ions to roots.
75. The finer the texture of the soil, the less rapid will be the movement of _______ and the diffusion of ions through the water.
76. $H_2PO_4^-$ and HPO_4^{2-} apparently have separate _______ and do not compete with one another for entry into the inner space.
77. Active ion absorption is thought to take place by _______ produced carriers which transfer the ions across otherwise impassable barriers.
78. _______ is confined to those nodule cells containing nitrogen fixing *Rhizobia*.
79. _______ is the nitrogen fixing *bacterium* on root surfaces of plants like maize, millet, rice and wheat etc. its energy demands are met with by carbonaceous root exudates from plants.
80. *Azotobacter* and _______ are asymbiotic nitrogen fixers.
81. _______ is the preferred nitrogen source since energy will be saved when it is used instead of nitrate in synthesis of protein.
82. A decline in pH of rhizosphere occurs when plants are fed NH_4^+ and the consequent _______ has an important effect on nutrient availability and microbial activity in the vicinity of roots.
83. High levels of ammonium can retard plant growth and restrict the uptake of _______.
84. An extremely wide N/S ratio say 20:1 or more could restrict _______ breakdown, if the soil was already deficient in this element.
85. Continued cultivation with the provision of adequate fertilization coupled with _______ incorporation not only maintains, but also augments soil organic matter status.
86. The ultimate objective of any farming enterprise is _______ maximum economic production.
87. With _______, crop residues are allowed to remain on the soil surface rather than being worked into the soil.
88. The physical nature of loose, coarse accumulations of _______ is also far from ideal for rapid turnover of organic materials and release of nitrogen and sulphur.
89. The mineralization of organic nitrogen compounds takes place in essentially three step-by-step reactions: aminization, _______, and nitrification.
90. The ammonifying microbial populations include both _______ microorganisms.
91. *Nitrosomonas* and _______ are usually referred to collectively as *Nitrobacteria.*
92. In well drained neutral to slightly acid soils, the rate of oxidation of NO_2^- to NO_3^- is normally higher than that of _______.
93. Enhancing nitrification during _______ of the crop is one of the means of ensuring higher yields.
94. The cationic nature of _______ permits its adsorption and retention by soil colloidal material.
95. It is essential that the soil have a sufficiently high exchange capacity to retain the added _______ or it will be removed in percolating water.
96. The _______ of nitrogen is completely mobile and within limits' moves largely with the water.
97. Immobilization of nitrogen is the reverse of _______ and occurs when large quantities of low nitrogen crop residues begin decomposition.
98. The fixed ammonium can be replaced by cations that expand the lattice (Ca^{2+}, Mg^{2+}, Na^+, H^+), but not by those that _______ it (K^+, Rb^+, Cs^+).
99. Potassium fertilization prior to ammonium application is advised, where ammonium fixation is a problem because potassium can also fill the _______.

100. Only a few particular kinds of facultative _______ are responsible for denitrification.
101. _______ of soil results in rapid denitrification due to impeded diffusion of oxygen to the sites of microbiological activity.
102. The rate of denitrification is very slow in _______ and very rapid in soils of high pH (8.0-8.6).
103. The supply of nitrate and/or nitrite in soil is a prerequisite for _______.
104. Fertilizer nitrogen enters a labile "pool" of soil nitrogen which must be subjected to continuous _______ losses to the atmosphere.
105. Losses of nitrogen from NO_2^- (nitrite) by _______ have been found to increase with increasing organic matter content.
106. Most of the ammonia in the world is produced _______ by reacting nitrogen and hydrogen gas and only some of it as a by-product of cooking coal.
107. Urea was first isolated in 1773 from _______.
108. Urea in Europe is considered a _______ fertilizer as it must undergo hydrolysis and nitrification before becoming available to plants.
109. _______ seems to be more waterproof and less subject to dissolution by light showers or heavy rain when urea is conditioned with surface dusts and powders.
110. Urea on application to soil is acted upon by the enzyme urease which hydrolyzes it to unstable _______.
111. Surface applications of urea are most efficient when they are worked into the soil or applied to soils of low _______.
112. The point placement urea of _______ will substantially increase its agronomic efficiency for rice production.
113. _______ appears to be the most suitable single component as a slow release nitrogen material.
114. At least 40 per cent of the nitrogen insoluble in cold water should be solube in hot water for an acceptable _______.
115. CDU (Crotonylidene Diurea) and IBDU (Isobutylidene) are _______ forms of nitrogenous fertilizers.
116. Among the sparingly soluble minerals _______ is the most familiar member of a group of compounds with general formula _______ $MNH_4PO_4 \cdot H_2O$ or $MKPO_4 \cdot H_2O$, where M represents a divalent metal like Cu, Co, Mn, Fe or Zn.
117. Coating, _______ and matrixes have been used to impede the dissolution of water soluble fertilizer materials containing nitrogen and other plant nutrients.
118. Nitrate is often dominant form of nitrogen taken up by crops since it is generally present in _______ concentrations than is ammonium in soil.
119. Localized placement of _______ fertilizers causes some drastic changes in soil condition within or near the retention zone.
120. Continued use of acid forming fertilizers will lead to a decrease in pH with an accompanying _______ in crop yields.
121. The inorganic phosphorus content of soil is frequently higher than that of _______ phosphorus except organic soils.
122. The phosphorus is absorbed by plants largely as primary and secondary _______ which are present in the soil solution.
123. Absorption rates of $H_2PO_4^-$ by plant roots can be described by _______ kinetics.
124. The quantity of solid phase phosphorus that acts as a reserve is frequently referred to as _______ factor.

125. Most naturally occurring organic forms of phosphorus are ______ orthophosphoric acid.
126. ______ is a homocyclic sugar like compound, which can form a series of phosphate esters ranging from monophosphates to hexaphosphates.
127. Nucleic acids are probably released into soil ______ than the inositol phosphates.
128. Phosphatidylcholine (lecithin) and ______ are the dominant phospholipids in soil.
129. Retention of phosphorus is most frequently a problem in acid soils high in finely divided ______.
130. The extent of phosphorus desorption is dependent on the nature of the complex at the surface of the hydrous ______ oxides.
131. Divalent cations enhance ______ sorption relative to monovalent cations.
132. Anions of tricarboxylic acids are more effective in reducing phosphorus sorption than are those of ______ or ______ acids.
133. It is generally agreed that turning under of stable or green manures results in better utilization of phosphorus by ______ crops.
134. The time period of availability of soil applied phosphorus determines its application at one time in the crop rotation or ______, more frequent applications.
135. ______ reduces the surface of contact between the soil and fertilizer with a consequent reduction in phosphorus fixation.
136. The compound in rock phosphate deposits is ______.
137. Ammonium polyphosphate has been developed by ______ of the United States of America.
138. ______ *bacterium* increases the plant availability of native and applied soil phosphorus.
139. Under wet conditions, response to granular phosphates of high water solubility is superior to that from ______ materials.
140. Among the essential, elements ______ accounts for at least one-half of the total number of ions being absorbed by a plant.
141. Phosphorus concentration in earth's crust is only 0.11 per cent, whereas that ______ averages about 1.9 per cent.
142. ______ has been proposed for a satisfactory characterization of availability of potassium to crops.
143. ______ could be a major factor in the potassium nourishment of crops grown in soil either naturally high or receiving water soluble potassium through fertilizers.
144. ______ diffusion to roots is limited to very short distances in soil, usually only 1-4 mm from the root surface during a growing season.
145. Like other exchangeable cations, the K^+ ion is held around negatively charged soil colloids by ______ attraction.
146. In general, the relation between exchangeable potassium and soil solution potassium is a good measure of the availability of the more ______ in soils to plants.
147. Potassium fixation results in a conservation of this which otherwise might be lost by leaching on ______ and tends to become available with the passage of time.
148. Minimum tillage or no-till system reduces the availability of ______ due to increased compaction, lessened aeration, lower temperature and positional availability.
149. Potassium present in soil solution and held in an ______ has been classified as available.
150. The quantities of chloride in excess of 30-40 kg/ha (approximately) impairs the ______ of tobacco.

151. In potato, sweet potato and citrus high quantities of chloride must be ________.
152. High availability of potassium ________ root development.
153. Root ________ are two major factors effecting soil potassium availability to crops.
154. Agronomic effectiveness of the principal potassium fertilizers is approximately equal in cropping situations where only ________ potassium is called for.
155. The average sulphur, the thirteenth most abundant element has been estimated to vary between ________ per cent.
156. ________ emissions are partly responsible for acid rain and snow.
157. Exposure to as little as 0.5 ppm of SO_2 for three hours can cause visible injury to the foliage of ________.
158. The reduction of SO_4^{2-} to H_2S is both ________ and pH dependent.
159. ________ minerals retain more sulphur than the montmorillonite group of clays.
160. Phosphate will either displace or reduce the adsorption of ________, but it has only little effect on phosphate.
161. Molybdates ________ sulphate adsorption.
162. Sulphur-oxidizing organisms are the autotrophic bacteria belonging to the genus ________
163. Sulphides and ________ do not exist in well-drained upland soils.
164. Wherever straw, stover or other organic materials are returned to the soil, adequate nitrogen and ________ should be available for their rapid decomposition.
165. Rape and alfalfa require relatively higher concentrations of ________.
166. In soils containing 5 ppm or more of soluble SO_4^{2-}, virtually all of the sulphur requirement of most of the crops can be met with by
167. Representative levels of calcium in the soil solution of ________ region soils are 30 to 300 ppm.
168. The capacity of plants for uptake ________ is limited because it can be absorbed only by young root tips in which the cell walls of the endodermis are still unsuberized.
169. The indirect deficiencies of calcium are caused by its shortage in ________ organs which grow rapidly with restricted internal supplies of calcium.
170. High ________ is indicative of a favourable pH for growth of most of the plants as well as for microbial activity.
171. The impaired plant uptake of magnesium in many ________ soils is caused by high levels of exchangeable aluminium.
172. Maize, cotton and tobacco are ________ to magnesium.
173. High levels of ________ can interfere with magnesium uptake of a crop.
174. Plant deficiencies of ________ can occur in soils with wide ratios of exchangeable Ca or Mg.
175. The cattle consuming grasses of low magnesium content suffer from ________.
176. The high protein content of ingested forages (other feeds too) will depress absorption of ________ by the animal.
177. ________ is the only non-metal among the micronutrient elements having the constant valence of +3 coupled with a very small ionic radius.
178. Boron in most of the soils ranges from 2 to 200 ppm (frequently 7 to 80 ppm), but less than ________ of the total soil boron is generally available.
179. ________ boric acid (H_3BO_3) is the predominant species expected in soil solution at pH values ranging from less than 5 to 9.

180. A significant quantity of plant available boron in soils is held in the _______ fraction.
181. Coarse textured, ________ and sandy soils are low in boron and crops like alfalfa respond to its external application.
182. ________ to boron occurs when plants have low calcium supply.
183. Potassium application in alfalfa may accentuate ________ symptoms.
184. Liberal nitrogen applications have been useful in controlling excess of ________ in citrus and other crops.
185. Susceptibility of tomato to, ________ is controlled by a single recessive gene.
186. Foliar feeding of boron is practised in perennial tree fruit crops, usually in combination with pesticides other than those formulated in ________
187. Cobalt in plants is essential for symbiotic ________ and rumen microorganisms need it to synthesize vitamin B_{12}.
188. ______ deficiencies in ruminants are often associated with forages produced on soils having its content less than 5 ppm.
189. Cobalt availability to plants decreases due to a-soil treatment that allows conversion of ________ to insoluble oxides.
190. ________, which contains small amounts of $COSO_4$ is a fertilizer source of cobalt used in Australia and New Zealand.
191. Because of immobility of copper in soil, it is supplied to plant roots mainly by ________.
192. Copper is capable of ________ substitution in octahedral positions of crystalline silicate clays.
193. ______acids contain multiple binding sites for, with COO^- carboxyl groups playing a prominent role.
194. Ploughing unharvested *Brassica* root crops into soil has been observed in England to aggravate ________ in the succeeding crop.
195. Iron comprises about 5 per cent of the earth's crust and is the ________ most abundant element in the lithosphere.
196. The low solubility of compounds containing Fe^{3+} severely limits the ________ and uptake of Fe^{3+}.
197. Each unit increases in pH causes 1000-fold and 100-fold decrease in solubility of ________, respectively.
198. It has been observed that the iron chelated by sorghum plant metabolites enhanced the iron uptake by 100 per cent on a moderately deficient soil whereas, by more than ______ on a severely deficient soil.
199. Any compact heavy texture soil that is ________ in reaction is potentially iron deficient.
200. Flooding and submergence of soils in which HCO_3^- formation is of no concern, can improve iron availability by enhancing the ______ form.
201. ________with iron chelating properties have been extracted from poultry manure.
202. The ability of plants to absorb and translocate iron appears to be genetically controlled adaptative process that responds to ________.
203. Correction of iron deficiency is mainly done by______ of 2-3 per cent ferrous sulphate solution mixed with several drops of a mild detergent.
204. Injection of ________ directly into trunks and limbs of fruit-tree species like pears and plums have been very effective to control chlorosis due to its deficiency.
205. For a satisfactory manganese nutrition of crops levels of water soluble, exchangeable and easily reducible manganese should be of the order of 2-3, 0.5-5.0 and _______ ppm, respectively.

206. The continuous flux of organic matter and decomposition of plant residues is thought to contribute significantly to the maintenance of ______ manganese.

207. In extremely acid soils, Mn^{2+} solubility can be sufficiently great to cause ______ problems in sensitive plant species.

208. High levels of Cu, Fe or ______ in the growth medium will impede Mn uptake by plants.

209. Soil submergence and waterlogging lowers the ______ and increase the amount of soluble manganese (Mn^{2+}) in soils.

210. ______ capacity at the root may be the factor restricting uptake and translocation of manganese.

211. Molybdenum in lithosphere is about 2 ppm, while typically ranging ______ ppm in soils, (averages approximately 2 ppm).

212. Plants absorb molybdenum as ______.

213. Diffusion becomes the dominant means for molybdenum transfer to ______ when the concentration is less than 4 ppb.

214. Molybdenum deficiency has been found more severe under ______ due to its inadequate supply to the growing plant.

215. Legumes, ______ and citrus are very sensitive to insufficient molybdenum.

216. The total ______ in soil is no more a criterion of its availability to plants than is the case for other plant nutrients.

217. Diffusion is believed to be dominant mechanism for transporting zinc to ______.

218. Most of the pH induced zinc deficiencies occur within the range 6 to 8 pH and ______ are particularly prone to this nutritional problem.

219. Zinc reversibly bound by ______ minerals is an exchangeable cation and should be of value to plants.

220. There are widespread reports that phosphorus availability in soils induces ______.

221. Acid forming nitrogenous fertilizers are expected to augment the uptake of both ______ zinc.

222. Sugarbeets respond to sodium fertilization when readily exchangeable sodium (Na^+) in soils is ______ 0.05 meq per 100g.

223. The beneficial effects of sodium on plant growth tend to be the greatest when ______ is the poorest.

224. The potassium concentration above 3.0-3.5 per cent generally tend to keep sodium levels ______.

225. Sodium nitrate (Chilean saltpeter) and Rhenania phosphate contain ______ per cent of sodium.

226. The concentration of chlorine (Cl^-) in precipitation drops off in the interior direction, with areas about ______ miles inland averaging about 0.2 ppm.

227. The Cl^- anion is bound ______ by most soils in the mildly acid to neutral pH range and becomes negligible at pH > 7.

228. The rate and extent of ______ of Cl^- in soil are dependent on water circulation.

229. Lowering of NO_3^- uptake by ______ levels of Cl^- has been observed in barley.

230. The fertilizer sources of silicon include calcium silicate slag ($CaAl_2\ Si_2O_8$ with $CaSiO_3$), calcium silicate ($CaSiO_3$) and sodium metasilicate (______).

231. Though selenium is apparently not needed by ______, it must be present in fodder crops since it is essential for animals.

232. Even when selenium is consolidated in lithospheric materials, it rarely exceeds ______.

233. ______ developed from Cretaceous shale tend to have higher concentrations of selenium ranging from 2 to 10 ppm.

234. Soluble organic selenium compounds are liberated through the decay of ________.

235. It should be noted that SO_4^{2-} and SeO_4^{2-} ions can act ________ toward one another.

236. Certain species of ________ absorb many times as much selenium as do other plants growing in the same soil.

237. Metal chelates are defined as ________ of a metal atom and an organic component in which the two components are held together with varying degrees of strength.

238. Urea (carbamide), a nonionic nitrogen material is used industrially by to manufacture ________ and as a protein to supplement feed of ruminant animals.

239. Deflourination refers to drive off flourine from phosphate rock by heating either in a gas or an oil-fired chamber to around ________.

240. Ordinary superphosphate is manufactured by mixing ________ parts of sulphuric acid and rock phosphate.

241. ________ is literally workhorse of the fertilizer industry, as more than 60 per cent of it is accounted for by the fertilizer industry alone.

242 The terms ferti-herbicides, ferti-insecticides and ferti-fungicides respectively refer to the fertilizers containing a herbicide, insecticide and a ________.

243. The pH* is defined as the logarithm of the ________ of the H^+ ion activity.

$$* ph = \log \frac{I}{AH^+} = -\log AH^+$$

AH^+ = Hydrogen ion activity in moles per litre.

244. Marls represent the soft, unconsolidated deposits of calcium carbonate embodying a neutralizing value between ______.

245. _______ or _______ is the by product of the basic open-hearth method of making steel from pig iron, which, in turn, is produced from high phosphorus iron ores.

246. The reactivity of limestones is related in part to the fineness with which they are ground because the _______ of the limestone exposed, the faster is its reaction with the soil.

247. Lime is seldom needed in those areas where rainfall is low and _______ is minimal.

248. Rapeseed is tolerant to excessive amount of manganese, but very _______ to its toxicity.

249. It is possible to derive the maximum benefit from the applied phosphorus between _______ soil pH.

250. The increased ________ concentration due to calcium dissolution prevents the clays dispersion and losses in hydraulic conductivity of sodic soils.

251. No-tillage cropping system in the surface few centimeters makes the soil ________ in a few years, primarily due to the surface application of nitrogen fertilizers.

252. _______ refers to a situation in which a crop needs more of given essential nutrient element, yet has shown no deficiency symptoms.

253. The critical nutrient concentration (CNC), for practical purposes represents the level of nutrient ________ crop yield, quality or performance is unsatisfactory.

254. _______, is a new comprehensive system to interpreting leaf or plant analysis which identifies all the nutritional factors limiting crop production.

255. An excellent example of the use of plant analysis in crop production is the _______ carried out for sugarcane in Hawaii.

256. In case of nitrogen and phosphorus as much as 65-75 per cent of total uptake can be accounted for in just the _______.

257. _______ movement from the point of placement is generally limited, as its iron is only slightly mobile in soil.
258. The nitrogen salts move _______ in the soil solution, depending upon the direction of water movement.
259. Excessive concentration of soluble salts in contact with roots/germinating seeds causes injurious effects due to _______, restricted moisture availability or actual toxicity.
260. Some of the nitrogen bearing compounds contribute more to damage of _______ than appears to be explained by the osmotic effects.
261. The starter response to N-P-K is often _______ of soil fertility.
262. Phosphorus might be applied in a band at planting in sufficient amounts for _______ of optimum levels of available soil phosphorus.
263. Phosphorus should generally be placed in the zone of _______.
264. Small amounts of nitrogen are important in starting plants off, but it must be kept well _______ from plant roots.
265. Micronutrients are applied in small amounts and _______ are directed toward greatest efficiency.
266. The application of fertilizer in irrigation water in either closed or open system is termed as _______.
267. _______ are the principal nutrients applied through fertilizers especially in U.S.A.
268. In areas having problem of soil fixation of nutrients _______ constitutes the most effective means of fertilizer placement.
269. The aim of all cropping systems should be _______ productivity and profits.
270. Maintenance of organic matter for the sake of maintenance is not a practical approach to _______.
271. _______ were a mainstay of some rotations for many years.
272. _______ is an important approach for control of nematodes feeding on the roots of annual crops.
273. The interest in crop rotations for the control of insects has been renewed due to _______ to chemicals and increased cost of inputs.
274. Rotation was a common practice for _______, but its use declined with the development of cheap and effective organic insecticides in the 1950s.
275. Rotation can greatly improve the _______ and tilth of many medium and fine-textured soils.
276. Forests are an excellent example, in the tropics and subtropics, of a crop that transports _______ to the surface.
277. Decomposition of green manure crops is rapid, but the _______ are well recognised.
278. Sewage effluence may be a valuable water and nutrient resource for crops or a _______ to land and water.
279. Through _______ it is feasible to monitor land cover changes, both natural and those resulting from human activities.

II. Tick mark (✓) the correct answer:

280. The humus myth was effectively deposed by _______ by presentation of a paper at a prominent scientific meeting.

(*a*) Justus Senebier (*b*) Jean Young
(*c*) Justus von Liebig (*d*) Justus Billright

281. Rothamsted Agricultural Experiment Station, England was founded by _______.

(*a*) J.B. Lawes (*b*) J.H. Gilbert
(*c*) J.B. Lawes & J.H. Gilbert (*d*) Lord Hastings

282. Some specialists have identified ________ factors that influence crop growth,

(*a*) 32 (*b*) 42

(*c*) 52 (*d*) 22

283. It has been suggested that the ________ of sunlight is generally most satisfactory for plant growth.

(*a*) Full spectrum (*b*) Half spectrum

(*c*) Little more than full spectrum (*d*) None of these

284. The maximum carbon dioxide concentration at normal atmospheric levels occur in relatively low light intensities of ________ footcandles for some plants.

(*a*) 2500-5000 (*b*) 6000-7500

(*c*) 1000-2000 (*d*) 2150-2450

285. Tomato plants grown on soils with low bulk densities of tended to be ________.

(*a*) High in sugar (*b*) Low in protein

(*c*) High in anthocyanin (*d*) Showed no effect

286. ________ in 1909 developed an equation that related growth to the supply of plant nutrients.

(*a*) V.J. Kilmer (*b*) R.B. McKercher

(*c*) J.W. Friedrich (*d*) E.A.Mitscherlich

287. The principle similar to that developed by E.A. Mitscherlich was also independently developed several years later by ________.

(*a*) F. Steenbjerg (*b*) W.J. Spillman

(*c*) M.E. Summer (*d*) J.G. Shannon

288. Based on dark metabolism, glucose consumption for protein production is about ________ percent when nitrogen is provided as nitrate rather than as ammonium.

(*a*) 20 (*b*) 30

(*c*) 40 (*d*) 50

289. The sequence in which amino acids are linked in proteins depends on ________.

(*a*) Climatic control (*b*) Agronomic control

(*c*) Genetic control (*d*) None of these

290. The tendency of the young upper leaves to remain as the lower leaves yellow or die is an indication of nitrogen ________ in the plant.

(*a*) Mobility (*b*) Immobility

(*c*) Stability (*d*) Degradability

291. Build up of soluble sugars and amino acids (due to inadequate potassium), low molecular weight compounds encourage the activity of ________.

(*a*) Plant hormones (*b*) Plant pathogens

(*c*) None of these (*d*) Both of these

292. Blossom-end rot in tomato has been found to be caused by the deficiency of ________.

(*a*) Nitrogen (*b*) Phosphorus

(*c*) Calcium (*d*) Sulphur

293. Affinity of the enzyme RuDP carboxylase for carbon dioxide is enhanced by ________.

(*a*) Sulphur (*b*) Phosphorus

(*c*) Nitrogen (*d*) Magnesium

294. The sufficiency range of iron is normally between _______ ppm.
(*a*) 10-40 (*b*) 50-250
(*c*) 300-400 (*d*) None of these

295. The presence of ectotrophic mycorrhiza enhances the uptake of nutrients in general, but particularly of _______.
(*a*) Molybdenum (*b*) Calcium
(*c*) Magnesium (*d*) Phosphorus

296. The quantity of nutrients that can come in direct contact with the plant roots is the amount in a volume of soil _______ the volume of roots.
(*a*) Equal to (*b*) Less than
(*c*) More than (*d*) No relation with

297. _______ ion effect represents the effect of adsorbed ion on the release of another from the surface of a colloid.
(*a*) Supplementary (*b*) Complementary
(*c*) Coordinated (*d*) Integrated

298. The movement of nutrients, ions by mass flow is reduced at low temperatures because of _______
(*a*) Low respiration (*b*) Low photosynthesis
(*c*) Low transpiration (*d*) None of these

299. Organic matter content under well drained conditions is higher under _______.
(*a*) Field crops (*b*) Fruit crops
(*c*) Grasslands (*d*) Forest covers

300. The _______ oxidation of ammonia has been termed as nitrification.
(*a*) Physical (*b*) Chemical
(*c*) Biological (*d*) Physico-chemical

301. _______ is considered to be most important of the soil organisms bringing about the conversion of NH_4^+ to NO_2^-
(*a*) *Nitrosomonas* (*b*) *Nitrobacter*
(*c*) *Azotobacter* (*d*) *Azospirillum*

302. The rapid increase in denitrification at the elevated soil temperatures suggests that _______ microorganisms play a major role in denitrification.
(*a*) Chemophilic (*b*) Photophilic
(*c*) Thermophilic (*d*) Hydrophilic

303. Application of urea, aqua-ammonia, anhydrous ammonia and diammonium phosphate form alkaline microsite at the point of application, and in rice _______ encourage the taking up of nitrite.
(*a*) High NH_4^+ concentration (*b*) High pH
(*c*) Both of these (*d*) None of these

304. _______ of the NH_4^+ in a region of alkaline microsite helps to restore the conditions suitable for the normal conversion of NO_2^- to NO_3^-.
(*a*) Diffusion (*b*) Dilution
(*c*) Both of these (*d*) None of these

305. The losses of ammonia usually become greater with ________.
(a) Increase in soil pH (b) Decrease in soil pH
(c) Decrease in calcium (d) Decrease in temperature

306. The highest percentage content of nitrogen among the commonly used nitrogenous fertilizers is embodied by
(a) Urea (b) Urea sulphate
(c) Ammonium nitrate (d) Anhydrous ammonia

307. Permissible biuret level, in most of urea fertilizers is ________ per cent.
(a) 5 (b) 4
(c) 3 (d) 2

308. In the fertilized soil with soil solution concentration of one ppm of phosphorus, mass flow contribution to phosphorus nutrition of crops could approach ________ per cent.
(a) 0 (b) 40
(c) 30 (d) 20

309. The quantity of solid phase phosphorus that acts as reserve is often referred to as ________.
(a) Intensity factor (b) Quantity factor
(c) Quality factor (d) None of these

310. Phosphotase enzymes play a major role in ________ of organic phosphates in soil.
(a) Mineralization (b) Immobilization
(c) Mass transportation (d) None of these

311. The mineralization of organic phosphorus has been studied in relation to ________ ratio.
(a) C/N/S (b) C/N/K
(c) C/N/P (d) C/N/Ca

312. The surfaces on which phosphate ions enter into sorption reactions are ________.
(a) Surfaces of constant charge (b) Surfaces of variable charge
(c) None of these (d) Both of these

313. The mineral calcite develops a negative charge due to ________ tendency for Ca^{2+} ions than CO_3^{2-} ions to go into solution.
(a) Lower (b) Greater
(c) Equal (d) None of these

314. Clays such as kaolinite will fix larger quantities of phosphorus with ________ SiO_2 / R_2O_3 ratio.
(a) Low (b) High
(c) Equal (d) None of these

315. Amorphous aluminosilicate minerals like allophane have ________ negative charge which is partly or entirely balanced by complex aluminium cations.
(a) Small (b) Zero
(c) Large (d) None of these

316. A minor portion of the phosphorus sorption capacity of soils originates from ________.
(a) Sodium bicarbonate (b) Sodium carbonate
(c) Calcium oxide (d) Calcium carbonate

317. The maximum phosphorus availability in most of the soils is in the pH range ________.
(*a*) 4.0-4.5 (*b*) 5.0-5.5
(*c*) 6.0-6.5 (*d*) 7.0-7.5

318. In a predominantly biological system, mineralization of phosphorus from organic matter or crop residues is dependent on soil ________ activity.
(*a*) Chemical (*b*) Physical
(*c*) Physico-chemical (*d*) Biological

319. ________ generally augments the utilization of phosphorus which is water soluble.
(*a*) Broadcast (*b*) Broadcast and incorporation
(*c*) Band placement (*d*) None of these

320. Rock phosphate is treated with ________ to break the apatite bond and to render the contained phosphate more soluble.
(*a*) Acid alone (*b*) Alkali alone
(*c*) Heat alone (*d*) Either acid or heat

321. Various potassic fertilizers embody nearly an equal effectiveness in ________ situations requiring its supplemental application.
(*a*) Climatic (*b*) Edaphic
(*c*) Cropping (*d*) Economic

322. The concentrations of ________ ppm of SO_4^{2-} ion in the soil or solution cultures have proved adequate for the growth of many plant species.
(*a*) 1-2 (*b*) 3-5
(*c*) 6-8 (*d*) 9-11

323. Proper ________ nourishment for cabbage, potato and sugarbeet *etc.*, is essential since these are known to have its high requirement.
(*a*) Sulphur (*b*) Manganese
(*c*) Zinc (*d*) Calcium

324. The essentiality of copper for higher plants was first recognised in ________.
(*a*) 1911 (*b*) 1921
(*c*) 1931 (*d*) 1941

325. "Reclamation disease" due to copper deficiency occurs in plants grown on newly reclaimed acid ________.
(*a*) Histosols (*b*) Alfisols
(*c*) Aridosols (*d*) Ultisols

326. Among small grain crops ________ has an exceptional tolerance to low levels of soil copper supply.
(*a*) Barley (*b*) Wheat
(*c*) Rye (*d*) Oats

327. Repeated use of Bordeau mixture, sewage sludge, pig and poultry manures and/or mine wastes may cause ________ toxicities.
(*a*) Iron (*b*) Aluminium
(*c*) Zinc (*d*) Copper

328. The accessibility and utilization of soil applied copper can be enhanced by ________.
(*a*) Reducing particle size (*b*) Reducing number of granules
(*c*) Reducing droplets per unit soil volume (*d*) None of these

329. Each unit increase in pH brings about a decrease in solubility of Fe^{2+} of ________ folds.
(*a*) 50 (*b*) 75
(*c*) 100 (*d*) 150

330. The total soluble iron concentration becomes sufficient to supply iron adequately to roots only at pH ________.

(*a*) 2 (*b*) 3
(*c*) 4 (*d*) 5

331. It has been observed that the iron chelated by sorghum plant metabolites, on a moderately deficient soil, enhanced iron uptake by ________ per cent.

(*a*) 25 (*b*) 50
(*c*) 75 (*d*) 100

332. Low total iron content of soil is ________ the basis for plant deficiencies.

(*a*) Commonly (*b*) Often
(*c*) Seldom (*d*) Mostly

333. Iron deficiency usually occurs in soil in the pH range of ________.

(*a*) 5.4-6.5 (*b*) 7.4-8.5
(*c*) 9.0-9.5 (*d*) 9.6-10.1

334. There can actually be a build up of toxic concentrations of Fe^{2+} in the soil solution of ________.

(*a*) Aridosol (*b*) Histosol
(*c*) Latosol (*d*) Vertisol

335. For each unit increase in pH, the concentration of Mn^{2-} decreases by ________ folds.

(*a*) 50 (*b*) 100
(*c*) 150 (*d*) 200

336. Silicon is the ________ most abundant element in the earth's crust.

(*a*) Third (*b*) Fourth
(*c*) Sixth (*d*) Second

337. Properties of the silicon-deficient Hawaiin soils include ________.

(*a*) High total aluminium content (*b*) High base saturation
(*c*) High pH (*d*) High total silicon

338. It is generally accepted that the Gramineae members contain ________ times the silicon concentration normally found in legumes and other dicotyledonous plants.

(*a*) 5-10 (*b*) 10-20
(*c*) 20-30 (*d*) 30-40

339. Superphosphate containing ________ selenium may provide enough of it to the plants in selenium deficient areas.

(*a*) 10 ppm or more (*b*) 20 ppm or more
(*c*) 30 ppm or more (*d*) 40 ppm or more

340. In the room and pillar pattern of mining potassium ________ rooms are mined out and the pillars of ore are left for support.

(*a*) Hexagonal (*b*) Spheroidal
(*c*) Rectangular (*d*) Square

341. ________ is probably the most important growth limiting factor in acid soils especially those having pH below 5.0-5.5.

(*a*) Nitrogen (*b*) Calcium
(*c*) Potassium (*d*) Aluminium

342. At pH ________ H^+ ion toxicity is lessened by the removal of these ions.
(*a*) 4.5 or less (*b*) 5.5 or less
(*c*) 6.0 or less (*d*) 5.0 or less

343. If an acid soil is limed to the pH level ________ it enhances nitrification.
(*a*) 3.5-4.5 (*b*) 4.5-5.5
(*c*) 5.5-6.5 (*d*) 6.5-7.5

344. When the phosphorus is either band placed or broadcast, the relative efficiency is related to ________.
(*a*) Its soil status (*b*) Its applied quantum
(*c*) Both of these (*d*) None of these

345. Crops during any season are generally able to recover only ________ of the added fertilizer phosphorus.
(*a*) Less than 25 % (*b*) Less than 30 %
(*c*) Less than 35 % (*d*) None of the these

346. Potassium salts are ________.
(*a*) More mobile than nitrates (*b*) Less mobile than nitrates
(*c*) Less mobile than phosphorus (*d*) As mobile as nitrates

347. Broadcast potassium is ________ than banded.
(*a*) More efficient (*b*) As efficient as
(*c*) Less efficient than (*d*) None of these

348. Winter application of phosphorus is followed in ________.
(*a*) Warm areas (*b*) Cool areas
(*c*) Both of these (*d*) None of these

349. Potassium is utilized more efficiently if applied ________.
(*a*) Before/at planting (*b*) Sidedressed
(*c*) Topdressed (*d*) None of these

350. Tillage of the soil ________ rate of disappearance of organic matter.
(*a*) Reduces (*b*) Increases
(*c*) Maintains (*d*) Has no effect

Do You Know That

1. Approximately 100 kg of organic material is required to fix one kg of N by a reductant.
2. Estimates have shown that soybean and alfalfa might fix as much as 500 kg N per hectare.
3. Ammonical fertilizers should be applied in reduced zone.
4. Zinc and Ferrous are micro nutrients.
5. Sulphur is essential nutrient for oil seed crops.
6. White tip and white bud of maize occurs due to zinc deficiency.
7. Nitrogen content in F.Y.M and urban compost is 0·5 and 1·4% respectively.
8. Nitro bacteria are bacteria which change nitrite to nitrate.

9. On hydrolysis of urea the first product is Ammonia carbonate.
10. Azotobacter is the free living nitrogen fixing organism.

KEY

1. More efficient	2. Macedonia	3. Legumes
4. Marl	5. Sufficient	6. Taste-test
7. Modern agronomy	8. John Wynn Baker	9. Annals of agriculture
10. Theodore de Saussure	11. Jean Baptiste Boussingaúlt	12. Justus von Liebig
13. 1843	14. Bacterial action	15. Ammonia
16. Nitrogen fixation	17. M.W. Beijerinck	18. Growth
19. 45	20. Environment	21. – 273°C
22. Agricultural plans	23. Partial pressure	24. Fluctuations
25. Low levels	26. Water use efficiency	27. Water use efficiency
28. Less than	29. Liebig's law	30. Physiological relationship
31. Proportional	32. One baule unit	33. 45 and 76
34. Quantitative agrobiology	35. Bray's nutrient mobility	
36. Functional or metabolic nutrient	37. Nitrogen	38. Nucleoproteins
39. Reduces	40. Nucleic acid	
41. Energy currency	42. Winter damage	43. Stomatal
44. Potassium	45. Translocation	46. Free amino acids
47. Oxidoreduction	48. Sulphur	49. Detoxification
50. Rumen	51. Phytohormonal	52. Chelates
53. Photosynthetic	54. Magnesium	55. Manganese
56. 400 ppm	57. Nitrate reductase	58. Nitrogenase
59. Chlorine	60. Take-all	61. Chlorine
62. Ribonucleotide	63. Scenedesmus vanadium	64. Sodium
65. Sugarbeet	66. Monosilicic acid, Si $(OH)_4$	
67. Hydrated polymer or silica gel	68. 75	69. Soybeans
70. Minimum	71. Deprotonation or dissociation	
72. New roots	73. Complementary ion effect	74. Retard
75. Soil moisture	76. Separate	77. Metabolically
78. Leghaemoglobin	79. *Azospirillum*	80. *Clostridium*
81. Ammonium-NH_4^+	82. Acidification	83. Potassium
84. Organic matter	85. Crop residues	86. Sustained
87. Zero tillage	88. Crop debris/residues	89. Ammonification
90. Aerobic and anaerobic	91. *Nitrobacter*	92. NH_4^+ to NO_2^-
93. Growing season	94. Ammonium-NH_4^+	95. Ammonium nitrogen
96. Nitrate form. NO_3^-	97. Mineralization	98. Contract
99. Fixation sites	100. Aerobic bacteria	101. Waterlogging
102. Acid soils (pH 3.6-4.8)	103. Denitrification	104. Denitrification
105. Chemodenitrification	106. Synthetically	107. Urine
108. Slow-release	109. Formaldehyde-treated	110. Ammonium carbamate
111. Ureolytic activity	112. Supergranules	113. Trimethylene urea
114. Agronomic response	115. Slow nitrogen release	

116. Magnesium ammonium phosphate
117. Encapsulations
118. Higher
119. Ammonium-containing/forming
120. Decrease
121. Organic
122. Orthophosphate ions ($H_2PO_4^-$ and $H_2PO_4^{2-}$)
123. Michaelis-Menten
124. Capacity or quantity
125. Esters
126. Inositol
127. More rapidly
128. Phosphatidyethanol-amine
129. Sesquioxide
130. Iron and aluminium
131. Phosphorus
132. Dicarboxylic or monocarboxylic
133. Subsequent/succeeding
134. In smaller
135. Band placement
136. Apatite (its general formula is $Ca_{10}(PO_4 \cdot CO_3)_6$ (F, Cl, OH)$_2$
137. TVA
138. *Bacillus megatherium* var-*Phosphaticum*. The Russian term is *Phosphobacterin*
139. Powdered
140. Nitrogen
141. Potassium
142. Electroultra filtration or EUF
143. Mass flow
144. Potassium
145. Electrostatic
146. Labile potassium
147. Sandy soil
148. Potassium
149. Exchangeable state
150. Burning quality
151. Avoided
152. Enhances
153. Type and density
154. Supplemental
155. 0.06 and 0.10
156. Sulphur
157. Sensitive vegetation
158. Redox potential
159. Kaolinite
160. Sulphate
161. Depress
162. *Thiobacillus*
163. Polysulphides
164. Sulphur
165. Sulphur
166. Mass flow
167. Temperate
168. Ca^{2+}
169. Fruit and storage
170. Calcium saturation
171. Strongly acid
172. Highly responsive
173. Exchangeable potassium
174. Magnesium
175. Hypomagnesemia, commonly called Grass Tatany
176. Magnesium
177. Boron
178. 5 per cent
179. Undissociated
180. Organic matter
181. Well drained
182. Low tolerance
183. Boron-deficiency
184. Boron
185. Boron-deficiency
186. Oils and emulsions
187. Nitrogen fixation
188. Cobalt
189. Mn^{2+} ions
190. Cobaltized superphosphate
191. Root interception
192. Isomorphous
193. Humic and fulvic
194. Copper deficiency
195. Fourth
196. Availability
197. Fe^{3+} and Fe^{2+}
198. 200 per cent
199. Calcareous and basic
200. Active Fe^{2+} ionic
201. Ligands
202. Iron deficiency/stress
203. Foliar feeding
204. Iron salts
205. 25-65
206. Water soluble
207. Toxicity
208. Zn
209. Redox potential
210. Reductive
211. 0.2 to 5 (averages approximately 2 ppm)
212. MoO_4^{2-}
213. Plant roots
214. Dryland conditions
215. Crucifers (broccoli, cauliflower, cabbage, rapesed *etc.*)
216. Zinc concentration
217. Plant roots
218. Calcareous Soils
219. Silicate clay
220. Zinc deficiency
221. Native and supplemental
222. Less than
223. Potassium nutrition
224. Below 3 per cent
225. 25 and 12
226. 500
227. Very slightly
228. Migration and accumulation
229. Increasing
230. $NaSiO_3$
231. Plants
232. 100 to 500 ppm
233. Seleniferous soils
234. Seleniferous plants
235. Antagonistically
236. Astragalus

237. Cyclic structures
238. Plastics and fertilizers
239. 1500-1600°C
240. Gravimetrically
241. Sulphuric acid
242. Fungicide
243. Reciprocal
244. 70 and 90 per cent
245. Basic slag or Thompson slag
246. Greater the surface
247. Leaching
248. Sensitive
249. 5.5 and 6.8 to 7.0
250. Electrolyte
251. Quite acid
252. Hidden hunger
253. Below which
254. DRIS = Diagnostic and Recommendation Integrated System
255. Crop logging
256. Harvest of grain
257. Phosphorus
258. Up and down
259. Plasmolysis
260. Germinating seds
261. Independent
262. Maintenance
263. Root development
264. Away
265. Placement methods
266. Fertigation
267. Nitrogen and sulphur
268. Foliar application
269. Sustained
270. Farming
271. Forage legumes
272. Crop rotation
273. Insect resistance
274. Insect management
275. Soil structure
276. Nutrients
277. Residual effects
278. Pollutant
279. Satellite imaging
280. (c)
281. (c)
282. (c)
283. (a)
284. (c)
285. (c)
286. (d)
287. (b)
288. (d)
289. (c)
290. (a)
291. (b)
292. (c)
293. (d)
294. (b)
295. (d)
296. (a)
297. (b)
298. (c)
299.. (c)
300. (c)
301. (a)
302. (c)
303. (c)
304. (c)
305. (a)
306. (d)
307. (d)
308. (d)
309. (b)
310. (a)
311. (c)
312. (d)
313. (b)
314. (a)
315. (c)
316. (d)
317.. (c)
318. (d)
319. (c)
320. (d)
321. (d)
322. (b)
323. (d)
324. (c)
325. (a)
326. (c)
327. (d)
328. (a)
329. (c)
330. (b)
331. (d)
332. (d)
333. (b)
334. (c)
335. (b)
336. (d)
337. (a)
338. (b)
339. (b)
340. (c)
341. (d)
342. (a)
343. (c)
344. (c)
345. (a)
346. (b)
347. (c)
348. (a)
349. (a)
350. (b)

SECTION 7

CROP AND SEED PRODUCTION

I. Fill up the blanks :

1. Woman, probably by her intrinsic insight, first observed that ________ come up from seed.
2. The subsistence form of agriculture was based on the principle ________.
3. The ________ agricultural village was the least common denominator of a permanent human society.
4. ________ started during the early eighteenth century.
5. Agriculture today is not merely production oriented, but has become sustainable ________.
6. The word ________ has been derived from Greek words-*agros* meaning field and *nomos* meaning to manage.
7. The word ________ has originated from a Roman word Ceres, the name of a Roman Goddess who was the "giver of grain".
8. The classification of crops in annual, biennial and perennial classes is known as ________. classification.
10. In ________ dormancy comprises a survival mechanism that prevents the fall-germination of species that are not winter hardy.
11. ________ weeds need some stimuli from their host plants for germination.
12. The plants of canary grass (*Phalaris minor*) if pulled out during flowering, can set about 50 per cent of ________.
13. ________ means putting a seed (s) or seed materials in a hole or pit or pocket made at a predetermined distance and depth.
14. Dropping of seeds in furrows of predetermined dimensions, at a predetermined distance and depth, covering with soil followed by compacting is known as ________.
15. The usually recommended proportion of N:P:K per square meter of ________ aera is 8-14:8-17:10-18 grammes respectively.
16. ________ $= \frac{\text{True density} - \text{Apparent density}}{\text{True density}}$
17. Repeated tillage operations over a long period of time prove detrimental to surface soil ________.
18. The first cutting and inverting of soil during turn-around period is known as ________.
19. Seasonal ________ occurs when the actual seasonal rainfall is defined by more than twice the mean deviation.
20. ________ drought is a period of four consecutive weeks from May to Mid-October or six consecutive weeks during rest of the year.

21. ________ cropping mean cultivation of different crops of different canopy heights simultaneously in a field.
22. Intercropping refers to growing of two or more crops ________ in alternate rows in the same field during the same period either by replacement or addition to the recommended plant density of the base crop.
23. Mixed cropping means growing of two or more crops simultaneously in the same field without keeping their ________ with respect to field area.
24. ________ $= \dfrac{'A'\text{ harvest} / 'A'\text{ sown}}{'B'\text{ harvest} / 'B'\text{ sown}} = 1$
25. Rotational intensity of a crop refers to the ________ of times the crop recurs in a total rotational cycle.
26. Rotational intensity of maize in maize-potato-greengram and maize-mustard-summer vegetables respectively in first year will be ________.
27. Rotational cropping intensity (per cent) represent the ________ of crops grown on a piece of land in one rotation-cycle and multiplied by 100.
28. Relative Yield Index (RYI) refers to the yield of a crop in a district expressed as percentage of the whole ________.

$$\text{That is, RYI} = \frac{\text{Mean yield of a crop in a district}}{\text{Mean all India yield of that crop}} \times 100$$

29. ________ is that part of the formulated product that principally responsible for herbicidal effects.
30. The ________ of an active ingredient is often influenced by the reactions between active ingredient and inert material.
31. ________ contains finely divided solid particles measuring less than 3 microns that can be readily suspended in water to formulate suspension.
32. Emulsification is done primarily to disperse the small volume phase (concentrate) in the large ________.
33. ________ are volatile chemicals applied into confined spaces or into the soil to produce gas to destroy weed-seeds (an organism) or to act as soil sterilant.
34. The ________ is designed to allow safe application of specifically effective herbicides to tough-to-control weeds.
35. In an electrodynamic sprayer, the spray liquid is ________ by an electric field and the droplet is charged and spray liquid is propelled away from the nozzle.
36. The foliage applied post-emergence herbicides effective against ________ are barban, asulam, diclofop methyl, difenzoqat, and, benzoylprop methyl.
37. The seed ________ aims at ensuring genuineness and quality of seed and propagating material to a purchaser.
38. The system of seed certification grew out of the increased concern for the rapid loss of ________ in early part of twentieth century.
39. ________ refers to the seed or the propagating material directly controlled by originating or sponsoring plant breeder.
40. Certified seed is the seed certified by the certification agency under Section 8 of the ________
41. The minimum genetic purity of ________ should be 99 per cent as against 99.5 per cent for the foundation seed.

42. According to European philosophy for regulation of seed quality "exclude low, or uncertain quality seed from _________" policy is followed.
43. _________ philosophy for regulating seed quality aims at truthful labelling.
44. Control legislation regulates the _________ sold in the market.
45. _________ Committee is the main source to advise Government (India) on administration of Seed Act.
46. The residual heterozygosity in the variety becomes better visible through _________ within the progeny.
47. In _________ the amount of variability observed in varieties is relatively higher than that of wheat.
48. In pulses viz., mungbean, urdbean, and chickpea a minimum of 500 plants should be planted for the production of _________.
49. In maize a single cross in the hybrid progeny from a cross between two _________ inbreeds.
50. Breeder's seed of male sterile, restorer and inbred lines is highly homozygous, while that of _________ is highly heterozygous.
51. In cross-pollinated crops, field inspections are essential during _________ to verify freedom genetic contamination.
52. _________ Lot Certificates can be issued when sampling has been done according to the rules by an official body approved by the seed testing station.
53. The most commonly used instrument for seed sampling is _________.
54. _________ shall include seeds and seed-like structures of any plant species other than that of pure seed.
55. Though light is not usually essential for seed germination, it may be required for some kind of a seed like _________.
56. _________ is the sum of those properties which determine the potential level of activity and performance of the seed or seed lot during germination and seedling performance.
57. Ageing refers to the accumulation of _________ which ultimately results in death or the failure of the seed to germinate.
58. Speed of germination represents the _________ of number of seeds (n) newly germinating at time t, and time (t) equals days or hours from sowing.

or

Speed of germination $= \sum(nt)$

59. MGT is the summation of numbers of seeds newly germinating at time t multiplied by number of days or hours _______ (n) divided by sum of n

or

Mean germination time $(MGT) = \sum(nt) / \sum N$

60. Coefficient of velocity of _________ is equal to sum of number of seeds newly germinating at time t multiplied by 100 divided by the sum of product of t and number of seeds newly germinating at time t (n)

or

Coefficient of seed germination $= (MGT) = \sum n \times 100 / \sum(nt)$

61. Conductivity test technique of seed testing is based on the _________ of solutes that occurs from all seeds in water.

62. __________ test is essentially an assessment of dehydrogenase enzyme activity.
63. The __________ seeds that have a high germination after __________ are those which emerge and store well.
64. The kind of seeds which require specifically red (*R*) irradiance to germinate are known as __________ seeds.
65. __________ is also an effective method of breaking hard-seededness in legumes.
66. Coleoptile in cereals is either colourless or contains a red colour of __________.

II. Tick mark (3) True or False:

67. A seed, strictly speaking, is an 'embryo', a living organism embedded in the supporting or the food storage tissue.
68. Seed certification is a legally sanctioned system for quality control of seed multiplication and production.
69. Foundation seed is the progeny of breeder seed or produced from foundation seed clearly traceable to breeder seed.
70. Certified seed produced from certified seed shall be eligible for further seed increase under certification.
71. On 29th December, 1966, the Seeds Act (India) was passed which came into force on 2nd October, 1969.
72. The nucleus seed of pulses should not be planted in .paired rows to raise breeder seed plots.
73. Cross pollinated plant species are highly homozygous and homogeneous.
74. Field inspections aim at the confirmation that the seed produced from a crop grown for seed is of a designated variety satisfying the genetic and physical limits of purity.
75. The Green Seed Lot Certificate requires the seed testing by an authorized station in a country (place) other than where the lot is situated.
76. Blue Seed Sample Certificate refers to official sampling and seed testing by a testing station of the quality represented .
77. A pure seed refers to the species stated by the sender or found predominant in the test, and shall include all botanical varieties and cultivars of that species.
78. In groundnut the germination is hypogeal.
79. In field pea the germination is epigeal.
80. More sophisticated assessments of the rate of germination can be made by including more frequent counts of germination.
81. Seedling growth has been assessed based both on dry weight and linear measurements.
82. Any physical or chemical treatment that weakens the seed coat is called scarification.
83. Acetone, ethanol, chloroform and methylene blue cannot be used to break seed dormancy.
84. Fungus *Colletotrichum gloeosporioides* provides satisfactory control of northern jointvetch (*Aeschynomene virginicia*) and paved the way for the development of mycoherbicides.
85. The introduction of bordeaux mixture in 1896 stimulated interest in chemical weed control.
86. The herbicide terbacil belongs to the chemical group phenols.
87. Herbicides enter the root *via* the same pathway and by identical mechanism as inorganic ions.
88. Besides roots, the soil applied herbicides are also absorbed by the developing seed, shoots and coleoptile.
89. Herbicides like picloram and dalapon are translocated through xylem when absorbed by roots and through phloem when absorbed by phloem.
90. Paper aqueous spray are repelled by most plant surfaces, their droplets are spherical and tend to runoff.
91. Generally, herbicides formulated in oil or oil emulsion are more affected by rain than the aqueous solution.

92. Light has no effect on herbicide penetration even due to stimulation of stomatal opening.
93. Soil water potential has no influence on herbicide uptake, translocation and phytotoxicity.
94. Generally, herbicides exist in ionic form in the soil between pH 4.3 and 7.5.
95. Generally, anionic agents perform better in cold water and best in soft water, while nonionic agents work well in warm water and hard water.
96. The spreading agent increases the angle of contact between the liquid drop and leaf surface.
97. Emulsifiers occupy the interface between oil and water surfaces by coupling them together to maintain the stability of the emulsion.
98. Some sticking agents are water soluble polymers which dry on leaf surface and form water resistant film.
99. Fluchloralin is absorbed by the plant tissues and thus its translocation is promoted.
100. Nitrogen is absorbed by germinating seeds and the roots of the emerging seedlings.
101. Phenoxyacids (group of herbicides), when applied to foliage, penetrate the cuticle by diffusion.
102. Metribuzin, primarily a pre-emergence herbicide, is readily taken up by the roots through diffusion.
103. Terbutryn a pre-emergence herbicide, penetrates the foliage but does not accumulate in growing regions.
104. The absorption of linuron (herbicide) occurs through active uptake.
105. Herbicides affect mitochondrial activity by coupling the reactions responsible for ATP synthesis
106. High concentrations of GA_T overcame the inhibition of α-amylase and protease by alachlor, but failed to remove it.
107 2, 4-Diaffects all types of RNA (mRNA, rRNA, tRNA) and DNA as well as ribonuclease (RNase).
108. Triazine herbicides also have growth stimulating effect on plants
109. Monuron, a herbicide produces normal meiotic cells in root tips.
110. Conjugation of a parent compound or a metabolite is not a common pathway of herbicide transformation in plants.
111. Many volatile herbicides show a direct relationship between volatilization and soil moisture.
112. The vapours of herbicides emitted during volatilization could not be phytotoxic.
113. The most important property of a herbicide governing its absorption and deactivation in soils is the electric charge of its molecules.
114. Paraquat desorbed by montmorillonite clay had little toxicity, while that adsorbed by kaolinite and vermiculite was immediately available.
115. The addition of organic matter to soils of low organic matter content increases the activity of herbicides.
116. Beans, potato, sugarcane and soybean have recorded stimulatory response to 2,4-D.
117. Treatment of soybean plant tissues with 2,4-D increased polisomal to ribosomal RNA ratio.
118. Atrazine and simazine enhanced chlorophyll content of maize leaves and decreased protein content of grain.
119. Simazine has been found to decrease protein content in rice.
120. Maleic hydrazide is widely known to inhibit suckering in tobacco and decrease yield.
121. Atrazine has been found to have antagonistic effect with dexon (a fungicide) in many plants species.
122. 2,4-D degrades rapidly in presence of MCPA.
123. Emulsifiable concentrates (EC) upon dilution with water give stable emulsions suitable for spraying plant surfaces.

124. Controlled droplet application technique is used to make ultra low volume (ULV) spraying of herbicides possible.
125. Maize and citrus seeds are monoembryonic and polyembryonic, respectively.
126. Seed quality index refers to the vigour of germination or percentage of germinated seeds with normal seedlings.
127. Dormancy is the arrested development and irreversible rest period of a plant organ, a seed or a vegetative part.
128. In seed bearing plants, the dormant seeds are much less resistant to unfavorable conditions than the mother plant.
129. The dormancy of weed seeds is a characteristic that enables weeds to persist for decades and even for centuries.
130. Cut or pulled panicles of *Avena* sp. at milk stage of seed development, already have 30 per cent viable seeds but not dormant.
131. The chronological age of the seed is not much less important than the environment in which it is held.
132. To rice nursery in an alkali soil, apply 2,4 and 2.5-7.5 grammes/m^2 of ferrous sulphate and zinc sulphate, respectively.
133. Blind tillage is done after sowing and germination (emergence of seedlings).
134. Clean tillage means working of the soil of the entire field in a way that no living plant is left undisturbed.
135. Mulch tillage refers to tilling of soil in a way that the mulch materials, surface clods and crop residues are fully disturbed.
136. According to IMD, drought is a situation occurring in any area in a year when the annual average rainfall is less than 75 per cent of the normal.
137. When the deficiency of the rainfall in an area in a year is above 50 per cent, it is referred to as a severe drought.
138. Multiple cropping is a philosophy of maximum production per unit area of land with a maximum of soil deterioration.
139. Land Equivalent Ratio (LER) is the relative land area under sole crop(s) that is required to produce the yield achieved in intercropping.
140. "When two crops are grown together and their yields on area basis are higher than their pure cropping" it is known as synergetic cropping.

III. Fill up the Blanks:

141. Phalaris minor came to India through ________ in 1960.
142. The success of biological control of weeds through insects and pathogens depends upon ________.
143. *Melanagromyza cucutae* has been found useful against the weed ________.
144. The organic chemicals for weed control took roots with the introduction of ________ an selective herbicides in 1935.
145. The discovery of ________ in early 1940's revolutionized the chemical weed control.
146. In 1941, 2,4-D was found ________ as fungicide and insecticide.
147. ________ (1944) reported selective weed control by 2,4-D in a bluegrass lawn in U.S.A.
148. Hammer and Tukey (1944) successfully used 2,4-D in ________.
149. ________ refers to the killing of the target plant species in a mixed population without harming or only slightly affecting other plants.

150. Volatility factor has been found responsible for lethal effect of trifluralin on foxtailmillet (*Setaria italica*) and ________.
151. Most of the soil applied herbicide is usually concentrated in the upper ________ cm of top soil.
152. Once a herbicide is absorbed into the plant system, it moves either ________.
153. ________ ,uraceil and urea herbicides embodying low ability to enter symplast in leaves, move acropetally *via* apoplast to the leaf mesophyll very rapidly with water.
154. A herbicide moves ________ in young plants than in old ones.
155. The increase in absorption and translocation of a herbicide at higher humidity is due to increased ________ transport.
156. The herbicides *viz*., paraquat and 2,4-D ester penetrate leaf surface rapidly and are not seriously affected by ________ falling even within an hour of application.
157. ________ are non-herbicidal compounds which enhance the absorption of aqueous solution of polar herbicides.
158. Hydrophilic and ________ balance is expressed as an arbitrary number used to categorize surfactants.
159. Penetration agents improve absorption of a herbicide by solubilizing ________ of cell wall or the membrane of plant tissues.
160. MSMA when foliarly applied, moves primarily in the xylem ________.
161. The absorption of paraquat/diquat by the leaves is influenced by their ________ properties.
162. The herbicides which inhibit or block oxygen evolution also inhibit noncyclic ________.
163. Acrolein, a general contact aquatic herbicide kills the plant through its ________ activity destroying vital plant cell enzyme system.
164. Triazine herbicides inhibit ________ reduction causing its accumulation in plants.
165. It is widely known that substituted urea herbicides inhibit the ________ of photosynthesis.
166. In simazine ________ takes place by replacing the chlorine molecules at the second position.
167. Intraspecific response to atrazine is due to a soluble enzyme, glutathione, S-transferase to detoxicify by catalyzing the formation of ________ conjugate in maize.
168. In India, pundia canes have been found more susceptible to 2,4-D than CO 419 and ________.
169. In ________, horticultural and plantation crops various herbicides or their combinations are to be used.
170. In minimum tillage foliar application of herbicides is followed by their ________ application.
171. ________ refers to the total effect of a combination which is equal to the sum of the effects of the component independently.
172. The average amount of solar energy reaching the outer limits of the atmosphere is called ________
173. The rain drops that reach the ground range from ________ in diameter.
174. Precipitation is associated with ________ cooling and condensation in rising air.
175. At sea, tornadoes are known as ________.
176. The principle of uniformitarrianism govern a wide variety of geologic and climatic studies that involve ________.
177. ________ is the process by which human beings and other animals as well as organisms become adapted to an unfavorable set of climatic conditions.
178. ________ days old seedlings are ready for transplanting of short duration varieties of rice.

179. Delayed transplanting leads to poor tillering, ________ flowering of main tillers and reduction in yield.
180. ________ seedlings per hill are transplanted at 20 × 10 cm distance under normal conditions.
181. In over aged seedlings, the number of seedlings per hill should be ________ .
182. Relatively older rice seedlings establish better than young seedlings in ________ soils.
183. The transplanting of rice seedlings deeper than 2-3 cm delays and inhibits ________ .
184. Depth of sowing is a very important aspect in successful cultivation of ________ of wheat.
185. The length of coleoptile of dwarf wheat varieties is ________ as compared to tall varieties.
186. The seeds of dwarf wheat varieties should not be sown deeper than ________ .
187. In late sown wheat, deep sowing delays emergence of seedlings by 2-3 days and ________ by 5-6 days.
188. Soybean grows well in ________ and moist climate.
189. The temperature of 26.5 to ________ °C appears to be optimum for growth and development of most of the varieties of soybean.
190. The soil temperature of ________ °C growth of soybean.
191. The lower temperature tends to delay ________ in soybean.
192. ________ is the key factor in most of the soybean varieties as they are short day plants and are sensitive to photoperiods.

IV. Tick mark (3) the correct answer :

193. Dispersing agents reduce ________ between similar particles.
(*a*) Adhesion (*b*) Cohesion
(c) Tension (*d*) None of these
194. Addition of ammonium sulphate to a herbicidal spray solution enhances the ________ against *Agropyron repens.*
(*a*) Glyphosphate (*b*) Amylase
(*c*) Reductase (*d*) Oxi-reductase
195. Uptake and translocation of alachlor by ________ germinating and emerging seedlings is faster at higher day and night temperatures than at lower temperatures
(*a*) Wheat (*b*) Castor
(*c*) Mustard (*d*) Snap beam
196. Propanil, a post-emergence herbicide is readily absorbed by the ________ .
(*a*) Stem (*b*) Root
(*c*) Leaf (*d*) None of these
197. Once the phenoxy herbicide penetrates the cuticle, it moves inside the plant ________
(*a*) Only apoplastically (*b*) Only symplastically
(*c*) By both mechanisms (*d*) None of these
198. Thiocarbonates *viz*., EPTC, a soil-incorporated herbicide is readily absorbed by roots and coleoptile and translocated ________ .
(*a*) Only upward (*b*) Only downward
(*c*) Both of these (*d*) None of these
199. It has been observed that propanil (a herbicide) interfered with ATP generation and electron transport in ________ mitochondria.
(*a*) Wheat (*b*) Barley
(*c*) Sorghum (*d*) Greengram

200. Triazines and phenoxy acids are subject to ring cleavage, triazine, heterocyclic ring can be cleaved resulting in liberation of _________ .

(*a*) Chlorine (*b*) Oxygen
(*c*) Hydrogen (*d*) Nitrogen

201. The accumulation of dinitramine in the plant tissue is believed to be _________ .

(*a*) Significant (*b*) Negligible
(*c*) Unchanged (*d*) None of these

202. The _________ acids which undergo b-oxidation are MCPB; 2, 4-DB, and 2,4, 5-TB.

(*a*) Phenoxyacetic (*b*) Phenoxyoxalic
(*c*) Phenoxymaleic (*d*) Phenoxybutyric

203. Urea herbicides undergo conjugation with _________ .

(*a*) Lipids (*b*) Carbohydrates
(*c*) Proteins (*d*) All of these

204. Glyphosphate has been reported to be metabolized to aminomethylphosphonic acid and glyoxalate in _________ .

(*a*) Maize (*b*) Sugarcane
(*c*) Sunflower (*d*) Safflower

205. The _________ structure of the herbicide also has a great influence on its volatility through adsorption to soil.

(*a*) Biological (*b*) Chemical
(*c*) Physical (*d*) Biophysical

206. _________ comprises an important mechanism of herbicide detoxification in soil under field conditions especially surface incorporation subsequent to rainfall or irrigation.

(*a*) Thermodecomposition (*b*) Biodecomposition
(*c*) Chemodecomposition (*d*) Photodecomposition

207. Photodecomposition plays an important role in the loss of urea herbicides from the soil surface in _________ areas.

(*a*) Moist (*b*) Wet
(*a*) Dry (*b*) Non of these

208. Most of the herbicides embody _________ phytotoxicity at lower soil moisture content.

(*a*) Higher (*b*) Lower
(*a*) Equal (*b*) Unchanged

209. _________ degradation plays a major role in the persistence and behaviour of herbicides in the soil.

(*a*) Microbial (*b*) Physical
(*c*) Chemical (*d*) Thermal

210. The organisms involved in herbicide detoxification include _________ .

(*a*) Earthworms (*b*) Nematodes
(*c*) Algae (*d*) None of these

211. Triazine-tolerant broadleaf weed biotypes include _________.

(*a*) Lambsquarter (*Chenopodium album*)
(*b*) Morning glory (*Convolvulus arvensis*)
(*c*) Sweet clover (*Melilotus indica*) (*d*) None of these

212. Oxyfluorfen has been found to inhibit apical bud growth in young ________ plants to better bush formation.

(*a*) Coffee (*b*) Tea
(*c*) Cacao (*d*) Coconut

213. Butylate stimulates germination in ________ seed by enhancing gibberellic activity or by changing membrane or seed permeability.

(*a*) Potato (*b*) Pigeonpea
(*c*) Safflower (*d*) Barley

214. Application of propanil after ________ in rice-paddies causes prohibitive vegetative injury

(*a*) DDT (*b*) Endosulfan
(*c*) Carbofuran (*d*) Sevin

215. There are ________ seed certification agencies in India at present

(*a*) 11 (*b*) 15
(*c*) 19 (*d*) 23

216. The recommended isolation distance (meters) for foundation seed production of radish, turnip and cauliflower is ________.

(*a*) 800 (*b*) 1200
(*c*) 1600 (*d*) 2000

217. The isolation distance required to produce the certified seed of chickpea, lentil, mungbean and urdbean is ________ meters.

(*a*) 25 (*b*) 15
(*c*) 10 (*d*) 5

218. The number of plants per hectare to be observed in taking one count in seed production of pearlmillet, sorghum, rice-paddies and wheat is ________ as recommended.

(a) 500 (b) 1000
(c) 1500 (*d*) 2000

219. The sampling lot in agricultural seed of large size should not exceed ________ kg except that of maize (where 40,000 kg is allowed).

(*a*) 5,000 (*b*) 10,000
(*c*) 15,000 (*d*) 20,000

220. Use of linear measurements of plumule growth as a vigour test for cereals and sugarbeet was first suggested by ________.

(*a*) S. Mathews in 1992 (*b*) J.S. Burris in 1939
(*c*) Germ in 1949 (*d*) Hegarty in 1959

221. The seed, the progeny of which comes from foundation seed or registered seed, is handled to maintain genetic purity, approved and certified by certifying agency is called ________

(*a*) Certified seed (*b*) Foundation seed
(*c*) Nucleus seed (*d*) Registered seed

222. The seeds of oil palm require as high as ________ °C temperature to break the dormancy.

(*a*) 30-40 (*b*) 40-50
(*c*) 50-60 (*d*) 60-70

223. The seeds of _________ are positively photoblastic.

(*a*) Tomato (*b*) Tobacco

(*c*) Chillies (*d*) Cucurbits

224. Heteromorphic seeds of the plant families Asteraceae and Chenopodiaceae do not permit _________ exchange.

(*a*) Water (*b*) Chemical

(*c*) Gaseous (*d*) Light

225. For raising a healthy nursery of tobacco on highly leached soils, besides other nutrients, borax are _________ g/m^2 is also recommended.

(*a*) 0.4-0.5 (*b*) 0.6-0.7

(*c*) 0.1-0.2 (*d*) 0.3-0.4

226. A basal dose of phosphorus at _________ g/m^2 of tobacco nursery area has been recommended.

(*a*) 5.5-6.5 (*b*) 7.5-8.0

(*c*) 9.0-9.5 (*d*) 10.0-10.5

227. Zero tillage system was first used successfully in 1950 in pasture renovation in _________.

(*a*) Germany (*b*) Japan

(*c*) United Kingdom) (*d*) U.S.A.

228. Though tilth is dynamic in nature, can be measured by _________.

(*a*) Aggregate analysis (*b*) Chemical analysis

(*c*) Biological analysis (*d*) None of these

229. The areas where drought has occurred in _________ per cent of year during the period are considered drought areas

(*a*) 10 (*b*) 20

(*c*) 30 (*d*) 40

230. The areas where drought has occurred in more than _________ percent of year is called chronic drought areas.

(*a*) 30 (*b*) 40

(*c*) 50 (*d*) 60

231. The Central Arid Zone Research Institute, Jodhpur (Rajasthan. India) was established in _________

(*a*) 1952 (*b*) 1957

(*c*) 1959 (*d*) 1961

232. The International Centre for Agricultural Research in Dry Area (ICARDA) was established in _________.

(*a*) 1957 (*b*) 1967

(*c*) 1977 (*d*) 1987

233. Mustard crop planted at a spacing of 50 × 20 cm will have _________ plants/ha.

(*a*) 75,000 (*b*) 1,00,000

(*c*) 1,25,000 (*d*) 1,50,000

234. Sorghum was planted at a plant spacing of 12.5 cm with a population of 1,60,000 plants/ha, its row spacing will be _________.

(*a*) 30 cm (*b*) 40 cm

(*c*) 35 cm (*d*) 50 cm

235. The seed rate of cotton would be _________ kg/ha, if the planting geometry is 75 × 50 cm, and test-weight, germination and purity percentages are 140, 90 and 95g, respectively.

(*a*) 2.17 (*b*) 3.37
(*c*) 4.37 (*d*) 5.21

236. If the germination and purity percentage, and test weight of seed are 95, 90 and 46 g, respectively and the wheat crop was planted at 20 × 3 cm. The seed rate of wheat per hectare will be _________.

(*a*) 50.67 kg (*b*) 60.12 kg
(*c*) 79.67 kg (*d*) 89.67 kg

237. The seed rate of potato tubers would be _________ q/ha, if the crop spacing, average weight of tubers and rottage loss of tubers during storage are 60 × 25 cm,. 35 kg and 5 per cent, respectively.

(*a*) 20.5 (*b*) 22.5
(*c*) 24.5 (*d*) 26.5

238. The quantity of urea needed for supplying 69 kg nitrogen to sorghum crop will be _________.

(*a*) 100 kg (*b*) 125 kg
(*c*) 150 kg (*d*) 175 kg

239. The application rates of nitrogen and phosphorus are 64 and 46 kg/ha to an experimental crop of wheat as basal, for that the quantity of urea and diammonium phosphate will be _________.

(*a*) 50 kg urea, 100 kg DAP (*b*) 75 kg urea, 75 kg DAP
(*c*) 75 kg urea, 100 kg DAP (*d*) 100 kg urea, 100 kg DAP

240. To supply 100 kg nitrogen and 50 kg potassium, the quantity of ammonium chloride and muriate of potash will be _________.

(*a*) 299.12 kg AC, 73.3 kg MoP (*b*) 384.61 kg AC, 73.3 kg MoP
(*c*) 2909.12 kg AC, 83.3 kg MoP (*d*) 384.61 kg AC, 83.3 kg MoP

241. Potato tuber yield will be _________ q/ha, if crop was spaced at 60 × 25 cm, and average number of tubers/plant and average weight of tubers are 14 and 35 g, respectively.

(*a*) 286.17 (*b*) 317.29
(*c*) 326.67 (*d*) 356.87

242. If the average panicle density per square meter is 260, the average number of filled grains per panicle and test weight of rice are 136 and 20 g, respectively. The rice crop will yield _________

(*a*) 5.98 t/ha (*b*) 7.08 t/ha
(*c*) 9.12 t/ha (*d*) 10.46 t/ha

243. The yield of wheat grain will be _________ t/ha from the following observations, spacing 20 × 3 cm, effective tillers/plant, 3, number of grains/car, 32, 1000-grain weight, 40 g.

(*a*) 5.8 t/ha (*b*) 6.2 t/ha
(*c*) 6.4 t/ha (*d*) 6.8 t/ha

244. The dapog method of raising rice nursery was introduced in India from _________.

(*a*) Philippines (*b*) Bangladesh
(*c*) Burma (*d*) Japan

245. The area needed to raise rice seedlings by dapog method sufficient for transplanting one hectare area is _________.

(*a*) 250-300 sqm (*b*) 25-30 .sqm
(*c*) 40-50 sqm (*d*) 400-500 sqm

246. Dapog seedlings would be ready for transplanting within ________.

(*a*) 8-10 days (*b*) 18-20 days
(*c*) 21-24 days (*d*) 11-14 days

247. The seed rate of bold grain varieties of rice to raise seedlings enough for one hectare is ________.

(*a*) 40-45 kg (*b*) 20-25 kg
(*c*) 30-35 kg (*d*) 50-55 kg

248. Under late sown conditions area of nursery, sufficient for transplanting one hectare rice field is ________.

(*a*) 800-1000 sqm (*b*) 500-600 sqm
(*c*) 1000-1200 sqm (*b*) 600-700 sqm

249. '*Aman*' rice is sown in ________.

(*a*) April-May (*b*) June-July
(*c*) Nov.-Dec. (*d*) May-Jun

250. In Orissa summer or spring season rice is known as ________.

(*a*) *Dalua* (*b*) *Boro*
(*c*) *Aman* (*d*) *Aus*

251. In parts of eastern region and peninsular India two or three crops of rice are taken in a year because of ________.

(*a*) Favourable mean temperature (*b*) High rainfall.
(*c*) Soils having good water retention capacity (*d*) Prolonged sunshine

252. To assure adequate population in rice, the number of hills per square meter area should be maintained at ________.

(*a*) 50 (*b*) 80
(*c*) 40 (*d*) 60

253. Anaerobic environment in paddy soil is responsible for gaseous loss of fertilizer nitrogen by ________.

(*a*) Denitrification (*b*) Volatilization
(*c*) Nitrification (*d*) Ammonification

254. Denitrification losses of nitrogen in paddy field can be prevented by incorporating ammoniacal nitrogen into the ________.

(*a*) Oxidized zone (*b*) Reduced zone
(*c*) Calcified zone (*d*) Hydronized zone

255. Recommendation of nitrogen, phosphorus (P_2O_5) and potassium (K_2O) for high yielding varieties of rice in UP is ________.

(*a*) 120 + 60 + 60 (*b*) 120 + 60 + 45
(*c*) 100 + 60 + 60 (*d*) 120 + 60 + 30

256. The technique, used for minimizing the nitrogen losses in paddy field under Indian conditions comprises ________.

(*a*) Use of pre-incubated urea (*b*) Use of neem seed cake
(*c*) Use of mud ball (*d*) All of these

257. The zinc deficiency in rice cause by ________ disease.

(*a*) Bacterial leaf streak (*c*) Bacterial leaf blight
(*c*) Sheath blight (*d*) *Khaira*

258. The most critical stage of rice for moisture stress is ________.
(*a*) Germination-tillering (*b*) Tillering-flowering
(*c*) Panicle initiation-flowering (*c*) Flowering-ripening

259. Weed competition in rice is more in the ________.
(*a*) Transplanted crop (*b*) Direct seeded crop
(*c*) Flooded crop (*c*) Crop sown in rows

260. The centre of origin of wheat is ________.
(*a*) South-western Asia (*b*) South-eastern Asia
(*c*) India (*d*) China

261. High yielding dwarf varieties of wheat were developed by ________.
(*a*) Dr. B.P. Pal (*b*) Dr. Norman E. Borlaug
(*c*) Dr. E.W. Burton (*a*) Dr. M.S. Swaminathan

262. The maximum area under wheat is in ________.
(*a*) USSR (erstwhile) (*b*) India
(*c*) China (*d*) USA

263. The production of wheat is the highest in ________.
(*a*) USSR (erstwhile) (*b*) India
(*c*) USA (*d*) China

264. The *Triticum aestivum* is ________ wheat.
(*a*) Diploid (*b*) Tetraploid
(*c*) Hexaploid (*d*) Monoploid

265. The optimum temperature range for ideal germination of wheat varies from ________.
(*a*) 25-30°C (*b*) 20-25°C
(*c*) 15-20°C (*c*) 10-15°C

266. In rainfed conditions one of the suitable varieties of wheat is ________ for Central India.
(*a*) Mukta (*b*) Bijaga red
(*c*) VL-421 (*d*) K-65

267. The seed of wheat should be treated with ________ against seed born pathogens.
(*a*) Vitavex (*b*) Thiram
(*c*) Both of these (*d*) Any one of these

268. Dibbling (sowing) of wheat requires ________ of seed.
(*a*) 15-20 kg/ha (*b*) 25-30 kg/ha
(*c*) 30-40 kg/ha (*d*) 20-25 kg/ha

269. A crop of wheat yielding 50 quintals of grain per hectare removes ________ from soil.
(*a*) 80-100 kg N + 50-60 kg P_2O_5 + 100-120 kg K_2O
(*b*) 100-150 kg N + 70-80 kg P_2O_5 + 125-150 kg K_2O
(*c*) 150-180 kg N + 100 kg P_2O_5 + 160-180 kg K_2O
(*d*) 160-200 kg N + 80-100 kg P_2O_5 + 150-170 kg K_2O

270. Wherever only two irrigations are available, the wheat crop should be irrigated ________.
(*a*) CRI and tillerin (*b*) CRI and flowering
(*c*) CRI and milking (*d*) CRI and late jointing

271. The *Phalaris minor* can be controlled by using the weedicide called _________ at 0.75-1.25 kg a.i./ha depending upon soil type.
(*a*) 2, 4-D
(*b*) Isoproturon
(*c*) Basalin
(*d*) Simazine

272. The causal organism of brown rust in _________.
(*a*) *Pucinia recondita tritici*
(*b*) *Puccinia streiformis*
(*c*) *Puccinia graminis tritici*
(*d*) *Ustilago nuda tritici*

273. Karnal bunt or partial bunt was first observed in experimental seed plots at _________.
(*a*) Karnal
(*b*) Pantnagar
(*c*) New Delhi
(*d*) Hisar

274. Maize protein is deficient in _________.
(*a*) Betadine
(*b*) Tryptophane and lysine
(*c*) Lysine
(*d*) Tryptophane

275. The country ranking first in respect of area in maize (corn) is _________.
(*a*) India
(*b*) China
(*c*) Brazil
(*d*) USA

276. The largest maize producing country in the world is _________.
(*a*) USA
(*b*) Mexico
(*c*) India
(*d*) Canada

277. The dent corn is also known as _________.
(*a*) *Zea mays indentata*
(*b*) *Zea mays indurata*
(*c*) *Zea mays tunicata*
(*d*) *Zea mays everta*

278. The major part of nitrogen uptake by the maize is over by the _________.
(*a*) Knee high stage
(*b*) Tasselling stage
(*c*) Silking stage
(*d*) Grain filling stage

279. Deficiency of nitrogen in maize causes _________.
(*a*) Yellowing of leaves from tip to base in V shaped pattern
(*b*) Chlorotic spots at base of leaves near the margins
(*c*) Yellow streaking of leaf edges
(*d*) Whitish-yellow spots on leaves

280. The optimum rainfall range for growing maize is _________.
(*a*) 360-500 mm
(*b*) 560-700 mm
(*c*) 300-400 mm
(*d*) 460-600 mm

281. The rate of application of atrazine in maize under heavy soils varies from _________ kg a.i./ha.
(*a*) 0.75-1.0
(*b*) 1.25-1.50
(*c*) 1.75-2.00
(*c*) 1.00-1.25

282. Brown stripe downy mildew of maize can be controlled by use of _________.
(*a*) Bordeaux mixture (4:4:50)
(*b*) Bavistin
(*c*) Karathane-453
(*d*) Diathane M-45

283. The temporary roots in maize root system are ________.
(a) Seminal roots (b) Aerial roots
(c) Crown roots (d) Coronal roots

284. The pH range for successful cultivation of maize ranges from ________.
(a) 6.5-8.5 (b) 7.5-8.5
(c) 7.5-9.5 (d) 5.5-7.5

285. All India Coordinated Maize Improvement Project was started in ________.
(a) 1957 (b) 1955
(c) 1965 (c) 1967

286. The maize crop should be planted at the distance of ________.
(a) 30 × 20-25 cm (b) 60 × 20-25 cm
(c) 30 × 10-15 cm (d) 60 × 10-15 cm

287. The seed rate for composites of maize varies from ________ kg/ha.
(a) 18-20 (b) 20-25
(c) 28-30 (d) 30-35

288. Under high rainfall conditions maize should be planted ________.
(a) In narrow furrows (b) On a flat bed
(c) On the side of ridges (d) In widely spaced furrows

289. Hybrid maize should be fertilized with ________ kg/ha of N + P_2O_5 + K_2O, respectively
(a) 120 + 30 + 15 (b) 80 + 40 + 20
(c) 120 + 60 + 40 (d) 120 + 30 + 30

290. Temperature requirement for optimum growth of sorghum ranges from ________.
(a) 16-20°C (b) 20-25°C
(c) 30-35°C (d) 26-30°C

291. Seed rate of sorghum is ________ kg/ha
(a) 12-15 (b) 10-12
(c) 8-10 (d) 15-20

292. To attain maximum yield of sorghum per hectare, plant population should be maintained at ________.
(a) 1,50,000 (b) 1,60,000
(c) 1,75,000 (d) 1,25,000

293. The sensitive stages to moisture stress in sorghum are ________.
(a) Flowering (b) Grain filling
(c) Both of these (d) None of these

294. Herbicide used for weed control in sorghum is ________ kg a.i./ha
(a) Atrazine at 0.5-1.0 (b) Atrazine at 1.25-1.5
(c) Basalin at 0.5-1.0 (d) Basalin at 1.25-1.5

295. The causal agent of anthracnose disease in sorghum is ________.
(a) *Puccinia purpurea* (b) *Helminthosporium turcicum*
(c) *Colletotrichum graminicola* (d) *Gleourcospora sorghi*

296. The best time for sowing of chickpea in northern India is ________.

(*a*) Second fortnight of October (*b*) First fortnight of October

(*c*) First fortnight of November (*d*) Second fortnight of September.

297. The starter dose of nitrogen for chickpea is recommended as ________ kg/ha.

(*a*) 20 (*b*) 10

(*c*) 30 (*d*) 40

298. The critical stages for irrigation in chickpea are ________.

(*a*) Branching and pre-flowering

(*b*) Branching and pod development

(*c*) Pre-flowering and pod development

(*d*) Branching, pre-flowering and pod development

299. The recommended herbicide for weed control in chickpea is ________.

(*a*) Basalin (*b*) Butachlor

(*c*) Alachlor (*d*) 2, 4-D

300. The chickpea wilt is caused by ________.

(*a*) *Fusarium orthocerus* (*b*) *Ascochyta rabi*

(*c*) *Botrylis cinerea* (*d*) *Sclerotinia sclerotiorum*

301. Chickpea pod borer can be controlled by the spray of ________.

(*a*) Monocrotophos @ 1 ml/litre of water (*b*) Aldrin (5%) @ 15 kg/ha

(*c*) Seed treatment by Captan (0.25%) @ 4 g/kg of seed

(*d*) BHC @ 10 kg/ha

302. The protein percentage in lentil has been estimated at ________.

(*a*) 25 (*b*) 20

(*c*) 30 (*d*) 35

303, ________ ranks first in respect of linseed production

(*a*) Pakistan (*b*) Burma

(*a*) Spain (*b*) India

304. The optimum sowing time for lentil in N.W. India is ________.

(*a*) Middle of October (*b*) Last week of October

(*c*) First week of October (*d*) Last week of September

305. The recommended optimum seed rate for lentil, in general, varies from ________ kg/ha

(*a*) 20-30 (*b*) 40-50

(*c*) 30-40 (*c*) 10-20

306. Lentil under late sowing situations should be seeded with ________.

(*a*) Ehanced seed rate (*b*) Reduced seed rate

(*c*) Widened row space (*d*) Widened plant space

307. A lentil crop grown with improved package of practices may record the yield upto ———— t/ha

(*a*) 1.0-1.5 (*b*) 3.0-3.5

(*b*) 1.5-2.0 (*d*) 2.0-2.5

308. The scientific name of field pea is ________.
(*a*) *Pisum sativum var. arvense* (*b*) *Pisum sativum var. hortense*
(*c*) *Pisum sativum var. leguminosarum* (*d*) *Pisum sativum var. esculentum*

309. The type of germination in field pea is called ________.
(*a*) Hypogeal (*b*) Epigeal
(*c*) Hypo-epigeal (*d*) Epihypogeal

310. High humidity is harmful to field pea as it accentuates ________.
(*a*) Incidence of insects (*b*) Excessive vegetative growth
(*c*) Incidence of disease (*d*) Delays flowering.

311. In north Indian conditions field peas should be sown in ________.
(*a*) First fortnight of November (*b*) Second fortnight of September
(*c*) First fortnight of October (*d*) Second fortnight of October

312. The recommended optimum row spacing for planting of field pea is ________ cm.
(*a*) 30 (*b*) 20
(*c*) 15 (*d*) 25

313. In phosphorus and potassium deficient soils, field pea crop should be fertilized with ________ kg/ha of P_2O_5+ K_2O, respectively.
(*a*) 30-40+20-30 (*b*) 50-60+20-30
(*c*) 60-70+30-40 (*d*) 50-60+30-40

314. *Arhar* (pigeonpea) is commonly known as ________.
(*a*) Redgram (*b*) Blackgram
(*c*) Bengalgram (*d*) Greengram

315. The second most important Indian pulse crop is ________.
(*a*) Chickpea (*b*) Pigeonpea
(*c*) Cowpea (*d*) Field pea

316. The *arhar* (pigeonpea) grows well in ________ climate.
(*a*) Tropical and subtropical (*b*) Temperate
(*c*) Humid and temperate. (*d*) Sub-humid and temperate.

317. The recommended optimum sowing time of arhar (pigeonpea) is ________.
(*a*) Second fortnight of July (*b*) First fortnight of July
(*c*) Second fortnight of June (*d*) First fortnight of June

318. The recommended optimum seed-rate for pigeonpea is ________ kg/ha.
(*a*) 12-15 (*b*) 20-25
(*c*) 8-10 (*d*) 18-20

319. Zinc deficiency in *arhar* (pigeonpea) can be rectified by spraying of ________.
(*a*) 5. kg $ZnSO_4$ + 2.5 kg lime/ha (*b*) 20 kg $ZnSO_4$ + 2.5 kg lime/ha
(*c*) 5 kg $ZnSO_4$ + 5 kg lime/ha (*d*) 10 kg $ZnSO_4$ + 5 kg lime/ha

320. Two hand weedings have been found adequate to control weeds in pigeonpea reasonably well ________ days after sowing.
(*a*) 25-30 and 45-60 (*b*) 40-45 and 60-65
(*c*) 15-20 and 35-40 (*d*) 30-35 and 60-65

321. The type of germination in mungbean is known as _________.
(*a*) Epigeal (*b*) Hypogeal
(*c*) Hypo-epigeal (*d*) Epi-hypogeal

322. Sow summer mungbean in _________ for reasonably good productivity.
(*a*) Middle of April (*b*) Middle of March to middle of April
(*c*) Middle of March (*d*) Middle of February to middle of March

323. The recommended optimum seed rate of *kharif* season mungbean is _________ kg/ha.
(*a*) 18-20 (*b*) 8-10
(*c*) 22-25 (*d*) 12-15

324. _________ a.i./ha has been recommended for the control of weeds in mungbean.
(*a*) Basalin @ 1 kg (*b*) 2,4-D @ 1 litre
(*c*) Simazine @ 1 kg (*d*) Atrazine @ 1 kg

325. It has been found that _________ incorporation of basalin provides relatively more effective control of weeds in mungbean.
(*a*) Pre-flowering spray (*b*) Post-emergence (20 days after sowing)
(*c*) Pre-emergence (*d*) Post-emergence (40 days after sowing)

326. Mungbean cultured with the package of improved package of technological practices may yield _________ q/ha.
(*a*) 22-25 (*b*) 12-15
(*c*) 18-20 (*d*) 8-10

327. The place of origin of urdbean is _________.
(*a*) India (*b*) Bunna
(*c*) Bangladesh (*d*) Ceylon

328. The scientific name of early maturing bold and black seeded urdbean varieties is _________.
(*a*) *Vigna mungo var. viridis* (*b*) *Vigna mungo var. niger*
(*c*) *Vigna mungo var. macropode* (*d*) *Vigna mungo var.* micropode

329. For urdbean, the suitable climate is _________.
(*a*) Hot and humid (*b*) Cool and humid
(*c*) Cool and dry (*d*) Hot and dry

330. For kharif season urdbean, the recommended optimum seed rate is _________ kg seed/ha.
(*a*) 15-20 (*b*) 8-10
(*c*) 12-15 (*d*) 22-25

331. Recommended row spacing for summer season, urdbean is _________ cm.
(*a*) 10-15 (*b*) 15-20
(*c*) 20-25 (*d*) 30-35

332. If urdbean is being grown for the first time in a field, the seed should be inoculated with _________
(*a*) *Azospirillum* (*b*) *Rhizobium*
(*c*) *PSB* (*d*) *Clostridium*

333. The recommended dose fertilizers for urdbean is _________ N + P_2O_5 + K_2O kg/ha. respectively.
(*a*) 15-20 + 50-60 + 30-40 (*b*) 15-20 + 20-30 + 8-10
(*c*) 40-80 + 50-60 + 30-40 (*d*) 15-20 + 0 + 30-40

334. Sufficient soil moisture _________ stage is essential for optimum productivity of urdbean.
(*a*) Branching and pod-development (*b*) Branching and flowering
(*c*) Pod development and maturity (*d*) Flowering and pod development

335. Cowpea grown for grain purpose should be seeded at _________ kg/ha.
(*a*) 10-15 (*b*) 20-25
(*c*) 15-20 (*d*) 25-30

336. The recommended row and plant spacing for *kharif* cowpea is _________ cm.
(*a*) 30-45 × 8-10 (*b*) 30-45 × 4-6
(*c*) 25-30 × 8-10 (*d*) 25-30 × 4-6

337. Application of nitrogen in cowpea at the time of planting is known as _________.
(*a*) Basic dose (*b*) Synergistic dose
(*c*) Starter-dose (*d*) Additional dose

338. Soybean besides good quality protein also contains about _________ per cent of oil
(*a*) 10 (*b*) 20
(*c*) 30 (*d*) 40

339. The protein content of soybean is about _________ per cent
(*a*) 40 (*b*) 20
(*c*) 30 (*d*) 10

340. The grain legume which is also grown as an oilseed is _________.
(*a*) Chickpea (*b*) Urdbean
(*c*) Lentil (*d*) Soybean

341. The _________ is considered to be a progenitor of soybean.
(*a*) *Glycine max* (*b*) *Glycine sinensis*
(*c*) *Glycine ussuriensis* (*d*) *Glycine usitattisimum*

342. The bacteria responsible for nitrogen fixation in soybean is _________.
(*a*) *Rhizobium japonicum* (*b*) *Rhizobium phaseoli*
(*c*) *Rhizobium leguminosarum* (*d*) *Rhizobium glycicum*

343. The pH range suitable for soybean cultivation is _________.
(*a*) 5.0-6.0 (*b*) 7.0-8.5
(*c*) 5.5-6.5 (*d*) 6.0-7.5

344. The soybean crop can be intercropped with _________.
(*a*) Wheat (*b*) Chickpea
(*c*) Maize (*d*) Tobacco

345. The optimum time for kharif soybean planting is _________.
(*a*) First fortnight of June (*b*) First fortnight of July
(*c*) Second fortnight of June (*d*) Second fortnight of July

346. The usually recommended plant to plant distance for soybean is ________.

(*a*) 2-3 cm (*b*) 4-5 cm

(*c*) 5-7 cm (*d*) 8-10 cm

347. The optimum seed rate of soybean for normal planting is ________ kg/ha:

(*a*) 50-60 (*b*) 60-70

(*c*) 70-80 (*d*) 80-90

348. For spring crop of soybean seed should be ________ than that of kharif planting.

(*a*) More (*b*) Less

(*c*) Similar (*d*) Double

349. Normally recommended N + P_2O_5 + K_2O dose for soybean is ________ kg/ha, respectively.

(*a*) 20-30 + 70-80 + 50-60 (*b*) 20-30 + 100-120 + 50-60

(*c*) 50-60 + 70-80 + 50-60 (*d*) 50-60 + 70-80 + 80-100

350. Soybean crop should be free from weed competition during first ________ days for its good productivity.

(*a*) 10-20 (*b*) 20-30

(*c*) 30-40 (*d*) 40-50

351. Fluchloralin can be used for weed control in soybean as ________.

(*a*) Pre-emergence (*b*) Pre-plant incorporation

(*c*) Post-emergence (*d*) Through herbigation

352. The ideal moisture content in soybean seed at the time of threshing has been estimated at ________ per cent.

(*a*) 10-11 (*b*) 11-12

(*c*) 13-14 (*d*) 14-15

353. Among the oilseed crops, groundnuts ranks ________ in India.

(*a*) First (*b*) Second

(*c*) Third (*d*) Fourth

354. Groundnut seed normally contains protein and oil ________ per cent, respectively.

(*a*) 25 and 45 (*b*) 22 and 43

(*c*) 45 and 26 (*d*) 43 and 22

355. The scientific name of erect type of groundnut is ________.

(*a*) *Arachis hypogaea* subspecies *fastigiata*

(*b*) *Arachis hypogaea* subspecies *procumbens*

(*c*) *Arachis hypogaea* subspecies *oleifera*

(*d*) *Arachis hypogaea* subspecies *gigantea*

356. The gynophore of groundnut is commonly referred to as the ________.

(*a*) Perianth (*b*) Peg

(*c*) Ovate (*d*) Monadelph

357. The most suitable soil for groundnut is ________.

(*a*) Sandy and sandy loam (*b*) Clayey loam

(*c*) Loamy clay (*d*) Silty loam and clay loam

358. Deep ploughing of soil in a groundnut field should normally be avoided because it ________
(*a*) Makes harvesting difficult
(*b*) Makes pegging difficult in upper layers
(*c*) Delays germination
(*d*) Delays pegging and pod development

359. The recommended row to row spacing for bunch type of groundnut is ________ cm.
(*a*) 20-30
(*b*) 30-40
(*c*) 40-50
(*d*) 45-60

360. The recommended row spacing for spreading type of groundnut is ________ cm.
(*a*) 25-30
(*b*) 35-50
(*c*) 45-60
(*d*) 55-70

361. Bunch type of groundnut is recommended to be seeded at ________ kg/ha.
(*a*) 60-80
(*b*) 80-100
(*c*) 100-120
(*d*) 70-90

362. Fertilizer dose recommended for a crop of groundnut is N + P_2O_5 + K_2O kg/ha, respectively ________.
(*a*) 20-40 + 50-60 + 30-40
(*b*) 40-50 + 50-60 + 30-40
(*c*) 20-40 + 60-80 + 30-50
(*d*) 40-50 + 60+80 + 30-50

363. For nitrogen and phosphorus application in groundnut ________ fertilizers are normally preferred.
(*a*) Urea and single superphosphate
(*b*) Ammonium sulphate and single superphosphate
(*c*) Urea and diammonium phosphate
(*d*) Ammonium sulphate and diammonium phosphate

364. Ammonium sulphate is preferred for nitrogen application in groundnut because it also ________ provides .
(*a*) Calcium
(*b*) Magnesium
(*c*) Sulphur
(*d*) Boron

365. Use of ________ provides effective control of weeds in groundnut.
(*a*) 2,4-D
(*b*) Simazine
(*c*) Isoproturon
(*d*) TokE-25

366. Sesamum cake contains ________ per cent of N + P_2O_5 + K_2O, respectively.
(*a*) 6.0-6.2 + 2.0-2 + 1.0-1.2
(*b*) 2.0-2.2 + 6.0-6.2 + 1.0-1.2
(*c*) 6.0-6.2 + 1.0-1.2 + 2.0-2.2
(*d*) 2.0-2.2 + 1.0-1.2 + 6.0-6.2

367. Quadricarpellatum capsule of sesamum contains ________ carpels.
(*a*) Two
(*b*) Three
(*c*) Four
(*d*) Six

368. Sesamum belongs to the family ________ .
(*a*) Leguminoseae
(*b*) Papilionaceae
(*c*) Pedaliaceae
(*d*) Chinipodeaceae

369. In South India sesamum is grown in ________ .
(*a*) *Rabi* season only
(*b*) *kharif* season only
(*c*) *Rabi* and *kharif* seasons only
(*d*) Summer season only

370. The recommended planting geometry for sesame is _________ cm.

(*a*) 25 × 15 (*b*) 30 × 15

(*c*) 30 × 10 (*d*) 4 × 15

371. The seed normally required for planting of sesamum is _________ kg/ha

(*a*) 2-3 (*b*) 3-4

(*c*) 4-5 (*d*) 5-6

372. Castor belongs to _________ family.

(*a*) Compositae (*b*) Euphorbiaceae

(*c*) Leguminoseae (*d*) Gramineae

373. High temperature above 41°C at flowering of castor results in _________.

(*a*) Rotting of pollens and poor fertilization

(*b*) Blasting of flowers and poor seed-set

(*c*) Delayed pollination and poor-fertilization

(*d*) Reduced pollination and rotting of seed

374. The optimum time for planting of castor varies between _________.

(*a*) 20th May and 5th June (*b*) 5th June and 20th June

(*c*) 20th June and 5th July (*d*) 5th July and 20th June

375. The recommended optimum depth of sowing of castor is _________ cm.

(*a*) 4 (*b*) 6

(*c*) 8 (*d*) 10

376. The recommended seed rate of castor varies from _________ kg/ha.

(*a*) 10 to 12 (*b*) 14 to 16

(*c*) 16 to 18 (*d*) 18 to 70

377. Irrigated crop of castor should normally be planted at a row and plant distance of _________ cm

(*a*) 45 × 45 (*b*) 60 × 45

(*c*) 60 × 60 (*d*) 90 × 45

378. Fertilizer requirement of castor has been recommended at _________ of N + P_2O_5 + K_2O kg/ha. respectively.

(*a*) 60 + 40 + 40 (*b*) 120 + 60 + 60

(*c*) 120 + 40 + 40 (*d*) 60 + 60 + 30

379. Under irrigated conditions, nitrogen should be splitted in castor as _________ day after sowing.

(*a*) Half basal plus half at 60 (*b*) Half plus half at 30

(*c*) Three-fourth as basal and one-fourth at 60 (*d*) Three-fourth as basal and one-fourth 30

380. The largest producer of rapeseed and mustard in the world is _________.

(*a*) China (*b*) Japan

(*c*) India (*d*) Canda

381. Rapseed and mustard belong to the family _________.

(*a*) Leguminoseae (*b*) Compositeae

(*c*) Euphorpiaceae (*d*) Cruciferac

382. The 2*n* chromosome number in *Rugosa* is ________.
(*a*) 20 (*b*) 24
(*c*) 32 (*d*) 36

383. The fruit of rapeseed and mustard is known as ________.
(*a*) Pod (*b*) Silique
(*c*) Grain (*d*) Caryopsis

384. The crop of ________ is more liable to suffer from frost and cold.
(*a*) *Toria* (*b*) *Pahari rai*
(*c*) *Sarson* (*d*) *Banarsi* rai

385. The optimum time of sowing of toria in N. India varies between ________.
(*a*) First and second week of September (*b*) First and second week of October
(*c*) Mid and last week of October (*d*) Mid and last week of September

386. Thinning of rapeseed and mustard is done to maintain a plant to plant distance of ________ cm.
(*a*) 5-10 (*b*) 10-15
(*c*) 15-20 (*d*) 20-25

387. Irrigated rapeseed and mustard is recommended to be fertilized with ________ of $N + P_2O_5 + K_2O$ kg/ha, respectively.
(*a*) 60-90 + 60 + 40 (*b*) 90-120 + 60 + 40
(*c*) 60-90 + 90 + 40 (*d*) 90-120 + 90 + 40

388. The mustard crop is regarded ready for harvest when its pods turn ________ in colour.
(*a*) Greenish-yellow (*b*) Greenish-black
(*c*) Yellowish green (*d*) Yellowish-brown

389. Linseed can be used as ________ crop.
(*a*) Oilseed (*b*) Fibre
(*c*) Oilseed and fibre (*d*) None of these

390. The protein content in linseed cake has been estimated at ________ per cent.
(*a*) 12 (*b*) 24
(*c*) 36 (*d*) 48

391. Linseed crop belongs to the family ________.
(*a*) Compositeae (*b*) Euphorbiaceae
(*c*) Leguminoceae (*d*) Linaceae

392. The fruit of linseed is known as ________.
(*a*) Pod (*b*) Canum
(*c*) Seedball (*d*) Dutum

393. Linseed is a ________ season crop.
(*a*) Warm (*b*) Cool
(*c*) Hot (*d*) Dry

394. The recommended row to row spacing for linseed planting is ________ cm.
(*a*) 20 (*b*) 30
(*c*) 40 (*d*) 50

395. Linseed has been recommended to be fertilized with _________ kg of P_2O_5 / ha to raise a good crop.

(a) 10 (b) 20
(c) 30 (d) 40

396. First irrigation to linseed is normally recommended _________ after sowing.

(a) 30-40 (b) 40-50
(c) 20-30 (d) 50-60

397. The weeds can be controlled in linseed by the application of MCPB @_________ kg a.i./ha.

(a) 0.5 (b) 1.5
(c) 1.0 (d) 2.0

398. Safflower is a _________ season crop.

(a) Dry (b) Summer
(c) Arid (d) Cool

399. Safflower can be grown as an intercrop with _________.

(a) Wheat (b) Urdbean
(c) Maize (d) Sorghum

400. The seed of safflower should be treated with Agrosan G.N. @ _________ /kg of seed.

(a) 30 g (b) 30 mg
(c) 30 decigram (d) 100 decigram

401. The recommended row spacing normally maintained for safflower planting is _________ cm.

(a) 25 (b) 35
(c) 45 (d) 55

402. Nitrogen application of safflower influences _________.

(a) Seed yield (b) Seed composition
(c) Both of these (d) None of these

403. Irrigated safflower is recommended to be fertilized with _________ kg/ha of N + P_2O_5 + K_2O, respectively.

(a) 80 + 60 + 20 (b) 80 + 40 + 20
(c) 40 + 20 + 20 (d) 40 + 40 + 20

404. Wherever only one irrigation is available, it should be given at _________ stage in safflower.

(a) 20 days (b) 30 days
(c) 40 days (d) 50 days

405. The identified critical stages for .irrigation of safflower are _________.

(a) Rosette and stem elongation (b) Rosette and flowering
(c) Flowering and grain filling (d) Stem elongation and flowering

406. Two hand weedings in safflower are required for its good growth at _________.

(a) 15 and 30 days stages (b) 20 and 40 days stages
(c) 25 and 50 days stages (d) 30 and 60 days stages.

407. Topping of safflower plants is beneficial _________.

(a) To reduce the lodging (b) To reduce the water losses
(c) To promote branching and flowering (d) To reduce losses of seed and fruit

408. Safflower rust can be controlled by ________.

(a) Spray of Zineb
(b) Treatment of seed with thiram
(c) Destroying the infected material
(d) Following the 3 to 4 years crop rotation.

409. Safflower as an oilseed crop was introduced into India in ________.

(a) 1965
(b) 1969
(c) 1972
(d) 1985

410. Sunflower is a ________ crop.

(a) Self-pollinated
(b) cross-pollinated
(c) Self and cross-pollinated
(d) Parthenocarpous

411. The sunflower crop requires cool climate from ________.

(a) Germination to seedling stage
(b) Seedling to flowering stage
(c) Flowering to maturity stage
(d) Seedling to maturity stage

412. If temperature is high during maturation of sunflower, the linoleic acid ________.

(a) Remains unaffected
(b) Increases with slow rate
(c) Decreases
(d) Increases with rapid rate

413. During kharif season sunflower takes ________ days to mature.

(a) 80-90
(b) 100-110
(c) 120-130
(d) 105-130

414. The optimum pH range for sunflower is ________.

(a) 5.5-7.5
(b) 6.5-8.5
(c) 7.5-9.5
(d) 7.0-9.0

415. The optimum time of sowing of sunflower during *kharif* in India is ________.

(a) First fortnight of June
(b) Second fortnight of June
(c) First fortnight of July
(d) Second fortnight of July

416. The recommended seed rate of sunflower varies from ________ kg/ha.

(a) 6-8
(b) 8-10
(c) 10-12
(d) 12-14

417. The sunflower crop is recommended to be planted at ________ cm spacing.

(a) 45×20
(b) 60×20
(c) 45×30
(d) 60×30

418. The fertilizer use recommendation for sunflower is ________ kg/ha of $N + P_2O_5 + K_2O$, respectively.

(a) $30 + 60 + 40$
(b) $30 + 30 + 20$
(c) $70 + 40 + 30$
(d) $70 + 60 + 40$

419. The most sensitive stages of sunflower to water stress lie between ________.

(*a*) Germination and seedling
(*b*) Germination and flowering
(*c*) Seedling and flowering
(*d*) Flowering and grain filling

420. Cotton belongs to the ________ family

(*a*) Malvaceae
(*b*) Compositeae
(*c*) Crucifereae
(*d*) Lineaceae

421. The number of known species in genus *Grossypium* have been estimated at ________.

(*a*) 10
(*b*) 15
(*c*) 20
(*d*) 25

422. Heavy rainfall or irrigation during fruiting periods of cotton may cause ________.

(*a*) Lodging of crop
(*b*) Shedding of flowers and young bolls
(*c*) Yellowing of young bolls
(*d*) Heavy incidence of boll worm

423. Delinting of cotton seed may be done with ________.

(*a*) Sulphuric acid
(*b*) Citric acid
(*c*) Sodium hydroxide
(*d*) Ammonium chloride.

424. Delinting of cotton helps in ________.

(*a*) Grading the seed
(*b*) Killing of hibernating boll worm larvae and disease pathogens
(*c*) Quicker germination
(*d*) All of these

425. Treatment of cotton-seed with organo-mercurial compound(s) helps to minimise the ________ diseases.

(*a*) Soil borne
(*b*) Air borne
(*c*) Water borne
(*d*) Seed borne

426. American cotton should normally be planted at the distance of ________ cm.

(*a*) 45 × 30
(*b*) 60 × 30
(*c*) 60 × 45
(*d*) 90 × 45

427. The optimum plant population for cotton has been estimated at ________ plants/ha.

(*a*) 25,000-50,000
(*b*) 30,000-60,000
(*c*) 50,000-80,000
(*d*) 80,000-1,00,000

428. The optimum sowing time of cotton in northern regions of India is ________.

(*a*) First fortnight of May
(*b*) Second fortnight of May
(*c*) First fortnight of June
(*d*) Second fortnight of June

429. Jute belongs to the family ________.

(*a*) Malvaceae
(*b*) Compositeae
(*c*) Lineaceae
(*d*) Tiliaceae

430. The best observed pH for jute cultivation is ________.
(*a*) 5.0-6.5 (*b*) 6.0-7.5
(*c*) 7.0-8.5 (*d*) 8.0-9.5

431. The optimum period of sowing for *Capsularis* jute is ________.
(*a*) February-March (*b*) March-April
(*c*) April-May (*d*) May-June

432. The optimum period of sowing for *Olitorius* jute is ________.
(*a*) February-March (*b*) March-April
(*c*) April-May (*d*) May-June

433. *Tossa* jute is to be sown at a row spacing of ________ cm
(*a*) 15 (*b*) 20
(*c*) 25 (*d*) 30

434. For fibre purposes, jute crop may be harvested at any time ________.
(*a*) After pod formation (*b*) After flowering
(*c*) Before flowering (*d*) Before pod formation

435. Retting is a process by which ________.
(*a*) The poor fibre stalk is sorted-out
(*b*) The fibres in the bark get loosened and separated from woody stalk
(*c*) The good quality fibres are sorted out
(*d*) Fibres are differentiated into various retted groups.

436. The observed best temperature for retting is ________ °C.
(*a*) 14 (*b*) 24
(*c*) 34 (*d*) 38

437. Green manuring of sannhemp adds approximately ________ kg N/ha to the soil on decomposition.
(*a*) 20-40 (*b*) 40-60
(*c*) 60-80 (*d*) 80-100

438. Sannhemp belongs to the family ________.
(*a*) Leguminoseae (*b*) Compositeae
(*c*) Liniaceae (*d*) Tiliaceae

439. For a fibre crop of sannhemp, recommended seed rate for one hectare ________ is kg/ha.
(*a*) 5-10 (*b*) 10-15
(*c*) 15-20 (*d*) 20-25

440. Sannhemp should be planted at a distance of ________ cm to raise a fibre crop.
(*a*) 20 × 7-10 (*b*) 25 × 5-7
(*c*) 30 × 7-10 (*d*) 30 × 5-7

441. Sugarcane belongs to the family ________.

(*a*) Gmmineae (*b*) Cruciferae
(*c*) Leguminoceae (*d*) Compositeae

442. Sugarcane is a ________ plant.

(*a*) Annual (*b*) Perennial
(*c*) Triennial (*d*) None of these

443. The roots emerging from a sugarcane sett are known as ________.

(*a*) Sett roots (*b*) Shoot roots
(*c*) Primary roots (*d*) Secondary roots

444. The inflorescence of sugarcane is called a ________.

(*a*) Spike (*b*) Tassel
(*c*) Panicle (*d*) Arrow

445. The average yield of sugarcane in north India is low as compared to that in the southern parts mainly due to ________.

(*a*) Climatic conditions (*b*) Varietal status
(*c*) Soil fertility status (*d*) Level of management

446. Which portion of sugarcane-stalk should normally be used for seed purpose ________.

(*a*) Top one-fourth portion (*b*) Top one-third to half portion
(*c*) Bottom one-fourth portion (*d*) Bottom one-third 'to half portion.

447. Sugarcane cut for seed-setts essentially have ________.

(*a*) One bud (*b*) Two buds
(*c*) Three buds (*d*) Four buds

448. The number of setts needed for planting one hectare of sugarcane is ________.

(*a*) 25,000-30,000 (*b*) 35,000-40,000
(*c*) 45,000-50,000 (*d*) 55,000-60,000

449. Treat the sugarcane seed setts with ________ against fungal diseases.

(*a*) Diathane M-45 (*b*) Zineb
(*c*) Thiram (*d*) Aretan

450. Late planting of autumn sugarcane reduces the germination due to ________.

(*a*) Short day (*b*) Frost
(*c*) Low temperature (*d*) High humidity

451. The planting of sugarcane by trench method ________.

(*a*) Improves germination (*b*) Reduces lodging
(*c*) Improves tillering (*d*) Saves seed setts

452. The water requirement of sugarcane is the maximum during _________ phase.
(*a*) Germination and formation
(*b*) Formation phase and grand growth
(*c*) Grand growth phase and maturity
(*d*) Formation phase and maturity

453. The most destructive disease of sugarcane _________.
(*a*) Red rot
(*b*) Wilt
(*c*) Smut
(*d*) Albino

454. Sugarbeet is a _________.
(*a*) Vegetable crop
(*b*) Forage crop
(*c*) Tuber crop
(*d*) Sugar crop

455. The family of sugarbeet is _________.
(*a*) Chenopodiaceae
(*b*) Crucifereae
(*c*) Euphorbiaceae
(*d*) Compositeae

456. Sugarbeet is a _________ plant.
(*a*) Annual
(*b*) Biennial
(*c*) Perennial
(*d*) None of these

457. The sucrose is found in _________ of sugarbeet.
(*a*) Stem
(*b*) Leaves
(*c*) Roots
(*d*) Inflorescence

458. Sugarbeet is grown during _________ season.
(*a*) *Rabi*
(*b*) *Kharif*
(*c*) *Zaid*
(*d*) *Rabi and Kharif*

459. The seed _________ kg/ha is required for sugarbeet planting.
(*a*) 6-8
(*b*) 8-10
(*c*) 10-12
(*d*) 12-14

460. The recommended spacings for sugarbeet planting are _________ cm.
(*a*) 30×15
(*b*) 50×15
(*c*) 30×25
(*d*) 50×25

461. Recommended dose of $N + P_2O_5 + K_2O$ kg/ha is _________ respectively for sugarbeet.
(*a*) $120 + 80 + 80$
(*b*) $90 + 60 + 40$
(*c*) $120 + 60 + 40$
(*d*) $90 + 80 + 60$

462. The annual broad leaf and grassy weeds in sugarbeet can be controlled effectively by use of _________ kg a.i./ha.
(*a*) Basalin @ 1.0
(*b*) 2,4-D @ 1.5
(*c*) Butachlor @ 2.0
(*d*) Pyramin @ 3.0

463. Out of the following _________ is commonly cultivated potato.

(*a*) *Solanum demissum* (*b*) *Solanum stenotonum*

(*c*) *Solanum tuberosum* (*d*) *Solanum andigenum*

464. A tuber represents _________.

(*a*) Enlarged underground root (*b*) Enlarged underground stem

(*c*) Enlarged underground nodules (*d*) None of these

465. Potato belongs to the family _________.

(*a*) Solanaceae (*b*) Compositeae

(*c*) Leguminoceae (*d*) Euphorbiaceae

466. The soil temperature for satisfactory growth of potato tuber should be _________ °C.

(*a*) 7-9 (*b*) 11-13

(*c*) 17-19 (*d*) 20-23

467. To avoid rotting in early planting of potato, seeds should be treated with _________.

(*a*) 0.5 per cent Diathane M-45 (*b*) 2.0 per cent Diathane M-45

(*c*) 1.5 per cent Aretan (*d*) 2.0 per cent Tafasan

468. The time of planting of main crop of potato in northern plains is _________.

(*a*) 10-15 October (*b*) 15-25 October

(*c*) 10-15 November (*d*) 15-25 November

469. The recommended seed rate of main crop of potato in northern plains is _________ q/ha.

(*a*) 15-20 (*b*) 20-25

(*c*) 25-30 (*d*) 30-35

470. A good crop of potato yielding about 400 q/ha on an average removes _________ $N + P_2O_5 + K_2O$ kg/ha, respectively.

(*a*) 170-180 + 100 + 250 (*b*) 170-180 + 25 + 250

(*c*) 170-180 + 50 + 125 (*d*) 170-180 + 25 + 100

471. Tobacco has been classified as a _________ crop.

(*a*) Cash (*b*) Catch

(*c*) Inter (*d*) Relay

472. *Nicotiana rustica* has been derived as an amphidiploid from a cross between _________.

(*a*) *Nicotiana tabacum* × *Nicotiana paniculata*

(*b*) *Nicotiana paniculata* × *Nicotiana sylvestris*

(*c*) *Nicotiana undulata* × *Nieotiana sylvestris*

(*d*) *Nicotiana undulata* × *Nieotiana paniculata*

473. Tobacco belongs to the family ________.

(*a*) Compositeae (*b*) Solanaceae

(*c*) Cruciferеae (*d*) Leguminoseae

474. Nicotine content of the leaves of *Nicotiana rustica* ranges between ________ per cent

(*a*) 2.0 and 5.5 (*b*) 3.0 and 4.5

(*c*) 3.5 and 8.0 (*d*) 5.0 and 10.5

475. Tobacco requires ________ °C temperature for uniformly rapid germination.

(*a*) 17-22 (*b*) 19-25

(*c*) 27-32 (*d*) 29-42

476. Rainfall at the time of maturity of tobacco is undesirable as it causes ________.

(*a*) Lodging (*b*) Leaves to get rotten

(*c*) Leaves to get shattered (*d*) Washing down of gums and resins from leaf

477. The optimum time for sowing nursery of tobacco is ________.

(*a*) First fortnight of August (*b*) Second fortnight of August

(*c*) First fortnight of September (*d*) Second fortnight of September

478. The seed rate of tobacco to raise seedlings for one hectare varies from ________ kg/ha.

(*a*) 0.5-1.0 (*b*) 1.0-2.0

(*c*) 1.5-2.5 (*d*) 2.0-3

479. Excess of chlorides in tobacco ________.

(*a*) Inhibits the leaf burn and reduces leaf storage capacity

(*b*) Reduces the leaf size and aroma

(*c*) Increases the leaf storage capacity and leaf burn

(*d*) Increases the leaf size and aroma

480. Topping in tobacco means a, process of ________.

(*a*) Removal of the buds in the axil, of leaves (*b*) Removal of leaves

(*c*) Removal of terminal buds (*d*) Burning of leaves

481. The aim of topping and desuckering in tobacco is ________.

(*a*) To reduce the plant height

(*b*) To divert energy and nutrients from flower head to leaves

(*c*) To increase the horizontal branching of plant

(*d*) To protect the plants against lodging

482. The first irrigation in wheat is normally recommended at _________.

(*a*) Tillering stage (*b*) Crown root initiation stage

(*c*) Flowering stage (*d*) Seedling stage

483. One of the following stages of rice is not critical in respect of irrigation _________.

(*a*) Seedling (*b*) Panicle initiation

(*c*) Flowering (*d*) Maturity

484. The identified critical stage of irrigation in barley is _________.

(*a*) Tillering (*b*) Flowering

(*c*) Both of these (*d*) None of these

485. 2, 4-D is a _________ herbicide.

(*a*) Selective (*b*) Non-selective

(*c*) Contact (*d*) None of these

486. One of the following herbicides is a selective herbicide _________.

(*a*) Simazine (*b*) Bisulphide

(*c*) Pentachlorophenol (*d*) Sodium chlorate

487. The critical period of weed control in upland rice varies between _________ days after sowing.

(*a*) 15-20 (*b*) 20-25

(*c*) 25-30 (*d*) 30-35

488. For mungbean the period between _________ days after sowing has been regarded as critical for weed control.

(*a*) 0 and 30 (*b*) 5 and 25

(*c*) 15 and 40 (*d*) 25 and 45

III. Match the following :

489. Match the following crops with their class.

(*a*) Rose and onion (*i*) Plantation crops

(*b*) Coffee and tea (*ii*) Food crops

(*c*) Rice and wheat. (*iii*) Garden crops

(*d*) Berseem and lucerne (*iv*) Forage crops

490. Match the families with the crop plants.

(*a*) Graminae (Poaceae) (*i*) Safflower and sunflower\

(*b*) Cruciferae (*ii*) Maize and sugarcane tobacco

(*c*) Solanaceae (*iii*) Mustard and cabbage

(*d*) Compositae (Astaraceae) (*iv*) Tomato and tobacco

491. Match the crops with their families.

(*a*) Jute	(*i*) Chenopodiaceae
(*b*) Castor and tapioca	(*ii*) Papilionaceae
(*c*) Spinach and sugarbeet	(*iii*) Tiliaceae
(*d*) Groundnut and chickpea	(*iv*) Euphobiaceae

492. Match the following crops with their agrarian or economic or agricultural class.

(*a*) Wheat and rice	(*i*) Field/forage crops
(*b*) Teosinte and stylo	(*ii*) Sugar/starch crops
(*c*) Asparagus and tapioca	(*iii*) Narcotic/fumitories/masticatories
(*d*) Tobacco and opium poppy	(*iv*) Cereal crops

493. Match the following crops with the method of their harvesting.

(*a*) Tobacc	(*i*) Cutting
(*b*) Mustard	(*ii*) Reaping
(*c*) Okra	(*iii*) Priming
(*d*) Amaranth	(*iv*) Picking

494. Match the purpose of growing or the special purpose served by the following crops

(*a*) *Lathyrus* (*khesari*)	(*i*) Sod/turf crop
(*b*) Sorghum	(*ii*) Exhaustive crop
(*c*) Bermuda grass	(*iii*) Paira cropping
(*d*) Linseed	(*iv*) Trap crop (for *Striga*)

495. Match the classes with the crops given below.

(*a*) Nurse crops	(*i*) Sugarcane and tapioca
(*b*) Riparian crops	(*ii*) *Tephrosia* and *Crotolaria*
(*c*) Energy crops	(*iii*) *Gliricidia* and pigeonpea
(*d*) Avenue crops	(*iv*) Pepperwot and water bind weed

496. Match the nursery area required for transplantation of one hectare of the following crops.

(*a*) Rice, dry bed	(*i*) 1250-1500 m^2
(*b*) Rice, wet bed	(*ii*) 50 m^2
(*c*) Rice-Dapog technique	(*iii*) 1000 m^2
(*d*) Tobacco	(*iv*) 75-80 m^2

497. Match the nursery area required with the crops for one hectare.

(*a*) 50 m^2	(*i*) Tomato
(*b*) 100 m^2	(*ii*) Cauliflower
(*c*) 150 m^2	(*iii*) Onion
(*d*) 500 m^2	(*iv*) Tobacco

498. Match the type of tillage with the climate and/or agropractice (s).

(*a*) Post-harvest (*i*) Uncropped land

(*b*) Summer (*ii*) Crop harvest

(*c*) Winter (*iii*) Tropical zones

(*d*) Fallow (*iv*) Temperate zone

499. Match the ploughs with the working of soil and operation.

(*a*) Country plough (*i*) Walking type

(*b*) Disc plough (*ii*) Soil turning type

(*c*) Bose plough (*iii*) Riding type

(*d*) Gang plough (*iv*) Soil stirring type

500. Match the nitrogen content (%) on green matter basis with the green manuring crops.

(*a*) Mungbean (*i*) 0.43

(*b*) *Sesbania* (*dhaincha*) (*ii*) 0.49

(*c*) Clusterbean (*iii*) 0.53

(*d*) Cowpea (*iv*) 0.34

501. Match the $N + P_2O_5 + K_2O$ content (%) with the manures containing them.

(*a*) $0.5 + 0.2 + 0.5$ (*i*) Castor cake

(*b*) $4.3 + 1.8 + 1.3$ (*ii*) Neem cake

(*c*) $5.2 + 1.0 + 1.4$ (*iii*) Blood meal

(*d*) $10.5 + 2.5 + 0$ (v) Farmyard manure

502. Match the cakes with their $N + P_2O_5 + K_2O$ content (%).

(*a*) $7.3 + 1.5 + 1.3$ (*i*) Rapeseed cake

(*b*) $4.0 + 1.4 +. 1.3$ (*ii*) Groundnut cake

(*c*) $5.2 + 1.8 + 1.2$ (*iii*) Linseed cake

(*d*) $2.5 + 0.8 + 1.8$ (*iv*) *Mahua* cake

503. Match the nitrogenous fertilizers and their N-content (%).

(*a*) Ammonium sulphate (*i*) 82

(*b*) Ammonium chloride (*ii*) 20-25

(*c*) Anhydrous ammonia (*iii*) 20-21

(*d*) Ammonia solution (*iv*) 24-26

504. Match the phosphatic fertilizers with their P_2O_5 content (%).

(*a*) Single superphosphate (*i*) 14-18

(*b*) Dicálcium phosphate (*ii*) 34-39

(*c*) Rock phosphate (*iii*) 16

(*d*) Basic slag (*iv*) 20-40

505. Match the compound fertilizers with N + P_2O_5 content (%).

(*a*) Nitrophosphate	(*i*) 11+48
(*b*) Monoammonium phosphate	(*ii*) 12.9+12.9
(*c*) Crude ammonium phosphate	(*iii*) 21+54
(*d*) Diammonium phosphate (*iv*)	16+20

506. Match the micronutrient fertilizers with their nutrient content (%)

(*a*) Ferrous sulphate (Fe)	(*i*) 23-35
(*b*) Manganese sulphate (Mn)	(*ii*) 23
(*c*) Zinc sulphate (Zn)	(*iii*) 37-39
(*d*) Sodium molybdate (Mo)	(*iv*) 20

507. Match the sulphur content (%) with the following micronutrient fertilizers.

(*a*) 18.8	(*i*) Copper sulphate
(*b*) 12.4	(*ii*) Ferrous sulphate
(*c*) 17.8	(*iii*) Manganese sulphate
(*d*) 12.8	(*iv*) Zinc sulphate

508. Match the crops with their critical stages for irrigation.

(*a*) Tobacco	(*i*) Pre-flowering, capsule development
(*b*) Rapeseed and mustard	(*ii*) Topping
(*c*) Pearlmillet	(*iii*) Seedling, flowering
(*d*) Sorghum	(*iv*) Flowering

509. Match the crops with their critical stages for irrigation.

(*a*) Rice-paddies	(*i*) Silking, cob development
(*b*) Maize	(*ii*) Flowering, grain formation
(*c*) Fingermillet	(*iii*) Emergence, tiller formation, elongation
(*d*) Sugarcane	(*iv*) Tiller initiation, flower primordia, flowering

510. Match the crop with the critical stages for irrigation.

(*a*) Chickpea	(*i*) Pegging to pod formation
(*b*) Pigeonpea	(*ii*) Preflowering, flowering
(*c*) Field pea	(*iii*) Flower initiation, pod filling
(*d*) Groundnut	(*iv*) Start of flowering, pod formation

511. Match the critical stage (s) for irrigation with crop.

(*a*) Flowering, grain filling	(*i*) Safflower
(*b*) Branching, flowering	(*ii*) Linseed
(*c*) Preflowering, capsule development	(*iii*) Oats
(*d*) Ear emergence	(*iv*) Sunflower

512. Match the soil moisture storage capacity (mm) with broad soil groups.

(*a*) 300/m	(*i*) Alluvial deep, loam
(*b*) 140-180/m	(*ii*) Submontane, deep, loamy sand
(*c*) 100-140/m	(*iii*) Black deep (90 cm)
(*d*) 90-100/m.	(*iv*) Submontane, deep, sandy loam

513. Match the effective cropping season (weeks) with the regional centre.

(*a*) 8	(*i*) Anantpur
(*b*) 11	(*ii*) Bellary
(*c*) 17	(*iii*) Jodhpur
(*d*) 13	(*iv*) Bijapur

514. Match the following regional centre with the effective cropping seasons (weeks).

(*a*) Jhansi	(*i*) 23
(*b*) Solapur	(*ii*) 27
(*c*) Anand	(*iii*) 25
(*d*) Akola	(*iv*) 21

515. Match the regional centres with the effective cropping seasons (weeks).

(*a*) Varanasi	(*i*) 35
(*b*) Hoshiarpur	(*ii*) 51
(*c*) Ranchi	(*iii*) 32
(*d*) Dehradun	(*iv*) 45

516. Match the isolation distance (meters) from the fields of other prescribed crops for the production of foundation seed with the crops.

(*a*) Wheat	(*i*) 1000
(*b*) Pearlmillet	(*ii*) 1600
(*c*) Cauliflower	(*iii*) 50
(*d*) Cotton	(*iv*) 150

517. Match the crop with the diseases designated for seed certification.

(*a*) Rape and mustard	(*i*) Phyllody
(*b*) Cabbage	(*ii*) Early blight
(*c*) Cowpea	(*iii*) Alternaria blight
(*d*) Tomato	(*iv*) Anthracnose

518. Match the weed species designated objectionable with the crops in seed production.

(*a*) *Convolvulus arvensis* (morning glory)	(*i*) Okra
(*b*) *Chicorium intybus* (chicory)	(*ii*) Wheat
(*c*) *Cuscuta* spp. (dodder)	(*iii*) Berseem
(*d*) Wild *Abelmoschus* spp.	(*iv*) Lucerne

519. Match the seed sampling intensity from a stream of seed entering the containers.

(*a*) At least 5 individual samples (IS)	(*i*) 501-3,000 kg
(*b*) One IS for each 300 kg, but not less than 5 samples	(*ii*) >20,000 kg
(*c*) One IS for each 500 kg, but not less than 10 samples	(*iii*) Upto 500 kg
(*d*) One IS for each 700 kg, but not less than 40 samples	(*iv*) 3,001-20,000 kg

520. Match the maximum permissible weight of a seed-lot with the plant species given below.

(*a*) 10,000	(*i*) *Vigna unguiculata*
(*b*) 20,000	(*ii*) *Oryza sativa*
(*c*) 25,000	(*iii*) *Zea mays*
(*d*) 40,000	(*iv*) *Brassica juncea*

521. Match the minimum size of a working pelleted seed sample with the quality character to be determined.

(*a*) 2500 pellets	(*i*) Size grading
(*b*) 400 pellets	(*ii*) Determination of other seeds
(*c*) 2000 pellets	(*iii*) Germination
(*d*) 7500 pellets	(*iv*) Purity analysis

522. Match the PSD (Pure Seed Definitions) of the following genus.

(*a*) *Avena* (Oats)	(*i*) 13
(*b*) *Gossypium* (cotton)	(*ii*) 12
(*c*) *Cichorium* (chicory)	(*iii*) 3
(*d*) *Daucus* (carrot)	(*iv*) 11

523. Match the prescribed number of days for final count for germination with the crop seeds.

(*a*) 14 days	(*i*) Sorghum
(*b*) 8 days	(*ii*) Wheat
(*c*) 10 days	(*iii*) Okra
(*d*) 21 days	(*iv*) Rice-paddies

524. Match the method of scarification practised with the seeds given below.

(*a*) Manually or mechanically scarified by rubbing *etc.*	(*i*) Bitter gourd (*Momordica charantia*)
(*b*) Piercing of seed coat or incision at abexial end	(*ii*) Cotton (*Gossypium* spp.)
(*c*) Seed coat completely removed by breaking	(*iii*) Subabul (*Leucaena leucocephala*)
(*d*) Treated with diluted sulphuric acid	(*iv*) Rubber (*Heavea* spp.)

525. Match the following chemicals used to break the dormancy of seeds with their major chemical group.

(*a*) Gibberellins	(*i*) Sulphydryl
(*b*) Indole acetate	(*ii*) Oxidant
(*c*) Hypochlorite	(*iii*) Growth regulators
(*d*) Dithiothreitol	(*iv*) Respiratory inhibitors

526. Match the major chemical group with the chemicals used to break the dormancy in seeds.

(*a*) Plant products	(*i*) Dinitrophenol
(*b*) Nitrogenous compound	(*ii*) Cotylenol
(*c*) Growth regulators	(*iii*) Thiourea
(*d*) Respiratory inhibitors	(*iv*) Ethylene

527. Match the carbohydrate content (%) with seeds of the following.

(*a*) 65-75	(*i*) Sorghum
(*b*) 56-59	(*ii*) Flax
(*c*) 50-60	(*iii*) Wheat
(*d*) 20-25	(*iv*) Chickpea

528. Match the following seeds with their protein content (%).

(*a*) Wheat	(*i*) 20-25
(*b*) Chickpea	(*ii*) 8-9
(*c*) Sorghum	(*iii*) 26-41
(*d*) Sunflower	(*iv*) 10-14

529. Match the following seeds with their fat content (%).

(*a*) Sunflower	(*i*) 1.5-2.0
(*b*) Flax	(*ii*) 40-45
(*c*) Chickpea	(*iii*) 3-4
(*d*) Sorghum	(*iv*) 35-45

530. Match the tocopherol (Vitamin E) content (mg/kg of fresh weight) of the following seeds having 87 per cent of dry weight.

(*a*) Wheat	(*i*) 6.2
(*b*) Barley	(*ii*) 1.5.8
(*c*) Rice	(*iii*) 0.4
(*d*) Maize	(*iv*) 7.2

531. Match the quality component with the recommended standard percentage for hybrid cotton.

(*a*) Germination (minimum)	(*i*) 98
(*b*) Physical purity (minimum)	(*ii*) 90
(*c*) Genetic purity (minimum)	(*iii*) 10
(*d*) Self-plants (maximum)	(*iv*) 60

532. Match the following insect predators with the weed which they have been found to feed upon.

(*a*) *Acroclita* spp. (*i*) *Cyperus rotundus* (nutgrass)

(*b*) *Orseoliella javanica* (*ii*) *Euphatorium adenophorum*

(*c*) *Bactra vermosana* (*iii*) *Imperata cylindrica* (thatchgrass)

(*d*) *Procecidochares utilitis* (*iv*) *Cuscuta* spp (dodder)

533. Match the organisms and weed controllable by it.

(*a*) Cochinial mealy bug (*Dactylopius indicus*) (*i*) *Striga* spp.

(*b*) Mexican gallfly (*Procecidochares utilitis*) (*ii*) *Eupatorium adenophorum*

(c) Gall-forming weevil (*Smlcronyx albovariegatus*) (*iii*) *Parthenium hysterophorus*

(*d*) Larval of Diacrisia obliqua (*iv*) *Opuntia vulgaris*

534. Match the herbicide with their chemical group.

(*a*) Dalapon (*i*) Amides and acetamides

(*b*) Butacblor (*ii*) Bypyridilium

(*c*) MSMA (*iii*) Aliphatics

(*d*) Paraquat (*iv*) Arsenicals

535. Match the chemical group with the herbicide.

(*a*) Carbamates (*i*) Nitrogen

(*b*) Benzoice and phenyacetates (*ii*) Problem

(*c*) Dinitroanilines (*iii*) TIBA

(*d*) Diphenyl esters (*iv*) Pendimethalin

536. Match the chemical group with the herbicide.

(*a*) Nitriles (*i*) PCP

(*b*) Phenols (*ii*) Norflurazon

(*c*) Phenoxy acids (*iii*) MCPA

(*d*) Pyridazinones (*iv*) Ioxynil

537. Match the herbicide with the chemical group.

(*a*) Benthiocarb (*i*) Benthiazuron

(*b*) Triazines (*ii*) Thiocarbamates

(*c*) Triazoles (*iii*) Terbutryn

(*d*) Ureas (*iv*) Amitrole

538. Match the soil organic matter percentage with the proposed rate of trifluralin application (kg/ha).

(*a*) 2% OM (*i*) 4.48 trifluralin

(*b*) 4% OM (*ii*) 0.56 trifluralin

(c) 8% OM (*iii*) 2.24 trifluralin

(*d*) 10% OM (*iv*) 1.12 trifluralin

539. Match the weeds with their botanical name.

(*a*) Star bur	(*i*) *Achyranthes aspora* L.
(*b*) Prickly chaff flower	(*ii*) *Aerva tomentosa* Forsk
(*c*) Javanese woolplant	(*iii*) *Acanthospermum hispidim* (L.) DC
(*d*) Camel thorn	(*iv*) *Alhagi camelorum* Fisch.

540.

Weed	**Botanical name**
(*a*) *Khaki* weed	(*i*) *Boerhaavia diffusa* L.
(*b*) Spreading hog weed	(*ii*) *Alternanthera echinata* Smith
(*c*) Hog weed	(*iii*) *Brassica arvensis* Kuntze
(*d*) Wild mustard	(*iv*) *Blumea wightiana* DC.

541.

Weed	**Botanical name**
(*a*) *Madar*	(*i*) *Chrozophora rottlerii* Klot.
(*b*) Wild safflower	(*ii*) *Cannabis sativa* L.
(*c*) Hog weed	(*iii*) *Brasciica arvensis* Kuntze.
(*d*) Wild mustard	(*iv*) *Blumia wightiana* DC.

542.

Weed	**Botanical name**
(*a*) Chicory	(*i*) *Chichorium intybus* L.
(*b*) Cleome	(*ii*) *Coix lachryma* L.
(*c*) Conch flower creeper	(*iii*) *Cleome chelidonii* L.
(*d*) *Sankru*	(*iv*) *Clitoria ternatea* L.

543.

Weed	**Botanical name**
(*a*) Jew's mallow jute	(*i*) *Crotolaria striaia* DC.
(*b*) Rattle box	(*ii*) *Corchorus olitorius* L.
(*c*) Bulb grass	(*iii*) *Cyperus iria* L.
(*d*) Yellow sedge	(*iv*) *Cyperus bulbosus* Vab.

544.

Weed	**Botanical name**
(*a*) Crow foot grass	(*i*) *Datura fastuosa* L.
(*b*) Thorn apple	(*ii*) *Elephantopus scaber* L.
(*c*) False daisy	(*iii*) *Dactyloctenium aegyptium* Beauv.
(*d*) Elephant's foot	(*iv*) *Eclipta alba* Hassk.

545.

Weed	**Botanical name**
(*a*) India lovegrass	(*i*) *Gynandropsis gynandra* (L.) Brig.
(*b*) Horseweed	(*ii*) *Hydrocotyle asiatica* L.
(*c*) Caravelleseed	(*iii*) *Erigecron canadensis* L.
(*d*) Asiatic pennywort	(*iv*) *Eragrostis pilosa* Beauv.

546. **Weed** — **Botanical name**

(*a*) Indigo — (*i*) *Mimosa pudica* L.

(*b*) Ivy-leaved morning glory — (*ii*) *Ipomea hederacea* Jacq.

(*c*) Leucas — (*iii*) *Indigofera glandulosa* Willd.

(*d*) Touch-me-not — (*iv*) *Leucas aspera* Spreng.

547. **Weed** — **Botanical name**

(*a*) Carpet weed — (*i*) *Ocimum canum* Sims.

(*b*) Hoary basil — (*ii*) *Oxalis corniculata* L.

(*c*) Prickly pear — (*iii*) *Mollugo lotoides*

(*d*) Indian sorrel — (*iv*) *Opuntia dillenii* Haw.

548. **Weed** — **Botanical name**

(*a*). Knot grass — (*i*) *Polygonum convolvulus* L.

(*b*) Passion flower — (*ii*) *Paspalum sanguinale* Lamk.

(*c*) Wild buck wheat — (*iii*) *Potamogeton pectinatus*

(*d*) Pond weed — (*iv*) *Passiflora foetida* L.

549. **Weed** — **Botanical name**

(*a*) Yellow foxtail — (*i*) *Sida spinosa* L.

(*b*) Mallow — (*ii*) *Setaria glauea* Beauv.

(*c*) Prickly sida — (*iii*) *Silene* spp.

(*d*) Sleepy catch fly champion — (*iv*) *Sida rhombifolia* L.

550. **Weed** — **Botanical name**

(*a*) White horse nettle — (*i*) *Spergula arvensis* L.

(*b*) Corn spurry — (*ii*) *Trianthema portulacastrum* L.

(*c*) Horse purslane — (*iii*) *Trihulus terrestris* L.

(*d*) Ground burnet — (*iv*) *Solanum elaegnifolium*

551. **Weed** — **Botanical name**

(*a*) Cattails — (*i*) *Xanthium strumariuni* L.

(*b*) Ash-coloured flea bane — (*ii*) *Typha latifolia* L.

(*c*) Cocklebur — (*iii*) *Salvinia auriculata*

(*d*) Water fern — (*iv*) *Vernonia cinerea* Lers.

552. Match the crop with its scientific name.

(*a*) Rice — (*i*) *Zea mays* L.

(*b*) Wheat — (*ii*) *Sorghum bicolor* L. Moench

(*c*) Maize — (*iii*) *Triticum aestivum* L.

(*d*) Sorghum — (*iv*) *Oryza sativa* L.

553. **Crop** — **Scientific name**

(*a*) *Bajra* (pearlmillet) — (*i*) *Elcusine coracana* Gaertn.

(*b*) *Mandua* (fingermillet) — (*ii*) *Panicum miliaceum* L.

(*c*) *Cheena* (prosomillet) — (*iii*) *Echinochloa frumentacea* L.

(*d*) *Sawan* (Barnyard millet) — (*iv*) *Pennisetum typhoides* L.

554. **Crop** | **Scientific name**
(*a*) Gram (chickpea) | (*i*) *Cajanus cajan* L. Millsp.
(*b*) Lentil | (*ii*) *Cicer arietinum* L.
(*c*) *Arhar* (pigeonpea) | (*iii*) *Setaria italica* (L.) Beauv.
(*d*) *Kakun* (foxtail millet) | (*iv*) *Lens eseulenta* Moench

555. **Crop** | **Scientific name**
(*a*) Greengram | (*i*) *Vigna mungo* L. Hepper
(*b*) Blackgram | (*ii*) *Arachis hypogaea* L.
(*c*) Cowpea | (*iii*) *Vigna radiata* L. Wilczek
(*d*) Groundnut | (*iv*) *Vigna sinensis* L

556. **Crop** | **Scientific name**
(*a*) Barley | (*i*) *Pisum sativum*
(*b*) *Kodo* (kodomillet) | (*ii*) *Hordeum vulgare* L.
(*c*) Soybean | (*iii*) *Glycine max* L. *Merrill*
(*d*) Field pea | (*iv*) *Paspalum scrobiculatum* L.

557. **Crop** | **Scientific name**
(*a*) Sesamum | (*i*) *Ricinus communis* L.
(*b*) Castor | (*ii*) *Linum usitatissimum* L.
(*c*) Linseed | (*iii*) *Carthamus tinetorius* L.
(*d*) Safflower | (*iv*) *Sesamum indicum* L.

558. **Crop** | **Botanical name**
(*a*) Oats | (*i*) *Cyamopsis tetragonoloba* L.
(*b*) Berseem (Egyptian clover) | (*ii*) *Avena sativa* L.
(*c*) Lucerne | (*iii*) *Trifolium alexandrinum* L.
(*d*) *Guar* (clusterbean) | (*iv*) *Medicago sativa* L.

559. **Crop** | **Scientific name**
(*a*) Sugarcane | (*i*) *Beta vulgaris* L.
(*b*) Sugarbeet | (*ii*) *Nicotiana tabacum*
(*c*) Potato | (*iii*) *Saccharum officinarum* L.
(*d*) Tobacco | (*iv*) *Solanum tuberosum* L.

560. **Crop** | **Scientific name**
(*a*) *Desi* cotton | (*i*) *Corchorus olitorius*
(*b*) American cotton | (*ii*) *Gossypium herbaceum*
(*c*) White jute | (*iii*) *Corchorus capsularis*
(*d*) Tossa jute | (*iv*) *Gossypium hirsutum*

561. **Crop** | **Scientific name**
(*a*) Sunflower | (*i*) *Crotolaria juncea* L.
(*b*) Napier grass | (*ii*) *Pennisetum purpureum*
(*c*) Sannhemp | (*iii*) *Nicotiana rustica*
(*d*) Tobacco | (*iv*) *Helianthus annus* L.

562. **Crop** — **Scientific name**

(*a*) Indian rape — (*i*) *Brassica juncea*
(*b*) Mustard — (*ii*) *Gossypium barbadense*
(*c*) Black mustard — (*iii*) *Brassica campestris var yellow toria*
(*d*) American cotton — (*iv*) *Brassica nigra*

563. Match the weed with its scientific name.

Weed — **Scientific name**

(*a*) Lantana — (*i*) *Echinochloa colonum* L. Link
(*b*) Kans grass — (*ii*) *Saccharum spontaneum* L.
(*c*) Jungli rice — (*iii*) *Eleusine indica* L. *Gaertn.*
(*d*) Goose grass — (*iv*) *Lantana camera* L.

564. **Weed** — **Scientific name**

(*a*) Saw thistle — (*i*) *Parthenium hysterophorus* L.
(*b*) Wild carrot weed — (*ii*) *Cuscuta chinensis* Damk.
(*c*) Common purslane — (*iii*) *Sonchus oleraceus* L.
(*d*) Dodder — (*iv*) *Portulaca oleracea* L.

565. **Weed** — **Scientific name**

(*a*) Canary grass — (*i*) *Axonopus compressus* (*Sw.*) Beauv.
(*b*) Carpet grass — (*ii*) *Commelina benghalensis* L.
(*c*) Day flower — (*iii*) *Phalaris minor*.
(*d*) Bermuda grass — (*iv*) *Cynodon dactylon* L. Pers.

566. **Weed** — **Scientific name**

(*a*) Witch weed — (*i*) *Azolla caroliniana*
(*b*) Water velvet — (*ii*) *Sorghum halepense* L. Pers.
(*c*) Johnson grass — (*iii*) *Cyperus rotundus* L.
(*d*) Nut grass — (*iv*) *Striga* spp.

567. **Weed** — **Scientific name**

(*a*) Sourgrass — (*i*) *Pennisetum clandestrium Hachst.*
(*b*) Morning glory — (*ii*) *Paspalum conjugatum Berg.*
(*c*) Kikuyu grass — (*iii*) *Salvia auriculata Aubl.*
(*d*) Water fern — (*iv*) *Ipomea* Spp.

568. **Weed** — **Scientific name**

(*a*) Hairy beggar ticks — (*i*) *Ageratum conyzoides* L.
(*b*) Barnyard grass — (*ii*) *Bidens pilosa* L.
(*c*) Tropic ageratum — (*iii*) *Echinochloa crusgalli* L. Beauv
(*d*) Pimpernel — (*iv*) *Anagallis arvensis* L.

569. **Weed** — **Scientific name**

(*a*) Quack grass — (*i*) *Argemone mtixicana.* L.
(*b*) Prickly poppy — (*ii*) *Digitaria sanguinaus.* L. Scop.
(*c*) Broom rape — (*iii*) *Agropyron repens* L. Beauv.
(*d*) Crab grass — (*iv*) *Orobanche cernua Loeft.*

570.

Weed	Scientific name
(*a*) Torepedograss	(*i*) *Borreria hispida* (L.) K. Schumb
(*b*) Black night shade	(*ii*) *Panicum repens* L.
(*c*) Wild oat	(*iii*) *Avena fatua* L.
(*d*) Button weed	(*iv*) *Solanum nigrum* L.

571.

Weed	Scientific name
(*a*) Lambsquarters	(*i*) *Mikania micrantha HBX.*
(*b*) Garden spurge	(*ii*) *Chemopodum albin*
(*c*) Thistle	(*iii*) *Euphorbiahitra* L
(*d*) Climbing hempvine	(*iv*) *Cirsium arvense* (L.) Scop.

572.

Weed	Scientific name
(*a*) Cox comb	(*i*) *Amaranthus viridis* L.
(*b*) Thatch grass	(*ii*) *Oxalis corymbosa* L.
(*c*) Wood sorrel	(*iii*) *Celosia argentina* L.
(*d*) Amaranth	(*iv*) *Imperata cylindrica* (L.) Beauv.

573.

Weed	Scientific name
(*a*) Water lettuce	(*i*) *Lemma minor*
(*b*) Common duck weed	(*ii*) *Pistia stratiotis*
(*c*) Fragrant water lilly	(*iii*) *Eichhornia crassipes Sol.*
(*d*) Water hyacinth	(*iv*) *Nymphata odorata*

574.

Weed	Scientific name
(*a*) Water nut	(*i*) *Hydrilla vesticillata Casp.*
(*b*) Hydrilla	(*ii*) *Luphar advena*
(*c*) Yellow water lilly	(*iii*) *Pontederia sogittaria*
(*d*) Arrow head	(*iv*) *Nelumbo lutea*

575. Match the disease with its causal organism:

Disease	Causal organism
(*a*) Blast of rice	(*i*) *Helminthosporium oryzae*
(*b*) Brown spot	(*ii*) *Erwinia carotovora var. zea*
(*c*) Bacterial stalk rot	(*iii*) *Cercospora sesami*
(*d*) Cercospora leaf spot	(*iv*) *Pyricularia oryzae*

576.

Disease	Causal organism
(*a*) Bacterial pustula	(*i*) *Glomerella cingulata*
(*b*) Twig blight	(*ii*) *Peronospora brassiceae*
(*c*) Seedling blight	(*iii*) *Xanthomonas phaseloli*
(*d*) Mustard downy mildew	(*iv*) *Phytophthora parasitica*

577.

Disease	Causal organism
(*a*) Bacterial blight	(*i*) *Xanthomonas malvacearum*
(*b*) *Scelerotium* rot	(*ii*) *Fungi and bacteria*
(*c*) Rosette	(*iii*) *Sclerotium rolfsii*
(*d*) Boll rot	(*iv*) *Virus*

578. **Disease** — **Causal organism**

(*a*) Red rot — (*i*) *Virus*

(*b*) Smut — (*ii*) *Collectrotrichum falatum*

(*c*) Wilt — (*iii*) *Ustilago scitaminea*

(*d*) Albino — (*iv*) *Cephalosporium sacchari*

579. **Disease** — **Causal organism**

(*a*) Bacterial blight — (*i*) *Erysiphe polygoni*

(*b*) Powdery mildew — (*ii*) *Collectotrichum truncatum*

(*c*) Pod blight — (*iii*) *Cercospora kikuchii*

(*d*) Purple seed stain — (*iv*) *Xanthomonas vignicola*

580. **Disease** — **Causal organism**

(*a*) White blister — (*i*) *Ustilago nuda trilici*

(*b*) Loose smut — (*ii*) *Gleacercospora sorghi*

(*c*) Sorghum Anthracnose — (*iii*) *Albugo candida*

(*d*) Zonate leaf spot — (*iv*) *Colletotrichum graminicola*

581. **Disease** — **Causal organism**

(*a*) Late blight of potato — (*i*) *Pseudomonas solanacearum*

(*b*) Early blight of potato — (*ii*) *Phytophithora infestans*

(*c*) Black scurf — (*iii*) *Alternaria solani*

(*d*) Bacterial wilt — (*iv*) *Rhizoctonia solani*

582. Match the following with each other suitably.

(*a*) Gall midge — (*i*) Soil borne

(*b*) Root rot — (*ii*) White fly

(*c*) Anthracnose — (*iii*) Onion leaf

(*d*) Yellow mosaic — (*iv*) Seed borne

583. Match the disease with the chemical used for its control.

(*a*) Bacterial bundle disease — (*i*) Brassicol

(*b*) Sclerotium rot — (*ii*) Zineb

(*c*) Anthracnose — (*iii*) Thiram

(*d*) Yellow mosaic — (*iv*) Mixture of metasystox and malathion

584. Match the weedicide/fungicide with its method of application.

(*a*) Basalin — (*i*) Pre-emergence application

(*b*) Nitrofen — (*ii*) Seed treatment

(*c*) Ceresan — (*iii*) Post-emergence

(*d*) 2, 4-D — (*iv*) Pre-plant incorporation

585. Match the disease with its causal organism

(*a*) *Tikka* — (*i*) *Tolyposporium penicillaria*

(*b*) Phyllody — (*ii*) *Cercospora*

(*c*) Ergot — (*iii*) *Mycoplasma*

(*d*) Pearlmillet smut — (*iv*) *Claviceps fusiformis*

586. Match the following crops with the scientific practices

(*a*) Gram	(*i*) Earthing
(*b*) Potato	(*ii*) Topping
(*c*) Sugarcane	(*iii*) Tying
(*d*) Tobacco	(*iv*) Nipping

587. Match the following with each other suitably.

(*a*) Maize	(*i*) Curing
(*b*) Groundnut	(*ii*) Batoning
(*c*) Tobacco	(*iii*) Tasseling
(*d*) Sunflower	(*iv*) Pegging

588.

Herbicides	**Chemical class**
(*a*) Diallate	(*i*) Ureas
(*b*) Metoxuron	(*ii*) Phenoxy fatty acid
(*c*) Nitrofen	(*iii*) Ethers
(*d*) 2,4-D	(*iv*) Thiocarbamates

589.

Herbicides	**Chemical class**
(*a*) Propanil	(*i*) Dipyridyls
(*b*) MCPA	(*ii*) Amides
(*c*) Tricamba	(*iii*) Phenoxy fatty acid
(*d*) Paraquat	(*iv*) Acids

590.

Herbicides	**Chemical class**
(*a*) Linuron	(*i*) Anilines
(*b*) Trifluralin	(*ii*) Triazines
(*c*) Diquat	(*iii*) Ureas
(*d*) Atrazine	(*iv*) Dipyridyls

591. Match the crop/weed with the scientific name.

Crop/weed	**Scientific name**
(*a*) Wild oat	(*i*) *Zea mays indurata*
(*b*) Flint corn	(*ii*) *Avena fatua*
(*c*) Kabuli gram	(*iii*) *Cicer arietinum*
(*d*) Chickpea	(*iv*) *Cicer /cabulium*

592.

Crop/weed	**Scientific name**
(*a*) Garden peas	(*i*) *Brassica compestris Var. yellow sarson*
(*b*) Indian colza	(*ii*) *Linum angustifolium*
(*c*) Wild flax	(*iii*) *Linum usitatissimum L.*
(*d*) Linseed	(*iv*) *Pisum sativum* Var. *hortense*

593. Match the following crops with their Scientific name

(*a*) American cotton	(*i*) *Corchorus capsularis*
(*b*) Sea- island cottons	(*ii*) *Corchorus olitorius*
(*c*) *Tossa* jute	(*iii*) *Gossypium hirsutum*
(*d*) White jute	(*iv*) *Gossypium barbadense*

594. Match the following crops with their product class.

(*a*) Sannhemp	(*i*) Forage crop
(*b*) *Guar*	(*ii*) Pulse crop
(*c*) Castor	(*iii*) Fibre crop
(*d*) Soybean	(*iv*) Oilseed crop

595. Match the following with each other suitably.

(*a*) Maize kernel	(*i*) Stalk
(*b*) Castor inflorescence	(*ii*) Caryopsis
(*c*) Cotton square	(*iii*) Raceme
(*d*) Cotton fibre	(*iv*) Braceteoles

596. Match the following terms with the process.

(*a*) Desuckeing	(*i*) Removal of moisture from tobacco
(*b*) Priming	(*ii*) Removal of fibre from jute stems
(*c*) Curing	(*iii*) Harvesting method of tobacco leaves
(*d*) Extraction	(*iv*) Removal of buds in the axil

597. Match the following with each other.

(*a*) Steeping	(*i*) Fuel
(*b*) Retting	(*ii*) Sugarcane
(*c*) Bagasse	(*iii*) Sunnhemp
(*d*) Molasses	(*iv*) Jak

598. Match the following crops with their sowing period.

(*a*) Autumn sugarcane	(*i*) February-March
(*b*) *Adsali* sugarcane	(*ii*) July
(*c*) Spring sugarcane	(*iii*) October
(*d*) Sugarbeet	(*iv*) October-November

599. Match the following with each other.

(*a*) Lenticeles	(*i*) Red rusty spots
(*b*) Tuber	(*ii*) Respiratory structure
(*c*) Sugarbeet	(*iii*) Underground stem
(*d*) Spangles	(*iv*) Root

600. Match the following crop with the family.

Crop	**Family.**
(*a*) *Phalaris minor*	(*i*) Compositae
(*b*) Safflower	(*ii*) Leguminoceae
(*c*) Jute	(*iii*) Gramineae
(*d*) Pea	(*iv*) Tiliaceae

601.

Crop	**Family.**
(*a*) Wheat	(*i*) Gramineae
(*b*) Blackgram	(*ii*) Cruciferae
(*c*) Sesamum	(*iii*) Pedaliaceae
(*d*) Mustard	(*iv*) Leguminoceae

602. Match the crop with its critical period for weed control.

(*a*) Rice (upland)	(*i*) 25-30 days after sowing
(*b*) Rice (Transplanted)	(*ii*) 15-25 days after sowing
(*c*) Groundnut	(*iii*) 15-20 days after sowing
(*d*) Urdbean	(*iv*) 20-25 days after sowing

603. Match the following:

(*a*) Leaf area index	(*i*) Increase in plant dry weight/unit dry weight/unit time
(*b*) Crop growth rate	(*ii*) Increase in plant weight/unit leaf area/unit time
(*c*) Relative growth rate	(*iii*) Leaf area/unit land area
(*d*) Net assimilation rate	(*iv*) Increase in plant dry weight/unit time

604. Match the following soils with their chemical properties

(*a*) Saline soil	(*i*) $EC < 4\ dsm^{-1}$, ESP 15%, $pH > 8.5$
(*b*) Non-saline alkali soil	(*ii*) $pH < 7.0$
(*c*) Saline-alkali soil	(*iii*) $EC > 4\ dsm^{-1}$, $ESP < 15\%$, $pH < 8.5$
(*d*) Acid soil	(*iv*) $EC > 4\ dsm^{-1}$, $ESP > 15\%$, $pH > 8.5$

605. Match the residence time of water with the time period required.

(*a*) Rivers	(*i*) 2-50 weeks
(*b*) Soil	(*ii*) 3-600 years
(*c*) Ground water	(*iii*) 2-weeks
(*d*) Oceans	(*iv*) 1-10,000 years

606. Match the estimated annual average precipitation (cm) with the continents.

(*a*) Indian	(*i*) 69
(*b*) African	(*ii*) 60
(*c*) Asia	(*iii*) 133
(*d*) Pacific	(*iv*) 117

607. Match the estimated annual evaporation (cm) with the continents wherein it occurs.

(*a*) Indian	(*i*) 126
(*b*) Europe	(*ii*) 132
(*c*) Altantic	(*iii*) 124
(*d*) Global (world)	(*iv*) 39

608. Match the estimated annual average runoff (cm) with the continents of its occurrence.

(*a*) South America	(*i*) 25
(*b*) India	(*ii*) 93
(*c*) Asia	(*iii*) 8
(*d*) Europe	(*iv*) 29

609. Match the land use with the monthly evapotranspiration (mm).

(*a*) Grassland	(*i*) 36
(*b*) Farmland, dry	(*ii*) 40
(*c*) Farmland, wet	(*iii*) 31
(*d*) Deciduous forest	(*iv*) 43

610. Match the threshold temperature with the crops given below.

(*a*) 4°C (*i*) Potato

(*b*) 7°C (*ii*) Cotton

(*c*) 17-18°C (*iii*) Oats

(*d*) 6°C (*iv*) Peas

611. Match the appropriate effects of urbanization on climatic elements as compared with rural environment

(*a*) Gaseous pollution (*i*) 10 times more

(*b*) Solid particle pollutants (*ii*) 5-20% more

(*c*) Ultraviolet radiation (winter) (*iii*) 5-25 times more

(*d*) Calms (*iv*) 30% less

612. Match the estimated kinetic energy (ergs) with atmospheric motion system.

(*a*) 10^{22} (*i*) Extratropical cyclone

(*b*) 10^{23} (*ii*) Small thunderstorm (life)

(*c*) 10^{25} (*iii*) Large thunderstorm (life)

(*d*) 10^{26} (*iv*) Hurricane (instantaneous)

613. Find out the expected growth inhibition E (%) by combination, if the growth inhibition (x) by herbicide $A = 30$, and growth inhibition (y in %) by herbicide B = 50

According to Growing (1960), $E = x + y\left(\frac{100 - x}{100}\right)$

$$E = 30 + 50\left(\frac{100 - 30}{100}\right)$$

$$E = 30 + 50\left(\frac{100 - 30}{100}\right)$$

This can also bse computed by Limpel *et al.* (1962) formula which is ________

$$E = x + y - \frac{xy}{100}$$

$$= 30 + 50 - \frac{30 \times 50}{100}$$

Colby (1967) suggest to convert the data on % inhibition of control to compute combination response as ________.

$$E_1 = \frac{X_1 Y_1}{100}$$

where, E_1 = Expected dry weight as % of total

X_1 and Y_1 = Dry weights as obtained from application of herbicides A (70) and B (50) alone,

Therefore, $E_1 = \frac{70 \times 50}{100} = 35\%$ of control

and ________.

614. Determine the spray volume per hectare, if 80 meters are covered while spraying solution of 3.6 liters with a swath width of 1 meter.

Since, $$\text{Volume pplied / ha} = \frac{\text{Water used (litres)} \times 10{,}000}{\text{Distance covered (meters)} \times \text{Width of spray swath (meters)}}$$

Therefore, $\frac{3.6 \times 10{,}000}{80 \times 1} = \frac{36000}{80} =$ ________.

615. Compute the total product required to apply diuron at 2.0 kg a.i./ha, when the commerical formulation contains 80 per cent active ingredient.

Since, $$\text{Total (gross) product} = \frac{\text{Rate of a.i. kg / ha} \times 100}{\text{Active ingredient (\%)}}$$

Therefore, $= \frac{2.0 \times 100}{80}$

616. If spraying is done at spray volume of 500 liters per hectare while covering a swath of 1 meter wide and maintaining a walking speed of 1 km per hour, compute the pump capacity

Since, Pump capacity (liters/min.)

$$= \frac{\text{Spray vol. (l / ha)} \times \text{swath width (m)} \times \text{walking speed (km / hr)} \times \text{metres / km}}{\text{metres / ha} \times \text{minutes / hr}}$$

Therefore, $= \frac{500 \times 1.0 \times 1000 \times 1}{1000 \times 60}$

Pump capacity = ________

617. Compute the area covered by a person walking at 2 km/hr covering a swath of 0.6 m wide in one go with a sprayer.

Since, $$\text{Area (hectare) / hr} = \frac{\text{Walking speed (km / ha)} \times \text{m / km} \times \text{spray width (m)}}{\text{m / ha}}$$

$$= \frac{2 \times 1000 \times 0.6}{10{,}000} = \frac{1.2}{10} = \text{\_\_\_\_\_\_\_\_}$$

IV. Tick mark (✓) the correct answer :

618. The volume of water required to spray one hectare of land would be ________ liters if the distance sprayed, width of spray and water required to refill are 100 m, 1.6 m and 8 liters, respectively.

(*a*) 325 (*b*) 375

(*c*) 385 (*d*) 415

619. If the volume of tank is 250 liters and rate of spray per hectare is 170 -liters, the area sprayed by a full tank would be ________.

(*a*) 1.47 (*b*) 1.52
(*c*) 1.43 (*d*) 1.54

620. The volume of alachlor (50%) needed for spraying 1 hectare land area of urdbean at the rate of 0.75 litre a.i./ha would be ________.

(*a*) 1.00 (*b*) 1.25
(*c*) 1.50 (*d*) 1.75

621. The quantity of simazine to spray one hectare maize would be ________ kg wettable powder ha if the rate of application and active ingredient of simazine are 2.5 kg a.i./ha and 80%, respectively.

(*a*) 2.15 (*b*) 3.00
(*c*) 3.02 (*d*) 3.13

622. If 30 kg of 2, 4-D is mixed with 2000 litre of water, the concentration of solution in ppm will be ________.

(*a*) 15,000 (*b*) 20,000
(*c*) 25,000 (*d*) 30,000

623. The depth of irrigation would be ________ cm, if the Persian wheel with an average discharge of 280 liters/minute irrigates 1 hectare wheat crop in 40 hours.

(*a*) 6.72 (*b*) 6.92
(*c*) 6.98 (*d*) 7.10

624. If the net amount of irrigation is 7 cm and the field efficiency is 70 per cent, the gross amount of water to be applied to the field is ________ cm.

(*a*) 10.00 (*b*) 10.62
(*c*) 10.73 (*d*) 10.90

625. A tube well having a capacity of 4000 liters/hr operates for 20 hours each day during the irrigation season. The area commanded by it would be ________ ha if the irrigation interval is 20 days and depth of irrigation is 7 cm.

(*a*) 20.86 (*b*) 21.86
(*c*) 22.86 (*d*) 23.86

626. A wheat crop evaporated 40 cm water during whole period and yielded 4.0 t/ha of grain. The water use efficiency would be ________ kg/ha-mm

(*a*) 8 (*b*) 10
(*c*) 12 (*d*) 14

Do You Know That

1. The first synthetic organic chemical introduced in 1932 for selective weed control in crops was 2-methyl-4, 6-dinitrophenol.
2. Estimates have shown that soybean and alfalfa might fix as much as 500 kgN per hectare.
3. Jethro Tull (1674-1741) invented a horse-hoe and a seed-drill for row crops with a view to carry out interculture operations effectively.
4. In 1855, sulphuric acid in Germany was used to control weeds in cereals and onions.
5. The first use of sound for weed control was patented in 1895.
6. Mercurous chloride was used as a fungicide and for seed treatment in 1755.
7. About 3,000 of the 350,000 + recognized plant species are or have been cultivated and one might assume that the rest of them are weeds.
8. National Seeds Corporation (NSC) was established in 1963.
9. Water use efficiency is the highest in case of Drip Irrigation.
10. Water hyacinth (*Electronia crassipes*), a troublesome aquatic weed constitutes an economically viable and environmentally sound proposition to mitigate energy crisis.
11. Water requirement of irrigated wetland rice is about 1500 mm.

KEY

(1) Plants
(2) Grow it and eat it
(3) Self sufficient
(4) Modem agriculture
(5) Agribusiness
(6) Agronomy
(7) Cereal
(8) Ontogenic
(9) Real value
(10) Temperature zones
(11) Parasitic
(12) Viable seeds
(13) Dibbling
(14) Drilling
(15) Nursery
(16) Pore space per cent
(17) Granules
(18) Primary tillage
(19) Drought
(20) Agricultural
(21) Multi-storeyed
(22) Simulatneously
(23) Identity
(24) Relative Reproductive Rate or RRR
(25) Number
(26) 200
(27) Total number
(28) Country
(29) Active ingredient, "ai"
(30) Chemical stability
(31) Wettable powder, 'wp'
(32) Volume phase (spray carrier)
(33) Fumigants
(34) Herbicide glove
(35) Atomised
(36) Wild oats
(37) Certification
(38) Variety
(39) Breeder's seed
(40) Seeds Act, 1966
(41) Certified seed
(42) Market
(43) North American
(44) Quality of seed
(45) Central seed
(46) Segregation
(47) Rice-paddies
(48) Nucleus seed
(49) Homozygous
(50) Composites and synthetics (varieties)
(51) Flowering
(52) Orange seed
(53) Sleeve-type trier/stick trier
(54) Other seeds
(55) *Lactua sativa*
(56) Seed vigour
(57) Degenerative changes
(58) Summation or speed of germination = $\sum(n/t)$
(59) After sowing
(60) Germination
(61) Leakage
(62) Tetrazolium
(63) Controlled Deterioration or CD

(64) Phytochrome
(65) Hot water treatment
(66) Anthocyanin
(67) True
(68) True
(69) True
(70) False
(71) True
(72) False
(73) False
(74) True
(75) True
(76) False
(77) True
(78) False
(79) False
(80) True
(81) True
(82) True
(83) False
(84) True
(85) True
(86) False
(87) True
(88) True
(89) True
(90) True
(91) False
(92) False
(93) False
(94) True
(95) True
(96) False
(97) True
(98) True
(99) False
(100) True
(101) True
(102) True
(103) False
(104) False
(105) False
(106) True
(107) True
(108) True
(109) False
(110) False
(111) True
(112) False
(113) True
(114) False
(115) True
(116) True
(117) True
(118) False
(119) False
(120) False
(121) True
(122) True
(123) True
(124) True
(125) True
(126) True
(127) False
(128) False
(129) True
(130) True
(131) False
(132) False
(133) False
(134) True
(135) False
(136) True
(137) True.
(138) False
(139) True
(140) True
(141) Imported wheat
(142) Host specificity
(143) *Cuscuta* spp. or dodder
(144) Nitrophenols
(145) 2.4-D
(146) Ineffective
(147) Marth and Mitchell
(148) Field weed control
(149) Herbicidal selectivity
(150) *Panicum miliaceum* (*kutki*)
(151) 2-8
(152) Apoplastically or symplastically
(153) Triazine
(154) Faster
(155) Phloem
(156) Rain
(157) Surfactants
(158) Lipophilic
(159) Waxy cuticle/ Lipoidal part
(160) Acropettaly
(161) Cationic and polar
(162) Photophosphorylation
(163) Sulphahydryl
(164) Nitrites
(165) Hill reaction
(166) Hydroxylation
(167) Atrazine glutathione
(168) POJ 2878
(169) Multiple cropping
(170) Soil
(171) Additive effect
(172) Solar constant
(173) Less than 1 mm to 5 mm
(174) Adiabatic
(175) Waterspouts
(176) Organic residues.
(177) Acclimation
(178) 20-25
(179) Early
(180) 2-3
(181) Increased
(182) Alkaline
(183) Tillering
(184) Dwarf variety
(185) Dwarf
(186) 5 cm

(187) Heading	(188) Warm	(189) 30°C
(190) 15.5°C	(191) Flowering	(192) Day length
(193) (*b*)	(194) (*a*)	(195) (*d*)
(196) (*c*)	(197) (*c*)	(198) (*c*)
(199) (*d*)	(200) (*b*)	(201) (*b*)
(202) (*d*)	(203) (*c*)	(204) (*a*)
(205) (*b*)	(206) (*d*)	(207) (*c*)
(208) (*b*)	(209) (*a*)	(210) (*c*)
(211) (*a*)	(212) (*b*)	(213) (*d*)
(214) (*c*)	(215) (*c*)	(216) (*c*)
(217) (*d*)	(218) (*b*)	(219) (*d*)
(220) (*c*)	(221) (*d*)	(222) (*c*)
(223) (*b*)	(224) (*c*)	(225) (*c*)
(226) (*b*)	(227) (*d*)	(228) (*a*)
(229) (*b*)	(230) (*b*)	(231) (*c*)
(232) (*c*)	(233) (*b*)	(234) (*d*)
(235) (*c*)	(236) (*d*)	(237) (*c*)
(238) (*c*)	(239) (*d*)	(240) (*d*)
(241) (*c*)	(242) (*b*)	(243) (*c*)
(244) (*a*)	(245) (*b*)	(246) (*d*)
(247) (*a*)	(248) (*a*)	(249) (*b*)
(250) (*a*)	(251) (*a*)	(252) (*a*)
(253) (*a*)	(254) (*b*)	(255) (*a*)
(256) (*d*)	(257) (*d*)	(258) (*b*)
(259) (*b*)	(260) (*a*)	(261) (*b*)
(262) (*a*)	(263) (*a*)	(264) (*c*)
(265) (*b*)	(266) (*a*)	(267) (*d*)
(268) (*b*)	(269) (*b*)	(270) (*b*)
(271) (*b*)	(272) (*a*)	(273) (*a*)
(274) (*b*)	(275) (*d*)	(276) (*a*)
(277) (*a*)	(278) (*b*)	(279) (*a*)
(280) (*d*)	(281) (*b*)	(282) (*a*)
(283) (*a*)	(284) (*d*)	(285) (*a*)
(286) (*b*)	(287) (*a*)	(288) (*c*)
(289) (*c*)	(290) (*d*)	(291) (*a*)
(292) (*a*)	(293) (*c*)	(294) (*a*)
(295) (*c*)	(296) (*a*)	(297) (*a*)
(298) (*c*)	(299) (*a*)	(300) (*a*)
(301) (*a*)	(302) (*a*)	(303) (*d*)
(304) (*a*)	(305) (*c*)	(306) (*a*)
(307) (*d*)	(308) (*d*)	(309) (*a*)
(310) (*c*)	(311) (*d*)	(312) (*a*)

(313) (c) (314) (a) (315) (b)
(316) (a) (317) (d) (318) (a)
(319) (a) (320) (a) (321) (a)
(322) (b) (323) (d) (324) (a)
(325) (a) (326) (b) (327) (a)
(328) (b) (329) (a) (330) (c)
(331) (a) (332) (b) (333) (a)
(334) (d) (335) (b) (336) (a)
(337) (c) (338) (b) (339) (a)
(340) (d) (341) (c) (342) (a)
(343) (d) (344) (c) (345) (b)
(346) (b) (347) (c) (348) (a)
(349) (a) (350) (c) (351) (b)
(352) (c) (353) (a) (354) (a)
(355) (a) (356) (a) (357) (a)
(358) (a) (359) (b) (360) (c)
(361) (b) (362) (a) (363) (b)
(364) (c) (365) (d) (366) (a)
(367) (c) (368) (c) (369) (c)
(370) (d) (371) (b) (372) (b)
(373) (b) (374) (c) (375) (c)
(376) (d) (377) (b) (378) (a)
(379) (a) (380) (d) (381) (d)
(382) (d) (383) (b) (384) (a)
(385) (d) (386) (b) (387) (a)
(388) (d) (389) (c) (390) (c)
(391) (d) (392) (c) (393) (b)
(394) (b) (395) (d) (396) (a)
(397) (a) (398) (d) (399) (a)
(400) (c) (401) (b) (402) (c)
(403) (d) (404) (b) (405) (c)
(406) (b) (407) (c) (408) (b)
(409) (b) (410) (b) (411) (a)
(412) (c) (413) (a) (414) (b)
(415) (c) (416) (b) (417) (b)
(418) (d) (419) (d) (420) (a)
(421) (c) (422) (b) (423) (c)
(424) (d) (425) (d) (426) (c)
(427) (c) (428) (a) (429) (d)
(430) (b) (431) (b) (432) (c)
(433) (b) (434) (c) (435) (b)
(436) (c) (437) (b) (438) (a)

(439) (*b*)	(440) (*c*)	(441) (*a*)	
(442) (*b*)	(443) (*a*)	(444) (*d*)	
(445) (*a*)	(446) (*b*)	(447) (*c*)	
(448) (*b*)	(449) (*d*)	(450) (*c*)	
(451) (*b*)	(452) (*b*)	(453) (*a*)	
(454) (*d*)	(455) (*a*)	(456) (*a*)	
(457) (*c*)	(458) (*a*)	(459) (*b*)	
(460) (*b*)	(461) (*a*)	(462) (*d*)	
(463) (*c*)	(464) (*b*)	(465) (*a*)	
(466) (*c*)	(467) (*a*)	(468) (*b*)	
(469) (*a*)	(470) (*b*)	(471) (*a*)	
(472) (*d*)	(473) (*b*)	(474) (*c*)	
(475) (*c*)	(476) (*d*)	(477) (*b*)	
(478) (*d*)	(479) (*a*)	(480) (*c*)	
(481) (*b*)	(482) (*b*)	(483) (*d*)	
(484) (*c*)	(485) (*a*)	(486) (*a*)	
(487) (*c*)	(488) (*b*)		
(489) (*a*)-(*iii*)	(*b*)-(*i*)	(*c*)-(*ii*)	(*d*)-(*iv*)
(490) (*a*)-(*ii*)	(*b*)-(*iii*)	(*c*)-(*iv*)	(*d*)-(*i*)
(491) (*a*)-(*iii*)	(*b*)-(*iv*)	(*c*)-(*i*)	(*d*)-(*ii*)
(492) (*a*)-(*iv*)	(*b*)-(*i*)	(*c*)-(*ii*)	(*d*)-(*iii*)
(493) (*a*)-(*iii*)	(*b*)-(*ii*)	(*c*)-(*iv*)	(*d*)-(*i*)
(494) (*a*)-(*iii*)	(*b*)-(*iv*)	(*c*)-(*i*)	(*d*)-(*ii*)
(495) (*a*)-(*ii*)	(*b*)-(*iv*)	(*c*)-(*i*)	(*d*)-(*iii*)
(496) (*a*)-(*iii*)	(*b*)-(*i*)	(*c*)-(*iv*)	(*d*)-(*ii*)
(497) (*a*)-(*iv*)	(*b*)-(*iii*)	(*c*)-(*i*)	(*d*)-(*ii*)
(498) (*a*)-(*ii*)	(*b*)-(*iii*)	(*c*)-(*iv*)	(*d*)-(*i*)
(499) (*a*)-(*iv*)	(*b*)-(*ii*)	(*c*)-(*i*)	(*d*)-(*iii*)
(500) (*a*)-(*iii*)	(*b*)-(*i*)	(*c*)-(*iv*)	(*d*)-(*ii*)
(501) (*a*)-(*iv*)	(*b*)-(*i*)	(*c*)-(*ii*)	(*d*)-(*iii*)
(502) (*a*)-(*ii*)	(*b*)-(*iii*)	(*c*)-(*i*)	(*d*)-(*iv*)
(503) (*a*)-(*iii*)	(*b*)-(*iv*)	(*c*)-(*i*)	(*d*)-(*ii*)
(504) (*a*)-(*iii*)	(*b*)-(*ii*)	(*c*)-(*iv*)	(*d*)-(*i*)
(505) (*a*)-(*ii*)	(*b*)-(*i*)	(*c*)-(*iv*)	(*d*)-(*iii*)
(506) (*a*)-(*iv*)	(*b*)-(*ii*)	(*c*)-(*i*)	(*d*)-(*iii*)
(507) (*a*)-(*ii*)	(*b*)-(*iii*)	(*c*)-(*iv*)	(*d*)-(*i*)
(508) (*a*)-(*ii*)	(*b*)-(*i*)	(*c*)-(*iv*)	(*d*)-(*iii*)
(509) (*a*)-(*iv*)	(*b*)-(*i*)	(*c*)-(*ii*)	(*d*)-(*iii*)
(510) (*a*)-(*ii*)	(*b*)-(*iii*)	(*c*)-(*iv*)	(*d*)-(*i*)
(511) (*a*)-(*iv*)	(*b*)-(*i*)	(*c*)-(*ii*)	(*d*)-(*iii*)
(512) (*a*)-(*iii*)	(*b*)-(*i*)	(*c*)-(*iv*)	(*d*)-(*ii*)
(513) (*a*)-(*ii*)	(*b*)-(*iii*)	(*c*)-(*iv*)	(*d*)-(*i*)

(514) (*a*)-(*iv*) (*b*)-(*i*) (*c*)-(*iii*) (*d*)-(*ii*)

(515) (*a*)-(*iii*) (*b*)-(*i*) (*c*)-(*iv*) (*d*)-(*ii*)

(516) (*a*)-(*iv*) (*b*)-(*i*) (*c*)-(*ii*) (*d*)-(*iii*)

(517) (*a*)-(*iii*) (*b*)-(*i*) (*c*)-(*iv*) (*d*)-(*ii*)

(518) (*a*)-(*ii*) (*b*)-(*iii*) (*c*)-(*iv*) (*d*)-(*i*)

(519) (*a*)-(*iii*) (*b*)-(*i*) (*c*)-(*iv*) (*d*)-(*ii*)

(520) (*a*)-(*iv*) (*b*)-(*i*) (*c*)-(*ii*) (*d*)-(*iii*)

(521) (*a*)-(*iv*) (*b* (*iii*) (*c*)-(*i*) (*d*)-(*ii*)

(522) (*a*)-(*iii*) (*b*)-(*i*) (*c*)-(*iv*) (*d*)-(il)

(523) (*a*)-(*iv*) (*b*)-(*ii*) (*c*)-(*i*) (*d*)-(*iii*)

(524) (*a*)-(*iii*) (*b*)-(*i*) (*c*)-(*iv*) (*d*)-(*ii*)

(525) (*a*)-(*iii*) (*b*)-(*iv*) (*c*)-(*ii*) (*d*)-(*i*)

(526) (*a*)-(*ii*) (*b*)-(*iii*) (*c*)-(*iv*) (*d*)-(*i*)

(527) (*a*)-(*iii*) (*b*)-(*i*) (*c*)-(*iv*) (*d*)-(*ii*)

(528) (*a*)-(*iv*) (*b*)-(*i*) (*c*)-(*ii*) (*d*)-(*iii*)

(529) (*a*)-(*ii*) (*b*)-(*iv*) (*c*)-(*i*) (*d*)-(*iii*)

(530) (*a*)-(*ii*) (*b*)-(*i*) (*c*)-(*iv*) (*d*)-(*iii*)

(531) (*a*)-(*iv*) (*b*)-(*i*) (*c*)-(*ii*) (*d*)-(*iii*)

(532) (*a*)-(*iv*) (*b*)-(*iii*) (*c*)-(*i*) (*d*)-(*ii*)

(533) (*a*)-(*iv*) (*b*)-(*ii*) (*c*)-(*i*) (*d*)-(*iii*)

(534) (*a*)-(*iii*) (*b*)-(*i*) (*c*)-(*iv*) (*d*)-(*ii*)

(535) (*a*)-(*ii*) (*b*)-(*iii*) (*c*)-(*iv*) (*d*)-(*i*)

(536) (*a*)-(*iv*) (*b*)-(*i*) (*c*)-(*iii*) (*d*-(*ii*)

(537) (*a*)-(*ii*) (*b*)-(*iii*) (*c*)-(*iv*) (*d*)-(*i*)

(538) (*a*)-(*ii*) (*b*)-(*iv*) (*c*)-(*iii*) (*d*)-(*i*)

(539) (*a*)-(*iii*) (*b*)-(*i*) (*c*)-(*ii*) (*d*)-(*iv*)

(540) (*a*)-(*ii*) (*b*)-(*iv*) (*c*)-(*i*) (*d*)-(*iii*)

(541) (*a*)-(*iii*) (*b*)-(*iv*) (*c*)-(*ii*) (*d*)-(*i*)

(542) (*a*)-(*i*) (*b*)-(*iii*) (*c*)-(*iv*) (*d*)-(*ii*)

(543) (*a*)-(*ii*) (*b*)-(*i*) (*c*)-(*iv*) (*d*)-(*iii*)

(544) (*a*)-(*iii*) (*b*)-(*i*) (*c*)-(*iv*) (*d*)-(*ii*)

(545) (*a*)-(*iv*) (*b*)-(*iii*) (*c*)-(*i*) (*d*)-(*ii*)

(546) (*a*)-(*iii*) (*b*)-(*ii*) (*c*)-(*iv*) (*d*)-(*i*)

(547) (*a*)-(*iii*) (*b*)-(*i*) (*c*)-(*iv*) (*d*)-(*ii*)

(548) (*a*)-(*ii*) (*b*)-(*iv*) (*c*)-(*i*) (*d*)-(*iii*)

(549) (*a*)-(*ii*) (*b*)-(*iv*) (*c*)-(*i*) (*d*)-(*iii*)

(550) (*a*)-(*iv*) (*b*)-(*i*) (*c*)-(*i*) (*d*)-(*iii*)

(551) (*a*)-(*ii*) (*b*)-(*iv*) (*c*)-(*i*) (*d*)-(*iii*)

(552) (*a*)-(*iv*) (*b*)-(*iii*) (*c*)-(*i*) (*d*)-(*ii*)

(553) (*a*)-(*iv*) (*b*)-(*i*) (*c*)-(*ii*) (*d*)-(*iii*)

(554) (*a*)-(*ii*) (*b*)-(*iv*) (*c*)-(*i*) (*d*)-(iii)

(555) (*a*)-(*iii*) (*b*)-(*i*) (*c*)-(*iv*) (*d*)-(*ii*)

(556) (*a*)-(*ii*) (*b*)-(*iv*) (*c*)-(*iii*) (*d*)-(*i*)

(557) (a)-(iv) (b)-(i) (c)-(ii) (d)-(iii)
(558) (a)-(ii) (b)-(iii) (c)-(iv) (d)-(i)
(559) (a)-(iii) (b)-(i) (c)-(iv) (d)-(ii)
(560) (a)-(ii) (b)-(iv) (c)-(i) (d)-(iii)
(561) (a)-(iii) (b)-(ii) (c)-(i) (d)-(iv)
(562) (a)-(iii) (b)-(i) (c)-(iv) (d)-(ii)
(563) (a)-(iv) (b)-(ii) (c)-(i) (d)-(iii)
(564) (a)-(iii) (b)-(i) (c)-(iv) (d)-(ii)
(565) (a)-(iii) (b)-(i) (c)-(ii) (d)-(iv)
(566) (a)-(iv) (b)-(i) (c)-(ii) (d)-(iii)
(567) (a)-(ii) (b)-(iv) (c)-(i) (d)-(iii)
(568) (a)-(ii) (b)-(iii) (c)-(i) (d)-(iv)
(569) (a)-(iii) (b)-(i) (c)-(iv) (d)-(ii)
(570) (a)-(ii) (b)-(iv) (c)-(iii) (d)-(i)
(571) (a)-(ii) (b)-(iii) (c)-(iv) (d)-(i)
(572) (a)-(iii) (b)-(iv) (c)-(ii) (d)-(i)
(573) (a)-(ii) (b)-(i) (c)-(iv) (d)-(iii)
(574) (a)-(iv) (b)-(i) (c)-(ii) (d)-(iii)
(575) (a)-(iv) (b)-(i) (c)-(ii) (d)-(iii)
(576) (a)-(iii) (b)-(i) (c)-(iv) (d)-(ii)
(577) (a)-(i) (b)-(iii) (c)-(iv) (d)-(ii)
(578) (a)-(ii) (b)-(iii) (c)-(iv) (d)-(i)
(579) (a)-(iv) (b)-(i) (c)-(ii) (d)-(iii)
(580) (a)-(iii) (b)-(i) (c)-(iv) (d)-(ii)
(581) (a)-(ii) (b)-(iii) (c)-(iv) (d)-(i)
(582) (a)-(iii) (b)-(i) (c)-(iv) (d)-(iii)
(583) (a)-(iii) (b)-(i) (c)-(ii) (d)-(iv)
(584) (a)-(iv) (b)-(i) (c)-(ii) (d)-(iii)
(585) (a)-(ii) (b)-(iii) (c)-(iv) (d)-(i)
(586) (a)-(iv) (b)-(i) (c)-(iii) (d)-(ii)
(587) (a)-(iii) (b)-(iv) (c)-(i) (d)-(ii)
(588) (a)-(iv) (b)-(i) (c)-(iii) (d)-(ii)
(589) (a)-(ii) (b)-(iii) (c)-(iv) (d)-(i)
(590) (a)-(iii) (b)-(i) (c)-(iv) (d)-(ii)
(591) (a)-(ii) (b)-(i) (c)-(iv) (d)-(iii)
(592) (a)-(iv) (b)-(i) (c)-(ii) (d)-(iii)
(593) (a)-(iii) (b)-(iv) (c)-(ii) (d)-(i)
(594) (a)-(iii) (b)-(i) (c)-(iv) (d)-(ii)
(595) (a)-(ii) (b-(iii) (c)-(iv) (d)-(i)
(596) (a)-(iv) (b)-(iii) (c)-(i) (d)-(ii)
(597) (a)-(iv) (b)-(iii) (c)-(i) (d)-(ii)
(598) (a)-(iii) (b)-(ii) (c-(i) (d)-(iv)
(599) (a)-(ii) (b)-(iii) (c)-(iv) (d)-(i)

(600) (*a*)-(*iii*)	(*b*)-(i)	(*c*)-(*iv*)	(*d*)-(*ii*)
(601) (*a*)-(i)	(*b*)-(*iv*)	(*c*)-(*iii*)	(*d*)-(*ii*)
(602) (*a*)-(*iii*)	(*b*)-(*i*)	(*c*)-(*iv*)	(*d*)-(*iv*)
(603) (*a*)-(*iii*)	(*b*)-(*iv*)	(*c*)-(*i*)	(*d*)-(*iv*)
(604) (*a*)-(*iii*)	(*b*)-(*i*)	(*c*)-(*iv*)	(*d*)-(*ii*)
(605) (*a*)-(*iii*)	(*b*)-(*i*)	(*c*)-(*iv*)	(*d*)-(*ii*)
(606) (*a*)-(*iv*)	(*b*)-(*i*)	(*c*)-(*ii*)	(*d*)-(*iii*)
(607) (*a*)-(*ii*)	(*b*)-(*iv*)	(*c*)-(*iii*)	(*d*)-(*i*)
(608) (*a*)-(*ii*)	(*b*)-(*iii*)	(*c*)-(*iv*)	(*d*)-(*i*)
(609) (*a*)-(*iii*)	(*b*)-(*i*)	(*c*)-(*iv*)	(*d*)-(*ii*)
(610) (*a*)-(*iv*)	(*b*)-(*i*)	(*c*)-(*ii*)	(*d*)-(*iii*)
(611) (*a*)-(*iii*)	(*b*)-(*i*)	(*c*)-(*iv*)	(*d*)-(*ii*)
(612) (*a*)-(*ii*)	(*b*)-(*iii*)	(*c*)-(*iv*)	(*d*)-(*i*)
(613) 65 per cent	(6s14) 450 Liters	(615) 2.5 kg/ha	
(616) 0.83 Liters/minute	(617) 0.12 ha/hr	(618) (*b*)	(619) (*a*)
(620) (*c*)	(621) (*d*)	(622) (*a*)	(623) (*a*)
(624) (*a*)	(625) (*c*)	(626) (*b*)	

SECTION 8

OLERICULTURE, HORTICULTURE AND FLORICULTURE

I. Fill up the blanks :

1. All vitamins are found in small or large quantities in common ________ crops.
2. Vitamin A is abundantly found in ________ vegetables.
3. Deficiency of vitamin A causes ________ and some eye diseases like corneal ulcer, conjunctivitis and neurophthalmia.
4. Onion bulbs and green onions are good source of vitamin ________.
5. ________ vegetables contain less of vitamin C than fresh ones.
6. Vitamin D regulates the use of calcium and ________ by the body in the process of growth of bones and teeth.
7. Vitamin E has an important effect on generative functions and promotes ________.
8. Besides vitamins, the ________ needs at least ten minerals.
9. Phosphorus can be had from milk and vegetables supply calcium and ________.
10. Vegetable *viz.*, fenugreek, spinach and mountain spinach are rich in ________.
11. Carrot, bitter gourd, onion and tomato comprise good source of ________.
12. Onion, okra,. asparagus and summer squash supply ________.
13. Fibrous framework of leaves, stems and even bulbs, tubers and roots of vegetables yields ________ which satisfies appetite and prevents constipation.
14. Dieticians recommend inclusion of ________ grammes of vegetables in our daily diet.
15. Vegetable growing is generally more lucrative than any other type of ________.
16. Cauliflower is sensitive to high ________.
17. Cauliflower has a high requirement of boron and ________.
18. June-July sown cauliflower should be transplanted in new beds before their final transplantation into the ________.
19. The defects noticed in cauliflower are premature heading, ________ of plants and production of under-sized heads.
20. In Nasik division of Maharashtra, Ootacamund region of Tamil Nadu and parts of Kerala cabbage is grown during ________ also.
21. Cabbage is heavy feeder of nitrogen and ________.
22. Ganga, Kaveri and Yamuna are ________ of cabbage.

23. Heavy irrigation to cabbage after development of heads causes ________ within 24 hours.
24. Premature seeding and/or failure of the leaves to form a ________ are common defects of early cabbage.
25. In ________ method of seed production in cabbage, selected true to type fully matured plants are uprooted during November-December and are reset in new beds
26. The commercial production of cabbage is done by ________ method.
27. Knolkhol (*Brassica oleracea* var.________, is little known in India.
28. White Vienna, Purple Vienna and King of North are the cultivars of ________.
29. The seed rate of knolkhol to raise seedlings for one hectare is ________ grammes
30. Pusa Early Bunching and Kasuri Selection are the cultivars of ________.
31. Although a ripe tomato is 94 per cent water, it is a good source of vitamin ________ and excellent source of vitamin C.
32. Immature tomato blossoms drop rapidly during ________ due to increased transpiration.
33. Cracking of the skin of tomato-fruits has been associated with the deficiency of ________.
34. The tomato varieties can be broadly classified into ________ categories.
35. ________ and training of tomato plants is a common practice in certain parts of USA.
36. Spraying of tomato plants at ________ using 25 and 50 ppm of GA_3 improves the quality of fruits.
37. In early varieties of tomatoes concentric cracking ________ is more common owing to their light, open foliage.
38. ________ of tomatoes is caused by *Stemphylian solani* Weber and *Alternaria solani* Ellis & Martin.
39. Bordeaux mixture (4:4:50 or 4:2:50), ________ and copramat give a control of defoliation in tomatoes.
40. Egg-plant (brinjal) contains vitamins A and B and is an ________ vegetable.
41. Brinjal crop yielding ________ of produce removes from soil 175 + 40 + 300 kg/ha of $N + P_2O_5 + K_2O$ and 30 + 10 kg/ha of MgO and sulphur, respectively.
42. Ash gourd (*Benincasa hispida* Cong.) is considered to be of great ________ value.
43. Watermelon (*Citrullus vulgaris*) is grown in USA since ________.
44. Ripe watermelon fruit when thumped with finger(s) gives out a ________ sound as against metallic and ringing sound by an immatured one.
45. When colour of ground spot (white spot) where the watermelon fruit rests on the ground assumes ________, is indicative of its maturity.
46. Coccinia (*Coccinia indica* W & A), a semi-perennial cucurbit is propagated by ________ 25-30 cm long and 1.5-2.0 cm thick.
47. Muskmelon (*Cucumis melo*) is a native of ________ India.
48. Ripening of muskmelon fruits begins first from the ________ accompanied by a change in skin colour.
49. "Muskmelon fruits on ripening when part completely and easily from the stem leaving a circular depression," it is said to be at ________.
50. Long melon is usually sown in ________ and overwintered under artificial protection from frost.
51. Long melon variety Selection-3 is from ________ principles.
52. Cucumber (*kheera*) is one of the oldest ________ vegetable crops having its origin probably in India.
53. Pusa Sanyog is a ________ of cucumber (*kheera*).
54. Summer squash (*Cucurbita pepo* L.) like pumpkin is of ________ origin and was first of the squashes to be introduced in Europe.

55. Arka Suryamukhi and Arka Chandan are the cultivars of ________.
56. Bitter gourd (*Memordica charantia*) is generally considered to be an old-world species with its native home in the ________ and Asia.
57. Bitter gourd has got heating and ________ effect on the body.
58. In ________ after first shower, when shoots come out from root-tubers is the best planting time for sweet gourd (*Memordica cochinchenesis*) in Assam.
59. Snake gourd (*Trichosanthes anguina* L.) is found growing wild in India and the Indian ________ is thought to be its source of origin.
60. Pointed gourd (*Trichosanthes diocia*) is a native of India and ________ is considered to be the primary centre of its origin.
61. Pointed gourd is easily digestible, diuretic, laxative, invigorates the ________, and is useful in disorders of the circulatory system.
62. Planting root materials are usually collected from old planting of pointed gourd during ________.
63. Turnip greens are a good source of minerals such as ________ and iron and vitamin A.
64. ________ types of turnip are relatively sweeter and more palatable.
65. The original home of radish is probably ________.
66. Radish is found growing wild in ________ region
67. White Iscle, Scarlet Globe and Pusa Himani are ________ of varieties of radish.
68. The cultivated carrot probably originated in the hills of the Punjab and Kashmir, with a secondary centre of distribution in ________ and North Africa.
69. Carrot is an excellent source of vitamin ________ and is rich in sugar.
70. Sweet potato contains 16 and 4 per cent of starch and sugar, that is, ________ per cent alcohol producing material.
71. ________ is the most important insect-pest of sweet potato.
72. ________ tubers of sweet potato store better than the white-skimed ones.
73. Potato (*Solanum tuberosum*) is a native of South America and was cultivated by ________.
74. Potato was introduced in Europe by the early ________ explorers during sixteenth century.
75. It is estimated that potato in Nilgiri Hills of Tamil Nadu was introduced in ________.
76. In Bihar, Himachal Pradesh and Nilgiri Hills (India) potato is grown as a ________ crop.
77. Per capita estimated consumption of potato in ________ is about 13 kg per annum.
78. Main crop of potato in Hills of Himalayan region (India) is. planted in ________.
79. Potato crop removes large amount of potassium followed by ________.
80. The potato variety Kufri Kuber has been developed at Potato Breeding Station (now CPRI) Shimla in ________.
81. In Nilgiri Hills, Tamil Nadu (India) potato is rotated ________ in alternate years.
82. Scientific name of potato tuber moth is ________.
83. Potato stored at –1–0°C suffers from internal break-down known as ________.
84. A preharvest spray of potato with ________ controls sprouting.
85. Elephant yam's botanical name is ________.
86. Elephant yam is common in ________ in valleys of Tapti, Purna and Ambika.
87. The ________ in onion is due to a volatile oil known as allyl propyl-disulphide.

88. The onion originates from the region comprising N-W India, Afghanistan, Tajikistan, Uzbekistan (former USSR) and ________.
89. The Western Asia and areas around ________ are onion's secondary centres of development.
90. Onion does not thrive well in areas receiving more than ________ of annual average rainfall.
91. Punjab Selection, Pusa Ratnar, and Arka Kalyan are the varieties of ________ onion.
92. S-48, Arka Pragati, and Hissar-2 are the varieties of white ________.
93. Garlic is supposed to have originated from Central Asia and ________ regions.
94. The seed rate of garlic varies from 340 to 570 kg/ha of ________.
95. The original races of pea came from ________.
96. It is believed that small seeded peas originated from ________, while large seeded ones from Mediterranean.
97. Double bean (*Phaseolus lunatus*) is a native of ________ and reportedly grown by American Indians.
98. Pusa Sadabahar and Pusa Naubahar are the varieties of cluster bean mainly grown for ________ purposes.
99. French bean an ancient crop is probably a native of ________.
100. Cultivated cowpeas consist of three groups *viz*., asparagus or yard long bean, the ________ and Sourthen pea.
101. Faba bean reached India probably from ________ and was grown in North (Kashmir and Punjab).
102. Wine is also made from ________ beside grapes.
103. Faba bean is tolerant to water stress due to higher ________ accumulation.
104. Indian bean (*Dolichos lablab*), in west is known as ________.
105. Perennial and annual types of Indian bean are known as *Typicus* and ________, respectively.
106. Indian bean is grown throughout tropical regions of Asia, ________ and America.
107. The seed rate of lettuce for nursery and direct sowing is 500-750 and ________ g, respectively.
108. The place of origin of celery *(Apium graveolens)* extends from Sweden Southward to Algeria, Egypt, ________ and in Asia to Caucasus, Baluchistan, Egypt, and the mountains of India.
109. Exclusion of light from stalks while plants are still growing makes them devoid of chlorophyll, is referred to as ________.
110. The seed rate of celery is about ________ per hectare.
111. Fruits may be either a garden or a ________.
112. Successful orcharding consists of not only yield, but also ________ production and efficient disposal.
113. Mango varieties of Southern India fail to fetch ________ in the North.
114. The ________ involves the flow of air from areas of high elevation to areas of low elevation.
115. The ________ fruit trees suffer more from frost than the deciduous fruit trees.
116. The descending order of salt-tolerance of different fruit trees is grape, olives, figs, almonds, oranges, pears, ________ prunus, apricot, lemons and mulberry.
117. Date-palm has been placed in ________ salt tolerant group.
118. The plants bend towards ________ side under the stress of high winds.
119. The plant nutrients leach in the following order Ca > Mg > – > K > N > P.
120. Fruit crop enterprise suffers more from ________ than any thing else.
121. Sod system is not favourable for ________, tree growth and fruit yield.

122. In orchards ________ are active in the sod system and still more in mulch system.
123. ________ crops need not be used as cover crops in orchards.
124. Intercrops preferably leguminous or ________ crops can be successfully grown till the fruit trees attain the bearing age.
125. Lack of optimum soil moisture supply during bloom and fruit development stage is commonly highly ________.
126. Nitrogen deficiency causes yellowing of vein in monocot leaf, while entire leaf becomes yellowish green in ________.
127. Boron deficiency causes ________ in sugarbeet.
128. ________ in turnip is due to deficiency of boron.
129. Molybdenum has been shown essential for ________ seedlings of plum besides tomato and cabbage.
130. The blue colour of the flowers of *Hydron macrophylla* is due to presence of more ________ than in the pink ones.
131. The control on the direction of growth of a plant is known as ________.
132. Training has little effect on ________ bearing.
133. Thinning out is the process of removal of twig or a ________ according to need.
134. ________ consists of climbing and spreading of vines in the trellised roof.
135. In open centre system of tree training ________ branches of approximately equal diameter at the base are developed.
136. ________ denotes training of fruit trees, to walls, trellises and fences.
137. Pruning is based on scientific principles to augment the overall performance of ________ trees/plants.
138. Pruning in effect improves the size and ________ of fruits.
139. In loquat and mango fruit buds are borne terminally containing flower parts and give rise to ________ without leaves.
140. ________ and pears' fruit buds are borne terminally that unfold to produce leafy shoots terminating into flower clusters.
141. In citrus, peach and plum etc., fruit buds are borne laterally containing ________ only and give rise to inflorescence without or with small leaves.
142. American strain of ________ has succeeded in the control of San Jose Scales (*Aspidiotus perniciosus* Coms.)
143. *Ascyltus pterygodes* is known to have controlled the outbreak of ________ in Fiji.
144. *Coccinella septempunctata* L. is very commonly used against ________.
145. ________ phylloxera (*Phylloxera vitifoliae*) menace was combated by use of resistant rootstocks.
146. Plants which bleed profusely should not be pruned when cell sap is at ________.
147. ________, the development of seeds without complete sexual process is a form of nonsexual or vegetative propagation.
148. Polyembryonic stock induces more ________ than monoembryonic ones.
149. Tip layerage is done ________ for black raspberries.
150. When the branches are alternatively covered and exposed over their entire length, the layerage is known as ________ layerage.
151. Air layerage is also known as "Chinese layerage", "pot layerage", "Circumportion", "Marcotage" or ________.

152. In ________ layerage the young tip shoot should not be covered with soil at any stage, but may be covered half the way.
153. ________ aims at cambial union.
154. The success of graftage depends on combatibility, ________ and closeness between the scion and the rootstock.
155. In veneer grafting a shallow downward and inward cut of about 3-4 cm length is made above the ________ of the stock plant.
156. ________ grafting method is especially adopted for top worked trees.
157. Bridge grafting is generally useful for the purpose of ________.
158. ________ is a common method of propagation of mango and loquat.
159. In budding it is essential to use ________ and not flower buds.
160. Ring budding is practised with jujube and peach on ________.
161. ________ is commonly practised in guava.
162. Forket method of budding is common in ________ and has been recommended for mango in India.
163. A series of 16 vegetatively propagated apple rootstocks at ________ comprises a classified example of effect of rootstock on plant-vigour.
164. Malling II, a ________ rootstock tends to have vigorous plants embodying good spreading habit and early bearing.
165. The tomato scion produced ________ fruits when grafted on *Datura strammonium*.
166. Sour orange (*C. aurantium*) when budded on Eureka lemon suffered much more from ________ injury than the unbudded seedlings.
167. Defective graft unions are many times due to failure to maintain ________ continuity.
168. ________ in grafting of *Cucumis melo* on *Cucurbita fictifolia* can be prevented by retaining few leaves of the stock (*C. fictifolia*).
169. Cracking of fruits may also occur due to high absorption of water coupled with low transpiration exerting enhanced pressure on ________.
170. ________ buds have higher maximum temperature requirement than leaf buds.
171. A capsule (dry fruit) arises out of ________ with either superior or inferior ovary.
172. ________ is a single seeded, small, dry fruit with seed attached to the wall of the ovary at one point.
173. ________ resembles the achene except that thin seed coat and the pericarp unite to form a single unit.
174. Indehiscent dry, 1-2 seeded fruit developing from a superior or tricarpellary ovary with flattened wing like out-growth are ________.
175. In fruits developed from pistil of superior bi- or polycarpellary ovary where pericarp is hard and woody are known as ________.
176. Cypsela is a dry one-chambered fruit developing from an inferior ________ ovary with the pericarp and the seed coat free as in composital.
177. A ________ refers to a fruit derived from superior (sometimes inferior) ovary in which the entire ovary wall develops into a fleshy, often juicy and edible pericarp.
178. Date-palm is a ________ berry.
179. The citrus fruits are regarded as modified berries called ________ in which the rind is not edible.
180. Pepo is a type of berry in which the outer wall which is the ________ becomes hard as in Cucurbitaceae family.

181. A ________ is a fleshy one or more chambered and one or more seeded fruit developing from monocarpellary or syncarpous pistil.
182. Pomes denote fleshy fruits embodying pericarp differentiated into epicarp, ________ and endocarp.
183. An aggregate fruit is a collection of simple fruits and fruitlets developing from ________ pistil of a flower.
184. A pollenizer must be a heavy pollen producer to ensure better chances of ________ fertilization.
185. Generally, 11 per cent ________ trees are considered sufficient for deciduous fruit trees..
186. Large blocks of ________ trees improve in pollination when some of big trees are grafted over with pollenizer varieties.
187. Apple fruits develop ________ quite successfully, but such development is not associated with any particular variety.
188. Peach can be successfully grown even with a single ________ variety except the self-barren varieties.
189. ________ is not important for fruit development in persimmon.
190. In strawberry early maturing flowers are ________ than those maturing late.
191. Filbert varieties of chestnut show both ________ and self-incompatibility.
192. Loquat varieties Golden Yellow, Pale Yellow and California Advance are ________.
193. Fruiting in mango can be augmented by mixed planting due to ________.
194. Staminant constants are those which bear ________ flowers each year along with some staminate flowers.
195. Of the ________ plants the pure staminate flowering ones are essentially barren.
196. Ringing leads to ________ only due to greater concentration of nutrition at the point of bearing on tips.
197. The tomatoes supplied with rich nutrition fail to produce ________.
198. Jonathan apple in Australia, though mostly self-sterile on rich soils became ________ on poor soils.
199. The production of ________ pistil is known to be a changing character associated with locality.
200. The change of end-season fertility to self-sterility in tomato, mango and grape plants or end-season sterility to self-fertility in strawberry are indicative of the effect of ________.
201. The flower buds of apple are formed mostly on the ________.
202. Mangoes blossom generally on the old ________ growths.
203. The pear are quite large and conspicuous forming a wider angle with the ________.
204. Pruning of nitrogen deficient trees induces more of ________.
205. Supply of the required minimum of carbohydrate and nitrogen to plants brings the C:N ratio to the forefront to control ________.
206. ________ developed fruits of tomato are seedless.
207. Growth substances have been used to increase size of the ________.
208. Auxins also bring about the ________ of the developed or developing embryos leading to fruit thinning.
209. Long and short day plants accelerated flowering only in excess of ________, respectively.
210. Diploid tissues from mother plant, the ________ and diploid tissues of new embryo compose the fruit.
211. All the fruits do not have the same amount of increase in weight during the same period of ________.
212. Maleic hydrazide spray, possibly due to its effect as check of ————, lowers fruit drop.
213. 2, 4, 5 ________ acetic acid is known to check fruit drop.

214. ________ inhibitors prevent fruit ripening.
215. ________ are synthesized at increasing rates in apples during ripening.
216. Unsaturated hydrocarbons (ethylene) can stimulate the process of fruit ________.
217. Addition of methanol to persimmon fruits ________ ripening.
218. Pick the fruits preferably at 1600 hours for home consumption as ________ is the maximum at that point of time.
219. Fruits have waxy cuticles (apple), while tubers have ________ (potato) to cut down the water losses.
220. Yeast ferments fruit-sugars and their products into ________ and carbon dioxide.
221. Bacteria found in fruits and ________ are destroyed by exposing to temperatures of 212 and 240°F for 15-30 and 30-60 minutes, respectively.
222. The temperature fluctuations of the ________ must not vary by more than 0.5°C at any time.
223. Most of the fruits in store are harmed when the ________ concentration exceeds 1 per cent.
224. ________ (1:2000) contained in muslin bags when introduced in crates of grape wards off decay and augments storage life.
225. Short-period preservation of fruits and vegetables is achievable by ________ activity of enzymes and microbes by refrigeration, exclusion of moisture and addition of salt and sugar (other chemicals too).
226. Any product containing more than 65 per cent sugar can be permanently ________.
227. Common salt at ________ per cent is required for permanent preservation.
228. Most of the auxins do not only stimulate stem and coleoptile growth, but also affect ________ and abscission.
229. ________ propagation is preferred due to ease of maintenance of hereditary characters of the mother plant.
230. Growth substances or regulators accelerate the ________ of cuttings in vegetative plant propagation.
231. Quick-dip and Lanolin methods denote the application of growth substances to aid vegetative ________.
232. ________ is mobilized to the morphological basal end of the cutting for root formation.
233. Iodine substituted benzoic acids like, TIBA (2, 3, 5-triodobenzoic acid) is good for inducing profuse ________ in many crops.
234. The best time for pruning of *ber* (jujube) in northern India is ________.
235. Chiku (*Achras sapota*) is grown in the moist ________ of peninsular India.
236. The cultivated species of citrus are believed to be natives of tropical and subtropical regions of ________ Asia.
237. According to De Candolle citrus originated somewhere in the ________ parts of India.
238. Sweet orange is very susceptible to ________ footrot.
239. Lemon is widely used as a ________ in China and Japan.
240. Grape-fruits are closely related to ________.
241. Kinnow is the first generation hybrid of the ________ orange.
242. Proper ripening of date-palm fruits needs a temperature of over 30°C for no less than ________.
243. The optimum offshoot size of date-palm for planting is ________ or more as 6-8 kg in Punjab.
244. The area in the neighbourhood of ________ is considered to be the place of origin of grapes.
245. Litchi is indigenous to South East ________.

246. Plants of litchi raised by seeds are not ________ and may take 8-20 years for bearing.
247. Loquat varieties Golden Yellow and Janaka are ________.
248. Flowering panicle of mango with 100 to 4000 flowers may develop only ________, as large number of flowers are with male functional parts.
249. Mango variety Amrapali is a hybrid of the cross between Dashehri and ________.
250. Mango ________ is due to an imbalance between growth promoters and growth inhibitors.
251. The amount of RNA, DNA and proteins are always ________ is healthy panicles than in malformed ones in mango.
252. Unripe papaya fruit is rich in ________, an enzyme helpful in digestion of proteins.
253. Papain is useful in the treatment of stomach ulcers ________ and even cancer.
254. Pomegranate barks and rinds are commonly used in dysentery and ________.
255. The flowers form a soul of ________ and convey the message of nature to man.
256. Ashok trees (*Saraca indica*) were the dominant plants in ________ where Sita was held captive.
257. Lord Krishna's association with ________ is well known.
258. The great Emperor Ashok (264-277 B.C.) adopted ________ as one of the state policies.
259. Vatsayana (300-400 A.D.) narrated four kinds of gardens Promododyan, Udyan, Vrikshvatica and ________.
260. ________, the famous Chinese pilgrim wrote "the Hindus needed flowers every morning for worshipping".
261. ________ laid a garden at Agra, now known as Rambagh.
262. Moghul Emperor, Akbar, the Great established ________ close to Dal lake in Kashmir (India).
263. A small but pretty garden at Chashma Shahi in Kashmir was laid by one of the governors of ________.
264. Sher Shah Suri constructed the famous Grant Trunk Road and planted ________ on both sides.
265. "Floriculture is the art and knowledge of growing flowers to ________."
266. Acclimation and ________ are not enough for improving the plant wealth of India.
267. A natural mutant bougainvillea, ________ evolved spontaneously in a Calcutta garden.
268. The dried fruit of *Vanilla planifolia* syn. *V. fragrans* yield the ________ of commerce.
269. Underground stem of ________ is a popular vegetable in N. India.
270. ________ wood cuttings are used for propagation in jasmine and hydrangeas.
271. Lateral shoots pulled off from the stem containing a portion of it (stem) are called ________.
272. Cuttings embodying a small portion of the woody branch attached to the base are known as ________.
273. Node cuttings are inserted ________ in sand.
274. Root cuttings should be taken from ________ of average thickness and the length may vary from 2.5 to 15.0 cm with one or a few buds.
275. The cuttings longer than 7 cm (7 cm too) are placed ________.
276. Plants like *Saintpaulia, Peperomia, Bryophyllum* and *Sedum spectabile* etc., are propagated by ________.
277. Leaf-cuttings or leaf-bud cuttings are raised in hot-humid and partially ________ places.
278. Chinese or pot layerings are identical to ________.
279. ________ is a subterranean stem arising from a lateral bud from the main stem at ground level and extending underground near the surface horizontally.

280. A tuber comprises a short and thickened part of a ________ branch storing a large quantity of plant food, mainly starch.

281. The tubers embody ________ in the axils of reduced leaves.

282. In bulbs, the stem is reduced extremely to a ________ around which leaf scales remain attached.

283. A corm is an ________ stem with a short, fleshy, vertical axis with dried leaf bases.

284. ________ are tiny buds or small bulbs in axils of the leaves which on planting into ground develop into bulbs.

285. In ornamental horticulture mostly "T" or "Shield" budding is employed for ________.

286. The propagation of orchid clones through meristem culture (mericlones) was the first commercially successful venture in ________ technique.

287. The success of *in vitro* ________ depends much on the chemical composition and physical qualities of the nutrient media.

288. It is essential to gain sufficient knowledge about the trend in abnormal plant production before large scale plant production through ________.

289. Actual pathogenecity tests are absolutely essential to claim actually disease pathogenfree plants through ________.

290. Soil sterilization can be done either with heat or with chemicals to eliminate ________ diseases.

291. Pinching or stopping means removal of the ________ of a shoot along with a few leaves.

292. Chrysanthemum, carnation, brachycome and marigold etc., require ________.

293. The stakes can be interlinked with strings, forming an interlacing mesh, as is done in ——— method of chrysanthemum growing.

294. A planned removal of branches, twigs, shoots, limbs or roots is called ________.

295. The rust anti-auxin was possibly ________.

296. In ________ method the basal portion is dipped from 5 seconds to 2 minutes depending upon the nature of the cuttings.

297. SADH is very effective in controlling ________ of chrysanthemum.

298. Transferring of the young seedlings to another pan or tray is known as ________.

299. Sand-verbena (*Abronia umbellata* syn. A. *rosea*) of family *Nictaginaceae* originated from ________.

300. Sweet Alison (*Alyssum maritimum* syn. *Lobularia maritima*) has its origin from Europe and West Asia and belongs to family ________.

301. ________ (*Anchusa capensis*) of family *Borgginaceae* has its origin in South Africa.

302. Both annual and perennial lupins (*Lupinus* family Leguminosae) are grown in ________.

303. Lady's lace (*Pimpinella monoica*) has its origin in ________.

304. Indian ________ belongs to family *Tropaeolaceae* and 'its place of origin is Mexico/South America.

305. Garden pansy (Heart's Ease). *Viola tricolor hortensis* originated in ________.

306. Moonflower (*Calonyction aculeatum*) is of tropical origin and belongs to family ________.

307. Morning Glory (*Pharbitis purpurea, P. tricolor*) is a native of ________.

308. Black-eyed susan (*Thumbergia alata*) and canary bird-flower (*Tropaeolum perigrinum*) are natives of South Africa and ________ respectively.

309. Veni is a special kind of flower arrangement used in S. India to decorate long ________.

310. Rangoli has a ________ overtone.

311. In a bouquet gladiolus in one plane and roses sholuld be arranged in ________ on different planes.

312. *Thusa* and *Asparagus* plumosus are most commonly used in ________.

313. Gladiolus corms should be treated with 0.1 per cent of ________ for about 15 minutes and then air-dried before planting.

314. In carnation rooted ________ have been found to give better results.

315. The purpose of ________ is to restore the turgidity of flowers.

316. ________ is a preshipment treatment employed by growers.

317. ________ is a method in which flowers are harvested at a stage earlier than the one considered as 'cutting stage'.

318. The first Japanese style garden was laid out in the ________ Delhi.

319. ________ Baroda (Gujarat) was established by Maharaja Sayajirao III in 1879.

320. *Ficus benghalensis* belonging to family ________ is a native of India and Tropical Africa.

321. *Juniperous bermudiana* is a densely branched ________ tree.

322. *Pongamia glabra* (*karanj*) is a medium tall ________ tree with trifoliate, bright-green, glossy leaves.

323. *Putranjiva roxburghii*, Child-Life-Tree belongs to family ________.

324. *Arjun* (*Terminalia arjuna*) is a large (20-25m), ________ shade tree.

325. *Jamun* (*Eugenia jambolana*) fruits are ________ oblong to roundish and edible.

326. *Bauhinia purpurea* syn. *B. triandra* (*gulabi kachnar*) flower is rosy purple or lilac or ________.

327. *Bombax malabaricum* syn. *B. ceiba* (*shimbal*) has egg-shaped fruit pods which yield ________.

328. Flame of the Forest (*Butea monosperma.* syn. *B. frondosa*) can withstand both frost and ________.

329. Bottle brush (*Callistemon lanceolatus* syn *C. citrinus*) bears crowded ________ flowers.

II. Tick mark (✓) True or False:

330. Knolkhol is a hardy winter vegetable.

331. In seed-to-seed method of seed production of cabbage, the plants are allowed to over-winter in their original position.

332. All Green, Jobner Green and Pusa Jyoti are the improved cultivars of fenugreek.

333. The recommended seed rate for spinach is about 60 kg/ha.

334. *Amaranthus lividus* L. and *A. caudatus* are known as Kolsa and Siliara, respectively.

335. *Purslane* (*kulfa*), *Portulaca oleracea* occurs in several forms during cool weather both in wild and cultivated forms.

336. The seed-rate of purslane is 2250-3825 g/ha.

337. Chekurmanis (*Sauronus androgynus* Merr.) is commonly known as 'multivitamin and multimineral packed leafy vegetable.

338. Both hardwood and semi-hardwood cuttings of Chukurmanis of 20-30 cm length are used as planting material.

339. Muskmelon fruit should not be picked at full slip stage for home consumption.

340. Long melon (*Cucumis melo* var. *utilissimus*) can stand cool climate better than muskmelon.

341. In cucumber (*kheera*) a small portion of the stem-end is cut crosswise and rubbed together to remove the black substance that comes out.

342. The cucumber (*kheera*) seed retains viability for about five years and good seed gives 80-90 per cent germination.

343. Arka Harit and Pusa Do Mausami are the cultivars of cowpea.
344. Sweet gourd (*Memordica cochinchenesis*) is mainly grown in Cochin.
345. In sweet gourd male and female flowers occur on the same plant.
346. The leaves and tender shoots of pointed gourd (*Trichosanthes diocia*) are used to prepare the soup for convalescents.
347. Pointed gourd ratoon crop flowers 10-15 days earlier than the planted crop.
348. Do propagate pointed gourd by seeds only.
349. Turnip is found growing wild in Russia and Siberia.
350. Arka Nishant, Punjab Safed and Pusa Reshmi are Asiatic or tropical type of radish varieties.
351. Though Nantes is an European variety of carrot, its seed can be produced in plains.
352. Pusa Kesar, a cultivar of carrot is a selection from cross between Local Red and Nantes half long.
353. Sweet potato (*Ipomea batata* Lam.) is a native of tropical America.
354. Sweet potato does best on slightly to highly acidic soils.
355. Potato in India was introduced in the seventeenth century.
356. Potato varieties *viz*., Phulwa, DRR, Satha and Hellora are not chance survivals of early introductions.
357. Early maturing potato varieties are favoured by relatively short days, while late ones are better adapted to long days.
358. The tuber production in potato totally stops at 36°C.
359. Potato tubers, stored in cold storage should be kept for 12-24 hours at 15°C before exposure to atmosphere.
360. Elephant yam species are found in tropical Asia and America, and about 14 species occur in India.
361. Elephant yam is not as rich in minerals and vitamins A and B as potato.
362. Occasionally, flowering is also seen in elephant yam.
363. Onion can be cultivated as a rainfed crop between April and August even at 1525-2134 m elevations.
364. Onion seed remains viable for more than one year.
365. Premature producing of seed stocks in onion is known as bolting.
366. Garlic is a spice or a condiment used to flavour and season vegetable and meat preparations.
367. French bean is tolerant to acid soils, but pH should not be lower than 3.5.
368. French bean does well at places 3000-4000 m above mean sea level.
369. Cowpea is probably the native of Central Africa.
370. Indian bean Hebbal Avare-l has been evolved from the segregating material of *Local Avare* × *Red Typicus*.
371. Hebbal Avare-3, Wal Konkan-l and Arka *Jay* are the vegetable varieties of faba bean.
372. Lettuce is probably a native of Europe and Asia, and has been in cultivation for at least 2,000 years.
373. Pear, apple, orange, grape-fruit, plum, apricot, strawberry, lemon and avacado are medium salt tolerant fruit trees.
374. Broad leaved evergreen trees may not be successful in regions where temperature falls below 5°C.
375. Deciduous plants pass winters in active vegetative phase and can tolerate temperate climatic conditions.
376. Safe temperature limits for higher plants is considered between 5 and 22°C with no marginal adjustments.
377. The optimum and maximum temperatures for most of the plants are 22-27 and 40-52°C, respectively.

378. Sunshine is essential for fruit plants for pollination, development and colouring of fruits.
379. Leaffall in potato occurs due to deficiency of boron.
380. Training controls the distribution of fruiting wood.
381. Heading back must be done within a distance of 15-25 cm from the place where first branches are not desired.
382. The observation, "Pruning may be done (in plants) any time the knife is sharp" is still scientifically tenable.
383. Annual pruning is the rule for all the fruit trees.
384. The woolly apple aphid (*Eriosoma lanigerum* Hausm.) has been controlled in W. Himalayas by *Aphelinus mali* Hald.
385. The percentage of germination of polyembryonic seeds is higher than the monoembryonic ones.
386. The sexual embryos develop larger seedlings than the asexual ones.
387. Stem cuttings usually prepared during the dormant season are generally unsuccessful.
388. Asexual method of propagation is used generally to increase the planting stock, while sexual for hybridization.
389. Certain varieties of citrus (*Citrus medica*) root easily, while others (*Citrus aurantium*) with difficulty.
390. Grafting or budding is not chiefly employed for perpetuation of clones.
391. In saddle grafting diagonal cuts of equal length are made on stock and scion of equal girth in the form of a saddle to match each other.
392. In side grafting scions are placed laterally on the side of an above stock.
393. Chip method of budding is practised when the bark does not slip easily.
394. Bracing is a method to afford "natural brace" in young trees by grafts identical to inarching and bridge grafting.
395. In stock-scion union there exists a zone of blended, intermediate or hybrid tissue with mixed characteristics.
396. Malling XII forms a very vigorous rootstock.
397. The effect of rootstock on immaturity of wood is not uncommon.
398. Decreased yields of grape varieties like *Vitis labrusca* were obtained when grafted on vigorous rootstocks *vis-a-vis* own rooted plants.
399. Stock-fruit characteristics are generally carried over to the fruits of the scion variety.
400. Tomato fruits have been detected to contain nicotine when grafted on tobacco rootstock.
401. Lower and higher mean temperatures favour degradation and accumulation respectively of sugars in fruits.
402. A green leaf in light generally fixes less carbon dioxide than that released by its own respiration.
403. In plants like *Brassica* temperature controls flowering.
404. A follicle is a dry monocarpellary, superior, one chambered fruit splitting along the adaxial or ventral side only.
405. Silique is a long narrow multi-seeded fruit developed from a superior bicarpellary ovary with two parietal placentae.
406. Pistillate constant varieties of plants do not produce only pistillate flower.
407. Heterostyly is relatively more important factor in dioecious plants.
408. A protoandrous variety of walnut does not need interplanting with other varieties to ensure fruiting.

409. Flower abortion is more common in case of determinate inflorescence.
410. The pollen of mango is defective, while that of plums abortive.
411. Hybridity is associated with sterility, but not with unfruitfulness.
412. Unequal distribution of chromosomes during pollen tetrad formation in many raspberry forms is the cause of sterility.
413. In tobacco when mature pollen reaches immature pistil, it may germinate, enter the immature ovule and the flower falls.
414. Ringing is commonly followed in mature fruit trees to stimulate bud formation artificially.
415. Root pruning, in principle, reduces the entrance of nutrients and water, thus retards the growth of shoots and spurs.
416. It has been observed that only 5-10 per cent of blossoms develop into fruits on a full blossoming apple or pear tree.
417. In fruits RNA synthesis has been generally associated with their maturation.
418. A number of hydrolytic enzymes show decreased activity during fruit ripening.
419. During fruit ripening, starch is degraded to sugars adding sweetness to the fruits.
420. Sometimes lipase activity increases free fatty acid content in fruits.
421. Enzymes undergo quantitative changes during the process of fruit ripening.
422. Gases coming out in the fumes of kerosene stoves were used some six decades ago to improve the colouring of lemons.
423. Ethylene could strongly promote ripening activities by stimulating the climacteric rise.
424. Ethylene even in non-climacteric fruits like lemons and oranges stimulates respiration.
425. Immersion of banana stems in a solution containing 1000 ppm sodium 2,4-D, 2,4,5-T or parachlorophenoxy acetic acid retarded ripening.
426. Potatoes should be stored at 5°C because storage at 0°C makes them more sweet.
427. Acetic acid at 1-4 per cent preserves vinegar prickles permanently.
428. Properly canned fruits and vegetables can be kept for 1-3 years.
429. Frozen foods are not better than canned ones.
430. Vegetables need sterilization as heat resistant bacteria remain unaffected of water boiling at 115.5°C or more.
431. The vegetables are not blanched before filling into cans or bottles sterilized under 10 lb pressure and containing 3 per cent solution of salt and sugar each.
432. For every 12.5 M height, the time of sterilization is increased by two minutes.
433. In any squash 10-25 per cent of fruit juice should be present.
434. For pasteurization heat the fruit juice to 80°C and bottle, then wrap them in a thick cloth and place in cool water.
435. When fruit juice is totally clear free from pulp or part the fruit and moderately sweetened, it is referred to as cordial.
436. A syrup contains more than 65 per cent sugar, usually has high acid content and small quantity of pulp of the fruit.
437. Proper setting of fruit jelly depends upon correct proportion of pectin, sugar and acid.
438. The amount of extracted pectin may be tested by spirit test and Jel-meter test.
439. Marmalade is slightly sweet in taste as shreds from orange or Mosambi peel are added ti it.

440. Preserves are prepared by cooking whole or cut fruit with syrup and in the finish product the sugar concentration is 85 per cent.

441. Cordial, jelly and squash can be prepared from apple.

442. Squash can be prepared from papaya and pineapple.

443. Marmalade cannot be made from apple, orange and malta.

444. Auxins cannot reduce alternate bearing of some fruit trees such as apples.

445. Gibberellins overcome genetic and physiological dwarfism in plants.

446. Certain seeds that require light to germinate need cytokinin for their germination.

447. Aonla plants when raised from seed bear fruits of inferior quality.

448. Avocado (butter fruit), a staple food and native of tropical America was introduced in India almost 1000 year ago.

449. Mexican race (*Persea drymofolia*) avocado has, large fruits.

450. Robusta bunches of banana take 3 to 4 weeks for ripening without any outside aid.

451. Champa, Rasthali, Dwarf Cavendish are the dessert banana varieties.

452. Culinary bananas can be used even before cooking.

453. Jujube is indigenous to the area streching from India to South Western China and Malaya.

454. Grape is considered to be one of the important temperate fruits of the world.

455. *Karonda* (*Carissa carandas* L., family *Apocynaceae*) is also known as 'Christ's Thorn'.

456. Flowers are symbolic of beauty, love and tranquility.

457. Vertical cuttings are inserted in the medium to a depth of 2.5-3.0 cm after removal of bottom leaves for propagation.

458. Any plant that can readily produce sucker may be propagated by stem cuttings.

459. Horizontally placed cuttings are covered adequately and firmed for propagation.

460. Budding is a form of grafting wherein instead of a scion twig, only a single bud is implanted in the stock.

461. Sterilization with steam is not the best to kill fungal, bacterial spores and nematodes as well as to destroy unwanted seeds and tubers.

462. Root regeneration of a transplanted seedling is conditioned by the stored carbohydrates in the tissue.

463. Besides annual and herbaceous perennials, stopping is needed in flowering trees too.

464. Flowering shrubs such as rose and jasmine can be wintered in northern and eastern India.

465. Topiary is considered as "tree sculpture" and is free from controversy.

466. Most ,commonly used shrubs for topiary are *Clerodendron inerme* and *Duranta plumieri.*

467. The term phytochrome is specifically applied to the hormones produced exclusively outside the living plant.

468. The combination of fruit and flower arrangement is called Morimono by Japanese.

469. The NBRI popularly known as Sikander Bagh was laid out by Nawab Saadat Ali Khan.

III. Tick mark (✓) the correct answer:

470. Spinach produces seed stalks in about ________ and seed can be harvested in about 150 days.

(*a*) 45 days (*b*) 55 days

(*c*) 65 days (*d*) 75 days

471. ________ variety of *Brassica pekinensis* is a useful leaf vegetable for plains and hills of N. India.
(*a*) Chinese (*b*) American
(*c*) Canadian (*d*) Japanese

472. Orach or *chakwat* (*Atriplex hortensis* L.) or mountain spinach is mainly grown on small scale during winters in ________.
(*a*) Maharashtra and Karnataka (*b*) Gujarat and Madhya Pradesh
(*c*) Tamil Nadu and Kerala (*d*) Himachal Pradesh and J & K

473. The optimum temperature for brinjal-germination is ________ °C
(*a*) 5 (*b*) 10
(*c*) 15 (*d*) 20

474. An isolation distance of ________ between varieties of watermelon is considered enough for pure seed production.
(*a*) 100-200 m (*b*) 200-300 m
(*c*) 300-375 m (*d*) 400-500 m

475. Squash melon (*Citrullus vulgaris*) seed should be sown when the temperature (air) warms upto ________ °C.
(*a*) 15.6 (*b*) 20.6
(*c*) 24.6 (*d*) 26.6

476. In squash melon 100 g of seed accounts for about ________ seeds.
(*a*) 100 (*b*) 200
(*c*) 250 (*d*) 350

477. The cold storage temperature for melons is 0°C and relative humidity ________ per cent.
(*a*) 50-60 (*b*) 60-70
(*c*) 40-50 (*d*) 80-90

478. The seed rate of long melon is ________ kg/ha.
(*a*) 1-2 (*b*) 2-3
(*c*) 3-4 (*d*) 4-5

479. Cucumber (*Cucumis sativus* var. *kheera*) was domesticated by the ancient Greeks and Romans in about ________ B.C.
(*a*) 100 (*b*) 200
(*c*) 300 (*d*) 400

480. Cucumber (*kheera*) was known in France in ninth century and was common in England in ________.
(*a*) 927 (*b*) 1127
(*c*) 1227 (*d*) 1327

481. Flowering in pumpkin (*Cucurbita moschata*) starts ________ days after sowing.
(*a*) 30-40 (*b*) 50-60
(*c*) 60-80 (*d*) 85-95

482. Bottle gourd (*Legenaria siceraria*) was being cultivated in India even before ________ B.C.
(*a*) 500 (*b*) 1000
(*c*) 1500 (*d*) 2000

483. ________ is the cultivar of bottle gourd.

(*a*) Pusa Meghdoot (*b*) CO-1

(*c*) Australian Green (*d*) Straight Eight

484. The ________ is probably a native of South Asia and perhaps also of Africa, Australia and Polynesia.

(*a*) Smooth sponge gourd (*b*) Bottle gourd

(*c*) Pointed gourd (*d*) Bitter gourd

485. The number of seeds of bitter gourd per 100-g are about ________.

(*a*) 350 (*b*) 450

(*c*) 550 (*d*) 650

486. About 3 kg of seed or ________ root tubers of pointed gourd are enough to plant an area of one hectare.

(*a*) 20,000 (*b*) 30,000

(*c*) 40,000 (*d*) 50,000

487. Turnip (*Brassica campestris*) was introduced into England probably in ________, while in 1606 in U.S.A.

(*a*) 1590 (*b*) 1490

(*c*) 1390 (*d*) 1290

488. One gramme of turnip seed holds ________ seeds.

(*a*) 460-500 (*b*) 360-400

(*c*) 560-660 (*d*) 260-360

489. Radish seems to have reached England in about 1548 but, introduced in America in ________.

(*a*) 1429 (*b*) 1529

(*c*) 1629 (*d*) 1729

490. One gramme radish contains about ________ seeds.

(*a*) 700-1000 (*b*) 500-600

(*c*) 600-675 (*d*) 1100-1150

491. One gramme carrot contains about ________ seeds.

(*a*) 550 (*b*) 650

(*c*) 750 (*d*) 850

492. Carrot seed will not germinate below ________ °C.

(*a*) 7.9 (*b*) 6.9

(*c*) 5.9 (*d*) 3.9

493. The length of sweet potato cutting should normally be ________ with 4-5 sound (healthy) buds.

(*a*) 40 cm (*b*) 30 cm

(*c*) 20 cm (*d*) 10 cm

494. On weight basis ________ kg of cuttings of sweet potato are required per hectare for planting.

(*a*) 300 (*b*) 400

(*c*) 500 (*d*) 600

495. Potato tuber production is the maximum at ________ °C.

(*a*) 15 (*b*) 20

(*c*) 25 (*d*) 30

496. The young potato plant grows the best at ________ °C.

(*a*) 16 (*b*) 20
(*c*) 24 (*d*) 28

497. In general, potato needs ________ mm of irrigation water for the optimum production.

(*a*) 500 (*b*) 600
(*c*) 700 (*d*) 800

498. Elephant yam corms ("buds") weighing 100-200 g are used for planting of the ________ years crop.

(*a*) First (*b*) Second
(*c*) Third (*d*) Fourth

499. Elephant yam corms at the end of ________ year weigh 6.8 - 9.0 kg.

(*a*) Second (*b*) Third
(*c*) Fourth (*d*) Fifth

500. One gramme of onion, as estimated, generally contains ________ seeds.

(*a*) 180 (*b*) 240
(*c*) 300 (*d*) 360

501. Garlic freezes at the average temperature of ________ °C.

(*a*) –5 (*b*) –4
(*c*) –3 (*d*) –2

502. The best storage temperature for garlic is 0 to 2.2°C with ________ per cent of relative humidity.

(*a*) 60 (*b*) 50
(*c*) 40 (*d*) 3

503. Garden pea was an important crop in eleventh century in ________.

(*a*) Holland (*b*) Poland
(*c*) England (*d*) New Zealand

504. Garden pea was probably distinguished from field pea in 1536, but their common use began after ________.

(*a*) 1586 (*b*) 1600
(*c*) 1675 (*d*) 1700

505. One gramme of celery seed holds about ________ seeds.

(*a*) 1570 (*b*) 2070
(*c*) 2270 (*d*) 2470

506. Celery seed takes nearly ________ to germinate.

(*a*) 10 days (*b*) 20 days
(*c*) 30 days (*d*) 40 days

507. Pomegranate, fig, olive and grape have been placed in ________ salt tolerant group of fruit trees.

(*a*) High (*b*) Low
(*c*) Medium (*d*) Very high

508. Browning of cauliflower is caused by the deficiency of ________.

(*a*) Zinc (*b*) Manganese
(*c*) Iron (*d*) Boron

509. The citrus diseases namely 'Reclamation Disease' and 'Dieback Disease' are caused by the deficiency of ________.

(*a*) Zinc (*b*) Iron
(*c*) Copper (*d*) Molybdenum

510. Fastening of vines to a upright support of a tree called *panagara* (*Erithrina indica*) is known as ________.

(*a*) Kniffen system (*b*) Head system
(*c*) Single stake system (*d*) Cordon system

511. In whip tongue grafting the length of the cut should be about ________ times the diameter of the plants in question.

(*a*) 3 (*b*) 4
(*c*) 5 (*d*) 6

512. It has been observed that the Malta sweet orange budded on rough lemon produced trees ________ times larger than those budded on citrus (*C. medica*).

(*a*) Two (*b*) Three
(*c*) Four (*d*) Five

513. A fruit that develops from a hollow pear-shaped fleshy receptable (inflorescence: *hypanthodium*) Which encloses a number of minute male and female flowers is known as ________.

(*a*) Aggregate fruit (*b*) Hesperidium
(*c*) Pome fruit (*d*) Syconus fruit

514. The budded plants commence bearing in ________ year.

(*a*) Second (*b*) Third
(*c*) Fourth (*d*) Fifth

515. Mandarins reached Europe in ________.

(*a*) 1605 (*b*) 1700
(*c*) 1790 (*d*) 1805

516. For hand pollination in date-palm 10 male trees are sufficient for ________ female plants.

(*a*) 50 (*b*) 75
(*c*) 100 (*d*) 125

517. Hillawi is very popular variety of ________ throughout the world due to adaptability to high humidity and rains.

(*a*) Coconut (*b*) Date-palm
(*c*) Cashewnut (*d*) Arecanut

518. Fig in India is grown in ________.

(*a*) Madhya Pradesh (*b*) Punjab
(*c*) Kerala (*d*) Gujarat

519. Guava is a native of ________.

(*a*) Tropical South-east Asia (*b*) Tropical Africa
(*c*) Tropical America (*d*) Sub-tropical India

520. Allahabad Safeda is the variety of ________.

(*a*) Mango (*b*) Guava
(*c*) Loquat (*d*) Grapes

521. ________ is grown as a shade tree in coffee, areca and cardamom plantations ________.
(*a*) Jack-fruit (*b*) Coconut
(*c*) Mango (*d*) Guava

522. The stone, bark, leaves etc. of ________ are used as an effective medicine against diabetes.
(*a*) Litchi (*b*) Mango
(*c*) Indian blackberry (*jamun*) (*d*) Jujube (*ber*)

523. The first school of Ikebana called Ikenobo meaning "the arrangement of flowers of the hermitage along a pond" was started by Buddhist Monk Semmu around ________ A.D.
(*a*) 421 (*b*) 521
(*c*) 621 (*d*) 721

524. The *Moribana* meaning "Piled flowers" denoted the arrangement of flowers in ________.
(*a*) Shallow containers (*b*) Deep containers
(*c*) Paper wrappings (*d*) Papercones

525. Rose cut flower must be cut at tight bud stage at least ________ cm stem length for export.
(*a*) 20 (*b*) 40
(*c*) 60 (*d*) 80

526. The Mandor Garden, Jodhpur (Rajasthan) was established by Raja ________ (1724-1749).
(*a*) Abhai Singh (*b*) Ajay Singh
(*c*) Hari Singh (*d*) Man Singh

527. Lloyd Botanical Garden, Darjeeling (West Bengal) was laid out by ________ on a piece of land donated by William Lloyd.
(*a*) Sir Robert Llyod (*b*) Sir George King
(*c*) Sir Peter Hunt (*d*) Sir Holdgate Baird

528. *Lantana camara* syn. L. *aculeata* belong to family ________ and is a native of Jamaica.
(*a*) *Lythraceae* (*b*) *Rosaceae*
(*c*) *Acanthaceae* (*d*) *Verbenaceae*

529. *Aristolochia*, family *Aristolochiaceae*, represents a group of ________.
(*a*) Herbaceous annuals (*b*) Perennial shrubs
(*c*) Annual flowering plant (*d*) Climbers

530. Golden shower (*Cassia fistula*) may take ________ years to flower.
(*a*) 5 (*b*) 10
(*c*) 15 (*d*) 18

531. In *Cassia nodosa* ________ flowers appear in bunches from the nodes all along the branches.
(*a*) Yellow (*b*) Red
(*c*) Pink (*d*) Purple

532. In potato tree (*Solanum macranthum* syn. S. *maroniense*) flowers 2.5 cm across and resemble ________ flowers.
(*a*) Tomato (*b*) Eggplant
(*c*) Potato (*d*) Sweet potato

533. Madonna lily is ________.

(a) *Lilium candidum* (b) *L. pardalimum*

(c) *L. tigrinum* (d) *L. auratum*

IV. Match the following:

534. **Common name** — **Scientific name**

(a) Artichoke — (i) *Cinchorium intybus*

(b) Head lettuce — (ii) *Cynara scolumus*

(c) Safflower — (iii) *Lactua sativa* var. *capitata.*

(d) Chicory — (iv) *Carthamus tinctorius*

535. Match the family with the vegetable which it belongs to-

(a) *Compositae* — (i) Lady's finger

(b) *Cucurbitaceae* — (ii) Celery (*Apium graveolens*)

(c) *Malvaceae* — (iii) Head lettuce

(d) *Umbelliferae* — (iv) Snap melon

536. **Family** — **Common vegetable**

(a) *Amaryllidaceae* — (i) Asparagus

(b) *Liliaceae* — (ii) Taro

(c) *Araceae* — (iii) Pigweed

(d) *Chenopodiaceae* — (iv) Garlic

537. **Family** — **Common vegetable**

(a) *Cruciferae* — (i) Pepper

(b) *Leguminosae* — (ii) Turnip

(c) *Umbelliferae* — (iii) Fnugreek

(d) *Solanaceae* — (iv) Parsley

538. Match the mustard (*sarson*) species with the main growing states of India

(a) *Brassica campestris* var. brown *sarson* — (i) U.P., Bihar, Bengal

(b) *B.c.* var. sarson plain yellow *sarson* — (ii) N. Bengal, Assam

(c) *B. juncea* (*banga sarson*) — (iii) Punjab

(d) *B.c.* var. cuneifolia (*lai*) — (iv) Delhi

539. Match the common name of the vegetables with their scientific name.

(a) Parsnip — (i) *Ipomea batata*

(b) Sweet potato — (ii) *Solanum melongena*

(c) Potato — (iii) *Pastinaea sativa*

(d) Brinjal — (iv) *Solanum tuberosum*

540. **Common name** — **Scientific name**

(a) Tomato — (i) *Cucurbita pepo*

(b) Pepper — (ii) *Lycopersicon esculentum*

(c) Pungent pepper — (iii) *Capsicum annum*

(d) Summer squash — (iv) *Capsicum frutescens*

541. **Common name** — **Scientific name**
(*a*) Wax gourd — (*i*) *Citrullus vulgaris*
(*b*) Watermelon — (*ii*) *Cucumis melo* var. *reticulatus*
(*c*) Cucumber — (*iii*) *Benincasa hispida Cong.*
(*d*) Muskmelon — (*iv*) *Cumunis sativus* var. *kheera*

542. **Common name** — **Scientific name**
(*a*) Snap melon — (*i*) *Citrullus vulgaris* var. *fistulosus*
(*b*) Long melon — (*ii*) *Cucumis melo* var. *memordica*
(*c*) Squash melon — (*iii*) *Luffa cylindrica,* L. *acutangula*
(*d*) Sponge gourd — (*iv*) *Cucumis melo* var. *utilissimus*

543. **Common name** — **Scientific name**
(*a*) Bitter gourd — (*i*) *Trichosanthes diocia*
(*b*) Pointed gourd — (*ii*) *Lagenaria siceraria*
(*c*) Snake gourd — (*iii*) *Trichosanthes angunia*
(*d*) Bottle gourd — (*iv*) *Memordica charantia*

544. **Common name** — **Scientific name**
(*a*) Taro (*arbi*) — (*i*) *Allium cepa*
(*b*) Aspargus — (*ii*) *Colocasia esculentum*
(*c*) Onion — (*iii*) *Allium sativum*
(*d*) Garlic — (*iv*) *Asparagus officinalis*

545. **Common name** — **Scientific name**
(*a*) Spinach beet — (*i*) *Spinacia oleracea*
(*b*) Spinach — (*ii*) *Brassica oleracea* var. *capitata*
(*c*) Pigweed — (*iii*) *Beta vulgaris*
(*d*) Cabbage — (*iv*) *Chenopodium album*

546. **Common name** — **Scientific name**
(*a*) Cauliflower — (*i*) *Brassica campestris* var. *rapa*
(*b*) Turnip — (*ii*) *Raphanus sativus*
(*c*) Radish — (*iii*) *Brassica juncea*
(*d*) Leaf mustard — (*iv*) *Brassica oleracea* var. *botrytis*

547. **Common name** — **Scientific name**
(*a*) Garden pea — (*i*) *Vicia faba*
(*b*) Broad bean — (*ii*) *Cyamopsis psoraloides*
(*c*) Lima bean — (*iii*) *Pisum sativum*
(*d*) Cluster bean — (*iv*) *Phaseolus lunatus*

548. **Common name** — **Scientific name**
(*a*) Fenugreek — (*i*) *Daucus carota*
(*b*) Okra — (*ii*) *Trigonella foenum, T. graecum, T. corniculata*
(*c*) Carrot — (*iii*) *Petroselinum crispum*
(*d*) Parsley — (*iv*) *Abelmochus esculentus*

549. Match the following varieties of *chaulai* (Amaranthus) with the species.

(*a*) *Badi chaulai*	(*i*) *Amaranthus magnostanus* L.
(*b*) *Leotia chaulai*	(*ii*) *Amaranthus blitum* L.
(*c*) *Chhoti chaulai*	(*iii*) *Amaranthus dubius* Mart.
(*d*) *Khada sag*	(*iv*) *Amaranthus tricolor* L.

550. Match the per capita consumption of potato in different countries.

(*a*) 124 kg/annum	(*i*) West Germany (erstwhile)
(*b*) 146 kg/annum	(*ii*) Austria
(*c*) 174 kg/annum	(*iii*) Denmark
(*d*) 132 kg/annum	(*iv*) Belgium

551. Match type of potato crop with plant time.

(*a*) Autumn	(*i*) July-August
(*b*) Winter	(*ii*) September-November
(*c*) Main	(*iii*) September-October
(*d*) Monsoon	(*iv*) December-January

552. Match the following potato varieties with the duration (days of maturity).

(*a*) Kufri Alankar	(*i*) 85-95
(*b*) Kufri Chandramukhi	(*ii*) 95-100
(*c*) Kufri Jyoti	(*iii*) 110-120
(*d*) Kufri Chamatkar	(*iv*) 75

553. Match the row spacing with number of potato seeds needed when plant to plant spacing is 15 cm.

(*a*) 30	(*i*) 34,848
(*b*) 45	(*ii*) 87,120
(*c*) 60	(*iii*) 58,080
(*d*) 75	(*iv*) 43,560

554. Row spacing number of seeds/acre in seed to seed spacing of 22.5 cm.

(*a*) 30 cm	(*i*) 23,232
(*b*) 45 cm	(*ii*) 58,080
(*c*) 60 cm	(*iii*) 38,720
(*d*) 75 cm	(*iv*) 29,040

555. Match fungal diseases of potato with the causal fungus.

(*a*) Dry rot	(*i*) *Corticium solani* and *Rhizoctonia solani*
(*b*) Black scurf	(*ii*) *Synchtrium endobioticum*
(*c*) Charcoal rot	(*iii*) *Fusarium oxysporum*
(*d*) Wart	(*iv*) *Corticium rolfsil* and *Sclerotium rolfsil*

556. Match the bacterial diseases of potato with the causal bacterium.

(*a*) Brown rot	(*i*) *Corneybacterium sepedonicum*
(*b*) Ring rot	(*ii*) *Streptomyces scabies*
(*c*) Black leg	(*iii*) *Erwinia carotobora*
(*d*) Scab	(*iv*) *Pseudomonas solanacearum*

557. Match the viral diseases of potato with the causal virus (es).

(*a*) Leafroll	(*i*) Virus X and Virus Y
(*b*) Mild mosaic	(*ii*) *Solanum* virus 14 (potato virus I)
(*c*) Rugose mosaic	(*iii*) Potato virus X and potato virus A
(*d*) Crinkle of potato	(*iv*) Potato mottle virus X, *Solanum* virus I

558. Match the crop area of elephant yam in different advancing years of cropping with the number of corms needed for planting.

(*a*) First (nucleus area) year 0.50 ha	(*i*) 13,750
(*b*) Second year 0.75 ha	(*ii*) 8,750
(*c*) Third year 1.25 ha	(*iii*) 17,500
(*d*) Fourth year 2.50 ha	(*iv*) 11,250

559. Match the seed rate of elephant yam with the yield in different advancing years, both expressed in quintals per hectare.

(*a*) First year 45.35	(*i*) 283.50
(*b*) Second year 68.05	(*ii*) 453.60
(*c*) Third year 124.75	(*iii*) 1134.00
(*d*) Fourth year 113.25	(*iv*) 1814.50

560. Match the approximate removal of nutrients by onion yielding 350 q/ha.

(*a*) 50 kg/ha	(*i*) K_2O
(*b*) 160 kg/ha	(*ii*) Sulphur
(*c*) 15 kg/ha	(*iii*) P_2O_5
(*d*) 20 kg/ha	(*iv*) MgO

561. Match the following pod vegetables with the botanical name.

(*a*) Sword bean	(*i*) *Dolichos lablab*
(*b*) Velvet bean	(*ii*) *Phaseolus lunatus*
(*c*) Indian bean	(*iii*) *Mucuna cochinchinensis*
(*d*) Double bean	(*iv*) *Canavalia ensiformis*

562. Match the percentage of yield of the total yield of pea with the picking.

(*a*) 5	(*i*) Second picking
(*b*) 14	(*ii*) First picking
(*c*) 8	(*iii*) Fourth picking
(*d*) 4	(*iv*) Third picking

563.

Percentage yield	**Rank of picking**
(*a*) 8	(*i*) Seventh picking
(*b*) 14	(*ii*) Eighth picking
(*c*) 40	(*iii*) Fifth picking
(*d*) 4	(*iv*) Sixth picking

564. Match the soil characteristic with the weed usable as plant indicator.

(*a*) Heavy clay soil	(*i*) *Polygonum aviculare*
(*b*) Damp soil	(*ii*) *Primula vulgaris*
(*c*) Light sandy soil	(*iii*) *Chrysanthemum segetum*
(*d*) Acid soil	(*iv*) *Juncus effusus*

565. **Soil characteristic** — **Indicator weed**

Soil characteristic	Indicator weed
(*a*) Chalk soil	(*i*) *Spergula arvensis*
(*b*) Soil needing lime	(*ii*) *Papaver rheas*
(*c*) Damp soil	(*iii*) *Chichorium intybus*
(*d*) Light sandy soil	(*iv*) *Lychnis Flos-cuculi*

566. Match the pH range with fruit crop for which it has been found favourable.

(*a*) Blue berry	(*i*) 4.5-7.0
(*b*) Apple	(*ii*) 5.2-6.7
(*c*) Citrus	(*iii*) 5.8-8.0
(*d*) Grape	(*iv*) 4.5-5.0

567.

Fruit crop	**Favourable pH-range**
(*a*) Pear	(*i*) 5.0-5.5
(*b*) Peach	(*ii*) 5.6-7.2
(*c*) Pineapple	(*iii*) 5.2-6.7
(*d*) Red raspberry	(*iv*) 5.1-6.7

568.

Fruit crop	**Favourable pH-range**
(*a*) Strawberry	(*i*) 5.8-7.5
(*b*) Plum	(*ii*) 4.5-7.0
(*c*) Cherry	(*iii*) 5.0-6.0
(*d*) Citrus	(*iv*) 5.8-7.0

569. Match the following fruits with the soil found suitable for their cultivation.

(*a*) Almond	(*i*) Medium / light loam with slightly heavier subsoil
(*b*) Apple	(*ii*) Deep, rich, alluvial loamy soils
(*c*) Banana	(*iii*) Light loam/deep organic loam
(*d*) Citrus sp.	(*iv*) Light loam

570.

Fruit	**Suitable soil**
(*a*) Pear	(*i*) Light loam to heavy clay
(*b*) Pomegranate	(*ii*) Deep moist
(*c*) Date palm	(*iii*) Light sandy loam
(*d*) Guava	(*iv*) Deep loam/alluvial

571.

Fruit	**Suitable soil**
(*a*) Litchi	(*i*) Well drained, rich deep alluvial
(*b*) Jackfruit	(*ii*) Sandy loam to heavier soil, well drained light loam
(*c*) Grapes	(*iii*) Well drained clayey loam
(*d*) Loquat	(*iv*) Welll drained, shallow medium black loamy

572.

Fruit	**Suitable soil**
(*a*) Pineapple	(*i*) Loamy, deep and well drained
(*b*) Papaya	(*ii*) New alluvial, lateritic hill soils, old alluvium
(*c*) *Jamun*	(*iii*) Red sandy and also rocky soils
(*d*) Custard apple	(*iv*) Rich loam, medium black and alluvial

573. Match the choice of legume for sod in orchards with the soil or climatic conditions which these are suitable for.

(*a*) *Sesbania* sp.	(*i*) Well drained soils
(*b*) *Sannhemp*	(*ii*) Moderate conditions
(*c*) Vetch	(*iii*) Waterlogged conditions
(*d*) Clover (*Trifolium* sp.)	(*iv*) Cold region

574. Match the tree(s) given below with their estimated longevity.

(*a*) Sweet chestnut	(*i*) 100-300 years
(*b*) Walnut, pecan	(*ii*) 30-70 years
(*c*) Persimon, avocado	(*iii*) 1000 years
(*d*) Apricot, fig	(*iv*) 50-100 years

575.

Tree	**Longevity**
(*a*) Strawberry	(*i*) 20-40 years
(*b*) Peach, plum, pomegranate	(*ii*) 25-30 years
(*c*) Currant, goose / raspberry	(*iii*) 30-70 years
(*d*) Walnut, pecan	(*iv*) 4-5 years

576. Match the water content with the plant parts given below

(*a*) 93%	(*i*) Dry beans
(*b*) 40-50%	(*ii*) Barley roots
(*c*) 10-15%	(*iii*) Sunflower stem
(*d*) 80%	(*iv*) Woody tissues

577. Match the percentage of light with the mode of utilization of light by plants.

(*a*) 50%	(*i*) Transmitted
(*b*) 30%	(*ii*) Reradiated
(*c*) 19%	(*iii*) Use in photosynthesis
(*d*) 1%	(*iv*) Transpiration

578. Match the types of fruits below with the plant bearing it.

(*a*) Samara	(*i*) Rice
(*b*) Siliqua	(*ii*) Tree of heaven
(*c*) Caryopsis	(*iii*) Almond
(*d*) Nut	(*iv*) Mustard

579. Match the fruits with its edible part.

(*a*) Apple, pear (pome)	(*i*) Endosperm
(*b*) Banana	(*ii*) Peduncles and cotyledons
(*c*) Cashewnut	(*iii*) Fleshy thalamus
(*d*) Coconut-palm	(*iv*) Meso- and endocarp

580.

Fruit	**Edible part**
(*a*) Cucumber (pepo)	(*i*) Pericarp
(*b*) Custard apple (etaerio of berries)	(*ii*) Mesocarp, endocarp and placentae
(*c*) Date-palm	(*iii*) Fleshy pericarp
(*d*) Fig	(*iv*) Fleshy receptacle

581. **Fruit**	**Edible part**
(*a*) Guava	(*i*) Pericarp and placentae
(*b*) Grape	(*ii*) Bracts, perianth and seed
(*c*) Jackfruit	(*iii*) Mesocarp including epicarp
(*d*) Indian plum	(*iv*) Thalamus and peri carp

582. **Fruit**	**Edible part**
(*a*) Litchi	(*i*) Outer Portion of receptable bracts and perianth
(*b*) Mango	(*ii*) Fleshy aril
(*c*) Citrus	(*iii*) Juicy placental hairs
(*d*) Pear (pome)	(*iv*) Mesocarp

583. **Fruit**	**Edible part**
(*a*) Tomato	(*i*) Succulent thalamus
(*b*) Strawberry	(*ii*) Fleshy thalamus
(*c*) Papaya	(*iii*) Pericarp and placentae
(*d*) Pineapple	(*iv*) Mesocarp

584. **Fruit**	**Edible part**
(*a*) Pomegranate	(*i*) Endosperm
(*b*) Melon (pepo)	(*ii*) Fleshy receptable
(*c*) Coconut palm	(*iii*) Mesocarp
(*d*) Fig	(*iv*) Juicy out seed coat

585. Match the storage-life of fruits with the temperature.

(*a*) Ripe banana, 3 weeks	(*i*) 6-8°C
(*b*) Coorg orange, 10-12 weeks	(*ii*) 2-5°C
(*c*) Nagpur santara, 10-14 weeks	(*iii*) 12-13°C
(*d*) Punjab santara, 4-6 weeks	(*iv*) 5-6°C

586. **Fruit and average life**	**Temperature (°C)**
(*a*) Mosambi, 16 weeks	(*i*) 2-5
(*b*) Common malta, 16 weeks	(*ii*) 8-9
(*c*) Blood red malta, 16 weeks	(*iii*) 5-6
(*d*) Lemons, 8-12 weeks	(*iv*) 7-8

587. **Fruit and average life**	**Temperature (°C)**
(*a*) Grapes, 6-8 weeks	(*i*) 11-13
(*b*) Guava, 3 weeks	(*ii*) 8-9
(*c*) Jackfruit, 6 weeks	(*iii*) 0-2
(*d*) Mango, 4-7 weeks	(*iv*) 9-10

588. **Fruit and average life**	**Temperature (°C)**
(*a*) Papaya, 1-2 weeks	(*i*) 0-2
(*b*) Watermelon, 2-4 weeks	(*ii*) 9-10
(*c*) Apple, 16-32 weeks	(*iii*) 0-1
(*d*) Pear, 12-26 weeks	(*iv*) 2 4

589. Match the plant part used for propagation with the growth substance and the concentration normally used.

(*a*) Lemon, cuttings	(*i*) IAA (week solution)
(*b*) Sweet lime, hardwood cutting	(*ii*) NAA (0.2%)
(*c*) Trifoliate orange cuttings	(*iii*) Hortomone A
(*d*) Guava, Gootee	(*iv*) IBA (200 mg/l with 2% surose)

590.

Plant part	**Growth substance**
(*a*) Tomao, seeds	(*i*) 2, 4-D
(*b*) Orange, seeds	(*ii*) Heteroauxinaques solution and IBA
(*c*) Peach, seeds	(*iii*) IBA
(*d*) Vine, seeds	(*iv*) IAA

591.

Plant part	**Growth substance, concentration**
(*a*) Jackfruit, Marcoting tests	(*i*) IBA (3%)
(*b*) Mango, ringed part of marcots	(*ii*) IBA and NAA (3-5% in linolin)
(*c*) Papaya, shoots	(*iii*) Heteroauxin solution
(*d*) Olive, cuttings	(*iv*) IBA (1%)

592.

Plant part	**Growth substance**
(*a*) Grape cuttings	(*i*) 2, 4-D
(*b*) Vine (*Vitis vinifera*), cuttings	(*ii*) IAA
(*c*) Coconut seeds	(*iii*) IBA
(*d*) Fig cuttings	(*iv*) NAA with honey (10 mg/l)

593. Match the common name with scientific name and family.

(*a*) Aonla	(*i*) *Persea americana* Mill, *Lauraceae*
(*b*) Avocado	(*ii*) *Zizyphus mauritiana* Lamk, *Rhamnaceae*
(*c*) Banana	(*iii*) *Phyllanthus emblica* L., *Euphorbiaceae*
(*d*) *Ber* (Jujube)	(*iv*) *Musa paradisiaca* var. *Sampientum, Musaceae*

594.

Fruit tree	**Scientific name and family**
(*a*) Bread-fruit	(*i*) *Citrus* spp., *Rutaceae*
(*b*) Chiku	(*ii*) *Annona squamosa* L., *Annonaceae*
(*c*) Citrus	(*iii*) *Achras sapota* L., *Sapotaceae*
(*d*) Custard apple	(*iv*) *Artocarpus altilis,* Fosberg, *Moraceae*

595.

Fruit tree	**Scientific name and family**
(*a*) Date-palm	(*i*) *Vitis vinifera* L., *Vitaceae*
(*b*) Fig	(*ii*) *Phoenix dactylifera* L., *Palmae*
(*c*) Grape	(*iii*) *Psidium guajava* L., *Myrtaceae*
(*d*) Guava	(*iv*) *Ficus carica* L., *Moraceae*

596.

Fruit tree	**Scientific name and family**
(*a*) Jack-fruit	(*i*) *Syzygium cumuni* L., *Skeels, Myrtaceae*
(*b*) *Jamun*	(*ii*) *Eriobotrya japonica* Lindl, *Rosaceae*
(*c*) Litchi	(*iii*) *Artocarpus heterophyllus* Lamk, *Moraceae*
(*d*) Loquat	(*iv*) *Litchi chinensis* Sonn., *Sapindaceae*

597. **Fruit tree** — **Scientific name and family**

(*a*) Mango — (*i*) *Morus* species, *Moraceae*

(*b*) Mangosteen — (*ii*) *Carica papaya* L., *Caricaceae*

(*c*) Mulberry — (*iii*) *Garcinia mangostana* L., *Guttiferae*

(*d*) Papaya — (*iv*) *Mongifera indica* L., *Anacardiceae*

598. **Fruit tree** — **Scientific name and family**

(*a*) Passion fruit — (*i*) *Grewia asiatica* L., *Tiliaceae*

(*b*) *Phalsa* — (*ii*) *Passiflora edulis* Sims, *Passifloraceae*

(*c*) Pineapple — (*iii*) *Punica granatum* L., *Punicaceae*

(*d*) Pomegranate — (*iv*) *Ananas comusus* Merr., *Bromeliaceae*

599. **Fruit tree** — **Scientific name and family**

(*a*) Apple — (*i*) *Malus pumila* Mill., *M. sylvestris* Mill., *Rosaceae*

(*b*) Apriot — (*ii*) *Prunus persica* Stokes, *Rosaceae*

(*c*) Cherry — (*iii*) *Prunus armeniaca* L., *Rosaceae*

(*d*) Peach — (*iv*) *Prunus avium* L., *P. cerasus* L., *Rosaceae*

600. **Fruit tree** — **Scientific name and family**

(*a*) Japanese persimmon — (*i*) *Prunus* species. L., *Rosaceae*

(*b*) Pear — (*ii*) *Fragaria* species, *Rosaceae*

(*c*) Plum — (*iii*) *Diospyros kaki*, L.f., *Ebenaceae*

(*d*) Strawberry — (*iv*) *Prunus domestica* L., *Rosaceae*

601. **Fruit tree** — **Scientific name and family**

(*a*) Almond — (*i*) *Corylus avellana* L., *Bitulaceae*

(*b*) Cashewnut — (*ii*) *Prunus amygdalus* Stokes syn., *Amygdalus communis* Lion., *Rosaceae*

(*c*) Hazlenut — (*iii*) *Carya illinoensis* Koch, *Juglandaceae*

(*d*) Pecan nut — (*iv*) *Anacardium occidentale* L., *Anacardiaceae*

602. **Fruit tree** — **Scientific name and family**

(*a*) Walnut — (*i*) *Citrus aurantium* L., *Rutaceae*

(*b*) Sour orange — (*ii*) *Citrus limon* Burm. F.Po.C. *trifoliate* Raf., *Rutaceae*

(*c*) Lemon — (*iii*) *Citrus aurantifolia* Swing, *Rutaceae*

(*d*) Lime — (*iv*) *Jugulans regia* L., *Juglandaceae*

603. Match the number of buds in each spur of grape varieties

(*a*) Seedless beauty — (*i*) 2-3

(*b*) Thompson seedless — (*ii*) 4-5

(*c*) Early-Moscut — (*iii*) 5-6

(*d*) Anab-e-Shahi — (*iv*) 8-10

604. Match the fruit with the place of origin as known todate.

(*a*) Loquat	(*i*) Brazil
(*b*) Mango	(*ii*) Malaya
(*c*) Mangosteen	(*iii*) South Asia
(*d*) Passion-fruit	(*iv*) Japan and China

605.

Fruit	**Place of origin**
(*a*) Apple	(*i*) China (probably)
(*b*) Apricot	(*ii*) South-West Asia
(*c*) Peach	(*iii*) N. America and Japan
(*d*) Plum	(*iv*) Armenia

606. Match the fruit with its protein content (per cent).

(*a*) Litchi	(*i*) 0.5
(*b*) Papaya	(*ii*) 12.5
(*c*) Cashewnut (nuts)	(*iii*) 1.15
(*d*) Peacun nut	(*iv*) 20.0

607. Match the flower (plant) with place of origin.

(*a*) Hollyhock (*Althaea rosea*)	(*i*) South Africa
(*b*) Sweet allyssum (*Alyssum maritimum Lobularia maritima*)	(*ii*) Orient, China
(*c*) Forget-me not (*Anchusa capensis*)	(*iii*) Europe
(*d*) Snapdragon (*Antirrhinum majus*)	(*iv*) Europe, W. Asia

608.

Flower plant	**Place of origin**
(*a*) African daisy (*Aretotis*)	(*i*) South America
(*b*) Browallia (*Browallia demissa, B. elata*)	(*ii*) Tropical Asia
(*c*) Pot marigold (*Calendula officinalis*)	(*iii*) South Africa
(*d*) Cockscomb (*Celosia argentea, C. plumosa*)	(*iv*) South Europe

609.

Flower plant	**Place of origin**
(*a*) Snapdragon (*Antirrhimum Majus*)	(*i*) California (USA)
(*b*) Golden star (*Bartonia aurea*)	(*ii*) Tropical Asia
(*c*) Calendula (*Calendula officinalis*)	(*iii*) Europe
(*d*) Cockscomb (*Celosia argentea / plumosa*)	(*iv*) S. Europe

610.

Flower plant	**Place of origin**
(*a*) Sweet sultan (*Centaurea moschata*)	(*i*) Tropical America
(*b*) Wall flower (*Cheiranthus cheiri*)	(*ii*) Europe
(*c*) Giant spider flower (*Cleome spinosa* syn. *C. pungens*)	(*iii*) Australia
(*d*) Glory pea (*Clianthus dampieri / formosus*)	(*iv*) Europe

611.

Flower plant	**Place of origin**
(*a*) Mexican aster (*Cosmos bipinnatus*)	(*i*) Great Britain
(*b*) Fox glove (*Digitalis purpurea*)	(*ii*) South Europe
(*c*) Larkspur (*Delphinium ajacis / consolida*)	(*iii*) N. France
(*d*) Sweet William (*Dianthus barbatus*)	(*iv*) Mexico

612. **Flower plant** | **Place of origin**

(*a*) Blanket flower (*Gaillardia pulchella*) — (*i*) Caucasus

(*b*) Backelor's button (*Gamphrena globosa*) — (*ii*) Sicily and S. Italy

(*c*) Baby's breath (*Gypsophila elegans*) — (*iii*) America

(*d*) Sweet pea (*Lathyrus odoratus*) — (*iv*) India

613. **Flower plant** | **Place of origin**

(*a*) Scarlet flax (*Linum gradiflorum* var. *rubrum*) — (*i*) S. America

(*b*) Feverfew (*Matricaria eximia* syn. *Chrysanthemum parthenium*) — (*ii*) N. Africa and Europe

(*c*) Nemesia (*Nemesia strumosa*) — (*iii*) N. Temperate Regions

(*d*) Petunia (*Petunia hybrida*) — (*iv*) S. Africa

Do you know that

1. Botanical name of Mango is Mangifera Indica.
2. Mango has high contents of Vitamin-A.
3. Sweetest variety of Mango is Chausa.
4. Propagation of Mango is done by Veneer Grafting.
5. Propagation method of Banana is sword suckers.
6. Propagation method of Grapes is hard wood cutting.
7. Propagation method for Guva is strooling/mound layering.
8. Strawbery fruit is propgated by runners.
9. Apple is propagated by shield budding and grafting.
10. Edible part of cauliflower is curd.
11. Origin of vegetable Tomato was country Peru.
12. Banana is a moisture loving plant.
13. Ripe Banana contain about 26% of sugar.
14. Pappaya is polygamous plant.
15. Guava can be harvested throughout the year except the months of May and June.
16. Citrus fruit have a special kind of fruit skin referred as 'leathery rind'.
17. Kinnow var of citrus was developed by H.B. Frost in 1935.
18. Mg deficency is universal in grapes.
19. Aonla contain maximum amount of Vitamin C.

KEY

(1) Vegetable	(2) Leafy	(3) Night-blindness
(4) B	(5) Wilted	(6) Phosphorus
(7) Fertility	(8) Human body	(9) Iron
(10) Calcium	(11) Iron	(12) Iodine
(13) Fibrous mass	(14) 285	(15) Farming
(16) Acidity	(17) Molybdenum	(18) Field
(19) Buttoning	(20) *Kharif* season	(21) Potassium
(22) Hybrids	(23) Bursting/splitting	(24) Solid head
(25) Head-to-seed	(26) Seed-to-seed	(27) Gongylodes

(28) Knolkhol (29) 1250 (30) Fenugreek
(31) A and B (32) Heat and drought (33) Boron
(34) Determinate and indeterminate (35) Pruning
(36) Flower initiation (37) Netting or russeting (38) Defoliation
(39) Dithane Z-78 (40) Appetizing (41) 60 tonnes/ha
(42) Medicinal (43) 1629 (44) Muffled dull/dead
(45) Yellow tinge (46) Stem cuttings (47) North-West
(48) Blossom-end (49) Full slip stage (50) November
(51) Bitter (52) Cultivated (53) F-1-hybrid
(54) American (55) Pumpkin (56) Tropical Africa
(57) Wormicidal (58) April-May (59) Archipelago
(60) Assam (61) Heart and brain (62) December and January
(63) Calcium (64) European (65) China and India
(66) Mediterranean (67) European/temperate rype (68) Ethiopia
(69) A and iron (70) 20
(71) Sweet potato weevil (*Cylas formicarius*) (72) Red skinned
(73) Incas (74) Spanish (75) 1822
(76) Rainfed (77) India (78) March-April
(79) N and P_2O_5 (80) 1943 (81) Fingermillet
(82) *Gnorimoschema operculelia* Zell (83) Black heart (84) Maleic hydrazide
(85) *Amorphophallus companulatus* Blum. (86) Gujarat
(87) Pungency (88) Tien Shan (89) Mediterranean
(90) 750-1000 mm (91) Red (92) Onion
(93) Mediterranean (94) Cloves/bulblets (95) Ethiopia
(96) South Asia (97) South America (98) Vegetable
(99) South America (100) Catjung (101) Near East
(102) Faba bean (103) Protein (104) BonavistiHyacinth bean
(105) Lignosus (106) Africa (107) 1875-2500
(108) Abyssinia (109) Blanching (110) 125
(111) Field crop (112) Economic (113) Economic value
(114) Air drainage (115) Evergreen (116) Peaches
(117) High (118) "Lee-ward" (119) S
(120) Erosion (121) Foliage colour (122) Rodents
(123) Small grain (124) Vegetables (125) Detrimental
(126) Dicots (127) 'Heart rot' (128) 'Brown heart'
(129) Myrobalan (130) Aluminium (131) Training
(132) Fruit (133) Part thereof (134) Bower system
(135) Diverging (136) Espalier (137) Fruit/flower
(138) Colour (139) Inflorescence (140) Apple/peccan/quince

(141) Flower parts (142) *Prosopaltella perniciosi* Tower (143) Coconut moths
(144) Cabbage aphid (145) Grape (146) High pressure
(147) Apomexis (148) Scion-vigour (149) Commercially
(150) Compound (151) 'Gootee' (152) Mound
(153) Graftage (154) Cambiuin content (155) Crown
(156) Cleft (157) Repairs (158) Inarching
(159) Vegetative (160) Commercial lines (161) Patch budding
(162) Indonesia (163) East malling (164) Semi-dwarfing
(165) Poisonous (166) Winter (167) Cambium
(168) Incompatibility (169) Cell walls (170) Flower
(171) Pistil (172) Achene (173) Caryopsis
(174) Samara (175) Nuts (176) Bicarpellary
(177) Berry (178) Single-seeded (179) Hesperidium
(180) Receptacle (181) Drupe (182) Mesocarp
(183) Apocarpous (184) Cross (185) Pollenizer
(186) Self-unfruitful (187) Parthenocarpically (188) Self-fertile
(189) Pollination (190) Less fertile (191) Dichogamy
(192) Self-incompatible (193) Crosspollination (194) Pistillate
(195) Unisexual (196) Parthenocarpy (197) Normal flowers
(198) Self-fruitful (199) Defective (200) Season
(201) Spurs (202) Spring and summer (203) Shoots
(204) Unfruitfulness (205) Flowering (206) Parthenocarpically
(207) Fruit (208) Abortion (209) Carbohydrates and nitrogen
(210) Endosperm (211) Growth (212) Respiration-rate
(213) Trichlorophenoxy (214) Respiratory (215) Proteins
(216) Ripening (217) Aid (218) Sugar content
(219) Corky epidermis (220) Alcobol (221) Vegetables
(222) Storage chamber (223) CO_2 (224) Potassium metasulphide
(225) Retarding (226) Preserved (227) 15-20
(228) Differentiation (229) Vegetative (230) Rooting
(231) Propagation (232) Rhizocaline (233) Flowering
(234) Mid-May to Mid-June (235) Coastal tracts (236) South-east
(237) North-eastern (238) Maida Goma (239) Root stock
(240) Pummelo (241) King sweet (242) 30 days
(243) 3 kg (244) Caspian Sea (245) China
(246) True to type (247) Self-incompatible (248) One fruit
(249) Neelam (250) Malformation (251) Higher
(252) Papain (253) Diphtheria (254) Diarrhoea
(255) Garden (256) Ashok-van

(257) Kadamba (*Anthocephalus indicus*) (258) Arboriculture
(259) Nandanavana (260) Hiuen Tsang (261) Ibrahim Lodi, 1526 AD
(262) Nasim Bagh (263) Shah Jahan (264) Avenue trees
(265) Perfection (266) Introduction (267) 'Mary Palmer'
(268) Vanilla (269) Lotus (*Nelumbium*) (270) Semi-hard
(271) Heel cuttings (272) Mallet cuttings (273) Horizontally
(274) Young roots (275) Vertically (276) Leaf cuttings
(277) Shaded (278) Gootee/air layering (279) Rhizome
(280) Subterranean (281) Buds (282) Disc
(283) Underground (284) Bulbils (285) Propagation
(286) Tissue culture (287) Propagation (288) Tissue culture
(289) Tissue culture (290) Soil-borne (291) Growing-point
(292) Pinching (293) Sen rin tsukuri (294) Pruning
(295) γ-phenyl butyric acid (296) Quick-dip (297) Height
(298) Pricking (299) California (USA) (300) Cruciferae
(301) Cape Forget-me-not (302) Gardens (303) India
(304) *Tropaeolum majus* (305) Southern France (306) Colvolvulaceae
(307) Tropical America (308) Peru (309) Plait to hair
(310) Religious (311) Layers (312) Buttonholes
(313) Benlate/Bavistin (314) Cuttings (315) Conditioning/hardening
(316) Pulsing/Loading (317) Bud-opening (318) Roshanara Park
(319) Sayaji Park (320) Moraceae (321) Pyramidal
(322) Deciduous (323) Euphorbiaceae (324) Evergreen
(325) Purple-black (326) Deep pink (327) Silk cotton
(328) Drought (329) Scarlet (330) True
(331) True (332) False (333) False
(334) True (335) False (336) True
(337) True (338) True (339) False
(340) True (341) False (342) True
(343) False (344) False (345) False
(346) True (347) True (348) False
(349) True (350) True (351) False
(352) True (353) True (354) False
(355) True (356) False (357) False
(358) True (359) True (360) False
(361) False (362) True (363) True
(364) False (365) True (366) True
(367) False (368) False (369) True
(370) True (371) False (372) True

(373) False (374) True (375) False
(376) False (377) True (378) True
(379) True (380) True (381) False
(382) False (383) False (384) True
(385) False (386) True (387) False
(388) True (389) True (390) False
(391) True (392) False (393) True
(394) True (395) False (396) True
(397) False (398) False (399) True
(400) True (401) False (402) False
(403) True (404) True (405) True
(406) False (407) False (408) False
(409) False (410) True (411) False
(412) True (413) True (414) False
(415) True (416) True (417) True
(418) False (419) True (420) True
(421) False (422) True (423) True
(424) True (425) False (426) True
(427) True (428) True (429) False
(430) False (431) False (432) True
(433) True (434) False (435) True
(436) False (437) True (438) True
(439) False (440) False (441) False
(442) True (443) False (444) False
(445) True (446) True (447) True
(448) True (449) False (450) False
(451) True (452) False (453) True
(454) False (455) True (456) True
(457) False (458) False (459) True
(460) True (461) False (462) True
(463) False (464) True (465) False
(466) True (467) False (468) True
(469) True (470) (*c*) (471) (*d*)
(472) (*a*) (473) (*b*) (474) (*d*)
(475) (*d*) (476) (*d*) (477) (*d*)
(478) (*b*) (479) (*c*) (480) (*d*)
(481) (*c*) (482) (*d*) (483) (*a*)
(484) (*a*) (485) (*d*) (486) (*d*)
(487) (*a*) (488) (*a*) (489) (*c*)

(490) (*a*) (491) (*d*) (492) (*d*)
(493) (*b*) (494) (*d*) (495) (*b*)
(496) (*c*) (497) (*c*) (498) (*b*)
(499) (*c*) (500) (*b*) (501) (*b*)
(502) (*a*) (503) (*a*) (504) (*d*)
(505) (*d*) (506) (*c*) (507) (*c*)
(508) (*d*) (509) (*c*) (510) (*c*)
(511) (*c*) (512) (*c*) (513) (*d*)
(514) (*d*) (515) (*d*) (516) (*c*)
(517) (*b*) (518) (*d*) (519) (*c*)
(520) (*b*) (521) (*a*) (522) (*c*)
(523) (*c*) (524) (*a*) (525) (*c*)
(526) (*a*) (527) (*b*) (528) (*d*)
(529) (*d*) (530) (*b*) (531) (*c*)
(532) (*c*) (533) (*a*)
(534) (*a*)-(*ii*) (*b*)-(*iii*) (*c*)-(*iv*) (*d*)-(*i*)
(535) (*a*)-(*iii*) (*b*)-(*iv*) (*c*)-(*i*) (*d*)-(*ii*)
(536) (*a*)-(*iv*) (*b*)-(*i*) (*c*)-(*ii*) (*d*)-(*iii*)
(537) (*a*)-(*ii*) (*b*)-(*iii*) (*c*)-(*iv*) (*d*)-(*i*)
(538) (*a*)-(*iii*) (*b*)-(*i*) (*c*)-(*iv*) (*d*)-(*ii*)
(539) (*a*)-(*iii*) (*b*)-(*i*) (*c*)-(*iv*) (*d*)-(*ii*)
(540) (*a*)-(*ii*) (*b*)-(*iii*) (*c*)-(*iv*) (*d*)-(*i*)
(541) (*a*)-(*iii*) (*b*)-(*i*) (*c*)-(*iv*) (*d*)-(*ii*)
(542) (*a*)-(*ii*) (*b*)-(*iv*) (*c*)-(*i*) (*d*)-(*iii*)
(543) (*a*)-(*iv*) (*b*)-(*i*) (*c*)-(*iii*) (4)-(*ii*)
(544) (*a*)-(*ii*) (*b*)-(*iv*) (*c*)-(*i*) (*d*)-(*iii*)
(545) (*a*)-(*iii*) (*b*)-(*i*) (*c*)-{*iv*) (*d*)-(*ii*)
(546) (*a*)-(*iv*) (*b*)-(*i*) (*c*)-(*ii*) (*d*)-(*iii*)
(547) (*a*)-(*iii*) (*b*)-(*i*) (*c*)-(*iv*) (*d*)-(*ii*)
(548) (*a*)-(*ii*) (*b*)-(*iv*) (*c*)-(*i*) (*d*)-(*iii*)
(549) (*a*)-(*iv*) (*b*)-(*i*) (*c*)-(*ii*) (*d*)-(*iii*)
(550) (*a*)-(*ii*) (*b*)-(*iv*) (*c*)-(*i*) (*d*)-(*iii*)
(551) (*a*)-(*iii*) (*b*)-(*iv*) (*c*)-(*ii*) (*d*)-(*i*)
(552) (*a*)-(*iv*) (*b*)-(*i*) (*c*)-(*ii*) (*d*)-(*iii*)
(553) (*a*)-(*ii*) (*b*)-(*iii*) (*c*)-(*iv*) (*d*)-(*i*)
(554) (*a*)-(*ii*) (*b*)-(*iii*) (*c*)-(*iv*) (*d*)-(*i*)
(555) (*a*)-(*iii*) (*b*)-(*i*) (*c*)-(*iv*) (*d*)-(*ii*)
(556) (*a*)-(*iv*) (*b*)-(*i*) (*c*)-(*iii*) (*d*)-(*ii*)
(557) (*a*)-(*ii*) (*b*)-(*iv*) (*c*)-(*i*) (*d*)-(*iii*)

(558) (*a*)-(*iii*)	(*b*)-(*i*)	(*c*)-(*iv*)	(*d*)-(*ii*)
(559) (*a*)-(*iii*)	(*b*)-(*iv*)	(*c*)-(*i*)	(*d*)-(*ii*)
(560) (*a*)-(*iii*)	(*b*)-(*i*)	(*c*)-(*iv*)	(*d*)-(*ii*)
(561) (*a*)-(*iv*)	(*b*)-(*iii*)	(*c*)-(*i*)	(*d*)-(*ii*)
(562) (*a*)-(*ii*)	(*b*)-(*i*)	(*c*)-(*iv*)	(*d*)-(*iii*)
(563) (*a*)-(*iii*)	(*b*)-(*iv*)	(*c*)-(*i*)	(*d*)-(*ii*)
(564) (*a*)-(*ii*)	(*b*)-(*iv*)	(*c*)-(*i*)	(*d*)-(*iii*)
(565) (*a*)-(*iii*)	(*b*)-(*i*)	(*c*)-(*iv*)	(*d*)-(*ii*)
(566) (*a*)-(*iv*)	(*b*)-(*iii*)	(*c*)-(*i*)	(*d*)-(*ii*)
(567) (*a*)-(*ii*)	(*b*)-(*iv*)	(*c*)-(*i*)	(*d*)-(*iii*)
(568) (*a*)-(*iii*)	(*b*)-(*i*)	(*c*)-(*iv*)	(*d*)-(*ii*)
(569) (*a*)-(*iv*)	(*b*)-(*iii*)	(*c*)-(*ii*)	(*d*)-(*i*)
(570) (*a*)-(*ii*)	(*b*)-(*iv*)	(*c*)-(*i*)	(*d*)-(*iii*)
(571) (*a*)-(*iii*)	(*b*)-(*i*)	(*c*)-(*iv*)	(*d*)-(*ii*)
(572) (*a*)-(*ii*)	(*b*)-(*iv*)	(*c*)-(*i*)	(*d*)-(*iii*)
(573) (*a*)-(*iii*)	(*b*)-(*i*)	(*c*)-(*iv*)	(*d*)-(*ii*)
(574) (*a*)-(*iii*)	(*b*)-(*i*)	(*c*)-(*iv*)	(*d*)-(*ii*)
(575) (*a*)-(*iv*)	(*b*)-(*i*)	(*c*)-(*ii*)	(*d*)-(*iii*)
(576) (*a*)-(*ii*)	(*b*)-(*iv*)	(*c*)-(*i*)	(*d*)-(*iii*)
(577) (*a*)-(*iv*)	(*b*)-(*i*)	(*c*)-(*ii*)	(*d*)-(*iii*)
(578) (*a*)-(*ii*)	(*b*)-(*iv*)	(*c*)-(*i*)	(*d*)-(*iii*)
(579) (*a*)-(*iii*)	(*b*)-(*iv*)	(*c*)-(*ii*)	(*d*)-(*i*)
(580) (*a*)-(*ii*)	(*b*)-(*iii*)	(*c*)-(*i*)	(*d*)-(*iv*)
(581) (*a*)-(*iv*)	(*b*)-(*i*)	(*c*)-(*ii*)	(*d*)-(*iii*)
(582) (*a*)-(*ii*)	(*b*)-(*iv*)	(*c*)-(*iii*)	(*d*)-(*i*)
(583) (*a*)-(*iii*)	(*b*)-(*i*)	(*c*)-(*iv*)	(*d*)-(*ii*)
(584) (*a*)-(*iv*)	(*b*)-(*iii*)	(*c*)-(*i*)	(*d*)-(*ii*)
(585) (*a*)-(*iii*)	(*b*)-(*i*)	(*c*)-(*iv*)	(*d*)-(*ii*)
(586) (*a*)-(*iv*)	(*b*)-(*iii*)	(*c*)-(*i*)	(*d*)-(*ii*)
(587) (*a*)-(*iii*)	(*b*)-(*iv*)	(*c*)-(*i*)	(*d*)-(*ii*)
(588) (*a*)-(*ii*)	(*b*)-(*iv*)	(*c*)-(*i*)	(*d*)-(*iii*)
(589) (*a*)-(*ii*)	(*b*)-(*iv*)	(*c*)-(*i*)	(*d*)-(*iii*)
(590) (*a*)-(*iii*)	(*b*)-(*i*)	(*c*)-(*iv*)	(*d*)-(*ii*)
(591) (*a*)-(*iv*)	(*b*)-(*i*)	(*c*)-(*ii*)	(*d*)-(*iii*)
(592) (*a*)-(*ii*)	(*b*)-(*iv*)	(*c*)-(*i*)	(*d*)-(*iii*)
(593) (*a*)-(*iii*)	(*b*)-(*i*)	(*c*)-(*iv*)	(*d*)-(*ii*)
(594) (*a*)-(*iv*)	(*b*)-(*iii*)	(*c*)-(*i*)	(*d*)-(*ii*)
(595) (*a*)-(*ii*)	(*b*)-(*iv*)	(*c*)-(*i*)	(*d*)-(*iii*)
(596) (*a*)-(*iii*)	(*b*)-(*i*)	(*c*)-(*iv*)	(*d*)-(*ii*)

(597) (*a*)-(*iv*)	(*b*)-(*iii*)	(*c*)-(*i*)	(*d*)-(*ii*)
(598) (*a*)-(*ii*)	(*b*)-(*i*)	(*c*)-(*iv*)	(*d*)-(*iii*)
(599) (*a*)-(*i*)	(*b*)-(*iii*)	(*c*)-(*iv*)	(*d*)-(*ii*)
(600) (*a*)-(*iii*)	(*b*)-(*i*)	(*c*)-(*iv*)	(*d*)-(*ii*)
(601) (*a*)-(*ii*)	(*b*)-(*iv*)	(*c*)-(*i*)	(*d*)-(*iii*)
(602) (*a*)-(*iv*)	(*b*)-(*i*)	(*c*)-(*ii*)	(*d*)-(*iii*)
(603) (*a*)-(*ii*)	(*b*)-(*iv*)	(*c*)-(*i*)	(*d*)-(*iii*)
(604) (*a*)-(*iv*)	(*b*)-(*iii*)	(*c*)-(*ii*)	(*d*)-(*i*)
(605) (*a*)-(*ii*)	(*b*)-(*iv*)	(*c*)-(*i*)	(*d*)-(*iii*)
(606) (*a*)-(*iii*)	(*b*)-(*i*)	(*c*)-(*iv*)	(*d*)-(*ii*)
(607) (*a*)-(*ii*)	(*b*)-(*iv*)	(*c*)-(*i*)	(*d*)-(*iii*)
(608) (*a*)-(*iii*)	(*b*)-(*i*)	(*c*)-(*iv*)	(*d*)-(*ii*)
(609) (*a*)-(*iii*)	(*b*)-(*i*)	(*c*)-(*iv*)	(*d*)-(*ii*)
(610) (*a*)-(*ii*)	(*b*)-(*iv*)	(*c*)-(*i*)	(*d*)-(*iii*)
(611) (*a*)-(*iv*)	(*b*)-(*i*)	(*c*)-(*ii*)	(*d*)-(*iii*)
(612) (*a*)-(*iii*)	(*b*)-(*iv*)	(*c*)-(*i*)	(*d*)-(*ii*)
(613) (*a*)-(*ii*)	(*b*)-(*iii*)	(*c*)-(*iv*)	(*d*)-(*i*)

SECTION 9
PLANT PROTECTION

I. Fill up the blanks:

1. ________ are arthropods with three pairs of legs belonging to invertebrate phylum Arthropoda.
2. A ________ refers to an insect whose population increases to an extent that causes economic losses to crops or a nuisance or health hazard to human beings and other animals ________.
3. Dead human lice have been discovered in the hair of ________ mummies.
4. Natural barriers like mountain ranges. large water bodies and deserts prevent pest ________.
5. Soil types also limit the distribution and ________ of soil insects.
6. Among the insects themselves, there exists a large number of ________ species.
7. Entomophagous insect species may be either ________.
8. ________ pathogens produce fatal diseases in insects.
9. Crop rotation usually affects those insects which have a limited ________ and relatively immobile in some stage of their development.
10. Intercropping/mixed cropping helps in control of ________.
11. Tillage tends to reduce ________.
12. ________ method of pest control is specifically useful against vegetable and field crops.
13. Insect (pest) resistance of a plant is derived from certain ________ and/or morphological characteristics.
14. Light traps are used to attract ________ insects which are strongly phototaxic.
15. ________ produce differential heating in the hosts (grains) and infesting pests.
16. The insects, responsive range to solar spectrum lies between below UV to ________.
17. ________ radiations either kill the insect-pests outrightly or sterilize them.
18. Insecticides can exist in three forms *viz*., pure, ________ forms and formulations.
19. Pure form of an insecticide is synthesized by scientists with 99 per cent purity (gramme quantity) in lab for analytical and ________ studies.
20. The ________ refers to a toxicant manufactured in bulk by a basic manufacturer after satisfactory lab-tests.
21. After commercial manufacture, the ________ add various additions to prepare formulations.
22. Generally, basic manufacturers themselves prefer to be also formulators to avoid the risk of ________.
23. When an insecticide is adsorbed on the particle surface of the insecticide of the diluent, the latter is called a ________ otherwise a filler.
24. A solvent (spray additive) should be highly soluble, inflammable and ________.
25. ________ are used to suppress the unpleasant odour of certain insecticides when used for household purposes.

26. ________ are chemicals embodying no insecticidal property of own, but an addition to an insecticide enhances, its toxicity manifold.

27. ________ stabilize the droplet size of insecticides spray solution to ensure persistent contact with insect's body for augmented kill.

28. Most of the insecticides are ________ in water.

29. An emulsion is a ________ dispersion involving water and an immiscible solvent.

30. The technique of low volume concentration was first conceived soon after World War II during ________ in East Africa.

31. ________ in 1963 demonstrated the efficacy of ULV spray on crops.

32. Insecticides used in gaseous form are called ________.

33. Insecticides ________ are referred to as the quantities of persistent insecticides that pollute environment and foodstuffs.

34. Median residual life (RL_{50}) or half-life of an insecticide is the time required for half of its residues to react and kill 50 per cent of the ________.

35. Insect poisoning in ________ insecticides occurs due to inhibition of acetylcholinesterase (AChE) enzyme causing accumulation of transmitter acetylcholine (ACh).

36. Organophorus insecticides produce two types of symptoms *viz.*, muscarinic and ________.

37. Poisoning due to carbamate insecticides occurs due to AChE inhibition, by ________ unlike phosphorylation of organophorus group.

38. Death due to PCP is due to ________ or respiratory failure.

39. Arsenites are derived from arsenious acid, while arsenates from ________.

40. Paris green is ________.

41. Seeds and leaves (dried) of ________ serve as locust repellant and protect stored grains against store-pests.

42. DDT was first described by a German Chemist, ________ in 1874, but Paul Muller (of Switzerland) in 1939 discovered its insecticidal property.

43. The complete chemical name of DDT is ________.

44. Marked male moths are known to have been attracted to a trap baited with the female ________ from a distance of two miles.

45. The pheromone produced by gypsy moth female has been estimated at 0.01 mg, it is enough to ________ one billion males of its species.

46. The pheromones induce aggregation or congregation of ________ for protection, reproduction, and feeding or combinations thereof.

47. ________ pheromones are primarily an antipredator device.

48. The ant (*Camponotus*), when attacked ejects ________ in its own defence (as an allomone).

49. The formic acid ejected by one ant is utilized by another ant (*Myrmecia gulosa*) to ________ of this ant (*Camponotus*).

50. Neurosecretary cells (NSC) are neurons in the central nervous system that are specialized to secrete ________.

51. *Corpora cardiaca* are small paired bodies immediately behind the ________ and are believed to be modified ganglia (in insects).

52. *Corpora allata* are ________ organs and may fuse into one in some insects.

53. Any chemical that can inhibit the growth gonads or interfere with reproductive capacity of an insect in any other way is called ________.
54. BHC (Gemmexane, $C_6H_6C_{16}$) is ________.
55. Most of the ________ are esters of alcohols with phosphoric acid or anhydrides of phosphoric acid with some other acid.
56. In woody plants absorption of an insecticide has been more effective through ________ than through roots.
57. Decomposition of systemic insecticides into different compounds inside the plant body is known as ________.
58. Thimet (phorate) and disystox are used as ________ either directly or through soil treatment.
59. Inflammable fumigants should be mixed with ________.
60. Fumigation should be carried out during ________ hours.
61. Pest ________ occurs either due to development of resistance or due to destruction of parasites or both.
62. DDT "fallout" is the second ________ after the nuclear fallout.
63. Chemicals present in the host plants act as attractant (phagostimulants) and those in the non -host plants as ________.
64. "Malus yields a phenolic substance, phlorizin that stimulates probing in the apple feeding aphids and acts as feeding deterrent for non-apple feeding aphids (*Myzus persicae*)" is known as ________.
65. ________ alkaloids extracted from some species of *Solanum* reduce feeding and survival time in potato leafhopper, *Empoasca devastans*.
66. *Rodonalia cardinalis* from Australia was introduced into California (U.S.A.) in 1888 to control ________ a serious pest of citrus.
67.. ________ comprises a method of controlling pests by exposing them to their natural enemies.
68. Helping to make imported species establish itself in a new environment (area/country) is known as ________.
69. ________ bacteria are more promising in insect control than the non-sporeforming ones.
70. Toxins produced by entomogenous fungi are known as ________.
71. Aflatoxins cause serious changes in ________ activity of the vertebrates and insects.
72. Destruxins (Destruxin A and Destruxin B) cause ________ and death in insects.
73. The Panel of FAO-Experts (1967) defined Integrated Pest Management (IPM) "as a system, that, in context of the associated environment and the population dynamics of the ________, utilizes all suitable techniques and methods in as compatible a manner as is possible and maintains the pest populations at levels below those causing economic injury".
74. The insects and some of their arthropod relatives are the ________ who can breathe in free air besides reptiles, birds and mammals.
75. The ________ ants capture other ants who act as slaves to them doing all the chores of their nest.
76. In honeybee hive as the temperature falls in winter, they consume ________, become active, vibrate the wings to generate energy raising the inside temperature by many degrees.
77. ________ are the main transmitters of viruses to the plants.
78. A phytophagus insect, a leaf feeder nibbles the leaves either on ________ or the surface that can be easily seen.

79. ________ will produce stunted growth, bunchy tops and dead hearts.
80. Root borer renders the ________ of the plant so weak that they can be easily pulled out or can be felled by gust or wind.
81. ________ are not easy to detect.
82. The ________ refers to the level of pest population above which crop losses occur and below which the pest has no significance.
83. The damage threshold has to be separately determined for different ________.
84. Ladybird has no special structural ________ as their preys are largely immobile.
85. The desirable substitutes for cyanide bottle (usually used for insect collection) are ethyl acetate, ammonium hydroxide, benzene, ________, carbon tetrachloride, and trichloro-ethylene.
86. Relaxing is the process of ________ the insect.
87. The knowledge of ________ of insects helps in prediction of pest-outbreak and population buildup.
88. Life histories of insects make one important component of information about their biology that is crucial to their ________.
89. ________ is a specialized condition of suspended activity with body metabolism at its minimum.
90. Preventing the insects from. entering the diapause is to force them to face ________ climatic condition and perish.
91. ________ means broods or generations, but it is mainly used in reference to silkworm races.
92. A race producing single race a year is called ________.
93. Eulophid (*Tetrastichus nyemitawus*) and chalcid (*Callitula bipartius*) are the larval parasites of ________.
94. ________ is parasited by *Scolia aureipennis.*
95. White grub adults are parasitised by the fungus ________.
96. *Perilissus cingulator* is the parasite of mustard sawfly (________).
97. Pink bollworm (*Pectinophora gossipiella*) eggs are preyed upon by anthocorid bug (________).
98. The mosquito bug (*Helopeltis theivora*) nymphs are parasitised by ________, nematode.
99. Though cockroaches are ________ in distribution, they thrive in tropical and sub-tropical climates.
100. *Periplaneta americana* (a cockroach) is the ________ and dark brown in colour.
101. Locusts ________ eat *Calotropis procera* (*aak*), *Datura stramonium* (*dhatura*), *Melia azadirachta* (*neem*), *Psidium cuminii* (*jamun*), *Dalbergia sissoo* (*sheesham*) and *Ficus carica* (*anjeer*).
102. Some individuals are so sensitive to locusts and grasshoppers sight and touch that they suffer from bouts of ________ attack.
103. The expansion of termite queen's abdomen to accommodate reproductive organs is known as ________.
104. Termites, commonly but ________ called white ants, are neither white nor are related to ants.
105. The termite workers develop from ________, but remain stunted (smallest in size) because they are reared on ordinary food.
106. The termite king and queen of a colony are forced to live in ________ located in the centre of the nest, 0.5 m below the ground.
107. The termite king develops from ________ and is smaller than queen in size.
108. Silk is the product of a pair of silk glands which are the ________ of the larva present in its thoracic cavity.

109. The silk (fibre) is composed of fibroin and ________ (proteins).
110. The nest (comb) of a honey bee has three types of hexagonal cells, worker cells, ________ and queen cells.
111. All honey bee eggs hatch in three days, but the period of ________ of larva and pupa differ among the castes.
112. In honey bee, transformation of three castes depends on the amount of ________.
113. Brood-food is produced by the ________ salivary glands of the workers.
114. Honey bees employ both dance and sound in their ________.
115. ________ bees drink all the honey of their nest and leave behind empty combs, brood and sometimes even food.
116. ________ is obtained from the combs of the wild hives, frame hives and cappings.
117. ________ is the ability of a pathogen to cause disease.
118. ________ is a measure or degree of pathogenicity of an isolate or race of a pathogen.
119. ________ speaks of the capacity of a pathogen to invade and grow in its host plant and to reproduce on or in it.
120. Elicitors are signals, presumably chemical signals, generated by an organism to bring about ________ in another organism.
121. Vraksha-Ayurveda, a book by Surapal in ancient India is the ________ in which much light has been thrown on plant diseases.
122. In 1675, the Dutch worker ________ developed the first microscope and in 1683 used it to describe bacteria seen with this.
123. The French scientist Prevost proved in 1807 that ________ are caused by microorganisms.
124. During 1830-1845 ________ of potato spread fast in England, Ireland and continental Europe.
125. Tulasne brothers of France (R.L. Tulasne and C. Tulasne) produced illustrated descriptions of ________ causing fungi.
126. In 1878 the downy mildew of grapevines was introduced into Europe from ________.
127. The presence of nematodes or similar organisms in human body was known to ________ as early as 1553 B.C.
128. As early as 1898, Nocard and Roux discovered another group of disease incitants in animals similar to virus in size that was known as ________.
129. In 1967, Japanese scientists found that mycoplasma-like organisms could be responsible for most of the ________ supposed to be caused by virus in plants.
130. The first Indian Universities established in 1857 at Calcutta, Bombay, and Madras emphasized ________ of fungi.
131. During 1850-1875, A.D. Cunningham and A. Barclay started ________ of fungi in India itself.
132. ________ was first Indian scientist who collected and identified fungi in this country.
133. T.S. Sadasivan's school contributed to the concept of ________ and worked out the mechanism of wilting in cotton due to *Fusarium vasinfectum*.
134. Typical plant diseases are caused by inanimate (non-living) or ________ causes.
135. A ________ is a compact, often hard mass of dormant fungus mycelium.
136. ________ diseases are characterized by drying of the entire plant.
137. In die-back or whither tip diseases plant organs especially stem or branches dry from the ________.

138. Certain infectious pathogens, such as viruses, are neither seen nor can be grown on ________.
139. ________ parasites are basically saprophytic in their feeding mechanism.
140. The infection by ________ parasites never kills the host.
141. The chain of events leading to disease development is referred to as ________
142. When the pathogen survives on only one genus or species of plants, it is called ________.
143. Most of the wilt causing species of *Fusarium* are ________.
144. When a pathogen present in the host does not produce symptoms, the host is regarded as its ________.
145. In citrus, canker is caused by ________ and the bacterium survives in cankers on the standing trees.
146. In red rot of sugarcane, causal fungus is *Colletotrichum falcatum* and its primary infection comes from ________.
147. The primary inoculum of rice leaf spot (*Helminthosporium oryzae*) and blast (*Pyricularia oryzae*) is believed to come from ________.
148. ________ fungi over-summer in hills from where comes the primary inoculum through wind or insects.
149. The role of alternate hosts is not as important as of ________ hosts.
150. Generally, the soil microflora reduce saprophytic activity in the process of ________ survival of fungi.
151. ________ fungi have declining saprophytic phase limiting their survival in soil.
152. ________ have no resting stage and are transmitted through a continuous infection chain.
153. A majority of ________ nematodes, survive through their dormant structures.
154. The ________ are the main structures for dormant survival.
155. When the dormant mycelium is present in the embryo, the disease is known as ________.
156. Fungi species like *Pythium, Phytophthora* etc. form zoospores provided with ________ for locomotion in films of soil water.
157. The growth of ________ fungi in soil is either extremely slow or non-existent.
158. The nematode of ________ of wheat may remain viable in the galls in quiescent state for 26 or more years.
159. The primary inoculum of cucurbit (*Erwinia tracheiphila*) by striped and spotted cucumber beetles in their ________.
160. The most common insect vectors are ________.
161. The ________ can carry the fungal propagules on their body and help in entry through punctures for their own entry.
162. The ________ of nematodes is so far known to act as vector.
163. Stem segments of dodder (*Cuscuta*) are carried by ________ to prepare nest and is thus transported to new sites.
164. Dissemination of red rot fungus and wilt organisms in active or dormant state may be ________ by agency of water.
165. The uredospores of *Puccinia graminis* are disseminated by ________.
166. The uredospores of *Puccinia graminis* var. *tritici* have been detected as high as 1400 feet above ________ wheat fields.
167. In Australia, the introduction of *Puccinia graminis* (rust causing fungus) has been suspected due to wind-borne spores from ________ and elsewhere.
168. The pathogens embodying enzyme-based success have to produce adequate ________ to produce needed quantum of enzymes.

169. Rhizomorphic fungus, ________ can produce sufficient amount of hyphae to produce desired amount of enzymes success.

170. The ________ fungi are usually more aggressive and endoparasitic nematodes also attack roots.

171. Pathogens for direct penetration have to neutralize the natural ________ to establish in the host-plant system.

172. ________ and nematodes are the only group of plant pathogens employing force for direct penetration into the host.

173. The glands in leaf hairs of chickpea contain ________ which is antifungal and provides resistance against rust fungus.

174. "The tendency of treatments and conditions, acting before inoculation or introduction of incitant to affect susceptibility to biotic or abiotic pathogens" is referred to as ________.

175. The energy of growth of a parasite available for infection of a host at the surface of the host organ to be infected is known as ________.

176. The manifestation of resistant reaction of the host at a particular stage of growth is termed as ________.

177. ________ deals with outbreaks and spread of disease in a population.

178. The ________ develop in the same manner as the rise in human population.

179. The period of incubation and ________ is short in epiphytotic.

180. Stem rust of wheat (*Puccinia graminis tritici*) serves as an example of ________ nature of disease spread.

181. In simple nature of disease-spread ________ infection rarely occurs during the same season.

182. ________ is the best method for the control of slow epidemics.

183. Longer the distance from the source of survival of the pathogen, the longer will be time required for build up of epiphytotic in a ________ crop.

184. Continuous use of susceptible variety occupying large contiguous area help in build up of inoculum and augments chances of ________.

185. High birth rate coupled with low rate- of mortality enhances the chances of occurrence of ________ at a high level.

186. Disease severity is the product of inoculum potential and ________.

187. Inoculum and disease potentials *vis-a-vis* environment favourably or unfavourably influence the development of ________.

188. As a system, epidemic exists in a relatively very small compartment of a much bigger system, the ________.

189. A system is regarded as an interlocking complex of processes characterized by many reciprocal ________ pathways.

190. ________ model could simulate, imitate or mimic an epidemic on a computer provided complete information about the epidemic is fed to the computer.

191. Harmful effects of infection on host physiology comprise the chief causes of ________ expression and loss.

192. The most common symptoms of plant diseases are those caused by ________ of tissues.

193. It is believed that the ________ enzymes mainly help in penetration of infection thread by pressure.

194. Fungi, bacteria and nematodes embody pectic or pectinolytic enzymes which degrade the components of middle ________ and cell wall.

195. ________ DNA is not degraded, but cytoplasmic DNA can be degraded by pathogens.

196. ________ enzyme separates the amino groups from nucleotides and makes them available to the parasite.

197. Indole acetic acid (IAA) is produced either by the pathogen in small quantities or by ________ the plant to produce more of it.

198. Due to the effect of IAA on oxidative enzyme system of the plant, there may occur an abnormal increase in ________ of the tissues.

199. The fungi causing late blight of potato, smut of maize, panama diseases of banana, downy mildew of maize and pearlmillet and nematodes causing root knot not only induce to produce, but also produce ________.

200. The crown gall caused by *Agrobacterium tumefasciens* has served as a classic model to study the role of auxins, IAA and related compounds in plant ________.

201. The ________ were discovered by Japanese, while investigating *bakanae* (foolish seedling) disease of rice caused by *Gibberella fujukuroi.*

202. The loss from disease is owing to reduction in ________ of the plant.

203. The injury or wounds caused by pathogens to plant roots reduce their effective number and proportionately the water ________.

204. The fungi or bacteria causing damping off, stalk rot, and canker can enter the ________ vessels.

205. Bacteria and fungi are capable of producing polysaccharides that can induce wilt symptoms ________

206. Tyloses are outgrowth of ________ adjacent to xylem and appear as peg-like structure.

207. The toxin hypothesis with experimental evidence was first provided by metabolites of *Cochliobolus* (*Helminthosporium*) *victoriae*, a fungus which causes ________ of oats.

208. A ________ toxic is a metabolic product of a pathogenic microorganism, selectively toxic only to susceptible host of the pathogen.

209. In cereal rusts ________ the penetrates through the stoma.

210. The species of ________ invade only juvenile tissues in which secondary thckening has not yet developed

211. The ________ and post-infectionally produced metabolites inducing resistance.

212. ________ leaves are known to excrete chemicals that provide resistance to attack of *Botrytis cinerea.*

213. ________ leaves resistant to *Cercospora* leaf spots possess toxic substances that inhibit the gemination of *Conidia.*

214. Marigold (*Tagetes erecta*) has been used in biological control of ________.

215. *Asparagus officinalis* produces ________ acid (a toxic material) against the nematode *Tichodorus christici.*

216. Cucurbits (bitter cucumber) produce a compound named cucurbitacin which is a repellent for ________.

217. Gum deposition in cells along the border of ________ often serves as a protective mechanical barrier.

218. The cytoplasmic defence reactions weaken, localize, and eliminate the ________ bacteria or the endomycorrhizal fungi.

219. Compatible (susceptible) soybean - *Phytophthora* produce very little ________, a pterocarpanoid phytolexin.

220. Elicitors are cell wall components of the pathogen capable of inducing ________ synthesis.

221. *Xanthomonas malvacearum* is ________ more similar to its host cotton than to other species of *Xanthomonas*..

222. Chemically different crops' residues in rotation help in environmental modification in favour of ________ and against pathogen.

223. Chemically zineb is called zinc ________ disdithiocarbamate.

224. Maneb is chemically known manganese ethylene ________.

225. When ________ is added to maneb it forms Dithane M-45 (Mancozeb).

226. Bordeaux paste, ________ and chestnut compounds are copper based home-made fungicides.

227. ________ paste contains 800 g of copper carbonate, 800 g red lead and one litre of raw linseed oil or lanolin.

228. Quinones are naturally present in plants and often exhibit ________ activity.

229. Sugar-beet sickness in Europe, yellows disease of pepper in Indonesia and decline of citrus in California (U.S.A.) are now established ________ problems.

230. *Anguina tritici* on ________ causes crinkling of leaves.

231. *Anguina tritici* (nematode) larvae enter the flower primordia which instead of normal development into seed, change to ________.

232. *Anguina tumafaciens* causes ________ on *Cynodon transvalensis.*

233. *Anguina picridis* causes galls on the stem of ________.

234. Root galls are characteristically produced by ________ nematodes.

235. 'Bearding' or 'hairy root' and 'witche's broom' are caused by ________ of nematodes.

236. The juveniles of *Tylenchulus semipenetrans*, as estimated can last as long as nine years without ________.

237. *Hirschmanniella mucronata* nematode penetrates rice roots for feeding and ________ inside the cortex.

238. *Pratylenchus penetrans*, *P. vulnis* and *P. coffeae* are bisexual nematodes with ________ reproduction.

239. *Tylenchorhynchus agri*, nematode has been mainly reported as a parasite of ________ and graminaceous plants.

II. Tick mark (✓) True / False:

240. Wilt of cotton (*Fusarium oxysporum* f. sp. *vasinfectum*) and tomato (*F. oxysporum* f. sp. *lycopersici*) is favoured by acidic soils.

241. Most of the nematodes grow best at pH values of 5-6 except *Heterodera avenae*, the cause of molya disease of wheat and barley.

242. Bean bacterial blight (*Xanthomonas phaseoli*) spreads through irrigation and drainage water.

243. Sugarcane red rot (*Collectotrichum falcatum*) cannot spread through drainage and irrigation. water.

244. Nematodes *viz*., *Meloidogyne* spp., *Tylencnulus semipenetrans* (on citrus), *Heterodera schachtii* (beet) and *H. avenae* (wheat) spread by irrigation and drainage water.

245. Irrigation and drainage waters are not helpful in spread of downy mildew of maize (*Peronoclerospora sacchari*).

246. Angular leaf spot of cotton (*Xanthomonas malvacearum*) and black shank of tobacco (*Phytophthora nicotianae* var. *nicotianae*) do not spread through irrigation and drainage waters.

247. Foot and stem rot of papaya (*Pythium aphanidermatum* and *phytophthora parasitica*) spread through drainage and irrigation water.

248. Cucurbitaceous weeds aid in survival and spread of the pathogens causing powdery mildew and mosaic in them.
249. Banding of stem is usually employed to prevent insect-pests from climbing to tree-tops.
250. Nymphs of grasshoppers and locusts have the habit of moving in bands.
251. Basic manufacturer and formulators do not need separate government licences.
252. The insecticides need not be mixed with additives as these are needed in large quantities to kill the pests.
253. If a synergist is applied later than the insecticide, there is no synergism.
254. The finished product of a dust formulation of an insecticide may contain 0.1-25 per cent of the toxicant.
255. In general, the toxicity of an insecticide decreases with the decrease in its particle size.
256. Insecticide dusts embodying particle size larger than 0.25-2.4 mm are called granular formulations.
257. Median lethal dose is a unit to calculate the acute oral or dermal toxicity of an insecticide on a test animal, usually white rats.
258. The toxicity of an insecticidal spray cannot be enhanced by its mixing with oil.
259. Development stage of an insect plays no role in its susceptibility to insecticides.
260. Dense hairy growths on the foliage encourage penetration by insecticides.
261. The insecticides which on mixing with others react and change to lose their effectiveness are called incompatible.
262. Pyrethrins, rotenone and nicotine are botanical insecticides.
263. Sweettlag's (*Acorus calmus*) powdered rhizomes and seeds afford protection of stored grains against pests (insects).
264. The absorption of insecticides by roots occurs the best in solution.
265. Fumigants can be applied both in closed and open areas alike.
266. Vacuum fumigation is done in case of cotton bales.
267. Antifeedants produce phytotoxicity or pollution.
268. Chinese farmers employed predaceous red ant (*Oecophylla*), centuries ago, to control the insect-pests feeding on mandarin (orange) trees.
269. Aldrovandi (1602), an Italian noted the hymenopteran parasite, *Apanteles glomeratus* laying eggs in the pupae of the cabbage butterfly, *Pieris brassicae*.
270. "The study and utilization of parasites, predators and pathogens for the regulation of host (= pest) population densities" is biocontrol.
271. Colonization is not the most critical operation in biological pest-control.
272. Natural enemy of insects are host specific and therefore, do not attack the non-targets.
273. Among the organisms *Bacillus thuringiensis* has been most extensively tried and found effective against many *lepidopterous* insects of field crops and forests.
274. A pheromone is a chemical or a mixture of chemicals released by an organism in the environment.
275. A pheromone causes a specific reaction in a receiving organism of the other species.
276. More than 150-insect-species are known in which females produce pheromones and 50-male species do so.
277. The dead, dry and powdered bodies of cactus scale insects yield a crimson colour dyestuff cochineal, used to dye robes of kings and nobles.

278. Britishers grew cactus scale insect in Bihar and held the monopoly earning huge profits.
279. Insects do not destroy weeds.
280. Insects have never catered to the aesthetic needs of man.
281. Some 150 diseases, some of them quite serious, are known to be exclusively transmitted by insects and their arthropod relatives.
282. Insects possess an exoskeleton made up of chitin.
283. Parental care in insects is an indication of lower evolution.
284. Ants carry European beetle's (*Clythra*) eggs covered with their excrement by mistaking them as vegetable bits, they (eggs) hatch in their nests and live as guests (inquilines).
285. The sand-wasp (*Ammophila*) injects only such a quantity of poison in the caterpillar (future food of its larvae) that would just paralyse and not kill it.
286. Most of the parasites attack a wide range of hosts.
287. Parasites by themselves are immune to parasitic attack.
288. Insects do not abound anywhere and everywhere.
289. The cyanide is since a deadly poison should be handled by a chemist.
290. Temporary development arrest largely of eggs in summer is referred to as aestivalion.
291. The lady beetles (*Coccinella septempunctata* and *Menochilus sexmaculata*) have been found predating on the larvae of stem borer (*Chilo zonellus*).
292. Damage by shoot borer is done by caterpillars feeding outside the stem.
293. Typical symptoms of stem borer are dead hearts, and frass and weakening of the plants.
294. The house cricket (*Gryllodes sigillatus*) is dull straw coloured insect with deep brown spots on the body.
295. Crickets can be controlled (killed) by any poison-bait prepared from any bitter starchy substance.
296. The winged sexual forms of ants (*Monorium indicum*) appear at the first rains.
297. Wasps (*Polistes hebraeus* and *Vespa. orientalis*) are found in hilly areas of India.
298. Clothe-moths (*Tinae pellionella* and *T. pachyspila*) and are straw coloured and tiny (less than 1.25 cm across the wings) in size.
299. In carpet beetles (*Anthrenus scrophulariae. A. flavipes* and *Attagenus piceus*) damage is done by adults and larvae feed outdoor.
300. Cigarette beetle (*Lasioderma serricorne*) is a very serious insect-pest of stored tobacco.
301. In India, Lefroy (1905-1906) was first to investigate silkworms and sericulture at Pusa Institute (Indian then Imperial) Agricultural Research Institute, New Delhi.
302. J.C. Luthra and his associates developed the solar treatment of wheat seed for control of loose smut.
303. M.J. Thirumalachar successfully introduced antibiotics in plant diseases control.
304. Sporadic diseases are those which occur at very regular intervals.
305. An epiphytotic disease is one which occurs widely but periodically.
306. Association of a specific pathogen is not essential with infectious diseases.
307. Nematodes can be cultured on artificial media.
308. The virus is not maintained on its original host, but on artificial media.
309. The total number of plant diseases may be more than 80,000.

310. The facultative saprophytes live on dead organic matter.
311. Usually the obligate parasites are not host specific.
312. The means of survival are the first link in disease cycle.
313. Externally seed-borne organisms (mycelium, spores, bacterial cells) remain in the seed.
314. Germination of spores brings about antagonistic elimination of the pathogen (s).
315. The movement of propagules of animate pathogens through wind is not common for soil or seed-borne pathogens.
316. The green ear is a common disease of pearimillet and occurs in several countries including India, Iran, Israel, China, Fiji, Japan, the U.S.A. and European and African countries.
317. Autonomous dispersal of pathogens is accomplished through soil, seed, and plant organs during normal agronomic operations.
318. No fungal pathogen first grow on the surface of the host before causing penetration.
319. *Rhizoctonia solani* (attacking radish/tomato roots) on coming in contact with root surface, forms *infection cushions* and *appressoria* and from these no multiple infections occur through infection pegs.
320. Nematodes cannot multiply outside the host as they depend for nutrition solely on the host.
321. Many fungal pathogens first grow on the surface of the host before causing infection.
322. In *Colletotrichum* species even the hyphae of the fungus within the host cells do not form appressoria.
323. In indirect infection, the germ tubes of the infection threads enter the host through wounds and / or through natural openings.
324. The infection occurring through wounds is known as trauma infection.
325. Most of the pathogens do not use wounds as portal of entry into the host.
326. Insect vestors either bite the leaves or insert their proboscis to suck juice cause wounds there on.
327. In many host-specific pathogens like rust and powdery mildew entry of fungi through *stomate*s is a rule to infect a non-cereal host.
328. The entry of the pathogen into the host plant always ensures infection and disease development.
329. The virus particles do not absorb nutrients from. the cell protoplasm, but their nucleic acid induces self-duplication.
330. The time lapses between penetration by pathogen and appearance of symptoms is known as incubation period.
331. The pathogens unable to produce mycelium are ectobiotic as the thallus is entirely contained within a host cell.
332. Fungi after growing for some time in the host tissues produce branched spore bearing hyphae when conditions are favourable to cause primary infection.
333. Genetic response of the plant to the pathogen is an innate plant factor determining success of infection.
334. "Predisposition is the action of set of environment, prior to penetration and infection, which makes the plant vulnerable to attack by pathogen".
335. Ontogenic disposition plays no role in the infection by many pathogens.
336. Temperature predisposes infection chiefly by producing injury, a real predisposing agent.
337. Humidity is a major predisposing factor in as much as its effect on the plant is concerned.
338. Dark treatment before inoculation decreases susceptibility of potatoes to infection by *Macrophomina phaseolina* and *Fusarium coeruleum*.

339. Resistance of cotton to wilt in zinc amended soil has been assigned to its vigorous growth.
340. The plant exudates are rich in sugars, amino acids, and other nutrients unsuitable for parasitic growth.
341. The presence of sugars in wrinkled seeded pea varieties enhance their susceptibility to infection of *Pythium*.
342. "Any phenomenon, structural or functional, having two or more separate components and some interaction between these components" represents a system.
343. The activity of pectic enzymes may not be aggravated by synergistic action of other enzymes and metabolites.
344. The 'foolish seedling' disease of rice entails abnormal elongation of stem due to excessive elongation of internodes.
345. Gibberellins are considered as normal constituents of green plants and are not found in microorganisms.
346. The best known cytokinin is kinetin (6-furfurl-amino-purine).
347. Dormin can function as antagonist of gibberellins in the plant.
348. The pathogen or its growth regulators, toxins and enzymes alter cell wall permeability of roots.
349. The decreased suction tension due to increased transpiration may result in collapse of vessels or formation of tyloses.
350. Rust and mildew fungi are known to cause accumulation of carbohydrates and minerals away from infection site.
351 The pentose pathway of respiration dominates in diseased plants.
352. There is evidence that the Kreb's cycle is activated in infected plants due to decrease in conçentration of coenzyme A (Co A).
353. Leaf blights, spots and identical disease pathogens reduce the assilative surface in plants and hence the photosynthesis.
354. Like the bacteria and viruses, fungal pathogens do not obstruct photosynthesis by adversely affecting chloroplasts.
355. In blight affected potato, tuber growth ceases when 75 per cent foliage is killed.
356. In 1954, Ernet Gaumann had boldly asserted that a microorganism cannot be pathogenic unless it is toxigenic.
357. A toxin represents microbial metabolites excreted (*exotoxin*) or released by lysed cells (*endotoxin*) which in very low concentration is directly toxic to cells of suscept.
358. The concentration of glucosides in roots, stems, leaves, flowers, and seeds of different plants vary from 1-5 mg / gramme of fresh weight.
359. Fungal invasion of oat roots triggers release of avenacins from protoplasts simultaneously with leakage of electrolytes and nutrients.
360. Root rot of cotton (*Phymatotrichum omnivorum*) is favoured by dry soil or water deficiency.
361. Common scab of potato (*Streptomyces scabies*) incidence is favoured by water deficiency or dry soil.
362. Bare patch of wheat (*Rhizoctonia solani*) infestation is favoured by high relative humidity or wet soil.
363. Stalk rot maize (*Fusarium moliniforme*) infection is favoured by wet soil or high relative humidity.
364. Wet soil or high relative humidity favours the occurrence of safflower root rot (*Phytophthora cryptogea*).
365. Black root rot of tobacco (*Thielaviopsis basicola*) is favoured by wet soil or high relative humidity.
366 Wilt of pea (*Fusarium oxysporum* f. sp. *pisi* race 1) incidence is favoured by alkaline soils.

367. Acidic soil favours the incidence of common scab of potato (*Streptomyces scabies*).

368. Club root of cabbage (*Plasmodiophora brassicae*) infestation is favoured by acid soils.

III. Tick mark (✓) the correct answer·

369. The nematode *Paratylenchus* Microletzky (1992) members measure ________ mm in size.
(*a*) 0.10-0.20 (*b*) 0.25-0.50
(*c*) 0.7-0.8 (*d*) 0.9-0.10

370. *Paratylenchus projectus* nematode has been found to cause considerable damage in red clover yield at ________ nematodes / kg of soil.
(*a*) 2-7 (*b*) 8-13
(*c*) 14-19 (*d*) 20-25

371. *Xiphinema cobbi* (nematode) has been described after 1980 from ________.
(*a*) Brazil (*b*) South Africa
(*c*) India (*d*) Italy

372. It has been estimated that insects had existed on this earth for at least ________ million years.
(*a*) 100 (*b*) 150
(*c*) 200 (*d*) 250

373. Stored grain pests can be killed by ________ hours exposure to 51.5-54.5°C.
(*a*) 2 (*b*) 3
(*c*) 5 (*d*) 7

374. Most of the insects cannot survive the temperatures above ________ °C.
(*a*) 29.9 (*b*) 39.9
(*c*) 49.9 (*d*) 59.9

375. Ultra-low volume (ULV) or low volume concentration (LVC) refers to the use of spray volume (liquid) less than ________ litres.
(*a*) 5 (*b*) 7
(*c*) 9 (*d*) 11

376. Malathion is a ________ insecticide.
(*a*) Slow fumigant (*b*) Contactplus systemic
(*c*) Contactplus stomach (*d*) Systemic

377. Metasystox-R is a insecticide.
(*a*) Systemic (*b*) Fumigant
(*c*) Contact (*d*) Contact-plus stomach

378. Phorate is a ________ insecticide.
(*a*) Systemic (*b*) Contact-plus systemic
(*c*) Contact (*d*) Contact-plus stomach

379. Phosdrin is a ________ insecticide.
(*a*) Slow fumigant (*b*) Systemic
(*c*) Systemic plus contact (*d*) Contact

380. A minimum period of ________ years is to be given before assessing the effectiveness of an important biocontrol agent.
(*a*) 2 (*b*) 3
(*c*) 4 (*d*) 5

381. The queen termite produces ________ eggs per second.

(a) 40
(b) 50
(c) 60
(d) 70

382. Honey bee queen produces ________ thousand eggs per day.

(a) 0.5-1.5
(b) 2-3
(c) 4.0-4.5
(d) 5.0-5.5

383. An average locust swarm spreads over ________ square kilometers.

(a) 5
(b) 10
(c) 15
(d) 20

384. One kilometer of locust swarm weighs as much as ________ tonnes of locusts.

(a) 100
(b) 200
(c) 300
(d) 400

385. The duration of locust plague period lasts for ________ years.

(a) 2-3
(b) 3-4
(c) 5-10
(d) 11-16

386. A locust swarm as large as ________ square kilometers is on record.

(a) 100
(b) 200
(c) 300
(d) 400

387. The ________ botanist Micheli (1679-1737) was the first scientist who in 1729 studied fungi and saw their spores.

(a) German
(b) Dutch
(c) Italian
(d) Austrian

388. In ________ the French botanist Tillet published a paper on bunt or stinking smut of wheat.

(a) 1555
(b) 1655
(c) 1755
(d) 1855

389. By 1857, Berkley and Schacht discovered root knot nematodes and cyst nematode in ________.

(a) Sweet sorghum
(b) Sugarcane
(c) Potato
(d) Sugarbeet

390. The discovery of ________ mosaic by Meyer in 1886 was the beginning of studies on viruses as incitants of diseases in plants.

(a) Tomato
(b) Mung bean
(c) Tobacco
(d) Soybean

391. ________, before 1910 initiated exhaustive study of Indian fungi and diseases caused by them.

(a) E.J. Butler
(b) J.G. Moseman
(c) R.E. Nelson
(d) A. Livney

392. Dr. K.C. Mehta of Agra College made an outstanding contribution to plant pathology by discovering the disease cycle of cereal ________ in India.

(a) Smuts
(b) Rusts
(c) Wilts
(d) Blights

393. In bacterial brown rot and wilt of potato the amount of ________ produced by pathogens are proportional to severity of symptoms.

(*a*) Gibberellins (*b*) Lipids
(*c*) Polysaccharides (*d*) Proteins

394. Some ________ varieties of apple exude toxic wax on leaf surface to prevent germination of conidia of *Podosphaera leucotricha.*

(*a*) Scab resistant (*b*) Leaf blight resistant
(*c*) Powdery mildew resistant (*d*) Rust resistant

395. Red scales of ________ (red varieties) contain protocatechuic acid and catechol which may exude in drops to resist the attack of *Colletotrichum circinans.*

(*a*) Garlic (*b*) Onion
(*c*) Leek (*d*) Celery

396. Some varieties of ________ are resistant to wilt due to the presence of hydrocyanides (HCN) in root exudates.

(*a*) Sunflower (*b*) Safflower
(*c*) Castor (*d*) Linseed (flax)

397. Oil from American elm seed contains 55 per cent capric acid toxic to *Ceratocystis ulmi*, the pathogen causing the famous ________ disease.

(*a*) English elm (*b*) Dutch elm
(*c*) American elm (*d*) French elm

398. The epidermal cells of ________ plant become filled with toxic terpenoid aldehyde after they are few days old and these cells are rarely penetrated by pathogens.

(*a*) Jute (*b*) Flax
(*c*) Cotton (*d*) Okra

399. In *P. coffeae* (nematode) a ________ species, the optimum temperature for multiplication is reported to be 29.5°C on rough lemon.

(*a*) Temperate (*b*) Tropical
(*c*) Humid (*d*) Sub-humid

400. Strawberry plants infected with *P. penetrans* (nematode) have been successfully treated with exposure in hot water at ________.

(*a*) 49.4°C for 17.5 min. (*b*) 52.8°C for 6 min.
(*c*) 54.4°C for 4 min. (*d*) 56°C for 2 min.

401. Genus *Radopholus* of nematode was first described in 1893 on the basis of a male specimen obtained from necrotic roots of ________ growing in Fiji Islands.

(*a*) Sugarbeet (*d*) Sugarcane
(*c*) Banana (*d*) Coconut

402. The nematode *Radopholus similes* has shown the maximum numbers at a soil depth of ________.

(*a*) 5-15 m (*b*) 20-30 m
(*c*) 32-42 m (*c*) 1-4 m

403. Nematode genus *Hoplolaimus* Daday was first recorded in ________ from an Island in the Paraguay river.

(*a*) 1900 (*b*) 1905
(*c*) 1910 (*d*) 1915

IV. Match the following:

404. Match the following insecticides with the discoverer and his/her nationality

(*a*) DDT, 1939	(*i*) Schrader, Germany
(*b*) Parathion, 1944	(*ii*) Geigy, Switzerland
(*c*) Chlordane, 1945	(*iii*) Muller, Switzerland.
(*d*) Carbamates, 1947	(*iv*) Julius Hayman, USA/Riemschneider, Germany

405. Match the following insecticides (pesticides) with the country where these were developed and used first.

(*a*) Paris Green, 1867	(*i*) Caucasus
(*b*) Chloropicrin, 1918	(*ii*) China
(*c*) Arsenite, 1900	(*iii*) France
(*d*) Pyrethroids, 1800	(*iv*) USA

406. Match the following pesticides with their generation as has been grouped.

(*a*) Petroleum products	(*i*) Third generation
(*b*) Dinitro compounds	(*ii*) First generation
*(*c*) Juvenile hormone	(*iii*) Fourth generation
*(*d*) Precocene	(*iv*) Second generation

*Insecticides

407. Match the insecticides with time interval (days) between application and consumption/harvesting of an edible crop or a part thereof.

(*a*) All chlorinated hydrocarbons	(*i*) 4
(*b*) Malathion	(*ii*) 30
(*c*) Parathion, gusathion	(*iii*) 14
(*d*) Phospdrin	(*iv*) 7

408. Match the LD_{50} values of the following insecticides, oral for rats given in mg/kg of body weight.

(*a*) Nicotine	(*i*) 570
(*b*) Pyrethrins	(*ii*) 750-1200
(*c*) Rotenone	(*iii*) 70
(*d*) Ryania	(*iv*) 25-132

409.

Insecticide	**LD_{50}**
(*a*) Aldrin	(*i*) 283
(*b*) BHC (Lindane)	(*ii*) 40-50
(*c*) Chlordane	(*iii*) 250-500
(*d*) DDT	(*iv*) 200

410.

Insecticide	**LD_{50}**
(*a*) DDE (TDE, Rothane)	(*i*) 110
(*b*) Endosulfan (Thiodan)	(*ii*) 3-6
(*c*) Endrin	(*iii*) 40
(*d*) Heptachlor	(*iv*) 400-3400

411. **Insecticide** — **LD_{50}**

Insecticide	LD_{50}
(*a*) Methoxychlor	(*i*) 10-100
(*b*) Toxaphene	(*ii*) 5,000
(*c*) Calcium arsenate	(*iii*) 283
(*d*) Lead arsenate	(*iv*) 35-100

412. **Insecticide** — **LD_{50}**

Insecticide	LD_{50}
(*a*) Dimeton (systox)	(*i*) 25-30
(*b*) Diazinon (Basudin)	(*ii*) 150-220
(*c*) Dichlorvos (DDVP, Nuvan)	(*iii*) 137
(*d*) Dimethoate (Rogor)	(*iv*) 3-5

413. **Insecticide** — **LD_{50}**

Insecticide	LD_{50}
(*a*) Malathion	(*i*) 3-5
(*b*) Mevinphos (Phosdrin)	(*ii*) 20
(*c*) Monocrotophos (Nuvacron)	(*iii*) 57
(*d*) Oxydemeton (Metasystox R)	(*iv*) 1400-1900

414. **Insecticide** — **LD_{50}**

Insecticide	LD_{50}
(*a*) Parathion	(*i*) 2-3
(*b*) Parathion-methyl	(*ii*) 15
(*c*) Phorate (Thimet)	(*iii*) 3-6
(*d*) Phosphamidon (Dimicron)	(*iv*) 12-16

415. **Insecticide** — **LD_{50}**

Insecticide	LD_{50}
(*a*) Trichlor (Diptrex)	(*i*) 50-90
(*b*) Aldicarb (Temic)	(*ii*) 650
(*c*) Carbaryl (Sevin)	(*iii*) 6.2
(*d*) Pyrolan	(*iv*) 400

416. Match the following insecticides with their RL_{50} when used on different plants/plant products.

(*a*) DDT on citrus	(*i*) 150-190
(*b*) Malathion on stored grain	(*ii*) 5-6
(*c*) Parathion on apple	(*iii*) 28
(*d*) Pyrethrum on stored wheat	(*iv*) 50-58

417. Match the antidote with the following insecticides.

(*a*) Atropine	(*i*) PCP
(*b*) Potassium permanganate	(*ii*) Nicotine
(*c*) Magnesium sulphate	(*iii*) OP-insecticides
(*d*) Cold packs tepid water	(*iv*) Arsenals

418. Match the following inorganic insecticides with their chemical formula.

(*a*) Sodium fluosilicate	(*i*) $Na_2B_4O_7$
(*b*) Cryolite	(*ii*) Na_2SiF_6
(*c*) Sodium selenate	(*iii*) Na_2AlF_6
(*d*) Borax	(*iv*) Na_2SeO_4

419. Match the following natural (organic) insecticides with their chemical composition.

(a) Nicotine (i) $C_{21}H_{30}O_3$
(b) Pyrethroids (ii) $C_{23}H_{22}O_6$
(c) Rotenoids (iii) $C_{32}H_{49}N$
(d) Cevadine (iv) $C_{10}H_{14}N_2$

420. Match the following insecticides with their chemical formula.

(a) Endrin (i) $C_{10}H_6C_{18}$
(b) Endosulfan (ii) $C_{10}H_5Cl_7$
(c) Heptachlor (iii) $C_6H_8Cl_6O$
(d) Chlordane (iv) $C_9H_6Cl_6O_2S$

421. Match the organophosphate group of insecticide with, its formula as indicated below.

(a) Phosphonate (i) 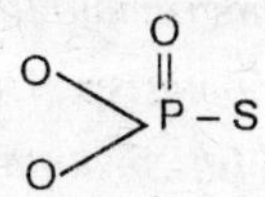

(b) Phosphorothionate (ii) 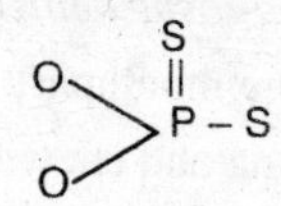

(c) Phosphorodithioate (iii) 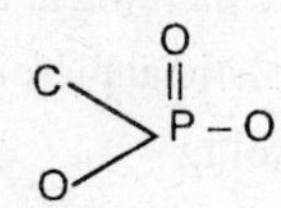

(d) Phosphoramidate (iv) 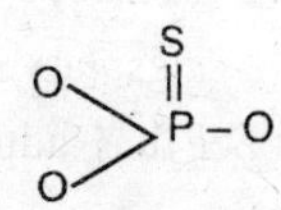

422. Match the following insects with its food lure.

(a) Onion fly (i) Sugar, molasses
(b) Housefly (ii) Methyl eugenol
(c) Oriental fruitfly (iii) Heptyl butyrate
(d) Yellow jacket wasp (iv) Propylmercaptan

423. Match the insects with the repellent.

(a) Mosquito (i) Diacetyl pthalate
(b) Ticks, fleas (ii) Dimethyl pthalate
(c) Cattle fleas (iii) Benzyl benzoate
(d) Mites (chiggers, Trombicula) (iv) N-butylacetanilide

424. Match the insect-pest with the scientific names.

(a) Cucurbit stinking bugs (i) *Palpita indica*
(b) Pumpkin caterpillar (ii) *Mylabris pustulata*
(c) Plume moth (iii) *Coridius janus*
(d) Blister beetle (iv) *Sphenarches caffer*

425. Match the biological control stations with the country of their location.

(*a*) CSIRO	(*i*) India (Bangalore)
(*b*) CIBC	(*ii*) Japan (Fukoda)
(*c*) FAKU	(*iii*) Australia (Canberra, Sydney)
(*d*) IBS	(*iv*) Germany (Dermstadt)

426. Match the pest and crop with the natural enemy with source and year.

(*a*) San Jose Scale, apple	(*i*) *Capidosoma uruguayensis*, South America
(*b*) Cotton bollworm	(*ii*) *Aphytis diaspidis*, USA (1960)
(*c*) Paddy stem borer	(*iii*) *Trichogramma brasiliensis*, S. America, 1965
(*d*) Potato tuber moth	(*iv*) *Telenomous alecto*, Colombia (S. America), 1966

427. Match the natural insect-enemy with the place where established in India.

(*a*) *Trichogramma fasciatum*, Sugarcane	(*i*) A.P. (Hyderabad)
(*b*) *Telenomus* sp., Castor	(*ii*) Orissa, Tamil Nadu
(*c*) *Rodolia cardinalis*, Citrus	(*iii*) West Bengal, U.P., Bihar
(*d*) *Spoggosia beniziana*, Coconut	(*iv*) Tamil Nadu, Kerala

428. Match the mouthpart type with the insects mentioned below.

(*a*) Biting and chewing	(*i*) Thrips and mites
(*b*) True piercing and sucking	(*ii*) Pea-moth and cutworms
(*c*) Superficial piercing and sucking	(*iii*) Larvae of diptera
(*d*) Rasping	(*iv*) Hemiptera of all kinds

429. Match the predatory stage of insects with their main prey.

(*a*) Lacewings, larvae and adults	(*i*) Plant feeding mites
(*b*) Robber flies, adult and some larvae also	(*ii*) Aphids
(*c*) Predatory mites, juvenile and adults	(*iii*) Various soft-bodied insects
(*d*) Predatory bugs, nymphs and adults	(*iv*) Various insects

430. Match the main group of insect pathogens with their examples cited below.

(*a*) Bacteria	(*i*) Nuclear *polyhedrosis* causing agent
(*b*) Virus	(*ii*) *Entomophthora* spp.
(*c*) Nematode	(*iii*) *Bacillus papilliae*
(*d*) Fungi	(*iv*) *Neoaplectana carpocapsae*

431. Match order of classification with the popular name of the insect.

(*a*) *Ephemeropea*	(*i*) Stoneflies
(*b*) *Odonata*	(*ii*) Mayflies
(*c*) *Plecophera*	(*iii*) Earwigs
(*d*) *Dermaptera*	(*iv*) Dragonflies

432.

Order	**Popular name**
(*a*) *Orthoptera*	(*i*) Leaf insects, stick insects
(*b*) *Phasmida*	(*ii*) Web spinners
(*c*) *Embioptera*	(*iii*) Cockroaches, mantids
(*d*) *Dictyoptera*	(*iv*) Grasshoppers, locusts, crickets

433. **Order** — **Popular name**

(*a*) *Isoptera* — (*i*) Booklice, psocids
(*b*) *Psocoptera* — (*ii*) Thrips
(*c*) *Siphuculata* — (*iii*) Termites
(*d*) *Thysanoptera* — (*iv*) Sucking lice

434. **Order** — **Popular name**

(*a*) *Neuroptera* — (*i*) Beetles
(*b*) *Coleoptera* — (*ii*) Stylopids
(*c*) *Strepsiptera* — (*iii*) Scorpion flies
(*d*) *Mecoptera* — (*iv*) Lacewings, antlions

435. **Order** — **Popular name**

(*a*) *Lepidoptera* — (*i*) Ants, bees, wasps, sawflies
(*b*) *Trichoptera* — (*ii*) Butterflies and moths
(*c*) *Hymenoptera* — (*iii*) Fleas
(*d*) *Siphonaptera* — (*iv*) Caddisflies

436. Match the common names of locusts with scientific names.

(*a*) Desert locust — (*i*) *Locusta migratoria* L.
(*b*) Migratory locust — (*ii*) *Chortoicetes terminefera* Wlk.
(*c*) Bombay locust — (*iii*) *Schistocerca gregaria* Forskall.
(*d*) Australian locust — (*iv*) *Patanga succincta* L.

437. **Common name** — **Scientific name**

(*a*) Italian locust — (*i*) *Schistocerca paranensis* Burm.
(*b*) Red locust — (*ii*) *Nomadacris sepetemfasciata* Serv.
(*c*) Brown locust — (*iii*) *Locustana pardalina* Wlk.
(*d*) South American locust — (*iv*) *Calliptamus italicus* L.

438. Match the following viruses with transmitter aphid (s)

(*a*) Potato leaf-roll Y virus — (*i*) *Brevicoryne brassicae*
(*b*) Sugarcane mosaic virus — (*ii*) *Myzus persicae*
(*c*) Mosaics of crucifers — (*iii*) *M. persicae* and *A. gossypii*
(*d*) Bean mosaic virus — (*iv*) *Aphis maidis*

439. Match silkworms with their main host plant (s).

(*a*) Mulberry silkworm — (*i*) *Ricinus communis* (Castor), *Heteropanax fragrans* (*kasseru*)
(*b*) Tasar silkworm — (*ii*) Mulberry (*Morus* spp.)
(*c*) Muga silkworm — (*iii*) *Terminalia tomentosa* (*asan*), *T. arjuna* (*arjun*)
(*d*) Eri silkworm — (*iv*) *Machilus bombycina* (*Som*), *Litasaea poly antha* (*soalu*)

440. In India total loss due to pests, diseases and weeds is 18 per cent (Mehta, 1976), match the share of different agencies.

(*a*) Weeds — (*i*) 26%
(*b*) Diseases — (*ii*) 13%
(*c*) Insect-pests — (*iii*) 33%
(*d*) Rates and storage losses — (*iv*) 20%

441. Match the crop with nematode vector.

(*a*) Grapevine	(*i*) *Trichodorus christiei*
(*b*) Strawberry	(*ii*) *Xiphinema index* and *X. americanum*
(*c*) Potato	(*iii*) *Longidorus elongatus*
(*d*) Red currant	(*iv*) *Xiphinema diversicaudatum*

442. Match the viruses transmitted by nematodes with crop.

(*a*) Raspberry ring spot	(*i*) Lucerne
(*b*) Tobacco rattle	(*ii*) Red currant
(*c*) Arabis mosaic	(*iii*) Potato
(*d*) Early browning	(*iv*) Strawberry

443. Match the fungi with the virus disease transmitted by them.

(*a*) *Olipidium brassicae*	(*i*) Oat mosaic
(*b*) *Polymixa graminis*	(*ii*) Potato mop top
(*c*) *Spongospora*	(*iii*) Pea false leaf roll
(*d*) *Pythium ultimum*	(*iv*) Lettuce big vein

444. Match disease and host with the parasite.

(*a*) Small maize	(*i*) *Synchytrium andobioticum*
(*b*) Wart, potato	(*ii*) *Gymosporangium juneperivirginianae*
(*c*) Canker, apple	(*iii*) *Ustilago maydis*
(*d*) Rust, cedar apple	(*iv*) *Nectria galligena*

445.

Disease, host	**Parasite**
(*a*) Downy mildew, sugarcane	(*i*) *Puccinia graminis*
(*b*) Bakanae disease, rice	(*ii*) *Sclerospora sacchari*
(*c*) Rust. wheat	(*iii*) *Gibberella fujukuroi*
(*d*) Leaf blight, cherry	(*iv*) *Gnomonia erythrostroma*

446.

Disease, host	**Parasite**
(*a*) Rust, safflower	(*i*) *Omphalia flavida*
(*b*) Leaf spot, coffee	(*ii*) *Sclerospora sacchari*
(*c*) Downy mildew, maize	(*iii*) *Corynebacterium fasaiens*
(*d*) Witches broom, sweetpea	(*iv*) *Puccinia carthami*

447. Match the pathogen with the toxin produced by it.

(*a*) *Helminthosporium victoriae*	(*i*) T-toxin
(*b*) *H. maydis, race* T	(*ii*) HS-toxin
(*c*) *H. carbonum*	(*iii*) Victorin
(*d*) *H. sacchari*	(*iv*) HC-toxin

448.

Pathogen	**Toxin**
(*a*) *Alternaria kikuchiana*	(*i*) PM-toxin
(*b*) *Periconia circinata*	(*ii*) Phytoalternarin
(*c*) *Phyllosticta maydis*	(*iii*) Fumaric acid
(*d*) *Rhizopus* spp	(*iv*) PC-toxin

449. **Pathogen** | **Toxin**

(*a*) *Alternaria tenuis* — (*i*) Juglone
(*b*) *Fusarium* spp — (*ii*) Tentoxin
(*c*) *Pseudomonas tabaci* — (*iii*) Marticin
(*d*) *Juglans nigra* — (*iv*) Tabtoxin / wild fire toxin

450. Match the formation of appressoria with epidermal cells.

(*a*) 53.0% — (*i*) Long cells
(*b*) 16.2% — (*ii*) Hairs
(*c*) 12.8% — (*iii*) Motor cells
(*d*) 1.7% — (*iv*) Short cells

451. Match the antimicrobial compound with the crop(s) producing it.

(*a*) Allyl sulphoxides — (*i*) Pear and walnut
(*b*) Glucosinolate — (*ii*) Onion and garlic
(*c*) Gyanogenic glucosides — (*iii*) Cabbage
(*d*) Para-hydroquinone glucosides — (*iv*). Sorghum, limabean, peach

452. **Toxin** | **Crop**

(*a*) Benzoxazines — (*i*) Green skin of potato tubers
(*b*) Solanin — (*ii*) Potato leaves
(*c*) Chaconin — (*iii*) Tomato
(*d*) Tomatin — (*iv*) Maize, wheat, rye

453. Match the lignification agent imparting fungal resistance with the crop.

(*a*) *Alternaria japonica* — (*i*) Wheat
(*b*) *Septoria nodorum, S. tritici* — (*ii*) Radish
(*c*) *Cladosporium cucumerinum* — (*iii*) Sweet potato
(*d*) *Helicobasidim mompa* — (*iv*) Cucumber

454. Match the phytolexins with the plant (host) producing it.

(*a*) Rishitin — (*i*) Tobacco and pepper
(*b*) Phytuberin — (*ii*) Tobacco
(*c*) Capsidiol — (*iii*) Potato and tomato
(*d*) Glutinosone — (*iv*) Potato

455. **Phytolexin** | **Host**

(*a*) Hirinol — (*i*) Oats
(*b*) Ipomeamarone — (*ii*) Orchids
(*c*) 6-methoxy mellein — (*iii*) Sweet potato
(*d*) Avenalumin I, II & III — (*iv*) Carrot

456. Match the varieties of stem rust fungus *Puccinia graminis* with uredospores size (microns).

(*a*) *tritici* — (*i*) 22×16
(*b*) *secalis* — (*ii*) 32×20
(*c*) *avenae* — (*iii*) 25×17
(*d*) *agrostis* — (*iv*) 28×20

457. Match the host-parasite relationship given below.

(*a*) *Triticum* — (*i*) *Helminthosporium victoriae* (Victoria blight of oat)
(*b*) *Avena* — (*ii*) *Cladosporium fulvum* (Leaf mould of tomtoes)
(*c*) *Lycopersicon* — (*iii*) *Venturia inequalis* (Scab of apple)
(*d*) *Malus* — (*iv*) *Puccinia striiformis* (yellow rust of wheat)

458. **Host** — **Parasite**

(*a*) *Zea* — (*i*) *Hemileia vastatrix* (coffee rust)
(*b*) *Solanum* — (*ii*) *Puccinia sorghi* (Rust of maize)
(*c*) *Gossypium* — (*iii*) *Globodera rostochiensis* (Cyst nematode)
(*d*) *Coffea* — (*iv*) *Xanthomonas malvacearum* (Black arm of cotton)

459. Match the predisposing soil temperature with the pathogen.

(*a*) 30-35°C — (*i*) *Drechslera graminae* (Barley stripe)
(*b*) 10°C — (*ii*) *Fusarium culmorum* (wheat root rot)
(*c*) 17-23°C — (*iii*) *Sclerotium rolfsii* (Apple root rot)
(*d*) 24-28°C — (*iv*) *Thielaviopsis basicola* (Tobacco root rot)

460. Match the nematode infestations with the development of fungal and bacterial diseases which they enhance.

(*a*) *Criconematoides xenoplax* — (*i*) Cotton wilt
(*b*) *Meloidogyne* spp. — (*ii*) Bacterial canker in plum
(*c*) *Meloidogyne javanica* — (*iii*) Root rot of tomato
(*d*) *Meloidogyne incognita* — (*iv*) Tomato wilt

461. **Nematode** — **Disease**

(*a*) *Tylenchulus semipenetrans* — (*i*) Potato wilt
(*b*) *Pratylenchus thornei* — (*ii*) Root rot of tobacco
(*c*) *Meloidogyne incognita* — (*iii*) Soybean root rot
(*d*) *M. incognita & Heterodera glycines* — (*iv*) Root rot of citrus

462. Match the disease with the pathogen exhibited by suppressive soils.

(*a*) Wilt of bean — (*i*) *Fusarium oxysporum* f. sp. *cucumerinum*
(*b*) Wilt of cucurbits — (*ii*) *Streptomyces scabies*
(*c*) Root rot of lettuce — (*iii*) *Fusarium solani* f. sp. *phaseoli*
(*d*) Common scab of potato — (*iv*) *Olpidium brassicae*

463. **Disease** — **Pathogen**

(*a*) Black root rot, cucurbits — (*i*) *Pseudomonas solanacearum*
(*b*) Damping off, vegetables — (*ii*) *Phomopsis sclerotioides*
(*c*) Wilt, vegetables — (*iii*) *Rhizoctonia solani*
(*d*) Bare patch, wheat — (*iv*) *Pythium ultimum, Pythium* spp.

464. Match the decoy crop (s) which reduce the pathogen populations.

(*a*) Ryegrass, *Papaver rhoeas, Reseda ordorata* — (*i*) *Plasmodiophora brassicae*
(*b*) *Datura stromonium* — (*ii*) *Striga asiatica*
(*c*) Sudan grass — (*iii*) *Heterodera avenae*
(*d*) Maize — (*iv*) *Spongospora substerranea*

465. **Decoy crop** — **Pathogen population**
(*a*) *Crotolaria spectabilis* — (*i*) *Meloidogyne javanica*
(*b*) Groundnut — (*ii*) *Pratylenchus alieni*
(*c*) *Sesamum orientale* — (*iii*) *Pratylenchus* spp.
(*d*) Bean, chrysanthemum — (*iv*) *Meloidogyne incognita*

466. Match the effect of crop(s) grown in short-term rotation on reduction or elimination of the pathogen.
(*a*) Rice-sesame/wheat, India — (*i*) *Gaeumannomyces graminis*
(*b*) Tobacco-groundnut, U.S.A. — (*ii*) *Pratilenchus indicus.*
(*c*) Wheat-pea, France — (*iii*) *Meloidogyne incognita*
(*d*) Cotton-paddy-rice, U.S.A. — (*iv*) *Verticillium dahliae*

467. **Rotation** — **Pathogen reduced / eliminated**
(*a*) Tomato-Sudangrass, U.S.A. — (*i*) *Meloidogyne incognita*
(*b*) Cotton-barley, U.S.A. — (*ii*) *Pratylenchus penetrans*
(*c*) Cereals-beet, France — (*iii*) *Pratylenchus indicus*
(*d*) Rice-sesame/wheat, India — (*iv*) *Pseudomonas solanacearum*

468. Match the nematodes with the crop(s) or disease which they are associated with.
(*a*) *Meloidogyne* spp. — (*i*) Citrus nematode
(*b*) *Tylenchulus semipenetrans* — (*ii*) Cereal root nematode
(*c*) *Heterodera avenae* — (*iii*) Root knot of tomato okra / brinjal
(*d*) *Heterodera tobacum* — (*iv*) Tobacco cyst nematode

469. **Nematode** — **Disease**
(*a*) *Globodera rostochiensis* — (*i*) Lesion nematode
(*b*) *Heterodera sachachtii* — (*ii*) Potato cyst nematode
(*c*) *Praylenchus penetrans* — (*iii*) Sting nematode
(*d*) *Belonolaimus longicaudatus* — (*iv*) Sugarbeet cyst nematode

470. Match the antagonistic pathogens with each other.
(*a*) *Penicilium vermiculatum* — (*i*) *Ophiobolus graminis*
(*b*) *Didymella exitialis* — (*ii*) Conidia of many fungi
(*c*) *Gliocladium roseum* — (*iii*) Sclerotia of *Sclerotinia sclerotiorum*
(*d*) *Coniothyrium minitans* — (*iv*) *Rhizoctonia solani*

471. Match the pathogen with organic amendment of soil.
(*a*) *Fusarium oxysporum* f. sp. *Cubense* (Banana wilt) — (*i*) Green manure with pea, *Melilotus*
(*b*) *Streptomyces scabies* (Potato scab) — (*ii*) Oat straw, maize stover, lucerne hay
(*c*) *Phymatotrichum omnivorum* (cotton root rot) — (*iii*) Sugarcane residues
(*d*) *Thielavicopsis basicola* (Bean root rot) — (*iv*) Green manure with soybean

472. **Pathogen** — **Amendment**
(*a*) *Aphanomyces euteiches* (Pea, root rot) — (*i*) Barley straw
(*b*) *Verticillium albo-atrum* (Potato wilt) — (*ii*) Wheat straw, sawdust, oilcakes
(*c*) *Rhizoctonia solani* (Potato black scarf) — (*iii*) Green manure with rape, pea mixed grass legume
(*d*) *Gaeumannomyces graminis* (wheat lake-all) — (*iv*) Crucifer tissues

473. Match the crops with their variety/source of resistance against reniform nematode. (Reniform nematodes in the genus Rotylenchulus are semiendoparasitic (partially inside roots) species in which the females penetrate the root cortex, establish a permanent-feeding site in the stele region of the root and become sedentary or immobile. The anterior portion (head region) of the body remains embedded in the root whereas the posterior portion (tail region) protrudes from the root surface and swells during maturation. The term 'reniform' refers to the kidney-shaped body of the mature female.)

(*a*) Cotton	(*i*) Kalyanpur Selection I
(*b*) Cowpea	(*ii*) Lousiana 33
(*c*) Tomato	(*iii*) Fulghum
(*d*) Oats	(*iv*) V-16

474.

Crop	**Resistant variety/source**
(*a*) Onion	(*i*) IPCL-95
(*b*) Pigeonpea	(*ii*) La rouge
(*c*) Potato	(*iii*) Gold rush
(*d*) Sweet potato	(*iv*) Evergreen

475. Match *Hirschmanniella* species with the host (s).

(*a*) *H. mucronata*	(*i*) *Colocasia esculenta*
(*b*) *H. miticausa*	(*ii*) Pearlmillet
(*c*) *H. areolata*	(*iii*) Rice
(*d*) *H. pomponiensis*	(*iv*) Lily, water chestnut

476. Match the species of *Xiphinema* nematode described by a country after 1980.

(Xiphinema Doagger nematode is a genius of plant parastic roundworms. Family Longidondae)

(*a*) *algeriense*	(*i*) Fiji
(*b*) *bacaniboia*	(*ii*) Italy
(*c*) *barbercheckae*	(*iii*) Algeria
(*d*) *barense*	(*iv*) South Africa

477.

Species	**Country, reported by**
(*a*) *clavicaudatum*	(*i*) India
(*b*) *colombiense*	(*ii*) Nigeria
(*c*) *dolosum*	(*iii*) U.K.
(*d*) *hydrabadensis*	(*iv*) Brazil

478.

Species	**Country, reported by**
(*a*) *incertum*	(*i*) Portugal
(*b*) *kosaigudensis*	(*ii*) Bulgaria
(*c*) *lusitanicum*	(*iii*) Malawi
(*d*) *malawiense*	(*iv*) India

479.

Species	**Country, reported by**
(*a*) *manmillocaudatus*	(*i*) Canada
(*b*) *occiduum*	(*ii*) Germany
(*c*) *pseudocoxi*	(*iii*) Botswana
(*d*) *stockeri*	(*iv*) India

480. Match the duration of life cycle of *Xiphinema* species (nematode) with duration of life cycle.

(*a*) *x. americanum*	(*i*) Two years
(*b*) *x. brevicolle*	(*ii*) One year
(*c*) *x. diversicaudatum*	(*iii*) 4-7 months at 20-23°C
(*d*) *x. vuitenezi*	(*iv*) Three years

V. Computations:

481. How much of 50% WDP of DDT will be required to prepare 100 litres of solution of 0.5% concentration?

Ans. Since, $\frac{\text{Total spray needed} \times \text{per cent strength needed}}{\text{Given percentage of strength}}$ = Amount of DDT needed

Therefore, $\frac{100 \text{ liters} \times 0.5 \text{ per cent}}{50 \text{ per cent}}$ = ------

482. **What will be the strength of a 20 per cent endrin emulsion if 1 litre of it is diluted to 100 litres?**

Ans. Since, percentage concentration of end product

$$= \frac{\text{Quantity of emulsion to be diluted} \times \text{emulsion strength}}{\text{Quantity of the finished product}}$$

$$= \frac{1 \text{ litres} \times 20 \text{ per cent}}{100 \text{ litres}} = \text{------}$$

483. **Compute the amount of 20 per cent aldrin emulsion required to apply 50 g of aldrin per hectare (give only final answer).**

Ans. Since, quantity of insecticide required

= 100 percent purity of insecticide used × quantity of actual insecticide used

Strength of the given formulated insecticide

$$= \frac{100 \times 50}{20} = 250g$$

484. **Compute the infection rate of powdery mildew of barley using the formula**

$$r = \frac{1}{t_2 - t_1} \log e \frac{x_2}{x_1} \quad \textbf{Ans.}$$

where, r = average infection rate

x_1 = assessed at time t_1 (x = infection per cent)

and x_2 = assessed at time t_2 (t = time of assessment)

Therefore, if assessments are,

– 0.5 % powdery mildew in the crop at 45 days after sowing.

– 3.5 % powdery mildew in the crop at 55 days after sowing

$x_1 = 0.005, \; x_2 = 0.035$

$$t_2 - t_1 = 10 \text{ days}$$

Hence, $$r = \frac{1}{10} \log e \frac{0.035}{0.005}$$

Note: When disease intensity is high, 1-*x* factor is brought into compute *r* as shown below

$$r = \frac{1}{t_2 - t_1} \log e \frac{x_2(1-x)}{x_1(1-y)}$$

485. **Work out the percentage acreage affected by disease, if average number of foci / ha is 5, and average of foci is 1m².**

Ans. Percentage ha affected $= \frac{5 \times 100}{10{,}000}$ -----

486. **Compute the per cent infection index if sum of disease rating is 495, total ratings are 200 and maximum disease grade is 9.**

Ans. $$\% \text{ infection index} = \frac{\text{Sum of all disease ratings}}{\text{Total no. of ratings} \times \text{Max. disease grade}} \times 100$$

$$= \frac{495}{200 \times 9} \times 100 = \text{------}$$

487. **Determine the loss of grain yield in kg/ha if the infected ears in a wheat field are 10 per cent (p_r) and the actual yield is 4500 kg/ha (p_a).**

Ans. $$\text{Loss (kg / ha)} = \frac{P_r}{100 - P_r} \times 4500 = \frac{10}{90} \times 4500 = \text{-------}$$

Do you know that

1. In 1906, carbon bisulphide was introduced as a soil fumigant for the control of Canada thistle and field bindweed.
2. Dithiocarbamate compounds were first patented as fungicides in 1934.
3. Nuclear polyhedrosis virus (NPV) is the most effective for control of *Helicoverpa armigera.*
4. Bordeaux mixture was discovered in the year 1885 by Millardot at *Bordeaux, France.*
5. Sh E.J. Butler was the first person to discover dowrey mildew in India.
6. The Fungicide most widely used for smut fungi disease is Vitavax.
7. Algae is the main source for Agar-Agar.
8. Reinform nematodes in the genus *Rotylenchulis* are semiendoparasitic species in which females penetrate the root cortex, establish a permanent feeding site in the stele region of root and become sedentary or immobile.
9. Tools of Integrated Pest Management are, (*i*) monitoring (*ii*) Cultural pest control (*iii*) Mechanical control (*iv*) Biological control (*v*) Chemical control (*vi*) Pest resistant varities

10. Term Integrated Pest Management was coined by Geiger and Clark in the year 1961.
11. Father of Insect Physiology is Wiggelsworth.
12. Allelopathy is the ability of one species to inhibit or prevent the growth of another species through the production of toxic substances.
13. Insecticides Act was pased in the year 1968.
14. Central Plant Protection Training Institute is situated at HYDERABAD.

KEY

1. Insects
2. Pest
3. Egyptian
4. Migration
5. Multiplication
6. Entomophagous
7. Predators or parasites
8. Entomogenous
9. Host-range
10. Pests
11. Soil-insects
12. Clean culture
13. Biochemicals
14. Nocturnol / night
15. Radio frequencies
16. red (253-700 nm)
17. Ionising
18. Technical (commercial)
19. Toxicological
20. Technical insecticides
21. Formulation
22. Disrepute
23. Carner
24. Non-phytotoxic
25. Deodorant/masker
26. Synergist
27. Pseudosynergists
28. Insoluble
29. Two-phase
30. Locust
31. USDA
32. Fumigants
33. 'Residues'
34. Insect-population
35. Organophosphorus
36. Nicotinic
37. Carbamylation
38. Myocardial
39. Arsenic, acid
40. Copper acetoarsenate
41. Neem (*Azadirachta indica*)
42. Othmar Zeidler
43. Dichlorodiphenyl trichloroethane
44. Sex pheromone
45. Sexually stimulate
46. Insects
47. Alarm
48. Formic acid
49. Locate workers
50. Hormones
51. Brain
52. Pavied
53. Chemosterilant
54. Benzene hexachloride
55. Organophosphates (insecticides)
56. Bark
57. Detoxification
58. Seed systemics
59. Carbon tetrachloride (CCl_4)
60. Morning
61. Resurgence
62. Biggest
63. Antifeedants
64. Apple-factor
65. Solanum
66. Cottony cushion scale (Iserapurchasi)
67. Biological or biocontrol
68. Colonization
69. Spore forming
70. Aflatoxin / destruxins
71. Metabolic
72. Paralysis
73. Pest species
74. Invertibrates
75. Slave-hunting
76. Stored honey
77. Aphids
78. Margins
79. Stem borer
80. Moorings
81. Fruit borers
82. Damage threshold
83. Pests
84. Modifications
85. Chloroform
86. Re-sorfening
87. Life-history
88. Rational control
89. Diapause
90. Unfavourable
91. Voltinism
92. Univoltine
93. Sorghum shoot fly (*Atherigona soccata*)
94. *Holotrichia consanguinea*
95. *Metarrhizium anisophiae*
96. *Athalia lugens proxima*
97. *Orius tantilus*

98. *Agamermis paradecoudate*
99. Cosmopolitan
100. Largest
101. Do not
102. Allergic
103. Physogastry
104. Wrongly
105. Fertilized eggs
106. Royal chamber
107. Unfertilized egg
108. Salivary glands
109. Sericin 110. Drone cells
111. Development
112. Royal jelly / brood food
113. Pharyngeal
114. Language
115. Absconding
116. Beeswax
117. Pathogenicity
118. Virulence
119. Aggressiveness
120. Metabolic shifts
121. First book
122. Leeuwenhoek
123. Diseases
124. Late blight
125. Rust and smut
126. America
127. Egyptians
128. Mycoplasma
129. Yellows disease
130. Taxonomy
131. Identification
132. K.R. Kirtikar
133. Vivotoxin
134. Animate (living)
135. Sclerotium
136. Wilt
137. Tip backwards
138. Artificial media
139. Facultative
140. Obligate
141. Pathogenesis or disease cycle
142. Homogeneous infection chain.
143. Host specific
144. Carrier
145. *Xanthomonas citri*
146. Diseased setts
147. Wind-borne spores
148. Cereal rusts
149. Collateral
150. Saprophytic
151. Root inhabiting
152. Plant viruses
153. Phytophagous
154. Spores
155. Internally seed-borne
156. Flagella
157. Pathogenic
158. Ear cockle
159. Body
160. Aphids
161. Nematodes
162. *Dorylaimoidea*
163. Birds
164. Transported
165. Wind
166. Infected
167. India
168. Hyphae
169. *Armillariella mellea*
170. Vascular wilt
171. Barriers
172. Fungi
173. Maleic acid
174. Predisposition
175. Inoculum potential
176. Latent infection
177. Epidemiology
178. Epiphytotics
179. Sporulation
180. Compound interest
181. Secondary
182. Crop sanitation
183. Susceptible
184. Epiphytotics
185. Epiphytotics
186. Disease potential
187. Epidemics
188. Agroecosystem
189. Cause-effect
190. EPIDEM
191. Symptoms
192. Disintegration
193. Cuticular
194. Lamella
195. Chromosomal
196. Deaminases
197. Induce
198. Respiration
199. IAA
200. Pathogenesis
201. Gibberellins
202. Reproductivity
203. Uptake
204. Xylem
205. in vitro
206. Parenchyma
207. Victoria blight
208. Host specific
209. Infection-tube
210. *Pythium*
211. Phytoalexins
212. Tomato
213. Cowpea
214. Nematodes (*Meloidogyne* and *Pratylenchus*)
215. Asparaguisic
216. Nematodes
217. Diseased tissues
218. Endophytic nodule
219. Glyceollin
220. Phytoalexins
221. Antigenically
222. Host
223. Ethylene
224. Disdithiocarbamate

225. Zinc
226. Burgundy mixture
227. Chaubattia
228. Antimicrobial
229. Nematodes
230. Wheat
231. Rounded galls
232. Leaf galls
233. *Aeroptilon picris* (orchid)
234. Root-knot
235. *Nacobbus* species
236. Host
237. Ovisets
238. Amphimictic
239. Leguminous
240. True
241. True
242. True
243. False
244. True
245. False
246. False
247. True
248. True
249. True
250. True
251. False
252. False
253. True
254. True
255. False
256. True
257. True
258. False
259. False
260. False
261. True
262. True
263. True
264. True
265. False
266. True
267. False
268. True
269. True
270. True
271. False
272. True
273. True
274. True
275. False
276. True
277. True
278. True
279. False
280. False
281. True
282. True
283. False
284. True
285. True
286. False
287. False
288. False
289. False
290. True
291. True
292. False
293. True
294. True
295. False
296. True
297. False
298. True
299. False
300. True
301. True
302. True
303. True
304. False
305. True
306. False
307. False
308. False
309. True
310. True
311. False
312. True
313. False
314. True
315. False
316. True
317. True
318. False
319. False
320. True
321. True
322. False
323. True
324. True
325. False
326. True
327. False
328. False
329. True
330. True
331. False
332. False
333. True
334. True
335. False
336. True
337. False
338. False
339. True
340. False
341. True
342. True
343. False
344. True
345. False
346. True
347. True
348. True
349. False
350. False
351. True
352. False
353. True

354. False 355. True 356. True
357. True 358. True 359. True
360. False 361. True 362. True
363. False 364. False 365. True
366. True 367. False 368. True
369. (*b*) 370. (*a*) 371. (*c*)
372. (*c*) 373. (*b*) 374. (*d*)
375. (*a*) 376. (*c*) 377. (*c*)
378. (*b*) 379. (*a*) 380. (*b*)
381. (*c*) 382. (*b*) 383. (*b*)
384. (*c*) 385. (*c*) 386. (*c*)
387. (*c*) 388. (*c*) 389. (*d*)
390. (*c*) 391. (*a*) 392. (*b*)
393. (*c*) 394. (*c*) 395. (*b*)
396. (*d*) 397. (*b*) 398. (*c*)
399. (*b*) 400. (*a*) 401. (*c*)
402. (*b*) 403. (*b*)

404. (*a*)-(*iii*) (*b*)-(*i*) (*c*)-(*iv*) (*d*)-(*ii*)
405. (*a*)-(*iv*) (*b*)-(*iii*) (*c*)-(*ii*) (*d*)-(*i*)
406. (*a*)-(*ii*) (*b*)-(*iv*) (*c*)-(*i*) (*d*)-(*iii*)
407. (*a*)-(*ii*) (*b*)-(*iv*) (*c*)-(*iii*) (*d*)-(*i*)
408. (*a*)-(*iii*) (*b*)-(*i*) (*c*)-(*iv*) (*d*)-(*ii*)
409. (*a*)-(*ii*) (*b*)-(*iv*) (*c*)-(*i*) (*d*)-(*iii*)
410. (*a*)-(*iv*) (*b*)-(*i*) (*c*)-(*ii*) (*d*)-(*iii*)
411. (*a*)-(*ii*) (*b*)-(*iii*) (*c*)-(*iv*) (*d*)-(*i*)
412. (*a*)-(*iv*) (*b*)-(*ii*) (*c*)-(*i*) (*d*)-(*iii*)
413. (*a*)-(*iv*) (*b*)-(*i*) (*c*)-(*ii*) (*d*)-(*iii*)
414. (*a*)-(*iii*) (*b*)-(*iv*) (*c*)-(*i*) (*d*)-(*ii*)
415. (*a*)-(*ii*) (*b*)-(*iii*) (*c*)-(*iv*) (*d*)-(*i*)
416. (*a*)-(*iv*) (*b*)-(*i*) (*c*)-(*ii*) (*d*)-(*iii*)
417. (*a*)-(*iii*) (*b*)-(*ii*) (*c*)-(*iv*) (*d*)-(*i*)
418. (*a*)-(*ii*) (*b*)-(*iii*) (*c*)-(*iv*) (*d*)-(*i*)
419. (*a*)-(*iv*) (*b*)-(*i*) (*c*)-(*ii*) (*d*)-(*iii*)
420. (*a*)-(*iii*) (*b*)-(*iv*) (*c*)-(*ii*) (*d*)-(*i*)
421. (*a*)-(*iii*) (*b*)-(*iv*) (*c*)-(*ii*) (*d*)-(*i*)
422. (*a*)-(*iv*) (*b*)-(*i*) (*c*)-(*ii*) (*d*)-(*iii*)
423. (*a*)-(*ii*) (*b*)-(*iv*) (*c*)-(*i*) (*d*)-(*iii*)
424. (*a*)-(*iii*) (*b*)-(*i*) (*c*)-(*iv*) (*d*)-(*ii*)
425. (*a*)-(*iii*) (*b*)-(*i*) (*c*)-(*ii*) (*d*)-(*iv*)
426. (*a*)-(*ii*) (*b*)-(*iii*) (*c*)-(*iv*) (*d*)-(*i*)
427. (*a*)-(*iii*) (*b*)-(*i*) (*c*)-(*iv*) (*d*)-(*ii*)
428. (*a*)-(*ii*) (*b*)-(*iv*) (*c*)-(*i*) (*d*)-(*iii*)
429. (*a*)-(*ii*) (*b*)-(*iv*) (*c*)-(*i*) (*d*)-(*iii*)

430. (a)-(iii)	(b)-(i)	(c)-(iv)	(d)-(ii)
431. (a)-(ii)	(b)-(iv)	(c)-(i)	(d)-(iii)
432. (a)-(iv)	(b)-(i)	(c)-(ii)	(d)-(iii)
433. (a)-(iii)	(b)-(i)	(c)-(iv)	(d)-(ii)
434. (a)-(iv)	(b)-(i)	(c)-(ii)	(d)-(iii)
435. (a)-(ii)	(b)-(iv)	(c)-(i)	(d)-(iii)
436. (a)-(iii)	(b)-(i)	(c)-(iv)	(d)-(ii)
437. (a)-(iv)	(b)-(ii)	(c)-(iii)	(d)-(i)
438. (a)-(ii)	(b)-(iv)	(c)-(i)	(d)-(iii)
439. (a)-(ii)	(b)-(iii)	(c)-(iv)	(d)-(i)
440. (a)-(iii)	(b)-(i)	(c)-(iv)	(d)-(ii)
441. (a)-(ii)	(b)-(iv)	(c)-(i)	(d)-(iii)
442. (a)-(ii)	(b)-(iii)	(c)-(iv)	(d)-(i)
443. (a)-(iv)	(b)-(i)	(c)-(ii)	(d)-(iii)
444. (a)-(iii)	(b)-(i)	(c)-(iv)	(d)-(ii)
445. (a)-(ii)	(b)-(iii)	(c)-(i)	(d)-(iv)
446. (a)-(iv)	(b)-(i)	(c)-(ii)	(d)-(iii)
447. (a)-(iii)	(b)-(i)	(c)-(iv)	(d)-(ii)
448. (a)-(ii)	(b)-(iv)	(c)-(i)	(d)-(iii)
449. (a)-(ii)	(b)-(iii)	(c)-(iv)	(d)-(i)
450. (a)-(iii)	(b)-(i)	(c)-(iv)	(d)-(ii)
451. (a)-(ii)	(b)-(iii)	(c)-(iv)	(d)-(i)
452. (a)-(iv)	(b)-(i)	(c)-(ii)	(d)-(iii)
453. (a)-(ii)	(b)-(i)	(c)-(iv)	(d)-(iii)
454. (a)-(iii)	(b)-(iv)	(c)-(i)	(d)-(ii)
455. (a)-(ii)	(b)-(iii)	(c)-(iv)	(d)-(i)
456. (a)-(ii)	(b)-(iii)	(c)-(iv)	(d)-(i)
457. (a)-(iv)	(b)-(i)	(c)-(ii)	(d)-(iii)
458. (a)-(ii)	(b)-(iii)	(c)-(iv)	(d)-(i)
459. (a)-(iii)	(b)-(i)	(c)-(iv)	(d)-(ii)
460. (a)-(ii)	(b)-(i)	(c)-(iv)	(d)-(iii)
461. (a)-(iv)	(b)-(i)	(c)-(ii)	(d)-(iii)
462. (a)-(iii)	(b)-(i)	(c)-(iv)	(d)-(ii)
463. (a)-(ii)	(b)-(iv)	(c)-(i)	(d)-(iii)
464. (a)-(i)	(b)-(iv)	(c)-(ii)	(d)-(iii)
465. (a)-(iii)	(b)-(iv)	(c)-(i)	(d)-(ii)
466. (a)-(ii)	(b)-(iii)	(c)-(i)	(d)-(iv)
467. (a)-(iv)	(b)-(i)	(c)-(ii)	(d)-(iii)
468. (a)-(iii)	(b)-(i)	(c)-(ii)	(d)-(iv)
469. (a)-(ii)	(b)-(iv)	(c)-(i)	(d)-(iii)
470. (a)-(iv)	(b)-(i)	(c)-(ii)	(d)-(iii)
471. (a)-(iii)	(b)-(iv)	(c)-(i)	(d)-(ii)
472. (a)-(iv)	(b)-(i)	(c)-(ii)	(d)-(iii)

473. (*a*)-(*ii*)	(*b*)-(*iv*)	(*c*)-(*i*)	(*d*)-(*iii*)
474. (*a*)-(*iv*)	(*b*)-(*i*)	(*c*)-(*ii*)	(*d*)-(*iii*)
475. (*a*)-(*iii*)	(*b*)-(*i*)	(*c*)-(*iv*)	(*d*)-(*ii*)
476. (*a*)-(*iii*)	(*b*)-(*i*)	(*c*)-(*iv*)	(*d*)-(*ii*)
477. (*a*)-(*iv*)	(*b*)-(*iii*)	(*c*)-(*ii*)	(*d*)-(*i*)
478. (*a*)-(*ii*)	(*b*)-(*iv*)	(*c*)-(*i*)	(*d*)-(*iii*)
479. (*a*)-(*iv*)	(*b*)-(*i*)	(*c*)-(*ii*)	(*d*)-(*iii*)
480. (*a*)-(*ii*)	(*b*)-(*iii*)	(*c*)-(*iv*)	(*d*)-(*i*)

481. 1 kg or 1 litre for solid or liquid formulations 482. 0.2 per cent 483. 205 g

484. 0.194 units of disease/day 485. 0.5 % 486. 27.5 % 487. 500 kg/ha

SECTION 10
AGRICULTURAL ECONOMICS AND EXTENSION

I. Fill up the blanks :

1. The economic depression of 1890 generated considerable interest in farm management problems, this field of interest was later designated as ________.
2. Agricultural economics attends to all the aspects of problems of ________.
3. Agricultural economics is the science in which the principles and methods of ________ are applied to the special conditions of agricultural industry.
4. An agricultural economist has to formulate the methods, ________ to tackle the problems of agriculture.
5. The identification, description and classification of the ________ of agriculture to the end that these may be solved.
6. The domain of agricultural economics covers the examination of each ________ of agricultural production.
7. Agricultural economics is both a social science as also a ________.
8. In no other phenomenon than agriculture ________ is so directly and strongly involved.
9. Agriculture is a unique ________ in which the mode of life and business enterprise are combined together.
10. The large scale ________ and its benefits, typical of industry are less applicable to agriculture due to its small-sized units.
11. Agriculture must also generate export surplus to earn________.
12. It is only in agriculture that the________ nature along with man and by bounty yields which beside labourers and the farmer, society gets nourishment.
13. Only agriculture turns out________ over and above its cost of production.
14. The creation of an agricultural surplus is *sine-qua-non* for generating________ for other goods.
15. In Ricardo's vision of economic society, there are three major groups of actors *viz.* landlords, and ________ labours.
16. Rate of wages, according to Ricardo is determined by the cost of ________.
17. ________ economists turned their attention to short-run problems.
18. The intellectuals started showing more interest in the theories of economic development only after the revolution ________ in 1930.

19. Most of the underdeveloped countries have abundant of labour but ________ of labour being negligible or approaching zero.
20. The key to the process of economic expansion is the ________ of the capitalist system.
21. The ________ model also focuses attention on the transfer of labour from agricultural to nonagricultural sector as central to economic development.
22. Non-redundancy ratio is directly proportional to labour utilization ratio and inversely proportional to the ________.
23. Henry Carey and his father ________ though strong exponents of industrialization, affirmed the significance of prosperous agriculture.
24. Farming in India is less a ________ than a tradition.
25. It is the surplus generated by agricultural sector that "would help Indian economy to "________"
26. The total savings fund consists of savings from ________ sector and from agricultural sector.
27. In the absence of a developed agricultural sector, the base for "Take off" into a ________ economy would be weak and Indian economy would remain pitiable.
28. Agro-industries and agro-based industries hold a great promise for ________ in India.
29. Agricultural progress is normally a ________ for industrial development.
30. Increase in agricultural productivity raises agricultural incomes and ________ purchasing power.
31. The failure of agriculture sector would spell disaster to the entire ________ process.
32. The man's urge to own more land has been due to lack of ________ possibilities of employing the labour and capital.
33. The desire for more land is also stimulated by its permanent value, ________ and immovability.
34. ________ is basic to agriculture.
35. Food production and the ________ of mankind go together.
36. Changing technologies and tastes of people have led to frequent changes in ________ all over the world.
37. The productivity of pastures and grazing lands can be improved considerably by promoting ________ pasture land.
38. Malthusian thinking on population and food supply was greatly influenced by the ________ of land.
39. In the amount produced and the amount consumed by the producer relationship, negative or zero values are not in tune with ________ development.
40. Labour is the primary factor in enhancing the production of ________ agriculture.
41. Transformation from traditional to dynamic agriculture does not depend only on farm labour force, but also on technological ________.
42. Lewis-type models visualized ________ from agriculture.
43. The ________ school of theories on population growth emphasizes the factors like fecundity, fertility, sterility, food supply, physical resources, population density and standards of living as the growth influencing factors.
44. Sociological school of theories of population growth lays stress on ________ devised by human beings and emphasizes social rather than environmental factors as influencing factors.
45. The naturalistic school on population growth is founded on ________ on population growth.
46. Malthus in his thinking faltered on man's ________ and acceptability of a cultural pattern of a controlled birth-rate.

47. Malthus failed to foresee the possibilities of ________ revolution enabling man to produce more per unit of inputs including land.
48. The size of population can also be regulated by formulating ________ relative to population.
49. The suitability of otherwise of ________ of population growth is being debated and investigated.
50. The size of population depends upon the difference between births and corrected by in- and out-migration from a ________ territory.
51. For the world as a whole ________ are of no effect.
52. The marriages at younger age enlarge the ________ age span and hence augment the rate of population growth.
53. The level of medical technology is probably the most important single factor influencing the ________.
54. The farm size, system of farming and ________ development influence the demand for agricultural labour.
55. ________ system of farming generally need more labour per unit of land than that needed by extensive system.
56. ________ method of milking entails less demand for labour than indoor hand milking system.
57. The demand of agricultural labour depends upon the nature of operation (s) and ________ sensitivity of crops.
58. Farming need to be scientifically managed to permit reasonable avoidance of shortage and redundancy of labour to minimise ________ and overburden.
59. There is an advantage in using ________ labour as it is self-organized and need no continuous supervision.
60. ________ labour has a special place in agriculture owing to its peculiar nature *vis-a-vis* industrial sproduction.
61. Japanese experience postulates that technological advancement in agriculture can ________ in character.
62. The income effect is associated with ________ effect.
63. Physical quality of labour force refers to sound health, stamina and ________ characteristics.
64. ________ quality of labour force shall depend upon the level of education, extension services and agricultural training programmes.
65. Improved agri-technology enhances employment per unit of land and also ________ per unit of employment.
66. The amulgamation of farm ________ effects labour efficiency.
67. A ________ agricultural production involves acquisition of land and its preparation for agri-activities, seeds and agro-chemicals, tools and implements and organization of workers.
68. More acquisition of land is not enough unless it is prepared to suit agricultural ________.
69. ________ in agriculture is generally used to augment output per worker.
70. The productivity per worker does not merely depend on the ________ of capital per worker, but also on quality of other inputs.
71. The nature of crops and the duration of the crop season are also the ________ of the use of capital in agriculture.
72. Less developed countries lack ________ to develop agriculture at a desired rate of growth.
73. ________ of capital refers to its ownership either by an individual or groups of individuals.

74. Farming is highly dynamic and receptive to ________ innovations.
75. A higher rate of accumulation of capital relative to the rate of population growth adds to the real ________ of capital of a nation.
76. Saving decisions are conditioned by the ________ and power to save.
77. Capacity to save is limited by ________ competence and the level of personal income.
78. The accumulation and use of capital coupled with suitable technologies does not contribute only to the growth of agriculture, but also to ________ as a whole.
79. The people in underdeveloped countries generally believe in the philosophy of ________ and do not have high expectations from life.
80. The agricultural sector in most of the underdeveloped countries is particularly very weak to shed its ________.
81. The level of saving in underdeveloped countries is low due to low level of ________ itself.
82. If the level of income does not rise, social values, attitudes and ________ may not come through.
83. Lenders are naturally guided by the rate of ________ both at home and abroad.
84. The returns on capital in various sectors of economy act as a strong ________ in the competition for capital.
85. A number of lending agencies may lend credit to a single agency that pools them and makes available for ________.
86. Government either directly or through some agency makes loans available on more ________ terms to the farm-operators.
87. The introduction of new capital also calls for the study of ________ of associated risks and uncertainties.
88. If the new capital restricts the freedom of the farmer to choose a crop or a variety or any other input, naturally an alternative with less or no ________ is sought for.
89. The allocation of capital is guided by the maximum ________ criterion.
90. Equalization of marginal gains on diverse farm activities is bidirection, that is, achieved either through reallocation of existing stocks or acquiring ________ units of capital.
91. The capital allocation decisions are more oftenly based on practical wisdom than on postulates.
92. Production denotes the process of conversion of certain inputs/resources into a ________ forms.
93. ________ relationship explains the *modus operandi* of the various factors of production as converted into final farm products.
94. ________ relationship is concerned with the determination of type of crops to grow or breed of livestock to rear and their suitable combination at a given amount of resources.
95. As long as technology remains constant, the ________ remains unchanged and indicates the greatest output from a given input mix.
96. No single production function can be used to characterize ________ production under all environmental conditions.
97. The power of *v* of *k* is called the degree of ________ of the production function and serves as a measure of the returns of scale.
98. The Cobb-Douglas function is based on the ________ study of the American manufacturing industry undertaken by Paul H. Douglas and C.W. Cobb.
99. When the average product (AP) is, marginal product (MP) is equal to AP; when AP starts falling, MP falls faster than AP.

100. A farmer with limited funds may operate in a range of ________ returns to capital, is, however, not an irrational producer.

101. F. Benham defined the law of ________ proportions, "As the proportion of one factor in a combination of factors is increased, after a point, first the marginal and then the average product of that factor will diminish".

102. The constant marginal return function does not generally exist when inputs per unit (land/animal) are ________.

103. The phenomenon of diminishing marginal returns has played a crucial role in shaping the classical ________ of production.

104. ________ can be expressed as (*i*) average physical product = output/input (Y/X), (*ii*) marginal physical product = additional output/additional input (DY/DX).

105. When average product attains the maximum value and is constant, the ________ product is equal to it.

106. When average product is rising, marginal product rise ________ than average product.

107. Elasticity of production is less than one between the ________ average product and the maximum total product.

108. A production function with an elasticity of 1.0 throughout indicates ________ returns.

109. A profit maximizing farmer will maximize the ________ for given level of outlay.

110. A production with two substitutable variables for one another within limits can be represented by a family of ________

111. Perfectly ________ factors replace each other at a constant rate regardless of level of output or proportion of combination.

112. The factors substitute each other at a diminishing rate are the factors of production are ________ substitute for each other.

113. An isoquant curve is ________ inclined.

114. The arithmetical method, though simple, may not be helpful in locating the true ________ combination.

115. Competitive products are those which compete for the use of farmer's ________.

116. When output of one production be increased without gain or sacrifice in another product at constant level of resources, the relationship is called ________.

117. If a farmer raises rice-paddies instead of maize, the ________ of raising it will be the amount of maize sacrificed in the process.

118. Economic cost equals accounting or explicit cost plus ________.

119. Total fixed cost represents the sum of ________ which will be incurred.

120. ________ is the total fixed cost divided by the number of units of output produced.

121. ________ correspond to those factors of production whose supply is variable in the short period and change with the output.

122. The ________ of farm together with its costs determines the profits realized by the farmer.

123. ________ is the value received in exchange of goods and services and distinguished from money, merely a medium of exchange.

124. The ________ for a commodity is a schedule of quantities that a buyer would be willing to purchase at different prices at any given time or period.

125. The ________ states that a commodity will be demanded more at a lower price and less when the price is higher.

126. If two goods are not substitutes at all, the value of ________ will be zero.
127. Income elasticity of demand is equal to the percentage change in the quantity demanded divided by the percentage change in ________
128. Law of ________ can be defined as the quantity of a commodity produced and offered for sale.
129. At ________ price both buyers and sellers are satisfied and no one can benefit from further recontracting.
130. The response of supply and demand to price changes in ________ may not exactly match the law of demand and supply.
131. In ________, there is complete interdependence among the sellers with regard to their price output policies.
132. The ________ competition involves both the monopoly and competitive elements.
133. most profitable price, the rate of increase of marginal revenue must be less than the rate of increase of the ________.
134. price is the price at which the government would be under obligation to buy the entire stocks offered to it for sale.
135. The Foodgrains Procurement Committee (1950) recommended the continuation and extension of the system of ________ in India.
136. Terms of trade simply denote terms on which two ________ exchange their goods.
137. Farmers terms of trade equal the farm price divided by ________ goods price.
138. The doctrine that in countries farmers either are indifferent or respond perversely to changes in prices is patently false and harmful price policies on it always impair the efficiency of ________.
139. The farmers settled into a traditional agriculture, the rate at which they accept a new factor of production depends upon profit with due allowance to risk and uncertainty and in this respect the response is similar to that in ________.
140. The ________ method approach involves derivation of supply functions from available data and information relating to production functions and individual behaviour.
141. While making ________ in response to changes in economic environment, a farmer is faced with a number of constraints.
142. ________ is one of the many factors affecting supply response of agricultural commodities.
143. Unmindful of price changes, the farmers ________ their crop to sustain soil fertility.
144. Large-sized farms are more economical in working and conducive to greater ________ than small sized ones.
145. During a ________, the unpaid family labour serves as a cushion on many small farm units.
146. The relationship Log $Y = \text{Log } a + b \text{ Log } X$ has been estimated between yield per hectare/ acre (Y) and the average of holding (X) for all ________
147. Economic holding is the one which provides full employment to the farmers family and allows a reasonable ________.
148. Chief Ministers Conference on ceiling of agricultural holdings was held in July, 1972 and the ________ were laid down.
149. The defective implementation of land reforms policy has created more ________ than were abolished.
150. The legal protection granted to tenants has often been ________.
151. The policy of imposing a ceiling on land would be able to meet the desire to posses land and reducing the ________ in ownership and use.

152. "Farm management is a study of the principles underlying the function of the _______ as a business proprietor.

153. Farm management is an art of applying business and scientific principles to the organization and _______ of a farm.

154. Planning requires intellectual effort, reflective thinking, foresight and _______.

155. Planning describes the courses of actions to be adopted and _______.

156. It is generally believed that the technique of linear programming is the product of, _______.

157. The problems of planning form the core of _______ economics.

158. In linear programming model, a fanner is interested in maximizing the profits or minimizing the cost of production with fixed and _______ quantities of factors of production.

159. The _______ method is the most accepted procedure of solving a linear programming problem.

160. In practice, not much use has been made of the linear programming technique in _______ countries.

161. Output of agriculture is largely a _______ material.

162. _______ output comes from many small units operating independently.

163. Processing is often excluded from the list of marketing _______ as it is essentially a form changing activity.

164. Dispersion is the process exactly the opposite to that of _______

165. _______ believed that agriculture alone is productive, for it yields the subsistence of its workers.

166. The principle sources of the high productivity of modern agriculture are _______ sources.

167. The real development in land development banking was made by _______ state in 1979.

168. The cooperative credit structure is criticized as the small and _______ farmers do not get their fair share.

169. In India, there has been disparity in the expansion of the cooperative credit societies and their _______.

170. The agricultural _______ in India is one of the largest in the world.

171. Too much of diversification may lead to _______.

172. _______ refers to the practice of grazing animals on the public lands.

173. The application of _______ pertains to a situation in which two competitive farm firms are involved.

174. In Gurgaon Attempt village people were never made a party to the _______ planned for them.

175. The Sevagram Attempt was started under the guidance of _______ in 1920.

176. The main activities of Sevagram Attempt comprised organization of training centres for cottage industries, _______ and removal of untouchability.

177. In the earlier days rural development was considered synonymous with _______ development.

178. Rural development is the result of many _______ forces and education is one of them.

179. _______ is designed to provide literacy, an elementary understanding of science and environment.

180. The education designed to develop a specific knowledge and the skills associated with economic activities beneficial to make respectable living is called _______.

181. _______ should be conceived as a lifelong process of learning.

182. Formal education is highly _______, chronologically graded and hierarchically structured to begin with primary school upto university education.

183. Non-formal education denotes any organized, systematic educational activity carried outside the _______ of the formal system.

184. ________ education is the education for rural people outside the regularly organized schools and classrooms to bring about social and cultural development.
185. Philosophy is a body of general ________ as a field of knowledge.
186. An extension worker should utilize the ________ goodwill of the people in extension programmes.
187. The extension workers should have faith in ________ values and should try to educate people.
188. ________ development is accorded priority in programmes of rural development.
189. The basic ________ of extension is directed towards changing the outlook of persons by educating them.
190. Need and interest based programmes yield better results than the ________ ones.
191. Extension programmes should be ________ programmes with government aid.
192. The rural people should ________ participate in the extension work.
193. An extension worker is. also learning, while giving the learning ________ to the people.
194. The leadership ________ are developed in rural people, if they participate in extension programmes.
195. The ability and capability of an individual should be brought out and sharpened by an ________ worker.
196. Extension work cannot thrive without trained ________.
197. The success of the extension work lies in ________ of the people.
198. Neglect of one member of a family by extension worker may lead to ________ of an innovation.
199. Results of programme ________ greatly help in improving the quality of programme (s).
200. Extension has to carry research findings to the ________ and establish their relevance in fulfilling their needs.
201. The first principle of extension service rests on, "citizen is ________ in the democracy".
202. The home is the fundamental unit of civilization, family is the first training group of human race and the average farm is ________ with great resources and facilities comprise principles of extension besides the sovereignity of the citizen in democracy.
203. In some cases use of progressive leader farmers is made to produce the ________ effect.
204. The training approach emphasizes more systematic and deeper learning of specific ________ and related knowledge.
205. The ________ system comprises an excellent example of the training approach.
206. Extension workers with superior knowledge and wisdom can help in solving problems of ________ and lead them on the voyage to modernization.
207. The messages or the impact points for each crop are prepared in coordination with ________ university specialists and the staff of the departments of agriculture.
208. The technical messages are carefully selected and are relayed during the visit to the ________.
209. Drive is defined as a tendency initiated by shifts in the ________ balance in the body.
210. In psychology ________ refers to some internal activator within an individual.
211. ________ is energy mobilization towards the attainment of goals.
212. ________ denotes the degree of positive or negative feelings associated with some psychological object towards which people differ in varying degrees.
213. Intelligence quotient is equal to mental age divided by ________ age and multiplied by 100.
214. If a child of 8 can do all tests meant for the 10 years old then his I.Q. will be ________.

215. ________ is the process of inducting the individual into the social and cultural world to play his role as a member of society.
216. Personality is the dynamic organizations within the individual of those ________ systems that determine the unique adjustments to his environment.
217. Successful teaching contributes to effective ________.
218. Action follows when desire, conviction and the prospect of ________ make it easier for the person to act rather than not to act.
219. Learning is effected by physical and ________ environment.
220. ________ calls for effective communication.
221. The extension worker should understand the basic wants and ________ of the people with be/she has to work.
222. In extension educational ________ the change agents are more concerned with the adult or grown up people.
223. It is necessary to base the extension education programmes on the psychology of the ________ to make them effective.
224. A single communication model consists of source (S), message (M), Channel (C), receiver (R) and ________ (E).
225. An ________ is an idea, practice or object perceived as new by an individual.
226. Friends and neighbours are first in importance in the ________, trial and adoption stages of innovation (s).
227. ________ is the degree to which an individual is relatively earlier in adoption of new ideas than others of his social system.
228. Films are one of the most effective means of ________ interest.
229. Radio belongs to the ________ word means of communication.
230. All the ________ listeners may or may not be educated in formal sense.
231. A prepared ________ should be divided into different parts depending upon the nature of the message to be conveyed.
232. In presentation of a talk just talk to the people and do not ________.
233. The advantage of the ________ projector is that a teacher can always face the class.
234. In the sound track sound is ________ on the photographic film.
235. The means by which sound is ________ from a sound motion picture film is practically the reverse of the way it is recorded.
236. A screen is to provide the maximum possible ________ of the image with minimum glare or strain on the eyes.
237. A tape stored under normal room temperature and humidity is not ________, but holds sharp and clear quality for many years.
238. Next to camera and film the most important ingredient for ________ is a good imagination.
239. Imagination will put new ________ on old things and will lead to seek new and better viewpoints.
240. Facts are the foundation stones on which the community leaders and the ________ build and carry out their programmes.
241. Objectives represent the directions of movement, while a goal is the ________ in a given direction one expects to go during a given period of time.

242. ________ objectives are the specific items which are to be achieved.

243. Plan of work comprises a ________ of procedure for solving the different problems of an extension programme.

244. A decision is a choice among ________.

245. ________ is an assignment of values to alternatives.

246. Evolution should be in line with the overall ________ of the agency.

247. The participation of the people in the programme planning process normally gives them a ________ interest in seeing that an action programme is carried out.

248. Administration refers to the guidance, leadership and control of efforts of a group of individuals towards some ________.

249. POSDCORB denotes planning, organization, staffing, directing, ________, reporting and budgeting.

250. Rural sociology is the systematic study of people living in rural areas and who are living by or are immediately dependent on ________.

251. Rural society is more homogeneous in nature, relatively independent and with a low degree of ________.

252. The persons in the ________ group have face-to-face relationship, such as a family and play group.

253. The members of a secondary group has little ________ affection and their relationship is governed by the fulfilment of some objective.

254. ________ group is a group of persons whom an individual consults before taking an important decision.

255. ________ are organized for particular purposes.

256. The ________ is the primary institution of society.

257. The Janpads referred to in Valmiki Ramayana were a kind of federation of ________ republics.

258. In the Mahabharta and Manusmriti, there is a mention of ________.

259. ________ planning denotes planning for possible future environments which are not expected to occur but which may occur; if this possible future is widely different from that premised, alternative premises and plans are required.

260. ________ in an organization is the power in a, position to exercise discretion in making decisions affecting others.

261. ________ is a small group of persons to whom some matter is referred to mainly for detailed examination and decision.

262. The basic personal skills needed for effective ________ are technical, human and conceptual.

263. Spontaneity and creativity are important parts of ________.

264. ________ is the process of influencing people so that they will strive willingly and enthusiastically toward attainment of the organizational goals.

265. A new concept of budgeting is ________, the introduction of which has been recommended by the Administrative Reforms Commission.

266. Efficiency-cum-________ Audit is a technique of audit adopted to assess and evaluate the economy, efficiency and effectiveness of development projects in an organization.

267. Extension programme is a ________ of situation, objectives, problems and solutions.

268. ________ denotes an intense educational activity for motivating and mobilizing a community to action, to solve a problem or satisfy a need urgently felt by it.

269. An exhibition is a systematic display of models, specimens, charts, posters, information *etc.* in a ________ around a theme to create interest in the community.

270. ________ is the capacity to see oneself in other fellow's situation.

271. Homophily is the degree to which ________ of individuals who interact are similar in certain attributes, such as beliefs, values, education, social status and the like.

272. ________ to degree to which pairs of individuals who interact are different in certain attributes.

273. The number of ________ villages in India in 1981 (excluding Assam) was 557,137.

II. Tick mark (3) True or False:

274. The process of capital formations begins when capital accumulation catches up with population.

275. Failure to provide food could seriously limit the process of economic expansion.

276. The strategic nature of agriculture sector in India is only to its preponderant size, but also to peculiar production and consumption conditions attached to agricultural goods.

277. An increase in the output of agriculture in and of itself represents a rise in the product of a country.

278. The product contribution can be examined as a contribution to the growth of total, net or gross product and the product per capita.

279. The economic development is characterized by a substantial decrease in the demand of agricultural products.

280. Expansion of exports may be one of the most promising means of increasing expenditure and foreign exchange earnings.

281. Rising net cash incomes of the farm population may be important as a stimulus to industrial expansion.

282. Adam Smith in his "Wealth of Nations" took vigorous exception to the notion, "agriculture is the only productive activity" yet ranked it as the highest wealth creating powers.

283. T.R. Mathews in his rust essay on population, which appeared in 1798 laid pronounced emphasis on agriculture.

284. Increased agricultural productivity supplies the major wage-good (food) to industrial workers at a favourable price to the disadvantage of new industry.

285. All the growth models for surplus labour countries have underlined the importance of agriculture to develop the industrial sector in initial stages.

286. It has been estimated that the industries drawing raw material from agricultural sector contribute nearly 50 per cent of the income generated by manufacturing sector in India.

287. Agricultural exports earn substantial share of foreign exchange without draining it away through ex-ports.

288. Forests offer no possibility of intensive fodder production.

289. Industrialization exerts no pull towards urban migration.

290. To a given piece of land, other things remaining constant, additional input units show positive, but diminishing response to each additional unit of input.

291. Expansion in the area of cultivation accentuates the incidence of the law of diminishing returns.

292. Changes in productivity of labour are connected with the process of transformation from static to dynamic agriculture.

293. The static agri-technology and rise in labour force cause fall in wages below minimum subsistence level, finally resulting in increased death rate and reduced birth rate of growth of population.

294. Modem agriculture has no longer remained static in character.

295. The possibilities of monocropping have increased due to new seed-fertilizer technology.

296. Agriculture offers as much division of labour as does a manufacturing industry.
297. Farm workers, efficiency is not effected by his/her family background.
298. Technical improvements have greatly influenced labour efficiency by pervading in all fields of farming.
299. Mechanical improvements alone can raise labour efficiency.
300. Historically, the gap between farm and non-farm wages have been justified on the ground that rise in farm wages leads to more than a proportionate rise in non-farm wages.
301. At initial stages of industrial growth, the farm sector is the only supplier of urban. workers.
302. Farm workers have bargaining power equal to industrial workers.
303. State legislations in developed countries of the world have not improved the status and lot of farm workers.
304. Capital as a productive resource assumes a number of forms.
305. Psychological impulses and social values have so developed as would often induce an individual, landlord, farm owner to spend.
306. Future expectations are so high that every one has a strong motivation to save.
307. Repayment of loans depends upon the nature and terms of a loan, its size, but not the modalities of repayment.
308. The loans, sometimes, are paid in fixed instalments comprising the principal and the interest.
309. During periods of economic depression, private agencies are not nervous of making loans to farm operators.
310. It is essential that under depressing economic conditions, the government should not come to the rescue of the farmers.
311. The loans from commercial banks in agriculture have been a traditional phenomenon.
312. Insurance companies have started issuing loans to the farm sector in the developed countries of the world.
313. Insurance companies in less developed countries have recently taken up crop insurance schemes.
314. Insurance companies do not recruit trained agricultural personnel to deal with agricultural credit.
315. Due to a number of malpractices and inefficiency, the cooperative credit schemes have so far achieved only limited success.
316. The increase in both quality and quantity of farm products augments farm receipts and the wage-bill.
317. The positive difference between net gains and the additional cost would definitely suggest a decision in favour of using additional capital.
318. The technical and trained personnel problems involved in introduction of new capital deserve a decideratum to make a final decision.
319. Farm production refers to producing food, fibre and livestock by using s several different kinds of outputs.
320. Agricultural production economics is concerned with qualitative relationships which are basic to production processes in agriculture.
321. The agricultural production is concerned with levels of factor costs and product prices, and the nature of production patterns.
322. Resource-Resource Factor-Factor relationship refers to the most profitable combination of resources to produce a specific amount of a given output.
323. Production function is a mathematical relationship indicating the way in which the quantity of a product depends upon the qualities of particular inputs used.

324. "Consideration of activities like selling, settling strikes and anticipating future styles of product involve business knowledge and talents unattainable in best engineering schools.

325. A production function which is homogeneous of the first degree is known as linear homogeneous production function.

326. Monotonic relationships do not share even a single feature of the linear relationships.

327. Non-monotonic relationships share one feature of the linear relationship, that is, throughout they are increasing or decreasing.

328. The elasticity of substitution between the two factors of production is not infinite.

329. An isoquant does not cross or cut the lower or the lower isoquant.

330. The slope of the iso-cost line is equal to the ratio of the prices of the factors of consumption.

331. "When an increase in output of one, with resources held constant in amount, also causes increase in the output of other" are. known as complementary enterprises.

332. The constant of substitution refers to substitution of two crops for each other at constant rate if an increase in one necessitates the same increase in the quality of the other.

333. Increasing rate of substitution means an increase in one product requires small and smaller sacrifice of the other product produceable within the same resource mix.

334. Iso-revenue line or price line (*TR*) may be defined as the *locus* of product combinations on production possibility curve

$$\left[\begin{array}{l}(TR = y_1 \,.\, Py_1 \,.\, y_2 \,.\, Py_2)\\ y_1 \text{ and } y_2 = \text{total price of two outputs}\\ Py_1 \text{ and } Py_2 = \text{total revenue}\end{array}\right]$$

335. The term "cost" generally refers to the outlay of funds for productive services.

336. Average total cost can be computed by dividing the total cost by the number of units of the output produced.

337. Marginal cost is the deduction from the total cost by the last unit of output.

338. Price policy must ensure that the agricultural production is economic both in the widest and strictest sense of the term.

339. In Simple Ratio and Link Relatives methods price and area or output are converted into index numbers and then the price index of previous year is related to the current year area or output index.

340. Regression analysis cannot be expressed in terms of exponential model or Cobb-Douglas type of production function.

341. According to Third Report of UN on progress of Land Reforms (LR), "LR is an integrated programme of measures designed to eliminate obstacles to economic and social development arising out of defects in the agrarian structure".

342. The policy of land ceiling would be reducing inequalities in agricultural incomes and self-employment.

343. The ceiling is applicable to a family of five consisting of husband, wife and three minor children.

344. The 'Task Force' of the Planning Commission concluded in 1972 that no tangible progress in land reforms is possible without requisite political will.

345. Rising land rents may not prove burdensome if productivity per hectare decreases *pari passu*.

346. The negative effect of tenancy farming which does not help in increasing agricultural productivity is absentee landlordism.

347. Insecurity of tenure in tenancy farming is an obvious stimulant to any kind of long-term improvement by the tenant.

348. The tenant is necessarily poor due to high rate of land-rent and low productivity.

349. The tenant in traditional societies is rarely an independent entrepreneur.

350. Adapt Smith considered large ownership and servile tenure as encouragement to progress.

351. J.S. Mill advocated the demerits of the peasant proprietorship on grounds of income equality and social justice.

352. Agricultural production is expected to rise by redistribution of agricultural land.

353. Any increase in the purchasing power of the cultivator will be of great benefit to developing secondary and tertiary industries.

354. The relationship between land reforms and capital formation is always direct and positive.

355. The possibilities of land reforms as an aid to agricultural development clearly define limitations.

356. Farm management deals with the problems of resource allocation in agricultural sector encompassing farm business and economic efficiency of the farm.

357. Farm management is a science of organization and management of farm enterprises for the purpose of securing the maximum continuous progress.

358. According to the Committee of American Marketing Association, "Marketing includes all activities having to do with effecting changes in the ownership and possession of goods and services".

359. "Marketing is that part of economics which deals with the creation time and place and possession - utilities and that phase of business activities through which human wants are satisfied by the exchange of goods and services for some valuable consideration.

360. The least important cause of rural indebtedness in India is mass poverty of the farmers.

361. The Indian farmer never takes unproductive loans from the moneylenders.

362. The transformation problem of traditional Indian agriculture, basically is not an investment problem.

363. Delayed attention to the economic potentials of Indian agriculture has been due to economists' neglect of the industrial sector in less developed countries.

364. The old doctrines did not recognize the importance of agriculture in the process of economic development.

365. Schultz hypothesised "There are comparatively few significant inefficiencies in the allocation of factors of production in traditional agriculture".

366. The reproducible material capital is relatively less as a factor of production in many poor agricultural communities.

367. Farm technology may be distinguished from farm mechanization and farm technical knowledge.

368. No significant advances have been made in farm technology yet yields have increased beyond expectations.

369. Most of the empirical studies in India have postulated that the benefits of Green Revolution have been equally shared by different categories of rural households.

370. Dryland farming is the key to stability of agri-production in India.

371. Farm mechanization decreases the productivity of land and labour and hence cost of production.

372. Technical progress and industrial development contribute to increasing the ease to add capital to labour.

373. The promotion of farm mechanization in developing countries is neither a pure agricultural production, nor a pure agricultural technology function.

374. The motive of specialized farming is profit, but that of diversified farming is self-sufficiency.

375. A specialized farmer consciously or unconsciously gets involved in international trade.

376. Education is the projection of desirable changes in human behaviour.
377. The behaviour of an individual is influenced, controlled and directed by culture.
378. With the changes in time and environment, the patterns of culture remain uninfluenced.
379. Extension education widens the gap created by cultural lag through adjustments in new environment.
380. Extension education brings out the changes in knowledge, skills and attitudes in human behaviour.
381. An extension agency interprets the research results to the farmers and feeds back the research institutions with farmer's problems.
382. Extension uses autocratic methods in educating the farmers.
383. Extension helps in adoption of innovations.
384. The philosophy of life has no relevance with the actions of the people.
385. A farmer invariably tests the messages *vis-a-vis* own philosophy of life.
386. The blueprint for the extension programme evolved for one area will be applicable equally well to another area.
387. The extension work has to be changed with the growth and development to commensurate with cultural changes.
388. All the principles of extension are universally applicable.
389. Extension service operates within the broad framework of national agricultural policies and objectives.
390. An extension service is only concerned with the transfer of technology.
391. In Comilla Project (Bangladesh) involved an extension service in which much of the efforts moved from bottom up. instead of from top down.
392. Integrated Development Approach emphasizes upon rational development and coordination of all principal factors required for industrial and urban development.
393. The IADP used the integrated development approach in tackling the problem of rural development.
394. Community development consists of advising the individual and the community to avoid self-improvement, making use of available government assistance and obtaining peoples participation.
395. Community development aimed at securing the minimum development of material and human resource in the area and to stabilize the standard of living of rural community.
396. Instincts are complex inherited tendencies common to all members of a species compelling each individual to perceive, to experience and to act.
397. Need refers to a condition of lack or deficiency in the organism.
398. The favourable attitudes towards the family planning programme of an individual is not likely to participate and follow the programme recommendations.
399. A change in attitude may preclude action.
400. Individuals in any community range from idiots to a very brilliant level of intelligence.
401. Culture is defined as the socially standardized way of feeling.
402. A well-organized group discussion conducted properly is the best way to learn individual group action.
403. Encourage speech makers as speeches induce group thinking.
404. The presentation will be interesting if the subject in question is of interest to the people.
405. The extension worker need not visit his demonstrator in the beginning and plan demonstration of his own.
406. Many papers or periodicals going to the villages do not welcome the "service type" information.

407. Literature is the basis of any teaching programme.
408. Circular letters can teach, but cannot save time of the extension worker.
409. Photographs are particularly suitable to teach the literates.
410. A poster as a visual aid is always used alone.
411. A poster, generally speaking, should contain announcement, set out the conditions and recommend action.
412. The assembling of facts pertaining to local situations is a continuous activity.
413. Interpretation of facts involves casual reasoning backed up by experience and judgement.
414. Objectives are the expressions of the 'beginnings' towards which efforts are directed.
415. The evaluation of all the stages could be done at one time *i.e.*, at the end of the programme year.
416. Non-agricultural jobs are few and are not of much economic importance.
417. The poor move to rural areas in search of job opportunities to augment their income.
418. The rural contacts may be frequent, but they tend to be more cursory, formal and impersonal.
419. In rural areas, control is more by formal, impersonal means of law-prescribed rules and regulations with penalties for violation.
420. The cohesion and unity in rural areas is due to common tracts, similarity of experience and common objectives which are shared by rural people.
421. The communication and interaction should not be one way, but it should be from both the persons.
422. The term management stems from French word '*minage*' meaning 'housekeeping'.
423. "Historically, five basic functions forming the core of studying management are planning, decision making, organizing, directing and controlling.".
424. "Planning is decision making, and involves selecting and integrating the courses of action that an organization will follow to attain its objectives".
425. The RSR programme should include specific attention to the training of men in new skills.
426. Knowing of something pertaining to others need or arousing need in others is called awareness.
427. 'DIORAMA' is scenic representation of the original, with specimen, model and painting.
428. Translides are transparent small size photographs which are displayed without light at the back.

III. Tick mark (✓) the correct answer :

429. The _______ Year Plan sought to maintain a clear-cut distinction between the minimum support price and the procurement price.
(*a*) Second (*b*) Third
(*c*) Fifth (*d*) Sixth

430. Following the support price policy, the Government of India in 1984-85 raised the price of rice-paddies (paddy) by _______ per cent.
(*a*) 32.2 (*b*) 44.2
(*c*) 36.8 (*d*) 26.7

431. The Food Corporation of India was set up in _______.
(*a*) 1960 (*b*) 1962
(*c*) 1965 (*d*) 1967

432. Land holdings of either 10 or more hectares have been classified as _______ in India.
(*a*) Semi-medium (*b*) Medium
(*c*) Semi-large (*d*) Large

433. Land reforms have been equated with total _______ development.
(*a*) Urban (*b*) Agrarian
(*c*) Industrial (*d*) Educational

434. Profits are defined as $\pi = R - (FC + VC)$, where, FC = total fixed cost and VC = total variable cost and _______.
(*a*) R = Revenue (*b*) R = Reduction
(*c*) R = Regression (*d*) R = Coefficient

435. According to Hung-Chao Tai land reforms aim at attaining just relationship among _______ population.
(*a*) Urban (*b*) Industrial
(*c*) Traders (*d*) Agricultural

436. The "term land reform" should be used in broadest sense to serve as _______ for action.
(*a*) Inscription (*b*) Prescription
(*c*) Description (*d*) Formulation

437. *Zamidari*-system was based on _______ to support British Imperialism in India.
(*a*) Exploitation (*b*) Elimination
(*c*) Regulation (*d*) Augmentation

438. The main objective of land reform measures undertaken after independence was removal of institutional and _______ obstacles.
(*a*) Emotional (*b*) Motivational
(*c*) Conventional (*d*) National

439. In *Zamidari* abolition, the elimination of intermediaries led to excessive burden of _______.
(*a*) Revenue (*b*) Reservation
(*c*) Supplementation (*d*) Compensation

440. The reform of tenancy laid down that the rent should not exceed _______ per cent of gross produce.
(*a*) 20-25 (*b*) 10-15
(*c*) 25-30 (*d*) 35-40

441. According to the Directorate of Marketing and Inspection _______ per cent may be taken as the average marketing margin for all surplus food grains in India.
(*a*) 15 (*b*) 20
(*c*) 25 (*d*) 35

442. Major commercial banks were nationalized in _______.
(*a*) 1965 (*b*) 1967
(*c*) 1969 (*d*) 1971

443. NABARD Act was passed in _______, 1979.
(*a*) January (*b*) February
(*c*) March (*d*) April

444. NABARD came into existence on July 12, _______.
(*a*) 1980 (*b*) 1981
(*c*) 1982 (*d*) 1983

445. The authorized share capital of NABARD is Rs. ______ million

(*a*) 5,000 (*b*) 4,000

(*c*) 3,000 (*d*) 2,000

446. The paid up capital share of NABARD is Rs.______ million.

(*a*) 400 (*b*) 600

(*c*) 800 (*d*) 1,000

447. According to the 1951-52 survey, the proportion of indebtedness was about 60 per cent for all the families, of which ______ per cent were cultivators.

(*a*) 70 (*b*) 60

(*c*) 80 (*d*) 90

448. The average debt for an indebted cultivator's family during 1951-52 and 1961-62 rose by ______ per cent.

(*a*) 60 (*b*) 45

(*c*) 35 (*d*) 25

449. The spurt to Zero Marginal Productivity type of exercise was given by ______ in 1954.

(*a*) W. Arthur Lewis (*b*) W. David Hopper

(*c*) W. Nelson Michael (*d*) W. Benzene Shoemaker

450. Gurgaon Attempt was organized by F.L. Bryne, Collector of Gurgaon district in Punjab in ______.

(*a*) 1915 (*b*) 1920

(*c*) 1925 (*d*) 1930

451. Based on the recommendations of the Grow More Food Enquiry Committee, ______ Community projects were taken up in 1952.

(*a*) 25 (*b*) 35

(*c*) 45 (*d*) 55

452. Extension education is ______ process.

(*a*) Only teaching (*b*) Only learning

(*c*) Teaching and learning (*d*) None of these

453. The Comilla Project approach was first used by the Academy of Rural Development at Comilla, in ______.

(*a*) Pakistan (*b*) Bangladesh

(*c*) Mauritius (*d*) Nepal

454. Balwantrai Mehta Team stimulated an active consideration of ______ through democratic bodies.

(*a*) Centralization (*b*) Mobilization

(*c*) Stabilization (*d*) Decentralization

455. Maharashtra government appointed a committee in ______ under the chairmanship of Vasantrao Naik to examine the question of democratic decentralization in Maharashtra.

(*a*) 1961 (*b*) 1959

(*c*) 1957 (*d*) 1955

456. Maharashtra Zila Parishads and Panchayat Samiti Act was enacted in ______.

(*a*) 1967 (*b*) 1965

(*c*) 1963 (*d*) 1961

457. In _______ village panchayats were established under the Mumbai Village Panchayat, Act, 1958.
(*a*) Madhya Pradesh (*b*) Gujarat
(*c*) Rajasthan (*d*) Maharashtra

458. The objectives of education are decided by _______.
(*a*) Biological Science (*b*) Physical Science
(*c*) Normatic Science (*d*) Social Science

459. The extension practice varying in operation to varying extents and the results are showy is named as _______.
(*a*) Complexity (*b*) Visibility
(*c*) Divisibility (*d*) Utility

460. If a new practice represents a real major improvement over the existing one, the content of such an innovation embodies _______.
(*a*) Compatibility (*b*) Visibility
(*c*) Utility (*d*) Complexity

461. The leaflet, is a single sheet of paper folded usually to make _______ page piece of printed paper.
(*a*) Two (*b*) Four
(*c*) Six (*d*) Eight

462. A _______ mm camera is necessary for making slides that fit most of the projectors.
(*a*) 25 (*b*) 35
(*c*) 45 (*d*) 70

463. The motion picture camera, actually a device for recording a series of still pictures at the rate of _______ exposures per second.
(*a*) 12 (*b*) 24
(*c*) 36 (*d*) 48

464. The beliefs the agriculture is the basic industry, and any philosophy invented to go with it was named as "Agricultural Fundamentalism" by Dr. S. Davis in _______.
(*a*) 1895 (*b*) 1905
(*c*) 1920 (*d*) 1935

465. _______ and the group viewed, "the wealth and welfare of nations depend upon many complex conditions and not only on agriculture".
(*a*) T.S. Davis (*b*) C.C. Bishop
(*c*) J.W. Meller (*d*) W.J. Foreman

466. _______ and Shultz believe that there is interdependence and close relationship among the various sectors of economy.
(*a*) W.W. Wilcox (*b*) Z.R. Davis
(*c*) A.J. Anderson (*d*) N.W. Cummings

467. According to 1981 census, _______ of working force was still engaged in the primary sector.
(*a*) 61 (*b*) 67
(*c*) 71 (*d*) 77

468. One of the significant models of economic development of a labour surplus economy has been advanced by _______.
(*a*) Hung-Chao Tai (*b*) Huag P. Lewis
(*c*) Chan K. Heady (*d*) Foe C. Gray

469. In an expanding industrial sector, technological developments in industry tend to _______ labour.
(*a*) Displace (*b*) Replace
(*c*) Engage (*d*) No change

470. In countries of_________ labour problem has become all the more serious owing to demographic explosion.
(*a*) America (*b*) Europe
(*c*) Asia (*d*) Whole world

471. The problem of allocation of capital is essentially a farm management problem aiming at ________ utilization of the available production resources.
(*a*) Maximizing (*b*) Optimizing
(*c*) Stabilizing (*d*) Minimizing

472. ________ production function is expressed as Y = m – arx, where, Y = total production, x = quantity of variable factor, m = maximum output attained from fixed technical unit, r = ratio of addition of increments to production and a = maximum output added by the particular variable factor.
(*a*) Douglas (*b*) Bruce
(*c*) Spillman (*d*) Hillman

473. The constant elasticity of substitution function (CES) was used by J.W. Swan and R.M. Solow in ______.
(*a*) 1926 (*b*) 1936
(*c*) 1946 (*d*) 1956

474. Input- output production function is based on the general equilibrium model of _______(1874).
(*a*) Leon Walras (*b*) Leon Michael
(*c*) Wilson Arrow (*d*) David Solow

475. "According to law of _______ proportion, "if equal increments of one input are added, the inputs of other production services being held constant, beyond a certain point, the resulting increments of the product will decrease, that is, marginal product will diminish".
(*a*) Constant (*b*) Linear
(*c*) Variable (*d*) Inverse

476. ________ rightly remarked, "Let divisibility enter through door, the law of variable proportions rushes out through the window".
(*a*) M.M. Bober (*b*) C.A. Watson
(*c*) T. Sutovsky (*d*) R.M. Solow

477. When fertilizer input is increased from one to two units, total output increases from 103 to 174, that is, the output has increased only by _______ per cent.
(*a*) 90 (*b*) 85
(*c*) 61.9 (*d*) 71.9

478. ________ was the nest economist to give a clear formulation of price elasticity (Ep) which is the ratio of a relative change in quantity of relative change in price (Ep = relative change in quantity or relative change in price).
(*a*) Alfred Marshall (*b*) A.M. Khusro
(*c*) E.J. Long (*d*) P. Dorner

479. Foodgrains Price Committee was constituted in India in ______.
(a) 1951 (b) 1953
(c) 1947 (d) 1950

480. The Foodgrains Price Committee was appointed in ______ by the Govt. of India.
(a) 1954 (b) 1958
(c) 1962 (d) 1964

481. The Agricultural Price Commission (APC) was set up in ______ to evolve a balanced and integrated price structure
(a) 1955 (b) 1965
(c) 1970 (d) 1973

482. Among the different types of motion picture projectors, ______ mm projector is most suitable for class-room teaching.
(a) 16 (b) 70
(c) 8 (d) 20

483. The ______ situation is the bench-mark from where people should start the process of programme planning.
(a) Regional (b) Local
(c) National (d) None of these

484. Execution of a plan assumed that a programme is planned, and a plan of work is ______.
(a) to be thought of (b) to be developed
(c) already developed (d) being modified

485. The execution of plan should be carried out ______.
(a) Without change (b) With change
(c) After a lapse of time (d) In presence of leader

486. There are ______ development blocks in India.
(a) 2,000 (b) 3,000
(c) 4,000 (d) 5,000

487. Voluntary agencies are characterized by ______ among the community.
(a) Greater continuity (b) Less acceptability
(c) Less commitment (d) Less intensity

488. Rural sociology is expected to develop greater understanding of the behaviour of ______ people and society.
(a) Urban (b) Rural
(c) Both of these (d) None of these

489. Rural population is about ______ of the world population and lives mainly in developing countries.
(a) One-third (b) One-fourth
(c) One-fifth (d) Two-thirds

490. In India ______ of the population lives in villages.
(a) Half (b) One-third
(c) Three-fourths (d) Two-thirds

491. National Extension Service was launched in ________.
(*a*) 1952 (*b*) 1953
(*c*) 1954 (*d*) 1955

492. Efforts to revive *panchayats* in India were made in ________ by introducing Village Panchayat Act in several States.
(*a*) 1945 (*b*) 1935
(*c*) 1925 (*d*) 1915

493. The Village Panchayat Act came into being in ________.
(*a*) 1956 (*b*) 1958
(*c*) 1960 (*d*) 1954

494. ________ concentrates on a rational structure with universal applications in social institutions.
(*a*) Bureaucracy (*b*) Autocracy
(*c*) Anarchy (*d*) Monarchy

495. Formations of clique ________ an organization.
(*a*) Damages (*b*) Improves
(*c*) Stabilizes (*d*) None of these

496. Staffing denotes ________, maintaining and developing personnel in position to fulfill the organizational objectives.
(*a*) Rejecting (*b*) Eliminating
(*c*) Selecting (*d*) Upgrading

497. Programme Evaluation Organization (PED) was set up in 1952 as an independent organization under general guidance and direction of ________.
(*a*) Reserve Bank (*b*) Ministry of Agriculture
(*c*) Finance Commission (*d*) Planning Commission

498. ORPs were initiated in ________.
(*a*) 1970-71 (*b*) 1972-73
(*c*) 1974-75 (*d*) 1975-76

499. The first KVK was established in 1974 at ________.
(*a*) Nagpur (*b*) Nilokheri
(*c*) Ludhiana (*d*) Pondicherry

500. LLP was launched by the ICAR in 1979 as a part of its ________ Jubilee Celebrations.
(*a*) Silver (*b*) Golden
(*c*) Diamond (*d*) Platinum

501. The University Education Commission was headed by ________, recommended the establishment of 'Rural Universities'.
(*a*) Dr. Rajendra Prasad (*b*) Dr. S. Kothari
(*c*) Dr. S. Radhakrishnan (*d*) Shri C. Rajgopalacharee

502. The first agricultural university came into existence at ________ in 1960.
(*a*) Ludhiana, Punjab (*b*) Pantnagar, Uttar Pradesh
(*c*) Rahuri, Maharashtra (*d*) Hyderabad, Andhra Pradesh

503. Two Joint Indo-American Teams on Agricultural Research and Education recommended setting up of Agricultural Universities in the states on the pattern of Land Grant Colleges of _______.

(*a*) Germany (*b*) France

(*c*) U.K. (*d*) U.S.A.

504. The Government of India reorganized the ICAR and charged with the responsibility of coordinating, directing and promoting agricultural research and education in India in _______

(*a*) 1962 (*b*) 1964

(*c*) 1966 (*d*) 1968

505. The government sponsored Firka Development Scheme of _______ was launched in 1966.

(*a*) Bombay state (*b*) Madras state

(*c*) Punjab state (*d*) U.P. state

506. The Government of India set up Planning Commission in _______.

(*a*) 1949 (*b*) 1950

(*c*) 1951 (*d*) 1952

507. The term community development appears to have originated from Cambridge in England in _______.

(*a*) 1950 (*b*) 1948

(*c*) 1946 (*d*) 1944

508. Implementation of CD and NES was brought to sharp focus by the Report of the Team for the Study of Community Projects and NES by _____ in 1957.

(*a*) Balvantrai G. Mehta (*b*) Bhalerao N. Khuspe

(*c*) Dadajibhai R. Mehta (*d*) Chinnani M. Bathkal

509. IADP implementation should be so phased that in the first year 20 per cent and by the end of fifth year _______ per cent area is covered.

(*a*) 85 (*b*) 75

(*c*) 65 (*d*) 55

510. The key village scheme was initiated in _______ 1952 comprising first systematic attempt to improve the quality and productivity of cattle and buffaloes in India.

(*a*) June (*b*) July

(*c*) August (*d*) January

511. NERP was started in _______.

(*a*) 1975 (*b*) 1977

(*c*) 1979 (*d*) 1981

512. The Institute of Development Studies, University of Sussex, _______ developed the Farmer First (FF) method in late 1980s.

(*a*) U.K. (*b*) U.N.

(*c*) U.S.A. (*d*) E. Germany

513. The Rural Systems Research idea was motivated by _______ in 1988.

(*a*) David E. Benor (*b*) Ralph W. Cummings

(*c*) Guy B. Barid (*d*) M.S. Swaminathan

514. In India, slightly less than half the villages are inhabited by less than _______ persons.

(*a*) 200 (*b*) 300

(*c*) 400 (*d*) 500

515. Slightly less than three-fourths Indian villages have a human population of less than ______.

(a) 1,000 (b) 900

(c) 800 (d) 700

IV. Match the following:

516. Match the agricultural income expressed as percentage of total national income 'during the following periods.

(a) 48.4 (i) 1980-81

(b) 41.5 (ii) 1985-86

(c) 39.8 (iii) 1970-71

(d) 37.2 (iv) 1983-84

517. Match the GDP percentage with the sector as estimated during 1983-84.

(a) 39.8 (i) Transport and Communication

(b) 21.8 (ii) Agriculture and allied sectors

(c) 6.9 (iii) Services

(d) 32.0 (iv) Mining and manufacturing

518. Match x_1 with $PX_1 . X_1$ if $PX_1 = 0.75$

(a) 10 (i) 22.50

(b) 30 (ii) 52.50

(c) 50 (iii) 7.50

(d) 70 (iv) 37.50

519. Match $PX_1 \cdot X_1$ $(PX_1 = 0.75)$ with PX_2, X_2 $(PX_2 = 1{\cdot}00)$

(a) 15.00 (i) 12.00

(b) 30.00 (ii) 7.20

(c) 45.00 (iii) 7.00

(d) 67.50 (iv) 27.00

520. Match $PX_2 \cdot X_2$ if PX_2 = Re. 1·00 with cost

(a) 44.00 (i) 46.10

(b) 17.00 (ii) 51.50

(c) 8.60 (iii) 58.60

(d) 6.00 (iv) 39.00

521. Match the enterprise relationship with the marginal rate of substitution when $\Delta Y_1 / \Delta Y_2$ or $Y_2/\Delta Y_1$ = ______ (Y = output)

(a) Competitive (i) More than zero

(b) Supplementary (ii) More than zero

(c) Complementary (iii) Equal to zero

522. Match the following with their abbreviated expressions when Y = output and X = input.

(a) Output (i) $(X/Y).(DY/DX)$

(b) Elasticity of production (ii) PX_2/PX_1

(c) Marginal substitution ratio (iii) $Y = A + BX$

(d) Price ratio (iv) DY_1/DX_2

523. Match the Index Number with period taking 1952-53 equal to 100.

(*a*) 110 — (*i*) 1955-56
(*b*) 88 — (*ii*) 1956-57
(*c*) 104.5 — (*iii*) 1957-58
(*d*) 107.4 — (*iv*) 1950-51

524. **Index Number** — **Period**

(*a*) 1958-59 — (*i*) 123.8
(*b*) 1959-60 — (*ii*) 114.0
(*c*) 1960-61 — (*iii*) 115.5
(*d*) 1961-62 — (*iv*) 116.5

525. Match the years with the percentage increase/decrease in Index Number with base, 1961-62 = 100, weight 33.2.

(*a*) 1962-63 — (*i*) +20.8
(*b*) 1963-64 — (*ii*) +2.3
(*c*) 1964-65 — (*iii*) +6.0
(*d*) 1965-66 — (*iv*) +8.3

526. **Year** — **Increase / Decrease (IN)**

(*a*) 1966-67 — (*i*) +3.2
(*b*) 1967-68 — (*ii*) −4.7
(*c*) 1968-69 — (*iii*) +17.3
(*d*) 1970-71 — (*iv*) 13.0

527. Match the years with Index Number, base 1970-71 = 100.

(*a*) 1971-72 — (*i*) 158.4
(*b*) 1976-77 — (*ii*) 236.5
(*c*) 1981-82 — (*iii*) 330.1
(*d*) 1986-87 — (*iv*) 100.4

528. Match the general index of wholesale prices with the year.

(*a*) 111.8 — (*i*) 1980-81
(*b*) 124.9 — (*ii*) 1970-71
(*c*) 181.1 — (*iii*) 1950-51
(*d*) 257.3 — (*iv*) 1960-61

529. Match the year with the index of agricultural commodities.

(*a*) 1955-56 — (*i*) 141.7
(*b*) 1965-66 — (*ii*) 88.0
(*c*) 1975-76 — (*iii*) 309.6
(*d*) 1985-86 — (*iv*) 157.3

530. Match the National Sample Survey on number and size of operational holdings' 'round number' with the year

(*a*) 8th round — (*i*) 1959-60
(*b*) 16th round — (*ii*) 1970-71
(*c*) 17th round — (*iii*) 1953-54
(*d*) 26th round — (*iv*) 1960-61

531. Match the class of land-holding as specified in the census reports with their actual hectarage in India.

(*a*) Marginal holdings — (*i*) 4-10 hectares
(*b*) Small holdings — (*ii*) Less than 1 hectare
(*c*) Semi-medium holdings — (*iii*) 2-4 hectares
(*d*) Medium holdings — (*iv*) 1-2 hectares

532. Match the category of holdings with their per cent of the total number of holdings in 1980-81 in India.

(*a*) Marginal — (*i*) 14.0
(*b*) Small — (*ii*) 9.1
(*c*) Semi-medium — (*iii*) 56.4
(*d*) Medium — (*iv*) 2.1
(*e*) Large — (*v*) 18.0

533. Match the total area operated (million hectares) with the categories of holdings as estimated in 1980-81 in India.

(*a*) Marginal — (*i*) 34.6
(*b*) Small — (*ii*) 37.1
(*c*) Semi-medium — (*iii*) 148.9
(*d*) Medium — (*iv*) 19.8
(*e*) Large — (*v*) 23.0

534. Match the category of holding with the average area operated per holding based on estimates of 1980-81 in India.

(*a*) Marginal — (*i*) 17.7 hectares
(*b*) Small — (*ii*) 2.8 hectares
(*c*) Semi-medium — (*iii*) 1.4 hectares
(*d*) Medium — (*iv*) 6.0 hectares
(*e*) Large — (*v*) 0.4 hectare

535. Match the category of holdings with the per cent of the total area operated as per the estimates of 1980-81 in India.

(*a*) Marginal — (*i*) 29.7
(*b*) Small — (*ii*) 12.2
(*c*) Semi-medium — (*iii*) 22.8
(*d*) Medium — (*iv*) 14.1
(*e*) Large — (*v*) 21.2

536. Match the state with the prevalent rates of fair rent on agricultural lands in India.

(*a*) Andhra Pradesh — (*i*) 33%
(*b*) Jammu and Kashmir — (*ii*) 30 and 25% on irrigated and drylands
(*c*) Jammu and Kashmir — (*iii*) 25% on lands less than 5 hectares and wet
(*d*) Punjab — (*iv*) 33% on drylands

537. Match the marketable surplus of various commodities in India with the percentage of the total production

(*a*) Rice — (*i*) 35
(*b*) Wheat — (*ii*) 25
(*c*) Millet — (*iii*) 90-95
(*d*) Cash crops — (*iv*) 32

538. Match the years with the scheduled bank advances (Rs. crores) to agriculture.

(*a*) 1960-61	(*i*) 3.95
(*b*) 1962-63	(*ii*) 5.48
(*c*) 1964-65	(*iii*) 4.30
(*d*) 1966-67	(*iv*) 4.09

539. Match the gross domestic savings (Rs. billions) during 1985-86 at the prices prevailing that time with sectors of business.

(*a*) Domestic savings	(*i*) 435.03
(*b*) Private corporate	(*ii*) 22.2
(*c*) Household sector	(*iii*) 74.81
(*d*) Public sector	(*iv*) 44.47

540. Match the year with human population in India expressed in millions.

(*a*) 1951	(*i*) 548.2
(*b*) 1961	(*ii*) 685.2
(*c*) 1971	(*iii*) 361.1
(*d*) 1981	(*iv*) 844.3
(*e*) 1990 (excluding Jammu and Kashmir)	(v) 439.2

541. Match the year with the rural population per cent of the total population of India.

(*a*) 1951	(*i*) 80.1
(*b*) 1961	(*ii*) 82.7
(*c*) 1971	(*iii*) 76.7
(*d*) 1981	(*iv*) 74.3
(*e*) 1991	(*v*) 82.2

542. Match the year with the percentage of cultivators of the total human population of India.

(*a*) 1951	(*i*) 38.8
(*b*) 1961	(*ii*) 49.9
(*c*) 1971	(*iii*) 37.8
(*d*) 1981	(*iv*) 52.8
(*e*) 1991	(*v*) 43.4

543. Match the year with per capita net availability of foodgrains (grammes per day) in India.

(*a*) 1951	(*i*) 468.8
(*b*) 1961	(*ii*) 511.0
(*c*) 1971	(*iii*) 394.9
(*d*) 1981	(*iv*) 468.7
(*e*) 1991	(*v*) 454.8

542. Match the year with the Investment in Agriculture in crore of rupees

Year	GDP from Agriculture
(*a*) 1981	(*i*) 48593
(*b*) 2001	(*ii*) 407176
(*c*) 2004	(*iii*) 441183
(*d*) 2005	(*iv*) 239678
(*e*) 2006	(*v*) 468013

543. Match the year with per capita net availability of foodgrains (grammes per day) in India.

(*a*) 1951	(*i*) 468.8
(*b*) 1961	(*ii*) 511.0
(*c*) 1971	(*iii*) 394.9
(*d*) 1981	(*iv*) 468.7
(*e*) 1991	(*v*) 454.8

544.

Year	**Cereals**
(*a*) 1951	(*i*) 399.7
(*b*) 1961	(*ii*) 334.2
(*c*) 1971	(*iii*) 417.3
(*d*) 1981	(*iv*) 470.7
(*e*) 1991	(*v*) 417.6

545.

Year	**Cereals**
(*a*) 1951	(*i*) 51.2
(*b*) 1961	(*ii*) 40.3
(*c*) 1971	(*iii*) 37.5
(*d*) 1981	(*iv*) 60.7
(*e*) 1991	(*v*) 69.0

546. Match the following extension attempts with the founder and the year of organization.

(*a*) Etawah Attempt	(*i*) Hatch in 1921
(*b*) Martandum Attempt	(*ii*) P.L. Bryne
(*c*) Sriniketan Attempt	(*iii*) Albert Mayer in 1948
(*d*) Gurgaon Attempt	(*iv*) Rabindranath Tagore with Elmhirst in 1921

547. Match the audio-visual techniques with the acceptor's class.

(*a*) Written material	(*i*) Who attend
(*b*) Radio programmes	(*ii*) Who see
(*c*) Meetings	(*iii*) Who can read
(*d*) Demonstrations	(*iv*) Who listen to radio

548. Match the intelligence quotient (mental age/chronological age × 100) of child of 8 years old with tests performed by the child of the following ages.

(*a*) 12 years	(*i*) 125
(*b*) 10 years	(ii) 100
(*c*) 8 years	(*iii*) 62.5
(*d*) 6 years	(*iv*) 150
(*e*) 4 years	(*v*) 75

549. Match the elements of innovation diffusion with their components.

(*a*) Receivers	(*i*) Origin
(*b*) Channels	(*ii*) New ideas
(*c*) Message	(*iii*) Members
(*d*) Source	(*iv*) Adoption/Rejection
(*e*) Effects	(*v*) Spreaders

550. Match the category of an adopter with the percentage of the total (100) adoption of an innovation by these categories

(*a*) Innovators	(*i*) 34
(*b*) Early adopters	(*ii*) 16
(*c*) Early majority	(*iii*) 13.5
(*d*) Late majority	(*iv*) 2.5
(*e*) Laggards	(*v*) 3.4

551. Match the social classes with the examples given below.

(*a*) Defined class	(*i*) Farmer
(*b*) Economic class	(*ii*) Gathering of marriage function
(*c*) Self-identified class	(*iii*) Hindu
(*d*) Cultural class	(*iv*) Tribals
(*e*) Prticipation class	(*v*) Rotary club

552.

Class	**Representative group**
(*a*) Defined class	(*i*) Mohammedan
(*b*) Economic class	(*ii*) Lion's club
(*c*) Self-identified class	(*iii*) Non-tribal
(*d*) Cultural class	(*iv*) Congress (I)
(*e*) Political class	(*v*) Business

553. Match the training method with its *modus operandi.*

(*a*) Lecture	(*i*) Discussion, learning and application under supervision
(*b*) Seminar	(*ii*) Modified panel discussion
(*c*) Colloquium	(*iii*) Formal group discussion
(*d*) Symposium	(*iv*) Verbal presentation on a topic
(*e*) Workshop	(*v*) Presentation of short papers by a small group

554. Match the development agencies with the year of their initiation in India.

Community development	**Year**
(*a*) CDP	(*i*) 1953
(*b*) NES	(*ii*) 1957
(*c*) CDB	(*iii*) 1994
(*d*) Panchayati Raj	(*iv*) 1979
(*e*) IRDP (Integrated rural development)	(*v*) 1954
(*d*) PMRY (Pradhan Mantri Rozgar Yojna)	(*iv*) 1952

555.

Technological development	**Year**
(*a*) IADP	(*i*) 1964-65
(*b*) IAAP	(*ii*) 1960
(*c*) ICDP	(*iii*) 1966
(*d*) HYVP	(*iv*) 1964

556.

Development with, social justice	**Year**
(*a*) SFDA. MFAL, DPAP	(*i*) 1972-73
(*b*) PPTD	(*ii*) 1974
(*c*) T & V	(*iii*) 1978-79
(*d*) IRDP	(*iv*) 1970-71

557. **Development, with social justice** **Year**

(*a*) TRYSEM (*i*) 1980

(*b*) NREP (*ii*) 1983

(*c*) DWCRA (*iii*) 1979

(*d*) NAEP (*iv*) 1986

(*e*) TMO (*v*) 1982

558. Match the district with state where IADP was launched in India from *kharif* 1960.

(*a*) Thanjavur (*i*) Madhya Pradesh

(*b*) West Godavari (*ii*) Tamil Nadu

(*c*) Sahabad (*iii*) Andhra Pradesh

(*d*) Raipur (*iv*) Bihar

559. **District** **State**

(*a*) Aligarh (*i*) Punjab

(*b*) Ludhiana (*ii*) Madhya Pradesh

(*c*) Pali (*iii*) Uttar Pradesh

(*d*) Raipur (*iv*) Rajasthan

560. Match the size of population with the percentage of villages in India as estimated in 1989, by Directorate of Economics and Statistics, Ministry of Agriculture (GOI).

(*a*) Less than 200 (*i*) 16.96

(*b*) 200-499 (*ii*) 21.55

(*c*) 500-999 (*iii*) 8.42

(*d*) 1000-1999 (*iv*) 24.40

(*e*) 2000-4999 (*v*) 27.05

561. Following were established or founded in year.

Institute **Year**

(*a*) First Agricultural University (*i*) 1963

(*b*) First ICVIC (*ii*) 1969

(*c*) N.S.S (*iii*) 1974

(*d*) National Seeds Corportion (*iv*) 1934

(*e*) Indian Socioty of Soil Seeds (*v*) 1960

562. Tenth Five Year Plan 2002-2007 achieved the % share in GDP was

(*a*) 11% (*b*) 8%

(*c*) 12% (*d*) 5%

563. The target for the 11th five year plan (2007-2012) set by Planning Commision (GOI) is

(*a*) 12% (*b*) 9%

(*c*) 10% (*d*) 7%

564. Plan Holiday was observed during the period

(*a*) 1990-92 (*b*) 1993-95

(*c*) 1989-91 (*d*) 2001-03

Do you know that

1. Tribal Area Development Programme (TADP) was started in 1971-72.
2. Food Corporation of India (FCI) was founded in 1970.
3. Cotton Corporation of India (CCI) was established in 1970.
4. Jute Corporation of India (JCT) was founded in 1971.70.
5. Small Farmers Development Agencies (SFDA) for the benefit of small farmers (1-2 ha holders), marginal farmers (less than 1 ha holders) and agricultural labourers (having a homestead and 50 per cent income from agriculture) were started during 1970-71.
6. Hill Area Development Programme (HADP) was started in 1973-1974.
7. First Five Year Plan was initiated for the period from 1951 to 1956.
8. Command Area Development (CAD) was launched in 1974-75.
9. Voluntary Action Scheme (VAS) was undertaken in 1974-75 to benefit the rural people
10. Banks were nationalized in 1969.
11. Intensive Agricultural District Programme (IADP) was introduced in 1960-61.
12. Intensive Agricultural Area Programme (IAAP) was initiated in 1964.
13. Panchayati Rajya was first introduced in India in the state of Tamil Nadu.
14. Samproon Grameen Rojgar Yojna was started in the year 2001.
15. First irrigation commision was appointed in the year 1901.
16. Indira Mahila Yojna started in the year 1995.
17. SGSY (Swarne Jayanti Gram Swarojgar Yojna) was started in the year 1999 and it merges IRDP, TRYSEM, DWCRA and SITRA.
18. NATP (National Technology Project was started in the year 1999.
19. NABARD came into exitence in the year 1980.
20. National food for work programme was implemented in the year 2004.
21. K. N. Singh is considered as father of extension in India.

KEY

(1) Agricultural economics
(2) Agriculture
(3) Economics
(4) Techniques and procedure
(5) Economic problems
(6) Element
(7) Natural science
(8) Nature
(9) Industry.
(10) Organization
(11) Foreign exchange
(12) Labours
(13) Net product
(14) Demand
(15) Capitalists
(16) Subsistence
(17) Neo-classical
(18) Keynesian
(19) Marginal productivity
(20) Reinvestment
(21) Fei- Ranis
(22) Endowment ratio
(23) Mathew Carey
(24) Business
(25) Golden stage
(26) Industrial
(27) Mature
(28) Employment
(29) Pre-requisite
(30) Rural
(31) Planning
(32) Alternative
(33) Industructivity
(34) Land
(35) Existence
(36) Cropping patterns
(37) Permanent
(38) Scarcity
(39) Economic
(40) Traditional
(41) Innovations
(42) Double-benefit
(43) Naturalistic
(44) Institutional setup
(45) Malthusian theory
(46) Inventive competence
(47) Technological
(48) Public goals

(49) Zero-rate (50) Geographical (51) Migrations
(52) Reproductive (53) Death rate (54) Technological
(55) Intensive (56) Mechanical (57) Seasonal
(58) Waste (59) Contract (60) Overtime
(61) Labour-intensive (62) Substitution (63) Race
(64) Mental (65) Productivity (66) Enterprises
(67) Structural (68) Operations/occupations (69) Capital
(70) Quantity (71) Determinants (72) Capital
(73) Accumulation (74) Technological (75) Stock
(76) Desire (77) Risk-taking (78) Economy
(79) Contentment (80) Traditional values (81) Income
(82) Saving motivation (83) Interest (84) Incentive
(85) Farm-investment (86) Favourable (87) Nature and magnitude
(88) Restrictions (89) Return (90) Additional
(91) Theoretical (92) Consumable (93) Resource / Factor-Product
(94) Product-Product (95) Production-function (96) Agricultural
(97) Homogeneity (98) Empirical (99) Maximum and constant
(100) Increasing (101) Variable (102) Intensified
(103) Theory (104) Factor productivity (105) Marginal
(106) More (107) Maximum (108) Constant
(109) Output (110) Isoproduct curves / isoquants / production indifference curves
(111) Substitutable (112) Incomplete (113) Negatively
(114) Least cost (115) Resources (116) Supplementary
(117) Social cost / opportunity cost (118) Implicit cost (119) Expenditures
(120) Average fixed cost (121) Total variable costs prime/special/direct costs
(122) Revenue. (123) Price (124) Demand
(125) Law of demand (126) Cross elasticity (127) Income
(128) Supply (129) Equilibrium (130) Agriculture
(131) Oligopoly (132) Monopolistic (133) Marginal cost
(134) Support (135) Rationing (136) Sectors
(137) Manufactured (138) Agriculture (139) Modern agriculture
(140) Constructure (141) Production-decision (142) Price
(143) Rotate (144) Efficiency (145) Depression
(146) Crop production (147) Standard of living (148) National guidelines
(149) Feudal landlords (150) Ineffective (151) Inequalities
(152) Farmer (153) Operation (154) Imagination
(155) Followed (156) World War II (157) Modern
(158) Limited (159) Simplex (160) Underdeveloped
(161) Raw (162) Agricultural (163) Functions
(164) Assembling (165) Physiocrats (166) Reproducible
(167) Madras (168) Medium (169) Coverage
(170) Credit system (171) Mismanagement (172) Ranching
(173) Game theory (174) Programme (175) Mahatma Gandhi
(176) Prohibition (177) Community (178) Interacting
(179) Basic education (180) Occupational education

(181) Education
(182) Institutionalized
(183) Framework
(184) Extension
(185) Principles / laws
(186) Latent
(187) Democratic
(188) Economic
(189) Philosophy
(190) Imposed
(191) People
(192) Voluntarily
(193) Experience
(194) Qualities
(195) Extension
(196) Specialists
(197) Satisfaction/participation
(198) Rejection
(199) Evaluation/assessment
(200) Rural people
(201) Sovereign
(202) Endowed
(203) Multiplier
(204) Basic skills
(205) Training and visit
(206) Rural society
(207) Agricultural
(208) Farmers
(209) Physiological
(210) Motive
(211) Motivation
(212) Attitude
(213) Chronological
(214) 125
(215) Socialization
(216) Psychological
(217) Learning
(218) Satisfaction
(219) Social
(220) Learning
(221) Incentives
(222) Psychology
(223) Rural people
(224) Effects of communication
(225) Innovation
(226) Evaluation
(227) Innovativeness
(228) Arousing
(229) Spoken
(230) Rural
(231) Script
(232) Speak naturally
(233) Overhead
(234) Photographed
(235) Reproduced
(236) Visibility
(237) Erased
(238) Picture-taking
(239) Glitter
(240) Problem committee
(241) Distance
(242) Working
(243) Definite outline
(244) Alternatives
(245) Judgement
(246) Purposes
(247) Proprietary
(248) Common goal
(249) Coordination
(250) Agriculture
(251) Social differentiation
(252) Primary
(253) Personal
(254) Reference
(255) Associations
(256) Family
(257) Village
(258) Gramsanghs
(259) Contingency
(260) Authority
(261) Committee
(262) Administration
(263) Brain forming
(264) Leading
(265) Performance budgeting
(266) Performance
(267) Statement
(268) Campaign
(269) Sequence
(270) Empathy
(271) Pairs
(272) Heterophily
(273) Inhabited
(274) False
(275) True
(276) False
(277) True
(278) True
(279) False
(280) False
(281) True
(282) True
(283) True
(284) False
(285) True
(286) True
(287) True
(288) False
(289) False
(290) True
(291) False
(292) True
(293) True
(294) True
(295) False
(296) False
(297) False
(298) True
(299) False
(300) False
(301) True
(302) False
(303) False
(304) True
(305) False
(306) True
(307) False
(308) True
(309) False
(310) False
(311) False
(312) True
(313) True

(314) False (315) True (316) False
(317) True (318) True (319) False
(320) False (321) True (322) True
(323) True (324) False (325) True
(326) False (327) False (328) True
(329) True (330) False (331) True
(332) False (333) False (334) True
(335) True (336) True (337) False
(338) True (339) True (340) False
(341) True (342) False (343) True
(344) True (345) False (346) True
(347) False (348) True (349) True
(350) False (351) False (352) True
(353) True (354) False (355) True
(356) True (357) True (358) True
(359) True (360) False (361) False
(362) False (363) False (364) False
(365) True (366) False (367) True
(368) False (369) False (370) True
(371) False (372) False (373) True
(374) True (375) True (376) True
(377) True (378) False (379) False
(380) True (381) True (382) False
(383) True (384) False (385) True
(386) False (387) True (388) False
(389) True (390) False (391) True
(392) False (393) True (394) False
(395) False (396) True (397) True
(398) False (399) False (400) True
(401) True (402) False (403) False
(404) True (405) False (406) False
(407) True (408) False (409) False
(410) False (411) True (412) True
(413) False (414) False (415) True
(416) True (417) False (418) False
(419) False (420) True (421) True
(422) True (423) True (424) True
(425) False (426) False (427) True
(428) False (429) (*c*) (430) (*b*)
(431) (*c*) (432) (*d*) (433) (*b*)
(434) (*a*) (435) (*d*) (436) (*b*)
(437) (*a*) (438) (*b*) (439) (*d*)
(440) (*a*) (441) (*a*) (442) (*c*)
(443) (*c*) (444) (*c*) (445) (*a*)

(446) (*d*)		(447) (*a*)	(448) (*c*)	
(449) (*a*)		(450) (*b*)	(451) (*d*)	
(452) (*c*)		(453) (*b*)	(454) (*d*)	
(455) (*a*)		(456) (*d*)	(457) (*d*)	
(458) (*c*)		(459) (*b*)	(460) (*c*)	
(461) (*b*)		(462) (*b*)	(463) (*b*)	
(464) (*d*)		(465) (*a*)	(466) (*a*)	
(467) (*c*)		(468) (*b*)	(469) (*d*)	
(470) (*c*)		(471) (*b*)	(472) (*c*)	
(473) (*d*)		(474) (*a*)	(475) (*c*)	
(476) (*a*)		(477) (*d*)	(478) (*a*)	
(479) (*c*)		(480) (*d*)	(481) (*b*)	
(482) (*a*)		(483) (*b*)	(484) (*c*)	
(485) (*a*)		(486) (*d*)	(487) (*a*)	
(488) (*b*)		(489) (*d*)	(490) (*c*)	
(491) (*b*)		(492) (*b*)	(493) (*b*)	
(494) (*b*)		(495) (*a*)	(496) (*c*)	
(497) (*d*)		(498) (*c*)	(499) (*d*)	
(500) (*b*)		(501) (*c*)	(502) (*b*)	
(503) (*d*)		(504) (*c*)	(505) (*b*)	
(506) (*b*)		(507) (*c*)	(508) (*a*)	
(509) (*c*)		(510) (*c*)	(511) (*b*)	
(512) (*a*)		(513) (*d*)	(514) (*d*)	
(515) (*a*)				
(516) (*a*)-(*iii*)	(*b*)-(*i*)	(*c*)-(*iv*)	(*d*)-(*ii*)	
(517) (*a*)-(*ii*)	(*b*)-(*iv*)	(*c*)-(*i*)	(*d*)-(*iii*)	
(518) (*a*)-(*iii*)	(*b*)-(*i*)	(*c*)-(*iv*)	(*d*)-(*ii*)	
(519) (*a*)-(*iv*)	(*b*)-(*i*)	(*c*)-(*ii*)	(*d*)-(*iii*)	
(520) (*a*)-(*ii*)	(*b*)-(*iv*)	(*c*)-(*i*)	(*d*)-(*iii*)	
(521) (*a*)-(*ii*)	(*b*)-(*iii*)	(*c*)-(*i*)		
(522) (*a*)-(*iii*)	(*b*)-(*i*)	(*c*)-(*iv*)	(*d*)-(*ii*)	
(523) (*a*)-(*iv*)	(*b*)-(*i*)	(*c*)-(*ii*)	(*d*)-(*iii*)	
(524) (*a*)-(*ii*)	(*b*)-(*iv*)	(*c*)-(*i*)	(*d*)-(*iii*)	
(525) (*a*)-(*ii*)	(*b*)-(*iii*)	(*c*)-(*i*)	(d)-(*iv*)	
(526) (*a*)-(*iii*)	(*b*)-(*iv*)	(*c*)-(*ii*)	(*d*)-(*i*)	
(527) (*a*)-(*iv*)	(*b*)-(*i*)	(*c*)-(*ii*)	(*d*)-(*iii*)	
(528) (*a*)-(*iii*)	(*b*)-(*iv*)	(*c*)-(*ii*)	(*d*)-(*i*)	
(529) (*a*)-(*ii*)	(*b*)-(*i*)	(*c*)-(*iv*)	(*d*)-(*iii*)	
(530) (*a*)-(*iii*)	(*b*)-(*i*)	(*c*)-(*iv*)	(*d*)-(*ii*)	
(531) (*a*)-(*ii*)	(*b*)-(*iv*)	(*c*)-(*iii*)	(*d*)-(*i*)	
(532) (*a*)-(*iii*)	(*b*)-(*v*)	(*c*)-(*i*)	(*d*)-(*ii*)	(*e*)-(*iv*)
(533) (*a*)-(*iv*)	(*b*)-(*v*)	(*c*)-(*i*)	(*d*)-(*iii*)	(*e*)-(*ii*)
(534) (*a*)-(*v*)	(*b*)-(*iii*)	(*c*)-(*ii*)	(*d*)-(*iv*)	(*e*)-(*i*)
(535) (*a*)-(*ii*)	(*b*)-(*iv*)	(*c*)-(*v*)	(*d*)-(*i*)	(*e*)-(*iii*)

(536) (*a*)-(*ii*) (*b*)-(*iii*) (*c*)-(*iv*) (*d*)-(*i*)

(537) (*a*)-(*iv*) (*b*)-(*i*) (*c*)-(*i*) (*d*)-(*iii*)

(538) (*a*)-(*ii*) (*b*)-(*iv*) (*c*)-(*i*) (*d*)-(*iii*)

(539) (*a*)-(*ii*) (*b*)-(*iv*) (*c*)-(*i*) (*d*)-(*iii*)

(540) (*a*)-(*iii*) (*b*)-(*v*) (*c*)-(*i*) (*d*)-(*ii*) (*e*)-(*iv*)

(541) (*a*)-(*ii*) (*b*)-(*v*) (*c*)-(*i*) (*d*)-(*iii*) (*e*)-(*iv*)

(542) (*a*)-(*iv*) (*b*)-(*ii*) (*c*)-(*iii*) (*d*)-(*v*) (*e*)-(*i*)

(543) (*a*)-(*iii*) (*b*)-(*iv*) (*c*)-(*i*) (*d*)-(*v*) (*e*)-(*ii*)

(544) (*a*)-(*ii*) (*b*)-(*i*) (*c*)-(*v*) (*d*)-(*iii*) (*e*)-(*iv*)

(545) (*a*)-(*iv*) (*b*)-(*v*) (*c*)-(*i*) (*d*)-(*iii*) (*e*)-(*iv*)

(546) (*a*)-(*iii*) (*b*)-(*i*) (*c*)-(*iv*) (*d*)-(*ii*)

(547) (*a*)-(*iii*) (*b*)-(*iv*) (*c*)-(*i*) (*d*)-(*ii*)

(548) (*a*)-(*iv*) (*b*)-(*i*) (*c*)-(*ii*) (*d*)-(*v*) (*e*)-(*iii*)

(549) (*a*)-(*iii*) (*b*)-(*v*) (*c*)-(*ii*) (*d*)-(*i*) (*e*)-(*iv*)

(550) (*a*)-(*iv*) (*b*)-(*iii*) (*c*)-(*i*) (*d*)-(*v*) (*e*)-(*ii*)

(551) (*a*)-(*iv*) (*b*)-(*i*) (*c*)-(*v*) (*d*)-(*iii*) (*e*)-(*ii*)

(552) (*a*)-(*iii*) (*b*)-(*v*) (*c*)-(*ii*) (*d*)-(*i*) (*e*)-(*iv*)

(553) (*a*)-(*iv*) (*b*)-(*iii*) (*c*)-(*ii*) (*d*)-(*v*) (*e*)-(*i*)

(554) (*a*)-(*vi*) (*b*)-(*i*) (*c*)-(*v*) (*d*)-(*ii*) (*e*)-(*iii*)

(555) (*a*)-(*ii*) (*b*)-(*iv*) (*c*)-(*i*) (*d*)-(*iii*)

(556) (*a*)-(*iv*) (*b*)-(*i*) (*c*)-(*ii*) (*d*)-(*iii*)

(557) (*a*)-(*iii*) (*b*)-(*i*) (*c*)-(*v*) (*d*)-(*ii*) (*e*)-(*iv*)

(558) (*a*)-(*ii*) (*b*)-(*iii*) (*c*)-(*iv*) (*d*)-(*i*)

(559) (*a*)-(*iii*) (*b*)-(*i*) (*c*)-(*iv*) (*d*)-(*ii*)

(560) (*a*)-(*ii*) (*b*)-(*v*) (*c*)-(*iv*) (*d*)-(*i*) (*e*)-(*iii*)

(561) (*a*)-(*v*) (*b*)-(*iii*) (*c*)-(*ii*) (*d*)-(*i*) (*e*)-(*iv*)

(562) (*b*)

(563) (*c*) (564) (*c*)

SECTION 11
AGRICULTURAL STATISTICS

I. Fill up the blanks:

1. Chi-square is an index ________.
2. A student tossed a coin, 800 times, getting 440 heads. What will be the value of chi-square in relation to hypothesis that heads and tails are equally likely.
3. The use of 5 per cent and 1 per cent levels of significance is simply a working ________.
4. ________ inference is concerned with attempts to make quantitative statements about the properties of a population from a knowledge of the results given by a sample.
5. A point estimate is stated ________ as an estimate of some quantitative property of the population.
6. An interval estimate is a statement that a population ________ has a value lying between two specified limits.
7. The ________ population denotes the aggregate about which an investigator tries to make inference from the sample.
8. In a ________ distribution, the values in the sample are grouped into a limited number of classes.
9. A test of ________ is, in general terms, a calculation by which the sample results are used to throw light on the truth or falsity of a null hypothesis.
10. A ________ hypothesis is a specific hypothesis about a population that is being tested by means of the same results.
11. Chi-square = Σ (observed-expected) / (expected) is a test ________ for the null hypothesis that the population with some attribute in the population has a specified value.
12. Normal ________ is completely determined by two constants (parameters) *viz*., mean (μ) which locates the centre of distribution and standard deviation (σ) which measures the spread or variation of the individual measurements.
13. The rescaled measurement is given by the relation ________.
14. The quantity Z in rescaled measurement is known as ________.
15. What is the probability that a normal deviate lies between – 2.67 and – 0.59. In this case we take the area from – 2.67 to 0, namely 0.4972, and subtract from it the area from – 0.59 to 0, namely 0.224 giving ________.
16. The sample ________ denoted by s, is most widely used in statistical work and

$$s = \sqrt{\frac{\sum\left(x-\bar{x}\right)^2}{n-1}} = \sqrt{\frac{\sum x^2}{n-1}}$$

17. In five patients with pneumonia, treated with sodium pencillin *G*. the number of days required to bring the temperature down to normal were 1, 4. 5, 7. 3; compute *s* for these data and compare it with the estimate based on the range.

18. The *standard deviation* of $\bar{x}$, δ is often called alternatively, the __________ $\bar{x}$.

19. Standard error and __________ are synonymous.

20. In estimating the mean height of large group of boys with a standard deviation of 1.5 inches, a sample of __________ must be taken if the standard error of mean height is to be 0.2 inch.

21. Compute the mean (μ) and standard deviation (δ) when perfect dice are thrown, the probability is 1/6 that each of the faces 1, 2, 3, 4, 5, 6 turns up = __________.

22. If the boys and girls are equally likely, the probabilities that a family of size two contains 0, 1, 2 boys respectively 1/4, 1/2 and 1/4. The mean and standard deviation for this population will be __________ respectively.

23. The heights of a random sample of 16 persons from a population with δ = 2.6 inches, the confidence probability (*p*), the *x* does not differ from μ by more than 1 inch will be __________.

24. If you wish to estimate the monthly house rent in a city correct to within ± Rs. 20, apart from a 1 in 20 chance, and standard deviation (δ) is about Rs. 60 ; __________ houses must be included in the sample.

25. The "students" *t*-distribution was discovered by __________ in 1908 and perfected by R.A. Fisher in 1926.

26. An investigative survey on growth of school children revealed the sample mean height of 265 boys of 13.5-14.5 years was 63.84 inches, with standard deviation $s = 3.08$ inches, the 95 per cent confidence interval for μ will be __________.

27. In describing the amount of variation in a population, a measure often used is __________.

28. The coefficient of variation is often between __________.

29. Coefficient of variation denotes the ratio of averages having the same unit of measurement and hence is __________ of unit.

30. In an experiment on 20 rats gave $\Sigma X^2 = 23{,}000$, $s = 35$ g as suspected, as a check test of null hypothesis: $\delta = 26$ g, against the alternative, $\delta > 26$ g, $X^2 = 23{,}000$ __________ $= 34.02$, d.f. = 19.

31. In a sample of 61 patients, the amount of an anaesthetic to produce anaesthesia required for surgery was found to have a standard deviation of $s = 10.2$ mg (from patient to patient), the 90 per cent confidence limit will be __________ mg by using $X^2 = 0.950$ and $X^2 = 0.50$.

32. If $3 + 4 + 5 + 8 + 2 + 3 = 25$ samples have $|t| > 2.262$; X^2 value to test the hypothesis that 5 per cent of the population values are more than 2.262 will be __________.

33. It has been observed that the frequency distribution of the heights of 8,585 persons arranged in ten classes of 2 inches width ; the number of classes is too small for accurate work yet gives as easy exercise, compute $\overline{X}$ and *s* using a convenient coding.

34. In X^2 __________, the data are grouped into classes to form a frequency distribution and the sample mean $\overline{X}$ and standard deviation s are computed.

35. In a population, a measure of __________ is the average values of $(X - \mu)^4$ divided by δ.

36. K. Pearson produced a family of theoretical __________ curves intended to simulate the shapes of frequency distributions having any special values of λ_1 and λ_2 provided, the non-normality was not too extreme.

37. The investigations are often designed to discover and evaluate ________ between effects rather than the effects themselves.
38. In an investigation when two groups or two procedures are compared, these ________ are called treatments.
39. The objective of ________ is to enhance the precision of the comparison of the two procedures.
40. The variables on which the pair, should predict accurately the performance of the subjects on the measurement by which the effects of ________ are to be judged.
41. ________ variations often calls for pairing.
42. A population ________ is defined as the average, over the population, of the squared deviations from the population mean.
43. The pH readings of a soil with a modified quinhydrone electrode were 5.78, 5.74, 5.84 and 5.80, while with modified Ag/AgCl$^-$ electrode, the readings were 5.82, 5.87, 5.96 and 5.89; with the hypothesis that $\mu_1 - \mu_2 = 0$, compute t = ________.
44. Two sets of maize grains (kernels) harvested at full maturity (*A*) and dough stages (*B*) were tested for crushing resistance, the resistance (pounds) for set *A* were 50, 36, 34, 45, 56, 42, 53, 25, 65, 33, 40, 42, 39, 43, 42 and for set *B* were 43, 44, 51, 40, 29, 49, 39, 59, 43, 48, 67, 44, 46, 54, 64; test the significance of the difference between the two means.
45. Randomization does not guarantee to balance out the ________ between the members of a pair exactly.
46. ________ gives each treatment an equal chance of being allotted to any subject giving unusually good or poor response exactly as assumed in the theory of probability.
47. Randomization serves primarily to protect against sources of bias that are ________.
48. If $\delta_D = 5$, how many pairs are needed to make the half-width of the 90 per cent confidence interval for the difference between the two population means = 2.
49. ________ methods are needed when sampling from populations far from normal is done.
50. ________ like t-test assumes a normal distribution and has become popular particularly in industrial work.
51. Range-test is more sensitive than t-test to ________ in the population and to the appearance of gross errors.
52. The ________ of a population has the property that half the values in population exceed it and half fall short of it.
53. If the distribution is ________ about its mean, the mean and the median, coincide.
54. In reporting on frequency distribution from large samples, the investigators often quote ________ of the distribution.
55. For the 179 cows, the 90th percentile is estimated by order statistic whose number i = (180) (90)/ ________ = 162. .
56. The t-test is sometimes called a ________, while the sign-test is called non-parametric.
57. In sampling from normal distribution the efficiency of the ________ relative to the t-test is about 65 per cent.
58. The sign test save time at the expense of a loss of ________ in the test.
59. The ________, due to Wilcoxon, is another substitute for the t-test in paired samples.
60. The ________ test applies to unequal group sizes as well as to equal group sizes.
61. The practice of quoting the test that agrees with ones ________ vitiates the whole technique.

62. In a paired two-sample, the ten values of differences D were 3, 3, 2, 1, 1, 1, 1, 0, 0, –1. Show that the randomization test gives $P = 3/64 = 0.047$, while the value of t for continuity is ________ corresponding to a P value of about 0.036.

63. In his studies of inheritance ________ developed the idea of regression.

64. Calculate $S_b = 0.409$ cm per week; set 95 per cent confidence interval for the population regression (S_b has 5 d.f.).

65. When X is 0, 2, 3, 7, 8 and 10 ; x is – 2.5, – 1.5, – 1.0, 1.0, 1.5 and 2.5, compute estimates for sample regression, Y on X ________.
   (*a*) $\Sigma X^2 =$ ________.
   (*b*) $\Sigma XY =$ ________.
   (*c*) $\Sigma Y^2 =$ ________.

66. The correlation coefficient (r) is a measure of the degree of ________ between two variables.

67. Correlation coefficient (r) is a pure number without units or dimensions and always lies between ________.

68. The population correlation coefficient P and its estimate r are intimately connected with a bivariate population known as the bivariate normal ________.

69. If $\overline{X} = 83$g, $\overline{Y} = 60$ mg, $\Sigma X^2 = 1000$, $\Sigma Y^2 = 6854$, $XY = 2302$, calculate the regression of body weight X on comb weight Y of chicks.

70. A convenient way to draw samples from a normal bivariate population is by use of an old device called ________.

71. Assuming that μ_1, μ_2, μ_3 are independent draws from the same population, and that $X_1 = 3\mu_1 + \mu_2, X_2 = 3\mu_1 + \mu_3$: determine the correlation P between X_1 and X_2.

72. The study of ________ began around three hundred years ago.

73. If an event is satisfied by any of a group of mutually ________, the probability of the event is the sum of the probabilities of the outcomes of the group.

74. In second of probability, the condition of mutual ________ is essential.

75. In a series of independent trials, the ________ that each of a specified series of events happen is the product of the probabilities of the individual events.

76. A bag contains the letters *A, B, c, D, f, e, G, h, I*; if each letter is equally likely to be drawn, what will be the probability drawing (*a*) a capital letter (*b*) a vowel, (*c*) either a capital or a vowel.

77. Ordered ________ are common in the study of human behaviour and preferences, and more generally whenever different degrees of some phenomenon can be recognized.

78. The variance ratio F was first tabulated by ________ in whose honour the criterion was name F by Snedecor.

79. ________ design is often desirable to get precise information on one factor and on the interaction of this factor with a second, but to forego such precision on the second factor.

80. The essential feature of the split-plot experiment is that the sub-plot treatments are not ________ over the whole large block, but only over the main plots.

81. With more than two variables, an extension of the bivariate normal distribution called ________ normal distribution forms the basic model in correlation studies.

82. The coefficient is the correlation between variables 1 and 2 in a cross-section of individuals all having the same value of variable 3; the third variable is held constant so that only 1 and 2 are involved in the correlation.

83. The ________ coefficient applies to the situation in which one variable, say Y, has been singled out to

examine its joint relation with the other variables.

84. The analysis of ________ is a technique that combines the features of analysis of variance and regression.

85. The discovery of a precise description of the relation between two or more quantities is one of the problems of curve fitting, known as ________.

86. The law that the rate of increase at any stage is proportional to the size already attained is described mathematically as ________ where c is the constant.

87. The probability of selection need not be equal for all members of the ________: it is sufficient that these probabilities be known.

88. In order to apply ________, have someway of subdividing the population into units, called sampling units, which form the basis for the selection of the sample.

89. If a sample of 4 from the 16 townships of a count has a standard deviation 45, show that the ________ of the mean is 19.5.

90. Systematic sampling is easier to draw, since only one random number is required, and it ________ the sample more evenly over the listed population.

91. In ________ sampling, the size of the sample chosen to be taken from any stratum.

II. Tick mark (✓) the correct answer:

92. In a normal distribution,
    (*a*) Mean and median are equal (*b*) Median and mode are equal
    (*c*) All the three are equal

93. If fertility variation in the field is in two directions at right angles, which of the experimental design is suitable.
    (*a*) CRBD (*b*) RBD (*c*) Latin Square

94. As a general rule, the number of classes in the frequency distribution should be about,
    (*a*) 30 (*b*) 15 (*c*) 6

95. Range of distribution is,
    (*a*) The difference between largest and smallest observations
    (*b*) Averages of all observations (*c*) Middle of the series

96. Correlation coefficient is,
    (*a*) More than +1 (*b*) Less than –1 (*c*) Lies between –1 and +1

97. Coefficient of variation is useful for comparing,
    (*a*) Comparison between different populations (*b*) Same population
    (*c*) None of these

98. In an experimental plot, 7 rows were sown with 50 cm row spacing and 5m length, while harvesting one row on either side of the plots were discarded. The net plot size will be;
    (*a*) 2.0 × 5.0 m (*b*) 2.5 × 5.0 m (*c*) 3.5 × 5.0 m

99. In a field experiment, the net plot size was 2.5 × 4.0 m and the yields were recorded in kg. What is the conversion factor for q/ha?
    (*a*) 10 (*b*) 100 (*c*) 50

100. In a fertilizer trial, 40 kg N/ha has to be applied to the plot of 10.0 sq.m. area. What quantity of urea is needed?
    (*a*) 95 g (*b*) 89 g (*c*) 115 g

101. Biometry deals with,
(*a*) Observation with living things (*b*) Collection of observations
(*c*) Interpretation of data

102. Arithmetic mean is most commonly used because,
(*a*) Based on all the observations (*b*) Largest and smallest observations
(*c*) Located in the middle of the series

103. Standard deviation is,
(*a*) Expressed in the same unit of measurements (*b*) Free from unit of measurements
(*c*) It is in percentage

104. The test of significance of differences between two means in small samples is known as
(*a*) *t*-test (*b*) *F*-test (*c*) On the basis of normal deviate

105. *F*-test can be used for testing the significance of
(*a*) Serval differences (*b*) A single difference (*c*) Not used for testing the difference

106. When two variables change together in such a way that an increase in one variable is accompanied by an increase in the other. The variables are said to be,
(*a*) Independent (*b*) Positively correlated (*c*) Negatively correlated

107. X^2 test is applied to
(*a*) Quantitative observations (*b*) Qualitative observations (*c*) In both the cases

108. The randomization of treatments in the field experiments is essential:
(*a*) The statistical procedures hold good only when randomization is done
(*b*) To average out the effects of environment differences
(*c*) For comparison of treatment effects

109. Local control helps in
(*a*) Reducing the experimental error (*b*) Homogeneity of experimental units (*c*) Both these

110. ANOVA table of an experiment done in split plot design is given below, fill up the gaps therein ____.

Source	D.F.	SS	MS
Main-plots:			
Varieties	2	0.1781	0.0890
Blocks	5	4.1499	0.8300
Error (*a*)	10	1.3622	0.1362
Sub-plots:			
Dates of cutting	3	1,9262	____ (II)
Date × Varieties	6	0.2105	0.0351
Error (*b*)	____ (I)	1.2586	____ (III)

111. ANOVA table of a split plot is presented below, fill up the gaps therein ________

Source	DF	Error (*b*)	_____ (I)
Main-plots : Block	3	Sub-sub plots:	
Irrigation	31	Fertilizer, F	2
Error (*a*)	3	IF	2
Sub-plots : stands, *s*	2	SF	4
I × S	2	ISF	4
		Error (*c*)	_____ (II)

True and False

1. The regression coefficient lies between –1 to +1.
2. The correlation coefficient lies between – –∞ to ∞.
3. The value of χ^2 (chi square) always lies between 0 to ∞.
4. The value of standard deviation may vary between 0 to ∞.
5. The minimum sample size for using chi square test is 50
6. The most commonly used measure of central tendency is median.
7. When Mean > Median > Mode skewness will be negative.
8. When two variables move in the opposite direction corelation is said to negative.
9. Harmonic mean is reciprocal of the arithmetic mean.
10. In normal distribution mean, mode and median are not equal.

Do you know that

1. Student '*t*' distribution was discovered by W.S. Gooset in the year 1908.
2. The father of vital statistics is Captain John Grant.
3. The normal distribution was discovered by De Moivre.
4. Predictor variables are also known Independant variable.
5. The definition of mathematical probability was given by Von-Mises.
6. Student '*t*' test was perfected by R. A. Fisher.
7. Ogive is a method of graphical representation.
8. ANOVA is a tool by which total variation can split up into several physical assignable components.
9. Kolmogrov Smirnov test of N.P. is similar to χ^2 (chi square) test of goodnen of fit.
10. The square of standard deviation is variance.
11. Poission distribution was developed by S. D. Pearson in 1837.
12. Normal distribution was developed by De Moivre.
13. Idea of regression was developed by Sir Francis Galton.

KEY

1. Dispersion
2. 8
3. Convention
4. Statistical
5. Single number
6. Parameter
7. Target
8. Frequency
9. Significance
10. Null
11. Criterion
12. Distribution
13. $Z = X - \mu / \delta$
14. Standard normal variate/deviate or a normal deviate is a standard measure or a standard score in education and psychology
15. 0.2748
16. Standard deviation
17. S = 2.24 days: Range estimate = 2.58 days
18. SE (standard error)
19. Standard deviation
20. 56 boys
21. $\mu = 3.5$ and $\delta = 1.71$
22. $\mu = 1$, $\delta = 0.71$
23. 0.876
24. $n = 36$
25. W.S. Gosset
26. 63.5 to 64.2 inches
27. Coefficient of variation ($c = \delta / \mu$)
28. 5 and 15 per cent
29. Independent
30. $(26)^2$
31. 8.9 and 12.0
32. 0.0124
33. $\overline{X} = 67.53$ inches and S = 2.62 inches
34. Goodness of fit test
35. Kurtois
36. Non-normal
37. Differences
38. Procedures
39. Pairing
40. Treatments
41. Environmental
42. Variance
43. 2.66
44. $t = 1.38$
45. Natural differences
46. Randomization
47. Unsuspected
48. $n = 17$
49. Distribution-free
50. Range-test
51. Skewness
52. Median
53. Symmetrical
54. Percentiles
55. 100
56. Parametric test
57. Sign-test
58. Sensitivity
59. Signed rank-test
60. Mann-Whitney
61. Predicted
62. 2.457
63. Galton
64. 5.09 – 7.20 cm per week
65. (*a*) 76, (*b*) 35.6 (*c*) 22.43
66. Closeness
67. – 1 and +1
68. Distribution
69. $\hat{X} = 83 + 0.336 (Y - 60)$ g
70. Common elements
71. 0.9
72. Probability
73. Exclusive outcomes
74. Exclusiveness
75. Probability
76. (*a*) 4/9, (*b*) 1/3, (*c*) 5/9
77. Classifications
78. Fisher
79. Split-plot/nested
80. Randomized
81. Multivariate
82. Partial correlation
83. Multiple correlation
84. Covariance
85. Curvilinear regression
86. $dW/dX = cW$ (c = constant)
87. Population
88. Probability sampling
89. Standard error
90. Distributes
91. Stratified
92. (*c*)
93. (*c*)
94. (*a*)
95. (*a*)
96. (*c*)
97. (*a*)
98. (*b*)
99. (*a*)
100. (*b*)
101. (*a*)
102. (*a*)
103. (*a*)
104. (*a*)
105. (*a*)
106. (*b*)
107. (*b*)
108. (*a*)
109. (*c*)
110. (*I*) = 45, (*II*) = 0.6542, (*III*) = 0.0280
111. (*I*) = 12, (*II*) = 36

True and False

1. F	2. F	3. T	4. T	5. T
6. F	7. F	8. T	9. T	10. F

SECTION 12
ANIMAL HUSBANDRY

I. Fill up the blanks :

1. Most of the Indian animal breeds are well known for their _______ qualities and to withstand diseases and parasites.
2. The rainfall map of India shows that it is in the _______ of the country, and in the humid areas like those of Assam, West Bengal, Bihar, Orissa and Kerala that cattle are small and non-descript.
3. A group of animals related by _______ and similar in most characters like general appearance, features, size, configuration, etc. are said to be a breed.
4. The _______ of the breed is maintained by confining the mating of animals to within the breed.
5. Pure Sahiwal cattle breeds were maintained at N.D.R.I., Karnal, _______,Government Dairy Farm, Lucknow and B.R. College Farm, Agra.
6. Loose _______ are common in females of Sahiwal breed of cattle.
7. General colours in Sahiwal cattle are various shades of red, pale red and dark brown _______ with white.
8. Sahiwal is one of the best _______ breeds in India.
9. The home of _______ breed of Indian cattle is Karachi and Hyderabad (Sindh) in Pakistan.
10. Sindhi breed of cattle has medium size and is compact, it has well proportioned body and is extremely_______.
11. The Gir (also called Kathiawarhi Surti or Desan) breed of Indian cattle probably originated in the Gir forests of _______.
12. The ears of Gir breed of cattle are markedly long,_______ resembling a tiny curved leaf.
13. Ears of Deoni (Dongarpatti) breed of cattle unlike _______ have no notch near the tip.
14. Bullocks of Deoni breed are well _______ for heavy work.
15. Haryana breed of cattle have _______ body and compact graceful appearance.
16. Haryana cattle breed animals have small and sharp ears, fine textured skin _______ to the body.
17. Ongole breed of cattle is also known as _______.
18. Ongole breed animals are greatly alert and _______ with good gait.
19. Tharparkar breed of cattle are also known as_______.
20. Tharparkar breed of cattle are medium sized, deep built and embody short, straight and_______.
21. The tail of Tharparkar breed of cattle is fine with _______ switch.
22. Kankrej breed of cattle are also known as Banniai or Vagadia or _______.
23. The Kankrej breed of cattle is one of the _______ of Indian breeds.

24. Kankrej cattle have broad chest, their forehead is dished in the centre, have strong curved horns accompanied by skin upto some length, powerful body and ________ back.
25. Amrit Mahal breed of cattle have compact body frame with short straight back, well arched ribs, ________ quarters .
26. Long sweeping horns of ________ breed are typical of Myosre type cattle.
27. Amrit Mahal breed of cattle have well developed ________ and hump, very small sheath and close skin.
28. Amrit Mahal breed of cattle have grey coloured body with ________, neck, hump and quarters.
29. Kangayam breed of cattle are also known as Kongu or ________.
30. Kangayam breed of bullocks/bulls are excellent type for ________.
31. The Kangayam breed of animals have moderate sized hump, ________ strong limbs, small dewlap, fire skin, very small sheath, well developed quarters and a fine tail.
32. The colour of the Kangayam bull is of grey with dark grey to black markings, while the cow is white with ________ just in front of the fetlocks on all the four legs sometimes on the knees.
33. The Malvi breed of cattle is also known as Mahadespuri or ________.
34. The Malvi breed of cattle have deep, short and compact body, their ears are ________ in size, horn short but thick tapering to a blunt point.
35. The general colour of the Malvi breed of cattle is ________ black in the neck and quarters.
36. The Malvi breed bullocks are good for road and field work, economical feeders and have good ________.
37. The Siri breed of cattle are found in ________ hill tracts, Sikkim and Bhutan.
38. The Siri breed cattle have ________ body, small head, squarecut, wide and flat forehead, presenting no convexity.
39. Sharp horns, relatively small ea , well placed hump covered with a ________ at the top, stronglegs and feet, and tight sheath are some of the characters of Siri breed of animals. '
40. The best known breeds of Indian buffaloes are ________, Jaffarabadi, Nili and Bhadawari.
41. Murrah buffaloes have deep ________ with short, broad back and a comparatively light neck and head.
42. Murrah buffaloes have short, characteristic ________ horn, well developed under and a long tail with a white switch reaching the fetlock.
43. The popular colour of murrah buffaloes is jet black with ________ on the tall, face and extremities.
44. The ________ breed of buffalo is the most efficient producer of milk, not only in India but probably in the world.
45. Jaffarabadi breed of buffaloes in their purest form are seen in ________ of Kathiawar where they are bred in large numbers , almost solely for *ghee* (butter-oil) production.
46. The noticeable feature of Jaffarabadi buffalo-breed is the very prominent forehead and ________ inclined to droop on each side of the neck and then turn up at the points.
47. It has been observed that ________ breeds of buffalo are distinct without difference and are officially treated as one. breed.
48. Nili and Ravi breeds of cattle are medium sized, have deep frame with an elongated, coarse and ________ bulging at the top, depressed between the eyes and ending in a fine muscle.
49. It is the ________ of Nili and Ravi buffaloes that distinguish this breed mainly from the murrah.
50. Bhadawari breed of buffaloes is found scattered in surroundings of ________ and Chambel rivers.
51. Bhadawari buffaloes have medium size and ________ shaped body.
52. Comparatively small head bulging towards horns, short but stout legs, hooves of hind quarters more backward than those of fore quarters, short but well barrel, slightly broad forehead deep in the middle, are main characteristic of ________ breed of buffalo.

53. In animal biology, the term cell refers more specifically to the individual units of ________.
54. Most cells range in diameter from about 10 to 100 micra with cells that are about ________ in diameter.
55. With the exception of yolks of bird's egg the distance from the interior of the cell to some portion of the cell membrane (surface of the cell) is seldom more than ________.
56. In multicellular organisms the cells are differentiated to carry out the specific functions, creation, ________ maintaining structure and conveying impulses.
57. The endoplasmic reticulum and ________ of the cytoplasm are continuous with pores of the plasma membrane.
58. The cell membrane itself produces an almost ________ barrier between the aqueous portion of the cytoplasm and the aqueous solution surrounding the cell
59. The nucleus is roughly a ________ body in the cell with a diameter between 5-7 micra.
60. In most tissues, one ________ is found in each cell.
61. The nucleus is surrounded by a double membrane, the outer membrane being continuous with the endoplasmic ________.
62. The chromatin of nucleus is primarily, DNA (deoxyribonucleic acid) that is complexed with a basic protein, ________.
63. The combination of DNA and histone is known as ________.
64. The DNA molecule, which has molecular weight in millions, contains a combination of four bases, a pentose, sugar-deoxyribose, and a ________ group.
65. The four bases of a DNA molecule are composed of two purines-adenine and guanines and two ________ and thiamine.
66. Each of the four bases of a DNA molecule is attached to the one carbon position of ________.
67. The pentose sugars in a DNA molecule are joined in a strand by a ________ bond between 3 and 5 carbon atoms of the adjacent pentose sugar.
68. Prior to mitosis the chromatin material (of a nucleus) congregates into the chromosomes, the number being specific for each ________.
69. DNA is responsible for the activity of the cytoplasm and accomplishes this by the synthesis of ________.
70. RNA is comparable to DNA, except the pyrimidine, uracil replaces the thiamine of DNA and the pentose ribose replaces ________.
71. A triplet of bases on in-RNA serves as the code for the placement of amino acid, *i.e.*, a triplet of ________ is the code for lysine, an amino acid.
72. The second RNA is the ribosomal RNA, which becomes part of the ribosomes living ________ reticulum.
73. The third RNA is transfer RNA or soluble RNA recognizes specific ________ in the cytoplasm, activates them, and carries them to the specific site on the m-RNA.
74. The nucleoli intermeshed with chromosomal-DNA appear to be the primary sites for protein and ribosomal ________ synthesis.
75. The principal function of the nucleus is to serve as the site for the regulation and transmission at ________ characteristics.
76. The endoplasmic reticulum (ER) is a series of membrane bounded tubules, vesicles and ________. that extend from the nuclear membrane outward to the plasma membrane.
77. The dense particles embodied by tubules are ribosomes and take up ________ dyes because of their high RNA content.

78. The entire cytoplasm consists of membranes and much of the secretion process and functional work of the cell is done by the passage of ________ through membranes.
79. The vacuoles as a part of the endoplasmic reticulum or Golgi apparatus are located throughout the cell may be reservoirs for essential ________ of the cell.
80. Golgi apparatus is a series of smooth lined membrane tubules and cavities that are continuations of the ________ membranes of the endoplasmic reticulum.
81. The zymogen granules of the pancreatic cells take on an identifiable form in the ________ by the progressive concentration of secretary products, which then move to centrally located condensing vacuoles.
82. The zymogen granules from the condensing vacuoles move away from Golgi Zone and accumulate in the apical region of the cell and wait to be released into the ________ after the intake of food.
83. The surface of both the outer and inner membranes and cristae are sprinkled with small particles that carry out the chemical activities of ________.
84. The inner membranes of mitochondria contain enzymes of the citric acid cycle ________.
85. Mitochondria can actively accumulate certain ions from surrounding cytoplasm in a process that appears to be related to the respiratory chain ________.
86. Lysosomes are slightly small than mitochondria and contain most of the active degradative or ________ enzymes of the cell.
87. The rupture of the lysosomal membrane causes the release of the enzymes which can cause a ________ of the cell.
88. Somatic, zygotic or diploid number (characteristics of body cells of the species) is $2n$; the ________ number is designated by n
89. Only one member of the chromosome pair enters into each gamete by the process of ________.
90. In mitosis two daughter nuclei are formed whose ________ number is the same as that of the original parent nucleus.
91. The mitotic cell division is divided into six stage *viz.*, interphase, prophase, prometaphase, metaphase, ________ and telophase.
92. Avery, Mc Leod and Mc Carty (1944) demonstrated that the component of the cell responsible for the phenomenon of transformation in the bacterium *Diplococcus pneumonia* (Pneumococcus) is ________.
93. Viruses have been extremely useful in studying many genetic processes because of their simple structure chemical composition and very rapid ________.
94. Tobacco mosaic virus (TMV) is a small virus composed of a single molecule of RNA encapsulated in a ________ coat.
95. Different strains of TMY can be identified on the basis of differences in the ________ composition of their protein coats.
96. Certain DNA sequences have been shown to exist in a unique ________ double helical form called Z-DNA (Z = zigzagged path of the sugar-phosphate backbones of the structure).
97. When a heavy density solution such as 6 M Cs Cl is centrifused at very high speeds (30,000 50,000 r.p.m.) for 48-72 hours an ________ is formed.
98. DNA replication is ________, and have extended it to many other organisms including higher plants and animals.
99. ________ is a method to detect and localize radioactive isotopes in cytological preparations or macromolecules by exposure to a photographic emulsion that is sensitive to low-energy radiation.

100. Autoradiography is particularly useful in studying DNA metabolism because DNA can be specifically labelled by growing cells on ________.

101. ________ is the process of breaking of the hydrogen and hydrophobic bonds that hold the complementary strands together in the double helix configuration on exposure of DNA molecules to high temperature (100°C) or high pH (pH 11.4).

102. The rate of DNA replication in Drosophila is about 2,600 nucleotide pairs per minute at ________°C.

103. Arthur Kornberg (Nobel Prize winner in 1959) isolated an enzyme from *Escherichia coli* (initially called DNA polymerase or Kornberg enzyme) known as ________ that catalyzes the covalent addition of nucleotides to pre-existing DNA chains.

104. DNA Polymerase does not contain sequence specificity, that is, the enzyme requires a ________ chain.

105. An exonuclease is an enzyme that degrades ________ from the ends, as opposed to an endonuclease that degrades it by making internal cuts.

106. The 3'-5' exonuclease activity of DNA polymerases carries out a critical "proofreading" "editing" function that is necessary for the high degree of ________ characteristic of DNA replication.

107. Highly repetitive DNA sequences are located in ________, the chromatin that remains condensed during interphase and is genetically inactive.

108. ________ is not visible during interphase with the light microscope; it contains most, if not all, of the structural genes.

109. ________ replication is accomplished by a complex replication apparatus composed, of many different proteins and enzymes.

110. The process of cell division may be broadly divided into ________ and cytokinesis (Cytoplasmic division).

111. Each chromosome builds a copy of itself out of the materials in the protoplasm and thereby duplicates itself during ________.

112. The nucleoli during ________ gradually decrease in volume.

113. ________ disappears at prometaphase stage of cell division.

114. At metaphase stage of cell division the chromosomes, which are now very short and thick, orient themselves in the ________ region of the spindle.

115. In anaphase stage of cell division, the ________ of each chromosome divided into two, and the two sister chromatids are converted into two independent chromosomes' which move to opposite poles.

116. In the cell division, the chromosomes ________ in the telophase nucleus.

117. In cell division, the prophase is subdivided into leptonerna, zygonema, pachynema, diplonema and ________.

118. During leptonema stage the chromosomes are stretched and bead like structures, ________ are often visible.

119. Paring or synapsis of ________ chromosomes takes place during zygotene phase.

120. ________ is the stable stage of chromosome pairing.

121. Homologous chromosomes (which have divided into chromatids) of a bivalent start separating during ________ stage.

122. The chiasmata move towards the end of the bivalent during diplonema stage and this process of movement is called ________.

123. The bivalents become shorter and thicker during the ________ stage of cell division.

124. The process of terminalization is ________ during the diakinesis stage of cell division.

125. ________ traits (characters) are transmitted from parent to progeny.

126. ________ are composed of DNA molecules (the genetic material) surrounded by histones.

127. ________ chromosomes mean the two chromosomes one inherited from sire (male) and dam (female) each, which pair and synapse at meiosis, have the identical morphology and embody genes governing the same characteristics.

128. A ________ in molecular terms is a segment of a DNA molecule (chromosome) which codes for the formation of a specific amino acid.

129. ________ is the term used to describe corresponding gene locations on like (homologous) chromosomes.

130. ________ are those genes which may appear at the same locus in homologous chromosomes.

131. The sudden and discrete change of a gene from allelic form to another is known as ________.

132. ________ is the normal chromosome compliment for somatic cells of most animals.

133. ________ are haploid cells which receive, by meiotic division, one chromosome from each homologous pair of their diploid parent cell.

134. The diploid cell formed by fertilization of an ovum by a sperm is called a ________.

135. An individual is said to be ________ if the alleles at a single gene locus are identical.

136. A ________ gene expresses its characteristic effect both in the heterozygote and homozygote.

137. A ________ represents an individual which is heterozygous for one pair of allelic genes.

138. The same (one particular) ________ may produce a different phenotype in one set of environment than in another.

139. A ________ represents a group of animals, which can be interbred, and thus produce simal genotypes.

140. A ________ is a group of individuals of common ancestry which are genetically identifiable because all members of the group possess certain genes.

141. Phenotypic, cellular and ________ levels have been integrated to provide the present knowledge of genetic mechanism.

142. ________ (11822-1884), an Austrian monk, has been called the "father of genetics" because he was the first to uncover and record the laws of inheritance.

143. In the shorthorn breed of cattle red (RR) when crossed with white (rr) produce an F_1 with roan (Rr) ________.

144. Roan coat colour in shorthorn breed of cattle is produced due to a mixture of ________ hair.

145. Monohybrid cross with incomplete dominance is found in the cross of black and white feather types of fowl where the F_1 is of blue ________ type.

146. Mendel crossed yellow round (RR) seeded pea with green wrinkled (rr) seeded pea plants, F_1 plants were all ________ seeded and on selfing they produced F_2 generation with yellow rounds, yellow wrinkled, green round and green wrinkled seeded plants in 9:3:3: 1 ratio.

147. The law of ________ can be enunciated as, if two pairs of unrelated contrasting characters are combined in a hybrid they group themselves independently of each other during gamete formation.

148. Sutton and Bovery (1902-1904) summarized the ________ basis for Mendel's laws of inheritance.

149. Biochemists discovered that ________ were strands of DNA surrounded by histones, and that DNA was genetically active portion.

150. The ________ model rêpresented the DNA molecule as two strands coiled around each other to from a double helix.

151. The property of information storage clearly lies in the order of the purine and ________ bases in the

DNA molecule.

152. Storage of genetic information is analogous to a book written in a language which contains only ______ and three letter words.

153. The change in the sequence of bases in a DNA molecule which causes coding for the formation of a protein different from that produced by the original gene represents ______.

154. The switching on and off genes is also controlled ______.

155. The study of genetic defects due to mutation has provided most of the knowledge on ______.

156. Human-disease, ______ exemplifies the genetic control of a specific chemical reaction.

157. The deficiency anaemia disease is confined largely to all population in areas where ______ is prevalent.

158. The deficiency anaemia disease is confined largely to the population in areas where ______ is prevalent.

159. "When one condition of a character is contrasted with another form or condition of the same character", the genes responsible for the conditions are called ______ with one another.

160. More than two alternative forms of the same gene are known as ______.

161. ______ gene produces several superficially unrelated effects.

162. The converse of pleiotrophy, many genes affecting one character, is known as ______ inheritance.

163. Quantitative traits are usually characterized by ______ inheritance and large environmental effects.

164. Dominance model of quantitative inheritance is more complex than the additive model due to the involvement of ______ genes.

165. In dominance model of quantitative inheritance, ______ as produce progeny some of which are smaller than themselves, but most of which are larger.

166. The phenomenon by which the parental types appear in greater frequency than is expected in F_2 is known as ______.

167. According to Morgan (1910) ______ are but two aspects of a single phenomenon called linkage.

168. The presence of a gene in a particular combination blocks certain vital developmental or metabolic processes of the organism concerned, such a gene is called ______.

169. In certain strains of horse, there are approximately twice as many females as males at birth due to ______ recessive lethal gene.

170. In swine during pregnancy, embryonic death losses increase due to inbreeding suggesting that the genes with ______ effects are involved.

171. In male calves of Angus and Jersy cattle, the lower jaw is several centimeters shorter than upper, this or the aguatha condition may be ______ recessive.

172. The Holstein-Friesian calves, there is an opening in the skull due to failure of ossification of the frontal bones and the brain tissue protrudes, such calves are ______.

173. Mc Clung associated X-body discovered by Henking with sex determination, but erroneously considered it to be peculiar to ______.

174. ______ succeeded in following oogenesis and spermatogenesis in genus Protenor (an insect) and observed that the unreduced cells of male carried 13 chromosomes and those of the female carried 14.

175. The invertebrate hormones are not functionally comparable with steroid hormones in birds and mammals, such as chickens and mice were primarily used in experimental work on ______ characteristics.

176. C.B. Bridges demonstrated in Drosophila that female determiners were located in the x chromosomes, while male determiners in the ______.

177. The ________ theory of sex determination was devised as a more detailed explanation of the mechanics of sex determination.

178. *In Bracon hebetor,* ________ many occur in the anterior-posterior plane, giving rise to wasps with such peculiar arrangement as male heads with female abdomens and female heads with male abdomens.

179. M.L. Barr observed that ________ in the nerve cells female cats that were not present in the cells of male.

180. The sex chromatin body and ________ in mammals is determined by inactivation of one x-chromosome in the normal female.

181. Autosomal genes responsible for horns in some breeds of sheep may behave differently in the presence of the male and female ________.

182. Like the *y* chromosome in *Drosophila,* supernumerary chromosomes in some species of animals and plants (mealy bugs and maize) are composed mostly of ________.

183. ________ syndrome disease follows the pattern of X-linked recessive inheritance.

184. ________ denotes a sudden discrete and heritable change in the genotype of an organism or alteration in the chemical structure of a gene.

185. The best known mutant among farm animals is ________.

186. Mutation from a normal type to a new allele is called direct mutation, and from ________ back to the normal type is called reverse mutation.

187. Unlike ________ inversion does not result in loss of genes.

188. Occurrence of ________ in a sex chromosome brings about the formation of a new sex linkage.

189. The seminiferous tubules are lined by ________ that charges into sperms by the process of spermatogenesis.

190. The mucous membrane in the urethra contains fine ________ and are surrounding by muscular and erectile tissues.

191. The ________ (in bulls) which is attachedto the anterior arms of the flexure helps in pulling the erected and exposed penis back into thesheath for protection against injury and infection.

192. The oviduct (fallopian tube or ovarian tube) has a diameter of about 0.1 cm in case of the cow and it widens into a funnel shaped tube at the ovarian end which is called the ________.

193. The thick walled portion of the reproductive tract lying between the uterus and the vagina is known as ________.

194. The muscular folds of the cervix project into the uterus and vagina as the uterine and vaginal os respectively; in cow its is about ________ cm long and 2.5 cm or more thick.

195. The female organ extending from the cervix posteriorly upto the urogenital sinus or vestibule from which it is separated by the hymen or the hymenal constriction is the organ of ________ in females.

196. The vagina of a cow is constricted at the junction with the urinogenital sinus or vestibules, peculiarly also embodies a constriction or ________ just at the back of the externals.

197. A small rod-like structured organ though represents the penis of male (in cattle), is solid unlike the penis, is sensory and eretical ________.

198. The cells which supply nutrition to the maturing spermatids are known as ________.

199. The primitive germ cells after numerous cell divisions become ________.

200. At a later stage of transformation of spermatids into sperms which is known as ________, the nucleus condense and the acrosomal head spreads over its anterior surface to form the acrosome.

201. The matured eggs are discharged from the ovary once in most of the vertebrates, but once a month in the human and bovine species.

202. The number of ova discharged at a single ovulation varies from one, as in ________ , to thousands in the frog and even millions in fish.

203. The contraction of the delicate bands of involuntary muscle fibres (as in frog and rat) may aid in the rupture of the ________ and the liberation of the eggs.

204. In some vertebrates (notably birds), a whitish linear area devoid of flood vessels on the surface of the follicle along which its rupture occurs is known as ________.

205. The movement of sperms towards the egg attracted by some chemical substances from the egg or female organs is known as ________.

206. In ________ the sperms swim in a spiral path, and when they approach a small solid body, they may move directly towards it.

207. The sperm after penetration and when at rest against the plasma membrane produces a coagulation called ________ of the egg.

208. Vitelline membrane finally changes into ________ membrane which is considered to be a bar to the entrance of extra sperm cells.

209. Diestrum or dioestrum periods are transmitted by activities which normally occur at the end of pregnancy such as nest making and the secretion of milk and these periods are known as ________ periods.

210. The secretions discharged directly into the blood (ductless glands) by ________ organs usually contain hormones.

211. Oxytocin and Vasopressin are produced by ________ neurosecretory cells.

212. Pituitary has frequently been described as, "the conductor of the ________ orchestra"

213. The active principle of the thyroid gland was first isolated by Kendall who named it thyroxine, found in a protein material called ________.

214. ________ isolated from the beef adrenals which acts like the male six hormones.

215. Estradiol, estrone, estariol, equilin and equilenin are called ________.

216. The anterior pituitary secretes F.S.H. in increasing quantities bringing about the multiplication of granulosa cells and stimulates the ovaries to produce graafian follicles on the attainment of ________.

217. The ovulation in cows takes place by the action of ________.

218. In cows and she buffaloes cessation of estrus, sluggish temperament, easier tractability and increase in body weight are some of the signs of ________.

219. The most reliable method of pregnancy diagnosis in bovine animals is ________ of the uterus per rectum.

220. Uterine abnormalities like pyometra of uterus may be confused for ________.

221. The examination of vagina by means of a speculum shows that the vaginal walls are ________ because the secretion of the cervical glands becomes gelatinous and tough to form a plug to seal the canal.

222. The presence of ________ hormones in the urine of pregnant women and the blood of pregnant mares helps in detection of pregnancy by laboratory tests.

223. Parturition is presumably caused by an increase in the level of estrogen, a decrease in the level of progesterone, increase in the size of foetus, and inadequacy of ________.

224. The expulsion of the young one is achieved by plain muscle of the uterus wall and by contraction of abdomen walls which raises the ________ pressure.

225. In the process of parturition and expulsion, the ________ shape of the young completes the dilation of the genital canal to make the delivery possible.

226. The udder secretion, immediately before parturition changes from ________ secretion to an yellowish one, known as colostrum.

227. The stages of parturition (a continuous act) comprises the stages *viz*, *preliminary* ________, foetus expulsion and after-birth stage.

228. The maternal dystokia may be due to uterine abnormalities like torsion of uterus, uterine inertia, and ________.

229. In anterior presentation the foetus is wedge-shaped, whereas in the posterior presentation compression of the ________ causes expansion of ribs and the coastal arch enlarges abruptly.

230. In cryptorchids or rigs (males), there is undescended condition of the ________ into the scrotal sac.

231. When a female calf is born as a twin to a male calf, a sterile female is known as ________.

232. In case of ________ the hymen is a thick bond of tissues between the vagina and vestibule in virgin females, cannot be easily broken and bars reproduction.

233. Reversion of vagina and at times of uterus and its protrusion out through the vulva is known as ________.

234. The deficiency of ________ hormones may limit or retard. reproduction in either sex.

235. The silent or shy breeder cows and buffaloes go through the normal ovarian changes in the estrous cycle but show no signs of beat and ________ to males.

236. A chronic buller or the cow having nymphomania will not usually breed until it passes one or two ________ periods.

237. The deficiency of fat leads to a number of troubles in animals namely, lack of ________ in males, reabsorption of the foetus, abortion or dead births etc.

238. Vitamin A deficiency causes ________ of the mucous membrane, that is, what is otherwise known as unfavorable uterine environment.

239. Brucellosis (Bang's disease) caused by *Brucella abortus* is usually found in ________ uterus, but may also localize in udder or testes.

240. Bovine venereal trichomoniasis is caused by a single called protozoa, ________ which brings about the destruction of embryo within 3-5 weeks after conception.

241. Hybrids of distant crosses like horse × ass = male and horse × zebra = zebroid are mostly ________.

242. Exposure of ________ to artificial light brings them to heat, but darkness induces late maturity and reduces oestrus.

243. Milk production increase rapidly following ________, reaches a peak 2-4 weeks where it remains for a short period and then gradually declines.

244. The ________ and intra-mammary pressure are two important factors influencing the level at which lactation is maintained.

245. ________ provide optimal level of calcium, while insulin regulates carbohydrate metabolism during lactation period.

246. The colostrum contains greater percentage of protein, a large part of which is due to the presence of ________, the antibody proteins.

247. In the milk of ruminants, fatty acids are also synthesized in the mammary cells from ________ and about 25 per cent of them are derived from fatty acids coming from dietary fat.

248. The random nature of ________ and recombination makes selection a slow and complex process.

249. The animals homozygous for gene c (cc) are ________ as the gene blocks the formation of pigments in the hair: and. skin.

250. The differential influence on environment on candidates leads to commission of errors in choosing the best ________.

251. The progenies far superior to their parents are produced by ________ of genes for quantitative traits.

252. If the dominance, epistasis, or random environmental influences have affected the ________ the progeny will tend to average nearer to the group average than their parents.

253. Use of ________ individuals for parents will produce the progeny superior to any other parents.

254. The amount of practical selection within a herd is limited by the ________ and the success in raising replacements.

255. Cousins are ________ relatives as they have some ancestors in common.

256. The average percentage increase in homozygosity or decrease in heterozygosity is an inbred animal in relation to an average animal of the same breed of the foundation stock is known as the ________ of inbreeding.

257. The rate of attainment of homozygosity in line breeding is not as quick as in ________ breeding.

258. ________ breeding has become quite common in pigs and in the production of hybrid chickens.

259. ________ breeding is proposed for utilizing the heterosis in both dam and progeny.

260. ________ is no widely used by animal breeds.

261. The King Ranch of Kingsville, Texas (U.S.A) created the first American breed of cattle, ________ from a crossbred foundation of shorthorn and Brahman cattle.

262. First crosses of Sahiwal cow and Ayrshire bull were high milk yielders, but susceptible to ________ disease.

263. Holstein-Friesian had proved superior to ________ breed in India for breeding to augment milk productivity.

264. Stallion (male horse) × Jannet (female ass) = ________ which is generally inferior to mule.

265. ________ is phenomenon in which the crosses of the unrelated individuals often result in progeny with increased vigour much above their parents.

266. ________ is the practice of breeding sires of a given breed to non-descript females and their offspring for generation after generation.

267. The ________ test is only an estimate, and not a measure, of genetic value.

268. The accuracy of the estimate of performance test depends on the ________ of the trait.

269. ________ evaluation is essentially, only an extension of the performance testing since each individual is performance tested and the performance records are used in evaluation.

270. The contribution of each parent to the phenotypic variation is 0.25 h^2 (h^2 = heritability) because the ________ are modified by the environment.

271. ________ selection provides information when performance tests are not available for the candidates.

272. In ________ the average method of animal breeding, it is assumed that all parents have an equal number of progeny, the rates of each candidate for selection are equal and equivalent environments are provided to all progeny groups.

273. Animal selection on conformation has ________ because a part of sale price is determined by the conformation of the individual.

274. ________ is more or less restricted in its application to the female or groups such as breed, strain or heard.

275. ________ is the potential capacity of a female to produce functional ova, regardless of what happens to them after they are produced.

276. In ________ the period of ovulation seems to be 14 hours after the end of heat.

277. The ________ mortality may be due to hormone deficiency or imbalance, failure of implantation of fertilized ova, death due to lethal genes, accidents in development, insufficient nutrition, overcrowding or infection in the uterus.

278. Repiquet (1894), a French veterinarian, recommended the artificial insemination as a means of curing sterility in ________.

279. The Indian Veterinary Research Institute, Izatnagar, started experimental work on artificial insemination under the direction of ________ in 1942.

280. The Government of India started artificial insemination centres at Kolkata, Hissar, Channai, Bangalore and Nagpur in ________.

281. ________ in Australia developed a method of semen collection from rams by electric stimulation of spinal cord.

282. The best known and commonly used method of semen collection is ________.

283. The mature spermatozoa, in the majority of species have a filiform structure due to the presence of a flagellate appendage, although, non-flagellar forms of sperms are not uncommon among ________.

284. The high degree of ________ is responsible for speedy exchange reactions between the spermatozoa and seminal plasma or an artificial pabulum.

285. In the bull the spermatozoon is about ________ in length (head is 9m (mu) long and 5.5m (nu) wide and about 65m in length).

286. The main part of the spermatozoon is occupied by the nucleus, filled by closely packed chromatin largely composed of ________.

287. *Galea capitis*, a loose protoplasmic structure enveloping the apical part of the sperm head breaks away spontaneously to form ________.

288. The ________ plasma, a composite mixture of secreted fluids in higher species comprises epididymis, vas deferens, ampullae, prostrate, seminal vesicles, cowpea's glands and other glands located in urethral canal wall.

289. In rats and guinea-pigs ________ is formed due to semen coagulation after mating.

290. ________ is a suspension of spermatozoa in seminal fluid, it is opaque, white to light cream-coloured fluid.

291. The spermatozoa are generated in the testes and stored in epididymis whereas ________ is contributed by these cretory fluids reduced in accessory orgns.

292. The average specific gravity of whole semen is 1.028, 1.011 and 1.03 in man, dog and ________ respectively.

293. The specific gravity of the bull spermatozoa (1.28) considerably exceeds that of ________ and other cells of animals body.

294. It is certain that ________ charge is associated with the sperm cell.

295. Observing the change of frequency of ________ to electric charge one of the method to determine the quality of semen.

296. Fructose is not utilized by either azoospermic or mecrospermic semen and hence ________ may be employed to distinguish its normal activity from abnormal activity.

297. Hydrogen peroxide and pure oxygen have detrimental influence on spermatozoa of mammalian semen due to lack of ________.

298. One of the first diluent of semen in veterinary science for the insemination of cattle in Russia was ________.

299. Phillips and Lardy (1939-40) introduced an advance technique of semen storage known as ________.

300. U.D. Sharma (1957) used the semen dilutor known as ________ to preserve it at room temperature.

301. Different ________ along with different dilutors have been used to check the multiplication of bacteria in semen.

302. The ________ hormone stimulates the elaboration of seminal plasm and ejaculation.

303. Guinea grass is a native of ________ ,but it is now popular in many tropical countries as a perennial grass.

304. The term ________ is applied to that group of feeds which are relatively high in total digestible nutrients and. low in crude fibre.

305. Lucerne (alfalfa) besides protein is also rich in calcium and ________.

306. Among the bye-product of grains, ________ contains the maximum (13.2 per cent) of fat content.

307. ________ is not palatable to cattle and sheep still should be given with concentrate mixtures as it contains nearly 4, 55 and 25 per cent of fat, proteins and mineral matter respectively besides vitamin A and D, iodine, riboflavin and nicotinic acid.

308. ________ is well balanced calcium-phosphorus mineral supplement as it contains. 30, 15,7 and 3 per cent of calcuim. phosphorus, protein and fat respectively.

309. It has been observed that animals may live for more than 100 days with organic food but they die in 5-10 days when deprived of ________.

310. ________ forms a major form of source of supply in incubating chick and hibernating animals.

311. Conversion of one gramme of water into one gramme of vapour without any change in temperature requires ________ which is also called latent heat of evaporation.

312. The factors *viz*., endorine, autonomic nervous system, renal regulation, respiration and skin, and phenomenon of thirst are involved in regulation of ________ in an animal body.

313. The injection of ________ reduces the urine volume by constriction of renal vessels and the consequent reduction of renal circulation.

314. An obscure function of ________ is its role in the structure of certain biologically important compounds like heparin, nucleic acids, glycolipids. and glycoproteins etc.

315. ________ established the concept to dynamic state of ________ which led to a new appreciationof adipose tissue.

316. Ether extract consists of glycerides of fatty acids, free fatty acids, ________, lecithin chlorophyll, alkali substances, volatile oils and resins in general.

317. Proteins comprise cell's structural components, antibodies and many hormones, but as much as 90 per cent of cellular proteins are the ________ upon which fundamental function depends.

318. The properties and characteristics of a protein depend upon the ________ present, their position in the molecule and the special arrangement of the molecule.

319. All the amino acids are ________ in nature.

320. Uncharged or dipolar ions structure is known as ________.

321. Hormones of ________ glands maintain the calcium concentration of flood.

322. Deficiency of ________ causes pica in cattle.

323. A hormone of adrenal cortex called ________ regulates the sodium metabolism by promoting its reabsorption from kidney tubules.

324. Excess iron in body is deposited in all but specially in liver cells forming ferritin in combination which is also known as ________.

325. Apoferritin excess of capacity of storage pool is stored in the extremely insoluble form known as ________.

326. Most of the zinc in blood is present in the ________.

327. The animal specially cattle diseases *viz*., "Salt sick" and "lechsucht" are caused by ________ deficiency.

328. The most sensitive index of copper deficiency is ________ involves a syndrome consisting of achrometrichia, alopecia and dermatitis.

329. Excess of ________ and deficiency of copper causes ________ disease in cattle.

330. ________ disease of chickens is due to the deficiency of manganese.

331. Hydrolysis of ________ releases thyroxin and other iodinated compounds into the blood stream.

332. Iodine deficiency delays ________ development which results in "cretinism" in humans.

333. The essentiality of ________ as a mineral nutrient was first recognized by a group of Australian investigators.

334. The ________ anaemia factor in liver designated as vitamin B_{12} is a cobalt containing (almost 4 per cent) compound.

335. Complete remission of all signs of cobalt deficiency in ________ was secured with parental injections of vitamin B_{12}.

336. Xanthine oxidase and liver aldehyde oxidase contain ________ as an essential part of the molecule.

337. A condition in cattle called ________ has been identified as molybdenum poisoning.

338. Keeping sheep on a low molybdenum diet causes a rapid accumulation of ________ resulting to its typical deficiency.

339. Mc Collum and Davis (1913) established by adding egg to carbohydrates, protein, fats and salts based diet of experimental rats that the growth promoting component was ________ substance.

340. Mori (1922) clearly established that the disease ________ (an eye disease) is due to deficiency of vitamin ACO (a fat soluble factor).

341. Vitamin A molecule contains a ________ ring with an unsaturated side chair.

342. Mellanby (1916) observed rickets in milk fed dogs, while Huldschinsky (1919) demostrated marked clinical improvement in severely rachitic children by playing ________ light on their body.

343. For nutritional purposes the two most important *D* vitamins are D_2, ergocalciferol and D_3 ________.

344. Vitamin D_4 is activated 22 - dehydroergosterol, while vitamin D_5 is activated ________.

345. Bishop and Evans (1922) observed factor X in certain foods for normal reproduction in rats and later on Evans termed this active substance as ________.

346. Vitamin E acts as an antioxidant in the cellular level, participates in normal tissue respiration, is involved in the synthesis of ________ and ubiquinine (coenzyme) and in the metabolism of nucleic acid and sulphur amino acid..

347. Severely K-deficient chicks may ________ to death from slight bruise or other injury.

348. Anaemia in K-deficient chicks may be due to loss of blood or to the development of a ________ bone marrow.

349. The disease "sweet clover poisoning" or "bleeding disease" in cattle and other ruminants has been shown to be caused by the antivitamin K action of ________.

350. The disease scurvy caused most of the deaths during long-term explorations and times of ________.

351. In the late nineteenth century, ________ working in a hospital laboratory in Batavia, Dutch East Indies, discovered that a polyneuritis in chickens with symptoms similar to beriberi in humans was produced by feeding polished rice.

352. ________ is a complex nitrogenous base composed of a pyrimedine and a thiazole ring and is available commercially in hydrochloride form.

353. In humans, the most characteristic feature of beriberi is '*percipheral neuritis*' and is often accompanied by contractions of feet, severe wrist weakness and affected brain, under these conditions, it is termed as "cerebral beriberi" or ________.

354. In beriberi, evidence indicates that the myelin sheath of the nerves and the ________ of the brain are the tissues most seriously affected.

355. Paralysis in animals and birds on account of beriberi appears due to accumulation of ________ in the brain and muscles.

356. ________ was synthesized independently by Kuhn *et al.* (1935) and Karrer *et al.* (1935).

357. ________ in humans produces cheilosis, angular somatitis, glossitis and seborrheic dermatitis.

358. Severe riboflavin deficiency in chicks causes swelling and softening of the sciatic and brachial nerves producing a contraction of toes and typical symptoms known as ________.

359. Funk isolated nicotinic acid from ________ as early as 1914, but did not realize that it was a vitamin.

360. Christian could cure black tongue in dogs with niacinamide isolated from liver, niacin was firmly established as the ________ preventive factor.

361. The name ________ was proposed by Mitchell *et al.* (1941) for a compound isolated from spinach and shown to be necessary for growth of *Streptococcus faccalis* R.

362. Rickes *et al* (1940) in U.S.A. and Smith and Parker (1941) in U.K. independently isolated ________ which was shown to be active in the treatment of pernicious anaemia.

363. In chicks and other animals, ________ deficiency is characterized by poor growth and reproductive failure, with only slight. or no anaemia.

364. The antibiotic vitamin B_{12} feed supplement is largely included in the commercial ________ for chicks, pigs and dairy calves for their growth and fattening.

365. ________ is more effective than other antibiotics as feed supplement to poultry ration especially for growing chicks and turkey poults.

366. Addition of aureomycin feed supplement to rations of fattening lambs has been found to reduce the incidence of ________.

367. At the junction of omasum and abomasum is an arrangement of folds of mucous membrane, the *vela terminalia*, derived from omasum in the cow, but from the abomasum in the ________.

368. The terminal part of the ileum (of small intestine) joins the cecum in ________ or coecum and colon in other animals in the right caudal part of the abdominal cavity.

369. The distention of rumen may be so much due to bloat (gas accumulation) that the animal may die due to high pressure of the ________ towards heart.

370. The enzyme pepsin can digest any kind of protein, but not to completion to amino acids, that is, it simply splits ________ and converts protein into proteoses, peptones and some small peptide chains.

371. There is no ________ enzyme source in the rumen wall unlike that in simple stomached animals.

372. The carboxyl part of the bile salt is highly soluble in water, whereas the ________ portion in fat.

373. The free glycerol released in the intestinal lumen is not reutilized but passes directly to the ________.

374. Mixed microorganisms of the ________ rumen produce enzyme and galactosidases which liberate galactose from galactolipids.

375. Glycerol fermenting bacteria isolated from sheep rumen contents have been identified as ________ they did not show lipolytic activity.

376. The ________ may be defined as the percentage of the total amount consumed which is digested and absorbed or

$$\frac{\text{Amount digested and absorbed}}{\text{Amount consumed}} \times 100$$

$$\frac{\text{Amount consumed} - \text{amounti n feaces}}{\text{Amount consumed}} \times 100$$

377. The digestibility of a specific nutrient can be computed as ________.

378. ________ idea of feeding animals on the basis of net energy rather than by TDN was first recognized in Germany in 1905 and in England in 1909.

379. The best time for cutting a crop for hay making is when it is ________ in blossom.

380. Foundation soil for dairy building as a as possible should not be too ________.

381. Dairy building should he so located that it is maximum and minimum exposed to ________ respectively and very well protected from prevailing wind currents.

382. In tail to tail system of barn arrangement, any sort of minor disease or any change in the ________ of the animals can be detected quickly and even automatically.

383. The three main types of dairy barn stalls are ________, the tie and the comfort stalls.

384. The cement concrete continuous manger with removable partitions is the best from the point of view of ________ and cleanliness.

385. The confinement of a bull onto a hard floor with inadequate exercise leads to ________ of hoofs creating difficulty in mounting and the loss in the breeding power.

386. The exercise yard of a bull shed should communicate with a service crate *via* a swing gate to economise an attendant needed otherwise to bring the bull to the ________.

387. The mixture of grasses in a good pasture should have high percentage of ________ grasses (forage crops).

388. The method of keeping and operating ________ was standardized at an International Convention signed in Rome in October, 1936.

389. A cow prefers laxative diet, but some dairyman advise a light dose of alcoholic drink which acts as stimulant, when it is milked after sometime of ________.

390. Feed the calf enough of ________ for the first four days following its birth.

391. Colostrum contains higher proportion of globulin than does normal milk, it contains 3-5 and 5-15 times more protein and ________, respectively.

392. Dehorning of a calf should be done before it is 10 days old because ________ upto this age remains unattached to skull.

393. ________ enhances the rate of gain, enables to produce more desirable type of meet and makes the animal more docile.

394. Castration with the help of a Burdizzo's castrator is also known as ________.

395. Fatty sires are often indifferent and may even embody ________.

396. It has been recommended that sows should be mated on the ________ of heat for the optimum fertility.

397. ________ is a common genital disease in swine and is dangerous to man.

398. Most of the mares are bred to foal in spring, the length of estrus cycle is 15-24 days and the heat period is ________ days.

399. The main problem in ________ is the usually long heat period and the variation in ovulation time.

400. ________ should he valued largely by the amount of milk and butterfat they produce.

401. Beating of a cow is not only cruel, but it also ________ milk production.

402. A cradle or bull ring is put in ________ cows and then 2 or 3 other rings are attached to it.

403. The term ________ is used to designate groups of poultry breeds developed in certain areas.

404. The first breed of poultry named ________ was exhibited at America's first poultry show, held at Boston in 1849.

405. The varieties of Wyandotte (poultry) originated between ________ and is a general purpose breed.

406. Aseel (poultry) embodies noble qualities of fighting, is a superior ________ and has good parental qualities.

407. A few ova (in hen) after attaining a diameter of 6 mm, add 4 mm per twenty-four hours, until full size of ________ in diameter is reached.

408. The sperms, in case of a hen, remain in the oviduct for ________ after mating, but the newest sperm is the one most likely to fertilize the egg.

409. It is desirable to produce infertile eggs at all times except when they are needed for hatching because in fertile eggs above ________ further germ development takes place.

410. The percentage of thick white in egg tends to ________ from about April to July in most of the flocks.

411. Meat or blood spots may result due to degenerated blood in general or of clots due to ________ of small blood vessel in the ovary or oviduct.

412. ________ eggs may be due to ripening of two ova at the same time or one ovum being pushed back into the oviduct at the same time when another ovulation takes place.

413. ________ in eggs finds way into the oviduct and gets included in the albumen, passes through egg formation stages and gets embodied in the egg.

414. success in ________ is just as dependent upon use of good breeding stock as it is in crop production.

415. ________ with coarse, phlegmatic, masculine, or "beefy" heads are not likely to lay many eggs.

416. Birds ________ the tendency to shed their plumage annually, and an early moulter, under normal conditions, is a poor layer.

417. During the periods of growth of new plumage, the late moulters are timid and dislike handling due to the active ________ and sensitive nerve development in the feather follicles.

418. A good ________ is among the first off the perch in the morning and among the last on it at night.

419. Broodiness in birds is the external evidence of the ________ and is a dominant sex linked character.

420. Beginning of early moult signals the lack of ________.

421. The eggs having a proportion of white to yolk of about ________ usually hatch better than those having either wider or narrower ratio.

422. On 19th or 20th day of hatching, fertile eggs when but in hot water (exactly at 102 °F wriggle as ________ endeavour to make escape from the shell.

423. In Southern Australia, a bird, ________ incubates its eggs by preparing a nest of vegetable matter in the sand, which later provides by fermentation sufficient heat to incubate its eggs.
424. Evaporation from of the moisture from the egg contents, supply oxygen and removal of gases formed by respiration govern the ________ development.
425. On the ________ of incubation approximately 140-150 times as much air is needed as on the first day.
426. The spread of ________ disease may he excessive in incubation unless precautionary disinfection is applied to minimize the spread.
427. ________ must he properly grown out it they are to become economical producers of eggs.
428. Bigger the pen more is actual usable floor space ________.
429. Light in a poultry house does not only destroy disease germs and supplies Vitamin D, but also makes the birds ________.
430. A hundred hens will drink ________ gallons of water, depending on size of birds, rate of production, salt contents of .the ration and weather conditions.
431. Flowers of ________ should be added to the ashes (of dust bath) and also some dry coarse tobacco leaves.
432. The ________ system of housing of poultry is suitable whenever limited land area is at one's disposal, however, allowing the birds out for an hour and occasional feeding of 2 per cent of cod liver oil are required.
433. The hens kept in ________ produce vegetative eggs.
434. Start the ________ pen when weather is dry and start new litter with each year's pullet.
435. A well built up deep litter in operation for about one year has been found to contain ________ per cent of nitrogen, phosphorous and potassium, respectively.
436. ________ are the male birds whose testicles have been removed either surgically of chemically.
437. Cockerels from ________ weeks of age and weighing about 0.5-1.0 kilogram are considered the best subjects for the capsonizing operation.
438. ________ in hens may be by inheritance, deficiency in ration, and by close confinement.
439. Dislike to feed, shaking of tail and restlessness *etc.*, are ________ in doe (she goat).
440. ________ ameliorates palatability of meat, accelerates the rate of increase in weight and improves the quality of skin in goats.
441. Goat, having their origin from open mountains like plenty of fresh air, love a clean and dry ________ place.
442. Many hardly ever drink water, if they have plenty of natural green feeds.
443. In selection of gilt or sow, the period between weaning and attainment of market weight of about 225 pounds is referred to as ________.
444. Reasonable development of ________, and rear quarters and bacon characterize a good gilt.
445. A ________ should be 4-6 months of age at the time of selection, as no serious defects are to develop after this age.
446. The ovaries of a sow are rounded and the surface is lobulated with ________ and cropora lutea.
447. The ________ of the pigs at birth should be removed with a small pair of pliers or with strong forceps very close to the gums.
448. Creep feeding of pigs and other animals since it is said, "________"
449. As the lactation in sow proceeds, there is decrease in the efficiency of the utilization of ________ by the piglets.

450. The study of the behaviour of the ________ before selecting the pair for a single pen comprises a good practice.

451. The young boars that take to excessive ________ may go off the feed and become shieldy.

452. The main change in feed lipids in pigs stomach is a result of ________ which by churning and kneading turn the lipids into a coarse emulsion.

453. ________ produced in the caecium and colon of pigs are rapidly absorbed in the blood system and are readily utilized by the animal.

454. The ________ resembles human beings perhaps more than any mammalian species in quantitative and qualitative requirements of nutrition.

455. The ________ acquired antibodies persist in the serum for at least six weeks after birth in pigs weaned at two or eight weeks of age.

456. The digestibility of milk protein and fish meal is high, over 90 per cent, and changes little with increase in the age of the ________.

457. The recommended ________ ratio for reproduction in pigs is approximately 1.5:1.

458. The potassium deficiency in pigs reduces heart rate, increases ________ and deforms the QRS complex.

459. ________ deficiency is of special significance in the newborn pig since its placental transfer is rather poor and mammary transfer is grossly inadequate.

460. A deficiency of ________ causes liver necrosis, a yellowish brown discoloration of body fat and death in young pigs.

461. Large doses of ________ leads to histological anomalies of the eyes, pronounced malformation of heart and lungs and hypertrophy of the pulmonary artery in pigs.

462. Deficiency of ________ depressed the absorption of magnesium.

463. ________ and selenium protect pigs from liver necrosis and muscular dystrophy.

464. The time spent in the uterus is about ________ the total life a growing pig destined for meat production.

465. At birth, pigs weight between ________ kilograms.

466. To provide ________, 2.6 kg is needed of a diet with 11.5 MJ DE / kg, while only 2.2 kg is needed of a diet with 13.5 MJ DE / kg in a pig diet.

467. Dietary protein may be measured either as crude protein or as ________.

468. ________ = Lysine in diet (g / kg) / CP in diet (g / kg) / / 0.07 or = {[Lysine in diet (g / kg) 80.85] / DCP in diet (g / kg)} /0.07.

469. If the DE to DCP ratio remains unchanged then an increase in DE density will be exactly matched by a *pro rata* increase in ________.

470. There are two areas of concern in rationing ________ animals (pigs); mothers body condition in relation to rebreeding and the growth rate of youngs.

471. One of the uses of the ________ pig is to look at aspects of production strategy and financial optimization.

472. A sow's ability to produce piglets is of no practical consequence if there are too few ________.

473. In pig improvement, central testing can offer help to pedigree breeders by providing facilities at which ________ and their relatives can be grown and assessed.

474. Foot-and-mouth, swine fever, swine vesicular disease, tuberculosis, brucellosis, Teschen disease, anthrax and rabies are unusual in ________ herds.

475. Two complex syndromes in breeding female pigs, MMA (________) and SMEDI (Still births, mummified foetus, embryo death and infertility) are caused by a variety of organisms.

476. The wool of the majority of British mountain breeds with dark faces and the fleece of most of the African and Asiatic sheep are classed as ________.

477. Introduction of Finnish Landrace 'blood' into British and the ________ Booroola into New Zealand constitute good examples of raising fertility of sheep stocks.

478. ________ denotes low ground sheep farming practice of increasing fertility by pulling the ewes on to a higher plane of nutrition before introducing them to the rams.

479. The watchword for ewes, as for all breeding stock, is that they should be fit but not ________.

480. The sheep breed like East Friesland milk yield may be as much as 500-600 liters in a ________ lactation.

481. Ewe's milk on an average has a much higher solid content than ________ and goat milk.

482. Ewe's like cows need ________ to give good milk yield in early lactation.

483. Mating of large rams, on small owes, big-headed, square shouldered rams tends to increase the number of ________.

484. Both milk and permanent sets of teeth in sheep, all the incisors are on the lower jaw and these teeth bite against a ________ dental pad on the upper jaw.

485. A sheep is able to bite individual blades of grass unlike a cattle beast because it embodies ________ lip.

486. The stomach of sheep, a ruminant is divided into four sections viz., rumen, reticulum, ________ and abomasum.

487. The low ________ content sheep herbage causes sway-back or neonatal ataxia or emzootic ataxia.

488. Deficiency of ________ lends to a wasting disease in sheep known as pine, vanquish, bush sickness and known by other various names.

489. ________ is an essential trace element for sheep and its deficiency is associated with muscular dystrophy, infertility and poor wool growth.

490. Moving sheep long distances by truck often 'sparks off' pneumonia, while cold wet weather is associated with ________ in ewes.

491. One of the chief villains causing sheep diseases is the bacterium called ________.

492. The process to dispose of ewes after three, four, or five crops of lambs is known as ________.

493. The sheep breed ________ was developed in Spain and its largest and famous herds were owned by the King.

494. The systematic cross breeding of sheep on a regional scale is called ________.

495. Lambs that are weaned from their mothers and go for further feeding prior to slaughter are known as ________.

496. ________ is a specific iron-binding protein.

497. The swam water buffalo (*Bubalus bubalis*) is indigenous to Southeast Asia, Southeast China and ________ in India.

498. ________ originate from the Indian subcontinent, have a chromosome number of 2n = 50 and are improved domesticated animals with high milk and meat production.

II. Tick mark (✓) the True or False:

499. Sahiwal and Sindhi are milch breeds of Indian cattle.

500. Giri and Deoni breeds are dual purpose breeds of Indian cattle.

501. Hariana, Ongole, Tharparkar and Kankrej are dual purpose breeds of Indian cattle.

502. Amrit Mahal, Kangayam, Malvi and Siri are milch breeds of Indian cattle.

503. Sahiwal breed of Indian cattle has deep body, loose skin (hence the name *lola*), short legs, stumpy horns and broad head and are lethargic.

504. The males of Sindhi breed of Indian cattle are lighter red in colour than the females.

505. In Sindhi breed of cattle, capacious udder with a tendency to become pendulous is a characteristics in heavy milkers.

506. The head of Giri breed of cattle is massive in appearance with prominent bony forehead, straight and levelled back are its most marking characters.

507. The skin of Giri breed of cattle is rough and tough, and hip bones are prominent.

508. The bullocks of Giri breed are light but powerful, fast paced and unsuitable for drought.

509. Deep chest, well arched ribs, straight back, strong quarters heavy dewlap and pendulous sheath are special characters of Deoni (Dongarpatti) breed of cattle.

510. Bullocks of Hariana breed are good work animals for fast ploughing and road transport.

511. The hump in Ongole breed of cattle is well developed and drooping, filled up on both sides with leaning.

512. Ongole breed bullocks are powerful and suitable for cart and road work and also fast paced.

513. The Tharparkar breed of cattle are strong have well proportioned frame, broad poll and their head is slightly convex with medium sized horns.

514. Tharpar breed cows are good yielders, but the bullocks are unsuitable for carting and ploughing.

515. Kankrej cattle are highly prized as milch cattle.

516. Gait is particular to Kankrej breed known as 1.25 spaces (*Sawai chal*) with smooth movements of the body and head noticeably high.

517. The Kankrej breed cattle are energetic and vigorous, excitable and nervous with strangers.

518. Amrit Mahal breed of cows are very good milkers.

519. Amrit Mahal is one––of the best draught breeds of India.

520. The name Kangayam breed of cattle is derived from the Kangayam division of Dharampuram taluk of Coimbatore district where the breeding of this breed is a traditional affair.

521. Kangayam breed heifers, on an average start calving at the age of three years and two months.

522. The Malvi breed of cattle takes its name from the Malwa tract, named after the family kings called Malawa in Madhya Pradesh.

523. There are two recognized types of Malvi cattle *viz.*, Agar type and Mandsaur or Bhopal type.

524. The Malvi breed is not essentially a good draught breed.

525. Siri breed of cows are heavy milkers.

526. Buffaloes in countries other than India, though have distinct types, no type has the specific physical characters.

527. Good, well defined, milk breeds of buffaloes are found only in Punjab, Rajasthan, Haryana and Gujarat, but in Central and Southern India, there is a noted draught breed.

528. Murrah breed of buffaloes have long massive limbs with good bone, narrow hoofs and drooping quarters.

529. The skin of murrah buffaloes is soft, smooth and with dense hair.

530. Jaffarabadi buffalo do not embody well developed dewlap and udder.

531. Nili and Ravi are two types of buffaloes found in the valley of Montgomery and Ferozepur.

532. Nili and Ravi are considered to be one of the best breeds of buffaloes in India next only to murrah.

533. The udder not so well developed but milk veins are fairy prominent in Bhadawari buffaloes.
534. Diverse kinds of cells serve the specialized purpose of the various tissues.
535. The nucleus is connected with the endoplasm by a system of pores in the double layer membrane.
536. The nucleus contains the genetic material which is made up of chromatin material.
537. The genetic information is coded by the sequence of bases on the polynucleotide.
538. The DNA is composed of two strands that curl around each other to form a triple helix.
539. RNA is a double strand unit.
540. There is at least one specific soluble RNA (s-RNA) for each amino acid.
541. The triplet bases on the s-RNA pairs with the triplet on the m-RNA, and in this way, the m-RNA determines the sequence of amino acids in protein.
542. DNA can be demonstrated in the nucleus by the Feulgen stain or other basic stains.
543. It is generally believed that the amount of DNA per cell is constant for a species.
544. The nucleus contains one or more nucleoli, which show thin granular textures.
545. The nucleoli have membrane to separate them from the nucleus and are intermeshed with the chromosomal-DNA.
546. The endoplasmic reticulum allows the cell to maintain efficient contact with its environment.
547. Ribosomes from animals consist of approximately equal amounts of RNA and protein.
548. The Golgi apparatus plays a direct part in protein synthesis and is also involved in exporting protein synthesized by the ribosomes.
549. The membrane of the Golgi vacuole does not become the limiting membrane of the zymogen granule.
550. The zymogen granule is released into the lumen after the rupture of the cell membrane.
551. Mitochondria contain DNA that can be used as template to synthesize messenger RNA for carbohydrate formation.
552. Mitochondria arise from *de novo* synthesis within the cell.
553. Mitochondria also reduce and actively synthesize fatty acids.
554. The lysosomes have a dense matrix with vacuoles or droplets in them.
555. Lysosomes can also function as scavengers for removing unneeded or foreign material from the cell.
556. Mitosis takes place in the gonads and precedes gametogenesis. ,
557. Pneumococci (bacteria) like all other living organisms, exhibit genetic variability that can be recognized by the existence different phenotypes.
558. DNA contains phosphorus but no sulphur, whereas proteins contain sulphur but no phosphorus.
559. Viruses are the smallest living organisms and are acellular obligate parasites that can reproduce only in appropriate host cells.
560. Nucleins are macromolecules composed of repeating subunits called nucleotides, each of them composed of a phosphate group, a five carbon sugar (pentose), and a cyclic nitrogen containing compound called an acid.
561. The helices of A- and B-from DNA are bound in right-handed manner.
562. The replication of DNA is central to all of biology because the genetic information is stored in DNA.
563. The density of most DNAs is about the same as the density of concentrated solutions of light salts such as cesium chloride (CsCI).
564. DNA polymerase I can initiate the synthesis of DNA chains *de novo*.

565. No known DNA polymerase can initiate the synthesis of a new strand of DNA

566. The synthesis of the RNA primers is catalyzed by enzymes called primerases.

567. Karyokinesis succeeds cytokinesis.

568. Cytokinesis takes place before the unclear cell division.

569. Mitotic cell division does not help in maintaining the constancy of species.

570. The process of meiosis or reduction division (of cells) occurs during the gametogenesis of animals.

571. The nuclear membrane reappears and the bivalents are arranged at the equator during Metaphases I phase of cell division.

572. The two heterologous chromosomes constituting a bivalent separate and move to the opposite poles during Anaphase-I phase of cell division.

573. The separated chromosomes reconstitute four daughter nuclei during Telophase-I phase of cell division.

574. Cell Division- II is an equational like usual mitotic division.

575. In a heterozygous individual, the two alleles at a single gene locus are not identical.

576. The exchange of corresponding segments of genetic material by heterologous chromosomes has been termed as crossing-over.

577. A gene is said to be recessive when it characteristic effect is not expressed when paired with some other allelic gene.

578. A dihybrid is an individual which is homozygous at two *loci*, for two pairs of allelic genes.

579. Filial is a Latin word meaning progeny and is generally denoted Fi with the subscript to denote the generation after crossing.

580. A phenotype for a character is the actual expression of that particular character as determined by the genes and the environment in which the living organism has lived.

581. An animals genotype for a character is the combination of genes one possesses which influence this character.

582.. Several different genotypes may produce the same phenotype.

583. Fertilization in plants and animals is effected by the union of egg and sperm.

584. Only the nucleus of the sperm takes part in fertilization but it must contain the female hereditary factors.

585. The chromosomes are the only elements which divide exactly and are distributed unequally to the daughter nuclei during cell division.

586. The chromosome occur in pairs of somatic cells.

587. DNA duplicates by separation of two strands of the helix.

588. Black urine colour in alcaptonuria patients (humans) is caused by homogentistic acid accumulation.

589. All types of gene action probably are not present among the genes affecting quantitative traits.

590. The eggs fertilized by sperm containing the x chromosomes product zygotes with two X chromosomes, which become makes.

591. The eggs receiving sperm without an X chromosome produced zygotes with one X, which became females.

592. In XY type of sex determination XX and XY zygotes became females and males respectively.

593. Genes are in chromosomes has been postulated by sex determination by a particular chromosome.

594. In Drosophila also Y determines the sex as in animals.

595. In a number of species of Hymenoptera, females develop parthenogenetically and have haploid chromosome number.

596. It has been demonstrated by experiments that the homozygous, heterozygous or hemizygous (genes present in single dose) status of certain chromosome segments controls sex determination.

597. Males and females have similar genotype, but stimuli from environmental sources initiate the development toward one sex or the other.

598. Sex hormones are limiting factors in the expression of some genes.

599. A number of mutant genes such as the Xg^a blood alleles in cattle have been identified in the X chromosome.

600. A man defective in green colour vision has a single dominant allele (g) in his X chromosome.

601. The Y chromosome carries colour vision locus in humans yet the single allele is expressed, causing colour blindness.

602. An X-linked allele is never transmitted directly from father to son and affected females have an affected father and a carrier or affected 'mother.

603. Juvenile muscular dystrophy does not depend on a sex-linked recessive gene.

604. The mutants of a beneficial character appear so rarely as to have no practical significance.

605. Any system of herd improvement founded on the search for and utilization of mutants is hardly doomed.

606. A suitable modification in the environmental conditions is capable of changing the complete expression of hereditary characters.

607. The interstitial or the leying cells are contained between the seminiferous tubules and produce female hormones.

608. The epididymis consists of a very long selender tube lying very much coiled on the three sides of the testes (in bulls) and has a caput (head), the corpus (body) and the cauda (tail)

609. The mutants of a beneficial character appear so fairly that they have great practical significance.

610. Vasa *differentia* originates from the cauda epididymis running vertically along the spermatic cords through inguinal canal into the pelvic cavity and opens at the base of the urethra along with urinary bladder and seminal vesicles.

611. Both the ovaries are functional in all the farm animals inculding poultry.

612. In the non-pregnant animals the uterus lies in the pelvic cavity which ascends into the abdomen during pregnancy.

613. The diameter of the vulva is considerably smaller than that of the vagina.

614. The gonia first undergo a period of rapid growth, and thereafter they are known as auxocyte or meocytes, called oocytes and spermatocytes in male and female, respectively.

615. There occur no quantitative changes, so far as is known, during the transition from a spermatogonium to a primary spermatocyte.

616. In equation division, the members of each diad draw close to each other.

617. The females auxocyte or primary oocyte is very mush like the primary spermatocyte in respect of period of growth to the maturation division as well as nature of the maturation division.

618. In mammals follicular fluid is secreted in the cavity of the follicle surrounding the egg.

619. In none of the vertebrates, ovulation can be inducted at any stage through hormone injection by the anterior part of the pituitary gland.

620. It has been shown that in sea fish the enzyme fertilizin is emitted only after egg-maturation, but before its fertilization.

621. The union of two pronuclei to form a common cleavage nucleus is known as conjugation.

622. The vaginal smears, taken when an animal is in heat, usually possess a few large polymorphonuclear and mononuclear leucocytes, a few nucleated epithelial cells and no confirmed cells.

623. In hyperfunction of the pituitary growth of arms, legs, and face exceeds that of the trunk.

624. The injection of thyrotropic hormone into animals causes enlargement of pituiry glands and symptoms of toxic goiter may appear.

625. Addison's disease, rheumatic arthritis, rhumatic fever and various allergies cannot he treated by the use of adrenocortico tropic hormone (A.C.T.H).

626. The four adrenal glands are usually located between the kidneys and abdominal part of the aorta.

627. Virilism develops in women due to reduced production of male sex hormones.

628. The injection of adrenaline into the blood stream causes a sharp and temporary rise in blood pressure owing to shifting of blood from active to inactive body organs.

629. In animals like sheep and horse, adrenaline stimulates certain glands and secretion of sweat.

630. Estrogens have effects antagonistic to androgen action.

631. The hormone prosterome is produced after the development of a corpus luteum, but before the discharge of the ovum of grafian follicle.

632. The placenta with the help of hormone stimulates the growth of mammary glands. lactation, ovulation and growth of uterus.

633. The observations on sows have brought out that estrongen neither causes a cessation pf F.S.H. secretion nor does it stimulate the secretion of LH. (leutenizing hormone).

634. The hormone called testosterone has been considered to be the primary sex hormone.

635. In the bovine, the corpus luteum of pregnancy persists in the ovary at its minimum size through a part of gestation period.

636. An early discharge of the placental membrane is imperative to rule out the putrefaction of placenta which may bring about uterus infection.

637. Feed the full dose of concentrates to a cattle immediately after parturition.

638. Disproportion of foetus rarely occúrs in crossbreds.

639. In bovine animals relative as well as absolute oversize of the foetus are common.

640. Lowered fertility in animals is more troublesome than sterility as it is more expensive to handle.

641. The male born twin to a female calf does not breed normally.

642. Iodine deficiency and reproductive troubles are related to insufficient secretion of thyroxine.

643. The organism *Vibrio foetus* interferes with the circulation of blood in the placenta but causes no abortion.

644. Each secretary tissue of the udder consists of numerous alveoli or tiny chambers.

645. Milk "let down" mechanism is greatly influenced by sensory and different motor sympathetic nerve fibres.

646. It is believed that parasympathetic nerve fibres are present within the mammary gland of the cow.

647. In the Holstein cow, between birth and two months of age, there is large growth of the udder.

648. The largest part of mammary growth takes place during pregnancy, but duct system proliferates during first six months.

649. Prolactin alone has the ability to produce considerable lobule-alveolar-growth.

650. The epithelian cells of the mammary gland begin to secrete milk during the early phase of pregnancy.

651. Most of the milk is stored in alveoli and the smaller ducts where capillary forces prevent its drainage.
652. The calf can absorb gamma globulins during its first day of life to build up antibody titer (measure of constration) which protects it from common calfhood diseases.
653. Glucose comprises the primary source of fatty acids in the case of ruminants.
654. Cows freshening shortly before winter months produce less total milk than those calving at other times of the years.
655. The breeds of cattle which produce tremendous volumes of milk have evolved from foundation stock which produced largely enough of milk to support one calf.
656. The wide variety of colours in pelts and high efficiency of egg laying have largely been achieved not by creation of new genes but by locating existing genes.
657. The reproductive rate places a limit beyond which selection intensity can increase. .
658. Heritability is defined to be the fraction of the superiority of parents which is, on the average, transmitted to their parent.
659. Simultaneous selection for several traits enhances the selection intensity for any single trait.
660. The relationship between two animals can be defined as the fraction of genes obtained from common ancestors.
661. It has been noted that the death rates in the inbred animals are higher than those in outbred ones.
662. Holstein-Sahiwal crosses are good for very heavy yield of milk.
663. Ayrshire breed was failure in India as it did not have the characteristic which blend with the characteristics of the Indian breeds.
664. It is advisable to use an imported breed for animal grading up programme.
665. The pure breed dairy cattle from humid zones often degenerate when used in temperate climate.
666. Performance test permits only small selection differential.
667. Milk yield and egg production are sex-linked traits.
668. Accuracy, relative to alternative selection procedures is usually high in pedigree method of selection.
669. High heritability accentuates the genetic process both in pedigree and performance testing.,
670. In daughter-dam comparison method of animal improvement method the sire whose progeny excel their dams by the largest amount are left out.
671. The sire is half of the herd. (Since in male parent of an animal)
672. Good proven sires are often not available by artificial insemination.
673. Breeding efficiency measures the reproducing ability of an adult animal.
674. The age at which females are bred greatly hamper the development of their mature size in dairy cattle.
675. Cows can be re-bred in 9-12 weeks after parturition.
676. Identical twins in animals are of great practical importance to the breeder.
677. Neck-piece is the most vulnerable and fragile part of the spermatazoon.
678. A cap-like structure covering the anterior parts of the nucleus is known as acrosome.
679. The prostatic secretion is rather low in zinc content.
680. The invention of the deep freezing method of semen preservation, failed to usher in a new era in the field of articial insemination.
681. The cervical semen insemination results in lower rate of conception than its vaginal deposition
682. The seasonal fluctuations in the intensity of light impulses, relayed through optic nerves, are probably responsible for the change associated with the so called male sex-cycle.

683. Most of the straws (dry fodder mostly non-leguminous) contain very little protein, but fairly large amount of phosphorus.

684. An excess of potassium in rice straw not only leads to non-absorption of calcium, but , it also drives out the sodium.

685. Alkali treated wheat straw is relatively richer in energy content yet failed to find favour with livestock owners.

686. Blood meal is commonly used as a cattle feed in India

687. Bound water freezes at low temperature and evaporates at high temperature or under dry conditions.

688. The nature of food taken by an animal has no relationship with the amount of water taken.

689. Increased deficiency of essential fatty acids markedly enhances the water consumption in animals.

690. Ether extract is undoubtedly the sole source of essential amino acids.

691. Amino acids in solution and blood are mostly present as uncharged molecules.

692. All the Amino acids including glycine are optically active.

693. Phosphorus deficiency is more common in sheep and goat than in cattle.

694. Nerves and muscle cells are specially rich in potassium.

695. Zinc important for the conversions of pyruvic and lactic acids.

696. Zinc deficiency in pigs and cattle causes parakeratosis.

697. The copper content of body of a new born calf is poorer in copper than that of any of the other species.

698. Copper deficiency in sheep produces abundance of black wooled sheep and the characteristic loss of 'crimp' from the fibres of all wool.

699. All the plant and animal materials used as farm animal feed contain only traces, but legumes, in general, comprise a richer source of cobalt.

700. Vitamin A exists in animal products largely as the alcohol, Retinol and it is stored in animal body in combination with fatty preferably palmitic acid.

701. Ultraviolet light is the main power which converts the pro-vitamins into vitamin C.

702. Vitamin D stimulates the uptake of calcium by kidney mitochondria.

703. Purified Vitamin K was isolated from alfalfa by Dam *et all* (1939).

704. Menaquinone is about 3.3 times as active biologically as the naturally occurring vitamins.

705. Mammals (like man and monkey) can synthesize vitamin C (ascorbic acid) and hence do not need it from deitary source.

706. Animal product as a whole are rich sources of vitamin C.

707. In general, microbial synthesis of the B complex in the digestive tract can meet the entire requirement of all the monogastric animals.

708. William *et al.* (1936) identified the structure of the vitamin B_1 and its synthesis.

709. All the plant products constitute a rich source of vitamin B_{12}

710. Biotin deficiency in chicks leads to dermatitis identical to that occurring in pantothenic acid deficiency.

711. The addition of aureomycin supplement to cow ration augments both milk production and fat percentage.

712. Use of a combination of antibiotics has been more effective than that of a single antibiotic.

713. Antibiotics should be used in the food of ruminants, breeding pigs, and breeding and laying poultry stock.

714. In ruminants, the rumen is the largest, while the reticulum is the most cranial compartment in the stomach.

715. All non-ruminants have only one stomach unlike four compartment's stomach in ruminants.

716. Horse has the largest and most complex large intestine of any of the domestic animals.

717. The enzyme ptyalin is contained in the saliva of cat, dog, horse and all ruminant animals.

718. When animals are on soft green pasture during rainy season, about 35-45 per cent of dry matter consists of cellulose and hemicellulose.

719. Lactic acid is a normal intermediate of carbohydrate metabolism in the rumen, and is usually present in high concentration.

720. In rumen, whether the feed contains protein or non-protein nitrogenous compounds, the end product of each compound is ammonia.

721. Ruminants have the privilege to utilize both protein and non-protein nitrogenous compounds to meet their protein requirement.

722. An increase in the amount of grain fed to cows leads to an increase in unsaturated and saturated acids.

723. Feeding fat or fat rich feeds enhances the fat content of milk and it is sustained by continuous feeding of such feeds.

724. The amino acids entering the ruminant animals blood bears no relationship to the protein quality of ration.

725. Sudden changes in animal diet cause a number of digestive troubles notably like tympanitis and impaction *etc.*

726. Between 300 and 500 gallons of blood must be passed through the udder for every gallon of milk.

727. Cows make a better showing in face to face system of barn arrangement for visitors when beads are together. but they (cows) feel (difficult to get into their stalls.

728. Burning of grazing lands can be recommended in all places and under specified conditions only.

729. Thorough tearing of a sod greatly helps in forming a fine and firm seed bed.

730. Ear tagging method of animal identification is most common in India.

731. Branding of animals should be done at an early age, preferably before the weaning.

732. The unborn calf makes most its growth during the last 2 or 3 months before birth.

733. Constipation in pregnant cows decreases the possibility of dystokia.

734. Cows need but only limited exercise or else milk production slides down.

735. Both thin and fleshy cows are provided an equally long dry period.

736. The poultry breed Rhode Island Red is one of the hardiest of all the breeds, but it is not popular.

737. Brahma breed of poultry was developed in U.S.A and U.K., and imported into India.

738. Cochin breed of poultry originally hails from the Shanghai district of China, while Langshan in Langshan district.

739. The appearance of leghorn is the worst of all the birds.

740. Minorca breed of poultry produces small white eggs.

741. Hens generally lay and shed feathers at the same time.

742. Early moulter takes a longer vacation and should be culled.

743. For brown coloured eggs, medium and dark brown eggs hatch better than light brown eggs.

744. Soiled egg should be washed well with water before setting for hatching.

745. Birds grow relatively faster and record higher yield, when kept in a 24 hour lighted house.

746. Gable type of poultry house requires more material, but less labour for construction.

747. Corrugated iron and zinc sheets are as satisfactory a construction material for constructing poultry house and its cost is higher than that of cement-asbestos.

748. All vaccinations should be completed at least a month before the flock is due to lay.

749. Fertility is not so good in pen mating as in flock mating.

750. Stud mating is no good where hens are kept in laying batteries.

751. Mating of birds at least once a week helps to maintain good fertility.

752. A specified amount of a nutrient regardless of its source is important in poultry nutrition.

753. The white and the yolk of the egg can be frozen together with addition of 5 per cent glycerine.

754. Less light reduces the secretion of hormones from pituitary glands and decreases egg production.

755. Indian goats commonly kid twice in one year and usually thrice in two years.

756. Shortening length of the day induces reproductive activity in goats unlike that of sheep.

757. In India in region with little seasonal difference, the oestrus cycle in goats recur only once in a year.

758. Bringing the buck near the female goats for a short time every morning during breeding season does not help in picking up the shy breeders.

759. Ovulation without external manifestation of estrus is rare in swine.

760. Though external signs of estrus last for 3-4 days or more, but the female accepts the boar usually during 2-3 days.

761. Parity, age, nutrition level and breed do not influence the rate of ovulation in swine.

762. The domesticated pigs have a longer gestation period than that of wiled ones.

763. A high plane of nutrition immediately following breeding enhances embryonic mortality in swine.

764. Farrowing appears to follow pattern, parturition is rare in the morning and early afternoon, more frequent in late afternoon and most frequent at neight.

765. Breeding immediately after farrowing results in very high fertility in sows.

766. Young boars should be limited to one service per day and more than four times a week

767. Rye or wheat straw is preferred to oat straw for bedding of the farrowing pen.

768. Boars should not be allowed to become fat.

769. No lipase are secreted from the stomach glands in pigs.

770. Manganese is not related with normal production in pig.

771. Iodine deficient pigs are stillborn, but with lot of hair.

772. Production efficiency necessitates weaning earlier for fruitful pig rebreeding.

773. Most conventional pig diets fall within the rage of 12-14 MJ DE / kg.

774. Increasing diet protein concentration in pregnant pigs may slightly decrease liveweight gain during pregnancy, but within the normally feasible range CDE : DCP, 1:8-14; DE : CO, 1:9 – 17 will have no effect on number of pigs nor on their birth weights.

775. Biological value governs the effective utilizability of the dietary DCP.

776. The feed allowance, or ration, is the control value for both rate of output and product quality in grown up, but breeding pigs.

777. As young growers (pigs) embody a high potential for lean growth in comparison to appetite, the common problem is one of overeating.

778. A ready guide to weight is the pigs age: specifically, the time spent on a known feed intake.

779. Pregnant females (pigs) are seldom rationed to a flat rate, the amount depending on body condition and environmental circumstances.

780. In pigs, at feeding levels lower than 2 kg, it is possible that the maternal body would need to be used up for purposes of supporting foetal gain.

781. With pigs, reproductive qualities are of high heritability.

782. A housed pig is more environmentally comfortable than a feral pig.

783. Most pigs are farmed intensively, and intensivism is prone to generate animal welfare problems.

784. Feeding arrangements have no relationship with the designs of houses for growing pigs.

785. In housing of pigs, wire mesh floor deals with exereta more conveniently than a deep straw bed.

786. The density of stocking is positively related both with the air temperature and likelihood of one pig being able to lie alongside another to provide a source of mutual warmth.

787. Cold animals (pigs) grow faster, convert food more efficiently and become fatter than warm ones.

788. At cold temperature the pigs divert nutrients from productive processes into body heating.

789. Cold tolerance in pigs is more related to body size than to feed intake.

790. Pregnant females (Pigs) become cold at about 15°C if the floor is solid and there is medium ventilation rate.

791. The sheep breed Wiltshire Horn have heavy fleeces of very fine wool.

792. Merinos breed of sheep has virtually no wool, and that which it has is regularly being cast.

793. The sheep attains sexual maturity at an age of seven months regardless of the type of nutrition.

794. The onset of heat in a ewe is mainly controlled by day length, sexual activity being induced by a shortening of the day length.

795. The mating season in sheep ends when the day length rises above 13-14 hours.

796. Ulike the sow and the cow, ewes show less obvious signs of being in season and the only reliable way to detect heats is to run a ram with the flock.

797. In sheep the permanent incisors are used as a precise guide and measure of age.

798. Two-toothed females (sheep) are also referred to as gimmers or shearling ewes, while the males as shearling rams.

799. The sheep embodies an entire upper lip unlike a cattle beast that has a split upper lip.

800. Volatile fatty acids *viz*., acetic, propionic and butyric acids make no significant contribution as far as total energy needs of the sheep are concerned.

801. The disease lamb dysentery effects only adults, while the parasite nematodirus is lethal to lambs.

802. In sheep, diseases such as scrapie and Johne's disease are present subclinically at an early age, are only manifest in older animals.

803. The sheep grazed for generations on tick infested land have lost hereditary resistance to tick-borne fever.

804. The organism *Fusiformis nodosus* attacks only sheep and goats.

805. Mastitis, in sheep is most commonly caused by *Staphylococcus aurelts*.

806. Enzootic abortion or kebbing (in sheep) is fairly widespread only in United Kingdoms and in no other country.

807. Hypocalcaecia or milk fever in sheep is often associated with hypomagnesaemia.

808. Keeping ewes in good, well-fleshed and firm but not fat condition minimises the incidence of twin lamb disease pregnancy toxaemia.

809. The true wool fibre of the sheep is not shed as is hair but grows continuously.

810. The sheep kept under conditions of limited nutrition as in some semi-arid areas tend to produce coarser wool than similar sheep kept on lush pastures.

811. The fineness of wool is not related to the number of secondary follicles present along with primary follicles in the sheep skin.

III. Tick mark (✓) the correct answer:

812. The bulls of ________ breed of buffalo are extensively used for upgrading inferior stock.
(*a*) Ravi (*b*) Bhadawari
(*c*) Murrah (*d*) Jaffarabadi

813. There are about ________ breeds of cattle in India besides hybrids.
(*a*) 14 (*b*) 20
(*c*) 26 (*d*) 32

814. There are ________ breeds of buffaloes in India, in addition to a large number of non- descripts.
(*a*) 4 (*b*) 6
(*c*) 10 (*d*) 12

815. An examination of the rainfall map of India will show that it is invariably in the higher elevations, and in humid areas that the cattle are ________.
(*a*) Large and non-descript (*b*) Large and well-descript
(*c*) Small and well descript (*d*) Small and non-descript.

816. ________ is a breed of cattle.
(*a*) Bhadawari (*b*) Tharparkar
(*c*) Kashmiri (*d*) Landrace

817. ________ is a breed of buffalo.
(*a*) Berkshire (*b*) Beetal
(*c*) Jaffarabadi (*d*) Sindhi

818. ________ is a breed of goat.
(*a*) Berari (*b*) Large White Yorkshire.
(*c*) Sahiwal (*d*) Nili

819. ________ is a breed of swme.
(*a*) Malvi (*b*) Ravi
(*c*) Gaddi (*d*) Chester White

820. Hereford is a breed of ________.
(*a*) Cattle (*b*) Goat
(*c*) Swine (*d*) Buffalo

821. Durock is a breed of ________.
(*a*) Swine (*b*) Cattle
(*c*) Buffalo (*d*) Goat

822. Tamworth and Middle White Yorkshire are breeds of ________.

(a) Buffalo (b) Goat
(c) Cattle (d) Swine

823. Jamunapari and Barabari are breeds of ________.

(a) Cattle (b) Buffalo
(c) Swine (d) Goat

824. Surti and Beetal are breeds of ________.

(a) Swine (b) Goat
(c) Cattle (d) Buffalo

825. The discovery of living cells would have been difficult, if not impossible; before the compound microscope was invented by Zachaias Jansen of ________ in 1590.

(a) England (b) Poland
(c) France (d) Holland

826. ________ of England applied the term "cell" to the cavities he saw in sections of cork.

(a) Robert Hooke (b) William Winter
(c) Ralph Turner (d) Kleiber Baird

827. Marcello Malpighi in ________ published "Anatomy of Plants", the first systematic study of cell structure.

(a) 1575 (b) 1675
(c) 1775 (d) 1875

828. In 1839, ________, an animal anatomist, formulated the cell theory which set forth the concept that the elementary parts of all tissues are formed of cells though highly diversified in manner.

(a) Robert Hooke (b) Marcello Malphighi
(c) Jheodor Schwam (d) Alred White

829. The nucleus contains ________ per cent of the RNA in the cell.

(a) 4-10 (b) 6-12
(c) 7-71 (d) 8-20

830. The ribosome is composed of two sub-units and has an approximate size of ________ A

(a) 230 (b) 210
(c) 200 (d) 195

831. The Golgi apparatus plays a role in the export of steroids and protein in the ________, since lipoproteinmolecules apparently are exported through the Golgi apparatus.

(a) Cow-liver (b) Goat liver
(c) Rat liver (d) Swine liver.

832. Mitochondria, located throughout the cytoplasm are fried rice shaped objects measuring about ________ Angstrom in length.

(a) 15.000 (b) 12,000
(c) 9,000 (d) 6,000

833. Mitochondria, located throughout the cytoplasm are fried rice shaped objects measuring ________ Angstrom in diameter

(a) 2,000 (b) 3,000
(c) 4,000 (d) 5,000

834. The mitochondria are considered the power house of the cell in the way that they supply over ________ per cent of the energy requirements.

(*a*) 60 (*b*) 70

(*c*) 80 (*d*) 90

835. It has been calculated that mitochondria make up for 18 per cent of the total volume and ________ per cent of the total cytoplasmic volume of the rat liver cell.

(*a*) 16 (*b*) 18

(*c*). 20 (*d*) 22

836. The details of cell reproduction were elucidated in animal cells in the latter part of nineteenth century by ________, and in plants cells by Edward Strasburger and others.

(*a*) F. Haguenau (*b*) A.H. Sparrow

(*c*) Walther Flemming (*d*) A. Zimmerman

837. The first direct evidence showing that the genetic material is DNA rather than protein or RNA was published by O.T. Avery, C.M. Mgc Leod, and M.Mc Carty in ________.

(*a*) 1924 (*b*) 1934

(*c*) 1944 (*d*) 1954

838. The phenomenon of transformation in pneumococcus was discovered by ________ in 1928.

(*a*) Frederick Griffith (*b*) Zimmerman

(*c*) Kornberg Taylor (*d*) Hershey Britten

839. F. Miescher in ________ isolated nucleic acids from the cell nuclei and first called them 'nuclein'.

(*a*) 1849 (*b*) 1869

(*c*) 1889 (*d*) 1909.

840. The correct structure of DNA was first deduced by ________ in 1953.

(*a*) R.I. Britten & C.M.F. Mac Leod (*b*) W. Dressler & M.N.M. Chase

(*c*) J.D. Watson & F.H.C. Crick (*d*) C.R Cantor & F.G.N. Klick.

841. The Visualization of replicating chromosomes was first accomplished by ________ in 1963 using the technique called autoradiography.

(*a*) R.J. Britten (*b*) C.R Cantor

(*c*) A.D. Hershey (*d*) J. Cairns

842. The chromosomes of *Drosophila embryo* replicate within ________ minutes, and the nuclei divide once every 9 to 10 minutes during the early cleavage divisions.

(*a*) 1-2 (*b*) 3-4

(*c*) 5-6 (*d*) 7-8

843. The in *vitro* synthesis of DNA was first accomplished by and his co-workers in 1957.

(*a*) Bill Britten (*b*) Guy Contor

(*c*) Gordon Minor (*d*) Arthur Kornberg

844. DNA containing sequences that repeated more than ________ times is called highly repetitive DNA.

(*a*) 10^3 (*b*) 10^5

(*c*) 10^7 (*d*) 10^9

845. Mendel experimented with crosses among inbred lines of garden pea (*Pisum sativum*) duringthe years ________.

(*a*) 1844-1852 (*b*) 1852-1860

(*c*) 1856-64 (*d*) 1862-70

846. Mendel's experiments were forgotten until 1900 when three Botanists, Corrents (Germany), De Vries (Holland) and Tschermak (Austria) independently rediscovered his paper published in ________..

(*a*) 1866 (*b*) 1868

(*c*) 1870 (*c*) 1872

847. There are only ________ types of bases in a D molecule.

(*a*) Two (*b*) Four

(*c*) Five (*d*) Six

848. Each gene is though to contain 1,000 to 1,500 pair, thus there are at least ________ different ways in which these bases would be ordered into sequences.

(*a*) 4^{100} (*b*) 4^{1000}

(*c*) $4^{10,000}$ (*d*) $4^{100,000}$

849. There are ________ different alleles in the white eye series of *Drosophila.*

(*a*) 4 (*b*) 8

(*c*) 12 (*d*) 16

850. The cellular antigens in cattle have a long series of multiple alleles, numbering about ________...

(*a*) 100 (*b*) 200

(*c*) 300 (*d*) 400

851. The classical Mendelian dihybrid ratio is ________.

(*a*) 9:3:3:1 (*b*) 9:2:3:1

(*c*) 9:2:2:1 (*d*) 9:2:2:2.

852. ________ (1906) first reported an exception to Mendel's law of independent assortment in *Lathyrus odoratus* (sweet pea).

(*a*) White and Haudler (*b*) Batison and Punnet

(*c*) Winter and Funk (*d*) Jurner and Smith.

853. Jersey calves suffering from ________ have broad skull, large eye-sockets, short and broad nasal bones and forehead broader than normal.

(*a*) Aguatha (*b*) Cerebral hernia

(*c*) Umblical hernia (*d*) Bulldog head (prognathism)

854. H. Henking, a ________ biologist in 1891 discovered that a particular nuclear structure (identified as X body) could be traced throughout spermatogenesis of certain insects.

(*a*) Polish (*b*) Dutch

(*c*) German (*d*) French.

855. Sex linkage has two been indicated for more than 200 traits in ________.

(*a*) Cattle (*b*) Sheep

(*c*) Horse (*d*) Humans

856. The sac of the scrotum in bulk is thermoregulatory in function, that is, it provides protection to the testes and maintains them at a temperature lower by ________ °F than the abdomen which is necessary for active spermatogenesis.

(*a*) 2-4 (*b*) 5-7

(*c*) 8-10 (*d*) 11-13.

857. In the case of bulls the seminal vesicles are about ________ cm long 5 cm wide.

(*a*) 16.0-13.5 (*b*) 10.0-12.5

(*c*) 14.0-15.5 (*d*) 13.0-14.5

858. In each ovary (of farm animals) there may be as many ________ folliciles.

(a) 25,000 (b) 50,000

(c) 75,000 (d) 100,000

859. In case of ________, the ovaries are-enclosed by membranous covering which is continuous with the wall of the tube to ensure that the discharged ova passes into the tubes and is not lost into the body.

(a) Dog (b) Cow

(c) Goat (d) Rabbit.

860. In case of cow, the vagina is about ________ cm long.

(a) 7.5-10.0 (b) 12.5-15.0

(c) 16.5-19.0 (d) 20.0-25.0

861. The process of spematogenesis in the male and oogenesis in female finally gives rise to ________ daughter cells.

(a) 2 (b) 4

(c) 6 (d) 8

862. The egg, after the formation of fertilization membrane decreases in diameter by ________ per cent due to the secretion of some fluid.

(a) 4 (b) 8

(c) 11 (d) 14

863. The parathyroid glands were discovered by sondstorm in ________.

(a) 1840 (b) 1860

(c) 1880 (d) 1900

864. ________ compounds have been isolated from the adrenal cortex which are all sterol derivatives.

(a) Twenty-eight (b) Twenty-six

(c) Twenty-four (d) Twenty-seven

865. The cortical hormones control electrolytes as well as water metabolism which helps in retention of ________ in the body.

(a) Iodine (b) Sulphur

(c) Sodium (d) phosphorus

866. The ovary can be examined upto ________ months of pregnancy after which it sinks deeper into abdominal cavity.

(a) one (b) Two

(c) Three (d) Four

867. Dystokia, among the domesticate species is mostly met with in ________.

(a) Dogs (b) Cats

(c) Monkeys (d) Dairy cattle

868. The amount of ________ needed by an adult cow for efficient reproduction is about 10-12 g per day.

(a) Potassium (b) Phosphorus (c) Calcium (d) Sodium

869. The Calcium to phosphorus ratio for the maximum reproduction efficiency in cattle should b tween ________.

(a) 1:2 and 2:1 (b) 1:1 and 3:1

(c) 1:3 and 3:1 (d) 1:4 and 4:1.

870. Vitamins ________ are synthesized by the ruminants in their body.

(a) A and D (b) B and K

(c) E and D (d) C and D

871. ________ per cent of animals contracting bang's disease become either temporarily or permanently sterile.

(a) 10-15 (b) 15-20

(c) 18-23 (d) 25-30

872. The milk exudes from ________ separate gland tubes that open at the base of the "mammary hairs".

(a) 50-95 (b) 100-150

(c) 40-80 (d) 155-195

873. The udder usually increases about ________ in size between milking, depending upon the quality of the udder and the amount of milk secreted.

(a) One-fourth (b) Half

(c) One-third (d) Two-thirds

874. In Holstein cow, between two months and the time of puberty (7-10 months), the mammary gland grows three and half times faster than the body weight and reaches the peak pubertal development at ________ months of age.

(a) 6-8 (b) 10-12

(c) 11-13 (d) 14-16

875. It is estimated that ________ volumes of blood flow through the mammary gland for each volume of milk synthesized.

(a) 600 (b) 500

(c) 400 (d) 300

876. An acceptable record is 70 per cent non-returns upto 60 days after breeding, or 60 per cent non-returns upto ________ days after breeding.

(a) 70 (b) 80

(c) 90 (d) 100

877. A fertile herd takes less than ________ months between calving.

(a) 13 (b) 14

(c) 15 (d) 16

878. A cow during her productive life must remain pregnant only for ________ months in every year

(a) 6 (b) 7

(c) 8 (d) 9

879. In unipara as the cow, mare etc., usually single ovum is released, in sheep one or two and occasionally three, whereas in swine several ova upto ________ are released in a single ovulation.

(a) 15 (b) 20

(c) 25 (d) 30

880. According to legend artificial insemination had its origin in ________ at which time an Arab Chieftain used it to impregnate a prized mare with semen stealthily collected by night from the sheath of an enemy's stallion.

(a) 1310 (b) 1315

(c) 1319 (d) 1322

881. The first scientific research on artificial insemination of domestic animals was conducted with ________ by the Italian psychologist, Lazarro Spallanzani in 1780.

(*a*) Dogs (*b*) Sheep
(*c*) Goats (*d*) Cows

882. The discovery of spermatozoa dates back to ________ when the compound microscope was invented by Leewenhock, the Dutch Naturalist.

(*a*) 1627 (*b*) 1677
(*c*) 1697 (*d*) 1707

883. Mikhail Fyalorovich Ivanoy, a Russian physiologist commenced his investigations on artificial insemination in farm animals as early as ________...

(*a*) 1879 (*b*) 1889
(*c*) 1897 (*d*) 1899

884. In Denmark, Edward Sorensen and Jens Gylling Ham organized the first Cooperative Artificial Breeding Association in ________.

(*a*) 1916 (*b*) 1926
(*c*) 1936 (*d*) 1946

885. Dr Sampath Kumaron employed artificial insemination method for the first time in India in ________ at the Palace Dairy Farm, Mysore.

(*a*) August, 1939 (*b*) September, 1939
(*c*) August, 1938 (*d*) September, 1938

886. "Broad helix" of "Spiral body" or mitochondrial sheath is ________ rich structure believed to be derived from mitochondria.

(*a*) Carbohydrate (*b*) Lipid
(*c*) Protein (*d*) Minerals

887. The human prostatic secretion contains fibrinolysin that is so powerful that 2 cc of the same can liquefy 100 cc of clotted blood in ________ hours at 37°C.

(*a*) 18 (*b*) 16
(*c*) 14 (*d*) 12

888. The prostatic secretion represents the main source of citric acid and acid phosphate for whone ________ semen.

(*a*) Stallion (*b*) Bull
(*c*) Human (*d*) Dog

889. The identification of the seminal sugar as ________ by Mann (1956) opened up the way for detailed studies on its generation capacity of the accessory tissues.

(*a*) Glucose (*b*) Fructose
(*c*) Sucrose (*d*) Ribulose

890. In species viz., ________ semen after ejaculation remains liquid unlike in others wherein it tends to gelate or coagulate shortly after ejaculation

(*a*) Horse and Ass (*b*) Sheep and Goat
(*c*) Bull and Dog (*d*) Cat and Camel

891. Haemacytometer contains in the centre 16 big squares divided into ________ small squares.

(*a*) 128 (*b*) 256
(*c*) 384 (*d*) 512

892. The percentage of abnormal semen in a normal bull should not exceed ________.

(*a*) 21-26 (*b*) 5-12
(*c*) 15-20 (*d*) 26-30

893. Roughages are feeds embodying more than ________ per cent of crude fibre.

(*a*) 24 (*b*) 22
(*c*) 20 (*d*) 18

894. In practice, the food value of ether extract has been taken as yielding ________ Kcal of gross energy per gramme of the product while carbohydrates and proteins yield about five Kcal per gramme.

(*a*) 6.35 (*b*) 7.35
(*c*) 8.35 (*d*) 9.35

895. The term protein (from Greek word *protrus*) was suggested in 1840 by ________.

(*a*) Mulder (*b*) Shudder
(*c*) Coleure (*d*) Watemail

896. There may be about upto ________ different enzymes in a single cell.

(*a*) 250 (*b*) 500
(*c*) 750 (*d*) 1,000

897. Wool is rich in cystine and contains ________ per cent of sulphur.

(*a*) 1.5 (*b*) 2.0
(*c*) 3.0 (*d*) 4.0

898. About ________ per cent of the plasma copper is firmly bound to an alpha-2 globulin as ceruloplasmin, the form in which it is transported in the body.

(*a*) 96 (*b*) 94
(*c*) 92 (*d*) 90

899. As early as ________, a Swiss physician, J. Francois Coindet, first recommended iodine as a remedy for goiter.

(*a*) 1800 (*b*) 1820
(*c*) 1840 (*d*) 1860

900. By late ________ synthetic vitamin A became available on the commercial market.

(*a*) 1925 (*b*) 1930
(*c*) 1935 (*d*) 1940

901. Vitamin K was identified by ________ in 1935 as a factor present in green leaves.

(*a*) Dam (*b*) Dixon
(*c*) Dukes (*d*) Diggins

902. Jansen and Donath in ________ succeeded in crystalizing vitamin B_1 in pure form.

(*a*) 1906 (*b*) 1916
(*c*) 1926 (*d*) 1936

903. Vitamin B_6 (pyridoxine) was isolated by Kerestezy (1938) and its synthesis was accomplished by ________ in U.S.A.

(*a*) Elvehjem and Funk (*b*) Christian and Williams
(*c*) Harris and Folkers (*d*) Kerestezy and Gyorgy

904. Pantothenic acid was isolated by ________ (1930) and synthesized by Merk and company in 1940.
(*a*) Harris et al (*b*) Williams et al
(*c*) Funk et al (*d*) Christian et al.

905. Folic acid deficiency was first described by ________ as a "tropical macrocytic anaemia" observed in pregnant women patients in Mumbai (India) whose diet consisted primarily of white rice and bread.
(*a*) Wills, 1911 (*b*) Willis, 1921
(*c*) Wills, 1931 (*d*) Wills, 1941

906. The intestine represents a long tube approximately ________ feet long in average dairy cattle.
(*a*) 180 (*b*) 160
(*c*) 200 (*d*) 220

907. Rumination is a long process and occupies about ________ hours out of 24 ...hours.
(*a*) 6 (*b*) 7
(*c*) 8 (*d*) 9

908. The large intestine of ________ is the shortest and simplest of all the domestic animals.
(*a*) Cat (*b*) Dog
(*c*) Cow (*d*) Horse

909. The rate of gas production in the rumen is most rapid immediately after meal and in the cow may exceed ________ per hour.
(*a*) 15 (*b*) 20
(*c*) 25 (*d*) 30

910. It has been estimated that the human stomach wall is. replete with ________ glands.
(*a*) 100,000.000 (*b*) 150,000,000
(*c*) 300,000,000 (*d*) 350,000,000

911. In bovine ________ per cent of the total rumen bacteria. have a proteolytic activity.
(*a*) 32 (*b*) 34
(*c*) 36 (*d*) 38

912. In tail to tail system of barn arrangement ________ per cent of time is spent behind the cows.
(*a*) 40 (*b*) 50
(*c*) 60 (*d*) 70

913. The central walk (of a cow stall) should have a width of 5-6 feet exclusive of gutters when cows face out, and ________ feet when they face in.
(*a*) 2-3 (*b*) 3-4
(*c*) 4-5 (*d*) 1.5-2

914. The manure gutter should have a gradient of one inch for every ________.feet length.
(*a*) 15 (*b*) 14
(*c*) 12 (*d*) 10

915. A calving box should have an area of about ________ square feet with ample of soft bedding.
(*a*) 100s-50 (*b*) 75-95
(*c*) 60-75' (*d*) 45-55

916. An area of 100 square feet per head for an young stock of ________ calves and an increase of 50 square feet for every additional calf makes a good *paddock*.

(*a*) 12 (*b*) 10
(*c*) 8 (*d*) 6

917. A system of grazing known as Henbenhein system was developed in ________.

(*a*) Holland (*b*) Poland
(*c*) England (*d*) Germany

918. Bone meal upto ________ q/ha is supposed to be the best fertilizer for pastures.

(*a*) 7-8 (*b*) 5-6
(*c*) 3-4 (*d*) 2-3

919. The digestibility of colostrum increases when it is given at a temperature between ________ of

(*a*) 89-92 (*b*) 93-98
(*c*) 97-98 (*d*) 99-102

920. In electrical dehorning the rod embodies an automatic control to maintain the temperature at about ________ °F and its application to horn button for 10 seconds destroys the horn cells.

(*a*) 1,000 (*b*) 900
(*c*) 800 (*d*) 700

921. The best time for castration of calves, lambs and pigs is between ________, 2 and 1 weeks respectively.

(*a*) 2-4 (*b*) 5-7
(*c*) 8-10 (*d*) 11-13

922. On attainment of maturity, between first and second year a bull can serve ________ cows if properly spaced in respect of time interval.

(*a*) 18 (*b*) 20
(*c*) 23 (*d*) 25

923. Ordinarily, lambs are not used for servicing until ________ months of age.

(*a*) 20 (*b*) 18
(*c*) 16 (*d*) 14

924. Boars reach sexual maturity between ________ days.

(*a*) 60-90 (*b*) 100-180
(*c*) 190-200 (*d*) 210-220

925. Cows come in heat regularly at intervals of 16-24 days and heat losts ________ hours.

(*a*) 8-12 (*b*) 13-15
(*c*) 16-20 (*d*) 21-24

926. In most of the cows ovulation occurs ________ hours after the end of heat.

(*a*) 5-9 (*b*) 10-14
(*c*) 15-17 (*d*) 18-20

927. Ewes remain in heat for about ________ hours and ovulate shortly before the end of heat.

(*a*) 20 (*b*) 25
(*c*) 30 (*d*) 33

928. A lose of 10 per cent of water causes restlessness, trembling and weakness, and loss of ________ per cent of water results in death through thirst.

(*a*) 14-16 (*b*) 17-19
(*c*) 20-22 (*d*) 23-25

929. Dairy cows and buffaloes require ________ gallons of water per diem and an additional amount of about one kilogram need be allowed for each pound (nearly half a kilogram) of milk produced.

(*a*) 4-5 (*b*) 5-6
(*c*) 7-8 (*d*) 9-10

930. Barned variety of Plymoth Rock was developed in about ________ from the cross of the Dominique and Black Cochin breeds.

(*a*) 1835 (*b*) 1845
(*c*) 1855 (*d*) 1865

931. The poultry breed New Hampshire was developed both for meat and egg production in New Hampshire from single comb Rhode Island Red and Red and Red Stock during ________.

(*a*) 1910 (*b*) 1920
(*c*) 1930 (*d*) 1940

932. The poultry breed New Hampshire developed in ________ about 200 years ago, primarily as a table bird.

(*a*) Poland (*b*) Holland
(*c*) New Zealand (*d*) England

933. The commercial egg farms in India maintain Austro White, a cross between ________.

(*a*) Australorp male × White Leghorn female (*b*) Australorp male × Langshan female
(*c*) Australorp male × New Hampshire female (*d*) Australorp male × Wyandotte female

934. Artificial hatching was practised some ________ years ago in China and Egypt.

(*a*) 2,500 (*b*) 3,000
(*c*) 3,500 (*d*) 4,000

935. In 1770, an Englishman named ________, hatched chicks by passing hot air through the room where the eggs were located.

(*a*) John Watchman (*b*) John William
(*c*) John Champion (*d*) John Laggard

936. Bonneman, a French physician, in ________ hatched chicks by heating a hatching oven with circulated hot water.

(*a*) 1770 (*b*) 1777
(*c*) 1779 (*d*) 1787

937. The most convenient folding unit to house poultry is the one made for ________ hens.

(*a*) 15 (*b*) 20
(*c*) 25 (*d*) 30

938. It takes a bout 2.5 hours for feed to go from mouth to cloaca in the laying hen, and ________ hours in a non-laying hen.

(*a*) 4 (*b*) 6
(*c*) 8 (*d*) 10

939. By Water-glass and lime-water methods eggs can be preserved' for about ________ months.

(*a*) 2 (*b*) 4
(*c*) 6 (*d*) 8

940. Dipping of eggs in hot water at a temperature of 135-145 °F of for about ________ minutes kills the germ of the egg.

(*a*) 10 (*b*) 15
(*c*) 20 (*d*) 25

941. Provision of ________ hours of light artificial or natural maximizes egg' production.

(*a*) 10 (*b*) 12
(*c*) 14 (*d*) 16

942. Exposure of hens to brilliant light say ________ watt-bulb flashed on for 15 seconds effectively stimulates winter egg production.

(*a*) 750 (*b*) 1,000
(*c*) 1,250 (*d*) 1,500

943. In goats oestrus is usually 24-48 hours, but in certain breeds like Indian Beetal may be as short as ________ hours on an average.

(*a*) 18 (*b*) 16
(*c*) 14 (*d*) 12

944. Breeding of goats at the age from ________ months yields good results.

(*a*) 8-12 (*b*) 14-18
(*c*) 10.13 (*d*) 19-22

945. The average life of a goat is usually ________ years and should give milk for about ten lactations.

(*a*) 8 (*b*) 10
(*c*) 12 (*d*) 14

946. A well fed buck keeps fit for breeding till ________ years of age.

(*a*) 5-7 (*b*) 8-10
(*c*) 11.13 (*d*) 14-16

947. The ________ is the most economical animal to keep.

(*a*) Cow (*b*) buffalo
(*c*) Swine (*d*) Goat

948. ________ are excellent feed convertors

(*a*) Goats (*b*) Sheep
(*c*) Pigs (*d*) Hens

949. One kilogram of work can be produced on ________ kilograms of feed.

(*a*) 1.5-2.0 (*b*) 2.5-3.5
(*c*) 4.0-4.5 (*d*) 5.0-5.5

950. The best single measures of the ability of a sow to produce is the weight of her litter at ________ day. the usual weaning time.

(*a*) 60 (*b*) 58
(*c*) 56 (*d*) 54

951. The diameter of mature follicles is about ________ mm.

(*a*) 4-5 (*b*) 7-8

(*c*) 9-10 (*d*) 11-12

952. The diameter of sow-corpora lutea is about 15-18 cm, while the body of the uterus is about ________ cm long.

(*a*) 3 (*b*) 4

(*c*) 5 (*d*) 6

953. Most of the gilts reach puberty between ________ months.

(*a*) 4-5 (*b*) 6-8

(*c*) 9-10 (*d*) 11-12

954. The mammary glands in sow are ________ number, are arranged along the belly in two rows.

(*a*) 14-16 (*b*) 10-12

(*c*) 6-8 (*d*) 17-19

955. In sow fertilization occurs only ________ hours after mating.

(*a*) 2-5 (*b*) 6-10

(*c*) 11-13 (*d*) 14-15

956. The pH of the duodenal juice from pigs ranges from ________.

(*a*) 4.5-5.6 (*b*) 6.2-7.9

(*c*) 8.4-8.9 (*d*) 8.0-8.2

957. A value of ________ per cent of calcium in the diet is probably adequate in both male and female breeding swine.

(*a*) 0.45 (*b*) 0.55

(*c*) 0.65 (*d*) 0.75

958. The role of zinc in preventing skin lesions (parakeratosis in pigs) was first reported by Tucker and Salmon in ________.

(*a*) 1935 (*b*) 1945

(*c*) 1955 (d) 1965

959. The onset of puberty in a female (swine) normally occurs at around ________ days of age and 90 kg of liveweight.

(*a*) 160 (*b*) 170

(*c*) 180 (*d*) 190

960. Most of the growth of the unborn young pig is during last ________ days of pregnancy.

(*a*) 20 (*b*) 30

(*c*) 40 (*d*) 50

961. The energy value of swine milk is ________ MJ/R and total solid contents of 20g / 100g of fresh milk.

(*a*) 2.5 (*b*) 3.5

(*c*) 4.5 (*d*) 5.5

962. Pig milk contains ________ per cent fat, 5 per cent milk sugar, and 6 per cent protein.

(*a*) 10 (*b*) 8

(*c*) 6 (*d*) 5

963. The lactating pig can produce ________ g of protein in her milk every day.

(*a*) 50-100 (*b*) 110-220

(*c*) 350-375 (d) 400-500

964. The quantitative production of pig response to a change in feed dose. lies at the core of a computer model developed at the university of ________ in 1970.

(*a*) Michigan (*b*) Kansas

(*c*) Edinburgh (*d*) California

965. It has been estimated that half a dozen average-size pigs win throw off the energy at the rate of about 1 kWh which should be actively dispersed to maintain normal body temperature at ________ °C

(*a*) 39 (*b*) 38

(*c*) 37 (*d*) 40

966. Gestation period in pregnant ewes last ________ days.

(*a*) 135 (*b*) 140

(*c*) 147 (*d*) 170

967. The number of lambs born per ewe, on an average rise until the age of ________ years.

(*a*) 6 (*b*) 5

(*c*) 4 (*d*) 3

968. For most of the farm animals the ratio is of the order of ________ parts by weight of water to every one part of dry matter eaten.

(*a*) 1-2 (*b*) 3-4

(*c*) 5-6 (*d*) 7-8

969. ________ poisoning is common in areas of U.S.A. where it is known as alkali disease, or blind staggers.

(*a*) Cobalt (*b*) Chlorine

(*c*) Magnesium (*d*) Selenium

970. The finest woolled sheep of the Down breeds and the South down (of Britain), has a count of ________ microns - (1000000 microns = 1 meter).

(*a*) 27-28 (*b*) 25-26

(*c*) 23-24 (*d*) 29-30

971. Wool yields vary from about 1.3 kg for a Welsh ewe to 2.6 kg for a Suffolk and ________ kg for an English Leicester.

(*a*) 3 (*b*) 4

(*c*) 5 (*d*) 6

IV. Match the following :

972. Match the somatic chromosome number with species

(*a*) 4	(*i*) Horse
(*b*) 38	(*ii*) Dog
(*c*) 64	(*iii*) *Ascaris megalocephala*
(*d*) 78	(*iv*) Pig

973. *Somatic chromosome number* — *Species*

(*a*) 78 — (*i*) Sheep
(*b*) 54 — (*ii*) Cattle
(*c*) 60 — (*iii*) Human beings
(*d*) 46 — (*iv*) hens

974. Match the time-period of gene expression of the following:

(*a*) Short tail in sheep-lamb — (*i*) After maturity (25-30 years of age)
(*b*) Eye colour in humans — (*ii*) Past 50 years of age
(*c*) Hereditary boldness (humans) — (*iii*) Embryonic life
(*d*) Huntington's chorea (Humans) — (*iv*) A few weeks after birth

975. Match the sex chromosome number with the animals embodying it :

(*a*) 23 pairs — (*i*) Cattle
(*b*) 30 pairs — (*ii*) Sheep
(*b*) 27 pairs — (*iii*) Wheat
(*d*) 21 pairs — (*iv*) Human

976. Match the transformative process of spermatids into sperms with each as given below:

(*a*) Golgi bodies plus centrosomal material forms a complex body — (*i*) An inner chromophobic mass forms a complex body.
(*b*) Golgi idiosomes comprise (heavily staining) — (*ii*) Numerous granular mitochondria
(*c*) An outer chromophilic (heavily staining) — (*iii*) Idiosomes lying next to nucleus
(*d*) Throughout the cytoplasm are in ting vacuole. — (*iv*) Two chomosomes and paracrosomic granules each

977. Match tbe beat-period with the animal.

(*a*) 12-24 Hours — (*i*) Ewe
(*b*) 1-2 days — (*ii*) Mare
(*c*) 4-5 days — (*iii*) Sow
(*d*) 2-3 days — (*iv*) Cow

978. Match the hormone with its function.

(*a*) Pancreatropic — (*i*) Antagonistic to insulin
(*b*) Ketogenic — (*ii*) Stimulates smooth muscles
(*c*) Diabetogenic — (*iii*) Controls growth and activity of islets of langerhans
(*d*) Oxytocin — (*iv*) Mobilizes fats

979. Match the term used in parturition with the animal.

(*a*) Foaling — (*i*) Ewe
(*b*) Lambing — (*ii*) Sow
(*c*) Farrowing — (*iii*) Bitch
(*d*) Whelping — (*iv*) Marc

980. Match the disease with the symptom (s).

(*a*) Salpingitis — (*i*) Uterus inflammation
(*b*) Piosalpingitis — (*ii*) Pus accumulation in uterus
(*c*) Metritis — (*iii*) Fallopian tube-inflammations
(*d*) Pyometra — (*iv*) Pus-filled fallopian tube

981 Match the percentage with the component as estimated in colostrum.

(*a*) 14.0	(*i*) sugar (lactose)
(*b*) 2.7	(*ii*) Fat
(*c*) 6.7	(*iii*) Total solids
(*d*) 23.9	(*iv*) Protein

982.

Per cent component	*Cow's milk (Indian)*
(*a*) 13.52	(*i*) Fat
(*b*) 2.78.	(*ii*) Total solids
(*c*) 4.56.	(*iii*) Lactose (sugar)
(*d*) 3.67.	(*iv*) Protein

983.

Per cent component	*Cow's milk (Western)*
(*a*) 4.83	(*i*) Sugar (lactose)
(*b*) 3.42	(*ii*) Total solids
(*c*) 4.78	(*iii*) Fat
(*d*) 12.69	(*iv*) Protein

984.

Per cent component	*Human milk*
(*a*) 11.8	(*i*) Sugar (lactose)
(*b*) 3.7	(*ii*) Total solids
(*c*) 1.3	(*iii*) Fat
(*d*) 6.8	(*iv*) Protein

985.

Per cent component	*Goat's milk*
(*a*) 4.5	(*i*) Fat
(*b*) 3.2	(*ii*) Protein
(*c*) 3.9	(*iii*) Total solids
(*d*) 12.1	(*iv*) sugar (lactose)

986. Match the reproductive rate (s) with the animals (s).

(*a*) One offspring/year	(*i*) Sheep and goat
(*b*) One to three progeny/year	(*ii*) Swine
(*c*) Ten progeny twice/year	(*iii*) Poutry
(*d*) 100 or more progeny/year	(*iv*) Cattle, buffalo, horse

987. Match the relative selection intensity with the number of traits when it is $1/\sqrt{n}$.

(*a*) 0.71	(*i*) 4
(*b*) 0.58	(*ii*) 2
(*c*) 0.50	(*iii*) 16
(*d*) 0.25	(*iv*) 3

988. Match the animals breed with the parents.

(*a*) Hisardale, sheep	(*i*) Lincoln rams × lRambouilletewes
(*b*) Columbia	(*ii*) Tamworth × Landrace
(*c*) Panama	(*iii*) Bikaneri owes × Merino rams
(*d*) Minnesota No.1, swine	(*iv*) Rambouillet rams × Lincoln ewes

989. Match the worker and with the observation/scientific attempt in the field of artificial insemination.

(*a*) Provest and Dumas, 1824	(*i*) Investigated problems of telegony in a bitch
(*b*) Hunter. 1792	(*ii*) Studied biochemical nature of spermatozoa
(*c*) Plonnis, 1876	(*iii*) Produced pregnancy in a human female
(*d*) Miescher, 1897	(*iv*) Proved spermatozoa as main agent for fertilization

990. Match the year with the event in the artificial insemination

(*a*) 1939	(*i*) Experimental work started on A.I.
(*b*) 1942	(*ii*) Establishment of AI. centers by GOI
(*c*) 1945	(*iii*) Sahiwal cows impregnated by A.I. successfully
(*d*) 1940	(*iv*) First A.I. in cows

991. Match the animal with the average volume of ejaculate per CC

(*a*) Bull	(*i*) 5-100
(*b*) Ram	(*ii*) 200-250
(*c*) Stallion	(*iii*) 4.0
(*d*) Boar	(*iv*) 0.1-1.5
(*e*) Cock	(*v*) 1.0

992. Match the animal with average concentration of ejaculated semen per C.C. in million.

(*a*) Bull	(*i*) 800-4000
(*b*) Ram	(*ii*) 25-1000
(*c*) Stallion	(*iii*) 600-1200
(*d*) Boar	(*iv*) 0.5-0;6
(*e*) Cock	(*v*) 50-200

993. Match the animal with ejaculated semen storage survival time with retention of fertilizing capacity expressed in days.

(*a*) Bull	(*i*) 1-2
(*b*) Ram	(*ii*) 4-6
(*c*) Stallion	(*iii*) Always use fresh
(*d*) Boar	(*iv*) 0.25
(*e*) Cock	(*v*) 5-7

994. Match the animal with the number of females impregnable artificially particulate.

(*a*) Bull	(*i*) 40-100
(*b*) Ram	(*ii*) 4-8
(*c*) Stallion	(*iii*) 6-10
(*d*) Boar	(*iv*) 8-12
(*e*) Cock	(*v*) 100-600

995. Match the shape of the head of spermatozoa with the animal which pertains to ________.

(*a*) Ovoid	(*i*) Fowl
(*b*) Like elongated cylinder	(*ii*) Human species
(*c*) Like a hook	(*iii*) Bull, ram, boar and rabbit
(*d*) Fattened oval body	(*iv*) Mouse and rat

996. Match the average semen-volume per ejaculation with the animal.

(*a*) Bull	(*i*) 0.6 ml
(*b*) Ram	(*ii*) 100 ml
(*c*) Stallion	(*iii*) 1 ml
(*d*) Boar	(*iv*) 200 ml
(*e*) Cock	(*v*) 5 ml

997. Match the osmotic pressure expressed in terms of freezing point depression (°C) with the animal.

(*a*) 0.55-0.58	(*i*) Ram
(*b*) 0.54-0.73	(*ii*) Man
(*c*) 0.55-0.70	(*iii*) Rabbit
(*d*) 0.58-0.62	(*iv*) Bull
(*e*) 0.55-0.59	(*v*). Stallion

998. *Osmotic Pressure* *Animal*

(*a*) 0.55-0.59	(*i*) Dog
(*b*) 0.56-0.60	(*ii*) Jack, ass
(*c*) 0.59-0.63	(*iii*) Rabbit
(*d*) 0.56-0.62	(*iv*) Boar
(*e*) 0.54-0.73	(*v*) Bull

999. Bernstein and Shergin (1936) detennined the electro-conductivity values of semen at 25°C expressed in reciprocal ohms × 10^{-4}, match the value with the animal.

(*a*) 89.5-116.3	(*i*) Stallion
(*b*) 48.5-80.5	(*ii*) Dog
(*c*) 111.3-129.5	(*iii*) Man
(*d*) 129.0-138.0	(*iv*) Bull
(*c*). 88.0-107.0	(*v*) Ram

1000. *E.C* at 25°C (*Reciprocal ohm* × 10^{-4}) *Animal*

(*a*) 123.3-134.6	(*i*) Stallion
(*b*) 85.5-101.4	(*ii*) Boar
(*c*) 89.5-116.3	(*iii*) Dog
(*d*) 111.3-129.5	(*iv*) Rabbit
(*c*) 129.0-138.0	(*v*) Bull

1001. Match the frequency of occurrence or its effect on the bacterium in the semen of a bull.

(*a*) *Diptheroids*	(*i*) Frequently
(*b*) *Staphylococci*	(*ii*) Detrimental
(*c*) *Psedomonas aeriginosa*	(*iii*) Predominast
(*d*) *E. Coli*	(*iv*) Occasionally

1002. Match the source of development with the semen diluent.

(*a*) Egg-yolk phosphate	(*i*) Salisbury et al. (1941)
(*b*) Egg-yolk citrate	(*ii*) Almquist (1952)
(*c*) Homogenized cow's milk	(*iii*) Roy and Bishop (1954)
(*d*) Glycine plus egg-yolk	(*iv*) Phillips and Lardy (1939-40)
(*e*) Colloidon-filtered sea-water	(*v*) In France, (1958)

1003. Match the protein contents (per cent) with the concentrate (feed).

(*a*) Wheat bran	(*i*) 20.0
(*b*) Rice bran	(*ii*) 25.0
(*c*) Chikpea *Chuni*	(*iii*) 12.0
(*d*) Linseed cake	(*iv*) 46.0
(*e*) Groundnut cake	(*v*) 10—15

1004. Match the feeding stuff with digestibility coefficient.

(*a*) Egyptian clover	(*i*) 61
(*b*) Gucnea grass	(*ii*) 45
(*c*) Maize (feed)	(*iii*) 81
(*d*) Mixed grass hay	(*iv*) Zero
(*e*) Rice/wheat straw	(*v*) 58

1005.

Constituent (grain/seed)	*Digestibility coefficient*
(*a*) Barley and Oats	(*i*) 68
(*b*) Maize	(*ii*) 78
(*c*) Chickpea	(*iii*) 70
(*d*) Cotton seed	(*iv*) 74
(*e*) Cowpea hay	(*v*) 66

1006.

Constituent	*Digestibility coefficient*
(*a*) Mustard cake	(*i*) 92
(*b*) Rape cake	(*ii*) 84
(*c*) Sesame cake	(*iii*) 90
(*d*) Groundnut cake	(*iv*) 55
(*e*) Maize silage	(*v*) 85

1007.

Constituent	*Crude protein* (*Per cent*)
(*a*) Fish meal	(*i*) 14.0
(*b*) Rice bran	(*ii*) 17.4
(*c*) Wheat bran	(*iii*) 51.8
(*d*) Berseem (feed)	(*iv*) 70.1
(*e*) Groundnut cake	(*v*). 11.4

1008.

Constituent	*Crude protein* (*Per cent*)
(*a*) Sesame Cake	(*i*) 18.1
(*b*) Rape Cake	(*ii*) 36.1
(*c*) Mustard Cake	(*iii*) 46.3
(*d*) Cottonseed	(*iv*) 36.4
(*e*) Chikpea grain	(*v*) 18.0

1009.

Constituent	*Crude protein* (*Per cent*)
(*a*) Oats grain	(*i*) 9.5
(*b*) Barley grain	(*ii*) 3.3
(*c*) Rice straw	(*iii*) 10.1
(*d*) Wheat straw	(*iv*) 14.0
(*e*) Rice bran	(*v*) 3.8

1010. *Constituent* — *Crude protein (Per cent)*

(*a*) Cowpea hay — (*i*) 7.9
(*b*) Mixed grass hay — (*ii*) 17.4
(*c*) Maize feed — (*iii*) 7.6
(*d*) Maize silage — (*iv*) 15.3
(*e*) Berseem — (*v*) 5.1

1011. *Constituent* — *Digestibility coefficient total carbohy drate (per cent)*

(*a*) Berseem feed — (*i*) 57
(*b*) Guinea grass — (*ii*) 72
(*c*) Maize feed — (*iii*) 70
(*d*) Maize silage — (*iv*) 59
(*e*) Cowpea hay — (*v*) 72

1012. *Constituent* — *Digestibility coefficient total carbohy-drate (per cent)*

(*a*) Wheat straw — (*i*) 60
(*b*) Barley grain — (*ii*) 74
(*c*) Oats grain — (*iii*) 52
(*d*) Chickpea grain — (*iv*) 90
(*e*) Cotton seed — (*v*) 88

1013. *Constituent* — *Digestibility coefficient total carbohy drate (per cent)*

(*a*) Mustard cake — (*i*) 77.
(*b*) Rape cake — (*ii*) 66
(*c*) Cotton cake — (*iii*) 80
(*d*) Wheat bran — (*iv*) 42
(*e*) Fish meal — (*v*) 70

1014. *Constituent* — *Nutritive ratio*

(*a*) Berseem feed — (*i*) 10.5
(*b*) Guinea grass feed — (*ii*) 16.8
(*c*) Maize feed — (*iii*) 22.0
(*d*) Maize silage — (*iv*) 3.6
(*e*) Mixed grass hay. — (*v*) 13.2

1015. *Constituent* — *Nutritive ratio*

(*a*) Cowpea hay — (*i*) 9.0
(*b*) Barley grain — (*ii*) 3.9
(*c*) Oats grain — (*iii*) 10.5
(*d*) Maize grain — (*iv*) 6.0
(*e*) Chickpea grain — (*v*) 10.7

1016. *Constituent* — *Nutritive ratio*

Constituent	Nutritive ratio
(*a*) Cotton seed	(*i*) 1.7
(*b*) Mustard cake	(*ii*) 1.0
(*c*) Rape cake	(*iii*) 0.7
(*d*) Sesame cake	(*iv*) 1.8
(*e*) Groundnut cake	(*v*) 6.1

1017. *Constituent* — *Nutritive ratio*

Constituent	Nutritive ratio
(*a*) Wheat bran	(*i*) 0.2
(*b*) Rice bran	(*ii*) 22.0
(*c*) Fish meal	(*iii*) 7.1
(*d*) Mixed grass hay	(*iv*) 9.0
(*e*) Oats grain	(*v*) 7.3

1018. Match the one gramme of substance oxidized with the metabolic water produced (gramme)

Substance	*Metabolic water*
(*a*) Glucose	(*i*) 0.77
(*b*) Starch	(*ii*) 1.11
(*c*) Tributrin	(*iii*) 0.56
(*d*) Tristearin	(*iv*) 0.42
(*e*) Protein (average)	(*v*) 0.60

1019. Match the saturated fatty acids with its common source.

(*a*) Butyric acid (C_3H_7COOH)	(*i*) Coconut oil
(*b*) Caproic acid ($C_5H_{11}COOH$)	(*ii*) Palm oil
(*c*) Caprylic acid ($C_7H_{15}COOH$)	(*iii*) Not known
(*d*) Lauric acid ($C_{11}H_{23}COOH$)	(*iv*) Milk fat
(*e*) Palmitic acid ($C_{15}H_{31}COOH$)	(*v*) Mutton tallow
(*f*) Stearic acid ($C_{17}H_{35}COOH$)	(*vi*) Butter fat.
(*g*) Arachidic acid ($C_{19}H_{39}COOH$)	(*vii*) Laurel kernel oil

1020. Match the unsaturated fatty acids with its common source.

(*a*) Palmetoleic acid ($C_{15}H_{29}COOH$)	(*i*) Linseed oil
(*b*) Oleic acid ($C_{17}H_{33}COOH$)	(*ii*) Glandular organs
(*c*) Linoleic acid ($C_{17}H_{31}COOH$)	(*iii*) Milk fat.
(*d*) Linolenic acid ($C_{17}C_{29}COOH$)	(*iv*) soybean oil
(*e*) Arachidonic acid ($C_{19}H_{31}COOH$)	(*v*) Pork fat

1021. Match the chemical structure with the amino acid.

(*a*) Proline (*i*)

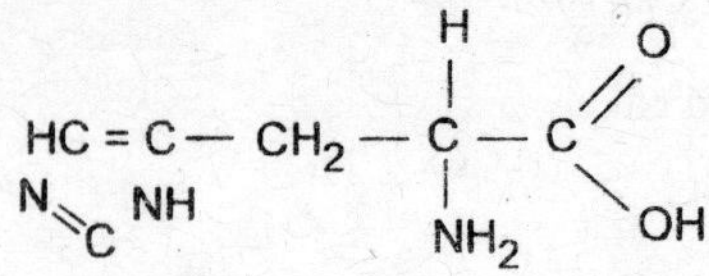

(*b*) Methionine (*ii*)

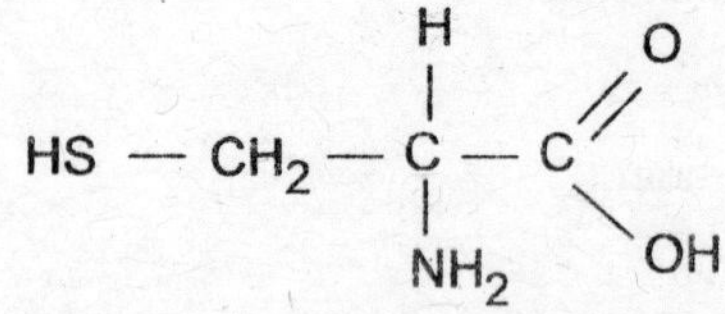

(*c*) Lysine (*iii*)

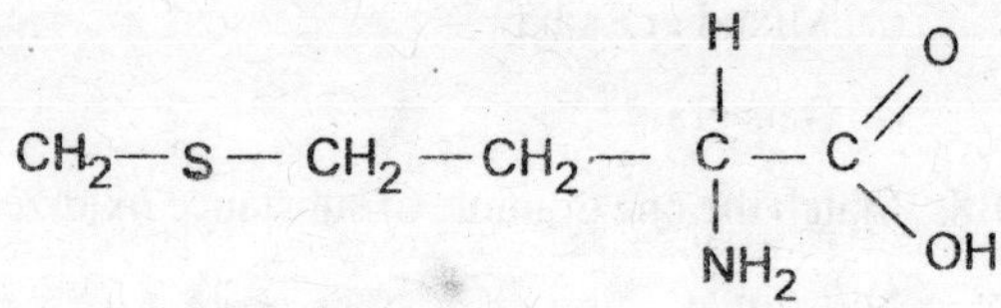

(*d*) Histidine (*iv*)

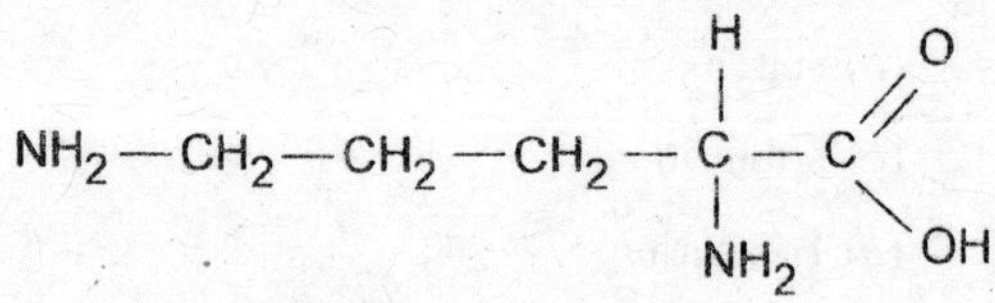

(*e*) Cysteine (*v*)

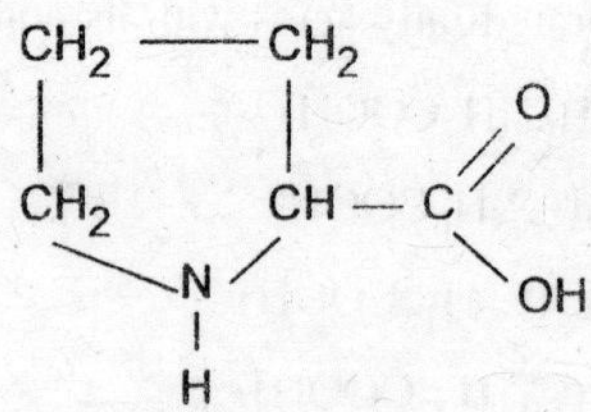

1022. *Chemical structure* *Amino acid*

(*a*) Aspartic (*i*)

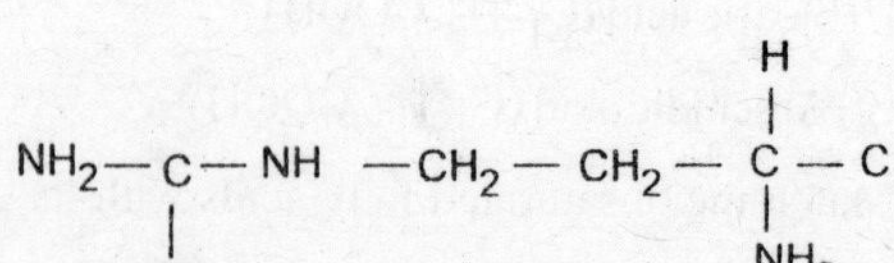

(*b*) Glutamic (*ii*)

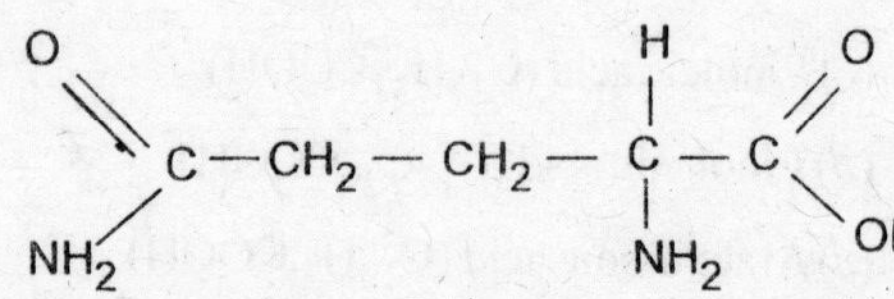

(*c*) Arginine (*iii*) 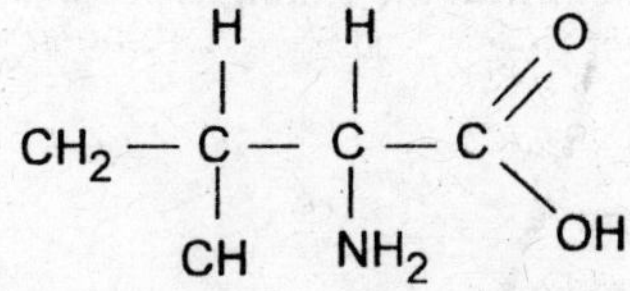

(*d*) Glutamine (Asp H_2) (*iv*) 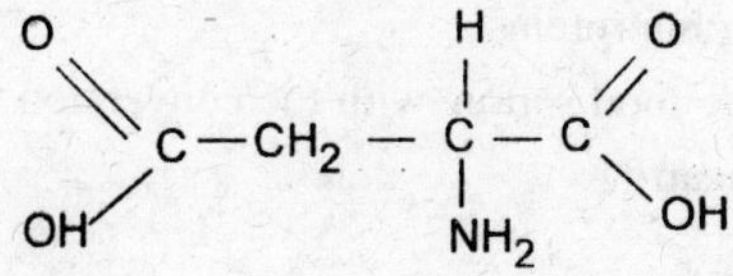

(*e*) Threonine (*v*) 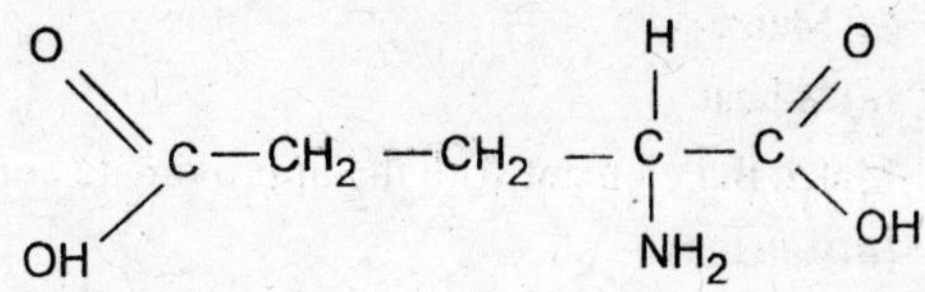

1023. *Chemical structure* *Amino acid*

(*a*) Glycine (*i*) 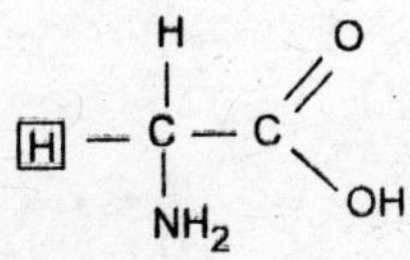

(*b*) Alanine (*ii*) 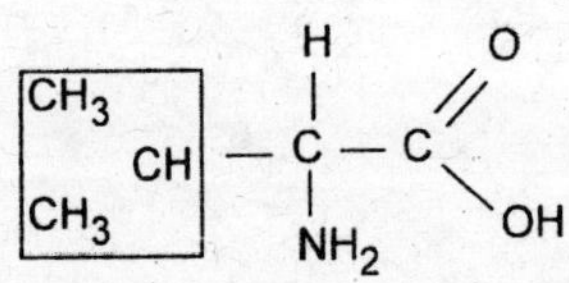

(*c*) Valine (*iii*) 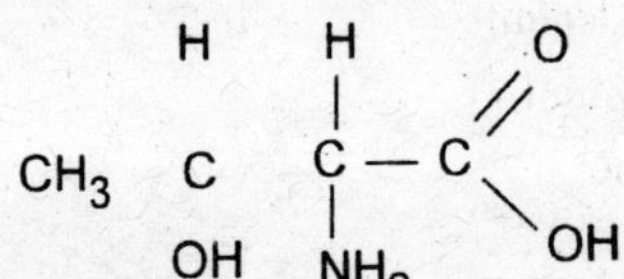

(*d*) Leucine (*iv*) 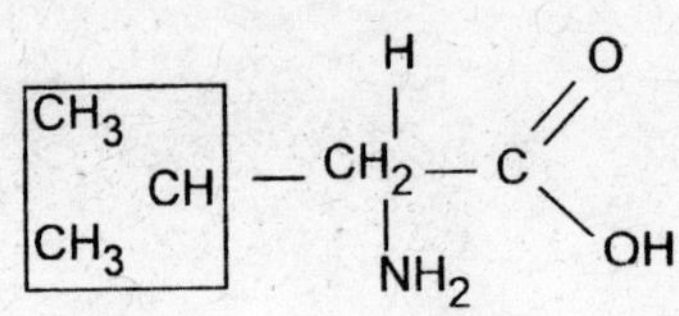

(*e*) Threonine (*v*) 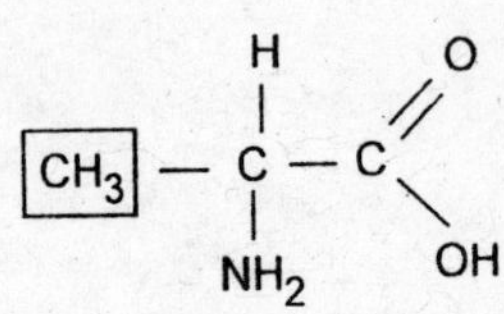

1024. Match the protein with the example/occurrence.

(*a*) Histones	(*i*) Serum alpha and beta
(*b*) Collagens	(*ii*) Casein of milk
(*c*) Glycoprotein	(*iii*) Tendons
(*d*) Chromoproteins	(*iv*) Nucleoprotein
(*e*) Phosphoproteins	(*v*) Hemoglobin

1025. Match the food source with the conversion factor for converting nitrogen into crude protein.

(*a*) Soybean	(*i*) 5.30
(*b*) Milk	(*ii*) 6.25
(*c*) Cotton seed	(*iii*) 5.71
(*d*) Maize	(*iv*) 5.83
(*e*) Wheat	(*v*) 6.38

1026. Match the element with the approximate concentration (per cent) found in animal body.

(*a*) Calcium	(*i*) 0.2
(*b*) Phosphorus	(*ii*) 0.16
(*c*) Potassium	(*iii*) 1.0
(*d*) Sodium	(*iv*) 0.15
(*e*) Sulphur	(*v*) 1.5

1027.

Element	*Approximate concentration (ppm)*
(*a*) Iron	(*i*) 1-5
(*b*) Zinc	(*ii*) 20-80
(*c*) Copper	(*iii*) 0.2-0.5
(*d*) Manganese	(*iv*) 0.3-0.6
(*e*) Iodine	(*v*) 10-50

1028.

Element	*Approximate concentration*
(*a*) Cobalt	(*i*) 0.11 per cent
(*b*) Molybdenum	(*ii*) 0.3-0.6 ppm
(*c*) Magnesium	(*iii*) 1-4 ppm
(*d*) Chlorine	(*iv*) 0.04 per cent
(*e*) Iodine	(*v*) 0.02-0.1 ppm

1029. Match the calcium content (per cent) with the source.

(*a*) 0.12	(*i*) Whole rice
(*b*) 0.05	(*ii*) Milk
(*c*) 0.02	(*iii*) Fish meal
(*d*) 5.50	(*iv*) Wheat or rice bran
(*e*) 0.10	(*v*) Whole egg

1030. Ca-content (per cent)

(*a*) 30	(*i*) Dicalcuim phosphate
(*b*) 38	(*ii*) Meat and bone meal
(*c*) 26	(*iii*) Limestone
(*d*) 27	(*iv*) Steamed bone meal
(*e*) 10.6	(*v*) Rock phosphate

1031. Match the source with the estimated phosphorus content (per cent).

(*a*) Milk — (*i*) 0.21
(*b*) Whole egg — (*ii*) 1.40
(*c*) Wheat bran — (*iii*) 0.14
(*d*) Rice — (*iv*) 0.09
(*e*) Whole rice — (*v*) 1.20

Source	*Phosphorus content (per cent)*
(*a*) Fish meal	(*i*) 14.0
(*b*) Meat and bone meal	(*ii*) 9.0
(*c*) steamed bone meal	(*iii*) 2.8
(*d*) Disodium phosphate	(*iv*) 20.0
(*e*) Dicalcium phosphate	(*v*) 5.1

1032. Match the name of the disease caused by cobalt deficiency with the country where in it has been called as ________.

(*a*) Bush sickness — (*i*) South Australia
(*b*) Coast disease — (*ii*) Kenya
(*c*) Wasting disease — (*iii*) Great Britain
(*d*) Nakuruitis — (*iv*) Western Australia
(*e*) Pinning — (*v*) New Zealand

1033. Match the molybdenum content (ppm) determined by *xanthine oxidase* method with the food/feed stuff.

(*a*) 1.00 — (*i*) Whole soybeans
(*b*) 1.80 — (*ii*) Dehydrated alfalfa meal
(*c*) 2.50 — (*iii*) Cabbage
(*d*) 1.40 — (*iv*) Liver and glandular meal
(*e*) 0.35 — (*v*) Peas

1034. Match the animal with the requirement of vitamin *D* expressed in I.U./day (.0.025 microgramme of pure crystalline vitamin D_3 is equal to one International Unit).

(*a*) Man — (*i*) 200
(*b*) Dairy cattle — (*ii*) 400
(*c*) Sheep — (*iii*) 200
(*d*) Growing poultry — (*iv*) 500
(*e*) Laying lbreeding poultry — (*v*) 350

1035. Match the pathological condition caused by the deficiency of vitamin *E* with the animal (s) affected.

(*a*) Reproductive failure — (*i*) Ewe
(*b*) Embryonic degeneration — (*ii*) Rat, pig
(*c*) Sterility — (*iii*) Chick, turkey
(*d*) Liver necrosis — (*iv*) Female: rat, hen, turkey
(*e*) Blood protein loss — (*v*) Male: rat, dog. cock, hamster, guinea pig

1036. *Pathological condition* — *Animal(s)*

(*a*) Encephalomalacia — (*i*) Rat, monkey, mink
(*b*) Exudative diathesis — (*ii*) Calf, Sheep, mouse, mink
(*c*) Kidney degeneration — (*iii*) Chick
(*d*) Steatitis — (*iv*) Chick, turkey
(*e*) White muscle disease — (*v*) Pig, Chick, mink

1037. Match the food or feed stuff with a-tocopherol content (mg/100g)

(*a*) Wheat germ oil — (*i*) 13
(*b*) Brown rice — (*ii*) 145
(*c*) Whole sunflower seed — (*iii*) 0.8-2.0
(*d*) Dehydrated clover — (*iv*) 1-2
(*e*) Fish meal — (*v*) 10

1038. Match the vitamin K_1 contents (mg) per 100 g of edible portion with its source.

(*a*) 275 — (*i*) Wheat bran
(*b*) 334 — (*ii*) Soybean
(*c*) 80 — (*iii*) Grass meal
(*d*) 190 — (*iv*) Cauliflower
(*e*) 20 — (*v*) Spinach

1039. Match the food stuff with the respiration quotient (R.Q).

(*a*) Glucose — (*i*) 0.7
(*b*) Body and food fats — (*ii*) 0.97
(*c*) Tripalmitin — (*iii*) 1.00
(*d*) Triolein — (*iv*) 0.704
(*e*) Protein — (*v*) 0.712

1040. Match the form of sugar with the absorption value taking glucose absorption value as 100.

(*a*) Galactose — (*i*) 19
(*b*) Fructose — (*ii*) 110
(*c*) Mannose — (*iii*) 9
(*d*) Xylose — (*iv*) 43
(*e*) Arabinose — (*v*) 15

1041. Match one kilogram of digestible nutrient with starch equivalent.

(*a*) True protein — (*i*) 1.00
(*b*) Crude fibre — (*ii*) 2.10
(*c*) Fat (roughages) — (*iii*) 2.40
(*d*) Fat (cereals) — (*iv*) 0.94
(*e*) Fat (oil cakes) — (*v*) 1.90

1042. Match the animal protein food with biological value.

(*a*) Whole milk — (*i*) 67
(*b*) Whole egg — (*ii*) 94
(*c*) Potato — (*iii*) 83
(*d*) Oats — (*iv*) 65
(*e*) Egg white — (*v*) 85

1043. Match the breed (s) of cow (s) or buffalo(es) with the year of beginning of herd book by the Indian Council of Agricultural Research, New Delhi.

(*a*) Sindhi and Sahiwal (*i*) 1942
(*b*) Hariana and Murrah (*ii*) 1947
(*c*) Gir and Kankrej (*iii*) 1941
(*d*) Tharparkar, Kangayam and Ongole (*iv*) 1945

1044. Match the animal with its daily water requirement expressed in gallons.

(*a*) Cows and buffaloes (*i*) 20-25
(*b*) Camel (Watered daily) (*ii*) 1-5
(*c*) Pig (*iii*) 1
(*d*) Elephant (*iv*) 7-8
(*e*) Dog (*v*) 4-8

1045. Match the class with the breed of poultry.

(*a*) American (*i*) Orpington
(*b*) Asiatic (*ii*) Wyandotle
(*c*) English (*iii*) Ghagus
(*d*) Indian (*iv*) Langshan
(*e*) Mediterranean (*v*) Minorca

1046. Match the description with the body part (s) of a hen (poultry).

(*a*) Largest bone of the limb (*i*) Backbone
(*b*) Scapulae, coracoids, clavicle make (*ii*) Drumstick (tibia)
(*c*) Shows fusion of vertebrates (*iii*) Pelvic girdle
(*d*) Is large, project back beyond ribs (*iv*) Pectoral girdle
(*e*) Consists of ilia, ischia and pubes (*v*) Sternum

1047. Match the gland with the hormone produced in hens.

(*a*) Anterior pituitary (*i*) Cortical hormones
(*b*) Posterior (*ii*) Androgen
(*c*) Adrenal (*iii*) Insulin
(*d*) Islets of langerhans (*iv*) Thyrotrophic hormone
(*e*) Jests (*v*) Oxytocin

1048. Match the age of a chick (in weeks) with brooding temperature of °F (measured about 5 cm) above the floor at the age of the brooder.

(*a*) 0-1 (*i*) 78-80
(*b*) 1-2 (*ii*) 70
(*c*) 2-3 (*iii*) 93-95
(*d*) 3-4 (*iv*) 83-85
(*e*) 5-6 (*v*) 68-90

1049. Match the ration ingredient with protein contents (per cent).

(*a*) Sesame cake (*i*) 5.2
(*b*) Rice polish (*ii*) 1.8
(*c*) Maize (*iii*) 1.5
(*d*) Maize gluten meal (*iii*) 4.5
(*e*) Wheat bran (*iv*) 1.6

1050. *Ration ingredient* — *Lysine (per cent)*

(*a*) Sesame cake — (*i*) 0.10

(*b*) Maize gluten meal — (*ii*) 0.13

(*c*) Fish meal — (*iii*) 0.27

(*d*) Maize/wheat bran — (*iv*) 0.06

(*e*) Rice polish — (*iv*) 0.01

1052. *Ration ingredient* — *Calcium (per cent)*

(*a*) Sesame cake — (*i*) 0.15

(*b*) Fish meal — (*ii*) 0.01

(*c*) Wheat bran — (*iii*) 0.08

(*d*) Molasses — (*iv*) 0.26

(*e*) Bone meal — (*v*) 0.2

1052. *Ration ingredient* — *Phosphorus (per cent)*

(*a*) Sesame cake — (*i*) 0.04

(*b*) Fish meal — (*ii*) 0.05

(*c*) Wheat bran — (*iii*) 0.02

(*d*) Molasses — (*iv*) 0.13

(*e*) Bone meal — (*v*) 0.10

1053. Match the popular terms used in swine husbandry (SH) with the meaning thereof.

(*a*) Swine — (*i*) A domesticated animal with long broad shout, thick fat body and coarse bristles

(*b*) Pig — (*ii*) Female swine having produced piglets

(*c*) Hog — (*iii*) Young female intended for breeding

(*d*) Sow — (*iv*) A pig or hog usually used colectively

(*e*) Gilt — (*v*) Denotes entire swine family or weighs more than 120 lb.

1054. *Popular term (SH)* — *Meaning*

(*a*) Litter — (*i*) Castrated male swine before attaining sexual maturity

(*b*) Ratling — (*ii*) To bring forth a number of young at one time

(*c*) Boar — (*iii*) Male swine castrated on becoming a mature boar

(*d*) Stag — (*iv*) An uncastrated male swine

(*e*) Barrows — (*v*) The smallest in a litter, the last born, called rit, erit or cad pig

1055. *Popular term (SH)* — *Meaning*

(*a*) Bacon — (*i*) The part of the leg behind knee (back of thigh).

(*b*) Ham — (*ii*) Fat melted out from fresh, fatty pork tissue

(*c*) Sausage — (*iii*) Feeding concentrates to young in enclosures away from dam

(*d*) Lard — (*iv*) Chopped fine highly seasoned, stuffed ordinarily in prepared intestine tube

(*e*) Creep feeding — (*v*) Salted and smoked meat from hog's back or sides.

1056. Match the breed of the pig with its place or origin.

(*a*) Land race	(*i*) Central England
(*b*) Bershire	(*ii*) Northeastern U.S.A.
(*c*) Tamworth	(*iii*) Denmark
(*d*) Duroc	(*iv*) South Central England
(*e*) Hereford	(*v*) Missouri, U.S.A.

1057.

Pig breed	*Place of Origin*
(*a*) Chester White	(*i*) Northern England (Yorkshire)
(*b*) Large White Yorkshire	(*ii*) Southeastern Pennsylvania; U.S.A.
(*c*) Middle White Yorkshire	(*iii*) South Central England
(*d*) Berkshire	(*iv*) Denmark
(*e*) Landrace	(*v*) Yorkshire, England

1058. Match the amino acid requirement expressed as percentage of diet of weaning pigs.

(*a*) Isoleucine	(*i*) 0.60
(*b*) Leucine	(*ii*) 0.40
(*c*) Lysine	(*iii*) 0.20
(*d*) Valine/threonine	(*iv*) 1.00
(*e*) Arginine/tryptophan	(*v*) 0.70

1059. Match the vitamin with the deficiency symptoms in pigs.

(*a*) Vitamin B_{12}	(*i*) Diarrhea necrotic enteritis
(*b*) Pantothenic acid	(*ii*) Dematitis
(*c*) Niacin	(*iii*) Microcytic anaemia
(*d*) Riboflavin	(*iv*) Liver necrosis
(*e*) Vitamin *E*	(*v*) Loss of hair follicles

1060. Match the diet ingredient with the commonly considered dry matter percentage thereof.

(*a*) Root crops	(*i*) 15-25
(*b*) Fish meal	(*ii*) 85-90
(*c*) Liquid milk by products	(*iii*) 87
(*d*) Cereal/soybean mixes	(*iv*) 10-25
(*e*) Drymatter of commonly used diet	(*v*) 6-13

1061. Match the lower limits for energy density range with the type of pig.

(*a*) 14 MJ DE/kg	(*i*) Grower (20-60 kg)
(*b*) 13 MJ DE/kg	(*ii*) Pregnant breeders
(*c*) 12 MJ DE/kg	(*iii*) Lactating breeders
(*d*) < 11 MJ DE/kg	(*iv*) Grower (60-100 kg)
(*e*) 12.5 MJ DE/kg	(*v*) Baby pig (5-20 kg)

1062. Match the type of pig with the nutrient concentration of diet.

(*a*) Young grower (20 kg)	(*i*) 13
(*b*) Pregnant breeder	(*ii*) 13
(*c*) Lactating breeder	(*iii*) 14
(*d*) Improved entire male grown	(*iv*) 14
(*e*) Unimproved entire male grown	(*v*) 12.5

1063.

Type of Pig	*DCP density (g/kg)*
(*a*) Young grower (20 kg)	(*i*) 182
(*b*) Pregnant breeder	(*ii*) 200
(*c*) Lactating breeder	(*iii*) 140
(*d*) Improved entire male grower (40 kg)	(*iv*) 140
(*e*) Unimproved breeder	(*v*) 153

1064.

Type of Pig	*DCP density (g/kg)*
(*a*) Young grower (20 kg)	(*i*) 120
(*b*) Grower (40 and 60 kg)	(*ii*) 170
(*c*) Grower (80 kg)	(*iii*) 115
(*d*) Grower (100 kg)	(*iv*) 155
(*e*) Improved entire male grower	(*v*) 130

1065.

Type of Pig	*DE :CP ratio*
(*a*) Young grower (20 kg)	(*i*) 1:11
(*b*) Pregnant .breeder	(*ii*) 1:14
(*c*) Lactating breeder	(*iii*) 1:13
(*d*) Improved entire male grower (40 kg)	(*iv*) 1:12
(*e*) Grower (40 and 60 kg)	(*v*) 1:12

1066. Match the food with degradability of protein (per cent)

(*a*) Oats and barley	(*i*) 60-70
(*b*) Maize	(*ii*) 65-85
(*c*) Soybean meal (extracted)	(*iii*) 85-95
(*d*) Ground nut meal (decorticated) (W)	(*iv*) 25-45
(*e*) Fish meal	(*v*) 45-65

1067

Food	*Protein degradability (per cent)*
(*a*) Dried sugar beet pulp	(*i*) 30-50
(*b*) Clover hay	(*ii*) 75-90
(*c*) Very leafy dried grass	(*iii*) 35-65
(*d*) Hay of early flowered ryegrass	(*iv*) 70-80
(*e*) Formic acid added grass silage	(*v*) 80-90

1068 Match the diseases with the causal organism as commonly observed in sheep.

(*a*) Coccidiosis	(*i*) *Clostridium Welchii type D*
(*b*) Johne's disease	(*ii*) *Fusiformis necrophorus*
(*c*) Pulpy Kidney (in lambs)	(*iii*) *Clostridium Welchii type B*
(*d*) Lamb dysentery	(*iv*) Protozoan parasite
(*e*) Lameness	(*v*) *Mycobacterium paratuberculosis*

1069. Match the poisonous plant(s) found to cause poisoning in sheep with the country where such observations have been made.

(*a*) Yew, rhododendron, laurel	(*i*) New Zealand
(*b*) Ragwort	(*ii*) Scotland
(*c*) Laurel	(*iii*) Britain
(*d*) Bog asphodel	(*iv*) Eastern Canada
(*e*) Some strain of subterranean clover	(*v*) Australia

1070.

Type of pig	*Lower limit for biological value*
(*a*) Baby pig	(*i*) 0.65
(*b*) Grower (20-60 kg)	(*ii*) 0.60
(*c*) Grower (60-100 kg)	(*iii*) 0.70
(*d*) Pregnant breeder	(*iv*) 0.65 .
(*e*) Lactating	(*v*) 0.60

1071. Match the temperature in respect of housing standards for pigs with the body weight or sex.

(*a*) 26-30°C	(*i*) 10-20 kg
(*b*) 22-26°C	(*ii*) 50-100 kg
(*c*) 18-22°C	(*iii*) < 10 kg
(*d*) 16-20°C	(*iv*) 20-50 kg

1072. Match the basic physical and physiological properties of sheep with each other.

(*a*) Average temperature	(*i*) 16 days
(*b*) Average pulse rate	(*ii*) 147 days
(*c*) Oestrus cycle	(*iii*) 75-80 / minute
(*d*) Natural life time	(*iv*) 40°C
(*e*) Natural life time	(*v*) 8-10 years

1073. Match the age with the name given according to sex of the sheep.

(*a*) Birth to weaning (0-14/16 weeks)	(*i*) Wether hogget (castrated male)
(*b*) Weaning to shearing (4/16 weeks to 5 months)	(*ii*) Gimmer (female)
(*c*) First to second shearing	(*iii*) Full mouthed tup (entire male)
(*d*) Second to third shearing	(*iv*) Ewe lamb (female)
(*e*) After fourth shearing	(*v*) Two shear ram (entire male)

1074. Match the Britain's common breeds and cross with the mature ewe body weight as estimated by Meat and Livestock Commission.

(*a*) South Country Cheviot (Hill breed)	(*i*) 50 kg
(*b*) Scottish blackface (Hill breed)	(*ii*) 86 kg
(*c*) Kerry Hill (Hill breed)	(*iii*) 75 kg
(*d*) Border Leicester (Long wools)	(*iv*) 48 kg
(*e*) Dorset Down (Down breed)	(*v*) 47 kg

1075. *Breed/Cross*	*Weight*
(*a*) Devon closewool (Short wools)	(*i*) 32 kg
(*b*) Masham (Crossbred fat lamb mother)	(*ii*) 98 kg
(*c*) Welsh Mountain (Crossbred fat lamb mother)	(*iii*) 72 kg
(*d*) Oxford (Crossbred fat Lamb mother)	(*iv*) 69 kg
(*e*) Mule (Crossbred fat Lamb mother)	(*v*) 57 kg

1076 Match the food with the metabolizable energy (M.J) per kilogram of dry matter.

(*a*) Oats	(*i*) 13.7
(*b*) Barley	(*ii*) 12.3
(*c*) Maize	(*iii*) 11.5
(*d*) Soybean (extracted)	(*iv*) 11.1
(*e*) Fish meal	(*v*) 14.7

1077. *Food*	*Metabolisable energy (MJ)*
(*a*) Very leafy, dry grass	(*i*) 10.1
(*b*) Clover hay	(*ii*) 10.8
(*c*) Hay of ryegrass leafy	(*iii*) 12.8
(*d*) Molasses	(*iv*) 7.3
(*e*) Barley straw	(*v*) 9.6

1078. Match the digestible crude protein (g) per kg of dry matter of the food.

(*a*) 84	(*i*) Barley
(*b*) 82	(*ii*) Hay of ryegrass leafy
(*c*) 78	(*iii*) Early flower, dried grass
(*d*) 96	(*iv*) Oats
(*e*) 90	(*v*) Maize

1079. *D C P* (*g*)	*Food*
(*a*) 113	(*i*) Dried grass, early flower
(*b*) 136	(*ii*) Dried grass, very leafy
(*c*) 128	(*iii*) Grass silage, leafy (high digestibility)
(*d*) 116	(*iv*) Dried grass, leafy
(*e*) 96	(*v*) Clover hay

1080. Match Ca (g) per kg of dry matter with the food.

(*a*) 0.8	(*i*) Groundnut meal (decorticated)
(*b*) 2.2	(*ii*) Swedes roots
(*c*) 6.4	(*iii*) Clover roots
(*d*) 9.6	(*iv*) Barley straw
(*e*) 3.4	(*v*) Oats

1081. Match the food with P (g) per kg of dry matter.

(*a*) Maize	(*i*) 3.3
(*b*) Soybean meal (extracted)	(*ii*) 0.6
(*c*) Very leafy, dried grass	(*iii*) 7.5
(*d*) Barley straw	(*iv*) 5.8
(*e*) Dried sugar beet pulp	(*v*) 0.9

1082. Computation of nutritive ratio (NR) is shown below, fill up the blanks there in.

$$NR = \frac{\text{Dig N - free extract + Dig. fibre + (Dig. fat} \times 2.25)}{\text{Digestible crude protein (DCP)}}$$

When a ratio contains

DCP = 6.0 per cent

Digestible ether extract = 3.0 per cent

Digestible N-free extract = 60.0 per cent

Digestible crude fibre = 1.5 per cent

$$NR = \frac{60.0 + 1.5 + (3.0 \times 2.25)}{60} = \_\_\_\_\_\_$$

1083. Fill up the blank in the formula to compute biological value (BV) of a protein for maintenance and growth of the rat.

$$BV = \frac{\text{N - intake} - (\text{faceal N + urinary N}) - (\text{urinary N - EUN})}{\text{N} - \text{intake} - \text{faceal N}}$$

Food consumed daily (g)	6.000
N-in food (per cent)	1.043
Daily N-intake (mg)	62.6000
Total N-excretion in urine (mg)	22,000
Total N-excretion in excreted daily (mg) 2	0.900
Metabolic faecal N excreted daily (mg) 1	10.700

$$BV = \frac{62.6 - (20.9 - 10.7) - (32.8 - 22.0) \times 100 = 79}{62.9 \cdot (\_\_\_\_\_\_\_)} \times 100 = 79$$

1084. Fill up the blank in the following showing the computation of egg replacement value (RV) of wheat protein, one source of protein is egg (BV nearly 100) and the other is wheat. Daily nitrogen intake is 50 g in each ration and N balances are + 25 and +19, respectively.

$$RV = 100 - \frac{\text{(Difference in N - balance)}}{\text{N} - \text{intake}} \times 100$$

$$\text{or Egg RV of wheat protein} = 100 - \frac{(25 - \_\_\_\_\_)}{50} \times 100$$

$$= 88 \text{ per cent}$$

1085. Selection index (*I*) weight and accuracy are computed from the following equations. Fill up the blanks in these equations.

(*a*) $I = -(X - H)$

(*b*) Selection index weight $= b = \dfrac{2nh^2}{4 + (-)h^2}$

(*c*) Accuracy of index $= \sqrt{\dfrac{\_\_\_\_\_\_}{4 + (n-1)h^2}}$

Where,

n = progeny each have one performance record

X = the average for the n progeny record

H = the average of contemporary herdmates of progeny

h^2 = heritability

1086. Digestible DM (g) = DM intake (g) – ________ .

1087. Digestible DM (%) $= \frac{\text{\_\_\_\_\_\_\_\_ – DM in faces}}{\text{DM intake}} \times 100$

1088. TDN (%) $= \frac{\text{(DM intake} \times \text{Chemical composition)} - \text{\_\_\_\_\_\_}}{\text{DM intake}} \times 100$

1089. TDN (g) (DM intake × Chem. Composition) – (________ × Chem. Composition)

Do You Know That

1. The smallest breed of cows in the world, the "Santa Rosalia" with an average height of 80 cm is at Sitio Novo Ranch at Italiaicu, Brazil.
2. Santa rosalia breed of cows consumes 30 per cent less than other normal breeds and produces an average of seven litres of milk per day.
3. The Brazilian rancher Mario Cisar Reda has the bovine mix miniature ponies and donkeys, dwarf pigs, tiny Guernsey cocks and hens.
4. Mammals appeared on earth about 150 million years ago and are believed to have evolved from an advanced type of reptiles.
5. The mammary gland of the cow is probably the most advanced form from an evolutionary point of view.
6. The pigeons produce a white slimy substance in their crop called pigeon "milk" which they regurgitate into the mouth of their young.
7. The duckbill platypus embodies mammary glands similar that of cow morphologically, but has no nipples.
8. The first artificial insemination centre was established in 1907 at the request of Royal Study Authorities in U.S.S.R.
9. The disease *beriberi* is characterized by extensive damage to the nervous and cardiovascular system and may be accompanied by severe muscle wasting (dry beriberi) or edema (wet beriberi).
10. Rice said, "The bird carries its health certificate on top of its head."
11. The first animal to be domesticated, by early Stone Age man was the dog.
12. The archaeologists, estimates reveal that hunters and gatherers became herdsman probably in the highlands of Anatolia and Iran, in the mesolithic period of some 12,000 years ago.
13. The first sheep domesticated in the Middle East has been supposed to be Urial (*Ovis vignei*).
14. Two premier sheep countries of Europe are Spain and Britain.
15. India ranks first among the countries of the world in goat population.
16. Gestation period in buffalo is about 310 days
17. Gestation period in swine is about 114 days
18. Two humped camel is called / known as *camelus bacterianus.*

20. Gestation period of sheep is about 145 days
21. Tallest breed of sheep is from Nellore (A.P.)
22. Per capita availability per day of milk in India during year 2007-08 was 250 gm / day
23. The average fertile life of egg is about 12-24 hours.
24. Incubation period in chicken is about 21 days.

KEY

1. Draught resisting
2. Higher elevations
3. Descent
4. Purity
5. I.A.R.I., New Delhi
6. Horns
7. Splashed
8. Dairy
9. Sindhi or Red Sindhi or sciendhi
10. Docile
11. South Kathiawar
12. Pendulous
13. Gir breed
14. Suited
15. Proportionate
16. Close
17. Nellore
18. Docile
19. Thari
20. Strong limbs
21. Black
22. Wadhiar
23. Heaviest
24. Straight
25. Sloping
26. Amrit Mahal
27. Dewlap
28. Dark head
29. Konganad
30. Hard Work
31. Wide muzzle
32. Black markings
33. Manthani
34. Alert and short
35. Grey to iron grey
36. Adaptability
37. Darjeeling
38. Massive
39. Tuft of hair
40. Murrah
41. Massive frame
42. Tightly curled
43. White markings.
44. Murrah
45. Gir forest
46. Heavy horns
47. Nili and Ravi
48. Heavy head
49. face and forehead
50. Jamuna
51. Wedge
52. Bhadawari
53. Living structures
54. 20 to 30 micra (1 micra = 1/1000 millimeter)
55. 50 micra
56. Absorption
57. Golgi apparatus
58. Impermeable
59. Spherical
60. Nucleus
61. Reticulum
62. A histone
63. Nucleo histone
64. Phosphate
65. Pyrimidines-cytosine
66. Deoxyribose
67. Phosphodiester
68. Specific species
69. RNA (Ribonudic acid)
70: Deoxyribose
71 Adenine-Adenine-Adenine
72. Endoplasmic
73. Amino acids
74. RNA
75. Heredity
76. Cisternae
77. Basophilic
78. Micromolecules
79. Secretary materials or waste products
80. Lipoprotein
81. Golgi apparatus
82. Lumen
83. Mitochondria
84. Metabolites
85. Phosphorylation
86. Hydrolytic
87. Breakdown
88. Gametic or haploid
89. Meiosis or reduction division
90. Chromosome
91. Anaphase.
92. DNA
93. Reproduction
94. Protein
95. Chemical
96. Hand-handed
97. Equilibrium-density gradient
98. Semiconserative
99. Autoradiography
100. ^{3}H-thymidine
101. Denaturation
102. 25

103. DNA polymerase I
104. DNA template
105. Nucleic Acids
106. Fidelity
107. Heterochromatin
108. Euchromatin
109. Chromosome
110. Karyokinesis
111. Interphase
112. Prophase
113. Nucleolus
114. Equatorial
115. Centromere
116. Uncoil
117. Diakinesis
118. Chromomeres
119. Homologous
120. Pachynema
121. Diplonema
122. Terminalization
123. Diakinesis
124. Completed
125. Hereditary
126. Chromosomes
127. Homologous
128. Gene
129. Locus (Loci, plural
130. Alleles
131. Mutation
132. Diploid
133. Gametes
134. Zygote
135. Homozygous
136. Dominant
137. Monohybrid
138. Genotype
139. Species
140. Breed
141. Molecular
142. Gregor Johann Mendel
143. Coat colour
144. Red and White
145. Andalusian
146. Yellow and round
147. Independent assortment
148. Cytological
149. Chromosomes
150. Waston-Crick
151. Pyrimidine
152. Four letters
153. Mutation
154. Genetically
155. Gene action
156. Alcaptonuria
157. Bacterial
158. Malaria
159. Allelic
160. Multiple alleles
161. Pleiotrophic
162. Polygenic
163. Polygenic
164. Two dominant
165. Small parents
166. Linkage
167. Coupling and repulsion
168. Lethal gene
169. Sex linked
170. Non-additive
171. Sex linked
172. Stillborn or die soon after birth
173. Males (grass hopper)
174. E.W. Wilson
175. Secondary sex
176. Autosomes
177. Genetic balance
178. Gynandromorphs
179. Chromatin body
180. Dosage compensation
181. Sex hormones
182. Hetero chromatin
183. Hunter
184. Mutation
185. *Polledness* or hornlessness
186. Mutant allele
187. Deletion
188. Translocation
189. Germinal epithelium
190. Elastic fibres
191. Retractor muscle
192. Infundibulum
193. Cervix or neck of the womb
194. 10
195. Copulation
196. Anterior sphincter
197. Clitoris
198. Sustenacular/nurse/sertoli's celles
199. Spermatogonia
200. Spermiogenesis/Spermiteleosis
201. One year
202. Man or Fowl
203. Follicles
204. Stigma
205. Chemotaxis
206. Thigmataxis
207. Vitelline membrane
208. Fertilization
209. Pseudopregnant
210. Endocrine
211. Hypothalmic
212. Endocrine
213. Thyroglobulin
214. Adrenosterone
215. Estrogen or estrogenic hormones
216. puberty
217. Leutenizing hormone
218. Pregnancy
219. Palpation
220. Pregnancy
221. Dry and wrinkled
222. Gonadotropic
223. Nutrients
224. Intra-abdominal
225. Wedge
226. Honey-like
227. Dilation
228. Uterine hernia

229. Foetal abdomen
230. Testes
231. Free-martin or neuter
232. White heifer disease
233. Ballooned vagina
234. F.S.H and L.H
235. Receptivity
236. Normal heat
237. Libedo
238. Cornification
239. Pregnant
240. Trichomones Foetus
241. Sterile
242. Ewes
243. Parturition
244. Suckling stimulus
245. Parathormone
246. Gamma globulins
247. Acetate
248. Segregation
249. Albinos
250. Genotype
251. Recombination
252. Phenotype
253. Outstanding
254. Reproductive rate
255. Collateral
256. Coefficient
257. Close
258. Cross
259. Criss-Cross
260. Back-crossing
261. Santa Gertrudis
262. Foot and Mouth
263. Ayrshire
264. Hinny
265. Hybrid vigour or heterosis
266. Grading
267. Performance
268. Heritability
269. Pedigree
270. Genetic values
271. Pedigree
272. Progeny or daughter
273. Economic value
274. Prolificacy
275. Fecundity
276. Dairy cattle
277. Embryonic
278. Mares
279. Dr. P. Bhattacharya
280. 1945
281. Gunn
282. Artificial vagina or AV methode.
283. Crustacae and nematodes
284. Permeability
285. 80 μ
286. Deoxyribonucleo protein
287. Spermatic veil or Floating cap
288. Seminal
289. Vaginal plug
290. Semen
291. Seminal plasma
292. Bull
293. Erythrocytes (1.1)
294. An electric
295. Impedance
296. Fructolysis
297. Catalase
298. Milovanov's "SGE-2 dilutor"
299. Egg-yolk phosphate EYP-diluent
300. IVT (Illine Variable Temp.)
301. Antibiotics
302. Testicular
303. Tropical Africa
304. Concentrate
305. Phosphorus
306. Rice bran
307. Fish meal
308. Bone meal
309. Water
310. Metabolic water
311. 589 calories
312. Water balance
313. Adrenaline
314. Carbohydrate
315. Lipid metabolism
316. Cholesterol
317. Enzymes
318. Amino acid
319. Amphoteric
320. Zwitter ion
321. Parathyroid and thyroid
322. Phosphorus
323. Aldosterone
324. Storage ion
325. Hemosiderin
326. Erythrocyte
327. Copper
328. Rabbit
329. Scouring disease or peat scours
330. Perosis or slipped tendon
331. Thyroglobulin
332. Osseous
333. Cobalt
334. Anti-pernicious
335. Lambs
336. Molybdenum
337. Teartness
338. Copper
339. Fat soluble
340. Xerophthalmia
341. b-ionine
342. Ultra-violet
343. Cholecalciferol
344. 7-dehydro site sterol
345. Vitamin *E*
346. Ascoribic acid
347. Bleed
348. Hypoplastic
349. Decumarol
350. Famine and war
351. Eijkmann
352. Thiamine (an eurine, vitamin B_1)
353. Wernicke's encephal opathy
354. White matter
355. Lactic acid

356. Riboflavin
357. Ari bo flavinosis
358. Curled-toe paralysis
359. Rice polishings
360. Pellagra (from the Italian *pelle agra* means rough skin
361. Folic acid
362. Crystanine, B_{12}
363. Vitamin B_{12}
364. "Fornula feeds"
365. Penicillin
366. Enterotoxaemia or "over eating disease"
367. Sheep
368. Horse
369. Diaphram
370. Polypeptide chain
371. Proteolytic
372. Sterol
373. Portal vein
374. Sheep
375. *Selenomonas ruminartium* var loctilyticus
376. Digestibility, coefficient
377. 100
378. Kellner's
379. 33-50 per cent
380. Dehydrated or desiccated
381. North and South
382. Hind quarters
383. Stanchion
384. Durability
385. Over-growth
386. Service crate
387. Leguminous
388. Herd Book
389. Calving
390. Colostrum
391. Vitamin *A*
392. Horn button
393. Castration
394. "Bloodless castration
395. Low fertility
396. Second day
397. Brucellosis
398. 3-7
399. Horse-breeding
400. Cows and buffaloes
401. Reduces
402. Suckling
403. "Class"
404. Plymouth rock
405. 1970 and 1905
406. Sitter
407. 40 mm
408. 2-3 weeks
409. 82°F
410. Decrease
411. Haemorrhages
412. Double yolked
413. Foreign matter
414. Poultry production
415. Hens
416. Inherit
417. Circulation
418. Layer
419. Maternal instinct
420. Persistency
421. 2:1
422. Live chickens
423. *Leipoa Ocellata*
424. Embroynic
425. 21st day
426. Pullourm
427. Pullets
428. Per bird
429. Happy
430. 3-6
431. Sulphur
432. Intensive
433. Battery system
434. Deep litter
435. 3, 2 and 2
436. Capons
437. 6-8
438. Cannibalism
439. Heat signs
440. Castration
441. Sleeping
442. Goats
443. Growing-fattening
444. Back and loin
445. Boar
446. Follicles
447. Needle teeth
448. Young gains are cheap gains
449. Sow's milk
450. Boars
451. Ranting
452. Gastric motility
453. Volatile fatty acids
454. Pig
455. Colostrum
456. Pig
457. Calcium-phosphorus
458. Wave-interval
459. Iron
460. Selenium
461. Vitamin A
462. Vitamin *D*
463. Vitamin *E*
464. Half
465. 0.75-1.75
466. 30 MJ DE
467. Digestible crude protein
468. Biological value
469. DCP concentration
470. Lactating
471. Edinburgh Model
472. Nipples
473. Candidate males
474. European
475. Mastitis, Metritis and Agalactia
476. Carpet woods
477. Australian
478. Flushing
479. Fat
480. 200 - day
481. Cow
482. 'Steaming up'
483. Dystocias
484. Carilagenous
485. Split upper
486. Omasum

487. Copper	488. Cobalt	489. Selenium
490. Hypomagenesaemia	491. *Clostridium welchi*	492. Casting for age
493. Merino	494. Stratification	495. Store Lamb
496. Transferrin	497. Assam	498. River buffaloes
499. True		
500. False	501. True	502. False
503. True	504. False	505. True
506. True	507. False	508. False
509. True	510. True	511. False
512. False	513. True	514. False
515. False	516. True	517. True
518. False	519. True.	520. True
521. True	522. True	523. True
524. False	525. False	526. True
527. True	528. False	529. False
530. False	531. True	532. True
533. True	534. True	535. False
536. True	537. True	538. False
539. False	540. True	541. True
542. True	543. True	544. False
545. False	546. True	547. True
548. False	549. False	550. False
551. False	552. True	553. False
554. True	555. True	556. False
557. True	558. True	559. True
560. False	561. True	562. True
563. False	564. False	565. True
566. True	567. False	568. False
569. False	570. True	571. False
572. False	573. False	574. True
575. True	576. False	577. True
578. False	579. True	580. True
581. True	582. True	583. True
584. False	585. False	586. True
587. True	588. True	589. False
590. False	591. False	592. True
593. True	594. False	595. False
596. True	597. True	598. True
599. False	600. False	601. False
602. True	603. False	604. True
605. False	606. False	607. False
608. True	609. False	610. True
611. False	612. False	613. False
614. False	615. True	616. False
617. False	618. True	619. False

620. True	621. True	622. True
623. True	624. False	625. False
626. False	627. False	628. False
629. True	630. True	631. False
632. False	633. True	634. True
635. False	636. True	637. False
638. False	639. True	640. True
641. False	642. True	643. False
644. True	645. True	646. False
647. False	648. False	649. True
650. False	651. True	652. True
653. False	654. False	655. True
656. True	657. False	658. False
659. False	660. True	661. True
662. True	663. True	664. False
665. False	666. False	667. True
668. False	669. True	670. False
671. True	672. False	673. True
674. False	675. True	676. False
677. True	678. True	679. False
680. False	681. False	682. True
683. False	684. True	685. True
686. False	687. False	688. False
689. True	690. False	691. True
692. False	693. False	694. True
695. True	696. True	697. False
698. False	699. True	700. True
701. False	702. False	703. True
704. True	705. False	706. False
707. False	708. True	709. False
710. True	711. False	712. False
713. False	714. True	715. True
716. True	717. False	718. True
719. False	720. True	721. True
722. False	723. False	724. True
725. True	726. True	727. False
728. False	729. True	730. False
731. True	732. True	733. False
734. True	735. False	736. True
737. False	738. True	739. False
740. False	741. False	742. True
743. True	744. False	745. True
746. False	747. False	748. True
749. True	750. False	751. True
752. True	753. False	754. True
755. True	756. False	757. False

758. False	759. True	760. True
761. False	762. False	763. True
764. True	765. False	766. False
767. True	768. True	769. True
770. False	771. False	772. True
773. True	774. False	775. True
776. False	777. False	778. True
779. False	780. True	781. False
782. True	783. True	784. False
785. True	786. True	787. False
788. True	789. False	790. True
791. False	792. False	793. False
794. True	795. True	796. True
797. False	798. True	799. False
800. False	801. False	802. True
803. False	804. True	805. True
806. False	807. True	808. True
809. True	810. False	811. False
812. (*c*)	813. (*c*)	814. (*b*)
815. (*d*)	816. (*b*)	817. (*c*)
818. (*a*)	819. (*d*)	820. (*c*)
821. (*a*)	822. (*d*)	823. (*d*)
824. (*b*)	825. (*d*)	826. (*a*)
827. (*b*)	828. (*c*)	829. (*d*)
830. (*a*)	831. (*c*)	832. (*a*)
833. (*d*)	834. (*d*)	835. (*d*)
836. (*c*)	837. (*c*)	838. (*a*)
839. (*b*)	840. (*c*)	841. (*d*)
842. (*b*)	843. (*d*)	844. (*b*)
845. (*c*)	846. (*a*)	847. (*b*)
848. (*b*)	849. (*c*)	850. (*c*)
851. (*a*)	852. (*b*)	853. (*d*)
854. (*c*)	855. (*d*)	856. (*b*)
857. (*b*)	858. (*c*)	859. (*a*)
860. (*d*)	861. (*b*)	862. (*d*)
863. (*c*)	864. (*a*)	865. (*c*)
866. (*c*)	867. (*d*)	868. (*b*)
869. (*a*)	870. (*b*)	871. (*d*)
872. (*b*)	873. (*c*)	874. (*b*)
875. (*b*)	876. (*c*)	877. (*a*)
878. (*d*)	879. (*c*)	880. (*d*)
881. (*a*)	882. (*b*)	883. (*d*)
884. (*c*)	885. (*a*)	886. (*b*)
887. (*a*)	888. (*c*)	889. (*b*)
890. (*c*)	891. (*b*)	892. (*c*)
893. (*d*)	894. (*d*)	895. (*a*)

896. (*d*) 897. (*d*) 898. (*a*)
899. (*b*) 900. (*d*) 901. (*a*)
902. (*c*) 903. (*c*) 904. (*b*)
905. (*c*) 906. (*a*) 907. (*c*)
908. (*b*) 909 (*d*) 910. (*d*)
911. (*d*) 912. (*c*) 913. (*c*)
914. (*d*) 915. (*a*) 916. (*b*)
917. (*d*) 918. (*b*) 919. (*d*)
920. (*a*) 921. (*c*) 922. (*d*)
923. (*b*) 924. (*b*) 925. (*c*)
926. (*b*) 927. (*c*) 928. (*c*)
929. (*c*) 930. (*d*) 931. (*c*)
932. (*d*) 933. (*a*) 934. (*d*)
935. (*c*) 936. (*b*) 937. (*c*)
938. (*d*) 939. (*c*) 940. (*b*)
941. (*c*) 942. (*d*) 943. (*a*)
944. (*b*) 945. (*c*) 946. (*b*)
947. (*d*) 948. (*c*) 949. (*b*)
950. (*c*) 951. (*b*) 952. (*c*)
953. (*b*) 954. (*b*) 955. (*b*)
956. (*c*) 957. (*d*) 958. (*c*)
959. (*c*) 960. (*b*) 961. (*d*)
962. (*b*) 963. (*d*) 964. (*c*)
965. (*a*) 966. (*c*) 967. (*d*)
968. (*b*) 969. (*d*) 970. (*a*)
971 (*c*)
972. (*a*)-(*iii*) (*b*)-(*iv*) (*c*)-(*i*) (*d*)-(*ii*)
973. (*a*)-(*iv*) (*b*)-(*i*) (*c*)-(*ii*) (*d*)-(*iii*)
974. (*a*)-(*iii*) (*b*)-(*iv*) (*c*)-(*i*) (*d*)-(*ii*)
975. (*a*)-(*iv*) (*b*)-(*i*) (*c*)-(*ii*) (*d*)-(*iii*)
976. (*a*)-(*iii*) (*b*)-(*i*) (*c*)-(*iv*) (*d*)-(*ii*
977. (*a*)-(*iv*) (*b*)-(*i*) (*c*)-(*ii*) (*d*)-(*iii*)
978. (*a*)-(*iii*) (*b*)-(*iv*) (*c*)-(*i*) (*d*)-(*ii*)
979. (*a*)-(*iv*) (*b*)-(*i*) (*c*)-(*ii*) (*d*)-(*iii*)
980. (*a*)-(*iii*) (*b*)-(*iv*) (*c*)-(*i*) (*d*)-(*ii*)
981. (*a*)-(*iv*) (*b*)-(*i*) (*c*)-(*ii*) (*d*)-(*iii*)
982. (*a*)(*ii*) (*b*)-(*iv*) (*c*)-(*iii*) (*d*)-(*i*)
983. (*a*)-(*iii*) (*b*)-(*iv*) (*c*)-(*i*) (*d*)-(*ii*)
984. (*a*)-(*ii*) (*b*)-(*iii*) (*c*)-(*iv*) (*d*)-(*i*)
985. (*a*)-(*iv*) (*b*)-(*ii*) (*c*)-(*i*) (*d*)-(*iii*)
986. (*a*)-(*iv*) (*b*)-(*i*) (*c*)-(*ii*) (*d*)-(*iii*)
987. (*a*)-(*ii*) (*b*)-(*iv*) (*c*)-(*i*) (*d*)-(*iii*)
988. (*a*)-(*iii*) (*b*)-(*i*) (*c*)-(*iv*) (*d*)-(*ii*)
989. (*a*)-(*iv*) (*b*)-(*iii*) (*c*)-(*i*) (*d*)-(*ii*)
990. (*a*)-(*iv*) (*b*)-(*i*) (*c*)-(*ii*) (*d*)-(*iii*)

991. (*a*)-(*iii*) (*b*)-(*v*) (*c*)-(*i*) (*d*)-(*ii* (*e*)-(*iv*)
992. (*a*)-(*iii*) (*b*)-(*i*) (*c*)-(*v*) (*d*)-(*ii*) (*e*)-(*iv*)
993. (*a*)-(*ii*) (*b*)-(*v*) (*c*)-(*i*) (*d*)-(*iv*) (*e*)-(*iii*)
994. (*a*)-(*v*) (*b*)-(*i*) (*c*)-(*iv*) (*d*)-(*ii*) (*e*)-(*iii*)
995. (*a*)-(*iii*) (*b*)-(*i*) (*c*)-(*iv*) (*d*)-(*ii*)
996. (*a*)-(*v*) (*b*)-(*iii*) (*c*)-(*ii*) (*d*)-(*iv*) (*e*)-(*i*)
997. (*a*)-(*ii*) (*b*)-(*iv*) (*c*)-(*i*) (*d*)-(*v*) (*e*)-(*iii*)
998. (*a*)-(*iii*) (*b*)-(*i*) (*c*)-(*iv*) (*d*)-(*ii*) (*e*)-(*v*)
999. (*a*)-(*iv*) (*b*)-(*v*) (*c*)-(*i*) (*d*)-(*ii*) (*e*)-(*iii*)
1000. (*a*)-(*ii*) (*b*)-(*iv*) (*c*)-(*v*) (*d*)-(*i*) (*e*)-(*iii*)
1001. (*a*)-(*iii*) (*b*)-(*i*) (*c*)-(*iv*) (*d*)-(*ii*)
1002. (*a*)-(*iv*) (*b*) -(*i*) (*c*)-(*ii*) (*d*)-(*iii*) (*e*)-(*v*)
1003. (*a*)-(*v*) (*b*)-(*iii*) (*c*)-(*i*) (*d*)-(*ii*) (*e*)-(*iv*)
1004. (*a*)-(*iii*) (*b*)-(*v*) (*c*)-(*i*) (*d*)-(*ii*) (*e*)-(*iv*)
1005. (*a*)-(*ii*) (*b*)-(*iv*) (*c*)-(*v*) (*d*)-(*iii*) (*e*)-(*i*)
1006. (*a*)-(*ii*) (*b*)-(*v*) (*c*)-(*i*) (*d*)-(*iii*) (*e*)-(*iv*)
1007. (*a*)-(*iv*) (*b*)-(*i*) (*c*)-(*v*) (*d*)-(*ii*) (*e*)-(*iii*
1008. (*a*)-(*iii*) (*b*)-(*iv*) (*c*)-(*ii*) (*d*)-(*v*) (*e*)-(*i*)
1009. (*a*)-(*iii*) (*b*)-(*i*) (*c*)-(*v*) (*d*)-(*ii*) (*e*)-(*iv*)
1010. (*a*)-(*iv*) (*b*)-(*v*) (*c*)-(*i*) (*d*)-(*iii*) (*e*)-(*ii*)
1011. (*a*)-(*ii*) (*b*)-(*iv*) (*c*)-(*v*) (*d*)-(*iii*) (*e*)-(*i*)
1012. (*a*)-(*iii*) (*b*)-(*iv*) (*c*)-(*ii*) (*d*)-(*v*) (*e*)-(*i*)
1013. (*a*)-(*ii*) (*b*)-(*v*) (*c*)-(*iv*) (*d*)-(*i*) (*e*)-(*iii*)
1014. (*a*)-(*iv*) (*b*)-(*i*) (*c*)-(*v*) (*d*)-(*ii*) (*e*)-(*iii*)
1015. (*a*) -(*ii*) (*b*)-(*v*) (*c*)-(*i*) (*d*)-(*iii*) (*e*)-(*iv*)
1016. (*a*)-(*v*) (*b*)-(*i*) (*c*)-(*iv*) (*d*)-(*ii*) (*e*)-(*iii*)
1011. (*a*)-(*iii*) (*b*)- (*v*) (*c*)-(*i*) (*d*)-(*ii*) (*e*)-(*iv*)
1018. (*a*)-(*v*) (*b*)-(*iii*) (*c*)-(*i*) (*d*)-(*ii*) (*e*)-(*iv*)
1019. (*a*)-(*vi*) (*b*)-(*iv*) (*c*)-(*i*) (*d*)-(*vii*) (*e*)-(*ii*)
(*f*)-(*v*) (g)-(*iii*)
1020. (*a*)-(*iii*) (*b*)-(*v*) (*c*)-(*iv*) (*d*)-(*i*) (*e*)-(*ii*)
1021. (*a*)-(*v*) (*b*)-(*iii*) (*c*)-(*iv*) (*d*)-(*i*) (*e*)-(*ii*)
1022. (*a*)-(*iv*) (*b*)-(*v*) (*c*)-(*i*) (*d*)-(*ii*) (*e*)-(*iii*)
1023. (*a*)-(*i*) (*b*)-(*v*) (*c*)-(*ii*) (*d*)-(*iv*) (*e*)-(*iii*)
1024. (*a*)-(*iv*) (*b*)-(*iii*) (*c*)-(*i*) (*d*)-(*v*) (*e*)-(*ii*)
1025. (*a*)-(*iii*) (*b*)-(*v*) (*c*)-(*i*) (*d*)-(*ii*) (*e*)-(*iv*)
1026. (*a*)-(*v*) (*b*)-(*iii*) (*c*)-(*i*) (*d*)-(*ii*) (*e*)-(*iv*)
1027. (*a*)-(*ii*) (*b*)-(*v*) (*c*)-(*i*) (*d*)-(*iii*) (*e*)-(*iv*)
1028. (*a*)-(*v*) (*b*)-(*iii*) (*c*)-(*iv*) (*d*)-(*i*) (*e*)-(*ii*)
1029. (*a*)-(*ii*) (*b*)-(*v*) (*c*)-(*i*) (*d*)-(*iii*) (*e*)-(*iv*)
1030. (*a*)-(*iv*) (*b*)-(*iii*) (*c*)-(*i*) (*d*)-(*v*) (*e*)-(*ii*)
1031. (*a*)-(*iv*) (*b*)-(*i*) (*c*)-(*v*) (*d*)-(*ii*) (*e*)-(*iii*)
1032. (*a*)-(*v*) (*b*)-(*i*) (*c*)-(*iv*) (*d*)-(*ii*) (*e*)-(*iii*)
1033. (*a*)-(*iii*) (*b*)-(*iv*) (*c*)-(*i*) (*d*)-(*v*) (*e*)-(*ii*)

1034. (*a*)-(*ii*)	(*b*)-(*v*)	(*c*)-(*i*)	(*d*)-(*iii*)	(*e*)-(*iv*)
1035. (*a*)-(*iv*)	(*b*)-(*i*)	(*c*)-(*v*)	(*d*)-(*ii*)	(*e*)-(*iii*)
1036. (*a*)-(*iii*)	(*b*)-(*iv*)	(*c*)-(*i*)	(*d*)-(*v*)	(*e*)-(*ii*)
1037. (*a*)-(*ii*)	(*b*)-(*iv*)	(*c*)-(*i*)	(*d*)-(*v*)	(*e*)-(*iii*)
1038. (*a*)-(*iv*)	(b)-(*v*)	(*c*)-(*i*)	(*d*)-(*ii*)	(*e*)-(*iii*)
1039. (*a*)-(*iii*)	(*b*)-(*i*)	(*c*)-(*iv*)	(*d*)-(*v*)	(*e*)-(*ii*)
1040. (*a*)-(*ii*)	(*b*)-(*iv*)	(*c*)-(*i*)	(*d*)-(*v*)	(*e*)-(*iii*)
1041. (*a*)-(*iv*)	(*b*)-(*i*)	(*c*)-(*v*)	(*d*)-(*ii*)	(*e*)-(*iii*)
1042. (*a*)-(*v*)	(*b*)-(*ii*)	(*c*)-(*i*)	(*d*)-(*iv*)	(*e*)-(*iii*)
1043. (*a*)-(*iii*)	(*b*)-(*i*)	(*c*)-(*iv*)	(*d*)-(*ii*)	
1044. (*a*)-(*iv*)	(*b*)-(*v*)	(*c*)-(*ii*)	(*d*)-(*i*)	(*e*)-(*iii*)
1045. (*a*)-(*ii*)	(*b*)-(*iv*)	(*c*)-(*i*)	(*d*)-(*iii*)	(*e*)-(*v*)
1046. (*a*)-(*ii*)	(*b*)-(*iv*)	(*c*)-(*i*)	(*d*)-(*v*)	(*e*)-(*iii*)
1047. (*a*)-(*iv*)	(*b*)-(*v*)	(*c*)-(*i*)	(*d*)-(*iii*)	(*e*)-(*ii*)
1048. (*a*)-(*iii*)	(*b*)-(*v*)	(*c*)-(*iv*)	(*d*)-(*i*)	(*e*)-(*ii*)
1049. (*a*)-(*iv*)	(*b*)-(*i*)	(*c*)-(*ii*)	(*d*)-(*v*)	(*e*)-(*iii*)
1050. (*a*)-(*ii*)	(*b*)-(*v*)	(*c*)-(*i*)	(*d*)-(*iv*)	(*e*)-(*iii*)
1051. (*a*)-(*v*)	(*b*)-(*i*)	(*c*)-(*ii*)	(*d*)-(*iii*)	(*e*)-(*iv*)
1052. (*a*)-(*ii*)	(*b*)-(*v*)	(*c*)-(*i*)	(*d*)-(*iii*)	(*e*)-(*iv*)
1053. (*a*)-(*iv*)	(*b*)-(*i*)	(*c*)-(*v*)	(*d*)-(*ii*)	(*e*)-(*iii*)
1054. (*a*)-(*ii*)	(*b*)-(*v*)	(*c*)-(*iv*)	(*d*)-(*iii*)	(*e*)-(*i*)
1055. (*a*)-(*v*)	(*b*)-(*i*)	(*c*)-(*iv*)	(*d*)-(*ii*)	(*e*)-(*iii*)
1056. (*a*)-(*iii*)	(*b*)-(*iv*)	(*c*)-(*i*)	(*d*)-(*ii*)	(*e*)-(*v*)
1057. (*a*)-(*ii*)	(*b*)-(*v*)	(*c*)-(*i*)	(*d*)-(*iii*)	(*e*)-(*iv*)
1058. (*a*)-(*v*)	(*b*)-(*i*)	(*c*)-(*iv*)	(*d*)-(*ii*)	(*e*)-(*iii*)
1059. (*a*)-(*iii*)	(*b*)-(*v*)	(*c*)-(*i*)	(*d*)-(*ii*)	(*e*)-(*iv*)
1060. (*a*)-(*iv*)	(*b*)-(*i*)	(*c*)-(*v*)	{*d*)-(*ii*)	(*e*)-(*iv*)
1061. (*a*)-(*v*)	(*b*)-(*i*)	(*c*)-(*iv*)	(*d*)-(*ii*)	(*e*)-(*iii*)
1062. (*a*)-(*iii*)	(*b*)-(*v*)	(*c*)-(*i*)	(*d*)-(*iv*)	(*e*)-(*ii*)
1063. (*a*)-(*ii*)	(*b*)-(*iii*)	(*c*)-(*v*)	(*d*)-(*i*)	(*e*)-(*iv*)
1064. (*a*)-(*ii*)	(*b*)-(*v*)	(*c*)-(*i*)	(*d*)-(*iii*)	(e)-(*iv*)
1065. (*a*)-(*ii*)	(*b*)-(*i*)	(*c*)-(*v*)	(*d*)-(*iii*)	(*e*)-(*iv*)
1066. (*a*)-(*iii*)	(*b*)-(*i*)	(*c*)-(*v*)	(*d*)-(*ii*)	(*e*)-(*v*)
1067. (*a*)-(*v*)	(*b*)-(*iii*)	(*c*)-(*ii*)	(*d*)-(*iv*)	(*e*)-(*i*)
1068. (*a*)-(*iv*)	(*b*)-(*v*)	(*c*)-(*i*)	(*d*)-(*iii*)	(*e*)-(*ii*)
1069. (*a*)-(*iii*)	(*b*)-(*i*)	(*c*)-(*iv*)	(*d*)-(*ii*)	(*e*)-(*v*)
1070. (*a*)-(*iii*)	(*b*)-(*i*)	(*c*)-(*v*)	(*d*)-(*ii*)	(*e*)-(*iv*)
1071. (*a*)-(*iii*)	(*b*)-(*i*)	(*c*)-(*iv*)	(*d*)-(*ii*)	
1072. (*a*)-(*iv*)	(*b*)-(*iii*)	(*c*)-(*i*)	(*d*)-(*v*)	(*e*)-(*ii*)
1073. (*a*)-(*iv*)	(*b*)-(*i*)	(*c*)-(*ii*)	(*d*)-(*v*)	(*e*)-(*iii*)

SECTION 13
AGRICULTURAL ENGINEERING

I. Fill up the blanks :

1. The two general classes of surveying represent __________ and plane surveying.
2. Geodetic surveying is also denoted as __________ surveying which considers the curvature of the earth because large distances and areas are surveyed.
3. __________ surveying comprises laying out of contour terrace, drainage, profile lines, establishment and preparation of property-maps, computation of farm and field areas as well as laying out farm buildings and roads.
4. The scale of a map is the __________ that every distance on the map bears to the corresponding distance on the ground.
5. "The ratio between any length on the drawing and the corresponding length on the ground which is independent of units of measurements" is denoted as __________.
6. Levels and theodolites are usually equipped with two horizontal cross hairs known as __________ besides the levelling cross hair.
7. __________ means establishment of intermediate points on a straight line between the terminal points.
8. The measurements recorded with a smaller or longer chain can be corrected as :

$$\text{Correct Distance} = \frac{\text{Incorrect length}}{\text{-------------}} \times \text{observed distance}$$

9. __________ method is commonly used to lay out a right angle.
10. The head of a Cross Staff is fixed to the top of an iron shod staff of about __________ m long.
11. The __________ is a compact hand instrument used to set out right angles with greater accuracy than a cross staff.
12. __________ denotes the perpendicular distance taken from any point of a chain line to any object or feature.
13. The head of a Cross Staff is fixed to the top of an iron __________ about 1.2 to 1.5 m long.
14. A compact hand instrument called optical square used to set out __________ with more accuracy than a cross staff.
15. Magnetic __________ denotes the angle between the true meridian and the magnetic meridian.
16. Magnetic __________ of the line represents the angle which a line makes with the magnetic meridian.
17. The sum of the two angles called __________ angles formed due to meeting of two lines at a point is 360°.
18. The bearing of a line in the direction of progress of survey is known as __________.

19. The deviation of compass needle due to various factors from the magnetic meridian is called ________.
20. The local attraction in ________ survey can be corrected by taking the unaffected line as the baseline.
21. Radiation, ________ and traversing are three common methods of plane tabling.
22. Hand levels are used for running of guideline for ________ farming or approximate determination or land slope.
23. In Abney hand levels, the slope angle or the slope percentage is read on the ________.
24. The ________ level is the most commonly used level.
25. The ________ are the two supports in which the telescope rests on the wye level.
26. The maximum permissible error in millimetres for an ordinary levelling is $\pm$________.
27. The ________ system is quicker and involves less of calculations; there is no check to mistakes made in computing elevations of intermediate stations.
28. In ________ after plotting the elevations to a selected scale, studies on grades, depths, high and low spots and quantitative estimations of cuts and fills can be made.
29. The horizontal scale commonly used to plot the profile is 10 or 20 m to 1 cm, while the vertical scale is ________ to 1 cm.
30. ________ is the level to which the earth work will have to be carried out.
31. Fly levels, taken at certain representative points, provide an approximate idea of the nature of ground enabling the engineer to select the line along which to take the detailed levels to prepare ________.
32. A ________ is an imaginary line of a constant elevation on the surface of the ground.
33. The contours and the contour lines differing by a fixed vertical distance are known as ________.
34. In a reservoir, if the water surface areas at elevations 90 and 100 m, are respectively 20,000 and 30,000 sq m, the volume of water between two contours will be ________.
35. In levelling, ________ points are marked by short and long stakes respectively.
36. The ________ method is commonly used to compute the volume of earth till or earth excavation.
37. Land development programme must the planned prior to ________.
38. The centroid of a rectangular field is located at the point of intersection of its ________.
39. The elevation of the centroid of a rectangular field surveyed for levelling by selecting 20 grid points at intervals of 25 m and sum of elevations of the these 20 stations is 2150.75 m, will be ________.
40. Formation level at a grid point at 0.2 per cent slope will be ________ when the station is 50 m from the north-south line passing through the centroid.
41. Cut to fill ratio of more than one means a ________ of cut than fill must be allowed.
42. The soil acts as a reservoir, while water is always in transitory storage in soil in the ________.
43. Canals run from higher to lower elevations, and water flows in them by the
44. The water used for hydro power generation navigation, pollution control, recreation, fish culture etc., has been classified as ________ of water.
45. The great ________ are often uncertain and capricious in their behaviour.
46. The northern stope of the Himalayas drain into Indus, Sutlej and Brahmaputra, while the southern slopes drain into the mighty ________.
47. The large ________ plain between Himalayas in north arid peninsula plateau in south and extending through whole of India support a major part of country's population.

48. __________ and its tributaries drain the heavy rainfall areas of India lying in the eastern and north-eastern regions.

49. Central and southern rivers are the most stable since they flow through __________ stable areas.

50. The rivers contributing to the Ganga in north, Narmada and Tapi in the west, Damodar and Mahanadi in the east and the tributaries of Godavari in the south; originate from the __________ and flow in all the directions.

51. Most of the __________ originate from the Western Ghats stretching along the entire Western coast from north to south.

52. The rivers draining the __________ are short in length, have high flow velocity and carry large volume of water.

53. The planned and rapid development irrigation was forced by two great famines of 1897-98 and __________.

54. The period between 1836 and 1866 witnessed investigations, development and completion of upper Ganga Canal, the upper Bari Doab canal, the Krishna and __________ system.

55. First, Second and Third Five year plans witnessed an increase in irrigation potential of __________ .2.1 and 2.1 million hectares, respectively.

56. The capacity of main Indian canals varies from __________ cubic metres per second.

57. A branch canal, major and minor distributaries carry per second discharge measuring 8.5-4.0 and 5.5-0.75 cubic metres, and __________, respectively.

58. In northern India, outlets used commonly in canals are adjustable proportionate module, pipe outlets, siphon outlets and __________ outlets.

59. Commonly fixed outlet capacity is __________ of the channel.

60. According to Northern India canal and Drainage Act, any channel receiving water from a canal but which is not maintained at the cost of the state including all the subsidiary works of such a channel is known as a __________.

61. The actual area irrigated from outlet denotes __________ of irrigation.

62. The volume of irrigation water divided by the area irrigated is equal to __________.

63. Warabandi (turn) in northern India is fixed by dividing the __________ per week by total area irrigated in hectares from an outlet.

64. The alluvial terrains of the Indo-Gangetic plains comprise one of the richest __________ bearing formations of the world.

65. The place of ground water use along the sub-mountains of Jammu and Kashmir, Himachal Pradesh, Uttar Pradesh, Assam and Meghalaya is usually at __________ location from the point of ground water extraction.

66. A narrow band of __________ ground water extends from Himachal Pradesh through Uttar Pradesh to Bihar.

67. Planned conjunctive use of surface and ground waters may boost canal supply, combat __________ and facilitate use of poor quality ground water for irrigation.

68. A committee of the Planning Commission of India conducted investigations during 1955-61 and advocated that the __________ ratio should be used to assess the feasibility of a new irrigation project.

69. In irrigation project areas wherein the cultivators are unfamiliar with irrigated agriculture and water-demand is inadequate, the Irrigation Commission (1972) supported the implementation of system of __________.

70. Either a porous soil or a geological formation capable of yielding significant volume of water has been denoted as ________.
71. The aquifer lying below an impervious layer and wherein water is under pressure is known as ________.
72. Underground water unlike that in large free bodies lies in soil pores and rock ________.
73. The water rises to a height equal to the piezometric level and this level (piezometric) is higher than the ground level, water flows out due to its own pressure and such a well originating from a broken ________ is known as artesian well.
74. The boundary between a shallow and deep well is ________ because that is about the maximum height to which water could be lifted in practice.
75. After completion of excavation of a well graded ________ is created, each layer of which is held in position by the slightly coarser material above it.
76. Usually, pumps of the ________ type are employed to draw water from the driven wells.
77. In situations where a clay layer lies over a sandy water bearing formation, a ________ is installed therein.
78. In Cauvery delta of Tamil Nadu and the Krishna and Godavari deltas of Andhra Pradesh ________ have been successfully sunk.
79. The piezometric surface around a well existing in the form of an inverted cone which is devoid of water has been named as cone of ________.
80. Wells of 10-60 cm diameter through consolidated rock materials are drilled by ________ method.
81. A tube well, regardless of the drilling method should be ________ as much as is possible.
82. In tube well making, while doing gravel packing the size of the (gravel) should be slightly larger than the size of the ________ opening.
83. In developing a tube well, ________ should be started slowly first and then the speed be increased as the operation proceeds.
84. Dug out farm ponds are usually built where there is no satisfactory ________ site.
85. An improvement in traditional counterpoise lift is the addition of a ________ device.
86. One man can lift nearly 16,000 litres of water from a height of 50 to 100 cm by ________.
87. The discharge of a paddle wheel of 2.4 m diameter with 12 wades operated by a man is approximately ________ litres per hour.
88. A shallow well reciprocating pump can lift water to a height of about ________ at standard atmospheric pressure of one kilogramme per square centimetre.
89. Deep well plunger pumps are usually ________.
90. In diffuser type of pumps, the velocity head of the liquid leaving the impeller is more completely converted into pressure head than that in the ________.
91. In rural areas where electricity is not available, a well designed ________ has been found suitable to pump water from the open wells.
92. In case of a centrifugal pump, at the point where head and efficiency curve intersect, the discharge is 1110 litres per minute, against a head of 27 metres and efficiency of 60 per cent, and the power required is ________.
93. Design and proportionate well the suction lines to minimise the friction losses and submerge sufficiently to avoid formation of ________ and sucking of air into the pump.
94. The centrifugal pumps on account of being non-positive action, need the ________ before they are operated.

95. The efficiencies of __________ are comparable with those of a good horizontal centrifugal pump.
96. If a pump has an incorrect rotation of the driver or if the pumping head is too high, or if pump speed is too low or if suction pipe is clogged such a pump will not __________.
97. A motor made of smaller diameter and is much longer than an ordinary motor for an easy insertion in small diameter tube-wells is __________.
98. A submersible pump is especially suitable for the deep and crooked wells as it embodies __________.
99. The flow from the impeller of a propeller type of pump is __________ to the axis of the drive shaft.
100. A propeller pump is usable in special conditions as for pumping from canals, rivers *etc.*, and pumping from drainage of its __________ characteristics.
101. When an airlift pump is in action, the rising air bubbles and layers of air with the pressure of liquid acting on the inlet of the rising main, forces the liquid to rise a distance, depending upon the amount of submergence and __________.
102. The __________ is the most efficient one since it entails no loss of power in transmission but calls for identical speed of this and the pump.
103. In float method, the average rate of water flow is the product of and the average cross-sectional area of the stream.
104. The discharge through an orifice is calculated using the formula __________ (Do not expand Q, a, g and h).
105. The basic formula to determine the discharge through a weir is __________ (Do not explain Q, C, L, H and m).
106. Commonly used formulae to work out the discharge from rectangular, contracted rectangular Cipolleti weirs are respectively Q = 0.0184 LH 3/2, __________ and Q = 0.186 LH 3/2.
107. Sometimes hydraulic gradient is expressed as __________ by friction per given length of pipe and is equal to head lost due to friction divided by the total length of pipe.
108. The velocity of stream tends to be when the __________ is larger for the same area of the cross-section of the stream.
109. The wetted perimeter and hydraulic radius are minimum and maximum respectively, when the most efficient cross-section of an open channel is a __________.
110. The control of gradient and the flow-velocity either through the use of drops or by building up channel beds, would make it possible to use __________ on steep slopes.
111. Though __________ reduce the seepage losses, are safe against breaks and embody a number of other advantages the physical factors and cost relationships dictate their disability.
112. An irrigator has essentially to carry water across roads, hillsides, and natural depressions and hence needs conveyance structures to combat the natural obstacles; these structures are __________.
113. Building of an inverted siphon (only siphon), in case of a stream upstream has been found essential to act as a __________ measure of slowing down the velocity of flowing water to work as the __________.
114. The sitting of a siphon occurs due to upstream erosion but the tanks of a siphon slow down the velocity of flowing water as these (tanks) function as __________.
115. The provision of erosion control structures in case of irrigation channels involves the __________ of flowing water.
116. The water flows at high velocities which is reduced by providing sufficiently large stilling basins in case of __________.
117. The discharge from a siphon tube can be measured by the formula __________ (Do not expand symbols).

118. Pipelines operate under pressure and hence can be laid __________.
119. The underground pipelines are not very suitable in canal command areas on account of silt laden water and __________.
120. The discharge through a pipeline can be computed by using the __________.
121. The size of the concrete pipe on which an air vent is mounted should be at least half of the size of the __________.
122. When gated pipes are connected to the underground pipelines through hydrants, gated pipes permit the conveyance of water in an enclosed system from the source head end of the __________.
123. Either the constant or nearly constant rate at which the soil takes in water after an extended period of time denotes the __________.
124. The water requirement of crops denotes the __________ and the supply comprises contributions from any source of water.
125. Net irrigation requirement divided by field efficiency of the system under field conditions equals __________.
126. The uniform distribution of water in a border strip is ensured by recession and __________ curves.
127. The vertical distance along the border (furrow) between the advance and recession curves at the point denotes __________ time.
128. A useful thumb rule in check basin design is that the water spread in the entire basin should be covered in __________ the time required to infiltrate the net depth of irrigation water.
129. Though the upper basins receive more water, construction of basins with __________ between successive basins on impermeable soils facilitates irrigation from one turn out to head ditch, with the water overflowing from basin to basin successively and economizes the labour needed for water application.
130. Water infiltrates into soil and spreads laterally in __________ method of irrigation.
131. The __________ to flow of water may be owing to the effect of roughness of the wetted surface of the furrow as well as the resistance offered by the crop.
132. Furrows should be spaced in a way that the spread of water takes place to the sides, into the ridge and the root zone before its movement down below the __________.
133. Large furrows are usually made with a lister or a __________ board plough.
134. The corrugations should be spaced at about 35-40 cm to allow the moistening of the surface soil between the corrugations on relatively __________ soil.
135. The soil should embody uniform texture, sufficient permeability for movement of water horizontally and vertically, within as well as below the crop root zone for successful execution of __________ design.
136. Flexibility of the equipment coupled with efficient water application control make __________ of irrigation adaptable to most of the topographic situations without much of land preparation.
137. Drip irrigation method economizes on water use and also gives relatively higher yields with poor quality water and hence it is becoming popular in __________.
138. A smooth flow of water takes place through the drip nozzles provided there is efficient performance of the __________.
139. The spacing of drip nozzles within a lateral is a dependent function of the type of the crop and the nozzle __________.
140. On account of flat topography, frequent floods, canal irrigation and obstruction to natural drainage ways, the drainage problems are more acute in the __________.
141. The percolation of one centimetre of water below crop root zone may raise the water-table by about

142. In order to provide gravel packing in a water-table observation well of 2.5 cm diameter, an auger hole is first drilled and its diameter is ________.

143. Isobath lines to the water-table are drawn by standard mapping procedure, that is, ________.

144. Deep open ditches have been found suitable for sub-surface drainage which involves the lowering of water-table below the root zone and these are unlined ________.

145. In order to lead excess surface water of surface drain laterals from crowned strips of lands into dead furrows, then to collection drains and finally to an out, it is necessary to design, construct and maintain the ________.

146. The minimum depth and the cross-sectional area of the ditch in parallel field ditch system are ________ respectively.

147. Removal of ________ both from the surface and below the surface of a farm land in order to create the conditions favourable for plant growth is known as agricultural drainage.

148. The design and layout of the cross-slope ditches are essentially similar to ________.

149. ________ of the formation immediately around the drain greatly influence the flow of water into the sub-surface drains.

150. In a situation wherein the soil texture is medium, potential soil productivity and the value of crops to be grown are high and the potential design factors entail only moderate cost, the most needed and justified drainage system is ________.

151. If the water flows horizontally through the sides of an auger hole, the rate at which the hole fills with water is ________ to its cross-sectional area.

152. The rate of rise of water in the auger hole due to circumferential flow at time t is ________.

153. The equation of ellipse as shown by J.N. Luthin (1973) is ________.

154. When the diameter of the perforations in a drainage pipe are increased from 6 to 12 mm at 120 cm depth, the water flow will increase by 68 and 36 per cent for ________ respectively.

155. The main advantage of PVC pipes for drainage is the feasibility of ________.

156. It is imperative that the filter material should be more pervious than the base soils since it avoids the building up of ________.

157. The limits of the filter material to be satisfied for a specific base material have been established based on design criteria by the U.S. Bureau and the ________ of Engineers.

158. In digging of tile drains with hand tools, an open spade is used in ________.

159. The selected drainage coefficient should hold good for the entire contributing watershed when the surface water is admitted through ________.

160. If a grassed water way and a tile drain discharges at the same place, it would be essential to provide a ________ headwall.

161. Flap gates hinged at the top are used to protect the tile outlet from backwater when the level of water in the outlet rises above the ________.

162. When the quantity of surface water is small or when the sendiment load is too large, the drains likely to be installed are called ________.

163. Wherever degree of slope of tile line calls for reduction or surface water enters the tile or several lateral join the main at one station, it is necessary to provide ________.

164. A mole plough has a long blade like shank to which is attached a ________ plug called mole.

165. The drained water is conducted through vertical well for penetration into the ________ in case of vertical drainage.

166. Mesopotamia had well developed land in the time of the Babylonians, Assirians, Chaldeans and Persians it is now virtually a desert due __________.

167. In Syria where 1-2 metres of topsoil has been washed off most the hillsides, there are hundreds of __________.

168. In India, the civilizations which became extinct due to neglect of land management were __________.

169. There are four factors involved in the process of soil erosion and these comprise detaching capacity of the erosive agent, soil detachability, transporting capacity of the erosive agent and soils __________.

170. Erosive capacity of the raindrops is governed by the quantum and intensity of rainfall, soil-striking velocity of raindrops and their __________.

171. Soil loss by erosion is proportional to __________ to the 0.5 power.

172. The effects of climate, topography and soil on erosion may be completely negated by the provisions of a good __________.

173. Mainly heavy implements like ploughs, harrow ploughs and at times harrows are used for __________.

174. In India there are about 40 or more types of indigenous ploughs which are basically identical but vary widely in their __________.

175. Indian (indigenous) ploughs, the __________ of the share in some designs (especially in Gujarat and Rajasthan) passes through a slot especially provided in the body.

176. In __________ method of ploughing, a single ploughman would normally divide one hectare of area in 8-10 small blocks.

177. Most of the one-way walking types of mould board ploughs are designed to throw the furrow slice to only __________ in the direction of motion.

178. The share point of __________ share is a small replacement unit and can be changed before the complete share becomes unserviceable.

179. In adjustment of plough, the straight edge is placed under the point of the share and the land side, a clearance of 0.3 to 0.5 cm should be measured and this is known as __________.

180. Vegetative canopy and well distributed as well as close growing vegetation minimise the soil loss due to water erosion by absorption of impact of raindrops and the prevention of __________.

181. It depends on the soil structural relationships of the immediate soil surface and the intensity of soil loss through water erosion since the latter is a dependent function of a soil's __________.

182. Allison from the study of four soils observed that the relative soil loss for an half hour rainfall period varies of the __________.

183. The four stages involved in the development of a gully are, formation, development, __________ stages.

184. It applies to the lower end to the stream tributaries and streams embodying continuous flow and relatively flat gradients and thus __________ is different from the gully erosion.

185. Most of the multipurpose reservoirs in India have been designed on the basic of sediment inflow into them to the tune of __________ of the watershed area.

186. An instrument consisting of a galvanized iron cylinder 225 cm in diameter and 60 cm high with a funnel top equipped with a brass knife edge periphery commonly is known as __________.

187. The ordinate of __________ rainfall at any time represents the total rainfall that has occurred from zero time up to that time.

188. It is essential to design an economical size of a soil conservation structure that the due weightage cis accorded to the recurrence of the storms of varying __________.

189. The water available for infiltration or overland runoff is known as________.

190. The formula in metric terms (based on the equation proposed by C.E. Ramser) representing the rational method of prediction of runoff rates is ________ (Do not explain the symbols).

191. An empirical formula applicable to estimate the time of concentration (Tc) is ________.

192. When time of concentration (Tc) is expressed in FPS unit, then $Tc = 0.0078K^{0.77}$ and if Tc = time of concentration in minutes, K = ________.

193. The erosive wind is turbulent at all heights except in a paper thin zone along the surface projections where the flow is ________.

194. It has been observed that there exists a gradient in velocity as the wind moves over the soil surface, the velocity is the minimum near the ground and increases in proportion to ________ of the height above the surface.

195. The saltation movement of soil results due to the pressure of the wind on soil particles as well as collision of a particle with other particles and particles moving by this process ranges from ________.

196. The percentage of weight of soil carried in saltation, suspension and surface creep is 50-75, ________, respectively.

197. A typical sand dune on windward and leeward sides embodies the slopes of ________ respectively.

198. Soil erodibility can be conveniently related with the equivalent diameter which is equal to ________.

199. Strip cropping traps the saltating soil particles and consequently reduces soil ________.

200. The crop residues for the control of wind erosion can be best handled with the implements having sweep type of ________.

201. The sub-surface tillage implements equipped with straight or V-shaped blades or rods undercut land and may maintain 80-90 per cent of the crop residues on the surface after a ________.

202. It has been brought out by the investigations that when the wind direction is at right angles to the shelter-belt, the reductions in wind velocity range from ________ near and to the leeward of the belt.

203. Graded terraces have been classified as interception and diversion types, and level terraces as ________.

204. An American farmer, in 1885 introduced the broad based terraces in order to carry out the tillage operations over the entire structure, these are also referred to as ________.

205. Though there is no maximum length limit for a level terrace, it would be desirable to make check dams at ________ intervals in its channel.

206. If erosion can be controlled, it is possible to direct the outflow from terraces either into a waste land or into a ________.

207. It is imperative to remove the surplus vegetation when one has to construct the terraces using either ________.

208. A relatively more efficient construction of terraces is possible by V-ditcher in conjunction with a mould board or ________.

209. Farming operations done as nearly parallel to the terrace as possible aid in moisture conservation and erosion control by producing a series of miniature ________.

210. Though bench terraces on steep slopes retard the erosion and make cropping both possible and safe, it is economically viable in situation where the available land is ________.

211. ________ is scarce relative to need for agricultural production.

212. A freeboard of at least 15 cm, side slopes 1:1 and height of about 30 cm and the bottom width of 75 cm comprise the common dimensions of the ________.

213. A triangular channel can be easily constructed using a V-ditcher, while a trapezoidal one with a V-ditcher and a ________.

214. In planning for gully control, it is essential to take into account not only the possible benefits downstream and the adjacent area, but also on-site benefits to determine its ________.

215. The storage capacity of contour furrows depends on their spacing and ________.

216. Diversion ditch located immediately below the inadequately protected fields from sheet erosion need a closely growing vegetation embodying a minimum width of 15 metres and it is called permanent ________.

217. Permanent structures are designed to carry the runoff from the heaviest rain that may be expected once either in 25 or in 50 years or even more depending the estimated ________.

218. The free flow capacity for drop spillways can be estimated by weir formula. If the value of Coefficient C_∞ is assumed as 0.6, the formula in metric units can be written as ________ (Do not explain the symbols).

219. The ratio of the inertia force to gravity forces is known as Froude Number and can be written as ________.

220. In a straight inlet drop spillways the dissipation and conversion of energy are accomplished either in a straight apron or a ________.

221. Chute spillways are frequently used in combination with earth dams to drop water from farther than is feasible with ________.

222. The length L_B (in chute spillways) of the stilling basin for Froude numbers between 1.7 and 17 can be determined by ________.

223. The capacity of a pipe spillway is designed following the formula ________.

224. The use of low-pressure pneumatic tyres became popular in tractors during ________.

225. During 1930s the first Ferguson system tractors incorporating three-point linkage with ________ control were introduced.

226. A significant improvement in 4-wheel drive systems have enabled the manufacturers to extend the power range of tractors of convention shape up to about ________.

227. In tractors more than 200 h.p., equal size wheels are usual and the general shape is commonly a two-section ________.

228. The improvement in 4-wheel drive have removed a number of earlier limitations of conventional tractors in respect of ________.

229. One significant remaining difference between the multi-purpose and systems tractors is whether the vehicle incorporates a load plateform or ________.

230. Driver's seats are improved to reduce spinal and intestinal injuries due to excessive vibrations and intensity of noise at drivers ears and the controls designed to improve of ________ tractor driving.

231. ________ enables the tractor driver to continue to raise a loaded manure fork as the backs away from the heap and manoeuvres his tractor either towards the spreader or the trailor.

232. The simplicity, ease of use and low coast of use of ________ applicators comprise a preferred wipe-on technique over other complex devices.

233. The section of the shoulder banks or bunds along the outer edges of terraces should be designed to be stable against ________.

234. Biplanes designed military trainers are widely used for spraying and dusting, but the trend is towards especially designed ________.

235. In a centrifugal pump water enters at the centre of the casting, and the motion of the impeller pushes up the delivery pipe, which is attached _______ to the outer rim of the casting.

236. The semi-rotary pumps are light in weight and easily portable and hence these are useful for work where _______ cannot be used.

237. Modern power-driven diaphragm pumps used on spraying machines normally used a _______ diaphragm.

238. The sum of static head and the friction head representing all friction losses is the _______ head.

239. Piston pumps usually cost slightly less to run than the centrifugal but the latter are less subject to _______.

240. Power steering is fitted as standard on almost all the high power tractors, and comprises a necessity on all the large _______.

241. Hydrostatic transmission system has become less important with the advent of finger-tip controlled _______ and synchromesh gears which make it easy to change the gear on the move.

242. John Deere (1960) designed a quick hitch for use between the standard 3-point linkage and slightly modified implements, after its study an _______, applicable in different sizes to three categories of 3-point free-link hitches, was agreed and published.

243. Most of the countries work to international (150) standards for features concerned with interchangeability between the _______.

244. The further development of specialized vehicles is essential for some complex harvesting operations and for handling unit loads because low priced all purpose tractors cannot be technically as efficient as specialist _______ machines.

245. The general farm-work using a medium-powered tractor employed regularly to transport and to do all kinds of fieldwork, the best tyred wheels are _______.

246. The net power on engine or a tractor means the power the engine can deliver for the performance of work at the _______.

247. The modern _______ used in agricultural engineering research and testing are almost invariably of the strain gauge type.

248. Belt power is exactly equal to the _______ if the pulley is directly mounted on the engine crankshaft.

249. The complete OECD Test Code had by 1980 became very long and expensive, but the develop-ment of _______ later on was adopted since it covers the essential major characteristics sufficiently.

250. The Nebraska tractor tests determine the powers of the tractors according to the code laid down by ASA and SAE which is called the _______.

251. The manufactures under the widely used OECD Test Code nominates a _______ which is intended to be employed for continuous operation.

252. In the process of tractor testing in accordance with OECD test code besides power at p.t.o. and at the drawbar, the corresponding _______ is also measured.

253. Within limits, with pneumatic tyres on firm ground the addition of 454 kg ballast to the rear wheels will usually increase the maximum drawbar pull by about _______.

254. In testing of a tractor, agricultural tests are important because in Nebraska test or the British Standard, 150 or OECD test, it would be possible for a tractor fitted with wheels to put up an excellent drawbar performance but actually may be unsuitable for normal _______.

255. The maximum drawbar power in pneumatic tyred tractor is attainable at fairly high speeds and low drawbar pulls, but the limiting factor at the higher speed(s) is engine power and not _______.

256. In a situation where it is impracticable to increase either the width of work or the speed or to high implements in tandem, the best solution will be to run the tractor in a higher gear, with the engine __________.

257. The distance travelled without load minus the distance travelled when working divided by the distance travelled without load multiplied by 100 is equal to percentage__________.

258. The maximum drawbar power that can be developed generally falls off rapidly at speeds exceeding 4.8-6.4 km/hr in a __________ tractor.

259. In case of engine speed of tractor a good, flexible __________, is made capable of adjustment to give, in normal working conditions, over 50 per cent more or less than the standard governed engine speed.

260. It has been observed that most tractor engines show the lowest __________ at about 75 per cent of the maximum power and engine speed.

261. Most of the operators manuals devote a considerable proportion of space to describe the operation and the use of modern tractors due to the complexity of the __________.

262. The improvement in tractor can reduce or sometimes even eliminate the possible dangers like the provision of a reliable __________ hitch makes it possible to hitch an equipment safely by an unaided driver without leaving the safety cab.

263. A rear-wheel-drive tractor can safely be driven up a slope that is dangerous to drive down, partly because there is effective __________ to the driven and braked wheels only when going up hill.

264. The Tractor Safety Cabs (Amendment) Regulations, 1973 require that the maximum noise at the driver's ear as measured by the specified test for new tractors is __________.

265. Use of __________ tractors calls for bigger and heavier equipment and also involves some significant problems of matching as well as balance between the two.

266. The availability of effective __________ implement linkages and p.t.o. makes it certain that this feature will be increasingly demanded.

267. Besides reasonably high clearance and easy alteration of wheel tract width, ease of __________ is also essential where both high clearance and low-ground-pressure work is expected of one vehicle.

268. Small tractors fundamentally use the mechanisms like the ones on __________.

269. In case of fully hydrostatic systems there is no __________ between the steering wheels and the steered wheels.

270. The rapid development of __________ tractors and fully hydrostatic steering stimulated a number of improvements in front wheel drive systems.

271. The adjustment of __________ on a crop tractor for open field-work can be adjusted by fixing the rear wheels with a sliding wheel hub fixed to the axle shaft by means an easily loosened clamp.

272. The oil-immersed type of __________ in a tractor provides effective cooling, reduces fade and completely eliminates the entry of water and dirt.

273. Hydraulic __________ operated tractor brakes require to provide a suitable valve and hydraulic outlet at the rear for operation of trailer brakes.

274. The __________ system is sometimes a nuisance in the field-work because the major portion of power may be delivered to the wheel meeting the least resistance.

275. A four-wheel drive (tractor) transmission system embodying a positive power-shift gear box easily engageable rear differential lock augments safety on slopes due to assured __________.

276. So far as the gear change system in a tractor is concerned __________ offers more choices with fingertip change.

277. In a tractor, one type of synchromesh *e.g.* Marshall employs high-torque synchrocones on the layshaft on forward and reverse gear-change system in conjunction with three speed (high, medium, low) ________.

278. It is an advantage to have a transmission system that provides instantaneous shuttling from forward to reverse for regular work with a ________.

279. A number of rough-terrain handling vehicles employ a combination of a fairly simple three forward with one reverse mechanical transmission in conjunction with an automatic power shift torque converter which permits rapid ________ on the move.

280. When torque convertor is found in automobile transmission system, the energy is transmitted by the oil impelled at high speed to impinge on the blades of turbine, such a transmission system is known as ________.

281. Whenever change in direction of power transmission is called for, this is easily achievable with hydraulic motor and its ________ couplings.

282. Ground speed p.t.o. drive (in power take-off) at a British Standard speed of one revolution per ________ of forward travel can provide a useful drive for drills, distributors and sprayers but generally it is not offered by tractor manufactures as similar results can be easily achieved by controlled hydraulic drive.

283. Some tractors are designed from the start with ________ and p.t.o. at both front and rear.

284. Radial tyres compared with crossply have an increased footprint area-leading to improved floatation, lower rolling resistance and an increased ________.

285. In addition to water ballasting in the drive wheels of a tractor to aid traction ________ can be bolted to the wheel centres or heavy cast iron wheel centres can be used.

286. Among the tractor engines ________ four-stroke is the most common one.

287. One of the most important features of agricultural tractor is ________ acting through three point linkage.

288. In the 'open-centre' hydraulic lift system a constant displacement pump supplies oil to a ________.

289. Most of the modern implement control systems are applied through a three-point linkage consisting of one upper and two lower links which in ________, respectively.

290. The variations in the pull exerted by the tractor on the implement deflect the load spring, and result in a corresponding movements of the hydraulic control valve in an ________ control.

291. In draft control, moving of control lever forwards and rearwards puts the valve in ________, the implement depth increases and decreases respectively to return the valve to neutral.

292. An oil enters the external cylinder of a remote depth central hydraulic system from the pump, an equal amount of oil is displaced from behind the external ram piston and is forced into the main ________.

293. The elimination of inefficiency due to friction, elasticity and wear of mechanical components can be accomplished by employing ________ in control of three-point linkage systems.

294. In monitoring the performance of a tractor, use of a combined meter with two needles, one of which displays engine r.p.m. via impulses from the alternator; the other exhibits output via exhaust gas temperative, helps in ________.

295. An advanced 'Tractometer' suitable to fitting to any tractor make or model (RDS) measures forward speed by ________.

296. Direct control of application rate by microprocessor can be fairly easily arranged where the fertilizer is metered by a hydraulic drive to central metering feed rollers, as in many ________ systems.

297. Hydraulic power available from a pump may be computed in Imperial units from ________ formula.

298. In high-power-tractors built to carry implements weighing more than one tonne, the linkage is heavier and more difficult to manipulate by hand, and hence additional refinements like ________ are added.

299. 'Essentially an overrun ratchet keeping the front wheels locked together while they are running at the same speed, but releases the outer wheel when it needs to run faster during turns' is in effect the ________.

300. Most of the very high-powered articulated-steer tractors are fitted with eight tyres and are so wide that their use case in Britain is Subject to ________ 'use' regulations.

301. 'The purpose-designed cab and a console comprising seat and driving controls which rotate as a single unit through 180 degrees after the release of one locking device' comprise an important feature of ________ tractors.

302. The engine and the transmission are compactly arranged over the rear driving axle in case of ________ tool-bars.

303. It is essential that a constant fairly high forward speed (8-15 km/hr) be maintained during working of vehicles primarily for the application of ________.

304. A essential feature of motorcycle-based ATVs as the wide ________ with tread pattern designed to carry reasonable loads and to provide traction to pull a trailer or equipment on soft surfaces without serious damage to the soil or to the growing crop.

305. Tracklaying tractors when ploughing normally run with both tracks on unploughed ground; this gives the advantage of ________ of the furrow bottom.

306. The interest in ________ assemblies suitable for fitting in place of or around the rear wheels of a general purpose tractor to provide an outfit capable to overcome difficult conditions and substantial drawbar pull in situation where any type of wheel would be unsatisfactory.

307. Lower-powered tractor of conventional design and small overall dimensions are often described as ________ tractors.

308. Some European narrow-track tractors embody engines of 33 kW have four-wheel drive by equal-sized wheels, and ________ steering of a type to provide a very small turning cycle.

309. As far as simple tractors 'single or two cylinder engine of 15-30 h.p.' are concerned, the main interest centres on a type with a ________ channel construction, with two large wheels at the rear and two small steering wheels on a centre privoted front axle.

310. Soils vary widely in their suitability for 'minimum' cultivation in its extreme from ________.

311. The body (of a plough) *viz.*, general purpose, semi-digger and digger implies suitability for unbroken shallow work (up to about 200 mm), partly broken medium-depth work (up to about 250 mm) and to produce broken work at a depth up to ________, respectively.

312. The changes of angle if the main beam (of plough) and of the individual bodies provide for quick changes of ________.

313. The share of the ________ has a definite 'neck' that has the effect of placing the cutting edge well in advance of the mouldboard.

314. The part of plough which inverts furrow slice in a general purpose plough and pulverises it in the digging type is the ________.

315. The softer the soil, the less ________ are required to keep the plough running smoothly and cutting its full depth and width.

316. An efficient use of very large skimmers is allowed in some new designs of ploughs like ________ plough.

317. All the forces acting upon a plough at work may be considered as balanced about a theoretical point located between the mouldboard and the landslide is called ________.

318. The vertical hitch adjustment of a plough is always influenced by the length of the hitch and ________.

319. The centre of resistance of a plough engaged in deep ploughing with a tracklaying tractor lies much nearer the ploughed land than the line drawn through the centre of power parallel to the direction of travel leads ________.

320. Rear wheel setting is very important on all the disc ploughs, and on a mounted disc plough it must be adjusted in conjunction with the setting of ________.

321. A system of ploughing popular especially in Fens (U.K.) for deep work, where the fields are well shaped and must be left level is known as ________.

322. With a trailed or semi-mounted plough it is the best, when ploughing from outside, to leave the diagonals unploughed until finish for square ploughing with ________.

323. Square ploughing with cross lands is certainly the fastest for trailed ploughs, and probably the fastest for any type of ________ plough.

324. Tractors fitted with 'load-monitor' can employ a special draught-regulating remote cylinder at the rear of long ________ plough.

325. The main reason for front mounting of a plough is usually to secure maximum ploughing efficiency from ________ 4-wheel drive tractor rather than to carry out two or three operations simultaneously.

326. Variable ________ of a plough is particularly advantageous to work up and down the slopes, making finishes, and to plough round obstacles and up to wary field edges.

327. Time on marking out, setting and closing ridges is saved, open furrows on junctions between lands are eliminated, turning time is saved and running along headlands is reduced by a ________.

328. Where under-body subsoiler blades are fitted or ploughs are used on rocky soils, automatic reset mechanisms are increasingly used to save time and to reduce ________.

329. Multiple legs are commonly staggered on a 2-beam implement; some are arranged in a single line of blunt arrow shape on soil ________.

330. Early attempt to reduce drought and improve the effectiveness of subsoils by employing a p.t.o. drive to reciprocate the points underlined the need for strength and durability in the main components and good engineering design of the ________.

331. Replaceable wearing plates on shin and landslide and an improved easy-fit type of point is provided in ________.

332. The disc in disc ploughs is set at an angle to the line of travel, and it turns a furrow slice to one side with a ________.

333. Main advantage of the mounted implement is its easy transport and ________.

334. Usually very wide, embodying moderately small discs in gangs of six and capable of independent vertical movement on the main frame is a popular mounted implement called ________.

335. There are no essential differences between deep cultivators and subsoilers on the one hand and shallow cultivators and ________ on the other.

336. Any type of cultivator that is capable of working compacted soil at moderate depth is indiscriminately called a ________.

337. Sets of seeds harrows and slightly heavier 'light' harrows from 6 to 9 m wide are easily drawn with the capacity of ________.

338. In case of combination cultivators with wide implements, it is also imperative to allow for independent floating of adjacent sections to ensure constant work-depth over ________ surfaces.

339. The spring-tined harrow can be adopted to produce very variable effect and in fact it is a ________.

340. An implement with ground-driven spiked wheels, with curved teeth embodying slicing action is a typical ________.

341. The discs (of harrows) are generally 457-610 mm in diameter that rotate as the harrow is pulled along, and the action on the soil is unlike that of small ________ plough.

342. The transport problems with heavy implements of semi-mounted or trailed type may be solved by the use of pneumatic-tyred road wheels and external ________.

343. It is useful under some situations to have a disc harrow which can be off set from the tractor to work beneath ________ trees.

344. The heavy 'one-way' discs with a single axle can effectively replace ploughs for ________.

345. Working depth is generally shallow, but may be up to 180 mm in ground-driven ________.

346. A forward speed of 10-12 km/hr is advantageous in case of ________ tillage implements with gearing between rotors.

347. Modem furrow presses are mainly designed for simultaneous use when ploughing, often with a ________ plough.

348. Heavy crumbler rollers with large diameter with narrow sections of heavy beams projecting from the cylinders at right angle to the travel-direction are powerful ________.

349. Good levelling work can be done by employing tractor-mounted land smothers attached to a vertically converging ________.

350. Modern tractor-driven rotary cultivators are usually fully mounted, the largest machines being fitted with a ________ to facilitate handling the heavy machine.

351. Some of the useful powered cultivators of the horizontal rotary axis type employ also un-driven tines and often a rotary crumbler in the form of combined ________ machine.

352. Reciprocating motion always involves vibrations and the bearings have to work very close to the soil and it was an arduous task to obtain reasonably long life from ________.

353. Change of broadcasting to drilling was primarily brought about by Jethro Tull's (1674-1740) publication entitled ________ which came in 1733.

354. Ridging work can also be done by concave discs suitably angled or by a ________ ridger.

355. A raised flat-topped bed can be produced by using a short-tined ________ in the centre.

356. A rear-attached tool-bar has a much higher labour productivity where in the grooves in cut soil when drilling a crop are followed by ________.

357. A rotary-head type of thinning machine tends to be preferable for dealing with ________.

358. Regardless of the type of thinner (of plants), the forward speed should not usually be higher than about ________.

359. The mechanism of the modern external force-feed drill consists essentially of a fluted roller rotating just below the seed box to draw seed from the bottom of the box into hoppers at the tops of the ________.

360. On a typical seed drill the baffle gates or feed gates can be set in three quarters for large seeds, half open for medium seeds and ________ for small seeds.

361. In pneumatic or jet-drills, sowing rate is set by adjusting the effective length of the metering barrel by a screw which sets the position of a sliding ________.

362. The general design features entail the use on large-scale medium of heavy-land farms in working width of 6 or 12 m, where 4-wheel-drive tractors of 90 to 200 h.p. are available to run ________ drills.

363. In single-disc drill coulter a ________ hardened steel disc cuts the furrow to deliver the seed to boot attached to the convex side of the disc, just below and behind its centre.

364. A number of modern drills provide for spacing down to 100-125 mm achieved with small _______.

365. Gearing of drill is relatively simple where means of adjustment of seed rate are provided in the feed mechanism, as in the _______.

366. Some modern drills provide a large number of speeds through the use of oil-bath _______ boxes.

367. A control box operated by pressure switches from the tractor cab is provided on modern multi- purpose drills normally offered with _______ equipment.

368. Drill-wheels are used to drive the mechanism, and putting the drill out of gear simply by lifting whole machine bodily off the ground is practised in _______ drills.

369. Coulter design include extra large diameter (365 mm) single concave discs capable of cutting through trash in case of equipment for _______.

370. The compactness of many power harrows and rotary cultivators and the very small amount of extra power needed to drill immediately behind such machines make _______ combinations attractive.

371. If the headlands are left unsown until last, it is difficult to cover the seed owing to the effect of _______.

372. When a drill is being stopped or started there is always a lag between the operation of the feed mechanism and arrival of the seed at the _______.

373. At the time of putting away the drill at the end of the season, it is advisable to lower the coulters in order to remove _______ from the coulter springs.

374. Unit-drills for root and vegetable crops are _______ of two types in which feed hole and agitator comprise feed mechanism to keep the seed flowing and those in which there is _______ mechanism.

375. The seed is carried round in the slot and is positively ejected when it arrives over the furrow opener in _______ drills.

376. Single-seeding of lettuce and very small seeds like that of petunia is done by multi-row units made on the application of _______.

377. When a gang of 'single-seed' drill units is employed a shaft which drives the individual feed mechanisms is better than that wherein the drive is by the _______.

378. In maize drills, the rotating plate lies at the bottom of a _______.

379. Suspension of seeds in a suitable gel to make metering seeds of irregular shapes easy, and facilitates gemination in controlled conditions with application of advocated agro-chemicals comprise the steps in _______.

380. The _______ seeding head has lines of probes which are lowered into the liquid container and suck a single pre-germinated seed on to the hole of appropriate size at end of each probe; withdraw from the liquid, deliver the row of seeds into peat blocks, release the vacuum and withdraw, leaving the seeds in the block.

381. One type of _______ applicable to any fluid seed drill employs a photo-sensitive element which detects the seeds as they drop through a section of transparent tubing or through specially designed sensor unit.

382. A typical modern-drill with studded or fluted roller feed and attached harrows is well suited for _______ drilling.

383. In potato planting, automatic planters of the belt feed type tend to give a less even distribution than hand-fed some automatic machines or _______.

384. With senti-automatic potato planters, the operator sitting on the machines, has to place the _______.

385. Two potato planters are usually mounted, 4-row either mounted or trailed, but six row are normally _______.

386. A number of unmanned potato harvesters are capable of dealing easily with flat-topped beds at 1.83 m centres and about 1.53 m __________.

387. A simple 2-row potato planter for chitted seed employs __________ corrugated conveyor sections to transfer the tubes laterally from the two hoppers to a valuable-speed hydraulic drive metering belt.

388. The Smallford 'Setwell' is a more basic model designed for high-speed work producing the most uniform result possible, using graded seed, without any __________ system.

389. A system of potato planter filling developed by the SIAE, the units are placed by fork-fit on two pivoting goalpost-type frame which are fitted to the plant-hopper and can be opened or closed by __________.

390. In the process of stone and windrowing, whole of the soil to be lifted at harvest is passed through the windrower, the stones are removed by __________ of the required spacing.

391. In a situation where the quantity of stones to be windrowed exceeds about 250 tonnes/ha, stone removal as a preliminary operation on the worst area can be carried out by some machines fitted with a __________.

392. In a hand-fed transplanting machine, the plants directly dropped in the furrows made by hollow coulters followed by a pair of __________.

393. With mechanical planters, the operators place the plants in trays or between fingers on an __________, and from this point the plants are dealt with entirely mechanically.

394. Some of the mechanical planters embody a __________ especially for use under dry ground conditions.

395. When the external hydraulic ram is operated in a bulk fertilizer spreader, the scoop is automatically raised over the vertical position, to a point where the fertilizer falls into the __________.

396. Liquid fertilizers are sometimes applied by very simple type of ground-driven peristaltic pump which provides a __________ effect.

397. Simultaneous loading of fertilizer and seed for __________ maintains the weight balance, and speeds up the work of liquid fertilizers.

398. Ammonia is handled as a liquid under pressure in special cylinders or large pressure tanks of __________.

399. A __________ distributor for general use should be capable of uniformly distributing the quantities varying from 125 to more than 1900 kg/ha.

400. One of the simplest in operation and best for sowing basic slag or any other free-flowing material is the delivery roller called __________ type.

401. A broadcasting machine embodying a hopper, often of truncated cone shape, situated above a disc which rotates at high speed is __________ delivery type.

402. The provision of a reliable bout marking procedure is done by employing the __________ systems.

403. __________ delivery mechanism dealing effectively with most fertilizers consists essentially of a tappered spout oscillating fairly rapidly throwing out the fertilizer.

404. Late application of nitrogen to tramlined cereals can be done by the __________ embodying a correct width.

405. The varying size of seed and fertilizer hoppers in a combined grain and fertilizer drill may be done by reversing top-to-bottom a dividing plate containing along its length a __________.

406. The mechanical loaders include rear-mounted __________, most of which are usable with either a digging bucket or a clam-shell type of grab.

407. Rough-terrain __________ with a typical medium powered vehicle fork-loads of over one tonne can be quickly extracted from yard or heap and transferred to the transport or spreading vehicle.

408. The beaters tear the manure into small fragments, and additional cylinder scatters over a strip wider than the machine in case of __________.

409. The vacuum-fill pressure-discharge type of slurry tanks can work effectively with any other equipment provided that the slurry is __________ liquid.

410. The gravity-fill mechanical-discharge type of slurry tanks can handle thick slurries provided that they can be delivered into the tank either by gravity or by an independent __________.

411. In hydraulic agitation of spray solution, a pump of fairly large capacity (90-135 litres/min.) is preferred, and after refilling the tank, but before spraying the full __________ is first used to circulate the contents.

412. The diaphragm pump principle is attractive on account of the complete absence of __________ in the pumping mechanism.

413. In a swirl type of nozzle, the spray solution is given a whirling as it approaches the orifice and the spray pattern is __________.

414. The ratio between VMD and NMD reflects the __________ of drop production.

415. The term __________ has become widely applied to the production of spray droplet by a whole variety of rotary atomizers.

416. In tractor-operated CDA sprayer-designs where part of the spray is returned to the supply inevitably add to operation problems due to increased __________.

417. On large sprayers boom length is often 24 m and then there are usually __________ to allow compact folding by hydraulic power.

418. One of the basic factors for good boom performance is stiffness to avoid the extreme __________ due to boom whip and yaw.

419. A microprocessor in spray booms for ground crop sprayers integrates the signals and __________ operates controlling the hydraulic rams to maintain vertical position.

420. In spray booms for ground crop sprayers, it can be useful to position the __________ markers at the boom ends.

421. The smaller-tractor mounted spray-machines are designed only for __________ appliation of solution.

422. In cereal growing system, sprayer specification call for greater clearance beneath axles, a maximum of boom height (up to about 2 m) and ability to follow accurately on turns.

423. Expensive chemicals can be saved while spraying row crops, by the use of __________.

424. An old and simple automatic spray regulation system relying on a positive displacement pump, often of piston type, driven by land wheel is __________.

425. Once the regulating orifice system spray machine has been calibrated by fitting suitable discs, output to the boom depends, within reasonable limits, only on __________ speed.

426. One of the simplest servo-operated systems entails the use of a mechanically driven __________ to regulate spray pressure.

427. The correct functioning of tractor-operated and self-propelled sprayers is increasingly indicated to drivers in 'Q' cabs through __________ devices.

428. A speedometer using a __________ (*e.g.* Dickey John; RDS) gives a true measure of speed of a spray machine regardless of soil conditions.

429. Blower or air-carrier sprayers are mobile, automatic machines which employ an air-stream to carry the droplets to the trees, rather than depending on the energy of __________.

430. __________ nozzles are designed to operate at low or very low volume.

431. In most pums, a small amount of leakage at the glands is a normal occurrence and no attempt should be made to eliminate leakage completely by __________ the glands.

432. Alkathene tube of 25 nun bore can be used as a spray line without nozzles, the holes can be pierced by means of a punch about __________ of the hole required.

433. In case of rotating boom with sprinklers wets an area of 100 m in diameter and gives an effective application of 25 mm in four hours on approximately __________ meters.

434. An automatic irrigation system designed primarily for extensive farming in very dry regions is __________.

435. Power in field is normally supplied to linear irrigation machines by a __________ generator on the main 4-wheeled mobile end tower at the supply end of the irrigation line.

436. Automatic water by a linear machine can be provided on a round-the-clock basis by using hydraulic sequence values in conjunction with a __________ irrigation layout.

437. Modern __________ are essentially power driven machines and often tractor mounted on the 3- point linkage.

438. The cutting mechanism consists of finger-bar containing a reciprocating steel knife, made up of __________ revited to a steel bar.

439. Some of the direct-mounted mowers embody a safety device which stops the tractor automatically when the __________ mechanism operates.

440. It is usual to employ p.t.o. driven rear-mounted machines consisting of two, three, four or five large diameter rotors, with flexible connections in case of __________ mowers.

441. Tractor-mounted gang mowers, which can be raised clean of the ground by __________, have obvious advantages of transport from field to field, and turning at the ends.

442. The term __________ is normally applied to mowers employing a horizontally arranged shelf with swinging cutting blades rotating, at high speed in a direction opposite to that of the tractor wheels.

443. A bruising-bar or rough surface concave retards the crop flow at first, to assist conditioning action by the angled spokes in case of a rotary __________.

444. Cylindrical rotors fitted with tufts of stiff plastic bristles have been found very effective at providing type of __________ suitable for grassy crops (in case of rotary brush conditioners).

445. The cylindrical reel combined haymaking machines embody the teeth mounted on three or more bars, which rotate in plane at __________ to the axis of the cylinder.

446. In rotating-head machines, the replacement of steel tines by suitably designed __________ can result in less breakages and more importantly in less forage harvester troubles following tine loss.

447. The mechanism used in some single-row maize-harvesters for silage entail feed chains a power-driven knife and a chopping cylinder identical to those employed on __________ harvesters.

448. The work rate and chap length in __________ can satisfy a wide range of needs, and availability of trailer on its own for substantical part of the year can be of real value in countries like U.S.A. and U.K.

449. Loader wagons, originally designed for handling hay on family farms in Central Europe, have been redesigned and strengthened for making __________ silage.

450. In the most common type of silo top-unloaders, the electric motor drives an auger fitted with knives which tease out the silage and convey it to the centre, where an impeller sucks it up and throws it __________.

451. All types of __________, after a short period of use, cut only at the edges of silo, and work beneath a dome that contains a mixture of silo gases and air.

452. A __________ suitable for use between the silo unloader and feeding equipment consist of a chain-and-flight conveyor pivoted at the feed end and supported at the delivery end on a load cell.

453. In the process of unloading horizontal silos, close tine spacing and crowding grab help to minimize ________.

454. A simple silage ________ cuts and picks up rectangular blocks of silage, working layer by layer across and down the silo face.

455. Side-emptying of combined mounted unloader-feeders either to right or left is by a hydraulically driven moving floor and ________.

456. A common type of mixer-feeder-wagon or ________ developed in the U.S.A. specially for feeding beef cattle incorporates three large-diameter horizontal augers running longitudinally in a V-shaped hopper.

457. As a general guide it is necessary to limit chop length of silage to about 25 mm, to 'tub-grind' any straw fed, and to run the machine during ________.

458. Where part bales need to be separately handled, a manoeuvreable rear-mounted twin-blade fingerless cutter with hydraulic drive can be used to slice bales held in position by ________ spikes.

459. The most widely practised method of hay bailing is use of a ________ bales of the type that makes compact, rectangular bales of a size small enough to be lifted by hand when necessary.

460. A typical knot-tying medium-sized machine has a potential output of about ________ bales per minute, equivalent to 6-10 tons/hour in hay or 3.6 tons/hour in straw.

461. On the return stroke of the, ram, the compressed hay is held by a variable number of fixed wedges and sometimes by ________ dogs that project into the bale chamber.

462. Most modern bale sledges incorporate automatic guides which assemble the bales in 'flat 8s', ready for handling from above by a ________ loader.

463. Some of the wheeled bale group accumulators use hydraulically operated mechanisms to arrange ________.

464. A bar on one side of the loader can be used by a good tractor driver to squeez adjacent ________ together.

465. Flat 10 groups can be assembled by the tined loader into cross-tied groups of up to 100 and transported on a specially designed ________ carrier.

466. The ________ with clamp arms open, is reversed up to the group; the hydraulically operated clamp arms are closed to grip the bales, the load is then lifted round the axle, until it is moved through approximately 90° to rest securely on transporter's drawbar.

467. In the process of stacking, the deflectors may be set to unload them at the required points, and in some situations it may be worthwhile to consider ________.

468. A rotary feeder operating in a semi-cylindrical charge chamber is driven in conjunction with the plunger, feeding the crop into the ________.

469. In Vermeer roll-type big baler, a pick-up reel feeds the windrow between a steel roller and an endless platform belt to a point where the crop is peeled off by the ________.

470. Core formation by rolling by New Holland 841 baler is initialed by six positive-action floor chains as soon as the crop comes in contact with the main ________.

471. A fixed chamber-size type of attractively simple design (*e.g.* Krone) employs a pair of sturdy endless chains running in channels and connected by ________.

472. A unique type combining the ________ principles (*e.g.* Lely-Bale) has a floor and lower back of embossed steel plate rollers and a front, top and upper back formed by three pivoting arms of chains and slats.

473. The hay wafering machines currently available in the U.S.A. require a crop containing approximately 15 per cent of moisture content and absorb a considerable amount of __________.

474. A type of self-propelled windrower used in Britain for large-scale and contract work (Shellbourne Reynolds) has a transmission by __________ giving a high road speed in addition to stepless range of working speeds.

475. Simple trailed __________ combines with bagging attachment remain of interest in less developed countries where bulk handling facilities are not available.

476. In some modern __________ harvesters, it is possible to make a number of adjustments like that of concave clearance without stopping the machine, alteration of drum speed during work, independent hydraulic control of both the cutter-bar height and the height and fore-and-aft positioning of the pick-up reel and infinitely variable forward speed at full engine speed.

477. An electro-hydraulic __________ immediately disengages the table clutch and the feed mechanisms and activates reverse drive by a 6 h.p. combine machine.

478. The drive to the knife (in a combine machine), reel, auger and elevator can be immediately stopped when required, by a foot operated combine throw-out and __________.

479. Mechanisms designed for a combine machine to improve the grain separating efficiency of straw walkers include __________ (John Decre).

480. Side-mounted __________ on a combine machine can provide a lower centre of gravity than one centrally mounted.

481. Recently the mechanisms that level __________ combines both transversely and to it lesser extent fore-and-aft have been provided with fully automatic control.

482. Most modern combine machines also provide for a wide range of fan speed adjustment by means of __________ pulley.

483. Most monitors on combine machines have __________ that detect the sounds of the grains striking them.

484. Augers running beneath the rotor delivered the grain and chaff to sieve separators of conventional type, and tailings are delivered back for rethreshing in __________ threshing.

485. Rotary separation systems have been developed to replace strew walkers after primary threshing in a drum and concave of conventional __________.

486. A powerful air blast is employed in conjunction with a pre-cleaning sieve to get rid of most of the fight straw and chaff before the grain reaches the conventional sieves in __________.

487. The __________, relying primarily on centrifugal forces, is unaffected by side slopes.

488. Grain capacity of combine harvesters in the rating run equals to straw output multiplied by __________.

489. With less expensive combine cabs, a low cost solution of the dust problem is provided by a suitable __________ helmet (*e.g.* Racal Airstream).

490. In __________ potato diggers, the forks are attached directly to the revolving shaft.

491. The conventional type of __________ has a strongwide share that passes beneath the potato rows and completely loosens the soil and tubers.

492. The elevator digger consists essentially of a broad share, behind which rises a metal elevator chain composed of parallel links, running on __________.

493. In conditions, where abrasion is particularly severe with the hook-link type of web, it is worthwhile to use a __________ type of web with the flattened ends of the rods attached to endless belts.

494. Electro-hydraulic control of agitators below the webs in unmanned 2-row potato harvesters allows rapid adjustment from the cab to suit changes of __________ often encountered within the length of a single row.

495. Because of the low work rate of complete harvesters with hand sorting, use of a bunker hopper on the harvester may be preferable to use of a continuous ________ delivery.

496. One type of clod separators consists of a __________ inclined studded belt which runs horizontally quite slow.

497. The pallets may be designed for loading on the harvester, and for setting down by a __________ platfom without stopping the harvester.

498. The most widely used type of haulm pulverizer employs beaters attached to horizontal __________ and usually contoured to match the ridges.

499. Separation of stones from potatoes by X-ray sensor channels and high speed __________ acting on a carefully regulated flow ribbon has become mainly confined to stationary machines.

500. Main dust size to provide ventilation to potato stores over 2.1 m deep, should be such that air speed does not exceed __________.

501. The air-flow needed to distribute potato __________ at the recommended rate is very low, and distribution should be spread over a long period.

502. Potato sorting machines with reciprocating riddles rotary screen, __________ rollers etc., were once widely used.

503. Automatic separation of stones and clouds can be reliably effected by stationary __________ housed in good operating conditions at the potato store.

504. Five or six-row 3-stage sugar-beet harvesting systems were formerly widely used in France, but have many disadvantages and are tending to be replaced by multi-row __________.

505. Sugar-beet row widths for convenient mechanical harvesting with tractor should be about 50 cm to accommodate __________ rear wheels.

506. The use of flails or pre-toppers running of the feeler wheels makes, it easier for the feeler to adjust the __________ effectively.

507. One of the most widely used beet lifting devices, used mainly on, __________, consists of a pair of inclined lifting wheels called 'Oppel', which pull, the roots and can result in low dirt tares.

508. On harvesters that rely for cleaning mainly on chain and __________, provision is usually made for extra rubbing by passing the roots between two webs driven at different speeds.

509. Harvesters that top the beet after lifting have a poor of __________ elevators chains to grasp the beet tops at the same time as the roots are loosened by a small share running beneath the row.

510. Armer and FMC carrot and other root vegetable harvester employs a __________ lifting system basically similar to that used on the Armer and Scott-Urschell sugar-beet harvesters.

511. Field is irrigated to encourage germination of weed to kill them subsequently by __________.

512. Boilers commonly used for soil sterilization purpose include portable loco-types, preferably with forced draught and high __________ capacity.

513. A typical compost shredder and mixer has an inclined :hopper, the lower side of which consists of a __________ combing belt.

514. Some ordinary farm manure handling equipment may be used with advantage either to apply compost (manure) to land or to make __________ beds.

515. Soil __________ machines consist essentially of a mould and a press, designed to make moist potting compost into firm blocks for planting of seedlings for propagation.

516. A typical pruning machine has four banks of __________ which pass between interceptor bars in order to produce a thorough chopping action.

517. Mechanism employed to assist sorting of fruits for quality include __________ conveyors, which turn the produce over it passes in front of, operators, who pick out rejects.
518. In general, that machines that grade by __________ tend, to have higher throughputs, or to be rather less expensive for a given throughput, than which grade by weight.
519. The graders in large-scale apple-packing stations are often fed by first immersing the boxes in water and then handling the fruit on to the drier by __________.
520. In the size fruit grading machines in which the produce falls through a circular hole of fixed size, the crop is carried along by means of a series of wooden laths operated by __________.
521. In weight graders, each fruit rests in an individual hinged cup, and for much of the journey along the conveyor the cup and fruit are supported in an upright position by a fixed __________.
522. A number of vegetable washing machines employ a soak tank, either before or during the washing process and most continuous-process machines employ a final __________ conveyor which enables any blemished vegetables to be removed before packing.
523. In __________ to wash vegetables, a pre-soak tank assists the action of the spray jets, and can be fairly easily incorporated in some type of endless belt machine.
524. The water has cushioning effect, and tumbler machines, with a mechanism designed to handle crops gently, can be __________ used for a number of vegetables.
525. The mechanism involved in designing scrubbers to wash carrots employs __________ cylindrical brushes may work inside the cylinder just above the layer of carrots.
526. Prefabricated steel sumps complete with necessary drainage __________ for delivering the tubers to the washer are available.
527. The introduction of a successful tractor-mounted bine loader has revotionized the field-work at harvest on farms where __________ are used.
528. When the pea freezing industry was first established alongside canning, the first __________ machines used were stationary Viners.
529. The output of a haulm-threshing mobile pea Viner is 3000 m^2 per hour or __________ per hour.
530. The trend in pea harvesting is strongly towards __________ that pick the pods from the uncut crop, through and clean in one operation in advanced crop production systems.
531. One of the simplest types of sprout harvester is a tractor 3-points-linkage-mounted __________ with a few essentials for safe use.
532. Many of the complex cleaning and grading machines currently in use on farms or by seedsmen, employ a combination of __________.
533. The main components comprise a large diameter rotary drum with a slightly inclined axis having interchangeable round holes or slotted screens and a __________ base in a drum rotary grader.
534. Hairy type of wild oats may be separated from grain by means of an __________ machine.
535. Buhr-stone or plate mills have been so termed because of the grooves (buhrs) which cut on the grinding faces of the two __________ stones.
536. A suitable mixer weigher can provide the nucleus for an automated medium-size farm-scale batch milling and mixing installation capable of following __________.
537. A simple arrangement for batch mixing of molasses involves spraying a pre-heated measured quantity into the mixer by means of __________.
538. Grass initially embodying moisture content of 80, 70 and 60 per cent, 3.5, __________ tonnes of water has to be evaporated to produce one tonne of dried grass, respectively.

539. A simple and effective endless-belt conveyer (drier) consists of a pair of chains and angle-iron slats which move-over a stationary inclined steel bed, made up of __________.

540. Grass drying temperature at the inlet end, second and the inlet end, second and third stages may be 150-177, __________, respectively.

541. Insufficient time allowed for moisture to diffuse out from stemmy grass-parts makes single-stage __________ driers inefficient.

542. When dried grass is for sale, a number of drying plants employ __________.

543. Axial-flow fans are used in storage drying with perforated floor, capable of operating against __________ are generally used.

544. The approximate that requirement for 5.5°C temperature rise in a __________ is 3 kW per 0.47 m^3/second of air for drying of grains.

545. Different types of sweep augers are currently available for emptying __________ circular silos.

546. Generally, it is believed that the first commercial frozen food ever produced was __________ prepared with the help of salt-ice mixture.

547. In meat packing plants the most common system is the __________.

548. The butter worked and packed in tubes and chilled to – 4° to 2 °C is converted into prints at the temperatures varying from __________.

549. In can method of rice making, water is frozen by immersion of cans (blocks) in brine kept at – 12° to – 4 °C by __________ of the refrigeration system.

550. In the process of hot watch soaking of paddy grains generates heat energy which weakens the starch granule structure by disturbing __________.

551. Parboiled rice' develops more rancidity than raw rice during parboiling there occurs the destruction of some natural __________.

552. The saturated steam supplies heat in parboiling for __________ of starch.

553. Soaking of paddy in ordinary water for 24-72 hours and its subsequent transfer to cylindrical kettles for steaming in small batches under atmospheric pressure is __________ method.

554. The temperature of paddy-water mixture after dumping paddy into the parboiling tanks stays around 70 °C in __________ process.

555. In Kisan continuous parboiling method, the paddy flows vertically down the angular steam chamber into steaming cylinder and steam flows outwards radially in a __________ to heat and gelatinize the grain.

556. Rapid drying of parboiled paddy established a steep moisture gradient between the kernel surface and centre setting up a stress which at, a certain stage is relieved by the kernel resulting in __________.

557. In India, only a very small percentage of rice millers purchase paddy and/or market rice and hence the major impact on industry is achievable by augmenting their earnings through higher out-turn of rice, better utilization of by-products and __________ of rice and by-products.

558. Milling equipment of high efficiency, based on the choice of __________ have been imported from Japan and Germany in India.

559. Though huller rice mills give the lowest out-turn both in terms of quantity and quality and products of lesser value, are in use as they serve __________.

560. Efficient milling of paddy coupled with added efficiency of yield of out-turn of rice and better by-products of better quality is done by __________.

561. "When paddy grain is pressed between its two ends and rubbed slightly, its husk splits apart and the kernel comes out" is the guiding principle in case of __________.

562. Roller diameter should neither be more than 260 mm nor less than 220 mm and the output is decided by the length of the rollers in case of ________.

563. Grinding type of rice whitening machine has the peripheral speed of 900 m/min and the pressure of ________.

564. The abrasive surface of the cone, crib lining and rubber can be made of the material purchased from the market as and when so required in case of ________ rice whiteners.

565. The abrasive roller is set to rotate at a linear speed of approximately 800 m/min in ________ rice whiteners.

566. Diversion of runoff through the natural outlet is most commonly done via diversion ditches and ________.

567. The objective of gully control is not only their stabilization but also to establish an ________ cover of plants.

568. The construction of temporary ________ across the bed of gully leads to collection of water enough to support protective vegetation and to check channel erosion until protective vegetation is established.

569. Spillway capacities of temporary dams are designed to handle ________ that may be expected over 5-10 year period.

570. Woven wire dam is commonly built in a ________ shape with the open end upstream allowing for a longer spillway than that with a straight dam.

571. In case of ________ posts are set in a row across the gully to a depth of about 1 m and about 1.2 m apart.

572. A reconnaissance of the area, collection and analysis of available data and outline survey comprise prerequisites in the overall planning of a permanent ________ structure.

573. The determination of the design runoff rates and flood volumes which the structure is expected to handle deserve involvement in ________.

574. A structural ________ design is to provide the required strength and stability to the component parts of the structure.

575. In a ________ the water flows through a weir and falls over an apron in which the energy of the water is dissipated.

II. True or False :

576. The plane surveying takes into account the curvature of earth as these surveys extend to small areas only.

577. A graphical scale need not be drawn on the map for an accurate determination of distance.

578. A chain is made up of thick galvanized wire and consists of 100 or 150 links.

579. Chaining should be done before ranging.

580. Chaining refers to the operation of measuring distance between two points using a chain only.

581. The process called 'chain breaking' or stepping is used for the measurement of too steep lands.

582. The bearing of a line in opposite direction of survey is known as back/reverse bearing.

583. Back bearing is equal to fore bearing minus 180 as a rule.

584. Plane tabling is a method of surveying in which the field-work and plotting are not done simultaneously.

585. Plane tabling method of survey is very accurate and highly suitable for wet climate.

586. Farm level is though not manufactured in India at present, holds good promise in agricultural surveying.

587. The maximum transmission of information between the levelman and rodman in the process of survey is done though vocal signals.

588. The telescope of the theodolite/transit can be revolved either in horizontal or vertical planes, but not in both planes.

589. The hydrologic cycle is always punctual in delivering the precipitation to the earth's surface.

590. A river basin has a defined watershed boundary.

591. An analysis of water resource potential, utilization and requirement determined on national basis also paints a clear picture of the regional needs.

592. Base (of irrigation) is independent of the duration of the crop season.

593. The ratio between the area irrigated and the quantity of water used is known as duty of water.

594. Irrigation water charges are uniform in all the states of Indian Union.

595. The continuance of promotional rates of irrigation water-charge entail no or little loss of revenue.

596. A free, phreatic, non-artesian or unconfined aquifer overlies an impervious stratum wherein water is under pressure.

597. Artesian wells are also denoted as cavitation wells.

598. Multiple well systems have been found suitable in areas suffering from waterlogging.

599. The vertical distance to which the water column is lowered is denoted as drawndown.

600. The provision of at least on antiseep collar along the pipe spillway shall not prevent seepage losses.

601. In constructing a dam, it is regarded a good practice to lessen the slope around the shore line.

602. A sod spillway should have a minimum grade of about 15 cm in 30m.

603. Water by swing basket can seldom be lifted to a height more than 1.0 to 1.2 m and the discharge varies from 6,000 to 7,000 litres per hour.

604. All the irrigation pumps involve all the four basic principles *viz.*, atmospheric pressure, centrifugal force, positive displacement and movements of columns of water caused by differences in specific gravity.

605. The single suction impeller has been found more practical than the double suction in small pumps.

606. Closed instead of non-clog impellers are commonly used to pump sewage water.

607. The gate valve is used in priming and starting when pump is operated against a low static head.

608. A turbine pump shaft may be either oil lubricated or water lubricated.

609. The maximum impeller diameter of a turbine pump is determined by the diameter of the bowl which, in turn, is restricted by the well diameter.

610. The wells producing sand or clay need not be necessarily equipped with oil lubricated pumps.

611. The mixed flow propeller pump is designed especially for small capacities with moderate heads.

612. The vertical distance between the water level and the centre line of the pump is called static suction head, while the distance between the centre line of the pump and the point of free delivery of water is known as fruition head.

613. Equation of continuity is written as $Q = a_1 v_1 = a_2 v_2$, while Bernoulli's theorem as $Q = \frac{P}{20} + \frac{V^2}{B} + Z$

614. The fall of the energy gradient in both open channel and pipe flow for a specified length of channel and pipe denotes loss of energy by friction.

615. Hydraulic perimeter decreases with a decrease in the wetted perimeter for a given cross-sectional area.

616. The velocity of flow in a channel varies directly as the hydraulic slope.

617. Non-reinforced concrete linings with vertical sides have been found suitable for depths exceeding 0.45 metre.

618. Proper curing of concrete line is imperative to reduce the possibility of shrinkage crakes while the concrete is still plastic.

619. The soil layer with the lowest transmission rate located only at the surface determines the infiltration rate.

620. Most of the evaporation formulae are based on Dalton's theory (1802 AD).

621. Evaporation pan data denote the measurements of soil moisture and not the approximations of consumptive use.

622. The size of the check basins may vary from one metre square to 10,000-20,000 metres square.

623. Furrow grades for most of the Indian conditions have been advocated as 0.6-0.9 per cent.

624. The direction of flow through contour furrow is across the slope rather down the slope.

625. The water having high sand content can be used for sub-irrigation by modifying its design and layout suitably.

626. The irrigation water embodying sand and debris can also be efficiently used in sprinkler method of irrigation.

627. Cost of installation of semi-permanent sprinkler method of irrigation is less than that of the permanent one.

628. The drip or trickle method of irrigation has originally been developed in America.

629. Drainage problems are assuming increasingly serious proportions in new river or canal command areas.

630. The drainage coefficient to be used in the design of the ditch with leeves remains unchanged from that for the ordinary open ditches.

631. From design and layout viewpoint, the parallel field ditch system is similar to bedding system of surface drainage.

632. The shape of the water-table between the two tile drains is circular.

633. Iso-conductivity map is greatly helpful so far as designing of the tile drainage system is concerned.

634. The equation $\frac{y^2}{\frac{S^2V}{4R}} + \frac{x^2}{\frac{S^2}{4}} = 1$ is the equation of anellipse embodying semi-major and semi-minor axes by S/2 and (S/2) $\sqrt{V/k}$ respectively.

635. Joint covering of plastic pipes laid for drainage is usually laid around the upper one-third of the tile to check sediment from entering the lines.

636. The capillary forces and fluctuating ground water flows lead to soil conditions different from the ordinary concept of a sharp break from saturation to a much lower moisture content, such as, field capacity.

637. The amount of cover over the top of the tiles, in order to protect them from heavy surface loads and to check their shifting, should not be less than 40 cm.

638. Drainage tile spacing closer than 30 cm usually entails too much of cost and renders it economically unacceptable unless high value crops are involved.

639. The commonly recommended size of the tile is 10 cm though 12.5 and 15 cm tiles are also used, with a slights increase in price a 12.5 cm tile augments capacity by about 80 per cent over that of 10 cm tile.

640. The changes in the direction of tiles are provided by curves as well as by sharp angles keeping curves regular with, the outside of the joints covered with pieces of a broken tile.

641. Drainage wells are often used to control the water in potential seepage areas and simultaneously to push up irrigation water supply either in the same area or in the nearby one.

642. A number of large and costly irrigation systems have either failed or are threatened with failure on account of fall of water-table and salt accumulation.

643. Drainage coefficients for an irrigated area located in arid or semi-arid climates are intimately related with rainfall of the region.

644. The sub-surface drains in arid and semi-arid regions are deeper than those in humid areas.

645. The revolution of 1789 A.D. made the royal forests and gam. reserves accessible to common people which led to their denudation and their use had to be limited by 1803 A.D. in Poland.

646. The studies have brought out that a single raindrop may splash a wet soil as much as 60 cm high and 1500 cm from the spot where the raindrop strikes at.

647. A watershed denotes the total land area above a given point on a water-way that contributes runoff water commonly to the flow at that point but it cannot be commonly interchangeably used either with drainage area or catchment area.

648. Rainfall intensity-time, curve is obtainable by plotting its intensity for increments of time.

649. The hydrology of surface runoff from a watershed concerning small and large watersheds is known as upstream and downstream hydrology respectively.

650. The minimum velocities required to produce and initiate soil movement are known as fluid and impact threshold velocities, respectively.

651. The threshold velocity to initiate movement of soil particles larger than 0.15 mm increases with the increase in the size of soil particles, while for very fine particles less than 0.05 mm it decreases with the decrease in the size of the soil particles.

652. Deep tillage leaves more cloddy material of greater stability against erosion on the surface than does the shallow tillage.

653. The rate of soil movement varies inversely with the roughness of the surface and even ordinary plough furrow if aligned at an angle of 45 degree to the prevailing winds will reduce the soil movement appreciably.

654. Bench terraces make it possible to grow the cultivated crops in mountainous regions.

655. As a general rule the drainage area above the top terrace should not exceed one hectare.

656. The provision of a parabolic channel and earthen bund along a suitable grade has been found suitable for less steeper slopes.

657. In case of graded bunds a freeboard of 25 cm or 25 per cent of design depth, whichever is more essential.

658. Greater the height of a graded bund, more should be its top width so far as stability is concerned.

659. In clayey, sandy loam and sandy soils, the slope of the seepage line (horizontal to vertical) should be 3, 5 and 6 is to one, respectively.

660. The cultivation is permissible neither on earthen embankments nor on graded bunds.

661. Contour bunds are also successful in shallow soils embodying a depth less than 7.5 cm.

662. The normal practice of bunding in India calls for providing sufficient capacity to take care for the runoff from the rains expected in 25 year recurrence interval.

663. The cross-section area (CSA) of the storage space required in constructing bunds is equal to the runoff measured in centimetres into bund HI expressed in centimetres divided by hundred.

664. It is not only the steepness of the slope, but also its length that augments the flow velocity of water.

665. In the process of construction of bunds, the burrow pits should be both wide and deep.

666. Wherever suitable natural depressions are unavailable, waterways should preferably be located along field boundaries.

667. Grassed waterway is a wasted area.

668. Even if no suitable outlet is possible, the concentrated runoff in the diversion channel should not be spread on vegetated area.

669. A gully located in a drainage way constituting a part of the surface runoff disposal system may have to be used to convey the runoff, but calls for a full control on water.

670. A stabilized gully can be used as a woodland or pasture land or habitat for wildlife or as a drainageway for water, but ordinarily should not be used to grow cultivated crops.

671. It has been observed that a number of check dams comprise a better choice for the control of gullies than one large structure.

672. In order to reduce the number of checks in a gully bed, a grade of 0.2 per cent is usually allowed in fine sand and silt loam soils, while up to 0.7 per cent in silt and clay soils.

673. In the construction of the woven-wire dam, a row of posts is set along the curve of the proposed dam at an approximate interval of 1.75 metres at a depth of 60 to 90 cm.

674. Brush dams are equally permanent like other types of check dams constructed (in control of gullies but they entail relatively lower cost and greater ease in their building up.

675. In the construction of loose stone dams in the gullies, the irregularly shaped stones should preferably be so placed that the voids are brought down to the base minimum.

676. The incorporation of a load platform or passenger accommodation in a tractor rightly tends to be linked to the provision of a spring suspension and a high road-speed capability.

677. The 1000 r.p.m. p.t.o. speed is an ISO standard.

678. The only factor determining the choice of a tractor is the cultivation performance.

679. Tractors in developing countries have steadily become more versatile, safer and more efficient.

680. For ploughing of wet soils tracklayer instead of a wheeled tractor may be better since it may cause relatively less damage to soil structure because it runs out of the furrow.

681. It is possible to use a simple dynamometer to measure pulls where three-point linkage hitch is employed.

682. A weir in its simplest form consists of a weir wall or bulkhead of either timber on metal or concrete with an opening of variable dimensions cut in its top edge.

683. Usually hydraulic dynamometer is used to test the power of a tractor at the p.t.o.

684. Wheel slip in a tractor can always be eliminated and can also be minimized by lightening the load and working in a higher gear.

685. From 1977 no employed person in England is permitted to drive a tractor without safety cab.

686. Design with seat and controls on a turntable providing 145 degree rotation enhance multipurpose capability and enable tractors to compete with specialist self-powered machines for work like forage harvesting and heavy duty loading.

687. Provision of electronic sensing and control permits more rapid action of hydraulic draught control systems, and gives a good basis for use of performance monitors and manual controls.

688. In four-wheeled tractor, the rigid frame gives freedom from misalignment of the transmission and may at the same time provide a casing that is dust and waterproof.

689. A number of modern tractors have 10-20 forward gears, giving speeds of about 0.8 to 32 km/hr.

690. A simple method of providing the differential dock in a tractor is by means of manual engagement of dent-type clutches.

691. In respect of gear-change system in a tractor, an easy change-on-the more on an automatic basis is provided by synchromesh.

692. A dual power unit is housed within the clutch bell housing and is directly coupled to the output shaft of the eight speed transmission in a tractor.

693. In a tractor, the ring gear is directly connected to the input from the main clutch.

694. It is claimed that the straight gate synchro change direct from forward one to reverse is robust enough (in a tractor) for regular and continuous loader use, and that it absorbs less power than more sophisticated hydraulically activated systems.

695. In a hydrostatic transmission the torque depends on the dynamic pressure of the oil, the small quantities of which are pumped at low pressures to the hydraulic motor.

696. In case of hydraulic motors, the pumping fluid drives the piston and thus transmits motive power to the drive-shaft, which then becomes the driven shaft.

697. The standard belt pulley speed is 90 m/min with a tolerance of 40 m/min at the engine recommended for the belt work.

698. The distribution of tractor weight and location of the drawbar must be such that there is always sufficient weight on the front wheels to make steering possible.

699. In a four-wheeled tractor, the design of the traction wheels should aim at securing the best possible adhesion with the maximum absorption of power.

700. It has been found that closer the tread bars, the longer will be vehicle-tyre last.

701. A tyre supports its load by deforming until the ground contact area multiplied by the inflation pressure equals the load applied.

702. In a diesel-tractor, the filters normally made of impregnated paper should be cleaned and used instead of their replacement at servicing periods.

703. In a tractor, the automatic type of filters provide either an electrical warning signal or automatic fuel cut-off if the water in the bowl fall below a critical level.

704. In an oil bath air cleaner abrasive particles are entrapped while air is deflected up through the filtering element carrying a little oil to augment its effectiveness.

705. Usually, the filtering element of an oil filter consists of a fire material like fine filter felt or impregnated paper and cannot be cleaned by the operator.

706. With 'bypass' type, the filtering element itself is often spring-mounted, and is automatically bypassed if excessive pressure develops.

707. 'Open-centre' hydraulic lift system is well suited to operation of servo mechanisms including 'draught control' systems.

708. A too-rapid automatic lowering of the implement removes transferred weight from the tractor and results in loss of traction.

709. The position control is made for mowers, sprayers, buckrakes, hoes etc., calls for a constant working position influenced by draught.

710. The main function of the pressure control system is to provide a controlled degree of weight transfer on to the tractor rear wheels when towing trailed implements.

711. The method of controlling the pressure by means of restricting the flow to the pump avoids unnecessary pumping and consequent rise in temperature of the transmission oil.

712. When a 'closed-centre' hydraulic system is employed it is practicable to employ lower-link sensing for load control and it has the advantages in case of long fully-mounted equipments.

713. Load monitor instead of draught control can be used with long fully mounted implements.

714. A sensing system of advanced design internal an internal hydraulic control unit mounted on the rear mudguard.

715. The American standard hitch ASAES 287-1 comprises a simple attachment for the tractor which requires the minimum modification of the standard implement hitch to accept it.

716. In tractors, the 'limited slip' employs a pair of pre-loaded clutch which clamps the drive shafts to the differential.

717. Pivot steering is often used on very high-powered tractors, especially 8-wheel types.

718. The disadvantages of pivot steering include some complexicity in electrical transmission of power round the articulation axis.

719. Commercial LPG vehicles should have successful coordination between the load carried, tyre or track size, and soil conditions especially softness and moisture content.

720. The load of an LPG vehicle is carried mainly by the air pressure in tyres and in their case the ordinary tyres are preferred over the radial tyres.

721. Though an independent suspension improves spray boom stability, makes heterogeneous spread of granule distribution by commercial LGP.

722. It would be essential to maintain competitiveness with four-wheel drive, track layers that these are able to carry out stubble cultivation and seedbed preparation with moderately low forward speed.

723. The best tractor seats now provide a good compromise between the soft springing and light damping that can provide smooth riding, and the necessity to avoid small movements making safe operation controls impossible.

724. Tillage and weathering modify the air spaces in the soil, as well as the size of the soil particles.

725. Ploughing is often the most important operation of the arable farmer, not only because of the basic nature of the work but also from the standpoint of the power required.

726. The cutting edge of the digging ploughshare is close to the forward part of the mouldboard and often almost at sixty degree angles to the line of draught.

727. The method of sharpening of the plough shares of soft centre and crucible steel are widely different.

728. 'Bar-point' plough shares consist of a steel bar passing through the form to form the point of the share used on rocky or hard and stony land.

729. The 'pitch measurement' is usually reckoned to be the horizontal distance from underside of the plough share to the bottom of the beam.

730. Modern disc coulters have a fitting that allows them to be tilted.

731. Diamond plough uses coulters of conventional type and makes inclined cut with a shin on the mouldboard.

732. The depth regulating wheel on a mounted plough functions in the manner identical to that on a trailed plough.

733. The pitch of the complete plough may be enhanced by shortening the top link, and the adjustment has the same effect as due to raising the hitch at the hake of a trailed plough.

734. Most of the tractors employing three-link system are attached to the ends of the upper links by pins which form the ends of a cranked cross-shaft.

735. With a well-designed reversible plough, hitch adjustments made for right hand work should not need alteration when the left-hand body is at work, but it is essential that tractor wheel settings should be correct for the plough and the work being done or else setting is almost impossible.

736. At no point of time in the past, there has been any controversy regarding the merits of different shapes of furrow slice for lea work, especially with regard to the 'crest' style.

737. The most effective application of power by modern tractor outfits calls for speeds of 6.4-8.0 km/hr but such speeds may be too high, with normal mooldboards.

738. Long, 5-12 furrow semi-mounted ploughs cannot be hydraulically controlled and lifted out of work at both front and rear.

739. The reversible ploughs often turn with great momentum, and it is necessary to ensure that nobody is standing near the plough when the bodies are forwarded.

740. A typical shallow plough with a tractor of 60 kW has eight 300 mm furrows and can be used at a high forward speed.

741. In a sub-soiling plough the vertical L-shaped steel blade running about 150 mm below the furrow bottom has a minimum power requirement.

742. The hydraulic reset mechanism in a subsiding plough incorporates a nitrogen accumulator to provide the required 'spring' force in the hardest conditions.

743. Soil looseners and subsoilers models for the work deeper than 350 mm employ a horizontal extension of the top of the leg.

744. Lines with right and left-hand spirals are provided and these should be used in uneven numbers on the right and left sides of the cultivator to keep the implement running straight.

745. It has been observed that a smooth finish of a spring line by shot peening is of value in extending their life under repeated bending stresses.

746. The points and shares on cultivators are generally made of cast iron, but some of the very heavy ones have massive cast-steel points.

747. Heavier and wider harrows for use with tractors of about 75 kW may be fully-mounted.

748. Mounted implements up to about 8 m side, suitable for use with 40-50 kW tractors, may be carried on a frame embodying hydraulic folding of outer sections to give transport width of about 3 m.

749. With the harrow on level ground at normal working depth each of the ram cylinders is fully-filled with oil.

750. Some of the chain harrows have turf blade on one side and arable land tines on the other.

751. Scalloped discs penetrate better than plain, and hence there is an increasing tendency to use them for the front gangs of tandem implements.

752. When disc harrows are used with medium to heavy tractors, it is advantageous to enhance the load on the tractor when turning.

753. The off-set disc has four gangs set in opposite direction and working independently.

754. The greater the diameter of a roll for a given weights the lower are the draught and consolidation if other factors remain constant.

755. Flat rolls consist of steel or cast iron cylinders made in two or three sections to facilitate turning.

756. Typical rotor speed range for machine with rotor 457 mm in diameter is about 150-350 r.p.m. giving a blade speed of up to 22 km/hr.

757. A typical power-driven rotary harrow has uneven number of rotors arranged in a single line with adjacent rotors-rotating.

758. The short length of power-driven harrows makes it practicable to hitch another implement such as light seeddrill directly behind the harrow.

759. The most favoured types of grubber units float independently on a front toolbar.

760. Mid-mounted hoes, which respond immediately to steering of the tractor cannot be satisfactory.

761. The seed is delivered from seed box by feed mechanism driven by gearing only from one land wheel.

762. A flutted roller was used as the feed mechanism on some of the earliest English drills.

763. The internal force-feed mechanism for seed drills was developed in the U.S.A. and is especially efficient for sowing large-seeded crops.

764. In an internal double-run force feed seed drill, each feed disc is housed in a casting fitting well at the top of the seed box.

765. The internal double-run force feed mechanism of a seed drill embodies the advantages of providing a more continuous flow of seed than the external feed type.

766. One of the main advantages of studded roller feed type in a seed drill is its wide adaptability.

767. 'Wing' coulters are available for sowing of cereals on drills originating in America.

768. In semi-mounted tractor drills, the headlands can be wide and drilling can be started or stopped to an accurate line.

769. The rule for setting markers for high speed work is, "distance of marker from outside coulter equals half drill width plus one row width".

770. Some of the 'Single-seed' drills which give satisfactory performance at 3.2 km/hr record equally good spacing on doubling of speed.

771. Modern pelleted monogerm sugar-beet seed produces less than 15 per cent double, while 90 per cent of singles can be guaranteed with most polyploid varieties.

772. The advent of multi-purpose drills has tended to make most specialized grass seed drills obsolete.

773. The widespread use of fertilizer broadcasting machines also capable of sowing seeds made it more essential to have special purpose seed broadcasting machines.

774. A small broadcasting device called the 'fiddle' is not preferred by some farmers especially on hillside work.

775. In a common working system the separator in stone and windrowing works on pair of ridges or a bed immediately ahead of the 2-row planter, and delivers the stones by cross conveyor into a furrow beyond the two rows just planted.

776. An effective clod reduction mechanism consists of two steeply inclined short elevator chains with another web suspended above, and a reversible conveyor for cold delivery.

777. In a typical windrower a power-driven rotor works below the share, and is driven at a speed high enough to assist the intake of ridges or bed, reduce draught and break up clods.

778. The fertilizer tanks to place liquid fertilizers are usually forward or saddle mounted on the tractor to counter the balance the substantial weight.of a mounted planter with full elevator.

779. Fully automatic planting generally restricts the choice of methods to either 'bandolier' or 'chain-pot' systems applicable to all the machines and crops.

780. Lack of uniformity at moderate fertilizer application levels should not exceed 20 per cent.

781. Most fertilizer distributors are broadcasting machines, and the object is to secure a uniform broadcasting of manure over and below the surface.

782. Big fertilizer bags of about 750-1000 kg capacity provide a quick turn-around and are well suited to a specialist contract service.

783. The usual flying height of an aircraft distributing fertilizers is little more than 9 m, and the swath covered, is about 12 m.

784. The problems of scorching in application of liquid fertilizers to growing crops can be minimized by the use of a suitable spray nozzle in place of dribble bar.

785. Even with a good distributor which has a symmetrical distribution pattern, considerably more fertilizer is delivered over the central part of the bout than at the edges.

786. An accurate fertilizer distribution by pneumatic distributors with wide booms naturally depends on maintenance of the inlets at uniform height and an absence of appreciable yawing.

787. Best of the line distributing machines may not be used for distributing fertilizers even if maintained in good condition.

788. An early type of fertilizer metering mechanism used on combine drills consists of a series of horizontal notched wheels called 'star wheels'.

789. Liquid fertilizer cannot be placed when drilling or planting a crop.

790. The front-mounted tractor loaders are normally operated by the tractor's built-in hydraulic lift pump.

791. Typical tipping angles for clean emptying of a front-mounted tractor loader are about 80 and 70 or more for bucket and fork respectively.

792. Though hydraulic loaders are simple machines and have only short life even if used carefully.

793. The loader should work on the yard bottom, kept free from spilled muck in order to reduce wheel spin.

794. A handy type of slurry scrapper is rear-mounted on a 3-point linkage and, is equipped with reversible wings and with wings projecting both to front and rear.

795. The spreading rates of a trailer spreader can usually be carried from about 7,500-50,000 kg/ha of manure.

796. A successful dual purpose spreader employs a hopper with a V-shaped bottom, and a half length flighted rotary vertical conveyor running near the bottom to carry manure forward to variable width opening on one side near the front.

797. One of the most efficient manure-handling systems, both as regards minimum capital investments and labour economy is the 'two-men' system.

798. In case of dribble bar type of slurry tankers, a transverse box across the rear of the spreader receives the slurry at low pressure and delivers it between the closely spaced pair of heavy-gauge polythene sheets joined to the spring loaded front and rear halves of the bottom of the box.

799. The advantages of the slurry injector system, widely used on heavy-land arable soils are avoidance of atmospheric and run-off pollution and effective use of the nutrients contained in the manure.

800. Two-stage slurry separator systems are preferable, the objective is a stackable solid with dry matter content of 20 per cent.

801. Either vibrating screens or centrifuges can produce stackable high dry matter solids from normal agricultural slurries economically.

802. One simple type of slurry aeration equipment of only 3 h.p. has automatically operated valves directing the compressed air in turn to a number of different nozzles suitably located in the storage tank.

803. Mechanical agitation of spray solution in a spray tank is provided usually by a horizontal shaft with flat blades.

804. In low-volume work much less proportion of pump output is normally needed for distribution than that ill high volume work.

805. Good hydraulic mixing of spray solution is achievable in curved bottom (an oval or cylindrical section), and the pump running horizontally near the top, but offset about 60 degrees from the centre-tine.

806. Modern methods of spray distribution do not call for the as high pressures (up to 41 bar) as were formerly used in some of the hydraulic orchard sprayers.

807. Work rate on high volume spray-work may be limited by the requirement of mechanical agitation.

808. High-pressure and medium-pressure piston pumps were formerly widely used for the low performance machines.

809. Nylon roller pumps are used mainly for medium and high-volume sprayers.
810. Fan type of nozzles are usually designed for low-volume work, but the selection of nozzles with suitable apertures, high application rates are achievable
811. In radar control system in spray machines like Air PAM (Sands) the speed sensor signal is converted to an air pressure signal proportional to forward speed.
812. A speedometer developed exclusively for use with sprayers essentially consists of an electronic sensor attached to the kingpin housing of tractor front wheel, and magnets fixed to the inside of the wheel centre as RDS.
813. Air-carrier sprayer is preferable to a hydraulic sprayer for top fruit spraying.
814. A 1 h.p. mist-blower weighing barely 5 kg can apply an oil-based spray without the addition of water at the rate of one hectare per hour.
815. The simplest type of granule applicator consists of a unit like a spacing drill, usually without agitator, a simple force feed, and adjustable delivery spouts.
816. A Dutch machine (for below-ground application of chemicals) consists essentially of a compressor which delivers and atomizes beneath a number of broad shares.
817. In case of submersible electric pumps, current is conveyed to the motor by rubber-sheathed cable.
818. A normal type of deep well jet pump capable of working at fairly low pressure, standing on the surface, delivers water through a pipe at the bottom of the well.
819. Rotary pumps are generally used for water supply or for pumping gritty fluids.
820. Roller Vane pumps are widely used on simple spraying machines and are typically mounted directly on p.t.o. and driven at a speed of 400-600 r.p.m.
821. In case of moving hose-reel and sprinklers like Rainamatic, a wheeled carriage carries a fixed boom with sprinklers along its width.
822. Frost-protection sprinkler systems are usually designed for British conditions to apply about 3.2 mm of water per hour to protect fruit crops against radiation frost of cup to 5-6 °C.
823. A pump specially designed to deliver liquid manure to rainers is a multi-cylinder piston type in which the poppet valves will handle a considerable amount of straw without blocking.
824. Centrifugal pumps for handling slurry use a simple impeller with less clearance than those used for pumping pure water.
825. Rainers dealing with slurry need a fairly large aperture, minimum of 9 mm diameter and the relatively more suitable-one is that of unstretchable rubber.
826. Finger-bar mowers have not been altered in principle since the days when horses were used to pull them.
827. The knife must be gently and firmly pressed on to the ledger plates by tapping the malleable 'guides' for clean cutting by a mower.
828. Many modern mowers designed for high speed cutting have a stroke appreciably longer than the distance between centres of fingers, *e.g.* 95-120 mm and 76.2 mm.
829. The double-knife system lands itself to use as a lightweight hydraulically driven front-mounted mower on high-powered tractors.
830. The knife carriers of drum type of rotary grass cutters tend to be of smaller diameter than those of disc mowers.
831. Drum mowers much over 2 m wide tend to be heavier than disc mowers of common width.
832. The drums or discs of a mower must be set horizontal so no uncut strip of grass is left between each pair.

833. The finger-wheel machines should be set with the bottoms of the wheels slightly forward and just touching the ground.

834. Rotor speed of flail (a tool with longhandle with a stick swinging from it, used especially to seprate grains of wheat from their dryouter covering by bearing the crop) type of harvester has much more effect than forward speed, which should usually be as high as practicable.

835. A typical double-chop flail of harvesting machine with a maximum output of 30-35 t/hr absorbs 20-30 kW at the p.t.o. when used at optimum efficiency.

836. A typical flywheel type of harvesting machine with heavy duty flywheel about 1.75 m diameter may be fitted with 2, 5, 7 or 12 radial concave knives.

837. Multiple knife cylinder type of harvesting machines are designed to avoid serious damage by foreign bodies to the complete cylinder.

838. With all high-output forage harvesters, effective and rapid adjustment of the discharge chute angle and of the flap are essential.

839. Easy control of operations of self-loading forage wagons is provided by a cab-mounted mechanical control box, giving pick up height adjustment, steering by stationary drawbar, activation of chain-and-slat floor conveyor and operation of tailgate.

840. A front-mounted push-off buckrake in the equipment for filling horizontal silos makes the driver's work difficult in some respects, but the requirements for a satisfactory performance are large front tyres, 4-wheel drive with power steering, and a small counter-balance weight at the rear.

841. Capital, depreciation and maintenance costs, added to occasional breakdowns of unloading and feeding equipment, tend to make tower system compare favourably with the best of horizontal systems of tower silos.

842. In cases where crops have to be transported long distances to the silo, provision of stationary dump box and use of tipping trailers is likely to be most economic especially where trailers are already available.

843. The pipes of the forage blowers must be as nearly as possible vertical, and the projecting ends of the sections which occur inside the pipe always pointing downward, to prevent blocking of the material at the junctions.

844. Top-unloaders, in case of silos, can be automatically regulated by means of electronic control.

845. Intermediate types of auger feeders work inside a cylinder which has a series of oval slots.

846. Chain-and-paddle auger feeder is in principle similar to the endless-chain type of cowshed gutter cleaner.

847. One endless-belt feeder consists of 400 mm wide rubber belt running on rollers at about 30 m/min and a plough comprising an angled blade and brush which move to and fro above it.

848. A belt feeder using 300 mm wide belt running at1.5 m/sec sweeps the feed from the belt by a rotary brush that is winched to and fro at half belt-speed.

849. In practice, density of typical silage roll bales in polythene bags is about 300-344 kg/m^2; this is only half that of typical settled clamp silage.

850. Regardless of the type of pick-up hay baler used, the work goes better if the windrows have been made straight and uneven.

851. Most commercially available chemical (additives) applicators for use on conventional pick-up balers have the spreading devices located below the baler pick-up.

852. Most modern machines make a compact bale with a section usually about 450 × 350 or 400 mm and length is variable from 60-120 cm.

853. In a ram type of pick-up baler (machine) the plunger has a stroke of about 70 cm and works at about 80-90 cycles/min.

854. The European design (Vicon HP 1600) relies on mechanically controlled hydraulic pressure for compression.

855. In the process of bale wrapping, a magnetic switch activates a knife across the full width and the bale is ready for ejection about five seconds after initiation.

856. Hydraulically operated spikes are used from mountings on trailers for lifting and carrying a number of hay bales on long-distance road transport.

857. An American loose hay stacker compresses the stacks by means of a hydraulically operated curved roof.

858. At buildings, the hay is blown or mechanically conveyed into a bay or a special container for drying.

859. Tractor-mounted swathers used for harvesting crops such as peas have similar characteristics.

860. Conventional combine machines have shakers or straw walkers, but now there are machines in which the straw-walkers are replaced by rotary grain separation devices.

861. Modern British and European combine machines invariably incorporate a pick-up reel for dealing with laid crops.

862. The range of adjustment for stubble length is typically-from about 75 to 600 mm.

863. There is no fore-and-aft levelling in a simpler hillside combine machine.

864. It should be remembered that the rate of combining is governed by weight of straw handled, rather than the volume of the grain.

865. In correct setting of the pick-up reel can lead to severe cutter-bar losses, particularly in laid or under ripe crops.

866. If increasing the drum speed is not effective, the concave clearance must be enhanced in a combine machine.

867. Modern high-speed combines can pose a difficult handling problem where transport or reception facilities are inadequate.

869. Rational method of prediction of runoff rates is applicable to watersheds of area less than 1300 hectares.

870. Potato-spinners are usually p.t.o. driven tractor mounted machines invariably with a single depth wheel.

871. The web, rollers and agitators of an elevator digger should not be lubricated, but all rollers should be inspected occasionally to ensure that they are rotating.

872. With the help of specialized potato handling equipment (in case of an elevator digger) larger boxes (one tonne capacity) can be handled in good conditions, but cannot be stacked for storage.

873. The simplest harvester is in effect little more than a side-loading potato elevator digger; but the most complex types rely on many automatic sorting devices.

874. With one-row harvesters where an attempt is made to remove all contaminants in the harvester, work rate, is usually slow.

875. Gene pyrameding dates back to the traditional plant breeding era.

876. The teleselector of potatoes employs a TV camera to view the produce on a specially designed roller conveyor.

877. Potato brushing machine is seldom located between the end of the grading line and weighing machinery.

878. The 'Lowerator' (Fyson) vehicle loading aid machine consists of a shallow-flighted enclosed driven conveyor which is hinge-attached below the end of a suitable main elevator, and only releases the crop at the bottom of the extension.

879. When separate toppers are used the beet must be topped too for ahead of the lifter, otherwise serious loss of sugar from roots is likely.

880. Spring-steel bars which make up the cages a cleaning mechanism in a 3-row complete harvester (Standen 'Seepre') are located in angled slots in the support discs.

881. Guide-type row-finders of a beet digger act as sensors and are connected to a valve which directs the flow from the tractor to a single-acting hydraulic ram.

882. A good cleaner-loader needs to be equipped with a fairly large, sturdy hopper suitable for receiving the beet from a mechanical front-loader.

883. Harvesting swedes (Yellow root of vegetable) and turnips is a relatively complicated operation compared with sugar-beet harvesting.

884. A typical turnip topping unit consists of a multi-bladded rotor that floats on and is centralized by tapering skids.

885. One type of carrot and other root vegetable harvester uses a share and elevator web little different from that normally employed for potatoes.

886. Carrot and similar tops are squeezed off by a well-proved rotary bar system; and a reverse drive to the lifting belts minimizes blockage difficulties.

887. A cutter bar in a market-garden tractor can be attached to the front of some machines which are primarily small rotary cultivators.

888. A typical hand-type hedge trimmer unit employs a 110-volt generator and 0.5 kW electric motor.

889. Most modern fruit shakers (in the operation of harvesting) are of the 'inertia' type and vibration is usually produced by eccentric counter-rotating weights which are seldom coaxial and one below the other.

890. Bulbs are now usually lifted in European countries by a specially modified potato elevator digger or complete potato harvester.

891. Most vegetable harvesters are general purpose machines designed for all type of crops.

892. Self-propelled tracklaying sprout harvesters embody a number of labour saving devices *e.g.* automatic braking, opening of trimming knives, electronic sensor, hydraulically tipper bunker hopper and automatic stalk shredding.

893. Drumhead-type cabbages can be easily harvested on a bulk-handling system

894. After drying seed-impurities are much more easily removed, and a final dressing can produce a clean and well graded seed sample.

895. Sieve cleaners which achieve separation without using an air blast are common and were installed as pre-cleaners in conjunction with tower-type grain dryers.

896. In endless woven-wire pre-cleaners, the grain (seed) sample is introduced into the machine in such a way that long pieces of straw, string etc., tend to lie vertical on the belt.

897. The dressing of seeds can be controlled by the choice of sieves, the strength of the air blast and the rate at which the grain passes through the machine.

898. A number of simple pre-cleaners rely for separation on passing the crop in a horizontal air current which lifts the chaff, dust and other heavy contaminants allowing the sound grain to fall through the air-stream.

899. Indented cylinders type of machines are used mainly for separation of impurities on the basis of their size.

900. The specific gravity table (of a separator) consists of an oscillating deck covered with fabric, woven, wire or perforated metal and with the upper end and one side adjustable for height.

901. The air blast in a seed cleaner can be controlled by adjustment of fan blinds and sometimes by varying the speed of rotation.

902. The available grinding, kibbling and crushing machines include a wide range of grinders and mixers suitable for attended operation.

903. The fineness of grinding is controlled by the nature of the corrugations and by the clearance between the two plates, which are mounted on a vertical shaft.

904. High speed corrugated roller mills may be used for crushing only dry grains.

905. The grinders are especially suited for receiving big round bales which can easily and quickly be handled into it by tractor loader.

906. One popular type of hammer mill in Europe requires only 2.25 kW.

907. In meal bins, the filter cloth is fitted tight, so that it balloons upwards when the mill operates.

908. In medium-pressure (mix milling) system the feed to air ratio is 10-20 : 1 by weight, compared with 3 : 1 for the normal low-pressure system.

909. Capacities of wet-wash molasses mixers range from 50 to 1500 kg.

910. The die ring of a tubing machine has a large number of radially located holes which are tapered from outside to inside of the ring.

911. With grass driers, the standard operating conditions are drying from an initial moisture content of 80 per cent to a final moisture content of 10 per cent.

912. It has been estimated that a good efficiency for a grass drier is 9-10 kg of water evaporated per litre of fuel.

913. High temperature driers are usually of either rotary type or may employ a pneumatic tower and a rotary drum.

914. In 'Dutch' horizontal air-flow system of drying if stack is oblong in shape formation of branch ducts running towards closer parts is necessary to equalize distances from the duct to the outside.

915. 'Cascade' grain driers in some respects are intermediate between tower driers and horizontal conveyor machines.

916. Though horizontal and inclined driers require more space than tower driers of equivalent capacity, can be housed in lower buildings.

917. When the grain drying progresses in a ventilated bin there are three layers one : dry grain at the bottom, two : drying in the middle and three the layer wherein drying has just commenced.

918. 'Air-sweep' method using suitably louvred ducts in combination with a vertical conveyor located below the main duct, or a pair of conveyors at its each side, can be employed for emptying floor stores.

919. Most continuous farm driers are rated at throughputs of from 5-10 tonnes per hour, for a reduction of moisture contents of grain from 21 to 15 per cent at a hot air temperature of 66 °C.

920. Among the grain conveying equipment, the pneumatic conveyors are advantageous due to their self cleaning and adaptability to irregular layouts.

921. Air speed for grain conveyance should be approximately 21 m/sec and pressure usually more than 50 m bar, but a high-output conveyor may operate at 225 m bar.

922. Low-speed auger comprises a very useful type of general purpose grain conveyor for the movement of grain at an angle.

923. Conventional halocarbon condensing units may be used in quick freezing where temperatures below about –40 °C are required.

924. An indirect air circulation system of refrigeration permits a more rapid change in temperature as well as the control of humidity.

925. In larger cold storage plants a number of smaller compressors are preferred to provide more flexibility to handle varying refrigerating loads.

926. In refrigerated trucks and trailers liquid nitrogen instead of ice, chilled brine or solid carbon dioxide may be used to hold low temperature for a short period of time.

927. Rice bran from parboiled rice contains higher oil percentage than that from raw rice bran.

928. Shelled parboiled rice embodies lower mill throughput capacity than shelled raw rice.

929. Pressure parboiling method was developed at Tiruvarur in later half of 1970.

930. Breakage of rice during milling is avoidable by drying of parboiled paddy in three phases.

931. Tempering equalizes the moisture in paddy and after tempering it can be again dried in second pass safely to 13 per cent moisture level.

932. Both hydrolytic and oxidative rancidities in parboiled rice may take place under high and low temperature situations.

933. It has been observed and practically experienced that the modern parboiling units (CFTRI parboiling tank and LSU oil fired mechanical dryers) involve the cost competitive with that of conventional units.

934. Most of the Modern Rice Mills, with mechanization of various operations have the milling capacity of 2-4 tonnes per hour.

935. Louisiana State University (LSU) design of mechanical dryer has been fabricated in U.S.A.

936. The greater the difference in speed in rubber roller sheller, the weaker is the stripping effect.

937. The hullers each driven by 20-25 h.p. motor using belt drive are used first for shelling of rice by keeping a wide clearance between the cylinder and the blade.

938. Horizontal rice whitening machine is grouped as the grinding type of unit.

III. Tick mark (✓) the correct answer :

939. Each link of a metric chain is __________ cm long.

(*a*) 10 (*b*) 15
(*c*) 20 (*d*) 25

940. The tag at the centre of an Engineers Chain is __________.

(*a*) Oval (*b*) Square
(*c*) Rectangular (*d*) Circular

941. The Gunter's or Surveyor's Chain was introduced by Edmund Gunter of England in __________ A.D.

(*a*) 1620 (*b*) 1610
(*c*) 1625 (*d*) 1630

942. Surveyor's Chain in __________ feet long and is divided into 100 links.

(*a*) 50 (*b*) 66
(*c*) 70 (*d*) 75

943. Ten square Gunter's chain is equal to __________ acre.

(*a*) 0.50 (*b*) 0.75
(*c*) 1.00 (*d*) 1.25

944. The size of a level is specified by the focal length of the objective which are __________ and __________ cm.

(*a*) 10 and 15 (*b*) 20 and 25
(*c*) 30 and 35 (*d*) 40 and 45

945. The size of a theodolite, generally, varies from __________ cm.

(*a*) 5.0 to 7.5 (*b*) 7.5 to 9.5

(*c*) 10 to 25 (*d*) 30-45

946. The magnifying power of the telescope (of theodolite) varies from __________ times of its diameter.

(*a*) 2-14 (*b*) 4-16

(*c*) 5-17 (*d*) 18-30

947. In the process of construction of contour maps of the free-hand drawn smooth lines, usually each __________ is made heavier than the rest of them.

(*a*) Third line (*b*) Fourth line

(*c*) Fifth line (*d*) Sixth line

948. Fills because of settling are made about __________ per cent higher than the stake marking.

(*a*) 2.5-5.0 (*b*) 5.5-7.0

(*c*) 7.5-9.5 (*d*) 10.0-15.0

949. The average annual rainfall of India is about __________ mm.

(*a*) 1194 (*b*) 1200

(*c*) 1175 (*d*) 1210

950. The utilizable quantum of surface water in India has been estimated at __________ million hectare-metres.

(*a*) 55 (*b*) 60

(*c*) 65 (*d*) 70

951. India annually receives about __________ million hectare-metres of water through rainfall and snow-fall.

(*a*) 400 (*b*) 375

(*c*) 350 (*d*) 325

952. Viranarayana and Gangaikonda-Cholapuram tanks in Tamil Nadu were constructed as early as __________ century.

(*a*) 9th (*b*) 10th

(*c*) 11th (*d*) 12th

953. Anantaraja Sagara was constructed in __________ in thirteenth century.

(*a*) Kerala (*b*) Karnataka

(*c*) Andhra Pradesh (*d*) Madhya Pradesh

954. The first Irrigation Commission in India was appointed in __________.

(*a*) 1899 (*b*) 1901

(*c*) 1903 (*d*) 1904

955. The most potential ground water reservoirs in India are found in the drainage basins of the major rivers of __________ India.

(*a*) Northern (*b*) Southern

(*c*) Eastern (*d*) Western

956. Assessment of water resources of India was attempted as early as __________.

(*a*) 1895 (*b*) 1898

(*c*) 1900 (*d*) 1901

957. The finance policy of Government of India pertaining to irrigation projects is traceable to ________.

(*a*) 1846 (*b*) 1856

(*c*) 1866 (*d*) 1876

958. Mud is pumped into the well through drilling shaft by a reciprocating pump in ________ drilling method of tube well making.

(*a*) Cable tool (*b*) Direct rotary

(*c*) Reverse circulation rotary (*d*) Rotary air percussion

959. The most common animal operated water lift in India to draw water from deep wells is ________.

(*a*) Rope and bucket lift (*b*) Two bucket lift

(*c*) Persian wheel (*d*) Chain pump

960. Windmills can be successfully installed in ________.

(*a*) Punjab (Ludhiana and Hoshiarpur districts)

(*b*) Karnataka (Raichur and Bijapur districts)

(*c*) Tamil Nadu (Coimbatore and Kanyakumari districts)

(*d*) Haryana (Rohtak and Hissar districts)

961. V-belt drive is more efficient than flat belt drives and its efficiency has been estimated at 90-95 per cent as against ________ per cent of the latter.

(*a*) 50-60 (*b*) 60-70

(*c*) 70-80 (*d*) 80-90

962. The standard power-take-off speed of a tractor is 540 ± 10 and irrigation pumps are commonly operated at or more and hence an speed increaser is necessary to use a tractor for this purpose.

(*a*) 1050 (*b*) 1250

(*c*) 1450 (*d*) 1150

963. One of the standard conditions for installing a weir is that the centre line of the weir box should be ________ to the direction of flow.

(*a*) Parallel (*b*) Perpendicular

(*c*) At right angle (*d*) At 75°

964. The depth of water flowing over the rectangular weir should not be less than ________ and not more than two-third the crest width.

(*a*) 3 cm (*b*) 4 cm

(*c*) 5 cm (*d*) 6 cm

965. For lining of channels, often recommended ratio among cement, sand and gravel is ________.

(*a*) 1:2:4 (*b*) 1:3:4

(*c*) 1:4:4 (*d*) 1:2:5

966. The use of brick, flat clay tile or stones as a lining material for irrigation channels using cement-sand ratio of 1:3 has been recommended for channels where through the discharge is more than about ________.

(*a*) 10 LPS (*b*) 20 LPS

(*c*) 30 LPS (*d*) 15 LPS

967. The size of the tank commonly used in inverted siphons is ________ cm.

(*a*) 45 × 30 (*b*) 45 × 45

(*c*) 50 × 45 (*d*) 60 × 60

968. Riser values installed on the surface of the pipe and saddled over the openings in the pipeline are usually spaced at ________.

(*a*) 20 cm (*b*) 40 cm

(*c*) 60 cm (*d*) 80 cm

969. Evaporation pans mostly used are ________ cm in diameter and 20 cm deep, made of mild steel sheet and painted white and requires a water depth of 17-20 cm.

(*a*) 80 (*b*) 100

(*c*) 120 (*d*) 140

970. The value of the crop factor for the common cultivated crops varies from ________.

(*a*) 1.9-1.7 (*b*) 1.6-1.8

(*c*) 0.9-1.2 (*d*) 0.4-0.7

971. The Manjari Drainage Scheme near Pune was initiated in ________.

(*a*) 1920 (*b*) 1930

(*c*) 1950 (*d*) 1965

972. The minimum spacing between the individual piezometers in a battery is ________.

(*a*) 30 cm (*b*) 40 cm

(*c*) 50 cm (*d*) 60 cm

973. Lateral outlet ditches in an open drainage system are spaced nearly ________ kilometres apart.

(*a*) 1.5 (*b*) 2.0

(*c*) 2.5 (*d*) 3.0

974. The capacity of a temporary check dam, terrace outlet and vegetated watering is usually designed to handle peak runoff of a ________.

(*a*) 10-year frequency (*b*) 25-year frequency

(*c*) 35-year frequency (*d*) 50-year frequency

975. The rational method of prediction of runoff rates is applicable to watershed covering an area of less than ________.

(*a*) 2000 hectares (*b*) 1800 hectares

(*c*) 1600 hectares (*d*) 1300 hectares

976. Soil-erosion by wind brings about the serious damage in soil by changing the ________.

(*a*) Soil structure (*b*) Soil texture

(*c*) Soil permeability (*d*) Soil plasticity

977. It has been observed that for ordinary, wind velocities 93 per cent of the total windborne soil is carried at a height less than ________.

(*a*) 60 cm (*b*) 50 cm

(*c*) 40 cm (*d*) 30 cm

978. The minimum length of a shelter belt is approximately ________ its height.

(*a*) 16 times (*b*) 20 times

(*c*) 24 times (*d*) 28 times

979. The minimum width of the terrace may be assumed as 3m for slopes between ________ per cent.

(*a*) 10-14 (*b*) 15-25

(*c*) 25-33 (*d*) 34-36

980. The vegetated waterways are designed to carry the maximum runoff from a rainstorm of __________ recurrence interval.

(*a*) 10-year (*b*) 20-year

(*c*) 25-year (*d*) 35-year

981. The shaping of natural depressions into watercourses calls for a __________ cross-section as it approximate to that of the natural channels.

(*a*) Triangular (*b*) Trapezoidal

(*c*) Parabolic (*d*) Tetragonal

982. A sod-flume may be successfully used to control overfalls in gullies with heads less than 3 metres and the drainage area less than __________.

(*a*) 5.0 hectares (*b*) 7.5 hectares

(*c*) 10.0 hectares (*d*) 12.5 hectares

983. The maximum depth of water flow over a sod-flume ordinarily should not exceed __________.

(*a*) 25 cm (*b*) 30 cm

(*c*) 35 cm (*d*) 40 cm

984. The maximum torque is __________ higher than the torque at the maximum power.

(*a*) 10 per cent (*b*) 12 per cent

(*c*) 14 per cent (*d*) 16 per cent

985. In an engine of type A, with a very flat torque speed curve (maximum torque only 4 per cent greater than the torque at the maximum power) __________ overload will cause the tractor to stall with very little warning.

(*a*) 8 per cent (*b*) 10 per cent

(*c*) 12 per cent (*d*) 14 per cent

986. A tractor capable of pulling three 360 mm furrows can generally handle three times the width of cultivator or disc harrow, six times the width of heavy harrow and __________ width of drill.

(*a*) 4 times (*b*) 5 times

(*c*) 2 times (*d*) 7 times

987. In accordance with the Nebraska test of tractors, the rated belt horse-power should not exceed __________ of the maximum belt horse-power developed continuously on test and that the horsebar rating must not exceed 75 per cent of the maximum drawbar horse-power.

(*a*) 80 per cent (*b*) 85 per cent

(*c*) 70 per cent (*d*) 90 per cent

988. It has been observed that a small to medium powered tractor pulling two-furrows at 4.8 km/hr exerts a drawbar pull of 8.896 kW, it is developing only __________ on the drawbar.

(*a*) 16 kN (*b*) 14 kN

(*c*) 12 kN (*d*) 10 kN

989. The trials on tillage have brought out that the increase in th speed of ploughing from 4 to 6.4 km/hr adds to the draught by __________.

(*a*) 5-9 per cent (*b*) 10-20 per cent

(*c*) 8-12 per cent (*d*) 21-25 per cent

990. It has been estimated that for heavy draught work at normal speeds modern tractors need about __________ of weight on wheels per kW of power and this power to weight ratio is more easily available in 4-wheel drive tractors than rear-wheel drive.

(*a*) 75 kg (*b*) 90 kg
(*c*) 100 kg (*d*) 110 kg

991. Whenever high drawbar pulls are needed from 2-wheel drive tractors the fitting of a larger or dual tyres can usefully be considered, for example, a __________ tractor might be fitted with 20.8-34 singles or 16.9-34 dual wheels.

(*a*) 40 kW (*b*) 50 kW
(*c*) 60 kW (*d*) 70 kW

992. A road speed of an all-purpose medium powered tractor up to __________ is invaluable for quick movement to the scattered fields or for some sort of road transport.

(*a*) 20 km/hr (*b*) 24 km/hr
(*c*) 28 km/hr (*d*) 32 km/hr

993. Small size and weight of hydraulic pumps and motors so far as their power input is concerned comprise an important factor, for example, a radial piston hydraulic motor with a maximum output of 7 kW weighs only 7 kg, while a typical 5.6 kW three phase electric motor weighs __________.

(*a*) 80 kg (*b*) 90 kg
(*c*) 100 kg (*d*) 110 kg

994. In a tractor p.t.o. speeds and shaft details are standardized on an international basis, the current 150 types, which are also British standards, according a __________ splines embodying a diameter of 35 nun to give 540 r.p.m. and has been found suitable for p.t.o. power rated speed up to 48 kW.

(*a*) 6 straight (*b*) 8 straight
(*c*) 21 involute (*d*) 20 involute

995. British diesel tractor engines are usually of the full diesel full-stroke multicylinder water cooled type and run at about 2000 r.p.m. rated speed, with the maximum torque at about __________.

(*a*) 800-1000 r.p.m. (*b*) 1200-1400 r.p.m.
(*c*) 1500-1600 r.p.m. (*d*) 900-1100 r.p.m.

996. High compression petrol engines are used in some tractors, and have high performance in __________.

(*a*) Holland (*b*) Poland
(*c*) Germany (*d*) U.S.A.

997. In the manufacture of tractors, there is a trend towards the adoption of the British standard working pressure of __________ bar.

(*a*) 140 ± 20 (*b*) 150 ± 25
(*c*) 160 ± 14 (*d*) 170 ± 10

998. A three-point system (in power-lift linkage) with check chains is often used in conjunction with a triangular frame quick hitch of Accord A - frame type for equipment requiring a lift capacity of up to about __________ kg.

(*a*) 1000 (*b*) 1200
(*c*) 1400 (*d*) 1600

999. Heavy duty front hitches may carry loads of 1500-3500 kg and cater for p.t.o. powers of over __________ h.p.

(*a*) 70 (*b*) 80
(*c*) 90 (*d*) 100

1000. The wheel motors embody a limited power input needing no more than __________ per cent of oil flow, a proportion nearly always available in draught work where the front-wheel drive is required.

(*a*) 65 (*b*) 70
(*c*) 75 (*d*) 80

1001. A British specialist S-P tool-bar for drilling, hoeing and spraying has a 15 kW two cylinder engine with hydrostatic drive to wheel motors, giving speed range up to __________ km/hr.

(*a*) 10.5 (*b*) 12.5
(*c*) 14.5 (*d*) 16.5

1002. Multi-purpose power frames have been developed in a number of countries in order to use them as the power unit for a variety of __________ operations.

(*a*) Harvesting (*b*) Threshing
(*c*) Grading (*d*) Winnowing

1003. An average ground pressure beneath the tracks of a typical medium-powered agricultural track layer with footprint 1.88 by 0.4 m is about __________.

(*a*) 48 kN/m^2 (*b*) 44 kN/m^2
(*c*) 40 kN/m^2 (*d*) 36 kN/m^2

1004. The __________ type of coulter is usually set with its point slightly forward, so that it forms an angle of from 55 to 85 degrees with the slade.

(*a*) Knife (*b*) Disc
(*c*) Skim (*d*) None of these

1005. The centre of resistance with a trailed plough body of ordinary proportions is generally about __________ back from the point of the share, while 50 nm each from edge of the landslide and bottom of the slade respectively.

(*a*) 150 mm (*b*) 200 mm
(*c*) 250 mm (*d*) 300 mm

1006. The resistance of soil per unit area of furrow section with well-designed and constructed ploughs varies from about 34.5 kN/m^2 on light, loose, sandy land to about __________ on hard heavy clays.

(*a*) 90.5 kN/m^2 (*b*) 100.5 kN/m^2
(*c*) 110.5 kN/m^2 (*d*) 115.5 kN/m^2

1007. As a general rule, draught of a disc plough is lowest at a disc angle of about __________, and up to this angle, increasing the angle tends to increase the penetration.

(*a*) 50 degree (*b*) 45 degree
(*c*) 40 degree (*d*) 35 degree

1008. A rolling cultivator is commonly seen in use in __________.

(*a*) America (*b*) China
(*c*) Britain (*d*) India

1009. A typical medium-right disc harrow model weighs about __________ kg/m.

(*a*) 330 (*b*) 350
(*c*) 370 (*d*) 390

1010. The heaviest agricultural type with 760 mm diameter discs 8 mm thick may weigh around __________.

(*a*) 200 kg/disc (*b*) 180 kg/disc
(*c*) 160 kg/disc (*d*) 140 kg/disc

1011. A power-driven rotary action strip seeder (Hinter) employs a line of independent chain-driven horizontal-axis rotors to cut ________ mm wide slots at 229 mm centres.

(*a*) 70 (*b*) 72

(*c*) 74 (*d*) 76

1012. Features which are desirable in a 'single seed' drill are any appreciable proportions of doubles indicated by about one per cent doubles and any peak at ________ or above.

(*a*) 30 cm (*b*) 40 cm

(*c*) 50 cm (*d*) 60 cm

1013. The speed of the hand-fed planters is governed by the fact that an operator cannot handle more than ________ potatoes per minute at a spacing of 460 mm, and the resultant forward speed is not more than 3.2 km/hr.

(*a*) 80 (*b*) 100

(*c*) 120 (*d*) 140

1014. By an automatic cup feed type of four-row planter up to ________ per row can be planted giving a potential work of about 1.5 ha/hr at 6.5 km/hr allowing 30 per cent 'turn-around' time.

(*a*) 800 Tubers (*b*) 700 Tubers

(*c*) 600 Tubers (*d*) 500 Tubers

1015. The distribution of fertilizers by aircraft is widely practised in ________.

(*a*) New Zealand (*b*) Holland

(*c*) England (*d*) Poland

1016. Application rates of liquid fertilizers are usually 168-1100 litres/hr and provides for dressing equivalent to about ________.

(*a*) 108-1200 kg/hr (*b*) 158-1500 kg/hr

(*c*) 208-2000 kg/hr (*d*) 188-2550 kg/hr

1017. Fertilizer distributors may be classified as ________.

(*a*) Half-width type (*b*) Full-width type

(*c*) Semi-hopper type (*d*) Quarter-hopper type

1018. A delivery roller of a fertilizer distributor rotates at the bottom of the box with an action similar to that of ________ drill.

(*a*) External force-feed (*b*) Internal double-run force-feed

(*c*) Internal single-run force-feed (*d*) External air-delivery type

1019. A machine working on 12 m tramlines needs to provide overlap by working along every tramline at a spread width with a measured amount delivered to ________.

(*a*) 24 m width (*b*) 26 m width

(*c*) 20 m width (*d*) 30 m width

1020. For handling of slurry through the piped systems, the minimum dilution required is normally about ________.

(*a*) 2 : 1 (*b*) 3 : 1

(*c*) 4 : 1 (*d*) 4.5 : 1

1021. A typical pipeline slurry distribution system with a 20 m boom has ________ of 99 mm hose.

(*a*) 200 m (*b*) 210 m

(*c*) 220 m (*d*) 230 m

1022. In a spray tank paddle tip speeds exceeding ________ per minute may bring about foaming.

(*a*) 1100 m (*b*) 125 m

(*c*) 150 m (*d*) 175 m

1023. A VMD less than ________ mm typically results in over 40 per cent of the spray volume in the form of small drops (159 mm or less).

(*a*) 220 (*b*) 240

(*c*) 290 (*d*) 190

1024. One of the proven advantages of CDA at 40 l/ha *vis-a-vis* ________ l/ha is that the reduction in spray-volume to be handled can augment the overall work rate by 50 per cent.

(*a*) 225 (*b*) 210

(*c*) 200 (*d*) 190

1025. A type of orchard sprayer formerly in general use was a two-wheeled tractor-trailed p.t.o.- driven machine having a fairly large tank and a multi-cylinder high-pressure piston pump with an output of about ________ l/min.

(*a*) 140 (*b*) 120

(*c*) 110 (*d*) 90

1026. A typical 0.75 kW plunger pump operating with 70 mm cylinder at 45 strokes/min. in 41/m deep well against a total head of 69 m may be expected to deliver about ________ l/hour.

(*a*) 1230 (*b*) 1030

(*c*) 1430 (*d*) 1530

1027. A typical piston installation with 0.25 kW motor will deliver 1350 l/hour against a total head of ________ m.

(*a*) 44 (*b*) 40

(*c*) 36 (*d*) 32

1028. A portable centrifugal pump built of aluminium weighing less than 25 kg is capable of pumping 13,500 l/hour with a section lift of 4.5 m and against total head of ________.

(*a*) 8 m (*b*) 9 m

(*c*) 10 m (*d*) 11 m

1029. When a propeller pump is driven by a 540 r.p.m. p.t.o., it is usually essential to arrange a speed increase of about ________.

(*a*) 2 : 1 (*b*) 2.5 : 1

(*c*) 3 : 1 (*d*) 3.5 : 1

1030. Conventional pitman drive mowers normally operate at crank speeds of about ________.

(*a*) 400-600 r.p.m. (*b*) 800-1000 r.p.m.

(*c*) 1100-1200 r.p.m (*d*) 1300-1400 r.p.m.

1031. The power requirement of a typical intermeshing notched roller conditions for dealing with 2.4 m swath is in the region of ________.

(*a*) 25 kW (*b*) 35 kW

(*c*) 45 kW (*d*) 55 kW

1032. The flails in harvester (flail type) rotate in the opposite direction to the ground wheels, at a peripheral speed in the region of ________.

(*a*) 60 m/sec (*b*) 50 m/sec

(*c*) 40 m/sec (*d*) 35 m/sec

1033. The cylinder speed of a cylinder type full-width knives harvesters is usually about __________ r.p.m. for average diameters and attainable chop length can be down to 5 mm.

(*a*) 800 (*b*) 1000
(*c*) 1200 (*d*) 1400

1034. The peripheral speed of a forage blower in the region of __________ m/sec are needed for a height of about 24.4 m with an easily handled crop.

(*a*) 550 (*b*) 450
(*c*) 350 (*d*) 250

1035. Wire-tying balers manufactured in Britain, use wire to a similar British Standard and follow __________ design.

(*a*) German (*b*) French
(*c*) Dutch (*d*) American

1036. A rear beater is almost invariably employed just behind the drum to free straw from the drum and open it out on its way to the __________.

(*a*) Shakers (*b*) Separators
(*c*) Elevators (*d*) Mixers

1037. A combination of a gearbox and hydrostatic drive can provide a widely variable forward speed to both slow work in heavy laid crops and high forward speed in __________ in combine machine.

(*a*) Light laid crops (*b*) Heavy standing crops
(*c*) Light standing crops (*d*) Medium laid crops

1038. As a general rule, in laid crops, the reel should be set well forward with the tines just brushing the ground when the cutter-bar is about __________ above the ground level.

(*a*) 25 mm (*b*) 50 mm
(*c*) 75 mm (*d*) 100 mm

1039. As a guide, one wheat or barley grain kernal per 0.09 m^2 is equivalent to a loss of about __________.

(*a*) 6.5 kg/ha (*b*) 5.5 kg/ha
(*c*) 4.5 kg/ha (*d*) 3.5 kg/ha

1040. A typical performance of a modern single-row potato harvester with three men working on the machine is __________.

(*a*) 800 m^2/hr (*b*) 1000 m^2/hr
(*c*) 1200 m^2/hr (*d*) 1400 m^2/hr

1041. A 2-row potato harvester, working in good conditions with 4 or 5 men on the machine, can do __________ ha per day.

(*a*) 0.75-0.90 (*b*) 1.2-1.4
(*c*) 1.6-1.7 (*d*) 1.8-1.9

1042. An unmanned 2-row potato harvesting machine can harvest __________ in 8 hours.

(*a*) 1.0-1.5 ha (*b*) 2.0-3.0 ha
(*c*) 3.5-4.0 ha (*d*) 4.5-5.0 ha

1043. A steam boiler with an output of 270 kg/hr can work at a pressure of 0.7 bar with a 50 mm main up to __________ long and a grid of two pipes only on the soil sterilization operation.

(*a*) 60 m (*b*) 50 m
(*c*) 40 m (*d*) 30 m

1044. The dimensions of soil blocks normally used for tomato seedlings are 75 mm across the parallel sides of hexagon, and about 100 mm high in Britain, for other crops smaller block of ________ may be employed.

(*a*) 30 × 30 mm
(*b*) 40 × 40 mm
(*c*) 50 × 50 mm
(*d*) 60 × 60 mm

1045. Self-propelled fruit harvesters in general, can harvest over ________ of fruits per day.

(*a*) 20 tonnes
(*b*) 18 tonnes
(*c*) 16 tonnes
(*d*) 14 tonnes

1046. Most tractor mounted fruit harvesting machines use a frequency in the region of ________ of a length of about 38 mm.

(*a*) 600 cycles/min
(*b*) 800 cycles/min
(*c*) 1000 cycles/min
(*d*) 1200 cycles/min

1047. Modern mobile root feeders include a tractor-operated root feeding trailer (*e.g.* Boswell) with a body capable of holding about ________ of roots.

(*a*) 0.5 ton
(*b*) 1.0 ton
(*c*) 1.5 ton
(*d*) 2.0 tons

1048. In grain driers, temperature of the mixture may be controlled at from below 388-105 °C, in low temperature grass driers 105-105 °C are common, while in high temperature grass driers initial temperature may be well above ________ °C.

(*a*) 338
(*b*) 438
(*c*) 538
(*d*) 638

1049. Studies have brought out that with a grass of 75 per cent moisture dried to 10 per cent, an average figure of ________ of fuel is reasonable.

(*a*) 500 l/tonne
(*b*) 400 l/tonne
(*c*) 300 l/tonne
(*d*) 250 l/tonne

1050. In a central-duct drying system the air speed required to pass through the crop is about ________.

(*a*) 0.23 m^3/m^2 per second
(*b*) 0.3 m^3/m^2 per second
(*c*) 0.18 m^3/m^2 per second
(*d*) 0.2 m^3/m^2 per second

1051. For sweep augers, the typical operating speeds are ________ and the power requirement is 3-4 h.p.

(*a*) 700-800 r.p.m.
(*b*) 900-1000 r.p.m.
(*c*) 1100-1200 r.p.m.
(*d*) 1300-1400 r.p.m.

1052. Sharp freezing of fish and poultry has been in vogue since about ________.

(*a*) 1845
(*b*) 1855
(*c*) 1865
(*d*) 1875

1053. A committee to study and evaluate the overall performance of seven modern rice mills was constituted by the Government of India in ________.

(*a*) 1961
(*b*) 1962
(*c*) 1963
(*d*) 1964

1054. The modern mills recorded an increase in total rice out-turn averaging 2.5 per cent over sheller type of units and ________ over huller units in respect of raw paddy as revealed by the studies.

(*a*) 4.6 per cent
(*b*) 5.6 per cent
(*c*) 6.6 per cent
(*d*) 7.6 per cent

1055. In a friction type of rice whitening machine the peripheral speed is 300 m/min and the pressure is ________.

(*a*) 500 g/m^2 (*b*) 400 g/m^2

(*c*) 350 g/m^2 (*d*) 300 g/m^2

1056. The recommended maximum depth of paddy grain for drying is ________ cm and the minimum air flow rate is 3-4 cu m/cu m of paddy.

(*a*) 100-125 (*b*) 125-150

(*c*) 150-175 (*d*) 200-250

1057. The standard sizes of drains are 10 and 12.5 cm, the capacity of laterals has been found adequate to carry the drained water, but when the length exceeds ________, it becomes essential to work out the size.

(*a*) 150 m (*b*) 120 m

(*c*) 110 m (*d*) 100 m

1058. Breathers or vents should be provided at every ________ on long tile mains.

(*a*) 200 m (*b*) 300 m

(*c*) 400 m (*d*) 600 m

1059. Mole drainage is practised extensively in ________.

(*a*) U.S.A (*b*) China

(*c*) Japan (*d*) New Zealand

1060. The great flood of 1856 A.D. in the Rohne Valley made it essential for the ________ Forestry Laws of 1860 and 1864 laying down measures for revegetation of mountain sides.

(*a*) French (*b*) German

(*c*) Polish (*d*) Syrian

1061. The *Chos Act* was passed by the Government of Punjab to check denudation by closure of eroded areas to grazing and cutting of grass in ________.

(*a*) 1898 (*b*) 1900

(*c*) 1902 (*d*) 1904

1062. There are ravine lands adjoining most of the Indian rivers yet the worst offender in this regard is ________.

(*a*) Ganga (*b*) Jamuna

(*c*) Chambal (*d*) Kaveri

1063. Soil particles in water rise by saltation only about ________ of distance of water as they do in air.

(*a*) 1/900th (*b*) 1/1000th

(*c*) 1/1100th (*d*) 1/800th

IV. Match the following :

1064. Match the nature and the form of the object with the conventional sign used in land surveys :

(*a*) Culvert	(*i*) ///////////////////////////
(*b*) Silo	(*ii*) ________________
(*c*) Rail road	(*iii*) - - - - - - - - - - - - - -
(*d*) Crop boundary (no fence)	(*iv*)] [
(*e*) Farm boundary (no fence)	(*v*) Ⓢ

1065. **Object** **Sign**

(*a*) Terrace (*i*) 

(*b*) Well (*ii*) 

(*c*) Grain/hay stack (*iii*)

(*d*) Terrace outlet (*iv*) 

(*e*) Road (v) 

1066. Match the volume of utilizable water-quantity with the resource as assessed by the Irrigation Commission in 1972.

(*a*) 49,300 m cu m (*i*) The Ganga system

(*b*) 123,400 m cm m (*ii*) Narmada, Tapti, Godavari, Krishna, Cauvery and other Southern rivers

(*c*) 185,000 m cu m (*iii*) The Brahmaputra system

(*d*) 246,700 m cu m (*iv*) The Indus system

(*e*) 12,300 m cu m (*v*) Mahanadi and other east flowing rivers

1067. Match the soil formation and texture with the radius of influence of a well.

(*a*) Fine sand layers with some silt and clay (*i*) 90-180 m

(*b*) Fine sand layers, fairly clean, free from silt and clay (*ii*) 180-300 m

(*c*) Coarse sand, fine gravel layers free from silt and clay (*iii*) 300-600 m

(*d*) Coarse sand and gravel without silt and day (*iv*) 30-90 m

1068. Match the width of the throat of a Parshall flume with the free flow limit Hb/Ha.
Throat width (cm) Free flow limit Hb/Ha

(*a*) 3-15 (*i*) 0.7

(*b*) 2.5-7.5 (*ii*) 0.6

(*c*) 30-240 (*iii*) 0 8

(*d*) 15-22.5 (*iv*) 0.5

1069. The diameter of a pipe is 22.5 cm, the friction factor (f) is 0.00710 of a 150 metres pipe, match the operating head with the discharge expressed in litres per second.

Operating head (m) **Discharge (l/sec)**

(*a*) 2.0 (*i*) 70.1

(*b*) 2.5 (*ii*) 90.5

(*c*) 3.0 (*iii*) 81.0

(*d*) 4.0 (*iv*) 57.2

(*e*) 5.0 (*v*) 64.0

1070. Pipe diameter and length are 15 cm and 100 metres respectively while f is equal to 0.009. Match the operating head with the discharge.

Operating head (m) **Discharge (l/sec)**

(*a*) 2.0 (*i*) 31.8

(*b*) 2.5 (*ii*) 25.0

(*c*) 3.0 (*iii*) 35.5

(*d*) 4.0 (*iv*) 27.5

(*e*) 5.0 (*v*) 22.6

1071. The diameter of the pipe is 30 cm and its length is 500 metres and f value is 0.00595. Match the operating head with the discharge.

Operating head (m)	**Discharge (l/sec)**
(*a*) 2.0	(*i*) 86.1
(*b*) 2.5	(*ii*) 99.4
(*c*) 3.0	(*iii*) 70.3
(*d*) 4.0	(*iv*) 111.1
(*e*) 5.0	(*v*) 78.6

1072. Match the soil type and border slope with the flow (litres/second) per metre width of the border strip slope (per cent).

(*a*) Sandy loam, infiltration rate 2.5 cm/hr, border slope 0.2-0.4	(*i*) 2-4
(*b*) Loamy sand infiltrating rate 1.8-2.5 cm/hr, border slope 0.44-0.60	(*ii*) 4-6
(*c*) Clay sand infiltration rate 0.2-0.6 cm/hr, border slope 0.10-0.20	(*iii*) 2-3
(*d*) Clay loam infiltration rate 0.6-0.8 cm/hr, border slope 0.30-0.40	(*iv*) 10-15
(*e*) Sandy loam infiltration rate 1.2-1.8 cm/hr, border slope 0.40-0.60	(*v*) 5-8

1073. Match the tile drainage system with the situations wherein it is commonly installed.

(*a*) Random	(*i*) Main/sub-main in a narrow depression
(*b*) Herringbone	(*ii*) Seepage water from hillsides
(*c*) Gridiron	(*iii*) Scattered wet areas in a field in isolation
(*d*) Interceptor	(*iv*) Flat, regularly shaped field, uniform soil

1074. Match the cross-sectional area (A), wetted parameter (P), hydraulic radius (R) and top width (t) of a trapezoidal channel with the formula to determine each of them.

(*a*) A	(*i*) $b+2d\sqrt{rx^2+1}$
(*b*) P	(*ii*) $b+2dx$
(*c*) R	(*iii*) $bd+xd^2$
(*d*) t	(*iv*) $\dfrac{bd+xd^2}{b+2d\sqrt{x^2+1}}$

1075. Match the formula with the parameter of a parabolic channel.

(*a*) $\dfrac{A}{0.67d}$	(*i*) Wetted parameter
(*b*) $\dfrac{1+8d^2}{3t}$	(*ii*) Hydraulic radius
(*c*) $\dfrac{t^2d}{1.5t^2+4d^2}$	(*iii*) Cross-sectional area
(*d*) $\dfrac{2}{3}td$	(*iv*) Top width

1076. Match the landmark in the history of tractors with year.

(*a*) Use of internal combustion engine	(*i*) 1901
(*b*) Ivel tractor	(*ii*) 1917
(*c*) American Ford	(*iii*) 1923
(*d*) International Farmall	(*iv*) 1890

1077. Match the following plough parts with the function/feature.

(*a*) Landslide	(*i*) Makes vertical cut to separate furrow slice from the unploughed land
(*b*) Coulter	(*ii*) The part to which power is applied
(*c*) Transhboards	(*iii*) Makes horizontal cut to separate furrow slice from soil below
(*d*) Beam	(*iv*) Receives the side thrust due to turning of furrow slice
(*e*) Share	(*v*) Is used for purposes similar to skim coulter

1078. Match the working condition with type of work done by a single-disc drill coulter.

(*a*) Hard ground	(*i*) Cutting through
(*b*) Presence of rubbish	(*ii*) Better cleaning
(*c*) Poor tilth	(*iii*) Fair penetration
(*d*) Sticky ground	(*iv*) Pulverization

1079. Match the time-gap between cutting and feeding from common type of silo with an average dry matter loss.

(*a*) Unwalled clamp	(*i*) 15-25 per cent
(*b*) Small walled horizontal silo	(*ii*) 10-20 per cent
(*c*) Large walled horizontal silo with plastic seal	(*iii*) 30-45 per cent
(*d*) Large tower silo	(*iv*) 25-40 per cent

1080. Match the commonly recommended temperature with the crop which it has been found suitable for unless high temperature has been experimentally observed appropriate:

(*a*) 105 °C	(*i*) Barley for malting, or seed corn up to 24 per cent m.c.
(*b*) 66 °C	(*ii*) Mustard, linseed etc.
(*c*) 49 °C	(*iii*) Barley for malting, or seed corn over 24 per cent m.c.
(*d*) 44 °C	(*iv*) Feed corn for home consumption
(*e*) 46 °C	(*v*) Wheat for milling

1081. Match the temperature requirement of livestocks housed in controlled ventilation conditions.

(*a*) 15-25 °C	(*i*) Turkeys
(*b*) 16-18 °C	(*ii*) Broilers
(*c*) 10-24 °C	(*iii*) Porkers
(*d*) 18-24 °C	(*iv*) Heavy hogs

1082. Match the vegetable(s) with the recommended ventilation rates with their storage:

(*a*) Potato	(*i*) 0.4 m^3/s tonne
(*b*) Onions	(*ii*) 0.03-0.05 m^3/s tonne
(*c*) Carrots	(*iii*) 0.05 m^3/s tonne
(*d*) Chilling potatoes	(*iv*) 0.01-0.03 m^3/s tonne

1083. Match the crop with the recommended storage temperature:

(*a*) Green beans	(*i*) 8 °C
(*b*) Cucumbers	(*ii*) 4-7 °C
(*c*) Tomatoes	(*iii*) 3 °C
(*d*) Red beet	(*iv*) 7-10 °C

1084. Match the ultimate strength in terms of tension with the material given below:

(*a*) 138 N/mm^2	(*i*) Malleable iron
(*b*) 240 N/mm^2	(*ii*) Wrought iron
(*c*) 379 N/mm^2	(*iii*) Timber
(*d*) 83 N/mm^2	(*iv*) Cast iron

1085.

Tension	**Material**
(*a*) 448 N/mm^2	(*i*) Chrome nickel steel
(*b*) 725 N/mm^2	(*ii*) Brass castings
(*c*) 200 N/mm^2	(*iii*) Steel (0.15% c)
(*d*) 1380 N/mm^2	(*iv*) Steel (0.8% c)

1086.

Tension	**Material**
(*a*) 103 N/mm^2	(*i*) Timber
(*b*) 241 N/mm^2	(*ii*) Aluminium castings
(*c*) 379 N/mm^2	(*iii*) Bronze: gun-metal
(*d*) 83 N/mm^2	(*iv*) Wrought iron

1087. Match the ultimate strength (compression) with the material.

(*a*) 655 N/mm^2	(*i*) Malleable iron
(*b*) 290 N/mm^2	(*ii*) Wrought iron
(*c*) 345 N/mm^2	(*iii*) Bronze: gun-metal
(*d*) 207 N/mm^2	(*iv*) Cast iron

1088.

Compression	**Material**
(*a*) 83 N/mm^2	(*i*) Cast iron
(*b*) 41 N/m^2	(*ii*) Timber
(*c*) 345 N/mm^2	(*iii*) Brass castings
(*d*) 655 N/mm^2	(*iv*) Wrought iron

1089.

Shear	**Material**
(*a*) 138 N/mm^2	(*i*) Bronze: gun-metal
(*b*) 276 N/mm^2	(*ii*) Cast/malleable iron/Brass castings
(*c*) 241 N/mm^2	(*iii*) Steel (0.8% c)
(*d*) 552 N/mm^2	(*iv*) Wrought iron

1090. Match the material with its elastic strength (tension).

(*a*) Wrought iron	(*i*) 69 N/mm^2
(*b*) Chrome nickel steel	(*ii*) 207 N/mm^2
(*c*) Cast iron	(*iii*) 49 N/mm^2
(*d*) Aluminium castings	(*iv*) 1170 N/mm^2

1091.

Material	**Elastic Strength (Compression)**
(*a*) Cast iron	(*i*) 24 N/mm^2
(*b*) Steel (0.15% C)	(*ii*) 272 N/mm^2
(*c*) Steel (0.8% C)	(*iii*) 276 N/mm^2
(*d*) Aluminium castings	(*iv*) 434 N/mm^2

1092. Match the cooled constituent iron carbide ($Fe_{24}C$) with the function which it accomplishes in cast iron.

(*a*) Pearlite — (*i*) Produces soft spots in castings

(*b*) Cementite — (*ii*) Gives low tensile strength, high resistance to compression

(*c*) Ferrite — (*iii*) Makes castings hard, but brittle

(*d*) Graphite — (*iv*) Gives toughness to castings

1093. Match the following materials with their typical hardness expressed in. kg f/mm^2.

(*a*) Soil (flint quartz) — (*i*) 450

(*b*) Typical steel components — (*ii*) 1200

(*c*) Typical hard facing — (*iii*) 1100

(*d*) Alumina ceramic — (*iv*) 700

1094. Match the synchronous speeds of an AC-electric motor with the actual speed at full loads.

Synchronous Speed (r.p.m)	Actual Speed (r.p.m)
(*a*) 3000	(*i*) 1480
(*b*) 1500	(*ii*) 450
(*c*) 1000	(*iii*) 710
(*d*) 500	(*iv*) 2800

1095. Match the type of roof with its estimated U-value (thermal transmittance, W/m^2 °C)

Roof type	U-value
(*a*) Corrugated Steel sheeting	(*i*) 2.04
(*b*) Corrugated asbestos sheeting	(*ii*) 8.5
(*c*) Corrugated asbestos lines with 12.5 mm boards	(*iii*) 1.02
(*d*) Corrugated asbestos lined 25 mm polystyrene slabs	(*iv*) 7.95

1096.

Roof-type	U-value
(*a*) Corrugated asbestos and 30 cm straw	(*i*) 1.14
(*b*) Double aluminium with glass fibre infill	(*ii*) 1.19
(*c*) Corrugated steel sheeting with 25 mm glass fibre mat fixed above purlins	(*iii*) 0.68
(*d*) Corrugated asbestos pitched with ceiling of wire mesh, building paper and 25 mm glass fibre mat	(*iv*) 0.57

1097.

Wall-type	U-value
(*a*) Brick work, 112 mm	(*i*) 2.67
(*b*) Dense concrete, 150 mm	(*ii*) 3.63
(*c*) Brick work, 225 mm	(*iii*) 3.41
(*d*) Cavity brick work	(*iv*) 1.70

1098.

Wall-type	U-value
(*a*) Solid brick work, 355 mm	(*i*) 2.38
(*b*) Clinker breeze blocks, cement reinduced outside	(*ii*) 1.82
(*c*) Hollow clinker concrete blocks cement rendered outside, 225 × 225 × 450 m	(*iii*) 0.96
(*d*) Clinker breeze blocks, cement rendered outside, lined with 25 mm fibre board	(*iv*) 1.70

1099. Match the crop weight per bushel (lb) with the volume per ton expressed in m^3.

Crop and Bu.wt (lb)	Volume/ton
(*a*) Wheat, 63	(*i*) 1.98
(*b*) Oats, 42	(*ii*) 1.22
(*c*) Barley, 56	(*iii*) 1.30
(*d*) Beans, 66	(*iv*) 1.45

1100.

Crop and Bu.wt (lb)	Volume/ton
(*a*) Potatoes, 50	(*i*) 1.45
(*b*) Peas, 63	(*ii*) 1.53
(*c*) Rye, 57	(*iii*) 1.98
(*d*) Oats, 42	(*iv*) 1.30

1101. Match the refrigeration requirements with candy making process.

Temperature (°C)	Process
(*a*) 18°	(*i*) Chocolate
(*b*) 02°	(*ii*) Cast chocolate
(*c*) 15°	(*iii*) Storage-nuts
(*d*) 12°	(*iv*) Dipping/packing rooms
(*e*) 07°	(*v*) Hard candy

1102. Match the refrigeration requirements in bakeries with the temperature.

Requirement	Temperature (°C)
(*a*) Cold work rooms	(*i*) 25°
(*b*) Bread cooler	(*ii*) –15°
(*c*) Mixer cooling	(*iii*) 4°
(*d*) Flour storage	(*iv*) 18°
(*e*) Frozen ingredient storage	(*v*) 22°

1103. Match the type of refrigeration with the temperature recommended for commercial refrigerators.

Type of Refrigeration	Recommended Temperature
(*a*) Reach-in/dairy/vegetable refrigerator	(*i*) –30 to 15°C
(*b*) Frozen food cabinet	(*ii*) 2-7°C
(*c*) Ice cream cabinet	(*iii*) 2-5°C
(*d*) Bottle beverage cooler	(*iv*) –17 to –12 °C

1104. Match the crop (s) with the equilibrium moisture contents of grain at 25°C and 63 per cent humidity.

Crop (grain)	Moisture contents (%)
(*a*) Maize/pearlmillet/sorghum	(*i*) 11.6
(*b*) Wheat	(*ii*) 12
(*c*) Soybean	(*iii*) 11.9
(*d*) Peas	(*iv*) 9.3

1105. Match the machine with the expected annual hours.

Machines	Expected annual hours
(*a*) Electric motors	(*i*) 10,000
(*b*) Wheeled tractors	(*ii*) 5,000
(*c*) Power chaff cutter	(*iii*) 2,500
(*d*) Puddler	(*iv*) 15,000

1106. **Machine** | **Expected annual hours**

Machine	Expected annual hours
(*a*) Self-propelled combine	(*i*) 1,200
(*b*) Seed-drill	(*ii*) 3,000
(*c*) Seed-cum-fertilizer drill	(*iii*) 2,500
(*d*) Seed cleaner	(*iv*) 1,500

1107.

Machine	Expected annual hours
(*a*) Ridger	(*i*) 2,500
(*b*) Planters	(*ii*) 3,000
(*c*) Power thresher	(*iii*) 1,500
(*d*) Cultivators	(*iv*) 1,000

1108.

Machine	Expected annual hours
(*a*) Power tillers	(*i*) 5,000
(*b*) Tractor (Crawler)	(*ii*) 8,000
(*c*) Agricultural trailer	(*iii*) 3,000
(*d*) Disc harrows	(*iv*) 10,000

1109.

Machine	Expected annual hours
(*a*) Centrifugal pump	(*i*) 1,000
(*b*) Dozer	(*ii*) 1,500
(*c*) Power sprayer	(*iii*) 2,000
(*d*) Ridger	(*iv*) 10,000

1110. Match the estimated post-harvest losses during different operations in South and South-East Asia.

Operation	Range of losses (per cent)
(*a*) Harvesting	(*i*) 2-7
(*b*) Handling	(*ii*) 2-10
(*c*) Storing	(*iii*) 1-3
(*d*) Milling	(*iv*) 2-6

1111.

Operation	Range of losses (per cent)
(*a*) Threshing	(*i*) 1-3
(*b*) Drying	(*ii*) 2-6
(*c*) Harvesting	(*iii*) 2-7
(*d*) Handling	(*iv*) 1-5

1112. Match the product (for drying) with the value of C (MKS units).

Product	'c' °k^{-1}
(*a*) Wheat	(*i*) 6.12×10^{-6}
(*b*) Sorghum	(*ii*) 5.76×10^{-5}
(*c*) Maize	(*iii*) 1.22×10^{-5}
(*d*) Paddy	(*iv*) 10.62×10^{-7}
(*e*) Soybean	(*v*) 1.98×10^{-5}

1113. Match the product (for drying) with the value of 'h' in MKS units.

Product	'h'
(*a*) Wheat	(*i*) 1.90
(*b*) Sorghum	(*ii*) 3.03
(*c*) Maize	(*iii*) 1.35
(*d*) Paddy	(*iv*) 1.32
(*e*) Soybean	(*v*) 2.31

1114. Match the floor space (L × W in m) required for different machines.

(*a*) 3 × 5 m	(*i*) Tractor drawn harrow
(*b*) 3 × 3 m	(*ii*) Power operated thresher
(*c*) 2 × 3 m	(*iii*) Engine operated sprayer
(*d*) 1.5 × 1.5 m	(*iv*) Tractor drawn cultivator
(*e*) 8 × 3 m	(*v*) Trailed type of mowers

1115. Match the type of structure with the proportion of aggregates by volume.

(*a*) Beams	(*i*) 1 : 3 : 6
(*b*) Dams	(*ii*) 1 : 2 : 2.4
(*c*) Water tanks	(*iii*) 1 : 1.5 : 3
(*d*) Columns	(*iv*) 1 : 2 : 4

V. Answer the following (computation method on rough attached sheet of the answer book :

1116. Give the correct length of the line measuring 250 m when measured with 20 m chain which was 10 cm too long.

1117. The distance between two points measured by Gunter's chain was 950 links, if the chain was too short by 0.9 link, in date the true distance.

1118. A rectangular field measured 150 and 175 m, respectively when measured with 30 m chain which was 10 cm too short, find out the correct lengths.

1119. What will be power requirement of pumping 900 litres of water per minute against a head of 50 metres of a pump having 65 per cent efficiency; specify the size of the electric motor.

1120. If the yield of well is 18,000 litres per hour, static and pumping water levels are 20 m each, friction loss is 20 per cent, pump and drive efficiencies are 60 per cent each. What will be the pump-size and BHP of engine required ?

1121. Determine the quantity of the earth work needed to fill a trapezoidal bund measuring 80 metres in length. The bottom width is 3 metres and top width is 1.2 metres. The height of one end is 1.5 while 1.7 metres of the other.

1122. The following elevations were observed at grid points of a topographic survey of an area. Determine the elevation of the centroid of the area. Guiding stakes are put in a play ground. Compute the cut or fill at the grid points.

STATION	LINES				
	I	II	III	IV	V
A	9.50	10.30	9.75	10.80	9.95
B	9.75	10.37	9.85	10.20	10.15
C	10.10	10.90	9.70	11.20	10.27
D	9.25	9.90	10.20	11.15	11.25
E	10.50	9.80	11.00	11.30	11.35

1123. The discharge of tube well was collected in a drum of 300 litres capacity. The water was pumped and the time was noted to fill up the drum to its capacity, the measured time intervals were 40, 42 and 38 seconds, compute the discharge rate of the well.

1124. Determine the head lost due to friction in a pipe 15 cm in diameter and 400 metres long when water flows at 2 metres/second. (f = 0.005, g = 9.81/m/sec^2)

1125. Work out the head lost in friction when water is flowing through a 10 cm diameter pipe 75 metres long at a velocity of 4 metres per second. Value of f = 0.0056.

1126. Determine the velocity of flow and the carrying capacity (Q) of the earth channel on a grade 0.1 per cent, depth of water is 120 cm, bottom width 60 cm and side slopes are 1 : 1.

1127. Work out the carrying capacity of a channel section, the channel specifications are, bottom and top width and height are 17.5, 20.0 and 17.5 cm, respectively.

1128. A persian wheel discharges water @ 10000 litres per hour and works for 8 hours. How much area (hectares) of a crop could be irrigated if the depth of irrigation is 5 cm and the interval between two irrigations is 15 days.

1129. Determine the time required to irrigate a 100 × 5 m border strip if the depth of irrigation is 6 cm. The available discharge of water is 12.5 litres per second and the water conveyance efficiency is 75 per cent.

1130. A sample was taken with an open side tube and collected in a moisture box and, weighed. The weight of the box with moist soil is 180.04 g, with oven dry soil it weighed 167.15 g. The empty moisture box weighed 42.20 g. Find out the moisture content of the soil.

1131. Compute the time required to give 6 cm irrigation to a potato plot measuring 80 × 55 m with a rope and bucket lift yielding a discharge of 9,500 litres per hour. Water is conveyed through a lined channel.

1132. Determine the storage efficiency based on the following parameters:

Stream size: 30 *l*/sec, Water application efficiency : 60 %,

Area irrigated: 10,000 m^2, Depth of the root zone : 1 m,

Time required: 10 hours, Soil moisture holding capacity: 16 cm/m,

Irrigation was given at : 50% available moisture.

1133. The estimated discharge of a canal is 0.25 cubic metres of water per second and drains an area of 300 hectares. Determine the drainage coefficient.

1134. If the drainage coefficient is 10 mm, what will be the capacity required at the outlet end of the drainage ditch draining a watershed of 400 hectares.

1135. Work out the flow velocity (m/sec) based on the following parameters :

Flow to be carried	: 2.2 m deep
Soil type	: Sandy loam
Slope	: 0.20 per cent
Carrying capacity	: 13.4 cu. m./sec.

1136. An area having 15 cm tile drains and a slope of 0.15 per cent if the drainage coefficient is taken as 15 cm, determine area which can be drained.

1137. Find out the slope required to provide flow velocity of 0.5 m per second at a full flow in a 12.5 cm tile.

1138. Work out the peak runoff rate based on the following parameters :

Rainfall recurrence interval 10 years

Rainfall intensity per hour as expected is 6.3 cm. Watershed comprises:

(*a*) 20 hectares of cultivated crops on 3 per cent slope, c = 0.50.

(*b*) 30 hectares of pasture crops on 7 per cent slope, c = 0.36.

Soil type is silt loam

Maximum length of path of water is 700 m

Average slope of the path is 4 per cent

Average flow velocity of water is 1.2 m/second

1139. Determine the design peak runoff using the following details:

Rainfall recurrence 25 years

Cultivated clay loam on 1 per cent slope measures 20 hectares

Pasture land on 7 per cent slope is 35 hectares

Woodland on 12 per cent slope is 30 hectares

Most remote in watershed is 3.2 km away

Outlet located 8 m below the remote point

Rainfall intensity per hour is 7.5 cm

C-value for cultivated, pasture and woodland is 0.50, 0.36 and 0.50, respectively

Rainfall intensity for a 97.74 min. is 5.3 cm/hr when 1-hour intensity is 7.5 cm/hr

Time of concentration is 56.77 cm.

1140. In a watershed, the most remote point is 650, m away from the outlet which is 3.2 m below the most remote point, work out the time of concentration.

1141. Design the notch dimensions of a wooden slab dam to carry a peak flow of 600 litres/second. The notch has the rectangular opening width of gully channel is 250 cm.

1142. Work out the maximum capacity of a straight inlet embodying a crest length of 3 metres and depth of flow of one metre.

1143. Determine the discharge through a 90° V-notch under 19 cm head.

1144. How much will be the discharge a Cipolleti weir having crest width of 60 cm and the head of water flowing over the crest is 30 cm.

1145. Determine the discharge of 2.5 cm siphon tube when the surface in the channel is 30 cm above that in the field.

1146. A murrah buffalo weighs 700 kg and is to be fed @ 4 kg of silage per 100 kg of body weight,.Compute the quantity of silage required 10 feed 50 such buffaloes.

1147. Cows and heifers numbering 25 each have the body weight of 450 and 200 kg respectively. Determine the total quantity of silage in terms of volume (One cu. m = 650 kg) required to feed them all, if the feeding rate is 3 kg per 100 kg of body weight.

1148. Work out the number of bags of standard size (100 × 60 × 30 cm) of 75 kg of paddy to store 247.5 tonnes.

1149. The first Irrigation Commission was appointed in 1901.

1150. Grow More Food Campaign was launched in 1943.

1151. Rajasthan desert (India) convers an area of 2,08,000 km^2.

1152. Dr. Diesel (1892) patented a cycle in which the fuel was caused to ignite spontaneously on its injection into the cylinder, owing to the high temperature set up by the compression of the air.

1153. The term 'diesel' is generally applied today to the solid (or airless) injection, compression-ignition (C.I.) engine.

1154. Regular tractor testing dates back to 1920, when a scheme for the compulsory testing of all types of tractors marked in the State Nebraska (USA) was inaugurated.

1155. More complex systems of implement control (on tractors) began with the Ferguson system.

Do you know that :

1. Ten dams with one hectare catchments will store more water than one dam of ten hectare.
2. India recieves most of rainfall in just 100 hrs. out of 8760 hrs in a year
3. Sprinkler irrigation is also known as head irrigation.
4. When electric conductivity of a soil exceed 4 desi somon per metere, the soil is classified as saline soil.
5. Average rainfall of world is about 850 mm; while that of India is 1200 mm
6. Cherapunji recieves 11 metre of rainfall annually.
7. About 100 districts in 14 states of India experience recurring drought
8. Mcormide reape was invented in the year 1834
9. Deere Mould board plough was made in the year 1837.

KEY

1. Geodetic
2. Trigonometrical
3. Agricultural
4. Fixed relation
5. Representative fraction of R.F.
6. Statia hairs
7. Ranging
8. Normal Correct length
9. Three-four-five
10. 1.2 to 1.5
11. Optical square
12. Offsets
13. Sho staff
14. Right angles
15. Declination
16. Bearing
17. Interior and exterior
18. Fore/Forward bearing
19. Local attraction
20. Traverse
21. Intersection
22. Contour
23. Vertical arc
24. Dumpy
25. Wyes
26. Distance in km
27. Collimation
28. Profile/longitudinal levelling/sectioning
29. 1, 2 or 3 m
30. Formation level
31. Project designs
32. Contour
33. Contour interval
34. $\frac{20.000 + 30.000}{2} \times 10 = 250,000$ cu m
35. Cut and fill
36. End area
37. Levelling design
38. Diagonals
39. 1075.375 m
40. 0.1 m below the centroid or 98.296 (98.296) m
41. Greater volume
42. Hydrologic cycle
43. Force of gravity
44. Non-consumptive use
45. Himalayan rivers
46. Ganga system
47. Indo-gangetic
48. Brahmaputra
49. Geologically
50. Central plateau
51. Southern rivers
52. West coast
53. 1899-1900
54. Godavari Delta
55. 1.3
56. 425 to 280
57. 750 litres
58. Open flume
59. Full supply level (FSL)
60. Water course
61. Intensity
62. Delta
63. Minutes
64. Water
65. Higher
66. Artesian
67. Waterlogging
68. Benefit-cost
69. Promotional rates
70. An aquifer
71. Confined aquifer
72. Interstices
73. Confining stratum

74. 6 metres
75. Sand filter
76. Reciprocating suction
77. Cavity well
78. Filter points
79. Depression
80. Cable tool
81. Perpendicular
82. Strainer
83. Surging
84. Impounding
85. Self-emptying
86. Archimedean screw
87. 18,000
88. 10 metres
89. Single acting
90. Volute type pumps
91. Vertical centrifugal pump
92. 11 horse-power (h.p.)
93. Vortexes
94. Primed
95. Turbine pump
96. Deliver water
97. Submersible motor
98. Short line-shaft
99. Parallel
100. Low lift
101. Air pressure
102. Direct drive
103. Average velocity
104. $Q = 0.61 \times 10^{-3}\ a\sqrt{2gh}$
105. $Q = CLH^m$
106. $Q = 0.0184\ (L\text{-}0.1nH)H^{3/2}$
107. Head lost
108. Wetted perimeter
109. Semi-circl
110. Earth channels
111. Lined channels
112. Flumes and inverted siphons
113. Stilling
114. Stilling basins
115. Dissipation of energy
116. Chutes
117. $Q = 0.65 \times 10^{-3}\ a\sqrt{2gh}$
118. Uphill or downhill
119. Insufficient head
120. Darcy's equation or $V = \sqrt{Hdg/2fl}$
121. Main pipeline
122. Irrigation strip
123. Basic infiltration rate
124. Demand
125. Gross irrigation requirement
126. Parallelism of advance
127. Infiltration opportunity
128. One-fourth
129. Overflow and drop structures
130. Furrow
131. Hydraulic resistance
132. Root zone
133. Double mould
134. Impervious
135. Sub-irrigation
136. Sprinkler method
137. Arid regions
138. Filter unit
139. Discharge
140. Northern Gangetic plains
141. 8-10 cm
142. 5 cm
143. Interpolation and extrapolation
144. Trapezoidal channels
145. Bedding system
146. 22.5 cm and 0.5 m^2
147. Free/Gravitational water
148. Terraces
149. Hydraulic characteristics
150. Underground drainage
151. Inversely proportional
152. $\frac{dy}{dt} = \frac{2\Pi ad}{\Pi a^2} \times \frac{y}{s}$
153. $S^2 = \frac{4kH}{V}(2d+H)$
154. 13 and 33 holes
155. Mechanical laying
156. Hydraulic pressure
157. U.S. Army Corps
158. Sticky soils
159. Surface inlets
160. Notched concrete
161. Tile line
162. French drains/Blind inlets
163. Sedimentation basin
164. Cylindrical bullet-nosed
165. Water-absorbing stratum
166. Soil erosion
167. Dead cities
168. Mohenjodaro and Harappa
169. Transportability
170. Diameter
171. Length of the slope
172. Vegetative cover
173. Primary tillage
174. Shape, size and weigh
175. Tang or shank
176. Side to centre
177. One-side
178. Slip-nose
179. Vertical suction
180. Water concentration
181. Infiltration capacity

182.	4.33 power of velocity	183.	Healing and stabilization	184.	Stream channel erosion
185.	3.52 m ha/100 km^2	186.	Rain gauge	187.	Mass curve of cumulative
188.	Intensity and duration	189.	Detention storage/surface detention		
190.	Q = 0.0276 CIA = 1/36. CIA.	191.	$T_c = 0.0195\, L^{0.77}\, S^{0.385}$	192.	$\sqrt{\frac{L^3}{H}}$
193.	Laminar/smooth	194.	Logarithm	195.	0.05 to 0.5 mm
196.	3 to 40 and 5 to 25	197.	5-10 and 30 degrees	198.	OD/2.65
199.	Avalanching	200.	Furrow openers	201.	Single operation
202.	60 to 80 per cent	203.	Absorption types	204.	Mangum terraces
205.	120-150 m	206.	Permanent pasture		
207.	Mouldboard plough/Whirlured terracer			208.	Disc plough
209.	Depressions and ridges	210.	Scarce	211.	Cultivable land
212.	Shoulder bund	213.	Buck scraper	214.	Economic feasibity
215.	Cross-sectional area	216.	Filter strip	217.	Life of the structure
218.	$Q = 2/3 \times 0.6 \sqrt{2 \times 9.81} \times LH^{3/2}$	219.	$Fn = \frac{V_1}{\sqrt{gD_1}}$	220.	Stilling basin
221.	Drop structure	222.	$LB - 4.5y_2/Fn^{0.176}$	223.	$V = \sqrt{Hdg/2ft}$
224.	1930s	225.	Hydraulic draught	226.	200 h.p. or 149 kW
227.	Articulated chassis	228.	Operating implements	229.	Passenger accommodation
230.	Ergonomic aspects	231.	Live hydraulics	232.	Rope-wick
233.	Slipping and overtopping	234.	Monoplanes	235.	Tangentially
236.	Power-driven pump	237.	Synthetic rubber	238.	Manometric
239.	Mechanical troubles	240.	4-wheel drive models	241.	Power shift system
242.	American Standard Quick Hitch	243.	Tractors and machines	244.	Self-propelled
245.	The pneumatic	246.	Crankshaft		
247.	Transmission dynamometers	248.	Engine power	249.	Restricted Standard Code
250.	Standard Farm Tractor Rating Code.			251.	Rated engine speed
252.	Fuel consumption	253.	2.224 kN	254.	Farm-work
255.	Wheel slip	256.	Throttled down	257.	Wheel slip
258.	Steel wheeled	259.	Governor control	260.	Specific fuel consumption
261.	Hydraulic services	262.	Automatic pick up	263.	Weight transfer
264.	90 dBA	265.	High powered	266.	Multi-purpose front
267.	Wheel changing	268.	Cars and trucks	269.	Mechanical linkage
270.	4-wheel drive	271.	Track widths	272.	Braking system
273.	Transmission system	274.	Differential lock	275.	Engine braking assistance
276.	Hydra-shift	277.	Constant-mesh range	278.	Front loader/Fork-lift
279.	Clutchless changes	280.	Hydro kinetic	281.	Flexible

282. 178 ± 13 mm 283. Quick-hitch 284. Pull capacity
285. Wheel weights 286. Vertical multi-cylinder 287. Hydraulic lift
288. Three position valve 289. Compression and tension 290. Automatic draught
291. Discharge and intake 292. Ram cylinder 293. Electronic sensing
294. Fuel saving 295. Radar 296. Pneumatic distribution
297. h.p. = flow (gal/min) × pressure (psi) × 0.0007 298. Telescopic lower links
299. 'No spin' 300. Specific restrictive 301. German
302. Self-propelled 303. Agro-chemicals 304. Balloon types
305. No compression 306. Half-track 307. Compact
308. Articulated-frama 309. Chassis of welded 310. Direct drilling
311. 300 mm 312. Furrow-width 313. Lea plough
314. Mould board 315. Pitch and land 316. Diamond
317. Centre of resistance 318. Hake setting 319. Side draught
320. Cross-shaft 321. Square ploughing 322. Cross-land
323. Right hand 324. Semi-mounted 325. High powered
326. Width capability 327. Reversible plough 328. Breakage
329. Looseners and sub soilers 330. Eccentric mechanism 331. Paraplow
332. Scooping action 333. Manoeuvrability 334. Discer
335. Harrows 336. Chisel plough 337. Small tractors
338. Undulating 339. Light cultivator
340. Rotary weeder/Rolling cultivator 341. Digging type
342. Lifting cylinders 343. Over handing 344. Stubble breaking
345. Rotary harrows 346. Ground-drive 347. Reversible
348. Clod-crushers 349. Three-link-hitch 350. 'Quick-hitch'
351. Seed-bed preparation 352. Reciprocating harrows 353. Horse hoeing husbandry
354. Power-driven rotary 355. Cylindrical rotor
356. Automatic ribbed wheel/Fin steerage
357. Adverse conditions 358. 4.8 km/hr 359. Seed-tubes
360. Quarter open 361. Blanking-off plate 362. Cultivator air-delivery
363. Saucer shaped 364. Shoe-type coulters 365. External force-feed
366. Spur-gear 367. Electronic tramlining 368. Tractor mounted
369. Direct drilling 370. Cultivator drill 371. Trampling
372. Coulters 373. Strain 374. Positive feed
375. Single seed 376. Vacuum principle 377. Wheels
378. Cylinder hopper 379. Fluid drilling
380. Trolly-mounted automated 381. Electronic monitor 382. Grass seed

383. Cup-feed type
384. Potato-in-cups
385. Trailed
386. Shoulder to shoulder
387. Reciprocating slow-moving
388. Automatic make-up
389. Hydraulic cylinders
390. Separator web
391. Side-loading elevator
392. Press wheels
393. Endless conveyor
394. Watering device
395. Distributor hopper
396. Positive displacement
397. Below ground placement
398. 8 bar at 22 °C
399. Liquid fertilizer
400. Agitator feed
401. Spinning disc
402. Drill tramline
403. Oscillating spout
404. Pneumatic distributors
405. U-shaped endentation
406. Hydraulic slewing grabs
407. Fork lift-loaders
408. Trailer spreaders
409. Free-flowing
410. Slurry pump/loader.
411. Pump output
412. Sliding friction
413. Cone shaped
414. Uniformity/Span
415. Controlled droplet applica tion (CDA)
416. Complexity
417. Five sections
418. Distribution irregularities
419. Servo valves
420. Foam blob
421. Low volume
422. Tramlines
423. Band sprayers
424. Metering pump, DPA
425. p.t.o.
426. Centrifugal governor
427. Electronic sensing
428. Radar velocity sensor
429. Hydraulic pressure
430. Spinning
431. Over-tightening
432. Twice the diameter
433. 5,000 square
434. Central-pivotal system
435. Diesel electric
436. 'Solid-set'
437. Reciprocating mowers
438. Triangular sections
439. Break back
440. Orchard
441. Hydraulic lift
442. Flail mowers
443. Mower conditioner
444. Surface treatment
445. Right angles
446. Plastic fingers
447. Multi-purpose
448. Metered chop harvester/Tippingg trailer combination
449. Wilted
450. Down the chute
451. Bottom unloader
452. Forage weigher/harvester
453. Spillage
454. Block cutter
455. Rotating drum
456. Complete diet feeder
457. Roughage loading
458. Rear mounted
459. Pick-up
460. Six full-length
461. Spring-loaded
462. Fork-type
463. Vertical columns
464. Group of bales
465. Two wheeled
466. Transfer-weight bale transporter
467. Tumble-stacking
468. Compression chamber
469. Upper belt
470. Apron chain
471. Steel rods
472. Fixed and variable
473. Power
474. Hydraulic variations
475. p.t.o. driven
476. Self-propelled combine
477. Fingertip control
478. Slip clutch
479. Cross-shaker system
480. 'Saddle tanks'
481. Hillside
482. Variable speed
483. Ultra-sonic sensors
484. Axial flow
485. Beater-bar type
486. Twin-flow system
487. Cylinder separation
488. Grain to straw ratio
489. Dust protective
490. Direct action
491. Potato spinner

492. Agitator sprockets	493. Continental	494. Soil conditions
495. Side-elevator	496. Transversely	497. Hydraulically actuated
498. Miller shaft	499. Pneumatic deflectors	500. 10.2 m/sec
501. Sprout suppressant	502. Adjustably-spaced	503. X-ray sorters
504. Self-propelled harvesters	505. 11-in-wide	506. Topping kinves
507. Complete harvesters	508. Rod-link conveyors	509. Rubber-faced
510. Gripping-belt	511. Shallow tillage	512. Steam-raising
513. High speed	514. Mushroom	515. Block-making
516. Heavy duty flails	517. Roller feed	518. Diameter
519. Floatation	520. Crank, mechanism	521. Guide rail
522. 'Picking over'	523. Jet washers	524. Satisfactorily
525. Contra-rotating	526. Cocks and elevator	527. Large pickers
528. Shelling	529. 1.5 to 2.0 tonnes	530. Self-propelled harvesters
531. Stripping head	532. Sieves and aspirations	533. Hopper shaped
534. Inclined endless belt	535. Disc shaped	536. Repeatable programmes
537. Air pressure	538. 2.0 and 1.5	539. Overlapping louvres
540. 120 and 105	541. High temperature	542. Cubing machines
543. 7.5 m bar	544. Ventilated bin	545. Flat-bottomed
546. Ice-cream	547. Ammonia compression	548. –9° to 7 °C
549. Expansion coils	550. Hydrogen bonds	551. Anti-oxidants
552. Gelatinization	553. Single parboiling	554. CFTRI
555. Horizontally flow	556. Cracking	557. Better quality
558. Three-man team	559. Local needs	560. Mini Modem Rice
561. Under-pressure disc sheller	562. Rubber roller shellers	563. 500 g/m^2
564. Vertical cone	565. Horizontal abrasive	566. Terraces
567. Erosion resistant	568. Check dams	569. Peak runoff
570. Crescent/half moon	571. Plank/slab dams	572. Soil conservation
573. Hydrologic design	574. Hydraulic	575. Drop spillway
576. False	577. False	578. True
579. False	580. False	581. True
582. True	583. False	584. False
585. False	586. True	587. False
588. False	589. False	590. True
591. False	592. False	593. True
594. False	595. False	596. False
597. True	598. True	599. True
600. False	601. False	602. True

603. False 604. False 605. True
606. False 607. False 608. True
609. True 610. False 611. False
612. False 613. False 614. True
615. False 616. True 617. False
618. True 619. False 620. True
621. False 622. True 623. False
624. True 625. False 626. False
627. True 628. False 629. True
630. False 631. False 632. False
633. True 634. True 635. False
636. True 637. False 638. False
639.True 640. False 641. True
642.False 643. False 644. True
645. False 646. True 647. False
648. True 649. True 650. True
651. False 652. True 653. False
654. True 655. True 656. False
657. False 658. True 659. True
660. True 661. False 662. False
663. False 664. True 665. False
666. True 667. False 668. False
669. True 670. True 671. True
672. False 673. False 674. False
675. True 676. True 677. True
678. False 679. False 680. True
681. True 682. False 683. False
684. False 685. True 686. False
687. False 688. True 689. True
690. False 691. False 692. False
693. True 694. True 695. False
696. False 697. False 698. True
699. False 700. True 701. True
702. False 703. False 704. True
705. True 706. False 707. False
708. True 709. False 710. True
711. True 712. False 713. True
714. False 715. True 716. True

717. True	718. False	719. True
720. False	721. False	722. False
723. False	724. True	725. True
726. False	727. False	728. True
729. False	730. True	731. False
732. True	733. True	734. False
735. True	736. False	737. True
738. False	739. False	740. True
741. False	742. True	743. False
744. False	745. True	746. False
747. False	748. True	749. False
750. True	751. True	752. False
753. False	754. True	755. True
756. False	757. False	758. True
759. False	760. False	761. False
762. True	763. False	764. False
765. True	766. True	767. False
768. False	769. True	770. False
771. False	772. True	773. False
774. False	775. True	776. True
777. False	778. False	779. False
780. True	781. False	782. True
783. False	784. False	785. True
786. False	787. False	788. True
789. False	790. True	791. False
792. False	793. True	794. False
795. True	796. False	797. False
798. True	799. False	800. True
801. False	802. True	803. True
804. True	805. False	806. True
807. False	808. False	809. False
810. True	811. True	812. False
813. True	814. True	815. False
816. True	817. True	818. False
819. False	820. True	821. False
822. True	823. True	824. False
825. False	826. True	827. True

828. True
829. False
830. False
831. True
832. False
833. True
834. True
835. False
836. False
837. True
838. True
839. False
840. False
841. False
842. True
843. False
844. True
845. False
846. True
847. True
848. True
849. True
850. False
851. False
852. True
853. True
854. False
855. False
856. False
857. True
858. True
859. False
860. True
861. True
862. True
863. True
864. False
865. False
866. False
867. True
868. False
869. False
870. False
871. True
872. False
873. True
874. False
875. True
876. True
877. False
878. False
879. False
880. True
881. False
882. False
883. False
884. True
885. True
886. True
887. True
888. False
889. False
890. True
891. False
892. True
893. True
894. True
895. False
896. False
897. True
898. False
899. False
900. True
901. True
902. False
903. False
904. False
905. True
906. True
907. False
908. True
909. True
910. False
911. True
912. True
913. True
914. False
915. True
916. True
917. False
918. False
919. True
920. True
921. True
922. False
923. False
924. True
925. True
926. False
927. True
928. True
929. False
930. False
931. True
932. True
933. False
934. True
935. False
936. False
937. True
938. False

V. Tick mark the (✓) correct answer

939. (*c*) 940. (*d*) 941. (*a*)
942. (*b*) 943 (*c*) 944. (*c*)
945. (*c*) 946. (*d*) 947. (*c*)
948. (*d*) 949. (*a*) 950. (*d*)
951. (*a*) 952. (*b*) 953. (*c*)
954. (*b*) 955. (*a*) 956. (*d*)
957. (*c*) 958. (*b*) 959. (*a*)
960. (*c*) 961. (*d*) 962. (*c*)
963. (*a*) 964. (*c*) 965. (*b*)
966. (*c*) 967. (*d*) 968. (*c*)
969. (*c*) 970. (*c*) 971. (*b*)
972. (*d*) 973. (*a*) 974. (*a*)
975. (*d*) 976. (*b*) 977. (*d*)
978. (*c*) 979. (*c*) 980. (*a*)
981. (*c*) 982. (*c*) 983. (*b*)
984. (*c*) 985. (*b*) 986. (*b*)
987. (*b*) 988. (*c*) 989. (*b*)
990. (*c*) 991. (*c*) 992. (*d*)
993. (*b*) 994. (*a*) 995. (*b*)
996. (*d*) 997. (*c*) 998. (*a*)
999. (*d*) 1000. (*c*) 1001. (*c*)
1002. (*a*) 1003. (*b*) 1004. (*a*)
1005. (*d*) 1006. (*c*) 1007. (*b*)
1008. (*a*) 1009. (*c*) 1010. (*c*)
1011. (*d*) 1012. (*c*) 1013. (*c*)
1014. (*d*) 1015. (*a*) 1016. (*d*)
1017. (*b*) 1018. (*a*) 1019. (*a*)
1020. (*b*) 1021. (*c*) 1022. (*c*)
1023. (*d*) 1024. (*a*) 1025. (*d*)
1026. (*a*) 1027. (*c*) 1028. (*b*)
1029. (*b*) 1030. (*b*) 1031. (*c*)
1032. (*b*) 1033. (*b*) 1034. (*c*)
1035. (*d*) 1036. (*a*) 1037. (*c*)
1038. (*c*) 1039. (*c*) 1040. (*b*)
1041. (*b*) 1042. (*b*) 1043. (*d*)
1044. (*d*) 1045. (*a*) 1046. (*c*)
1047. (*d*) 1048. (*c*) 1049. (*b*)

1050. (*d*) 1051. (*c*) 1052. (*c*)
1053. (*d*) 1054. (*c*) 1055. (*a*)
1056. (*d*) 1057. (*a*) 1058. (*c*)
1059. (*d*) 1060. (*a*) 1061. (*b*)
1062. (*c*) 1063. (*b*)
1064. (*a*) (*iv*) (*b*) (*v*) (*c*) (*i*) (*d*) (*iii*) (*e*) (*ii*)
1065. (*a*) (*iii*) (*b*) (*i*) (*c*) (*v*) (*d*) (*ii*) (*e*) (*iv*)
1066. (*a*) (*iv*) (*b*) (*v*) (*c*) (*i*) (*d*) (*ii*) (*e*) (*iii*)
1067. (*a*) (*iv*) (*b*) (*i*) (*c*) (*ii*) (*d*) (*iii*)
1068. (*a*) (*iii*) (*b*) (*iv*) (*c*) (*i*) (*d*) (*ii*)
1069. (*a*) (*iv*) (*b*) (*v*) (*c*) (*i*) (*d*) (*iii*) (*e*) (*ii*)
1070. (*a*) (*v*) (*b*) (*ii*) (*c*) (*iv*) (*d*) (*i*) (*e*) (*iii*)
1071. (*a*) (*iii*) (*b*) (*v*) (*c*) (*i*) (*d*) (*ii*) (*e*) (*iv*)
1072. (*a*) (*iv*) (*b*) (*v*) (*c*) (*i*) (*d*) (*iii*) (*e*) (*ii*)
1073. (*a*) (*iii*) (*b*) (*i*) (*c*) (*iv*) (*d*) (*ii*)
1074. (*a*) (*iii*) (*b*) (*i*) (*c*) (*iv*) (*d*) (*ii*)
1075. (*a*) (*iv*) (*b*) (*i*) (*c*) (*ii*) (*d*) (*iii*)
1076. (*a*) (*iv*) (*b*) (*i*) (*c*) (*ii*) (*d*) (*iii*)
1077. (*a*) (*iv*) (*b*) (*i*) (*c*) (*v*) (*d*) (*ii*) (*e*) (*iii*)
1078. (*a*) (*iii*) (*b*) (*i*) (*c*) (*iv*) (*d*) (*ii*)
1079. (*a*) (*iii*) (*b*) (*iv*) (*c*) (*i*) (*d*) (*ii*)
1080. (*a*) (*iv*) (*b*) (*v*) (*c*) (*i*) (*d*) (*iii*) (*e*) (*ii*)
1081. (*a*) (*iii*) (*b*) (*i*) (*c*) (*iv*) (*d*) (*ii*)
1082. (*a*) (*iv*) (*b*) (*i*) (*c*) (*ii*) (*d*) (*iii*)
1083. (*a*) (*ii*) (*b*) (*iv*) (*c*) (*i*) (*d*) (*iii*)
1084. (*a*) (*iv*) (*b*) (*i*) (*c*) (*ii*) (*d*) (*iii*)
1085. (*a*) (*iii*) (*b*) (*iv*) (*c*) (*i*) (*d*) (*ii*)
1086. (*a*) (*ii*) (*b*) (*iii*) (*c*) (*iv*) (*d*) (*i*)
1087. (*a*) (*iv*) (*b*) (*i*) (*c*) (*ii*) (*d*) (*iii*)
1088. (*a*) (*iii*) (*b*) (*ii*) (*c*) (*iv*) (*d*) (*i*)
1089. (*a*) (*ii*) (*b*) (*iv*) (*c*) (*i*) (*d*) (*iii*)
1090. (*a*) (*ii*) (*b*) (*iv*) (*c*) (*i*) (*d*) (*iii*)
1091. (*a*) (*ii*) (*b*) (*iii*) (*c*) (*iv*) (*d*) (*i*)
1092. (*a*) (*iv*) (*b*) (*iii*) (*c*) (*i*) (*d*) (*ii*)
1093. (*a*) (*iii*) (*b*) (*i*) (*c*) (*iv*) (*d*) (*ii*)
1094. (*a*) (*iv*) (*b*) (*i*) (*c*) (*iii*) (*d*) (*ii*)
1095. (*a*) (*ii*) (*b*) (*iv*) (*c*) (*i*) (*d*) (*iii*)

1096.	(*a*) (*iv*)	(*b*) (*iii*)	(*c*) (*ii*)	(*d*) (*i*)	
1097.	(*a*) (*ii*)	(*b*) (*iii*)	(*c*) (*i*)	(*d*) (*iv*)	
1098.	(*a*) (*iv*)	(*b*) (*i*)	(*c*) (*ii*)	(*d*) (*iii*)	
1099.	(*a*) (*iii*)	(*b*) (*i*)	(*c*) (*iv*)	(*d*) (*ii*)	
1100.	(*a*) (*ii*)	(*b*) (*iv*)	(*c*) (*i*)	(*d*) (*iii*)	
1101.	(*a*) (*iv*)	(*b*) (*iii*)	(*c*) (*i*)	(*d*) (*v*)	(*e*) (*ii*)
1102.	(*a*) (*iii*)	(*b*) (*v*)	(*c*) (*i*)	(*d*) (*iv*)	(*e*) (*ii*)
1103.	(*a*) (*ii*)	(*b*) (*iv*)	(*c*) (*i*)	(*d*) (*iii*)	
1104.	(*a*) (*ii*)	(*b*) (*i*)	(*c*) (*iv*)	(*d*) (*iii*)	
1105.	(*a*) (*iv*)	(*b*) (*i*)	(*c*) (*ii*)	(*d*) (*iii*)	
1106.	(*a*) (*ii*)	(*b*) (*iv*)	(*c*) (*i*)	(*d*) (*iii*)	
1107.	(*a*) (*iii*)	(*b*) (*iv*)	(*c*) (*i*)	(*d*) (*ii*)	
1108.	(*a*) (*ii*)	(*b*) (*iv*)	(*c*) (*i*)	(*d*) (*iii*)	
1109.	(*a*) (*iv*)	(*b*) (*i*)	(*c*) (*iii*)	(*d*) (*ii*)	
1110.	(*a*) (*iii*)	(*b*) (*i*)	(*c*) (*iv*)	(*d*) (*ii*)	
1111.	(*a*) (*ii*)	(*b*) (*iv*)	(*c*) (*i*)	(*d*) (*iii*)	
1112.	(*a*) (*iv*)	(*b*) (*i*)	(*c*) (*v*)	(*d*) (*iii*)	(*e*) (*ii*)
1113.	(*a*) (*ii*)	(*b*) (*v*)	(*c*) (*i*)	(*d*) (*iii*)	(*e*) (*iv*)
1114.	(*a*) (*iv*)	(*b*) (*i*)	(*c*) (*v*)	(*d*) (*iii*)	(*e*) (*ii*)
1115.	(*a*) (*iv*)	(*b*) (*i*)	(*c*) (*ii*)	(*d*) (*iii*)	

1116. 251.25 m 1117. 941.45 links 1118. 150.5 and 175.58 metres

1119. WHP 986 and Electric motor of 15 BHP

1120. Total head 24 m and engine of 4.1 BHP

1121. 268.8 Cubic metres 1122. Elevation = 10.33996 m, Σ cut = 7.2343 Σ Fill = 5.6136

1123. 7.5 litres/second 1124. 16.31 m 1125. 1037 m

1126. Velocity = 0.536 m/sec; q = 1.16 Cu. m./sec 1127. 58.2 litres/hour

1128. 3 hectares 1129. 53.3 minutes 1130. 10.3 %

1131. 27 hrs. 47 minutes 1132. Q 1 % 1133. 0.72 cm

1134. 0.463 cu. m./sec 1135. 1.19 m/sec 1136. 4.11 hectares

1137. 0.3 % 1138. 9.48 cm/sec 1139. 5.54 cu. m/sec

1140. 22.12 minutes 1141. Length = 2.5, and total depth = 32 cm

1142. 5.13 cu. m/sec 1143. 22 litres/sec 1144. 183 litres/sec

1145. 0.07 litre/sec 1146. 1400 kg 1147. 0.75 cu. m

1148. 3,300

SECTION 14
BIOTECHNOLOGY & BIOINFORMATICS

Multiple Choice Questions

1. DNA finger printing was invented by

(*a*) Eithovan (*b*) Naryanan

(*c*) A. Jeffreys (*d*) Manju Sharma

2. Important segments for DNA finger printing are short-repetitive nucleatide sequences which vary from person to person are called

(*a*) PCR (*b*) VNTR

(*c*) BCH (*d*) TNTR

3. Crop that contain one or more foreign genes and expresses them is called

(*a*) Somatic Hybridisation (*b*) Callus Culture

(*c*) Transgenic Crop (*d*) Improved Cultivar

4. Basic tools of Genetic Engineering

(*a*) Molecular scissors (*b*) Plasmids

(*c*) Both (*a*) and (*b*) (*d*) None of the above

5. Synthesis of a gene in a test tube and its transfer to a cell is called

(*a*) Genetic engineering (*b*) Cloning

(*c*) Mutation (*d*) Hybridization

6. The enzyme that cleaves DNA at specific sites, producing sticky ends is called

(*a*) Lyseing enzyme (*b*) Cleaving enzyme

(*c*) Exonuclease (*d*) Restriction endonuclease

(*e*) Endonuclease.

7. Structure involved in genetic engineering is

(*a*) Plasmid (*b*) Codon

(*c*) Plastid (*d*) Scissors

8. Which enzyme is useful in genetic engineering ?

(*a*) DNAase (*b*) Amylase

(*c*) Lipase (*d*) Restriction endonuclease.

9. Restriction endonubase used in genetic engineering

(*a*) They can degrade harmful proteins (*b*) They can join DNA fragments

(*c*) They can cut DNA at specific base sequences (*d*) They can cut DNA at variable. sites.

10. The transgenic animals are those which have

(*a*) Foreign DNA in some of their cells
(*b*) Foreign RNA in all of their cells
(*c*) Foreign RNA in all of their cells
(*d*) Both (*a*) and (*c*).

11. First artificial gene was synthesized by

(*a*) Nirenberg
(*b*) Mendel
(*c*) Morgan
(*d*) Khorana

12. Advancement in genetic engineering has been possible due to the discovery of

(*a*) Oncogenes
(*b*) Transposons
(*c*) Restriction endonuclease
(*d*) Exonucleases

13. Genetic engineering would not have been possible if which of the following were not known?

(*a*) DNA polymerase
(*b*) RNA synthetase
(*c*) DNA ligase
(*d*) Reverse transcriptase.

14. Restriction endonucleases are

(*a*) Synthesized by bacteria
(*b*) Present in mammalian cells for degradation of DNA
(*c*) Used for in-vitro DNA synthesis
(*d*) Used in genetic engineering.

15. The chemical knives of DNA are

(*a*) Ligases
(*b*) Polymerases
(*c*) Endonucleases
(*d*) Transcriptases

16. Bundess *et al.* (1996) defined.

(*a*) Biotechnology
(*b*) DNA
(*c*) Genetic engineering
(*d*) Vimamin

17. Plasmids occur in

(*a*) Viruses
(*b*) Chromosomes
(*c*) Bacteria
(*d*) Chloroplasts

18. One of the following is used to join the segments of DNA during genetic engineering

(*a*) Lipase
(*b*) Ligase
(*c*) Gyrase
(*a*) Helicase

19. The tool of genetic engineering which makes it successful is

(*a*) DNA polymerase
(*b*) Permease
(*c*) Restriction endonuclease
(*d*) Topoisomerase

20. Clones are stored in

(*a*) Gene bank
(*b*) Bookshelves
(*c*) Biological reserves
(*d*) All of these

21. Ligase helps in

(*a*) Removal of few genes
(*b*) Translation
(*b*) Inserting few genes in DNA
(*d*) Bringing transversion in chromosomes.

22. The enzyme used in polymerase chain reaction is

(*a*) Taq-polymerase
(*b*) Lyases
(*c*) Hydrolases
(*d*) Ligases

23. Which one of the following pair is transgenic organisms?

(*a*) Holly sheep and Tomato (*b*) Dolly sheep and Subabul

(*c*) Molly sheep and Banana (*d*) Dolly sheep and Tomato

24. DNA fingerprinting technique was discovered by

(*a*) Wilmut (*b*) A. Jeffreys

(*c*) Eithoven (*d*) Kary Mullis.

25. PCR (Polymerase chain reaction) was discovered by

(*a*) Wilmut (*b*) A. Jeffreys

(*c*) Eithoven (*d*) Kary Mullis

26. PCR method is useful for

(*a*) Amplification of DNA for forming billions of copies of itself

(*b*) Monoclonal antibody production

(*c*) Hybridoma production (*d*) All of the above

27. DNA probe is used for

(*a*) DNA finger printing (*b*) Detection of pathogenic bacteria

(*c*) Medical genetics to find whether a person carries a particular gene or not

(*d*) All of the above.

28. Restriction enzymes are

(*a*) Not always required in genetic engineering (*b*) Essential tool in genetic engineering

(*c*) Nucleases that cleave DNA at specific sites (*d*) Both (*b*) and (*c*)

29. Genetically identical individuals are

(*a*) Cybrids (*b*) Hybrids

(*c*) Clones (*d*) Plasmids

30. Collection of organisms as bacteria that all contain the same piece of recombinant DNA is called

(*a*) Gene cloning (*b*) Cell cloning

(*c*) Organ cloning (*d*) All of these.

31. The technique in which a foreign DNA is precipitated on the surface of tungsten or gold particle and shot into the target cells is known as

(*a*) Microinjection (*b*) Chemical mediated gene transfer

(*c*) Particle gun (*d*) Electroporation

32. The enzyme that cuts specifically recognition sites in DNA is known as

(*a*) DNA ligase (*b*) DNA polymerase

(*c*) Reverse transcriptase (*d*) Restriction endonuclease

33. Biologically functional gene coding for tyrosine tRNA of E. Colisynthesized by Khorana in 1979

(*a*) 333 nucleotides (*b*) 312 nucleotide pairs

(*c*) 207 nucleotide pairs (*d*) 77 nucleotide pairs.

34. The chemical knives of DNAs

(*a*) Ligases (*b*) Polymerases

(*c*) Endonucleases (*d*) Transcriptases.

35. When the genotype of an organisms is improved by the addition of foreign genes, the process is called

(*a*) Biotechnology (*b*) Tissue culture
(*c*) Genetic Engineering (*d*) Genetic diversity

36. Plasmids

(*a*) are circular protein molecules (*b*) are required by bacteria
(*c*) are tiny bacteria (*d*) confer resistance to antibiotics.

37. DNA can be introduced into any cell by

(*a*) injection (*b*) being complexed with calcium salts
(*c*) being placed along with the cell into a gene gun
(*d*) gel electrophoresis

38. In DNA finger printing

(*a*) a positive identification can be made
(*b*) multiple restriction enzyme digests/generate unique fragments
(*c*) the polymere chain reaction amplifies fewer DNA
(*d*) the variability of repeated sequences between two restriction sites is evaluated

39. Reproducing new plants by cells instead of seeds is known as

(*a*) Biofertilizer (*b*) Tissue culture
(*c*) Mutation (*d*) Antibiotics

40. Conversion of sugar into alcohol during fermentation is due to the direct action of

(*a*) Temperature (*b*) Micro-organisms
(*c*) Concentration of sugar solution (*d*) Zymase

41. First antibiotic isolated was

(*a*) Terramycin (*b*) Neomycin
(*c*) Penicillin (*d*) Streptomycin

42. Which of the following enzymes is secreted by yeast, responsible for fermentation ?

(*a*) Emolase (*b*) Gyno phase
(*c*) Zymase (*d*) Invertase

43. Tissue culture technique has been successfully used for producing

(*a*) Alcoholic beverages (*b*) Cheese
(*c*) Shikonin (*d*) Insulin

44. Utilisation of biological knowledge for producing materials useful to society is called

(*a*) Ecology (*b*) Pathology
(*c*) Applied Biology (*d*) Biotechnology

45. Discovery of restriction endonuclease was made by

(*a*) Crick Kornberg and Robert (*b*) Temin and Baltimore
(*c*) Arber Nathans and Nirenberg (*d*) Holley, Khorana and Nirenberg

46. Restriction endonuclease is

(*a*) Specific for each gene (*b*) Common to all genes
(*c*) Common to all RNAs (*d*) Common to all organisms

47. **Scientist associated with the discoveries in Genetic Engineering.**
(a) Chopra (b) Khorana
(c) Crick (d) Swaminathan

48. **Teminism is the synthesis of DNA on RNA template was observed in**
(a) TMV (b) Rice dwarf virus
(c) Reovirus (d) Rous sarcoma virus

49. **What is cDNA ?**
(a) Circular RNA
(b) Cloned DNA
(c) DNA produced from reverse transcription of RNA
(d) Cytoplasmic DNA

50. **The central dogma of molecular biology is**
(a) DNA $\rightarrow$ RNA $\rightarrow$ Protein (b) DNA $\rightleftharpoons$ RNA $\rightarrow$ Protein
(c) $\uparrow$ DNA $\rightleftharpoons$ RNA $\rightleftharpoons$ Protein (d) $\uparrow$ DNA $\rightleftharpoons$ RNA $\rightarrow$ Protein

51. **Germinating barley seeds are employed in the preparation of**
(a) Cheese (b) Wine
(c) Beer (d) Lactic acid

52. **Which enzymes are used for converting corn starch into high fructose syrup?**
(a) Glucoisomerases (b) Glucoamylases
(c) Amylases (d) All of these

53. **The number of enzymes known today is approximately,**
(a) 1220 (b) 2200
(c) 3050 (d) 4050

54. **Enzymes can be immobilised by**
(a) Cross-linking enzyme molecules (b) Covalently attaching to a solid support
(c) Entrapping them in gel (d) All the above

55. **The enzyme TPA is used to**
(a) Maintain turgor pressure (b) Strengthen tissues
(c) Increase plasma (d) Dissolve blood clots

56. **Which enzymes are used for manufacturing detergents ?**
(a) Proteases (b) Blucoamylases
(c) Amylases (d) Lactases

57. **The enzyme diastase was identified by**
(a) S. A. Waksman (b) Randhawa
(c) R. N. Singh (d) Payen and Persoz

58. **Rennet enzyme was purified by**
(a) A. Fleming (b) S. A. Waksman
(c) Payen and Persoz (d) Christian Hansen

59. **Humulin is**
(a) A form of chitin (b) A powerful antibiotic
(c) A new digestive enzyme (d) Human insulin

60. **Restriction enzyme was discovered by**
(a) Maheshwari (b) Smith and North
(c) Waksman (d) Mehta

61. **The foundation stone of Lal Bahadur Shastri Centre forAdvanced Research in Biotechnology and Plant Protection was laid by**
(*a*) Rajiv Gandhi (*b*) Indira Gandhi
(*c*) V.P. Singh (*d*) Chandra Shekar

62. **Lal Bahadur Shastri Centre for Advanced Research in Biotechnology is located at**
(*a*) Hyderabad (*b*) Bangalore
(*c*) New Delhi (*d*) Bombay

63. **Somaclone released for commercial cultivation in**
(*a*) Carrot (*b*) Indian mustard
(*c*) Tomato (*d*) Ehick pea

64. **Research on oncogenes, cell transformation, etc. is being carried at**
(*a*) Centre for Cellular and Molecular Biology, Hyderabad
(*b*) IARI, New Delhi
(*c*) Pune University, Pune
(*d*) Indian Institute of Science, Bangalore

65. **NBPGR holds over accessions of various crops**
(*a*) 1.0 lakh (*b*) 1.1 lakh
(*c*) 1.2 lakh (*d*) 1.3 lakh

66. **A co-enzyme can be**
(*a*) conjugated protein (*b*) organic molecule
(*c*) inorganic iron (*d*) metal

67. **Pepsin acts best at pH**
(*a*) 2 (*b*) 7
(*c*) 9 (*d*) none of the above

68. **Basic unit of protein is**
(*a*) Peptides (*b*) Peptones
(*c*) Helical strand (*d*) Amino acids

BIOINFORMATICS

It may be defined as information technology applied to management and analyes of biological data, this has implications in diverse areas like artificial intelligence and robotics to genome analysis. Bioinformatics was originally applied to computational manipulation and analysis of DNA or protein. But recent and rapid developments made it possible for manipulation and analysis of 3 dimensional structural data.

1. **The term bioinformatics was coined in the year**
(*a*) 1990 (*b*) 2000
(*c*) 1995 (*d*) 1980

2. **A unique number code given to made the entry of a sequence or pattern to a primary or secondary data base**
(*a*) Fhromosome number (*b*) Accession number
(*c*) Domain number (*d*) None

3. **The database consists of information on virolagy of animal cell lines and tissue culture is called**
(*a*) Animal virus information system.
(*b*) Tissue culture information system
(*c*) Both (*a*) and (*b*) (*d*) None

4. **A Protein that assist the correct non-covalent assembly of folding proteins is viva.**
   (*a*) Exons (*b*) Chaperone
   (*c*) Enzyme (*c*) None
5. **A partial sequence of a clone which is randomly selected from a cDNA library**
   (*a*) Expressed sequence tags (*b*) Gene sequence
   (*c*) Regular expression (*d*) None
6. **A pseudo sequence that summarises the residue information contained in a multiple alignment**
   (*a*) Conserved sequence (*b*) Consenus sequence
   (*c*) Multiple sequence (*d*) None
7. **A sequence of bases in a DNA molecule which remain unchanged during evolution**
   (*a*) Consensus sequence (*b*) Multiple sequence
   (*c*) Conserved sequence (*d*) None
8. **Protein-coding sequence of a gene**
   (*a*) Gene (*b*) Exons
   (*c*) Genmoe (*d*) None
9. **An alteration in the reading sense of DNA resulting due to inserted or deleted base is.**
   (*a*) File shift (*b*) Frame shift
   (*c*) False shift (*d*) None
10. **Genetic alternation where a segment of DNA is repeated**
   (*a*) Protein duplication (*b*) Frame duplication
   (*c*) Gene duplication (*d*) None

KEY

1. (*c*)	2. (*b*)	3. (*c*)	4. (*c*)	5. (*a*)
6. (*d*)	7. (*a*)	8. (*d*)	9. (*c*)	10. (*b*)
11. (*d*)	12. (*c*)	13. (*c*)	14. (*d*)	15. (*c*)
16. (*a*)	17. (*c*)	18. (*b*)	19. (*c*)	20. (*a*)
21. (*c*)	22. (*a*)	23. (*d*)	24. (*b*)	25. (*d*)
26. (*a*)	27. (*a*)	28. (*d*)	29. (*c*)	30. (*a*)
31. (*c*)	32. (*d*)	33. (*c*)	34. (*c*)	35. (*c*)
36. (*d*)	37. (*c*)	38. (*c*)	39. (*b*)	40. (*d*)
41. (*c*)	42. (*c*)	43. (*c*)	44. (*d*)	45. (*c*)
46. (*a*)	47. (*b*)	48. (*d*)	49. (*c*)	50. (*d*)
51. (*c*)	52. (*d*)	53. (*b*)	54. (*d*)	55. (*d*)
56. (*a*)	57. (*d*)	58. (*d*)	59. (*d*)	60. (*b*)
61. (*a*)	62. (*c*)	63. (*b*)	64. (*a*)	65. (*d*)
66. (*b*)	67. (*a*)	68. (*c*)		

BIOINFORMATICS

1. (*d*)	2. (*b*)	3. (*a*)	4. (*b*)	5. (*a*)
6. (*b*)	7. (*c*)	8. (*b*)	9. (*b*)	10. (*c*)

QUIZ TYPE QUESTIONS

Q. 1. Totipotency is

Ans. Capability of an isolated single cell to multiply and differentiate into multicellular organism.

Q. 2. RNA (ribonucleic acid) is a

Ans. Molecule similar to DNA, helps in process of decoding genetic information carried by DNA.

Q. 3. Methods used for determination of gene sequences

Ans. 1. Maxm and Gilbert method

2. Sangerdide oxynucleotide synthetic method

Q. 4. DNA (deoxyribonucleic acid)

Ans. Molecule encodes genetic information

Q. 5. Micropropgation is

Ans. In-vitro multiplication of plants from a small tissue explant

Q. 6. What is Electroporation.

Ans. A technique uses electric discharge to produce pores on cell membrane for intake of recombinant DNA

Q. 7. E-coli is a

Ans. Bacterium used in genetic engg. for its small size.

Q. 8. Agrobucterium rhizogenes

Ans. Soil bacteria often possesses R_i plasmids and cause the hairy root system in plants

Q. 9. Allele is

Ans. One of a number of different forms of a gene.

Q. 10. Anticodon

Ans. Triplet of nucleotides in transfer of RNA

Q. 11. Double haploids are

Ans. Individuals derived from haploid gametes and carry two identical chromosomes

Q. 12. Crossing of plants through fusion of somatic cell is

Ans. Somatic hybridization

Q. 13. DNA ligase is

Ans. An enzyme that closes nicks or discontinuities in one strand of double stranded DNA by creating a bond.

Q. 14. Father of genetic engineering

Ans. Paul Berg

Q. 15. Gene bank is a

Ans. Group of genes or cloned DNA fragments

Q. 16. Marker is

Ans. A sequence of bases at a unique physical location in genome

Q. 17. Molecular markers are

Ans. DNA fragments used as finger print in identification of any organism or species.

Q. 18. PCR technique uses

Ans. Bacterial enzymes for in-vitro amplification of DNA

Q. 19. Transgenics plants are

Ans. Genetically modified organisms

Q. 20. Transgenics or GMO are

Ans. Organisms with gene or genetic construct introduced by molecular or recombinant DNA.

Q. 21. Transcription is

Ans. Process during which the information in a sequence of DNA is used to construct m-RNA

Q. 22. Golden rice was developed by

Ans. Ingo Protrykus and Peter Bayeo

Q. 23. Golden rice provides

Ans. Higher β-carotene over normal rice

Q. 24. Biotechnology related to Agriculture is also called

Ans. Green biotechnology

Q. 25. Plant tissue culture is

Ans. Multiplication of cell of large number of plants placed in appropriate environment conditions with required nutrients.

Q. 26. Virus that live in bacteria is

Ans. Bacteriophage

Q. 27. Hybridization is

Ans. Crossing of two genotypically different plants, Genes from both plants are brought together

Q. 28. The insoluble RNA that constitutes the largest part of cellular RNA (About 80%).

Ans. r-RNA

Q. 29. Explant is

Ans. An excised fragment of a tissue or an organ used to start tissue culture

Q. 30. Process by which a cell monolayer or a plant explant is transferred without subdivision into a fresh medium

Ans. Reculture

Q. 31. A pheromone is

Ans. A small molecule secreted by one mating type of an organisms in order to interact with a member of the opposite mating type.

Q. 32. DNAs consist of repetitions of extremely short units (typically < 10 bp).

Ans. Microsatellite

Q. 33 Enzymes that attack bonds in DNA.

Ans. DNAases

Q. 34 DNA-synthesizing enzyme required specifically for replication.

Ans. DNA replicase

TRUE FALSE QUESTIONS

Q. 35. In plants, chromosome number is usually higher in dicots than in monocots

Ans. (True)

Q. 36. Circular chromosomes are found in bacteria and viruses

Ans. (True)

Q. 37. Plants usually have large chromosomes than in animals.

Ans. (True)

Q. 38 The term chromosome was coined by Waldyer in the year 1988

Ans. (True)

Q. 39. The condons which code for amino acids are called sense codons.

Ans. (True)

Q. 40. The chrosomes were first discovered by Strasbwger in the year 1875

Ans. (True)

SECTION-15
ENVIRONMENTAL SCIENCE

1. Important component (s) of environment are _________ components
   (*a*) Abiotic / non-living (*b*) Biotic / living
   (*c*) Energy (*d*) All of them
2. Abiotic environment consists of _________
   (*a*) Lithosphere (*b*) Hydrosphere
   (*c*) Atmosphere (*d*) All of them
3. Biotic component of environment consists of _________
   (*a*) Flora (*b*) Fauna
   (*c*) Flora and Fauna including man (*d*) All of them
4. If one plans for one year-plant rice, if for 10 years-grow trees but educate the people to plant for _________
   (*a*) 25 years (*b*) 50 years
   (*c*) 75 years (*d*) 100 years
5. UNESCO held Environmental Education Conference (EEC) at Belgrade in year _________
   (*a*) 1925 (*b*) 1950
   (*c*) 1975 (*d*) 1995
6. UNEP (United Nations Education Programs) held EEC in Tbilisi (U.S.S.R) in
   (*a*) 1930 (*b*) 1950
   (*c*) 1977 (*d*) 1987
7. An environmental education programme is based on the discipline (s) namely _________
   (*a*) Environmental studies (*b*) Environmental science
   (*c*) Environmental engineering (*d*) All of them
8. National Environmental Awareness Campaign (NEAC) or National Environmental Month (NEM) is observed from Nov.19 to Dec.18 every year since _________
   (*a*) 1866 (*b*) 1976
   (*c*) 1986 (*d*) 1996
9. World Environment Day (WED) is observed every year on _________
   (*a*) April 5 (*b*) May 5
   (*c*) June 5 (*d*) July 5

10. According to an estimate, by 2015 urban population of India would be ________
(a) 30%
(b) 40%
(c) 50%
(d) 60%

11. Cities, the engines of economic growth are inherently unsustainable in terms of environment inspite of the fact that their contribution to national income has been estimated at about ________
(a) 40%
(b) 50%
(c) 60%
(d) 70%

12. The estimate reveal that India's urban population living below poverty line is about ________
(a) 50%
(b) 40%
(c) 30%
(d) 25%

13. India's urban population living in slums has been estimated at about ________
(a) 35-40%
(b) 20-30%
(c) 15-19%
(d) 14-9%

14. Environment (Protection) Act was enacted in ________
(a) 1996
(b) 1986
(c) 1976
(d) 1966

15. Woman are seen inferior to men and nature to ________
(a) Culture
(b) Agriculture
(c) Olericulture
(d) Architecture

16. London smog killed 3000-4000 people in ________
(a) 1942
(b) 1952
(c) 1960
(d) 1965

17. Several people died by eating fish that caused Minamata disease in ________
(a) Japan
(b) Thailand
(c) China
(d) Indonesia

18. Atmosphere from earth's surface extends to a height of about ________
(a) 2000 km
(b) 1800 km
(c) 1600 km
(d) 1400 km

19. Every 6 square centimeter of our bodies feel an air pressure of about ________
(a) 9 kg
(b) 7 kg
(c) 5 kg
(d) 3 kg

20. The total mass of the atmosphere has been estimated at ________ tonnes.
(a) 2500 trillion
(b) 3500 trillion
(c) 4500 trillion
(d) 5500 trillion

21. Normal lapse rate of temperature upward in the troposphere per km above sea level has been observed as ________
(a) 2.5-3.5 °C
(b) 4.0-5.5 °C
(c) 6.0-6.5 °C
(d) 7.0-7.5 °C.

22. In the lithosphere, outer and inner core besides crust and mantle, core is the central fluid / vaporized sphere has a diameter of about ________ km.
(a) 15,000
(b) 17,000
(c) 20,000
(d) 25,000

23. In addition to nutrients and water, soil is also the medium of ________ food chain

(*a*) Detritus (*b*) Diactus

(*c*) Delrilus (*d*) Divisional

24. Sedimentary rocks cover world's area of about ________

(*a*) 25 % (*b*) 50 %

(*c*) 65 % (*d*) 75 %

25. Igneous rocks make up 95% of earth's upper (top) crust extending to ________

(*a*) 6 km (*b*) 12 km

(*c*) 16 km (*d*) 20 km

26. The most polluted continent of the world is ________

(*a*) US (*b*) UK

(*c*) Holland (*d*) Poland

27. The root cause of environmental pollution has been man's misbehavior with ________

(*a*) Water (*b*) Air

(*c*) Non-living components (*d*) Collectively called nature

28. There may occur marked decline in the population of birds that feed on the fish polluted with DDT in an amount as small as ________

(*a*) 2.5 ppm (*b*) 5.0 ppm

(*c*) 7.5 ppm (*d*) 10.0 ppm

29. " Christian ethic is responsible for pollution due to exploitation" according to Lynn White (1967) and ________

(*a*) Ian McHarg (1969) (*b*) Ian Han-Harg (1970)

(*c*) Ian DeHan (1972) (*d*) Ian Tan-Heug (1975)

30. " Pollution is an undesirable change in physical, chemical or biological characteristics of water, air, and that may harmfully effect human, animal and the plants life, industrial progress, living conditions and cultural assets" is the definition of pollution given by ________

(*a*) National Environmental Research Council (1976)

(*b*) U.S. Presidents Science Advisory Committee

(*c*) National Academy of Science, U.S.A. (1966)

(*d*) International Environmental Research Board.

31. " A pollutant is a harmful solid, liquid or gaseous substance present in such concentration in the environment which tends to be injurious for the whole living bioda" has been stated by ________

(*a*) Holdgate (*b*) EPA (Environmental Protection Act), 1986

(*c*) Odum (*d*) Holister and Porteus, creater of pollution

32. Copious use of agro-chemicals to usher in an Agricultural Miracle (AM) /Green Revolution (GN) made the life of fishes and other animals impossible due to as water was deficient in ________

(*a*) Nitrogen (*b*) Oxygen

(*c*) Hydrogen (*d*) Halogen

33. Lithosphere contains two chief elements viz, Si and Al, that is why the name SIAL is the material forming first ________ of the crust.

(*a*) 10 km (*b*) 15 km

(*c*) 20 km (*d*) 30 km

34. Earth's water supply coming from the oceans amounts to about .________
(*a*) 67% (*b*) 77%
(*c*) 87% (*d*) 97%

35. The lithosphere and hydrosphere are surrounded by the atmosphere upto ________
(*a*) 300 km (*b*) 250 km
(*c*) 200 km (*d*) 400 km

36. The zone of atmosphere above lithosphere and hydrosphere in which living organisms survive upto ________
(*a*) 30 km (*b*) 35 km
(*c*) 15 km (*d*) 20 km

37. For most of the organisms, the optimum temperature range lies between ________
(*a*) 0-20 °C (*b*) 0-40 °C
(*c*) 0-50 °C (*d*) 0-60 °C

38. Earth's surface is covered with about ________ of water.
(*a*) 60-65% (*b*) 70-71%
(*c*) 80-81% (*d*) 50-55%

39. Condensed liquid remains clouds in the form of small droplets measuring ________
(*a*) 0.001 (*b*) 0.002
(*c*) 0.003 (*d*) 0.004

40. The major store house of earth's water are oceans which constitute ________
(*a*) 67.5 (*b*) 77.5
(*c*) 87.5 (*d*) 97.5

41. Oceanic water distributed to terrestrial areas has been estimated at only ________
(*a*) 0.008 (*b*) 0.007
(*c*) 0.006 (*d*) 0.005

42. United Nations Conference on Environment and Development (UNCED), called the Earth Summit at Riode Janeiro (Brazil) from 3 to 14 June,________
(*a*) 1952 (*b*) 1982
(*c*) 1992 (*d*) 1997

43. The first U.N. Conference on Environmental Pollution was held in 5th and 6th June, 1972 at________
(*a*) New York (*b*) London
(*c*) N. Delhi (*d*) Stockholm

44. Men breath 22,000 times a day inhailing ________ kg of air.
(*a*) 24 (*b*) 20
(*c*) 16 (*d*) 12

45. Mass of the atmosphere comprising troposphere has been estimated at about ________
(*a*) 90% (*b*) 70%
(*c*) 60% (*d*) 80%

46. The ability to metabolize O_3 (0.2g/m^2) creates an optimum concentration gradient for further absorption in ________
(*a*) Bean (*b*) Alfalfa
(*c*) Grassland (*d*) Maize

47. It has been estimated that the amount of solar energy falling on atmosphere is ________
(*a*) 2000 J cm^{-2} (*b*) 4000 J cm^{-2}
(*c*) 5000 J cm^{-2} (*d*) 6000 J cm^{-2}

48. The height of the stratosphere from the earth's surface is ________
(*a*) 45.85 km (*b*) 120-300 km
(*c*) 30 km (*d*) 20 km

49. At sea level CO_2 content is 330 ppm, while that of water vapour is ________
(*a*) 40,000 ppm (*b*) 30,000 ppm
(*c*) 20,000 ppm (*d*) 15,000 ppm

50. Estimates reveal that the heat caused by all the tropospheric CO_2 may raise temperature of atmosphere by an extra ________
(*a*) 20 °K (*b*) 15 °K
(*c*) 10 °K (*d*) 50 °K

51. In stratosphere ozone concentration is ________
(*a*) 15 ppm (*b*) 10 ppm
(*c*) 20 ppm (*d*) 5 ppm

52. Each atom of chlorine liberated from CFC can decompose ozones as many as ________
(*a*) 75,000 (*b*) 50,000
(*c*) 100,000 (*d*) 150,000

53. A major constituent in smog formation is an excited state of oxygen that has ________ electrons.
(*a*) 16 (*b*) 14
(*c*) 12 (*d*) 10

54. The safety level of SPM for residential areas lies between ________
(*a*) 100 and 150 ppm (*b*) 50 and 175 ppm
(*c*) 95 and 200 ppm (*d*) 125 and 195 ppm

55. Metallurgical industries; chemical and rubber manufacturing plants; sugar, cotton, paper and pulp mills comprise major air pollution causing industries upto about ________ of the air pollution.
(*a*) one-third (*b*) one-fourth
(*c*) one-fifth (*d*) one-sixth

56. The most polluted city of India is ________
(*a*) New Delhi (*b*) Kolkata
(*c*) Nagpur (*d*) Bhopal

57. The watchman in Tokyo requires the need of oxygen chamber to inhale pure oxygen every.______
(*a*) 15 Minutes (*b*) 30 Minutes
(*c*) 45 Minutes (*d*) 60 Minutes

58. In Mumbay ocean is polluted every day due to sewage measuring roughly ________
(*a*) 700 million gallons (*b*) 550 million gallons
(*c*) 400 million gallons (*d*) 800 million gallons

59. Among occupation diseases according to ICMR, byssinosis is found in case of ________.
(*a*) Bihar miners (*b*) Coal miners
(*c*) Asbestos factories (*d*) Textile workers

60. Which of the following was banned in 1972 ?.

(*a*) PCB (*b*) DDT
(*c*) CFC (*d*) Dioxin

61. The most severe effects of dioxin are on ________

(*a*) Reproduction (*b*) Respiration
(*c*) Perspiration (*d*) Digestion

62. The first case of severe air pollution in modern times was in the Meuse Valley of Belgium in ______

(*a*) 1925 (*b*) 1930
(*c*) 1935 (*d*) 1940

63. Hundreds of people died due to killing smog along the Monongahela River in 1948 in ________

(*a*) Donora, Pennisyllvania (*b*) Washington, Districts of Columbia
(*c*) Morgan Town, West Virginia (*d*) Davis, California

64. The Poza Rica air pollution occurred due to an industrial accident at a refinery in ________

(*a*) September, 1950 (*b*) September, 1960
(*c*) November, 1960 (*d*) November, 1950

65. Los Angeles in California experienced serious air pollution during ________

(*a*) 1944 (*b*) 1954
(*c*) 1964 (*d*) 1974

66. Bhopal gas tragedy occurred on ________

(*a*) Oct.3,1984 (*b*) Nov.3,1984
(*c*) Dec.3,1984 (*d*) August. 3,1984

67. Carbondioxide traps heat in the atmosphere to cause ________

(*a*) Green house effect (*b*) Affects respiration
(*c*) Causes acid rain (*d*) Causes bronchitis

68. According to UN Environment Programme, there exit chemicals in the world today numbering ________ millions.

(*a*) One (*b*) Two
(*c*) Three (*d*) Four

69. Modern world employs chemicals for various purposes like increasing productivity, to maintain health, but many of these ________ are potentially toxic to living organisms.

(*a*) 30,000-35,000 (*b*) 40,000-50,000
(*c*) 60.000-70,000 (*d*) 75,000-85,000

70. Arsenic also occurs in micro-quantities is air and acts as a serious potent ________

(*a*) Cytoplasmic poison (*b*) Protoplasmic poison
(*c*) Augments thiolgrverp in plant enzymes (*d*) Safeguards soil properties.

71. SO_2 at 38 ppm caused 80 deaths and killing the majority of cattle in ________

(*a*) Donora Pennsyvania U.S.A. & Monongaheola river in Oct 1948
(*b*) London 5-9 Dec, 1952
(*c*) London Jan.1956 & Dec., 1957
(*d*) Meuse River Valley, Belgium, Dec.,1930

72. Tobacco came to India with Portuguese in ________
(a) 14th Century (b) 15th Century
(c) 17th Century (d) 18th Century

73. World wide tobacco use results in annual net loss of ________
(a) 75 billion USD (b) 150 billion USD
(c) 100 billion USD (d) 200 billion USD

74. The estimates revealed that the number of carcinogenic chemicals are ________
(a) 63 (b) 53
(c) 43 (d) 33

75. Tick mark the correct one of the following
(a) NO (nitrogen oxide) does not carry message to man's nervous system
(b) Alcohol does not cause oral cancer
(c) CO dilates blood vessels
(d) Vitamin does not prevent damage to white blood cells.

76. CO has as greater affinity for the haemoglobin as does oxygen, it is ________ times that of oxygen
(a) 50-100 (b) 125-150
(c) 350-450 (d) 200-300

77. A person may die in an atmosphere of CO_2 due to
(a) Lack of oxygen (b) CO_2 is poisonous
(c) Man's more susceptibility than animals and birds (d) Kills due to stench

78. Plants which mostly emit terpenes are ________
(a) Eucalyptus and oak (b) Sorghum and pearlmillet
(c) Pigeonpea and chickpea (d) Sunflower and safflower

79. Methane has mean residence time of ________ years
(a) 10-12 (b) 8-9
(c) 13-15 (d) 3-7

80. The quantity of methane contributed to the atmosphere by the animals has been estimated at ________ million tonnes
(a) 95-100 (b) 80-85
(c) 110-115 (d) 120-125

81. Estimate has shown that from fly ash from coal combustion, the maximum variation occurs in ________
(a) K_2O content (b) Na_2O content
(c) Titanium content (d) P_2O_3 content

82. The estimates show that thousands of people in Kolaghat area of Midnapore district of W.B. due to exposure to flyash / suffer from the disease ________
(a) Cerosis (b) Silicosis
(c) Megnosis (d) Calcosis

83. Annual addition of particulates injected into the atmosphere by man made activities has been estimated at ________ million tonnes
(a) 250 (b) 350
(c) 450 (d) 550

84. In U.S.A. alone the annual particulate emission is about ________

(a) 20×10^4 (b) 20×10^6

(c) 20×10^7 (d) 20×10^9

85. Black lung' disease is common in ________

(a) Coal miners (b) Iron miners

(c) Lead miners (d) Vanaduim miners

86. Textile workers frequently suffer from ________

(a) Grey lung disease (b) Red lung disease

(c) White lung disease (d) Orange lung disease

87. Particulate pollutant like finely divided cobalt when inhaled causes the lung disease called. ________

(a) Roentgeno (b) Hoentgeno

(d) Noentgeno (d) Oentgeno

88. Leakage of methyl isocynate in case of Bhopal disaster of 1984 coated the soil with dust within ______ km radius from Bhopal.

(a) 120 (b) 140

(c) 160 (d) 180

89. Which of the following technique to control particulate emissions is least expensive?

(a) Gravity Setling Chamber (b) Cyclone collector

(c) Filters (d) Scrubbers

90. Negative ion theory has been successful to treat the patients suffering from psychoneurosis and anxiety syndromes in the ________

(a) Catholic University of Buenos Aires, Argentina

(b) Prostant University of Buenos Aires, Argentina

(c) Catholic University of Madison, U.S.A.

(d) Prostant University of Madison, U.S.A.

91. The malaise produced in man by ill polluted winds is called ________

(a) Anxiety syndrome (b) Psychoneurosis syndrome

(c) Irritation syndrome (d) General allergy syndrome

92. Allergenic pollen of Parthenium (rag weed) is transmitted by wind and in India causes ________

(a) Hay fever (b) Yellow fever

(c) Diarrhoea (d) Bronchitis

93. Emission factor (g / km) of CO has been estimated at 40 g / km due to

(a) Motor cycles (LTV) (b) Petrol driven cars (MTV)

(c) Diesel driven cars (MTV) (d) Heavy duty diesel vehicles (HTV)

94. In Britain, pollutants primarily ground level zone registered a steep increase in ________

(a) June, 1994 (b) July, 1994

(c) September, 1994 (d) October, 1994

95. The maximum relative amount required of the antiknock additives is that of ________

(a) Ethanol (b) Aniline

(c) Tetra ethyl lead (d) Benzene

96. Super additive AK 33 × (methyl cyclo penta dienyl manganese-tricabonyl) is twice as effective as TEL but it is

(*a*) Photosensitive
(*b*) Both expensive and photosensitive
(*c*) Dangerous to use
(*d*) Corrosivé

97. The crankshaft of the Split Cycle Engine moves at about 300 revolutions per minute, which in comparison to conventional shaft is slower by ________ times

(*a*) 5.0
(*b*) 7.5
(*c*) 10.0
(*d*) 12.5

98. Apart from conventional curative measures to prevent further damage to earth and environment pollution due to vehicular traffic, innovative methods for urban transport which are ________

(*a*) Economic
(*b*) Efficient
(*c*) Environment friendly
(*d*) Economic, Efficient and environmental friendly

99. The compound extremely lethal to living organisms, the product of polluting property of NO_2 which acts its precursor is ________

(*a*) PAN & O_3
(*b*) PAN
(*c*) O_3
(*d*) VOCs

100. In a FAD report lowest observed effect level of NO_2 is ________

(*a*) 1.00 ppm
(*b*) 0.75 ppm
(*c*) 0.5 ppm
(*d*) 1.10 ppm

101. NO_2 poisoning in man results in dangerous ________

(*a*) Silofilter's disease
(*b*) Milofilter's disease
(*c*) Maxifilter's disease
(*d*) Minifilter's disease

102. NO_2 being most toxic in the blood is transformed into ________

(*a*) Nitroxy haemoglobin
(*b*) Mathemoglobin
(*c*) Hydroxemoglobin
(*d*) Nitroxemoglobin

103. Metabolic activity in plant tissues is checked if exposed vehicular exhaust containing NO_2 upto about ________

(*a*) 5.0 ppm
(*b*) 7.5 ppm
(*c*) 10.0 ppm
(*d*) 3.5 ppm

104. Epidemiological studies have shown that the average concentration of NO_2 should not exceed 0.05 ppm for normal plant growth over a period of ________

(*a*) 12 Hrs
(*b*) 16 Hrs
(*c*) 20 Hrs
(*d*) 24 Hrs

105. Inhalation of CO by man restricts transport of oxygen from lungs to cells since it reacts with haemoglobin to form ________

(*a*) Stable carboxy haemoglobin
(*b*) Stable hydroxy haemoglobin
(*c*) Stable nitroxy haemoglobin
(*d*) Unstable nitroxy haemoglobin

106. Breathing becomes difficult and irritation of mucous membrane resulting in unconsciousness and impaired vision perception when CO concentration is ________

(*a*) 100 ppm
(*b*) 75 ppm
(*c*) 50 ppm
(*d*) 25 ppm

107. Match the following

(*a*) Halogens	(*i*) Halons
(*b*) Hydrocarbons	(*ii*) Bromine
(*c*) Fluorocarbons	(*iii*) SOx
(*d*) Toxicants	(*iv*) Benzene
(*e*) Photochemical Oxidants	(*v*) PAN

108. Mach the nature of accident with place ________

(*a*) Shri Ram Foods Fertilizer, Delhi 1985	(*i*) Sulphur trioxide leak
(*b*) Bhorari Industrial area, Pune, 1987	(*ii*) Acid tanker overturned
(*c*) Kaluparbat, Bhubneshwar, 1987	(*iii*) Oleum gas leak
(*d*) Duse Town, Ahmedabad, 1988	(*iv*) Sulphuric acid leak
(*e*) Century Rayon, Sahad (MS)	(*v*) Ammonia gas leak

109. Match the following

(*a*) Jheni, U.P. (1994)	(*i*) Ammonia gas leak
(*b*) National Fertilizer Plant Panipat (Haryana)	(*ii*) Explosion in filling heat
(*c*) Behrampur, Ahmedabad (1987)	(*iii*) Oleum gas leak
(*d*) IPC Ltd, Gwalior (1991)	(*iv*) Explosion in a factory
(*e*) Dahanu, Maharashtra (1991)	(*v*) Chemical explosion from overturned tanker

110. Match the following

(*a*) CO	(*i*) 1430
(*b*) CxHy	(*ii*) 515
(*c*) SOx	(*iii*) 40,000 mg/m^3
(*d*) NOx	(*iv*) 375
(*e*) Particulates	(*v*) 19,300

111. Match the following

(*a*) Irrigation	(*i*) 4 %
(*b*) Domestic	(*ii*) 4%
(*c*) Industrial	(*iii*) 8%
(*d*) Thermal	(*iv*) 12%
(*e*) Electrical	(*v*) 2%

112. Match the component with average composition of the following:

(*a*) CO	(*i*) 0.0002
(*b*) O_3	(*ii*) 0.001
(*c*) NH_3	(*iii*) 0.1
(*d*) NO_2	(*iv*) 0.01
(*e*) SO_2	(*v*) 0.02

113. Match the SPM (microgram / cubic meter) with the cities in India

(*a*) Kalkata	(*i*) 249.3
(*b*) Delhi	(*ii*) 143.3
(*c*) Agra	(*iii*) 301.7
(*d*) Chennai	(*iv*) 430.6
(*e*) Jaipur	(*v*) 401.0

114. Match the following

(*a*) Kanpur	(*i*) 114.5
(*b*) Hyderabad	(*ii*) 190.6
(*c*) Cochin	(*iii*) 326.3
(*d*) Mumbai	(*iv*) 249.3
(*e*) Ahmedabad	(*v*) 248.7

115. Match the following

(*a*) Moraie soil	(*i*) Gravitational forces as landslides
(*b*) Alluvial soil	(*ii*) Wind
(*c*) Colluvial soil	(*iii*) Oceanic waves
(*d*) Aeolian soil	(*iv*) Glacier
(*e*) Marine soil	(*v*) Streams and rivers

116. Match the definitions of ecology with its author

(*a*) "A multidisciplinary science which deals with organism and its place to live and while fouses on the ecosystem"	(*i*) S.C.Kendeigh (1974)
(*b*) " The scientific study of relationships of living organisms with each other and to their environment"	(*ii*) Pinaka (1973)
(*c*) " The study of animals and plants in their relation to each other and to their environment".	(*iii*) Charles Southwick (1976)
(*d*) " The study of relations between organisms and totality of the biological and physical factors affecting them or influence by them".	(*iv*) M.E.Clark (1973)
(*e*) " A study of ecosystems or the totality of the reciprocal interactions between living organisms and their physical surroundings."	(*v*) R.L Smith (1977)

117. Match the percentage of the mixture of gases found in the atmosphere ________

(*a*) Oxygen	(*i*) Traces
(*b*) Nitrogen	(*ii*) 0.3 %
(*c*) Carbon dioxide	(*iii*) 0.1 %
(*d*) Water vapours	(*iv*) 78 %
(*e*) Argon	(*v*) 21 %

118. Match soil type with the its transportation agency ________

(*a*) Ealian	(*i*) Running water
(*b*) Glacial	(*ii*) Remains on parent rock
(*c*) Colluvial	(*iii*) Ice and glacier
(*d*) Alluvial	(*iv*) Winds
(*e*) Residual	(*v*) Gravity from hills and rivers

119. Match the following.

(*a*) Interspecific competition	(*i*) One species harmed without benefit to other
(*b*) Intraspecific competition	(*ii*) Beneficial to both
(*c*) Mutualism	(*iii*) Between same species
(*d*) Amanelism	(*iv*) Between different species
(*e*) Predation	(*v*) Killing of another

120. Match the composition (mg /m^3) with the particulate found in SPM

(*a*) Nitrate ions	(*i*) 10.5
(*b*) Ammonium ions	(*ii*) 13.4
(*c*) Sulphate ions	(*iii*) 10.4
(*d*) Silicon	(*iv*) 2.6
(*e*) Calcium	(*v*) 1.3

121. Match the emission factors (g /km) of pollutants for the Indian vehicles viz. Heavy Duty Diesel (HTV)

(*a*) CO	(*i*) 3.0
(*b*) HC	(*ii*) 21.0
(*c*) PM	(*iii*) 12.7
(*d*) NOxs	(*iv*) 1.5
(*e*) SO_2	(*v*) 2.1

122. Match the emission factors (g /km) of pollutants for Petrol Driven Cars (MTV) under Indian conditions.

(*a*) SO_2	(*i*) 3.2
(*b*) NOx	(*ii*) 6.0
(*c*) PM	(*iii*) 40.0
(*d*) HC	(*iv*) 0.08
(*e*) CO	(*v*) 0.33

123. Match estimated Global emissions of pollutant hydrocarbons with the source.

(*a*) Petroleum	(*i*) 38.5
(*b*) Gasoline	(*ii*) 0.4
(*c*) Refining	(*iii*) 55.05
(*d*) Oil	(*iv*) 3.3
(*e*) Coal	(*v*) 7.2

124. Match the Global emission of pollutants hydrocarbons with the source.

(*a*) Wood (Fuel and forest fire)	(*i*) 11.3
(*b*) Organic solvent Evaporation	(*ii*) 28.3
(*c*) Industrial ashes	(*iii*) 8.8
(*d*) Incinerators and Refuge Burning	(*iv*) 0.8
(*e*) Evaporation of Solvents in storage	(*v*) 2.2

125. Match the content of a hydrocarbon (ppm) with the associated adverse effect on human beings.

(*a*) Benzene 100 ppm	(*i*) Most fatal
(*b*) Benzene 7500 ppm	(*ii*) Induces cancer
(*c*) Benzene 20,000 ppm	(*iii*) Mucus membrane irritation
(*d*) Benzpyrene 100 ppm	(*iv*) Affects nervous system
(*e*) Toluene 600 ppm	(*v*) Lung cancer

126. Match the CO Hb level in blood of smokers

(*a*) Non-smoker	(*i*) 2.3%
(*b*) Pipe smokers	(*ii*) 5.9%
(*c*) Light smoker 10 cig/day	(*iii*) 1.3%
(*d*) Moderate cig. smoker (20 cig/day)	(*iv*) 6.9%
(*e*) Heavy cig. smoker 40 cig/day	(*v*) 1.7%

127. Match the most likely risk of cancer with the country /place.

(*a*) Liver cancer	(*i*) South-East Asia (also India)
(*b*) Stomach cancer	(*ii*) Caspian Sea
(*c*) Gullet cancer	(*iii*) Japan
(*d*) Mouth-throat cancer	(*iv*) Africans
(*e*) Breast cancer	(*v*) Western woman

128. Match CO concentration with its toxic effect

(*a*) 100 ppm	(*i*) Immediate death
(*b*) 500 ppm	(*ii*) Unconsciousness
(*c*) 750 ppm	(*iii*) Headache
(*d*) 1000 ppm	(*iv*) Death after few hours
(*e*) 250 ppm	(*v*) Vomiting

129. Match the concentration (parts per billion /ppp) by the automobile exhausts in the atmosphere.

(*a*) Methane	(*i*) 76
(*b*) Ethylene	(*ii*) 2400
(*c*) Acetylene & Propane	(*iii*) 35
(*d*) Butane	(*iv*) 102
(*e*) Isopentane	(*v*) 46

130. Match the pollutant with the causal agent.

(*a*) Metallic	(*i*) X-rays
(*b*) Carcinogenic	(*ii*) Kr 85
(*c*) Natural radio active	(*iii*) Benzidine
(*d*) Manmade radiation	(*iv*) Nuclides of U-238
(*e*) Gaseous waste	(*v*) Ba

131. Match the atmosphere concentration of pollutants

(*a*) CO_2	(*i*) 0.5 to 4 ppb
(*b*) SO_2	(*ii*) 6-20 ppb
(*c*) NO_2	(*iii*) 0.1 ppm
(*d*) NH_3	(*iv*) 320 ppm
(*e*) CO	(*v*) 0.2 ppb

132. Match the effect of SO_2 on man

(*a*) 1.0 ppm	(*i*) Throat irritation
(*b*) 3.0-5.0 ppm	(*ii*) Constriction of air passage
(*c*) 10.0 ppm	(*iii*) Maximum allowable exposure in 30 mins
(*d*) 20.0 ppm	(*iv*) Eye irritation
(*e*) 50-100 ppm	(*v*) Detectable by odour

133. Match the CO emmision with its contributor

(*a*) Motor vehicles	(*i*) 6.9%
(*b*) Industrial processes	(*ii*) 8.3%
(*c*) Forest fires	(*iii*) 2.5%
(*d*) Agriculture burning	(*iv*) 9.6%
(*e*) Air crafts	(*v*) 59.5%

134. Match the sulphur content with the fuels used in India.

(*a*)	Kerosene	(*i*)	3.5-4.5%
(*b*)	Fuel oil	(*ii*)	1.0%
(*c*)	Gasoline	(*iii*)	1.8%
(*d*)	HSD (Diesel)	(*iv*)	0.25%
(*e*)	LDO (Diesel)	(*v*)	0.25%

135. Match the particulates emissions (tonnes / day) from vehicle traffic in following Indian cities as indicated in WHO report of 1994.

(*a*)	Delhi	(*i*)	3.25
(*b*)	Mumbai	(*ii*)	2.34
(*c*)	Kolkata	(*iii*)	10.3
(*d*)	Chennai	(*iv*)	1.54
(*e*)	Hyderabad	(*v*)	5.59

136. Match the carbonmonoxide emission (tonnes / day) due to vehicular traffic in following Indian cities as indicated in WHO report of 1994.

(*a*)	Delhi	(*i*)	469.92
(*b*)	Kolkata	(*ii*)	49.22
(*c*)	Mumbai	(*iii*)	162.24
(*d*)	Pune	(*iv*)	651.01
(*e*)	Lucknow	(*v*)	188.24

137. Match the following:

(*a*)	Greece and Italy	(*i*)	Nuclear radiation
(*b*)	Taj Mahal	(*ii*)	Gas
(*c*)	Bhopal	(*iii*)	Acid rain
(*d*)	Hiroshima and Nagasaki	(*iv*)	SO_2

138. Match the following

(*a*)	Stratosphere	(*i*)	1600 km above earth surface
(*b*)	Mesosphere	(*ii*)	500 km above earth surface
(*c*)	Thermosphere	(*iii*)	50 km above earth surface
(*d*)	Exosphere	(*iv*)	80-90 km above earth surface

139. Match the following

(*a*)	Arctic ocean	(*i*)	38% Salinity
(*b*)	Baltic sea	(*ii*)	37% Salinity
(*c*)	Arabian sea	(*iii*)	11% Salinity
(*d*)	Bay of Bengal	(*iv*)	20% Salinity
(*e*)	Red Sea	(*v*)	30% Salinity

140. Match the following

(*a*)	The organisms who eat dead organic matter	(*i*)	herbivores
(*b*)	Bacteria that obtain both energy and material from organic sources	(*ii*)	decomposes
(*c*)	Plants which produce food themselves through photosynthes	(*iii*)	hetrotrophs
(*d*)	Organism who live in plants	(*iv*)	autotrophs

Do You Know That

1. Global annual average rainfall has been estimated at 857 mm.
2. About 77 and 23 per cent of rain-falls on ocean and land, respectively.
3. Oceans comprise 97 per cent of the total water supply on earth which is equal to 817 cubic miles or one quadrillion acre-feet.
4. India receives 73.7 per cent of the total annual rainfall through South-West monsoon.
5. Approximately 30 and 42 per cent of area receives 0-750 and 750-1150 mm of average annual rainfall in India, respectively.
6. When the annual average rainfall is more by 20 per cent, it is taken as excess rainfall.
7. If the annual rainfall is either 19 per cent less or more, it is regarded as normal rainfall
8. The highest magnitude of an earthquake recorded so far on Richter Scale was 8.9 on 2 March, 1933.
9. The most devastating earthquake ever was in Shaanxi (Shencil), Central China on 24 January, 1566 when an estimated 830,000 people were killed..
10. The most famous, Krakataku, Volcano erupted in 1883 with such a force that the resulting tidal wave killed 36,000 people and termour were felt as far away as Australia.
11. The longest drought occurred in Calama, N. Chile where no rainfall was recorded in 400 years to 1971
12. CFC_{12} has 25,000 times the heat absorption capacity of carbon dioxide, is present only as 0.00044 ppm
13. It has been estimated that due to heat-absorbing gases especially carbon dioxide, world atmospheric temperature will rise by 1.5^{b}C by 2020.
14. As much as 60 per cent of the world's crop lands and range lands are in some danger, with 6 million hectares lost altogether every year and a further 21 million hectares are rendered agriculturally worth-less.
15. Acid rainfall is caused when sulphur and nitrogen oxides in the air combine with water vapour to form sulphuric, nitric and other acids.
16. Prevailing wind patterns mean that the acids often fall many hundred kilometres from where the original pollutants were discharged.
17. Troposphere denotes the lower portion of atmosphere, subject to differential heating causing convection currents and turbulence; it extends to 16 km in tropics, but not more than 9.6 km 60° latitude.
18. Mixing of gases at sea level and at a height up to 80 km is identical.
19. Molybdenum is required in the smallest traces for the assimilation of nitrates and biological fixation of nitrogen in the root nodules of leguminosae family of plants.

KEY

1. (*d*)	2. (*d*)	3. (*c*)	4. (*d*)	5. (*c*)
6. (*c*)	7. (*d*)	8. (*c*)	9. (*c*)	10. (*c*)
11. (*c*)	12. (*b*)	13. (*d*)	14. (*b*)	15. (*a*)
16. (*b*)	17. (*a*)	18. (*c*)	19. (*b*)	20. (*d*)
21. (*c*)	22. (*d*)	23. (*a*)	24. (*d*)	25. (*c*)
26. (*a*)	27. (*d*)	28. (*d*)	29. (*a*)	30. (*c*)
31. (*b*)	32. (*b*)	33. (*c*)	34. (*d*)	35. (*c*)
36. (*d*)	37. (*c*)	38. (*d*)	38. (*d*)	39. (*d*)
40. (*d*)	41. (*b*)	42. (*c*)	43. (*d*)	44. (*c*)

45. (*b*)	46. (*d*)	47. (*b*)	48. (*c*)	49. (*b*)
50. (*a*)	51. (*b*)	52. (*c*)	53. (*c*)	54. (*a*)
55. (*c*)	56. (*b*)	57. (*b*)	58. (*c*)	59. (*d*)
60. (*b*)	61. (*a*)	62. (*b*)	63. (*a*)	64. (*d*)
65. (*a*)	66. (*c*)	67. (*a*)	68. (*d*)	69. (*c*)
70. (*b*)	71. (*d*)	72. (*c*)	73. (*d*)	74. (*c*)
75. (*c*)	76. (*d*)	77. (*a*)	78. (*a*)	79. (*d*)
80. (*b*)	81. (*d*)	82. (*b*)	83. (*c*)	84. (*b*)
85. (*a*)	86. (*c*)	87. (*a*)	88. (*c*)	89. (*b*)
90. (*a*)	91. (*c*)	92. (*c*)	93. (*b*)	94. (*b*)
95. (*d*)	96. (*b*)	97. (*c*)	98. (*d*)	99. (*a*)
100. (*c*)	101. (*a*)	102. (*b*)	103. (*c*)	104. (*d*)
105. (*a*)	106. (*a*)			
107. (*a*) (*ii*)	(*b*) (*iv*)	(*c*) (*i*)	(*d*) (*v*)	(*e*) (*iii*)
108. (*a*) (*iii*)	(*b*) (*i*)	(*c*) (*v*)	(*d*) (*ii*)	(*e*) (*iv*)
109. (*a*) (*iv*)	(*b*) (*i*)	(*c*) (*iii*)	(*d*) (*ii*)	(*e*) (*v*)
110. (*a*) (*iii*)	(*b*) (*v*)	(*c*) (*i*)	(*d*) (*ii*)	(*e*) (*iv*)
111. (*a*) (*iii*)	(*b*) (*v*)	(*c*) (*i*)	(*d*) (*ii*)	(*e*) (*iv*)
112. (*a*) (*iii*)	(*b*) (*v*)	(*c*) (*iv*)	(*d*) (*ii*)	(*e*) (*i*)
113. (*a*) (*iv*)	(*b*) (*v*)	(*c*) (*i*)	(*d*) (*ii*)	(*e*) (*iii*)
114. (*a*) (*iii*)	(*b*) (*v*)	(*c*) (*i*)	(*d*) (*ii*)	(*e*) (*iv*)
115. (*a*) (*iv*)	(*b*) (*v*)	(*c*) (*i*)	(*d*) (*ii*)	(*e*) (*iii*)
116. (*a*) (*v*)	(*b*) (*iii*)	(*c*) (*i*)	(*d*) (*ii*)	(*e*) (*iv*)
117. (*a*) (*v*)	(*b*) (*iv*)	(*c*) (*ii*)	(*d*) (*iii*)	(*e*) (*i*)
118. (*a*) (*iv*)	(*b*) (*iii*)	(*c*) (*v*)	(*d*) (*i*)	(*e*) (*ii*)
119. (*d*) (*iii*)	(*b*) (*iv*)	(*c*) (*ii*)	(*d*) (*i*)	(*e*) (*v*)
120. (*a*) (*iv*)	(*b*) (*v*)	(*c*) (*i*)	(*d*) (*ii*)	(*e*) (*iii*)
121. (*a*) (*iii*)	(*b*) (*v*)	(*c*) (*i*)	(*d*) (*ii*)	(*e*) (*iv*)
122. (*a*) (*iv*)	(*b*) (*i*)	(*c*) (*v*)	(*d*) (*ii*)	(*e*) (*iii*)
123. (*a*) (*iii*)	(*b*) (*i*)	(*c*) (*v*)	(*d*) (*ii*)	(*e*) (*iv*)
124. (*a*) (*v*)	(*b*) (*i*)	(*c*) (*iv*)	(*d*) (*ii*)	(*e*) (*iii*)
125. (*a*) (*iii*)	(*b*) (*v*)	(*c*) (*i*)	(*d*) (*ii*)	(*e*) (*iv*)
126. (*a*) (*iii*)	(*b*) (*v*)	(*c*) (*i*)	(*d*) (*ii*)	(*e*) (*iv*)
127. (*a*) (*iv*)	(*b*) (*iii*)	(*c*) (*ii*)	(*d*) (*i*)	(*e*) (*v*)
128. (*a*) (*iii*)	(*b*) (*v*)	(*c*) (*iv*)	(*d*) (*i*)	(*e*) (*ii*)
129. (*a*) (*ii*)	(*b*) (*iv*)	(*c*) (*i*)	(*d*) (*v*)	(*e*) (*iii*)
130. (*a*) (*v*)	(*b*) (*iii*)	(*c*) (*iv*)	(*d*) (*i*)	(*e*) (*ii*)
131. (*a*) (*iv*)	(*b*) (*v*)	(*c*) (*i*)	(*d*) (*ii*)	(*e*) (*iii*)
132. (*a*) (*ii*)	(*b*) (*v*)	(*c*) (*i*)	(*d*) (*iv*)	(*e*) (*iii*)
133. (*a*) (*v*)	(*b*) (*iv*)	(*c*) (*i*)	(*d*) (*ii*)	(*e*) (*iii*)
134. (*a*) (*v*)	(*b*) (*i*)	(*c*) (*iv*)	(*d*) (*ii*)	(*e*) (*iii*)
135. (*a*) (*iii*)	(*b*) (*v*)	(*c*) (*i*)	(*d*) (*ii*)	(*e*) (*iv*)
136. (*a*) (*iv*)	(*b*) (*v*)	(*c*) (*i*)	(*d*) (*iii*)	(*e*) (*ii*)
137. (*a*) (*iii*)	(*b*) (*iv*)	(*c*) (*ii*)	(*d*) (*i*)	
138. (*a*) (*iii*)	(*b*) (*iv*)	(*c*) (*ii*)	(*d*) (*i*)	
139. (*a*) (*iv*)	(*b*) (*iii*)	(*c*) (*i*)	(*d*) (*v*)	(*e*) (*ii*)
140. (*a*) (*ii*)	(*b*) (*iii*)	(*c*) (*iv*)	(*d*) (*i*)	

SECTION 16
DO YOU KNOW THAT

1. "A weed is a plant that originated in natural environment and, in response to imposed or natural environments, evolved and continues to do so as an interfering associate with our crops and activities." R.J. Aldrich, 1984).

2. "It is thus farming, if you do one thing late, you will be late in all your work" (Cato, the elder, *De Agri Cultura* second century B.C.).

3. A camel can lose upto 30% of its body weight in perspiration and continue to cross the desert while a man would die of shock after sweating away only 12% of body weight.

4. A day is divided into hours AM (*ante meridiem*) and PM (*post meridiem*) or forenoon and after- noon, respectively.

5. A green alga called Dundáliella, discovered in the Dead sea (Israel) produces glycerd, beta carotene and proteins as well.

6. A horse eats almost seven times its own weight each year.

7. A long fallow of tropical forest vegetation over a period of 12 years or more can accumulate as much as 500 kg N per hectare from lightning and biological N_2-fixing sources.

8. A normal human being excretes 10-12 g of protein per day.

9. Acid rainfall is caused when sulphur and nitrogen oxides in the air combine with water vapour to form sulphuric, nitric and other acids.

10. After a nuptial flight, the termites descend to the ground, cast off their wings and segregate in pairs, a male chasing a female

11. Agricultural Colleges at Coimbatore, Nagpur, Pune, Kanpur, Sabour and Lyallpur (now in Pakistan) were established in 1905.

12. An adult (human being) approximately requires 8 kJ/day of net energy.

13. An alga, *Botryococcus braunii* has been shown in Australia that it's extract produces a hydrocarbon liquid closely resembling crude oil.

14. Ancient people changed their food procurement habits some 9,000 to 10,000 years ago.

15. At Equator, the length of day and night are almost equal all the year round.

16. At latitude 30°, the day length varies 'from about 14 to 10 hours, while 50° from about 16 to 8 hours.

17. At the summer solstice in the northern hemisphere (21 June), the Arctic has total daylight and the Antarctic total darkness.

18. Atlantic, Indian, Pacific and Arctic are four oceans in the world.

19. Average yield of rough-rice in Australia in 1992 was 8.81 tonnes per hectare as against 2.61 tonnes per hectare in India.

20. Average yield of wheat in India in 1992 was 2.4 tonnes per hectare, while 7.25 tonnes per hectare in U.K. in the same year.

21. Balwantray Mehta Team was appointed in 1957 and the team recommended the establishment of Panchayati Raj Institutions, the statutory elective local bodies.

22. Beaufort wind scale in 19th century was devised by a British naval officer Beaufort.

23. Bentham and Hooker System of Plant Classification was jointly worked out by Bentham (1800-1884) and Hooker (1817-1911).

24. Biodegradable water can be converted to useful with the help of bacteria and earthworms.

25. Blue vitriol was foliarly fed to control diseases in 1803 and first used for weed control in 1821.

26. By 2050 India will most likely overtake China to become most populour country of the word

27. Carolus Linnaeus (1707-1778), the father of botany, was Professor of Botany at Uppsala (Sweden).

28. Celsius (°C) is equal to °F-32 multiplied by 5/9 and °F is equal to C multiplied 9/5 plus 32 (0°C = 32°F).

29. Central Rice Research Institute, Cuttack (Orissa) was founded in 1946.

30. Certain legume seeds have been found to germinate after 100-150 years of dry storage (Ohaga, 1926).

31. Chemicals sprayed on fruits and vegetables find their way into human bodies, thus leading to various serious ailments.

32. Cotton Corporation of India (CCI) was established in 1970.

33. Cotton Technological Laboratory, Matunga was set up in 1924

34. Deimos, one of the moons of Mars, rises and sets twice a day.

35. Diwan Bahadur Sir, T. Vijayraghavacharya was the first Vice-Chairman of ICAR.

36. Dolphins can swim and sleep at the same time.

37. Dr. A.B. Stewart from the Macaulay Soil Research Institute, Aberdeen, Great Britain visited India and after a study presented a report to the ICAR in 1946 on Soil Fertility Investigations in India with special reference to manuring.

38. Dr. B.P. Pal took up breeding for rust resistance and the wheat variety NP 809 (New Pusa) that was resistant to rust was released after 18 years of research work.

39. Dr. B.P. Pal was appointed as the first Director General of ICAR on May 14, 1965.

40. Dr. Charles A. Barber started sugarcane crossings in 1912 with Noble cane at Coimbatore (Tamil Nadu).

41. Dr. M.S. Swaminathan was the first agriculture scientist to become Secretary to the Government of India.

42. Dr. William Carey founded Royal Agri-Horticultural Society in 1820.

43. Earth revolves around the sun once a year on an 'anticlockwise' direction, tilted at a constant angle of 66.5°.

44. English agriculture witnessed a revolution during 17th and 18th century.

45. Estimates have shown that soybean and alfalfa might fix as much as 500 kgN per hectare.

46. *Euphorbia lathyrus* may be used for extraction of hydrocarbons having approximate molecular weight close to petroleum.

47. Europe and Central-North America apparently sustained four distinct ice invasions over a period of 1.0-1.5 million years.

48. Evolution was used as the basis of plant classification after the publication of Darwin's, "Origin of Species by Natural Selection" in 1859.

49. First Indian Irrigation Commission was appointed in 1901.

50. First Indo-American Team headed by K.R. Damle was constituted in 1955.

51. First woman to sail around the world solo in less than 100 days was Ellen MacArthur (English) in the year 2001.

52. Fluid Seeding Technology refers to planting of seeds/seedlings in a gel that prevents desiccation.

53. Grow More Food Committee was constituted in 1952.

54. Human skin has about 1,00,000 bacteria per square centimetre. 10% of human dry weight is due to bacteria.

55. IARI before independence (1947) was known as Imperial Agricultural Research Institute.

56. IARI, New Delhi was accorded the status of a "Deemed University" by the University Grants Commission in 1956.

57. ICAR was renamed as the Indian Council of Agricultural Research on June 10, 1947.

58. Imperial Bacteriological Laboratory, Mukteshwar and Indian Veterinary Research Institute, Izatnagar were set up in 1889.

59. Imperial Lac Research Institute, Namkum (Ranchi) was set up in 1925.

60. In 1763, nicotine was recommended for the control of aphids.

61. In 1855, sulphuric acid in Germany was used to control weeds in cereals and onions.

62. In 1871, the Department of Revenue, Agriculture and Commerce was established to take care for agriculture in India.

63. In 1941, 2, 4-D (2, 4-dichlorophenoxy acetic acid) was synthesized.

64. In 1962, agriculture universities on the pattern of land grant colleges of U.S.A. were set up at Udaipur (Rajasthan), Bhubaneswar (Orissa) and Ludhiana (Punjab).

65. In India economically non-viable holdings comprise 76 per cent of the total holdings.

66. In Iraq and Israel dog was domesticated 10,000 B.C., the first animal to be domesticated.

67. In Mali (Africa) the Sahara desert advanced 350 kilometres southwards in only 20 years.

68. In non-migratory aphids, the wingless, parthenogenetic and viviparous females continue to breed parthenogenetically throughout the year.

69. In U.S.A., 64 per cent of the total river pollution is caused by agriculture.

70. India has a coastal tidal belt of about 5,000 kilometres.

71. India is the second largest sugarcane sugar producer (19.7 per cent) after Brazil (22.4 per cent) in the world as estimated in 1989.

71. India produced 10 per cent of total world wheat production in 1989.

72. India accounts for a meager 2.4 % of world surface area and sustains whopping 16.7 % of the world population.

73. Indian lotus seeds obtained from a Manchurian lake bed germinated after, 1,000 years (Copeland, 1967).

74. Indian Society of Agronomy was established in 1955.

75. Indian Society of Seed Science was established in 1971.

76. Initial rural development projects in independent India (Post-1947) were:

    (*i*) Etawah Pilot Project (1948)

    (*ii*) Sarvodaya Programme (1948)

    (*iii*) Grow More Food Campaign (1949)

77. Ionosphere lies between 320 and 800 km above the earth and carries energy amounting to 20,000 to several million volts.

78. It has been estimated that an average arable soil has 30,000 to 350,000 weed seeds per square metre, that is 300 million to 3.5 billion per hectare.

79. It is believed that Aryans came around 1800 B.C. from South Russia and Central Asia to India.

80. Jute Corporation of India (JCT) was founded in 1971.

81. Jute Technological Research Laboratory, Kolkata was established in 1938.

82. Key Village Scheme was started in 1952.

83. Largest population of any country is that of China and lowest is that of Vatican City.

84. Leonard da vinci was the first person to record that number of rings in the cross section of a tree trunk to reveal its age.

85. Man and animals need Iodine and Fluorine for the formation of hormones and the development of teeth.

86. Millet production in India was 32.8 per cent of the total world production in 1989.

87. Mimosa (*Micmosa glomerata*) seeds from Herberia of the National Museum of Paris (France) demonstrated germinability after 221 years (Becqueral, 1934).

88. Most of the world's active volcanoes occur in a belt around Pacific Ocean, on the edge of the Pacific plate, called the "*ring of fire*",

89. Northern Autumn and Southern Spring Equinoxes fall on 21 September.

90. Northern Spring and Southern Equinoxes fall on 21 March.

91. Northern Summer and Southern Winter Solstices fall on 21 June.

92. Northern Winter and Southern Spring Equinoxes fall on 21 December.

93. Of the solar radiation absorbed during the daytime by a crop surface, 75-85 per cent is used to evaporate water, while 5-10, 5-10 and 1-5 per cent goes into sensible heat storage in soil, sensible heat exchange with the atmosphere by convection and into photosynthesis respectively.

94. On an average, bright sunny day each square metre of earth's surface receives approximately one K watt of radiant energy.

95. On an average, one kilogramme of dry wood or charcoal or any dry biomass can produce one k-watt per hour of energy.

96. On June 21 sun is directly overhead at the Tropic Cancer (23.5°N) and the Tropic of Capricorn (23.5°S) in northern and southern hemisphere respectively indicating midsummer.

97. One pound of nuclear fuel, if fully consumed may give energy equivalent to 3 million pounds of coal.

98. One tree neutralizes 60 pound of pollution in a year.

99. Only 13 per cent of the land in India is now covered with forests.

100. Paris Green (copper acetoarsenite) was used for the control of Colorado potato beetle in 1868.

101. People have been living on earth for about two million years.

102. Per capita land availability in India is likely to drop down to 0.15 hectare in 2000 from 0.48 hectare as estimated in 1951.

103. Petroleum oils were introduced for weed control along irrigation ditches and in carrots in 1914.

104. Planning Commission was set up in 1950.

105. Potassium plays a very important part as an antagonist to nitrogen and calcium.

106. Pre-independence (pre-1947) rural development works attempts were:
   (*i*) Gandhian Experiment in Rural Reconstruction (1920)
   (*ii*) Sriniketan Project (1921)
   (*iii*) Marthandom Scheme (1921)
   (*iv*) Gurgaon Project (1927)
   (*v*) Rural Reconstruction Movement (1932)
   (*vi*) Indian Village Upliftment Scheme (1945)

107. Rain water is the purest form of the water.

108. Ribulosebis phosphate-carboxylase is the most abundant enzyme on the earth.

109. Salt Water Fuel is generated at the juncture where river water enters the ocean, potential energy at this point is equivalent to the energy generated by an hydroelectric plant with a dam height of 216 metres due to difference in osmotic pressure.

110. Second Indo-American Team was set up in 1959 under the Chairmanship of Dr. M.S. Randhawa.

111. Seeds of lupine (*lupinus articus*) removed from a peat bog in Canada germinated after 10,000 years (Porslid and Harringtion, 1967).

112. Solanine at 20-25 mg/100 g of fresh weight of potato is considered toxic to human beings.

113. Solar constant is 2.00 cal. per square centimetre per minute (1395 W per square centimetre).

114. South India receives 5 kwh / m^2 / day of solar energy on horizontal surface which is equivalent to 1825 kwh / m^2 / annum, thus yielding 1.22 per cent more than the per capita consumption of 1500 kwh per annum..

115. *Spirilum lipoferum*, a grass embodies associated nitrogen fixing organisms.

116. Sugarcane Breeding Institute, Coimbatore (Tamil Nadu) was established in 1912.

117. Sulphur occurs in the plant as sulphate esters (in Agar Agar obtained from the red algae) as structural component of amino acids (cystin, methionin), and as reactive sulphur containing substances, as well as in some secondary products like oil of garlic and mustard oil.

118. Sun diameter is 109 times that of earth.

119. Sun generates power in the form of radiant energy at a phenomenal rate of 3.8 × 1023 k watts of which 1.8 × 1014 k watts equivalent reaches the earth surface annually amounting to the energy produced by 1.760 million-billion liters of oil.

120. Sun rotates on its axis about once every four weeks.

121. Sushruta, a specialist surgeon of fifth century B.C. made a mention of about 700 medicinal plants.

122. Synthetic rubber can be replaced by guayule (*Parthenium argentatum, extract*) rubber.

123. Tarai Development Corporation (TDC) was established in 1969 with the headquarters at Pantnagar, Uttar Pradesh.

124. Temperature of sun is believed to be 5750 K.

125. Temperature of sun is believed to be about 5750°K.

126. The All-India Coordinated Maize Improvement Project was formulated in 1957 with the collaboration of Rockefeller Foundation of USA.

127. The areas having 1-74 and 75-119 day's growing season are classified as arid and semi-arid, respectively.

128. The constitution changes in 1919 made the agriculture a provincial (state) subject.

129. The density of the interior mass of the sun is 80-100 times that of water.

130. The departments of agriculture were established in 1874 at provincial level in India.

131. The diameter of sun is 1.39 × 10^6 kilometres.

132. The earth's average temperature has risen by approximately 0.5°C since the beginning of the 20th century and is still rising.

133. The elate forms (primary reproductive) of termites come out during early monsoon showers and undertake short nuptial flight.

134. The estimates have postulated that one-trillionth (1012) of a gramme of C^{14} per gramme of ordinary carbon is found in all the living organisms.

135. The farming within the confines of regions with less than 750 mm annual rainfall is called dryland agriculture; whereas the one located in zones with more than 750 mm annual rainfall is designated as *rainfed agriculture*.

136. The global minimum rainfall of 0.02 inch is received by Africa in Chile as against the maximum of 905 inches (2262.5 cm) received by Cherrapunji in India.

137. The highest recorded temperature was in Al Aziziyah, Ribya, 58 °C (134.4°F) on 13 September, 1922.

138. The Imperial (now Indian) Council of Agricultural Research was established by a Resolution of the Government of India dated May 23, 1929 with its headquarters in the Ministry of Agriculture, New Delhi.

139. The Indian Agricultural Research Institute was founded in 1905 at Pusa, district Darbhanga (now Samastipur), Bihar.

140. The Indian Central Cotton Committee was constituted in 1921.

141. The Indian Central Sugarcane Committee was established in 1944.

142. The Indian National Science Congress was founded in 1914.

143. The largest single flower in the Raffesia. It is about three feet in diameter.

144. The monuments of Greece were dissolving in Athen's smog.

145. The National Commission on Agriculture was set up by' the Government of India in 1970.

146. The National Seeds Corporation (NSC) of India was founded in 1963 with the headquarters at New Delhi.

147. The net primary production of biomass of the total land is about 10.9 × 1010 tonnes per annum as against 5.5×10^{10} tonnes per year of the entire oceans.

148. The estimated global population in 2000 was 6055 million. World population is increasing 80 million per year and Asian population is 60.8 % of total population of the world.

149. The post-embryonic development in termites caters to the needs of the community.

150. The publication entitled, "History of Plants" by Theophrastus (372-287 B.C.), a student of Aristotle (344-322 B.C.) embodied the description of about 500 plants of food, medicinal and other economic utility.

15!. The rotation of sun at the equator and poles takes 27 and 30 days respectively.

152. The Royal Commission on Agriculture was appointed in 1926 and made recommendations in 1928.

153. The Secretariat of ICAR was declared as a Department of the Government of India in 1930.

154. The solar radiation at earth's surface, when that surface is perpendicular to sun rays is reduced from 2.0 to between 1.4 and 1.7 cal. per square centimetre per minute on a clear day.

155. The standing biomass for the entire earth at anyone time is about 185.5×10^{10} tonnes on weight basis.

156. The sun on average is 1.5×10^{8} kilometers away from the earth.

157. The sun radiates approximately 56×10^{26} calories of energy per minute.

158. The surface temperature of the sun is 5762°K and in the central interior it has been estimated to range between 8×10^{6} and 40×10^{6} °K.

159. The temperature at the core of the sun due to continuous thermonuclear of hydrogen into helium is estimated to be 15 million degrees celsius.

160. The temperature at the core of the sun due to continuous thermonuclear fusion of hydrogen into helium is estimated to be 15 million degrees Celsius.

161. The total cultivated lands occupy 14×10^{6} square kilometres and their total production is about 1×10^{10} tonnes.

162. The total reporting area of India is 304.8 million hectares.

163. The U.S. Army Corp of Engineers introduced sodium arsenate in 1902 for the control of water hyacinth in Lousiana.

164. The U.S. Department of Agriculture was established in 1862 and the first Agricultural Experiment Station in 1886.

165. The olive tree can live upto 1500 years.

166. The gas which does not pollute air is nitrogen oxide.

167. The Union Minister of Agriculture is the President of ICAR Society.

168. The word 'volcano' derives from the island of Vulcano off Sicily, in the Mediterranean Sea.

169. The world's land lows are Caspian and Dead seas, Assal and Eyre North lacks, Death Valley and Valde's Peninsula.

170. The world's windiest place is Commonwealth Bay, George V. Coast, Antartica, where gales reach over 320 kilometres per hour.

171. There are about 10 billion galaxies, and in each galaxy there are about 100 billion stars, the sun is such one star and earth is an insignificant spot in the map of universe.

172. There are about 70 areas in the world where deep underground heat is already serving the people.

173. Turner (1515-1568), and English physician-cum-botanist was regarded the father of botany at that time due to his monumental work on botany.

174. Until 1850, 90 per cent of man's energy requirement came from firewood and thereafter man's dependence shifted to fossil fuels, that is, the product of photosynthesis achieved about 250 million years ago.

175. Venus is the hottest planet of the solar system.

176.. Water hyacinth (*Electronia crassipes*), a troublesome aquatic weed constitutes an economically viable and environmentally sound proposition to mitigate energy crisis.

177. Water hyacinth is believed to have been introduced in Bengal in 1888.

178. Western Jamuna canal was restored in 1821.

179. When – 60 per cent or less. than .the total average annual rainfall is received, that year is termed as scanty rainfall year.

180. When the sun is 90° overhead, the number of atmospheres light must pass through equals one, while it is two and five atmospheres at 60° and 30°, respectively.

181. Whitney's Cotton Gin was invented in 1793.

182. William F. Libby, University of Chicago (USA) developed a method of estimating age of carbon.containing objects called Radio-Carbon dating during 1946 and 1954.

183. World oceans hold 97.4 per cent of water, while only 2.6 per cent is fresh water.

184. World population during 8000 B.C. and 1650 A.D. expanded from 5 millions to 500 millions.

185. World receives 3.4 Gg of water through rainfall annually.

186. World's 29.3 per cent of total area is occupied by land and 70.7 per cent by water.

187. Year means the time (365.24 days) taken by the earth to revolve around the sun.

188. Highest amount of rainfall received in India by south west monsoon.

189. First agricultural chemist of imperial agricultural station was Mr. J. W. Leather.

190. The highest award presented to an agricultural scientist in India is Rafi Ahmed Kidwai award.

191. India's first biotech crop technology approved for commercialization in the year 2002

192. Kissan Credit Card Scheme started in the year 1998.

193. National Food Security Mission started in the year 2007-2008

194. Agricultural Research Information Systems established by ICAR is 1995.

SECTION 17
ACRONYMS

AAR	Accumulated Assured Rainfall
AAS	Analytical Action Spectra
AAU	Assam Agricultural University, Jorhat (Assam)
ACIAR	Australian Centre for International Agricultural Research
ACP	Asian-Caribbean-Pacific (1963)
ACTHA	Dreno-Cortico-Tropic Hormone
AGMARK	Agricultural Marketing
AGMARK	Agricultural Product Market Regulation Act.
AGRIS	International Information System for Agricultural Sciences and Technology
AICPND	All-India Coordinated Project on National Demonstrations
AICRP	All-India Coordinated Research Project
AIFC	All India Farmers Council
AIFPA	All-India Food Preservers Association, Delhi (1946)
ALESCO	Arab Education, Cultural and Scientific Organization
AOAC	Association of Official Agricultural Chemists
APAU	Andhra Pradesh Agricultural University, Rajendranagar, Hyderabad (AP)
APC	Agriculatural Price Commission
APCF	Agricultural Produce Cess Fund
A.P.E.D.A.	Agriculture and Processed Products Dev. Authority
APHNET	Animal Production and Health Information Network
ARDC	Agriculture Refinance and Development Corporation
ARIC	Agricultural Reasearch Information Centre
ARISNET	Agricultural Research Information System Network
ARS	Agricultural Research Services
ASEAN	Association of South-East Asian Nations (1967)
ASRB	Agricultural Scientists Recruitment Board, ICAR, Anusandhan Bhawan, New Delhi-110012
ASRIC	Asian Small Ruminant Information Centre
ATMA	Agricultural Technology Management Agency
BARC	Bangladesh Agricultural Research Council, Dhaka

BAU	Birsa Agricultural University, Ranchi (Bihar)
BCKVV	Bidhan Chandra Krishi Vishwa Vidyalaya, Kalyani, Nadia (WB)
BDO	Block Development Officer
BIS	Bureau of Indian Standard
BPC	Block Planning Committee
BWRC	Biological Welfare Research Centre
CABARD	Centre for Agriculture, Biotechnology and Rural Development
CABI	Commonwealth Agricultural Bureaux International
CAD	Command Area Development
CAP	Catabolite Activator Protein
CARDS	Centre for Agriculture and Rural Development Studies
CARIBNGI	Central Agricultural Research Institute for Andaman and Nicobar Group of Islands, Port Blair
CASAS	Commonwealth Association of Scientific Agricultural Societies
CAZRI	Central Arid Zone Research Institute, Jodhpur (Rajasthan)
CCI	Cotton Corporation of India
CDP	Community Development Programme
CEP	Commission on Environmental Planning (of IUCN - Switzerland)
CEP	Cultural Exchange Programme
CEQ	Council of Environmental Quality (under US President)
CFTRI	Central Food Technological Research Institute, Mysore (Karnataka)
CGA	Central Ganga Authority (India)
CGIAR	Consultative Group of International Agricultural Research, Washington, D.C. (U.S.A.)
CIAE	Central Institute of Agricultural Engineering, Berasia Road Bhopal (MP)
CIAT	Centro International de Agriculture Tropical (International Centre for Tropical Agriculture), Coli, Columbia (South America)
CIBA	Central Institute of Brackishwater Aquaculture, Madras (TN)
CICFRI	Central Inland Capture Fisheries Research Institute, Barrackpore (WB)
CICR	Central Institute for Cotton Research, Nagpur (MS)
CIDA	Canadian International Development Agency, Cubac
CIFA	Central Institute of Freshwsater Aquaculture, Kausalyaganga (Orissa)
CIFE	Central Institute of Fisheries Education, Bombay (MS)
CIFRI	Central Inland Fisheries Research Institute, Barrackpore (WB)
CIFT	Central Institute of Fisheries Technology, Cochin (Kerala)
CIHNP	Central Institute of Horticulture for Northern Plains, Lucknow (UP)
CIMAP	Central Institute of Medicinal and Aromatic Plants, Lucknow
CIMMYT	Centro International de Mejoramiento de Maizy Trigo (International Maize and Wheat Improvement Centre), Mexico

CIP	International Potato Centre, Lima, Peru (South America)
CIPET	Central Institute of Post-harvest Engineering and Technology, Ludhiana (Punjab)
CIRB	Central Institute for Research on Buffaloes, Hisar (Haryana)
CIRG	Central Institute for Research on Goats, Makdoom, Mathura, (UP)
CITH	Central Institute for Temperate Horticulture, Srinagar, J & K
CMFRI	Central Marine Fisheries Research Institute, Cochin (Kerala)
COHMAP	Cooperative Holocene Mapping Project
COMECON	Council for Mutual Economic Assistance, founded in 1949 by Joseph Stalin
Commonwealth	The Commonwealth Nations evolved from the British Empire, comprised 18 nations recognizing the British Monarch as head of state and 32 with their own heads of state
CP	Colombo Plan
CPCB	Central Pollution Contral Board (India)
CPCRI	Central Plantation Crops Research Institute, Kasaragod (Kerala)
CPRI	Central Potato Research Institute, Shimla (HP)
CRIDA	Central Research Institute for Dryland Agriculture, Hyderabad (AP)
CRIJAF	Central Research Institute for Jute and Allied Fibre, 24-Parganas, Barrackpore (WB)
CRRI	Central Rice Research Institute,. Cuttack (Orissa)
CSAUAT	Chandra Shekhar Azad University of Agriculture and Technology, Kanpur (UP)
CSIR	Council of Scientific and Industrial Research, New Delhi
CSSRI	Central Soil Salinity Research Institute, Karnal (Haryana)
CSWCRTI	Central Soil and Water Conservation Research and Training Institute, Dehradun
CSWRI	Central Sheep and Wool Research Institute, Avikanagar (Malpura) (Rajasthan)
CTCRI	Central Tuber Crops Research Institute, Sreekariyam, Trivandrum (Kerala)
CTRI	Central Tobacco Research Institute, Rajahmundry (AP)
CTRL	Cotton Technological Research Laboratory, Bombay (MS)
CWC	Central Water Commission
DARE	Department of Agricultural Research and Education, New Delhi
DDP	Desert Development Programme
DES	Directorate of Economics and Statistics
DESCONAP	Desertification Council in Asia and Pacific
DPA	Debit Proportional Advancement
DPAP	Drought Prone Areas Programme
DPC	District Planning Committee
DPCC	District Planning and Coordination Committee
DRDA	District Rural Development Agency
DRR	Directorate of Rice Research, Hyderabad (AP)

DST	Department of Science and Technology, New Delhi
DWCRA	Development of Women and Children in Rural Areas (1982)
EARCAL	Eastern Africa Regional Cereals and Legumes Programme
EEC	European Economic Community (1957)
EFTA	European Free Trade Association (1960)
EPA	Environmental Protection Agency (USA)
ERA	Entomological Research Association, Udaipur (1985)
ESCAP	Economic and Social Commission for Asia and the Pacific
FAKU	Faculty of Agriculture University, Fukoda (Japan)
FAO	Food and Agricultural Organization, Rome (Italy)
FCI	Food Corporation of India.
FSH	Follicle Stimulating Hormone
FSR	Farming Systems Research
FSS	Farmers' Service Society
F.T.C.	Farmers Training Centre
G-6-PD	Glucose-6 Phosphate Dehydrogenase
GARP	Global Atmosphere Research Programme
GATT	General Agreement on Trade and Tarrifs
GAU	Gujarat Agricultural University, Sardar Krushinagar, Dantiwada (Gujarat)
GBPUAT	Govind Ballabh Pant University of Agriculture and Technology, Pantnagar (UP)
GIPME	Global Investigations on Pollution in Marine Environment
GIS	Geographic Information System
GMO	Genetic Modified Organism
GNP	Gross National Product
GPP	Gross Primary Productivity
GPR	Ground Penetrating Radar
GPS	Geographic Positioning System
HAD	Hill Area Deveplopment Programme
HAU	Haryana Agricultural University, Hisar (Haryana) (now CCSHAU)
HFAP	Hunger Free Area Programme
HGPRT	Hypoxanthine Guanine Phospho-Ribose Transferase
HPKVV	Himachal Pradesh Krishi Vishwa Vidyalaya, Palampur (HP)
HYVP	High Yielding Variety Programme
I.A.D.A.	Intensive Agricultural District Programme
IAAP	Intensive Agricultural Area Programme
IADP	Intensive Agricultural District Programme

IARI	Indian Agricultural Research Institute, New Delhi
IASRI	Indian Agricultural Statistics Research Institute, New Delhi
IBGE	Institute Brassiliero de Geografia-e-Estadistica (Brazile)
IBPGR	International Board of Plant Genetic Resources, Rome (Italy)
IBRD	International Bank for Reconstruction and Development. Washington, D.C. (U.S.A.)
IBSNAT	International Benchmark Soils Network for Agrotechnology Transfer, Hawaii
ICAR	Indian Council of Agricultural Research, New Delhi
ICARDA	International Centre for Agricultural Research in Dry Area, Alleppo, Syria
ICDP	Intensive Cattle Development Project
ICIA	International Crop Improvement Association (established in 1919)
ICITV	Instituto de la Carte International du Tapis Vegetale
ICM	International Marine Committee
ICRAF	International Council for Research in Agroforestry, Nairobi, Kenya
ICRISAT	International Crops Research Institute for the Seim-Arid Tropics, Patancheru (AP)
ICSH	Interstitial Cell Stimulating Hormone
ICSU	International Council of Scientific Unions
IDA	International Development Agency
IDRC	International Development Research Centre, Canada
IEEP	International Environmental Education Programme
IFAD	International Fund for Agricultural Development, Rome, Italy
IFDC	International Fertilizer Development Centre, Muscale Shoals, Alabama (U.S.A.)
IFFCO	Indian Farmers Fertilizers Cooperative Ltd., New Delhi
IFPRI	International Food Policy Research Institute, Washington D.C. (U.S.A.)
IGFRI	Indian Grassland and Fodder Research -Institute, Jhansi (UP)
IGWA	International Federation for Women in Agriculture
IHD	International Hydrological Decade (of UNESCO started in 1965)
IIASA	International Institute for Applied. Systems Analysis, Luxemberg, Vienna, Austria
IIHR	Indian Institute of Horticultural Research, Bangalore Karnatka
IISAT	International Information System for Agricultural Science and Technology
IISR	Indian Institute of Sugarcane Research, Lucknow (UP)
IISS	Indian Institute of Soil Science Nebri Bag (Bhopal)
IITA	International Institute of Tropical Agriculture, Ibadan, Nigeria
IJO	International Jute Organization
ILCA	International Livestock Centre for Africa.
ILO	International Labour Organization
ILRAD	International Laboratory for Research on Animal Diseases

ILRI	Indian Lac Research Institute, Namkum, Ranchi (Jharkhand)
IMF	International Monetory Fund
INRAL	Institute National de la Researche Agronomique
INSFFER	International Network on Soil Fertility and Fertilizer Evaluation on Rice (IRRI)
INTECOL	International Association for Ecology
INTSORMIL	International Sorghum, Millet Collaborative Research Support Programme (U.S.A.)
IOC	Intergovernmental Oceanographic Commission (for purity and protection of oceans)
I.O.D.P.	Intensive Oil Seed Development Programme
IPCC	Intergovernal Panel on Climate Change
IPM	Integrated Pest Management
IPNS	Integrated Plant Nutrient System
IPR	Intellectual Property Right
IRDC	International Research and Development Council
IRDP	Integrated Rural Development Programme
IRRI	International Rice Research Institute, Manila (Philippines)
IRTP	International Rice Testing Programme
ISI	Indian Standards Institution (now Bureau of Indian Standards), New Delhi
ISNAR	International Service for National Agricultural Research, The Hague, Netherlands (Holland)
ISO	International Organization for Standardization
ISRIC	International Soils Reference and Information Centre, Netherlands (Holland)
ISSS	International Society of Soil Science
ISTA	International Seed Testing Association
ISTE	International Society for Tropical Ecology
ISWS	Indian Society of Weed Science
ITEC	Indian Technical and Economic Co-operation
IUBS	International Union of Biological Sciences
IUCN	International Union for Conservation of Nature and Natural Resources, Switzerland
IUFRO	International Union of Forestry Research Organization (established in 1890), England (UK)
IVLP	Institute Village Link Programme
IVLP	Institute Village Link Programme
IVRI	Indian Veterinary Research Institute, Izatnagar (UP)
IWMI	International Water Management Institute
IYE	International Youth Federation for Environmental Studies and Conservation
JARI	Jute Agricultural Research Institute, Barrackpore (WB)
JASIN	Joint Air-Sea Interaction Experiment
JNKVV	Jawaharlal Nehru Krishi Vishwa Vidyalaya, Jabalpur (MP)

JRY	Jawahar Rozgar Yojana
JTRL	Jute Technological Research Laboratory, Kolkata (WB)
JVTM	Jai Vigyan Technology Mission
KAU	Kerala Agricultural University, Vellanikkara (Kerala)
KCC	Kissan Call Centre, Kissan Credit Card
KKV	Konkan Krishi Vidyapeeth, Dapoli, Ratnagiri (MS)
KRIBHCO	Krishak Bharati Cooperative Ltd., New Delhi
KVK	Krishi Vigyan Kendra
LAIA	Latin American Integration Association (1980)
LBS	Lead Bank Scheme
LDB	Land Development Bank
LH	Lutenizing hormone
LISNET	Land Information System Network
LLP	Lab to Land Project
LMOs	Living Modified Organism
LRDC	Land Resources Development Centre, England (UK)
LTPC	Long-Term Programme of Co-operation
MAU	Marathwada Agricultural University, Parbhani (MS)
MBP	Man and the Biosphere Programme (of UNESCO)
MCP	Multiple Cropping Programme
MFAL	Marginal Farmer's Agricultural Labourers Programme
MINAS	Minimum National Standards
MOA	Ministry of Agriculture
MPKV	Mahatma Phule Krishi Vidyapeeth, Rahuri (MS)
MPTS	Multi Purpose Trees
MSP	Minimum Support Rrice
MSSRF	M. S. Swaminathan Research Foundation (Chennai)
MSY	Mahila Samridhi Yojana
NAARM	National Academy of Agricultural Research and Management, Hyderabad (AP)
NABARD	National Bank for Agriculture and Rural Development
NADAMS	National Agriculture Drought Advisory and Management System
NAEE	National Association for Environmental Education
NAEP	National Agricultural Extension Project (1982)
NAFED	National Agricultural Co-operative Marketing Federation Ltd.
NARP	National Agricultural Research Project
NASA	National Aeronauts & Space Administration (USA)
NATP	National Agricultural Technology Project.

NATO	North Atlantic Treaty Organization (formed in 1949)
NBAGR	National Bureau of Animal Genetic Resources, Karnal (Harayna)
NBPGR	National Bureau of Plant Genetic Resources, New Delhi
NBRI	National Botanical Research Institute, Lucknow (UP)
NBSSLUP	National Bureau of Soil Science and Land Use Planning, Nagpur (MS)
NCA	National Commission on Agriculture
NCAER	National Council for Agricultural Economics and Research.
NCEPC	National Committee on Environmental Planning and Cooperation
NDDB	National Dairy Development Board
NDP	National Demonstrations Project
NDRI	National Dairy Research Institute, Karnal (Haryana)
NDUAT	Narendra Dev University of Agriculture and Technology, Faizabad (UP)
NEERI	National Environmental Engineering Research Institute, Nagpur
NFSM	National Food Security Mission.
NGOs	Non-Government Organisations
NHM	National Horticulture Mission.
NIAE	National Institute of Agricultural Engineering
NIAG	National Institute of Animal Genetics, Karnal (Haryana)
NIANP	National Institute of Animal Nutrition and Physiology Bangaluru (Karnatka)
NIH	National Institute of Hydrology
NII	National Institute of Immunology, New Delhi
NIN	National Institute of Nutrition, Hyderabad (AP)
NOVOD	National Oilseeds and Vegetable Oils Development Board
NRC	National Research Centre
NRCC	National Research Centre for Camels, Jorbeer, Bikaner (Rajasthan)
NRCE	National Research Centre for Equines, Hisar (Haryana)
NRDC	National Research Development Corporation
NRDP	National Rural Development Programme
NREP	National Rural Employment Programme (1980)
NRSA	National Remote Sensing Agency
NSC	National Seed Corporation
NWDB	National Wasteland Development Board (India)
OAS	Organization of American States (1949)
OECD	Organization for Economic Cooperation and Development (1961)
ORP	Operational Research Project
OUAT	Orissa University of Agriculture and Technology, Bhubaneswar (Orissa)

PARC	Pakistan Agricultural Research Council, Islamabad
PAU	Punjab Agricultural University, Ludhiana (Punjab)
PCARD	Philippines Council of Agricultural and Rural Development
PCR	Polymeric Chain Reactions
P.D.	Poultry Development
PGPB	Plant Growth Promotion Bacteria
PKV	Punjabrao Krishi Vidyapeeth, Krishinagar, Akola (MS)
PPTD	Pilot Project for Tribal Development
PTD	Participatory Technology Development
PVC	Poly Vinyl Chloride
RAU	Rajasthan Agricultural University, Bikaner (Rajasthan)
RAU	Rajendra Agricultural University, Pusa Samastipur (Bihar)
RFLP	Restriction Fragment Length Polymorphism
RLEGP	Rural Landless Employment Guarantee Programme
RMK	Rashtriya Mahila Kosh
RRI	Rubber Research Institute of India, Kerala
RUCHI	Rural Centre for Human Interests
SAARC	South Asian Association for Regional Co-operation
SADCC	Southern African Development Coordination Conference
SAICSAARC	Agricultural Information Centre
SAU	State Agricultural University(ies)
SBI	Sugarcane Breeding Institute, Coimbatore (TN)
SCAP	Special Commonwealth African Assistance Programme
SCOPE	Scientific Committee on Problems of the Environment (of ICSU)
SEAFDEC	Southeast Asian Fisheries Development Centre
SEASAT	Sea Satellite Monitoring Studies
SEMEO	South East Asian Ministers of Education Organization
SFAC	Small Farmers Agri-Business Consortion
SFDA	Small Farmers Development Agency
SFPP	Special Foodgrain Production Programme, Ministry of Agriculture (GOI)
SKUAST	Sher-e-Kashmir University of Agricultural Sciences and Technology, Srinagar (J&K)
SMS	Subject Matter Specialist
SPCBs	State Pollution Control Boards (23 in India)
SWCRDT	Soil and Water Conservation Research, Demonstration and Training Centres in India.
T & V	Training and Visit (Programme)
TCA	Technical Committee on Agriculture

TCS	Technical Co-operation Scheme
TFRI	Tropical Forest-Research Institude (Jabalpur)
TMO	Technology Mission on Oilseeds (1986)
TNAU	Tamil Nadu Agricultural University, Coimbatore (TN)
TRYSEM	Training of Rural Youth for Self-Employment
TTCs	Trainers Training Centres
TVA	Tennessee Valley Authority
UAS	University of Agricultural Sciences, Bangalore (Karnataka)
UEE	Union for Environmental Education (USA and Europe)
UGC	University Grants Commission, New Delhi
UNDP	United Nations Development Programme
UNEP	United Nations Environmental Programme
UNESCO	United Nations Educational, Scientific and Cultural Organization
UNICEF	United Nations Children's Educational Fund
UNO	United Nations Organization (New York, USA)
USAID	United States Agency for International Development
USIF	US-India Funds
UTI	Unit trust of India
VAM	Vesicular Ambuscular Mycorrhiza
VAMNICOM	Vaikenth Mehta National Institute of Co-operative Management
VPKAS	Vivekananda Parvatiya Krishi Anusandhan Shala, Almora (Uttarakhand)
WALMTARI	Water Agriculture Land Management Training and Research Institute HYDRABAD
WARDA	West African Rice Development Association
WASIP	West African Sorghum Improvement Programme
WBCIS	Weather Based Crop Insurance Scheme
WCED	World Commission or Environment and Development
WHO	World Health Organization (of UNO)
WMO	World Meteorological Organization (of UNO), Geneva, Switzerland
WNCF	World Natures Conservation Fund
WTO	World Trade Organization
WVDP	Whole Village Development Programme
WWF	World Wide Fund for Nature
YUPUHF	(Dr) Yashwant Singh Parmar University of Horticulture and Forestry, Solan (HP)
ZARC's	Zonal Agricultural Research Centres
ZEIL	Zero Economic Injury level

SECTION 18
AGRO-CLIMATIC ZONAL PLANNING

Crop yield is the function of many factors like weather, soil type and its nutrient status, management practices and other inputs available. Of these, weather plays an important role, probably more so in India where aberrant weather such as drought, flood, etc., is a rule rather than an exception. Efficient crop planning, therefore, requires proper understanding of agro-climatic conditions. This calls for collection, collation, analysis and interpretation of long-term weather parameters available for each region to identity the length of the possible cropping period taking into consideration the availability of water.

Indian agriculture has made an impressive progress since mid-sixties and fertilizer has been one of the essential inputs in this progress. Fertilizer consumption in the country has been increasing steadily over the years. The year 1988-89, in fact, was a record year with both foodgrain production and fertilizer consumption registering impressive growth. However, our past experience, irrespective of good or bad year, reveals that there exists a wide variation in foodgrain production and fertilizer consumption from season to season, region to region and even within the districts of the same state. Crop yield response to the level of fertilizer application may be different from one location to another due to differences in agro-climatic conditions and soil characteristics. Also the response of crops for the same level of fertilizer may not be the same from one year to another. Zoning of the country in such a manner that variation within a zone is less, is therefore, necessary.

In the past, several attempts including that of NCA (1976) and ICAR have been made to divide the country into different zones. Recently, the Planning Commission has delineated 15 agro-climatic zones based on the physical conditions, topography, soil type, geological formation, rainfall, cropping pattern and development of irrigation and mineral resources of the country. The agro-climatic zonal planning aims at scientific management of zonal resources to meet the increasing demand for the 4Fs (*i.e.,* food, fibre, fodder and fuel) without adversely affecting the status of natural resources and environment.

Constraints and thrust areas also differ from one zone to another. In the hill regions of Western and Eastern Himalayas (Zones 1 and 2), the vallleys receive good rainfall and have rich soils while the temperate areas of Ladakh in Western Himalayas and Sikkim and Darjeeling in Eastern Himalayas have to reckon with inadequate moisture and low temperatures limiting the crop growing period. In the Gangetic plain zones, the Lower and Middle Gangetic Plains (Zones 3, 4) are characterized by high rainfall, alluvial and deltaic soils and good ground water, whereas the Upper and Trans-Gangetic plains (Zones 5 and 6) are rich alluvial soil areas with medium to low rainfall and very good availability of water. The Plateau and Hill Regions (Zones 7, 8, 9 and 10) are characterized by comparatively poor soils, high slopes with high runoff and medium rainfall. The Plain and Hill regions (Zones 11, 12 and 13) have large variation of soil and rainfall. The Western Dry Region (Zone 14) receives highly erratic and uncertain rainfall. Underground water is scarce and saline. The Islands Region (Zone 15) is a typical equatorial climatic region with annual rainfall of over 3000 mm.

The zone-wise productivity (kg/ha) trends reveal that it is maximum in Zone 6 (Trans-Gangetic Plain Regions) having highest irrigated area (%) and fertilizer consumption. Productivity is lowest in Zone 14 (West Drylands) which suffers from scarcity of water and low use of fertilizer. Although, average consumption has gone up to about 86 kg/ha in 1999 & 98 (Festile stat.) in the country, region-wise disparities continue. The differences in consumption are likely to be much more pronounced if made on sub-zone basis.

Having realized the need for micro-level planning to obtain maximum benefit, 15 agro-climatic zones have been further subdivided into 73 sub-zones on the basis of more specific soil, topograph, climate and cropping pattern characteristics. The exercise further proposes to build a detailed resource profile for each of these sub-zones. In the long run, it is proposed to develop effective linkages between agro-climatic regional planning to provide technological backup to the district planning exercise and *vice versa*.

Results of experiments, national demonstrations and on-farm trials conducted in different parts of the country have shown that there exists a great potential for increasing crop production provided location specific constraints of production are identified and suitable remedial measures are taken.

AGRO-CLIMATIC REGIONAL PLANNING

Concept and Approach

Indian agriculture took a quantum jump in 1988-89 and is likely to maintain level in 1989-90. However, large regional disparities still exist in the country. Against this background, Planning Commission decided to introduce Agro-climatic Regional Planning approach to give a new direction to agricultural developmental planning. This multiple objective planning exercise aims at narrowing these imbalances along with sustainable use of natural resources to generate additional rural employment and maximize incomes. The paper attempts to elaborate on concept and approach of this planning exercise and its attempts to elaborate on concept and approach of this planning exercise and its relevance to fertilize use planning.

Indian agriculture has made impressive progress since the introduction of Green Revolution technology in the country in mid.-60's. The agriculture development strategies during this period also underwent constant changes from area approach to specific crop-oriented and problem oriented approach. Special production programmes for rice and pulses, Technology Mission for Oilseeds, National Project for Rainfed. Agriculture, special programmes for development of small and marginal farmers are a few of the new initiatives taken by the Government in 80' s to strength the technological base of Indian agriculture. As a result of these initiatives, an agricultural growth rate of about 2.32 per cent per annum was achieved between 1967-68 to 1986-87. When this impressive national performance is further evaluated in terms of regional growth, extreme regional disparities in agricultural production and rural incomes are observed.

A district level analysis prepared for the Planning Commission by Professor G.S. Bhalla, former Chairman of Agricultural Prices, reveals that 50% of the country's increase in food grain production has come from the highly-irrigated north-western region. The eastern and central states could only contribute to 17% of the incremental output. Further, the increases in production have been mainly limited to fine cereals and not in case of pulses and millets. This lopsided growth scenario coupled with severe drought of 1987-88 forced agricultural planners to look for more comprehensive agricultural development strategies so that more incremental output is contributed by regions with low productivity. The launching of Special Foodgrain Production Programme in 169 identified districts in 14 states covering five major crops in 1988-89 was seen as a departure from earlier approach of nursing better-off regions. The principal strategy was to capitalise on identified sources of immediate agricultural growth based on analysis of resources and agronomic possibilities. At the same time agricultural planners also started looking for strategies which are dependable and sustainable to maintain the momentum of growth in agriculture in longer term perspective. It was thought appropriate to replace traditional crop production approach with a holistic approach through an optimal mix of agriculture and allied activities. In this context introduction of Agro-Climatic Regional Planning approach was proposed for formulation of agricultural development plans for the 8th Five Year Plan.

Concept and Objectives:

The agro-climatic regional planning aims at scientific management of regional resources to meet the food, fibre, fodder and fuel wood without adversely affecting the status of natural resources and environment.

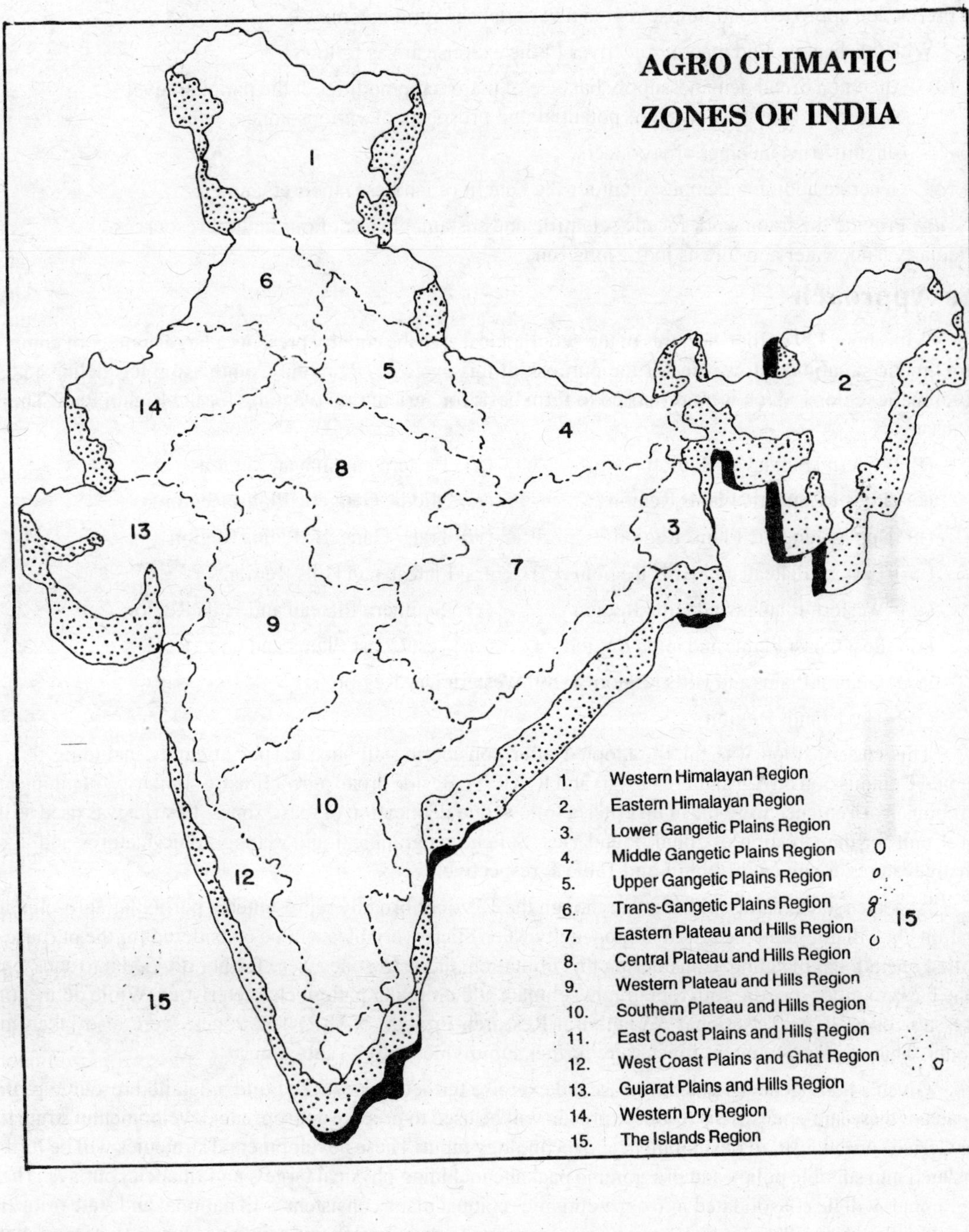

Source: Fertilizer News (Agronomic Special) 1990

While assessment of resource base will require holistic perspective, development will have to be achieved through an appropriate mix of crop production and allied activities including horticulture, forestry, animal husbandry and agro-processing, etc. Improved farming systems technologies will replace traditional crop production approach to minimise regional variations in rural incomes.

With this background macro objectives of the exercise are as follows:

(*a*) Attempt a broad demand-supply balance of major commodities at the national level based on a careful analysis of potential and prospects of various zones;

(*b*) Maximize net incomes of producers;

(*c*) Generate additional employment for the benefit of landless labourers; and

(*d*) Provide the framework for the scientific and sustainable use of our natural resources, particularly land, water and forests in the long run.

The Approach

With about 329 million hectares of the geographical area the country presents a large number of complex agro-climatic situations. However, for the purpose of this exercise, Planning Commission has delineated 15 agro-climatic regions which were proposed to form basis for agricultural planning for the Eighth Plan. The 15 regions are:

(*i*) Western Himalayan Region (*ii*) Eastern Himalayan Region

(*iii*) Lower Gangetic Plains Region (*iv*) Middle Gangetic Plains Region

(*v*) Upper Gangetic Plains Region (*vi*) Trans-Gangetic Plains Region

(*vii*) Eastern Plateau and Hills Region(*viii*) Central Plateau and Hills Region

(*ix*) Western Plateau and Hills Region (*x*) Southern Plateau and Hills Region

(*xi*) East Coast Plains and Hills Region (*xii*) est Coast Plains and Ghat Region

(*xiii*) Gujarat Plains and Hills Region (*xiv*) Western Dry Region

(*xv*) The Islands Region

This classification was finally adopted after considering all such earlier attempts including that of National Commission on Agriculture (1976) and ICAR (I). Beside broad agro-climatic similarity, planning and operational convenience were the main criteria followed in delineation of these zones. District was used as the lowest unit for demarcation of zonal boundaries. Salient geographical and demographic features and agro-climatic features are given in Table 1 and Table 2, respectively.

At a later stage, it was realized that though the 15 zones broadly represented a particular agro-climatic situation but will not stand the test of homogeneity when micro-variables will be considered for the purpose of detailed operational planning. Considering this limitation, these 15 zones were further divided into sub-zones on the basis of more specific soil, topography, climate and cropping pattern characteristics. While delineating these sub-zones, ICAR's National Agricultural Research Project (NARP) 127 zones, were also taken into account. Thus, 15 agro-climatic zones were further sub-divided into 73 sub-zones:

Given a homogeneous planning base the exercise further proposes to build a detailed resource profile for each of these sub-zones. This resource profile will be used to prepare appropriate developmental strategies considering current level of development and technology input. These developmental strategies will be further translated into suitable policy and programme package including physical targets and financial outlays. These programmes will be consolidated into agro-climatic regional plans consistent with national and state priorities for the 8th Five Year Plan. In the long run, it is proposed to develop effective linkages between agro-climatic regional planning to provide technological backup/input to the district planning exercise and *vice versa*.

Table 1. SALIENT GEOGRAPHICAL AND DEMOGRAPHIC FEATURE OF AGRO-CLIMATIC ZONES

Zone No.	*No. of Sub. zone*	*States Represented*	*No. of Dist.*	*Geographical Area (000' h)*	*Population Density (per sq. km)*	*Rural population (%)*
I	3	J & K. HP. UP	34	24574 (10983)	61.5	83.6
II	5	Assam. WB. Manipur, Meghalaya, Nagaland. A.P., Tripura and Mizoram	58	27533 (23325)	125.8	84.3
III	4	West Bengal	12	6940	684.3	71.6
IV	6	UP. Bihar	38	17033	531.2	84.9
V	3	UP	32	14344	464.2	78.4
VI	3	Punjab. Haryana. Delhi, Rajasthan	27	12508	328.9	63.3
VII	5	Maharashtra. M.P. Orissa. West Bengal	34	39503	136.1	84.6
VIII	14	MP. Rajasthan. UP	46	37592	136.8	78.8
IX	4	Maharashtra. MP. Rajasthan	34	33222 (32345)	169.3	74.3
X	6	A.P., Karnataka. Tamil Nadu	35	39410 (37949)	199.0	73.6
XI	6	Orissa. A P. Tamil Nadu. Pondicherry	25	19285	321.1	73.6
XII	4	Tamil Nadu, Kerala, Goa. Karnataka. Maharashtra	27	11419	414.0	63.8
XIII	7	Gujarat	22	19602 (20669)	174.3	68.9
XIV	–	Rajasthan	9	17580	58.2	78.1
XV	2	A & N and Lakshadweep Islands	3	832	28.8	70.2

***In case of significant difference between geographical and reporting area, latter has been indicated in parenthesis.**

The Planning Commission have taken adequate steps for effective operationalisation of work of this exercise. Beside constitution of 15 inter-disciplinary Zonal Planning Teams (ZPTs), one for each zone, an Agro-Climatic Regional Planning Unit (ARPU) has been set up at Ahmedabad to guide and coordinate activities of the Zonal Planning Teams. Necessary support from Ministry of Agriculture, ICAR, NIC, ISRO, NSSO, National Bureau of Soil Survey and Land Use Planning have been mobilised for providing information and guidance to the exercise. The ZPTs have been asked to work in close coordination with state agencies with necessary support from Central Government for integration of outcome of this exercise with the State Eighth Plans.

Emerging Strategies

In line with the approach, the agro-climatic regional planning exercise has already made substantial progress and has reached the stage of programme formulation. During the course of work a clear outline of future development strategies pertaining to agriculture and allied sector have emerged.

Core Strategies

Although, each Zonal Planning Team made an independent exercise to formulate strategies at zonal/ sub-zonal level but overall review of emerging strategies reveal certain similarities across zones. There are another set of strategies which are specific to each zone. The 'core strategies' for agricultural development which run across zones can be broadly grouped as below.

Land and Water Management

In the traditional approach of agriculture development land and water management has not received its due attention. The strategies suggested include increasing attention to soil conservation, improving farming practices in hilly and undulating areas. reclamation of problem soils and improving drainage systems to improve land productivity. This will be all important considering the fact that by the beginning of the next century the per capita availability of land will be hardly 0.15 hectare.

Similarly, management of water resources have been suggested through integrated watershed development approach for rain water, improving utilization of created irrigation potential, revival of tank irrigation and very high priority to ground water development so as to utilize greater part of available potential within next decade.

Horticulture Development

Horticulture offers immense scope in providing diversification and additional incomes to small and marginal farmers. The ZPTs have suggested that technology gap in this must be rapidly bridged with parallel improvement in marketing system.

Livestock Development

The livestock sector has capability to provide much needed impetus for growth provided milch animals stock of poor genetic quality is gradually replaced with parallel improvement in fodder availability and marketing infrastructure. The livestock development strategy should include optimum composition of animal population with a view to improve productivity and income particularly in case of weaker sections.

Agro-processing

Agro-processing of potential in ensuring remunerative prices to farmers and generate employment in the rural sector. In spite of available potential agro-processing units are not coming up in large numbers. The problems concerning growth of agro-processing industry needs to be examined in greater details for its planned growth in future.

The 'core strategies' suggest that last forty years of agricultural development effort has paid less attention to these areas than desired. The present planning exercise gives much larger reliance on above strategies with clear indications of stepping up investments in these areas.

Zone Specific Strategies

Besides these common strategies zone/sub-zone specific strategies have also been formulated. These zone specific strategies have suggested a framework for improvement in productivity, agricultural input delivery systems, afforestation-fisheries, poultry, sericulture, tribals oriented activities etc. The ZPTs are engaged in working out specific schemes and programmes in these areas besides indicating strategies which require further investigations before they are considered for any investment decision.

Table 2. SALIENT AGRO-CLIMATIC FEATURES OF 15 ZONES

Zone No.	*Rainfall Range in Sub-zone (mm)*	*Climate*	*Representative Soil*	*Major Crops*
I	165-2000	Cold arid to humid	Brown hill, Alluvial (recent) Mountain, Meadow, Skeletal	Wheat, Maize Rice, Potato
II	1840-3528	Per humid to humid	Alluvial, Red Loamy, Red Sandy, Brown hill soil	Rice, Maize, Jute, Rapeseed
III	1302-1607	Moist sub-humid to dry sub-humid	Red and Yellow Deltsic Alluvium Red Loamy	Rice, Jute, Wheat, Rapeseed
IV	1211-1470	Moist sub-humid to Dry sub-humid	Alluvial	Rice, Wheat, Maize
V	721-979	Dry sub-humid to semi-arid	Alluvial	Wheat, Rice, Maize, Tur
VI	360-890	Extreme arid to dry sub-humid	Alluvial (recent), Calcareous, Desert	Wheat, Maize, Rice, Sugarcane
VII	1271-1436	Moist sub-humid to dry sub-humid	Red Sandy, Red and Yellow	Rice, Wheat Maize, Ragi
VIII	490-1570	Semi-arid (drier half) to dry sub-humid	Mixed red and black, Red and yellow, medium black, Alluvial	Wheat, Gram, Jowar, Rice, Bajra
IX	602-1040	Semi-arid	Medium black, deep black, Jowar, Bajra,	Jowar, Bajra, Cotton, Wheat Cotton, Wheat
X	677-1001	Semi-arid	Medium black, deep black, Red sandy, Red loamy	Jowar, Rice, Ragi, Groundnut
XI	780-1287	Semi-arid to dry sub-humid	Deltaic Alluvium, Red loamy, Coastal Alluvium	Rice, Groundnut, Ragi, Jowar, Bajra
XII	2226-3640	Dry sub-humid per humid	Laterite, Red loamy, Coastal Alluvium	Rice, Ragi, Groundnut, Tapioca
XIII	340-1793	Arid to dry sub-humid	Deep black, Coastal Alluvium, medium black	Rice, Groundnut, Cotton, Bajra, Wheat
XIV	395	Arid to extremely arid	Desert, Grey, Brown	Bajra, Gram, Wheat, Rapeseed, Coconut
XV	1500-3086	Humid		

Compiled from sub-zonal description.

Source: Planning Commission, Agro-climatic Regional Planning: An overview (1989)

Relevance of Approach in Promoting Fertilizer Use

The revised strategy papers prepared by ZPT's have also reviewed the agricultural input supply system but problems in this area are zone/sub-zone specific, and therefore require location specific solutions. The ZPTs have raised greater concern with regard to inadequacy of seeds availability as compared to that of fertilizers.

The zone-wise fertilizer consumption pattern based on 1984-85 data is indicated below in Table . 3

The zone-wise trends show wide disparities in consumption on per unit area basis. The consumption ranges between 104.7 kg/ha in zone 6 (Punjab, Haryana, Delhi) to 5.4 kg/ha in zone 14 (Western Rajasthan). Although, average consumption has gone up in the country to about 86 kg/ha in 1997-98 but it is unlikely that consumptions trends have changed. The differences in consumption are likely to be much more pronounced when comparisons are done on sub-zone basis.

Table 3. Zone-wise fertilizer consumption during 1984-85

Zone No.	*Fertilizer Consumption (kg/ha)*	*Zone No.*	*Fertilizer Consumption (kg/ha)*
1	23.0	9	27.7
2	9.4	10	57.3
3	64.9	11	77.3
4	67.6	12	51.5
5	85.5	13	37.8
6	104.7	14	5.4
7	14.6	15	N.A.
8	15.9	All India	46.7

With reference to fertilizer use promotion zone/sub-zone will provide more homogeneous area with similar problems and remedies. The marketing and promotional programme effort of the industry can be tuned to requirement of each zone/sub-zone. The fertilizer consumption pattern across zones and observations of ZPT's with regard to fertilizers indicate that fertilizer use promotion efforts will have to be choosen and prioritised amongst following approaches:

(*i*) Promoting fertilizer use awareness in low consumption sub-zones.

(*ii*) Improving availability in sub-zones which lack accessibility or otherwise have avail ability problems.

(*iii*) Promoting balanced fertilizer use including uses of micro-nutrients to maintain soil fertility in long-term perspective.

(*iv*) Promote fertilizer use efficiency in areas with medium to high consumption level as compared to national average.

Anyone or combination of these initiatives can be taken depending on assessment of the problem in each sub-zone. To begin with, it will be appropriate to prepare a fertilizer use profile of each of 73 sub-zones. Depending on this detailed assessment, marketing effort and promotional programmes can be reoriented to achieve targeted fertilizer use in each sub-zone.

* Reproduced with permission from Fertilizer News, June, 1990 (Agronomy special).

SECTION 19
PLANTS
INDIAN CENTRE OF ORIGIN AND DIVERSITY OF CULTIVATED PLANTS

Dr. R.S. Rana, former Director, National Bureau of Plant Genetic Resources (NBPGR), New Delhi has described the above topic. A summary-thereof is presented here. It has been estimated that 15,000 species of flowering plants are native to Indian centre which includes more than 160 domesticated species of economic importance along with more than 320 species of their wild ancestral forms of close relatives. There are about 800 species of ethnobotanical interest. Agri-biodiversity comprises landraces and traditional cultivars of several cereals, millets, legumes, vegetables, fruits, forages, fibres, sugarcane, spices, condiments and medicinal and aromatic plants.

Crops in which rich diversity still occurs in India include rice (*Oryza sativa* var. *indica* and several wild species), wheat (*Triticum aestivum*, *T. durum*, *T. dicoccum*), barley (*Hordeun vulgare*), sugarcane (*Saccharum* species and allied genera). *Echinochloa*, *Panicum* species. *Setaria* species and *Paspalun* species, forage grasses, legumes (*Vigna radiata*, *V. mungo*, *V. aconitifolia*, *V. umbellata* and V. *unguiculata*, *Cicer arietinum*, *Cajanus cajan*, *Lablab purpureus*), several *Brassica* species, sesame (*Sesamum indicum*), okra (*Abelmoschus esculentus* and other allied species), egg plant (*Solanum melongena* and related types), *Citrus* species, banana and plantains (*Musa* species belonging to different genomic groups), jackfruit (*Artocarpus heterophyllus*, A. *integrifolia*), mango (*Mangifera indica*), *Phyllanthus emblica*, *Carissa carandus*, *Syzygium* species, jute (*Corchorus capsularis*), tree cotton (*Gossypium arboreum*), ginger (*Zingiber officinale*), turmeric (*Curcuma* species), pepper (*Piper* species), cinnamon and cardamom. Among tuber crops, rich variability exists in sweet potato (*Ipomoea batatas*), taros (*Colocasia* and *Alocasia*), yams (*Dioscorea esculenta*, *D. alata*, *D. deltoidea etc.*), *Coleus* species, swordbean (*Canavalia* species), velvet bean (*Mucuna* species), elephant yams and coconut (*Cocos nucifera*), particularly in Nicobar group of islands. Diversity also occurs in several minor fruits such as *Zizyphus jujube* and Z. *nummularia*, *Capparis decidua*, *Syzygium cuminii*, *Myristica fragrans*, *Aegle marmelos* and several species of the genera *Ribes*, *Rubus*, *Juglans*, *Pyrus* and *Prunus*.

The distribution pattern of wild plant genetic resources in different botanical/phytogeographical regions and the areas of their concentration where rich diversity of wild species still continues to perpetuate, are of special significance for undertaking programmes on collection as well as for *in-situ* conservation of biodiversity. The distribution pattern of wild species in different phytogeographical regions reveal seven zones as follows:

(*i*) Western Himalayas (125 species)

(*ii*) Eastern Himalayas (82 species)

(*iii*) North-Eastern region (132 species)

(*iv*) Gangetic Plains (66 species)

(*v*) Indus Plains-North-Western Plains (45 species)

(*vi*) Western Peninsular Region and Malabar Coast (145 species)

(*vii*) Eastern Peninsular Region Deccan Plateau (91 species).

The following may be noted:

– That the assessment and criticism of the preseat system of plant classification is very easy, but the synthesis of a new one is very difficult.

– That the subject is complex, knowledge is limited and an individual has only limited experience to reclassify the plants.

– That as a rule, there would be no last word on a scientific subject and plant classification is no exception.

– That the classification and distribution as done by Nikolai Vavilov (1887-1943), a great investigator in crop geography and genetics has been briefly dealt with. He was the President of Lenin Academy of Agricultural Sciences and Director of the Institute of Applied Botany.

– That from Darwin's time until about 1920, there was made practically no progress in determination of origin of plants.

– That Vavilov evaluated de Candole's method and observed:

(*i*) That many species do not occur outside the place of their origin.

(*ii*) That the progenitors and wild relatives possibly represent narrow group of forms, but a small number of varieties often isolated which fail to explain the diversity representing cultivated plants.

– That Vavilov (1926, 1951), recognized initially six, but later eight centres of plant origin.

Centres of origin and production:

Wheat	C. Asia	N.C. and N. U.S.A.
Maize	Tropical America	Mid-west U.S.A.
Groundnut	S. America	India, China
Soybean	NE Asia	U.S.A.
Potato	Peru	E. Europe
Citrus spp.	S.E. Asia	U.S.A.
Coffee	Ethiopia	C & S America
Cocoa	S. America	Ghana
Pineapple	Brazil	Hawaii
Rubber	Brazil	SE Asia

I. ***Crops in world food production:*** Wheat, rice, maize, potato, barley, sweet potato, cassava, grapes, soybean, oats, sorghum, sugarcane, millet, banana, tomato, sugar-beet, rye, oranges, coconut, cotton seed, apples, groundnut, watermelon, cabbage, onion, beans, peas, sunflower, mango.

II. ***Indo-Malayan Centre:*** Indo-China, Malay-Archipelago Species 55:

(*a*) ***Cereals and Legumes***

Job's tears (*Coix lachryma*), Velvet bean (*Mucura utilis*).

(*b*) ***Oil, sugar, fibre and spices:***

– Coconut palm, Candlenut, Sugarcane, Clove, Nugmeg, Black pepper, Manila/Abaca.

(*c*) ***Fruits:*** Pummelo (*Citrus grandis*), Banana, Bread-fruit (*Garçinia mangostansa*)

III. *Central Asiatic Centre* (Species 43):

N.W. India (Punjab, N-W Frontier Provinces and Kashmir), Afghanistan, Tadjikistan, Uzbekistan, Western Tian-Shan.

(*a*) *Grains and Legumes:* Common wheat, Club wheat, Shot wheat, Field pea, lentil, Horsebean (*Viciafaba*), Chickpea, Mungbean, Mustard, Flax, Sesame.

(*b*) *Vegetables:* Onion, Garlic, Spinach, Carrot.

(*c*) *Fibre plants:* Cotton, Hemp.

(*d*) *Fruit plants:* Apple, Grape, Pear, Almond, Pistachio.

IV. That the Near-Eastern Centre: Asia Minor, All of Transcaucasia, Iran, and highlands of Turkemenistan (Species 83).

(*a*) *Grasses* and *legumes:* Eikorn wheat, *Durum* wheat, Poulard wheat, Common wheat, Orien tal wheat, Persian wheat, 2-row barley, Rye (*secale cereale*), Mediterranean oats, Common oats, Lentil, Lupin.

(*b*) *Forage plants:* Alfalfa, Persian clover, Vetch, Hairy vetch, Fenugreek.

(*c*) *Fruits:* Apple, Pear, Pomegranate, Cherry, Fig, Quince, Hawthorn.

V. *Mediterranean Centre:*

Borders of Mediterranean sea (Species 84)

(*a*) *Cereals* and *Legumes*: *Durum* swheat, Emmer wheat, Polish wheat, Spelt wheat, Sand oats. Mediterranean oats, Canary grass, Grasspea (*Lathyrus sativus*), Bold seeded pea, Lupins (*Lupinus* spp.)

(*b*) *Forage plants:* Egyptian clover, White clover, Crimson clover, Serradella (*Ornithopus sativus*)

(*c*) *Oil and Fibre plants:* Rape (*Brassitca napus*), Black mustard (*B. migra*), Flax.

(*d*) *Vegetable plants:* Cabbage: Turnip, Lettuce, Garden beet, Celery, Asparagus, Chicory, Parsnip, *Rhubard*

(*e*) *Ethereal oil and spices:* Caraway, Pepper Mint, Anise, Sage, Thyme

VI. *Abyssinian Centre:* Abyssinia; Eritrea and parts of Somaliland (Species 88)

(*a*) *Grains and legumes:* Poulard, Emmer and Polish wheat, Barley, Grain sorghum, Pearlmillet, African millet (Finger millet), Cowpea, Flax.

(*b*) *Miscellaneous:* Sesame, Castor bean, Gardem cress, Coffee, Okra, Myrrh, Indigo.

VII. *South Mexican and Central American Centre:*

Guatemala, Costa Rice, Horduras, and S. Mexico.

(*a*) *Grains* and *legumes:* Maize, Common beam, Lima beam Grain amaranthus, Tepary bean, Jack bean,

(*b*) *Fibre plants:* Henequen/Sisal (*Agave sisalana*), Upland add Bourbon cotton

(*c*) *Melon plants*: Malabar gourd, Winter pumpkin

(*d*) *Miscellaneous:* Tobacco, Guava, Papaya, Sweet potato, Arrow root, Cashew, Wild black berry, Cacao, Cherry tomato, Cochenial, Pepper.

VIII. *South American Centre (Species. 62):*

(*i*) *Peruvian, Ecudorean, Bolivian Centre:* It includes High mountainous regions, Centre of megalithics pre-Inca civilization.

Grains and legumes: Starchy maize, Lima beans, Common bean.

Roots and Tubers: Edible canna, Potato, Andean potato, Edible naturtium.

Fibre plants: Egyptian cotton.

Vegetable plants: Tomato, Pumpkin, Pepper, Ground cherry, Pepino.

Fruits and *Miscellaneous:* Tobacco, Guava, Quinine, Heilbora, passion flower.

(*ii*) *Chio Centre:* Island near coast of S. Chile, Common potato, Wild strawberry.

(*iii*) *Brazilian-Peraguan Centre:* Groundnut, Pineapple, Cashew, Brazil nut, Rubber etc.

According to Vavilov's list, 400 out of 600 plants originated in S. Asia between 20 and 45 N. Latitude and nearly 100 in America. There may be smaller centres of origin within centres of origin which are called agro-ecological groups.

Man has played a commendable role in migration / introduction of plants *e.g.* Malaya produces much of rubber, but its tree *Hevea braziliensis* originated in S. America. Coffee originated probably in Africa, but has become popular all over the world. National and international bureaux have been established for plant introduction.

Cereals: Any gramineous plant yielding an edible farinaceous grain, as wheat, rye, rice, oats, maize etc. or the grain itself or some edible preparations of it especially breakfast food made from some of its grains or of pertaining to grain or the plants producing it (the term has been derived from the Latin word *cerealis* pertaining to *ceres*, the goddess of corn). However, the agronomic classification of the Common grain crops includes cereal or grain crops as one of the important group of field crops. Most of the cereals are members of grass family and are grown for grain. The term cereal denotes a plant or a grain including a number of manufactured and processed foods. The example includes wheat, barley, oats as well as sorghum (milo-too), pearl-millet, finger millet and the group of minor millets *viz*., harnyard millet, foretail millet, proso millet etc., as listed later here below: maize, sorghum and pearl millet are known as coarse grains. According to Mangelsdorf (1953) cereals among the grains occupy the most important position as would be evident from the statement, "No civilization worthy of the name has been founded on any agricultural basis other than the cereals".

The cereals are most extensively adaptable. Most of them are tillering type other than maize, sorghum (some types are tillering type as well) embody compact and drying grains easy to handle, transport and store. They have high carbohydrate, content, adequate proteins (7-10 per cent), in addition to fats, vitamins and minerals. It is important to note that it is easy to cultivate most of the cereals. Millets, teff and Job's tears are also included in this group of crops. Buck wheat and grain amaranthus though do not belong to the grass family, are included in the list of cereals. Some of the important cereals are presented below as stated earlier:

Wheat	*Triticum* L. ($x = 7$)
	T. aestivum L.
$n = 7$	*T. aegiloipes*, Wild einkorn
	T. monococcum (einkorn)
	T. dicoccoides (Wild emmer)
	T. durum (Macaroni wheat)
	T. persicum (Persian wheat)
$n = 14$	*T. turgidum* (Rivet wheat)
	T. polonicum (polish wheat)
	T. timopheevi
Hexaploid	*T. aestivum* (Common / bread wheat)

T. Sphaerococcum (Shot wheat)

$n = 21$ — *T. Compactum* (Club wheat)

T. Spelta (Spelt wheat)

T.

Macha (Macha wheat)

Rice — *Oryza Sativa* L. ($n = 12$)

O. glaberrima

O. longistaminata

O. perenisis

O. balunga

O. officinalis

Maize (Corn): Corn = a grain or a seed especially of cereals or growing of the cereal plants.

Zea mays L. ($n = 10$)

Dent corn	*Zea mays*	var.	*indentata*
Flint / yakeen	*Zea mays*	var.	*indurata*
Sweet corn	*Zea mays*	var.	*saccharata*
Flour corn	*Zea mays*	var.	*amylacea*
Waxy corn	*Zea mays*	var..	*ceratina*
Pop corn	*Zea mays*	var.	*everta*
Pod corn	*Zea mays*	var.	*tunicata*

Oats: *Avena fatua*

A. sterilis

A. byzatina

Rye:

Secale cereale

S. montanum

S. anatolicum

Triticale:

Manmade cereal

Wild grass × wheat

Sorghum:

Sorghum bicolor ($n = 20$)

S. versicolor (5 haploid chromosomes)

Sorghum groups:

Kafir	Hegari	Mils
Feterita	Durra	Shallu
Sorgo	Broomcorn	Sudan grass
	Johnson grass	

Pearl millet: Its other common names include cattail millet, bulrush millet, candle millet.

Pinnisetum glaucum

P. americanum syn. and *P. typhoidas*

Finger millet:

Eleusine coracana

Minor millets.

Foxtail millet	:	*Setaria italica*
Barnyard millet	:	*Echinocloa frumentacea*
Kado millet	:	*Paspalum scrobiculatum*
Proso millet	:	*Panicum miliaceum*
Browntop millet	:	*Panicum ramsum*
Little / millet	:	*Panicum miliare*
Fonio millet	:	*Digitaria* spp.
Jeff millet	:	*Eragrostus tef* and *E. abissinica*

Grain legumes: This group of crops are also called pulse crops/grains. Legumes comprise a very rich source of proteins and are an effective substitute of meat for the vegetarians. Their root tuburcles are commonly called *nodules* embodying nitrogen fixing bacterial capable of hauling down free nitrogen present in the atmosphere to produce nitrate and nitrite. Their protein content, a dietary essentiality of vegetarian sector of human and animal population generally ranges from 17-30 per cent. However, some of them like soybean embodies as high as 42 per cent of protein by weight. Though the grain legumes, by and large, contain as low as 2 per cent of fat, soybean embodies as much as 20 per cent of oil and hence its regarded as an oilseed crop as well. It must be noted that the pulses contain as per estimates 5 times more of riboflavin and 10 times more of thiamine than the commonly consumed cereals. All the same, the legume grain embodied protein is regarded as incomplete from nutritional viewpoint, but it is complemented by cereals. The sprouted legume grains make an excellent source of vitamin C. Some of the legumes contain toxic and biologically active substances *viz.* tripsin inhibitors, haemaglutinins, cynogenetic or cynogenic glucosides, saponins, goitrogens / goitrogenic substances, anticoagulants, toxic histones and substances that bring about disabilities like lathyrism and favism.

The common grain legumes , are:

Pigeonpea / Red gram / congpea:

Cajanus cajan ($n = 11$) estimated protein content is 22-23 per cent

C. indicus

C. cajan var. *bicolor*

C. cajan var. *flavus*

Chickpea / Bengal gram

Cicer arietinum

Phaseolus: Includes approximately 200 species

Phaseolus spp. ($x = 11, 12$)

Common beans: French beans / Kindney bean / Haricot bean

Phaseolus uilgaris ($n = 11$) protein 22-23 per cent

P. mungo, black gram ($n = 11, 12$) protein 23-24 per cent

urdbean

woolly pyrol

P. aureus mungbean ($n = 11$) protein 23-24 per cent

golden gram

green gram

Mothbean: Mothbeen ($n = 11$) protein 23-24 per cent

Field pea:

Pisum sativum ($n = 7$) protein 23-24 per cent

Goldenpea, *P. sativum* var. *hortense*

P. sativum var. *arvense*

Cowpea:

Vigna unguiculata ($n = 11$) protein 25-26 per cent

Catjuing cowpea, *V. unguiculata* var. unguiculata (Africa)

Common cowpea, *V. sinensis* (Africa)

Yard long cowpea, *V. sinensis*

or

Asparagus bean, *V. sesquipedalis*

Lentil:

Lens esculenta (Africa) protein 25-26 per cent

Masur / Maika:

Lens esculentus sub-sp. *macrospermae*

Masuri: L. esculenta sub-sp. *microsperma*

Grasspea: Checkling vetch / Lathyrus pea / Chickling pea

Lathyrus sativus ($n = 7$) protein 28-29 per cent

Cluster bean:

Cymopsis tetragonoloba syn. *psoraloides* protein 33-34 per cent

Horsegram:

Dolichos uniflorus ($n = 11, 12$) protein 24-25 per cent

Hyacinth bean: Bonavist bean Lhobia bean

Dolichos lab lab

Lab lab vulgaris

Lab lab niger

Lab lab bengalensis

Lab lab purpureus

Oilseeds crops: These crops yield vegetable oil which remains in liquid state at room temperature. On the contrary, fats remain either in fully solid or in nearly solid state at room temperature and are also known as "expressed or fixed oils". The oil of an oilseed remains in the form of small droplets within the plant cell predominantly in the seed and most commonly in the cotyledons and the endosperm. In the cereals the fats are exclusively contained in the embryo. The oils and fats are much less commonly located in roots, stems and leaves. These are triglycerides of the complex organic fatty acids. The fatty acids are either saturated or unsaturated.

The examples of fatty acids are capric, lauric, palmitic, stearic, myristic etc.

The unsaturated fatty acids include oleic, linoleic, linolenic, recinoloic, euric, etc.

Waxes unlike oils are fatty acid esters of mono-hydroxy alcohol. These usually cover the leaves and stem surfaces of the plants in order to minimise the transpirational water losses. However, these are seldomly located within the active / living plant cell. The most suitable ones for day-to-day use are *carnauba* and - *candililla* Vegetable oils are different from the essential oils since these oils do not volatilize at the room temperature and cannot be distilled. These oils leave greasy stains on clothes, paper and are used to make soap with alkali (caustic soda) embody no strong odour, are tasteless and become rancid on exposure to air for a long period of time.

Oil-yielding plants:

The important ones are given below.

Rape / Mustard and their relatives ($x = 8, 9, 9$) *Brassica* spp. 30-45 per cent oil content

(Includes 150 species both annual as well as biennial)

- Turnip rape ($n = 10$) *Brassica campestris* var. (brown sarson)
- Turnip rape ($n = 10$) *Brassica campestris* var. (yellow sarson)
- Indian rape (*toria*) *Brassica campestris* var. *toria*
- Indian mustard (Brown mustard / rai) *Brassica juncea* ($n = 18$)
- Black mustard (True mustard) *Brassica nigra* ($n = 18$)
- White mustard (True mustard) *Brassica alba* syn. *sinapsis alba* ($n = 12$)
- Rocket cress (*taramira*) *Eruca vesicaria* sub-sp. *sativa*
- Linseed (flax) *Linum utitatissimum* 33-43 per cent oil
- Castor (castor seed /bean) *Ricinus communis* 49-50 per cent oil

(Ricin, ricinine and allergen are embodied and ricin is a blood coagulant and hence cannot be fed to the livestock etc.)

- Coconut *cocos mucifera* 60-65 (75) copra per cent oil

[Toddy (contains 6 per cent alcohol), it is an exudate collected from unopened spadices, is usually drunk fresh, is also boiled to prepare jaggery or fermented to produce vinegar]

Niger seed or Ramtil: Guizotis abyssinica Cass; Compositae

Ramtil is a herb native to tropical Africa. It is an important plant from the viewpoint of the oil quality and potential. In India, it is grown in Madhya Pradesh, Andhra Pradesh, Karnataka, Bihar and Orissa. It is also grown in certain regions of Arunachal Pradesh, Gujarat, Uttar Pradesh (Mirzapur district), Rajasthan (Udaipur and Banaswara districts), West Bengal and Tamil Nadu. It is extensively grown on marginal and sub-marginal lands particularly in tribal areas on hill tops and slopes. However, it grows very well on well drained deep soils. It can be grown both in *rabi* and *kharif* seasons. Ramtil seeds yield semi-drying oil. It is used for cooking and in the manufacture of paints, varnishes and soaps. The seed cake is generally fed to the milch cattle. Its cake is also used as an organic manure. Its seeds are edible.

Jatropha species with their desirable attributes are presented below:

Attributes of Indian *Jatropha* Species

Scientific name	*Common name*	*Origin*	*Distribution in India*	*Desirable attributes*
J. gossypifolia L.	Bellyache Bush, Cotton-leafed physic eating caterpillars.	Brazil country	Throughout the mites and leaf	Resistant to scale. nut tolerant to saline soils
J. multifida L.	Coral plant, Fimon, Spanish physic nut	S. America (Barbados)	Throughout the country	Ornamental, photoperiod insensitive, non-dehiscent capsules
J. integerrima Jacq. (*J. panduraefolia Andr., J. acuminata Desv., J. hastata Griseb Manihot diversifolia Sweet*)	Fiddle-leaved Jatropha	Cuba	Throughout the country	Xerophytic adaptation, resistant to diseases and pests except leaf webber and scale. photoperiod insensitive
J. podagrica Hook	Guatemala Rhubarb, Tartago or Gouty-stemmed Jatropha, Hanuman nangtaen	Central America (Panama)	Throughout the country	Ornamental and adapts well to xerophytic conditions, photoperiod insensitive
J. curcas L.	Pinhao, French physic nut, purging nut, Sabudam, Barbados nut	South America (Peru)	Throughout the country	High oil content, drought resistant, frost tolerant, less attacked by insects and pests
J. glandulifiera Roxb (*J. glauca Vahl*)		India	S. India, Uttar Pradesh, Bengal	Resistant to pests and diseases
J. wightiana (*J. peltata, J. villosa*)	—	—	Deccan Peninsula Coimbatore	—
J. heterophylla (*J. heynii*)	—		S. India	Ephemeral
J. nana		—	Poona and Bombay	—

Source: Directorate of Oil-seeds Research, Rajendranagar, Hyderabad, A.P. (India).

The word Jatropha has originated from Greek word namely Jatros: Doctor, trophe: nutrition referring to its medicinal utility. It is a member of Euphorbiaceae family. It has $2n = 22$, rarely 44 too. It is morphologically diverse with 160-175 old and new world known species consisting of trees, shrubs, sub-shrubs and facultative annuls. A number of species are cultivated for ornamental purposes. Jatropha plant embodies an extensive environmental tolerance and is found both in the seasonal dry tropics as well as equatorial humid region. It is propagated both by seed and stem cuttings. It has been found that amongst the species listed above J. *curcas* and J. *gossypifolia* possess a potential which can be made use of commercially. Jatropha species are rich in oil content as indicated below:

Species	*Oil per cent*
J. curcas L.	48.5
J. gossypifolia L.	28.5
J. integerrima Jae q.	33.2
J. multifida L.	32.4
J. podagrica L.	34.1
J. glandulifera	27.2

Its oil is used for illumination and also as a lubricant. Cooked oil is mixed with iron oxide and is used as varnish for furniture. It is also used to make alkyds, plasticizers and as softener for hide. The oil is applied externally to cure rheumatism and paralysis affected areas. Dark blue dye from bark, yellow dye from roots and tan to brown colour dye from latex are variously used for colouring clothes, fishing nets and as marking ink. The sticky, opalescent, acrid and astringent latex is used for domestic medicine for healing ulcers, eczema, rheumatism and is antisyphilitic. Decoction of leaves and roots is given for diarrhoea.

Oil cake is rich in nitrogen and phosphorus and is used as a source of organic manure. Its green leaves and branches make an excellent green manure for coconut trees. Eri silk worm are fed on its leaves.

Jatropha as a source of fuel also compares well with diesel fuel as per estimates made in terms of Mj / kg as shown below:

Fuel type	*Mj / kg*
No. 2 Diesel Fuel	42.6-45
J. curcas	39.6-41.8
J. glandulifera	47.2
J. gossypifolia	42.2
J. multifida	57.1

Jojoba: pronouned as ho ho ba

***Simondsia chinensis* (Syn. *S. Californica*)**

Jojoba is an exotic shrub or a small tree. It is commonly found in the desert regions of Mexico and California and Arizona states of USA. It grows naturally on marginal soils like stony and gravelly (pabbly soils). It is an ever-green shrub, makes a slow growth, but has a long life varying from 40 to 200 years. It bears male and female flowers on different plants, *i.e.*, its population is composed of male plus female plants. In nature, the male and female plants occur usually in a ratio of 1 : 1. But when it is commercially cultivated, the recommended ratio is 1 : 4. This ratio is attainable by planting two seedlings in each pit and by removing the undesirable plants after one or two years when it starts flowering.

The male flowers are always borne in clusters of 7 to 36. On the contrary, the female flower appears only singly from one gland of a branch. It usually comes to flowering in October-November and seeds mature by April. However, sometimes flowering also takes place in April-May and the seeds are obtainable in October. It may be added that the seeds set in April-May give higher seed yield than those obtained from October-harvested plants. The seed is long, cylindrical and tapering. The oil content of the seed varies from 45 to 55 per cent. Its oil properties are identical to the whale sperm oil. It is used in the manufacture of cosmetics and adhesives. The oil is used in gears of the machines operating at high pressure and high temperature. One kg of jojoba contains 1000-1200 seeds. It is important to note that the seed viability is lost by about 80-90 per cent in one year and it is almost completely lost in 3-5 years. First flowering takes place within 3-4 years, but the seed yield of about 1 kg/plant is obtainable only after 10 years. It is recommended to have at least 1800 female plants / ha so that after 10 years an approximate seed yield of 1800 kg/ha is obtained:

– *Oil palm* (African oil palm) *Elaeis guineensis* 49-50 per cent oil.

– (Bunches bear 200-2000 fruits weighing 80-82 kg. contains β-carotene, a precursor of vitamin A.)

– Tunge relatives *Aleurites* spp. 50-60 per cent oil in kernel.

– (It yields the vegetable oil which contains alaeastearic acid, press cake contains toxalbumin, a toxic substance. It has not been commercially made use of in India so far.)

– Common olive: *Olea europaea* L. (Olearanceae)

Fruit contains 25-60 per cent oil

Mesocarp (pulp) contains 75 per cent oil

Kernel contains 12-28 per cent oil

– (A green plant contains a bitter glucoside called oleuropein which is removable by sodium hydroxide.)

– Safflower. *Carthamus tinctoius* L. contains 32-40 per cent oil

– Sunflower: *Helianthus annus* (Compositae) L. seed has 24-45 per cent oil

Kernel 45-55 per cent oil

– Perilla: *Perilla frutescens* (L.) Britt. (syn. P. *ocymoides* L.s).

Seed embodies 35-45 per cent oil

– Cramb / Abissinian crambi: *Crambe abissinica* contains 30-32 per cent oil (Cruciferae)

– Physic / Purging nut: *Jatropha curcas* L.

– Groundnut / peanut: *Arachis hytrogaea* L. (Papilionaceae)

It is either an erect or trailing herb grown for its underground pods. Peanut is believed to be a native to Brazil. But, in India, it is an important oilseed crop. The main groundnut growing Indian states are mainly in southern region. It is also an important crop in Maharashtra and Gujarat. Northern states have started growing groundnut especially knitted in various cropping systems. Peanut butter is prepared out of its seeds which are also called nuts. The nuts are roasted and consumed after adding salt and other likeable spices. A significant part of peanut oil is used to make vegetable ghee or vanaspati by hydrogenation nor refined as such as a cooking oil. Groundnut cake is a protein rich livestock feed. Its protein is used to manufacture a textile fibre called ardil. Peanut is a food rich in protein, vitamin B and nicotinic acid. Its high and low quality oil used to manufacture pharmaceuticals and soaps or as a lubricant respectively. Husk gives activated carbon and the shells make a source of fuel or are used to prepare coarse boards and cork replacements. Green haulms and stalks make a good hay and a source of fodder. Groundnut is a legume and fixes atmospheric nitrogen which augments soil fertility.

Soybean: *Glycine max* (L.) Merr. [syn. *G. soja* (L.) Sieb & Zuic ; *G. hispida* (Moench) Maxim. [*Soja max* (L.) Piper]

A native of S-E Asia, now grown in M.P., U.P., H.P., Punjab, M.S., Gujarat, Naga Hills, Manipur and Kashmir. It yields edible seeds. Its semi-drying oil is used to manufacture margarine and also to prepare oil sloth, linoleum, paints, printing inks, soaps, disinfectants, and insecticides. Lectin, phospholipids obtained as by-product of the oil industry is used as wetting and stabilizing agent in food, cosmetic, pharmaceutical, plastic, leather and soap industry. It is also used to prepare lipoxidase enzyme, extensively used in baking industry for bleaching. Soymeal, a residue after oil extraction is a rich source of protein and makes an excellent cattle-feed. Meal and soybean protein are used to manufacture synthetic fibre, adhesives and the textile sizes. Its germinated seeds provide a rich source of vitamin C. Incidentally, it may be added that isolates of beans are spun to make protein fibres used to prepare different kinds of food products.

A brief account of margosa tree or *neem* tree (*Melia azadirachta* L.) (See *Azadirachta indica* J. Juss) is given below:

Azadirachta indica A. Juss; Mellaceae.

It is a common road side tree bearing small, white and sweet scented flowers. It comes to flowering during early April in North Indian conditions. The tree is considered a good purifier of air on account of its large leaf area. The studies reveal that *neem* tree is a native of Burma, but it is grown everywhere in India. Oil cake is obtained from the seed and used as manure to slow down the availability of applied fertilizer nitrogen. Its green twigs are used as tooth brushes for cleaning teeth, and as a prophylactic for mouth and teeth complaints. Its different parts are used for medicinal purposes. The dried leaves are placed along with clothings to repel insects. The dried leaves greatly help in preservation of woollen clothings. An extract of leaves is used in tooth-pastes and soaps.

Neem seeds yield well known margosa oil embodying disagreeable garlic gas like flavours. The oil has been found effective to treat leprosy and other skin diseases. The oil is also used as a cure for mange in dogs. The poultice prepared of leaves help in healing of wounds. Ripe fruits are edible. Recently a number of insecticides have been prepared from the seed of this tree. It has a bitter taste and disagreeable odour which cannot be removed by conventional methods. A process has recently been developed to extract the bitter consequences from *neem* oil. The oil also has been found suitable for soap making and for hydrogenetic purposes. The oil is used as an anticeptic as well as for illumination purposes. The stolon separated from the fruits are used as beads and rosaries and necklaces. It is a common practice that a during the smallpox, garlands made of *neem* fruit stones are hung on the doors with the plea that such a practice precludes the spread of infection. *Azadirachtin*, a substance isolated from the tree has been found to embody insect repellent and insecticidal properties.

Its gum from the bark is used in different medicines as stimulant as well as for dyeing of silk. The bark has been found useful in fever, nausea, worms and skin diseases. The bitter substances of *neem* oil are reported to have been obtained by extraction with alcohol. The chief component of the oil is nimbidin which tastes very bitter. Nimbidin is used to make a number of pharmaceutical preparations including emulsions, liquors, ointments, cosmetics namely lotions, soaps, shampoos and also used for gargles. Its timber is used to prepare agricultural implements as well as furniture.

Bead Tree:

(Pride of India, China Tree)

Melia azedarach L. ($2n = 28$); Meliaceae.

It is a native of West Asia, naturalised throughout the length and breadth of the warm tracts. In India, tree is distributed both in plains and in the mountainous sub-Himalayan tracts. This species is mostly grown for ornamental and shade purposes due to its vast growing habit. The kernel content is 9.5 per cent of the whole fruit which has an oil content of 30 per cent. The fatty acid composition of bead tree oil is as follows:

Palmitic	8.4 per cent
Stearic	4.0 per cent
Oleic	23.7 per cent
Linoleic	62.9 per cent
Arachidic	0.5 per cent

The oil is very rich in unsaturated fatty acids to the extent of 87 per cent. Melia oil is more unsaturated than *neem* oil. It is used in the manufacture of soaps, detergents, alkyl resins, protective coatings, floor coverings, greases and floatation agents. The protein content of the fruit, seed and kernel has been estimated at 2.7, 2.4 and 18.2 per cent, respectively. Stones of fruits are used as beads in necklaces and rosaries. Its wood make a very good source of fuel. The wood seasons well and is easy to work and finish and is used for making toys, packing and museum cases, sportsware, agricultural implements etc. Wood and its bark can be used for controlling insect pests of crops. The leaves make a good source of fodder. The leaves, bark and drupes embody insect growth regulation and antifeedant activities. The bark and wood are used for different medicinal purposes, e.g., infusion of bark has anthelminthic activity. Aqueous extracts of heart wood has been found useful in asthama. The leaf juice is regarded as antheminthic, decoction of leaves is regarded as astringent and soomachic. The poultice of flowers is applied to eruptive skin diseases and for killing lice. The fruit is used as a disinfectant, while its seed consumption is prescribed in rheumatism.

Other species

The other species of Melia-M. *compositae* (Syn. M. *dubia* Hiern non cav.); Meliaceae.

It is distributed in eastern Himalayas, Assam, Western ghats, Gangetic plains and Deccan. The fruit pulp is useful for colic. The juice of green fruits with one third of its weight of sulphur and equal quantity of curd, heated and is applied to skin diseases and sores infested with maggots. The wood is used for making tea chests and for other identical purposes.

Fibre crops

A fibre means an elongated thick-walled cell found especially in the sclerenchyma tissue and providing support for the plant. It has also been defined as a thread or a structure or object resembling a thread like a slender root of a plant of grass family. In fact, a fibre represents an elongated tapering thick-walled plant cell void at maturity that imparts elasticity, flexibility and tensile strength. Thus, a fibre is a slender, and greatly elongated natural or synthetic filament like cotton, wool, gold, glass, asbestos or rayon. It is typically capable of being spun into yarn, that is, it can be spun, woven or felted. Further, botanically fibre comprises non-living plant cells embodying thick walls and small lumen providing strength and rigidity to the plant cells occurring either singly or in groups. The bundles are cemented together at the tapering ends dovetailing obliquely with the immediate next one forming the sheets of tissues. It has been estimated that the average fibre length varies from one to three millimeters. However, some fibres may be as long as 55 centimetres like that of ramie. A vegetative fibre is made chiefly of cellulose (64-94 per cent), but it also contains lignins, hemi-cellulose, resins, pectic substances, fats, waxes and mineral matter. On the contrary, animal fibre mainly consists of proteins and represents a thread like structure, as a muscle cell or nerve fibre. Dietary fibre denotes the indigestible element of foods derived from plants which adds bulk to the animal diet. This portion of animal diet is also called bulk or roughage and stimulates the intestine to peristalsis. Economically important fibres are derived from 44 plant families. The families *viz*., Gramineae, Malvacea, Palmae, Linaceae, Bombaceae and Cannabinaceae *etc*., are main contributors of vegetative fibre some of them are as follows:

Surface fibre	:	Cotton, Kapok
Soft fibre	:	Flare, Hemp, Jute, Ramie, Kenaf
Hard fibre	:	Abaca, Sisal, Coir
Cotton	:	Gossypium spp. ($x = 13$)
Old world cotton	:	($n = 13$)

Herbaceae: Egyptian cotton or sea-island cotton *Gossypium arboreum* L var. *nadam* (Watt) Prokh. (Syn. *G. barbadense* L.); Malvaceae.

– Asiatic cotton / Levant cotton: *Gossypium herbaceum* L. (Syn. *G. wightianum* Tod.; *G. obtusifolia* Roxb. p.p., Malvaceae. New World cotton ($n = 26$).

Hirsuta:

Upland cotton: *Gossypium hirsutum* L.

(Syn. *G. religiosum* L.); Malvaceae

Gossypium barbadense L. (*G. arboreum* L. var. *nadam* (Watt) Prokh.); Malvaceae.

(*Gossypium arboreum* L. (Syn. *G. nanking Meyen*; *G. indieum* Tod; *G. neglectum* Tod.

Tree cotton is cultivated all over India and main products of cotton seed are linter, hull, oil and meal or cake. all of these are of industrial value staple cotton is made use of in the manufacture of textiles, rubber-tyre fabrics and other woven products. Short fibres adhering to seed even after ginning are called 'linters' or 'fuzz'.Linters are used as high grade cellulose suitable to manufacture superior acetates and viscous rayon, cellulose esters and esters. nitrocellulose,.liqueurs and stuffing material. The hull (outer covering of seed) is used as cattle feed. manure, and soil conditioner, fillers in plastics, manufacture of insulating materials *etc.* cotton/seed oil (a semi-drying oil) is used to manufacture *vanaspati ghee*, soap, paint, varnish, toilet preparations, in leather industry and as a lubricant. Its seed meal is rich in protein and fit for human consumption. Three forms of its fibre are available to the paper industry *viz.*, rag fibres, second-cut cotton linters and cotton combers. The first one is used to manufacture finer papers.

Silk cotton (kapok) (n = 36-42) : *Ceiba pentandra* (L.) *Gaertn.* (Syn. *Eriodendron anfractuosum* DC; *Bombax pentandrum* L.; Bombacaceae.)

Silk cotton is a tree which is extensively distributed in the forest of western and southern India. It is also planted around villages and places of worship especially temples. *Kapok* means floss derived from the capsule (inner fruit wall) wherein seeds lie loose on fruit maturity. The fibres (hairs) are lustrous, resilient, elastic and buoyant. These are liable to bunch when used in upholstery and are made use of in the manufacture of life-belts and life-jackets on account of their high degree of buoyancy as well as resistance to waterlogging. These are also used in sound-proofing of rooms, manufacture of mattresses, pillows, cushions, surgical bandages and clothings made for aviators. In padded form, it is used for thermal and acoustic insulations in studios, hospitals, tanks and aeroplanes. The oil extracted from its seeds is edible and is also used to manufacture soaps as well as lubricants.

Flax (n = 15); *Linum usitatissimum* L. *Linaceae*:

Its plant is a herb and makes an important oilseed crop in M.P., U.P., M.S., Bihar and Rajasthan. Its oil is primarily non-edible yet used for edible purposes too. It is mainly used to prepare paint, soft soap, varnish, and printers ink. Its oil though only on a small scale, is also used in leather finishing compounds, lubricants, greases, polishes and plasticizers. Cake makes a good cattle feed and an organic manure. The oil is used as a laxative for cattle and horses. Linseed mucilage is used in cosmetic and pharmaceutical industries as demulcent poultice to apply on inflammations ulcers is made by crushing its seeds. Stem fibre is a raw material for linen textile manufacture, oil cloth, water-proof fabrics, twine, high grade paper pulp, cigarette, air-mail, bond and writing papers.

Hemp (n = 10); *Cannabis sativa* L.; Cannabinaceae:

Hemp is a tall and smelling type of herb originally a native of Central Asia, but now it is grown all over India. It is commonly self-seeded and grows in waste lands and grounds, along road and rail track sides. It becomes gregarious along irrigation channels leading specially to gardens and orchards Hemp plant yields three valuable products *viz.* fibre from stems, oil from seeds and narcotics including *bhang*, *ganja* and *charas* from leaves and flowers. Ropes, twines, canvas, nets and tarpaulins are made from fibre. Drying oil is used in paints, varnishes and soap manufacture. *Bhang* is made from dry leaves and flowering shoots of male as well as female plants both cultivated and wild. *Ganja* consists of dried unfertilized female inflorescences, and *charas* is crude resin. The active principle of these narcotics is resinous exudation from the gladular hairs of leaves, stems and inflorescences. *Ganja* and *charas* are two forms in which drug is used for smoking, but *bhang* is consumed in the form of a drink after proper grinding along with some other preferred eatables. The drug is also used as a stomachic, antispasmodic, analgesic and sedative.

Sannhemb sunnhemb L. (*Crotolaria juncea* L.; Papilionaceae)

It is a tall shrub cultivated throughout India. Stem fibre is used for unsized twine, fishing nets, cot stringing, matting, coarse canvas, bags and ropes. Its stem fibre is eminently suitable to use as a cigarette paper as well as high quality tissue paper owing to its high cellulose and low ash content. Flowers are used as vegetable. The stems make an excellent and very well known green manure. Its seeds also embody 15 per cent gum. Its other species are put to various commercially viable industrial uses. These species are, *crotolaria - anagiroides* H.B. & K.; Papilionaceae which is a native to venezuela, used as green manure to augment soil organic matter status and as a shade tree in tea and coffee plantations, makes an excellent mulch against splash and other hydro-erosion soil losses; *Crotolaria burhia* Buch-Ham ex Benth is a diffuse, profusely branched xerophytic undershrub found in Rajasthan, Gujarat, U.P. and Punjab and its branches and leaves make good fodder, while stem fibre is used to make ropes and cordage; *Crotolaria medicaginea* Lamk. var. *luxurians* (Benth.) Baker., Papilionaceae; is a common, perennial herb or undershrub, used as fodder for camels and goats, *Crotolaria retusa* Desv. (Syn. *C. stricata* DC.) called stripped *crotolaria*, Papilionaceae, is a herb grown all over India, makes an excellent cover and green manure crop, the gum content of seed has been estimated at 13 per cent; *Crotolaria retusa* L, golden yellow sweet pea, Papilionaceae, is grown all over India, stem bark fibre is used to make cordage and canvas, seeds embody 13 per cent gum, reported to cause liver cirrhosis in human beings and the cattle; *Crotolaria* sericea Retz. Papilionaceae, has been introduced from Argentina, this robust undershrub makes a very good green manure crop; *Crotolaria usaramoensis* Bak. f.; Papilionaceae; has been introduced from Australia and is used as green manure.

– Agave Sisal / Ramie (*Agave sisalana* Perr. ex Engelm.: Syn. A. *rigida Mill.* var. sisalana; Agavaceae; It is native to five space here be Mexico and Central America, is a xerophytic perennial embodied with a short thick stem. It is found in Assam, Bihar, Bengal, M.S., and South India, grows well on dry, sandy loam soils, is highly drought resistant. Leaf-fibre is used to manufacture ropes, twines and cordage, its wax resembles carnauba wax, required to prepare polishing compositions and the manufacture of carbon paper, sisal waste, leftover in manufacture of fibre makes a raw material to produce sisal wax, its fibre finds an extensive use in shipping industry owing to its excellent tensile strength and a high degree of resistance to sea-water attack, pulp is used to isolate hecogenin, a raw material to manufacture cortisone and sex hormones, its tow is used for padding materials to use in motor, cars, upholstery, etc., other species include century plant *Agave americana* L. Agavaceae which is a native of South America and is a stout shrub. It is an ornamental shrub, have a short stem and is a half woody plant, bearing a rosette of long, erect, pointed, and fleshy leaves. It is usually planted along railway embankments and roadsides, is suitable for hedging, fencing and preclusion of soil erosion. It is also suitable for seaside landscaping. Cantala, Manila Maguey, Aloe, *Agave cantala* Roxb; Agavaceae, is a native of Mexico, but now naturalized in eastern and western coasts in India, upper Gangetie plains and Punjab, leaf-fibre is used to manufacture ropes, cordage and twines, it is also grown as hedge, effectively controls soil erosion, its pulp, a waste by product left over after fibre separation is used for isolation of hecogenin which is used to manufacture steroid hormones. Blue elephant Aloe (*Agave vera-cruz* Mill, Agavaceae) is a native of Mexico, found all over India, leaf-fibre used to manufacture ropes, condage and mats, also useful as a hedge, and live fence and to check soil erosion.

– Coconut (*Cocos nueifera* L; Palmae):

It is a tall palm chiefly cultivated in Kerala, Tamil Nadu, and Karnataka in India. It yields a variety of commercially important products viz., items of food, drink, oil, fibre, fuel and timber. The fruit-wall consists of the layers *viz.*, a smooth outer exocarp, a fibrous mesocarp and a hard mesocarp. The outer two layers constitute the 'husk' and the endocarp of the coconut shell. The fibre extracted from the retted husk is used to manufacture mats, matting rugs, carpets, thermal insulating boards, while the inferior grades are used to prepare ropes and twines. The coir dust, leftover after the extraction of fibre is made use of as a rooting (plant) medium, as a mulching material for nurseries as well as for composting coupled with other compatible materials. The shell (the hard endocarp) is used for fuel, while whole shells are used for bottles and *hookahs* (Indian smoking pipe). The half shells are used for bowls, cups, measures and scoops. The shells are also carved and decorated and used to make buttons, combs, bangles, musical instruments and in preparations of gas absorbent charcoal which is used in gas masks. The finely ground shell has become an industrial produce and is used as filler in plastics. Its kernel is important as food and it is generally converted to 'copra' by drying, which is, in fact, a source of oil and oil-cake. The oil is used for cooking, lubrication and to manufacture soap, it (oil) also finds other numerous industrial uses including the manufacture of detergents, cosmetics, hair oils as well as a substitute of *ghee* (butter-oil commonly used in dining foods). The coconut-cake, a residue of oil-extracted / expressed residue makes a good cattle-feed. It is extensively used as cattle and poultry feed. The desiccated coconut is used in confectionery and bakery products. The water embodied in fresh green and unripe green fruit makes a likeable as well as useful beverage. The coconut plant embodies plant growth substances and hence is used in experimental culture of plant tissues. Toddy is produced by tapping unopened flower spathe. It is either drunk fresh or is boiled down to prepare jaggery or palm sugar. Arrack is made by fermentation of toddy after distillation. Palm cabbage, freshly cut tender terminal bud is treated as a delicacy. It is consumed either raw or after proper cooking. The plaited coconut leaves provide the material for thatching, making of mats, screens, hats, baskets and make-shift walls of temporary hutments as well as buildings. The leaves are often used for decoration and at festivals and religious functions The mid-ribs of the leaves are made into brooms, baskets and fences. Trinks are used for building purposes.

Substitutes of kapok:

– Red silk cotton or Simul (*Salmalia malabarica* DC) ; Scott & Endl.; *Bombax* ceiba L. (Syn. *B. malabaricum* DC); *Bombacaceae*

It is a tall tree which forms a spreading crown. The flowers are large in size and bright-red in colour. It is regarded as one of the finest trees in India. Though it is spread through the length and breadth of the country, fairly large supplies are available in Assam, the Andamans and Bengal. The flowers and the fleshy calyx, is edible. Its seeds are used as fodder silky floss is obtained from inner fruit-wall and is made use of for stuffing pillows and mattresses. The trunk yields gum as well as juice. Dried juice and gum are used as an adhesive. The main use of its wood is preparation of plywood. It is also used to manufacture matches, packing cases and the mechanical pulp for newsprint. Its other common uses include boarding for different purposes like making of ceiling-boards, picture / photo frames and for use in plywood tea-chests. The other species is *Salmalia insignis* (Wall.) Scott & Endl. (Syn. *Bombax insigne* Wall; Bombacaceae) which is also a large tree and occurs in Western Ghats, Assam and the Andamans. Its wood is used for matches, packing-cases, penholders, veneers and plywood.

– White silk cotton: *Cochlospermum religiosum* (L.) Alston (Syn. C. *gossypium* DC); *Cochlospermaceae*

This tree is native to India and is distributed in the rainfed (dry) forests of the country. The fibre which covers the seed makes a good stuffing material. It also yields edible gum.

– Madar: *Calotropis gigantea* Ait.; Asclepiadaceae

It is a perennial undershrub found everywhere in India. Floss is obtained from the seed and is used for stuffing. Bark of the stem also yields fibre which is used to prepare fishing-nets and twine. Root-bark is used as a herbal medicine in dysentery, acts as substitute for impecacuanha, diaphoretic, expectorant, emetic and makes on effective medicine to cure skin ailments. Leaf-tincture is made use of in intermittent fevers, while dried and powdered flowers are used to cure cold, cough and asthma. Fermented mixture of madar, *maida* (very finely ground wheat flour) and salt is used for unhairing of goat skins for preparation of '*nari*' leather and of the sheep skins to make leather used for cheap book-binding.

– Akund or swallow-wart: *Calotropis procera* (Willd.) Dryand ex W. Ait. (Syn. *Asclepias procera* Willd) Asclepiadaceae

Akund is an evergreen shrub found in Western and Central India. Stem-fibre is used to make cordage and floss from the seed is used as a stuffing material. Stem and leaves make a good green manure. Root-bark is used to cure dysentery. It resembles impecacuanha in its action and is used as diaphoretic, expectorant and emetic. Dried and powdered flowers are used as a medicine to cure cold, cough and asthma.

– Indian reed mace or cat's tail or elephant grass: *Typha elephantina* Roxb., non Grah.; nec. Schimp. ex Rohrb. Syn. T. *angustifolia* Watt, non L. Typhaceae.

It is a very tall growing perennial found in Kashmir and from D.P. to Assam in marshy lands; stagnant, fresh and brackish waters. It is also grown as an ornamental plant as well as a soil conservation agent. Young shoots and rhizomes are edible. It is fed to elephant and hence the name elephant grass. Leaves and stems are used for thatching, to make screens and soft mats as well as ropes. The dried stems are made into pens for writing purposes especially in rural areas where writing ink is used for this purpose.

Its other species *viz.*, Lesser Indian reed-mace. *Typha australis* Schum & Thonn. (Syn. T. *elephantina* Grah., non Roxb.; *T. angustata* Bory & Chaub.) is a tall marshy perennial, occurring throughout India in lakes, ponds, slow running rivers and streams. Its young shoots, inflorescence and rhizomes are edible. Leaves are planted into articles like ropes, chicks, winnowing baskets and mats. Silky florets of spikes make it very good stuffing material for pillows and cushions etc.

VEGETABLE CROPS

According to new Hamlyn Encyclopedia World Dictionary the word vegetable denotes *a herbaceous plant, annual, biennial or perennial whose fruits, seeds, roots, tubers, bulbs, stems, leaves or flower parts are used as food usually as a meal course.* The example includes beans, beet, potato, carrot, cabbage and the edible parts of such plants as leaves of the cabbage. In brief, a vegetable means a herbaceous plant like cabbage, beam or potato grown for an edible part and usually consumed as a part of meal.

Vegetable culture is also known as olericulture which represents a sub-division of horticulture. There are a number of local vegetables, while some of them are described worldwide. In recent years, vegetable culture has rapidly grown into an industry particularly after World War II on account of post harvest technology dovetailed with the means of transportation. As already indicated the word vegetable has not been satisfactorily defined. However, it is applicable to those plants or plant parts that are usually consumed with the main meal course. These are commonly salted and boiled before consumption or used for desserts and salads. Tomato, pepper, okra, egg plant, cucumber and squash etc. Rhubarb is botanically a petiole, commonly served as a dessert like fruit. Vegetables make an excellent source of vitamins and minerals. They also provide roughage. Most of the vegetables are annual and are consumed after harvest because of their very poor storability or shelf life due to high water content which is 80 per cent or more. The vegetables are classified as follows:

Root crops

These are also called earth vegetables. Food is stored in swollen underground parts viz., in true roots or modified stems, tubers, corms and bulbs. These vegetables produce relatively more calories per unit of land area. For instance, one hectare of potato produces 2-2.5 times as many calories as those produced by one hectare of either wheat or rice. The tuberous and rhizomatous crops commonly found in India include potato, cassava, sweet potato, arvids (*Colocasia, alocasia, Xanthosoma* and *amorphophallus coloeus* and arrow roots, miranta, curcuma and canna.

Potato or Irish Potato (x . 25): *Solanum tuberosum*; Solanaceae

It is a bushy herb native to South America. It is grown almost everywhere in India now. Tubers are used as vegetables and also as a raw material for preparing starch and ethyl alcohol.

Sweet Potato (n = 45) : *Ipomea batatas* (L.) Lamk. (Syn. *Convolvulus batata L. Batatas edulis Cloisy*), Convolvulaceae

It is diffusely spreading tuberous plant often rooting at the nodes. It is native to tropical America. Now it is cultivated throughout India for its edible tubers. The tubers are also used for manufacture of industrial alcohol, syrup, glucose and starch. Starch is used in textile, food, paper and cosmetic industries. Its tender tops and leaves are consumed as spinach. The vines and tubers embody fungicidal and bactericidal substances, active against gram-negative and gram-positive, bacteria as well as fungi. The leaves ground with salt are applied to whitlow, a painful inflammation of finger or toe specially near the nail.

Manioc or Tapioca or Cassava (n = 18): *Manihot esculenta* Grantz (Syn. *M. utilissima* Pohl): Euphorbiaceae.

It is a small shrub, native of Brazil. In India, it is grown in Kerala, Tamil Nadu and Karnataka. Tapioca tubers are made commercial use of to obtain starch, sago, samolina and flour.

White Yam or Greater Yam or Asiatic Yam: *Dioscorea alata* L. (Syn. *D. globosa*); Dioscoreaceae

It is a climbing shrub of a polymorphic species. It is a native to east Asia. In India, it is cultivated in Assam, Tamil Nadu, West Bengal, Madhya Pradesh and Gujarat. Tubers are used as a vegetable,

Potato Tam: *Dioscorea alata* L. (Syn. *D. saline* Thump) (*Diversicolor* Bud Ham); Dioscoreaceae.

It is also a climbing harbaceous perennial with large tuberous roots, distributed throughout India. Aerial bulbils or tubers are produced in leaf axils. These are fleshy and succulent. The tubers are detoxicated before consumption.

D. *deltoidea* wall ex Kunth:

It is cultivated in Kashmir, Punjab, Bangalore region of Karnataka and is also distributed throughout north-west Himalayas. Its tubers yield cortisome which is a steroid used in rheumatic diseases and ophthalmic disorders. The process for extracting laevulinic acid and starch with variable by products has been developed. The tubers yield steroidal sapogenins which are considered as a source material for manufacture of oral contraceptives. Clones with higher yields of diosgenin, 7 to 8 per cent on dry weight basis have been recently evolved.

Lesser Yam or Karenpotato: *Dioscorea esculenta* (Lour.) Burkill (Syn. *D. aculeata* L.; D.*fasciculata* Roxb.; *D. sativa*, ; *D. spinosa* Roxb. ex Wall); Dioscoreaceae

It is a prickly climbing shrub found in M.P., U.P., Bengal, Assam, Orissa, Eastern Himalayas, the Andamans, Khasi Hills and Nagaland. Its tubers are consumable. The rhizomes embody enough of diosgenin which may be made use of manufacture the precursors of steroid hormones.

Dioscorea hamiltonii Hook f. (Syn. *D. hookeri* Prain); Dioscoreaceae.

It is also a climbing shrub. It is found in Assam, Orissa, Bengal, Western Ghats and Sikkim. The tubers are edible.

– *Dioscorea pentaphylla* L. (Syn. *D. digitata* Mill; *D. triphylla* L.; *D. jacquemontii* Hook. f.); Dioscoreaceae.

Its place of origin is believed to be tropical region of Asia. However, it is now found allover India. Its tubers also edible. Other species are:

– *Dioscorea tomentosa* Heyne.; Dioscoreaceae.

It is found in southern regions of India. The tubers embody the steroid called sapogenins.

– *Dioscorea prazeri* Prain & Burk. (Syn. *D. clarkei* Prain & Burk.; *D. deltoidea* wall var. Sikkimensis Prain: *D. Sikkimensis* Prain & Burk); Dioscoreaceae

It is distributed in Eastern Himalayas, West Bengal, and Assam. Its tubers contain cortisone used in rheumatism and ophthalmic disorders. Rhizomes are used as a replacement of soap to wash the hair. Rhizomes also yield the steroidal sapogenins used to manufacture oral contraceptives.

Taro and relatives or cocoyam (x = 12, 24) or eddoe or dasheen/arum: *Colocasia erculenta* (L.) Schott. (Syn. *C. antiquorum* Schott var. *esculenta* Schott; *C. esculenta* var. *antiquorum* Hubb. & Rehd; Arum *esculentum* L.; *A colocasia*.); Araceae

It is a rhizomatous herb believed to have its origin from South East Asia. Taro is now grown almost all over India. Its rhizomes are tuberous, starchy and edible. Young leaves are used as a vegetable. Plantsap leaves behind a permanent black stain on the clothes.

Giant taro:

Alocasia cucullata (Lour.) Schott.; Araceae

It is a herb cultivated for edible rhiomes in Assam and West Bengal.

Elephant foot yam or Telugu potato:

Amorphophallus companulatus (Roxb.) Blume ex Dcne. (Syn. *Arum companulatum* Roxb.): Araceae

It is a perennial stemless herb. Belived to be a native to tropical rigions of Asia. Elephant foot yam is cultivated all over India for its large sized corms (looking like elephant foot and hence the name) consumed as vegetable. The tubers have medicinal properties and are used in acute rheumatism.

Tanni or tanier or yautia or cocoyam: *Xanthosoma sagittifoluim* Araceae

Onion (n = 8):

Alluim cepa L. ; Alliaceae.

Though onion is a biennial herb. is commonly grown as an annual throughout India. The important onion growing states include Maharashtra, Tamil Nadu, Karnataka and Madhya Pradesh. It is also an export crop. Its immature as well as mature bulb (rhizomes) are consumed both raw and cooked. It has become so popular and a common vegetable that its deficit brings about a chaotic situation and a political turmoil in India (commonly called *piyaz*-politics). It is extensively used to season the food. Onion embodies medicinal value too. Its bulbs are used as stimulant, expectorant, aphrodisiac and in fatulence as well as dysentery. It has been observed in studies that onion juice enhances diuresis in rabbits. The active principle is glycollic acid.

Top onion or Egyptian onion:

Alluim cepa L. var. *viviparum* (Metz.) Alef.; Alliaceae.

It has been introduced in Coimbatore (Tamil Nadu) and Conoor (Kerala). The rhizomes are made use of as a condiment.

Garlic:

Alluim sativum L.; Alliaceae.

It is believed that garlic is a native to Central Asia. Garlic is a good export crop. The bulbs (rhizomes) serve as a condiment as well as flavouring substance. Its powder makes an excellent condiment used extensively. It is used as carminative and gastric stimulant in the preparation of various medicines. Garlic embodies anti-bacterial properties and is hence made use of both to cure intestinal disorders and various infectious diseases. The anti-bacterial property is on account of allicin which has been observed .to inhibit the growth of a number of microorganisms. Garlic bulbs are used as a medicine to cure cough as well as fever. It also relieves rheumatism, clears chest and augments lungs. The juice is used as rubefacient in dermal ailments, as ear-drops in ear-ache as well as in colic and flatulence. Garlic plant has germicidal properties and exercises an inhibitory influence on gram-negative germs of typhoid-paratyphoid-enteretis group. Garlic is strongly antiseptic, taken internally, it destroys worms and externally, rids the skin of the parasites.

Shallot:

Allium ascalonicum L.; Alliaceae.

Its bulbs (rhizomes) are edible and the green leaves are also consumed. Shallot is mainly grown in Southern regions of India.

Chive:

– *Allium schoenoprasum* L.; Alliaceae.

Chive leaves and bulbs are used as condiment. It is a perennial herb which is distributed from Kashmir to Kumaon in Western Himalayas. It is also grown in hills of South India. The leaves are slender and used for seasoning of foods.

Leek:

Allium ampeloprasum L. var. *porrum* (L.) Gay (Syn. *A. porrum* L); Alliaceae.

It is a known bulb forming stout and tall herb. It is cultivated for its branches, stems and leaves. Leek is believed to be a native to Mediterranean region.

Welsh onion:

Allium fistulosum: Alliaceae.

Chinese chive, fragrant onion or Indian leek:

Allium tuberosum Rotls ex Spreng; Alliaceae.

It is grown in West Bengal for use as a flavouring substance.

Beet root or garden beet:

Beta vulgaris L. (Syn. B. *maritima* L.); Chenopodiaceae.

It is a biennial herb and embodies fleshy leaves and swollen roots. It is believed to be a native of South Europe. Beet root is cultivated in Northern parts of India. The roots and leaves are made use of as vegetable. The studies have revealed that it makes a good crop for sugar production and can be raised in Rajasthan, Sub-mountains, Western parts of Uttar Pradesh, Punjab and Haryana. However, its cultivation has so far not become as common as sugarcane.

Swiss chard:

B. vulgaris var. *Cicla*; Chenopodiaceae.

Garden beet:

B. vulgaris var. *Vulgaris*; Chenopodiaceae.

Turnip:

Brassica tapa (Syn. *B. campestris* L. var. *rapifera* Metz); Cruciferae ($n = 10$).

It is mainly grown in Punjab and Uttar Pradesh in India for its swollen roots which are eaten cooked as vegetables and also used as cattle feed. It is a branched annual.

Ruta baga / swede:

B. napobrassica; Cruciferae.

Carrot:

Daucus carota L. var. *sativa* DC: Umbelliferae.

It is an annual or biennial profusely branching herb. It is believed to have originated from Europe and the Mediterranean region. It is cultivated extensively in Punjab, Haryana. Uttar Pradesh and Madhya Pradesh for its fleshy tap roots which are eaten both raw or cooked or boiled. The tops of carrot make a good fodder for animals particularly the cattle and the horses. Its seeds are aromatic, stimulant, carminative and are useful to cure diseases namely, those pertaining to kidney and dreaded dropsy. The carrot makes an excellent source of carotene, a precursor of vitamin A. An essential oil is obtained from carrot seed. The oil is used in perfumery and for flavouring purposes.

Radish:

Raphanus sativus L; Cruciferae.

Radish is a herb. It is grown in Uttar Pradesh, Punjab; Maharashtra and Vadodra region of Gujarat. Its roots, young leaves as well as fruits are used as vegetable. Its preparation have medicinal value and have been found useful in liver and gall bladder ailments. It is also used for neuralgic headaches sleeplessness and chronic diarrhoea. The roots make a valuable medicine to cure urinary complaints, piles and gastrodynia. The juice of the fresh leaves is used as diuretic and laxative. Seeds are peptic, diuretic and carminative.

Rat-tailed radish:

Raphanus caudatus L. (*R. sativus* var. *caudatus* (L.); Vilmorin; *R. sativus* var. *Mougry* Helm; *R. raphanistrum* sub. sp. caudatus (L.) Thell: Cruciferae.

It is believed that rat-tailed radish has originated from Java. Its fruits are used as vegetables. The pods are used to prepare pickle.

Leafy vegetables

In case of leafy vegetables juvenil stems and foliage are used as vegetable. The leaves are consumed along with salad and are also cooked. Some of them are as follows:

Celery or garden celery:

Apium graveolens L. var. *dulce* (Mill.) DC (Syn. *A. dulce* Mill).; Umbelliferae.

It is believed to be a native of Europe and is now grown in north-western Himalayas and South India. Its seeds are used as stimulants, carminative, nervine sedative and tonic. Its long leaf stalks are used as salad as well as vegetable. The ripe fruits are dried and made use of as spice. Celery seed oil is highly valued as fixative and as an ingredient of perfumery. Its oil is also used for flavouring the food products, liquors and soaps.

Celeriac:

A. graveolens L. var. *rapaceum* (Mill.). DC (Syn. *A. rapacum* Mill.).

The roots of celeriac are eaten as vegetables. The oil is extracted from the fruits and is used as antispasmodic nerve stimulant and rheumatoid arthritis. The seed decoction is used as a popular medicine for rheumatism. It is cultivated mainly in hills of Uttar Pradesh and South India.

Asparagus or garden asparages:

Asparagus officinalis L.

It is believed to be a native of Europe and West Asia. Its young shoots are called spears. It is used as a vegetable.

Cabbage:

Brassica oleraceae L. var. *capitata* L.; Cruciferae.

It is believed to have originated from Europe but is now commonly cultivated in Northern India during winter season. It is an annual plant. Its stems are short and thick and the leaves are pucked into large bug or head which is consumed as a vegetable.

Brussels sprouts or bud brearing cabbage:

B. oleraceae L. var. *gemmifera* DC; Cruciferae.

It is classified as one of the rare vegetables cultivated during winter season in Northern India, Baroda region of Gujarat and Maharashtra State. The stems are tall and erect; axillary buds developed into long small heads which are consumed as a vegetable both raw and cooked. Its young leaves are edible.

Chinese cabbage or shantung cabbage:

B. pekinensis (Lour.) Rupr. (Syn. *B. petsai* Bailey); Cruciferae.

It is mostly grown in Northern regions of India on a very small scale. Its leaves are used as a vegetable.

Broccoli:

B. oleraceae L. var. *botrytis* L.; Cruciferae.

Broccoli and cauliflower have been treated alike. It is becoming an increasingly popular vegetable and is highly nutritive. It is believed to have originated from Western Europe. Cauliflower is grown mainly in Uttar Pradesh, Karnataka, Punjab, Haryana and West Bengal during cool season for its immature inflorescence which are consumed as a vegetable. The inflorescence is called as curd which is also pickled.

Borecole or cole couards broccoli :

B. oleraceae L. var. *acebhala* DC; Cruciferae.

It is grown in Assam, Kashmir, Maharashtra and Baroda region of Gujarat. The young shoots and leaves are consumed as vegetable.

Kohlrabi or knol-khol

B. oleraceae L. var. *gongylodes* L. var. *caulorapa* Pasq.; Cruciferae.

It is grown in Maharashtra, Baroda region of Gujarat, Uttar Pradesh and Punjab. Short and swollen stems are consumed raw or cooked. It is included in the group of kole vegetables.

Rhubarb:

Rhubarb is a French word which denotes *Reubarbarum* alter, of *rha barbarum* lit. Barbarian rhubarb; Rhubarb represents any of the herbs of the polygonaceus genus *Rheum* of Asian plants of the buck wheat family having large leaves with thick succulent petioles often used as food. The dried rhizomes and roots of any of rhubarbs grown in China and Tibet and used as a purgative and stomachic.

Rheum officinale (valued for medicinal rhizomes), *Indian rhubarb* or *Himalayan rhubard*:

Plant with edible leafstalks.

Rheum emodi Wall ex Melissn; Polygonaceae.

It is a herb found in sub-alpine Himalayas. Roots and rhizomes provide drug used as laxative, tonic as well as purgative. Flowers, leaves and leaf-stalks are edible. Powdered roots make a good tooth-powder. The powder also helps in healing of ulcers. Roots along with maddler and potash make red-dye for fabrics.

Garden rhubarb or rhapontic rhubarb or pie-plant:

Rheum rhaponticum L.; Polygonaceae.

It is believed to be a native of Siberia and China. In India it is grown in West Bengal, Nilgiris and Khasi Hills. Pie-plant embodies thick leaf stalks which are used as vegetable.

Nobil-rhubarb:

Rheum nobile Hook. f. & Thomas.; Polygonaceae.

It is a herb which is found in the Himalayas in India. Its stem is consumed as salad; dried leaves provide a replacement of tobacco.

Spinach:

Spinacia oleraceae L.; Chemopodiaceae.

Spinach is belived to be a native of South-West Asia. It is a common herb. Its succulent leaves are used as vegetable. Spinach has been identified as a good source of minerals, vitamin-B-complex, vitamin K, ascorbic acid and carotine.

Palak ($2n = 18$):

Beta vulgaris var. *bengalensis* Roxb.; Chenopodiaceae

In China, it has been known since 647 A.D. (as persian green). It is believed that *palak* originated from Indo-China region. It is a popular leafy vegetable especially in Northern parts of India. Tender leaves are consumed as a vegetable. This herb contains good content of protein, calcium, iron and other minerals. The plant is also valued as a source of a number of medicines.

Fenugreek ($2n = 16$):

Trigonella foenum-graecum L.; Papilionaceae.

Fenugreek is believed to be native of South Europe and Euthopia. Its wild species are seen in North Western parts and is chiefly cultured in Northern regions of India as a winter season annual. The green leaves are used both as a vegetable and fodder. The seeds make a good spice and condiment. Its pod-husk contains some tannins as well as alkaloid substances. The seeds are also used for medicinal purposes as carminative and tonic, and is used as a poultice externally to cure boils, ulcers and abscesses. Seeds embody diosgenin which is precursor of steroids including sex hormones and oral contraceptives. *T. foenum graecum* makes faster growth than *T. corniculate* (*kasuri* or *champa methi*).

Wild fenugreek:

Trigonella polycerata L.; Papilionaceae.

It is found in Northern India and the leaves are used as a vegetable.

Amaranth ($2n = 34$):

Its important species are:

Amaranth:

Amaranthus blitum var. *oleraceae* Duthie; Amaranthaceae.

(It is a herb- which is cultured for vegetable purposes).

Grain amaranth or African spinach or velvet flower; *Amaranth cruentus* L. (Syn. *A. hybriolus* L.) Sub/sp. *cruentus* (L.) Thell. var. *paniculatues* (L.) Theil. : *A. paniculatus* L.; Amaranthaceae.

It is a branching type tall growing herb grown in North India as a vegetable.

Prickly amaranth:

Amaranth spinosus L.; Amaranthaceae.

It is a diffuse, spinous herb or undershrub found in cultivated fields, waste places and along roadsides. It is used both as fodder and vegetable.

– Tender amaranth or Chinese spinach or Tempala:

Amaranthus tricolor L. (Syn. *A. gangeticuss* L.; *A. polygamus* L.; *A oleraceus* Willd); Amaranthaceae

Tempala is grown all over India. Both the leaves and young stems are used as a vegetable. Its plant is astringent, and is used as a medicine in diarrhoea, dysentery and haemorrhage and is used externally in ulcerated conditions of throat and mouth, and as a wash for ulcers.

– Lettuce ($2\ n = 18$) or Head & Cabbage lettuce or Romane / Cos asparagus lettuce:

Its important species are as follows:

Lettuce:

Lactua sativa L. (Syn. L. *scariola* L. var. *sativa* C.B. Clarke); Compositae.

It is a leafy herb believed to be a native of Southern Europe and West Asia. The studies have evinced that it has been in cultivation for 2500 years; while in Europe, Iran, Turkey and Asia minor, evidence about its culture even 500 B.C. has been obtained. Lettuce is commonly cultivated in Europe and America. In India, it is grown in kitchen gardens. The leaves make a good source of protein, carbohydrate, vitamin A, vitamin C and minerals especially calcium, phosphorus, sodium, sulphur, magnesium and potassium. Radical leaves are consumed as a raw vegetable. Leaves yield lactuarium which is used in medicines as hypnotic in bronchitis and asthma.

Lactua runcinata DC. (Syn. L. *heyneana* DC); Compositae.

It is glabrous herb embodying radical leaves, a common weed in a number of regions in India. The plant has diuretic, tonic and slightly aperient properties. Generally, it is an animal-fodder, but it is also used as a vegetable.

Indian lettuce:

Lactua indica L. (Syn. L. *brevirostris* Champ); Compositae.

This herb is believed to be native of China and Southern Japan. In India it is found in Assam, Meghalaya and Sikkim. Leaves embody tonic, digestive and depurative properties. Its dried latex is used as a replacement of opium.

Lactua remotiflora DC.; Compositae

Its leaves are smaller and more delicate than those of L. *rununata.* It is found in Western Uttar Pradesh, Rajasthan, Maharashtra and Deccan Peninsula; used for chronic obstructions of liver and bowels, and as a diuretic calculus affections.

– Wild lettuce or prickly lettuce:

Lactua scariola L.; Compositae

It is found in Western Himalayas. The seeds embody semi-drying oil used in soap, paints and varnish industries. Its refined oil is considered fit for human consumption. It is reported to contain hypnotic and antipyretic properties.

Fruits and Seeds vegetables

This group of vegetables includes true fruits. Most of the vegetables belonging to this group contain proteins, fats and vitamins A and C, Carbohydrates and a number of minerals. They are an inferior source of proteins, carbohydrates and fats. They belong to Cucurbitaceae and Solanaceae families and can be grouped as follows:

Vine Crops:

Cucurbits:

It is believed that this group of vegetables have originated from the tropical regions of Asia probably from India, China, Africa and Malaya. However S. gourd is believed to be a native to Japan and Jawa. In India and China, it has been in cultivation since ancient times. Its remains have been found in Mexico dated 7000-5000 BC. According to some authors bottlegourd has originated from Africa from where it has reached Southern America through sea waves. Some of the wild relatives are found in Africa.

Bottlegourd of Calabash cucumber: *Lagenaria siceraria* Standley (Syn. *Cucurbita siceraria* Molina; *C. lagenaria* L., *C. lencantha* Duch, *Lagenaria vulgaris* Ser); Cucurbitaceae

It is a climbing or trailing herb and believed to be a native to Africa. However, it is now cultivated throughout India for its fruits used as vegetable. Its seeds are also edible and are used as a medicine in dropsy as an anthelmintic. Its hard dried cells are made use of for a number of purposes like water bottles, ladder, bowls, pipes, playing horns and musical instruments. Its fruit pulp makes good source of vitamin B and ascorbic acid.

Spongegourd, Ribbed or Richgourd, Angled Looffa, Vegetable Sponge: *Luffa acutangula* (L.) Roxb. (Syn. *Cucumis* acutangulus L.); Cucurbitaceae

It is believed that its place of origin is tropical Asia and probably India. It is extensively trailing annual, cultivated throughout India for its tender fruits used as vegetable. The fibrous material obtained from ripe dried fruits provides a substitute for bath sponges.

Whitegourd, Ashgourd: ***Benincasa hispide* (Thunb.),** *Cogn*, (Syn. *B. cerifera* Savi; *Cucurbite hispida* Thump); Cucurbitaceae

It is a large trailing or climbing herb cultivated largely in Uttar Pradesh, Punjab, Rajasthan and Bihar. Its fruits are used as a vegetable. These are also candied with sugar to prepare *petha*, a common sweet in India. Its seeds are also edible.

Watermelon: *Citrullus lanatus* (Thunb.) Mansf. (Syn. *C. vulgaris* Schrad; *Colosynthis citrullus* (L.) O. Kuntze, *Cucurbita citrullus* L.; Cucurbitaceae.

It is a climbing or trailing hispid annual, believed to be a native to tropical Africa. It is cultivated throughout India for its cool and refreshing fruits. Its seeds are also edible and yield oil which is used both for cooling and illumination. Its aqueous and alcoholic extracts have been found to embody properties to cure paralysis. tapeworms and roundworms in cats.

Roundgourd: *C. lanatus* var. *fistulosia* (Stocks) Mansf. (Syn. *C. vulgaris* schard. var. *fistulosis* (Stock) Duch); Cucurbitaceae.

It is different from its main species since it embodies fistulous stems and petioles. Uttar Pradesh, Punjab, Haryana, Rajasthan and Bihar are the main growing states. Fruits are used as a vegetable and are also made into pickles.

Muskmelon: *Cucumus melo* L.; Cucurbitaceae

It is a creeping hispid annual believed to have originated from Africa. In India it is grown in high and dry western areas. Fruits are consumed as dessert, seeds are edible and have cooling diuretic properties.

Smallgourd: C. *melo.* var. *orgestis* Naud.; Cucurbitaceae.

Its fruits are edible.

Snapmelon: C. *melo.* var. *momordica* Duth & Full.; Cucurbitaceae

Its fruits are also edible.

Kakri: *C. melo.* L var. *utilissimus* Duth & Full. (Syn. C. *utilissimus* Roxb.); Cucurbitaceae

It is commonly grown in Punjab and Uttar Pradesh for its edible fruits. Seeds have cooling and diuretic properties.

Gherkin: *Cucumis anguria*; Cucurbitanceae

It is a trailing herb. Its fruits are used to prepare pickle and are also used as a vegetable.

Kheera cucumber: *C. sativus.*; Cucurbitaceae

Cucumber is a trailing and climbing annual. Its fruits are used as salad, vegetable and for consuming raw. The seeds are edible and diuretic. The seeds also contain edible oil.

Redgourd or red pumpkin: *Cucurbita maximna* Duch.; Cucurbitaceae.

It is grown as a fruit vegetable. Its seeds yield resin embodying vermicidal properties.

Summer squash, Pumpkin or Marrow: *C. pepo* L.; Cucurbitaceae

It is a hispid and hardy annual believed tó have originated from North Mexico and Eastern U.S.A., In North India, it is cultivated for fruits, consumed as a vegetable. The seeds are authelmintic and useful as taeniacide.

Squash: *C. moschata* (Duch). Poir, Cucurbitaceae

It is an annual, believed to be a native to Central America. Its fruits are used as a vegetable and also made use of to prepare jam.

Snakegourd, serpentgourd: *Trichosanthes anguine* L.; Cucurbitaceae

It is climbing or trailing herb grown throughout India specially in Southern parts of the country. Fruits are consumed as a vegetable. The roots and seeds are used in medicines for expelling worms, and for treating diarrhoea or syphilis.

Jangli chichinda: *T. cucumarina* L.; Cucurbitaceae.

It is cultivated through the length and breadth of India for use as a vegetable. The root is used for bronchitis and boils. Its leaves are used in biliousness. The seeds have been found to be anthelmintic and antifebrile.

Poundedgourd or parol : *T. dioica* Roxb.; Cucurbitaceae

It is grown in warmer regions of India specially Bihar, West Bengal, Uttar Pradesh arid Assam for its fruits consumed as a vegetable. Its leaves are also edible.

Chayote, Chocho, Christophine: *Sechicum edule* (Jacq.) Sw.; Cucurbitaceae

It is a trailing of climbing vine. It is mainly grown in hill regions of Northern India as well as Madurai and Nilgirihills in Tamil Nadu, Pune (Maharashtra) and some parts of Karnataka. Fruits are used as a vegetable.

Bittergourd: *Momordica charantia* L.; Cucurbitaceae

It is a climbing or trailing herb, cultivated all over India for its fruits consumed as a vegetable. It has a medicinal value as well. It is especially advocated for sugar patients.

Bhat karela: *M. cochinensis* Spreng (Syn. *M. mixta* Roxb.); Cucurbitaceae

It is cultivated throughout India for its fruits which are used as a vegetable.

Small bittergourd: *M. dioica* Roxb. ex. Willd.; Cucurbitaceae.

It is a common climbing and spreading herb. Its fruits are used as a vegetable.

Kadavacnchi: *M. tuberosa* Cogn. (Syn. *M. cumbalaria* Fenzl. ex. Naud, *Luffa tuberosa* Roxb.) Cucurbitaceae

It is also a trailing herb. Grown chiefly in Maharashtra and Tamil Nadu for its edible fruits.

Dish-cloth-gourd or Smooth Loofa. Vegetable Sponge: *Luffa aegyptiaca* Mull (Syn. *L. cylindrica* auct. pl. non M.J. Roem., *Momordica cylindrica* L.); Cucurbitaceae

It is believed to be a native of tropical Asia and probably India. The plant is a climbing or trailing annual grows all over India for its immature' fruits used as a vegetable. Its dried fruits yield fibrous substance, used as a replacement of bath sponges and is widely used for cleaning purposes. Luffa sponges make good baking material and are used for stuffing of pillows, mattresses, soldier pads and saddles. It is also used to manufacture sunhelmets on account of effective insulation against heat. Its dried fruits embody good shock and sound absorbing properties. The seeds also yield edible oil.

Ridge or ribbed gound or Angled loofah or Ridged gourd: *Luffa acutangula* (L.) Roxb. (Syn. *Cucumis acutangulus* L).; Cucurbitaceae

It is an extensively trailing annual believed to be native to tropical Asia, probably India. It is grown for its young and tender fruits which are used as a vegetable and is grown all over India. The fibrous material obtained from its dry fruits makes an excellent bath-sponges.

Chillies (2*n* = 24):

Red pepper chillies: *Capsicum annum* L.; Solanaceae

It is a herb believed to be a native to West Indies and tropical America. Now it is cultivated all over India. Chief producing Indian states include Andhra Pradesh, Karnataka, Tamil Nadu, Maharashtra, Madhya Pradesh, Bihar and Rajasthan. Its fruits are very pungent and are used both as spice and condiment. Green and red fruits are pickled. It is internally used as a strong stimulant and carminative particularly in fatulent dispepsia. Capsicum tincture is sometimes used as an ingredient of gargles to cure pharyngitis and to relax sore throat. It is externally used for lambago, neuralgia and rhematism. In rheumatoid arthritis, its ointment is applied to painful joints.

Chillies have a number of species *viz.*, *capsicum frutescence* L. *C. pendulum*, *C. pubescence*, *C. annum* var. *longum*, *C. annum* var. *grosum* (capsicum, bell pepper or Shimla mirch). *C. annum* and *C.* frutescence are grown all over the world. Chillies are cultivated in Brazil, U.S.A., Africa, Spain, China, Indonesia, India, Pakistan, Bangladesh and Japan. Green chillies contain vitamins A, B and C and embody enough of phosphorus and calcium. Pungency is due to the alkaloid called capsanin.

Tomato (2*n* = 11): *Lycopersicon lycopersicum* (L.) Karst. (Syn. *Lycopersicum esculentum* Mill.; *Solanum lycopersicum* L.), Solanaceae

Tomato is a herb. It is believed to be a native to Peru and Equador. In Mexico, it was known as zeeta tomato, but after 1695 came to be known as tomato. Spaniards introduced tomato in Europe in sixteenth century wherefrom it reached U.S.A. and Canada. In India tomato was brought by Portugese. Now it has become a very common vegetable allover India. It occupies third position from production viewpoint after potato and sweet potato. Tomato is consumed both raw and cooked. It is also used to prepare soup, juice, sauce and ketchup. Tomato fruits contain vitamin C (ascorbic acid), Vitamins A, B-1 and B-2. Its red colour is due lycopin. Its seeds contain semi-drying edible oil which is also used in the manufacture of soap. It is divided into two groups viz., determinate and indeterminate from vegetative growth point of view.

Brinjal or Egg-plant or Aubergine or Gooseberry or Pepino or Naranjilla (2 *n* = 24): *Solanum melongena* L.; Solanaceae.

It is believed to have originated in India as its sixteen wild species are found even today in various regions of the country. The tropical China is regarded as its second home. It is mainly grown in India, china, Pakistan. Bangladesh, Afghanistan, and Philippines. Fruits are used as vegetable. It embodies medicinal properties too.

Okra or Lady's finger or Gumbo (2*n* = 130): *Abelmoschus esculentus* (L.) Moench (Syn. *Hibiscus esculentus* L.); Malvaceae.

It is believed that tropical Africa or Asia are the homes of Okra. However, India cannot be ruled out as its place of origin since it is found growing wild. In Africa, okra has been grown before the discovery of America. It is a vegetable crop of world's tropical regions. The main Indian states cultivating okra in plains include Haryana, Punjab, Uttar Pradesh, Maharashtra, Tamil Nadu, Orissa, West Bengal and Assam. The fruits contain vitamins A, B, C, calcium, phosphorus and iron. The stem yields fibre. It is also used in paper industry. Its ripe seeds contain 20 per cent edible oil. The mucilage from stem and roots is used to clarify sugarcane juice in the manufacture of jaggery and sugar.

SECTION 20
SPICES AND CONDIMENTS

The spices and condiments have been defined as the natural or vegetable products or the mixtures thereof, used either in whole or ground form in order to impart a flavour, aroma and piquancy to food. They are also used for seasoning of foods and work as preservatives as well.

India is known as the land or home of spices. Their history is highly interesting. Indian spices in addition to perfumes and textiles were shipped to Mesopotamia, Arabia and Egypt even before the existence of Greece and Rome. These products attracted huge number of sailors to Indian seashores. The history reveals that the Greek merchants visited South Indian markets to buy spices and other commodities available in India that time even before the Christian era. It is said that Epicurean Rome spent a large amount of money on Indian spices. The Parthian wars by Rome were mainly fought in order to protect the trade route to India. The spices were so highly valued that once they were treated as a royal luxury. Numerous men risked their lives to obtain them. Christopher Columbus in 1492 though landed in the New World, initially undertook his voyage in search of India. Another important sailor Vasco da Gama in 1496 captained four ships from Lisbon ports. He was fortunate since he reached Calicut at the Malabar Coast of India. In his entire journey, he travelled a distance of 38,620 km in two years and had been to African continents and India. He finally reached Lisbon in 1498. Though only two out of the four ships could reach back home. These ships carried the spices and the other products estimated at 60 times the worth of the voyage. It shows that spices were highly priced. In fact, they continued to be extremely valuable and during middle ages one pound of ginger was treated equal to one sheep. Similarly, one pound of mace was equal either to three sheep or half a cow. The peppers during that period were sold by corn counts. It is said that one sack of pepper was treated worth man's life. The value and significanee of spices added to the internal power struggle to control the spices' trade. France, Great Britain, Holland, Portugal and Spain fought a number of bloody sea wars for 300 years to control the spice producing markets in the world. In nutshell, it may be said that the history of spices is the history of dreaded naval wars.

Spices have been hand and glove with culinary art to provide flavour to feeds and beverages. They add savour to insipid taste to the dishes and a tang to the beverages. The spices also function as appetizers. Some of them are used in perfumery, cosmetics and medicines/pharmaceuticals. The spices are preservatives and antioxygenic. The use of spices has remained unchanged even in modern times. In other words, they have been either to add or to mask tainted tastes of nutritious foods which otherwise would have been discarded because of their low palatability and acceptability. The spices are also used as food preservatives. In 16th century cloves were used to preserve foods without refrigerators. Its preservative properties have been assigned to eugenol, a bacterial growth inhibitor. Use of whole mustard and ground mustard is very well known to keep the quality of food intact for a long period of time. It makes an integral part of pickles as well. It is believed that in olden times the people would have gone hungry without spices since they did know neither the material nor the methods to preserve foods during summers to carry forward to winters for consumption.

Spices have been classified in the following four groups:

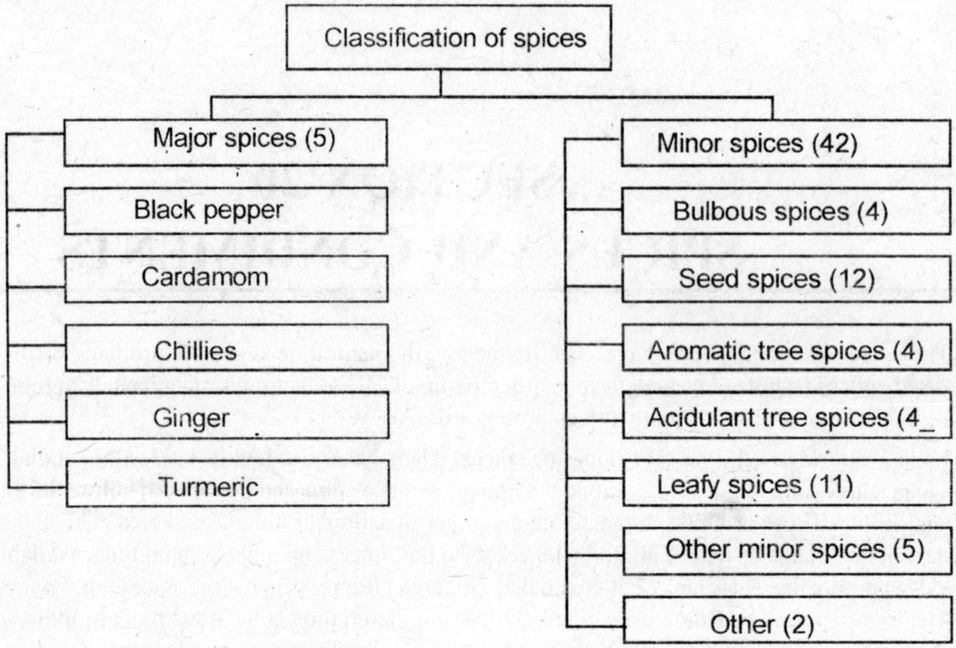

Major spices:

– Peppers:

Black pepper *Piper nigrum* L.

Green pepper *P. nigrum* L.

White pepper *P. nigrum* L.

Family: Piparaceae

– Chillies or Capsicums:

Capsicum annum L.

– Bird chilli

Capsicum frutescens

Family: Solanaceae

– Ginger:

Zingiber officinale Rosc.

Family: Zingiberaeceae

– Turmeric:

Curcuma longa L. Syn. *C. domestica* (Val).

Family: Zingiberaceae

– Cardamom:

True cardamom (Small cardamom):

Elettaria cardamom (L.) Maton (*a*) Minuscula Burkill (*b*) Major Thwaites

Family: Zingiberaceae

Large cardamom:

* Madagascar cardamom, *Aframomum augurstifolium* (Sonn) K. Schum.

* Cameroon cardamom *Aframomum hanburyi* K. Schum.

* Korarima cardamom *A. korarima*

A. Large Cardamom (*Aframomum* species):

	English Name	*Botanical Name*
1.	Madagascar cardamom	*Aframomum augustifolium* (Sonn) K. Schum.
2.	Cameroon cardamom	*Aframomum hanburyi* K. Schum.
3.	Korarima cardamom	*Aframomum koraima* (Pereira) Engler
4.	Grains of paradise or Guinea grains	*Aframomum melegueta* (Roscoe) K. Schum.

B. Greater Cardamom (*Amomum* species):

	English Name	*Botanical Name*
1.	Bengal cardamom	*Amomum aromaticum* Roxburgh)
2.	Round cardamom or Chester cardamom or Siam cardamom	*Amomum kepulaga* Sprague et Burkill Syn. *Amomum cardamomum* Roxburgh
3.	Cambodian cardamom	*Amomum krervanh* Pierre et Gagnipain
4.	Greater Indian cardamom or Nepal cardamom	*Amomum subulatum* Roxburgh

C. Lesser Cardamom (*Elettaria* species):

	English Name	*Botanical Name*
1.	Small cardamom or green cardamom ór true cardamom or Malabar cardamom or Ceylon cardamon	*Elettaria carrdamomum* (Linn). Maton var. *minuscula* Burkill var. major Thwaites
(*i*)	cardamom	
(*ii*)		

According to Bureau of Indian Standard (earlier known as Indian Standard Institute), New Delhi, India and the International Organization for Standards, Budapest, Hungary have classified and officially recognized the following 63 plants as spices and condiments included in four major groups:

List of spices and condiments

Sl No.	English Name	Botanical Name	Part Used
1.	Sweet flag	*Acorus calamus* Linn.	Rhizome
2.	Onion	*Allium cepa* Linn.	Bulb
3.	Garlic	*Allium sativum* Linn.	Bulb
4.	Greater galanga	*Alpinia galanga* (Linn.) Willd	Rhizome
5.	Greater Indian cardamom, Large cardamon Sikkim cardamom, Nepa cardamoml	*Amomum subulatum* Roxb.	Fruit and seed
6.	Dill	*Anethum graveolens* Linn.	Fruit and leaf
7.	Celery	*Apium graveolens* Linn.	Fruit
8.	Horse-radish	*Armoracia rusticana* Gaertn. Syn. *Cochlearia armoracia* Linn..	Root
9.	Indian mustard	Brassica juncea (Linn.) Czem. & Coss.	Seed
10.	Black mustard	*Brassica nigra* (Linn.) Koch.	Seed
11.	Caper	*Capparis spinosa* Linn.	Unopened flower bud
12.	Chillies, Paprika capsicums Bird chilli capsicums	(*a*) *Capsicum annuum* Linn. (*b*) *Capsicum frutescens* Linn,	Fruit Fruit
13.	Caraway Black caraway	(*a*) *Carum carvi* Linn. (*b*) *Carum bulbocastanum* Linn.	Fruit Fruit
14.	Cassia China or Cassia	*Cinnarmomum aromaticum* C.G. Ness	Bark
15.	Batavia cassia or Java cassia or Cassia vera or Padang cinnamon	*Cinnamomum burmanii* Blume	Bark
16.	Indian cassia lignea	*Cinnamomum tamala* (Buch Ham) Nees & Eberm	Bark and leaf
17.	Cinnamon	*Cinnamomum zeylanicum* Blume	Bark
18.	Coriander	*Coriandrum sativum* Linn.	Leaf and seed
19.	Saffron	*Crocus sativus* Linn.	Stigma
20.	Cumin	*Cyminum cyninum* Linn.	Fruit
21.	Turmeric	*Curcuma longa* Linn.	Rhizome

22.	Cardamom	*Elettaria cardamomum* (Linn.) Maton	Fruit and seed
23.	Clove	*Eugenia caryophyllus* (C. Sprengel) Bullock & Harrison Syn. *Syzygium aromaticum* (Linn.) Merril & Perry	Unopened flower bud
24.	Asafoetida (Hing)	*Ferula aliacea* Boiss Syn. F. *rubricaulis* Boiss	Oleogum resin from rhizome and thickened root
25.	Hingra	*Ferula foetida* Regel	Oleogum resin from rhizome and thickened root
26.	Fennel	*Foeniculum vulgare* Mill:	Fruit
27.	Cambodge	*Garcinia cambogia* (Gaertn.) Desrcusseaux	Pericarp-lobes
28.	Kokam butter tree	*Garcinia indica* Choisy	Peel of fruit (cured)
29.	Hyssop	*Hyssopus officinalis* Linn.	Leaves
30.	Common Juniper	*Juniperus communis* Linn.	Berry
31.	Sweet bay or true laurel leaves	*Laurus nobilis* Linn.	Leaf
32.	Lovage	*Levisticum officinale* Koch.	Fruit and root
33.	Sweet marjoram	*Majorana hortensis* Moench Syn. *Origanum majorana* Linn.	Leaf and flowering top
34.	Dried raw mango peeled slices or powder	*Mangifera indica* Linn.	Unripe fruit
35.	Japanese peppermint	*Mentha arvensis* Linn.	Leaf
36.	Mint	*Mentha longifolia* (Linn.) Hudson	Leaf
37.	Peppermint	*Mentha piperita* Linn. emend Hunds.	Leaf
38.	Spearmint	*Mentha spicata* Linn. Syn. *M. virdis* Linn.	Leaf
39.	Curry leaf	*Murraya koenigii* (Linn.) Sprengel.	Leaf
40.	Mace	*Myristica fragrans* Houttuyn	Aril
41.	Nutmeg	*Myristica fragrans* Houttuyn	Kernel
42.	Black cumin	*Nigella sativa* Linn.	Fruit
43.	Sweet basil	*Ocimum basilicum* Linn.	Leaf

44.	Marjoram	*Origanum vulgare* Linn.	Leaf and flowering top
45.	Opium poppy	*Papaver somniferum* Linn.	Seed
46.	Parsley	*Petroselinum crispum* (Mill) Airy-Shaw Syn. *P. sativum* Hoffm.	Seed
47.	Fimento or allspice	*Pimenta* dioica (Linn.) Merrill	Fruit and leaf
48.	Aniseed	*Pimpinella anisun* Linn.	Fruit
49.	Long pepper	*Piper longum* Linn,	Seed and leaves
50.	Black pepper, White pepper	*Piper nigrum* Linn.	Berry
51.	Pomegranate	*Punica granatum* Linn.	Seed (dried with flesh)
52.	Rosemary	*Rosmarinus officinalis* Linn.	Leaf
53.	Sage	*Salvia officinalis* Linn.	Leaf
54.	Summer savory	*Satureja hortensis* Linn.	Stem, leaf and flowering top
55.	White mustard or yellow mustard	*Sinapis alba* Linn. Syn. *Brassica alba* or *B. hirta*	Seed
56.	Tamarind	*Tamarindus indica* Linn.	Seed
57.	Wild thyme	*Thymus serpyllum* Linn.	Leaf and flowering top
58.	Common thyme	*Thymus vulgaris* Linn.	Leaf and flowering top
59.	Bishops weed	*Trachyspermum* ammi (Linn.) Sprague ex Turrill	Fruit
60.	Fenugreek	*Trigonella foenum-graceum* Linn.	Seed
61.	Vanilla	*Vanilla planifolia Andrews* Syn. *V. fragrans* Salishurry Ames	Pod
62.	Vanilla	*Vanilla pompons* Schneiden	Pod.
63.	Tahiti vanilla	*Vanilla tahitensis* Moore	Pod
64.	Dried ginger	*Zingiber officinale* Roscoe	Rhizome

Source: International Organization for Standardization (ISO) and ISI–Nomenclature of Spices and Condiments, 1972.

SECTION 21
FORAGE CROPS

The word feed means to furnish something essential to the growth, sustenance, maintenance or operation. In fact, there are four words namely feed, fodder, forage and provender which means feed for the animals. The feed is the general word and is used as pig feed or chicken feed *etc.* The word fodder is essentially applied to dry or green feed as opposed to pasturage, and fed to the horses, cattle *etc.*, like fodder for winter feeding. Further, forage represents a food which an animal obtains (usually grasses, leaves *etc.*) by searching about for it. A lost cattle can usually live on forage. Finally, the word provender denotes dry food such has hay, oat or corn. Regardless of the terms indicated above, grasses and legumes are extremely important in this regard. The forage consists of both of these components. These either grow or are grown as grasslands, meadow lands both occupy arable crop lands as well as barren lands. The forage crops are also grown in various agro-forestry systems. Climax grasslands are treated *on par* with prairies, steppes which are uncommon to Indian conditions. The estimates have revealed that the high, medium and low dry matter production varies from 20 to 40, 10 to 25 and 3 to 10 t/ha per annum. The studies have also brought out that elephant grass is capable of yielding up to 85-86 t/ha of dry matter every year. (J.P. Cooper, 1970, *Herb. abstr.* 40: 1-50).

The grasses are herbaceous annual or perennial graminacseous plants. Their root to shoot ratio plays an important part in their production. Generally, root to shoot ratio varies from 0.7 : 1 to 4 : 1. However, in most of them the ratio lies between 0.8 : 1 and 1.5 : 1. A ratio exceeding 1 : s1 indicates the drought resistance of grasses. It has been observed that in most of the cases 15-20 per cent of root mass is annually replaced, *i.e.*, 65-80 sper cent of the root mass in perennial grasses dies of every year. The grasses have six special families, 25 tribes, 600 genera and 7500 species as reported by F.W. Gould in 1968 (Grass Systematics – McGraw Hill, N.Y., USA). (Temperature and Light) requirement of C_3 group of grasses has been estimated at 15-20 °C and 15000-30000 lux, respectively. The respective requirement for C_4 grasses is 30-40 °C and 50000-60000 lux, as estimated by A.V. Bogdan in 1977 (Tropical Pastures and Fodder Plants, Longman, London, England). The grasses have been grouped into tropical and sub-tropical ones and the important ones are briefly described below:

Tropical grasses:

The tropical and torrid zone is located between and close to tropic of cancer and the tropic of capricon. World's tropical and subtropical regions lie between the latitude of 28° N and 30° S of the equator. According to Dabadghao and Shankarnarayan [(1973) P.M. Dabadghao and K.A. Shankarnarayan. The grassover of India, Indian Council of Agricultural Research, New Delhi] the following types of grass covers are met with in tropical and subtropical India:

– *Dicanthium / Cenchrus / Lasiurus — Sehimal / Dicanthium*

– *Themeda / A rundinella – Phragmites / Saccharum / Imperata*

Gamba grass/Sadabahar (2*n* = 40)*:* *Andropogon gayanus* Kunth. (Syn. *guineansis steud.*)*;* Gramineae *A* drought resistant and anti-erosion grass introduced in India from Africa. Gamba grass is palatable and is hence embodies high degree of palatability besides 6-12 per cent of crude protein and a potential to produce 400 q/ha per annum of dry matter. It can withstand low pH, low soil fertility, seasonal flooding as well as drought. It can be effectively propagated by root slips.

Beard grass ($2n = 20$): *Andropogon pumilus* Roxb. (Syn. *A. pachayarthrus* Hack ; *A. demissus* Steud); Gramineae.

It is found in drier parts of India. It is perennial and makes a profuse growth and makes a valuable fodder).

Banjura grass: *Apluda mutica* L. var. *aristata* Heckel ex Backer (Syn. *A aristata* L.); Gramineae

A perennial grass believed to be a native of S.E. Asia and Australia. It is associated with *sehima nervosum* (Rotle.) Staff. (Syn. *Andropogon nervosum* Rotte. ; *Ischaemum laxum* (R. Br.) Hook. f.) and *Zigiphus jujube* (L.) Lam. non Mill (Syn. of Z. mauritiana Lamk.) bushes ; grows in hedges, forests, open lands and bushes. It is used as a fodder. It has an ability to grow even on steeply slopy hillsides embodying rocky red and black clay soil. Its dry matter production protential has been estimated at 40-50 q/ha per annum.

Common needle grass ($2n = 22$): *Aristida adscensionis* L.; Gramineae.

It is an annual grass behieved to be a native of Africa and Asia. Adapts well to low fertility soils and grows well on bare lands. Other fodder species include *A. plumosa* L. [Syn. *Chaetaria depressa* (L.) Nees] and *A. pungens* Desf., sand-binder and a desert fodder. Crude protein content varies from 2 in mature hay to per cent (in early vegetative stage).

Bhangrola grass: *Arundinella nepalensis* Trin. Gramineae.

A perennial grass growing as a variable in *Themeda–Arundinella* cover. Found in mid-hills of Himachal Pradesh. Its other species *A. intricate* Hughes is found in Assam and Arunachal Pradesh and makes an excellent soil binder. The estimated production potential stands at 200 q /ha per annum of fresh fodder.

Mat grass or carpet grass ($2n = 80$): *Axonopus affinis* chase, Gramineae

It is believed to be a native of Central America and West Indies and is a stoloniferous perennial. One kilogramme of seeds–number has been estimated at 1.1 million. Its other species *A. compresses* (Swartz.) P. Beaure [Syn. *Milium compressum* Swartz.; *Paspalum compressum.* (Sw.) Poir] is also called Saiana grass. It is also native to Caribbean Islands and Central America. It makes an excellent pasture as well as a lawn grass and grows well on moist soils of Assam. Broad leaf carpet grass is tetraploid ($2n = 54$).

Forest blue grass ($2n = 40, 50, 60, 80$): *Bothriochloa blandhii* (Retz.) ST. Blake; Gramineae

It is believed to be a native of India, Africa and Australia. Embodies 5-6-13.6 per cent of crude protein as revealed by the estimates made at different growth stages. If cut thrice, dry matter yield per annum may amount to approximately 50 or 60 q/ha.

Indian blue grass ($2n = 40, 60$): *Bothriocohola pertusa* (L.) *A. camus* (Syn. *Andropogon pertusus* (L.) Willd.; *Holcus pertusus* L.; *Eliomurus pertusus* Nees ex Steud.) Gramineae

It is a tufted perennial grass growing to a height of about 70 cm. This grass is grown in Uttar Pradesh for fodder. It is capable of producing dry matter up to 150-155 q/ha and embodies nearly 1210-1220 seeds per gramme. It can withstand trampling resulting from heavy grazing.

Bothiochloa glabra (Roxb.) *A. Camus* (Syn. *Andropogon glaber* Roxb.; *A. punctatus* Trin.); Gramineae

It is an excellent fodder grass.

Sweet petted grass: *Bothriochloa insculpta* (Hochst.) *A. camus* (Syn. *Andropogon insculptus* Hochst. ex A. Rich ; *Amphilophis insculpta* (Hochst.) Stapf; Gramineae

It has been introduced from Brazil. It is perennial found in Nilgiris and used for soil conservation as well as for fodder purposes.

Bothriochloa intermedia (R. Br.) *A. camus* (Syn. *Andropogon intermedius* R. Br.); Gramineae

This grass is found all over India and is used for preparing paper pulp.

Bothriochloa odorata (Lisboa) *A. camus* (Syn. *Andropogon* odoratus Donna Lisboa; *Amphilophis odorata* (Lisboa) *A. camus*); Gramineae

It is usually cultured for its sweet scent and flavour in India.

Signal grass ($2n = 36$): *Brachiaria decumbens* Stapf.; Gramineae

Its other name is Surinam or Kenya sheep grass. It is believed to be a native of East and Central Africa. In Australia, Jamaica and Surinam, dry matter yield of 360 q/ha has been obtained as against the average which varies from 80 to 200 q/ha.

Paragrass or Mauritius grass: *Brachiaria mutica* (Forst.) Stapf. (Syn. *Panicum muticum*); Gramineae

It is a stoloniferous perennial, believed to be native of West Africa. However, it is also believed to be an indigeneous to South America. In India, it has been introduced in Assam, regions of South India and Maharashtra. It is used as a fodder grass containing 5.5 to 15 per cent of crude protein.

Ruzi grass: *Brachiaria ruziziensis* G.et. Ev; Gramineae

It is a broad-leaved perennial grass, believed to have originated from East and Central Africa. Its one kg of seed number has been estimated at 2.7 lakhs. Its dry matter yield varies from 20 to 25 q/ha per year and crude protein from 10 to 14 per cent.

Palisade grass: *Brachiaria brizantha* (Hochst. ex. A. Rich) Stapf. (Syn. *Panicum brazinthum* Hochst. ex. A. Rich); Gramineae

It is a perennial grass native to tropical Africa. It effectively suppresses the weeds, but is susceptible to swamp conditions. It is fairly resistant to drought conditions. Palisade grass is used both as a soil binder and as a fodder crop.

Brachiaria ramosa (L.). Stapf. (Syn. *Panicum ramosum* L.; *Panicum arvense* Kunth); Gramineae

It is an annual grass which grows wild as well as a cultivated good fodder crop.

Bunch grass or African Foxtail, Buffet grass ($2n = 32, 34, 36, 40, 44, 52$ and 54): *Cenchrus ciliaris* L. (Syn. *Panicum celiaria* Link; P. *cenchroides* Rich; *Setaria vulpina* (Willd). P. Beauv.; *Cenchrus longifolius* Hochst. ex. Steud.); Gramineae

Bunch grass is tufted and branches profusely. It is perennial by growth habit. It is cultivated for fodder and also for soil conservation purposes. Its rhiomatous perennial and forms tussock. Its home is believed to be Africa, India and Indonesia. The seeds are relatively bold as per estimates 400-450 grains weigh one per gramme. Seeds are also edible. Its dry matter yield varies from 20 to 80 q/ha per year and contains 6-7 per cent of crude protein. However, crude protein content in early growth stages has been estimated at 11 to 14 per cent.

Bird wood grass or Anjan grass (Tetraploids $2n = 36$; Hexaploids $2n = 54$): *Cenchrus setigerus* Vahl (Syn. *Pennisetum* vahlil Kunth; *Cenchrus montanus* Nees ex. Royle); Gramineae

It is an annual tufted grass distributed throughout India. It is one of the major as well as promising grasses of the arid zone pastures. It is also grown for soil conservation purposes. One kg contains 1.7-1.8. lakhs of seeds. The average annual dry matter yield varies from 4 to 21 q/ha. However, its protein content in early blooming stage has been estimated at 13.5 per cent.

Cenchrus biflorus Roxb. (Syn. *C. barbatus* Schumach. *C. Catharticus* Delike); Gramineae

It is generally grown in upper Gangetic plains. The seeds are consumed in times of scarcity, while the young shoots are fed to animals as fodder.

Cenchrus pennisetiformis Hochst. et. Steud. ex. Stend. (Syn. *Pennisetum cendoroides* var. *echinoides* Hook. f.; *Cenchrus lappaceus* Tausch; *C. aequilumis* Chiov.); Gramineae

It is an important fodder grass.

Cenchrus prieurii (Kunth) Maire (Syn. *Pennisetum prieurii* Kunth.; *Cenchrus macro-stachyus* Hochst. ex. Steud.); Gramineae

This grass occurs in semi-desert areas of north-west India and makes an excellent fodder for animal.

Rhodes grass ($2n = 20, 40$; Triploids $2n = 30$): *Chloris gayana* Kunth. (Syn. C. *abyssinica* Hochst ex. A. Rich; C. *glabrata,* Anders; *Eustachys gayana* (Kunth) Mundy; Gramineae

It is a stoloniferous creeping and at times a tufted perennial grass which is believed to be a native of south Africa. It grows well under drought conditions and in tropical climate, but has been found tolerant to cold as well. It is eminently suitable for preparing a nutritive hay. On an average, it yields 15 to 250 q /ha of dry matter. The protein content has been estimated at 4-13 per cent, but in young stages it has been found to contain 16-18 per cent of protein. One kg of rhodes grass contains 39 lakh seeds.

Chloris virgata Sw. (Syn. *Rhabdochloa virgata* (Sw). P. Beauv.; *Chloris pubescens* Ligasca; *C. compressa* DC; Gramineae

It is a grass adapted to saline soils of North-West India and makes an excellent fodder for the animals.

Guria grass ($2n = 20$, 40 and 80): *Chrysopogon fulvus* (Spreng.) Chiov. (Syn. *Pollinia fulva* Spreng; *Andropogon moutanus* Keen. ex. Trin; A. monticola Roem et. Schulz); Gramineae

It is a tufted tall growing both tropical and sub-tropical perennial grass. The protein content has been estimated at 4-6 per cent. Its dry matter yield varies from 25 to 45 q/ha.

Kufri: *Chrysopogon gryllis* (L.) Trin. (Syn. *Andropogon gryllus* L.) Holcus gryllus (L.) R. Br.; *Pollinia gryllus* (L.) Spreng; *Apluda gryllus* (L.) Presl; Gramineae

It is a tufted grass found in temperature Himalayas from Shimla eastwards, Khasi and Naga hills. It makes a good fodder.

Chrysopogon aciculatus (Retz.) Trin. (Syn. *Andropogon aciculatus* Retz. *A. acicularis* Retz. ex. Roem et. Schult; *Chrysopogon trivialis* Arn. et. Nees); Gramineae

Though it is not a fodder grass, has been mentioned here because its germinating seeds can sometimes be pressed out of the pus in dogs, flesh. The sharp basal callus of the ripe fruit makes its way into the flesh and causes ulceration to the grazing animals. The grass is a natural lawn grass in areas of high rainfall.

Makora grass, Rosha grass, Palmarosa:

Cymbopogon martinii (Roxb.) Wats. (Syn. *Andropogon martinii* Roxb.; *A. schoenanthus* L. var. *martinii* Hook. f., *Cymbopagon martinianus* Schult., *C. pachnodes* (Trin) Wats); Gramineae

It is a tall, perennial and seed scented grass found in Maharashtra, Andhra Pradesh, Karnataka, Madhya Pradesh and Uttar Pradesh. The most important centres of rosa grass oil production are located at Betul and Mimar in Madhya Pradesh and Nasik in Maharashtra. Its leaves are a source of an aromatic oil. The grass occurs in two forms namely *'motia'* and *'sofia'*. In case of *motia,* the upper surface of culm leaves makes an obtuse or right angle with culms. There are few radicle leaves at the base. It is found in scattered patches. Its requirements of light is higher, while that of moisture is lower than the *sofia.* The essential oil obtained from *motia* is of superior quality and is referred to as palmarosa oil or east Indian geranium oil. On the contrary, the oil from *sofia* is of an inferior quality and is popularly known as the ginger-grass oil. *Sofia* has upper surface of the culm leaves making an acute angle with the culm, radicles are many in number and it grows in dense masses. It has been found that palmarosa oil is next to sandal wood and lemon grass oils in terms of significance granted to essential oils produced in India. The palmarosa oil makes a source of finest quality of commercial, geraniol oil and emits rose like aroma. It is extensively used in cosmetics particularly in soaps and also in flavouring of tobacco. Geranial is highly valued as a perfume and as a basic material for large number of synthetic aromatic chemicals. Rosha oil is used in medicines for lumbago and skin diseases. It is also used in the manufacture of mosquito repellent ointments.

Bermuda grass or Bahama grass ($2n = 18, 27, 30, 36, 40$):

var. dactylon: Tetraploid $2n = 36$

var. aridus : Diploid $2n = 18$

var. elegans Tetraploid $2n = 36$

var. coursii Tetraploid $2n = 36$

Synodondactylon (L.) Pers. (Syn. *Panicum dactylon* L.; *Digitariadactylon* (L.) Scop.; *Paspalumdactylon* (L.) Lamk.; *Mulium dactylon* (L.) Moench.; *Chloris cynodon* Trin.; *Capriola dactylon* (L.) O. Kuntze); Gramineae

It is highly drought resistant omnipresent rhizomatous creeping perennial fodder as well as lawn grass embodying extremely variable growing habit. Bermuda grass is met with in almost all the tropical and subtropical regions of the world and makes an excellent forage and fodder which is both palatable as well as nutritive. The dry matter production and crude protein respectively range between 40 and 100 q /ha, and 8.3 and 22.0 per cent. It is highly resistant to burning, close grazing and drought conditions.

East African star grass or Giant star grass:

Cynodon plectostachyum (K. Schum.) Pilger (Syn. *Leptochloa plechtostachya* K. Schum. ex Engler); Gramineae

It is believed to be a native of Rift Valley in East Africa. The grass is stoloniferous, quick growing capable of producing 85 to 34.6 q /ha of dry matter spread over 3 to 5 cuttings. This grass is grown for soil conservation, fodder and lawn purposes.

Crowfoot grass ($2n = 20, 34, 36, 48$):

Dactyloctenium aegyptium (L.) P. Beauv. (Syn. *Eleusine aegyptiaca* (L.) Desf.; *Cynosures aegyptius* L.; *Chloris mucronata Willd.*); Gramineae

It is a drooping, tufted annual spread through the length and breadth of India. It makes an excellent forage crop. The seeds which are very small sized (estimated 2.7 million seeds/kg borne on 1.25 million spekelets) and used as food especially during the periods and in the regions of foodgrain scarcity (sometimes called as a famine food too). The protein content has been observed to vary from 7.4 to 15.8 per cent.

Dactylocteniunt scindicum Boiss. (Syn. *Eleusine scindica* Duth.; E. *aristata* Ehrenb. ex. Boiss.); Gramineae.

It is a perennial which is found in North India particularly in sandy areas and is regarded as a promising fodder grass.

Dactyloctenium australl Steud.; Gramineae

Initially, it was introduced as a lawn grass, but proved a highly effective soil binder.

Durva, Kusa grass: *Demostachya bipinnata* (L.) Stapf. (Syn. *Briza bipinnata* L.; *Eragrostis cynosuroides* (Retz.) P. Beauv.; *Uniona bipinnata* L.; *Poa cynosuroides* Retz.); Gramineae

It is a tall tufted perennial believed to a native to India and Africa which chiefly grows in sandy alluvial soils located in low moisture prockets. The culms are used for thatching to make rough rope, writing and printing-paper and brooms. It makes an excellent sand-binder, used in various Hindu ceremonies, makes an ingredient of medicines used to remedy dysentery, but it provides a coarse fodder embodying low palatability, acceptability and protein (about 4.5 per cent).

Marvel grass ($2n$ - 20, 40, 60): *Dichanthuium annulatum* (Forssk.) Stapf. (Syn. *Andropogon annulatus* Forssk.; *A comosus* Link.; *A. scandens* Roxb.; *Lepeocercis annulata* (Forssk.) Nees.); Gramineae

It is a densely tufted, erect, thin stemmed perennial grass found in Punjab, Rajasthan, Uttar Pradesh, Gujarat and Madhya Pradesh growing well both in summer and spring seasons; propagated by root slips. Fresh forage yield varies from 20 to 200 q/ha, while that of dry matter from 50-60 q/ha spread over two cuttings. The crude protein has been estimated at about 10.4 per cent in early stages which slides down to 2.6-2.8 per cent at maturity.

Dichanthium aristatum (Poir) C.E. Hubb. (Syn. *D. nodosum* Willem.; *Andropogon aristatus* Poir.; A. *mollicomus* Kunth.; *A. caricosus* L. Subsp. *mollicomus* Hack var. *mollicomus* (Kunth.) Hack.; *Diplasanthum lanosum* Desv.); Gramineae

It provides an excellent fodder both in terms of palatability and nutrition. The grass is commonly grown in South India, Maharashtra and Madhya Pradesh.

Dichanthium caricosum (L.) A. *camus* (Syn. *Andropogon caricosum* L.; *A. serratus* Retz; *Heteropogon concinnus* Thw.); Gramineae

It is a fodder grass commonly grown in South India.

Weeping love-grass (2 *n* = 20, 40, 50, 80):

Eragrostis curvula (Schrad.) Nees. (Syn. *Poa curvula* Schrad.); Gramineae

It is a densely tufted pasture and soil erosion preventing perennial grass native to tropics *viz*., South Africa, Tanzania and Rhodesia. Its dry matter yield has been observed to vary from 130 to 270 q/ha. Seeds are small and the estimated number per gramme is 3850.

Lehmann love-grass: *Eragrostis lehmanniana* Nees; Gramineae

The grass has been introduced from the United States of America. It is grown both for fodder and for the control of erosion.

Teff. *Eragrostis tef* (Zuccagni) Trotter. (Syn. E. *abyssinica* (Jacq.) Link, *Poa tef* Zucc.; *P. abyssinica* (Jacq.) Link.; Gramineae

It is believed to be a native to Ethiopia and grown for fodder in Uttar Pradesh, Maharashtra and Baroda area of Gujarat. Its grains are consumed especially in times of scarcity.

Eragrostis tremula Hochst. ex. Steud. (Syn. *Poa tremula* Lamk.) Gramineae.

It is a tufted annual grass used for fodder.

Eragrostis diarrhena (Schult.) Steud. and *E. interrupts* (Lamk.) Beauv,; Gramineae

Its culms are used for broomsticks.

Baibgrass or Sabai-grass: *Eulaliopsis binata* (Retz.) C.E. Hubb. (Syn. *Ischaemum angustifolium* (Trin.) Hack.; *Eulaliopsis angustifolia* (Trin.) Honda; *Andropogon binatus* Retz; *Pollinidium binatum* (Retz). C.E.Hubb.); Gramineae

A perennial tufted drought resistant grass found in a numebr of places in Northern regions of India, commonly seen in rangelands and forests as well as low hilly areas of Western Himalayas. It may yield 60-80 q/ha of dry matter in three cuttings. It is used to manufacture paper, ropes, strings and mats.

Panisharu grass (2*n* = 20, 18, 36, 40): *Hemarthria compressa* (L.f.) R.Br. (Syn. *Rottboellia compressa* Lf. *Hemarthria coromadeliana* Steud.): Gramineae

It is believed that this perennial creaping tropical grass is native to Africa and South-East Asia. Its culms are compressed and hence the second part of the scientific name is compreassa. It is palatable and acceptable in grazing lands to the animals. The estimated protein content at flowering stage stands at 7.0-7.5 per cent; while the dry matter yield spread over 3 to 4 cuttings has been estimated to vary from 40 to 50 q/ ha per year.

Common yellow day-lily: *Hemarthria protensa* Steud.; Gramineae

This grass is found in Assam, Meghalaya and West Bengal. It is highly relished by the cattle.

***Piligrass, Black spear grass or Spear grass* (2*n* = 20, 40, 44, 50, 60, 80)**; Gramineae

Heteropogon contortus (L.) P. Beauv. ex. Roem. et. Schult (Syn. *Andropogon contrortus* L.; *Heteropogon hirtus* Pers; *Andropogon allionii DC;* Gramineae

The grass is densely tufted, erect or decumbent perennial, extremely variable in growth habit. It is used for fodder. The culms are made into mats and the manufacture of paper and board. The grass has also been found useful for soil conservation purposes. Its estimated dry matter yield varies from 30 to 32 q/ha per annum. The estimated protein content varies between 4.0 and 9.5 per cent.

Cotton wool or Blady grass or Cogon grass (2*n* = 20): *Imperata cylindrica* (*L.*) Beauv. var. *major* (Nees) C.E. Hubb. ex. Hubb. & Vaughan (Syn. I. *arundinaceae* Cyr., *Lagurus cylindricus* L. *Saccharum cylindricum* (L.) Lamk; Gramineae

It is a perennial fodder grass believed to be native to India, Australia and Africa. It occurs through the length and breadth of India. Its stems are used for thatching and also as a raw material in the manufacture of paper. The fruits of this grass are used to stuff pillows and cushions. It is a soil stabilizer in high rainfall areas and effectively helps to combat soil erosion. The dry matter yield varies from 1.2 to 3.3 q/ha embodying a crude protein content of 3.8 to 9.9 per cent as estimated at various growth stages.

Batiki Blue grass (2*n* = 24, 36): *Ischaemum indicum* (Hontt.) Merrill (Syn. *I. aristatum*); Gramineae

This grass makes a member species in *Sehima/Dichanthium* cover. It covers the ground effectively by forming a dense mat. The grass is slender, erect or decumbent tufted one. It may yield up to 92 to 93 q/ha of dry matter containing approximately 8.3 per cent of crude protein.

Ischaemum molle Hook.f.; Gramineae

This fodder grass is mostly found in Central India, Maharashtra and South India.

Ischaemum muticum L. Syn. *I. repens* Roxb.; *Andropogon muticus* Steud., *A. repense* (Roxb.) Steud; Gramineae

This fodder grass is distributed in coastal region of South India. It has been found highly effective in stabilization of coastal sand-dunes.

Ischacemuni pilosum Hack; Gramineae

It is a tall perennial fodder grass found specially in Andhra Pradesh, Madhya Pradesh. It is fed to the cattle.

Ischaemum srigosum Salisb. (Syn. *I. colladoa Spreng ; I regetum* Trin.; *Mexchium rogosum* (Nees); Gramineae

Its variable species are found in wet areas of Indian plains. In its young stage, it is consumed by cattle and horses. Its grains are consumed as food in times of scarcity.

Manchuri grass (2*n* = 8, 24, 28, 36): *Ischaemum laxum* Hack; Gramineae

It is a tufted perennial grass believed to be a native of South-East Asia. It grows well in low lying situations and is also seen in waterlogged areas. The grass is very much relished by the livestock. It may yield 45.0 to 63.8 q/ha of dry matter annually containing only 3 per cent of crude protein at dead ripe stage. However, the protein content at pre-flowering stage has been recorded at 5.4 per cent.

Iseilema anthephoroides Hack.; Gramineae

This excellent fodder grass is found in South India and Maharashtra.

Iseilema prostraum (L.) Andress; Gramineae

It is a very good fodder grass which is distributed all over India.

Iseilema laxum Hack.; Gramineae

It is a perennial grass found all over India, used as fodder. It works as an effective soil binder.

Sewan grass (2*n* = 56): *Lesiurus hirsutus* (Forsk.) Boiss. (Syn. *Elionurus hirsutus* Munro ex. Bench); Gramineae

It is a perennial fodder grass believed to be a native to Africa, India and Pakistan. In India, it is distributed in sandy areas of Rajasthan and Punjab. The cattle like it only in its early growth stages. After maturity it is used for thatching purposes and seeds are consumed in times of scarcity. It may yield the dry matter varying from 15 to 120 q/ha having protein content of 6 to 6.5 per cent under natural conditions.

Molasses grass: *Meliais minutiflora* P. Beauv.; Gramineae

This perennial spreading grass is supposed to be a native to Africa, where from it has been introduced in India. It forms loose tussocks, staggling sward and smothers the associated plants by forming dense mat. The grass secretes the viscous oil with odour like that of cumin. Once the ainmals become accustomed they consume this grass with gusto. It is very widely known in Assam to keep away the mosquitoes and Anopheles. The dry matter yield may be 60.0 to 60.2 q/ha containing a protein amounting to 9.3 per cent.

Blue panicum (2*n* = 36, tetraploid; diploid 2*n* = 18) *Panicum antidotale* Retz.; Gramineae

This grass is also known as giant panicum and is believed to be a native to South-East Asia. In India this tall grass is found in Punjab, Uttar Pradesh and Western peninsula. It is used both as a fodder crop and also for stabilization and reclamation of sand-dunes.

Guinea grass (2*n* = 18, 32, 48): *Panicum maximum* Jacq.; Gramineae

This fodder grass is grown in Maharashtra, Tamil Nadu and Northern parts of India. It is believed to be a native to tropical Africa. It may yield 400-500 q/ha of dry matter in eight cuttings. Its protein content varies from 4-14 per cent.

Common millet: *Panicum miliaceum* L.; Gramineae

It is mostly grown in Uttar Pradesh. Its grains are edible and the straw is used as fodder.

Panicum paludorum Roxb. non Nees (Syn. *P. peliferum* auct. non Lam); Gramineae

This perennial grass is found all over India in marshy lands and still waters. The grass makes a fodder liked by elephants and the buffaloes. The hill tribes make the grains into cakes for consumption.

Panicum psilipodium Trin. var. *psilopodium* and var. *Coloratum* Hook f. Gramineae

It is used for fodder purposes. The grains are used in Assam for preparation of alcoholic beverages.

Torpedo grass: *Panicum repens* L.; Gramineae

It is useful as a coloniser of coastal flats.

Little millet: *Panicum sumatrense* Roth ex. Roem. & Schult (Syn. *P. miliare* Lam); Gramineae

This is grown basically for edible grains in Uttar Pradesh and Madhya Pradesh. It straw is used as fodder.

Panicum trypheron Schult.; Gramineae

It is a tufted annual grass found all over India. Its seeds are identical to those of Italian millet and are used to make bread for human consumption during the times of scarcity. Its straw is used as a fodder for livestock.

Panicum turgidum Forsk; Gramineae

It is mostly used for stabilization and reclamation of sand-dunes.

Sawan millet: *Echinochloa colona* (L.) Link (Syn. *Panicum colonum* L.; *Milium colonum* (L.) Moench, *Oplismenus colonum* (L.) H.B.K. *Echinochlon zonalis* (Guss.) Parl.; Gramineae

It is an annual tufted grass mainly cultivated in Maharashtra, Madhya Pradesh, Uttar Pradesh, Karnataka, Tamil Nadu, Bihar and Andhra Pradesh both for grain and fodder.

Barnyard grass: *Echinochloa crusgalli* (L.) Beauv. (Syn. *Panicum crusgalli* L. *Milium crusgalli* L. Moench; *Pannisetum crusgalli* (L.) Baumg; *Echinochloa hispidula* (Retz.) Nees ex. Royle; Gramineae

It is an annual grass and is grown mainly in Maharashtra, Madhya Pradesh, Karnataka, Tamil Nadu and Andhra Pradesh. It is grown as a forage crop; while grains are consumed as a human food in times of scarcity.

Klein grass: *Panicum coloratura* L.; Gramaneae

It is an erect and a tusky perennial grass. Usually its dry matter yield varies from 100-120 q/ha. In early stages its protein content has been recorded at about 19 per cent.

Dallis grass (2*n* = 50, 40): *Paspalum dilatatum* Poir; Gramaneae

It is a leafy, spreading and tuft forming fodder grass introduced in India from U.S.A., but it is believed to be a native to South America. The grass is drought tolerant and can withstand frost and is adapted well to subtropical situations. Though it makes a palable fodder, is infested by ergot at flowering and hence one has to be careful in avoiding to feed infested plants since ergot is poisonous.

Paspalum ancylocarpum Nees ex Steud.; Gramineae

The grass has been introduced into India from Brazil. It makes a very good fodder.

Hilo grass: *Paspalum conjugatum* Berg.; Gramineae

It is a perennial fodder grass.

Bahia grass: *Paspalum notatum* Fluegge; Gramineae

This fodder grass has been brought into India from U.S.A.

Kodo-millet: *Paspalum scrobiculatum* L. (Syn. P. *commersonii* Lam.; *P. commersonii* scrobic; *P. serobiculatum* var. *commersonii* Stapf: P. *serobiculatum* var. *frumentaceum* Stapf); Gramineae

It is commonly placed both in the group of foodgrains and fodders; though cultivated mainly as a grain crop in tribal and moisture scarcity areas of Madhya Pradesh, it is grown throughout India; grown for cattle fodder. A decoction of roots is used as an alternative in childbirth. The stem juice has been found useful for corneal opacity.

Seashore paspalum: *Paspalum vagitatum* Sw.; Gramineae

It is used as a soil stabilizer.

Broadleaf paspalum: *Paspalum wettsteinii* Hack., Gramineae

It is a tufted, stoloniferous broad leafed, semi-prostrate perennial grass believed to be a native to humid sub-tropics of Southern U.S.A. It has been found palatable and capable of producing 40-60 q/ha of dry matter.

Its other species inilude *P. plicatulum,* a species making an excellent forage; *P. orbiculare* is believed to be a native to Indian sub-continent and is generally found in grasslands in N-W India.

Kikuyu grass ($2n = 36$): *Pennisetum clandestinum* Hochst. ex.-Chiov.; Gramineae

It is a dense sward forming perennial grass grown in Nilgiri hills of Tamil Nadu and Assam. It is believed to be a native to East Afrcia. Grown both as a fodder crop as well as a soil stabilizer. It has a potential to produce upto 300 q/ha of dry matter, but on an average it ranges between 40 and 120 q/ha. The crude protein content has been observed to vary between 1 and 12 per cent. As a fodder, it has been classed as very highly palatable. This grass can withstand frost.

Birnalsia or Barijhan grass ($2n = 36$): *Pennisetum orientale* L.C. Rich, Gramineae

This fast growing perennial grass is adaptable to temperate and subtemperate climatic conditions. It has been found to tolerate drought as well as burning and is suitable for the soil conservation purposes.

Deenanath grass: *Pennisetum pedicellatum* Trin.; Gramineae

This, an annual fodder grass is believed to be a native to India and Africa. The grass has been found to show good performance on poor soils and in dry and humid climates. Its crude protein content vares from 7 to 13 per cent. The green fodder yield may be as high as 800 q/ha.

Napier grass or Elephant grass or Elefante grass or Infufu grass or Gigante grass ($2n = 27, 28, 56$): *Pennisetum purpureum* K. Schum; Gramineae

It is believed that the napier grass is a native to Zimbabwe (Africa). This grass is grown in Assam, Bengal, Bihar, Uttar Pradesh and Punjab. It embodies a potential to produce as much as 850 q/ha of dry matter. The protein content varies from 8 to 24 per cent as recorded at various growth stages.

Hybrid Napier ($2n = 20, 21$): *Pennisetum purpureum* XP. *americanum* ; Gramineae

Hybrid Napier is a triploid hybrid between Napier and pearlmillet and is sterile, that is, propagated vegetatively either by rooted slips or stem cuttings. The protential to produce dry matter ranges from 50 to 500 q/ha through multi-cuttings. The recorded range of crude protein is 5.2 to 22.8 per cent, but usually it varies from 8 to 11 per cent.

Pennisetum flaccidum Grisep.; Gramineae

It is found in temperate and alpine Himalayan regions from Kashmir to Western Nepal. This is reported to be an important fodder grass grazed by the sheep and goats.

Pennisetum lanatum Klotzsch.; Gramineae

It is distributed in Western Himalayas from Kashmir to Garhwal. It makes an excellent fodder grass as well as an effective soil stabilizer.

Bent-spike Pennisetum: *Pennisetum nervosum* Trin.; Gramineae

It has been introduced into India from Uruguay, is grown for fodder and is drought resistant.

Pennisetum villosum R. Br. ex Fresen; Gramineae

It is a tufted narrow leaved perrennial grass believed to be a native to Ethiopia where from introduced into India. The grass has been found to be drought resistant and classified excellent for grazing.

Pearl millet: *Pennisetum typhoides* (Burm. f.) Stapf. & C.E. Hubb. (Syn. P., *typhoideum* Rich.; *Alopecurus typhoides* Burm. f.), Gramineae

Basically it is classified as one of the coarse cereals and is cultivated as a food grain crop. Its dry stalks called *karvi* are used as a dry fodder. In India it is grown in Rajasthan, Maharashtra, Tamil Nadu, Andhra Pradesh, Harayana, Gujarat and Uttar Pradesh. It is also grown, purely as a green fodder crop.

White grass or Rats tail grass or Sain grass (2 n = 20, 34, 40): *Sehima nervosum* (Rottl.) Stapf. (Syn. *Andropogon nervosum* Rottl. ; *Ischalmum laxum* (R. Br.) Hook. f.); Gramineae

This perennial grass is found all over India and is densely tufted. It is believed to be a native to Africa, Asia and Australia. It tolerates droughty conditions, withstands annual burning, grows on undulating or hill or level lands soils which are medium to deep and makes the highest stage in succession in *sehima/Dichanthium* cover. The grass is relished by the livestock due to its high palatability; can produce 40-75 q/ha of dry matter. Its protein content varies from 5 to 7 per cent.

Sehima notatum (Hack). A. *Camas (Syn: Ischaemum notatum* Hack.); Gramineae

This valuable fodder grass is found in West Himalayas from Chamba (Himachal Pradesh) to Kumaon (Uttar Pradesh).

Sehima sulcatum (Hack.) A. *Camas* (Syn. *Ischaemum sulcatum* Hack.); Gramineae

This fodder grass is distributed in Southern India and Madhya Pradesh.

Golden timothy or Kayzngula grass (2n = 18): *Setaria anceps* Stapf. ex Massey (Syn. S. *sphacelata*) (Schumach.) Stapf. & Hubbard ex Mass); Gramineae

It is believed that this tussocky perennial grass is a native to tropical and sub-tropical Africa. But, S. *sphacelta* has been introduced into India from Brazil and is cultured as a fodder grass. It has been found to be tolerant frost and can also withstand waterlogging conditions. The dry matter productivity varies from 60 to 150 q/ha and the usual range of protein is 7 to 9 per cent.

Cat tail millet: *Setaria glauca* (L.) Beauv. (Syn. *Panicum glaucum* L.); Gramineae

It is an annual grass which is found all over India. It is also cultured as a fodder crop in Deccan Plateau. The grains are consumed as food and dry straw is used as fodder.

Kavatta grass: *Setaria pallide-fusca* (Schumach) Stapf. & C.E. Hubbard; Gramineae.

It occurs in North-West India, Tamil, Nadu, Gujarat and Maharashtra as a fodder crop. The grains are used for human consumption and straw is used as a fodder.

Palm grass: *Setaria palmifolia* (Koeing) Stapf. ; Gramineae

It is an important fodder grass.

Bristly fox tail: *Setaria verticillata* (L.) Beauv.; Gramineae

It is cultivated in Tamil Nadu and Andhra Pradesh as a food grain crop and the straw makes dry fodder for animals.

Italian millet: *Setaria italica* (L.) Beauv. (Syn. *Panicum italicum* L.; *Chaetochloa italica* (L.) Scribn); Gramineae

It is grown basically as a grain crop in Andhra Pradesh, Tamil Nadu, Gujarat, Maharashtra and Karnataka; also cultivated as a fodder crop. The grains embody medicinal properties and are used as diuretic and astringent as well as externally for rheumatism.

Columbus grass ($2n = 40$): *Sorghum almum* Parodi; Gramineae

It is believed to be a native to Argentina. The grass grows tall, robust and turssocky and is a short lived perennial. In first year, it gives more yield than that obtainable in second year. On matter basis (60-92 q/ha) the protein content varies from 12 to 14 per cent. The seeds are light in weight. One kilogram may have as many as 1,21,000 seeds.

Johnson grass ($2n = 40$, diploids $n = 20$): *Sorghum halepense* (L.) Pers. (Syn. *Holcus halepensis* L.; *Andropogon halepensis* (*L.*) Brot.); Gramineae

It is believed that though Johnson grass is a native to Mediterranean coast of Asia, it embodies extensive adaptability and is found well acclimatized to tropical climate too. It has adapted itself to tropical and subtropical conditions, has been found tolerant to frost, flooding and drought. It has been classified as a palatable fodder grass containing 7.4 to 13.5 per cent of protein. Like other sorghums, it embodies HCN in the form of dhurrin which shoots up under conditions of soil moisture stress especially in early growth stages prior to flowering which varies from 170 to 2600 ppm in different genotypes. HCN content exceeding 750 ppm proves toxic to animals. Nitrogen fertilization enhances HCN content. It may be added that Johnson grass in India is better known as an obnoxious weed rather than as a fodder crop.

Sorghum decanense Stapf. (Syn. *purpureosericeus*) (Hochst.) Aschers ex A. Rich; Gramineae

This fodder sorghum is chiefly grown in Central India and Maharashtra.

Durra: *Sorghum durra* (Forsk.) Stapf.; Gramineae

It is a tall grass grown for grain and fodder all over India.

Sorghum membranaceum Chiov; Gramineae

This is also a tall growing grass cultivated in parts of Maharashtra, Madhya Pradesh and Uttar Pradesh both for grain and fodder.

Sorghum roxburghii Stapf. (Syn. *Andropogon sorghum*) Brot. var. *roxburghii* (Hack.) Hook f.; Gramineae

This tall grass is grown in numerous regions of India especially in Maharashtra, Madhya Pradesh, Bihar and Southern parts both for grain and fodder.

Sorghum subglabrascens (Steud.) Schweinf. & Aschers. ; Gramineae

It is a stout grass. It is grown in Maharashtra, Madhya Pradesh, and several areas of Deccan Peninsula both for grain and fodder.

Sudan grass ($2n = 20$ (diploid), $2n = 40$ (tetraploid)): *Sorghum sudanense* (Piper) Stapf.; Gramineae

This annual grass grows fast. It is believed that its place of origin in Africa. A number of hybrids evolved by crossing with sorghum species embodying various desirable traits are in cultivation for fodder purposes. In India, it occurs in Assam, Maharashtra, Punjab, and Tamil Nadu as a fodder crop. The estimated / fodder productivity varies from 100 to 400 q/ha. It makes an acceptable and palatable fodder for the livestock. The protein content has been found to vary from 8.5 to 16.3 per cent. It is important to note that prussic acid poisoning risk is avoidable if fed after flowering.

Sorghum: *Sorghum vulgare* Pers. (Syn. *Andropogon sorghum* (L.) Brot.; *Holcus sorghum* L.); Gramineae

Sorghum is chiefly grown for grain, its stalks and leaves (both green and dry) are used for fodder; chief growing Indian states include Karnataka, Maharashtra, Madhya Pradesh, Andhra Pradesh, Tamil Nadu, Uttar Pradesh, Punjab and Rajasthan. Sorghum grain makes a raw material for malting industry and also serves as a source of starch needed in fermentation to manufacture industrial alcohol as well as acetone.

Sorgo or sugar sorghum: *Sorghum vulgare* Pers. var. *saccharatum* Koern. (Syn. *S. saccharatum* Pers.); Gramineae

Sweet juice is extracted from the stem. The leaves are used as fodder. The residue after juice extraction is usable both as a source of fuel as well as fodder. Its grains are consumed as a foodgrain by human beings especially in rural areas. The grain is also used as an animal feed (concentrate).

Dropseed grass: *Sporobolus marginatus* A. Rich.; Gramineae

Dropseed grass is tufted, stoloniferous and variable. It is commonly found in Northern parts of India, Western areas of Asia and Arabia. At flowering a protein content of about 23 per cent has been observed. The dry matter yield varies from 25-45 q/ha. One kilogramme has been found to contain 77 lakh of seeds.

Sporobolus diander (Retz.) Beauv.; Gramineae

It is a perennial fodder grass locally known as *chiriy aka dana.*

Sporobolus fimbriatus Nees.; Gramineae

It is a perennial fodder grass common to South and East Africa. The grass has reportedly been introduced into India.

Sporobolus maderaspatanus Bor. (Syn. *S. orientalis* Kunth); Gramineae

The grass is used to reclaim salt-affected (*leh*) soils and also makes good fodder.

Sporobolus tremulus Kunth; Gramineae

It is a common pasture and fodder grass and also serves as a sand-stabilizer.

Lunji grass: *Themeda anathera* (Nees.) Hack.; Gramineae

This grass is found in abundance in dry soils and makes an excellent component of *Themeda/Arundinella* cover. By habit, it is a weak, erect, and a perennial grass capable of producing about 65-70 q/ha of dry matter spread over three cuttings.

Elephant grass: *Themeda cymbaria* Hack. (Syn. *Anthistiria cymbaria* Rox.); Gramineae

It is a tall perennial grass found in Western Ghats used to manufacture writing and printing paper, also used as a fodder.

Kangaroo grass: *Themeda quadrivalvis* (L.) Kunth (Syn. *T. ciliata*) (L.t.). Hack.; *Anthistiria cilicata* U.); Gramineae

It has been reported to be used as cattle-feed, also used to prepare paper pulp and as a thatching material.

Rooi grass or Red oat grass ($2n = 20, 40, 60, 80$) and Somatic chromosome number 30, 50):

Themeda triandra Forsk. (Syn. *Anthistiria imberbes* Retz. *T. glauca* Desf. and *T. australis* (R. Br.) Stapf); Gramineae

This fodder grass is found in dry areas of India and believed to be a native to Africa and Asia. It also provides the basic material for the preparation of paper pulp and thatches. The grains are edible and the straw is used as fodder for livestock. It has been found resistant to burning and drought. In Himalaya, it is common in *Thermeda-Arundinella* cover. In three cuttings can produce 40-80 q/ha of dry matter. The protein content at different growth stages has been found to vary from 7 to 17 per cent. One gramme contains 280 seeds.

Themeda tremula (Nees ex Steud.) Hack. (Syn. *Anthistiria tremula* Nees ex Steud.); Gramineae It is a perennial pasture grass grown in South India. The grass is distributed in Deccan Peninsula.

Little parag grass or *Sabi* grass ($2n = 28$ (tetraploid) and $2n = 42$ (hexaploid):

Urochloa mosambicensis (Hack) Dandy ; Gramineae

It is a perennial fodder grass believed to be a native of tropical and South Africa, but has been introduced into India from Australia. The estimated crude protein content varies from 11 to 15 per cent and embodies the potential to yield 20-65 q/ha of dry matter. The seed count stands at 850,000 / kg.

Urochloa panicoides Beauv. (Syn. *Panicum javanicum* Poir); Gramineae

This fodder herb is distributed all over India. The grains are also edible.

Urochloa reptans Stapf = *Brachiaria reptans* (L.) Garod & C.E. Hubbard; Gramineae

This nutritious fodder perennial grass is distributed in Bihar, Bengal and Deccan Peninsula. The grains are also edible.

Urochloa pullulans Stapf; Gramineae

It is believed to be a native to Africa and has been introduced into India and is used for fodder.

Vetiver or khas-khas ($2n = 20$):

Vetiveria zizanioides (L.) Nash (Syn. *Phalaris zizanioides* L.; *Andropogon muricatus* Retz.; *A. squarrosus* Hook f., non L.f. *Anatheram zizanioides* (L.) Hitch-Cock and Chase ; Gramineae

It is densely tufted perennial grass believed to be a native of South-East Asia and Africa. In India, it is grown mainly in Rajasthan, Uttar Pradesh, Punjab and the West Coast. Its wild type is grown in North India and domesticated is grown in South India. It neither flowers nor sets seeds and is vegetatively propagrated. The dried roots are made into aromatic scented matsfans and ornamental baskets and also woven into curtains, which when moistened, cool and scent the air, mostly used in summer to beat the heat. An essential oil obtained from the roots is made used of in the manufacture of perfumes, cosmetics, soaps and to flavour *sherbats* the soft drinks). Its oil is a stimulant, diaphoretic and refrigerant. The dried roots are used to scent the linen clothes. This grass is also used in the manufacture of paper and board. A paste prepared out of roots is applied to cure swellings. The yield of forage obtainable through three cuttings varies from 50 to 72 q/ha of dry matter. The matured plants are used for thatching.

TEMPERATE GRASSES

The temperate climatic conditions prevail between tropics and polar circles are well as in high altitudes (above 2000 m) even in tropical regions as in Himalayan range. The Himalayan temperate and alpine cover measures 2500 and 250-400 kilometers between 27°N and 37°N latitude. The grass cover mostly festucoid (Poaoid) is found up to an altitude of 5000 m and embody C-3 pathway of photosynthesis. These are supposed to withstand chilling and frost. Their active growth takes place only in spring season which is spread over 2-3 months and are grazed by the animals of nomads. Some of them have been briefly dealt with here below:

Crested wheat grass ($2n = 40$): *Agropyron cristalum* (L.) Gaertn.; Gramineae

This grass is drought tolerant and is used for making hay. It also makes an important component of pastures. It is belived to be a native to Europe and is highly adaptable to wide range of soils as well as semi-arid climatic conditions. It can also withstand low temperature, but its productivity in such a situation slides down. Its production potential has been estimated at 40-50 q/ha of dry matter. It makes an excellent fodder when mixed with lucerne or sweet clover.

Twitchgrass or Couch grass: *Agropyron repens* (L.) P. Beauv. (Syn. *Triticum repens* L.); Gramineae

Besides fodder value the grass also has medicinal significance. The decoction of its rhizomes is made use of as a demulcent and diuretic in catarrhal diseases of Genito-urinary, tract.

Intermediate wheat grass ($2n = 42$): *Agropyron intermedium* (Host.) Beauv.; Gramineae

This rhizomatous turf forming perennial grass is believed to be a native to Europe and Asia. It may be grown for pasture hay as well as for soil stabilization. The palatability to animals decreases with the increase in the age of the plant. Its production potential spread over 3-4 cuttings has been estimated at 40-60 g/ha of dry matter. The seed count has been found as 197 seeds/gramme.

Drooping wheat grass ($2n = 28, 42$): *Agropyron semicostatus* Nees; Gramineae

It is also tufted perennial supposed to be a native to Eastern Asia. It is a common grass of temperature and alpine areas, makes good growth on moist, but well-drained soils. It may produce 35-50 q /ha of dry matter in 3-4 cuttings.

Commonbent, Rhode Island bent ($2n = 28$): *Agrotis tennis* Sibth (Syn. *A. vulgaris* With.; *A. hispida* Willd: *A. stolonifera* var. *vulgaris* (With.) Celak; *A. stolonifera* var. *hispida* (Willd), Farw.; *A. alba* var. tenuis (Sibth.) Fiori: Gramineae

This perennial leafy or densely tufted grass presumably has its home in Europe and temperate Asia. It is found in abundance on poor soils. Though it is considered to be a variable forage crop, its productivity is low (25-37.5 q /ha). It has been introduced in temperate regions of India and is extensively used for preparation of Cricket pitches and fine lawns. It has been found to grow well in drought hit, cold and arid areas. Each gramme has approximately 19,000 seeds.

Agropyroa myriantha Hook.f. (Syn. *A. playphylla* Mez.); Gramineae

This is an important pasture grass in Sikkim, Naga and Khasi hills.

Agropyroa nervosa, Nees ex. Trin (Syn. *A. clarkei* Hook. f.); Gramineae.

It is a grass distributed in high altitudes of Eastern Himalayas. It is also an important pasture grass.

Agropyroa procera Retz. (*Erichloa procera* C.E. Hubb.). Syn. *E. polystackya* Hook. f. non. H.B. & K.; *Agrostis procera* Retz.; *Paspalum annulanan* Fluegge; *Milium ramosum* (Retz.); Gramineae

It is a tufted grass used for fodder purposes.

White bent. Fiorin. *A. stolonifera* L. (Syn. *A. alba* auct non. L., *A. wightii* Nees ex. Steud.); Gramineae This is an important pasture grass and is found in hill areas of India. Other important forage grasses of this genus are: *A. alba, A. palastris, A. cannia.*

Meadow Foxtail grass ($2n = 28, 42$): *Alopecurus pratensis;* Gramineae

The place of origin of this grass is believed to be Europe and Asia. It is a tufted perennial grass capable of living for a long period of time. It grows well in cool and moist climates and has been found to be cold resistant. It is also tolerant to high temperatures. The production potential varies from 45-65 q/ha of dry matter obtainable in 3-4 cuttings. Each gramme as per observation contains about 2000 of seeds.

A. arundinaceus Poir (Syn. *A. ventricorus* Pers.); Gramineae

The grass is distributed in Himalayas from Garhwal to Kashmir and has been classified as an important alpine pasture grass.

A. himalaicus Hook. f.; Gramineae

It is an important component of alpine pastures and is found in North-West India.

Tall or False oat grass ($4n = 28$): *Arrhenatherum elatices* (L.) J. and C. Prest.; Gramineae

It is a tufted perennial hay grass. Its green plants are unpalatable and get destroyed in the process of grazing due to trampling. It is used as a component of mixtures of hay meadows on well drained soils. It has a potential to produce 35-55 q/ha of dry matter per annum. The seeds are very light and one kilogramme as per estimates contains approximately 330,000 seeds.

False brome grass (2*n* = 80): *Brachypodium sylvacticulm* Beauv; Gramineae

This is also a tufted perennial grass capable of producing 40-60 q/ha of dry matter per year. Its forage is of poor quality.

Prairie grass of Rescue grass (2*n* = 28, 42, 56): *Bronus catharticus* Vahn, (Syn. *B. unioloides* Kimth); Gramineae

It is beleved to be a native of South America and is a tufted perennial grass lasting only for a short period of time. Its production potential has been estimated as 45-65 q/ha spread over 3-4 cuttings taken in one year. Its crude protein content varies between 3.5 and 4.5 per cent. The estimated seed count is 135,000 seeds/kg.

Schrader brome, Rescue grass: *Bromus unioloides* H.B. & K. (Syn. *Fescuta unioloides* Willd. *Bromus catharticus* Vehl; *B. unioloides* (Willd.) Rasp. *Ceratochloa unioloides* (Willd.) P. Beauv; Gramineae

It is supposed to be a native to sub-tropical South America and has been classified as an important fodder grass of temperate regions.

Smooth brome grass (2*n* = 28, 42, 56, 70): *Bromus inermis Leyss;* Gramineae.

Its home place is believed to be Asia and Europe.

This temperate grass is densely tufted. It is leafy, perennial and thrives for a long period of time. It may produce 50 to 90 q/ha of dry matter. Its protein content varies from 4.5 to 26.5 per cent. It is generally grown mixed with clovers and lucerne.

Small Reed or Bush grass (2*n* = 28, 42, 56): *Calamagrostis epigejos* (L.) Roth.; Gramineae

This perennial grass is supposed to be a native to Europe, Asia and Africa. It is tufted one. Though its herbage is not classified as palatable, is grazed by hill cattles, sheep and goats. The production potential attainable in 3-4 cuttings is 45 to 55 q/ha per annum.

Crested Dog's tail (2*n* = 14): *Cynosures cristatus* L.; Gramineae

It has been introduced in India from Europe and is distributed in Western Himalayas and Assam. It has been classified as an important pasture grass. It can yield 15-25 q/ha. The seed count is 1600 per gramme.

Orchard grass or Cocks foot (2*n* = 28): *Dactylis glomerata* L. (Syn. *Bromus glomeratus* (L.) Scop.; *Festuca glomerata* (L.) All: *Trachypoa vulgaris* Babanii; Gramineae

Its home is believed to be Europe, North Africa and temperate Asia. It grows erect, makes turf during cool season. This perennial grass is tolerant to shade frost and drought. This multi-cut grass has a potential to produce 95-125 q/ha of dry matter through five cuttings per annum. The protein content varies from 9 to 18 per cent. In India, it is found, in Punjab, Kashmir, Assam and Nilgiri hills of Tamil Nadu.

Oat grass or Heath grass: *Danthonia jaquemontii* Bor; Gramineae

Heath grass is a tufted perennial distributed in temperate and alphine Himalayas on slopes at an elevation of 3000-4270 m. It usually inhabits sandy and peaty soils. It is frequently found on moorland, heaths and poor grasslands. It yields low quality fodder.

Tufted hair grass or Hassock grass (2*n* = 26, 28): *Deschampsia caespitosa* (L.) Beauv. (Syn. *Aira caespitosa* L.); Gramineae

It is believed to be a native to Europe and Asia and is densely tufted ornamental grass distributed in ill-drained and wet temperate Himalayas from Kashmir through Nepal to Sikkim. It is also found on marshy fields, rough grasslands and the moorlands. The estimated yield potential stands at 25-45 q/ha per annum. It is also called as tussock grass which embodies poor palatability.

Tall fescue (2*n* = 42): *Festuca arundinacea* Schreb.; Gramineae

This grass is native to Europe and temperate Asia and is tufted, bunchy, deep rooted, cool season and long lived. It is capable of tolerating drought, wet soil conditions and pH between 4.5 and 9.5. The grass has been classified as palatable. It embodies a yield potential of about 36-93 q/ha of dry matter per annum. The protein content recorded in spring, summer and fall season stands at 17, 19 and 22 per cent, respectively. The observed seed count is about 575 per gramme.

Meadow fescue (2*n* = 14): *Festuca pratensis* Huds. (Syn. / *elatior* L.); Gramineae

It is a perennial grass believed to be a native to Europe and South West Asia. In India, it is distributed in South India. The leaves are smooth, bright green, and make a leafy bottom growth. The grass is cold resistant and comprises an important component of pastures. The palatability rating is high similar to rye grass and embodies a good compatibility with clovers, lucerne, birds foot trefoil and other grasses *viz.*, timothy and orchard grass. It has a potential to produce 55-85 q/ha per year of dry matter containing 11-16 per cent of crude protein. The observed count is about 500 per gramme.

Giant fescue: *Festuca* gejantea (L.) Vill.; Gramineae

This fodder grass commonly occurs in Western Himalayas from Kashmir to Kumaon.

Sheep's fescue: *Festuca ovina* L.; Gramineae

It is a good fodder grass.

Red fescue (2*n* = 42, 56): *Festuca rubra* L.; Gramineae

This fodder grass is found in Himalayas and Khasi hills in India. It is perennial, creeping rhizomatous, found all over Europe and temperate Asia. Though regarded as a good bottom grass, the productivity is low 15-30 q/ha of dry matter per year having nearly 9.1 per cent of crude protein. The observed seed count is about 1350 per gramme.

Velvet grass or Yorkshire Fog (2*n* = 14): *Holcus lanatus* L.; Gramineae

This perennial tufted and softly haired grass is believed to be a native to Asia, Europe and Africa. The grass is found growing on both light and heavy textured soils in dry as well as wet conditions particularly on acid soils. The observed production potential varies from 25 to 45 q/ha. It makes a palatable fodder only while young since on maturity it becomes coarse. The observed seed count is 3300 seeds per gramme.

"*Holcus hatepensis* L. is nearly similar to *sorghum halephense* (L.) Pers."

Crested hair grass (2*n* = 28): Koeleria cristata (L.) Pers. (Syn. Aira cristata L.; *Airochloa cristata* (L.) Link.; *Dactvlis cristata* (L.) M.B.; *Festuca cristata* (L.) Vill.; Gramineae

It is a tufted perennial grass adapted to dry low meadows and pastures raised on sandy soils. The dry matter yield varies from 30 to 40 q/ha per annum. Its species *viz.; K. gracilis, K. britannica* and *K. albescens* appear similar to *K. cristata.* The grass is also a good soil- binder and hence embodies soil conservation value.

Koeleria phleoides Pers.; Gramineae

It is distributed in Punjab, Delhi and Kashmir. The grass provides a quality fodder.

Rye grass (2*n* = 14, 28): *Lolium multiflorum* Lam. (Syn. *L. italicunt* A. Br.; Gramineae.

This annual grass is believed to be native to Central and South Europe, North-West Africa and South-West Asia and has been introduced into Assam, India, basically for fodder purposes. It has the potential to produce 115-225 q/ha of forage (as dry matter) per year. The protein content depends upon the growth stage and lies between 10 and 25 per cent. It is ideally suitable for temporary pastures and hay-making and can easily, crossed with *L. perentic Festuca arundinacea* and *F. pratensis.* The observed seed count is about 460 per gramme.

Perennial rye grass (2*n* = 14, 28): *Loliunt perenne* L. (Syn. *L. brastilianum* Nees.), Gramineae

It is a tufted perennial grass distributed in Sikkim, Kashmir and Nilgiri hills. It imbodies a trait to regenerate quickly, tolerant to heavy grazing. frost and makes luxuriant growth on fertile heavy textured soils to produce 125/190 q/ha of dry matter per annum containing 14.5-21.5 per cent of crude protein.

The observed seed count is about 500 seeds per gramme.

Darnel grass: *Loluim temulentum* L.: Gramineae

In India, it is found in Western Himalayas, Punjab and upper Gangetic Plains and is used as a fodder.

Rice grass: *Oryzopsis aequizlumis* Duthie.; Gramineae

It is a robust, tufted, smooth, erect perennial grass commonly distributed in Himalayas. It may produce 30-40 q/ha of dry matter per year.

Pennisetum grass: *Pennisetum flaccidum* Griseb.; Gramineae.

This perennial grass is distributed in temperate and alpine areas from Kashmir to Western Nepal. The sheep and goats graze this grass. It can produce 30-40 q/ha of dry matter per year.

Reed canary grss (2*n* = 28, 42): *Phalaris arundinacea.* L., var. *pieta* L.; Gramineae

Reed canary grass is robust, coarse, sodformer, tall growing on poorly drained soils of 5 to 8 pH, organic matter rich sandy soils or fertile loams or clays. Embodies potential to produce 60-135 q/ha of dry matter contain 11-29 per cent of crude protein as estimated at various growth stages. Grazing in early stages is advocated when it is acceptably palatable.

Hardinge grass or Joowoomba canary grass (2*n* = 28): *Phalaris tuberosa* L.; Gramineae

This tall, hairless, deep rooted. rhizomatous (red colour rhizomes) is a perennial grass introduced into India from Mediterranean region and has been found suitable for pasturage in hilly areas. Studies have envinced that sole and continuous feeding in autumn and winter causes poisoning especially in sheep. This can be precluded by growing *Phalauris* in a mixture with legumes or by the administration of cobalt pellets to the consuming animals to avoid staggers especially in sheep.

Timothy grass (2*n* = 14, 42): *Phletan pratense* L.; Gramineae

Timothy grass is a perennial tufted one, a native of Europe and Asia. It is grown in India as a pasture grass. It is distributed in Shimla (Himachal Pradesh) and Shillong (Meghalaya). The estimated dry matter production varies from 32 to 70 q/ha depending upon the growth stage and has shown a production up to 350 q/ha or more. Its protein content varies from 6.5 to 16.3 per eent. Seed count has been observed to vary from 2400 to 2800 per gramme.

Smooth stalked meadow grass or Kentucky blue grass (2*n* = 28, 36, 124): *Poa pratense* L.; Gramineae

This grass is tufted, leafy, erect, long lived stoloniferous perennial found in temperate and alpine areas of Himalayas. It imbodies a shallow root system and is as such sensitive to low moisture and temperature conditions, however, grows oil ill-drained soils of low fertility. It has a productivity potential of 25-45 q/ha and the crude protein content is about 11-13 per cent. It is an excellent pasture and lawn grass relished by all classes of animals.

Alpine meadow grass: *Poa alpina* L.; Gramineae

It is a densely tufted, gregarious grass found in the Western Himalayas from Kashmir; to Garhwal and is used for fodder.

Dwarf or Annual meadow grass: *Poa annua* L.; Gramineae

It is also tufted grass believed to be a native to North Mediterranean region, found in Himalayas, Khasi hills and the Nilgiri. It is lopped for fodder.

Bulbous meadow grass: *Poa bulbosa* L. var. *elanata* Stapf; Gramineae

This tufted fodder grass is found in Western Himalayas.

Poa nepalensis Wall ex Duthie (Syn. P. *annua* var. *nepalensis*); Gramieae

It is a tall perennial grass found in Kumaon, Tehri-Garhwal and Kulu. The grass is used as a fodder.

– *Poa songarica* = *Eremopoa persica* (Trin.) Roschev. var. *songarica* Bor (Syn. *Poa persica* Trin. var. *songarica* Hook. f.); Gramineae

It is an annual grass found in Western Himalayas from Kunawar to Kashmir and Western Tibet.

The grasses listed below also yield importance essential oils used for different commercial and industrial purposes.

Citronella grass: C. *nardus* (L.) Rendle (Syn. *Andropoga nardus* L., A. *ampliflourus* Steud.), Gramineae; Camel hay-C. *pendilous;* Gramineae; and C. *Schoelanthus* L. (Spreng) (Syn. *Andropogon schoenanthus* L., C. *densiflorus* Stapf.; A. *laniger* (Desf.) *jwarancusa* subsp. *Laniger* (Desf.) Hook. (f.)

This fragrant grass is found in Southern Asia. It is cultivated as a source of an oil called citronella oil. The oil is used in the manufacture of liniment, perfumes and soaps. It has been named on the basis of its centron-like smell. The oil contains cetronellal, a liquid aldehyde found in essential oils, and is used as a flavouring agent and also in the perfume industry.

SECTION 22
LEGUMES

The word legume has been derived from *lengumen* which means a pulse. From literary point of view this word denotes something gathered or picked. Scientifically a legume is any plant belonging to family Leguminosae Syn. Fabaceae specially the one used for food, feed and for soil amelioration or improvement. The seed or the seed vessels of legumenous plant is usually dehiscent by both sutures which divide it into two parts of valves. It is said that this word has come from the French word Leguma; or Latin *Legumin* or Legumen which means a leguminous plant. As already indicated *Legere* in French means together. It may be briefly stated that the legumes are the dicotyledon herbs. shrubs or trees embodying fruits that are either legumes or dowments means pods. The legumes bear nodules on the roots which fix atmospheric nitrogen with the help of *Rhizobium* bacteria. The group includes important food and forage plants like peas, beans, clovers etc. which embody a dry dehiscent one celled fruit developed from a simple superior ovary and usually dehiscing into two valves with the seed attached to the ventral sutures. As already indicated, its fruit is called a pod. The legumes make a valuable forage as they have high protein content almost as mush as contained by grasses. They also fix atmospheric nitrogen in quantities varying from 60 to 450 kg N/ha. Half to two third of the fixed nitrogen is added to the soil as evinced by various studies and estimates. This group includes 650 genera and 14,000 species. Legumes like grasses are also divided into two groups *viz.*, tropical and temperate. The important members of each group commonly used for forage have been briefly discussed below:

TROPICAL LEGUMES

Most of the tropical legumes are the members of the tribes *viz.,* Stylosantheae, Desmodieae and Phaseoleae. Generally, this group of forage legumes grows larger than their temperate counterparts. However, their growth period is relatively shorter and hence have been classified as less regenerative. Tropical legumes are discriminative so far as the response to *Rhizobium* bacteria is concerned. It has been observed that this group of legumes fixes atmospheric nitrogen in a quantity which varies from 40 to 260 kg/ha. In pure plant densities their estimated dry matter yield varies from 100 to 1500 q /ha. They have been reported to embody 10-15 per cent of protein on dry matter basis. All the tropical legumes are sensitive to frost and prolonged winters or low temperatures. The frost may also bring about their mortality. These legumes *vis-a-vis* temperate legumes remain green relatively for a longer period of time and therefore, can be introduced into the grassland to upgrade forage quality and their palatability as well as acceptability to the animals. A brief account of the important tropical legumes is a follows:

Joint vetch or thornale as mimosa: *Aeschynomene americana* L.; Papilionaceae

This perennial legume is believed to be native to Central and South America. It competes well with the grasses on account of its deep root system. It performs well on the soils of poor and low fertility and is also adapted to unfertile wetlands. Its productive potential has been estimated at about 140 q/ha, while the protein content varies from 16 to 20 per cent. The estimated seed count stands at about 370 seeds/gramme.

Solapith: *Aeschynomene aspera* L.; Papilionaceae

It is a perennial tall growing shrub embodying spongy floating stems. It is commonly found in wet places of Uttar Pradesh, Bihar, Maharashtra, Orissa, Assam, Bengal and South India. Its soft wood has insulating properties and is used to prepare sun-hats, toys, artificial flowers, models *etc.* It also serves as a replacement for bottle corks and is used in the manufacture of swimming jackets and belts. Its leaves are edible, while the pith is made use of for embedding plant materials for cutting free sections. It is also cut into small pieces which are strung together and are worn by tribal people as ear ornaments.

Aeschynomenae indica L.; Papilionaceae

This shrub generally occurs along the canal banks. It is found in Kashmir, Bengal, Assam, South Andamans and South India. Its soft wood is used to prepare solar hats and the plants make a source of fodder for animals.

Alyce clover (2*n* = 16): *Alysicarpus vaginalis* (L.) DC; Papilionaceae

It is believed to be a native to India and other tropical countries. In Himalayas, it is found up to an elevation of 1500 metres. It has a capacity to yield 18-30 q/ha of dry matter annually. Its young plants embody 26 per cent of crude protein. It is non-specific to *Rhizobium* bacteria, but requires scarification of seed for induction of germination. It is well adapted to sandy loam soils and competes well with indigenous grasses both in tropics and subtropics.

Alysicarpus glumaceus (Vahl.) DC; Papilionaceae

It is found all over India and is used as fodder.

Alysicarpus longifolius Wight & Arn; Papilionaceae

This herb is distributed all over Indian plains and makes a good source of fodder.

Alysicarpus monilifer DC; Papilionaceae

It is a prostrate herb which profusely branches and is used as fodder.

Alysicarpus rugorus Will. DC; Papilionaceae

It is also an important fodder crop.

Ban Kulthi: *Athylosia scarabaeoides* (L.) Benth.; Papilionaceae

This perennial climber or trailing herb is believed to be a native to Asia and Africa. It annually yields 9 to 11 q/ha of dry matter containing 7-15 per cent of crude protein.

Calopo (2*n* = 36): *Calopogonium mucunoides* Desv.; Papilionaceae

It is a creeping herb or a woody climber. It is a native to tropics and sub-tropics of America. The estimated dry matter yield varies from 130 to 145 q/ha. Its palatability is low, but it grows well with *Brachiaria. Panicum* and *Setaria* species. The protein content on dry matter basis has been found to range between 14 and 18 per cent. The estimated seed count stands at 70-75 seeds / gramme. The herb is grown as a cover crop in rubber and other plantation crops. It also helps in the control of soil erosion.

Butterfly Pea or Centro (2*n* = 20): *Centrosema pubescens* Benth; Papilionaceae

This herb has been introduced in India from tropical South America as a cover crop for coffee plantations in Tamil Nadu and Karanataka. It makes a vigorous growth and embodies pubescent stems. It adapts well to humid and sub-humid tropics as well as sub-tropics. Its seeds remain dormant for about one year. The herbage is highly palatable and the plants have the capacity to withstand grazing. Its dry matter yield has been estimated at 25 to 125 q/ha. Its protein content as observed stands at 10-25 per cent. The estimated seed count is 40-41 seeds/gramme. It is used as a fodder as well as for the control of soil erosion.

Butterfly Pea (2*n* = 16): *Clitoria ternatea* L.; Papilionaceae

This rambling climber is perennial, grows in summer and is believed to be a native to tropical America. It may yield up to 340 q/ha of dry matter/annum containing 10-25 per cent of crude protein. It is also palatable to the livestock. Its dormancy can be broken by treating its seed with sulphuric acid of 1.8 specific gravity for 20 minutes. It is grown in hedges or on walls. Seeds are used as purgative, while the roots as cathartic, diuretic and purgative.

Desmodium green leaf (2*n* = 22): *Desmodium intortum* **(Mill.) Urb.; Papilionaceae**

It is a trailing perennial believed to be native to Central and South America. It has been found to fix nearly 300 kg of N/ha per annum. It has a potential to produce 85-125 q/ha of dry matter. Its protein content has been found to vary from 10-20 per cent at different growth stages. The seed count as observed stands at about 600 seeds/gramme.

Desmodium silver leaf: *Desmodium uncinatum* (Jacq.) DC; Papilionaceae

It is a large perennial herb which is believed to be a native to Central and South America. It is adapted to humid and sub-humid tropics and sub-tropics. Desmodium silver leaf can tolerate low pH, frost and embodies qualities to resume growth early in the season. Its production potential has been estimated at 45 to 65 q/ha per year, while the protein content lies between 10 and 25 per cent. One gramme has been found to have nearly 220 seeds.

Desmodium pallaceum Guill & Pers; Papilionaceae

It has been introduced into India from Nigeria. This perennial herb is grown for fodder.

Desmodium triflorum (L.), DC. / Syn. Hedyrarum *triflorum* L.; Papilionaceae

It is a profusely branched gregarious and a trailing herb. It is grown both for fodder and soil conservation purposes. It produces an excellent green turf.

Desmodium gangeticum (L.) /DC-; Papilionaceae

This shrub is found all over India. Its roots and seeds are used as febrifuge and anticatarrhalic medicines.

Desmodium tiliaefolium G. Don; Papilionaceae

It is found in Western Himalayas. Its bark fibre is used to prepare rope and baskets.

Desmodium tortuosum (Sw.) DC/ Papilionaceae

It has been introduced in Southern areas of India and makes a good fodder crop.

Lablab bean of Hycinth bean (2*n* = 22): *Lablab purpureus* (L.) Sweet (Syn. *Dolichos lablab; Lablab vulgaris* Sawi) ; Papilionaceae

It is a tall and twinning herb believed to be native to tropical Asia and probably India. It is cultivated all over the country and has been found to fix about 225-230 kg N/ha annually. It can produce 20-45 q/ha of dry matter containing 10-21 per cent of crude protein. Seeds are also consumable as a vegetable. This is also grown on an extensive scale to prevent soil erosion and as a cover crop. It makes a good quality fodder. The seeds are large in size and one kilogramme has been found to contain 4000 seeds.

White popinac, Horse tamarind, Leucaena (2*n* = 104): *Leucaena leucceophala* (Lam) de leucocephala Wit (Syn. L. *glauca,* L. Benth.; *Acacia glauca* Willd; *Mimosa leucocephala* Lamk.; Papilionaceae

This is a leguminous shrub or a small tree believed to be native to Central and South America and Pacific high lands. It has a very deep root system and is adapted to tropics and sub-tropics. The young fruits and seeds are edible. Its leaves and pods are fed to cattle, sheep and goats. However, it contains 2-5 per cent mimosine, an alkaloid which has been found to be harmful to the monogastric animals in whom sole feeding leads to hair shedding. It is recommended that Leucaena in animal forage should not be more than one-third of the total fodder. It has three types namely Hawaiian, Salvador or Arborial or Guatemala and Peru types. Its productivity varies from 65 to 225 q/ha. The herbage embodies 20-35 per cent crude protein. The estimated seed count is 24-25 gramme. It is also grown to provide shade and cover to tea, coffee rubber plantations.

Lotononis (2*n* = 36): *Lotononis bainesii* Baker; Papilionaceae

It is a creeping prostrate perennial pasture legume. Its place of origin is believed to be South Africa. It adapts well to moist tropical and sub-tropical climates. It is capable of tolerating frost and waterlogging. Its forage has been classified as highly palatable and nutritive. It has a potential to yield 25-55 q/ha of dry matter which contains 17-27 per cent of crude protein. It is absolutely essential to inoculate the seed to obtain a satisfactory plant density and subsequent growth. The estimated seed count is about 3.3 million seeds / kg.

Siratro, (2*n* = 22): *Macroptilium atropurpureum* (DC) Urb.; Papilionaceae

It is a deep rooted perennial legume. Its stems are trailing, somewhat hairy and throw roots at the nodes. It is adapted to tropical and subtropical climatic conditions. Siratro is drought resistant and can very well withstand grazing impact. Its dry matter yield and protein content as per estimates average from 20 to 85 q/ha and 15 to 24 per cent, respectively. Its seeds are hard coated and hence it is essential to soak them in water for about 24 hours followed either by mechanical scarification or submergence in sulphuric acid for 3-15 minutes to augment their germination. The estimated seed count is 75 seeds /gramme.

Phasey bean (2*n* = 22): *Macroptilium lathyroides* (L.) Urb.; Papilionaceae

It is believed to be a native to India. It is annual, grows erect, adaptable to subtropical climates, tolerant to low soil fertility, acid and poorly drained soil conditions. Its production potential varies from 23 to 65 q/ha embodying approximately 17 per cent of crude protein.

Archer axillaris (2*n* = 20): *Macrotyloma axillare* (E. Mey.) Verdc., Papilionaceae

Its place of origin is believed to be tropical Africa, by growth habit it is a twining type of perennial legume capable of producing 15-22 q/ha of dry matter. The estimated seed count is 100 seeds / gramme. It is moderately tolerant to trampling and grazing.

Velvet bean horse-eye bean: *Mucuna pruriens* (L.) DC. (Syn. *Stizolobium deeringianum* Bort.): Papilionaceae

It is believed that velvet bean has its home in Southern Asia and Malaysia. In tropics and subtropics this trailing vine is good for a temporary pasture. This bean is adaptable to moist climate, can grow on a variety of soils *viz.*; sands and clays, and makes satisfactory growth even on acid soils. It is capable of suppressing weeds due to its vigorous growth. It may produce 65-75 q/ha of dry matter containing 11.5-21 per cent of crude protein. Its one thousand grains (test-weight) weigh one kilogramme (each grain weighs one gramme).

Florida velvet bean: *Mucuna deeringiana* (Bort.) Merr. (Syn. *Stizolobium deeringianum* Bort.); Papilionaceae

In India, it has been brought from Australia. It is a herbaceous vine grown as a cover crop. This bean makes a quality fodder and is also used as a green manure crop.

Mucuna purita Hook. (Syn. *M. pruriens* Baker); Papilionaceae

It is a twining type of annual found almost all over India especially in Andaman and Nicobar Islands. It has been found useful both as a cover crop and for green manuring purposes. Its cultivation is done for pods which are used as a vegetable and the young tender leaves are used as a fodder. The seeds are used as a nervine tonic. Its strong infusion of roots, mixed with honey is administered to cure cholera.

Mucuna bracteata DC; Papilionaceae

It is also a twining herb which is both annual and perennial distributed in tropical Eastern Himalayas and Assam. The seeds and trichomes from pods embody medicinal properties identical to those of *Mucuna purita* as discussed above.

Mucuna capitata Wight & Arn. ; Papilionaceae

It is also a twining type of legume distributed in foot hills of Himalayas and Central India. The seeds are considered a good tonic.

Lyon bean: *Mucuna cochinchinensis* (Lour.) A. Cheval. (Syn. M. *nivea* DC.); Papilionaceae

It is primarily cultured as a cover crop to protect soil against loss and also for green manuring purposes. The fruits called pods are consumed as a nutritive vegetable.

Mucuna gigantea DC.; Papilionaceae

In India, it is distributed in Sunderbans, the Andamans and Malabar. The seeds are edible.

Mucuna monosperma DC.; Papilionaceae

It is distributed in Nepal, Khasi Hills, Deccan Peninsula and the Andamans. Its seeds embody medicinal properties and are used to cure cought, asthama and tongue- affections.

Mucuna nigricans (Lour.) Steud. (Syn. M. *imbricate DC.*); Papilionaceae

It is distributed in sub-Himalayan tracts, Bihar, North Bengal, Assam, Madhya Pradesh and the Andamans. Watery stem-sap in Philippines is used to cure cough and fever.

Perennial soybean or Rhodesian Kudzu vine (2*n* = 22, 44): *Neonotonia wightii* (Arn.) Lackey (Syn. *Glycine javanica* L.; *G. Wightii* (Arn.) Verde.); Papilionaceae

Perennial soybean is twining herb which is commonly found in Western Ghats. It makes an effective cover crop as well as a fodder crop. It is also used for soil conservation purposes. The protein content varies from 10 to 20 per cent and embodies a potential to produce 22 to 60 q/ha of dry matter. Its seed count is 154-155 seeds/gramme.

Soybean: *Glycine max* (L.) Merr. (Syn. *G. soja* (L.) Sieb. & Zucc.; *G. hispida* (Moench) Maxim.; *Soja max* (L.) Piper); Papilionaceae

This bushy herb is believed to be a native to South-East Asia. Now in India soybean is grown as a pulse crop in Punjab, Haryana, Uttar Pradesh, Himachal Pradesh, Maharashtra, Gujarat, Naga, Hills, Manipur and Kashmir. It has become an important oilseed crop mainly cultivated in Madhya Pradesh wherein its area in recent past has increased by leaps and bounds. The seeds yield an edible, semi-drying oil used to manufacture margarine, and also to prepare oil cloth, linoleum, paints, printing inks, soaps, disinfectants and insecticides. 'Lectin', phospholipids, the by-product of oil-industry is used as wetting and stabilizing agent in food, cosmetics, pharmaceuticals, plastic, leather and soap industries. Lipoxidase enzyme is prepared from soybean and is made use of in baking industry for bleaching flour. Its protein isolates are reported to have been prepared from beans, which have been spun to yield protein fibres used in preparation of various food products. Soymeal, the residue after oil extraction, is rich in protein and makes a valuable cattle feed. Meal and soybean protein are used to manufacture synthetic fibre, adhesives and textile sizes. Germinated soybean is rich in vitamin C. Straw is usable as fodder.

Puero or Tropical kudzu. (2*n* = 22, 24): *Pueraria phaseoloides* (Roxb.) Benth; Papilionaceae

Puero is believed to be a native to South-East Asia. In India, it is found in Eastern Himalayas, Assam and Khasi Hills. It makes a vigorous growth; is a robust perennial endowed with deep root system and climbing hairy shoots. It is grown as green manure and a fodder crop. Sterm fibre is made into ropes and twines. Its productivity potential has been estimated at 50-107.5 q/ha of dry matter containing 11-16 per cent of crude protein. Each gramme as per estimates has 80 seeds.

Thunberg Kudzu /Thunberg kudzu vine: *Pueraria lobate* (Willd.) Ohwi (Syn. *P. thunbergiana* Benth); Papilionaceae

Its home is believed to be China and Japan. This shrub is adapted to poor and eroded soils of warm and moist regions. It is grown for fodder and conservation of soil.

Paeraria tuberoses (Roxb). ex Willd. DC; Papilionaceae

It is distributed in Western Himalayas, Kumaon, Orissa and West Peninsula. The tubers and leaves are edible.

Rhynchosia (2*n* = 22): *Rhynchosia minima* (L.) DC; Papilionaceae

This climbing or trailing or prostrate legume as per prevailing belief is native to Indian subcontinent, tropical Africa and South America. In India, it is distributed throughout the plains and in the Himalayas. It has been found tolerant to mild frost. drought and grazing and to do well on soils of poor fertility. It embodies a potential to produce 20-40 q/ha of dry matter. Though classified of low palatability, protein is approximately 15-16 per cent which denotes its good level. Its leaves are reported to be used as abortifacient.

Rhynchosia capirata DC; Papilionaceae

It is a trailing herb and is used as fodder.

Brazilian Lucerne or Schofield stylo or Stylo (2*n* =20): *Stylosanthes guyanensis* (Aubl.) Sw. subsp. *guywiensis* (Syn. S. *gracilis* H.B. & K.); Papilionaceae

It is either a perennial herb or scandent shrub brought in from Brazil and introduced into Bihar, West Bengal and Tamil Nadu as a valuable component of a pasture. The observed productivity potential is 20-100 q/ha per annum containing 12-19.2 per cent of crude protein. It is tolerant to drought, can grow on acidic and ill-drained soils of low fertility in tropical conditions. One gramme has been found to contain 250 seeds.

Wild lucerne: *Stylosanthes fruticosa* (Retz.) Alston (Syn. *S. mucronata* Willd.; *S. bojeri* Vog.); Papilionaceae

Wild lucerne is a herb or a undershrub found in dry areas of Andhra Pradesh, Karnataka and Orissa. It is recommended as fodder for animals.

Townsville stylo: *Stylosanthes hulliilis* H.B.K. (Syn. *S. sundaica* Taub.); Papilionaceae

It is an annual and is self-regenerating. Its seed count is 440 gramme. Townsville stylo is adapted to semi-arid regions in tropics and subtropics and is susceptible to shade.

Other important species of stylo are:

*Carribean/ Verano stylo (*stylosanthes hamata*), its place of origin is believed to be South and Central America. It is drought tolerant and is capable of growing in sandy soils and sand dunes.

*Shrubby stylo (*stylosanthes scabra* Syn. *S. diarthra, S. gloides,* and *S. plicata* is a perennial highly, tolerant to drought and can produce 10-100 q/ha of dry matter having a seed count of 500 seed /gramme.

Rabbit vine: *Teramnius labialis* (L.f.) Spreng.; Papilionaceae

Rabbit vine is a climbing or widespreading hairy herb. It is believed to be a native of tropical and Subtropical areas. It production potential has been observed to vary from 12 to 130 q/ha per year of dry matter. Rabit vine is a pasture herb, embodying high acceptability and grows well both in pure and mixed swards.

Kenya white clover (2*n* = 16): *Trifolium semipilosum* Fres.; Papilionaceae

This perennial subtemperate pasture legume is native to African continent and looks like white clover, but is less frost tolerant. It is drought tolerant and is suitable for mixed growing with Italian millet, kodomillet, kikiya and rhodes grasses. It may yield 85-90 q/ha of dry matter annually. The estimates evinced that one kilogramme contains 700,000-1,000,000 seeds.

Dalrymple vigna (2*n* = 22): *Vigna lateola* (Jacq.) Benth.; Papilionaceae.

It is believed that dalrymple vigna is a native to coastal and swamply regions of Africa, Central and South Amierica. It is an annual grown in summer season having climbing and twining habit. Its dry matter yield is relatively low (15-20 q/ha) and contains about 17.5 per cent of crude protein at blooming. It has been classified as a highly palatable forage which can with stand heavy grazing. The estimated seed count is 37,000 seeds per kg kilogramme.

Sarawak bean:

Vigna hosei (Craib) Backer (Syn. *Dolichos hosei* Craib; *V. oligosperma* Backer); Papilionaceae

It is believed to be a native to Borneo and has been introduced in India in Tamil Nadu. It makes a good green manuring crop.

Vigna trilobata (L.) Verdcourt (Syn. *Dolichos trilobatus* L.; *Phaseolus trilobatus* (L.) Schreb.; P. *trilobus* Sensu Ait. & Owct., non *Dolichos trilobus* L.; Papilionaceae

It is grown throughout India mainly as a fodder crop.

Cowpea: *Vigna unguiculata* (L.) Walp. (Syn. V. *sinensis* (L.) Savi ex. Hassk.; V. *catjang* (Burm.f). Walp.; V. *cylindrica* (L.) Skeels.; V. *sesquipedalis* Frubw.); Papilionaceae

Cowpea is classified as a pulse crop, a vegetable and a fodder crop and also sometimes used as a green manure crop. It is cultivated all over India. Its young shoots and leaves are consumed as spinach.

Cowpea: *Vigna vexillata* (L.) A. Rich. (Syn. V. *capensis* (E. Mey.) Walp.); Papilionaceae This herbacious vine is cultivated all over India for its edible roots and seeds.

TEMPERATE LEGUMES

Most of the legumes used for fodder purposes are the members of sub-family Papilionoideae. Their flowers are zygomorphic, papilionaceous and corolla is imbricate. The process of cross-pollination takes place through tripping, or squeezing of pollen through piston mechanism or by insects which visit the flowers time and again. Generally, this group of forage legumes is frost resistant, but damaged by very low temperatures as well as snowfall. The extent of winter hardiness varies from one to other species and from one to the other cultivar. They are the most important components of ley farming system. These legumes are long day plants and the 12 hours or more is their critical photo-period requirement. These are very specific to *Rhizobium* bacterial requirement unlike tropical legumes. These legumes also make highly nutritive and palatable forage and fodder for the livestock.

Cicer milkvetch L.; *Astragalus cicer* L.; Papilionaceae

This perennial forage legume grows well in dryland conditions in temperate areas. It is also tolerant to acidity and alkalinity as well as drought and frost. The estimated dry matter production varies from 35 to 65 q/ha. Cicer milkvetch makes a slower germination and growth than lucerne.

Indian tragacanth: *Agstragalus heratensis* Bunge; Papilionaceae

It is a large sized shrub. Its stems make a source of gum locally called *Katira* gabina. It is mostly used for grazing purposes. Its tender twigs and leaves make a source of fodder.

Agstragalus prolixus Sieb; Papilionaceae

It is an undershrub mostly found in Punjab. The gum tragacanth is obtained by tapping the stems. This gum is used in the manufacture of cosmetic, calico printing and confectionery. The hydrophobic and colloidal properties of the gum are of significance in the manufacture of ice creams, lotions, liquor, sizing and number of other industrial products.

Agstragalus strobiferous Royle; Papilionaceae

It also yields gum from the stems which is used for confectionery. It is distributed in Western Himalayas and Kashmir.

The other important species of *Agstragalus* are – purple milkvetch (A. *danicus*).

Wild liquorice: *Agstragalus glycyphyllos;* Papilionaceae

These are low and tall growing perennials making an important component of grasslands.

Crown vetch: *Coronilla varia* L.; Papilionaceae

It is a long lasting perennial herb believed to be a native to South Europe, Asia Minor and Northern Africa. It is resistant to frost and drought and can produce 25 to 55 q/ha of dry matter. Its rate of regeneration is slower than lucerne. It grows well on permeable and well drained calcareous soils. It has been found to be more easily digestible than lucerne.

Sericea lespedeza, Perennial lespedeza:

Lespedeza cuneata (Dotinont) G. Don. (Syn. L. *sericea* Miq. non Benth); Papilionaceae

It is also a long lasting perennial erect to semi-erect growing leafy herb, or undershrub. It has been introduced in India. Its native place is believed to be China, Korea and Japan. It grows well on soils of poor fertility where neither clover nor lucerne can be grown. It can produce up to 60 q/ha of dry matter.

Korean lespedeza:

Lespedeza stipulacea Maxim; Papilionaceae

It is an annual legume grown for forage on small scale. It is also an exotic legume brought into India. It works well as a green manure crop and also for the control of soil erosion.

Japanese clover or Common lespedeza:

Lespedez striata (Thumb.), Hook. & Arn.; Papilionaceae

It is a pubescent herb and has been introduced in India from Uruguay. It is grown in a number of places in India. It is useful both as a fodder and makes an effective erosion controlling plant. It is also used for green manuring purposes and can be grown on soils having pH range of 4.5-6.5.

Birds foot trefoil ($2n = 12, 24$): *Lotus cornicalatus* L.; Papilionaceae

It is a perennial herb brought into India from Europe and parts of Asia. It is distributed in Western Himalayas. It grows well on soils of low fertility and has been classified as winter hardy plant. It is also tolerant to drought and alkalinity. Besides being a quality fodder legume also makes an excellent soil binder. It can produce 30-90 q/ha of dry matter annually. The studies have shown that it does not cause bloating in animals fed on it.

Greater or Big trefoil: L. *uligenosus* Schkuhr. (Syn. L. *pedunculatus* ; L. *major;* Papilionaceae

This fodder legume is adapted to wet and acidic soil conditions, but is relatively less winter hardy. It is drought tolerant and can also tolerate alkalinity.

Winged bean: *Lotus tetragonolobus* L.; Papilionaceae

Primarily it is a vegetable crop, but is used for fodder purposes as well.

Lotus hispidus Desf.; Papilionaceae

It is also grown for fodder purposes.

Alfalfa or Lucerne ($2n = 32$): *Medicago sativa* L.; Papilionaceae

This temperate perennial herb is believed to be native to Europe, Asia and North Africa. It is a widely cultivated forage crop used for pasturage, hay, silage and soiling. Lucerne seeds contain drying oil used in the manufacture of paints. Both the leaves and stems serve as a source of commercial chlorophyll. It is a rich source of vitamins namely A, C and E. Lucerne leaf meal in United States of America is used as a vitamin A supplement. It is capable of producing 125 to 150 q/ha of dry matter containing 15-20 per cent of crude protein. Its average seed count is 400/gramme.

Yellow lucerne or Sickle medick: *Medicago falcata;* Papilionaceae

It is used for covering banks, slopes and borders.

Black medick or Hop clover or Yellow trefoil: *Medicago lupulina;* Papilionaceae.

It is believed to be a native to Europe and Asia. In India, it is found in Punjab, Kumaon, Upper Gangetic Plains, Bihar and Northern Bengal. It is grown both as a fodder and as a green manure crop. It embodies lenitive properties.

Little bur clover or Small medick: *Medicago minima;* Papilionaceae

This is a herb used for pasturage and mostly found in Kashmir.

Medicago obscura Retz.; Papilionaceae

It is grown as a fodder crop.

California bur clover or Toothed bur clover or Toothed medick: *Medicago polymorphic* L. (Syn. *M. denticulata* Willd., *M. hispida* Gaertn.); Papilioneace

It is believed to be a native to Europe and Asia. It is distributed in Punjab, Kumaon. Upper Gangetic Plains, North Bengal and Tamil Nadu. It is grown both as a green manure and a fodder crop. Its leaves are a rich source of ascorbic acid.

Other important species of lucerne are:

Snail medic, *Medicago scutellata* or button clover or snail medic (*Medicago orbicularis*) *; noifton bur clover natals M. rigidula* and barrel medick **(M. truncatula /M. tribuloides)**

White flowered sweet clover or white sweet clover or hubam clover ($2n = 10$)*: Melilotus alba* Derr.; Papilionaceae

This herb is believed to be a native to Europe and Asia. In India, it is grown in Northern regions. It behaves both as an annual and a biennial. It is necessary to go for seed scarification to hasten the germination. Its observed seed count is 600 seeds / gramme.

Sweet clover: *Melilotus indica* (L.) All. (Syn. M. *parviflora* (Desf.)); Papilionaceae

It is an annual yellow flowered clover suitable for arable lands under irrigated conditions during winter season in tropical areas. It is believed to be native to Eurasia. It is mostly grown in Punjab, Haryana and Uttar Pradesh as a fodder crop on small scale.

Yellow seed clover (2*n* = 16): *Melilotus offinalis* (L.) Lamk; Papilionaceae

It is also a yellow flowered clover which is biennial having its place of origin in temperate Europe and Asia. It contains coumarin which is an aromatic substance and affects in palatability. The animals have to develop liking for this. However there are cultivars having only low coumarin content. It can produce 40-65 q/ha of dry matter containing approximately 14-15 per cent of crude protein.

Melilotus turbinata Willd.; Papilionaceae

It is also used as fodder.

Sainfoin (2*n* = 28): *Onobrychis viciifolia* Scop.; Papilionaceae

This deep rooted perennial does well on calcareous soils of dry regions. Though it performs well on deep and well drained soils, can, do reasonably well even on shallow soils. Sainfoin has been found to tolerate alkalinity as well as salinity. The legumes by rule does well on soils embodying good status of phosphorus, but this legume of dry temperate conditions adapts itself well to low phosphorus situatons. It can produce 30-65 q/ha of dry matter annually. It is important to note that sainfoin maintains its succulence up to maturity. Further, it has been observed that one gramme contains 70-72 seeds.

Egyptian clover or Berseem: *Trifolium alexandrinuni* L.; Papilionaceae

It is an important forage crop in Punjab, Kangra (Himachal Pradesh), Western Uttar Pradesh, and on small scale in Madhya Pradesh, Maharashtra, Bihar, Tamil Nadu and Karnataka. It is mainly grown for green fodder, hay and also as a pasture crop. It is highly nutritive as well as palatable. Berseem is also used as a green manure crop and for reclamation of alkalisaline soils. Berseem is grown during winter season in tropical climate.

Strawberry clover : *Trifolium frageferum* L.; Papilionaceae

This forage legume has been introduced into India from Australia.

Crimson clover: *Trifolium carnatum* L.; Papilionaceae

It has been brought in from U.S.A. for use as a fodder and a green manure crop.

Lappa clover: *Trifolium lappaceum* L.; Papilionaceae

This forage legume has been introduced into India from Uruguay.

Red clover: Trifolium pratense L.; Papilionaceae

This forage legume is found wild in Nilgiri Hills of Tamil Nadu and Western Himalayas.

Arrow-leaf clover: *Trifolium vesiculosum* Savi : Papilionaceae

It is an annual believed to be a native of mediterranean region. Arrowleaf clover embodies the capacity to thrive on well drained sandy as well as clay soils. It is less acidity tolerant and responsive to fertile soils. The annual dry matter production as per estimates ranges from 45 to 85 q/ha. The seed count is 880,000 / kg.

White clover or Dutch clover or Honey suckle clover (2*n* = 32): *Trifolium repens* L; Papilionaceae

This long-lived perennial clover is prostrate and shallow rooted and is also found wild in temperate Himalayas as well as Nilgiri Hills of Tamil Nadu. It is used as fodder and also for green manuring purposes. It is adapted to temperate and subtemperate areas and is very nutritive and a palatable forge capable of withstanding intense grazing cycle. The protein content varies from 18 to 25 per cent and dry matter yield from 53 to 155 q/ha. It is easily seedable in natural grasslands to augment their legume component. One gramme has been found to have approximately 1700 seeds.

Persian clover or Peshawar clover: *Trifolium resupinatum* L.; Papilionaceae

This forage legume is mainly cultivated in Punjab for green fodder.

Subterranean clover or Subclover: *Trifolium subterraneum* L.; Papilionaceae

In India, it has been brought in from Australia, but is a native to Mediterran Europe, Asia and Africa. It is cultivated for fodder and is also used as a soil-binder. It is suitable for subtropical and subtemperate areas and is adaptable to acid soils. It is highly tolerant to shade and grows well with phalaris, festuca. cocksfoot and / or rye grass. It may yield up to 330 q/ha of dry matter per year depending on the level of agronomic management.

Yellow Suckling clover: *Trifolium dubium;* Papilionaceae

It is also an important annual clover like other clovers suitable for cultivation in irrigated conditions on arable lands in tropical areas.

All the clovers listed above embody the production potential ranging between 40 and 170 q/ha per annum depending upon the level of production technology followed.

Winter vetch Hairy Vetch: *Vicia villosa* Roth; Papilionaceae

Winter vetch is an annual herbaceous legume believed to be a native to Asia and Europe. It is also called by the name of '*tare*'. Its estimated production potential ranges between 16 and 44 q/ha of dry matter per year. The studies have evinced that hairy vetch is eminently suitable as a component of pasturage. It makes an excellent cover crop and hence greatly helps in soil conservation.

Tufted vetch: *Vicia cracca;* Papilionaceae

It is a perennial legume like bush vetch. Tufted vetch makes a good component / complement of both temperate and alpine grasslands.

Purple vetch: *Vicia benghalensis* L.; Papilionaceae

It has been brought in India from Uruguay for cultivation as a fodder crop.

Vicia biennis L.; Papilionaceae

It has been introduced in India from Australia and is used as a fodder crop.

Vicia cassubica L.; Papilionaceae

It has also been introduced in India from Australia for fodder purposes.

Broad bean or Windser bean:

Viciafaba L. (Syn. *Faba vulgaris* Moench); Papilionaceae

This herb is believed to be a native of North Africa. It is mostly grown as a vegetable crop in North-Western parts of India. It is also cultivated for fodder and hay.

Tiny vetch: *Vicia hirsuta* (L.) S.F. Gray; Papilionaceae.

This herb is found in Punjab and Nilgiri Hills of Tamil Nadu. It is only occasionally grown as a fodder crop.

Vicia michauxii Spreng.; Papilionaceae

Like above-mentioned two species of *vicia,* it has also been introduced in India from Australia for cultivation as a fodder crop.

Common vetch:

Vicia sativa L.; Papilionaceae

It is believed that spring vetch is a native to Europe and West Asia. In India, it is grown both for fodder and green manure purposes in North Western parts of the country.

Yellow vetchling:

Lathyrus aphaca L.; Papilionaceae

It is a highly branched trailing herb used as fodder in Punjab, Uttar Pradesh, West Bengal and Madhya Pradesh.

Grass pea or Chickling pea or Tarosse: *Lathyrus sativus* L.; Papilionaceae

It is also a profusely branched hardy annual mainly cultivated in Madhya Pradesh, Eastern Uttar Pradesh, Bihar, West Bengal, Andhra Pradesh and Gujarat; is used as a fodder crop too. The seeds are consumed by poor class of people. It has been reported that the seeds consumed over a long period of time may cause lathyrism, paralysis of lower human-limbs. Its grains contain a toxic amino acid (BOAR) which is considered as a major factor to cause lathyrism.

SECTION- 23
COMMON TECHNICAL TERMS

2,4-D	2, 4-dichlorophenoxy acetic acid
2,4-DB	4 (2, 4-dichlorophenoxy) butyric acid
2,4,5-T	(2, 4, 5-trichlorophenoxy) acetic acid
AAR	Accumulated Assured Rainfall
AAS	Analytical Action Spectra
ACC	1-aminocyclopropane-1-carboxylic acid (precursor of ethylene)
ACTH	Adreno-cortico-tropic Hormone
ADP	Adenosine diphosphate
ALA	Delta aminolevunic acid
Allidochlor (CDAA)	N-N-diallyl-2-chloroacetamide
AM	Pyridine (2-amino-4-chloro-6-methylpyrimidine)
AMO1618	1- (N-piperidine carboxy)-2-isopropyl-5-methyphenyl-4-trimethyl ammonium chloride
AOA	Amino-oxyacetic acid
APP	Ammonium polyphosphate
APS	Adenosine-5-phosphosulfate
ATC	4-amino- 1, 2, 4-triazole hydrochloride
ATP	Adenosine triphosphate
ATPER	Area-Time-Price-Equivalency-Ratio
Atrazine	2-chloro-4-(ethylamino)-6-(isopropylamine)-s-triazine
AVG	Aminoeth oxyvinylglycine
B-Nine	N-dimethylaminosuccinamic acid
BAP	N5-benzylaminopurine
Benthiocarb	S- (4-chlorobenzy) N, N-diethylthio-carbamate
Biuret	NH_2-CO-NH-CO-NH_2
BOD	Biochemical or Biological Oxygen Demand
Butachlor	N-(butoxymethyl-2-chloro-2, 6-diethylacetanilide)
Calcite	$CaCO_3$
CAM	Crassulacean Acid Metabolism

CCC	2-chloroethyl-trimethyl-ammonium chloride (Cycocel)
CDTA	Cyclohexane diamine tetra-acetic acid
CEC	Calcium Carbonate Equivalent
CEPA	2-chloroethylphosphonic acid
$CFCl_3$	Freon
CFCs	Chloroflurocarbons
CGR	Crop Growth Rate
CH	Cychloheximide
CK	Cytokinin
CLIMP	Climate Long Range Investigation, Mapping and Production
COD	Chemical Oxygen Demand
COHMAP	Cooperative Holocene Mapping Project
CPAC	Chlorophenoxy acetic acid
CPIA	Chlorophenoxyisobutyric acid
Dalapon	2, 2-dichloropropionic acid
DAP	Diammonium phosphate
DCD	Dicyandiamide
DCPA	Dimethyl tetrachloroterephthalate
DCPD	Dicalcium phosphate dihydrate
DCS	N-2, 5-dichlorophenyl succinic acid
Diammonium phosphate	$(NH_4)_2$ - HPO_4
Dinitramine	N_4, N_4-diethyl-*x*, *x*-trifluro-3, 5-dinitrotoluene
DINOCAP	Dinitrocaprylphenol crotonate
Diuron	3- (3, 4-dichlorophenyl)- 1, 1-dimethyl urea
DMBA	3, 3. Dimethyl Ibutyl acetate
DNA	Deoxyribonucleic acid
DNOC	Dinitro-O-Cresol
DNOCHP	Dinitro-O-Cyclohexylphenol
DNOSPB	Dinitro-O-Butylphenol
DOM	Dissolved Organic Matter
DTPA	Diethylenetriaminepenta-acetic acid
ECC	Effective Calcium Carbonate
EDDHA	Ethylenediaminidi (O-hydroxyphenyl acetic acid)
EDTA	Ethylene diaminetetra-acctic acid
EPTC	S-ethyl dipropyl thiocarbamate
ESP	Enriched superphosphate
FAA	Formalin Acetic Acid
FAD	Flavin Adenine Dinucleotide (Flavoprotein)
Fluchloralin	N- (2-chloroethyl) - 2,6 - dinitro-N-propyl - 4 - (trifluoromethyl)

FMN	Flavin mono-nucleotide
FSH	Follicle Stimulating Hormone
Geothite	$Fe_2O_3 . H_2O$
Gibbsite	$Al_2O_3 . 3H_2O$
Glyphosate	N-(phosphynomethyl) glycine
GPP	Gross Primary Productivity
GPR	Ground Penetrating Radar
Guanylthiourea	1-amino-2-thiourea or ASU
Gypsum	$CaSO_4.2H_2O$
HCN	Hydrogen cyanide/hydrocyanic acid
HDPE	High Density Polyethylene
HGPRT	Hypoxanthine Guanine Phospho-Ribose Transferase
HMM	Hidden Markov Models
IAA	Indole Acetic Acid
IAN	Indole-3-acetonitrite
LAP	Indices of Atmospheric Purity
ICA	Indole-3-carboxylic acid
ICSH	Interstitial Cell Stimulating Hormone
ILA	Indole-3-lactic acid
IPYA	Indole-3-pyruvate
Kaolinite	$Si_2Al_2O_5 (OH)_4$
KMTB	Keto-r-methylthiobutyric acid
KN	Kinetic (6-furfuryl aminopurine)
KN/KNE	2-benzothiozolebutyric acid
KNAA	Potassium salt of naphthalene acetic acid
LAD	Leaf Area Duration
LAI	Leaf Area Index
LAR	Leaf Area Ratio
LC_{50}	Lethal Concentration (of a chemical that would kill 50% of the target animals)
LD_{50}	Lethal Dose (of a chemical that would kill 50% of the organisms)
LER	Land Equivalent Ratio
LH	Lutenizing Hormone
Linuron	3-(3, 4-dichlorophenyl)-methoxy-l-methylurea
MAC	Maximum Allowable Concentration (of pollutants in air)
MAI	Moisture Availability Index
MAP	Mono-ammonium phosphate: $(NH_4 . H_2PO_4)$
MAST	2-amino-4-methyl-6-tri-chloromethyl triazine
MCPA	2-methyl-4-chlorophenoxyacetic acid

MEC	Maximum Emission Concentration (from chimneys, expressed in g/m^3 or ppm or mg/cm^3
Metalachlor	2-chloro-N- (2-ethyl-6-methyl-phenyl) -N-(2-methoxy)-l-methylethyl) acetamide
Methabenzthiazuron	3-(2-benzothiazolyl)-I, 3-dimethylurea
Methazole	2-(3, 4-dichlorophenyl)-4-methyl-1, 2, 4-oxadiazolidine-3, 5-dione
MH	1, 2-dihydro-3, 6-pyridazinedione (Maleic hydrazide)
MLD	Minimun Lethal Dose (of a chemical that can cause death of a test organism)
MMC	Megaspore Mother Cell
MPN	Most Probable Number (usually for Coliform organisms/ 100 ml of water)
Monoammonium phosphate	$NH_4 . H_2PO_4$
MSMA	Monosodium methanearsonate
MT	3-marcapto-1, 2-4-triazole
N-Serve	2-chloro-6 (trichloromethyl, pyridine), referred to as nitrapyrin
NAA	Naphthalene Acetic Acid
NAA	Nicotine amide adeninedinucleotidephosphate
NAD	Nicotinamide Adenine Dinucleotide (Earlier called DPN Diphosphopyridine nucleotide)
NADP	Nicotinamide adenine dinucleotide phosphate
Napropamide	2-(x-napthoxy)-N-N-diethylpropionamide
Naptalam (NPA)	N-1-naphthylphathalamic Acid
NAR	Net Assimilation Rate
NCE	Net-CO_2 Exchange
Nitrofen	2, 4-dichlorophenyl p-nitrophenyl ether
NPP	Net Primacy Productivity
NR	Nitrate/Nitrite Reductase
NTU	Nephelometric Turbidity Unit
OAA	Oxalic Acetic Acid
OCP	Octacalcium phosphate
ODR	Oxygen Diffusion Rate
OMAI	Optimum Moisture Availability Index
Oxydiazon	2-tert-butyl-4-(2,4-dichloro-5-isopropoxyphenyl)-1-3-4-oxadiaon 5-one
PAA	Phenyl Acetic Acid
PAN	Peroxy Acetyl Nitrate
PAR	Photosynthetically Active Radiation
PAR	Potassium Absorption Ratio
Paraquat	1-1'-dimethyl-4,4'-bipyridinium

PCMB	P-chloromercurybenzene
PCO	Photorespiratory Carbon Oxidation
PCP	Pentachlorophenol
PCR	Photosynthetic Carbon Reduction
PCR	Polymers Chain Reactions
PEP	Phosphoenol pyruvate
PER	Price Equivalent Ratio
PGA	Phosphoglyceric acid
PIR	Protein Information Resource
PMC	Pollen Mother Cell
POM	Particulate Organic Matter
PPP	Pentose Phosphate Pathway
Prometon	2, 4-bis(isopropylamine)-6-rnethoxy-s-triazine
Pronamide	3, 5-dichloro(N-1, 1-dimethyl-2-propyny)benzamide
Propachlor	2-chloro-N-isopropylacetanilide
Propanil	3`4' -dichloropropionanilide
PSI	Pollutant Standard Index
PVC	Polyvinyl Chloride
RDP	Ribulose Diphosphate
RGR	Relative Growth Rate
RNA	Ribonuncleic Acid
RUBP	Ribulose 1, 5-Biphosphate
SAM	S-adenosylmethionine
SAR	Sodium Absorption Ratio
SCOP	Structural Classification of Proteins
SCU	Sulphur Coated Urea
SCUBA	Self-Contained Underwater Breathing Apparatus
Simazine	2-chloro-4, 6-bis(ethylamino)-s-triazine
SRS	Sequental Retrival System
SSP	Sexually/Seed Propagated Plants
ST	2-Sulfanilamidothiazole or sulfathiazole
Strengite	$FePO_4.2H_2O$
TCA	Tricarboxylic Acid
TCBA	2, 3, 6-Trichlorobenzoic Acid
TDS	Total Dissolved Solids
Terbutryn	2-(teri-butylamino-4-(ethylamino)-6-(methylthio)-s-triazine
Terrazole	5-ethoxy-3-trichloromsethyl-1, 2, 4-thiodiazole
TOC	Total Organic Content (in water expressed as mg C / litre)
TPP	Triammonium Phosphate Polyhydrate

Tricalciumphosphate	$Ca_3(PO_4)_2$
TSP or CSP	Triple superphosphate or concentrated superphosphate
TSS	Total Soluble Salts
UAP	Urea Ammonium Phosphate
Urea	$CO(NH_2)_2$
Urea phosphate	$CO(NH_2)_2 . H_3PO_4$
Vascite	$AlPO_4 . 2H_2O$
VIA	Video Image Analysis
VPP	Vegetatively/Asexually Propagated Plants
VSPP	Vegetatively and Sexually Propagated Plants
WDP	Water Dispersible Powder
WP	Wettable Powder
ZPG	Zero Population Growth

SECTION- 24

MEXICAN POPPY (ARGEMON MEXICANA L.)

Mexican poppy or prickly poppy sent shock waves during 1998 through the length and breadth of India due to a wide-spread incidence of a fatal disease known as dropsy. The disease is popularly known as *Epidemic dropsy* caused by the Mexican poppy seeds mixed with mustard seeds at the time of oil extraction. It's incidence occurred in 1926 as well, but the level of adulteration was only 0.01 per cent. The quantity of seeds adulterated slowly kept on increasing and has been estimated to vary from 10 to 30 per cent at present. Its seeds are mixed because the new mustard cultivars embody much less pungency than that contained by the traditional mustard varieties which were liked by the consumers in northern and north eastern parts of India. The pungency is due to the presence of allyl isothiocyanate found in the seeds of Mexican poppy. *Epidemic dropsy* attack takes place owing to consumption of the oil adulterated and expelled prickly seeds with those of the mustard. The incidence of the disease has earlier been noticed in Bengal (now West Bengal and Bangla Desh), Bihar, Orissa, Madhya Pradesh etc., the regions of maximum of mustard oil consumption. The symptoms of the disease vary from one to the other situation. The disease sets in with the gastric problem and loss of appetite followed by loose motions and swelling on feet. The disease as observed often commences with filling of pericardial cells with water and the pulse rate shoots up. The patient suffers from laboured breathing, condition deteguocates due to fatigue and consequently the liver gets enlarged. Sometimes, there develop fleshy, deep red spots inside the gums, tongue and the nose. These plump spots bleed sometimes. There is a reduction in eye-sight on account of this poisonous effect. It has been reported that in 1953 in Nadiad district of Gujarat a number of families fell prey to this disease. There is no prescribed routine medicine to treat this dangerous ailment, that is, the treatment is administered according to the symptoms. However, multivitamins have been found effective.

Common names:

Prickly poppy is known by different names in different countries as indicated below:

Argentina	Cardo santo
Australia	Mexican poppy
Bahamas	Donkey thistle, Mexican poppy
Bangla Desh	Bara silkanta
Burma (Mynamar)	Khy-ya
India	Mexican/prickly poppy
Pakistan	Sialkanta
U.S.A. (S. California)	Mexican/prickly poppy (Prickly poppies)

Distribution :

In India, it is widely distributed as would be evident from its different names like *kantakusum*, *kateli*, *satyanasi*, *bhadbhand*, *katara*, *banmirchay shilkanta*, *kandiars* etc. The plant is globally distributed as would be noted from the following:

United States of America (N. and C. America)

— Canada
— Mexico
— Brazil
— Argentina
— Chile
— Africa (South, Central, North and West Africa)
— Oceania

Philippines	Australia
New Zealand	Pacific Islands

— Bangla Desh	— Mynamar
— India	— Bahamas
— Pakistan	

It is believed that Mexican poppy has been introduced in India from Mexico. However, the ten species of this plant have originated from U.S.A. and Hawaii and five of them frequently occur globally. These species are :

— *Argemon mexicana*	— *A. ochroleuca*
— *A. corymbosa*	*A. munita*

A. Subsusiformis

In India, the most commonly occurring species is A. *mexicana.* However, *A. ochroleuca* has also been found in some areas of Punjab. The frequency of infestation (as a weed) has been observed as shown below:

"*A. mexicana* and *A. ochroleuca* occur in wheat up to 10 per cent, while *A. mexicana* infests jujube (*ber*) orchards from 40 to 90 per cents. Its occurrence (*A. mexicana*) in mango and guava orchards has been observed to be less than 40 per cent. A *corymbosa* and A. *munita* are the native herbs of southern California (U.S.A.)."

Botanical description :

Argemon mexicana (L.) belongs to the genus Papaver of Papaveraeea family. It is a prickly herb or undershrub and has naturalized throughout India. The English name is Mexican prickly poppy or simply prickly poppy. It is a winter annual and is a long day plant. Prickly poppy mostly grows on uncropped lands including field bunds, railway tracksides, air strips, roadside etc. But, it is also found in cropped fields, meadows and fallow lands. The plant embodies a deep tap root system and successfully survives in dryland areas. It makes very vigorous growth and is very difficult to be uprooted. The propagation takes place by the seeds which get scattered on the ground due to apical bursting of capsules. The seeds also get dispersed by a special mechanism known as censor mechanism wherein an itact plant swings due to the impact of wind forcing the matured capsules to release the seeds at a distance away from the mother plant. The number of seeds produced by a single plant varies from gust 10 to as many as 15,000. The seed diameter varies from 1.5 to 2.5 mm which is identical to the seed diameter of most of the mustard cultivars.

The stem is erect, stout, sparingly branched and usually prickly. Plant height varies from 3 to 8 dm and embodies yellow juice. Leaves are coarsely lobbed, spiny along the margin and midreb, often glaucous and blotched with white colour powdery substance and mostly clasping at the base. Its flowers measure 40-80 mm, are solitary, showy, calyx consists of 2-3 prickly sepals which fall down as the flowers open, corolla embodies 4-6 separate lemon yellow or cream coloured sepals (A. *orchroleuca* bears white flowers) which are 10-30 mm long. The stamens are many in number and distinct. The pistil is solitary having 3-6 sessile radiate stigmas on a very short style. The ovary matures into an ellipsoid, prickly capsule having 3-6 valves and many seeds as already mentioned. The seeds (2 mm long) are avoid, spherical, surface has angular depressions and a crest along one side and are grey or blackish-brown in colour. Other details of *A. mexicana* are:

(A, H) $n = 14, 2x$ (Malik and Grover, 1967, 1973-74; Malik and Mary 1969, 1976 and Mary *et al*, 1974).

$2n = 28, 2x$ (Bose, 1937; Malhotra and Mohra, 1944; Koul, 1966 and Bir and Sidhu, 1980).

$n = 28, 4x$ (Koul, 1966 and Mary *et al.*, 1974).

Uses:

The seeds of prickly poppy make a good quality of semi-drying oil which is used as an illuminant and a lubricant. The oil free from toxic impurities has been made use of to prepare liquid soap. Roots make an excellent cure for the chronic skin diseases. The seeds are laxative, expectorant and demulcent. Plant juice is administered to cure jaundice and cutaneous affections. It is oftenly used as mucilaginous substance/medicine or an agent for soothing or mollifying or for protecting irrigated mucous membrane.

The other uses include the use of the plant extract as an antifeedant and insecticide (Faeknath and Kawal, 1993). It was observed to embody an excellent potential to control the *Crocidolomia binotalis*, one of the most important pest of cauliflower. Hussain *et al.* (1983) isolated oxyhydrastirine isoquinolene, an alkaloid from the plant collected from Egypt and Pakistan. Harborne and Williams (1903) in U.K. re-examined the seed extract of A. *mexicana* for the newly reported 5, 7, 2, 6-tetrahydroxy flavone and found no new novel flavone, the major seed flavone was luteolin accompanied by the related flavone cariodictyol. One should not entirely rely on spectral measurements. Fletcher *et al.* (1993) in Australia observed that the seeds of A. *mexicana* contained dihydrosanguinarine as a major alkaloid. They also noticed that the alkaloid content varied with the maturity. The matured seeds contained the alkaloid more than that embodied by the immature seeds and exposure to light reduced its content. It also contained 11-oxo-octacosanoic acid and 11-oxotricontanoic acid as the major components. In 1989 in New York (U.S.A.) the leaf extracts of A. *mexicana*, P. *hysterophorus* and E. *alba* showed toxic effect on *Meloidogyne incognita* and M. *javanica* nematodes Cortez *et al.* (1993) observed in Mexico that A. *mexicana* and *Larrea tridenta* were less attractive to *Zebrotes subfasciatus* and hence can be used as a stored grain protectants. Rajesus (1992) in Philippines found A. *mexicana* as a host for the insects *Helicoverpa armigera* and H. *assulta* which later attack the tobacco crop.

In India also various aspects of *Argemone* Spp. have been studied. To illustrate, Misra *et al.* (1972) evaluated A. *mexicana* as an organic amendment to improve the soils composed of about 50, 40 and 11 per cent of silt, sand and clay respectively in Lucknow (U.P.). Ramkrishanan and Gupta (1972) in Punjab studied the effect of N and P on two species of *Argemon* and observed that A. *ochroeuca* made better growth at low N-levels; whereas shoot to root ratio decreased markedly in case of A. *mexicana* due to an increase in P-levels. These authors in 1980 reported from Shillong (Meghalaya) that addition of NPK to A. *mexicana* and A. *ochroleuca* reduced the survival rate of both of species of these premier weeds. Pandey *et al.* (1981) tested the effect of petroleum ether extract of seeds and leaves of A. *mexicana* on the control of H. *cajani* in cowpea (*vigna unguiculata*). They observed that the seed extract at 2 per cent caused 93 per cent mortality after 24 hours in laboratory and field conditions after 72 hours. The plant leaf extract at 2 per cent after 24 and 72 hours showed 86.7 per mortality in lab and field conditions respectively. Majumdar *et al.* (1989) noted 100 per cent mortality after 24 and 48 hours regardless of the concentration of leaf extract of A. *mexicana* used on the aforesaid insect. Nath *et al.* (1982) from Kanpur (U.P.) found the plant extract of A. *mexicana* to control 29 to 64 per cent infection caused by *Meloidogyne javanica* in okra. Its aqueous leaf leachate inhibited the germination of mustard under Bangalore (Karnataka) conditions (Leela, 1982).

Bhardwaj *et al.* (1982) of Delhi University isolated two new phenolic compounds *viz.*, 5, 7, 2, 6-tetrahydroxy flavone (argemexitin) and 5, 7-dihydroxychromone 7-neohesperidoside from the seeds of A. *mexicana.* Pandey *et al.* (1982) studied the ecological potential of A. *mexicana* on *Abelmoschus esculentus* and noted that the extracts of roots, leaves, stem and unripe fruits functioned as growth regulators. Root extract was more phytotoxic. The seeds of A. mexicana were found toxic to human beings (Paribar and Kanodia, 1987). Goswami and Vijaylakshmi (1986) from the Indian Agricultural Research Institute, New Delhi reported that dried extracts of A. *mexicana* reduced M. *incognita* gall formation and hatching on seedlings of tomato Pusa Rubi both in pots and in vitro experiments. Pathak *et al* (1989) found that aqueous leaf extracts of A. *mexicana* significantly suppressed the egg hatch of M. *incognita in-situ.* Das and Sukul (1988) reported that the oil obtained from A. *mexicana* seeds killed M. *incognita* in 17 minutes. They applied 0.2 per cent aqueous mixture of oil to the leaves of okra in the soil inouclated with M. *incognita.* Malhotra and Rai (1990) observed that its water extract when applied to soybean increased both the mycoflora and the level of seed germination. Hassan (1992) conducted a study at Faijabad (U.P.) and observed that the root extracts of A. *mexicana* significantly increased the percentage of second, third and fourth stage juveniles of the root knot nematodes (M. *incognitos*) and reduced the percentage of adult females associated with tomato roots. Soaking of seeds of chickpea in its leaf extract reduced the penetration of M. *incognita* juvenile (Majumdar and Misra, 1991).

A. *mexicana* has also been found to embody insecticidal properties. Katole and Mundiwale (1992) reported that monocrotophos 36 WSC applied to A. *mexicana* seeds was the most effective treatment to control the infestation caused by *Chilo partillus* on sorghum variety CSH-9. Its untreated seeds showed some insecticidal properties by reducing the extent of stem boring. Mixture of its extract with carbofuron controlled the *Atherigona soccata* in sorghun (Mote and Jadhav, 1993). Chitra *et al.* (1993) from Andhra Pradesh observed that 0.1 per cent petroleum ether extract of A. *mexicana* leaves was more effective (76 per cent) as compared to monocrotophos and endosufan for the control of *Henorepilachna vigintioctapunctata* (*Epilachna vigintioctopunctata*), *Aphis gassypii* and *Leucinodes orbondis* on aubergines.

Purnima *et al.* (1990) observed fungicidal properties of standard concentration of A. *mexicana* extract as it reduced the incidence of root caused by A. *niger* in stored tomato, fruits. Singh *et al.* (1993) from Bhagalpur (Bihar) found a good control of *Botryodiplodia theobromae*, *Fusarium oxysporum*, *Aspergillus flavus* with the aqueous leaf extract of this on banana.

Weed control measures (against *A. mexicana*) :

A. *mexicana* is undoubtedly a weed and the tested measures of its control are summarized below

	Recommended control measure (s)	***Author (s)***
1.	Pre-emergence application of phenmediphama @ 1.5-2.0 kg a.i./ha controlled *A. mexicana* well and recorded beet yield equal to hand weeding.	Robles (1977), Costa Rica
2.	Pre-plant incorporation of EPIC @ 2 and 4 kg a.i./ha gave a good control of weeds. But, neither alachlor nor stomp nor cabex gave satisfactory control of *A. maxicana.*	Mosha *et al.* (1980), Trop. Pestic. Res. Inst., Tanzania (Africa)
3.	Metoxuron @ 2 kg a.i./ha, metribuzn @ 0.5-1.0 kg a.i./ha, methabenzthiazuron @ 1.87-2.0 kg a.i./ha. terbutryne @ 0:5-1.0 kg a.i./ ha, methabenzthiazuron @ 0.93 kg a.i./ha plus fluchloralin @ 0.5 l/ha, fluchloralin @ 0.5 1/ha plus metribuzin @ 0.5 @ effectively controlled A. *mexicana* in peas. Fluchloralin and all the other herbicides were applied pre-planting and pre-emergence, respectively.	Randhava *et al.* (1981), PAU, Ludhiana
4.	Terbutryn @ 0.8 kg a.i./ha, oxadiazone @ 1.0 kg a.i./ha, Isp @ 1.0 kg a.i./ ha applied pre-emergence recorded a good control of *A. maxicana.*	Tiwari and Trivedi (1985), JNKVV, Jabalpur (M.P.)
5.	Three hanweedings and hoeings each 3, 6 and 9 weeks after sowing provided good control in cotton and *vigna mungo*.	Sheke *et al.* (1986) MAU, Parbhani (Maharashtra)
6.	Fluroxypyr @ 3-4 kg a.i./ha applied post-emergence in wheat gave good control.	Tiwari *et al.* JNKVV, Jabalpur (M.P.).
7.	Use of substituted benzthiazole nucleus containing compound was found more active in toxicating *A. mexicana.*	Chaurasia *et al.* (1989), DAV (PG) College, Dehradun (U.P.)

Fig. 1 Mexican Poppy with Flower and Fruit.

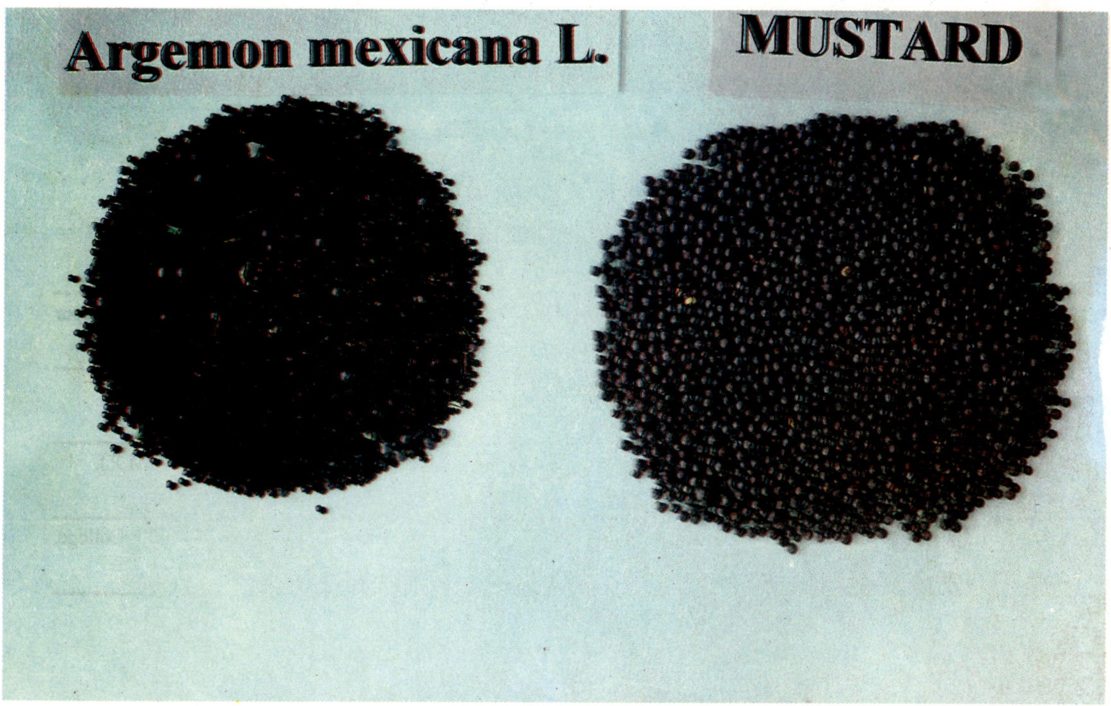

Fig. 2 Seeds of Mexican Poppy and Mustard.

SECTION- 25
EL NINO
NATURE'S VICIOUS CYCLE

It ROSE OUT OF THE TROPICAL PACIFIC in late 1997, bearing more energy than a million Hiroshima bombs. By the time it had run its course eight months later, the giant El Nino of 1997-98 had deranged weather patterns around the world, killed an estimated 2,100 people, and caused at least 33 billion dollars in property damage.

Isaias Ipanaque Silva knew none of that. All he and the other peasant farmers in the Peruvian hamlet of Chato Chico could see was that after weeks of incessant rain the adjacent Piure River had no stopped rising. The rainfall itself was no surprise. Every three to seven years, for as long as anyone could remember, the same rainfall had arrived after a pool of hot seawater the size of Canada appeared off the west coast of the Americas. The ocean would heat up right around Christmas time, so fishermen called the phenomenon El Nino, for the Christ Child. Then that titanic storm source would pour vast amounts of precipitation onto Peru's normally arid northwestern coast.

But few had ever seen this much rain-five of six inches a day in some places.

Finally, on February 15, 1998, the river broke its banks. The sudden ground could hold no more, and water swept into the riverside homes of Chato Chico. The swirling torrent was first knee-deep and soon chest high. "Suddenly we were surrounded from all directions," Ipanaque Silva says, "It took all the little animals. Then my house just fell down completely."

Hundreds of families splashed frantically through the muddy flood to save what they could. In most cases, says another villager, Roas Jovera Charo, "we just grabbed clothes for the children. "Everything else chickens and goats, pots and pans, religious icons and personal treasures washed away. Compared with other places in Peru and around the world. The residents of Chato Chico were fairly lucky. Some were evacuated on barges, a few in helicopters, to a barren but dry refugee camp in the desert. Nearly all survived.

That was not the case some 60 miles to the south, in a there area pocket of one-room houses called Motse outside the city of Chiclayo. "We thought that the water couldn't come here" says Flora Ramirez, "but we lost practically everything "Ramirez's neighbuorhood was overrun in a matter of minutes. "They strung ropes from one house to another to rescue people." recalls Manuel Guevara Sanchez. "Some spent three days on the roof. Those who knew how to swim brought them food. When the flood finally receded, they could begin to count the dead ten out of a village of just. 150.

The runoff from the floods poured into the coastal Sechura Desert. Where there had been nothing but arid hardscrabble waste for 15 years, suddenly amazingly-lay the second largest lake in Peru: 90 miles long, 20 miles. wide, and ten feet deep, with occasional parched domes of sand and clay poking up cerily from the surface.

In other areas the water simply pooled. The mosquitoes that thrived in these places caused rampant malaria—-some 30,000 cases in the Piura region alone, three times the average for its 1.5 million residents.

Peru was where it all began, but El Nino's abnormal effects on the main components of climate–sunshine, temperature, atmospheric pressure, wind, humidity, precipitation, cloud formation, and ocean currents changed weather patterns across the equatorial Pacific and in turn around the globe. Indonesia and surrounding regions suffered months of drought. Forest fires burned furiously in Sumatra, Borneo, and Malaysia, forcing drivers to use their headlights at noon. The haze travelled thousands of miles to the west into the ordinarily sparkling air of the Maldive Islands, limiting visibility to half a mile at times.

Temperatures reached 108 ° F in Mongolia; Kenya's rainfall was 40 inches above normal; Central Europe suffered record flooding that killed 55 in Poland and 60 in the Czech Republic; and Madagascar was battered with monsoons and cyclones. In the U.S. mudslides and flash floods flattened communities from California to Mississippi, storms pounded the Gulf Coast and tornadoes ripped Florida.

By the time the debris settled and the collective misery was tallied, the devastation had in some respects exceeded even that of the El Nino of 1982-83, which killed 2,000 worldwide and caused about 13 billion dollars in damage.

And that's not the end of it. It is not uncommon for an El Nino winter to be followed by a La Nino one– where climate patterns and worldwide effects are, for the most part, the opposite of those produced by El Nino. Where winter weather was abnormally mild, it turns abnormally harsh. La Ninas have followed El Ninos three times in the past 15 years–after the 1982-83 event and after those of 1986-87 and 1995. Signs of another La Nina began to show up by June 1998.

AT THE EXTREMES:

Influenced by countless variables, including variations in Earth's orbit, the strength of ocean currents, and possible human influences on the environment, no two El Nino or La Nina events are identical, Even within a single event, local conditions can change drastically over just a few days. Illustrated above are the most recent El Nino and La Nina events that have been fully studied, depicting the most extreme conditions of a each over a given month. All the conditions shown did not happen simultaneously.

While conditions during the past few events appear to have been more extreme than in earlier events, the evidence is not conclusive. Worldwide collection of detailed El Nino and La Nino does dates back only 13 years.

Highs and Lows of a Global Cycle

El NINO

For reasons still not entirely understood, atmospheric pressure periodically becomes abnormally low near Tahiti and unusually high over northern Australia. With the presence of the high-pressure system, Pacific trade winds that normally flow to the west become weak, allowing sun-warmed Pacific surface water to spread eastward. This creates a warm band of water that spans the equatorial Pacific. Along the Equator, where cloud formation is already heavy due to the convergence of northern and southern trade winds, more clouds that usually develop. Drawn south by the lower atmospheric pressure, the subtropical jet stream carries Pacific clouds eastward and increases the frequency of storms in that region. Continuing across Southern North America, the jet stream shears off the tops of westbound Atlantic storms, decreasing the development of Atlantic hurricanes.

LA NINA

In a reverse of the mechanism that triggers El Nino, atmospheric pressure is abnormally high over Tahiti and low over Australia. Westbound trade winds are intense, pushing warm surface water farther west than usual. The equatorial cloud formation splits, separated by the Tahiti high. Similarly split, the subtropical jet stream is weakened, allowing Atlantic hurricanes to move westward and gather strength.

OVER THE YEARS, the appearance of La Nina has been less predictable than that of El Nino, and fewer of its effects have been recorded. But both patterns are now far better understood than ever before. That is because the most recent El Nino will be the first to be remembered for more than just marked the first time in human history that climate scientists were able to predict abnormal flooding and droughts months in advance, allowing time for threatened populations to prepare. The U.S. National Oceanic and Atmospheric Administration

(NOAA) first announced a possible El Nino as early as April 1997; Australia and Japan followed a month later. By summer detailed predictions were available for many regions.

In northern Peru warnings allowed many farmers and fishermen to make the best of El Nino's effects. Grass grew on land that is usually barren, and farmers raised cattle. Rice and beans could be planted in areas normally too dry to support them; fishermen were able to plan for shrimp harvests in coastal waters, generally too cold for the shellfish.

"The potential uses of advance information are almost limitless," says Michael H. Glantz of the National Centre for Atmospheric Research (NCAR) in Boulder, Colorado, pointing out how governments and industries around the world can make planning for El Nino and La Nina pay off. For example, Kenyan coffee growers find their product in greater demand when droughts affect coffee harvests in Brazil and Indonesia. Palm oil production in the Philippines typically declines during El Nino, as does the squid catch off the California coast. Countries that anticipate these developments can fill the gaps and prosper.

At the very least, preparation can save lives in poverty ridden Peru constructing storm drains and stockpiling emergency supplies saved hundreds of lives during 1997 and 1998. Forewarning brought timely international aid to such places as Papua, New Guinea, where highland populations were threatened with starvation after frost and drought combined to destroy subsistence crops. Many affected areas could prepare for floods and fires, population migration, and the spread of disease.

THERE ARE WRITTEN records of El Nino's effects in Peru at least as far back as 1523, and researchers have found geologic evidence of El Ninos in Peruvian coastal communities from at least 13,000 years ago. We know the Inca knew about them, "says Adm. Giampietri Rojas of Peru's Institute of the Sea." They built their cities on the tops of hills, and the population kept stores of food in the mountains. If they built on the coast, it was not near rivers. That's why so many of their dwellings are standing today. "But it was not until about 25 years ago that the rest of the world began to pay attention to El Nino. And after the surprise devastation of 1982-83, climate experts intensified efforts to understand how the process works globally." Governments invested in equipment to monitor the particular conditions in the Pacific that trigger El Nino.

Perhaps the most important effort was the development of the TAO (Tropical Atmosphere/Ocean) array of 70 moored buoys to span the equatorial Pacific. Completed in 1994, the TAO buoys are now the world's premier early-warning system for change in the tropical ocean. They monitor water temperature from the surface down to 1,600 feet, as well as winds air temperature, and relative humidity.

The data collected by the buoys are transmitted to polar-orbiting satellites and then to NOAA's Pacific Marine Environmental Laboratory in Seattle. Supplemented with temperature measurements taken by research ships, the data help create a comprehensive portrait of the upper ocean and lower atmosphere.

Meanwhile the TOPEX/Poseidon satellite, a U.S-French mission began in 1992, orbits earth at a height of 830 miles, measuring sea-surface elevation and relaying information about ocean circulation, including the enormous rhythmic sloshings called Kelvin and Rossby waves that travel back and forth across the entire Pacific.

Thanks to the TAO buoys, the TOPER Poseidon satellite, and a variety of other tools, climate scientists now have information of unprecedented range and accuracy, which has enabled them to confirm and expand their theories about what occurs both during normal weather patterns and during sea changes that herald the periodic– and inevitable arrivals of El Nino and La Nina.

Weather is so variable that it's hard to call any situation normal. But in most years climate in the equatorial Pacific is governed by one generally dependable pattern. Sunlight heats the uppermost layer of seawater in the western ocean around Australia and Indonesia, causing huge volumes of hot, moist air to rise thousands of feet and creating a low-pressure system at the ocean's surface. As the air mass rises and cools, it sheds its water content as rain, contributing to monsoons in the area.

Now much drier and far aloft, the air heads east, guided by winds in the upper atmosphere, cooling even more and increasing in density as it travels. By the time it reaches the west coast of the Americas, it is cold and heavy enough that it starts to sink, creating a high-pressure system near the water's surface. The air currents then flow as trade winds back toward Australia and Indonesia. This giant circulatory loop, moving from west to east in the upper air and from east to west at low altitudes, is called the Walker circulation, for Sir Gilbert Walker, the British scientist who studied the process in the 1920s.

As the trade winds blow westward over the Pacific, they push the warm top layer of the ocean with them, causing the hottest water to pile up around Indonesia, where, because of both wind action and thermal expansion, the sea level is usually about 18 inches higher than that it is off the west coast of Mexico. All along the eastern Pacific, and especially off Ecuador and Peru, colder subsurface water wells up to replace the sheared-off top layer, bringing up a bevy of nutrients from the deep ocean. That chemical bounty sustains an enormous food web and makes the coastal water off Peru one of the worlds most prolific fisheries.

El Nino changes all that. For reasons that scientists still do not comprehend, every few years the trade winds subside or even disappear. The usual air-pressure pattern reverses itself in a phenomenon called the southern oscillation, making barometer readings higher in Australia than they are in the central Pacific. The resulting pattern–known as ENSO, for El Nino/Southern Oscillation–involves only one fifth of the circumference of the plane. But it transforms weather around the globe.

Without the trade winds the top layer of the eastern Pacific does not move west. It stays in place, getting hotter and hotter, swelling as it warms. Eventually it hits the threshold for what meteorologists call deep convection–the point at which the steamy surface air blasts into the upper atmosphere. (In some places during 1997-98, sea levels off South America were ten inches above normal and surface temperatures reached almost 86 °F.) When that happens, water in the upper atmosphere condenses and falls as torrential rain on the west coast of the Americas.

This, in turn, reduces the salinity of the coastal seas, where deep water upwelling has already declined or stopped. Marine life that customarily thrives off Ecuador and Peru, including economically essential anchovy populations, heads south in search of cooler, richer water to the great benefit of fishermen in Chile. Off North America exotic warm water species suddenly appear farther north. In 1997, apparently for the first time, a fisherman caught a marlin in the ordinarily chilly seas off Washington State. Californians started pulling in bonito and albacore tuna; species normally found only far offshore. Other tuna were netted in the Gulf of Alaska.

Because El Nino moves the rains that would normally soak the western Pacific toward the Americas, such places as Australia, Indonesia, and India may experience severs drought. According to historical records, 600,000 people died in just one region of India from the epic droughts of the 1789-1793 El Nino.

In Africa the altered wind, heat, and moisture patterns of El Nino portend drought generally in the east and extreme south. In particular, cooling of the southwestern Indian Ocean customarily strengthens a high pressure area that keeps rainfall from reaching the south.

Meanwhile, back in North America, the jet streams that travel five to eight miles above Earth's surface shift dramatically. The polar jet stream tends to stay farther north over Canada than usual; as a result, less cold air moves into the upper United States. In fact, northern tier states saves an estimated five billion dollars in heating costs during the 1997-98 El Nino.

At the same time upper-level tropical winds reverse themselves, blowing the tops off cyclones forming in the mid-Atlantic and usually reducing the number of hurricanes that strike land in the U.S. by half from an average of two a year to one or none, according to studies at Colorado State University and Florida State University. One study indicates that El Nino also generally reduces tornades in the southern Plains states.

AN UNEXPECTED GROUP of sardines off the coast of Chile ? Tuna in the Gulf of Alaska ? Lower heating bills in the U.S ? Fewer hurricanes in the Atlantic ?

Enter La Nina. During a La Nina event, an abnormal cooling in the eastern in the eastern Pacific produces conditions more or less the opposite of those created by El Nino–natures' way, perhaps, rectifying the heat imbalance that El Nino represents. As with El Nino, the effects of La Nina are most pronounced from December to March.

In La Nina years the easterly winds from the Americas are stronger than usual. That drives more than the normal amount of warm sea surface water westward, in turn causing larger than normal volumes of deep, chilly water to rise to the surface and producing a "cold tongue" that extends 3,000 miles along the Equator from Ecuador to Samoa.

With so much warm water flowing toward Asia, the Pacific's mightly heat engine remains firmly anchored in the west, causing heavier monsoon rains in India, higher than average precipitation in Australia, and wetter than normal conditions as far west as southern Africa. The huge air masses and cloud banks associated with the hot zone also change the part of the jet streams which move high-altitude air from west to east across the ocean.

The polar jet stream, which in an El Nino year stays high in Canada, moves farther south, driving frigid air down into the U.S. Winters are colder, especially in the northern-western and upper midwestern states. The subtropical jet stream that blows across Mexico and the Gulf during El Nino events weakens during La Nina; consequently, far less rain falls in the Gulf and southeastern states. Drought is common in the desert Southwest. Hurricanes in the tropical Atlantic encounter no westerly wind resistance and therefore are twice as likely to strike the U.S. The 1998 La Nina hurricane season was the deadliest in the past two centuries.

As experts use increasingly reliable data to comprehend the forces and patterns of these periodic weather cycles, they are making weather predictions of at least the broad contours of the cycle. There are two major ways of forecasting scale weather events such as El Nino, and climate scientists use both.

One method is statistical analysts pore over past weather records to determine what kind of conditions have the highest probability of occurring simultaneously. For example, lower barometric pressure and higher sea surface temperatures in, say, Tahiti usually mean more rain for Ecuador and less for northern Brazil. This technique yields results even if the analyst has no idea how the two coexisting conditions are related, and traditionally forecasters have preferred its reassuring mathematical solidity.

But statistical procedures provide very little information about what cause-and-effect relationships may by producing various climate conditions. Moreover, statistical analysis can only determine the likelihood that past conditions will recur-and no two El Ninos or La Ninas are the same.

With the advent of supercomputers, scientists have taken advantage of an alternative method of prediction called climate modelling. In this method, software incorporates the fundamental laws of oceanic and atmospheric physics into a simulate world where weather changes over time. Researchers then feed tens of thousands of specific pieces of information about the real world into the model and see how accurately the computer-generated results resemble what actually happens.

In theory, models can reveal the unique or idiosyncratic condition that will result from a given climate pattern and then fast-forward to see how events related to that pattern will unfold. In practice, most of the results have proved too broad and uncertain to predict weather on even a large regional scale, much less in local range of 100 to 200 miles.

So, historically, statistical predictions have been somewhat more accurate than computer generated models, until now. The 1997-98 El Nino "was one in which the full climate models were more successful than statistical predictions for the first time," according to NCAR climate analyst Kevin Trenberth. "The tropical Pacific," says Trenberth, "appears to be predictable for a year or so in advance."

In fact, "to a certain extent we underplayed what the models were telling us," says Ants Leetmaa, director of NOAA's Climate Prediction Centre. He believes that if scientists had relied on the models more and the statistical evidence less, thejr 1997-98 predictions would have been even more accurate.

As encouraging as the model results have been, there is still room for improvement. For example, most of the best models created in advance of the 1997-98 El Nino predicted much smaller monsoons in India than actually occurred and far less rain than actually fell in southeastern Africa and Australia. Kenya and Somalia had heavy and prolonged rains that provoked an epidemic of waterborne Rift Valley fever and dengue fever, among other maladies. "The big question is why," says Leetmaa. "That's the challenge for the future."

It would be far easier to tune the climate models if scientists were able to look through centuries of records. But "we just don't have hundreds of years of data," Leetmaa explains. And even if they were available, "data sets aren't going to give us the full answer. But analyzing the data in combination with computer-simulated experiments is where we're going to make progress."

Greater distribution of monitoring equipment would also increase the accuracy of climate-pattern prediction. No observation networks have been established yet for the equatorial Atlantic and Indian Oceans. Since part of the variability among El Ninos and their regional impacts can be attributed to activity in these ocean basins, the need for improved data reporting in these areas seems clear. Especially, experts note, if El Ninos are becoming more ferocious.

There is a consensus among climate scientists that El Ninos have become. more frequent and progressively warmer over the past century. Beyond that there is little agreement, particularly about whether human activity might be exacerbating their effects.

In the past 98 years there have been 23 El Ninos and 15 La Ninos. (That's according to NOAA's definitions. Other organizations get a slightly different count.) Of the century's ten most powerful El Ninos, four—the four strongest—have occurred since 1980. But no one knows whether this indicates a trend or is simply a meaningless random clustering.

And no one can know at this point. Even a hundred years of precise rainfall and temperature observations in the Pacific might not be sufficient to confirm a major tendency one way or the other. Moreover, many experts now suspect that El Ninos—and indeed many oceanic weather patterns—may alternate in form and severity on a time scale of decades or even centuries. "By and large," says NOAA's Leetmaa, "the El Nino patterns look a lot like the overall changes in U.S. rainfall and temperature patterns from decade to decade" But no matter what's happening. "the bottom line in the past 20 years are different from the previous 30.7

It is difficult to imagine how the global warming observed over the past hundred years, which amounts to about one-tenth of a degree Fahrenheit a decade, could have much effect on the stupefying volume of water in the equatorial Pacific. But it is plausible, some scientists believe.

"El Nino moves heat," says Tom Karl, one of NOAA's veteran climate experts, "both in terms of water temperature and in atmospheric convection. This heat is transported out of the oceans and the tropics during the peak of El Nino as global temperatures increase. As the heat is released, the whole El Nino cycle begins again, with less cloudiness in the tropics and with the oceans absorbing more heat. With global warming there is more heat available. So the cycle may be shortened because the recharge time is shorter or because the release of heat is less efficient."

Whatever the future may bring, the world need never again be taken completely off guard by El Nino or La Nino. Due to the unprecedented foresight that climate science has made possible, the ocean's thermal moods may not seem so unpredictable and diabolical, but rather an ordinary part of life on the planet. "We have to realize that it's something natural that's going to happen again and again," says Capt. Hector Soldi Soldi, a hydrographics expert with the Peruvian Navy. "And we have to be ready for that." "

Even Isias Ipanaque Silva—now living in one of the spare refugee camps in northern Peru, where homes are no more than four woven-straw walls with a plastic trap for a roof—knows it. He and his neighbours walk three miles each way, every day, to farm the riverside fields that lay right next to their homes before El Nino swept their hamlet away. "We can't go back," he says, sad but resigned. "It will happen again. If God wants to save us next time too, we say thanks. But right now, this is where we will stay."

SECTION- 26

INDIAN SCIENTIFIC SOCIETIES AND ASSOCIATIONS

Agricultural Society of India. Calcutta, 1957-58 (WB)

Association of Microbiologists of India (1938)

Entomological Research Association, Udaipur (1985)

Genetics Association of India, Bareilly (1968)

Horticultural Society of India, New Delhi (1942)

Indian Adult Education Association, New Delhi (1939)

Indian Association of Hydrologists (1976) _

Indian Association of Soil and Water Conservationists, Dehradun (1972)

Indian Botanical Society, Howrah (1920)

Indian Chemical Society, Kolkata (1924)

Indian Ecological Society, Ludhiana (1974)

Indian Economic Association, Mumbai (1918)

All India Food Preservers' Association, New Delhi (1939)

Indian Mycological Society, Kolkata (1954)

Indian Potato Association, Shimla (H.P.)

Indian Society for Cotton Improvement, Mumbai (1975)

Indian Society of Agricultural Chemistry, Allahabad (1968)

Indian Society of Agricultural Sciences, New Delhi (1979)

Indian Society of Agronomy, New Delhi (1955)

Indian Society of Coastal Agricultural Research, Canning Town, WB (1982-83)

Indian Society of Genetics and Plant Breeding, New Delhi (1941)

Indian Society of Mycology and Plant Pathology, Udaipur (1971)

Indian Society of Plant Genetic Resources, New Delhi (1987)

Indian Society of Plant Physiology, New Delhi (1958)

Indian Society of Pulses Research and Development, Kanpur (1987)

Indian Society of Soil Science. New Delhi (1934)

Indian Society of Weed Science. Hisar (1968)

Indian Virological Society, Hisar (1984)

Indian Water Resources Society, Roorkee (1980)

Nematological Society of India, New Delhi (1969)

Plant Protection Association of India, Hyderabad (1972)

Sugarcane Technologists Association of India (1925)

The Arid Zone Research Association of India, Jodhpur (1962)

SECTION- 27

INDIAN COUNCIL OF AGRICULTURAL RESEARCH

The Mandate

* To plan, undertake, aid, promote and co-ordinate education, research and its application in agriculture, agroforestry, animal husbandry, fisheries, home science and allied sciences.
* To act as clearing house of research and general information relating to agriculture, animal husbandry, home science and allied sciences and fisheries through its publications and information system and instituting and promoting transfer of technology programmes.
* To provide, undertake and promote consultancy services in the fields of education, research, training and dissemination of information in agriculture, agroforestry, animal husbandry, fisheries, home science and allied sciences.
* To look into problems relating to broader areas of rural development concerning agriculture, including post-harvest technology, by developing co-operative programmes with other organizations such as the Indian Council of Social Sciences Research, Council of Scientific and Industrial Research, Bhabha Atomic Research Centre and Universities.
* To do other things considered necessary to attain objectives of the Society.

At a Glance

* The Indian Council of Agricultural Research (ICAR) is an apex national organization for conducting and coordinating research and education in agriculture, including animal husbandry and fisheries.
* Born as the Imperial Council of Agricultural Research, an autonomous body (a registered society), on 16 July, 1929.
* The Union Minister of Agriculture is the President of the ICAR Society. The Director-General (DG) is the Principal Executive Officer and is also the Secretary to the Department of Agricultural Research and Education (DARE).
* The Governing Body, the chief executive and decision making authority, is chaired by the DG, which consists of eminent agricultural personalities.
* Standing Finance Committee, Standing Policy Planning Committee, Accrediation Board, Regional Committees and Scientific Panels assist the DG in carrying out his functions.
* The Council has its Headquarters at New Delhi, and a vast network of institutes all over the country, consisting of:
    * 45 Institutes
    * 5 National Bureaux
    * 30 National Research Centres
    * 10 Project Directorates
    * 80 All India Co-ordinated Research Projects
* 4 National Institutes with Deemed to-be University status, 1 Central Agricultural University.

* Functions on lines similar to those of University Grants Commission (UGC) in respect of agricultural education.
* 28 State Agricultural Universities, 4 deemed-to-be universities and one Central Agricultural University, work under the aegis of the ICAR.
* 261 Krishi Vigyan Kendras (KVKs: Farm clinics), 8 Trainer's Training Centres for Transfer of Technology.
* One of the leading agricultural research and development systems in the world having 30 thousand personal with more than 7,000 engaged in active research and management.

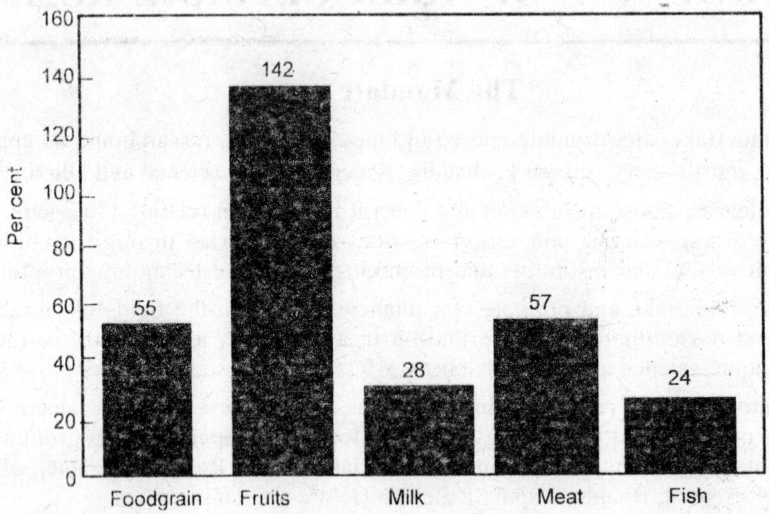

Fig. Required percent growth in production of various commodities over the 1994-96 average to meet the demand by 2020.

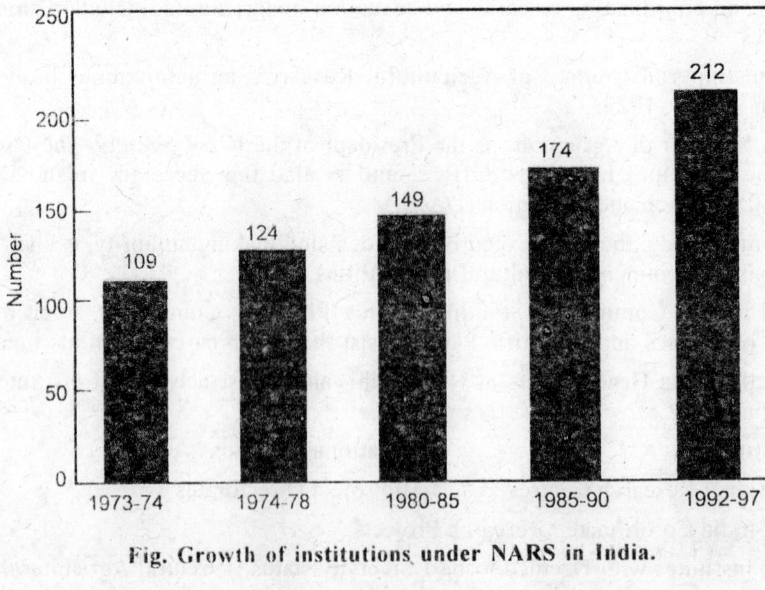

Fig. Growth of institutions under NARS in India.

The Goal

Sustainable growth of Indian agriculture by interfacing education research and extension initiatives complemented with efficient and effective institutional, infrastructural and policy support that will create a proper fit between humanity and its habitat.

Achievements

* More than 180,000 germplasm accessions of agri-horticultural crops and their wild relatives preserved in the National Gene Ban
* 2,300 HYVs/hybrids of field crops developed
* 460 HYVs/, hybrids of horticultural and plantation crops developed
* Developed region-specific IPM modules.
* Adequate breeder seed production to meet the national demand
* Use of biotechnology for production of clonal variants in rapeseed and mustard
* Developed high-yielding crossbred cows, buffaloes, sheep, goats and poultry breeds; and utilized superovulation techniques for quick production of calves from superior bovine females using biotechnology
* Soil maps of the country, states and agro-eco-regions developed
* IPNS (integrated plant nutrients system) and biofacilities developed and popularized
* Zero energy cooling chamber for on-farm storage developed
* Post-harvest technology developed for minimizing, wastes and by-product utilization and value addition in crops, animals and fishery
* A number of farm tools and implements for various field operations developed
* Transfer of technology through Krishi Vigyan Kendras (KVKs) and Institute Village-Linkage Programme (IVLP)
* Organized training courses for skill upgradation for national and international staff particularly in frontier sciences
* Developed computer based agricultural research information system
* MoU with different countries and 16 international organizations for international cooperation
* Enhanced partnership with NGOs, private sector in research and extension
* Vision 2020 document for all the institutes, SAUs and ICAR developed
* Organization and management (O&M) reforms for better work culture introduced

Vision

To harness science to ensure comprehensive and sustained physical, economic and environmental access to food and livelihood security to all Indians, through generation, assessment, refinement and adoption of appropriate technologies.

Strategy

The strategy to translate the vision into action is as follows:

Research Relevance

* Perspective Plans formulated up to 2020 AD
* Research planning and prioritization as a bottom up initiative
* Promote participatory approach for conducting research

Infrastructure

* Develop efficient infrastructure for agricultural research, education and extension education

Diversified Agriculture

* Diversify agriculture with focus on horticulture, livestock, fisheries, and agroforestry
* Special attention to post-harvest technology value-addition, agro-business management and trade

Efficiency

* Develop a research system that provides sufficient social benefits per unit of research inputs and add value for investment
* Achieve small farm mechanization and precision farming
* Ensure technological empowerment of women in agriculture
* Bring in decentralization of agricultural research management

Equity

* Removal of regional imbalance for institutional infrastructure and human resources

Environmental Sustainability

* System based interdisciplinary research thrust
* Concern for conservation and effective use of life-support systems (*e.g.* soil, water, flora, fauna and atmosphere)
* Organic recycling, and waste and by-product utilization
* Addressing global climate change

Enlightened Human Resources

* Training in frontier sciences, technologies and agricultural research management
* Enhancement in vocational skill
* Encourage entrepreneurship and equip-agricultural graduates to become job creators rather than job seekers
* Quality assurance in education
* Thrust on manpower planning
* Better Research-Extension-Farmer Linkage
* Technology assessment, refinement and transfer through more KVKs and IVLPs
* Suitable blending of traditional wisdom in farming with modern technology
* New extension approaches with ATICs (Agricultural Technology Information Centres), ATMAs (Agricultural Technology Management Agency), distance education, more use of non-media complimenting with group based extension and informatics.

Partnership

* Complemetarity in research efforts among institutions and agencies at national and international levels
* Public-private sector linkages
* Effective role of stakeholders (Farmers' Association, NGOs, Public and Private Sectors etc.)

Responsive and Responsible Governacnce

* O & M reforms
* Socio-economic and policy research

SECTION- 28

LAND STATISTICS

Table: 1. DISTRIBUTION OF AREA UNDER DIFFERENT SOIL EROSION, LAND DEGRADATION AND LAND UTILIZATION PROBLEMS (ESTIMATED)

(Area : Million hectares unless otherwise stated)

	Area under	*With 1976-77 Land utilisation Statistics and Reports till 1980-81*	*With 1981-82 Land utilisation Statistics and Reports till 1984-85*
1.	Geographical area	329	329
2.	Area subject to water and wind erosion	150	141.25
3.	Area degraded through special problems:-		
3.1	Waterlogged area	6.00	8.53
3.2	Alkali soils	2.50	3.58
3.3	Acid soils	–	4.50
3.4	Saline soils including coastal sandy areas	5.50	5.50
3.5	Ravines and gullies	3.97	3.97
3.6	Area subject to shifting cultivation	4.36	4.91
3.7	Riverine and torrents	2.73	2.73
	Total (3.1 to 3.7)	**25.06**	**33.72**
4.	**Total problem area (2 + 3)**	**175.06**	**174.97**
4A.	Annual average loss of nutrients from land is worth	5.37 to 8.4 million tonnes	5.37 to 8.4 million tonnes
5.	Average annual loss of production for not developing ravines is worth	3 million tonnes	3 million tonnes
6.	Average annual rate of encroachment of table lands by ravines	8000 ha.	8000 ha
7.	Average area annually subject to damages through shifting cultivation	1	1
8.	**Total flood prone area :**	**40**	**40 ****
8.1 a	Annual average area affected by floods	9	8
8.1 b	Maximum area affected in the worst year	17.6	18.6
8.2 *a.*	Annual average cropped area affected by flood	3.6	3.7
8.2 *b.*	Maximum cropped area affected in any year	10.0	10.0
9.	**Total drought prone area**	**260**	**260**
10.	Additional land needed by 2000 AD:		

10.1	For crop production (for each a maximum of 150 net sown area as per NCA)	10	10
10.2	For production of fuel wood (35/45 m.ha) and timber	40	40
10.3	For production of fodder	10	10
10.4	**Total (10.1 to 10.3)**	**60**	**60**
11.	Availability of land per capita :		
	Year	**Total cultivable land (including forest trees)**	
11.1	1951	0.89 ha.	0.48 ha.
11.2	1981	0.50 ha.	0.20 ha.
11.3	2000	0.33 ha.	0.15 ha.

** Flood Atlas of India, CWC of Water Resources Ministry, Govt. of India, New Delhi, dated 10th April. 1987

Source : *Indian Agriculture in Brief*. 25th Edition, DES, MOA, New Delhi.

Reproduced by permission

TABLE-2 CONVERSION RATIOS BETWEEN AGRICULTURAL RAW MATERIAL AND PROCESSED PRODUCT

Raw materials	*Processed products*
Rice	
Rice (cleaned) production	2/3 of paddy products
Cotton	
Cotton lint production	1/3 of *kapas* production
Cotton seed production	2/3 of *kapas* production 2 times of cotton lint production
1 Candy	355 kg or 782.42 lb
Jute	
100 yards of hessian	54 lb of raw jute
4,148 yards of hessian	1 ton of raw jute 5.55 bales of raw jute (of 180 kg each)
1 tonne of sacking	1.11 tonnes of raw jute 6.17 bales of raw jute (of 180 kg each)
1 tonne of hessian, sacking, etc.	1.05 tonnes of raw jute 5.85 bales of raw jute (of 180 kg each)
Groundnut	
Kernel to nuts in shell	70 per cent
Oil to nuts in shell	28 per cent
Oil to kernels crushed	40 per cent
Cake to kernels crushed	60 per cent
Sesamum	
Oil to seeds crushed	40 per cent
Cake to seeds crushed	60 per cent
Rapeseed and mustard	
Oil to seeds crushed	33 per cent
Cake to seeds crushed	67 per cent
Linseed	
Oil to seeds crushed	33 per cent
Cake to seeds crushed	67 per cent
Castor seed	
Oil to seeds crushed	37 per cent
Cake to seeds crushed	63 per cent
Cotton seed	
Oil to seeds crushed	14 to 18 per cent
Cake to seeds crushed	82 to 86 per cent
Coconut	
Copra to nuts	One tonne of copra = 6,773 nuts
Oil to copra crushed	62 per cent
Cake to copra crushed	38 per cent

Raw materials	Processed products
Niger seed	
Oil to seeds crushed	28 per cent
Cake to seeds crushed	72 per cent
Kardi seed	
Oil to seeds crushed	40 per cent
Cake to seeds crushed	60 per cent
Mahua seed	
Oil to seeds crushed	36 per cent
Cake to seeds crushed	64 per cent
Neem seed	
Oil to kernels crushed	45 to 50 per cent
Cake to kernels crushed	50 to 55 per cent
Soyabean seed	
Oil to soyabeen seeds crushed	18 per cent
Meal to soyabeen seeds crushed	73 per cent
Hull from soyabeen seeds crushed	8 per cent
Wastage from soyabeen seeds crushed	1 per cent
Sugar	
Gur from cane crushed	10 per cent
Crystal sugar from gur refined (gur refineries)	62.4 per cent
Crystal sugar from cane refined (cane factories)	9.97 per cent
Khandsari sugar from gur refined	37.5 per cent
Molasses from cane crushed	3.5 per cent
Cane thrash from cane harvested	10.0 per cent
Lac	
Seed lac	66.0 per cent of stick lac
Shell lac	57.4 per cent of stick lac or 87 per cent of seed lac
Cashew nuts	
Cashew kernels	25 per cent of cashew nuts
Butter and ghee	
Butter from mixed milk	6.9 per cent
Ghee from mixed milk	5.5 per cent

* This consists of leaves and a portion of the top of the stalk which are removed from the cane stalk while harvesting and before sending the cane for milling.

Source: *Indian Agriculture in Brief*, 25th Edition, Directorate of Economics and Statistics, Ministry of Agriculture, New Delhi.

Reproduced by permission.

APPENDIX-I

SOWING AND HARVESTING SEASONS OF PRINCIPAL CROPS IN MAJOR GROWING STATES

Zone/State	*Rice*					
	Autumn		*Winter*		*Summer*	
	Sowing	*Harvesting*	*Sowing*	*Harvesting*	*Sowing*	*Harvesting*
East						
Assam	Mid-Feb.-April	June-August	May-July	Nov. Jan.	–	–
Bihar	May-July	Sept.-Oct.	July-Sept.	Nov.-Dec.	Jan.-Feb.	May-June
Meghalaya	Mid-Feb.-April	June-August	March-July	Nov.-Jan.	–	–
Nagaland	March-May	June-August	May-July	Nov.-Jan.	–	–
Orissa	May-June	Sept.-Oct.	June-August	Dec.-Jan.	Dec.-Jan.	May-June
West Bengal	March-June (B) May-June (T)	July-Nov.	April-June (B) June-Aug.(T)	Nov.-Dec.	Oct.-Feb. (T)	April May
North						
Haryana	May-August	Sept.-Nov.	–	–	–	–
Himachal Pradesh	June-July	Sept.-Nov.	–	–	–	–
Jammu & Kashmir	–	–	April-July	Sept.-Dec.	–	–
Punjab	May-August	Sept-Nov.	–	–	–	–
Uttar Pradesh	May-July	Sept.-Nov.	June-August	Nov.-Dec.	Jan.-Feb.	April-June
South						
Andhra Pradesh	March-May	June-Sept.	June-Oct.	Nov-March	Dec.-Feb.	March-May

(B) = Broadcasting (T) Transplanting.

SOWING AND HARVESTING SEASONS OF PRINCIPAL CROPS IN MAJOR GROWING STATES

Jowar				*Bajra*		*Maize*	
Kharif		*Rabi*					
Sowing	***Harvesting***	***Sowing***	***Harvesting***	***Sowing***	***Harvesting***	***Sowing***	***Harvesting***
–	–	–	–	–	–	April-May	August-Sept.
April-August	Sept.-Dec.	–	–	April-August	Sept.-Dec.	June-July	Sept.-Oct.
–	–	–	–	–	–	April-May	August-Sept.
–	–	–	–	–	–	–	–
June-July	Sept.-Oct.	–	–	–	–	June-July	Sept. Oct.
–	–	–	–	–	–	April-June	July-August
June-July	Sept.-Nov.	–	–	June-August	Sept.-Nov.	June-July	Sept.-Nov.
–	–	–	–	–	–	April-June	Sept.-Oct.
–	–	–	–	June-July	Sept.-Oct.	April-June	Aug.-Oct.
June-July	Sept-Nov.	–	–	June-August	Sept.-Nov.	June-July	Sept.-Nov.
June-July	Oct.-Dec.	–	–	June-August	Sept.-Nov.	June-July	Aug.-Oct.
June-Oct.	Jan.-April	Nov.-Dec.	March-April	June-August	Sept.-Dec.	June-Aug. (K) Oct.-Dec. (R)	Sept.-Oct. (K) Jan.-March (R)

(K) = Kharif (R) = Rabi.

(Continued)

SOWING AND HARVESTING SEASONS OF PRINCIPAL CROPS IN MAJOR GROWING STATES (CONTINUED)

Zone/State	*Rice*					
	Autumn		*Winter*		*Summer*	
	Sowing	*Harvesting*	*Sowing*	*Harvesting*	*Sowing*	*Harvesting*
South (Concluded)						
Karnataka	May-August	Sept.-Dec.	June-Oct.	Nov.-March	Dec.-Feb.	April-July
Kerala	April-June	Aug.-Oct.	Aug.-Oct.	Dec.-Feb.	Nov.-Feb.	Feb.-May
Tamil Nadu	May-Nov.	Sept.-Feb.	Oct.-Jan.	Jan.-April	Feb.-April	May-June
West						
Gujarat	June-August	Oct-Dec.	–	–	–	–
Madhya Pradesh	10th June-15th Aug.	15th Sept.-15th Dec.	–	–	–	–
Maharashtra	June-July	Oct.-Dec.	–	–	–	–
Rajasthan	July-August	Oct.-Dec.	–	–	–	–
All India	March-Aug.	June-Dec.	June-Oct.	Nov.-April	Nov.-Feb.	March-June

SOWING AND HARVESTING SEASONS OF PRINCIPAL CROPS IN MAJOR GROWING STATES (CONTINUED)

Jowar				*Bajra*		*Maize*	
Kharif		*Rabi*					
Sowing	*Harvesting*	*Sowing*	*Harvesting*	*Sowing*	*Harvesting*	*Sowing*	*Harvesting*
May- July	Oct.- Dec.	Sept.- Nov.	Jan.- March	June- August	Sept.- Jan.	April- July Nov. (R)	July- Nov. Feb. (R)
–	–	–	–	–	–	–	–
June- Oct.	Sept.- Jan.	Nov.- May	Feb.- July	May- Dec.	Sept.- March	–	–
June- July	Nov.- Dec.	Sept.- Oct.	Feb.	June- July	Sept.- Nov.	June- July	Sept.- Nov.
10th June- 7th Aug.	Nov.- 15th Jan.	20th Sept.- Oct.	Jan.- March	15th June- 8th Aug.	10th Oct.- Dec.	June- July	15th Aug.- Sept.
June- July	Nov.- Jan.	Sept.- Nov.	Jan.- March	June- July	Oct.- Nov.	June- July (K) Nov.- Dec. (R)	Aug.- Nov. (K) March- April (R)
June- August	Oct.- Dec.	–	–	June- July	Sept.- Nov.	June- July	Sept. Nov.
April- August	Sept. Jan.	Sept.- Dec.	Jan.- April	June- August	Sept.- Dec.	June- Aug. (K) Oct. Dec. (R)	Aug.- Nov. (K) Jan. April (R)

(Continue)

SOWING AND HARVESTING SEASONS OF PRINCIPAL CROPS IN MAJOR GROWING STATES (CONTINUED)

Zone/State	Wheat		Gram		Potato	
					Hills	
	Sowing	Harvesting	Sowing	Harvesting	Sowing	Harvesting
East						
Assam	Nov.-Dec.	Mar.-Apr.	–	–	Oct.-Nov.	Jan.-Feb.
Bihar	Oct.-Dec.	Feb.-May	Oct.-Dec.	Feb.-May	–	–
Meghalaya	–	–	–	–	Oct.-Nov.	Jan.-Feb.
Nagaland	–	–	–	–	–	–
Orissa	Oct.-Nov.	Mar.-Apr.	–	–	–	–
West Bengal	Oct.-Dec.	Mar.-Apr.	Nov.-Dec	Mar.-Apr	–	–
North						
Haryana	Oct.-Dec.	Apr.-May	Sept.-Nov.	Mar.-Apr.	Sept.-Oct. Jan.-Apr.	Jan.-Feb. June.-Oct.
Himachal Pradesh	Oct.-Nov.	Apr.-June	Sept.-Nov.	Apr.-May	Jan.-Feb.	Jan-July
Jammu & Kashmir	Oct.-Nov.	Apr.-June	–	–	June-July Sept.-Oct	Oct.-Jan- Feb
Punjab	Oct.-Dec.	Apr.-May	Sept.-Nov.	Mar.-Apr.	Sept.-Oct Jan.-Apr.	Jan-Feb. June-Oct.
Uttar Pradesh	Oct.-Dec.	Mar.-May	Sept.-Nov.	Mar.-Apr.	Nov.-Dec.	Mar.
South						
Andhra Pradesh	–	–	Nov.-Dec.	Feb.-Mar.	–	–

SOWING AND HARVESTING SEASONS OF PRINCIPAL CROPS IN MAJOR GROWING STATES (CONTINUED)

(Winter)		*Potato (Summer)*				*sugarcane*	
Plains		***Hills***		***Plains***			
Sowing	***Harvesting***	***Sowing***	***Harvesting***	***Sowing***	***Harvesting***	***Sowing***	***Harvesting***
Oct.-Nov.	Jan.-Feb.	Feb.-Mar.	May-Jun.	–	–	Mar.-Apr.	Nov.-Jan.
Oct.-Feb.	Dec.-Mar.	–	–	–	–	Dec.-Feb.	Nov.-Mar.
Oct.-Nov.	Jan.-Feb.	Feb.-Mar.	May.-June	–	–	–	–
–	–	–	–	–	–	–	–
Oct.-Nov.	Jan.-Feb.	–	–	July-Aug.	Sept.-Oct.	Feb.-May.	Nov.-Feb.
Sept.-Nov.	Jan.-Apr.	–	–	–	–	Dec..-Apr.	Dec.-Mar.
Sept.-Oct. Dec.-Jan.	Nov.-Jan. Apr.-May	Nov.-Feb. Mar.-May	June Dec. -July	Sept.-Oct. Jan.-Feb.	Dec-July –	Feb.-Apr.	Dec.-Mar.
–	–	Apr.-May	Sept.-Oct.	–	–	Mar.-May	Oct.-Dec.
Sept.-Oct. June-July	Dec.-Feb. Oct.	Mar.-June	Sept.-Oct.	Mar.-June.	Sept.-Oct.	Feb.-Mar.	Oct.-Dec.
Sept.-Oct. Dec.-Jan.	Nov.-Jan. Apr.-May	Jan.-Feb. Mar.-May	June Dec.-July	Sept.-Oct. Jan.-Feb	Dec.-July –.	Feb.-Apr.	Dec.-Mar.
Sept.-Oct.	Nov.-Feb.	Sept.-Oct.	Nov.-Dec.	Sept.-Oct.	Nov.-Dec.	Sept.-Apr.	Oct.-June
Oct.-Nov.	Jan.-Feb.	–	–	–	–	June-May	Dec.-Apr.

(Continued)

SOWING AND HARVESTING SEASONS OF PRINCIPAL CROPS IN MAJOR GROWING STATES (CONTINUED)

Zone/State	Wheat		Gram		Potato	
					Hills	
	Sowing	Harvesting	Sowing	Harvesting	Sowing	Harvesting
South (Concluded)						
Kamaataka	Sept.- Nov.	Jan.-Mar.	Sept-Dec.	Dec.-Apr	–	–
Kerala	–		–	–	–	–
Tamil Nadu	–		–	–	Sept.-Dec.	Dec.-May
West						
Gujarat	Oct.-Nov.	Feb.-Mar.	Oct.-Nov.	Feb.-Mar.	Nov.-Dec.	Feb.-Mar.
Madhya Pradesh	Oct.-Nov.	15th Feb-Apr	Oct.-Nov.	Feb.-Mar.	Oct.-Dec.	15 Feb. -Mar.
Maharashtra	Oct.-Nov.	Feb.-Mar.	Sept.-Nov.	Jan.-Apr	–	–
Rajasthan	Oct.-Dec.	Mar.-May	Sept.-Nov.	Feb.-Apr.	–	–
All India	Sept.-Dec.	Feb.-May	Sept.-Dec.	Feb.-May	Aug.-Dec. (Sowing)	

SOWING AND HARVESTING SEASONS OF PRINCIPAL CROPS IN MAJOR GROWING STATES (CONTINUED)

(Winter)		*Potato (Summer)*				*sugarcane*	
Plains		*Hills*		*Plains*			
Sowing	***Harvesting***	***Sowing***	***Harvesting***	***Sowing***	***Harvesting***	***Sowing***	***Harvesting***
July-Jan.	Sept.-June	Apr.-May	Aug.-Sept.	June-Jan.	Sept.-Apr.	Dec.-Mar.	Nov.-Mar.
—	—	—	—	—	—	Nov.-Feb. Jan.-Mar.	Oct.-Dec. Dec.-Feb.
Oct.-Nov.	Feb.-Mar.	Apr.-July	July-Nov.	Apr.-May	Aug.-Sept.	Dec.-Sept.	Dec.-Aug.
Oct.-Nov.	Feb.-Mar.	—	—	—	—	Oct.-May	Dec.-Mar.
15 Oct.-Nov.	March- 15th May	June- 15th Aug.	21st Sept.- 15th Nov.	10th June- 15th Aug.	Sept.-Dec.	15th Dec.- 8th May	Oct.-Mar.
Nov.	Feb.	—		July	Oct.	Dec. Apr.	Oct.-Feb.
Aug.-Nov.	Dec.-Mar.	—		—		Jan..-May	Nov.-Feb.
Jan.-May (Harvesting)		Feb.-July (Sowing)		Jan.-May (Harvesting)		Dec.-May	Oct.-Apr.

(Continued)

SOWING AND HARVESTING SEASONS OF PRINCIPAL CROPS IN MAJOR GROWING STATES (CONCLUDED)

Zone/State	*Tobacco*		*Groundnut*		*Cotton*		*Jute*	
	Sowing	*Harvesting*	*Sowing*	*Harvesting*	*Sowing*	*Harvesting*	*Sowing*	*Harvesting*
East								
Assam	Oct.-Nov.	Feb.-Mar.	–	–	Apr.-May	Jan.-Mar.	Feb.-Mar.	July-Aug.
Bihar	–	–	July-Aug.	Dec.-Jan.	June-July	Nov.-Dec.	Mar.-July	July-Sept.
Meghalaya	Oct.-Nov.	Feb.-Mar.	–	–	Apr.-May	Jan.-Mar.	Feb.-Aug.	July-Aug.
Nagaland	–	–	–	–	–	–	–	–
Orissa	Sept.-Dec.	Nov.-Jan.	June-July	Nov.-Dec.	–	–	May-June	Aug.-Sept-
West Bengal	Sept.-Dec.	Feb.-Mar.	–	–	–	–	Mar.-June	July-Oct.
North								
Haryana	Nov.-Mar.	May-June	June-July	Nov.-Dec.	May-June	Sept.-Dec.	–	–
Himachal Pradesh	May-June	Oct.-Nov.	June	Oct.	–	–	–	–
Jammu & Kashmir	Mar.-July	June-July Sept.-Nov.	–	–	–	–	–	–
Punjab	Nov.-Mar. June-Aug.	May-June Oct.-Dec.	June-July	Nov.-Dec.	May-June	Sept.-Dec.	–	–
Uttar Pradesh	Sept.-Feb.	Jan.-May	May-July	Oct.-Dec.	Apr.-June	Sept.-Jan.	Jan.-July	July-Nov.
South								
Andhra Pradesh	Oct.	Feb.	May-Oct.	Sept.-Jan.	June-Oct.	Jan.-May	–	–

(Continued)

SOWING AND HARVESTING SEASONS OF PRINCIPAL CROPS IN MAJOR GROWING STATES (CONCLUDED)

Zone/State	Tobacco		Groundnut		Cotton		Jute	
	Sowing	Harvesting	Sowing	Harvesting	Sowing	Harvesting	Sowing	Harvesting
South (Concluded)								
Karnataka	Apr.-Sept.	Aug.-Feb.	June-Aug.	Sept.-Dec.	May-Sept.	Oct.-Apr.	–	–
Kerala	–	–	–	–	Aug.-Sept.	Feb.-Mar.	–	–
Tamil Nadu	Sept.-Jan.	Feb.-Apr.	Jan.-May July-Oct.	Apr.-May Oct.-Jan.	Feb.-Nov.	Oct.-Dec	–	–
West								
Gujarat	July.-Sept.	Nov.-Feb.	June.-July	Sept.-Nov.	June-Sept.	Dec.-Mar.	–	–
Madhya Pradesh	10 June-15 Nov.	Nov.-15 Mar.	10 June-July	21 Sept.-15 Nov.	20 May-July	15 Oct.-Feb.	–	–
Maharashtra	July-Sept.	Jan.-Mar.	June-July	Sept.-Dec.	June.-Sept.	Nov.-Apr.	–	–
Rajasthan	Nov.-Jan.	Apr.-May	June-Aug.	Oct.-Dec.	May-July	Oct.-Dec. Jan.-Aug.		
All India	July-Dec.	Jan.-May	May-Aug.	Sept.-Jan.	Mar.-Sept.	Sept.-Apr.	Feb.-July	July.-Nov.

Source : "*Area and Production Principal Crops in India*, 1993-94 to 1994-95, Directorate Economics and Statistics, Ministry of Agriculture, New Delhi.

Table 1.10 DISTRIBUTION OF AREA ACCORDING TO ANNUAL RAINFALL IN INDIA

Rainfall amount		*Approximate percentage of area receiving rainfall*
Dry	0-750 mm	30.0
Medium	750-1,150 mm	42.0
	1,150-2,000 mm	20.0
Assured	above 2,000 mm	8.0
Total		**100.0**

Table. 1.11. DISTRIBUTION OF ANNUAL RAINFALL ACCORDING TO SEASONS IN INDIA

Rainfall	*Duration*	*Approximate percentage of annual rainfall*
Pre-Monsoon	March-May	10.4
South-West Monsoon	June-September	73.7
Post-Monsoon	October-December	13.3
Winter or North-East Monsoon	January-February	2.6
Total		**100.0**

Source : Reported from India Meteorologcal Department, Pune.

Table. 1.12 DISTRIBUTION OF METEOROLOGICAL SUB-DIVISIONS ACCORDING TO EXCESS / NORMAL OR DEFICIENT/SCANTY RAINFALL SOUTH-WEST MONSOON PERIOD (JUNE-SEPTEMBER)

Item	1987	1988	1989	1990	1991	1992	1993	1994	1995	1996	1997	1998	1999
1. Excess/Normal	14	32	29	32	27	32	31	25	33	32	32	33	28
2. Deficient/Scanty	21	3	6	3	8	3	4	10	2	3	3	2	7
Total	**35**	**35**	**35**	**35**	**35**	**35**	**35**	**35**	**35**	**35**	**35**	**35**	**35**
3. % of districts having normal to excess rains	43	88	72	84	68	65	78	77	79	82	81	81	67
4. % of normal rainfall *	81	119	101	106	91	93	100	110	100	-103	102	106	96

Excess = +20% or more, Normal = +19% to –19%, Deficient = –20% to –59%,

Scanty = – 60% or less

* = Percentage of long term average value

Source : 1. *India Meteorological Department*, Pune.

2. *Economic Survey 1999-2000, * Ministry of Finance, New Delhi.

Table 1.13 PERFORMANCE OF TOTAL RAINFALL IN A YEAR

Year	*As percentage of normal rainfall*
1976	102
1977	104
1978	109
1979	81
1980	104
1981	100
1982	85
1983	113
1984	96
1985	93
1986	87
1987	81
1988	119
1989	101
1990	119
1991	91
1992	93
1993	100
1994	110
1995	100
1996	103
1997	102
1998	106
1999	96

Source : "Economic Survey, 1999-2000", Ministry of Finance, New Delhi.

Note: Five most bountiful rain years of the century :

1917:121%, 1933:117%, 1961:121%, 1988:119% and 1990:119%.

Table 1.14

	1997	1998	1999
1. Number of Reservoirs	63	68	68
2. Designed live capacity at full reservoir level (TMC)	124.6	129.4	129.4
3. Total Live Storage (TMC)	100.4	106.3	95.3.
4. Current year storage as per cent of the design storage	81	82	74

TMC = Thousand Million Cubic Metres.

Source : "Economic Survey - 1999-2000", Ministry of Finance, New Delhi.

Table 1.15 LIST OF DISTRICTS HAVING MEAN ANNUAL RAINFALL OF 760-1250 mm AND MOISTURE AVAILABILITY FOR AT LEAST 150 DAYS

1. Andhra Pradesh

(*i*) East Godavari
(*ii*) Krishna
(*iii*) Warangal
(*iv*) Srikakulam
(*v*) Visakhapatnam
(*vi*) Khammam
(*vii*) Prakasam
(*viii*) Nellore
(*ix*) Cuddapah

2. Bihar

(*i*) Palamau
(*ii*) Champaran
(*iii*) Dhanabad
(*iv*) Bhagalpur
(*v*) Patna
(*vi*) Rohtas
(*vii*) Gaya
(*viii*) Monghyr

3. Gujarat

(*i*) Surat
(*ii*) Bharuch
(*iii*) Baroda (Vadodara)
(*iv*) Ahmedabad
(*v*) Panchmahal

4. Haryana

Ambala

5. Karnataka

(*i*) Shimoga
(*ii*) Bidar
(*iii*) Bangalore
(*iv*) Hassan
(*v*) Mysore
(*vi*) Gulbarga

6. Jammu and Kashmir

Kargil

7. Madhya Pradesh

(*i*) Guna
(*ii*) Bhopal
(*iii*) Satna
(*iv*) Betul
(*v*) Chindwara
(*vi*) Ratlam
(*vii*) Indore
(*viii*) Damoh
(*ix*) West Nimar
(*x*) Gwalior
(*xi*) Morena
(*xii*) East Nimar

8. Maharashtra

(*i*) Nagpur
(*ii*) Kolhapur
(*iii*) Yeotmal
(*iv*) Amravati
(*v*) Buldhana
(*vi*) Akola
(*vii*) Jalgaon
(*viii*) Osmanabad
(*ix*) Aurangabad
(*x*) Parbhani

9. Orissa

Ganjam

10. Punjab

Patiala

11. Rajasthan

(*i*) Jhalawar
(*ii*) Kota

12. Tamil Nadu

(*i*) Madurai
(*ii*) Madras
(*iii*) North Arcot
(*iv*) Salem
(*v*) Tiruchirapalli

13. Uttar Pradesh

(*i*) Varanasi
(*ii*) Allahabad
(*iii*) Jhansi
(*iv*) Banda
(*v*) Fatehpur
(*vi*) Jalaun
(*vi*) Kanpur (Rural)
(*viii*) Lucknow
(*ix*) Agra
(*x*) Mainpuri
(*xi*) Hardoi
(*xii*) Bahraich
(*xiii*) Aligarh
(*xiv*) Lakhimpur
(*xv*) Bareilly
(*xvi*) Sharanpur

Source : "National Bank News Review" - November 1987 NABARD, Mumbai

Table 1.16: ALLINDIA AREA UNDER FOODGRAINS CULTIVATED AND IRRI GATED WITH LAND MANRATIO

(1950-51 to 1998-99)

Sl. No	Year	Area under food grains (Gross)		Share of area under food grains to (Gross)		Land Man ratio $
		Cultivated	Irrigated	Gross cultivated area #	Gross irrigated area #	
		← (000 hectares) →		← per cent →		
1.	1950-51	97,321	18,317	73.8	81.2	
2.	1951-52	96.61	18,560	72.8	80.1	0.34
3.	1952-53	102,088	19,040	74.2	81.7	0.35
4.	1953-54	109,065	20,020	76.5	82.2	0.35
5.	1954-55	107,858	20.140	74.9	80.7	0.35
6.	1955-56	110,560	20,626	75.1	80.4	0.35
7.	1956-57	111,136	20,450	74.3	79.6	0.34
8.	1957-58	109,480	21,160	75.1	79.5	0.33
9.	1958-59	114,764	21,460	75.7	79.6	0.33
10.	1959-60	115,823	21,840	75.8	79.6	0.33
11.	1960-61	115,581	22,065	75.7	78.9	0.32
12.	1961-62	117,232	22,450	75.0	78.9	0.32
13.	1962-63	117,844	23,390	75.2	79.4	0.32
14.	1963-64	117,421	23.340	74.8	78.6	0.31
15.	1964-65	118,112	23,943	74.2	78.0	0.31
16.	1965-66	114,103	24,032	73.5	77.8	0.29
17.	1966-67	115,302	25,760	73.3	78.8	0.29
18.	1967-68	121,421	26,170	74.2	78.8	0.37
19.	1968-69	120,430	28,100	75.5	79.2	0.28
20.	1969-70	123,570	29,080	76.2	78.6	0.28
21	1970-71	124,316	30,117	75.0	78.9	0.28
22.	1971-72	122,623	30,080	74.2	78.3	0.28
23.	1972-73	119,277	30,768	73.6	78.8	0.26
24.	1973-74	126,538	31,173	74.5	77.4	0.27
25.	1974-75	121,075	32,315	73.7	77.4	0.26
26.	1975-76	128,181	34,093	74.8	78.6	0.26
27.	1976-77	124,356	34,222	74.3	78.6	0.25
28.	1977-78	127,515	35.407	74.0	76.8	0.25

29. 1978-79	129,009	37,208	73.8	77.0	0.25
30. 1979-80	125,206	38,111	73.8	77.4	0.24
31. 1980-81	126,667	37,620	73.4	75.6	0.24
32. 1981-82	129,138	38,290	73.1	74.5	0.24
33. 1982-83	125,095	38,703	72.4	74.7	0.23
34. 1983-84	131,163	40,792	73.8	75.8	0.23
35. 1984-85	126,673	40,625	71.8	74.5	0.22
36. 1985-86	128,023	40,628	71.7	74.8	0.22
37. 1986-87	127,195	41,604	72.1	74.6	0.22
38. 1987-88	119,696	40,481	70.1	72.3	0.21
39. 1988-89	127,674	42,851	70.0	70.1	0.21
40. 1989-90	126,773	43,671	69.6	70.6	0.21
41. 1990-91	127,835	44,526	68.6	71.3	0.20
42. 1991-92	121,871	45,459	66.9	69.8	0.20
43. 1992-93	123,148	46,856	66.3	70.2	0.19
44. 1993-94	122,754	48,259	65.8	70.7	0.19
45. 1994-95	123,860	49,894	65.9	70.6	0.19
46. 1995-96	121,015	49,543	64.6	69.4	0.18
47. 1996-97	123,581	50,842	65.2	69.4	0.16
48. 1997-98	123,847				0.16
49. 1998-99	125,355				

$ = Land man ratio = Arable land and land under permanent crops/population.

Source: Directorate of Economics and Statistics, Ministry of Agriculture, New Delhi.

6.00 FIVE YEAR PLAN

TABLE 1.17 NINTH FIVE YEAR PLAN (LAND UTILIZATION AND FERTILIZER USE)

Item	Unit	2001-02 (9th Plan end)	2006-07 (10th Plan end)
Net sown area	Million hectares	142.0	142.0
Gross cropped area	,,	203.0	203.4
Cropping intensity	%	143.0	144.3
Area under food grains	Million hectares	126.0	135.0
Gross irrigated area	,,	91.5	114.0
fertilizer consumption	Million tonnes	20.0	30.0
($N + P_2O_5 + K_2O$)			
(*i*) For food grains	,,	16.6	21.0
(*ii*) Other than food grains	,,	7.1	9.0

Source: "*Agricultural Statistics at a Glance*. 2000", *Directorate of Economics* and *Statistics*, *Ministry of Agriculture*, *New Delhi*.

Table 1.18 TARGETED PRODUCTION, DOMESTIC CONSUMPTION OF AGRICULTURAL ACTIVITIES (million tonnes)

Item	2001-02 (9th Plan end)	
	Target Production	**Projected Consumption**
A) Food grains	234.00	227.16
i) Rice	99.00	94.29
ii) Wheat	83.00	78.37
iii) Coarse cereals	35.50	35.00
iv) Pulses	16.50	19.50
B) Oilseeds	30.00	25.75
C) Sugarcane	336.00	332.50
D) Fruits & vegetables	179.00	170.99
E) Other agricultural products		
i) Tea @	1000.00	877.00
ii) Coffee @	300.00	80.00
iii) Spices	3.36	2.75
iv) Rubber	0.83	0.79

@ = Million kg.

Source: "*Agricultural Statistics at a Glance*, 2000", *Directorate of Economics* and *Statistics*, *Ministry of Agriculture*, *New Delhi*.

TABLE 1.19: TARGET GROWTH RATE OF GDP, POPULATION AND AGRICULTURAL CROPS DURING 9th, 10th AND 11th PLAN PERIOD

Item	Per annum growth rate (per cent)		
	IX Plan	**X Plan**	**XI Plan**
GDP	**6.5**	7.7	**8.1**
Population	**1.57**	**1.57**	**1.45**
Agricultural crop	**3.82**	**4.54**	**4.27**
Food grains	3.05	3.57	2.73
Rice	2.75	3.08	2.73
Wheat	3.75	4.31	3.64
Coarse cereals	2.20	2.40	2.43
Pulses	3.50	4.93	5.66
Oilseeds	5.25	8.85	5.16
Sugarcane	4.00	6.16	5.07
Fruits and vegetables	7.00	8.01	7.89
Other agricultural products of which:	2.64	3.08	3.04
Tea	5.00	6.16	6.07
Coffee	5.00	6.16	6.07
Total agriculture	**4.50**	**5.30'**	**5.10**

Source: *Ninth Five Year Plan* (1997-2002). *Planning Commission, GOI, New Delhi.*

Table: 1.20 PROJECTED POPULATION, FOOD GRAINS PRODUCTION AND CONSUMPTION AND USE OF INPUTS BY THE END OF 11th PLAN

Item	Unit	2011-12
Population	Million nos.	1196.4
Per capita consumption of food grains	Kg.	223.35
Food grains production	Million tonnes	337.30
Rice	,,	128.16
Wheat	,,	130.45
Coarse cereals	,,	48.93
Pulses	,,	29.76
Oilseeds	,,	58.56
Sugarcane	,,	679.64
Net area sown	Million hectares	142.00
Gross area sown	,,	219.15
Gross irrigated area	,,	105.50
Fertilizer consumption ($N + P_2O_5 + K_2O$)		
Total	Million tonnes	45.48
Per hectare of gross cropped area	kg.	207.53

Source: *Ninth Five Plan* (1997-2002) *Planning Consumption, GOI, New Delhi.*

CONSUMPTION OF PLANT NUTRIENTS PER HECTARE ARABLE LAND AND LAND UNDER PERMANENT CROPS IN SELECTED COUNTRIES (Kg.) - 1998-99 & 1997-98

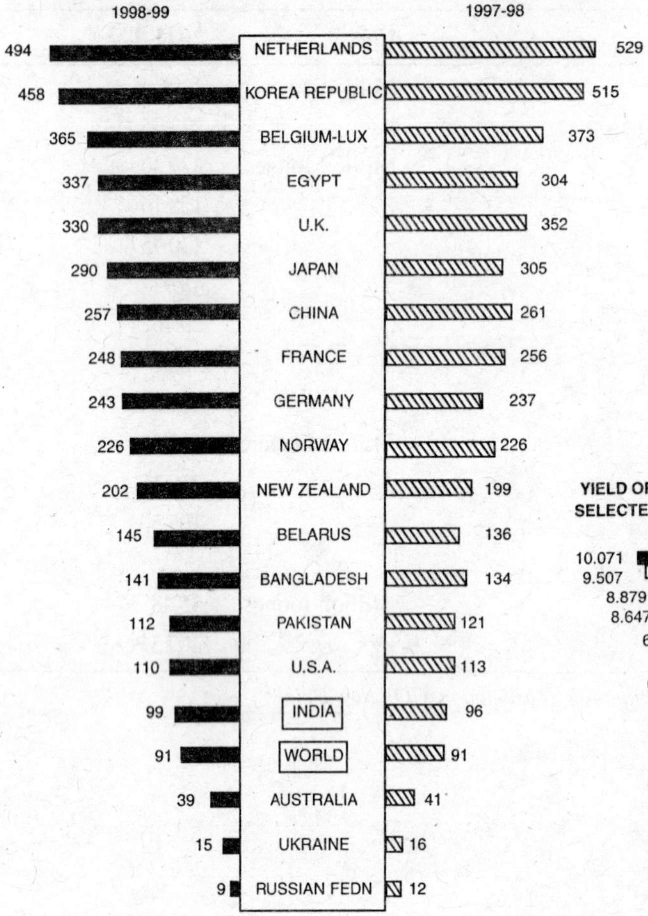

YIELD OF PADDY & WHEAT IN SELECTED COUNTRIES ('000 KG./hA)

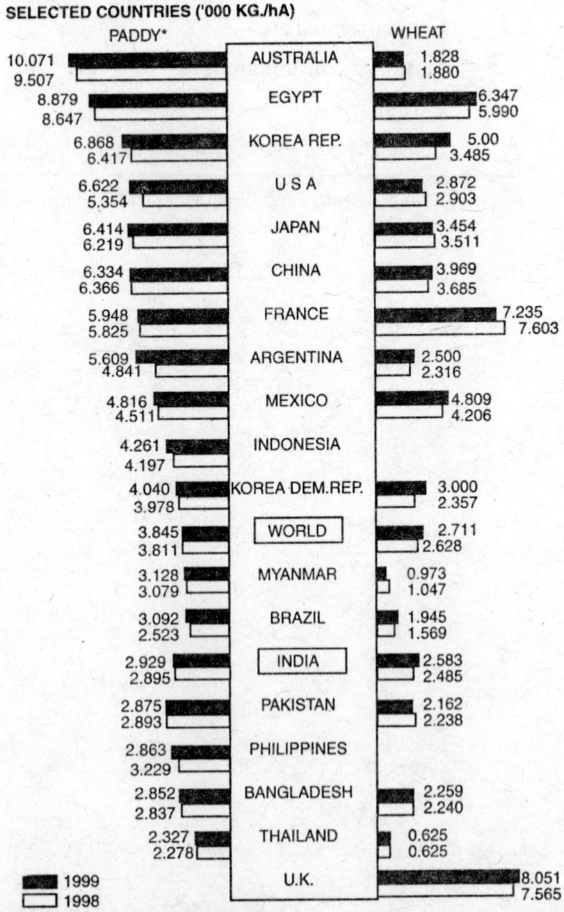

* Countries arranged in descending order of Paddy yield - 1999

IMPORTANT FORMULAE

1. Soil Moisture Content (SMC)

$$\text{SMC on volume basis} = \frac{\text{Volume of water}}{\text{Volume of soil}}$$

$$= \frac{\text{Weight of water}}{\text{Density of water}} \times \frac{BD \text{ of soil}}{\text{Weight of soil}}$$

$$= \frac{\text{Weight of water}}{\text{Weight of soil}} \times \frac{BD \text{ of soil}}{\text{Density of water}}$$

$$= \text{Weight basis} \times \text{Volume basis}$$

$$\text{On weight basis (Pw)} \frac{WS_1 - WS_2}{WS_2} \times 100$$

$$\text{On Volume basis (Pv)} = \frac{WS_1 - WS_2}{DW \times VS_1} \times 100$$

where, WS_1 = Weight of wet soil sample recorded on physical balance up to two decimal places and expressed in grammes;

WS_2 = Constant weight of oven dry soil, dried at 105°C for 12 hrs to a constant weight

VS_1 = Volume of the soil sample drawn either by a core sampler or tube auger of known volume

DW = Density of water.

"It is expressed in percentage"

2. Apparent Specific Gravity:

$$= \frac{\text{Weight of } ODS}{\text{Volume of } WS} \times \frac{1}{\text{Density of water}}$$

where, ODS = Oven dry soil,

WS = Wet soil

3. Maximum Water Holding Capacity (MWHC):

$$MWHC = \frac{b - c - d}{c - a} \times 100$$

where, a = Weight of the brass box plus filter paper placed inside on a perforated bottom

b = Weight of brass box, filter paper and the filled uniformly in the box after overnight saturation

c = Weight of the brass box and the soil dried at 105 °C in oven to a constant weight

d = Average weight of one filter paper (Weight five, filter papers, saturate them with water, roll a glass rod gently over the filter paper to squeez out uniformly, weigh again to determine overall weight of filter paper

4. Particle or Real Density (PD or RD)

$$PD / RD = \frac{WODSS}{VODSS}$$

$$VODSS = VDL = \frac{WDL}{DDL}$$

$$PD / RD = \frac{W_s - W_a}{[W_k + (W_s - W_a) - W_{sk}]} \times Dk$$

where, $WODSS$ = Weight of oven dry soil sample;

$VODSS$ = Volume of oven dry soil sample

VDL = Volume of displaced liquid;

WDL = Weight of displaced liquid

DDL = Density of displaced liquid;

PD = Particle density

W_a = Weight of air-filled pynometer;

W_k = Weight of xylene/kerosene filled pynometer

W_s = Weight of oven dry soil sample filled pynometer

W_{sk} = Weight of pynometer after filling completely with liquid after over-night exclusion of air in a vacuum desiccator

Dk = Density of displacing liquid

5. Total, capillary and non-capillary porosity:

$$SP_s = 1 - \frac{BD}{PD} \times 100$$

where, SP_s = Soil porosity;

BD = Bulk density;

PD = Particle density

Capillary porosity = FC on volume basis (per cent);

FC = Field Capacity

Non-capillary porosity = Total porosity – Capillary porosity

6. Hydraulic Conductivity (K):

Hydraulic Conductivity is the K factor in Darcy's Law and denotes the rate of flow of water in a porous medium under a unit hydraulic gradient.

Hydraulic Conductivity, $K = \frac{ql}{a\,(h_1 - h_2)}$

where, q = Volume/discharge per unit time;

l = Length of flow

$h_1 - h_2$ = Hydraulic head;

a = Cross sectional area through which water flows.

Intrinsic permeability:

$$K' = \frac{k_n}{d_g}$$

where, K' = Intrinsic permeability;

n = Liquid's viscosity

d = Density of liquid;

g = Acceleration due to gravity (scalar value).

Hydraulic conductivity under constant head.-

$$k = \frac{ql}{H_a t}$$

where, (Fig. 1)

k = Hydraulic conductivity under constant head;

q = Quantity of collected water

l = Length of flow;

H = Loss in head

a = Cross-sectional area of perimeter;

t = Time interval

Hydraulic Conductivity under variable water-head:

$$k = \frac{2.3\,al}{At} \log_{10} \frac{h_1}{h_2}$$

where, (Fig. 2)

a = Cross-sectional area of glass tube;

A = Cross-sectional area of cylinder;

l = Length of flow;

t = Time interval

h_1 = Initial water level;

h_2 = Final water level

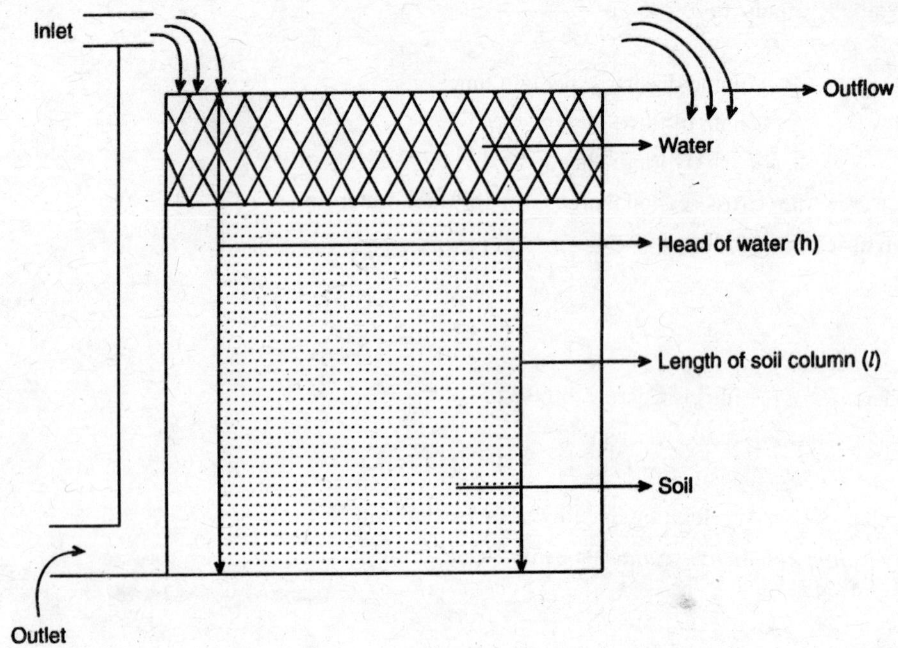

Fig. 1. Constant head perimeter

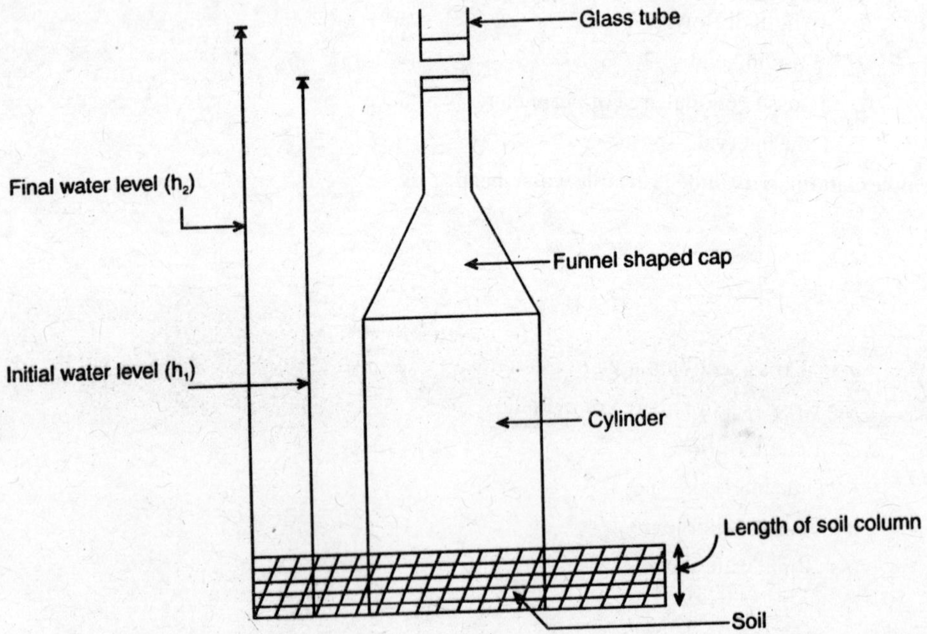

Fig. 2. Variable head perimeter

7. Irrigation efficiency:

$$I = \frac{MSSCG}{WA} \times 100$$

where, I = Irrigation efficiency (per cent)

$MSSCG$ = Moisture/water stored in soil for crop growth;

WA = Water applied.

8. Time required to irrigate an area:

$$Iqt = Ad$$

where, I = Irrigation efficiency;

q = Discharge (cusecs);

A = Area (acres)

t = Time in hours;

d = Soil moisture deficit.

9. Discharge

$$q = A \times V = AC\sqrt{rs}$$

where, q = Discharge (cusecs);

A = Cross sectional area (ft^2);

C = Discharge Coefficient

r = Hydraulic radius/ wetted perimeter/cross sectional area

s = Slope;

'C' value can be computed by Chezy Kutter formula:

$$C = \frac{\frac{1.811}{n} + 41.6 + \frac{0.0028}{s}}{1 + 41.6 + \frac{0.0028}{s} \cdot \frac{n}{\sqrt{r}}}$$

where, C = Discharge Coefficient;

n = Coefficient of roughness (from standard tables)

s = Slope (per cent);

r = Hydraulic radius (feet)

– *By Manning formula:*

$$q = A\frac{1.486}{n} r^{2/3} \times s^{1/2}$$

Where, q = Quality of discharge (Cusecs);

A = Cross-sectional area (ft^2)

n = Coefficient of roughness (from the standard tables);

s = Slope.

10. Tensiometer Calibration:

$$Y = c + b \log x$$

Y = Moisture (per cent)

x = Tensiometer reading

$$c = \bar{y} - b \log \bar{x} \text{ and } b = \frac{\sum y \log \bar{x}\left[\left(\sum y\right)\left(\sum \log x\right)n\right]}{\sum\left(\log x^2\right) - \left[\left(\sum \log x\right)^2 / n\right]}$$

$\bar{y}$ = Mean moisture content

x = Mean tensiometer reading

11. Water requirement:

$$WR = Cu + Al + WNSP$$

where, WR = Water requirement;

Cu = Consumptive use (of water)

Al = Application losses

$WNSP$ = Water needed for special purpose excluding Cu and Al.

12. Irrigation requirement:

$$IR = WR - (ER + GWC)$$

where, IR = Irrigation requirement;

WR = water requirement

ER = Effective rainfall;

GWC = Ground water contribution

13. Capillary rise of water:

$$Dgw = \frac{ECe \cdot ds \cdot Ds \cdot Sp}{dw \cdot ECgw \cdot 100}$$

where, Dgw = Depth of ground water removed / evaporated

Ec_e = Electrical conductivity of saturation extract mhos/cm at 25°C

ds = Soil density (g/cc)

D_s = Soil depth where accumulation occurs

Sp = Soil saturation percentage

dw = Density of water (g/cc)

$ECgw$ = Electrical conductivity of ground water (mhos/cm at 25°C).

14. Leaching requirement:

$$LR = \frac{Ddw}{Diw} \times 100 = \frac{ECiw}{ECdw} \times 100$$

where, D = Depth of water;

EC = Electrical conductivity;

dw = Drainage water;

iw = Irrigation water

15. Universal Soil Loss Equation

$$A = RKLSCP$$

where, A = Predicted soil loss;

R = Climate erosivity (rainfall and run off);

K = Soil erodibility;

L = Length of slope;

S = Steepness or slope gradient;

C = Cover and management;

P = Erosion control practice;

16. Acid neutralizing ability of liming materials:

Ca equivalent of $CaCO_3$ $$\frac{Ca}{CaCO_3} = \frac{40}{100} = 0.40$$

CaO equivalent of $CaCO_3$ $$\frac{CaO}{CaCO_3} = \frac{56}{100} = 0.56$$

CaO equivalent of $MgCO_3$ $$\frac{CaO}{MgCO_3} = \frac{56}{84} = 0.67$$

$CaCO_3$ equivalent of $MgCO_3$ $$\frac{CaCO_3}{MgCO_3} = \frac{100}{84} = 1.19$$

Mg equivalent of MgCO $$\frac{Mg}{MgCO_3} = \frac{24}{84} = 0.29$$

Mg equivalent of MgO_3 $$\frac{Mg}{MgO} = \frac{24}{40} = 0.60$$

17. Exchangeable Sodium Percentage (ESP):

$$ESP = \frac{\text{Exchangeable sodium (Cmol / kg)}}{\text{Cation Exchange Capacity (Cmol / kg)}}$$

18. Sodium Absorption Ratio (SAR)

$$SAR = \frac{\left[Na^+\right]}{\sqrt{y_2\left[Ca^{2+}\right] + \left[Mg^{2+}\right]}}$$

NUMBER OF SEEDS PER KG AND APPROXIMATE NUMBER OF RHIZOBIA PER SEED FOR DIFFERENT LEGUMES

Plant	*No. seeds 1 kg*	*Rhizobia No./seed*	*Kg seed 1 ha*	*Inoculum g/ha*
Vicia faba	1000	22×10^5	87	384
Arachis hypogaea	2000	11×10^5	44	194
Cicer arietinum	2000	11×10^5	33	145
Dolichos lablab	3000	7.3×10^5	27	119
Lupinus albus	3000	7.3×10^5	110	484
Pisum arvense	6000	3.7×10^5	98	431
Glycine max	9000	2.4×10^5	65	286
Cajanus cajan	17000	1.3×10^5	11	48
Lens esculenta	19000	1.2×10^5	15	66
Vigna radiata	22000	1×10^5	76	334
Cyanopsis tetragonoloba	44000	5×10^4	38	167
Vigna aconitifolius	44000	5×10^4	40	176
Vicia hirsuta	44000	5×10^4	49	215
Trigonella foenum-graecum	50600	4×10^4	33	145
Onobrychis viciifolia	66000	3×10^4	38	167
Coronilla cretica	242000	9×10^3	20	48
Ornithopus sativus	352000	6×10^3	22	97
Desmodium intortum	440000	5×10^3	11	48
Indigofera hirsuta	444000	5×10^3	10	44
Medicago sativa	444000	5×10^3	16	70
Trifolium incarnatum	605000	3.6×10^3	18	79
Lotus pedunculatus	1940000	1×10^3	4	18
Trifolium agrarium	2200000	1×10^3	4	18
Lotononis bainesii	3840000	6×10^2	2	9

WATER RESOURCES OF INDIA

1. Annual precipitation including snowfall is estimated of the order of 4000 cubic kilometres.

2. The water resources potential of India which occurs as natural runoff in the rivers is about 1880 cubic kilometres including surface and ground water (Central Water Commission 1995).

3. Ganga-Brahmaputra-Meghna system is the major contributor to total water resources potential of India accounting for more than 60 per cent of the total water resources potential of various rivers.

4. Per Capita availability of water is 2210 cubic metres.

5. Only 1140 cubic km of total 1880 cubic km can be put to beneficial use over space arid time due to constraints of topography and uneven distribution.

SURFACE WATER STORAGE IN INDIA

- Available is 162 cubic km.
- New projects to add 77 cubic km.
- Expected projects contribution 131 cubic km.
- Likely storage available will be 370 cubic km against total availability of 1880 cubic km.
- Total replenishable ground water potential is estimated at 453 cubic km/annum ; after the provision for drinking, industrial and other purposes (other then irrigation) which is about 15 per cent of total potential, the potential available for irrigation is 385 cubic km.
- Nearly 70 per cent of total potential still remains untapped.
- U.P. has the highest potential of ground water which is 84 cubic km and it mostly lies in Ganga basin.
- The total ultimate irrigation potential (UIP) of India is about 113.8 million hectares.
- Largest geographical area is in Africa which is 23 per cent of the total geographical area, but has 12 per cent of arable land.
- Asia (excluding erstwhile USSR) has 21 per cent, but arable land is 31.6 per cent followed by N.C. America having 20 per cent of world's arable land.
- India has 39 per cent of arable land of Asia's total arable land, but U.S.A. has more arable land than that of India.
- World's oceans cover about three-fourth's of earth's surface. According UN estimates, the total amount of water on earth is about 1400 million cubic km (m.cu.km) which is enough to cover the earth with a layer of 3000 metres depth.
- About 2.7 per cent of the total water available on the earth is fresh water of which about 75.2 per cent is frozen in polar regions and another 22.6 per cent is present as ground water.
- There 12 major rivers in India having the catchment area of 252.8 million hectares.
- The total navegable length of inland waterways in India is 15858 km which is more than 82 per cent of total length of inland waterways.

TABLE 1.1: WATER SECTOR AT A GLANCE

	Item		
1.	Estimated Annual Precipitation (including snowfall)	4000	Cu. Km.
2.	Average Annual Potential availability in Rivers	1869	Cu. Km.
3.	Per Capita Water Availability (2001)		1820 Cu. m.
4.	Estimated Utilizable Water Resources		
	(*i*) Surface	690	Cu. Km.
	(*ii*) Ground	432	Cu. Km.
	(*iii*) Total	1122	Cu. Km.
5.	Live Storage Capacities (2006-2007)		
	(*i*) Complete Projects	212.78	Cu. Km.
	(*ii*) Projects Under Construction	76.26	Cu. Km.
	(*iii*) Projects Under Construction	107.54	Cu. Km.
6.	Irrigation Potential		
6.1	At the time of Independence (Pre- Plan)		
	Created/ Utilized		
	(*i*) Major and Medium	9.7	Million Ha.
	(*ii*) Minor Irrigation	12.9	Million Ha.
	(*a*) Surface Water	6.4	Million Ha.
	(*b*) Ground Water	6.5	Million Ha.
	(*iii*) Total (*i* + *ii*)	22.6	Million Ha.
7.	**Number of Major and Medium Irrigation Projects**		
		Major Projects	**Medium Projects**
	(*i*) Completed in Pre-Plan	74	143
	(*ii*) Completed in Plan Period up to 1992	120	668
	(*iii*) On-going in VIII Plan	158	2226
	(*iv*) New in VIII Plan	14	50
8.	**CAD Programmes**		
8.1	Projects		
	(*i*) No. of Projects	203	Nos.
	(*ii*) Culturable Command Area	21.10	Million Ha.
	(*iii*) Total Irrigation Potential	20.19	Million Ha.
8.2	Physical Achievement (1995-96)		
	(*i*) Field Channels	368.5	Thousand Ha.
	(*ii*) Land Levelling	19.3	Thousand Ha.
	(*iii*) Warabandi	452.6	Thousand Ha.
	(*iv*) Field Drains	32.0	Thousand Ha.

9.	**Area Sown (1993-94)**		
	(*i*) Gross	186.4	Million Ha.
	(*ii*) Net	142.1	Million Ha.
10.	**Area Irrigated (1993-94)**		
	(*i*) Gross	68.4	Million Ha.
	(*ii*) Net	51.5	Million Ha.
11.	**Net Area Irrigated by Source (1993-94)**		
	(*i*) Canals	17.1	Million Ha.
	(*ii*) Tanks	3.2	Million Ha.
	(*iii*) Wells	27.8	Million Ha.
	(*iv*) Others	3.4	Million Ha.
	(*v*) Total	51.5	Million Ha.

12. Area and Production of Total Food grain

Year	Area (Million Ha.)	Production (Million Tonnes)
1950-51	97.3	50.8
2004-05	120.1	198.4
2005-06	121.9	208.6

13. Expenditure on Irrigation Sector

(Rs. Million)

Period		*Major and medium*	*Minor*	*CAD*	*Total*	*%age of Exp. on Irrgn. to Total*
First Plan	(1951-96)	3702	656		4418	23
Seventh Plan	(1985-90)	111073	61929	14475	187477	9
Annual Plan	(1990-91)	26348	14878	2856	44082	9
Annual Plan	(1991-92)	28240	15181	3338	46759	7
Annual Plan	(1992-93)	30471	18061	3228	51760	7
Annual Plan	(1993-94)	35714	19239	3749	58702	7
Annual Plan	(1994-95)	41591	21887	4221	67699	6
Annual Plan (Anticipated)	(1995-96)	44996	21007	4373	70376	6
Annual Plan (Target)	(1996-97)	70813	31564	5061	107438	7

14. Land Degradation	
14.1 Area Subject to Water and Wind Erosion	141.15 Million Ha.
14.2 Area Affected due to other problems	
(*i*) Waterlogging	8.51 Million Ha.
(*ii*) Alkali Soils	3.58 Million Ha.
(*iii*) Acidic Soil	4.50 Million Ha
(*iv*) Saline Soil including Coastal Sandy Area	5.50 Million Ha.
(*v*) Ravines and Gullies	3.97 Million Ha
(*vi*) Shifting Cultivation	4.91 Million Ha.
(*vii*) Riverine and Torrents	2.73 Million Ha.
Total	**33.70 Million Ha.**
15. Flood Damages during 1996	
(*i*) Area Affected	7.36 Million Ha.
(*ii*) Cropped Area Affected	3.35 Million Ha
(*iii*) Value of Damages to Crops	3839 Rs. Million
(*iv*) Population Affected	39.02 Million Nos.
(*v*) Human Lives Lost	1271 Nos.
(*vi*) Cattle lost	60171 Nos.
16. Area Protected at the end 2006-07 under Flood Management Programme	33.516 Million Ha.
17. Flood Forecasting Performance up to 3 / 2006	14.37 Million Ha.
(*i*) No. of Flood Forecasting Station Operated	9952 Nos.
(*ii*) No. of Flood Forecasting Station which issued forecast.	9745 Nos.
(*iii*) Total No. of Forecast issued	9952 Nos.
(*iv*) Total No. Correct Forecasts within	9745 Nos.
(+ / – 15 cm) / (+ / – 20 % cumes)	97.92%
18. Expenditure on Flood Management Works during 1994- 95	
(*i*) States/ UTs	2681 Rs. Million
(*ii*) Central Sector	397 Rs. Million
(*iii*) Total	3078 Rs. Million
19. Flood Management Measure under taken through the successive five year plans	
(*i*) Flood Embankments	34397.61 km
(*ii*) Drainage Channels	51317.50 km
(*iii*) Towns Protection Works	2400 Nos.
(*iv*) Village Raised	4721 Nos.

20. Status of Research Schemes

The present status of Research Schemes funded by Indian National Committee on Geotechnical Engineering (INCGE) is given as under:

1. Total No. of Research Schemes sanctioned	:	41
2. Sanctioned amount of grant-in-aid	:	Rs. 366.96 lakhs
3. Grant-in-aid released till date (3/2007)	:	Rs. 257.80 lakhs
4. No. of schemes completed	:	19
5. No. of schemes partially completed and closed	:	02
6. State of Art reports printed	:	03
7. No. of schemes closed	:	02
8. Schemes likely to be closed	:	05
9. On-going projects	:	13
10. New schemes under consideration	:	03

The present status of Research Schemes funded by Indian National Committee on Construc tion

Materials and Structures (INCCMS) is given as under

1. Total No. of Research Schemes sanctioned till date	:	21
2. Sanctioned amount of grant-in-aid	:	Rs. 247.36 lakhs
3. Grant-in-aid released till date (31/2007)	:	Rs. 173.54 lakhs
4. Grant released during the year 2004-2005	:	Nil
5. No. of schemes completed	:	12
6. No. of schemes under execution	:	08
7. No. of schemes discontinued	:	01
8. New schemes recommended for sanction	:	02

The fifth Annual Joint R & D Session of INCGE and INCCMS was held successfully at CSMRS.

TABLE 1.2 : WATER AVAILABILITY: BASINWISE

Sl. No.	*Name of the River Basin*	*Average annual availability*
1.	Indus (up to Border)	73.31
2.	(*a*) Ganga	525.02
	(*b*) Brahmaputra, Barak & Others	585.60
3.	Godavari	110.54
4.	Krishna	78.12
5.	Cauvery	21.36
6.	Pennar	6.32
7.	East Flowing Rivers between Mahanadi and Pennar	22.52
8.	East Flowing Rivers between Pennar and Kanyakumari	16.46
9.	Mahanadi	66.88
10.	Brahmani and Baitarni	28.48
11.	Subernarekha	12.37
12.	Sabarmati	3.81
13.	Mahi	11.02
14.	West Flowing Rivers of Kutch, Sabarmati including Luni	15.10
15.	Narmada	45.64
16.	Tapi	14.88
17.	West Flowing Rivers from Tapi to Tadri	87.41
18.	West Flowing Rivers from Tadri to Kanyakumari	113.53
19.	Area of Inland drainage in Rajasthan desert	NEG
20.	Minor River Basins Draining into Bangladesh and Burma	31.00
	Total	**1869.35**

TABLE 1.3 : CATCHMENT AREA OF MAJOR RIVER BASINS

Sl. No.	*Name of the River*	*Origin*	*Length (km.)*	*Catchment Area (Sq. km.)*
1	2	3	4	5
1.	**Indus**	Mansarovar (Tibet)	3180	321289+
2.	**(*a*) Ganga**	Gangotri (Uttra, Kashi)	2525+	861452+
	(*b*) Brahmaputra	Kailash Range (Tibet)	2960	194413+
	(*c*) Barak and other rivers flowing into Meghna, like Gomti, Muhari, Fenny etc.			41723+
3.	**Sabarmati**	Aravali Hills (Rajasthan)	371	21674
4.	**Mahi**	Dhar (Madhya Pradesh)	583	34842
5.	**Narmada**	Amarknatak (Madhya Pradesh)	1312	98796
6.	**Tapi**	Betul (Madhya Pradesh)	724	65145
7.	**Brahmani**	Ranchi (Bihar)	799	39033
8.	**Mahanadi**	Nazri Town (Madhya Pradesh)	851	141589
9.	**Godavari**	Nasik (Maharashtra)	1465	312812
10.	**Krishna**	Mahabaleshwar (Maharashtra)	1401	258948
11.	**Pennar**	Kolar (Karnataka)	597	55213
12.	**Cauvery**	Coorg (Karanataka)	800	81155
	Total			**2528084**

Source : *Central Water Commission*

Reassessment of Water Resources Potential of India, 2001.

Remark : '+' As in Indian Territory.

TABLE 1.4 : CATCHMENT AREA OF MEDIUM RIVER BASINS OF THE COUNTRY

Sl. No.	*Name of the River*	*Village/ Distt. (Origin)*	*State*	*Length (Km.)*	*Catchment Area (Sq. Km.)*
1	2	3	4	5	6
		WEST FLOWING RIVERS			
1.	**Ozat**	Kathiawar	Gujarat	128	3189
2.	**Shetrunjio**	Dalkania	Gujarat	182	5514
3.	**Bhadar**	Rajkot	Gujarat	198	7094
4.	**Aji**	Rajkot	Gujarat	106	2139
5.	**Dhadhar**	Panchmahal	Gujarat	135	2770
6.	**Purna**	Dhulia	Maharashtra	142	2431
7.	**Ambika**	Dangs	Maharashtra	142	2715
8.	**Vaitarna**	Nasik	Maharashtra	171	3637
9.	**Dammanganga**	Nasik	Maharashtra	143	2357
10.	**Ulhas**	Raigarh	Maharashtra	145	3864
11.	**Savitri**	Pune	Maharashtra	99	2898
12.	**Sastri**	Ratnagiri	Maharashtra	64	2174
13.	**Washishthi**	Ratnagiri	Maharashtra	48	2239
14.	**Mandvi**	Belgaum	Karnataka	87	2032
15.	**Kalinadi**	Belgaum	Karnataka	153	5179
16.	**Gangavati or Bedti (in Upper Reaches)**	Dharwar	Karnataka	152	3902
17.	**Sharavati**	Shimoga	Karnataka	122	2209
18.	**Natravati**	Dakshina Kannada	Karnataka	103	3657
19.	**Chalia or Baypore**	Elamtalvi Hills	Kerala	169	2788
20.	**Bharathapuzha (also known as Ponnani)**	Annamalai Hills	Tamil Nadu	209	6186
21.	**Periyar**	Sivajini Hills	Kerala	244	5398
22.	**Pamba**	Devamalai	Kerala	176	2235

	EAST FLOWING RIVERS				
23.	**Burhabalang**	Mayurbhanj	Orissa	164	4837
24.	**Baitarni**	Keonjhar	Orissa	365	12789
25.	**Rushikulya**	Phulbani	Orissa	146	7753
26.	**Bahuda**	Ramgirivillage	Orissa	73	1248
27.	**Vamsadhara**	Kalahandi	Orissa	221	10830
28.	**Nagavali**	Kalahandi	Orissa	217	9410
29.	**Sarda**	Vishakhapatnam	Andhra Pradesh	104	2725
30.	**Eleru**	Vishakhapatnam	Andhra Pradesh	125	3809
31.	**Vogarivagu**	Guntur	Andhra Pradesh	102	1348
32.	**Gundlakamma**	Kurnool	Andhra Pradesh	220	8494
33.	**Musi**	Nellore	Andhra Pradesh	112	2219
34.	**Raleru**	Nellore	Andhra Pradesh	104	2483
35.	**Muneru**	Nellore	Andhra Pradesh	122	3734
36.	**Swarnamukhi**	Koraput	Orissa	130	3225
37.	**Kandleru**	Vinukonda	Andhra Pradesh	73	3534
38.	**Kortalaiyar**	Chinglepet	Tamil Nadu	131	3521
39.	**Palar (including tributary Cheyyar)**	Kolar	Karnataka	348	17871
40.	**Varahandi**	North Arcot	Tamil Nadu	94	3044
41.	**Ponnaiyar**	Kolar	Karnataka	396	14130
42.	**Vellar**	Chithri Hills	Tamil Nadu	193	8558
43.	**Vaigai**	Madurai	Tamil Nadu	258	7031
44.	**Pambar**	Madurai	Tamil Nadu	125	3104
45.	**Gundar**	Madurai	Tamil Nadu	146	5647
46.	**Vaippar**	Tirunelvelli	Tamil Nadu	130	5288
47.	**Tambraparni**	Tirunelvelli	Tamil Nadu	130	5969
48.	**Subarnarekha**	Nagri/Ranchi	Bihar	395	19296
	Total			**248505**	

Source : Central Water Commission

TABLE 1.5: STATEWISE DETAILS OF INLAND AND WATER RESOURCES OF VARIOUS TYPES, 2001

(Lakh Hectares)

Sl. No.	Name of the State/UT	Rivers & Canals (Length (in Kms.)	Reservoir	Tanks, Lakes & Ponds	Beels, Oxbow Lakes & Derelict Water	Brachish Water	Total Water Bodies
1	2	3	4	5	6	7	8
1.	**Andhra Pradesh**	11514	2.34	5.17	–	0.64	8.15
2.	**Arunachal Pradesh**	2000	–	0.01	0.03	–	0.04
3.	**Assam**	4820	0.02	0.23	1.10	–	1.35
4.	**Bihar**	3200	0.60	0.95	0.05	–	1.60
5.	**Goa**	250	0.03	0.03	-	–	0.06
6.	**Gujarat**	3865	2.43	0.71	0.12	3.76	7.02
7.	**Haryana**	5000	NEG	0.10	0.10	–	0.20
8.	**Himachal Pradesh**	3000	0.42	0.01	–		0.43
9.	**Jammu & Kashmir**	27781	0.07	0.17	0.06	–	0.30
10.	**Karnataka**	9000	2.20	4.14	–	0.08	6.42
11.	**Kerala**	3092	0.30	0.30		2.43	3.03
12.	**Madhya Pradesh**	20661	2.94	1.19		–	4.13
13.	**Maharashtra**	16000	2.79	0.50	–	0.10	3.39
14.	**Manipur**	3360	0.01	0.05	0.40	–	0.46
15.	**Meghalaya**	5600	0.08	0.02	NEG	–	0.10
16.	**Mizoram**	1395	–	0.02		–	0.02
17.	**Nagaland**	1600	0.17	0.50	NEG	–	0.67
18.	**Orissa**	4500	2.56	1.14	1.80	4.17	9.67
19.	**Punjab**	15270	NEG	0.07	–	–	0.07
20.	**Rajasthan**	N.A.	1.20	1.80	–	–	3.00
21.	**Sikkim**	900	–	–	0.03	–	0.03
22.	**Tamil Nadu**	7420	0.52	6.91	N.A	0.56	7.99
23.	**Tripura**	1200	0.05	0.12	–	–	0.17
24.	**Uttar Pradesh**	31200	1.50	1.62	1.33	–	4.45
25.	**West Bengal (P)**	2526	0.17	2.76	0.42	2.10	5.45
	UNION TERRITORIES						
26.	**Andaman & Nicobar Islands**	115	0.01	0.03	–	0.37	0.41

27.	**Chandigarh**	2	–	NEG	NEG	–	–
28.	**Dadra & Nagar Haveli**	54	0.05				0.05
29.	**Daman & Diu**	12	–	–	–	–	–
30.	**Delhi**	150	0.04	–	–	–	0.04
31.	**Lakshadweep**	–	–	NEG	0.01	0.01	0.02
32.	**Pondicherry**	247	20.50	28.55	5.45	14.22	68.72
	Total						**185734**

Source : Fisheries Division, Department of Agriculture & Cooperation. Ministry of Agriculture.

N.A. : Not Available (P) : Provisional

NEG : Negligible * : Included in brackish water area

TABLE 1.6 : STATEWISE DETAILS OF NET IRRIGATED AREA (NIA), NET SOWN AREA (NSA) AND PERCENTAGE OF NIA TO NSA

Sl. No.	*States*	*Net Sown Area (NSA)*	*Net Irrigated Area (NIA)*	*% of NIA to NSA*
1.	Andhra Pradesh	11115	4528	40.73
2.	Arunachal Pradesh	164	42	25.61
3.	Assam	2734	170	6.22
4.	Bihar	7437	3625	48.74
5.	Chhattisgarh	4763	984	20.66
6.	Goa	141	23	16.31
7.	Gujarat	9443	2979	31.55
8.	Haryana	3526	2958	83.90
9.	Himachal Pradesh	555	126	22.70
10.	Jammu & Kashmir	748	311	41.58
11.	Karnataka	10410	2643	25.40
12.	Kerala	2206	381	17.27
13.	Madhya Pradesh	14664	4135	28.20
14.	Maharashtra	17636	2959	16.78
15.	Manipur	140	65	46.43
16.	Meghalaya	230	54	23.48
17.	Mizoram	94	9	9.57
18.	Nagaland	300	72	24.00
19.	Orissa	5829	1933	33.16
20.	Punjab	4264	3602	84.47
21.	Rajasthan	15865	4907	31.00
22.	Sikkim	95	17	17.89
23.	Tamil Nadu	5303	2888	54.50
24.	Tripura	280	37	13.21
25.	Uttar Pradesh	17612	12814	72.76
26.	West Bengal	5417	2354	43.45
	Total States	**140971**	**54616**	**38.74**
	Total UTs	130	66	50.77
	Grand Total	**141101**	**54682**	**38.75**

Note: Figures are as per Land Use Statistics brought out by Ministry of Agriculture for 2000-01 (latest) and are Provisional.

TABLE 1.7 : NUMBER OF ONGOING MAJOR, MEDIUM IRRIGATION PROJECTS

Sl. No.	*Name of State*	*Number of Projects*		
		Major	*Medium*	*Total*
1.	Andhra Pradesh	15	9	24
2.	Arunachal Pradesh	–	–	–
3.	Assam	5	5	10
4.	Bihar	9	3	12
5.	Chhattisgarh	3	5	8
6.	Goa	1	0	1
7.	Gujarat	3	18	21
8.	Haryana	4	0	4
9.	Himachal Pradesh	1	2	3
10.	Jammu & Kashmir	0	7	7
11.	Jharkhand	5	19	24
12.	Karnataka	16	18	34
13.	Kerala	4	4	8
14.	Madhya Pradesh	16	5	21
15.	Maharashtra	56	95	151
16.	Manipur	2	1	3
17.	Meghalaya	0	1	1
18.	Mizoram	–	–	–
19.	Nagaland	–	–	–
20.	Orissa	10	10	20
21.	Punjab	1	0	1
22.	Rajasthan	4	4	8
23.	Sikkim	–	–	–
24.	Tamil Nadu	0	2	2
25.	Tripura	0	3	3
26.	Uttarakhand	3	0	3
27.	Uttar Pradesh	9	0	9
28.	West Bengal	2	8	10
	Total	**169**	**219**	**388**

1.8 : PROGRESS OF PHYSICAL WORKS UNDER FLOOD MANAGEMENT PROGRAMME COMPLETED TILL MARCH 2006

Sl. No	*Name of State*	*Area benefited (m.ha)*	*Length of embankment (Km)*	*Length of drainage channel (km)*	*Town/ village protected (Nos.)*	*Villages on raised/ protected (Nos.)*
(1)	(2)	(3)	(4)	(5)	(6)	(7)
1.	Andhra Pradesh	1.0350	2600.58	17071.00	72	23
2.	Arunachal Pradesh	0.0033	6.93	8.50	18	22
3.	Assam	1.6361	4458.60	850.69	681	0
4.	Bihar	2.9490	3454.00	365.00	47	0
5.	Chattisgarh (Included in M.P.)					
6.	Delhi (NCT)	0.0780	83.00	453.00	0	0
7.	Goa	0.0030	17.07	31.77	2	0
8.	Gujarat	0.4827	104.12	271.00	805	30
9.	Haryana	2.0000	1144.00	4385.00	448	98
10.	Himachal Pradesh	0.0097	58.00	11.00	0	0
11.	Jammu & Kashmir	0.2173	230.00	14.00	12	5
12.	Jharkhand	0.0002	3.49	0.00	2	5
13.	Karnataka	0.0048	73.52	10.00	30	0
14.	Kerala	0.0555	116.70	29.55	4	6
15.	Madhya Pradesh	0.0040	26.00	0.00	37	0
16.	Maharashtra	0.0010	44.50	110.00	0	0
17.	Manipur	0.1300	360.00	126.00	1	1
18.	Meghalaya	0.0011	112.00	0.00	8	2
19.	Mizoram	0.0000	0.00	0.00	0	0
20.	Nagaland	0.0000	0.00	0.00	0	0
21.	Orissa	0.6300	6541.00	131.00	29	14
22.	Punjab	3.1900	1370.00	6622.00	3	0
23.	Rajasthan	0.0816	145.00	197.00	25	0
24.	Sikkim	0.0020	7.00	12.00	6	0
25.	Tamil Nadu	0.1220	87.00	19.00	46	4
26.	Tripura	0.0261	133.30	94.00	11	0
27.	Uttar Pradesh	1.5888	2810.00	13357.00	65	4511
28.	Uttarakhand (Included in U.P.)					
29.	West Bengal	2.2005	10350.00	7129.00	48	0
30.	A & N Islands	0.0000	0.00	0.00	0	0
31.	Chandigarh	0.0000	0.00	0.00	0	0
32.	Dadra and Nagar Haveli	0.0000	0.00	0.00	0	0
33.	Daman and Diu	0.0000	0.00	0.00	0	0
34.	Lakshadweep	0.0000	0.00	0.00	0	0
35.	Pondicherry	0.0040	61.00	20.00	0	0
	Total	**16.4557**	**34397.61**	**51317.51**	**2400**	**4721**

TABLE 1-9 : PLAN-WISE POSITION OF IRRIGATION POTENTIAL CREATED AND UTILIZED

(In million hectares)

Plan		*Potential created*					*Potential utilized*				
		Major & Medium	*Minor*			*TOTAL*	*Minor & Medium*	*Minor*			*TOTAL*
			S.W.	*G.W.*	*Total*			*S.W.*	*G.W.*	*Total*	
(1)	(2)	(3)	(4)	(5)	(6)	(7)	(8)	(9)	(10)	(11)	(12)
Upto 1951 (Pre-Plan)	Cumulative	9.70	6.40	6.50	12.90	22.60	9.70	6.40	6.50	12.90	22.60
I Plan	During	2.50	0.03	1.13	1.16	3.66	1.28	0.03	1.13	1.16	2.44
(1951-56)	Cumulative	12.20	6.41	7.63	14.06	26.26	10.98	6.43	7.63	14.06	25.04
II Plan	During	2.13	0.02	0.67	0.69	2.82	2.07	0.02	0.67	0.69	2.76
(1956-61)	Cumulative	14.33	6-45	8.30	14.75	29.08	13.05	6.45	8.30	14.75	27.80
III Plan	During	2.24	0.03	2.22	2.25	4.49	2.12	0.03	2.22	2.25	4.37
(1961-66)	Cumulative	16.57	6.48	10.52	17.00	33.57	15.17	6.48	10.52	17.00	32.17
Annual Plans	During	1.53	0.02	1.98	2.00	3.53	1.58	0.02	1-98	2.00	3.58
(1966-69)	Cumulative	18.10	650	12.50	19.00	37.10	16.75	6.50	12.50	19.00	35.75
IV Plan	During	2.60	050	4.00	4.50	7.10	1.64	0.50	4.00	4.50	6.14
(1969-74)	Cumulative	20.70	7.00	16.50	23.50	44.20	18.39	7.00	16.50	23.50	41.89
V Plan	During	4.02	0.50	3.30	3.80	7.82	2.77	0.50	3.30	3.80	6.57
1974-78)	Cumulative	24.72	7.50	19.80	27.30	52.02	21.16	7.50	19.80	27.30	48.46
Annual Plans	During	1.89	0.50	2.20	2.70	4.59	1.48	0.50	2,20	2.70	4.18
(1978-80)	Cumulative	26.61	8.00	22.00	30.00	56.61	22.64	8.00	22.00	30.00	52.64
VI Plan	During	1.09	1.70	5.82	7.52	8.61	0.93	1.01	4.24	5.25	6.18
(1980-85)	Cumulative	27.70	9.70	27.82	37.52	65.22	23.57	9.01	26.24	35.25	58.82
VII Plan	During	2.22	1-29	7.80	9.09	11.31	1.90	0.96	6.91	7.87	9.77
(1985-90)	Cumulative	29.92	10-99	35.62	46.61	76.53	25.47	9.97	33.15	43.12	68.59
Annual Plans	During	0.82	0.47	3.27	3.74	4.56	0.85	0.32	3.10	3.42	4.27
(1990-92)	Cumulative	30.74	11.46	38.89	50.35	81.09	26.31	10.29	36.25	46.54	72.85
VIII Plan	During	2.21	1.05	1.91	2.96	5.17	2.13	0.78	1.45	2.23	4.36
(1992-97)	Cumulative	3.295	1251	40.80	53.31	86.26	28.44	1.107	36.76	47.83	76.27
IX Plan	During	4.10	3.59		3.59	7.69	2 .5 7	1.22		1.22	3.79
(1997-2002)	Cumulative	37.05	16.10		56.90	93.95	31.01	18.04		49.05	80.06

SW: Surface Water; GW: Ground Water

APPENDIX-2
CONVERSION FACTORS

Length

1 kilometre = 0.6214 statute mile = 0.5396 nautical mile

1 metre = 1.0936 yards = 3.2808 feet = 39.37 inches

1 centimetre = 0.3937 inches ; 1 inch = 2.54 cm

1 micrometer = 1 micron = 10^{-6} metre = 10^{4} angstrom

1 nanometre = 1 millimicron = 10^{-9} metre = 10 angstrom

Area

1 hectare = 10^{4} square metres = 2.471 acres

1 square metre = 10^{4} square centimetres = 10.76 square feet

1 square centimetre = 0155 square inch

Volume

1 cubic metre = 1000 liters = 35.31 cubic feet = 264.2 U.S. gallons

1 litre = 1000 cubic centimetress = 33.81 fluid ounces = 1.057 U.S. quarts

Mass

1 metric tonne = 1000 kilograms = 2204.6 pounds (Ovoirdupois)

1 kilogram = 0.353 ounce = 0.0022 pound ; 1 pound = 0.45360

Mass Density

1 kg/m^{3} = 0.062428 lb/ft^{3}

1 m^{3}/kg = 16.0185 ft^{3} / lb

Momentum 1 kg m/s = 7.23301 lb ft/s

Angular momentum: 1kg m^{3}/s = 23.7304 lb ft^{2}/s

Temperature

1 Celsius degree = 1.8 Fahrenheit degree = 1 kelvin degree (Absolute)

Celsius temperature = $\frac{5}{9}$ (F – 32) = kelvin – 273.16

Fahrenheit temperature = $\frac{9}{5}$ C + 32

Degrees centigrade = $\frac{(°F - 32) \times 5}{9}$

Degrees Fahrenheit $= \frac{°C \times 9}{5} + 32$

Pressure

1 standard atmosphere = 1013.25 millibars = 101.32 kilopascals
= 760 millimetres mercury = 29.92 Hg inches
= 14.7 pounds per square inch

1 millibar = 1000 dynes per square centimetre = 100 newtons per square metre

1 newton per square metre = 1.4504×10^{-4} pounds per square inch

1 kilopascal = 10 millibars = 1000 newtons per square

Energy and power

1 kJ = 10^3 Nm = 101.972 kgfm = 737.562 ft lbf = 0.277778 Wh

$= \frac{1}{4.1868}$ kcal = 0.947817 Btu = 0.000372506 hp h

1 kW = 1kJ/s $= \frac{10^3}{9.80665}$ kgf m/s = 1.35962 metric hp = 1.34102 British hp

1 hp (metric) = 75 kgf m/s = 0.17569 kcal/s = 0.7355 kJ/s = 735.3 W = 0.98632 hp (British)

1 gramme calorie (thermochemical) = 4.184 joules = 4.184×10^7 ergs

1 British thermal unit = 252 gramme calories = 1054.35 joules

1 watt = 1 joule per second = 14.34 gramme calorie per minute = 0.057 British thermal unit per minute

1 kilowatt = 1000 watts = 1.341 horsepower

1 gramme calorie per minute = 0.0697 watt

1 langley = 1 gramme calorie per square centimetre = 3.67 British thermal per square foot

1 langley per minute = 697.33 watts per square metre

Table-1

Quantity	*Unit*	*Symbol*
Length	meter	m
Mass (not weight)	kilogram	kg
Time	second	s
Electric current	ampere	A
Temperature	kelvin	K (not °K)
Luminous intensity	candela	cd
Amount of substance	mole (Avogadro's number)	mol

Table-2

Quantity	*Unit*	*Symbol*	*Definition*
Force	newton	N	1 kg. m s^{-2}
Energy work, heat	joule	J	1 N-m
Power	watt	W	1 Js^{-1}
Pressure	pascal	Pa	1 N m^{-2}
Area	square metre	m^2	m.m
Volume	cubic metre	m^3	m.m.m.
Velocity	metre per second	ms^{-1}	ms^{-1}
Frequency	hertz	Hz	1 cycle s^{-2}
Voltage	volt	V	1 WA^{-1}
Electric resistance	ohm	Ω	1 VA^{-1}
Electric conductance	siemens	S	1 AV^{-1}
Concentration	mole per cubic metre	mol m^{-3}	mol m^{-3}
Irradiance (energy)	watt per square metre	Wm^{-2}	1 Js^{-1} m^{-2}
Irradiance (photons)	moles of photos per square meter per second	mol $m^{-2}s^{-1}$	mol $m^{-2}s^{-1}$
Spectral irradiance	moles of photons per square metre per second per nanometer	mol $m^{-2}s^{-1}nm^{-1}$	mol $m^{-2}s^{-1}nm^{-1}$

Table-3

Kilo K (10^3)	milli m (10^{-3})
mega M (10^6)	micro μ (10^{-6})
gigs G (10^9)	nano n (10^{-9})
tera T (10^{12})	pico p (10^{-12})
peta P (10^{15})	femto f (10^{-15})
exa E (10^{18})	atto a (10^{-18})

COMPATIBILITY CHART FOR COMBINATION SPRAYS

PESTICIDES ARE
TOXIC
OBSERVE
SAFETY
PRECAUTIONS

Pesticide	No.	Bordeaux Mixture	Captan Captafol	Copper-Fixed	Carbaryl	Carbophenothion	D D T Group	Demeton	Demeton-Methyl	Dicofol	Dichlorvos	Dicrotophos Group	Dinocap	Dimethoate	Dithiocarbamates	Endosulfan	Fenitrothion	Lime Sulphur	Malathion Group	Oxy Demeton-Methyl	Phosphamidon	Phasalone	Pyrethrine	Quinalphos	Sulphur Wettable	Streptomycin	Toxaphene	Urea	Zinc sulphate × Lime	2, 4-D
Bordeaux Mixture	1		N	Q	N	C	Q	N	N	N	N	N	N	N	C	N	N	N	N	N	N	Q	N	N	C	N	Q	C	C	C
Captan Captafol	2	N		Q	C	C	C	Q	Q	C	C	C	Q	C	C	C	Q	N	Q	C	C	C	C		Q	C	C	C	N	C
Copper-Fixed	3	Q	Q		N	C	C	C	C	C	C	C	N	C	Q		C	N	C		C	C	C		C	C	C	C	C	N
Carbaryl	4	N	C	N		C	C	C	C	C	N	N	C	C	C		C	N	C	C	C	C	C		C	C	C	C	N	C
Carbophenothion	5	C	C	C	C		C	C	C	C	C	C	N	C	C	Q	C	Q	C		C	C	C		C	C	C		C	C
D D T Group	6	Q	C	C	C	C		C	C	C	C	C	C	C	C	C	C	N	C	C	C	C	C		C	C	C	C	N	N
Demeton	7	N	Q	C	C	C	C			C	C	C	Q	C	C	C	C	N	C	C	C	C	C		C	C	C	C	N	C
Demeton-Methyl	8	N	Q	C	C	C	C			C	C	C	Q	C	C	C	C	N	C	C	C	C	C		C	C	C	C	N	C
Dicofol	9	N	C	C	C	C	C	C	C		C	C	C	C	C	C	C	N	C	C	C	C	C		C	N	C	C	N	C
Dichlorvos	10	N	C	C	N	C	C	C	C	C		C	C	C	C	C	C	N	C	C	C	C	C		C	C	C	C	N	C
Dicrotophos Group	11	N	C	C	N	C	C	C	C	C	C		C	C	C	C	C	N	C	C	C	C	C		C	C	C	C	N	C
Dinocap	12	N	Q	N	C	N	C	Q	Q	C	C	C		C	Q	C	C	N	Q	C	C	C	C		C	C	C			
Dimethoate	13	N	C	C	C	C	C	C	C	C	C	C	C		C	C	C	N	C		Q	C	C		C	C	C	C	N	C
Dithiocarbamates	14	C	C	Q	C	C	C	C	C	C	C	C	Q	C		C	C	N	C	C	C	C	C		C	C	Q	C	N	C
Endosulfan	15	N	C			Q	C	C	C	C	C	C	C	C	C		C	N	C	C	C	C	C		C	C	C			
Fenitrothion	16	N	Q	C	C	C	C	C	C	C	C	C	C	C	C	C		N	C	C	C	C	C		C	C	C	C	N	C
Lime Sulphur	17	N	N	N	N	Q	N	N	N	N	N	N	N	N	N	N	N		N	N	N	Q	N		C	C	N	N	C	C
Malathion Group	18	N	Q	C	C	C	C	C	C	C	C	C	Q	C	C	C	C	N		C	C	C	C		C	C	C	C	N	C
Oxy Demeton-Methyl	19	N	C		C		C	C	C	C	C	C	C	C	C	C	C	N	C		C	C	C				C			
Phosphamidon	20	N	C	C	C	C	C	C	C	C	C	C	C	Q	C	C	C	N	C	C		Q	C		C	C	C			
Phasalone	21	Q	C	C	C	C	C	C	C	C	C	C	C	C	C	C	C	Q	C	C	Q		Q		C		C			
Pyrethrine	22	N	C	C	C	C	C	C	C	C	C	C	C	C	C	C	C	C	C	C	C	Q			C		C	N	N	N
Quinalphos	23	N																												
Sulphur Wettable	24	C	Q	C	C	C	C	C	C	C	C	C	C	C	C	C	C	C		C	C	C	C			C	C	C	C	C
Streptomycin	25	N	C	C	C	C	C	C	C	N	C	C	C	C	C	C	C	C	C		C				C		C			
Toxaphene	26	Q	C	C	C	C	C	C	C	C	C	C	C	C	Q	C	C	N	C	C	C	C	C		C	C		C	N	C
Urea	27	C	C	C	C		C	C	C	C	C	C		C	C		C	N	C				N		C		C		C	C
Zinc sulphate × Lime	28	C	N	C	N	C	N	N	N	N	N	N		N	N		N	C	N				N		C		N	C		C
2, 4-D	29	C	C	N	C	C	C	C	C	C	C	C		C	C		C	C	C				N		C		C	C	C	

KEY TO SYMBOLS : C = Compatible N = Not compatible Q = Questionable because of any of the following reasons :— 1. Mixure with water decomposes soon. 2. Compatibility is doubtful. 3. Not normally combined : Blank square indicates information not available.

HOW TO USE THE CHART : 1. Locate one product in the vertical column. 2. In the horizontal column locate the other product to be combined. 3. Follow the two columns until they cross. 4. The symbol in the square where the columns cross indicates the compatibility.

GUIDE FOR MIXING FERTILIZERS

□ Fertilizers which can be mixed

□ Fertilizers which may be mixed shortly before use

□ Fertilizers which can not be mixed

	1. Muriate of potash	2. Sulphate of potash	3. Sulphate of ammonia	4. Calcium ammonium nitrate	5. Sodium nitrate	6. Calcium cyanamide	7. Urea	8. Superphosphate single or triple	9. Ammonium phosphate	10. Basic slag	11. Calcium carbonate
1. Muriate of potash	☒	□	□	☒	☒	☒	☒	□	□	□	□
2. Sulphate of potash	□	□	□	☒	☒	□	☒	□	□	□	□
3. Sulphate of ammonia	□	□	□	□	☒	■	☒	□	□	■	■
4. Calcium ammonium nitrate	☒	☒	□	□	☒	■	☒	☒	☒	■	□
5. Sodium nitrate	☒	☒	□	□	□	☒	☒	□	□	□	□
6. Calcium cyanamide	☒	□	■	■	☒	□	☒	■	■	□	□
7. Urea	☒	☒	☒	☒	☒	☒	☒	☒	☒	☒	☒
8. Superphosphate single or triple	□	□	□	☒	☒	■	☒	□	□	■	■
9. Ammonium phosphate	□	□	□	☒	☒	■	☒	□	□	■	■
10. Basic slag	□	□	■	■	□	□	☒	■	■	□	□
11. Calcium carbonate	□	□	■	□	□	□	☒	■	■	□	□

Note : The crossing point of the required vertical column and horizontal column indicates the possibility of mixing or otherwise of the fertilizer.

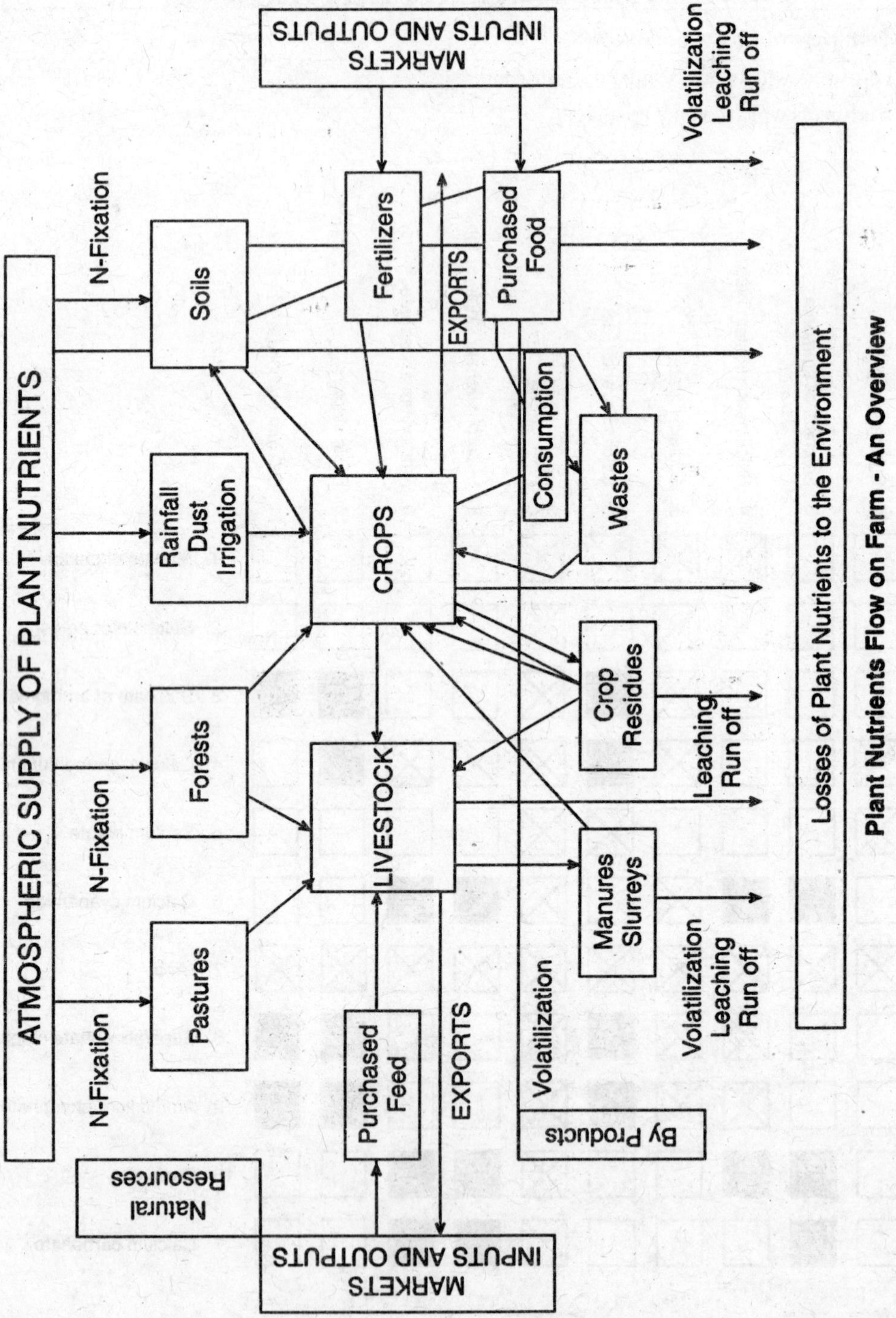

Plant Nutrients Flow on Farm: An Overview

MOST COMMONLY DETECTED PESTICIDES

Commodity	*Pesticides*	*Commodity*	*Pesticides*
Apples	Diphenylamine (?)	Oranges	Methidathion (?)
	Captan (✓)		Chlorpyrifos (?)
	Endosulfan (?)		Ethion (✓)
	Phosmet (✓)		Parathion (?)
	Azinphos-methyl (✓)		Carbaryl (✓)
Bannans	Diazinon (?)	Cantaloupes	Methamidophos (χ)
	Thiabendazole (✓)		Endosulfan (?)
	Carbaryl (✓)		Chlorothalonil (✓)
Bell Peppers	Methamidophos (χ)		Dimnethoate (✓)
	Chlorpyrifos (?)		Methyl Parathion (?)
	Dimethoate (?)	Carrots	DDT (✓)
	Acephate (χ)		Trifluralin (χ)
	Endosulfan (?)		Parathion (?)
Broccoli	DCPA (?)		Diazinon (?)
	Methamidophos (χ)		Dieldrin (?)
	Demeton (χ)	Cauliflower	Methamidophos (χ)
	Dimethoate (?)		Endosulfan (?)
	Parathion (?)		Dimethoate (?)
Cabbage	Methamidophos (χ)		Chlorothalonil (✓)
	Dimethoate (?)		Diazinon (?)
	Fenvalerate (?)	Celery	Dicloran (✓)
	Permiethrin (✓)		Chlorothalonil (✓)
	BHC (?)		Endosulfan (?)
Grapes	Captan (✓)		Acephate (χ)
	Dimethoate (?)		Methamidophos (χ)
	Dicloran (✓)	Cherries	Parathion (?)
	Carbaryl (✓)		Malathion (?)
	Iprodione (?)		Captan (✓)
Green Beans	Dimethoate (?)		Dicloran (✓)
	Methamidophos (χ)		Diazinon (?)
	Endosulfan (?)	Corn	Sulfallate (?)
	Acephate (χ)		Carbaryl (✓)
	Chlorothalonil (✓)		Chlorpyrifos (?)
Lettuce	Mevinphos (χ)		Dieldrin (?)
	Endosulfan (?)		Lindane (?)

Commodity	*Pesticides*	*Commodity*	*Pesticides*
	Permethrin (✓)	Cucumbers	Methamidophos (χ)
	Dimethoate (?)		Endosulfan (?)
	Methomyl (χ)		Dieldrin (?)
Onions	DCPA (?)		Chlorpyrifos (?)
	DDT (✓)		Dimethoate (?)
	Ethion (✓)	Grapefruit	Thiabendazole (✓)
	Diazinon (?)		Ethion (✓)
	Malathion (✓)		Methidathlon (?)
	Chlorobenzilate (✓)	Strawberries	Captan (✓)
	Carbaryl (✓)		Vinclozolin (?)
Peaches	Dicloran (✓)		Endosulfan (?)
	Captan (✓)		Methamidophos (χ)
	Parathian (?)		Methyl Parathion (?)
	Carbaryl (✓)		
	Endosulfan (?)	Sweet Potatoes	Dicloran (✓)
Pears	Azinphos-methyl (✓)		DDT (✓)
	Cyhexatin (?)		Phosmet (✓
	Phosmet (✓)		Dieldrin (?)
	Endosulfan (?)		BHC (?)
	Ethion (✓)	Tomatoes	Methamidophos (χ)
Potatoes	DDT (✓)		Chlorpyrifos (?)
	Chlorpropham (χ)		Chlorothalonil (✓)
	Diedrin (?)		Permethrin (✓)
	Aldicarb (χ)		Dimethoate (?)
	Chlordane (?)		
Spinach	Endosulfan (?)	Watermelon	Methamidophos (χ)
	DDT (✓)		Chlorothalonil (✓)
	Methomyl (χ)		Dimethoat (?)
	Methamidophos (χ)		Carbaryl (✓)
	Dimethoate (?)		Captan (✓)

✓ Residues can be reduced by washing.

χ Residues *cannot* be reduced by washing.

(?) It is not known if washing will reduce pesticides.

RAS Pre-examination, 1995

1. On the basis of total production which one is the most important crop in Rajasthan.
(*a*) Cotton (*b*) Wheat
(*c*) Bajra (*d*) Sorghum

2. The agricultural university named after the first President of India is in
(*a*) Bihar (*b*) M.P.
(*c*) U.P. (*d*) A.P.

3. Honey bees are used for
(*a*) Pisciculture (*b*) Sericulture
(*c*) Tissueculture (*d*) Apiculture

4. Per hectaré seed rate of mustard is
(*a*) 5 kg (*b*) 10 kg
(*c*) 15 kg (*d*) 20 kg

5. To get 30 q/ha yield of seed cotton with 50,000 plants per hectare and 20 bolls per plants the per boll yield of seed cotton should be
(*a*) 3 gm (*b*) 4 gm
(*c*) 6 gm (*d*) 8 gm

6. A wheat crop giving 5 tonnes/ha of grain yield will remove how many kgs of total plant nutrients from the soil
(*a*) 150 kg/ha (*b*) 200 kg/ha
(*c*) 250 kg/ha (*d*) 300 kg/ha

7. For the control of grassy weeds in paddy crop the most effective weedicide is
(*a*) 2,4-D (*b*) Butachlore
(*c*) Basalin (*d*) Benthiocarb

8. Cultivation of trees and grasses together is known as
(*a*) Agroforestry (*b*) Agrohorti
(*c*) Farm forestry
(*d*) Silvipasture/Silviculture

9. Average value of water use efficiency in case of irrigated paddy yielding 60 q/ha when grown at Udaipur will be about
(*a*) 10 kg/ha cm (*b*) 20 kg/ha cm
(*c*) 40 kg/ha cm (*d*) 80 kg/ha cm

10. Which one of the following occupations is most beneficial with sunflower farming
(*a*) Sericulture (*b*) Pisciculture
(*c*) Apiculture (*d*) Floriculture

11. Relationship between water and fertilizer as production factors in cereal crops is
(*a*) Synergestic (*b*) Additive
(*c*) Antagonistic (*d*) Negative

12. Growing of coconut, black pepper and ginger in same field, simultaneously is called
(*a*) Multiple cropping
(*b*) Relay cropping
(*c*) Multistoreyed cropping
(*d*) Inter-cropping

13. To get one tonne of oil from mustard variety Pusabold, the quantity of mustard seed required will be
(*a*) 2000-2200 kg (*b*) 2400-2600 kg
(*c*) 2700-2900 kg (*d*) 3300-3500 kg

14. Average weight of 1000 seeds of mustard, variety Varuna, is about
(*a*) 2 gm (*b*) 4 gm
(*c*) 6 gm (*d*) 8 gm

15. Growing of three crops of rice in a year in the same field in Tamil Nadu is known as
(*a*) Relay cropping (*b*) Multiple cropping
(*c*) Mono cropping
(*d*) Intensive cropping

16. Amongst micronutrients application of which one of the following has become necessary in paddy crop in north India
(*a*) Iron (*b*) Zinc
(*c*) Copper (*d*) Boron

17. Availability of phosphorus to crop plants is most affected by
(*a*) Soil pH
(*b*) Soil moisture stress
(*c*) Temperature
(*d*) Biological factors

18. Nitrogen in DAP is
(*a*) 9% (*b*) 18%
(*c*) 36% (*d*) 46%

19. In mustard crop gypsum is applied to supply
(*a*) Sulphur (*b*) Calcium
(*c*) Zinc (*d*) Nitrogen

20. Amongst oil cakes the highest nitrogen content is in
(*a*) Neem cake (*b*) Groundnut cake
(*c*) Coconut cake (*d*) Castor cake

21. Availability of iron to plants is relatively high at the following pH range:
(*a*) 6.0 to 6.5 (*b*) 6.6 to 7.0
(*c*) 7.1 to 7.5 (*d*) 7.6 to 8.0

22. Which one of the following fertilizer is suitable and economical to apply under acidic soil condition
(*a*) DAP
(*b*) Single super phosphate
(*c*) Rock phosphate (*d*) Basic slag

23. In saline soil major problem is due to
(*a*) High pH
(*b*) High exchangeable sodium
(*c*) High content of soluble salts
(*d*) Low soil pH

24. Symptoms of iron deficiency in plants are
(*a*) Yellowing of lower leaves
(*b*) Yellowing of young growing leaves
(*c*) Yellowing of whole plant
(*d*) Drying of lower leaves

25. Opening of stomata is related with
(*a*) Calcium (*b*) Potassium
(*c*) Magnesium (*d*) Iron

26. Bajra crop is
(*a*) Self pollinated (*b*) Cross pollinated
(*c*) Auto crossed (*d*) Out crossed

27. For increasing yield potential of crops which one is more effective method of crop improvement—
(*a*) Pure line selection
(*b*) Hybridization (*c*) Tissue culture
(*d*) Vegetative propagation

28. WCC-75 is a recommended variety for dry land condition of—
(*a*) Wheat (*b*) Sorghum
(*c*) Bajra (*d*) Cotton

29. Shortest duration variety of bajra is—
(*a*) HHB-68 (*b*) HHB-60
(*c*) MH-179 (*d*) HC-4

30. Gladiolus is raised by
(*a*) True seed (*b*) Bulbs
(*c*) Stem cuttings (*d*) Roots

31. Seed rate per hectare of garlic is—
(*a*) 250 kg (*b*) 500 kg
(*c*) 750 kg (*d*) 1000 kg

32. Optimum plant population per hectare in chillies is—
(*a*) 50,000 (*b*) 1,00,000
(*c*) 1,50,000 (*d*) 2,00,000

33. Neelam is a famous variety of—
(*a*) Mango (*b*) Guava
(*c*) Banana (*d*) Papaya

34. Snowball is famous variety of—
(*a*) Brinjal (*b*) Tomato
(*c*) Cauliflower (*d*) Cabbage

35. Honeydew is an important variety of—
(*a*) Water melon (*b*) Musk melon
(*c*) Papaya (*d*) Guava

36. Average seed rate per hectare of cauliflower is—
(*a*) 250 gm (*b*) 750 gm
(*c*) 1500 gm (*d*) 2500 gm

37. Which method is most commonly used in propagating good quality plants of citrus—

(*a*) Grafting (*b*) Budding

(*c*) Layering (*d*) Cutting

38. Which one is most serious insect of cotton crop—

(*a*) Pink ball worm (*b*) Jassisds

(*c*) Spotted boll worm

(*d*) Root rot

39. At what dose Malathion 50 EC is applied to control aphids in mustard—

(*a*) 100 ml/ha (*b*) 250 ml/ha

(*c*) 500 ml/ha (*d*) 1000 ml/ha

40. Painted bug is serious pest of—

(*a*) Gram crop (*b*) Mustard crop

(*c*) Cotton crop (*d*) Peas crop

41. Late blight of potato is caused by

(*a*) Alternaria solani

(*b*) Phytophthora infestans

(*c*) Rhizoctonia solani

(*d*) Rhizoctonia bacticola

42. Tikka disease in groundnut can be controlled by—

(*a*) Streptocyclin (*b*) Zeneb

(*c*) Diathane-M-45 (*d*) Thiaram

43. Inclusion of which one of these crops in rotation helps in reducing nematode problem

(*a*) Methi (*b*) Wheat

(*c*) Paddy (*d*) Bajra

44. Most important component in farm management is—

(*a*) Farm layout (*b*) Farm budgeting

(*c*) Marketing of produce

(*d*) Production unit

45. Success of TV programme of extension depends on—

(*a*) Quality of monthly workshops

(*b*) Regular visit of VEW

(*c*) Quality of fortnightly workshops

(*d*) Delivery of correct message to the farmers

46. How much growth rate was registered in gross domestic product during 1995-96 in the country ?

(*a*) 3 per cent (*b*) 5 per cent

(*a*) 7 per cent (*d*) 10 per cent

47. When was the first Agricultural University established in India ?

(*a*) 1950 (*b*) 1960

(*c*) 1965 (*d*) 1970

48. The impact of green revolution in India was largely noted in—

(*a*) Rice only (*b*) Wheat only

(*c*) Rice and Wheat

(*d*) Rice, wheat and pulses

49. Which of the following elements is part of the chlorophyll ?

(*a*) Iron (*b*) Zinc

(*c*) Maganese (*d*) Magnesium

50. Acid soils can be reclaimed by addition of—

(*a*) Gypsum (*b*) Lime

(*c*) Compost (*d*) Green manure

51. Which of the following mineral elements is essential for nitrogen metabolism in green plants ?

(*a*) P (*b*) K

(*c*) Zn (*d*) Mo

52. Which element is immobile in the plants ?

(*a*) Nitrogen (*b*) Potassium

(*c*) Phosphorus (*d*) Calcium

53. Hand refractometer is used to measure—

(*a*) Minerals

(*b*) Total soluble solids

(*c*) Sucrose (*d*) Fibre

54. Terrace cultivation is mostly practised

(*a*) In rural areas

(*b*) On slope of mountain

(*c*) In desert land (*d*) On slope of hill

55. The chemical characteristic feature of non-saline alkali soil is—

	EC ds/m	ESP	pH
(*a*)	<4	>15	>8.5
(*b*)	<4	<15	>8.5
(*c*)	>4	>15	>8.5
(*d*)	>4	<15	<8.5

56. What is the upper crops tolerable limit of biurett in urea ?

(a) 0.5% (b) 1.0%
(c) 1.5% (d) 3.0%

57. Which of the following is an igneous rock?

(a) Limestone (b) Slate
(c) Marble (d) Basalt

58. The crop plants transpire more when there is—

(a) High temperature and high humidity
(a) Low temperature and high humidity
(c) High temperature and low humidity
(d) High humidity and high wind velocity

59. Which state has the highest sugar production in the country ?

(a) Maharashtra (b) Tamil Nadu
(c) Uttar Pradesh (d) Punjab

60. The seed used for cultivation of mushroom is called—

(a) Mushroom seed (b) Fungal spores
(c) Mycelium (d) Spawn

61. Which of the following parasite can control rice stem borer ?

(a) *Trichogramma chilonis*
(b) *Trichogramma japonicum*
(c) *Cytobagous salvinia*
(d) *Neochetina eichhornica*

62. Current all India NPK use ratio is about

(a) 3 : 2 : 1 (b) 5 : 3 : 1
(c) 10 : 3 : 1 (d) 15 : 5 : 2

63. Who was awarded world food prize during 1995 ?

(a) Mr. Hans R. Herren
(b) Dr. M.G. Jackson
(c) Dr. K.R. Kurien
(d) Dr. M.S. Swaminathan

64. Which of the following legume crops do not fix atmospheric nitrogen ?

(a) French bean (b) Moong bean
(c) Khesri (d) Cluster bean

65. Which of the following crop is most suited for companion cropping with poplar ?

(a) Rice (b) Wheat
(c) Pea (d) Ginger

66. Rice is a:-

(a) Short day plant (b) Long day plant
(c) Day neutral plant
(d) Short day and long day plant

67. Match **List I** (institutions) with **List II** (place) and select the correct answer using the codes given below the lists :

List I	**List II**
A. CPCRI	1. Manila
B. CTCRI	2. Jodhpur
C. IRRI	3. Trivendrum
D. CAZRI	4. Kesargard

	A	**B**	**C**	**D**
(a)	III	I	II	IV
(b)	IV	III	I	II
(c)	I	II	IV	III
(d)	II	IV	III	I

68. A soil having bulk density of 1.65 g/collection centre exhibits 20.5 per cent moisture at field capacity and 8.5 per cent moisture at permanent wilting point. What would be the total moisture deficit in the soil in upper 30 cm layer ?

(a) 494×10^{-2} cm (b) 494×10^{-1} cm
(c) 594×10^{-2} cm (d) 59.4×10^{-2} cm

69. Gall formation of mango is caused by—

(a) Nutrient deficiency
(b) Fungus (c) Virus
(d) Insect

70. The removal of a ring of bark from trunk of plant eventually kills it because

(a) Water cannot go up
(b) Food does not travel down and roots starved
(c) The exposed part gets infected with pathogen
(d) Mineral salts cannot go up

71. What is the seed rate per hectare of pearl millet
(a) 8-10 kg (b) 10-12 kg
(a) 15-20 kg (d) 4-5 kg

72. An organism which converts nitrite to nitrate is—
(a) Azotobactor (b) Nitrobactor
(c) Nitrosomonas (d) Nitrogenase

73. Which of the following is major oil-seed crop of India ?
(a) Sunflower
(b) Rape-seed and mustard
(c) Groundnut (d) Castor

74. The efficiency of field irrigation would be more in
(a) Sandy loam (b) Loam
(c) Clay loam (d) Heavy loam

75. According to low variable proportions, total product will be maximum where
(a) Marginal product = 0
(b) Marginal product < 0
(c) Marginal product > 0
(d) Marginal product = Average product

76. Lucerne crop is a—
(a) Foliage crop (b) Root crop
(c) Stem crop (d) Cereal crop

77. Some states in India have imposed a ban on the consumption of Kesari dal (Lathyrus sativus) because it causes gradual loss of—
(a) Vision
(b) Movement of lower limbs
(c) Hearing (d) Red blood cells

78. The Central Rice Research Institute of India is located at
(a) Calcutta (b) Cuttack
(c) Bangalore (d) Mysore

79. Green plants evolve oxygen during the day rather than carbon dioxide. This means that
(a) Green plants do not respire
(b) Green plants respire only at night
(c) Green plants respire during the day also but the rate of respiration is very low
(d) The rate of photosynthesis is much higher than the rate of respiration

80. The fundamental role of hairs in plants is
(a) To protect the young root from damage by coarse soil particles
(b) To protect the root from soil microbes
(c) To absorb water and mineral salts from the soil
(d) To bind soil particles to the root for firm fixation of the plant.

81. Water and mineral salts are translocated in plants in the:-
(a) Collenchyma (b) Porenchyma
(c) Phloem (d) Xylem

82. Which of the following plants has the largest flower ?
(a) Chrysanthemum (b) Rafflesia
(c) Sunflower (d) Zenia

83. Which of the following bear the smallest seeds?
(a) Grasses (b) Legumes
(c) Orchids (d) Sedges

84. Which of the following is a true fruit ?
(a) Apple (b) Cashewnut
(c) Pineapple (d) Coconut

85. Which of the following plant hormones controls fruit ripening ?
(a) Auxins (b) Ethylene
(c) Gibbrellic acid (d) Zeatin

86. Seed dormancy can be broken by treating the seed with
(a) Abscisic acid (b) Acetic acid
(c) Coulmarin (d) Gibberellic acid

87. Seeds can best be preserved in—
(a) Cool and dry conditions
(b) Cool and wet conditions
(c) Hot and dry condtitions
(d) Hot and wet conditions

88. Which of the following plant diseases is caused by bacteria ?
(a) Citrus dieback
(b) Tundu disease in wheat
(c) Tikka disease in groundnut
(d) Leaf curl in tomato

89. On the basis of agroclimatic conditions, Rajasthan is divided into nine zones. Ajmer, Jaipur, Tonk and northern part of Swaimadhopur district in—

(*a*) Zone 3-A (*b*) Zone 2-A

(*c*) Zone 3-B (*d*) Zone I-B

90. The layers in soil are referred to as

(*a*) Horizons (*b*) Profile

(*c*) Hard pans (*d*) Pedocals

91. In late sown wheat crop irrigation are required—

(*a*) More frequently as compared to normal time sown crop

(*b*) Very late as compared to normal sown crop

(*c*) As per normal timings of normal time sown crop

(*d*) In less number as compared to normal time sown crop

92. Total cropped area of Rajasthan is approximately

(*a*) 342.44 lakh hectares

(*b*) 192.55 lakh hectares

(*c*) 162.32 lakh hectares

(*d*) 250.00 lakh hectares

93. Annual normal rainfall of which of the following district is highest ?

(*a*) Ganganagar (*b*) Ajmer

(*c*) Jhalawar (*d*) Udaipur

94. Which of the following chemical insecticide is a carbamate insecticide ?

(*a*) Aldecarb (*b*) Heptachlor

(*c*) Endosulphan (*d*) Malathion

95. In order to harvest a good crop of hybrid maize, at which of the following stages irrigation requirement is very much required?

(*a*) Plant growth and flowering stage

(*b*) Time of grain maturity

(*c*) Two weeks after sowing

(*d*) One month after sowing

96. Which is the correct order of treatment of seed leguminous crops with insecticides, culture and fungicides ?

(*a*) Culture, fungicide, insecticide

(*b*) Fungicide, insecticide, culture

(*c*) Insecticide, fungicide, culture

(*d*) Insecticide, culture, fungicide

97. Under the agriculture extension system, Krishak Mandal has been formed

(*a*) In every block

(*b*) In every chak

(*c*) At headquarter of agriculture supervision

(*d*) At headquarter of Panchayat

98. In order to get more returns from vegetable cultivation, farmer should

(*a*) Do timely sowing of early varieties

(*b*) Use heavy doses of fertilizers

(*c*) Do required interculture operations

(*d*) Control incidence of pests and diseases

99. Mustard production in Rajasthan during 1994-95

(*a*) 15.50 lakh tonnes

(*b*) 20.12 lakh tonnes

(*c*) 40.00 lakh tonnes

(*d*) 10.25 lakh tonnes

100. Which of the following is a suitable improved variety of bajra crop ?

(*a*) T-9 (*b*) S.P.V.-245

(*c*) M-13 (*d*) M.H.-179

JRF-1997 (Physical Science)

1. Total geographical area of India is—

(*a*) 328 million hectares

(*b*) 328 thousand hectares

(*c*) 327 million hectares

(*d*) None of the above

2. The period on which monsoon is onset in Kerala?

(*a*) 1-5th May (*b*) 1-5th July

(*c*) 1-5th June (*d*) 1-5th August

3. Which of the following statement is true?

(*a*) Protein does not exist in colloidal form

(*b*) Milk is an emulsion of fat in water

(*c*) Lactose is in emulsion form

(*d*) None of the above

4. Total food grain production of India during the year 1995-96 was—
(*a*) 185 million tonnes
(*b*) 192 million tonnes
(*c*) 176 million tonnes
(*d*) 180 million tonnes

5. Classification of soil in India is based on—
(*a*) Dokuchaeiv's classification
(*b*) USA soil classification
(*c*) Dr. Randhawa's classification
(*d*) None of the above

6. In North India which of the following crop is taken in rabi as well as kharif season.
(*a*) Moong (*b*) Maize
(*c*) Jowar (*d*) Bajra

7. Which of the following crop requires more water—
(*a*) Maize (*b*) Paddy
(*c*) Sugarcane (*d*) Wheat

8. Crop that can tolerate soil salinity is—
(*a*) Millets (*b*) Pulses
(*c*) Beans (*d*) Sugarcane

9. Limestone contains mainly—
(*a*) $CaCO_3$ (*b*) CaO
(*c*) $Ca(OH)_2$
(*d*) None of the above

10. 'B' horizon is also called as
(*a*) Illuvial horizone
(*b*) Eluviated horizone
(*c*) Both (*a*) and (*b*)
(*d*) None of the above

11. Fruit crop which occupies more than 50% area of total fruit cultivation is—
(*a*) Banana (*b*) Mango
(*c*) Papaya (*d*) Ber

12. Diammonium phosphate provides—
(*a*) Nitrogen (*b*) Phosphorus
(*c*) It is a N-P complex fertilizer
(*d*) Potassic fertilizer

13. Which of the following fertilizer can be absorbed as +ive and –ive ions?
(*a*) Phosphorus (*b*) Potassium
(*c*) Nitrogen (*d*) Calcium

14. Rediscovery of Mendalism was done by—
(*a*) Korens, Devries, Trchermark
(*b*) Darwin (*c*) Lammark
(*d*) None of the above

15. The river which has highest number of utilizable basins is—
(*a*) Ganga (*b*) Yamuna
(*c*) Kaveri (*d*) Brahmaputra

16. Main aim of zero tillage operation is—
(*a*) To improve soil structure
(*b*) To conserve soil moisture
(*c*) To maintain temperature of soil
(*d*) To increase pore space

17. Time required for an element to become 1/8 of it's original amount, half life is 20 minutes.
(*a*) 30 minutes (*b*) 60 minutes
(*c*) 90 minutes (*d*) 120 minutes

18. Geometric mean of number 2, 4, 5, is—
(*a*) 6 (*b*) 5
(*c*) 4 (*d*) 8

19. In north India, sometimes rains takes place in winter which is due to—
(*a*) Western depression
(*b*) Monsoon depression
(*c*) Eastern depression
(*d*) S-W depression

20. Which of the following country is highest producer of KNO_3—
(*a*) Russia (*b*) Canada
(*c*) U.S.A. (*d*) France

21. The erosion in which the upper layer of the soil surface is removed uniformly is known as
(*a*) Gully erosion (*b*) Sheet erosion
(*c*) Splash erosion (*d*) Rill erosion

22. Ogives are the
(*a*) Cumulative frequency curves
(*b*) Frequency polygon
(*c*) Histogram (*d*) Frequency curve

23. Bhopal Gas Tragedy was caused by the gas named as—
(*a*) Ethane (*b*) Methyl isocynate
(*c*) CCl_4 (*d*) $CHCl_3$

24. The deadly problem of soil that is increasing throughout the world is
(*a*) Soil salinity (*b*) Waterlogging
(*c*) Both (*a*) and (*b*)
(*d*) None of the above

25. The most concentrated fertilizer used for nutrient is—
(*a*) Urea (*b*) DAP
(*c*) Anhydrous Ammonia
(*d*) SSP

JRF-1997 (Agronomy)

1. Which of the following nitrogenous fertilizer provides maximum amount of P_2O_5?
(*a*) Mono Ammonium Phosphate
(*b*) Di-Ammonium Phosphate
(*c*) Poly Ammonium Phosphate
(*d*) APP

2. Which of the following tree leaves are used for green manuring in paddy crop ?
(*a*) Acacia nilotica (*b*) Casia fistula
(*c*) Azatirachta indica
(*d*) Polyanthus longifolia

3. Which of the following crop is highly resistant against salts ?
(*a*) Safflower (*b*) Castor
(*c*) Til (*d*) Linseed

4. Which of the following fruit having seed coat adherent to paricarp ?
(*a*) Achene (*b*) Drupe
(*c*) Pome (*d*) Haspiridium

5. To judge the maturity of sugarcane, the brix value should be—
(*a*) 16 (*b*) 18
(*c*) 20 (*d*) 21

6. Sugarcane planting in trenches is beneficial because it—
(*a*) Enhances germination
(*b*) Enhances tillering
(*c*) Reduce lodging
(*d*) Increases sugar percentage

7. The term 'crop lodging' (Sugarcane) has been given by—
(*a*) C.F. Clement (Hwai)
(*b*) H.F. Dastur (*c*) N. Mene
(*d*) J. Willey

8. Photoperiodically sugarcane is knwon as—
(*a*) Short day plant (*b*) Long day plant
(*c*) Day night plant (*d*) Night plant

9. Short duration crop grown between two main crops is known as-
(*a*) Companion crop (*b*) Catch crop
(*c*) Inter crop (*d*) Camel crop

10. Which of the following plays major role in persistance of herbicide in the soil—
(*a*) Photo decomposition
(*b*) Chemical decomposition
(*c*) Biological decomposition
(*d*) All of these

11. Which of the following crop is highly sensitive against 2, 4-D ?
(*a*) Maize (*b*) Cotton
(*c*) Green gram (*d*) None of these

12. Glyphosate is a-
(*a*) Selective translocated herbicide
(*b*) Non-selective translocated herbicide
(*c*) Non-selective non-translocated herbicide
(*d*) None of the above

13. Most common criterion used to determine the advantages of intercrops is known as—
(*a*) LER equivalent (*b*) MER equivalent
(*c*) MAL equivalent (*d*) ATER equivalent

14. Weight of one hectare furrow slice in kilo gram is-

(a) 2×10^{-6} (b) 2.24×10^{6}

(c) 2.16×10^{16} (d) 2.25×10^{-6}

15. Which of the following crops can develop small root penetration at wilting point---

(a) Lovegrass (b) Wheat

(c) Oat (d) Bajra

16. Which of the following crop requires maximum quantity of water ?

(a) Paddy (b) Maize

(c) Sugarcane (d) Wheat

17. Most critical stage of irrigation in maize crop is-

(a) Tillering stage (b) Silking stage

(c) Tesseling

(d) None of the above

18. Maximum loss of soil caused by saltation in ___ type of soil.

(a) Sandy loam (b) Sandy

(c) Laterite (d) Clay

19. Soil which gives big clodes is---

(a) Clay (b) Sandy clay

(c) Clay loam (d) Sandy

20. Which test is used to calculate differences in two means of the population ?

(a) 't' Test (b) 'Z' Test

(c) 'F' Test (d) All of these

21. Which of the following is not a measure of central tendency

(a) Frequency (b) Mean

(c) Range (d) Median

22. Which of the following catchment basin provides maximum irrigation ?

(a) Indus (b) Ganga

(c) Godavari (d) Brahamputra

23. Which gas has been released from paddy fields ?

(a) H_2S (b) CH_4

(c) CO_2 (d) NH_3

24. Flooded field have more concentration of-

(a) CH_4 (b) CO_2

(c) NH_3 (d) H_2S

25. Most important field crop growing in Rabi as well as Kharif season in North India is-

(a) Sorghum (b) Maize

(c) Bajra (d) Wheat

26. Most common cropping method prevailing in the dryland area is---

(a) Intercrop (b) Relay crop

(c) Mixed crop (d) Catch crop

27. Most important problem of alkali soil is---

(a) Toxic salts

(b) Low water deffloculation of soil colloids

(c) Low soluble salts

(d) Large quantity of soluble salts

28. Most common method in dryland area is---

(a) Single row method

(b) Paired row method

(c) Skip row method

(d) Broadcasting method

29. Which of the following is the most enhansive crop ?

(a) Maize (b) Jowar

(c) Potato (d) Sugarcane

30. Seed rate of rice in one hectare area through directly broadcasting in the field is---

(a) 40 kg/ha (b) 60 kg/ha

(c) 80 kg/ha (d) 100 kg/ha

31. Average milling percentage of rice is---

(a) 65-70 per cent (b) 70-75 per cent

(c) 60-65 per cent (d) 55-60 per cent

32. Area required for raising a nursery of one hectare paddy crop is---

(a) 250 sq.m (b) 500 sq.m

(c) 1000 sq.m (d) 750 sq.m

33. Area required for raising nursery for one hectare late sown paddy crop is-

(a) 750-1000 sq.m (b) 1/20 hectare

(c) 1/5 hectare (d) 1/15 hectare

34. Which of the following is day neutral plant—
(*a*) Tobacco (*b*) Red cover
(*c*) Sweet potato (*d*) Sunflower

35. Ratio between row to row and plant is known as—
(*a*) Rectangularity ratio
(*b*) Iquarity ratio
(*c*) Both (*a*) and (*b*)
(*d*) None ofthe above

36. Most suitable crop grown in black soil of dry land is—
(*a*) Linseed (*b*) Safflower
(*c*) Castor (*d*) Mustard

37. Humus theory was proposed by
(*a*) Jethro tull (*b*) Steven
(*c*) Loll and Bollag
(*d*) None of the above

38. Which of the following bacteria is an example of associate asymbiotic nitrogen fixation ?
(*a*) *Rhizobium* (*b*) *Azotobactor*
(*c*) *Clostridium* (*d*) *Nitrosomonas*

39. Which of the following is example of associate nitrogen fixation ?
(*a*) *Rhizobium* (*b*) *Azotobactor*
(*c*) *Clostridium* (*d*) *Nitrosomonas*

40. Most important factor considering inter cropping is—
(*a*) Duration of crop
(*b*) Temperature in relating crops
(*c*) Time of onset of competition
(*d*) Time of harvesting

41. Soyabean is a-
(*a*) Pulse crop (*b*) Oilseed crop
(*c*) Oilseed and pulse crop
(*d*) Cereal crops

42. *Cyprus rotendus* is propagated by -
(*a*) Stolons (*b*) Tuber
(*c*) Seeds (*d*) All of these

43. At present cropping intensity of India is -
(*a*) 120 per cent (*b*) 135 per cent
(*c*) 145 per cent (*d*) 140 per cent

44. Which of the following herbicide have zero persistence in the soil ?
(*a*) Glyphasate (*b*) Diquate
(*c*) Paraquate (*d*) All of these

45. Inactivation of herbicide in the soil is mainly due to—
(*a*) Organic matter (*b*) Temperature
(*c*) pH (*d*) All of these

46. First variety of rice released by India was—
(*a*) Jaya (*b*) Ratna
(*c*) Chambal (*d*) IR-8

47. Which of the following country having the highest per capita land in the world-
(*a*) India (*b*) China
(*c*) Canada (*d*) Australia

48. Photorespiration (fixation of NH_3) takes place in—
(*a*) Chloroplast (*b*) Cytoplasm
(*c*) Mitochondria (*d*) All of the above

49. Out of the following which crop is more resistant against drought-
(*a*) Cowpea (*b*) Black gram
(*c*) Green gram (*d*) Pigeon pea

50. What is botanical name of Indian mustard?
(*a*) *Brassica juncia* (*b*) *Brassica alba*
(*c*) *Brassica compestris*
(*d*) *Brassica carinata*

51. Which soil is the most productive having exchangeable sodium percentage of
(*a*) $<5\%$ (*b*) $<10\%$
(*c*) $<15\%$ (*d*) $<25\%$

52. 'Zn' recommended for wheat-rice rotation in each crop is at—
(*a*) Alternate season (*b*) Regular season
(*c*) After 2 years (*d*) After 4 years

53. If nodulation is less in any legume crop, which of the following nutrient shall be applied at pre-flowering stage ?
(*a*) Boron (*b*) Molybdenum
(*c*) Phosphorus (*d*) Nitrogen

54. The inter-cropping system is—
(*a*) Supplementary (*b*) Complementry
(*c*) Additive (*d*) Synergistic

55. Most efficient crop for potassium uptake is—
(*a*) Cereal crops (*b*) Oil seed crops
(*c*) Legume crops (*d*) Grasses

56. Percentage water available at wilting point is-
(*a*) 0 per cent (*b*) 2 per cent
(*c*) 10 per cent (*d*) 20 per cent

57. A soil provides highest percentage of organic matter in the
(*a*) Arable-crops (*b*) Grass-land
(*c*) Forest (*d*) None of these

58. Which of the following is a trap crop for striga-
(*a*) Cotton (*b*) Maize
(*c*) Soya-bean (*d*) Tobacco

59. Match the following:
(*i*) ***Crosps*** ***Varieties***
(*a*) Bajra → (*i*) C-J-104
(*b*) Sorghum → (*ii*) Swarna
(*c*) Maize → (*iii*) M-35-1
(*d*) Rice → (*iv*) Jaya
(*e*) Barley → (*v*) Kailash

60. (*ii*) ***Crops*** ***Test weight***
(*a*) Rice → (*i*) 22 g
(*b*) Cotton → (*ii*) 70 g
(*c*) Maize → (*iii*) 200 g
(*d*) Mustard → (*iv*) 4 g
(*e*) Green gram → (*v*) 25 g

61. (*iii*) ***Crops*** ***Water requirement***
(*a*) Wheat → (*i*) 500 mm
(*b*) Rice → (*ii*) 1680 mm
(*c*) Berseem → (*iii*) 900 mm
(*d*) Green-gram → (*iv*) 350 mm
(*e*) Cotton → (*v*) 700 mm

62. (*iv*) ***Critical stage*** ***Crops***
(*a*) Siliqua formation → (*i*) Mustard
(*b*) Tillering → (*ii*) Wheat
(*c*) Flowering → (*iii*) Pulses
(*d*) After each cutting → (*iv*) Berseem
(*e*) Silking → (*v*) Maize

JRF - 1998 (Agronomy)

1. Out of total net sown area (142 million hectares) of India, unirrigated area is—
(*a*) 30 million hectares
(*b*) 50 million hectares
(*c*) 80 million hectares
(*d*) 90 million hectares

2. Most critical stage of irrigation of wheat is—
(*a*) CRI stage (*b*) Tillering stage
(*c*) Jointing stage (*d*) Flowering stage

3. In maize crop dough stage comes at—
(*a*) Just after flowering time
(*b*) When grain becomes milky
(*c*) Just before harvesting
(*d*) Grain gets some hardness from softness

4. The state having largest area in the country is—
(*a*) Uttar Pradesh (*b*) Madhya Pradesh
(*c*) Rajasthan (*d*) Punjab

5. The state having highest area in paddy is
(*a*) Uttar Pradesh (*b*) West Bengal
(*c*) Punjab (*d*) Rajasthan

6. Which of the following state having highest production of wheat ?
(*a*) Punjab (*b*) Uttar Pradesh
(*c*) Madhya Pradesh (*d*) West Bengal

7. The insect "Boll Worm" commonly found on—
(*a*) Cotton (*b*) Mango
(*c*) Rice (*d*) Maize

8. Most destructive disease of sugarcane is—
(*a*) Red rot of sugarcane
(*b*) Hushy shoot
(*c*) RSD (*d*) GSD

9. Photophosphorylation means—
(*a*) Production of ATP
(*b*) Production of NADP
(*c*) Oxidation of CO_2 into carbohydrates
(*d*) Production of energy

10. Example of metamorphic rock is—
(*a*) Granite (*b*) Marble
(*c*) Gibbersite (*d*) Asbestos

11. First state Agricultural University of India was-
(*a*) Punjab Agricultural University, Ludhiana
(*b*) G.B. Pant Agricultural University, Pantnagar
(*c*) Rajasthan Agricultural University, Bikaner
(*d*) Gujarat Agricultural University, Vidhya Nagar

12. Which of the following is a short day plant-
(*a*) Wheat (*b*) Sugarcane
(*c*) Maize (*d*) Cotton

13. RNA is synthesized in—
(*a*) Nucleus (*b*) Nucleolus
(*c*) Protoplasm (*d*) Ribosomes

14. The term "Genetics" was given by—
(*a*) Mendel (*b*) Betson
(*c*) Corck (*d*) Hook

15. Per hectare seed rate of rapeseed in plant geometry 30 × 10 cm is—
(*a*) 3 kg/ha (*b*) 5 kg/ha
(*c*) 10 kg/ha (*d*) 20 kg/ha

16. Per hectare seed rate of direct seeded upland paddy is—
(*a*) 30 kg (*b*) 60 kg
(*c*) 80-100 kg (*d*) 150 kg

17. Number of sets required for planting one hectare sugarcane crop will be—
(*a*) 35,000-40,000 (*b*) 40,000-45,000
(*c*) 45,000-50,000 (*d*) 55,000-60,000

18. Seed rate of potato in mild season variety is—
(*a*) 20-25 q/ha (*b*) 15-20 q/ha
(*c*) 30-35 q/ha (*d*) 25-30 q/ha

19. The fodder crop berseem was originated from-
(*a*) Egypt (*b*) America
(*c*) Africa (*d*) China

20. Average hulling percentage of rice is—
(*a*) 30 per cent (*b*) 40 per cent
(*c*) 65 per cent (*d*) 80 per cent

21. In mustard white rust is caused by—
(*a*) *Phythuium* (*b*) *Albugo candida*
(*c*) *Phytopthera* (*d*) *Colectotricum*

22. Inflorescence of sugarcane is known as—
(*a*) Arrow (*b*) Tillering
(*c*) Silk (*d*) Tassel

23. Mostly gypsum is used in reclamation of—
(*a*) Alkali soils (*b*) Saline soils
(*c*) Acidic soils (*d*) None of these

24. Most common pulse crop sown in *Rabi* season in India is—
(*a*) Chick-pea (*b*) Black-gram
(*c*) Mung-bean (*d*) Horse-gram

25. 8.0 gram oxygen is equal to—
(*a*) 1.0 mole (*b*) 0.5 mole
(*c*) 2.0 mole (*d*) 5.0 mole

26. Plants move the water from roots to leaves because potential of leaves are—
(*a*) Greater than roots
(*b*) Lower than roots
(*c*) Equal to roots
(*d*) None of the above

27. Sowing time of rape (toria) is—
(*a*) June-July
(*b*) August-September
(*c*) October-November
(*d*) November-December

28. Fruit of guava is called as—
(*a*) Berry (*b*) Drupe
(*c*) Stone (*d*) Pome

29. Smallest unit of extension education is—
(*a*) Village panchayat (*b*) Village
(*c*) Cooperative bank (*d*) Tehsil

30. Botanical name of Barseem is
(*a*) Ezyptial clover
(*b*) Trifolium alexandrium
(*c*) Albuginia spp. (*d*) None of the above

31. Arkel is the variety of—
(*a*) Groundnut (*b*) Arhar
(*c*) Toria (*d*) Pea

32. T-9 is the variety of—
(*a*) Toria (*b*) Rape-seed
(*c*) Mustard (*d*) Black-gram

33. Generally average temperature required for growth of sugarcane is—
(*a*) 0-10°C (*b*) 10-20°C
(*c*) 20-30°C (*d*) 30-40°C

34. Adsali crop of sugarcane is sown in—
(*a*) July-August (*b*) January-February
(*c*) September-October
(*d*) November-December

35. Average yield of sugarcane adsali crop is
(*a*) 1000-1200 q/ha (*b*) 400-500 q/ha
(*c*) 800-900 q/ha (*d*) 100-200 q/ha

36. Average yield of sugarcane autumn crop is
(*a*) 700-800 q/ha (*b*) 300-350 q/ha
(*c*) 100-200 q/ha (*d*) 400- 500 q/ha

37. Khaira disease of Rice is caused by deficiency of—
(*a*) Boron (*b*) Sulphur
(*c*) Zinc (*d*) Molybdenum

38. White bud in maize is caused by deficiency of
(*a*) N_2 (*b*) P_2P_5
(*c*) Zn (*d*) Cl

39. Deficiency symptoms of nitrogen first appears on—
(*a*) Lower leaves (*b*) Lower roots
(*c*) Upper leaves (*d*) None of these

40. Deficiency symptom of phosphorus is first appears on
(*a*) Upper leaves (*b*) Lower leaves
(*c*) Roots (*d*) Stem

41. Test weight of Phalaris minor is—
(*a*) 5 gm (*b*) 2 gm
(*c*) 10 gm (*d*) 40 gm

42. Which of the following crop can survive between 4-6 ph ?
(*a*) Wheat (*b*) Paddy
(*c*) Tea (*d*) None of these

43. The weeds Cyprus rotendus and Cynodon dectylon are
(*a*) Annual dicot
(*b*) Perennial monocot
(*c*) Annual monocot
(*d*) Perennial dicot

44. The weed Cyprus rotundus is found in—
(*a*) 22 crops in 132 countries
(*b*) 52 crops in 100 countries
(*c*) 36 crops in 98 countries
(*d*) 52 crops in 92 countries

45. Sowing time of autumn crop of sugarcane is—
(*a*) October-November
(*b*) February-March
(*c*) November-December
(*d*) July-August

46. 'Pusa-Giant' is the variety of—
(*a*) Lucerne (*b*) Berseem
(*c*) Maize (*d*) Papaya

47. Botanical name of Indian Mustard is—
(*a*) *Brassica compestris* var
(*b*) *Brassica juncea*
(*c*) *Brassica nigra*
(*d*) *Brassica sativa*

48. Botanical name of Indian cotton is
(*a*) *Gossipium barbadence*
(*b*) *Gossipium hirsutam*
(*c*) *Gossipium arborium*
(*d*) *Gossipium herbarium*

49. 'Varuna' is a variety of—
(*a*) Yellow mustard (*b*) Toria
(*c*) Brown mustard (*d*) Indian mustard

50. Botanical name of Canada thistle weed is—
(*a*) *Cirrium arvensis*
(*b*) *Phyllanthus niruri*
(*c*) *Cirium arboreum*
(*d*) *Convolvulas arvensis*

51. The chemical which induce the stomata closing is—
(*a*) PMA (*b*) Kaoline
(*c*) Mustard oil (*d*) 2,4-D

52. Crop lodging was conducted in Hawaii
(*a*) Sugarcane (*b*) Cotton
(*c*) Mustard (*d*) Wheat

53. Quantity of simazine (a.i.) required for one hectare is—
(*a*) 0.5 kg (*b*) 1.0 kg
(*c*) 1.5 kg (*d*) 2.0 kg

54. Percentage of biuráte permissible in urea is—
(*a*) 2 % (*b*) 1.5%
(*c*) 3.0% (*d*) 5.0%

55. Generally Basalin is applied as—
(*a*) Pre-sowing (*b*) Pre-emergency
(*c*) After emergency
(*d*) None of the above

56. On an average per hectare nitrogen fixed by *dhaincha* crop per year is—
(*a*) 15 kg (*b*) 20 kg
(*c*) 30 kg (*d*) 40 kg

57. Amount of nitrogen obtained from environment from one hectare land in a year is—
(*a*) 10 kg/ha (*b*) 20 kg/ha
(*c*) 30 kg/ha (*d*) 40 kg/ha

58. Amount of P_2O_5 recovery is—
(*a*) < 35 % (*b*) < 45 %
(*c*) < 25% (*d*) < 15 %

59. A fertilizer having maximum amount of nutrient is—
(*a*) Urea
(*b*) Anhydrous ammonia
(*c*) CAN (*d*) DAP

60. Butachlor weedicide is used in paddy crop—
(*a*) At the time of sowing
(*b*) At pre-emergence
(*c*) At pre-sowing (*d*) After emergence

61. Which of the following fertilizer is used as top dressing in paddy crop—
(*a*) Diammonium phosphate
(*b*) Diammonium sulphate
(*c*) Single superphosphate
(*d*) None of the above

62. The cropping rotation of 200 per cent cropping intensity is—
(*a*) Maize-cotton
(*b*) Sugarcane-potato-wheat
(*c*) Sugarcane-mustard-cotton
(*d*) None of the above

63. Crop rotation of 150 per cent intensity is—
(*a*) Wheat-cotton-urd
(*a*) Groundnut-wheat-cotton-potato
(*c*) Sugarcane-mustard-maize-potato
(*d*) Sugarcane-potato-wheat

64. Cropping intensity of India is about—
(*a*) 50% (*b*) 100%
(*c*) 150% (*d*) 130%

65. Organic carbon can be converted into organic matter by multiplying with—
(*a*) 1.26 (*b*) 1.72
(*c*) 1.82 (*d*) 1.91

66. One cotton bale having weight of—
(*a*) 178 kg (*b*) 218 kg
(*c*) 190 kg (*d*) 160 kg

67. In greenhouses which of the following gas is not found abundantly—
(*a*) CO_2 (*b*) CH_4
(*c*) O_2 (*d*) N_2O

68. Malathion belongs to the group of
(*a*) Organo-phosphoide
(*b*) Organo-mercury
(*c*) Organo-chloride
(*d*) Pyrethroids

69. The disease occurs regularly in a specific area is known as—
(*a*) Hronic (*b*) Epidemic
(*c*) Epidemic (*d*) Sporodic

70. In double fertilization one male gamete is fused with egg cell and other fused with—
(*a*) Nuclei cells (*b*) Polar nuclei
(*c*) Antipodal cells (*d*) Synergids

71. Number of irrigations required for good maize crop are
(*a*) 3-4 (*b*) 5-6
(*c*) 6-7 (*d*) 1-2

72. FYM needed to supply 60 kg nitrogen is—
(*a*) 100 qt. (*b*) 120 qt.
(*c*) 60 qt. (*d*) 90 qt.

73. Hygroscopic coefficient at
(*a*) 1/3 bar (*b*) 3 bar
(*c*) 1000 bar (*d*) 10,000 bar

74. Most critical stage of maize is—
(*a*) Tillering stage (*b*) Silking stage
(*c*) Dough stage
(*d*) Pre-harvesting stage

75. Mustard fruit is called as—
(*a*) Siliqua (*b*) Berry
(*c*) Drupe (*d*) Hispiridium

76. Weedicide cannot be dust sprayed because
(*a*) Drift hazard (*b*) Not soluble
(*c*) Toxic (*d*) None of these

77. If mean and variances are equal in any distribution, this is called as—
(*a*) Poisson distribution
(*b*) Normal distribution
(*c*) Bionomial distribution
(*d*) None of the above

78. The term interspecific means—
(*a*) Two plants of same spp.
(*b*) Two plants of different spp.
(*c*) Two plants of different varieties
(*d*) None of the above

79. Water density is highest at the temperature of—
(*a*) 0 °C (*b*) 4 °C
(*c*) 100 °C (*d*) 39 °C

80. Isotopes means having—
(*a*) Same proton numbers
(*b*) Same neutron numbers
(*c*) Same proton and neutron numbers
(*d*) None of the above

81. 3 metre depth and 18 metre width with variable slope of a gully is known as—
(*a*) Medium gully
(*b*) Deep and narrow gully
(*c*) Small gully (*d*) Shrink gully

82. 50 quintal wheat is produced in one hectare area, how much nitrogen it will remove from the soil during the season?
(*a*) 50 kg (*b*) 100 kg
(*c*) 150 kg (*d*) 200 kg

83. Which of the following crop requires maximum water ?
(*a*) Maize (*b*) Sugarcane
(*c*) Barley (*d*) Rice or Paddy

84. If rain come at October-November, which crop should be grown—
(*a*) Sesamum (*b*) Black gram
(*c*) Moong (*d*) Fodder crops

85. Which of the following is early variety of pegion pea—
(*a*) UPAS-120 (*b*) Pusa-ageti
(*c*) T-9 (*d*) Prabhat

86. Which of the following fodder crop fixes the nitrogen—
(*a*) Berseem (*b*) Barley
(*c*) Moong (*d*) Bajra

87. At which stage of sugarcane internode elongation takes place—
(*a*) Jointing stage (*b*) Tillering stage
(*c*) Filling stage (*d*) Flowering stage

88. Seed rate of hybrid maize is—
(*a*) 10 kg/ha (*b*) 20-25 kg/ha
(*c*) 35-40 kg/ha (*d*) 50-60 kg/ha

89. Which of the following is the variety of chick pea—
(*a*) Ankur (*b*) Pusa G-124
(*c*) Pusa bahar (*d*) Pusa bold

90. Which of the following is a variety of castor-
(*a*) Neelam (*b*) K-851
(*c*) GAUCH-I (*d*) Jadia

91. Ezypt is origin of—
(*a*) Lucerne (*b*) Barseem
(*c*) Maize (*d*) Guar

92. In sugarcane the brix value of sugar is about-
(*a*) 10-12% (*b*) 20-21%
(*c*) 5-6% (*d*) 8-9%

93. Sonalika is variety of—
(*a*) Wheat (*b*) Barley
(*c*) Paddy (*d*) None of these

94. Most widely grown and edible spp. of wheat is—
(*a*) *Triticum duram*
(*b*) *Triticum aestivum*
(*c*) *Triticum vulgare*
(*d*) *Triticum spherococcum*

95. What should be optimum spacing of mustard in dryland areas ?
(*a*) 30-35 cm (*b*) 15-20 cm
(*c*) 10-15cm (*d*) 5-10 cm

96. The phenotypic pigment found in cotton seed that is toxic to animals is—
(*a*) Gossypol (*b*) Dhurin
(*c*) Solanin (*d*) None of these

97. Scientific name of macaroni wheat is –
(*a*) *Triticum duram*
(*b*) *Triticum aestivum*
(*c*) *Triticum dicocum*
(*d*) *Triticum vulgare*

98. Trench method of sugarcane sowing is commonly used because it—
(*a*) reduces Lodging (*b*) Increases yield
(*c*) Increases juice content
(*d*) All of these

99. Fluchloraline is used at—
(*a*) Pre-plant incorporation
(*b*) Pre-emergence
(*c*) Post-emergence
(*d*) Lay by application

100. Which of the following is family of sugarbeet?
(*a*) Chenopodiaceae (*b*) Rutaceae
(*c*) Convolvulaceae (*d*) Leguminosae

101. In up land paddy crop fluchloraline is applied with—
(*a*) Seed (*b*) Pre-emergence
(*c*) After-emergence,
(*d*) None of the above

102. Carbon-Nitrogen ratio of arable soil is—
(*a*) 10 : 1 (*b*) 20 : 1
(*c*) 15 : 1 (*d*) 50 : 1

103. Highly arable land is available in—
(*a*) India (*b*) Canada
(*c*) Australia (*d*) China

104. Maximum water is required by sugarcane at—
(*a*) Germination stage
(*b*) Grand growth period
(*c*) Juvenile phase (*d*) Maturity

105. If carrot is sown for seed production it is known as—
(*a*) Annual (*b*) Biennual
(*c*) Perennial (*d*) None of these

106. Which insect attacks on paddy crop at night?
(*a*) Gandhi bug (*b*) BPH
(*c*) Aphid (*d*) Rice stem borer

107. Which of the following crop is damaged by gandhi bug ?
(*a*) Wheat (*b*) Rice
(*c*) Cotton (*d*) None of these

108. Crop that survive at 4-6 pH is—
(*a*) Rice (*b*) Maize
(*c*) Tea (*d*) Mustard

109. Scientific name of the tea having broad leaves-
(*a*) *Camelis sinensis* (*b*) *Canichs sintex*
(*c*) *Camelis virescons* (*d*) *Comelis avelia*

110. Conversion of NH_4^+ into NO_2 is taken place through—
(a) Nitrobactor (b) Nitrosomonas
(c) Azatobactor (d) Clostridium

111. Which of the following crop requires maximum amount of nutrients?
(a) Maize (b) Rice
(c) Wheat (d) Sorghum

112. How much percentage of phosphorus is available in diammonuim phosphate?
(a) 30 % (b) 55%
(c) 20 % (d) 50%

113. Average standing water required in the field of paddy crop at sowing time is—
(a) 10 ± 5 cm (b) 15 ± 5 cm
(c) 20 ± 5 cm (d) Tilth level

114. Appropriate formula for mean of standard error is—
(a) $\sqrt{2MSE}$ (b) $\sqrt{MSE}$
(a) $MSE\frac{1}{2}$ (d) $\sqrt{\frac{2MSE}{r}}$

115. If fertility of the field changes towards one direction one should use experimental design of—
(a) Randomized block design
(b) Latin square design
(c) Complete randomized block design
(d) None of the above

116. Which of the following crop can survive in the copper deficit areas?
(a) Barley (b) Wheat
(c) Potato (d) Sugarcane

117. In a sloppy areas, pearl millet should be grown-
(a) On the top of slope
(b) On intermediate
(c) At the bottom of the slope
(d) Everywhere in the area

118. Terbutryn belongs to the group of-
(a) Atrazine (b) Fluchloralin
(c) Glyphosate (d) 2,4-D

119. The soil which have maximum quantity of water at wilting point is—
(a) Clay loam (b) Sandy loam
(c) Loamy sand (d) Silty loam

120. The soil which have maximum moisture at field capacity is—
(a) Clay loam (b) Loamy sand
(c) Sandy loam (d) Silty loam

121. Per capita land available is highest in—
(a) Australia (b) India
(c) America (d) France

Match the following

122. ***Fertilizers*** ***Nitrogen %***
CAN → 26
Ammonium Chloride → 20.5
Ammonium Sulphate → 20

123. ***Variety*** ***Year***
HB-1 → 1961
HB-2 → 1963

124. ***Crop*** ***Use***
Wheat → Food
Ground-nut → Oil Fibre
Jute
Sugarbeet → Sugar
Tea → Stimulant

125. ***Chemical name*** ***Chemical formula***
Gypsum → $CaSO_4.2H_2O$
Epson salt → $MgSO_4.7H_2O$
Nitel cake → $FeO(OH).nH_2O + Fe_2O_3$
Limonite → $NaHSO_4$
Olivane → $(MgFe)_2SiO_4$

126. ***Crop*** ***Weedicide***
Rice→ Alachlor
Maize → Simazine
Wheat → Isoproturon
Potato → TOK-E-20
Tea → Paraquat

127.

Growth regulator → 2,4-D
Fruit ripener → Etheral
Herbicide → Glyphosate
Slow release → DCD
Nitrification inhibitor → IBDU

RAS-pre-examination , 1998

1. Total cropped area in India is—
(a) 137 mha (b) 142 mha
(c) 147 mha (d) 152 mha

2. The average agricultural production from irrigated area is—
(a) 1.8 tonne/ha (b) 2.0 tonnes/ha
(c) 2.4 tonnes/ha (d) 2.8 tonnes/ha

3. Indian agriculture is facing the following major problems. Which is NOT correct—
(a) Land degradation
(b) Rising population
(c) Lack of bullock power
(d) Stagnant cultivable area

4. The area occupied by legume in India is—
(a) 24 mha (b) 29 mha
(c) 34 mha (d) 39 mha

5. The principle oil-seed crop of India is—
(a) Sesame (b) Mustard
(c) Linseed
(d) Groundnut

6. Which fibre crop occupies largest area in India ?
(a) Jute (b) Flax
(c) Cotton (d) Sunnhemp

7. First agricultural university was established at—
(a) Ludhiana (b) Pusa
(c) Kanpur (d) Pant Nagar

8. Nobel Prize for Peace was awarded to Dr. Norman Borlaug in—
(a) 1969 (b) 1970
(c) 1971 (d) 1972

9. Dr. Rajendra Singh Paroda has been felicitated with the award—
(a) Padam Shri (b) Padam Bhushan
(c) Padam Vibhushan
(d) Bharat Ratna

10. To be self reliant in agriculture the following growth rate per year is necessary—
(a) 3.0% (b) 3.5%
(c) 4.0% (d) 4.5%

11. On the basis of agroclimatic conditions Pali, Jalore. Sirohi and Jodhpur are included in Zone—
(a) II-B (b) II-A
(c) I-B (d) I-A

12. Which state is devoid of arid zone ?
(a) Punjab (b) Madhya Pradesh
(c) Maharashtra (d) Andhra Pradesh

13. Indian Institute of Soil Science is located at—
(a) Ludhiana (b) Hisar
(c) New Delhi (d) Bhopal

14. The irrigation water reuirement of onion is
(a) 60 cm (b) 50 cm
(c) 40 cm (d) 30 cm

15. Sowing of second crop in between the standard rows of the first crop before its removal is called—
(a) Inter-cropping (b) Multi-copping
(c) Intensive cropping
(d) Relay cropping

16. The cropping system beneficial to prevent soil erosion due to winds is—
(a) Mixed cropping (b) Strip cropping
(c) Relay cropping (d) Multi-cropping

17. The optimum temperature for sugarcane is—
(a) 21-27 °C (b) 14-29 °C
(c) 25-30 °C (d) 28-34 °C

18. Per hectare seed rate of guar is—
(a) 3 kg (b) 6 kg
(c) 9 kg (d) 12 kg

19. The production of oil-seeds in India during 1996-97 was--

(a) 22 million tonnes

(b) 25 million tonnes

(c) 24 million tonnes

(d) 26 million tonnes

20. The layer in the soil profile where material removed from the two overlaying horizones is deposited is called—

(a) A-horizon (b) B-horizon

(c) C-horizon (d) D-horizon

21. The diameter of very fine sand particles is—

(a) Below 0.002 mm (b) 0.05 - 0.002 mm

(c) 0.01 - 0.05 mm (d) 0.05 - 0.10 mm

22. The mineral weathering and clay formation are rapid where the climate is—

(a) Warm and moist (b) Warm and dry

(c) Cold and moist (d) Cold and dry

23. Alkali soils are treated with gypsum to correct the deficiency of—

(a) Sulphur (b) Calcium

(c) Magnesium (d) Zinc

24. Which micronutrient is most deficient in Indo Gangatic alluvium soils ?

(a) Iron (b) Zinc

(c) Copper (d) Manganese

25. Which fertilizer is most beneficial for alkali soils?

(a) Urea

(b) Ammonium sulphate

(c) Calcium ammonium nitrate

(d) Ammonium nitrate

26. The most productive normal soils have pH—

(a) 4-6 (b) 5-7

(c) 6-8 (d) 7-9

27. Which is the most harmful salt in salt affected soils ?

(a) Sodium chloride (b) Sodium sulphate

(c) Sodium bicarbonate

(d) Sodium carbonate

28. Which element is not phytotoxic ?

(a) Boron (b) Lithium

(c) Fluorine (d) Selenium

29. What happens when an saline-alkali soil is leached with water ?

(a) pH and EC both decrease

(b) pH and EC both increase

(c) pH increases and EC decreases

(d) pH decreases and EC increases

30. Which fraction of humus is insoluble both in alkali and alcohol ?

(a) Humin (b) Fluric acid

(c) Alkali acid soluble

(d) Hymatomelanic acid

31. Which of the following is NOT the advantage of using mixed fertilisers ?

(a) Economical (b) Require less care

(c) Reduce salinity

(d) Application is easier

32. Which crop has the maximum nitrogen fixing protential ?

(a) Pigeon pea (b) Soya-bean

(c) Groundnut (d) Guar

33. Rhizobium inoculation is effective only when an active and efficient strain is used under optimum

(a) EC (b) N

(c) Zn (d) PH

34. Maximum area of black soils in India is in

(a) Maharashtra (b) M.P.

(c) U.P. (d) Rajasthan

35. Which of the following is the variety of green gram ?

(a) T-2 (b) T-12

(c) T-49 (d) T-59

36. 'Triticale' is a cross between—

(a) Rye and mustard

(b) Barley and rye

(c) Barley and wheat

(d) Wheat and rye

37. Which country is the biggest producer of fruits ?
(*a*) China (*b*) Brazil
(*c*) India (*d*) Israel

38. What is the place of India in vegetable production
(*a*) First (*b*) Second
(*c*) Third (*d*) Fourth

39. Per capita availability of food grain in India is—
(*a*) 500 g/day (*b*) 450 g/day
(*c*) 400 g/day (*d*) 350 g/day

40. The content of total solids in sugarcane juice is—
(*a*) 20% (*b*) 25%
(*c*) 30% (*d*) 35%

41. Which fruit contains maximum calories of energy ?
(*a*) Dates (*b*) Karonda
(*c*) Custard apple (*d*) Aonla

42. Which fruit tree is sensitive to acidity and salinity ?
(*a*) Phalsa (*b*) Aonla
(*c*) Guava (*d*) Plum

43. Chuhara is an important variety of—
(*a*) Date palm (*b*) Grape
(*c*) Guava (*d*) Ber

44. 'Pusa Kranti' is a variety of—
(*a*) Tomato (*b*) Brinjal
(*c*) Potato (*d*) Ladies finger

45. The percentage of Vitamin *C* is maximum in—
(*a*) Grape fruit (*b*) Pummelo
(*c*) Lemon (*d*) Orange

46. The ideal intercrop in citrus orchard is—
(*a*) Bajra (*b*) Chillies
(*c*) Peas (*d*) Guar

47. Decrease in the rate of respiration in plants will—
(*a*) Decrease water absorption
(*b*) Increase water absorption
(*c*) Decrease transpiration
(*d*) Stop water absorption

48. Chlorosis in plants is caused due to deficiency of—
(*a*) Manganese and sulphur
(*b*) Boron and phosphorus
(*c*) Calcium and oxygen
(*d*) Nitrogen and magnesium

49. Fruit formation is suppressed due to deficiency of—
(*a*) Calcium (*b*) Sulphur
(*c*) Boron (*d*) Magnesium

50. In photosynthesis oxygen is liberated due to—
(*a*) Breakdown of CO_2
(*b*) Breakdown of chlorophyll
(*c*) Reduction of CO_2
(*d*) Oxidation of H_2O

51. The plants which manufacture their own food in presence of light are known as—
(*a*) Photophytic (*b*) Autophytic
(*c*) Photoautotrop (*d*) Phototropic

52. Photosynthesis does NOT take place in fungi due to absence of—
(*a*) Chlorophyll (*b*) Phosphorus
(*c*) Nitrogen (*d*) Potassium

53. Which hormone controls flowering ?
(*a*) Kinins (*b*) Gibberalins
(*c*) Florigen (*d*) Indole acetic acid

54. Energy obtained by a cell from metabolism is stored in the form of—
(*a*) ATP (*b*) DNA
(*c*) ADP (*d*) Pyruvic acid

55. 2,4-D is used as—
(*a*) Fungicide (*b*) Insecticide
(*c*) Pesticide (*d*) Weedicide

56. Application of auxins in higher concentration on plant will—
(*a*) Promote growth (*b*) Cause leaf fall
(*c*) Inhibit growth (*d*) Cause fruit fall

57. Which fruit tree is adversely affected by mealy bug—
(*a*) Mango (*b*) Papaya
(*c*) Banana (*d*) Guava

58. Treatment of bajra seed with Apron-35 S.D. controls the disease—

(*a*) Rust (*b*) Smut

(*c*) Ergot (*d*) Green ear

59. Wilting desease in cumin can be controlled by treatment of seed with—

(*a*) Diathane (*b*) Thiram

(*c*) Bavistin (*d*) Agrosan G.N.

60. Yellow mosaic virus in green gram is caused by—

(*a*) Caterpiller (*b*) White fly

(*c*) Termites (*d*) Jassids

61. The support price of groundnut for 1997-98 is

(*a*) 980 Rs./q (*b*) 930 Rs./q

(*c*) 880 Rs./q (*d*) 830 Rs./q

62. Name the state where agri cards have been issued in October 1997 to the farmers—

(*a*) Tamil Nadu (*b*) Maharashtra

(*c*) Kerala (*d*) Karnataka

63. What is the content of protein in *guar* meal?

(*a*) 21% (*b*) 28%

(*c*) 35% (*d*) 42%

64. Intensive cultivation of trees of fruits, gums, rasins etc. is called

(*a*) Arboriculture (*b*) Aboriculture

(*c*) Silviculture (*d*) Afforestation

65. The scientific study of grasses is called—

(*a*) Agrostology (*b*) Agrology

(*c*) Agroecology (*d*) Agrobiology

66. Albinism in corn is due to—

(*a*) Pathogen (*b*) Lethal gene

(*c*) Deficiency of minerals

(*d*) Deficiency of light

67. Which is the best chemical for inducing polyploidy ?

(*a*) Maleic hydrazide

(*b*) Acridine (*c*) Colchicine

(*d*) Ethylene

68. The first generation progeny hybrid is known as

(*a*) Parents (*b*) FI-plants

(*c*) Pure lines (*d*) Segregates

69. Crop insurance is done to provide against the crop loss due to—

(*a*) Weeds (*b*) Infertility

(*c*) Poor quality seeds

(*d*) Bad weather

70. Desert Development programme was started to develop the following. Which is not correct ?

(*a*) Industry

(*b*) Animal husbandry

(*c*) Horticulture (*d*) Afforestation

71. The method for establishing Mass 'Contacts' is—

(*a*) Farm and home visits

(*b*) National demonstration

(*c*) Bulletin (*d*) Conferences

72. Which is audio-visual aid ?

(*a*) Tape recorder (*b*) Drama

(*c*) Radio (*d*) Black-board

73. The demand for agricultural commodity depends on the following. Which is NOT correct—

(*a*) Price of a commodity

(*b*) Prices of related goods

(*c*) Tastes, habits and fashion

(*d*) Level of education

74. Which of the following is NOT important information in farm budgeting ?

(*a*) Resources (*b*) Cropping pattern

(*c*) Audio-visual aids

(*d*) Farm technology

75. The optimum dose of phosphorus for pulses in arid zone is ?

(*a*) 40 kg/ha (*b*) 30 kg/ha

(*c*) 20 kg/ha (*d*) 10 kg/ha

76. The optimum spacing for mustard plants is—

(*a*) 60 × 45 cm (*b*) 45 × 45 cm

(*c*) 45 × 10 cm (*d*) 30 × 10 cm

77. The soil remains most fertile below the tree—
(a) *Prosopis juliflora* (b) *Acacia tortilis*
(c) *Prosopis cineraria*
(d) *Eucalyptus hybrid*

78. Gum arabic is obtained from
(a) Acacia nilotica (b) Albizia lebbek
(c) Colophospermum mopane
(d) Acacia senegal

79. An important millet used as staple food in South Karnataka is—
(a) Sorghum (b) Ragi
(c) Maize (d) Bajra

80. Mixed farming includes—
(a) Several crop
(b) Vegetable and fruits
(c) Crops and livestock
(d) Trees and grasses

81. Central agricultural university is located in—
(a) Shillong (b) Itanagar
(c) Imphal (d) Gangtok

82. Indira Gandhi Viswa Vidyalaya is located at—
(a) Uttar Pradesh (b) Maharashtra
(c) Gujarat (d) Madhya Pradesh

83. Increase in production has caused 'Yellow revolution
(a) Sugar crops (b) Oilseed
(c) Pulses (d) Fruits

84. Which international institute is located in India—
(a) CIMMYT (b) ICARDA
(c) ICRISAT (d) ILCA

85. The waterl-ogged saline soils can be reclaimed through—
(a) Chemical amendment
(b) Farmyard manure
(c) Fertilizers (d) Biodrainage

86. "Parthenium weed" has been causing loss in crops on an average up to the extent of—
(a) 20% (b) 30%
(c) 40% (d) 50%

87. Which ICAR institute is located in Kasargod?
(a) CPRI (b) CRRI
(c) CPCRI (d) CARI

88. Which culture is possible with mustard farming—
(a) Floriculture (b) Pisciculture
(c) Sericulture (d) Apiculture

89. Which plant is most suitable for stabilising sand-dunes?
(a) Musk-melon (b) Water-melon
(c) Bottle-gound (d) Tumba

90. Total dissolved solids in a water having EC of 5 ds/m will be about—
(a) 3200 ppm (b) 3600 ppm
(c) 4000 ppm (d) 4400 ppm

91. The Sodium Absorption Ratio (SAR) of the soil containing Na, Mg and Ca ions as 100, 30 and 20 meq/L, respectively, will be—
(a) 5 (b) 10
(c) 15 (d) 20

92. The Residual Sodium Carbonate of a water containing Carbonate, Bicarbonate, Calcium and Magnesium ions as 5, 20, 10 meq/L, respectively, will be—
(a) 0 meq/L (b) 5 meq/L
(c) 10 meq/L (d) 20 meq/L

93. Which of the following mutants of Jadia Mothbean has been named Maru Moth-I ?
(a) JMM-259 (b) JMM-211
(c) JMM-60 (d) JMM-DBS-1

94. The variety of cluster-bean which is most suitable for the intercropping with pearl millet is—
(a) HG-75 (b) HG-182
(c) D Safed (d) FS 277

95. The variety of green gram which is suitable for both 'early and late' sown condition is—
(a) RMG 11 (b) K 851
(c) PDM 54 (d) P 7093

96. In limited moisture conditions, promising variety like ICCC-42 of gram may yield
(a) 10-12 q/ha (b) 12-14 q/ha
(c) 14-16 q/ha (d) 16-18 q/ha

97. What is the botanical name of "Yellow Sarson (mustard)"

(*a*) *Brassica juncea* (*b*) *Brassica rapa*

(*c*) *Brassica alba*

(*d*) *Brassica campestris*

98. Optimum plant population per hectare in bajra is—

(*a*) 1,50,000 (*b*) 1,75,000

(*c*) 2,00,000 (*d*) 2,25,000

99. At what concentration Thiram is applied to control severity of Ergot in bajra ?

(*a*) 0.2% (*b*) 0.3%

(*c*) 0.4% (*d*) 0.5%

100. At what rate application of sulphur powder can control powdery mildew disease in green gram ?

(*a*) 10-15 kg/ha (*b*) 15-20 kg/ha

(*c*) 20-25 kg/ha (*d*) 25-30 kg/ha

JRF-1999 (Plant Sciences)

1. Indias's food grain production in 1997-98 was—

(*a*) 191 million tonnes

(*b*) 196 million tonnes

(*c*) 182 million tonnes

(*d*) 190 million tonnes

2. Which of the following cereal, that occupies largest area in India ?

(*a*) Rice (*b*) Wheat

(*c*) Maize (*d*) Bajra

3. Dough stage of wheat refers to—

(*a*) State just before harvesting

(*b*) Change of stage from milking to watering fluid in grain

(*c*) Stage before harvesting

(*d*) None of the above

4. Most critical stage of wheat for irrigation is—

(*a*) Crown root initiation stage

(*b*) Panicle initiation stage

(*c*) Flowering stage

(*d*) Maturity stage

5. Total irrigated area of India in 1997-98 was—

(*a*) 45 million hectares

(*b*) 50 million hectares

(*c*) 55 million hectares

(*d*) 60 million hectares

6. Highest productivity of sugarcane is obtained from_____ in India.

(*a*) Punjab (*b*) Uttar Pradesh

(*c*) Tamil Nadu (*d*) Maharashtra

7. Which of the following country have highest arable land—

(*a*) Australia (*b*) Canada

(*c*) India (*d*) U.S.A.

8. The amino acid associated with water stress—

(*a*) Proline (*b*) Hydroxy proline

(*c*) Lysine

(*c*) None of the above

9. Guava is a ____ type of drifruit.

(*a*) Drupe (*b*) Pome

(*c*) Stone (*d*) Berry

10. Enzyme used while preparation of cheese in dairies—

(*a*) Rennin (*b*) Pepsin

(*c*) Trypsin (*d*) Amylase

11. Centres of origin were given by—

(*a*) N.I. Vavilov (*b*) Aristotle

(*c*) Darwin (*d*) None of these

12. Gene for gene hypothesis was given by-

(*a*) Batson and Punnet

(*b*) Johenson (*c*) Flor

(*d*) Bovari

13. Which of the following method is used for genetic purity?

(*a*) Mass selection

(*b*) Pure line selection

(*c*) Test cross (*d*) Grow-out test

14. Cynobacteria differs from bacteria in having—

(*a*) Photosynthetic activity

(*b*) Big in size (*c*) Non-motile

(*d*) None of the above

15. The pigment found in root nodules of legumes—
(*a*) Leg haemoglobin (*b*) Chlorophyll
(*c*) Haemoglobin (*d*) None of these

16. Seeds which retain viability for a long period of time even when dried to a low moisture content—
(*a*) Recacitrant seed (*b*) Orthodox seed
(*c*) Viable seed (*d*) Dormant seed

17. Brinjal is a—
(*a*) Self pollinated crop
(*b*) Cross pollinated crop
(*c*) Often self pollinated crop
(*d*) Often cross pollinated crop

18. Method used for improvement of self fertilized homozygous plants—
(*a*) Mass selection
(*b*) Pure line selection
(*c*) Bulk method (*d*) Pedigree method

19. Gene pyramiding is—
(*a*) Different lines with different genes for resistance
(*b*) Selection of desirable genes
(*c*) Locating genes
(*d*) None of the above

20. Gene deployment is—
(*a*) Used for recurrent selection
(*b*) Used for mass selection
(*c*) Used for disease resistance
(*d*) None of the above

21. Gene bank are meant for—
(*a*) Conservation of germplasm
(*b*) Exploitation of genes
(*c*) Both (*a*) and (*b*)
(*d*) None of the above

22. First virus isolated was—
(*a*) Potato mosaic virus
(*b*) Yellow mosaic virus
(*c*) TMV
(*d*) None of the above

23. Sugarcane is a —
(*a*) Long day plant (*b*) Short day plant
(*c*) Day neutral plant
(*d*) Intermediate plant

24. Sugarcane is propagated by—
(*a*) Seeds (*b*) Leaves
(*c*) Sets of stem (*d*) None of these

25. Director General of ICAR is—
(*a*) Dr. R.K. Randhawa
(*b*) Dr. A.L. Choudhary
(*c*) Dr. R.S. Paroda (*d*) Dr. J.S. Bhatia

26. National Bureau of Plant Genetic Resources is situated at—
(*a*) Kanpur (*b*) Ludhiana
(*c*) New Delhi (*d*) Pantnagar

27. Laboratory temperature for testing rice seeds should be
(*a*) 20°C (*b*) 25°C
(*c*) 30°C (*d*) 35°C

28. The predatory fungus is—
(*a*) Amanita (*b*) Arthopterix
(*c*) Both (*a*) and (*b*) (*d*) None of these

JRF-1999, (Social Science)

1. Food grain production of India in 1998-99 was—
(*a*) 190 million tonnes
(*b*) 192.6 million tonnes
(*c*) 196 million tonnes
(*d*) 202 million tonnes

2. National Bank for Agriculture and Rural Development was established in—
(*a*) July 1980 (*b*) July 1982
(*c*) July 1978 (*d*) July 1976

3. Training of rural youth for self employment programmes was started in—
(*a*) 15 August, 1979
(*b*) 26 January, 1979
(*c*) 2 Oct., 1979
(*d*) 15 August, 1978

4. Major part of commercial banks were nationalized in the year-

(*a*) 1 Oct. 1987 (*b*) 23 Sept. 1980

(*c*) 19 July 1969 (*d*) 3 Jan. 1972

5. Main objective of implementation of lab to land programme is to given benefits to—

(*a*) Marginal farmers

(*b*) Small farmers

(*c*) Land less farmers

(*d*) Large farmers

6. Food Corporation of India was established in—

(*a*) 1945 (*b*) 1955

(*c*) 1965 (*d*) 1975

7. Reserve Bank of India was established in

(*a*) 1928 (*a*) 1929

(*c*) 1930 (*d*) 1935

8. Marthendum project of extension education was started by—

(*a*) Albert Mayer

(*b*) Spencer Hatch (1928)

(*c*) R.N. Tagore (*d*) M.K. Gandhi

9. R.N. Tagore started Shri Niketan Programme in the year

(*a*) 1921 (*b*) 1920

(*c*) 1923 (*d*) 1924

10. Main objective of training and visit programme was---

(*a*) To provide training to the farmers

(*b*) To provide training and organize demonstration for farmers

(*c*) To conduct research

(*d*) None of the above

11. The extension programme TRYSEM was abolished under the cover of—

(*a*) IRDP (*b*) Antyodaya

(*c*) JRY (*d*) DPAP

12. Report on Panchayati Raj system made by Balwant Rai Metha was submitted in

(*a*) 1954 (*b*) 1955

(*c*) 1956 (*d*) 1957

13. Who gave the model of community development programme ?

(*a*) Balwant Rai Metha Committee

(*b*) Grow More Food Committee

(*c*) 1st Labour Enquiry Committee

(*d*) None of the above

14. All India Coordinated Project for Dry Land Agriculture was started in—

(*a*) 1970-71 (*b*) 1969-70

(*c*) 1971-72 (*d*) 1972-73

15. The word 'Extension' has been taken from ... language.

(*a*) Greek (*b*) Latin

(*c*) French (*d*) English

16. 1st KVK of India was established at

(*a*) Fatehpur (Rajasthan)

(*b*) Navsari (Gujarat)

(*c*) Pondicherry (*d*) Bhopal

17. When there is only one seller of the product in the market, situation is known as—

(*a*) Monopoly (*b*) Duopoly

(*c*) Monosonic (*d*) Monopolistic

18. When there are more than two but not much sellers in the market the situation is known as—

(*a*) Oligopsony (*b*) Oligopoly

(*c*) Duopoly (*d*) Duopsony

19. First KVK established in Rajasthan was at—

(*a*) Badgaon (Udaipur) 1983

(*b*) Fatehpur (Sikar) 1976

(*c*) Tabiji (Ajmer) 1956

(*d*) Argia (Bhilwara) 1975

20. First model of communication was given by--

(*a*) Albert Mayer (*b*) Spencer Hatch

(*c*) Berlo (*d*) R.N. Tagore

21. The government of India has been stressing the need for eliminating ullemployment since the—

(*a*) First plan (*b*) Second plan

(*c*) Third plan (*d*) Fourth plan

22. Indian concil of Agriculture Research was established in—
(*a*) 1935 (*b*) 1928
(*c*) 1929 (*d*) 1921

23. The headquarter of IARI was transferred from Pusa (Bihar) to New Delhi in the year —
(*a*) 1929 (*b*) 1936
(*c*) 1948 (*d*) 1945

24. The mental process through which an individual passes from the first knowledge of an innovation to a decision to adopt this process is known as—
(*a*) Motivation (*b*) Innovation
(*c*) Adoption (*d*) Diffusion

25. A process of spreading new Agricultural knowledge from its originating source to its final users is known as—
(*a*) Diffusion (*b*) Adoption
(*c*) Innovation (*d*) Motivation

26. Training and visit programme was first started by—
(*a*) James Stuart (1967)
(*b*) Smith Lever (1975)
(*c*) Denial Banner (1974)
(*d*) Seman A Nep

27. Who is a father of extension education ?
(*a*) James Stuart
(*b*) J. Paul Leagons
(*c*) August Comte
(*d*) Leonel Fielden

28. Total assets to the total liabilities is known as—
(*a*) Working ratio (*b*) Net capital ratio
(*c*) Current ratio (*d*) None of above

29. Curve showing various combinations of two commodities having equal satisfaction are known as
(*a*) Isoquants
(*b*) Isoproduct curve
(*c*) Indifference curve
(*d*) Iso cost lines

JRF-1999 (Agronomy)

1. Which of the following state having largest area in India ?
(*a*) Uttar Pradesh (*b*) Madhya Pradesh
(*c*) Rajasthan (*d*) Bihar

2. Which of the following state produces highest sugarcane per hectare ?
(*a*) Karnataka (*b*) Tamil Nadu
(*c*) Maharashtra (*d*) Uttar Pradesh

3. Which of the following is not a variety of lentil?
(*a*) Heera (*b*) Mukta
(*c*) Neelam (*d*) Sangam

4. Which of the following is a early variety pigeon pea ?
(*a*) Pusa Agrti (*b*) UPAS-120
(*c*) Innovation (*d*) Motivation

5. Botanical name of Canada thistle is—
(*a*) *Amaranthus arvensis*
(*b*) *Cirsium arvensis*
(*c*) *Tribulus terrestris*
(*d*) *Abulation* spp.

6. Sugarcane crop is a—
(*a*) Short day plant (*b*) Long day plant
(*c*) Day neutral plant
(*d*) Intermediate plant

7. For reclamation of saline and alkaline soils, one must use—
(*a*) Pyrite (*b*) Biotite
(*c*) Muscovite (*d*) None of these

8. Acid equivalent of ammonium phosphate
(*a*) 128 (*b*) 110
(*c*) 96 (*d*) 80

9. What will be the percentage moisture if wet soil is 100 gm and oven dry weight is 80 gm?
(*a*) 20 per cent (*b*) 25 per cent
(*c*) 30 per cent (*d*) 50 per cent

10. One cubic feet is equal to ____ cubic metre.
(*a*) 0.0288 (*b*) 0.0287
(*c*) 0.0289 (*d*) 0.0283

11. Critical stage of wheat at which irrigation is required essentially—
(*a*) CRI stage (*b*) Tillering stage
(*c*) Jointing stage (*d*) Flowering stage

12. If two irrigations are available, they should be applied at
(*a*) CRI and tillering stage
(*b*) CRI and milking stage
(*c*) CRI and flowering stage
(*d*) CRI and jointing stage

13. Toxic alkaloid found in the leaves of sorghum crop is—
(*a*) Papsin (*b*) Dhurin
(*c*) Capsasin (*d*) None of these

14. At what place seeds of bajra will be sown in slopy land—
(*a*) Top of furrow (*b*) Mid of furrow
(*c*) Bottom of furrow
(*d*) Anywhere in the furrow

15. The ratio of runoff water and absorbed water in catchment area is known as—
(*a*) Intensity (*b*) Index
(*c*) Coefficient (*d*) None of these

16. Food grain production of India in 1997-98 was-
(*a*) 180 million tonnes
(*b*) 190 million tonnes
(*c*) 200 million tonnes
(*d*) 220 million tonnes

17. Which of the following crop have highest productivity in the world ?
(*a*) Rice (*b*) Wheat
(*c*) Maize (*d*) Rye

18. Oxygen transfer in pith of xylum is found in
(*a*) Rye (*b*) Triticale
(*c*) Barley (*d*) Wheat

19. If fertility gradient of the land is in two directions, the experimental design choose will be-
(*a*) RBD (*b*) LSD
(*c*) CRD (*d*) Any of the above

20. The correct formula for calculating coefficient of variaton is—
(*a*) $\frac{\text{SD}}{\text{Mean}} \times 100$ (*b*) $\sqrt{\frac{X_1 - X_2}{N}} \times 100$
(*c*) $(\text{SD})^2$ (*d*) None of the above

21. The correct formula for calculating standard error is—
(*a*) $\frac{\sigma}{\sqrt{n}}$ (*b*) $\frac{\sigma^2}{n}$
(*c*) $\frac{\sqrt{n}}{\sigma}$ (*d*) None of the above

22. How much nitrogen will be removed from a wheat crop yielding 50 q/ha ?
(*a*) 60-70 kg/ha (*b*) 90-100 kg/ha
(*c*) 110-120 kg/ha (*d*) 130-140 kg/ha

23. If rainfall is 1200 mm, which land will be classified as dry land, where evaporation is—
(*a*) >50 mm (*b*) 1180 mm
(*c*) 1480 mm (*d*) >1500 mm

24. In waterlogged area which gas is found abundantly ?
(*a*) CO_2 (*b*) CH_4
(*c*) CO (*d*) O_2

25. Weight of top-soil of furrow slice will be—
(*a*) 2.24×10^6 (*b*) 2.25×10^6
(*c*) 2.25×10^4 (*d*) None of the above

26. Adsali sugarcane crop is sown in—
(*a*) March (*b*) July
(*c*) October (*d*) December

27. Iris famine in 1844, was caused due to
(*a*) *Phytopthera infestans*
(*b*) *Alternaria solani*
(*c*) *Macrophomina phaseoli*
(*d*) *Fusarium coerueum*

28. Adsali crop of sugarcane yields—
(*a*) 700 q/ha (*b*) 800 q/ha
(*c*) 900 q/ha (*d*) 1000-1200 q/ha

29. Loose smut of wheat is a—
(*a*) Seed-borne disease
(*b*) Soil-borne disease
(*c*) Air-borne disease (*d*) All of the above

30. Early blight of potato is caused by—
(*a*) *Alternaria solani*
(*b*) *Phytopthera infestans*
(*c*) *Erysiphe polygone*
(*d*) *Fusarium oxysporum*

31. Boll worm is a pest of—
(*a*) Mango (*b*) Cotton
(*c*) Tobacco (*d*) Rice

32. Fruit of guava is known as—
(*a*) Drupe (*b*) Berry
(*c*) Pome (*d*) Hespiridium

33. Fruit of mustard is known as—
(*a*) Berry (*b*) Pome
(*c*) Siliqua (*d*) Hespiridium

34. Flower of banana is called as—
(*a*) Spike (*b*) Corymb
(*c*) Spadix (*d*) Catkin

35. Scientific name of Indian mustard is—
(*a*) *Brassica juncia*
(*b*) *Brassica compestris*
(*c*) *Brassica nigra* (*d*) *Eurca sativa*

36. What is the name of marcony wheat—
(*a*) *Triticum duram*
(*b*) *Triticum destivum*
(*c*) *Triticum dicoccum*
(*d*) *Triticum saphracoccum*

37. Plants grown in drought condition should be-
(*a*) Drought tolerant
(*b*) Drought resistant
(*c*) (*a*) and (*b*) both (*d*) None of the above

38. In dry land of Rajasthan the best combination of sequence cropping is—
(*a*) Rice + Wheat (*b*) Gram + Mustard
(*c*) Maize + Chillies
(*d*) Groundnut + Maize

39. The term "Contingent Cropping" means—
(*a*) Crop grown for protecting from weather conditions
(*b*) Crop grown to achieve more soil fertility
(*c*) Crop grown to maintain soil fertility
(*d*) Crops grown to achieve nutritive production

40. Canopy temperature is measured by—
(*a*) Hygrometer (*b*) Irrometer
(*c*) Infra-red thermometer
(*d*) None of the above

41. Sandy soils having water at wilting point is—
(*a*) 5-10 mm (*b*) 10-20 mm
(*c*) 20-25 mm (*d*) 25-30 mm

42. Photorespiration means—
(*a*) Production of ATP
(*b*) Production of NADH
(*c*) Loss of ATP (*d*) None of above

43. Critical stage of maize crop is—
(*a*) Silking stage (*b*) Tesseling stage
(*c*) Milking stage (*d*) Dough stage

44. Which of the following roots are not permanent ?
(*a*) Seminal roots (*b*) Crown roots
(*c*) Tap roots (*d*) All of the above

45. Debt ratio means—
(*a*) $\frac{\text{Current liabilities}}{\text{Total assets}}$ (*b*) $\frac{\text{Total liabilities}}{\text{Total assets}}$
(*c*) $\frac{\text{Total assets}}{\text{Total liabilities}}$ (*d*) $\frac{\text{Current assets}}{\text{Total liabilities}}$

46. When EC > 4, ESP > 15 and pH = 8; the soil is called as—
(*a*) Saline soil (*b*) Alkaline soil
(*c*) Saline alkaline soil
(*d*) None of the above

47. Alternate wetting and drying in soil, changes—
(*a*) Soil texture (*b*) Soil structure
(*c*) Soil colour (*d*) Soil temperature

48. Which of the following soil have highest water content at wilting coefficient ?
(a) Sandy soils (b) Loam soils
(c) Clay soils (d) Sandy loam soils

49. Exchange of ions from high concentration to low concentration is known as—
(a) Diffusion (b) Osmosis
(c) Transpiration (d) Evaporataion

50. Plants absorb nutrients because potential of shoots is—
(a) Higher than roots
(b) Lower than roots
(c) Equal to roots
(d) None of the above

51. Ratio of volume of air and solids of soil is known as—
(a) Porosity (b) Void ratio
(c) Particle density (d) Bulk density

52. Green ear disease of bajra is suppressed by increasing the concentration of
(a) NO_3 (b) K
(c) P (d) Ca

53. Which of the following is semi-tolerant crop of salinity ?
(a) Beans (b) Mustard
(c) Rape (d) Tomato

54. Sodium (Na) is utilized essentially by the___ crop.
(a) Cabbage (b) Cauliflower
(c) Knol-Khol (d) Okra

55. In acidic soils toxicity is increased due to increasing—
(a) Alluminium (b) Potassium
(c) Sodium (d) Magnesium

56. Effect of higher plants to lower plants is known as—
(a) Allelopathy (b) Criptogamy
(c) Polygamy (d) None of these

57. Chemical formula of zypsum is—
(a) $CaSO_4.7H_2O$ (b) $CaSO_4.2H_2O$
(c) $CaSO_4$ (d) $CaSO_4.3H_2O$

58. Constituent of chlorophyll is—
(a) Nitrogen (b) Manganese
(c) Magnesium (d) Alluminium

59. In onion, smell is occur due to presence of—
(a) Sulphur (b) Phosphorus
(c) Ferrous (d) Calcium

60. Which of the following bacteria converts Ammonical form of nitrogen to nitrate ?
(a) Azotobacter (b) Nitrosomonas
(c) Clostridium (d) None of these

61. How much nitrogen is fixed per hectare by moong crop ?
(a) 20 kg (b) 30 kg
(c) 40 kg (d) 60 kg

62. At what level of atmospheric pressure free flowing of water is available ?
(a) > 1/3 atmospheric pressure
(b) < 1/3 atmospheric pressure
(c) < 2/3 atmospheric pressure
(d) None of the above

63. Light plough used in waterlogged area is—
(a) Mould bold (b) Turn wrest
(c) Deshi plough (d) Punjab plough

64. The erosion in which gully width is > 18 metre, depth 3 metre is classified as—
(a) Very small (b) Small
(c) Medium (d) Deep

65. Ploughing if done deplition of soil moisture be—
(a) 25-50% (b) 10-20%
(c) 12-14% (d) 10-12%

66. How much water is required per hectare for wheat crop ?
(a) 5-10 lac cu sec. (b) 10-15 lac cu sec.
(c) 15-20 lac cu sec
(d) 20-25 lac cu sec.

67. Which crop contributes highest percentage of oil production in India ?
(a) Mustard (b) Groundnut
(c) Soyabean (d) Sun flower

68. What will be seed rate of rape when spacing is 30 × 10 cm ?
(*a*) 5 kg/ha (*b*) 10 kg/ha
(*c*) 15 kg/ha (*d*) 20 kg/ha

69. Which of the following is a non-metallic nutrient ?
(*a*) Calcium (*b*) Chloride
(*c*) Boron (*d*) Magnesium

70. Deficiency symptoms of nitrogen occurs first on—
(*a*) Lower leaves (*b*) Upper leaves
(*c*) Anywhere on the plants
(*d*) None of the above

71. *Acacia catechu* can tolerate the pH up to—
(*a*) 7-8 (*b*) 8-8.5
(*c*) 9-9.9 (*d*) 10-12

72. Cheap nitrogen per unit volume can be obtained through—
(*a*) Calcium ammonium nitrate
(*b*) Urea
(*c*) Ammonium phosphate
(*d*) Ammonium chloride

73. Organic matter can be calculated by multiplying organic carbon—
(*a*) 1.72 (*b*) 1.82
(*c*) 1.92 (*d*) 0.58

74. Which of the following fertilizer provides highest potassium ?
(*a*) K_2SO_4 (*b*) KCl
(*c*) KNO_3 (*d*) K_2SO_4

75. Iron deficiency starts when it is
(*a*) < 55 ppm (*b*) 55-60 ppm
(*c*) 60-65 ppm (*d*) 80 ppm

76. Boron deficiency in fodder crops can be seen when boron is—
(*a*) <0.1% (*b*) 0.1-1%
(*c*) 1-2% (*d*) 2-3%

77. Boron is injurious to plant when irrigational water contains ____ concentration of boron.
(*a*) 1 ppm (*b*) 1-2 ppm
(*c*) 2-3 ppm (*d*) > 3 ppm

78. Per capita land availability is highest in which of the following country of the world ?
(*a*) India (*b*) China
(*c*) Australia (*d*) Canada

79. Binding of water with soil is called as—
(*a*) Adhesion (*b*) Cohesion
(*c*) Suspension (*d*) Dispersion

80. Hardening in sugarcane plants occurs while
(*a*) Increasing sugar content
(*b*) Decreasing bind water
(*c*) Decreasing soluble water
(*d*) None of the above

81. Scientific name of weed namely *Hirankhuri* is—
(*a*) *Convolvulus arvensis*
(*b*) *Cyprus rotendus* (*c*) *Parthinum* spp
(*d*) *Argemon maxicana*

82. Sugarcane is planted in furrows because—
(*a*) It reduces lodging
(*b*) It reduces soil-borne disease
(*c*) It avoid water losses
(*d*) All of the above

83. Which of the following is a metamorphic rock-
(*a*) Granite (*b*) Biotite
(*c*) Marble (*d*) Calcite

84. Out of 143 million hectares cultivated area of India, irrigated area is about—
(*a*) 50 million hectares
(*b*) 80 million hectares
(*c*) 100 million hectares
(*d*) 105 million hectares

85. If spacing of crop is 50 × 20 cm the per hectare plant population will be—
(*a*) 8000 plants (*b*) 10,000 plants
(*c*) 11,000 plants (*d*) 12,000 plants

86. Dough stage of a agricultural crop means—
(*a*) Preharvesting stage
(*b*) Milking to hardening stage
(*c*) After CRI stage
(*d*) None of the above

87. Most harmful insect of rice attacks on parical is—

(*a*) Rice hispa (*b*) Gandhi bug
(*c*) Rice weevil (*d*) None of these

88. Gandhi bug attacks rice at—

(*a*) Pre-flowering stage
(*b*) After-flowering stage
(*c*) CRI stage (*d*) Dough stage

89. How much farmyard mannure is required for obtaining 60 kg of nitrogen for a crop—

(*a*) 100 tonnes (*b*) 120 tonnes
(*c*) 140 tonnes (*d*) 160 tonnes

90. Percentage gur obtained from sugarcane is—

(*a*) 11-12% (*b*) 15%
(*c*) 20% (*d*) 22%

91. Optimum temperature required for growth of sugarcane is—

(*a*) 20-25 °C (*b*) 25-30 °C
(*c*) 30-35 °C (*d*) 10-12 °C

92. For sowing one hectare composite maize, seed requirement will be—

(*a*) 10-12 kg/ha (*b*) 20-25 kg/ha
(*c*) 18-20 kg/ha (*d*) 30-35 kg/ha

93. For planting of one hectare paddy crop, how much area is required for preparing nursery ?

(*a*) 0.05 hectare (*b*) 0.10 hectare
(*c*) 0.105 hectare (*d*) 0.2 hectare

94. Ooze test is helpful for detection of—

(*a*) Bacteria (*b*) Virus
(*c*) Fungus (*d*) All of these

95. A rice disease mostly occurs in cloudy weather and releases H_2S gas is—

(*a*) Khaira disease (*b*) Brown rust
(*c*) Leaf spot (*d*) Damping off

96. Which state of the country have highest area and production of wheat—.

(*a*) Punjab (*b*) Gujarat
(*c*) Uttar Pradesh (*d*) Haryana

97. Origin place of wheat is at—

(*a*) USA (*b*) Russia
(*c*) India (*d*) Mexico

98. Which of the following pulse crop have highest area in the country—

(*a*) Green gram (*b*) Black gram
(*c*) Chick-pea (*d*) Horse gram

99. Which of the following is a variety of chickpea—

(*a*) Pant G-114 (*b*) Pusa Baishakhi
(*c*) C-135 (*d*) Krishna

100. How much nitrogen is fixed by Dhaincha crop-

(*a*) 30 kg/ha (*b*) 50 kg/ha
(*c*) 70 kg/ha (*d*) 130 kg/ha

101. Origin place of Urd is—

(*a*) Burma (*b*) Pakistan
(*c*) India (*d*) Japan

102. Orgin place of berseem is—

(*a*) Burma (*b*) India
(*c*) Egypt (*d*) Japan

103. Scientific name of berseem is—

(*a*) *Medicago sativa*
(*b*) *Trifolium alexandrium*
(*c*) *Trifolium repens*
(*d*) *Trifolium betutata*

104. Photolytic seed is found in—

(*a*) Tobacco (*b*) Groundnut
(*c*) Tomato (*d*) None of these

105. Which of the following crop requires highest water ?

(*a*) Paddy (*b*) Sugarcane
(*c*) Maize (*d*) Potato

106. Critical stage of irrigation for sugarcane is—

(*a*) Germination stage
(*b*) Grand growth stage
(*c*) Formative stage (*d*) Flowering stage

107. For sowing of mid season potato, seed rate required will be—

(*a*) 15-20 q/ha (*b*) 20-25 q/ha
(*c*) 25-30 q/ha (*d*) 30-35 q/ha

108. Who is the Director General of ICAR ?

(*a*) Dr. A.L. Choudhary
(*b*) Dr. R.S. Randhawa
(*c*) Dr. R.S. Paroda (*d*) Dr. J.S. Bhatia

109. Weight of one bale is equal to—
(*a*) 177 kg (*b*) 180 kg
(*c*) 190 kg (*d*) 185 kg

110. In irrigated area crop losses water through—
(*a*) Evaporation
(*b*) Evapotranspiration
(*c*) Leaching (*d*) Erosion

111. Propanil herbicide is used at—
(*a*) Pre-emergence (*b*) Post-emergence
(*c*) At the time of sowing
(*d*) None of the above

112. Hulling percentage of rice is—
(*a*) 60 per cent (*b*) 70 per cent
(*c*) 65 per cent (*d*) 75 per cent

113. In which of the following crop rotation cropping intensity is 150 per cent—
(*a*) Maize, wheat
(*b*) Sugarcane, moong, wheat
(*c*) Bajra, mustard (*d*) Groundnut, wheat

114. Who has discovered the plant hormone Gibberellin?
(*a*) F.W. Went (*b*) Kogl
(*c*) Kurosawa (*d*) Skoog

115. Which of the following substance is used to reduce toxicity ?
(*a*) Reductant (*b*) Safener
(*c*) Absorbent (*d*) None of these

116. For manufacturing of K_2O, which of the following is used ?
(*a*) Kaolinite (*b*) Biotite
(*c*) Gibssite (*d*) Pyrite

117. 'Varuna' variety of mustard is—
(*a*) Indian mustard (*b*) Rape
(*c*) Black sarson (*d*) Brown sarson

118. Plants grown in saline soils are known as—
(*a*) Sciophyte (*b*) Halophyte
(*c*) Bryophyte (*d*) Xerophyte

119. According to Russian classification saline soils are classified as—
(*a*) Solon chacks (*b*) Solontra
(*c*) Solontez (*d*) None of these

120. Which of the following fertilizer provides maximum nitrogen—
(*a*) Urea (*b*) DAP
(*c*) Anhydrous ammonia
(*d*) Ammonium sulphate

121. At what pressure tensiometer is used ?
(*a*) 0-0.8 (*b*) 0.5-1.5
(*c*) 1.5-2.0 (*d*) 2.0-2.20

122. The term "intra-specific" means—
(*a*) Two plants of different varieties
(*b*) Two plants of different breeds
(*c*) One plant of different varieties
(*d*) None of the above

123. Whip tail disease is caused by the deficiency of—
(*a*) Mo (*b*) Mn
(*c*) Mg (*d*) S

124. In case of Zn deficiency in paddy how much zinc sulphate should be applied in one hectare of soil
(*a*) 15 kg (*b*) 20 kg
(*c*) 25 kg (*d*) 30 kg

125. Mean, mode and median are
(*a*) Simple distribution
(*b*) Piosson distribution
(*c*) Normal distribution
(*d*) None of the above

126. Which of the following is not measurement of central tendency—
(*a*) Mean (*b*) Mode
(*c*) Median (*d*) Range

127. Which of the following is not a measure of dispersion ?
(*a*) Mean deviation
(*b*) Stanadard deviation
(*c*) Coefficient of variation
(*d*) Range

128. The value of correlation coefficient lies dispersion—
(*a*) 0 to ∞ (*b*) 1 to 2
(*c*) -1 to $+1$ (*d*) Zero

129. Which of the following have R.Q. (Respiratory Quotient) value less than 1 ?

(a) Protein (b) Organic acid

(c) Carbohydrate (d) Fat

130. The term 'Isotops' mean

(a) Same number of protons

(b) Same number of neutrons

(c) Same number of electrons

(d) None of the above

131. Arid plants have high—

(a) Root to shoot ratio

(b) Root to top ratio

(c) Shoot to root ratio

(d) Top to root ratio

132. A disease occurs at a particular area regularly is known as—

(a) Endemic disease (b) Epidemic disease

(c) Both (a) and (b) (d) None of the above

133. Entry of water from air to soil is known as—

(a) Infilteration

(b) Percolation

(c) Water-logging

(d) None of the these

134. If carrot is grown for the purpose of seed production, it is known as—

(a) Annual (b) Biennial

(c) Perennial (d) None of these

135. Formula of SAR is

(a) $SAR = \dfrac{Na^+}{\sqrt{\dfrac{Ca^{++} + Mg^{++}}{2}}}$

(b) $SAR = \sqrt{\dfrac{Na^+}{Ca^{++} + Mg^{++}}}$

(c) $SAR = \dfrac{Na^+}{\sqrt{Ca^{++} + Mg^{++}}}$

(d) None of the above

136. In light soil fertilizer is applied—

(a) With seeds (b) Below seeds

(c) Spreading with seeds

(d) Top dressing

137. In which form urea provides nitrogen ?

(a) Ammonical form (b) Nitrate form

(c) Nitrite form (d) Amide form

138. Which of the following is a fruit ripening substance ?

(a) Acetylene (b) Ethane

(c) Ethylene (d) Methane

139. Which of the following cereal crop have highest area in India ?

(a) Wheat (b) Rice

(c) Groundnut (d) Gram

140. Which of the following alkaloid is found in tea ?

(a) Thelobrozen (b) Tasnine

(c) Cafine (d) Nicotine

141. How many sets are required for sowing of one hectare sugarcane ?

(a) 30,000 (b) 35,000

(c) 40,000 (d) 45,000

142. Weedicide Fluchloralin is applied at—

(a) Pre-planting (b) Pre-emergence

(c) Post-emergence (d) None of the above

143. Potassium is obtained through—

(a) Silkinite (b) Albite

(c) Biotite (d) None of these

144. Temporary roots found in maize is known as—

(a) Seminal roots (b) Crown roots

(c) Tap roots (d) None of these

145. Which of the following nutrient is absorbed in positive as well as negative form

(a) N (b) P

(c) Ca (d) K

146. Which of the following nutrient absorbed in compound form ?

(a) N (b) Ca

(c) Zn (d) K

Match the followings

147. **Fertilizers** — **% N**

(a) Anhydrous ammonia → 82
(b) Ammonium phosphate → 33
(c) Di ammonium phosphate → 20
(d) Ammonium chloride → 25
(e) Calcium ammonium nitrate → 12·5

148. **Herbicides** — **Trade names**

(a) Nitrofan → TOK-E-25
(b) Propanil → Stomp-F 34
(c) Fluchloralin → Basalin
(d) Isoproturon → Arelon-wp

149. **Particulars** — **Measuring instruments**

(a) Hygroscopic humidity → Irrometer
(b) Canopy temperature → Infra-red thermometer
(c) Atmospheric pressure → Barometer

150. **Weeds** — **Botanical names**

(a) Akra → *Vicia sativa*
(b) Hirankhuri → *Convolvulus arvensis*
(c) Kans → *Saccharum spontaneum*
(d) Motha → *Cyprus rotandus*
(e) Dub → *Cynodon dactylon*

151. **Scientist** — **Discovery**

(a) Mular Mutation through X-rays
(b) Disy → Vita-K
(c) Buckner → Enzymes
(d) Eujkman → Vita-B
(e) Duve → Lysosome

152. **Chemical** — **Use**

(a) Sodic soil → Illite
(b) Herbicide → 2.4-D
(c) Fruit repening → Etheline
(d) Nitrogen inhibitor → N - serve

153. **Soils** — **State**

(a) Red soil → Maharashtra
(b) Black soil → Kerala
(c) Laterite soil → Tamil Nadu
(d) Decan soil → U.P.
(e) Sandy soil → Rajasthan

154. **Weedicide** — **Crops**

(a) Atrazine → Maize
(b) Isoproturon → Wheat
(c) Stomp → Pea
(d) TOK-E-25 → Rice

155. **Origin** — **Crop**

(a) S. America → Potato
(b) Africa → Sorghum
(c) Asia minor → Soya-bean
(d) India → Wheat
(e) China → Rice

JRF - 1999 (Entomology)

1. The contribution of agriculture in national Income is—
(a) 30 % (b) 33%
(c) 28 % (d) 37 %

2. How many agro-climatic zones are there in India?
(a) 12 (b) 13
(c) 14 (d) 15

3. ICRISAT is situated at—
(a) Hyderabad (b) USA
(c) Mexico (d) Assam

4. National Research Centre of Integrated pest management is situated at—
(a) Kerala (b) U.P.
(c) Haryana (d) New Delhi

5. The total rainfall obtained from South- West monsoon in India is—
(*a*) 20-30% (*b*) 30-40%
(*c*) 40-45% (*d*) 75-85%

6. IRDP was established in—
(*a*) 2 October, 1989 (*b*) 2 October, 1980
(*c*) 2 October, 1979 (*d*) 2 October, 1981

7. "Durgamani" is the variety of—
(*a*) Sarson (*b*) Jowar
(*c*) Taramira (*d*) Coriander

8. DIP act/Quarantine Law was initiated in—
(*a*) 1914 (*b*) 1913
(*c*) 1912 (*d*) 1907

9. The disease which occurs occasionally but in very severe form is called—
(*a*) Endemic (*b*) Epidemic
(*c*) Sporadic (*d*) Pandemic

10. Systemic fungicide among the following is—
(*a*) Oxycarboxin (*b*) E.M.C.
(*c*) P.M.C. (*d*) Tetracydine

11. The casual organism of tungro disease of rice is—
(*a*) Bacteria (*b*) Fungi
(*c*) Virus (*d*) Nematode

12. Copper fungicide among the following is
(*a*) Cereson (*b*) Agallol
(*c*) Benomil (*d*) Blitox-50

13. Dagger nematode is—
(*a*) Xiphinemna (*b*) Trichodorus
(*c*) Longidorus (*d*) Anguina

14. Citrus nematode is—
(*a*) Dictylenchus (*b*) Heterodera
(*c*) Tylenculus (*d*) Longidorus

15. White tip disease of nematode is found in—
(*a*) Pearl millet (*b*) Sorghum
(*c*) Maize (*d*) Rice

16. Casual organism of ufra disease of rice is—
(*a*) *Dictylenchus angustus*
(*b*) *Heterodera rostreii*
(*c*) *Longidora* spp. (*d*) *Anguina* spp.

17. Which of the following is not a soil fumigant—
(*a*) D.D. Mixture (*b*) Nemagon
(*c*) Zireb (*d*) Vapam

18. The variety of tomato resistant to nematode is—
(*a*) S.I.-120 (*b*) Rajkiran
(*c*) Pusa Rubi (*d*) Azad

19. Which nematode is present in Banana—
(*a*) *Rodophilus* spp. (*b*) *Meloydigyne*
(*c*) *Trychodorus* (*d*) *Tylenchulus*

20. Molya disease was discovered by—
(*a*) Van (*b*) Taylor
(*c*) Vasudeva (*d*) Dastur

21. Word "Entomology" belongs to which language—
(*a*) Greek (*b*) Latin
(*c*) French (*d*) None of these

22. Which insect have complete metamorphosis-
(*a*) Bugs (*b*) Cricket
(*c*) Aphids (*d*) Butterflies

23. Sawfly belongs to the group—
(*a*) Hymenoptera (*b*) Coleoptera
(*c*) Lepidoptera (*d*) Isoptera

24. Chlorinated hydro-carbon is—
(*a*) Rogor (*b*) B.H.C.
(*c*) Phorate (*d*) Vitavax

25. Systemic fungicide among the following is—
(*a*) D.D.T. (*b*) B.H.C.
(*c*) Endosulphan (*d*) Gamoxen

26. Source of rotenon pesticide is—
(*a*) Darris elyptica (*b*) Nicotiana sp.
(*c*) Neem (*d*) Rynia spp.

27. Zoological name of sawfly is—
(*a*) Athelia proxima
(*b*) Virachda isocrates
(*c*) Aphis spp. (*d*) Benesia tabaci

28. Spilosoma obliqua is—
(*a*) Bihar hairy caterpillar
(*b*) Agrotis sp. (*c*) Chilo partillus
(*d*) Lipaphis irisici

29. *Atherigona soctata* is—
(*a*) Stem borer (*b*) Shootfly
(*c*) Army worm (*d*) Cut worm

30. Earis vitella is—
(*a*) Cotton whitefly
(*b*) Spotted boll worm
(*c*) Fruit borer (*d*) Aphids

31. Mango mealy bug is —
(*a*) *Drosicha* sp. (*b*) *Apsilla* sp.
(*c*) *Virachola* sp. (*d*) None of the above

32. *Virachola isocrates* is—
(*a*) Lemon butterfly
(*b*) Sorghum shootfly
(*c*) Anar butterfly
(*d*) Papaya butterfly

33. *Corcyra cephalonica* is—
(*a*) Rye moth (*b*) Grain borer
(*c*) Flour beetle (*d*) Pulse beetle

34. Field rat among the following is—
(*a*) *Mus musculus*
(*b*) *Rattus-rattus*
(*c*) *Rattus-meltoda*
(*d*) None of the above

35. Of which insect scientific name is *Rophalosyma media*—
(*a*) Aphid (*b*) Rat
(*c*) Sawfly (*d*) Grain beetle

36. Where does fruit fly lays its pupa ?
(*a*) In the soil
(*b*) In the pulp of fruit
(*c*) In the sheath of fruit
(*d*) On the leaves of the tree

37. The larvae which do not have locomotion apparatus is—
(*a*) Grub (*b*) Nymph
(*c*) Caterpillar (*d*) Maggot

38. To which group does the lac insect belongs?
(*a*) Homoptera (*b*) Orthoptera
(*c*) Diptera (*d*) Isoptera

39. Extension education is—
(*a*) Formal (*b*) Informal
(*c*) Non-formal (*d*) None of these

40. D.D.T. was first of all made by the scientist :
(*a*) Faraday (*b*) Zedler
(*c*) Hymen (*d*) D. Herelle

41. Central Honey Bee Research Station is situated at—
(*a*) Coimbatore (*b*) Hyderabad
(*c*) Pune (*d*) Haryana

42. Thé maximum amount of Sugar in honey is —
(*a*) 73% (*b*) 76%
(*c*) 62% (*d*) 69%

43. *Apis mellifica* is called as—
(*a*) Indian bee (*b*) European bee
(*c*) Little bee (*d*) Danar bee

44. The disease Acariopsis woodi R. spreads by
(*a*) Virus (*b*) Nematode
(*c*) Mite (*d*) Housefly

45. Foul brood disease of honey bee is caused due to—
(*a*) Fungi (*b*) Virus
(*c*) Nematode (*d*) Bacteria

46. Central Silk Research Station is situated at—
(*a*) West Bengal (*b*) U.P.
(*c*) Rajasthan (*d*) Maharashtra

47. Which of the following state ranks first in silk production—
(*a*) Kashmir (*b*) Karnataka
(*c*) Rajasthan (*d*) U.P.

48. The origin place of *Attacus ricini* is—
(*a*) Assam (*b*) Karnataka
(*c*) Kashmir (*d*) U.P.

49. Scientific name of green silkworm is—
(*a*) *Anthcrea assmensis*
(*b*) *Anthcraea paphial*
(*c*) *Attacus ricini* (*d*) *A. royley*

50. Vermiculture is associated with—
(*a*) Earthworm (*b*) Prawn
(*c*) Housefly (*d*) Lac insect

51. Lac Research Station is situated at
(*a*) W. Bengal (*b*) Bihar
(*c*) Bangalore (*d*) Lucknow

52. How much resin is found in lac insect—
(*a*) 52.1% (*b*) 59.2%
(*c*) 68% (*d*) 73.2%

53. Standard act of arithmetic mean is—
(*a*) $\frac{S.D}{\sqrt{n}}$ (*b*) $\frac{\sqrt{n}}{SD}$
(*c*) $\frac{SD}{n}$ (*d*) $\frac{SD}{n^2}$

54. The synonym of aldicarb is—
(*a*) Sevin (*b*) Rogor
(*c*) Carboryl (*d*) Temic

55. The insecticidal property in DDT was first of all discovered by the scientist—
(*a*) Paul Muller (*b*) D. Muller
(*c*) Faraday (*d*) Zidler

56. Carnivorous insect among the following is—
(*a*) Praying mantis (*b*) Cricket
(*c*) Cockroach (*d*) Honey bee

57. The I.L.R.I. was organised in—
(*a*) 1940 (*b*) 1925
(*c*) 1921 (*d*) 1920

58. At which humidity percentage should the cereal grains be stored ?
(*a*) 5-6% (*b*) 10-15%
(*c*) 8-10% (*d*) 7-9%

59. The per cent of CCl_4 and chlorine in EDB should be in the ratio of
(*a*) 1:3 (*b*) 3:1
(*c*) 2:1 (*d*) 1:2

60. Join each other—
(*a*) Spongy mouth parts (*a*) Housefly
(*b*) Piercing mouth parts (*b*) Mosquito
(*c*) Sucking mouth parts (*c*) Bug
(*d*) Siphoning mouth parts (*d*) Butterfly

61. Which insect have spongy mouth parts
(*a*) Housefly (*b*) Bugs
(*c*) Butterfly (*d*) Termite

62. Which type of mouth parts does butterfly have—
(*a*) Siphoning type
(*b*) Spongy type
(*c*) Bitting and piercing type
(*d*) Lapping type

JRF - 1999 (Biotechnology)

1. Endoplasmic Reticulum was discovered by—
(*a*) Benda (*b*) Portev
(*c*) Altmann (*d*) Park *et. al.*

2. What is phagocytosis ?
The process by which the cell takes in the solid food particles.

3. What is endo-osmosis ?
The process by which the solvent particles move from medium of high concentration to lower concentration through semi-permeable membrane.

4. What is endo-citosis ?
The process by which the cell takes in the solid food particles.

5. Cell lysis is brought about by the organelle
(*a*) Lysosome (*b*) Ribosome
(*c*) Centriole (*d*) Centromere

6. When does DNA replication occurs in eukaryotes and prokaryotes
(*a*) Before cell division
(*b*) After cell division
(*c*) During cell division
(*d*) None of the above

7. The rate of DNA replication is faster in-
(*a*) Eukaryotes (*b*) Prokaryotes
(*c*) Both (*a*) and (*b*) (*d*) None of these

8. Who discovered the cell ?
(*a*) Robert Brown (*b*) Robert Hook
(*c*) Watson (*d*) Strasburger

9. Nucleosome model was given by—
(*a*) Corberg & Thomas
(*b*) Ochawa (*c*) Batson
(*d*) Bulter E.J.

10. In which plant number of chromosome are lowest --

(*a*) Tradescantia (*b*) Haplopappus

(*c*) Pea (*d*) Onion

11. If $T = 15\%$ what will be value of C

(*a*) 35 (*b*) 45

(*c*) 55 (*d*) 25

12. The value of $A + T/G + C = 0.7$ in---

(*a*) Prokaryotes (*b*) Eukaryotes

(*c*) Algae (*d*) Fungi

13. The histones in chromosomes are of-

(*a*) Two types (*b*) Three types

(*c*) Four types (*d*) Five types

14. The nucleosome cone has base pairs

(*a*) 140 (*b*) 142

(*c*) 144 (*d*) 146

15. t-RNA attacks to—

(*a*) Enzyme (*b*) Amino acids

(*c*) DNA (*d*) Chromosome

16. Edible organism is—

(*a*) Fungi (*b*) Bacteria

(*c*) Algae (*d*) Yeast

17. In-vitro DNA synthesis discovered by-

(*a*) Kornberg (*b*) Watson

(*c*) Porter (*d*) Fleming

18. Casual organism of Irish famine—

(*a*) *Alternaria solani* (*b*) *Ustilago nuda*

(*c*) *Phytophora infestans*

(*d*) *Rhijoctonia* spp

19. Agriculture production of food grain in year 1998-99 was

(*a*) 180 mt (*b*) 190 mt

(*c*) 200 mt (*d*) 210 mt

20. **Duplication**— Refers to replication. It is a semi- conservative process in which each of two double helics of DNA formed from parental double strand have one old and new strand. It means during *S* phase of interphase.

21. **Plasmids**— Is a small circular DNA present in bacterial cytoplasm and is also known as extrachromosomal genetic material.

22. **Episome**— Sometimes fertility genes are present on plasmid also related as sex pilli. These are episomes.

23. **F^+**— In bacteria, the cell which transfers genetic material into another cell is known as For male cell or donor.

24. **F^-**—The cell which receives the genetic material from donor is called F- or female or recipient cell.

25. **HFr**— High frequency recombination— When episome attaches with genophore of F^+ bacteria, it is called HFr.

26. **F-Factor**— In bacteria, fertility factor which converts a cell into male cells with F factors have characteristic F-pilli.

27. **Frame Shift Mutation**— Either increase or decrease of nitrogenous base in the structure of DNA or m-RNA is called frame shift mutation. Acridine and proflavin induces this mutation.

28. **Transition**— Type or gene mutation in which one purine (AGRICULTURE) changes with the other pyrimidine (CT).

29. **Conjugation**— It refers to the unidirectional transfer of DNA from F^+ bacterial cell or donor cell to F^- or recipient cell through a specialized intercellular connection or conjugation tube.

30. **Transcription**— Protein synthesis from m-RNA is known as Transcription. The m-RNA formed during transcription moves out of nucleus and glides on surface of ribosome and participate in protein synthesis.

31. **Recon**— The unit of recombination; is present in nucleotide; the part of gene within which recombination takes place.

32. **Muton**— The unit of mutation; the smallest unit of a gene capable of undergoing mutation; represented by one nucleotide.

33. **Cistron**— A segment of DNA which codes for one polypeptide; the unit of function; identified by cis-trans or complementation test; usually, mutants within a cistron, do not show complementation; generally accepted as a synonym for gene.

34. **Heterosis**— The superiority of a heterozygote over both the concerned homozygotes in respsct of one or more characters, in practice; the superiority of F_1 over both its parents.

35. **Hemizygous**—A diploid organism having only one copy of a gene in place of the normal two, *e.g.* in case of sex linkage and in deletion heterozygotes.

36. **Gene Bank**— Large collection of germplasm representing material from various parts ofthe world.

37. **Gene pool**— Sum total of genes present in a Mendelian/Panmictic (random mating) population.

38. **Genome**— Genome consists of all the chromosomes of a diploid species that are distinct from each other with respect to their gene content and often morphology. Members of a genesome do not pair.

39. **Nucleosome**— The bead like structure of chromatin fibres; each composed of a histone octamer and 146 base pairs of DNA.

(Model Question Paper) Civil Services Examinations

1. Which of the following structure helps the fungi to survive under adverse conditions:
   1. Zoospores
   2. Chlamydospores
   3. Sclerotia
   4. Conidiospo res

   Select the correct answer using the codes given below:

   (*a*) 3 and 4 (*b*) 2 and 4
   (*c*) 1, 2 and 3 (*d*) 2 and 3

2. Modification of floral parts into leafy structures by pathogenic infection is called
   (*a*) Hyperplasia
   (*b*) Hypertrophy
   (*c*) Phyllody
   (*d*) Witch broom

3. Match **List I** (Diseases) with **List II** (Disease incitants) and select the correct answer using the codes given below the lists:

	List I		**List II**
A.	Kernel bunt of wheat	1.	*Sclerospora graminicola*
B.	Late blight of potato	2.	*Tilletia indica*
C.	Flax rust	3.	*Phytophthora infestans*
D	Downy mildew of bajra	4.	*Melamspora lini*

CODES

	A	B	C	D
(*a*)	3	2	4	1
(*b*)	2	3	4	1
(*c*)	2	3	1	4
(*d*)	3	2	1	4

4. Consider the following statements "Gundhi bug" causes damage to paddy crop by—
   1. sucking juice from the developing grains
   2. sucking juice from the leaves
   3. sucking juice from the culm
   4. affecting the quality and quantity of grain

   Of these statements
   (*a*) 2 and 4 are correct
   (*b*) 1, 3 and 4 are correct
   (*c*) 2 alone is correct
   (*d*) 1 alone is correct

5. Two of the more important diseases of potato whose spread in India has been successfully restricted through plant quarantine measures include—
   (*a*) Brown rot and late blight
   (*b*) Wart and golden nematode
   (*c*) Ring rot and mosaic
   (*d*) Bacterial wilt and charcoal rot

6. Severe incidence of red hairy caterpillar occurs at which one of the following sets of conditions-
(*a*) High temperature and high soil moisture
(*b*) High temperature and low soil moisture
(*c*) Low temperature and high soil moisture
(*d*) Low temperature and low soil moisture

7. Match **List I** with **List II** and select the correct answer using the codes given below the lists

List I (Pathogenic genera of fungi)	**List II (Symptoms and effects)**
A. Cystopus	1. Red rust
B. Protomyces	2. Green ear
C. Sclerospora	3. White rust
D. Taphrina	4. Leaf curl
	5. Stem gall

CODES

	A	B	C	D
(*a*)	1	5	2	4
(*b*)	3	5	4	1
(*c*)	4	1	2	3
(*d*)	3	5	2	4

8. Consider the following stages-
(*a*) Spore germination
(*b*) Embryo-infection
(*c*) Spore on flower stigma
(*d*) Infected grains
The correct sequence of these stages in the development of loose smut diseases in wheat is—
(*a*) 3, 1, 4, 2 (*b*) 1, 3, 4, 2
(c) 1, 3, 2, 4 (*d*) 3, 1, 2, 4

9. Which one of the following is the vector for yellow vein mosaic of Bhindi (okra)?
(*a*) Brown plant hopper
(*b*) Green plant hopper
(*c*) Aphids (*d*) White flies

10. Consider the following steps
1. Sampling 2. Surveillance
3. Control strategy
The correct sequence of these steps in the management of pests and diseases is—
(*a*) 1, 2, 3 (*b*) 2, 1, 3
(c) 2, 3, 1 (*d*) 1, 3, 2

11. Which one of the following statements correctly defines systematic insecticide ?
(*a*) An insecticide which enters into the system of insects
(*b*) An insecticide which is absorbed in the plant system
(c) An insecticide which is absorbed and translocated in the system of the plant
(*d*) An insecticide that possesses translammar activity

12. Which one of the following groups consists of systemic fungicides ?
(*a*) Bavistin, Topsin-M, Captan
(*b*) Plantvax, Emisan, Blitox
(c) Vitavax, Bavistin, Calixin
(*d*) Ziram, Plantvax, Blitox

13. Bordeaux mixture was discovered by P.A. Millardet of France during the year, 1882 following his chance observation of a farmer's practice for protection against
(*a*) Plasmopara viticola kon grapevine
(*b*) Uncinula necator on grapevine
(c) Podosphaera leucotricha on apple
(*d*) Venturia inequalis on apple

14. Which one of the following sprayers will cause more loss of spray droplets by drift?
(*a*) Low volume sprayer
(*b*) High volume sprayer
(c) Ultra low volume sprayer (*d*) Duster

15. Which of the following would determine the quantity of spray needed per hectare while using manually operated knapsack sprayers ?
1. Swath of spray
2. Walking speed of the person doing the spraying
3. Caliberation sprayer 4. Type of nozzle

Select the correct answer using the codes given below:

(*a*) 1, 2 and 4 (*b*) 1, 2 and 3

(*c*) 1, 3 and 4 (*d*) 2, 3 and 4

16. Which of the following safeguards are necessary for a proper operation and maintenance of plant protection equipment ?

1. Lubrication should be followed faithfully using the specified lubricant.
2. A multigrade motor oil should not be mixed with petrol as a fuel for 2-stroke engine.
3. The oil and fuel should be poured separately into the tank.

Select the correct answer using the codes given below :

CODES

(*a*) 2 and 3 (*b*) 1 and 2

(*c*) 1 and 3 (*d*) 1, 2 and 3

17. Which one of the following is to be suggested in case of failure of a manually operated sprayer to retain pressure ?

(*a*) Tightening of loose nuts and clamps and replacement of gaskets

(*b*) Tightening of the lid of the tank, replace ment of the gasket, if necessary

(*c*) Opening the nozzle and cleaing its various parts especially the orifice

(*d*) Straightening the plunger rod if found bent

18. While adopting a new innovation in agriculture, farmers go through the following four stages in the mental process:

1. Awareness 2. Interest

3. Action 4. Satisfaction

The correct sequence of these four stages is

(*a*) 1, 2, 4, 3 (*b*) 2, 1, 3, 4

(*c*) 1, 2, 3, 4 (*d*) 2, 1, 4, 3

19. The fruits of research and development findings could reach the poorest of the poor through

(*a*) Research personnel themselves

(*b*) NGO's

(*c*) A strong and devoted extension agency

(*d*) Agricultural universities and colleges

20. In a communication process, information flows through the following four elements:

1. Message 2. Communicator

3. Channel 4. Audience

The correct sequence of the flow of information is

(*a*) 2, 3, 1, 4 (*b*) 3, 2, 1, 4

(*c*) 1, 3, 2, 4 (*d*) 1, 2, 3, 4

21. For providing inputs like quality seeds, fertilizers and pesticides, the agency that is present at the Village Panchayat Samiti level is

(*a*) NABARD (*b*) Nationalised banks

(*c*) Cooperative societies

(*d*) Insurance companies

Directions:

The following fifteen items consist of two statements, one labelled as 'Assertion A' and the other labelled us 'reason *R*'. You are to examine these two statements carefully and decide if the Assertion *A* and Reason *R* are individually true and if so, whether the reason is a correct explanation of the Assertion. Select your answers to these items using the codes given below and mark your answer sheet accordingly

CODES

(*a*) Both *A* and *R* are true and *R* is the correct explanation of *A*

(*b*) Both *A* and *R* are true but *R* is NOT a correct explanation of *A*

(*c*) *A* is true but *R* is false

(*d*) *A* is false but *R* is true

22. Assertion (*A*): In India, area under wheat is more than what is necessary in a normal year, while area under oilseeds and pulses is still below the required level.

Reason (*R*): Area under pulses and oil-seeds have been shifted over to the production of wheat in recent years on account of higher prices and improved productivity potential of high yielding variety wheat seeds.

23. Assertion (*A*): Alkali soils need more puddling for the cultivation of rice when compared to normal soils.

Reason (*R*): Alkali soils have more exchangeable sodium on the exchange complex than the normal soil.

24. Assertion (*A*): Organic manures with wider C/N ratio when added to the soil decompose rapidly in soil and increase the plant available nitrogen.

Reason (*R*): Organic acids produced during the decomposition of organic manures.

25. Assertion (*A*): The complex and mixed fertilizers with the same nutrient contents are equally effective in crop production.

Reason (*R*): The complex fertilizers are granular, free flowing and easy to apply whereas fertilizer mixtures are physical blends of two or more straight fertilizers mechanically mixed.

26. Assertion (*A*): When light falls on guard cells of stomata, their osmetic potentials become more negative and they open.

Reason (*R*): Ligh causes an increase in the transport of k^+ ions from the accessory cells to the guard cells.

27. Assertion (*A*): In zinc deficient plants concentration of indole-acetic acid in the tissues drops well before visible symptoms appear.

Reason (*R*): Zinc is essential for the synthesis of tryptophan.

28. Assertion (*A*): Respiratory quotient for respiration of material rich in carbohydrates is usually about 1.

Reason (*R*): Carbohydrate molecules have the same number of carbon atoms as the oxygen atoms.

29. Assertion (*A*): Doubling the chromosomes of F_1 of an interspecific cross leads to fertility.

Reason (*R*): By doubling the chromosomes F_1 of an interspecific hybrid, each and every chromosome gets its homologue to form bivalent.

30. Assertion (*A*): $CoCl_2$ and $NiCl_2$ promote the vase life of chrysanthemum flowers

Reason (*R*): $CoCl_2$ and $NiCl_2$ act as antiethylene compounds.

31. Assertion (*A*): Self-incompatibility is a useful tool for the development of hybrid varieties in several crop species.

Reason (*R*): Production and maintenance of inbred lines is tedious and cosly in the case of self-incompatible species.

32. Assertion (*A*): Cultivation of maize is NOT recommended as inter-crop in a mango orchard.

Reason (*R*): Growth of maize remain spoor in a mango orchard.

33. Assertion (*A*): Vitamin C requirement of human body has to be met by exogenious sources such as fruit and vegetables.

Reason (*R*) : Vitamin *C* can neither synthesised nor stored in the human body.

34. Assertion (*R*) : Seed treatment with chlor pyriphos is done in groundnut.

Reason (*R*) : It helps in controlling white grub.

35. Assertion (*A*) : Integrated pest management is the best way of controlling diseases and pests of crop plants.

Reason (*R*) : This ensures that all the insects and pathogens are killed effectively.

36. Assertion (*A*) : Survey and surveillance is the backbone of integrated pest control.

Reason (*R*) : Integrated pest control can be achieved by integrating chemical, biological, cultural, regulatory and mechanical methods of pest control.

37. "Mechanisation in agriculture causes displacement of agricultural labour." Which one of the following statement DOES NOT fully support the viewpoint ?

(*a*) There is a greater outflow of agricultural labourers of the cities in search of jobs.

(*b*) The total number of man-days utilized, in fact increases after mechnisation.

(*c*) There is a tendency among agricultural labour to improve their skills.

(*d*) The marginal productivity of labour is declining

38. Consider the following statements :

An 'operational holding' is one which includes all lands used wholly or partially for agricultural production. The improvement in the size of operational holdings has largely been due to :

1. extension of irrigation facilities
2. land reclamation schemes
3. consolidation of holdings

Of these statements—

(*a*) 1 2 and 3 are correct

(*b*) 1 and 3 are correct

(*c*) 2 and 3 are correct

(*d*) 1 and 2 are correct

39. In terms of the area sown, which of the following crops occupies the most important position in India ?

(*a*) Jute (*b*) Cotton

(*c*) Mustard (*d*) Groundnut

40. Among the states growing cotton as rainfed crop, the one which obtains the highest yield in the country is

(*a*) Maharashtra (*b*) Haryana

(*c*) Gujarat (*d*) Punjab

41. North-east monsoon causes rainfall in the south-eastern part of the peninsular India during

(*a*) November-December

(*b*) February-March

(*c*) September-October

(*d*) May-June

42. Which of the following pairs of states dominates at present in pigeon pea cultivation in India,on account of favourable agro-climatic conditions ?

(*a*) Bihar and Haryana

(*b*) Uttar Pradesh and Maharashtra

(*c*) Madhya Pradesh and Rajasthan

(*d*) Karnataka and Andhra Pradesh

43. When instability of prices of a commodity is explained by the Cob-Webb model, which of the following conditions pertaining to the demand and supply functions should hold true?

1. The intercept of the demand function should be greater than the intercept of supply function
2. The intercept of the supply function should be greater than the slope of the supply function.
3. The slope of the demand function should be greater than the slope of the supply function
4. The slope of the supply function should be greater than the slope of the demand function.

Select the correct answer using the codes given below :

(*a*) 2 and 4 (*b*) 2 and 3

(*c*) 1 and 4 (*d*) 1 and 2

44. The following table relates to the productivity of crops for given bundle of resources in a unit area of land :

	USA	INDIA
Wheat	80	30
Rice	60	30

1. USA has absolute advantage in the production of wheat and rice.
2. USA has comparative advantage in the production of both rice and wheat
3. USA has comparative advantage in the production of rice and India in the production of wheat
4. USA has comparative advantage in the production of wheat and India in the production of rice

Based on the data given in the table which of the above statements are FALSE ?

(*a*) 1, 2 and 4 (*b*) 1 and 3

(*c*) 2 and 3 (*d*) 1 and 4

45. Match **List I** with **List II** and select the correct answer using the codes given below the lists

	List I		List II
A.	Minimum support price	1.	Farmer
B.	Registered finance	2.	Govt. of India
C.	Price taker	3.	NABARD
D.	Transportation	4.	Time utility
E.	Storage	5.	Space utility

CODES

	A	B	C	D	E
(*a*)	2	3	1	5	4
(*b*)	2	3	5	1	4
(*c*)	3	2	1	4	5
(*d*)	3	2	5	1	4

46. Which of the following principles will be applicable when a farmer is faced with the problem of purchase of heifers verses milch cows on his dairy farm

(*a*) Cost principle

(*b*) Opportunity cost principle

(*c*) Comparative advantage principle

(*d*) Time comparison principle

47. Match **List I** (Decision) with **List II** (Techniques) select the correct answer using the codes given below the lists :

List I		List II
(*A*) Capital investment	1.	Least cost combination
(*B*) Economically optimum level of resource use	2.	Payback period
(*C*) Economics of farm size	3.	Linear programming
(*D*) Optimum enter prise ombination under constraining resources	4.	Average cost curve

CODES

	A	B	C	D
(*a*)	2	1	3	4
(*b*)	2	1	4	3
(*c*)	1	2	4	3
(*d*)	1	2	3	4

48. Cropping intensity and gestation period of the crops grown are

(*a*) Inversely related (*b*) Directly related

(*c*) Exponentially related

(*d*) Not interrelated

49. Fruit stored in a cold chamber exhibit longer storage life because

(*a*) Exposure to sunlight is prevented

(*b*) The concentration of carbon dioxide in the environment is increased

(*c*) The rate of respiration is decreased

(*d*) There is an increase in humidity

50. Keeping in view the available technology for Kharif and Rabi crops, which one of the following patterns would be more in demand for crop planning ?

(a) Multiple cropping
(b) Monoculture
(c) Location specific cropping
(d) Mixed cropping

51. At present the farming system of India has become
(a) Export oriented
(b) Technology oriented
(c) Market oriented
(d) Domestic need oriented

52. The anti-quality constituent in young seedling of forage sorghum is
(a) Coumarins (b) Terpenses
(c) Acetic acid
(d) Hydrocyanic acid

53. Which of the following species belongs to pop maize ?
(a) Everta (b) Amylacea
(c) Indurata (d) Ceratina

54. High yield of maize is obtained in regions where the atmospheric temperature during the growing season is
(a) High during the day and low during the night
(b) High during the day and high during the night
(c) Low during the day and high during the night
(d) Low during the day and low during the night

55. Seed potato from the hilly regions of India is preferred because
(a) It is cheaper
(b) Good varieties are grown in those regions
(c) It has better germination percentage
(d) It is disease free

56. Which of the following pairs of common name and scientific name are correctly mached ?
(1) Prosomillet......Panicum miliaceum
(2) Kodo millet...Paspalum scorbiculatum
(3) Italian millet......Panicum antidotale
(4) Finger millet.....Elecucine coracana

Select the correct answer using the codes given below :
(a) 1, 2 and 3 (b) 1, 3 and 4
(c) 1, 2 and 4 (d) 2, 3 and 4

57. The dwarf wheat varieties should be
(a) Sown at the same depth at which the tall wheat varieties are sown
(b) Sown at a depth deeper than that for tall wheat varieties
(c) Sown at a depth shallower than that for tall wheat varieties
(d) Broadcast and incorportated in the top-soil

58. Which of the following chemicals used to treat potato to break its dormancy ?
(a) Ethral (b) Thiourea
(c) Indole acetic acid
(d) Naphthalene acetic acid

59. The interculture operation in standing broadcast rice crop is commonly known as
(a) Thinning (b) Spudding
(c) Rotation (d) Beushening

60. Consider the following statements :
In paddy, fertilizer application should be directed to be
(1) oxidised zone (2) reduced zone
(3) Surface
Of these statements
(a) 1 alone is correct
(b) 2 alone is correct
(c) 2 and 3 are correct
(d) 1 and 3 are correct

61. The following operations are practised in the cultivation of tobacco
(1) Priming (2) Topping
(3) Desuckering
The correct sequence of these operations in the field is
(a) 3, 2, 1 (b) 3, 1, 2
(c) 2, 3, 1 (d) 2, 1, 3

62. Consider the following statements :

A mulching material with albedo value is preferred because

1. it reflects back more of the incident radiation
2. it reduces considerably the downward transmission of heat
3. it has an evaporative cooling effect.

Of these statements

(*a*) 1 and 3 are correct
(*b*) 1 and 2 are correct
(*c*) 2 and 3 are correct
(*d*) 1, 2 and 3 are correct

63. Which of the following is NOT a mycoherbicide ?

(*a*) Bio-super (*b*) Collego
(*c*) Devine (*d*) Velgo

64. Match **List I** (Common names of weeds) with **List II** (Their scientific names) and select the correct answer using the codes given below the lists :

List I	**List II**
A. Nut grass	1. *Echnochloa crusgalli*
B. Bermuda grass	2. *Cyperus rotundus*
C. Yellow nut sedge	3. *Cynodon dactyon*
D. Barnyard grass	4. *Cyperus esculentus*

CODES

	A	B	C	D
(*a*)	1	3	4	2
(*b*)	2	3	4	1
(*c*)	2	4	3	1
(*d*)	1	4	3	2

65. If the land utilization index (LUI) of a crop is 0.50, then duration of that crop will be

(*a*) 183 days (*b*) 172 days
(*c*) 200 days (*d*) 135 days

66. If a farmer practises sugarcane-cotton-wheat the cropping intensity at his farm will be

(*a*) 100% (*b*) 150%
(*c*) 200% (*d*) 300%

67. The unconsolidated material on the underlying rock is called

(*a*) Regolith (*b*) Soil
(*c*) Solum (*d*) Earth

68. If a soil has a bulk density of 1.50 mg/m^3 and a particle density of 2.65 mg/m^3, then the percentage pore space of that soil will be

(*a*) 35.0 (*b*) 38.5
(*c*) 43.5 (*d*) 48.5

69. Active soil forming factors would include (*a*) Vegetation and topography

(*b*) Time, topography and climate
(*c*) Time and vegetation
(*d*) Vegetation and climate

70. The black cotton soils of Central India have been derived from

(*a*) Granites (*b*) Granodiorites
(*c*) Basalt (*d*) Rhyolife

71. Which one of the following minerals is LEAST weatherable in soil ?

(*a*) Olivine (*b*) Quartz
(*c*) Calcite (*d*) Biotite

72. Match **List I** (Microbial reaction) with **List II** (Soil organisms) and select the correct answer using the codes given below the lists :

List I	**List II**
A Sulphate reducton	1. Thiobacillus
B. Sulphate oxidation	2. Desulfotomaculum
C. Nitrate oxidation	3. Rhodosporium
D. Nitrogen fixation	4. Nitrobacter

CODES

	A	B	C	D
(*a*)	1	2	3	4
(*b*)	2	1	4	3
(*c*)	2	1	3	4
(*d*)	1	2	4	3

74. Properties of four different soils are given in the following table :

Soil property	*Soils*			
	Soil I	*Soil II*	*Soil III*	*Soil IV*
Organic matter (%)	3·1	0·8	2·0	0·4
Clay (%)	38·1	10·0	30·2	12·0
Sand (%)	51·2	74·0	50·1	70·0
Type of clay	2·1	1·1	2·1	1·1
pH	5·2	5·2	5·2	5·2

Which one of these soils will require the largest quantity of lime to raise its pH to 6.5 ?

(*a*) Soil I (*b*) Soil II

(*c*) Soil III (*d*) Soil IV

75. The best estimate of the available P in phosphatic fertilizers is obtained from the

(*a*) Water soluble fraction

(*b*) Citrate insoluble fraction

(*c*) Citrate soluble fraction

(*d*) Water soluble and citrate soluble fractions

76. E- value is

(*a*) Defined as the isotopically exchangeable P in the soil and soil solution as determined by crop uptake

(*b*) Defined as the isotopically exchangeable P in the soil as determined by ^{32}P

(*c*) The same as the L-value

(*d*) The difference betweell A and L value

77. Consider the following statements: Vermicompost is considered to be better because

1. It does not require tuning of compost material
2. It needs less composting time
3. It takes place at a comparatively low temperature
4. It has higher enzymatic activity

Of these statements

(*a*) 1, 2, 3 and 4 are correct

(*b*) 1 and 2 are correct

(*c*) 2, 3 and 4 are correct

(*d*) 1, 3 and 4 are correct

78. Match **List I** with **List II** and select the correct answer using the codes given below the lists

List I	**List II**
A. Gypsum	1. Magnesium fertilizer
B. 17 : 17 : 17	2. Micronutrient fertilizer
C. Serpentine	3. Calcium fertilizer
D. Chelates	4. Compound/complex fertilizer

CODES

	A	B	C	D
(*a*)	3	2	1	4
(*b*)	3	4	1	2
(*c*)	1	2	3	4
(*d*)	1	4	3	2

79. Sulphate of Potash is preferable of Muriate of Potash (MOP) for tobacco because

(*a*) The chlorine in the MOP affects the burning quality of tobacco

(*b*) The chlorine in the MOP increases the nicotine content of tobacco

(*c*) The application of MOP results in the luxury consumption of potassium

(*d*) The sulphate ion helps to increase the availability of the other nutrients

80. Match **List I** (reactants used for the preparation of fertilizers) with **List II** (fertilizer produced) and select the correct answer using the codes given below the lists:

List I	**List II**
A. Rock phosphate Phosphoric acid	1. Urea
B. Rock phosphate, Phosphoric acid, Nitric acid, ammonia	2. Ammonium sulphate
C. Ammonia, Gypsum, CO_2	3. Nitrophosphate
D. Ammonia, CO_2	4. Concentrated superphosphate

CODES

	A	B	C	D
(a)	4	3	1	2
(b)	4	3	2	1
(c)	3	4	2	1
(d)	3	4	1	2

81. Entry of potassium ions into root hair in soils having a low potassium ion content in the soil. is mediated through

(a) Ion exchange mechanism

(b) Mass flow phenomenon

(c) Donnan equilibrium process

(d) Utilization of metabolic energy

82. Consider the following statements :

According to cohesion theory for the ascent of sap, water moves from the roots through the stems to the leaves in tall trees because of

1. Forces of root pressure
2. The gradient in decreasing water potentials from the soil, through the plant to the leaves
3. Forces of adhesion of water to cell walls, especially in the leaves
4. Forces of cohesion between water molecules

Of these statements

(a) 1, 2 and 3 are correct

(b) 2, 3 and 4 are correct

(c) 1, 3 and 4 are correct

(d) 1, 2 and 4 are correct

83. Which one of the following physiological processes requires close coordination of three different organelles such as mitochondria, chloroplast and peroxisome ?

(a) Photosynthesis (b) Photorespiration

(c) Respiration (d) Protein synthesis

84. Which of the following are characteristic of C_4 plants ?

1. There are two CO_2 acceptors, namely PEP and RuBP
2. RuBP carboxylase is present in the mesophyll cells .
3. The first stable product is a 4-carbon compound
4. Oxygen does not have any inhibitory effect on the process

Select the correct answer from given below :

(a) 1, 2 and 4 are correct

(b) 1, 3 and 4 are correct

(c) 1, 2 and 3 are correct

(d) 2, 3 and 4 are correct

85. Which of the following is a set of high energy products of the light reaction of photosynthesis that are used in dark reaction?

(a) ATP and plastocynine

(b) ATP and NADP

(c) ATP and (NADHP + H^+)

(d) Plasoquinone and ferridoxine

86. Which of the following pairs of hormones and bioassay techniques are correctly matched ?

1. Cytokinin..........Radish cotyledon test
2. Gibberllic acid....Rice second leaf test
3. Indole-3 acetic acid..........coleoptile curvature test

Select the correct answer using the codes given below :

CODES

(a) 2 and 3 (b) 1 and 2

(c) 1 and 3 (d) 1, 2 and 3

87. Which of the following statement about carotenoids are correct ?

1. Carotenoids present in coleoptile affect the destruction of auxin by light.
2. Pollens generally carried by insects for pollination contain carotenes whereas carotenoid pigments are rarely detected in pollens of wind pollinated flowers.
3. They cause a suitable drop in light intensity leading to a gradient of increasing auxin concentrated from the lighted side to the darker side.
4. They absorb blue light to produce phototropic curvature in oat coleoptile in phycomyces and also certain blue-green algea.

Select the correct answer

(*a*) 2, 3 and 1 (*b*) 1, 2 and 4

(*c*) 1, 3 and 4 (*d*) 1, 2 and 3

88. Match **List I** (Source of character) with **List II** (Character exploited) select the correct answer using the codes given below the lists :

List I		List II
A. Norin-10	1.	Resistance to *Puccinia recondita* Causing leaf rust in wheat
B. Opaque-2	2.	Semi dwarfing habit in rice
C. Dee-gee woo-gen	3.	Protein content in maize
D. Lr genes	4.	Short stature in wheat

CODES

	A	B	C	D
(*a*)	4	3	1	2
(*b*)	4	3	2	1
(*c*)	3	4	1	2
(*d*)	3	4	2	1

89. Given that the somatic chromosome number of Triticum aestivum is $2n = 6x = 42$. Which of the following pairs is correctly matched ?

(*a*) Monosome..... $2n = 40$

(*b*) Trisome......... $2n = 42$

(*c*) Tetrasome...... $2n = 44$

(*d*) Nullisome....... $2n = 41$

90. When breaks occur in two chromosomes simultaneously in a nucleus and the broken chromosomes rejoin in a new manner, it results in

(*a*) Deletion (*b*) Duplication

(*c*) Translocation (*d*) Inversion

91. Consider the following statement:

1. Heterochromatin is concentrated near the nuclear envelop and near the nucleolus
2. Euchromatin is visible during interphase and is distributed throughout the nucleoplasm.
3. Euchromatin is concentrated near the nucleolus and near the nudear envelop.

Of these statement:

(*a*) 1, 2 and 3 are correct

(*b*) 1 and 2 are correct

(*c*) 2 and 3 are correct

(*d*) 1 and 3 are correct

92. The segregation of individuals in the F2 or in a later generation of a cross, which shows a more extreme development of a character than either parent is termed as

(*a*) Hybridization (*b*) Heterosis

(*c*) Linkage

(*d*) Transgressive segregates

93. Heritability may be defined as the

(*a*) Interaction product of genotype with environment

(*b*) Sum total of hereditary material present in a species

(*c*) Degree of resemblance between the original and the selected plants

(*d*) Proportion of phenotypic variability which is due to heredity

94. Evaluation of inbreds in maize is carried out in four stages. Open pollinated variety is in volved in the

(*a*) Phenotypic evaluation

(*b*) Top cross evaluation

(*c*) Single cross evaluation

(*d*) Double cross evaluation

95. Multiline varieties are mixtures of

(*a*) Several morphologically different plants having identical disease resistance genes

(*b*) Bulked progenies of different inbred lines

(*c*) Several similar pure lines having different genes for disease resistance

(*d*) Morphologically identical plants with different genetic make up

96. Consider the following statement :

The performance of advanced generation synthetic varieties, in theory, depends upon the—

1. Number of parental lines
2. Source of the parental lines included

3. Mean performance of the parental lines
4. Mean performance of all possible combinations among all the lines induded

Of these statements

(a) 1, 2 and 3 are correct

(b) 1, 3 and 4 are correct

(c) 2, 3 and 4 are correct

(d) 1, 2 and 4 are correct

97. The mechanism of male sterility in self-pollinated crops can be successfully utili sed to obtain

(a) Selfed seed

(b) Mutated seed without radiation treatment

(c) Hybrid seed without emasculation

(d) Sterile seed

98. The basic difference between a synthetic and composite variety lies in

(a) The differences in synthesis

(b) Testing for nicking ability

(c) The mode of pollination

(d) The number of components

99. Which of the following steps are involved in the utilization of hybrid vigour ?

1. Production of uniform homozygous in bred lines
2. Crossing inbreds in combination that give uniform and productive single cross (F_1) hybrids
3. Crossing single crosses in combination to give productive double cross hybrids.
4. Mixing single cross F_1 hybrids to give productive double cross hybrids

Select the correct answer using the codes given below :

CODES

(a) 1, 2 and 4 (b) 1, 3 and 4

(c) 1, 2 and 3 (d) 2, 3 and 4

100. A high yielding semi-dwarf variety of rice was first developed at

(a) CRRI, Cuttack (b) IARI, New Delhi

(c) ICRISAT, Hyderabad

(d) IRRI, Manila

101. The most popular extra early maturing variety in pigeonpea is

(a) UPAS-120 (b) Gulbarga

(c) Type-7 (d) Type-17

102. Varalaxmi is a hybrid developed in

(a) Rice (b) Cotton

(c) Brinjal (d) Brassica

103. Which of the following are the correet sets of crop, variety and breeding method employed to evolve the given variety ?

S.No.	*Crop*	*Variety*	*Breeding method*
1.	Wheat	Sharbati sonara	Mutation breeding
2.	Sunflower	APSH-11	Heterosis breeding
3.	Maize	Amber	Population improvement
4.	Groundnut	TMV-2	Pedigree selection

Select the correct answer :

(a) 2, 3 and 4 (b) 1, 3 and 4

(c) 1, 2 and 4 (d) 1, 2 and 3

104. Transfer of resistance gene to high yielding self-pollinated varieties is achieved by—

(a) Hybridization and pedigree selection

(b) Recurrent back crossing and selection

(c) Hybridization and bulk selection

(d) Hybridization and mass selection

105. To which of the following species does India's indigenous cotton being ?

(a) *Gossypium barbadence*

(b) *Gossypium hirsutum*

(c) *Gossypium arboreum*

(d) *Gossypium herbaceum*

106. Generally fruit plants bear fruit once a year but there are some in India which bear fruit twice a year. Which of the following belong to this category—

(1) Cashew (2) Grape

(3) Jack fruit (4) Pomegranate

Select the correct answer using the codes given below :

(*a*) 1, 2 and 3 (*b*) 1, 2 and 4

(*c*) 1 and 3 (*d*) 2, 3 and 4

107. Which of the following statements can be associated with the cultivation of mango as it is being practised in India ?

1. Varieties of fruit trees like mango being grown are inferior and they are often propagated by seeding.
2. Socio-economic status of most of the mango growers is low and they have small-sized holdings.
3. Marketing of mango is chaotic in most of the mango growing parts of India
4. Knowledge about right type of mango varieties and their cultural practices is not available

Select the correct answer using the codes given below :

CODES

(*a*) 1, 2 and 4 (*b*) 2, 3 and 4

(*c*) 1, 3 and 4 (*d*) 1, 2 and 3

108. Which of the following pairs are correctly matched ?

1. Date palm...........Monoecious
2. Papaya..........Polygamous
3. Walnut..........Monoecious
4. Pistachionut..........Dioecious

Select the correct answer using the codes given below :

CODES

(*a*) 2, 3 and 4 (*b*) 1, 2 and 3

(*c*) 1, 2 and 4 (*d*) 1, 3 and 4

109. Ratna variety of mango is a cross between-

(*a*) Alphonso and banganapalli

(*b*) Neelam and langra

(*c*) Neelam and alphanso

(*d*) Dashehri and neelam

110. Which of the following pairs are correctly matched ?

1. Ikebana..........Paved path in a garden
2. Pinjore garden..........Mughal garden
3. Topiary.....Clipping and shearing shrubs
4. Carnation..........Cut flower

Select th correct answer using the codes given below :

CODES

(*a*) 2, 3 and 4 (*b*) 1, 2 and 4

(*c*) 1, 3 and 4 (*d*) 1, 2 and 3

111. Consider the following species :

1. *Polyathia longifolia*
2. *Acalypha hispida*
3. *Pentas lanceolata*
4. *Ipomoea palmata*

Among these, the ones which can be planted in the shrubbery would include—

(*a*) 1 and 2 (*b*) 2 and 3

(*c*) 3 and 4 (*d*) 1, 2, 3 and 4

112. Which one of the following chemicals is used for the preservation of fruit products?

(*a*) Potassium sulphate

(*b*) Potassium manganate

(*c*) Potassium metabisulphide

(*d*) Potassium metabisulphite

113. Pollination of the fig flower by the blastophaga wasp takes through

(*a*) Fascination (*b*) Parthenogenesis

(*c*) Caprification (*d*) Apomixis

114. Multi-storey cropping system is practised in

(*a*) Jammu and Kashmir

(*b*) Karnataka and Kerala

(*c*) Bihar and Madhya Pradesh

(*d*) Rajasthan and Haryana

115. Which of the following statements regarding crop rotation are correct ?

(1) Susceptible vegetable to a particular pest should be followed by a resistant one

(2) Heavy feeder should be followed by low feeder

(3) Deep rooted crops should be followed by the same type of crop

(4) Legume must be followed by a non-legum

Select the correct answer using the codes given below :

CODES

(a) 2, 3 and 4 (b) 1, 2 and 3

(c) 1, 2 and 4 (d) 1, 3 and 4

116. Which one of the following vegetables gives maximum calories per 100 gram of edible matter ?

(a) Spinach (b) Water melon

(c) Sweet potato (d) Tomato

Net/ARS Question Papers 1999

Plant Breeding and Genetics
(Multiple choice questions)

1. The genetic basis of correlation is—

(a) Crossing over

(b) Linkage and pleiotropy

(c) Epistasis

2. If you self a plant with three heterozygous pairs of genes the total number of genotypes produced will be—

(a) Three (b) Sixteen

(c) Twenty seven

3. Who received 1962 Nobel Prize for chemical nature of DNA

(a) Watson and Crick

(b) Watson, Crick and Wilkins

(c) Watson and Khurana

4. Theory of pure line selection was proposed by—

(a) W.L. Johnssen (b) Louis de Vilmorin

(c) John Le Counteur

5. In pedigree method of plant breeding—

(a) Superior genotypes are selected in successive segregating generations and a complete record is maintained

(b) Only heterozygotes are favoured and complete record is maintained

(c) All the lines are retained in next generation maintaining complete record

6. Phenotypic disassortative mating indicates,

(a) Mating of individuals at random

(b) Mating of individuals on the basis of contrasting phenotypic characters

(c) Mating of individual which are more closely related

7. The dominance hypothesis for heterosis was proposed by—

(a) Davenport (1908) and Bruce (1910)

(b) Wilkins (1907) and Crick (1911)

(c) John Le Counteur (1917)

8. Ferridoxin is otherwise known as—

(a) Fe-P Protein (b) Fe-M Protein

(c) Fe-S Protein

(d) Fe-Mo Protein

9. Compared with most animal proteins, cereal grain proteins are low in lysin, while legume seeds are low in—

(a) Valine (b) Tryptophan

(c) Isoleucine (d) Methionine

10. The attraction between unlike molecules, water and other molecules is called—

(a) Cohesion (b) Adhesion

(c) Fusion (d) Absorption

11. The site of protein synthesis in a plant cell is—

(a) Mitochondria (b) Glyoxisome

(c) Ribosome (d) Mesosome

12. The sharp taste of oranges and lemons comes from the high concentration of citric acid in their—

(a) Cell wall (b) Cytoplasm

(c) Plasmalemma (d) Vacuole

13. It is an essential element and essential membrane component without which membranes lose their ability to transport solutes inwardly and become leaky for solutes they already contain—

(a) Manganese (b) Boron

(c) Calcium (d) Magnesium

14. The abundant and stable form of iron in leaves is stored in chloroplasts as an iron protein complex called—

(a) Pyridoxine (b) Phytoferritin

(c) Porphyrin (d) Ferricyanide

15. One of the non-aromatic amino acid present in plants is—
(*a*) Tryptophan (*b*) Glycine
(*c*) Tyrosine (*d*) Phenylalanine

16. The beautiful flower colours are due to the presence of—
(*a*) Chlorophyll-b (*b*) Cytochrome
(*c*) Anthocynin (*d*) Cryptochrome

Fill in the blanks

17. A beam of negatively charged particles is known as ....

18. A nucleotide consists of ....and ....

19. ....is mating of closely related organisms.

20. In RBD with three replications and four treatments the error degrees of freedom shall be ....

21. When F_1 is crossed with both the parents simultaneously it is called ....

22. The parent to which successive back crosses are made is called ....

23. Besides structural genes, an operon consists of .... and .... genes.

24. DNA synthesis occurs in the ....direction on the leading strand and in the ....direction on the lagging strand.

25. When a gene affect more than one character it is known to have ....effect.

26. Antibodies are produced by ....cells.

27. An individual once exposed to a pathogen normally does not get infected second time by the same pathogen because of ....cells.

28. Acquired immune deficiency syndrome is caused by ....

29. Protein 'X' has a molecular weight of 30,000 daltons. Assuming that the average molecular weight of an amino acid is 120 daltons, how many codons are found in the mRNA that code for this protein (include start and stop ....codon)

30. Insect resistant transgenic cotton plants have been obtained by transferring ....gene from *Bacillus thusingiensis*.

Animal Husbandry

Fill in the blanks

1. Chemically the DNA molecule is comprised a series of ....

2. Holandric genes are situated on ....chromosome.

3. One gene one enzyme hypothesis was proposed by ....

4. Turner syndrome is found in woman who have ....sex chromosome composition.

5. Giant chromosomes are found in ....of Drosophila larvae.

6. The main storage form of iron in the body is referred to as ....

7. Methyl groups from chlorine combine with ....to form methionine

8. The main storage polysaccharide in animal cells is ....

9. In folic acid deficiency ....type of anaemia is produced.

10. ....is the principal end product of nitrogen metabolism in mammals, while ....is the end product in birds.

11. ....RNA acts as carrier of specific individual amino acids during protein synthesis on'to the ribosomes.

12. Thiamine is primarily absorbed from ....

13. The physiologically active form of Vitamin D is ....

14. The ammonia released by the deamination units with carbon to form ....acid during urea formation.

15. The process transforming one mole of ammonia to one mole of urea requires ....ATPs.

16. The complete catabolism of glycerol to CO_2 and H_2O yields ....moles of ATO.

17. Heat of fermentation + ... = Heat increment.

18. The GE value of one g of fat is ....kcal whereas, its physiological fuel value is ....kcal/g.

19. Colostrum contains ....% protein.

20. Parakeratosis is caused by the deficiency of ....

21. Xerophthalmia is the pathological condition which occurs due to ....

Biotechnology (Agricultural Science)

Tick the correct answers

1. In plant cells, the chemical substance most abundantly present in the middle lamella is—
(*a*) Suberine (*b*) Pectine
(*c*) Cutin (*d*) Lignin

2. The organelle corresponding to mitochondria in bacteria is—
(*a*) Flagella (*b*) Nuclear body
(*c*) Mesosomes

3. The most abundant lipid in cell membrane is—
(*a*) Steroid (*b*) Phospholipid
(*c*) Cholestrol (*d*) Cutin

4. While formulating the DNA model Watson and Crick relied heavily on the result of—
(*a*) Wilikins
(*b*) Meselson and Stahl
(*c*) Hershey (*d*) Holley

5. In DNA replication, the helix is unwound by—
(*a*) Topisomerase (*b*) DNA polymerase
(*c*) Primase (*d*) Helicase

6. Which of the following amino acid has not even a single asymmetric carbon atom—
(*a*) Glycine (*b*) Proline
(*c*) Histidine (*d*) Leucine

7. Lecithin is a—
(*a*) Natural lipid (*b*) Proline
(*c*) Polar lipid

8. The backbone structure of waxes is constituted by—
(*a*) Glycerol-3-phosphate
(*b*) Nonpolar alcohols of high molecular weight
(*c*) Glycerol

9. For one turn of TCA cycle (starting from acetyl CoA) which of the following statement is false
(*a*) Two molecules of pyruvate are oxidized completely to CO_2
(*b*) One GTP is produced
(*c*) Two CO_2 are produced
(*d*) Three NADH are produced

10. Glucose labelled with the isotope ^{14}C in all the six carbon atoms is injected into a rat. The rat is sacrificed 30 minutes later. In which compound given below would you expect to find labelled carbon atoms.
(*a*) L-alanine isolated form
(*b*) Liver glycogen
(*c*) Liver fatty acids (*d*) All the above

Nematology

Fill in the blanks

1. Phanerogamic parasite with chlorophyll but no roots ....
2. A disease caused by *Trichodorus* ....
3. A disease caused by *Anguina* ....
4. A disease caused by *Rotylenchulus* ....
5. A nematophagus fungus ....
6. A bacterium that parasizes a plant pathogenic nematode ....
7. A disease caused by *Radopholus* ....
8. A fungus used for biological control of plant diseases ....
9. Antifungal antibiotic ....
10. A disease caused by *Pratylenchus* ....
11. Kernel bunt was first reported by ....
12. When the progress of disease is plotted against time, the curve obtained is commonly S-shaped. This curve is known as ....
13. Gray-speck disease of oats is caused by ....
14. The first report of plant parasite nematode was by ....
15. The scientific name of golden nematode of potato is ....
16. False smut of rice was incited by ....

Mark True or False against each statement

17. In the majority of virus, mycoplasma and nematode diseases, photosynthesis of infected plants is not reduced greatly.
18. Strains differing only in the plant species they in fact are called pathovars.
19. Water soaking of tissues during heavy rains greatly favours penetration and invasion by plant pathogenic bacteria.
20. MLO of plants cannot be grown on artificial nutrient media.
21. Most plant MLOs are transmitted from plant to plant by leafhoppers.
22. The body cavity of nematodes contain a fluid through which cirulation and respiration take place.
23. Many nematode species lack males.
24. In case of nematode-transmitted viruses, larval and adult nematodes can transmit a virus but the virus is not carried from one larval stage to another and to adult through moths.
25. Only the genetically controlled disease resistance should be considered as true resistance.
26. The resistance of a plant variety is broken due to change in the pathogen.
27. Wfra disease of rice is caused by *Tylenchus angustus.*
28. Diocious fungus cannot be homothallic.
29. Viruses posses Lipman system.
30. Butlar first used Bordeaux Mixture in India.
31. Tilletia caries is a smooth-spored bunt fungus.
32. Phytopathogenic bacteria are heterotrophs.

Horticulture

Write True, False or half true.

1. Abscissa acid (ABA) helps in the initiation of adventitious roots.
2. Cauliflower requires chilling for flower initiation.
3. Dahlia is propagated through bulbs and tuberose by tubers.
4. Climacteric fruits do not respond to the exogenous application of ethylene.
5. 'Whiptail of cauliflower is due to stenospermocarpy.

Fill in the blanks

6. Pungency in onions and chillies are due to ....and ....respectively.
7. 'Brown rot' and 'Whip tail' in cauliflower are caused by ....and ....respectively.
8. Two major methods of moisture conservation are ....and ....
9. Two major fungi that causes diseases in vegetable crops are ....and ....
10. In tomato two varieties suitable for processing are ....and ....
11. Fruit drop in mango is due to ....
12. What are various types of preservation methods ....

Give two examples or causes for each of the following as the case may be—

13. Climacteric fruits—
14. Monoecoious vegetable crops—
15. Determinate type of F_1 hybrids of tomat—
16. Chemicals for breaking dormancy—
17. Root inducing chemicals—
18. Insect transmitted diseases—
19. Self-pollinated vegetable crops—

Agricultural Economics

True or False

1. Consumers are indifferent between different indifference curves.
2. If the actual price is greater than the equilibrium price, there will be a shortage and price will rise.
3. An income elasticity coefficient of 0.80 means that consumers decrease their purchase of a good by 0.80 per cent when their income decreases by one per cent.
4. If an isoquant is convex to the origin more and more of one input is required to substitute for each successive unit reduction in the other input.
5. A monopolistically competitive firm will earn pure profits if price is above ATC curve at the profit if maximising quantity.

6. Profit maximising level of input happens when the AVP of the input is equal to its price.

7. The cost of producing a given level of output will be minimized when the MPP of all inputs are equal.

8. If an isoquant is convex to the origin, the producer will be indifferent between various input combinations because they will all yield the same profit.

9. The firm's supply curve is its MC curve.

10. A capital item is profitable to own, if its net MVP is at least as large and preferably larger than its interest plus depreciation.

11. In marginal rate of transformation is unity in the case of two products which are perfect substitutes.

12. Income elasticity of demand for foodgrains is lower than that for milk products.

13. With an increase in wages, the substitution effect pulls worker toward more work and less leisure.

14. Sales tax on sugar is a direct tax.

15. Production in traditional agriculture does not respond to price changes.

16. Traditional agriculture and backward agriculture are not synonymous.

17. A farmer in India is a price maker and not price taker.

18. The distinction between fixed and variable costs exists only in short run.

19. The solvency of a firm is assessed by computing current ratio from the balance sheet.

Write the correct answer

20. Slope of the income demand curve of a normal good is—

(*a*) Positive (*b*) Negative

(*c*) Both

21. A rational firm would stop further production when the MVP is :

(*a*) Lesser than MC (*b*) Equal to MC

(*c*) Higher than MC

22. A production possibility curve shows :

(*a*) Various combinations of resources that are available to an economy

(*b*) Various combinations of output that a society would like to produce if resources were available.

(*c*) The combinations of output that a society would like to produce from a given amount of resources

23. A good, highly demanded by consumers will exhibit :

(*a*) High price, giving producers an incentive to produce more of it

(*b*) Low price, giving producers an incentive to produce more of it

(*c*) Low price, giving producers an incentive to produce less of it

24. Production of foodgrains in India during last two years has been around :

(*a*) 18 crore tonnes (*b*) 85 crore tonnes

(*c*) 220 crore tonnes

25. A firm that faces downward sloping demand curve :

(*a*) Must reduce price if it wishes to increase output

(*b*) Must reduce output if it wishes to increase price

(*c*) Both (*a*) and (*b*)

26. Amortised method of repayment of LT loan refers to :

(*a*) Repayment in equated instalments

(*b*) Lumpsum repayment in single instalment

(*c*) Repayment of variable amounts in instalments.

27. Under which situation would the discounted present value of a machine be the highest:

(*a*) High net cash inflows and high interest rate

(*b*) High net cash inflows and low interest rate

(*c*) Low net cash inflows and low interest rate

28. The average product is at its maximum when :

(*a*) Marginal product is rising

(*b*) Marginal product is equal to average product

(*c*) Marginal product is falling

29. Inflation is defined as :
(*a*) A sustained rise in the price level
(*b*) A temporary spurt in the price level
(*c*) An equal increase in the price of all goods and services

30. Marginal proportion to cosumer is equal to:
(*a*) The proportion of income that is spent on cosumer goods and services
(*b*) The proportion of additional income spent on consumer goods and services
(*c*) A amount spent on consumer goods and services by the total population of the country

31. In the context of the simple Keynesian model, equilibrium income corresponds to the point where—
(*a*) Aggregate demand equals aggregate supply
(*b*) Consumer spending equals NNP
(*c*) Resources are fully employed

32. If MPC is 0.75 and government increases its spending by Rs. 100 million, equilibrium income will increase by Rs. :
(*a*) 400 million (*b*) 250 million
(*c*) 100 million

33. Different points on an isocline indicate :
(*a*) Same cost at which different levels of outputs are realized
(*b*) Minimum costs at which different levels of outputs are produced .
(*c*) Levels combination of two inputs that cost maximum

34. In a Cobb Douglas type production function, the sum of the coefficients indicate :
(*a*) Returns to scale (*b*) Marginal product
(*c*) Total product

35. Better measure of economic development is:
(*a*) Gross National Product
(*b*) Per Capita Income
(*c*) A development index of many economic and social variables

36. Marginal productivity of labour in under developed agriculture like India is :
(*a*) Negative (*b*) Positive
(*c*) Zero

37. Gross marketing margin is :
(*a*) The profit retained by the market middlemen
(*b*) The difference between the price received by the producer and that paid by the consumer
(*c*) the price paid by the consumer

38. Minimum support price for farm products announced by the Government of India is :
(*a*) The maximum price received by the farmers
(*b*) The price which traders are required to pay to the farmers
(*c*) The price at which Government agencies buy the produce from the farmers in case market price tends to go below that price and farmers offer their produce to the Government agencies.

39. Per capita availability of foodgrains in India in recent years had been estimated at around:
(*a*) 200 gml/day
(*b*) 460 gml/day
(*c*) 900 gml/day

Fill up the blanks with the one of the following :

40. Average output per worker is always ....than the average output per head of population. (lesser/greater)

41. A perfectly competitive firm sells a .... share of market. (smaller/larger)

42. Perfectly competitive employers of labour face a perfectly elastic ....labour. (supply of /demand of)

43. A shift in the demand curve refers to a ....in demand. (increase or decrease /change)

44. Short-run supply is ....elastic than long-run supply. (less/more)

45. Long-run demand is ....elastic than short- run demand. (less/more)

46. A perfectly competitive firm will earn normal profit if the price is above its ....cost at the profit maximising level of output. (AT/AV)

47. The law of comparative advantage demonstrates that trade is based on ....efficiency. (absolute/relative)

48. An isoquant cannot slope .... (upward/downward)

49. If the production possibility curve is horizontal X and Y are ....goods. (competitive/unrelated)

50. The capitalized value of a piece of land yielding a net return of Rs. 3000 per year is Rs. ....at an interest rate of 10 per cent. (30,000/33,000)

51. The amount of good A that must be given up to obtain more of good B is called ....cost. (variable/opportunity)

52. Inflation ....the real value of money. (enhances/reduces)

53. The unemployment that exists because of adjustments in the economy is called ....unemployment. (disguised/frictional)

54. India's foodgrains requirement by 2000 A.D. has been estimated at around ....million tonnes. (230/300)

55. During the last 40 years, the share of agricultural sector in the GNP has .... (increased/decreased)

56. Out of total cereals production in India, the share of wheat is ....than the share of rice. (more/less)

57. Prices of industrial goods fluctuate ....than the prices of farm products. (more/less)

Soil Science

Multiple choice questions

1. An aluminosilicate clay mineral in the smecite group with 2 : 1 expanding crystal lattice is
   (*a*) Illite (*b*) Montronite
   (*c*) Halloysite (*d*) None of these

2. Sodic soils generally exhibit soil structure of the type
   (*a*) Platy (*b*) Granulated
   (*c*) Subangular blocky
   (*d*) Prismatic/columnar

3. Soil water content (%) at field capacity is maximum/highest with—
   (*a*) Loam (*b*) Clayey soils
   (*c*) Silt loam (*d*) Clay loam

4. Carryover fertilizer effects are more pronounced in the case of
   (*a*) Urea (*b*) Calcium ammonium nitrate
   (*c*) Single superphosphate
   (*d*) Ammonium nitrate

5. Symbiotic nitrogen fixation in Cajanus cajan (tur/arhar) is mediated by—
   (*a*) Rhizobium phaseoli
   (*b*) Rhizobium leguminosarum
   (*c*) Rhizobium spp. (cow pea miscellany group)
   (*d*) Rhizobium lupini

6. Laterite soils occurs in the district of
   (*a*) Ratnagiri district of Maharashtra
   (*b*) Patiala district of Punjab
   (*c*) Indore district of Madhya Pradesh
   (*d*) Bikaner district of Rajasthan

7. The ionic form of phosphorus is determined by pH of the solution. At pH 4.0 the predominated ionic forms of phosphorus present are
   (*a*) HPO_4^{-2} (*b*) $H_2PO_4^{-1}$
   (*c*) $H_2PO_4^{-1}$ and HPO_4^{-1}
   (*d*) $H_2PO_4^{-1}$ and PO_4^{-1}

8. Journal of soil science is published from
   (*a*) India (*b*) Canada
   (*c*) USA (*d*) Australia
   (*e*) None of the above countries

9. X-ray diffraction technique (s) is used to study—
   (*a*) Tracer studies
   (*b*) Day mineralogy
   (*c*) Photosynthesis (*d*) None of these

10. Biurate content in urea fertilizer is permitted up to (by FCO)
    (*a*) Less than 2.5 %
    (*b*) Maximum up to 1.0 %
    (*c*) Between 2 to 3.0 %
    (*d*) Zero

11. Match items of column *A* with items in Column *B*

A	*B*
(*a*) Sodic soils	(*i*) Liming material
(*b*) Nitrification	(*ii*) Isomorphous substitution
(*c*) Negative charge on clay	(*iii*) Illite
(*d*) Nitrification inhibitor	(*iv*) Natric
(*e*) Mica	(*v*) Nitrosomonas
(*f*) Dolomite	(*vi*) N-serve
(*g*) Allophane	(*vii*) Marble
(*h*) Nitrogen fixation	(*viii*) Aridsols
(*i*) Desert soils	(*ix*) Nitrogenase
(*j*) Metamorphic rock	(*x*) Amorphous clay

(*a*) (*iv*) (*b*) (*v*)
(*c*) (*ii*) (*d*) (*vi*)
(*e*) (*iii*) (*f*) (*i*)
(*g*) (*x*) (*h*) (*ix*)
(*i*) (*viii*) (*j*) (*vii*)

12. The diagnostic horizon in Alfisol is termed
(*a*) Argillic (*b*) Spodic
(*c*) Mollic (*d*) Oxic

13. Which of the following soils has got the highest bulk density ?
(*a*) Sandy soil (*b*) Clay soil
(*c*) Loam (*d*) Silty clay

14. The equation of soil formation, $S = f(cl, o, r, p, t)$ was given by
(*a*) Dokuchaev (*b*) Glinka
(*c*) Jenny (*d*) Kellog

15. The structural rigidity of kaolinite is due to
(*a*) K-bridge
(*b*) Internal absorbed water
(*c*) H-bond (*d*) O-O bond

16. A soil formation process in which humus and sesquioxides become mobile and remain behind
(*a*) Pedoturbation (*b*) Calcification
(*c*) Laterization (*d*) Podsolization

17. Attraction of solid surface for water molecule is called
(*a*) Cohesion (*b*) Adsorption
(*c*) Adhesion (*d*) Absorption

18. Erosion caused by spattering of soil particles caused by the impact of raindrops is known as
(*a*) Sheet erosion (*b*) Rill erosion
(*c*) Splash erosion (*d*) Gully erosion

19. Which of the following is not a metamorphic rock ?
(*a*) Gneiss (*b*) Sandstone
(*c*) Conglomerate (*d*) Limestone

20. Which of the following is not a sedimentary rock ?
(*a*) Gneiss (*b*) Sandstone
(*c*) Conglomerate (*d*) limestone

True/False

21. The porous cup-tensiometer is used to measure soil moisture suction at the permanent wilting point.

22. The base saturation per cent of a soil is related to soil pH.

23. Most of the micronutrients are relatively more available in acidic soils.

24. Gypsum is best suited for the reclamation of saline soil.

25. A pressure membrane apparatus is used to measure metric potential at low soil moisture potential values as low as 100 bar.

26. The C.E.C. of a kaolinitic soil of pH 4.0 is 11 C/mol (p^+) kg. When limed to pH 6.0, the C.E.C. decreased.

27. The soil-buffering power is dependent on the colloidal content of a soil.

28. Molybdenum availability to plant increases with fall in soil pH.

29. Lime requirement of an acid soil is best measured by assessing its active acidity.

30. Loss of nitric oxide from soil into the atmosphere has harmful effect on the environment.

31. The thermal diffusivity of soil is of significance to describe heat flow in a non-isothermal soil under non-steady temperature distribution in soil.

32. One of the most effective method of peptisins clay suspensions involves reversal of positive edge charge into a negative one through adsorption of excess anions of the edge surfaces.

33. The SAR of a soil extract takes into consideration of adverse effect of Na ions in relation to the presence of Ca and Mg ions.

34. A soil having high potential buffer capacity for potassium will need a frequent application of potassic fertilizer in intensive agriculture.

35. The motted condition of soil colour indicates excellent drainage in a soil system.

36. The pH scale starts from 1 and ends at 14.

37. Sometimes sodic soils are called black alkali soils because of black crusts that appear on drying.

Fill in the blanks

38. Two new techniques used to improve the quality of soil surveys and to update old surveys are ....and ....

39. The saturated hydraulic conductivity of a loamy soil is ....than that of a silty clay loamy soil.

40. Tea plantation prefers soil pH in the range of .... to ....

41. Three types of acidity prevalent in a soil system are ...., ... and ....

42. The modern units of CEC, EC, ESP and ODR are respectively ...., ..., ... and ....

43. The chemical names of DTPA and EDTA are .... and ....

44. Molybdenum is a component of the enzyme .... which is essential for the process of nitrogen tixation.

45. Three main groups of organic phosphorus compounds found in soils are :.........., ...and ....

46. 15N is a ....isotope of nitrogen.

47. In a tracer-technique using ^{32}P radioisotope, the tracer is measured by ....counter.

48. A reasonable representative C : N : S ratio in soil is ....

49. Structure of clay minerals is essentially made up of two basic units, *viz.* (*a*) ....(*b*) ....

50. Value of correlation coefficient (*r*) can vary from ....to ....

51. One gram molecules of hydrogen contain ....hydrogen atoms.

52. Capillary is caused by two forces, *i.e* ....and ....

53. Sodic soils are characterized by pH ....and ESP ....

Entomology

True or False

1. All locusts are not grasshoppers.

2. White ants and black ants have identical colonies.

3. Honey bees and termites have similar mechanism of forming new colonies.

4. As in higher animals, in insects also, blood is the source of supply of oxygen to various organs.

5. Human lice and plant lice belong to the same. order.

6. In terrestrial insects temperature is the most important environmental factor to influence their development.

7. Insects meet their water requirement from the atmospheric moisture.

8. All insects of endopterygota have wings.

9. Higher the LD_{50} safer is the insecticidal poisoning.

10. Larvae of insects of order Hemiptera are called maggots.

11. In insects 1st and 2nd thoracic segments bear a pair of wings each.

12. Except insects there is no other animal, in any form which has 3 pairs of legs.

Fill in the blanks

13. The outermost layer of the insect cuticle is called ....

14. The outermost layer of eggs of insects is ....which has a delicate ....membrane underneath.

15. Malpighian tubules are absent in ....

16. Whitish spots on gram seed indicate infestation of ....

17. The most accurate method of detecting hidden infestation in stored grain is ....

18. When exposed to the atmosphere celphos releases ....

19. Three most important orders of insects from the pest point of view are ...., ...and ....

20. Insect blood is called ...., its most important function is ....

21. A General Text Book of Entomology has been written by ....

22. The full name of DDT is ....

23. Three species of locust recorded from India are ...., ..., and ...., Of these ...., ...are the most important.

Agronomy

Multiple choice questions

1. Formation of messenger RNA from a DNA template which carries the genetic information to the ribosome is called
(*a*) Transcription (*b*) Translation
(*c*) Translocation
(*d*) Genetic engineering

2. The pigment occurring in plastid, which is a precursor for vitamin A, is
(*a*) Flavin (*b*) Cholorphyll
(*c*) Carotene (*d*) Xanthophyll

3. An example of CAM plant is—
(*a*) Pineapple (*b*) Coconut
(*c*) Sunflower (*d*) Watermelon

4. Quantity of water required to produce one kg of dry matter is—
(*a*) Consumptive use (*b*) ET
(*c*) Water requirement
(*d*) Transpiration ratio

5. Soils that have no diagnostic pedogenic horizons are included in the order
(*a*) Inceptisol (*b*) Entisol
(*c*) Mollisol (*d*) Utisol

6. Average milling recovery of the commonly grown rice cultivars is—
(*a*) 60% (*b*) 50%
(*c*) 75% (*d*) 30%

7. The name of the organic compound occurring in cell walls of woody and fibrous species is-
(*a*) Cellulose (*b*) Hydroquinones
(*c*) Lignin (*d*) Xylum

8. An example of assortive, non-symbiotic nitrogen fixing organism is—
(*a*) Rhizobium (*b*) Azorhizobium
(*c*) Pseudomonas (*d*) Azospirillium

9. Beta decay of radioactive nuclei occurs resulting in the emission of—
(*a*) Protons (*b*) Electrons
(*c*) Neutrons (*d*) Mesons

10. Apatite is a mineral containing the plant nutrient—
(*a*) Potassium (*b*) Nitrogen
(*c*) Boron (*d*) Phosphorus

11. Akiochi desease in rice is due to the toxicity caused by
(*a*) Hydrogen sulphide
(*b*) Zinc (*c*) Bacteria
(*d*) Virus

12. The elastic substance found in wheat flour that gives adhesiveness of the dough is—
(*a*) Starch (*b*) Xylose
(*c*) Gluten (*d*) Cellulose

13. A cultivar developed by combining selected cross-pollinated lines is—
(*a*) Hybrid (*b*) Pure line selection
(*c*) Isoline (*d*) Synthetic

14. The NP fertilizer containing the highest amount of P_2O_5 is—
(*a*) Diammonium phosphate
(*b*) Ammonium polyphosphate
(*c*) Nitrophos
(*d*) Tripple superphosphate

15. The tetraploid species of cotton, known as American cotton, is
(*a*) G. hirsutam (*b*) G. arborium
(*c*) G. herbaceum (*d*) G. barbadense

16. The maximum oil yield per unit area can be obtained from
(*a*) Groundnut (*b*) Sesame
(*c*) Oil palm (*d*) Coconut

17. Nutrient mobility concept was propounded by—
(*a*) Liebig (*b*) Mitscherlich
(*c*) Bray (*d*) Baule

18. Water requirement of irrigated wetland rice is about
(*a*) 400 mm (*b*) 1500 mm
(*c*) 3000 mm (*d*) 800 mm

19. Measurement of sunlight intensity is expressed in—
(*a*) Calories (*b*) Megajoules
(*c*) Millibars (*d*) Lux units

20. Example of stem nodulating legume is—
(*a*) *Sesbania aculeata*
(*b*) *Crotalaria*
(*c*) *Aeschynomene afraspara*
(*d*) *Phaseolus tribobus*

21. The autotrophic bacteria involved in the nitrification process is—
(*a*) Thiobacillus (*b*) Azospirillum
(*c*) Rhizobium (*d*) Nitrosomonas

22. Moisture content at field capacity is approximately ..... per cent of the moisture content at saturation
(*a*) 100 (*b*) 50
(*c*) 75 (*d*) 30

True or False

23. Type 1 error is the rejection of hypothesis when it is actually true.

24. Quantity of water absorbed by a crop for its metabolic use is called its consumptive use.

25. Commercial muriate of potash contains 48.5 K_2O.

26. Fraction of light that is absorbed by a crop canopy is absorptivity coefficient.

27. Movement of water molecules/nutrient ions from regions of high concentration to low concentration is known as diffusion.

Plant Pathology

Multiple choice questions

1. The bacterium, *Corynebacterium michiganse*
(*a*) Gram negative bacterium
(*b*) Causes animal diseases
(*c*) Aquatic bacterium
(*d*) None of the above

2. Microbiology is the study of organisms
(*a*) With single cells
(*b*) With define nucleus
(*c*) Which cannot be seen by the unaided human eye
(*d*) Which move with the help of cilia

3. Prokaryotes are microorganisms
(*a*) With undefined nucleus
(*b*) With defined nucleus
(*c*) Which exhibit well defined mitosis
(*d*) Which contain a complete cytochrome chain

4. The early microscopes are simple microscopes because
(*a*) They were simple to operate
(*b*) They contained a single lens of short focal length
(*c*) They contained a single lens of a very long focal length
(*d*) They had double lens with high resolution

5. Electron microscope has the same principle as light microscope except
(*a*) The illumination system
(*b*) The lens system
(*c*) The fluorescent field
(*d*) All of the above

6. Discoverer of the microbial world was
(*a*) Louis Pasture (*b*) Robert Koch
(*c*) Winogradsky (*d*) All of the above

7. I have had several gentlemen in my house, who were keen on seeing the little eels in vinegar, but some of them were so disgusted at the spectacle, that they vowed they'd never use vinegar again. But what if one should tell such people in future that there are more animals living in the secum on the teeth in a man's mouth, than there are men in the kingdom ? Who made this statement ?
   (*a*) Antony Van Leewenhock
   (*b*) Louis Pasteur (*c*) Spallanzani
   (*d*) Martinus Willem Beijerinck
8. Cowpox postular contents when vaccinated to man, he was protected from smallpox: who invented this
   (*a*) Waksman
   (*b*) Alexander Fleming
   (*c*) Schwann (*d*) Edward Jenner
9. Bacteria and fungi are included under
   (*a*) Plant kingdom (*b*) Animal kingdom
   (*c*) Protista (*d*) None of the above
10. Mycoplasma or PPLO have
   (*a*) Incomplete cell structure
   (*b*) Controlled by antibiotics
   (*c*) Found in plants, animals and soil
   (*d*) All of the above
11. Bacterial flagella are
   (*a*) Made up of flagellin
   (*b*) Containing 9 : 2 fibres
   (*c*) Used inconjugation
   (*d*) All of the above
12. Protozoa belongs to animal kingdom and possess
   (*a*) Cell wall (*b*) Spore
   (*c*) Single cell with flagella
   (*d*) Mult-icellular body
13. A pure-culture isolation technique is
   (*a*) Streak plate method
   (*b*) Agar plate method
   (*c*) Batch culture method
   (*d*) Mass culture method
14. Streptomycin is effective against
   (*a*) Gram negative bacteria
   (*b*) All types of bacteria
   (*c*) Gram positive bacteria
   (*d*) Fungi and bacteria
15. The actinomycetes are characteristed by
   (*a*) Obligate existence with flagellar movement
   (*b*) Short rods with binary cell division
   (*c*) Prokaryotic and with gliding movement
   (*d*) Eubacteria and with mycellum
16. Spore forming anaerobic clostridia carry out fermentation with a common end product
   (*a*) Ethyl alcohol (*b*) Butyl alcohol
   (*c*) Propyl alcohol (*d*) All of the above
17. Bacterial photosynthesis is similar to plant photosynthesis except for the following factors:
   (*a*) Chlorophyll is different
   (*b*) Photolysis is absent
   (*c*) Oxygen is not evolved
   (*d*) All of the above

Fill in the blanks

18. Phanerogamic parasite with chlorophyll but no roots ....
19. A disease caused by *Trichodorus* ....
20. A disease caused by *Anguina* ....
21. A disease caused by *Xiphinema* ....
22. A disease caused by *Rodopholus* ....
23. A fungus used for biological control of plant diseases ....
24. A disease caused by *Pratylenchus* ....
25. Kernel bunt was first reported by ....
26. The first report of plant parasitic nematode was by ....
27. The virus particles were seen for the first time with the electron microscope by ....and his colleagues.

ANSWERS

RAS Pre-Examination 1995

1. (*b*)	2. (*a*)	3. (*d*)	4. (*a*)	5. (*a*)	6. (*c*)	7. (*d*)	8. (*d*)	9. (*c*)	10. (*c*)
11. (*a*)	12. (*c*)	13. (*b*)	14. (*c*)	15. (*d*)	16. (*b*)	17. (*a*)	18. (*b*)	19. (*a*)	20. (*b*)
21. (*a*)	22. (*c*)	23. (*c*)	24. (*b*)	25. (*b*)	26. (*b*)	27. (*b*)	28. (*c*)	29. (*a*)	30. (*b*)
31. (*a*)	32. (*b*)	33. (*a*)	34. (*c*)	35. (*c*)	36. (*a*)	37. (*a*)	38. (*a*)	39. (*d*)	40. (*b*)
41. (*b*)	42. (*c*)	43. (*a*)	44. (*b*)	45. (*d*)	46. (*b*)	47. (*b*)	48. (*c*)	49. (*d*)	50. (*b*)
51. (*d*)	52. (*c*)	53. (*b*)	54. (*b*)	55. (*a*)	56. (*b*)	57. (*d*)	58. (*c*)	59. (*a*)	60. (*d*)
61. (*b*)	62. (*c*)	63. (*b*)	64. (*a*)	65. (*d*)	66. (*a*)	67. (*b*)	68. (*c*)	69. (*d*)	70. (*b*)
71. (*d*)	72. (*b*)	73. (*c*)	74. (*c*)	75. (*a*)	76. (*b*)	77. (*b*)	78. (*a*)	79. (*d*)	80. (*c*)
81. (*d*)	82. (*b*)	83. (*c*)	84. (*d*)	85. (*b*)	86. (*d*)	87. (*a*)	88. (*b*)	89. (*c*)	90. (*a*)
91. (*a*)	92. (*c*)	93. (*c*)	94. (*a*)	95. (*a*)	96. (*e*)	97. (*b*)	98. (*a*)	99. (*b*)	100. (*d*)

JRF, 1997 (Physical Science)

1. (*a*)	2. (*c*)	3. (*b*)	4. (*b*)	5. (*b*)	6. (*b*)	7. (*c*)	8. (*c*)	9. (*a*)	10. (*a*)
11. (*b*)	12. (*c*)	13. (*c*)	14. (*a*)	15. (*d*)	16. (*b*)	17. (*b*)	18. (*c*)	19. (*a*)	20. (*c*)
21. (*b*)	22. (*a*)	23. (*b*)	24. (*c*)	25. (*c*)					

JRF, 1997 (Agronomy)

1. (*a*)	2. (*b*)	3. (*a*)	4. (*c*)	5. (*c*)	6. (*a*)	7. (*a*)	8. (*b*)	9. (*b*)	10. (*b*)
11. (*b*)	12. (*b*)	13. (*a*)	14. (*b*).	15. (*a*)	16. (*c*)	17. (*c*)	18. (*b*)	19. (*a*)	20. (*c*)
21. (*a*)	22. (*b*)	23. (*b*)	24. (*a*)	25. (*b*)	26. (*c*)	27. (*a*)	28. (*a*)	29. (*b*)	30. (*b*)
31. (*a*)	32. (*d*)	33. (*a*)	34. (*d*)	35. (*a*)	36. (*b*)	37. (*c*)	38. (*b*)	39. (*a*)	40. (*a*)
41. (*c*)	42. (*b*)	43. (*b*)	44. (*c*)	45. (*b*)	46. (*d*)	47. (*d*)	48. (*d*)	49. (*a*)	50. (*c*)
51. (*a*)	52. (*d*)	53. (*b*)	54. (*a*)	55. (*d*)	56. (*a*)	57. (*c*)	58. (*d*)		

JRF 1998 (Agronomy)

1. (*d*)	2. (*a*)	3. (*b*)	4. (*b*)	5. (*b*)	6. (*a*)	7. (*a*)	8. (*a*)	9. (*a*)	10. (*b*)
11. (*b*)	12. (*c*)	13. (*b*)	14. (*b*)	15. (*b*)	16. (*c*)	17. (*a*)	18. (*b*)	19. (*a*)	20. (*c*)
21. (*b*)	22. (*a*)	23. (*b*)	24. (*a*)	25. (*b*)	26. (*a*)	27. (*b*)	28. (*a*)	29. (*a*)	30. (*b*)
31. (*d*)	32. (*d*)	33. (*c*)	34. (*a*)	35. (*a*)	36. (*a*)	37. (*c*)	38. (*c*)	39. (*a*)	40. (*b*)
41. (*b*)	42. (*c*)	43. (*b*)	44. (*b*)	45. (*a*)	46. (*b*)	47. (*b*)	48. (*c*)	49. (*b*)	50. (*a*)
51. (*a*)	52. (*a*)	53. (*b*)	54. (*b*)	55. (*a*)	56. (*d*)	57. (*b*)	58. (*c*)	59. (*b*)	60. (*b*)
61. (*a*)	62. (*a*)	63. (*d*)	64. (*d*)	65. (*b*)	66. (*a*)	67. (*c*)	68. (*a*)	69. (*c*)	70. (*b*).

71. (*a*) 72. (*b*) 73. (*d*) 74. (*b*) 75. (*a*) 76. (*a*) 77. (*a*) 78. (*b*) 79. (*b*) 80. (*a*)
81. (*a*) 82. (*b*) 83. (*b*) 84. (*d*) 85. (*b*) 86. (*a*) 87. (*a*) 88. (*b*) 89. (*b*) 90. (*c*)
91. (*b*) 92. (*b*) 93. (*a*) 94. (*b*) 95. (*a*) 96. (*a*) 97. (*a*) 98. (*d*) 99. (*a*) 100. (*a*)
101. (*b*) 102. (*a*) 103. (*a*) 104. (*b*) 105. (*b*) 106. (*a*) 107. (*b*) 108. (*c*) 109. (*a*) 110. (*b*)
111. (*b*) 112. (*c*) 113. (*a*) 114. (*d*) 115. (*a*) 116. (*a*) 117. (*c*) 118. (*a*) 119. (*a*) 120. (*a*)
121. (*a*)

RAS Pre-Examination 1998

1. (*b*) 2. (*b*) 3. (*c*) 4. (*a*) 5. (*d*) 6. (*c*) 7. (*d*) 8. (*c*) 9. (*b*) 10. (*d*)
11. (*a*) 12. (*b*) 13. (*d*) 14. (*a*) 15. (*d*) 16. (*b*) 17. (*d*) 18. (*d*) 19. (*c*) 20. (*d*)
21. (*c*) 22. (*a*) 23. (*b*) 24. (*b*) 25. (*b*) 26. (*c*) 27. (*a*) 28. (*a*) 29. (*c*) 30. (*c*)
31. (*c*) 32. (*d*) 33. (*d*) 34. (*a*) 35. (*c*) 36. (*d*) 37. (*c*) 38. (*b*) 39. (*a*) 40. (*a*)
41. (*a*) 42. (*d*) 43. (*d*) 44. (*b*) 45. (*c*) 46. (*c*) 47. (*a*) 48. (*d*) 49. (*c*) 50. (*d*)
51. (*c*) 52. (*a*) 53. (*c*) 54. (*a*) 55. (*d*) 56. (*c*) 57. (*a*) 58. (*d*) 59. (*d*) 60. (*b*)
61. (*a*) 62. (*c*) 63. (*a*) 64. (*a*) 65. (*a*) 66. (*b*) 67. (*c*) 68. (*b*) 69. (*d*) 70. (*a*)
71. (*c*) 72. (*b*) 73. (*d*) 74. (*c*) 75. (*c*) 76. (*d*) 77. (*c*) 78. (*d*) 79. (*b*) 80. (*c*)
81. (*c*) 82. (*d*) 83. (*b*) 84. (*c*) 85. (*d*) 86. (*d*) 87. (*c*) 88. (*d*) 89. (*d*) 90. (*a*)
91. (*d*) 92. (*c*) 93. (*a*) 94. (*a*) 95. (*b*) 96. (*c*) 97. (*a*) 98. (*b*) 99. (*a*) 100. (*b*)

JRF, 1999 (Plant Science)

1. (*b*) 2. (*a*) 3. (*b*) 4. (*a*) 5. (*b*) 6. (*c*) 7. (*a*) 8. (*a*) 9. (*d*) 10. (*a*)
11. (*a*) 12. (*a*) 13. (*d*) 14. (*a*) 15. (*a*) 16. (*b*) 17. (*b*) 18. (*b*) 19. (*b*) 20. (*c*)
21. (*a*) 22. (*c*) 23. (*b*) 24. (*c*) 25. (*c*) 26. (*c*) 27. (*b*) 28. (*a*)

JRF, 1999 (Social Science)

1. (*b*) 2. (*b*) 3. (*a*) 4. (*c*) 5. (*a*) 6. (*c*) 7. (*d*) 8. (*b*) 9. (*b*) 10. (*b*)
11. (*c*) 12. (*d*) 13. (*b*) 14. (*a*) 15. (*b*) 16. (*c*) 17. (*a*) 18. (*a*) 19. (*b*) 20. (*c*)
21. (*d*) 22. (*c*) 23. (*b*) 24. (*c*) 25. (*a*) 26. (*c*) 27. (*b*) 28. (*b*) 29. (*c*)

JRF, 1999 (Agronomy)

1. (*b*) 2. (*a*) 3. (*d*) 4. (*b*) 5. (*b*) 6. (*a*) 7. (*a*) 8. (*c*) 9. (*b*) 10. (*d*)
11. (*a*) 12. (*c*) 13. (*b*) 14. (*c*) 15. (*a*) 16. (*b*) 17. (*c*) 18. (*c*) 19. (*b*) 20. (*a*)
21. (*a*) 22. (*c*) 23. (*d*) 24. (*b*) 25. (*b*) 26. (*b*) 27. (*a*) 28. (*d*) 29. (*a*) 30. (*a*)
31. (*b*) 32. (*b*) 33. (*c*) 34. (*c*) 35. (*a*) 36. (*a*) 37. (*a*) 38. (*b*) 39. (*a*) 40. (*c*)
41. (*b*) 42. (*a*) 43. (*a*) 44. (*a*) 45. (*b*) 46. (*c*) 47. (*c*) 48. (*c*) 49. (*a*) 50. (*b*)
51. (*b*) 52. (*b*) 53. (*c*) 54. (*b*) 55. (*a*) 56. (*a*) 57. (*b*) 58. (*c*) 59. (*a*) 60. (*b*)
61. (*c*) 62. (*b*) 63. (*b*) 64. (*c*) 65. (*a*) 66. (*b*) 67. (*b*) 68. (*a*) 69. (*c*) 70. (*a*)

71. (*b*) 72. (*b*) 73. (*a*) 74. (*b*) 75. (*a*) 76. (*c*) 77. (*d*) 78. (*c*) 79. (*a*) 80. (*a*)
81. (*a*) 82. (*a*) 83. (*c*) 84. (*a*) 85. (*b*) 86. (*b*) 87. (*b*) 88. (*d*) 89. (*b*) 90. (*a*)
91. (*b*) 92. (*c*) 93. (*b*) 94. (*a*) 95. (*a*) 96. (*c*) 97. (*c*) 98. (*c*) 99. (*a*) 100. (*d*)
101. (*c*) 102. (*c*) 103. (*b*) 104. (*a*) 105. (*b*) 106. (*c*) 107. (*b*) 108. (*c*) 109. (*b*) 110. (*b*)
111. (*a*) 112. (*c*) 113. (*b*) 114. (*b*) 115. (*b*) 116. (*b*) 117. (*a*) 118. (*b*) 119. (*a*) 120. (*c*)
121. (*a*) 122. (*a*) 123. (*a*) 124. (*c*) 125. (*c*) 126. (*d*) 127. (*c*) 128. (*c*) 129. (*c*) 130. (*a*)
131. (*a*) 132. (*a*) 133. (*a*) 134. (*b*) 135. (*a*) 136. (*d*) 137. (*d*) 138. (*b*) 139. (*b*) 140. (*a*)
141. (*c*) 142. (*a*) 143. (*c*) 144. (*a*) 145. (*a*) 146. (*a*)

JRF, 1999 (Entomology)

1. (*a*) 2. (*d*) 3. (*a*) 4. (*d*) 5. (*d*) 6. (*b*) 7. (*a*) 8. (*a*) 9. (*b*) 10. (*a*)
11. (*c*) 12. (*d*) 13. (*a*) 14. (*c*) 15. (*d*) 16. (*a*) 17. (*c*) 18. (*a*) 19. (*a*) 20. (*c*)
21. (*c*) 22. (*d*) 23. (*a*) 24. (*b*) 25. (*b*) 26. (*a*) 27. (*a*) 28. (*a*) 29. (*b*) 30. (*b*)
31. (*a*) 32. (*c*) 33. (*a*) 34. (*b*) 35. (*a*) 36. (*a*) 37. (*d*) 38. (*a*) 39. (*c*) 40. (*b*)
41. (*c*) 42. (*a*) 43. (*b*) 44. (*c*) 45. (*d*) 46. (*a*) 47. (*b*) 48. (*a*) 49. (*a*) 50. (*a*)
51. (*b*) 52. (*c*) 53. (*a*) 54. (*d*) 55. (*d*) 56. (*a*) 57. (*b*) 58. (*c*) 59. (*d*) 60. (*b*)
61. (*a*) 62. (*a*)

JRF, 1999 (Biotechnology)

1. (*b*) 5. (*a*) 6. (*a*) 7. (*a*) 8. (*b*) 9. (*a*) 10. (*b*) 11. (*a*) 12. (*a*) 13. (*d*)
14. (*d*) 15. (*b*) 16. (*a*) 17. (*a*) 18. (*c*) 19. (*b*)

Model Question Paper, Administrative Service Examination

1. (*d*) 2. (*c*) 3. (*b*) 4. (*d*) 5. (*b*) 6. (*a*) 7. (*d*) 8. (*d*) 9. (*d*) 10. (*b*)
11. (*c*) 12. (*c*) 13. (*a*) 14. (*c*) 15. (*d*) 16. (*b*) 17. (*b*) 18. (*b*) 19. (*c*) 20. (*a*)
21. (*c*) 22. (*c*) 23. (*a*) 24. (*b*) 25. (*b*) 26. (*a*) 27. (*a*) 28. (*c*) 29. (*a*) 30. (*a*)
31. (*b*) 32. (*c*) 33. (*b*) 34. (*a*) 35. (*c*) 36. (*b*) 37. (*a*) 38. (*c*) 39. (*d*) 40. (*d*)
41. (*a*) 42. (*c*) 43. (*a*) 44. (*b*) 45. (*a*) 46. (*a*) 47. (*a*) 48. (*a*) 49. (*b*) 50. (*c*)
51. (*a*) 52. (*d*) 53. (*a*) 54. (*a*) 55. (*d*) 56. (*c*) 57. (*c*) 58. (*b*) 59. (*b*) 60. (*b*)
61. (*c*) 62. (*b*) 63. (*d*) 64. (*b*) 65. (*a*) 66. (*b*) 67. (*a*) 68. (*c*) 69. (*b*) 70. (*c*)
71. (*b*) 72. (*c*) 73. (*a*) 74. (*a*) 75. (*b*) 76. (*a*) 77. (*b*) 78. (*b*) 79. (*a*) 80. (*c*)
81. (*b*) 82. (*b*) 83. (*c*) 84. (*c*) 85. (*d*) 86. (*a*) 87. (*b*) 88. (*b*) 89. (*c*) 90. (*b*)
91. (*d*) 92. (*d*) 93. (*b*) 94. (*c*) 95. (*c*) 96. (*c*) 97. (*b*) 98. (*c*) 99. (*d*) 100. (*d*)
101. (*b*) 102. (*b*) 103. (*b*) 104. (*c*) 105. (*d*) 106. (*d*) 107. (*a*) 108. (*a*) 109. (*a*) 110. (*b*)
111. (*d*) 112. (*c*) 113. (*c*) 114. (*b*) 115. (*c*) 116. (*c*)

Net/ARS Question Paper

Plant Breeding and Genetics : (Multiple choice Questions)

1. (*b*) 2. (*c*) 3. (*b*) 4. (*a*) 5. (*a*) 6. (*b*) 7. (*a*) 8. (*c*) 9. (*b*) 10. (*a*) 11. (*c*) 12. (*d*) 13. (*d*) 14. (*a*) 15. (*b*) 16. (*c*)

17. β-rays 18. Ribose sugar phosphoric acid and nitrogenous base 19. Inbreeding 20. 6 21. Backcross 22. Recurrent parent 23. Operator, Promotor 24. 5'-3', 5'-3' 25. Pleiotropic 26. White blood 27. White blood 28. Virus 29. 756 30. BT

Animal Husbandry

1. Nucleotides 2. *y* 3. Beadle and Tatum 4. *x* 5. Salivary glands of 6. Haemiglobin 7. Homocysteine 8. glycogen 9. Megaloblastic 10. Urea. Uric acid 11. (*t*) 12. Small and large intestine 13. Cholcaciferol 14. Carbamic acid 15. 4 16. 38 17. Heat nutrient metabolism 18. 9.4, 9 19. 15 20. Zinc 21. Vitamin A deficiency

Biotechnology : Tick (✓) mark the correct answer

1. (*b*) 2. (*c*) 3. (*b*) 4. (*a*) 5. (*a*) 6. (*a*) 7. (*c*) 8. (*b*) 9. (*d*) 10. (*a*)

Nematology

1. Loranthus 2. Stubby roots of sugarcane 3. Ear cockle disease of wheat 4. Discoloration of root system • 5. *Arthrobotrys/Trichothecium* 6. *Corynobacterium tritice* 7. Panama disease 8. *Streptomyces* fungus 9. *Griesofurim* by *Streptomyces zriesus* 10. Root usions 11. Munkar (1943) 12. Sigmoid curve 13. Magnesium deficiency 14. Needham (1743) 15. *Globodera rostockins* 16. Cooks (1878)

17. False	18. True	19. True	20. True	21. True	22. True
23. True	24. True	25. True	26. True	27. False	28. False
29. True	30. False	31. True	32. True		

Horticulture

1. True 2. True 3. True 4. False 5. False 6. Diallyl propyl disulphide, capsacin 7. Nitrogen and Molybdenum 8. Mulching and transpiration suppressants 9. *Rhizoctonia* spp. 10. Pusa Rubi and Pusa Gaurav 11. Physiological disorder 12. Radiation, Asepsis Filteration, Cold treatment 13. Banana, Mango. Papaya 14. Cucurbits *e.g.* Cucumbei, Spongezonard 15. Pusa Rubix Selection 120 16. Thiourea, Sulphuric acid 17. Indole Acetic Acid, Indole Butyric acid 18. Little leaf, leaf curl 19. Peas, Tomato

Biotechnology

1. True	2. True	3. True	4. True	5. True	6. False
7. False	8. False	9. True	10. True	11. True	12. True
13. True	14. True	15. True	16. True	17. False	18. True
19. True	20. (*a*)	21. (*a*)	22. (*b*)	23. (*a*)	24. (*a*)
25. (*c*)	26. (*a*)	27. (*b*)	28. (*a*)	29. (*a*)	30. (*b*)
31. (*a*)	32. (*a*)	33. (*a*)	34. (*a*)	35. (*b*)	36. (*c*)
37. (*a*)	38. (*c*)	39. (*b*)			

40. Greater 41. Smaller 42. Supply of 43. Increase/decrease 44. Less 45. None 46. AN 47. Relative 48. Upward .49. Unrelated 50. 30,000 51. Opportunity 52. Reduces 53. Frictional 54. 230 55. Decreased 56. Less 57. Less

Soil Science: Multiple Choice

1. (*c*)	2. (*d*)	3. (*d*)	4. (*d*)	5. (*b*)	6. (*a*)
7. (*b*)	8. (*c*)	9. (*b*)	10. (*a*)	11. (*a*) (*iv*)	11. (*b*) (*v*)
11. (*c*) (*ii*)	11. (*d*) (*vi*)	11. (*f*) (*i*)	11. (*g*) (*x*)	11. (*h*) (*ix*)	11. (*i*) (*viii*)
11. (*j*) (*vii*)	12. (*a*)	13. (*b*)	14. (*c*)	15. (*c*)	16. (*d*)
17. (*c*)	18. (*c*)	19. (*c*)	20. (*a*)	21. False	22. True
23. True	24. False	25. True	26. False	27. True	28. False
29. True	30. True	31. True	32. True	33. True	34. False
35. False	36. False	37. True			

38. Remote sensing and G/S 39. Higher 40. 5-6 41. Reserve, Active acid Potential 42. Cmoli/kg g/kz, mv 43. Diethylene triamine penta acetic acid, Ethylene diamino tetra acetic acid 44. Nitrogenase 45. Phospholipid nucleic acid, inociatol, Phytin 46. Radio 47. Greiger Muller 48. 10 : 10 : 1 49. Silica, Alumina 50. –1 to +1 51. Two 52. Adhesive, Cohesive 53. More than 8·5, More than 15%

Entomology

1. True	2. False	3. True	4. False	5. False	6. True
7. False	8. False	9. False	10. False	11. False	12. True

13. Epiculticle 14. Chorain, vitelline 15. Aphids

16. Callosobruchus 17. X-ray technique 18. Phosphine 19. Lepidoptera, Coleoptera, Isoptera 20. Haemolymph, Circulation 21. A.D. 9 mms 22. Dichlorodiphenyl trichloro ethane 23. *Schestocerca zragaria, locusta migratoria*, and *Patanga succinata*

Agronomy

1. (*b*)	2. (*c*)	3. (*a*)	4. (*a*)	5. (*b*)	6. (*a*)	7. (*c*)	8. (*d*)	9. (*a*)	10. (*d*)
11. (*a*)	12. (*c*)	13. (*a*)	14. (*b*)	15. (*a*)	16. (*b*)	17. (*c*)	18. (*b*)	19. (*d*)	20. (*c*)

21. (*d*) 22. (*c*) 23. True 24. False 25. False 26. True 27. True

Agronomy

1. (*d*)	2. (*c*)	3. (*a*)	4. (*b*)	5. (*c*)	6. (*a*)	7. (*c*)	8. (*d*)	9. (*a*)	10. (*d*)
11. (*a*)	12. (*c*)	13. (*a*)	14. (*b*)	15. (*b*)	16. (*a*)				

17. (*c*) 18. *Loranthus* spp. 19. Stubby roots 20. Wheat Ear cockle disease 21. Girdling of roots 22. Tunnel form of banana 23. Streptomyces 24. M. Mitra, 1931 25. Nedham, 1743 26. Kanche

GLOSSARY

Active Absorption means the ions cross the cytoplasmic membrane, plasmalema due to the energetics of high energy phosphate bonds like ATP produced in respiration. The vacuole, a storage reservoir inside the cell for water and ions, function to stabilize supply and demand balance.

Adaplation according to Daubenmire (1947) denotes any feature of an organism that is of definite value to its existence under the conditions of its habitat. Such features, permit the organism (plant) make better use of nutrients, moisture, light or may protect against adverse conditions. It may be direct *i.e.*, moulding in direct response to a particular need or indirect *i.e.*, by selective action of environment on the available genetic variations.

Adaptation denotes a feature of an organism which embodies survival value under the conditions of its existence in a habitat. The feature(s) may permit the plant to make fuller use of the nutrients, water, temperature and/or available light or may provide the protection against adverse factors *viz*., extremes of temperatures, detrimental diseases and insects (rather pests).

Agricultural Ecology is the study of the physical environment, climate and soil, in relation to the development of agricultural plants and to the yield of such plants from quantitative, qualitative and generative (characters of the seed) points of view.

Albedo represents the ratio of radiation reflected to the amount received on a surface. The earth's mean albedo also called the planetary albedo is about 30%. Its value is higher in polar region than that at the equator and is influenced by the angle of incidence and characteristics of the reflecting surface.

Alkaloids are cyclic nitrogenous storage compounds found in seeds and vegetative plant parts which cause strong flavours, odours and maybe toxic to other plants and animals. Some of the important ones are nicotine, caffeine, theobromine (in tea), morphine, strychnine, those in forage grasses reduce palatability, those in seeds inhibit germination and they may be allelochemicals.

Allelopathy is also known as antibiosis of allelochemical interaction. It is any direct or indirect inhibitory influence of one plant species usually due to exudation of chemicals from the roots on seed germination or the growth and development of the associated or succeeding plant species.

OR

"It is any direct or indirect harmful effect that one plant has on the other or mutually on each other through the production of chemical compounds that escape into the growth environment/medium (Rice, 1974) due to allo or auto-inhibition. It may be *true allelopathy* (active substances released causing inhibition in released form itself) and *functional allelopathy* (the substances may be released as precurssor(s) to be changed in an active substance to inhibit growth)."

Allometry denotes the relationship between the growth rates of an individual plant part or an organ or organism. The harvest index has relatively a high coefficient of allometry and is a stable temporal and spatial parameter. Though it is a physical parameter, logically follows physiological processes that are correlated.

Amino Acids : These are fundamental building blocks of proteins. There are 20 naturally occurring amino acids in animals and around 100 or more found in plants.

Annidation is the complementary use of environmental supplies of the growth factors (resources) by the intercrop or mixed crop components. It may be temporal as relay cropping of one component before the other is actually harvested (on full or physiological maturity) or spatial as intercropping in initial stages of orchard establishment or nutritional as inter/mixed cropping of a legume with a non-legume.

Antagonistic effect is the total effect due to combined application of active components amounting to less than the effect of a single active component.

Apoplastic Movement describes the movement along the cell wall as from cuticle to tracheid in leaves or from cortex to xylem in roots and also includes rapid transport in vessels and tracheids of the xylem in the transpiration stream and migration from the tracheids along walls to mesophyll in leaves. Like the symplastic movement, it also describes the transport processes in plants, that is, uptake and distribution and is used in case of systemic/translocated herbicides.

Atmosphere represents the gaseous envelope around the earth, the air consisting of a number of gases of which nitrogen, oxygen, carbon dioxide and water vapours are the most important. It exerts the pressure equal to 14.7 pounds per square inch or of mercury column equivalent to 760 millimetres.

Auxin is a generic term for the growth substances that typically stimulate not only the cell elongation, but also cause wide range of growth responses. Indole Acetic Acid (IAA) is the first natural substance isolated and identified to embody auxin activity. Indole Aceto Nitrile (IAN), Indole Pryruvic Acid (IPyA) and Indole Actaldehyde (IAAld) are intermediates in the synthesis of IAA from the amino acid precurssor tryptophane. Phenoxy Acetic Acid, Naphthalene Acetic Acid and Pecolenic and Benzoic Acids and Dinitrophenols are synthetic auxins.

Biofertilizers. These are organisms that enrich the nutrient quality of soil. Main sources of biofertilizers are bacteria, fungi and cyanobacteria (blue green algae).

Biological Control of pests (insects, diseases and weeds etc.) entails the deployment of insects and diseases or any other organism(s) to control them. It usually works well on species introduced free from natural predators and use of natural predators to prey upon them. The predators must be freed from parasites to make them functional unhempered of their natural enemy. Feeding habit/growing habit is predetermined of the predator by suitable tests as to starving test in case of insects. It needs be ensured that the introduction of the predator may not force it to turn into a pest itself later.

Biological magnification denotes a successive increase in the quantity of some chemicals on account of different food level organisms like that of DDT from water to algae to herbivore fish to carnivore fish to fish eating birds and to persons.

Biological Spectrum is the range and ratio of different life forms in an area like that of phanerophytes, therophytes etc., or the range of the various levels of biotic organization from sub cellular to cellular, to an organ, to an individual, to a population or to a community level.

Biomass Duration usually abbreviated as BMD is analogous to LAD. Mean BMD = $[(W_2 - W_1)/2] \times (T_2 - T_1)$ where, W = weight and T = time. The computation of area under the time curve for biomass production is done as for LAD, the value of biomass persistence with time is obtained.

Biotic Community means a functional unit held together by the interdependence of its members, consists of smaller groups or populations (usually composed of the individuals of the same species) of the members intimately associated with each other.

Bio-Toxicity represents the toxic influence owing to non-selectivity of the applied substance or its use in intolerable lethal concentrations.

Cardinal Growth Temperatures mean the minimum, optimum and maximum limits of not only the temperature, but also other factors of plant growth environment. Plant activities occur within more or less defined tolerance limits of temperatures and a minimum level of temperature is required for a plant to function, at some temperature its functioning is at the optimum rate which ceases to function at higher levels and hence the knowledge of cardinal limits is very essential for all growth factors.

Chemical Control as the name indicates, the method of pest control involves the use of a highly toxic and relatively inexpensive chemical(s). Though salt, ashes, smelter wastes and other industrial by-products have been in use for centuries, Liebig's chemical theory of plant nutrition, use of some chemicals leading to accidental control of pests, and selective control by some chemicals in mixed plant populations (iron sulphate, sulphuric acid and copper nitrate, in 1896 and 1997) aroused added interest and led to identification of a variety of chemicals to control pests.

Chemical Fallow entails use of chemicals for the control of unwanted vegetation either to eliminate or minimize tillage in order to maintain soil structure, permeability and penetration of water and gases, and also to minimize the loss of soil by water or wind erosion. It may become popular as less expensive (cost effective) chemicals become available for chemical elimination of weeds.

Chemosynthesis : Process of carbohydrate synthesis in which the organisms use chemical reactions to obtain energy from inorganic compounds. *Example* bacteria of the genus Nitrosomonas oxidise ammonia to nitrite.

Chromosomes : Thread or rod like structure in eukaryotes found in nucleus; made up of nucleoprotein and contain all the nuclear genes. The paired, self-replicating genetic structures of cells that contain the cellular DNA; the nucleotide sequence of the DNA encodes the linear array of genes.

Cistron : A unit function in DNA. One DNA cistron specifies one polypeptide chain in protein synthesis.

Climate represents the exchange processes within the atmosphere and between the atmosphere and earth accumulated over an extended period of time. The climate is thus an aggregate of the environmental conditions involving heat, moisture and motion and the climatic studies have necessarily to take into account the means, trends, fluctuations, probabilities, and also temporal as well as spatial variations.

Climatology consists of the Greek word *klima* (slope of the earth or say present day latitude) and *logos* (study or discourse). It is the science dealing with the description and explanation of nature of climatic variations from one to other place, ingredients of natural environment and the human activities.

Clone : All individuals derived by vegetative propagation from a single original individual.

Coenzymes : These are organic molecules that are required by certain enzymes to carry out catalysis. They bind to the active site of the enzyme and participate in catalysis but are not considered substrates of the reaction. They often function as intermediate carriers of electrons, specific atoms or functional groups that are transferred in the overall reaction. An example is the role of NAD in the transfer of electrons in certain coupled oxidation reduction reactions. Some examples are : Nicotine adenine dinucelotide (NAD), nicotine adenine dinucelotide phosphate (NADP), flavine adenine dinucelotide (FAD), Thiamine pyrophosphate (thiamine vit. B1) and biotin.

Cofactor : It is a non-protein chemical compound that is bound (either tightly or loosely) to a protein and is required for the protein's biological activity. These proteins are commonly enzymes and cofactors can be considered as "helper molecules/ions" that assist in biochemical transformations. Cofactors are often classified as inorganic substances that are required for, or increase the rate of, catalysis. Some examples are Zn^{++}, Fe^{+++} or Fe^{++}, Cu^{++} or Cu^{+}, K^{+} and Mg^{++}.

Combined Herbicides represent two or more herbicides combined together, many modern herbicide formulations contain an appropriate combination of toxicants to broaden their spectrum, to kill a greater variety of weeds like 2.4.D plus IPC, MCPA plus TCA, plus amitrol etc. These may embody synergistic action, may slow down or preclude detoxication of a more active toxicant or may inhibit delitarius action of other toxicant but need careful use.

Competition originated from the Latin word (verb) *competere* means to ask or sue for the same thing that another does. Etymologically, competition means seeking together in a situation when the combined demand of associate species for a particular growth factor cannot be met with when the plant species come together in the process of migration, ecesis and aggregation. It is purely a physical process with some exceptions like crowding of tuberous plants grown too closely (Clements *et al.* 1929). Two plants do not compete so long as water, nutrients, light and heat exceed their combined requirement.

Competition Relationship means *mutual inhibition* wherein the actual yield of each inter/mixed crop component (in 50:50 ratio) is less than the expected yield (occurs any rarely); *mutual co-operation* wherein the actual yield of each species exceeds the expected yield and compensation wherein the yield of one species is less than expected, while of the other species is more than expected. These have been based on replacement series.

Contact Herbicide means a herbicide which kills a plant by foliage contact action. It leads to the death of the cells in its immediate contact. It may be selective or- non-selective. Selective killing results from selective wetting and biochemical selectivity. Non-selective ones kill all the herbs which they come in contact with, these are used (contact herbicides) as per need of the control of weeds, that is, cropped or uncropped lands.

Control refers to a method employed to produce a profitable crop in spite of the infestation by weeds. It is a common procedure followed in field crop culture and horticultural crops or in situations where weed eradication entails the expenditure more than the cost the land concerned. Control comprises manual, mechanical, chemical, and biological methods used singly or in a suitable integrated manner.

Crop Ecology is the study of relationship between the crop plants and their environment. It includes the study of climate, soil, biotic and social factors. Their collective study is called ecological crop geography.

Crop Growth Rate is the gain in weight by a community of plants on a unit land area in a unit time. It is used in growth analysis of field crops. It is equal to $1/GA \times (W_2 - W_1) / (T_2 - T_1)$ weight (W) per unit area per unit time (T). CGR of 20 g/m^2/day = 200 kg/ha/day which is considered respectable for most of the field crops

OR

C.G.R is the rate of dry matter accumulation per unit land area per unit of time usually expressed in g/m^2/day. It comprises a most meaningful means of growth analysis of crop canopies and can be determined periodically. It is closely related to interception of solar radiation.

Crop Strategy Evaluation is done at three levels *viz.,* crop level, means the component technology is assessed to maximize the productivity of only a particular crop regardless of its consequences on the associated or the succeeding crop(s), cropping pattern level, means evaluation of the package of practices collectively for a cropping pattern to augment its total productivity and the farm level evaluation refers to the assessment of package of practices for a group (aggregate) of cropping patterns to maximize the farm productivity.

Cropping System denotes the cropping patterns used on a farm and their interactions with farm resources, other farm enterprises and available technology. These may be commerce/commodity oriented or merely for self-sustenance.

Crown Roots are also called adventitious, nodal, or coronal roots. They emerge from the basal nodes of the grass shoot immediately underneath soil surface. There are 3-6 nodes without internode growth to form the crown in plants of grass family. It gives rise to successive whorls of adventitious roots termed as crown roots. In case of wheat the emergence is by elongation of second internode, but in grasses, in general, of the first internode of mesocotyle as in maize and hence the crown in their case is positioned near the soil surface regardless of the seeding depth. Mesocotyle elongation ceases below the surface due to phytochrome, red light mechanism in coleoptile.

Cytokinins is a generic name for growth substances that typically stimulate cell division (cytokinesis) and also regulate and correlate a wide range of activities in morphogenesis. Young roots, immature fruits and seeds, and nurse tissues are rich in kinins, fruits of apple, banana, milky endosperm of coconut and immature maize seeds are especially rich in kinins. The purine base is common in both natural and synthetic kinins. Apparenthly, these are not transported and hence are presumably the sites of synthesis.

Darwinian fitness or adaptive value represents the reproductive efficiency of a genotype in a certain environment. In a populatioin of a mixture of genetically distinct types some of them (plants) may produce more surviving progeny than others.

Dew or white frost forms in a clear weather with little or no wind due to cooling of the surface layers of atmosphere at night. Rapid radiation from earths surface causes cooling of the adjacent air layer to the point of saturation and condensation takes place and the condensed water vapour is dew.

Doldrums refer to an equatorial belt of low pressure coinciding rather closely with the belts of the highest pressures. This is the region of ascending warm and moist air currents and heavy precipitation.

Dormancy denotes the suspended state of growth or rest and persists for an indefinite period despite the conditions favourable for seed germination. Quiescence is a more descriptive term for the seed rest resulting from an environmental condition non-supportive of germination. A dormant seed is the one that fails to germinate when provided with the environmental conditions supportive for the germination of non-dormant member of the seed population.

Ecotype represents the genetically distinct race within the framework of species and the variation in character/trait is associated with the variation in some environmental conditions. It is briefly defined as a group of biotypes (a homozygous or heterozygous group of an identical genetic constitution) adapted to a specific environmental niche. A niche means a place destined for an occupation by an organism.

OR

Ecotype denotes a group of biotypes specially adapted to a specific environmental niche (homestead). A biotype includes the members of a group having the same genetic constitution and may be either homozygous or heterozygous.

Ecological backlash is also known as ecological boomerang and denotes the unforeseen cancellation of projected gain or unforeseen adverse or catestrophic reaction from a natural system on account of human interference, management or the developmental activities.

Ecological Efficiency is the pecentage of ratios between energy flow at different points along the food chain. The ratios may have useful meaning in reference to the component populations in a biological community.

Ecological pyramid is the diagrammatic representation of number/counts, biomass, energy or productivity of different trophic level organisms with autotrophs at the base superimposed by those of herbivores, carnivores of the first order, second order and so on.

Ecology the word is derived from Greek word Oikos = dwelling/ homestead/ abode/ house and logos = study of; it has been defined as the study of the inter relationship between the plants, animals and microorganisms and their environment. Ecology as a scientific disciple is little more than a century old.

Ecosystem denotes an area of nature that includes living organisms and non-living substanes inseparably related and constantly interacting to produce an exchange of materials between living and non-living entities like a forest, lake, pond or a field. It consists of abiotic substances, producers, consumers and decomposers.

OR

Ecosystem denotes the structural and functional entity of the biotic communities and their physical dimensions or size. It is a basic funtional unit and may also be defined as the whole complex of plants and animals forming a community in the form of a single unit together with all the physical factors of environment.

Embryogenesis : Embryogenesis is a process whereby a plant is formed from one cell in a tissue, or callus by the normal zygotic pathway. Process is initiated by hormones or in the absence of hormones (*e.g.*, carrot, brome grass).

Environmental Resistance means the forces which tend to limit the population of an organism. The forces include the unfavourable physical factors of environment and unfavourable biotic factors of plant environment directly or indiretly related to the living organism ranging from soil microorganisms to man.

Equinoxes means that the lengths of day and night (on 21 March and 21 September) are approximately equal at all the latitudes. The day length at equator is 12 hours, while 30, 40, 60° north latitude and at north pole are 14, 15, 19 and 24 hours, respectively. The difference in day and night lengths as related to latitude constitutes a important factor in the natural distribution of vegetation.

Eradication of weeds means to grub them out and destruction of all the parts thereof to ensure that there is no recurrence of infestation. The infested area need be carefully watched and monitored as long as there comes no seedings of the destroyed weed species. It may be accomplished by use of chemicals (soil sterilants and fumigants or by manual method used singly or in a suitable combination).

Ethylene is a small gaseous molecule unique both chemically and physiologically among the phytohormones (Abeles, 1973). Beacuse of emission from ripening climacteric fruits like apple, banana stone fruits (having climax in ripening), the mixing of ripe fruits promotes more uniform ripening due to free movement from ripe to green tissues. Besides, climacteric fruits, it has also been found in leaves, stems, roots, flowers, fruits and seeds.

Explant : A plant organ or piece of tissue used to initiate a tissue culture.

Exponential Index its computation by Livingston and Livingston (1913) made use of the laws founded by van't Hoff and Arrhenius which state, "the velocity of chemical reaction doubles with each increase of about 10°C. The thermal efficiency index (μ) for each day of the season was computed as – μ = 2 (temp-40)" 18. This index recognises that the plant responses to increasing temperature are not linear, this index too postulates the efficiency of supra-optimal temperatures.

Farming System refers to an appropriate combination of farm enterprises *viz.*, cropping systems, livestock, inland fisheries, forestry, poultry, piggery, small scale cottage industry etc., and the means (resources), to raise them for sustainable profitablitity. They adequately interact with environment without dislocation of the ecological and socio-economic balance on one hand and endeavour to meet the national goal on the other. The usufructs of one constitutes the input of the other system-component and there results no waste or unfriendly residues.

Fermentation : It is the process of energy production in a cell under anaerobic conditions without oxygen.

Fog is formed when air masses of high moisture content close to the surface are cooled. Minute hygroscopic particles are effective as condensation nuclei about which waterdroplets form. Salt and smoke are among the most important of these fine particles.

Food chain has been defined as the transfer of food energy from the source in green plants through a series of organisms with repeated eating and being eaten by either predators or parasites or saprophytes.

formula is Index $(T-32/4)\,n$ or $TE = (T-32/4)\,n$ where, $n = 1$ and T = mean monthly temperature in °F. Thornthwaite (1948) also developed thermal efficiency index of evapotranspiration on this basis because the temperature is the primary variable in computation of evapotranspiration.

Fuzz : Non separable part of fiber attached to cotton seeds.

Gene duplication : Genetic alteration in which a segment of DNA is repeated. Duplications may appear anywhere, but where the duplicated segment is adjacent to the original one is called *tandem duplication.*

Genetic drift : It is the change in the relative frequency in which a gene variant occurs in a population due to random sampling and chance rather than natural selection. In genetic drift, a population experiences a change in the frequency of a given allele prompted by random luck rather than a need for adaptation.

Genotype-phenotype, a genotype denotes the heredity of an organism transmitted by parents to retain rather constantly through life. Phenotype refers to the appearance of the organism what it looks like-which is subject to change throughout life.

Germination is the resumption of active growth leading to the rupture of seed and emergence of the seedling and consists of physiological events *viz*., inhibition and absorption of water, tissues-hydration, oxygen absorption, enzymes and digestion activation, transportation of hydrolized molecules to embryo axis, increase in respiration and assimilation, cell division and enlargement-initiation and embryo emergence.

Gibberellins (GA) were discovered when a rice disease called *bakanae* (foolish seedling disease) in Japan led to the isolation and identification of the causative pathogen from the fungus Gibberella fujikuroi (*Fusartium moniliforme*). It was cell-free extract of *GA* like substances and later found that the GA are diterpenoids, which places them in the same chemical family as chlorophyll and carotene. The basic chemical moieties are gibbane skeleton and free carboxyl group.

Gibberellins : A group of plant hormones responsible for stimulation of the growth of leaves and shoots in general and internodal length of genetically dwarf plants in particular.

Gossypol ($C_{30}H_{30}O_8$) : It is a polyphenol derived from the cotton plant. It acts as a inhibitor for several dehydrogenase enzymes. It is a yellow pigment.

Gravitational Potential is always present but has only a little (or no) significance in case of short plants *vis*-a-*vis* other potentials. It can be significant in tall trees. It is due to the force of gravitation and is designated as ϕ g.

Greenhouse effect is the heating influence owing to trapping of the re-radiating heat waves, brought about by radiation reaching ground surface, allowed by atmosphere, dust, water vapours, carbon dioxide, ozone etc. The solar radiation enters a greenhouse (glass-house), but the re-radiating heat is trapped inside and results in rise of inside temperature. It is identical in sequence of events leading to rise in temperature and hence the name.

Gross production means the total enhancement in organic matter and energy fixation by photosynthesis per unit area or volume per unit time. The deduction of the loss due to respiration from the gross total (production) represents net production.

Growth denotes cell division, enlargement and differentiation leading to plant development and morphogenesis. It is measured in terms of dry matter accumulation. Fresh weight is less useful due to fluctuation, but the vegetables, fruits and flowers production measure growth in terms of fresh weight coupled with quality factors.

Growth Inhibitors represent a diverse group of substances that generally inhibit the plant growth. The commonest of them are aromatic compounds *viz*., phenols, lactones, and alkaloids, certain alcohols and fatty acids and even metallic ions can act as inhibitors. These have been grouped into three groups *viz*., phytohormones like terpenoid such as ABA, other natural inhibitors (phenolic and benzoic acid derivatives and lactones) and synthetics growth retardants are-phosfon-D and Amo-1618, daminozide.

Guttation: Loss of water in the liquid state from uninjured parts of plants is known as guttation. It usually occurs from tips and margins of leaves during night or early morning when there is high atmospheric humidity.

Half life represent the time required by the radioactive isotopes or by the pesticides fungicide (insecticide, herbicide or nematicide) to get reduced to its half strength or decay to reach half the level of strength of its initial strength.

Harvest Index is the proportion of biological yield (total dry matter accumulation) represented by economic yield (volume/weight of plant organs of economic/agricultural value) expressed in percentage.

$$\text{Harvest Index} = \frac{\text{Economic yield}}{\text{Biological yield}} \times 100$$

Heat Unit System This measure of thermal efficiency has been called by various names like remainder index system, temperature summation, day degrees, degree days, heat or thermal unit system. The direct summation of temperature above an established or vital temperature point provides a measure of temperature efficiency. However, no weighing is accorded to the efficiency of various levels of temperature and the detrimental thermal effects are also ignored.

Heaving is a term usually employed to define one of the effects of low temperature on plants. It means a upward lift of a plant from its normal position. Heaving pressure mounts (as much as 200 psi) with the decrease in soil particle size the free water forms filaments grouped in columns (oriented) vertically to the soil surface.

Herbarium : It is a collection of preserved plant specimens. There specimens may be whole plants or plant parts; these are usually in dry form, mounted on sheet or may be kept in alcohol or other preservative.

Homokaryon: A bi or multinucleate cell having nuclei of the same kind in a common cytoplasm.

Humidity is the measure of the moisture in the atmosphere expressed either as absolute or relative humidity. Absolute humidity represents the amount of water vapour present in a unit volume of air. Relative humidity means the amount of water vapour in the atmosphere as a percentage of that which could be held at saturation at a particular temperature and pressure.

Hybrid : Offsprings received from two genetically dissimilar individuals, strains, purelines etc.

Hydrolysis : A process that occurs when a large molecule is broken down into smaller parts by the addition of water.

Hydrothermal Index is also called moisture-temperature index and was evolved by Livingston (1914) using the following relationship: $I_{mt} = I_t (I_p / I_o)$ where I_t = index of temperature determined on the basis of physiological index, I_{mt} = moisture temperature efficiency index, I_p = intensity of precipitation and I_o = evaporating power of the atmosphere. It has been assumed that the plant growth increases proportionally to the value of rainfall index and retards proportionally to the index of evaporation and temperature index is correlated with the rates of activity manifested in plants.

Inoculum: A biological material (like a virus or toxin or immune serum) that in injected to increase immunity to a particular disease.

Inter/mixed Crop Durability has been defined as the extent to which the ecological basis of the system permits it to operate efficiently over a sufficiently long period of time. Long term persistence (say over a century) is the criterion of durability, therefore, it is to be adjudicated at the level of an agricultural system rather than that at an individual crop or cropping system level.

Inter/mixed Crop Resilience means the magnitude and extent of cropability to survive the stress or perturbation with the minimum ill effect on yield or (net returns). Recovery in a sole crop after shock involves compensation within and between the plants of an identical genotype, whereas in inter/mixed crop, the compensation is also between the components and hence embody relatively more resilience.

Inter/mixed crop Stability refers to the extent to which the aggregate yield or net returns of a mixed / intercop grown at a site remain constant year to year in the face of climate and other fluctuations. It can be measured as the reciprocal of the coefficient of variaton of either yields or net returns. The rotations, mixtures and proper monitoring strategies augment stability (Holling, 1973).

Intercopping denotes growing of usually two or more than two crops simultaneously on the same piece of land (field), one of them being the main/base crop sown using advocated seed rate to obtain/maintain the optimum pure crop density in recommended interand intra-row arrangement or in a suitably modified row (sowing/planting) geometry and the intercrop (component) is suitably pushed in between/among the main crop rows which entails better spatial and temporal crop intensification. It is denoted with a plus mark (+) like maize + mung bean and referred to as additive series. On the contrary, when one/two rows of the base crop is (are) replaced by the intercrop, it is called replacement series.

Interference refers to the interaction between two plants resulting in growth inhibition of either one or both of them. It consists of competition and allelopathy and deserves analytical decideratum especially in inter/mixed cropping systems and sequential cropping particularly multiple cropping for their stable and durable production (Muller, 1996).

Ion Carrier Theory indicates that the molecules in the plasmalema have binding sites specific to certain ions causing selectivity. A carrier ion complex formed at the membrane interface carries the ion across the membrane and subsequently discharges the same into the cell. It is mediated by ATP and the enzyme kinase (Mengel and Kirkby, 1979).

Ion Pump Theory means that the energy released by the conversion of ATP to ADP through AT Pase (causes) ions to move into the cell due to change in balance created as other ions leave the cell. Sodium potassium pump constitutes a common example.

Ionosphere is the uppermost layer of the atmosphere above the stratosphere wherein the phenomenon of Ionization takes place. Its lower limits in day and night times are 56 and 96 kilometres, respectively. It reflects the radio signals.

OR

Ionosphere denotes the layers (above 60 or 70 miles or 96 or 112 kilometres) extending from 40 or 50 miles (64 or 80 kilometres) outward for great distances and coincides with the lower limit of thermosphere. It is electrified due to electromagnetic radiation from the sun, contains heavy ions in numbers approximately equivalent to the number of electrons.

Jhum cultivation : A shifting cultivation usually practices in Bangladesh and Assam tract, remains at one place till the fertility is there otherwise change the place.

Lactones are phenolic compounds found in the seeds of some species. These include chlorogenic acid, coumarin acid, furelic acid and caffeic acid. These can inhibit germination and may serve as a dormancy mechanism.

Land Equivalent Ratio abbreviated as LER refers to the relative area under a sole crop that is required to produce the yield achieved in an intercropping system at an identical level of management of both of them. LER postulates relative and direct comparisons regardless of the crop, level and type of yield (but measures), both the competitive ability and actual advantage accruing from intercropping.

Law of Diminishing Returns, E.A. Mitscherlich (1909), a German Soil Scientist proposed the (law) which states, that "The increase in any crop produced by a unit increment of a deficient factor is proportional to the decrement of that factor from the maximum." The response is curvilinear instead of linear as suggested by B Jackm an (1905). The M itscherlich equation is: $dy/dx = C(A - Y)$, where d = the increment of change, dy = amount of increase in yield (y) due to increment of the growth factor dx, A = maximum possible yield and C is a proportionality constant. The increase in y is the maximum for the first increment of x, then the amount of yield increase becomes (progressively) smaller for each increment of x, theoretically nearly one half the response from the previous increment. The amount of a nutrient or any other factor required to obtain one half of the maximum yield is known as ***Baule Unit***

Law of Minimum was proposed by Justus von Liebig (1862) as "A deficiency of one necessary constituent, all others being present, renders the soil barren for crops for which that nutrient is needed." It is also known as "Barrel Concept". The law of the minimum is the best known of the limiting factor theory. The growth factor rate in the supply sets the capacity for yield.

Leaf Area Duration (LAD) denotes the magnitude and persistence of leaf area or leafiness during the period of crop growth. It measures the extent or seasonal integral of (light) interception. It has been postulated that LAD in wheat correlates highly with yield. It is computed from the leaf area from individual plants. LAD = $(LA_2 - LA_1)(T_2 - T_1)/2$; LA = leaf area and T = time.

Leaf Area Index (LAI) denotes the ratio of leaf surface (one side only) to the ground area occupied by the crop, is equal to $(LA_2 - LA_1) / 2 \times 1/GA$ (ground area). LAI of 3-5 is usually necessary for the maxium dry matter production in most of the field crops. The seasonal variation depends on species. The leaf shape, transmiscibility, inclination and vertical distribution effect the intercepted radiation (light) and so also the LAI.

Leaf Area Ratio or LAR represents the ratio between the area of leaf lamina or photosynthesizing tissue and the total respiring plant tissues or the biomass. LAR usually reflects leafiness of a plant. It can be approximately determined by dividing leaf area by weight. It has been estimated that among sunflower, beet root and pine, sunflower, all other factors being identical has strong competitive position in juvenile stages.

Length of Growing season comprises a measure of thermal efficiency and has been defined as the time period between the last kiling frost in spring season and the first in the fall season. The experience has revealed that the length of (frost) free period does not take into account the environmental factors other than temperature and as such the index could more appropriately be called as thermal growing season rather than thermal efficiency. Though it employs any measure in respect of thermal intensity, bears a high correlation with more complex temperature evaluation.

Lenticel : An opening in the cork of roots and stem of plants for exchange of gases.

Lichen : These are composite organisms consisting of a association of a fungus with a photosynthetic partner usually either a green alga (commonly *Trebouxia*) or (commonly *Nostoc*). The morphology, physiology and biochemistry of lichens are very different from those of the isolated fungus and alga in culture. Lichens occur in some of the most extreme environments on Earth, hot deserts, rocky coasts and toxic slag heaps.

Light Intensity Measurement is measured by comparison with a standard candle (SC). The amount of light received at a distance of one metre from *SC* is known as metre candle or lux, an accepted international unit of light and if measured at a foot distance from SC , it is called foot candle (10.764 luxes). Small quantum is measured in joules (J) or ergs and one gramme calorie equals 4.18 J or 41.8 million ergs.

Lux or metre candle means the amount of light received at a distance of one metre from a standard candle. Similarly, the light intensity at one foot from a standard candle is called foot candle which is equal to 10.764 luxes.

Matrix Potential is the force with which the water is held to plant and soil constituents by force of adsorption and capillarity. It can only be removed by force and as such has a negative value. ψ_m designates this potential.

Meristems are the specialized tissues wherein cell division and cell enlargement takes place. Their number is large, but only minor in terms of their total mass. The production of crop depends upon the management of meristem competition (increase in number of tillers, branches, inflorescence and leaf area).

Meteorology literally means a discourse on things above, and deals with day-to-day atmospheric conditions and the reasons thereof. It is oftenly defind as the physics of the atmosphere since the methods of physics are used to account for and explain the atmospheric processes and as such has been equated with or atmospheric science. Aerology and aeronomy represent the study of the upper atmosphere.

Micro-climate is the climate near the ground say within two metres of the ground surface. It is important to the plants, animals and man. This ground air layer is "plant climate" or "micro-climate" or "Photo-climate". It is influenced by the temperature near the ground, relative humidity, wind velocity and other factors *viz.*, nature of the ground surface, soil type, vegetative cover and topography of the area. Man has been destroying the micro-climate by cutting forests, ploughing arid lands, burning *etc.*

Microtubules : Submicroscopic, hollow tubes of protein that function throughout the cytoplasm to provide structural support and enable movement.

Mixed Cropping refers mostly to sowing of the seeds of two or more crops (at times as many as 5-7) mixed together in various pre-determined proportions usually in no distinct rows, that is, sown broadcast. Like intercropping, it is also denoted by a plus mark (+) as sorghum + pigeonpea + sesame or + ... The basic objective is an ensurance against vagaries of weather unlike intercropping that aims at an addition (bonus) yield/productivity. It is referred to as replacement series.

Molecular farming: The synthesis of certain chemicals through transgenic plants is known as molecular farming. The genes confirming quality characters are being transferred to get increased synthesis of some chemicals *viz.* Mannital dehydrogenage gene from *Escherichia coli* is transferred to tobacco for increased production of mannital.

Multiple Cropping means growing of more than one (or say several) crops on the same piece of land in one agricultural year (July to June). The component crops of a sequence in this system of cropping need be so planned and implemented jointly that the package of management practices for the same crop may be modified to commensurate with its position in the pattern and to maximise the productivity of the whole system.

Mycorrhiza. This term refers to symbiotic association between the fungus and the roots of higher plants. Some of these fungi are present on the root surface only whereas others enter into roots as well. These fungus solubilizes phosphorus, produce plant growth promoting substances and protect host plant from soil pathogens. Mycorrhiza is classified into two types (*i*) ecto and (*ii*) endo Mycorrhiza.

Mycotoxin : A deadly poison produced by fungi.

Net Assimilation Rate (NAR) denotes the rate of dry matter accumulation per unit leap area per unit of time expressed as g per m^2 (leaf area) per day. It is a measure of photosynthetic effeciency of leaves in a crop community. Non-laminate photosynthesis occurring in plant parts then other (leaves) is not taken into account. If it is multiplied by LAI, the product is CGR

OR

It is also called unit leaf rate. It means the net gain in assimilate (net photosynthetic gain per unit of leaf area and time, gain in minerals is also included though not large, only 5% or less). It is expressed as weight (W), per unit area (A), per unit time (T), is equal to $(W_2 - W_1) / (T_2 - T_1) \times (\ln LA_2 - \ln LA_1) / (LA_2 - LA_1)$. It is influenced by age, increase in size and competition for nutrients..

Nitrogenase : The enzyme used by some organisms to fix atmospheric gas (N2). It is the only known family of enzymes which accomplishes this process. Dinitrogen is relatively inert because each atom of nitrogen has three open orbitals in its outer electron shell to bond with another atom, so that if two nitrogen atoms bond to each other, they do so in all three of these orbitals.

Non-Selective Herbicide represents a chemical that kills all plants to which it is applied; those applied as spray or dust to the foliage are called general contact herbicides, and include water soluble chemicals, weed killing oils, fortified fuel oil or water emulsions, diquat (FB_2), chlorinated benzene, aromatic solvents, aqualin and aquathol *etc.*, usable in places where no plant growth is wanted, annually/perennially cropped fields and orchards *etc.*

Nucleic acid : Complex molecules that store and transfer information within a cell. They are constructed of fundamental monomers known as nucleotides.

Nucleoli : Nuclear structures composed of completed or partially completed ribosomes and the specific parts of chromosomes that contain the information for their construction.

Nucleoplasm : The liquid matrix of the nucleus composed of a mixture of water and the molecules used in the construction of the rest of the nuclear structure.

Nucleotide : A fundamental subunit of nucleic acid constructed of a phosphate group, a sugar, and an organic nitrogenous base.

Nutrient Essentiality denotes the essentiality of a nutrient when a plant fails to grow and complete its life cycle without that particular nutrient (excluding indirect and beneficial effects) and only then when it is a constituent of a necessary metabolite like sulphur in methionine amino acid. The essentiality is established by using the (technique) of hydroponics (growing a plant in water solution medium).

Nyctotemperature is also called effective night temperature and represents the summation of the minimum temperature and one-fourth of the difference between the maximum and the minimum temperature.

Oogenesis : The specific name given to the gametogenesis process that leads to the formation of eggs.

Optima and Limiting Factors: F.F. Blackman (1905) stated, "when a process is conditioned as to its rapidity by a number of separate factors, the rate of the process is limited by the pace of the slowest factor". According to "Blackman Response" the process ceases as soon as a factor becomes limiting. But, in nature the response is curvilinear (as in photosynthesis when either light or CO_2 is limiting) and reaches the maximum limit asymptotically.

Organelles : Cellular structures that perform specific functions in the cell.

Orthologues : Homologous proteins that perform the same function in different species.

Osmotic Potential: It means the potential energy of water as effected by solute concentration. The solutes lower the potential energy of water which results in solution with negative water potential. It is designated as ψ_s .

Ozone Layer. Ozone is found in natural form in atmosphere from ground surface to an approximate height of 60 km having the maximum concentration from 20 to 25 km and makes only a minute quantum of atmospheric gases (one out of ten lacs of molecules). If entire ozone is brought down to soil surface, it would make only 3 mm thick layer. It has three atoms of oxygen (O_3) as against two in oxygon (O_2). It prevents the filtration of ultra-violet rays and thus precludes them from coming to the land surface. And if all ultra-violet rays reach the land surface, sun shine will be brighter, the temperature will rise, the ice atop mountains will melt, sea level will rise, some regions will be submerged, there will occur skin diseases (cancer) and wrinkles, life-span will be reduced, photosynthesis will be hampered and seed germination and development will be slowed down, CFC (chlorofluro-carbon, Freon-$CFCl_3$) breaks into free chlorine atom which converts O_3 into O_2. A hole ruputure measuring equal to the area of U.S.A. was noted in O_3 layer over Antarctica in 1965. It is dangerous and since efforts are needed to maintain it (O_3-layer).

PAN is peroxy acetylene nitrate which is a secondary pollutant formed due to the action of light on hydrocarbons and nitrogen oxides present in air.

Partitioning Index or coefficient is the ratio of crop growth rate of economic yield to the crop growth rate of total productivity which leads to produce a useful quantity. It is a measure of the crop efficiency to convert the photosyntheses (assimilates) to economic yield. The high yielding dwarf varieties of wheat and rice embody higher partitioning coefficients than their older varieties or counter parts.

Passive Absorption is a physical process identical to absorption of water by a sponge, ions move with water without with the involvement of metabolism. Its total capacity depends on outer space (voids in root tissues and intercellular space) and Donnan free surface (roughly CEC of cell parts exposed to ions in water).

·**Pesticide** means a chemical (organic or inorganic) employed to kill the pests. A herbicide kills the herb(s), fungicide kills a fungers (fungi), insecticide kills insects, nematicide kills nematoades, rodenticide kills rats/mice and the like. A permanent pesticide continues to be effective even after one year of its application.

Photo Use Efficiency is an extension of resource use efficiency and has been defined as $PUF = P_i / P_o \times P_a / P_i \times B / P_a \times H$, where P_o = photosynthetically active radiation (*PAR*), P_i = *PAR* intercepted. P_a = *PAR* absorbed by a crop stand (GJ / m^2/ unit time. Instantaneous measurement of *PUE* that can be used before harvestable parts form a significant proportion of biomass. $PUE = P_i / P_a \times P_a \times P_i \times P_n / P_a$, where P_n = net photosynthetic rate. $PUE = P_i / P_o \times P_n / P_i$ since quantitative measurement is not possible.

Photoflux Density is the number of photons (a stream of light particles) striking a given surface area per unit time. Wave-length between 400 and 700 nm are most efficiently used in photosynthesis and hence light measurements for photosynthesis are usually based on photoflux density within those wave- lengths.

Photoperiodism means the response of plants to the relative length of day and night. The plants which develop and reproduce normally only when the photoperiod is greater than a critical minimum (12-14 hours) are called long day plants, whereas those needing less than the critical minimum (less than 12 hours) are called short day plants.

OR

Photoperiodism is the response of plants to the photoperiod or photo-climate which in turn means the length of exposure of plants to light. The long day plants like wheat, barley (which cereals) and potato etc., need a photoperiod of more than 14 hours to come to flowering. On the contrary tobacco, soybean, green gram, blackgram and millet (a group of coarse cereals like fingu millet, kodo millet, proso millet etc.) require less than 10 hours of exposure to light for flowering ; while day neutral plants like tomato, sweet potato, sunflower and cotton come to flowering regardless of the photo-climatic period.

Phototemperature is also known as the day-light temperature. It denotes the difference between the maximum temperature and one fourth of the difference between the maximum and the minimum temperature.

Phototropism refers to the plant growth movement or orientation brought about by light. Primary orientation refers to the position of the main axis which results due to gravity and has been termed as geotropism. The secondary response may occur as in growing plant tops towards the light, called positive phototropism as in sunflower since its response to changes in turgor is such that the tops and leaves tends to remain in the direction of sun.

Physiological Dormancy oftenly denotes embryo dormancy and has also been termed as deep dormancy. A physiologically immature embryo is regarded as physiological dormancy which may be caused either by growth inhibitors or deficiency or imbalance of hormones and deficiency of some other growth promoting substances. Coumarin is such a common inhibitor. Abscisic acid (ABA or dormin) lactones, alkaloids, ammonia, ethylene, hydrocyanic acid, essential oils etc. are other such chemicals.

Physiological Index of thermal efficiency was proposed by Lehenbauer (1914). It is based on the determination of the rate of elongation of maize shoots to account for the effects of supra-optimal temperatures. The index has only limited applicability since it is based on temperature growth relationship of a single plant species growth of plants as seedling only and mere measurement of shoot elongation at a constant temperature for a period of 12 hours.

Physiological Maturity is the steady state at the end of seed filling period, at which time the growth increments are in balance with metabolic losses. The time period required for seed growth depending upon the genotype and environment (particularly temperature) ranges between 20 and 40 days.

Phytochrome : A pigment which is a protein molecule, located within the plasma membranes of the leaf cells that is extremely sensitive to certain forms of light.

Phytochrome is a bluish-green protein pigment dictating light sensivity of seeds for their germination. Some seeds do need exposure to light for germination.

Phyto-toxicity, in general means the capability of a compound to kill vegetation at the dosage, of a part per million on fresh weight basis, that is, only a few microgrammes per plant. The chemical should have no or low mammalian toxicity.

Plant Evolution is the medium in which the picture of plant distribution is painted. The periodic production of new biotypes, ecotypes, species, genera and families has resulted in present day vast forms of the plant world.

Plant Growth Regulator means a broad category of organic substances (other than vitamins and trace elements) that in minute amounts promote, inhibit or otherwise modify physiological processes (Wareing and Phillips, 1970). These are also known as plant growth substances, growth hormones or phytohormones. Both endogenous or exogenous elicit essentially the same plant responses. These are divided in auxins, gibberellins, cytokinins or kinins, growth indibitors, and ethylene.

Plant Rectangularity in row crops refers to the ratio of distance between plants within the rows to the distance between the rows. It comprises a measure of unevenness of distribution in a broadcast sown crop. Its effect on yield depends on plasticity of an individual plant which, in turn, depends upon the plant species and increases either with the increasing seed rate or increaseing width of rows.

Plasmids : Small and circular DNA molecule which has self replicating property in the host cell or an extrachromosal genetic plant found in bacterial cell and can replicate independently of chromosomal DNA.

Polymerase chain reactions (PCR): A method for amplifying a DNA base sequence using a heat stable polymerase and two primers, one complementary to the (+) strand at one end of the sequence to be amplified and other complementary (–) strand at the other end. The faithfulness of reproduction of the sequence is to the fiedility of the polymerase. PCR was developed by Karl Mullis in the year 1980.

Precipitation means falling down of the water particles that become heavy due to condensation of water vapours floating in the air (called clouds) on account of adiabatic cooling to the level below the dew point. It may be in the form of rain or snow or any other form.

Pre-emergence Application means application of a chemical (herbicide) treatment of the weed seedlings that are likely to emerge before the emergence of the crop seedlings, that is, weeds are treated at their most vulnerable stage of development. The treatment may either be done at seeding or shortly thereafter or shortly before seeding (pre-planting) to kill the weeds as they emerge to keep the crop unharmed.

Pressure Potential also known as turgor pressure and represents the force caused by hydrostatic pressure. Since it is a force, it usually has a positive value. It has a minor importance in soils, but is of primary significance in plants. It is written as ψ_p.

Protoplast is a plant, bacterial or fungal cell that had its cell was completely or partially removed using either mechanical or enzymatic means.

Radiation constitutes the (though) the solar energy reaching the earth and the (loss) of engery by earth to the outer space. The global radiation budget consists of incoming solar radiation at atmosphere's outer limit (Q), planetary albedo (a) and out going long wave radiation from earth to space. (l) Radiation $Q\,(l - a) - l$.

Relay Cropping refers to growing of two or more annual crop(s) concurrently on the same piece of land in a manner that the succeeding crop is sown/planted before the preceding crop is harvested or reaches maturity or flowering. The technique was rediscovered and perfected by Dr. Sher Singh Bains (S. S. Bains) and the termed was coined by Dr. M.S. Swaminathan in late sixties at the Indian Agricultural Research Institute, New Delhi-110012 (India). It is denoted by a slash (/) *e.g.* maize / toria (an oilseed crop of Brassica group) or radish or turnip or carrot or potato-in maize-potato-wheat-mungbean or cowpea (for green pods or for fodder) cropping system. The succeeding crop is sown/planted in the standing (unharvested) preceding crop. Its objective is to enhance cropping intensity in areas of assured input supply or availability.

Resource Use Efficiency is the product of capture efficiency and resource conversion (whole plant biomass times harvest index) efficiency. Capture and conversion efficiencies are computed as, capture efficiency = $R / R_o \times R_a / R_i$ and conversion efficiency = $B / R_a \times H$, where R_i and R_a = resource quantum potentially intercepted and absorbed respectively, R_o = resource, quantity potentially available per unit land area, B = (whole) plant biomass and H = whole plant harvest index or the proportion of the whole plant present at harvest that provides economic yield.

Rhizobium. It is a symbiotic bacterium, and occurs in the root nodules of legumes. Rhizobium fixes atmospheric nitrogen in the presence of red pigment called leghaemoglobin. Rhizobium was first time isolated by Biejerinck in the year 1888.

Root weight is excluded due to difficulty to get those values.

Seed biologically a ripe, fertilized ovule is called a seed. Agriculturally in a number of species including grasses, the seed is a single ovule fruit that is dry and non-dehiscent (non-spliting of the fruit wall). In beet a seed is an aggregate of dry fruits, each with single ovule (a seed wall). There is a large variation in seeds of cultivated and wild species in physical appearance (size, shape and colour), biochemical properties and physiological characteristics.

Selectivity comprises an important selectivity of modern herbicides and represents the ability of a chemical to kill weed (pests) with little or no injury to the plants of economic utility. It may be accomplished either by differential killing in a mixed population or by selective destruction of mixed population or by selective destruction of weed seedlings (by pre-emergence herbicides) and is relative rather than absolute. It results either due to differential wetting and break down or due to selective effect on protoplasmic cells and ezyme inhibition *etc.*

Seminal Roots are also known as seed roots and emerge along with the radicle from the scuiteller or first node of the seed embryo axis. The cotyledon, scutellum, and the subtending node remains embeded in the seed and hence the name seed root. In wheat second node (coleoptilar) and scuteller node remain in the seed since emergence is from second node. The number of seminal roots contributes to adaptation and the competitive advantage in certainn enviromments.

Sequential Cropping refers to growing of two or more crops in a recurrent succession on the same field within 365 days (including turn-around period), by planting the (succeeding) crop only after the harvest of the preceding crop and minimum required tillage. Thus, a farmer (grower) has to manage only one crop at any one time in the same (one) field. It includes double, tripple, quadruple and ratoon cropping (culture of regrowth from the regenerative intact stalks of a preceding crop) and it is denoted by a hyphen (–) like rice-wheat-mungbean.

Shoot Root Ratio is the expression of allometry of top growth to root growth. It is physiologically important because it reflects the type of tolerance to moisture stress due to drought. Though genetically controlled, is greatly influenced by ervironment and (management) practices.

Smog this word has been coined from smoke and fog means an obnoxious concentration of air pollutants harmful to plants, enough to (facilitate) reduce visibility and to causes eyeirritation. The condensation nuclei *viz.*, dust particles, smoke, spores and salts facilitate smog-development.

Soil Structure refers to the arrangement of soil particles. (Primary) soil particles aggregate to form compound particles. It is modified by climate and the management practices and effects soil aeration.

Soil Texture refers to the relative fineness or coarseness, or the propotions of various size groups of soil particles. According to the International System of soil particle classificatin coarse sand and clay particle size is 2.00 - 0.20 and less than 0.002 mm, respectively. Surface of sand particles is much less exposed (23 cm^2/g) than of clay particles (11,342 cm^2/g).

Solar Constant is the amount of energy received on a flat surface that is perpendicular to the sun's rays and immediately outside the earth's atmosphere.

Soluble powder is wetable powder (WP)

Source & Sink source where the photosynthetic assimilates are synthesized or enter the plant, whereas sink means where they are utilized. Inter organ translocation of assimilates in the plant is primarily through xylem, (essentially) one way, acropetal or upward and pholem (bidirectional, acropetal or basipetal (downward), plasmodesmata in both of them allow some lateral movement as well.

Spot treatment means the application of a pesticide on a predetermined limited area seriously infested by pests either to (eliminate) or to minimise their spread below the defined economic threshold limit/level.

Stable Emulsion represents the emulsion in which the repelling and non-coalescing droplets are reduced to a small size by effective stirring (may be by thermal agitation) to homogenise their concentration throughout the mass of the emulsion. Water-oil interface stablization reduces surface tension and allows a low angle of attack on the waxy cuticle by a herbicidal emulsion in which wetting is essential as only the wet tissues are killed.

Stratosphere is the layer beyond the lowér atmosphere extending out into space, temperature is relatively constant (– 45 to – 75 °C), air in the upper region may be quite turbulent and there occurs a well marked layer approximately 32 km above sea level, which has increased concentration of ozone (O_3). It has a mean altitude of 50 km and mesosphere is beyond this and upto 80 km.

Surfactant is also called emulsion stabilizer or spreader. Surfactants tend to reduce interfacial tension between two (immiscible) liquids (oil and water), (comprising) a spray solution, and hence stabilize the surface in contact with foliage, it also serves as a wetting agent. It augments penetration and efficiency of the applied comprising (foliarly-fed/sprayed) chemical compound (s).

Synergistic effect is the total effect due to combined use of active components which is higher than their effect owing to their single/individual application.

Syniplastic Movement means transport within the living symplast and entails uptake by the ectoplast, movement about the cell in the streaming mesoplasm, cell to cell diffusion, release into sieve tubes, rapid translocation in the assimilate stream and includes migration in parenchyma of cambium, cortex and meristems. The terms is applicable in case of herbicides as it holds for the other chemicals (compounds).

Systemic herbicide is the herbicide which enters into the plant (weed) system through its absorption and paralyses its growth and development. Similar is the mode of action of all systemic pesticides.

Temperature indicates the relative degree of molecular activity or heat of a substance, is an index of sensible heat and not a direct quantitative measure of energy. It is indicated by an arbitrary scale of reference. The 'internationally accepted measure is Celsius scale named after a Swedish astromomer Ander Selsius to indicate air temperature. The zero of the scale is "triple point" temperature at which gaseous, liquid and solid states of water are at equilibrium under standard atmosheric pressure and boiling point of water under standard conditions is at 100°C. Another scale is Kelvin or aboslute based on absolute zero, the temperature at which theoritically molecular activity ceases, each Kelvin degree equals, a Celcius degree but absolute is at –273°C. addition of 273 to Celsius scale gives Kelvin temperature, yet another scale is Fahremheit, triple zero of water is at 32° and boiling point at 212°. Fahrenheit to Celsius is computed at – C = 5/9 (F - 32). The difference between the maximum and the minimum temperature is diurnal (daily) range.

Temporal and spatial complementarities repersent annidative resource utilization. The growth pattern of component crops in inter/mixed crop systems so differs in time dimension that the crops need growth resources at different times leading to their more efficient utilization and it is temporal complementarity. Combined leaf canopy makes better use of light and combined root systems make better spatial (space) use of water and /nutrients known as is and it spatial complementarity. Both of them are inseparable.

Theremoperiodism denotes the response of plants to a rhythmic fluctuation in temperature. Germination, stem elongation, floral development and increase in frost hardiness, may proceed most satisfactorily under a rhythm of alternating temperatures.

Thornthwait Temperature Efficieency Index. Thornthwaite (1931) evaluated the effects of temperature on linear basis. His index involves a linear transformation of the remainder method and the formula is Index $\sum_{n=1}^{12} (T-32/4)\, n$ or $TE = \sum^{12} (T-32/4)\, n$ where, $n = 1$ and T = mean monthly

Tolerance Theory means the tolerance of a species due to a specific character subject to the laws and processes of organic evolution. The range of tolerance of a taxonomic unit represents the sum total of ranges of tolerance of its constituent species.

OR

It means that each and every plant species is able to exist and reproduce sucessfully only within a definite range of climatic and edaphic conditions. This range denotes the tolerance of the species to external conditions. The tolerance of a species is a specific character subject to the laws and processes of organic evolution in the same way as its morphological characters, but the two are not necessarily linked. The change in tolernce may or may not be accompanied by morphological change and *vice-versa*.

Transgenic plants : These are genetically modified plants which have been created by mobilizing genes of interest from one species to another species by means of biotechnology.

Translocated Herbicide is a herbicide resulting in a kill due to translocation from the point of application. Translocation occurs either through xylem (wood) tissues or through phloem (bark) tissues along with the plant food materials. The former operates under the conditions of water deficit and the latter due to functioning of living cells needing high and low contact toxicities, respectively.

Troposphere is the lower portion of the atmosphere subject to differential heating and thereby causing convection currents and turbulences. This may extend to a height of 16 km in tropics, but at 60° (latitude) such turbulences may reach a height of not more than 9.6 km. it extends upto 8 and 16 km at poles and equator respectively and embodies three fourths of the atmospheric mass, is the realm of clouds, storms and convective currents.

Turnover number : The number of molecules of substrate that a single molecule of enzyme can react with in a given unit of time.

Vapour Pressure Deficit is the difference between the actual water vapour pressure and that required to saturate the air at the same (temperature).

Viets Effect denotes the availabity of an ion as influenced by the presence of other ions. that is, augmented by the pressure of certain ions, especially calcium. The uptake of (potassium), rubidium (Rb). bromine (Br), chlorine (Cl), sulphate (SO_4) and phosphate (PO_4) is accelerated by calcium.

Water Potential denotes the potential energy of water in plant and soil, expressed by Greek letter psi (ψ) as force per unit area. The unit of measurement is usually the bar or pascal (Pa) mean 1 bar = 10^5 Pa = 10^6 dynes/cm^2 = 0.99 atmospheres or 10^2 J/kg. Pure water has a water potential of zero bar and (ψ_w) in plants and soils is leess than zero bar. Water potential of plants and soils is a sum total of matric solute or osmqtic pressure or turgor and gravitational potentials.

Water Requirement is the reciprocal of water use efficency and is defined as

$$\text{Water Requirement} = \frac{\text{Evapotranspiration}}{\text{Dry matter production}}$$

It is usually expressed in weight of equal magnitude as g of water per g of dry matter.

Water use Efficiency of the field crops can be defined as

$$-\text{WUE} \ \frac{\text{Dry matter production (DM)}}{\text{Evapotranspiration}}$$

It is expressed as a DM per kg of water or kg DM per hectare per centimetre of water or lb DM per acre per inch of water. It can be measured on plants in containers or on individual plants in the field or on crop communities.

Watershed denotes an area of land and water bound by a drainage divide within which the surface runoff collects and flows out of the watershed through a single outlet into a larger river, lake or any other water body (Brown 1960). Resource conservation and its economically optimum deployment to sustain productivity constitutes the linch pinch pin of watershed. The management in totality, that is, the available resources (soil, water, crop, livestockhorticulture, agro-forestry, fisheries, piggeries, poulteries vis-a-vis human beinhgs) are (capacitated) with an overall prosperity and global peace.

Weather denotes the day-to-day state of atmosphere and entails the consideration of short term variation of energy and mass exchanges within the atmosphere and between the earth and the atmosphere. Thus, it is the result of the attempts made for equalization of the variation in the net radiant energy received from the sun.

Weed out of 300, 000 plant species inhabiting the earth, only relatively few are weeds defined by various workers with a common nature of their being out of place, unwanted and detrimental. "A hebaceous plant of little value for, use or beauty, growing wild, ranked and regarded as covering the ground and hindering the superior vegetation" (Onions, 1956)". Weed is a general term for any troublesome or otherwise undersirable plant usually introduced and grows without intentional cultivation (Herbert 1962. in Dictionary of (Ecology).

Yield Components. mean a number of sub-fractions contributing towards grain yield/biomass yield. Grain yield = No. of reproductive units (heads/ears/panicles) per unit ground area, No. of grains per reproductive unit and the average weight per grain. These are effected by genotype, management and environment.

PLANT STRESS

Literally stress means a force exerted when body part presses on/pulls on/pushes against or tends to compress/twist another body or body part. The intensity of this mutual force is commonly expressed in pounds per square inch or kilogramme per square centimetre. The force causes a deformation in the body or the body part. In case of plants, stress denotes an aberrant change in physiological changes due either to one or a combination of environment and biological factors. The change pertains to dislocation of plant metabolic processes *viz*., decreased growth, productivity or economic value or in extreme and unattended situations death of the plant or the plant part. The main sources of environmental stress have been summarized below.

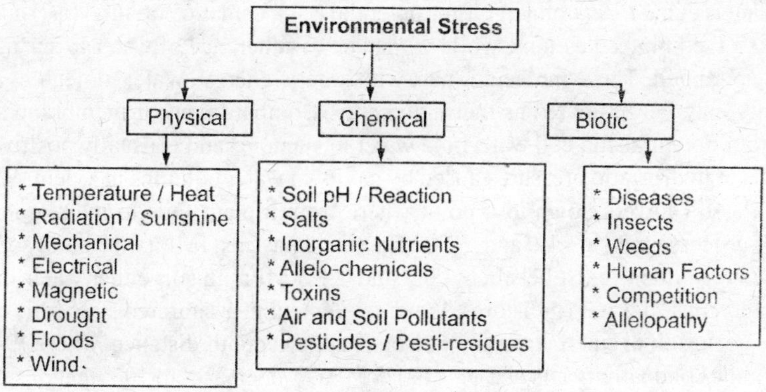

Fig.

The optimum environmental conditions cause zero stress which is theoretical. The extent of stress depends on the quantum of energy getting into the processes going on in a plant system. Stress caused injury may be clinical or subclinical. Plant may be resistant to stress or some plant parts *viz*., seeds, buds, dormant buds may be resistant. On the contrary, some plant parts like seedlings, succulent organs, and meristems may be susceptible. However, tolerant plants wholly or partially survive the impact of stress. The tolerance changes with the advancement of growth. The acclimated /plants are hardened and survive in the changed environment. Stress resistance can be divided into tolerance and avoidance. Avoidance means no thermodynamic equilibrium, but stress is excluded through physical or metabolic barrier. On the contrary, tolerance means that plant comes in equilibrium with stress, but no injury occurs or is made good (Leviff, 1980). The concept is based on stress-strain relationship as used in physics. It could not come in extensive use as recognition of category of strain is difficult. The individual stresses may be on account of one or more of the following factors:

Thermal stress : All the plants excepting a few attain ambient temperature of their environment of growth and development. These are poikilotherms and embody some suitable form to temperature stress.

Hydro-stress (Drought) **:** Avoidance of loss of turgor leads to resistance to moisture stress. Drought resistance consists of avoidance and tolerance of dehydration.

Photo-stress (Irradiation) **:** Plants cannot escape the penetration of radiation. The tolerance of irradiation is dictated by its intensity and duration and the energy absorbed.

Salt-stress : The root system of plants on high salt content soil embody low osmotic potential. They (plants) either have an inbuilt mechanism to exclude the salt(s) or to concentrate them in vacuoles.

Nutritional stress : The plants can tolerate the deficiency of an essential nutrient element either through exudation of metabolites to augment the uptake of that nutrient as in case of iron or through substitution as sodium for potassium. The nutrient toxicity is tolerated either by exclusion at the root or by concentration in vacuoles of leaf cells. Plants react to stress pathologically too. More than half the plant diseases are caused by unfriendly environment, nutritional and/or physical conditions. Phytodiseases are either infectious or non-infectious or abiotic or viral or physiogenic caused by pathogens. The phytodiseases caused by organisms develop through pathogenesis, while through physiogenesis due to physical environmental factors.

Drought stress : Drought is basically a meteorological connotation which means the lack of precipitation over a prolonged period of time. However, physiologically there may occur water stress for a relatively short periods of time and may effect plant growth and development. Drought stress here below is briefly discussed with a particular reference to water stress regardless of its cause(s) and its impact on physical and chemical changes in various processes of plant growth and development. Some conceptual parameters of water-plant relationships are highlighted when water loss exceeds water absorption. As it is well known that a living here baceous plant contains 85-90 fresh of its weight. When water absorption by plant roots is less than the loss through transpiration, conducting tissues are subject to tension / negative pressure, water potential slides down, plant tissues and organs suffer due to dislocated equilibria among the water potentials. Water potential (ψ_w) in a plant is equal to the total of turgor potential (ψ_p), osmatic potential (ψ_p) and metric potential (ψ_m). ψ_p is due to dissolved molecules/ions, while ψ_m is due to adherence of water to surfaces and interfaces and are more orderly arranged. These molecules part with kinetic energy. Water molecules lose their activity and the kinetic energy may be dissipated as thermal energy. Bombardment of membrane surfaces by water molecules causes turgor potential and cell walls hold water in vacuoles and is usually positive and opposed by membranes, cell walls or hydrostatic pressure caused by gavity in water columns in xylem. Water stress first of all effects ψ_p. $\psi\omega$ in a soil lowers down to a point where from a plant fails to make good the loss due to transpiration or other processes and at –1.0 and – 2.0 MPa (megapascals, IMPa = 10 bars) soil is at PWP at this water content. Incidentally, plants exist between – 0.3 and –1.5 MPa. In soil either water may move to plant roots or roots may intercept soil water (moisture). Water movement in a saturated state follows Darcy's law : $V = K \times$ change in total ψ_w in soil in cm of water divided by change in depth/distance, where V = flow velocity, K = coefficient of hydraulic conductivity and at a ψ_w of –1.5 MPa, K decreases to 10^{-3} that of saturated soil value. Water stress results in breakdown of continuity of water films. ψ_m contributes more to ψ_w leading to more contribution to ψ_p. Vapour movement now assumes higher significance and temperature gradient facilitates its movement among soil particles. Drought stress results since there is not enough available water in the rhizosphere and unfavourable atmospheric conditions add to the rate of transpiration and evaporation. Such a situation of stress may occur for a short period of time or for a prolonged period. It happens under the conditions of continued drought. Plant growth, yield and quality are adversely effected. Response of plants to drought have been placed in five categories by Hsiao (1973):

(*i*) Decline in ψ_w or the activity of cellular water,

(*ii*) Decrease in turgor pressure of plant cells,

(*iii*) Concentration of micro and macromolecules due to decrease in turgor,

(*iv*) Altered spatial relation among plasmalema, tonoplast and organelle membrane, and

(*v*) Structural change in macromolecules due to removal of water of hydration or due to modified structure of adjacent water. Water stress according to Hsiao (1973) may be—

(*i*) Mild stress (ψ_w is 0.1 of MPa and RWC (Relative Water Content) 8 or 10 %,

(*ii*) Moderate stress (ψ_w is –1.2 to (– 1.2 to – 1.5 MPa and RWC > 10 % but < 20 %) and

(*iii*) Severe stress (ψ_w > –1.5 MPa and RWC > 20 %). Plant desiccates if RWC > 50 %.

Water stress alters the source to sink relationships for assimilates. The effect on yield depends on the plant part of ecomomic value. Water distribution within plant body depends on the stage of growth and development. Protein creates ψ_m and helps in lowering of ψ_w and establishes strong gradient towards meristematic tissue vacuolation also needs water. Photosynthesizing leaves favourably complete for water under mild stress. Shaded leaves lose less water than the leaves directly exposed to incident radiation. Water stress during reproductive stage is important. In rice, the last 55-60% of the growth comprises panicle initiation, gamete production, anthesis and fertilization and grain filling. Gamete production and anthesis are the most sensitive as number of filled grains in a panicle depends on these growth processes. Loss of turgor reduces cell size accompanied by rseduction in leaf area which reduces the amount of photosynthates. Leaf expansion in sunflower ceases at ψ_w of – 0.2 to –0.4 MPa (Boyer, 1970), in maize at – 0.7 MPa (Acevedo *et al.*, 1979) and soybean at –1.2 MPa.

Anaerobic stress

Too much water condition creates an environmental stress for terrestrial plants in the form of oxygen deprivation. Wetlands which account for 6% of the world's terrestrial habitats. Very wet soils are common in large parts of world and *Anaerobic stress* is a problem for agriculture and forestry on flood plains and following irrigation as it is for natural plant populations. Rice is the most important crop of tropical and semitropical climates is cultivated pre-dominantly on flooded, anaerobic soils. In northern latitudes, water logging is common and low oxygen levels prevent oxygen diffusion. Water logging is a serious problem as when soils are flooded, air spaces and air packets in the soil are lost. For plants, **hypoxia** starts (hypoxia means oxygen limitation) when gaseous oxygen levels in the soil fall below 55 mmol/m^3 , generally after the one set flooding of land (*i.e.* submergence) the levels of available oxygen decline by 60% in an hour and 95% in a day although the precise rates depend upon the type of soil and prevailing temperature. Gaseous oxygen is displaced from the soil because of its low solubility and law rate of diffusion in water, and because soil microorganisms tend to consume all the readily available oxygen. Although all plants are obligate aerobes (*i.e.* they can not live without oxygen) some species can survive or even can grow with some or all of their organs in oxygen free (*anoxic*) environment and surrounding.

Low oxygen availability is signalled by ROP (RHO of plant) *G proteins* that are active in their GTP-bound forms and inactive in the GDP-bound forms, in a pathway similar to the RHO-GTP-dependent (RHO-GTPage) pathway in mammals.

Water Stress, and Photosynthesis: Water stress effects ultrastructure of a plant. Severe to mild water stress disrupts compartmentation with concomitant release of hydrolases that act on substrates. The released acid and alkali destroy membranes of susceptible plants, but the resistant ones remain intact (membrane keeps intact) and the little damage is repaired. However, there is reached a *point of no return* in both resistant and susceptible plants, if exceeded, plant dies. At "*point of no return* hydration aggravates the damage. In maize under mild stress tonoplast loses shape, releases vacuolar contents, chloroplast bursts when comes in contact of cell sap and fails to recover on hydration. In jackbean (*Canavalia ensiforme*) water stress slows down greening of leaves. The photosynthetic mechanism in chloroplasts changes. Free chloroplast showed reduced photosynthesis at ψ_w of –0.8 to –1.2 MPa (Boyer and Bowen, 1970). Chloroplasts of sunflower are irreversibly altered at –2.5 MPa presumably due to the changes in chloroplast membranes, but those of sorghum remained functional at –3.7 MPa.

Under the conditions of water stress stomates remain closed, radiant energy is intercepted, absorbed by leaves, CO_2 entrance into leaves is limited, reducing compounds are either stored and accumulated or used, carbohydrates are used and become deficient due to deficiency of carbon dioxide for growth and maintenance. The impact of stress is different in C_3 and C_4 plants. In C_3 plants metabolism, the first photosynthetic product is 3-phosphoglyceric acid (PGA), while it is four carbon organic acid in C_4 plants. Illuminated leaves of C_3 plants evolve CO_2 in photorespiration at or above 20% of the net photosynthesis, that is, are less efficient than C_4 plants. Dark respiration rates of mature leaves remained unaffected of the mild stress. However, the difference in the rates of photorespiration between C_3 and C_4 plants assumes significance in respect of survival during water stress. Concentration of CO_2 indicates the phostosynthetic rate, the CO_2 compensation concentration at which CO_2 leaves the leaf is equal to that getting into the leaf is 50 μL / CO_2 / L air for C_3 plants. The difference is due to the difference in photorespiration rates. Water stress alters exchange of CO_2 due to changes in stomatal aperture and resistance to CO_2 diffusion in the mesophyll cells. In C_3 plants photorespiration decreases loss rapidly than photosynthesis, leaf uses carbon sources instead of their synthesis resulting in death due to starvation. C_4 plants can withstand such a situation for a longer period of time due to lower rate of photorespiration in them. Both of them succumb to severe stress from causes other than starvation. Temperature also interacts but the mechanism is not well known so far. Temperature and O_2 concentration within the leaf also interact with water stress to effect photosynthesis, but call for studies io define these effects. In CAM plants (Crassulacean Acid Metabolism) malic acid is synthesized and stored until light energy is available to generate photosynthetic reducing power that fixes O_2 released from malate decarboxylation. *Mesembryanthemum crystallinum* shifts from C_3 to CAM metabolism as the growing season advances and the conditions change from mesic to xeric in the normal climatic cycle. Estimates reveal that CO_2 fixation is about 40 % less efficient in C_3 than in C_4 plants.

C_3 *Vs* C_4 Plants : In C_3 plants metabolism, the first product of CO_2 fixation is 3-phospoglyceric acid (PGA), a 3-carbon compound as shown in Fig. 1:

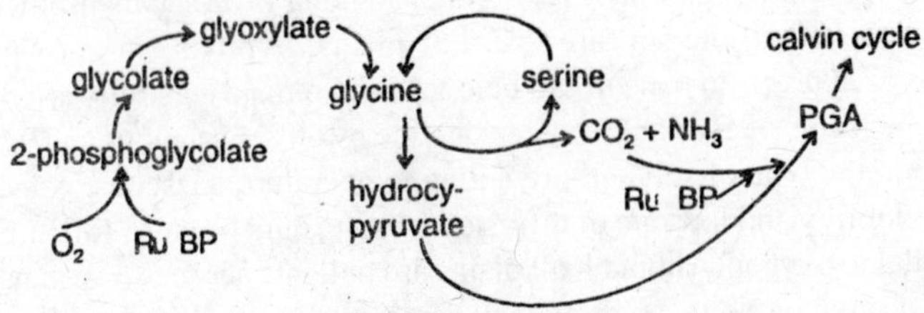

Fig. 1

In.C_4 metabolism the first product of CO_2 fixation are four carbon organic acid (Vide the Fig. 2)

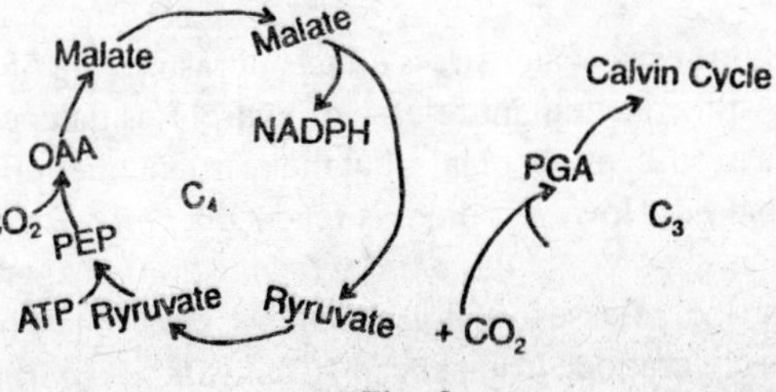

Fig. 2

C_3 and C_4 plants in respect of photosynthesis compare as described below :

C_3 plants	C_4 plants
(*i*) Photosynthesis is inhibited when little O_2 levels are more than 2%	(*i*) Photosynthesis increases to high irradiance, that is, it is little efrected by O_2.
(*ii*) Leaves *etc*, get saturated at light intensities above one-third of full sunlight.	(*ii*) Photorespiration is small, insensitive to O_2 or tem perature
(*iii*) Compensation concentration is 50/μL CO_2 per L of air.	(*iii*) Compensation concentration is less than 5 μL per L of air.
(*iv*) Illuminated leaves in air evolve CO_2 in photorespiration rates from 20 to 75 % of net photosynthesis.	(*iv*) Leaf cells visibly and functionally are differentiated into distinct tissue.

(*v*) Mesophyll cells (thin cytosol and large central vacuole) are not visibly and functionally differentiated	(*v*) Different enzymes complement bundle sheath, small cells with small vacuoles and many chloroplasts, mitochondria, peroxisomes closely adpressed to vascular tissue. Loosely packedmesophyll cells with large vacuole, scat tered chloroplats, cells between bundle sheaths.
(*vi*) Many temperate climate plants tolerate temperature from 5 to 30°C.	(*vi*) Tolerate temperature from 15 to 40°C.
(*vii*) Have lower productivity.	(*vii*) Have high rates of productivity
(*viii*) Have lower water use efficiency.	(*viii*) Have high water use efficiency.

Drought Resistance : Drought resistance can be divided into dehydration avoidance /tolerance (Ludlow, 1980) or dehydration postponement/tolerance (Kramer, 1980) or dehydration tolerance/avoidance (Levitt, 1980) or drought escape. When drought continues, a plant may face mild to severe stress. Extent of stress injury and plant survival depend on the state of occurrence of stress. A plant undergoes physiological changes due to stress leading to adjustment of osmotic pressure. An increase in osmotic potential initiates stress. A minor change in turgor may be regarded as the most probable changes that mean stress is transduced to metabolism. Lowered osmotic potential, active accumulation of solutes, cells/tissues elasticity and small cells help maintain the turgor. The adjustment of osmotic potential is influenced by

(*i*) Rate of stress development (ψ_m. decrease of – 0.1 to – 0.5 MPa / day permits adjustment, but a decrease of ψ_w of – 1.0 to – 1.2 MPa/day is regarded as too rapid)

(*ii*) Degree of stress early in the stress cycle full turgor may be maintained, but its continuance reduces the adjustment capacity of a plant,

(*iii*) Environmental conditions directly (temperature and sunlight intensity) and indirectly (factors effecting photosynthesis and production of solutes effect stress),

(*iv*) Difference in cultivar and in tissue or organ exposed, and

(*iv*) The age of the plant. Osmotic adjustment lead either to full or partial maintenance of turgor. Usually, increase in solute either at a water potential (ψ_w) of zero (turgor pressure = osmotic potential) or at zero turgor (turgor pressure = osmotic potential) and either of these conditions–osmotic potential = $\psi K_0\ V_0/V$ (V= osmotic volume, $\psi\pi_0$ and V_0 are at source reference value *e.g.* full or zero turgor). There may result confusion if two aspects of increasing solute concentration in the cells are not kept differentiated. Other terms used to describe this phenomenon are osmo-regulation, turgor regulation, water activity regulation, and osmotic adaptation. To illustrate, in wheat apex drought stress effects apecal meristems and the tolerance mechanism as follows : in the apex some tissues are enclosed in mature leaf sheaths, to some extent protected from the atmosphere, apex not connected to the body of the stem by functional xylem, that is, the reduction in transpiration and changes in water content witness only little change due to stress allowing osmotic adjustment. It has been noted that decrease in water potential by 0.5 MPa inhibits spikelet initiation leaf elongation and apex elongation. Accumulation of amino acids and soluble sugars have been correlated with the increase in resistance to stress.

Stress causes decrease in cell size accordingly by an increase in elasticity. A fourfold increase in cell size halves the elasticity. Further, increase in elasticity caused by the decrease in cell size enhances dry weight to turgid weight ratio. A plant escapes stress either by remaining dormant or by completion of its life cycle during the favourable conditions as noted in desert ephemerals. On the contrary, tolerance of stress at high tissue water potential is attributable either to reduced water loss or to maintenance of water uptake. The former is assigned to enhancement in stomatal and cuticular resistance, reduction in heat (radiation) absorption and leaf area. In drought stress, hydrostatic feedback control of stomatal aperature over-rides other controls like carbon dioxide concentration *e.g* in barrel cactus stomates close 40 days after stress and remain closed for seven months and water potential of cactus falls from – 0.1 to – 0.6 MPa, while soil water potential slides down to –0.9 MPa. In a number of crop plants stomates close at –0.8 to –2.8 MPa. In some crop plants stomates do not close completely. But the best advantagte is when all stomates close, cuticular resistance increases, culticle becomes

becomes thicker and offers increased resistance. Reduction in absorption of radiation is brought about by leaf movement to change angle of incidence to reduce the area of absorption, development of pubescence for leaf surface insulation, enhanced waxiness to change the quality of the leaf surface for radiation reflection, reduction in total leaf area due to reduced number of leaves, tillers, leaf abscission, morphological adaptation during stress like reduction in turgor and leaf area before decrease in stomatal aperture and photosynthesis, leaf rolling as in grasses and may reduce as much as 70 per cent of transpiration and the area exposed to radiation by 68 per cent (Begg, 1980). Water uptake is conditioned by root system. When roots grow more, root, to shoot ratio changes, there is less shoot growth, increased root length and density may change the ratio. Low resistance to water movement through roots and the conducting system to shoot due to increase in vessel number or diameter also help to maintain water uptake. The concept of tissue elasticity involves the relationship of turgor to cell volume. Small cells are more elastic than large ones, hence the tissues made of small cells are more tolerant to drought stress. In lichens, mosses, and resurrection plants tolerance occurs at protoplasmic level and has been named as desiccation tolerance. Seeds are resistant to drying as are some rhizomes and leafless plants. For resurrection plants, tolerance of desiccation is in the range of –160 MPa and below may occur. Foliage of some 83 angiosperms can tolerate these low levels of water potential and still survive and is likely to increase if stress develops slowly.

The method of measurement of drought resistance varies with its type and nature. The best measurement is that made on the plants themselves (Kramer, 1969). A measurement method should have good correlation between the rates of physiological processes and the stress, a given stress should produce identical physiological changes in wide range of plants, the units used should have a wide range usable on different plants and require the minimum of plant tissues.

Decrease in turgor and degree of stomal aperture measurement is an obvious measure of drought stress. Metabolic rates (accumulation of metabolites) are difficult to be correlated. Cuticle thickness, root density and size of conducting tissues from root to shoot are important. The fact is that measurement of drought stress is difficult due to osmotic adjustment, dehydration tolerance on account of synthesis of isozymes and metabolic repair of injury. Yield is a function of a combination of factors and is, thus, a poor measure of stress. The survival time has been used in various ways and has given rise to the terms like AUSDAUER unit (J. Levitt, 1980). *"An Ausdauer unit denotes the water content at complete stomatal closure divided by the cuticular transpiration rate."* Water content is equal to water content at death minus water content at stomatal closure. It (Ausdauer Unit) approximately measures relative order of resistance with a group of plants under one set of conditions, but not from one to the other population.

There are 'Water Saver' and 'Water Spender' plants. The concept of Water Use Efficiency or Water Requirement comprises grammes of dry weight produced divided by the kilogrammes of water used to produce the dry weight. A variation of measurement is to divide the net efflux of water by the net influx of carbon dioxide over a time period. A number of other concepts have been advanced to measure drought stress, *e.g.* stress at which 50 per cent plants are killed, measurement of energy level of water in stressed plants, water deficit or water saturation concept etc. Resistance can be measured by desiccation tolerance tests, field measurement of water potential or relative water content and by diffusive resistance or stomatal aperture.

A plant breeder needs some hints tor determine the drought resistance *viz.,* observations from single genotype, behaviour of species, races, or cultivars in contrasting environments, metabolic blocks/ reinforcements of some metabolic reactions, comparison between drought resistant and tolerant varieties, protein synthesis and use of mutants (with earliness, root growth, stomatal control and number, cuticular resistance, cell turgor and some chemical traits).

Heat Stress : Plants are poikilotherms, that is, they assume the temperature of their environment. Heat/ temperature stress is important in agriculture. It has been conjectured that a decrease of 1°C in the world temperature would cause 40 per cent reduction in rice production. A 2°C increase in frost hardiness would cause unimaginable increase in production of citrus trees, winter cereals, potatoes, deciduous fruit tree blossoms, and tender vegetables and would extend winter wheat to spring wheat areas. Currently, efforts are under way to research on mechanisms of freezing avoidance and tolerance, effective cryoprotectants, biochemical changes in nucleic acids, polyribosomes, amino acids, sugars and ultrastructural comparisons, changes in membranes, acclimatization, super cooling, survival traits and breeding for control of hardiness. Temperature stress causes chilling injury, freezing injury and high temperature (heat) injury.

Emerging seedlings, leaves and plant parts exposed to direct solar radiation embody high temperature. It causes necrotic lesions on stems and hypocotyls, chlorotic mottling of leaves, fruits and needles (of conifers), and finally (drying) leading to death. High temperature enhances the rate of respiration and decreases photosynthesis and causes the deficiency of life supporting energy in the tissues. Proteins or enzymes and membranes are altered. Enzymes function in a specific temperature range. Proteins may be denatured and aggrevated, membranes are disrupted, cells compartmentation is destroyed, enzymes come in contact with substrates, movement of ions, water and organic solute movement is altered. The basic metabolism of cells is changed due to liability of proteins. There occurs a change in viscosity of lipid components.

It has been observed that tolerance to high temperature can be augmented by the use of some chemicals that increase the ratio of saturated to unsaturated fatty acids. High temperature tolerance is usually expressed as the temperature required to produce a defined level of injury or a defined level of dead plants, usually 50%. Plasmolysis, cytoplasmic streaming and photosynthetic rate are also used as other criteria. The tolerance to high temperature indicates the ability of a plant to maintain high rates of photosynthesis, stability of proteins to resist conformotional changes, to repair or to synthesize structural proteins and embodiment of substances to protect the proteins from undesirable change. It has been postulated that lower hydration of protoplasm entails greater hydrogen bonding and tolerance to heat. The dormant tissues (seeds and buds) exhibit higher level of tolerance than the rapidly growing ones. Reduced use of nitrogen fertilization and cross linkages with devalent cations/augment tolerance. Some of the plants avoid high temperature injury because of angle and arrangement of leaves toward incident radiation. The colouration and refluctance properties of leaves play an important role in heat tolerance. The desert plant species may reflect as much as 70 % of the incident infra-radiation. Thick culticle and leaf hairs alter the reflectance properties and improve conductive cooling. Evaporative cooling due to transpiration when water is available also induces high temperature tolerance.

Temperature acclimatization : Acclimatization means physiological adjustment by an organism to an environmental change. Temperature acclimatization denotes the development of tolerance to injury either owing to low or high temperature. Its study paves the way to determine the process or structure involved in the process of acclimatization. The term 'hardy' is used to describe the tolerant and the process is known as 'temperature hardening'. The effects of acclimatization are postulated by exposure of plants to a slow change of temperature and the resultant change(s) in the metabolic processes like photosynthesis, respiration, protein synthesis etc., and studies on plants taken from different ecological temperature regimes. Time of exposure is controlled and exposure is carried out at various development stages. Controlled environmental conditions are necessary to conduct studies on temperature acclimatization.

It is suspected that high temperature would reduce the rate of photosynthesis and would enhance the rate of respiration leading to the reduction in accumulation of net photosynthates. A detailed information can be collected by deploying biochemical techniques of analysis and studies on enzyme systems. It has been observed that cold-adapted plant species embody much higher photosynthetic capacity than those adapted to heat. Desert plant species show much higher photosynthetic capacity at high temperature than the cold adapted plant species. The decrease in photosynthesis is attributable to an irreversible inactivation of photosynthesis at different temperature regimes. Photosynthetic machinery is directly effected and not the secondary changes leading to changes is membrane permeability and breakdown. Temperature acclimatization involves changes on account of low temperaure acclimatization due to enhanced capacity of a limiting temperature-dependent catalytic step, while high temperaure acclimatization occurs due to increased stability of one or several chloroplast components. Studies on enzymes comprise carbon dioxide fixation and photosystem II activity which indicates that the ribulose biphosphate carboxylase and fructose disphosphate phosphotase are probably limiting steps in carbon metabolism cycle at low temperatures and the heat stability of the thylokoid membranes constitute key component in the acclimatization to high temperatures. The response to change in temperature may be vertical movement of proteins in the bilayer toward the aqueous interface at low temperature while toward interior of the bilayer at high temperature. It causes an alteration in forces maintaining the tertiary structure of the proteins. Cold hardening in plants is effected by energy source, freezing rate, tissue water content, temperature, water deficit, salinity and nutrition.

Allelopathy : The biological entities in the environment compete for various growth resources *viz.,* for light, water and space on one hand, while on the other release a variety of chemical compounds which effect either own progeny or other associated plants in a community. The effect depends on the concentration of the released chemicals, their nature and time period of their continuance in the environment. Molisch (1937) coined the word *allelopathy* to describe the chemical interactions taking place among the living organisms. It is also called antibiosis of allelochemical interaction. Rice (1974) defined allelopathy *as any direct or indirect effect that one plant has on the other or mutually on each other through the production of chemical compounds due to their allo- or auto-inhibition that escape into the growth enviroment/medium.* The allelochemicals are the organic compounds involved in allelopathy. Allelochemicals may be both detrimental and beneficial-depending on their concentration and the length of time of exposure of a plant to them (Rice, 1974) either due to allo-inhibition or auto-inhibition. The allelopathy may be true or functional allelopathy. The allelopathic plants, or allelochemicals are usable in agro-ecosystem to manage plants pests by inter-planting, enhancement of allelopathic potential of crop plants by breeding or selection, their use as sources of pesticides, their elimination (if found as weeds) and identification and isolation of new compounds that appear as secondary metabolites of allelopathic plants. Allelopathic effects appear either due to addition of allelochemicals to soils through leaf litter, plant extracts, leaf washings/drips or decomposition of added allelopathic plant residues.

The best known example of allelopathy is the effect of walnut trees on herbaceous crops under its canopy or over the root system. The walnut's allelopathic effect on alfalfa and tomatoes (Massey, 1925) and on apple trees (Schreiderman, 1927) has been postulated. The compound 5-hydroxy-α-naphthaquinone from extracts of walnut leaves, roots and hulls named as *juglone* was identified in 1928 by Davis-after the generic name of walnut, *guglons.* The effect of guglone cannot be explained by competition since it is a depletion process unlike allelopathy which is an addition process. Further, an allelochemical is altered in its pathway to a donor organism as shown below by S.B. Horsley in 1976:

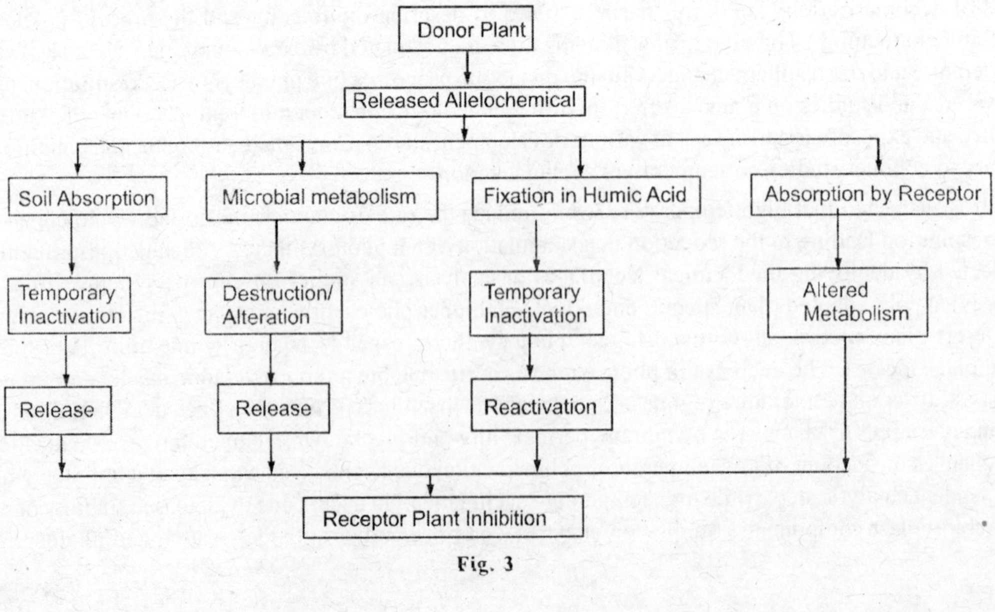

Fig. 3

Through allelochemicals (inhibitors) are contained in leaves, stems, roots, rhziomes, flowers, fruits and seeds, leaves and stems are very important in this regard. Different allelochemicais may be found in different parts of the same plant. These are released by volatilization or leaching by fog drip, rain, root exudation or degradation of dead plant parts. The growth inhibitors released into the rhizosphere, may be changed to other inhibitors by bacteria and fungi as shown by S.B. Horsley (1976):

Allelochemicals have been classified on the basis of their biological activity as phytotoxicants growth promoters, substrates for microorganisms, predisposer of diseases, root exuadation promoters and soil structure altering agents. Most of the allelochemicals arise from the activity of mevalonic acid meatbolic pathway as shown by Rice (1974). Many of them are secondary metabolites (more than 10,000 as shown by Swain, 1977) and a number of them function as protective agents against competitors, predators, and pathogens. The metabolic origin of allelochemicals from normal metabolism has been diagrammatically depicted by E.L. Rice (1974) in his book. *Allelopathy* published by Academis Press, New York as reproduced below.

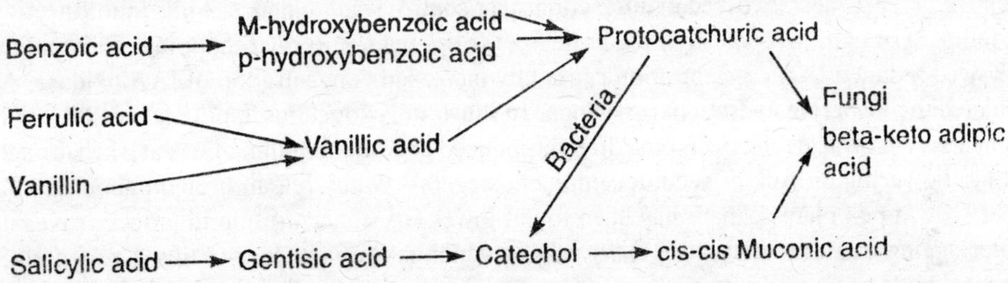

Fig. 4

A test for allelopathy must identify symptoms, rule out competition, isolate and assay the chemical, simulate interference, monitor the release and correlate the selectivity of the chemical with its role in the ecosystem.

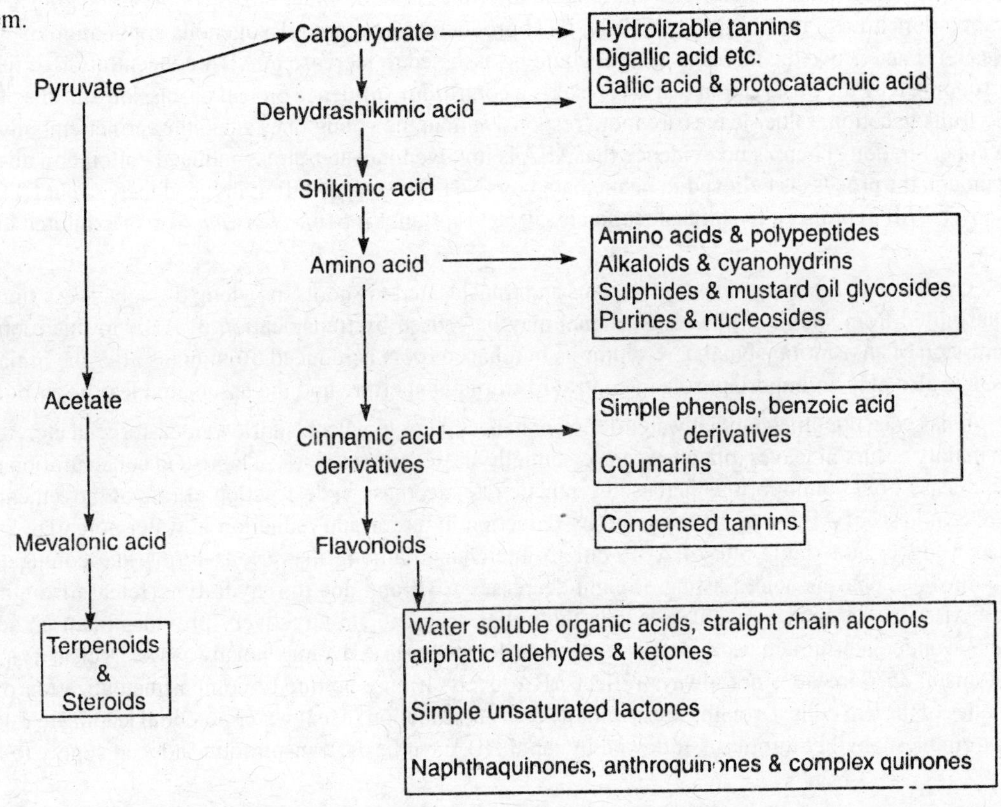

Selectivity of the chemical with its role in the ecosystem.

It may be added that in arid and semi-arid regions terpenoids, while in temperate regions benzoic acid, cinnamic acid and coumarins inhibit respiration, oxydative phosphorylation, photosynthesis, enzymic activity, protein synthesis, and cell division and elongation. Cucumber (*Cucumissativus* L.) accessions showed allelopathic effects of association of prosomillet (*Panicum miliaceum* L.) during first 10 days and its exposure to cucumber failed it to regain growth. Some cultivars of oats (*Avena sativum* L.) roots produce scopoletin and its production is increased by 25 times under drought/temperature stress. Scopoletin inhibits, the growth of the receptor only then when in association. Such plants comprise good plant improvement technique.

Phytohormones and Phytostress : Phytostresses may be on account of altered water relations, drought, temperature, nutrition, photoperiod and insect-pests which cause morphogenetic changes. These changes in effect cause changes in phytohormonal balance. The relationship between reactions to stress and hormones call for measurement, manipulation of levels and application to identify their impact on stressed plants. The maximum of available information lends support to the hypothesis that abscicic acid (ABA), cytokinins (CK), and ethylene (ETH) are most involved in interactions that control water balance, while indole acetic acid (IAA) and gibberellins (GA) are involved to a lesser degree. It has been observed that plum and apple trees under drought showed reduced IAA concentration caused by increased concentration of IAA oxidase. Auxins have been postulated to play a role in drought resistance. To illustrate, exogenous application of IAA or 2,4-D (2, 4-dichloro-phenoxy acetic acid) can overcome drought-induced growth inhibition of wheat when drought concided with heading, flowering or milk or seed development stage(s). Water defecit brought about the loss of polar transport of IAA in pea plants. There has been found lower GA concentration in lettuce leaves under water stress. Waterlogging causes reduction in GA synthesis which takes place in root tips. Exogenous application of GA to apical buds of tomato 7 days after flooding overcormes the inhibitory effect of waterlogging.

Water stress enhances synthesis of ethylene (ETH) from aminocyclo-propanecarboxylate (ACC) arising from S. adenosylmethionine (SAN). In cotton plants ETH increased at – 2.0 MPa, 10 % loss of water enhanced ETH in orange which occurred 2 hours after the onset of water stress. In broad bean, when water saturation deficit increased from 20 to 50 %, ETH production increared. Exogenous application of ABA increases ETH and hence the increase in ETH could be assigned to increase in ABA concentration of tissues. It is corroborated by the observation that ETH exerts a controlling influence on leaf abscission and abscission of young fruits in cotton. Older leaves are more responsive than the young ones since the former embody higher ABA concentration. There is no evidence that ABA is involved in water-stress-induced cotton boll abscission even though the process is believed to be mediated by ETH. The water-deficit induced increase in ETH (from – 0.8 to –1.2 MPa) reduced IAA translocation by 50 % in cotton. Fir (*Abies balsamea*) also exhibited identical effects.

Cytokinin (CK) are synthesized in roots and translocated to shoots in xylem; drought stress signal may be transmitted from shoots to the roots. Signal may be caused by translocation of ABA to this roots or by transmission of an osmotic-signal. CK synthesis in tobacco roots is reduced 30 minutes after the initiation of stress. CK also play an important role in control of stornatal aperture and the associated leaf water potential.

It has been documented that water deficit enhances ABA in wheat, sunflower, castorbean etc. Accumulation mainly occurs in leaves, but all organs essentially show some increase. The rise in concentration may be due to release from bound forms, increased synthetic rate, decrease in destruction or rate of movement out of tissues. Synthesis of ABA may be triggered by reduction in turgor and reduction in water potential. Drought induces a higher and stable rate of ABA due to interchange among its various forms like conjugates and metabolites *e.g.* phaseic acid. Lasting drought decreases ABA and due to rehydration (release from drought stress), ABA increases at a rate slower than the initial one. The slow recovery provides plant an adaptive advantage under intermittent water deficit conditions. Response to ABA may not always be as clear as in flacca and stomatal aperture does not always reflect ABA levels. It may be due to compartmentalization of ABA organelles of the leaf cells. Drought stress initially reflects reduction in leaf water potential leading to release of ABA from mesophyll chloroplasts followed by rapid ABA synthesis, transpiration-induced supply to leaves, on cessation of transpiraton, stomates open even at high ABA concentration in leaves as ABA is presumed to exist in compartments and hence unavailable to guard cells. Plants respond differently to subsequent stress due to previous stress. Some of the effects of drought can be explained by the effects of ABA concentration. Enhanced ABA concentration reduces shoot growth which may be due to consequently reduced-turgor. The effect on apical dominance influences dormancy of auxiliary buds as noticed in maize. Stress caused increase in ABA in cereals leads to an early ripening and cessation of growth. Flowering in some of them is inhibited, while initiated in others. Effects of ABA on roots are not yet known clearly.

Phytohormones and Temperature: Temperature stress depends upon plant species, organs/structures involved and stage of development. Thus, it is not an easy task to lay down specific temperature ranges which may cause stress. However, in general, suboptimal (nearing freezing) or supraoptimal (above 35-40°C) temperatures may be stressful to a number of plants specially herbaceous ones. The temperature extremes comprise important environmental signals to aid the plants to prepare them to face stress *e.g.*, induction of dormancy. Such temperature signals may be necessary for completion of life cycle of the plant *e.g.*, cold induction of flowering (vernalization), vegetative growth, seed germination, and breaking of dormancy. Some plants need heat treatment for flowering. Tobacco and tomato grow the best under conditions of differing day and night temperatures. The plants needing different day and night temperatures if grown at a single temperature may suffer temperature stress. The effects of temperature stress are difficult to be isolated as the plant growth and development are closely related to the environmental regimes of temperatures. Phytohormone concentrations are sensitive to temperature. Warm season crops like maize, okra, muskmelon, brinjal and beans showed high levels of ABA and conjugated forms of ABA at 10°C as compared to 25 or 40°C. On the contrary, in cool season crops like radish, pea, cabbage, beet and lettuce, only pea showed higher levels of ABA at 40 °C than at 10 or 25 °C. In other crops, low or high temperatures showed no difference in concentration of ABA. However, tomato seedlings subject to the temprature below/above optimum postulated increased concentration of free and conjugated ABA. Water stress was not a factor to enhance the ABA concentration. It has been observed that exposurre of roots of *Nicotiana rustica* and *Phaseolus vulgaris* for 2-minutes to 46 to 74°C reduced the CK in xylem exudates, but did not increase ABA. In maize, root inhibitor export was lowest at 33°C, but increased at 3°C. GA and CK levels were lowest at 3°C. A chilling temperature of 2.5°C given to cucumber fruits accelerated the synthesis of ACC, the precusor of ETH compared to that of fruits stored at 13°C. Chilling or heat stress appears to cause physical damage to cell and/or organelle membranes leading to decompart mentalization of the enzymes of ETH synthesis to bring about an increase in its production.

Phytohormones and Phytonutrition : Both deficiency and toxicity levels of nutrient elements are involved in phytohormone regulation resulting in alterations in plant growth and development. Supply of NO_3-N to sunflower pushed up zeatin and zeatin ribosides as compared to the plants supplied with ammonium nitrogen (NH_4-N). Potato plant roots in NO_3-supplemented plants embodied higher CK than those grown in NO_3 deficient media. Further, Mo is a part of NO_3- reductase enzyme, its availability effects phytohormone concentration through the synthesis of amino acid precursors. There has been observed correlations between CK synthesis, flowering and phosphorus levels in wheat, tomato, apple, and birck. Zn is also involved in nitrogen nutrition and phytohormone synthesis. Zn is needed in tryptophan synthesis which is a precusor of IAA. Zn deficiency symptoms can be corrected by application of tryptophan or Zn. Lack of IAA and Zn deficiency cause the rosette formation in some tree branches. ABA concentrations are also effected by nitrogen nutrition. Though the role of B is controversial, it has been observed that its deficiency depresses CK concentrations and increases IAA production. IAA accumulation in toxic concentration causes necrosis due to B deficiency. It may be assigned to reduction in IAA oxidase, an increase in bound IAA and reduction in free IAA. B is also involved in other aspects of metabolism, transport and activity of IAA. Ca stabilizes membranes, provides them differential permeability and its role in membrane-phytohormone interactions are also important. Ca deficiency disrupts integrity of membranes and synthesis action of phytohormones at receptor site is altered. IAA-induced hydrogen ion secretion which is a pre-requsite to IAA-induced growth in oat coleoptile is dependent on the presence of Ca in the medium. Ca has also been observed to stimulate ACC conversion to

ETH and uptake of ACC in mungbean and cucumber hypocotyls. Ca, IAA, ETH, membrane permeability and cell growth control are closely related. Further, high concentrations of Cu and Fe can increase ETH in some plants causing abscission of leaves. High level of CO increases ETH production in mungbean and cucumber hypocotyls and fruit mesophyll in apple. Phytohormones and nutrient elements are interdependent in respect of regulation of plant growth and development.

Phytohormones and Photoperiod : Photoperiod plays an important role in phyto-morphogenesis. Plants embody a number of light-sensing mechanisms and the pigment called phytochrome is related to several photoperiodic responses. Phytochrome is found in all the plant organs particularly in etiolated tissues localized in etioplasts. It also occurs in photosynthetic systems. Phytochrome consists of a protein and a chromophore sensitive to red and far-red light wavelengths, red-absorbing form of pigment (Pr) converted to far-red-absorbing form (Pfr) *via* rearrangement of a double bond in the chromophore of the phytochrome molecule. Endogenous phytohormones concentrations respond to direct light. Day length variations cause changes in phytohormones. Long and short days promote synthesis of growth regulators and inhibitors respectively. Light-mediated phytochrome action and changes their levels and/or ratios that control the plant response in terms of leaf expansion, light inhibition/stimulation of seed germination, flowering, photoperiodism light inhibition of root growth, hypocotyl hook opening, induction/breakdown of dormancy in buds, tubers and bulbs, light inhibition of stem elongation, light stimulation of cereal leaf rolling, phototropism, geotropism and translocation. Most of the available information on classical growth hormones pertains to IAA and GA, much less is known about the effect of light on ETH, CK and ABA. IAA decreases in tissues exposed to white or red light, while increases in dark or after exposure to far-red light. There occur interactions among phenolics, IAA, oxidase and IAA in respone to red light. It has been observed that bean plants grown in dark embodied more IAA and were taller than those exposed to red light. Red light reduces polar auxin transport in rice plant coleoptile, but enhances acropetal transport of IAA through root segments. Light (420 to 470 nm, blue to near UV effected lateral movement of IAA in oat coleoptile causing a positive phototropism. GA has been implicated in light mediated leaf expansion, seed germination, unrolling of cereal leaves and stem growth. Bean and pea plants grown in light showed more ABA than that in plants grown in dark. The relationships of light phytochrome and GA in seed germination is complex. Light is needed in seeds to make them germinate after inhibition. Light treatment followed by far-red treatment nullified germination though GA can replace light in light needing seeds for germination but not for all the such seeds. There is some evidence that hypocotyl hook opening is controlled light inhibition of ETH production. Exposure of bean and pea to light enhanced ABA content. However, light stimulated ABA production in pearlmillet. CK replaces red light in unrolling of wheat leaves, expansion of etiolated leaves in some plants and growth of duckweed, Lamina. CK increased in rose buds wrapped in aluminuim foil and decreased two days after exposurre to light after removal of foil.

Phytohormones, pathogens and insects : It has been observed the bacterial, fungal and viral infections of plant tissues often result from elevated levels of endogenous phytohormones, that is, a number of infection associated symptoms are hormone mediated and some cases can be duplicated by phytohormone manipulations. Symptoms comprise epinasty, adventitious root formations chlorosis, xylem hyperplasia, tylosis formation, shoot elognation, wilting and stunting. Plant pathogenic organisms are known to produce phytohormone in *vivo.* Host plants hormone synthesis is altered and the substances produced directly alter the physiological and biochemical processes. When green island of leaf tissue is surrounded by chlorotic ring of tissues in many plants it is induced by obligate parasites which cause mildew, dowry mildew and rust. Green island leaf formation could represent induction of CK synthesis, retention or resynthesis of chlorophyll and mobilization of nutrients to infection site as noted through the application of CK that delay senescence in detached leaves.

Green islands may also be due to parasitic insects like leaf minors. The following diseases are caused due to higher levels of CK (Hale and Orcutt, 1987):

Disease	***Incitant***	***Symptoms***
Fasciation disease	*Corynebacterium fascians*	Increase in numbers of shoots, shoots becoming thickened, fleshy and mis shapen
False broom rape	*Corynebacterium fascians*	Roots characterized by large white fleshy outgrowth from topped and debudded plants ; occurs in tobacco roots.
Crown gall	*Agrobacterium tumefaciens*	Tumour formation in a large number of species and families, mostly dicotyledenous.
Clubroof	*Plasmodiophora brassicae*	Roots and hypocotyl cells undergo abnormal enlargement and dense root gall formation with subsequent negative geotropism; occurs in cruciferae roots.
Rust gall	*Cronartium fusiforme*	Gall formation of pine stems.
Root knot	*Meloidogyne* spp.	Root disease caused by several species of Meloidogyne Stunted growth, root gall formation, wilting, giant cell formation.

Bacteria, fungi and viruses infected plant tissues generally show increase in IAA. Viral infection in tomato, bean, and beet (curly top virus) reduced IAA content. The following changes occur in IAA due to the aforesaid pathogens: (*i*) increase in IAA synthesis (*ii*) stimulation of host IAA synthesis and phenolic substanes that inhibit/stimulate IAA oxidase (*iii*) secretion of IAA from pathogen (*iv*) production of phenols, phenol oxidase and hydrolases due to infection, these inhibit the auxin-degrading enzymes (*v*) creation of water stress causing alteration in phytohormone balance. ETH production by infection is stimulated due to tissue injury. The symptoms of increased ETH are enhanced membrane permeability, epinasty, root growth inhibition, induction of senescence, leaf and fruit abscission and increased stem diameter. Wounding - produced ETH can also initiate production of peroxidases, polysaccharide hydrolases, chitinase, and polyphenoloxidases which degenerate the processes in cells. ETH may increase disease resistance due to production of antifungal quinones derived from oxidation of phenolic acid compounds. Involvement of GA in the fungal disease of rice called bakanae foolish disease, caused by *Gibberella fusikuroi* brings about stem elongation. The organism produced GA and stimulated the host to increase its endogenous level of GA. Bacteria and fungi produce GA like substances *in vivo.* Reduced GA has been observed in virus infected tobacco and cucumber by insects and mites change the endogenous levels of phytohormones. Increased IAA and CK lead to formation of galls. It has been correlated to IAA and CK content of saliva of *Stigmella Argentipodella.* Insect wounding causes production of ETH due to abscission of plant parts owing to change in phytohormone balance.

Available forms of nutrients : The form of the nutrients available to plants is given and relative amounts in soils and the relative concentrations found in plants are as follows. Nutrient concentrations in plants vary with age, plant part, species, and the rooting medium or soil type. The amounts of nutrients in soil very widely and depend upon the parent material from which the soil is derived and the processes in cycling the elements in natural or agricultural ecosystems.

Nutrient absorption from soil involves movement from soil to the root, from the exterior of the root to the interior, and the translocation within the plant. Movement through the soil to the root may be by diffusion in the soil solution, diffusion from soil particle to the root directly, diffusion from one particle to another, replenishment from the parent material or the adsorption surfaces to the soil solution, or by mass flow in the soil solution by capillary action or gravitational flow. Growth of roots through the soil also brings them into contact with fresh areas of soil and ions become available by interception. Plant roots exudate into the rhizosphere substances which effect the solubility of nutrients. Nutrient absorbed reduces the concentration of ions in the vicinity of roots and sets up a concentration gradient toward roots. The surface area of root relative to its volume is very important in the absorption process. Root hairs and mycorrhizal fungal hyphae play an important role in ion absorption as they increase the area for absorption. When there is abundance of ions bonded to exchange sites, then absorption is mainly through interception subject to root-soil contact. If concentration in solution is high, uptake is by replenishment. On the contrary, low concentration slows down the replenishment and the diffusion becomes the main mechanism of ion movement to the root surface. Regardless of the mechanism, any interference in the process of absorption of nutrients or change in the ion availability results in nutrient stress/deficiency. Some ions are mobile within plants, while others are immobile. Some ions like that of aluminium get concentrated in vacuoles of leaves. Ion movement in xylem occurs due to transpiration, and the pressure gradients caused by variation in water potential. In phloem, there are distinct differences for translocation resulting in deficiencies in some plant parts. Ca, B and Fe show the deficiency in younger plant parts due to little or no translocation and poor phloem mobility. Such nutrients when fed foliarly show little basipetal movements. Toxic ion concentrations often appear on older tissues due to accretion with time.

Essential Element	*Form Available to Plants*	*Source*	*Concentration in Dry Tissue*	*Concentration in Soils*
		Micronutrients		
Mo	MoO_4^-	Soil solids	0.1 ppm	2 ppm
Cu	Cu^+, Cu^{2+}	Soil solids	6 ppm	50 ppm
Zn	Zn^{2+}	Soil solids	20 ppm	100 ppm
Mn	Mn^{2+}	Soil solids	50 ppm	2,500 ppm
Fe	Fe^{2+}, Fe^{3+}	Soil solids	100 ppm	250,000 ppm
B	BO_3, B_4O_7	Soil solids	20 ppm	100 ppm
		Macronutrients		
S	SO_4^-	Soil solids	0.1 %	0.04 %
P	H_2PO_4	Soil solids	0.2 %	0.05 %
Mg	Mg^{2+}	Soil solids	0.2 %	0.03 %
Ca	Ca^{2+}	Soil solids	0.5 %	0.43 %
K	K^+	Soil solids	1.0 %	0.17 %

Deficiency causes and effects : A symptom in any perceptible change is known structure, appearance, or function. Such things as leaf yellowing (chlorosis), death (necrosis), lesions, malformations, or reduced growth and yield are all considered to be symptoms and occur as a result of nutrient deficiency. However, confusion occurs when one realizes that similar symptoms can be produced by deficiencies, toxic levels of nutrients, pathogenic organisms, air pollutants, and pesticides, and symptoms may vary with plant species or variety. Combinations of two or more causes of symptoms may result in a situation that is difficult to diagnose. Foliar deficiency symptoms on tobacco plants grown in sand culture in the greenhouse are presented below.

Symptom	*Deficient Element*
A. Parasitic and virus diseases disseminated by bacteria, fungi, or virus entities (excluded from present discussion).	
A. Nonparasitic troubles: never infectious; caused by element deficiencies.	
B. Older or lower leaves of plant mostly affected; effects localized or generalized.	
C. Effects mostly generalized over whole plant; more or less drying or firing or lower leaves; plant light or dark green.	
D. Plant light green; lower leaves yellow, drying to light brown colour; stalks short and slender if element is deficient in later stages of growth..................	NITROGEN
D. Plant dark green, often developing red and purple colours; lower leaves sometimes yellow, drying to greenish brown or black; stalks short and slender if element is deficient in later stages of growth.................................	PHOSPHORUS
C. Effects mostly localized; Mottling or chlorosis with or without spots of dead tissue on lower leaves; little or no drying up of lower leaves.	
D. Lower leaves mottled or chlorotic, without dead spots; leaf margins sometimes tucked or cupped upward or downward	
E. Mottled or chlorotic leaves typically, may redden, as with cotton; sometimes with dead spots; tips and margins turned or cupped upward; stalks slender..	MAGNESIUM
E. Mottled or chlorotic leaves with large or small spots of dead tissue.	
F. Spots of dead tissue small, usually at tips and between veins, more marked at margins of leaves; stalks slender..	POTASSIUM
F. Spots generalized rapidly enlarging, generally involving areas between veins and eventually involving secondary and even primary veins, leaves thick; stalks with shortened internodes..	ZINC
B. Newer or bud leaves affected; symptoms localized.	
C. Terminal bud dies, following appearance of distortions at tips or bases of young leaves.	
D. Young leaves of terminal bud at first typically hooked, finally dying back at tips and margins, so that later growth is characterized by a cut-out appearance at these points; stalk finally dies at terminal bud..................................	CALCIUM
D. Young leaves of terminal bud becoming light green at bases, with final break down here; in later growth, leaves become twisted; stalk finally dies back at terminal bud..	BORON
C. Terminal bud commonly remains alive; wilting or chlorosis of younger or bud leaves with or without spots of dead tissue; veins light or dark green.	
D. Young leaves permanently wilted (Wither-tip effect) without spotting or marked chlorosis; twig or stalk just below tip and seedhead often unable to stand erect in later stages when shortage is acute...	COPPER
D. Young leaves not wilted; chlorosis present with or without spots of dead tissue scattered over the leaf.	

E. Spots of dead tissue scattered over the leaf ; smallest veins tend to remain green, producing a checkered or reticulated effect.. MANGANESE

E. Dead spots not commonly present ; chlorosis may or may not involve veins, making them light or dark green in colour.

F. Young leaves with veins and tissue between veins light green in colour.................. SULFUR

F. Young leaves chlorotic, principal veins typically green ; stalks short and slender.. IRON

Source. J.E. McMurtrey, Jr. 1948. *Diagnostic Techniques for Soils and Crops.* American Potash Institute.

Nutrient and metal toxicity : The nutrient concentration difference between deficiency and toxicity is very narrow. It depends on environmental factors which effect nutrient and metal availability and growth of plants. The transition metals micrometallic nutrients are involved in causing toxicity which is influenced by chelation and pH-effects on solubility. Studies using isolated organelles have been useful, but concentrations used have been unrealistically high and species of chemicals and ions have been unknown. Toxicity denotes sensistisity of an "essential to life" process, processes. Zinc, copper and nickel usually embody toxic levels in soil. In unusual conditions lead, cobalt, beryllium and cadmium may have toxic concentrations. Lead and cadmium may have toxic concentrations. Lead and cadmium accumulation indroduces them in food chain. Aluminium and manganese toxicities have been studied in detail.

Aluminium toxicity effects resemble those of phosphorus deficiency. Thus, there may be a cause and effect relationship between these nutrients. Stunting, small dark green leaves, late maturity, purpling of leaves and stems are the effects of aluminium toxicity. Leaf tips become yellow and die. In some plants, calcium deficiency is induced causing curling and rolling of young leaves, growing points or petioles collapse. Roots are injured, become brittle, and stubby having speculate shape, root tips get thickened, become brown, and give rise to many stubby lateral roots having no fine branching. Such roots are susceptible to fungal diseases and have low absorption. Aluminium and phosphorus may precipitate octracellularly root surfaces or in the cell wall of root caps and first few cortical root cells. There are plants like wheat, barley and soybean which exclude aluminium. Rice, rye, alfalfa clones entrap it, while tea, some grasses, pine trees accumulate aluminium. Tolerance mechanism may be effected by pH in root zone. These pH changes may be related to source of nitrogen and release of organic acids. Tolerance could also be assigned to chelation. Most of the plants accumulate aluminium concentrations in 200 ppm range, that is, the range of micrometabolic nutrients. *Symplococcus spicata* showed a concentration of 72,300 ppm, while the range in other species was 2000-3000 ppm.

Manganese, an essential micrometabolic element shows a narrow, range between deficiency and toxicity. It gets accumulated in shoots and the level of accumulation dictates the injury. Marginal necrosis of leaves, leaf puckering, and necrotic spot formation are the symptoms. Roots later may become brown in colour. Its toxicity in cotton destroys auxim and causes an amino acid imbalance in potato. In some plants absorption is reduced, translocation to shots slides down, The tolerable concentrations may vary from 380 to 1600 ppm. Interaction with iron may cause deficiency and chelated iron forms may reduce manganese absorption. Thus, foliar feeding of iron may counteract its toxicity.

Copper is another transition element. There are a number of ligands which form chelates with copper and usual number of ligands per copper atom is four. Copper found as a prosthetic group of enzymes monodentate due to its affinity to organic ligands. Its toxicity causes chlorosis and stunting and appears first on root tips followed by the inhibition of lateral root development. Reduced root system leads to decreased absorption and growth inhibition. The effect on roots may be due to inhibition of IAA-oxidase activity. Copper toxicity induces iron deficiency and hence the chlorosis.

Chelation and stress tolerance mechanism : chelation means the coordination between a metal and a ligand to form a ring structure which needs two or more ligands. Ligands are bases having groups of atoms that share electrons with metals. These are bases with unshared electron pairs. The metals act as acids and accept electron pairs. The neutralization reaction between Lewis bases and Lewis acids is called coordination. The resultant bonding is unstationary and changes according to probability based on quantum mechanics. The ineraction with coordinating ligands depend on metal properties *viz*., valency, crystallization radius, mass and coordination number. The properties of a ligand include spatial requirement to ring size and configuration as well as the nature of the ligand molecules. In the formation of chelates the arrangements of electrons in the orbitals may he altered. Mineral element stress tolerance depends on strucwre and stability of the ring which, in turn, depends on number and size of the ring and composition of ligands. The chelation effects metal reactivity, so a plant may be protected from free ions concentration and may embody enhanced stabilization of structural elements. chelation leads to the formation of metalloenzymes to carry vital metabolic processes in a plant. Changed metabolism may be due to changes in enzyme composition owing to stress and effects the available ligands, metal ion concentration and protein associated enzymes. Some metalloenzymes may be in membranes where deficient/toxic concentrations of metal ions effect permeability *e.g.* calcium reacts with acid phosphatase or acid proteins in the membranes.

Stress tolerance and plant growth regulators: Plant growth regulators (PGR) may alter the expression of the genome of plants in a way that they tolerate a specific stress, but such a change is not heritable. Genetic engineering can cause a heritable trait enabling a plant to tolerate a specific stress. Use of PGRs alleviate stress and avoid injury or death oil one hand and on the other hand to understand the physiological effects of stress. These chemicals can alter drought, cold and salt stress tolerance as briefly discussed below:

Drought tolerance : Drought stress can be reduced either by decreasing the rate of transpiration or by augmenting water absorption rate by induction of root growth which, in effect, improves water absorption efficiency (WAE). Transpiration suppressants, stomata opening regulators, growth redardents / inhibitors and reflectance increasing chemicals have been used to increase drought tolerance. Film forming type of antitranspirants / suppressants include polymers like polyvinyl waxes, or polyethylene and vinylacrylate. Alcohols like hexadecanol have also been used for this purpose. These chemicals preclude physically a water vapour reaching the internal leaf tissue, and interfere with the exchange of carbon dioxide and oxygen. Thus, photosynthesis and other metabolic processes are altered in the leaves. These chemicals succeeded in reducing transpiration by 30-50 per cent with an average coating of 50 per cent leaf surface without impairing photosynthesis measeurably. Gas exchange can be controlled by the use of metabolic transpiration supressants (TS), but their activity extends beyond guard cells to mesophyll cells and thus, photosynthesis is effected to detrimental levels. Some of the metabolic TSs like ABA or those embodying anti-CK activity. ABA rapidly metabolises, is unstable in UV light and is costly to produce commercially. Natural metabolites and compounds resembling. ABA (phaseic acid, dihydrophaseic acid, xanteroxin and vomifoliol) have limited utility. Anti-CKs like such as 4- cyclopentylamino-2- metylthio-phyrolo (2, 3-d)-pyrimidine and 3 -methyl-7- pentylaminopyrazoli (4, 3- d)- pyrimidine are antagonists to CK- activity and prevent stomatl opening. ABA and anti-CK act synergistically to reduce transpiration when conibined and applied to detached wheat leaves, foliar spray on intact leavres showed no effectiveness. Certain fatty acids, phenylmercuric acetate, alkenylsuccinic acid, salicylaldoxine, and some photosynthesis inhibitors showed loss specific activity on stomatal movement. Some chemicals modify morphology through selective change in growth rate and have been used to reduce transpiration. These include chlorocholine chloride (CCC), AMO -1618, ammonium 5-hydroxycarvacryl) trimethyl chloride piperidine hydrochloride, CBBP (2, 4- dichlorobenzyltiributyl-phosphonicum chloride) and SADH (succinic acid 2, 2- dimethylhydrazide) and showed varied success. They inhibit growth in height (possibly by inhibiting GA), reduce leaf area, reduce the density of stomates, increase leaf thickness and produce greater root to shoot ratio. Further, change in membrane permeability and absorption rate may be a mechanism to conserve water in plants. CCC is a choline derivative and an important component of phospholipids, the latter may act as ion carrier across the membranes, and CCC may effect formation/functioning of phospholipids. The effects of growth retardants controlling water stress in various plant species have been listed by Hale and Orcutt (1987) as reproduced below

Plant	*Response*	*Growth Retardant*
Wheat	More shoots produced after rewatering	SADH & CCC
Barley	Used 1/2 H_2O as controls / more grain	CCC
Grape	Reduced water usage, less wilting, greater tolerance of drought	SADH
Bean	Reduced wilting	Phosfon & CCC
Apple	Water deficits lowered in fruits and leaves	SADH
Sunflower	Improved ability to recover from drought, improved yields	SADH & CCC
Gladiolus	Increased dry matter of corns under water stress	CCC & AMO - 1618
Corn	Decreased water usage, reduced transpiration in drought susceptible but not drought tolerant corn	CCC

Cold toelrance: SADH and CCC have been most frequantly used to enhance tolerance low temperatures and improvements to some extent have been observed in cabbage, tomato, young pear trees, wheat, raspberry, strawberry *etc.*

High concentrations (1,000 to 10,000 ppm) were used as foliar sprays or as soil drenches. Seed treatment of wheat with CCC to improve cold tolerance of seedlings is a common practice in the USSR. Maleic hydrazide has been used to improve frost tolerance in citrus trees because it reduces defoliation and deblossoming. It has also been used to increase cold tolerance of red raspberry, grape and mulberry. However, maleic hydrazide often causes leaf malformation as well which has made the use of the chemical less desirable.

Chilling temperatures may produce water stress accompanied by an increase in ABA and a decrease in GA. Exogenous application of ABA to cotton seedlings and cotyledonary discs prior to chilling prevented injury when exposure to 4°C was less than 5 days (Rikin, 1979). ABA also increased cold tolerance of *Acer negundo* and Rome Beauty apple trees. GA synthesis is apparently associated with decreased cold hardiness and can be countered by application of ABA and other inhibitors.

The chilling resistance of *Pisum sativum and Raphanus sativus* has been reported to be increased by applications of benzyladenine (BA), a synthetic CK, possibly by increasing mobilization of hardening promoters such as ABA, like inhibitors or complex sugars. In general, CK increases tolerance to low and high temperature extremes. Polyamines, such as long-chained alkylene diamines, have been effective in decreasing cold or frost damage in wheat, rice, barley, oats, maize, millet, soybean, piniabean, and snap beans, groundnut, spinach, lettuce, tomato, tobacco, mulberry, carnation, geranium *etc*.

Cold tolerance in wheat, cereals, tobacco and grapes has been reported by use of 2-amino-6-methyl benzoic acid and by NAA in orange trees. Many analogs of 5-chloro-4- quinoline carboxylic acid (zucchinic, mepiquat chloride (in citrus) and polyethylene glycol have also been used to induce cold tolerance.

Salt tolerance: Tolerance enhancement of plants to salt stress is important in dry land areas where irrigation is almost unavailable. The continued irrigation almost always increases soil salinity in the root zone or rhizosphere. The PGR chemicals decrease transpiration rates and the salinity problem and increase plant tolerance to saline soils.

Salts in a soil lower the water potential and make water less available to plants, responses of plants to salt stress are frequently similar to the responses to drought stress. In both types of stresses ABA concentration increases which causes stomates to close, but the CK levels decline. The ABA levels remain elevated for longer periods under salt stress than under drought stress even after the plants regain turgor.

There are reports of the use of AMO-1618, phosfon and CCC to increase salt tolerance in plants such as wheat, spinach, and soybean. Seed treatments with these compounds have also been effective. Naturally produced substances such as choline and betaine have been shown to act as "osmo-protectants" when

Escherichia coli was subjected to osmotic stress. The hardening of plants to drought stress or the use of PGR to increase tolerance to drought stress in some plants also leads to tolerance of low-temperature stress or high salt stress.

Nutrient stress : PGR can be used to improve nutrient uptake and their use efficiency. It can be accomplished by altered physiology, improvement in root growth and mycorrhizae associations. Chemicals are now available to inhibit nitrifying bacteria that inhabit the soil so that the available nitrogen is increased because the rate of leaching is reduced.

PGR effects accumulation of nutrients in tissues. GA has been reported to accelerate the uptake of K in wheat and 2, 4-D stimulates the accumulation of N and P in wheat and soybean. However, interfered with translocation of all three of the nutrients. SADH did not affect uptake, but stimulated translocation of N, R and K. Treatment with CCC resulted in higher concentrations of N, Ca, and Mg in the stem tissues of tomato and SADH caused all increase in N only. In wheat, CCC treatment caused a reduction of nitrogen levels and a retardation of protein accumulation. When CCC was combined with 2, 4-D, both N and protein accumulated and foliar application of CCC and SADH resulted in lower levels of N and P in the fruit of okra.

Air Pollutants : The information concerning the use of PGR to alleviate air pollution injury or to increase tolerance of crop plants to air pollutants is only limited. Ozone exposure causes leaf injury, reduction of growth and decreased yields of several crops such as potatoes, white beans, pinto beans, and tobacco. The chemical N-[2-(-oxo-1-imidazolidinyl), ethyl]-N-phenylurea (EDU) has been reported to increase ozone resistance of pinto beans by 30-fold when applied as a foliar spray. Antisenescence chemicals such as benzimadazole, N-6-benzyladenine and kinetin have reduced ozone damage in pinto bean and spinach. The increase in resistance was correlated with reduced losses of free sterols associated with the chloroplasts of the leaf tissue.

Use of Genetic Engineering : Recent advances in biotechnology used to explore and manipulate the genome of plants hold promise for increasing our understanding of mechanisms regulating stress responses. One method utilizes the bacterium *Agrobacterium tumefaciens,* which causes crown gall on many dicotyledenous plants. The infection results in the formation of gall-like swellings at the transition zone between the root which land shoot. When the bacterium infects the tissues, circular segments of DNA called plasmids which encompass several genes are inserted into the host cell DNA. The bacterium alters the genome of the plant and reprograms its metabolism. The technique of genetic engineering is used to remove plasmids from agrobacterium, modify them by inserting new DNA obtained from another organism and transfer the inserted code for desirable traits to a target plant.

Other bacteria are also known to produce plasmids and have been used in recombinant DNA research. To improve water stress tolerance in some legumes, genes responsible for proline synthesis have been introduced into rhizobia species that have been allowed to colonize and form nodules on the roots of plants. The gene modification prevents the feedback inhibition of proline synthesis and high concentrations of proline are produced and function as an osmoprotectant.

Genetic engineering also has been used successfully to develop herbicide-resistant plants. The active ingredient, glyphosate of Roundup (nonselective), blocks the enzyme that causes the synthesis of essential aromatic amino acids. If their synthesis of amino acids could be made to occur in the presence of glyphosate, plants would be rendered resistant to the herbicide.

It is quite possible that stress-resistance characteristics can be incorporated into plants but, the characterisics must first be identified and understood.

The use of a vector organism may be overcome by microinjection of DNA directly into a cell nucleus. The technique called *electroporation* has been used to transfer DNA into the protoplasts of corn. The protoplasts are subjected to an electrical current that temporarily opens the membrane pores and allows the DNA to penetrate the cell membrane. A better understanding of the physiology, biochemistry and development of stressed plants is needed if stress-tolerant plants are to be bioengineered.

Stressed Proteins and Tolerance : Heat shock proteins has were first discovered in the insect *Drosophila melanogaster* and later in plants. There are basically three different types known to occur in plants and they are grouped according to size as follows: group I, 68 to 104 kDa (found in bacteria, animlas, and plants); group II, 20 to 33 kDa; group III, 15 to 18 kDa (found only in higher plants). In *Drosophila* and in soybean, but not in cereal grains, hsp are the only proteins synthesized during the stress period. Induction of hsp can be initiated by subjecting plants to temperatures approaching 40°C.

Anaerobic stress proteins (hsp) are also expressed in plants subjected to anoxic conditions such as would occur in flooded fields. The asp produced in corn are different than the hsp produced as a result of heat stress except for one protein, but both groups are biphasic. The asp are continuously produced for upto 72 h, after which the cells begin to die. One of the asp produced in corn is alcohol dehydrogenase, the terminal enzyme in the pathway of fermentation. Fermentation occurs to a greater extent under anarobic conditions and is responsible for the survival of corn when flooded. Other causes of stress protein formation have been identified and include high concentrations of heavy metals, ultraviolet light and drought. Proteins produced by exposure to heavy metals may function as chelators of the metal causing detoxification. Proteins produced by exposure to UV light may be involved in the synthesis of the flavenoid pigments that absorb the potentially harmful irradiation. Considering the role of membranes in sensing environmental stresses and triggering defense mechanisms, it is interesting to speculate that stress proteins may be involved. Plant growth regulators that improve tolerance to stress may affect stress protein induction also.

Irradiation Stress : All life on earth is supported by the radiant energy from the sun, which plants convert into chemical energy by the process of photosynthesis. Light is one of the most important and variable components of the plant environment. The autotrophic plants are directly influenced by the intensity of light, which drives photosynthesis, and thereby, provides the chemical energy and carbon needed for plant growth and development. Thus, an alteration in light intensity, whether a deficit or excess, will result in a disruption of plant metabolic processes. Besides affecting photosynthetic rate, solar radiation also affects plant temperature and photomorphogenic responses in ways that can produce stress.

Unfiltered sunlight entering the ionosphere has an intensity of 1.39 kW/m^2 (the solar constant) and wavelengths from 225 to 3200 nm, with 41% of this radiation between the wavelengths of 400 and 700 nm, the physiologically active wavelengths in plants. The ozone layer in the stratosphere absorbs ultraviolet radiation while water vapour, carbon dioxide and oxygen in the trophosphere absorb the wavelengths of 1100 to 3200 nm. At sea level range of light wavelengths available to the plant is from 310 to 1100 nm with 46% of the radiation between wavelengths of 400 to 700 nm (visible light). See the data below for further details

Colour	*Wavelength Range (nm)*	*Representative Wavelength (nm)*	*Frequency (cycles/s) (Hz × 10^{14})*	*Energy (eV/photon)*	*kcal/mol of Photons*
Ultra-violet	Below 400	254	11.80	4.88	112.5
Violet	400-425	410	7.31	3.02	69.7
Blue	425-490	460	6.52	2.70	62.2
Green	490-560	520	5.77	2.39	55.0
Yellow	560-585	580	5.17	2.14	49.3
Orange	585-640	620	4.84	2.00	46.2
Red	640-740	680	4.41	1.82	42.1
Infrared	Above 740	1400	2.14	0.88	20.4

Distribution of Radiation in a Plant Community : In the plant community, photosynthesizing leaves form an overlapped and stacked arrangement. The incident light in these stands is progressively absorbed by the stacked leaves so that most of the light impinging upon a plant is utilized. The quantity and quality of light available to plant leaves will depend on the stand density, plant height and leaf shape. More light will be available to leaves at lesser heights in stands that contain plants with narrow leaves such as grain fields, meadows, or reed clumps compared to communities containing plants with broad leaves. Forests with closely packed tree crowns and dense foliage will intercept much more radiation than open stands of trees or tree species with sparse crowns. Light of several distinct wavelength ranges affect different photoprocesses and is absorbed by recognizable photoreceptors. A summary of the photoreactions of plants and the action spectra is given below:

Photo-process	*Reaction or Response*	*Photoreceptor*	*Action Spectra Peaks (nm)*	*Energy Conversion or Products*
Chlorophyll synthesis	Reduction of proto-chlorophyll	Photo-chlorophyll	Blue : 445 Red : 650	Chlorophyll *a* Chlorophyll *b*
Photosynthesis	Dissociation of water	Chlorophylls Carotenoids	Blue : 435 Red : 675	Reductant (H) Phosphorylated compounds
	Carbon reduction enhancement	Chlorophylls	Red : 650 Far-red : 710	Phosphorylated compounds
Blue light reactions	Phototropism	Carotenoids Other flavins	UV : 370 Blue : 445, 475	Oxidized auxin, auxin system,
	Protoplasmic viscosity	Unknown	Uncertain	other components of the cells
	Photo-reactivation	Pyridine nucleotide, riboflavin	Uncertain	
Red, far-red reactions	Seed germination	Phytochrome	Induction by red : 60	Research continues
	Growth Anthocyanin synthesis	Phytochrome	Reversed by far-red :	
	Chloroplast responses	Phytochrome	710 & 730	
	Other : heterotrophic growth, photoperiodism			

Source : R. B. Withrow, 1959. A kinetic analysis of photoperiodism. In R. B. Withrow (Ed.), *Photoperiodism and Related Phenomena in Plants and Animals.* Used with permission from the American Association for the Advancement of Science, Washington, DC.

Uptake of Radiation by Plants : Plants can either reflect, absorb, or transmit the solar radiation incident on their leaves. The degree of these three reactions will depend on the wavelength of the radiation, leaf structure and leaf orientation. The capacity of a plant to reflect visible light will depend on the leaf surface.

Modifications, such as hairs, will increase reflection of solar radiation. Leaves can reflect 70% of the infrared radiation, 6 to 12% of the visible radiation, but only 3% of the ultraviolet radiation. Green light tends to be reflected more strongly (10 to 20%) than orange or red light (3 to 10%). Radiation that penetrates the leaf can be absorbed by various components. Ultraviolet light is greatly absorbed by epidermal wax, cuticle and suberin as well as by phenolic compounds within the leaf. Chloroplast pigments determine the extent of visible light absorption. Infrared radiation above 700 nm (heat radiation) is readily absorbed by the plant. Transsmission of radiation depends mainly on leaf structure and thickness, thus, thin leaves will transmit more radiation than thick leaves. Wavelengths that are reflected tend to be more extensively transmitted with the result that there is an enrichment of the wavelengths around 500 nm and above 1800 nm.

Sun Vs. Shade Plants : In low light, photosynthesis is linearly dependent on light intensities where utilization (quantum yield) is at a maximum. At higher light intensities, photosynthesis becomes less than proportional and eventually does not increase with increased light intensity. The reaction of a plant to different intensities of solar radiation will differ depending on whether the plant is a shade or sun plant. Plants occupying sunny habitats (sun plants) require high light intensities to maintain a high photosynthetic rate and, consequently, show lower rates of photosynthesis at low light intensities. Plants occupying shaded habitats (shade plants) are capable of greater photosynthetic rates in low light intensities. Sun plants also have a higher light compensation point than shade plants. For the most part, the success of a plant depends on its ability to continue to photosynthesize under low light conditions.

Table-1

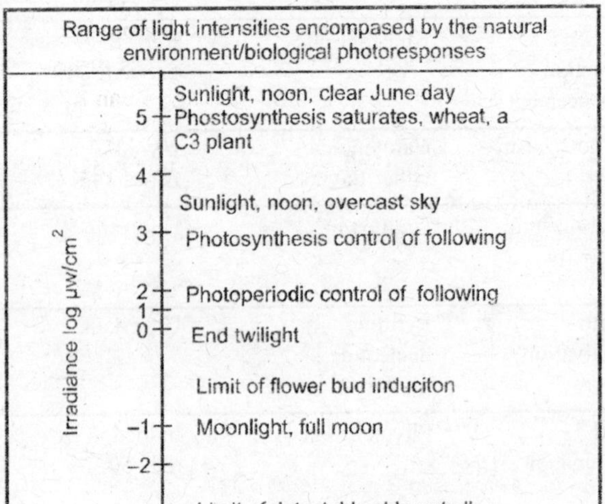

Diagram of the light intensities at which various plant reactions occur. From R.B. Withrow, 1959. A kinetic analysis of photoperiodism. In R.B. Withrow (Ed.), *Photoperiodism and Related Phenomena in Plants and Animals*. Used with permission of the American Association forAdvancement of Science, Washington, DC.

Typically, at light intensities below the compensation point, injury will occur in the plant as a result of starvation. The most rapid effect is a decrease in carbohydrate content followed by other alterations of metabolism. A summary of the range of intensities found in the natural environment and the physiological processes that are affected by the diffrerent intensities is shown in Table-1. A major difference between sun plants and shade plants occurs in the chloroplasts. Shade plants have large grana stacks with approximately 100 thylakoids per granum oriented irregularly with the chloroplast. Sun and shade plants also vary in the concentration of chlorophyll present and in the ratio of chlorophyll *a* to chlorophyll *b* in the chloroplasts. The light absorption efficiency of a plant depends on the amount of chlorophyll per unit leaf area that for a particular plant, remains constant over wide ranges of light intensities. The chlorophyll concentration and ratio of cholorophyll *a* to chlorophyll *b* of a plant can, however, adapt to changing environmental conditions.

Under low light intensities the chlorophyll *b* concentration increases in most plants whether they are shade or sun plants. The shift allows the capture and use of filtered light containing wavelengths that are enriched in the far-red region of the spectrum. In addition, shade plants normally have lower chlorophyll *a* to chlorophyll-*b* ratios than sun plants. Since chlorophyll *b* is a part of the light harvesting complex (LHC), differences in the ratio may be reflected in the proportion of LHC to total chlorophyll content. The light harvesting complex is associated with photosystem II (PS II), thus, shade plants may have a greater PS 11 to PS I ratio, enabling them to compensate for increases in the far-red light filtered through the canopy. In contrast to sun plants, shade plants contain less protein per unit of chlorophyll and per unit of leaf area.

Resistance to HLI-injury : Shade plants have a limited capacity for adjustment to high light intensities (HLI) and are usually injured or killed. Sun plants, on the other hand, gradually increasing the level of carbon metabolism enzymes, (2) increasing photosynthetic electron transport chain carriers, or (3) increasing the capacity for carbon dioxide transport. Resistance to high light stress also occurs in a number of ways. Increased suberin, wax, cuticle, and cell wall materials of the leaves can cause an increase in the amount of reflected light. The photodestruction of chlorophyll can be reduced by an increase in the content of β -carotene, xanthophyll and phospholipid of the leaves. An increase in the stacking of grana accompanied by a stabilization of the chloroplast membranes aids in preserving chlorophyll. And, the heliotropism of the leaves can cut down on the amount of light intercepted.

Ultraviolet Radiation and Plants : The electromagnetic radiation from the sun contains about 7% ultraviolet at sea level. Ultraviolet radiation is absorbed by plant chromophores, which include nucleic acids, proteins, lindolacetic acid, abscisic acid and flavoproteins. The role of chromophores has not been well established and their identification has been complicated by the secondary effects occurring in plants in response to irradiation by ultraviolet. Absorption by nucleic acids may alter protein synthesis but proteins are also absorbers of radiation and may react at a primary level. Alteration of protein and lipid membrane components by ultraviolet may alter membrane permeability and ionic balance. Such events also cause an inhibition of photosynthesis and respiration. The most common inactivation of nucleic acids by ultraviolet radiation is through photochemical lesions involving polymers of pyrimidine bases in the deoxyribonucleic acids (DNA). The result is the production of pyrimidine dimers and loss of DNA biological activity. It is evident that ultraviolet absorption can cause an acceleration in the mutation rates and aberrations of chromosomes. Repair systems for the DNA molecules have been found in plants, and involve the enzymatic splitting of the dimers formed by ultraviolet absorption. Such a repair system has been implicated in repairing epidermal tissue damage, restoration of growth rate and synthesis of chlorophyll and of nitrate reductase. In some cases, repair of ultraviolet radiation damage can be accomplished without light activation. The repair system consists of enzymatic reactions in which the DNA lesions are excised from the DNA strand and replaced by newly synthesized pieces. Or, undamaged DNA is replicated with gaps in the place of the lesions and a patch is synthesized from information within the cell and spliced into the new DNA strand. Unlike DNA, ribonucleic acid (RNA) and protein are better able to withstand ultraviolet radiation damage. Reduced plant growth with exposure to ultraviolet radiation can occur as a result of inhibition of photosynthesis or a reduction in leaf expansion.

Resistance to ultraviolet radiation damage consists of the ability of a plant to repair the damage to the DNA, or to synthesize screening compounds, such as flavanoids and flavones in the epidermis. Cuticular waxes may also be effective in absorbing harmful ultraviolet radiation. Changing the angle of the leaves to the incidence of radiation or increasing the reflecting properties of leaf surfaces are other mechanisms of resistance.

Ionizing Radiation as stress : Ionizing radiations are radiations that produce ions in the media they traverse. Energy is transferred from the moving particles and causes the ejection of an electron or of a proton or capture of the particle by the nucleus of the atom that gets in the way. Charged particles directly produce many ionizations per particle. Photons in X-rays, γ-rays, or neutrons produce few energetically charged particles but each in turn, produce many ionizations. In biological materials the production of electrons causes all of the ionizations. Excitation of matter is considered relatively unimportant in causing injury in biological material. It is the free radicals formed that are injurious. Free radicals contain unpaired electrons and are extremely reactive in chemical reactions within the system in which they are produced. The resultant injury to the plant may arise from alteration of essential components of protoplasm such as the genetic material in which mutations can be created. Alterations, deletions and additions to the DNA acid bases can occur. Such changes in the genetic potential of cells has been used in some breeding programmes to increase the rates of mutations.

Seeds are more susceptible to radiation when they have a high water content. Hydrated seeds have a low decay rate of the radiation-induced radicals. When oxygen is present, there is an increase of free radical production. Phosphorous and calcium deficiencies enhance radiosensitivity as does the presence of boron. Temperature has some effect on the ability of the plant to repair ionization radiation damage because low temperatures slow or prevent repair while relatively high temperatures enhance the recovery processes.

Salt Stress : Salinity has been an important factor in the history of mankind and in the agricultural systems upon which mankind has relied. Civilizations have been destroyed by the encroachment of salinity on the soils as a result of poor water management. If there is limited rainfall, salt is not leached out of the soil volume in which crop plants take root and yields are reduced as the salt concentration increases. Irrigation water contains dissolved salts that are concentrated as the water evaporates and build up in the soil over time. Vast areas of the land surface are rendered unfit for agriculture because of the present low tolerance of crop plants to salt and the lack of knowledge about the tolerance mechanisms available for plant breeders in the selection processes.

Many of the areas of restricted use because of salt are located where there is abundant solar energy that can be used by the plants to produce high yields. It is necessary, therefore, to better understand the ways that plants can tolerate salinity so that more use can be made of lands that would otherwise be wasted under conditions of an increasing, need for food and fibre by the increasing populations.

Plants are stressed in two ways in a high salt enviroment. In addition to the water stress imposed by the increase in osmotic potential of the rooting medium as a result of high solute content, there is the toxic effect of high medium as a result of high solute content, there is the toxic effect of high concentrations of ion. Some plants have evolved mechanisms for dealing with these stresses and others can become adapted to them. But, the majority of crop plants are susceptible and will not survive under conditions of high salinity or will survive, but with decreased yields.

In the saline environment, there is a preponderance of nonessential over essential ions. The plant must absorb the essential ions from a diluted source in the presence of highly concentrated nonessential ions. By studying plants usually grow in saline environments, it is possible to gain some knowledge of the mechanisms used to tolerate the conditions.

Native plants are frequently designated as halophytes or glycophytes by ecologists. Halophytes grow in saline soils, in high concentrations of salts, and are either facultative or obligate halophytes. Sometimes a finer classification is used by calling those that tolerate extreme salinity nonhalophytes and those that tolerate only moderate salinity oligohalophytes. Glycophytes, or nonhalophytes, cannot grow in the presence of high concentrations of salts or possess some mechanism by which the protoplasm is not exposed to high salt concentrations.

Mechanism of salt tolerance : Some of the characteristics of halophytes that may give clues as to the physiological mechanism involved in tolerance are;

Succulence that may lead to dilution of intracellular salt as it occurs in *Salicornia* sp.

The presence of salt excreting glands that reduce the concentration of salt in the plant, such as observed in species of *Frankenia, Cressa, Spartina* and *Glaux.*

Development of small leaves, water storage hairs, water storage hairs, and aerenchyma.

A water potential ranges from – 2 to – 4 MPa, which is equivalent to an ion concentration of 400 to 700 mM. (In the species *Salicornia rubra* the sodium and chloride ions make up 75 to 93% of the total osmotic potential.)

Species that rely mainly on a higher ion uptake and internal concentration of ions to maintain turgor.

Sometimes there is synthesis and accumulation of organic solutes that aid in the maintenance of turgor.

An understanding of the distribution of salt ions in the plant is necessary to understand tolerance. In the halophytes more than 90% of the sodium is in the shoot with the highest concentration in the leaves. Translocation out of leaves is nil. When sodium is applied to leaves, it remains there and is not translocated to other parts of the plant. This behaviour differs from that of potassium which is readily mobile. Sodium also accumulates in the vacuoles of cells where concentration may reach several thousand ppm.

The effect of salt stress on phosphorus metabolism varies with plant species and external phosphorus concentration in the rooting medium. Many data point to the fact that salinity damages mechanisms controlling intracellular phosphorus concentrations. Adverse effects on growth would be expected resulting death. For example, in kindney bean there is a decrease in phosphorus, adenosine triphosphate, and energy available for the young leaves. Salt stressed plants often look like phosphorus-deficient plants with small, dark green leaves, decreased shoot-to-root ratios, decreased tillering, prolonged dormancy of lateral buds, delayed and reduced flowering and fewer and smaller fruits.

Leaves of salt stressed plants frequently contain unusually high concentration of sugars as a result of the effects of the stress on phloem translocation or on reduced sink size because of reduced growth.

Under salt-stress conditions the osmotic potential of the soil solution is similar to that brought about by drought. Some of the symptoms of salt stress are those characteristic of water stressed plants. Although salt stressed plants are stunted, they are not wilted, which means that the cells must have water potentials that enable them to compete for water with the xylem. One of the ways the water potential may be lowered is by an increase in solutes. An accumulation of organic solutes in response to salt stress may in reality be a response to water stress caused by the differential in water potentials between the plant and the soil solution. Carbohydrates, amino acids or organic acids may accumulate. Oxalate may be as high as 50 to 100 meq/g by weight, while in crassulacean acid metabolism (CAM) malate is the acid that accumulates. Since halophytes are often C_4 plants, a shift from organic acid synthesis to amino acid synthesis may take place under salt stress.

Eflect of Specific Ions : The rate of uptake of ions by roots differs as a result of difference in membrane permeability, transport kinetics and selectivity, and feedback controls. Chloride ions contribute more to an osmotic adjustment than do sulfate ions because chloride is more readily absorbed. In the presence of predominantly monovalent cations and divalent anions, the cation uptake exceeds that of the anions. A balance of charges is achieved by the synthesis of organic anions within the cell or tissue. If the inorganic divalent anions are nitrate and sulfate, the balance is further disturbed by the metabolism of nitrate and sulfate. Sodium ions in a saline soil may exceed those of potassium by more than twice in magnitude but, the sodium to potassium ratio in plants is nearly 1 : 1. The root cells have a highly specific mechanism for absorbing potassium to the exclusion of sodium or else the cells secrete the sodium and retain more of the potassium. Some woody plants are susceptible to chlorine and their tolerance of saline conditions depends on their tolerance to chlorine and how much of the ion is absorbed and translocated.

Mycorrhizae to Alleviate Stress : Nutrient influx takes place across the soil-root interface including the complex of materials and organisms in the rhizosphere. Under conditions of limited nutrient supply, mycorrhizae may be formed and cause an increase in nutrient uptake. It has been estimated that more than 80% of the taxa of higher plants have mycorrhizal roots. It is the ectomycorrhizal association that increases mineral nutrient absorption and there are many factors involved in the relationship. The fungal hyphae increase the surface area in contact with the soil and pervade more volume of soil containing nutrients. The life of mycorrhizal roots is prolonged so that absorption from a soil site occurs over a longer period of time than would occur with nonmycorrhizal roots. Also, mycorrhizal roots absorb nutrients more rapidly per unit area than nonmycorrhizal roots. Because of the formation of a mantle of fungal hyphae over the root surface, it may be protected from invasion by pathogenic organisms. Mycorrhizae may also increase tolerance to toxic levels of essential metal ions in the rooting medium. The explanation is that the formation of precipitates and complexes of metals is greater in mycorrhizal roots than in nonmycorrhizal roots hence there is a decrease in foliar concentration of the metals. Mycorrhizal roots seem to form more abundantly in soils of low fertility and so they are of greater prominance in woody species than in crop species which grow on relatively fertile soil.

Foresters have known for some time that trees planted in areas where they have not grown for some time need by inoculated with fungi that form mycorrhizae or the trees will be stunted and lack vigour. The role of the mycorrhizal association in stress situations is an important one and its presence may make the difference between survival of the plant and death.

Consumptive Use Coefficient : The primary factors that influence ET for different species with water availability remaining high, are time of year (atmospheric demand) and rate of canopy development. The consumptive use coefficient (k), is calculated as follows,

$$\text{Consumptive use coefficient (k)} = \frac{\text{actual evapotranspiration}}{\text{potential evapotranspiration}}$$

It ranges from 0.65 to 0.87 and is primarily affected by the amount of ground covered by the crop canopy integrated over the growth period. Wheat has a low k because it is grown in the relatively cooler in the spring season and slowly develops leaf area from seeds. Alfalfa has a high k because in the spring it develops rapidly from reserve carbohydrates; although harvested during the year, it recovers leaf area rapidly from reserve carbohydrates of the root and crown and maintains a ground cover for a longer period of time during the growing season. Sorghum and soybean have intermediate k values because they are grown in the warm spring and summer seasons, but have relatively slow leaf area development from seeds.

Stem Vs root development

Root	*Stem*
Meristem apical	Meristem subapical
Lateral organs arise near apex of meristem	Lateral organs arise at some distance from apex
Lateral organs arise from surface layers	Lateral organs arise from internal tissue layers, normally the pericycle
Nodes and internodes present due to regularity of lateral organ formation	Nodes and internodes not present
Primary xylem and primary phloem are on the same radius	Primary xylem and primary phloem are on alternate radii; star-shaped
Vascular cambium arises from parenchyma cells between primary xylem and phloem	Vascular cambium arises both from parenchyma cells between primary xylem and phloem and from pericycle
Epidermis with stomata	Epidermis without stomata
Pericycle generally absent in seed plants	Pericycle generally present in seed plants
Endodermis generally absent	Endodermis almost universally present
Quiescent centre not present in apical meristem	Quiescent centre present

FOOD RESERVES AND THE MAJOR STORAGE STRUCTURES IN SOME CROP SEEDS

Species	*Average Composition (% dry wt)* *Protein*	*Fat*	*Nitrogen-free extract (major component)*	*Major Storage Structure*
Maize (*Zea mays*)	11	5	75 (starch)	Endosperm
Sweet corn (*Zea mays*)	12	9	70 (starch)	Endosperm
Oats (*Avena saliva*)	13	8	66 (starch)	Endosperm
Wheat (*Triticum aestivum*)	12	2	75 (starch)	Endosperm
Rye (*Secale cereale*)	12	2	76 (starch)	Endosperm
Barley (*Hordeum vulgare*)	12	3	76 (starch)	Endosperm
Broad bean (*Vicia faba*)	23	1	56 (starch)	Cotyledon
Flax (*Linum usitatissimum*)	24	36	24 (starch)	Cotyledon
Field pea (*Pisum arvense*)	24	6	56 (starch)	Cotyledon
Garden pea (*Pisum sativum*)	25	6	52 (starch)	Cotyledon
Peanut (*Arachis hypogaea*)	31	48	12 (starch)	Cotyledon
Soybean (*Glycine max*)	37	17	26 (starch)	Cotyledon
Cotton (*Gossypium* spp)	39	33	15	Cotyledon
Rape (*Brassica napus*)	21	48	19 (starch)	Cotyledon
Watermelon (*Citrullis vulgaris*)	38	48	5	Cotyledon
Brazil nut (*Bertholletia excelsa*)	18	68	6	Radicle, hypocotyl
Oil palm (*Elaeis guineensis*)	9	49	28	Endosperm
Ivory nut (*Phytelephas Macrocarpa*)	5	1	79 (galactomannan)	Endosperm
Date (*Phoenix dactylifera*)	6	9	58 (galactomannan)	Endosperm
Castor bean (*Ricinus communis*)	18	64	trace	Endosperm
Pine (*Pinus pinea*)	35	48	6	Megagametophyte

Source: Bewley and Blade, (1978).

Biological N_2 Fixation : Numerous free-living bacteria and associations between bacteria and higher plants have the capacity to reduce atmospheric N_2 to ammonia. The following reactions, mediated by the enzyme nitrogenase, is common to all organisms.

$$N_2 + 6H^+ + 6e^- + n\text{MgATP} \xrightarrow{\text{nitrogenase}} 2NH_3 + n\text{MgATP} + nP_i$$

The N_2-fixing organisms are primarily bacteria but also blue-green algae.

Classification of N_2-fixing organisms is as follows:

(*A*) Asymbiotic (free living)

(*a*) Bacteria

(*i*) *Aerobic.* Three genera of Azotobacteraceae, *Azotobacter, Azospirillum* and *Beijerinckia,* are of primary importance.

(*ii*) *Anaerobic.* The agriculturally important and widely distributed *Clostridium pasteurianum* and two photosynthetic genera, *Rhodospirillum* and *Chromatium* are anaerobic.

(*iii*) *Blue-green algae* (*Cyanobacteria*). Two genera, *Anabaena* and *Nostoc,* are the commonest. Cyanobacteria is a relatively new classification (Buchanan and Gibbons, 1974) and is not in common use so the term *blue-green algae will* be used here.

(*B*) Symbiotic (nodulating)

(*a*) Root nodulating

(*i*) *Rhizobium.* Associated with legumes

(*ii*) *Actinomycetes* (*e.g., Frankia*). Associated with woody angiosperms. *Alnus* (alder) is a well-known host plant.

(*iii*) Blue-green algae. Associated with gymnosperms. Nodules are formed on the surface roots (light required) of gymnosperm species.

(*b*) Leaf nodulating (phyllosphere). A number of bacteria, including some-free-living types, produce nodules on leaves of woody species in the humid tropics.

(*C*) Symbiotic (non-nodulating; associative)

(*A*) *Blue-green algae.* Associated with fern (*Azolla*) and with fungi (lichens).

(*B*) *Bacteria* (*Azotobacteraceae*). Associated with grasses. Bacteria include *Azospirullum barasilense, Spirillum lipoferum,* and *Azotobacter paspali,* which are commonly found in pastures of tropical and semitropical C_4 grasses.

Nodule Formation for N-Fixation: Following colonization of the root by compatible *Rhizobium* strains, the infection and nodulation process is more or less as follows:

1. Root hair deformation (*i.e.*, curling or branching), possibly as a response to indoleacetic acid (IAA), the production of which is stimulated by the bacterium, or perhaps as a response to ethylene stimulated by IAA.

2. Formation of the interconon thread for transference of the bacterial cells into the root cortex.

3. Release of bacteria into the cortex cells.

4. Formation of the nodule meristem and expansion of the nodule by division of the cortex cells.

5. Enlargement of the infected cortex cells inside the nodules see the figure below.

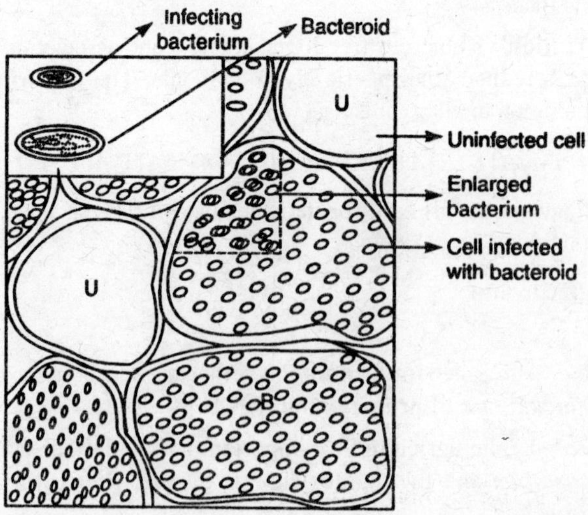

Fig. 5

6. In older nodules, loss of the *bacteroid* (nodule bacteria) envelope and mtrogenase activity as senescence commences.

Blackman : Optima and Limiting factors : F.F. Blackman's theory of "Optima and Limiting Factors" 1905) was stated as follows : "When a process is conditioned as to its rapidity by a number of separate factors, the rate of the process is limited by the pace of the slowest factor." Light and carbon dioxide are required for photosynthesis. The Blackman theory suggests that there is an abrupt cessation of the process, the "Blackman response," if one of factors becomes limiting (Fig. 6. below). However, nature seems to abhor angles and this type of response is seldom found.

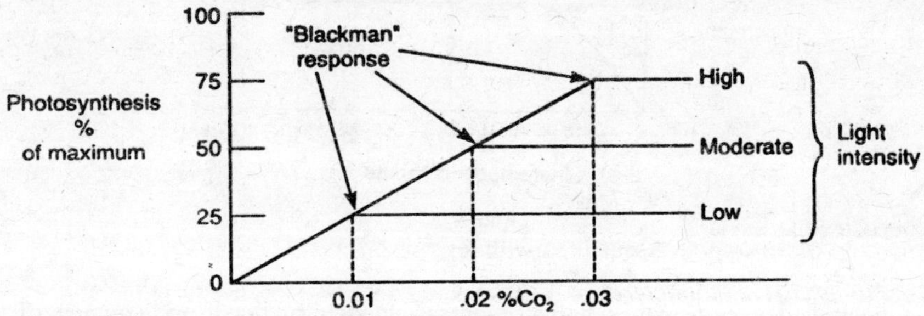

Fig. 6

Liebig : Law of the Minimum: The "law of the minimum", proposed by Justus von Liebig (1862), is probably the best known of the limiting factor theories. He stated it as follows: "A deficiency or absence of one necessary constituent, all others being present, renders the soil barren for crops for which that nutrient is needed." It is sometimes referred to as the "barrel concept." If a barrel has staves of different heights, the lowest one establishes the capacity of the barrel. Accordingly, the growth factor in lowest supply (whether climatic edaphic, biological or genetic) sets the capacity for yield as shown below by him.

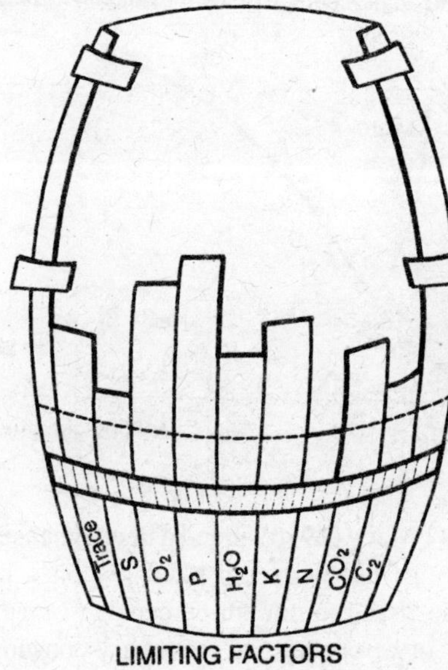

Fig. 7

Mitscherlich: Law of Diminishing Returns : A German soil scientist, E.A.Mitscherlich (1909), developed an equation that related growth to the supply of growth factors. He observed that when plants had adequate amounts of all, but one limiting element the growth response was proportional to the limiting element.

Plant growth increased with additional increments of a limiting factor, but not in direct proportion as shown in figure on the next page. The Mitscherlich "law of diminishing returns" states, "The incrsease in any crop produced by a unit increment of a deficient factor is proportional to the decrement of that factor from the maximum" The response is curvilinear instead of linear, as suggested by Blackman.

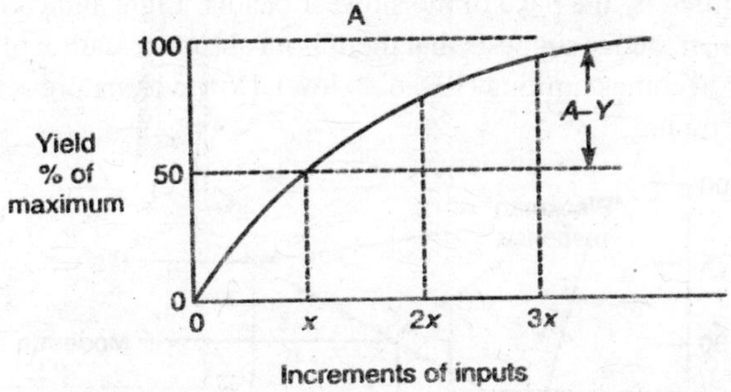

Fig. 8

The Mitscherlich equation is :

$dy/dx = C(A - Y)$

where d is the increment of change, dy is the amount of increase in yield (y) due to an increment of the growth factor (dx), A is the maximum possible yield obtained by unlimited supply of the limiting growth factor, Y is the yield obtained by a given quantity of factor x and c is the proportionality constant depending upon the nature of the growth factor. Increase in Y is the maximum for the first increment of x and thereafter progressively slides down, theoretically by one-half of the response from the previous increment. The amount of factor needed to obtain one half yield in this equation is called Baule unit. Yield curves, according to Mitscherlich, for a microelement and a macro-element in a simplified form are as follows:

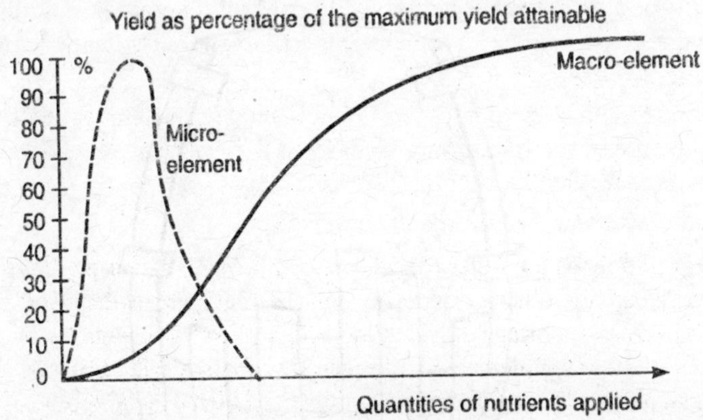

Fig. 9

Macy : Critical Percentages : Macy (1936) added a new dimension to these concepts by suggesting a relationship between the sufficiency of nutrients and plant response in terms of both yield and nutrient concentration of plant tissues. In the tissue minimum-percentage range, an added increment of a nutrient increases the yield, but not the nutrient percentage. In the luxury-consumption range, added increments of a nutrient have little effect on yield, but increase the composition percentage of the nutrient. He suggested that Liebigs, law holds in the tissue-minimum-percentage range because there is not enough of a nutrient to allow much plant growth. Liebig's law holds again in the luxury-consumption range because although there is a large supply of one nutrient, some other nutrient becomes limiting and stops growth. Mitscherlich's law of diminishing returns holds during the poverty-adjustment range because the response is curvilinear (*i.e.*, representing diminishing returns) to added increments. May proposed a critical percentage for each nutrient in each kind of a plant (see the Fig. 10 below).

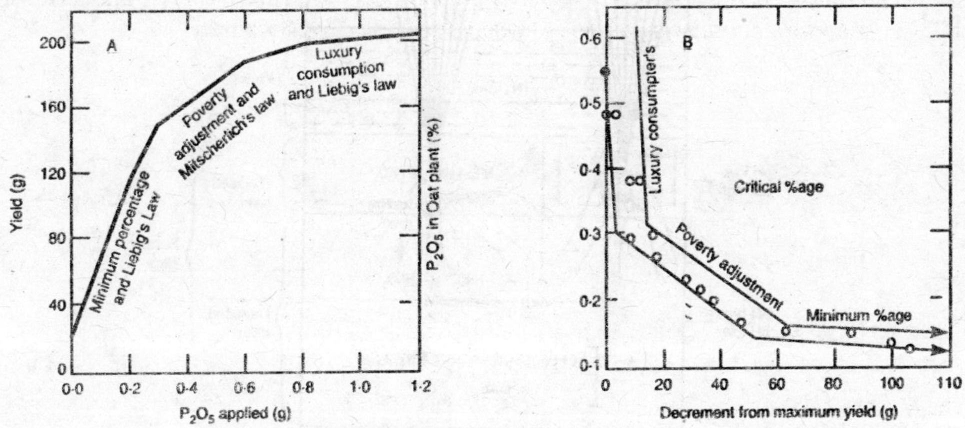

Fig. 10

Limiting Factor Qualifications : The following are the reasons as to why laws of *Minimum* and *Diminishing Returns* are theories and not accepted as laws :

* Biological reactions are complex and may proceed by more than a single pathway. Compound *A* can go to compound *B* and then to *C*, or directly to *C*, all reversibly. Slowing one pathway or lowering one reactant does not necessarily slow or stop the reaction.
* Factors substitute for factors. Sodium, for example, can partially substitute for potassium in certain species.
* Factors modify or affect other factors. Phosphorus decreases zinc uptake, and potassium decreases magnesium uptake, for example, increasing the irradiance increases temperature and decreases water availability.
* Plants affect factors, and factors in turn affect plants. For example, additional N increases plant growth and leaf area, which in turn reduces light to lower leaves. Soil temperature is decreased and humidity is increased by shading from additional growth.
* More than one factor may be limiting simultaneously.

Green Manures : So far as the water conditions permit, green manuring represents a cheap and effective way of improving soil fertility. Where water is the limiting factor, green manuring is not advisable since the following crop will suffer from a shortage of water. In so far as the green manuring plants are of Leguminosae family, considerable quantities of supplementary nitrogen are supplied to the soil. The more the soil is supplied with phosphoric acid and potash, the more nitrogen can be fixed by the leguminosae. It is generally profitable, therefore, to treat the green manuring plants with P and K, especially since these nutrients will also later benefit the following crop. The importance of legumes as green manuring plants is based on the following points:

* They supply organically combined nitrogen of a slow and long-lasting favourable action,
* They release and mobilise the inorganic substances in the soil.
* They promote crumb and soil structure,
* They promote microbial activity.
* They supply organic matter, even to the sub-soil.
* They loosen the sub-soil naturally.
* They act as a protection against erosion.

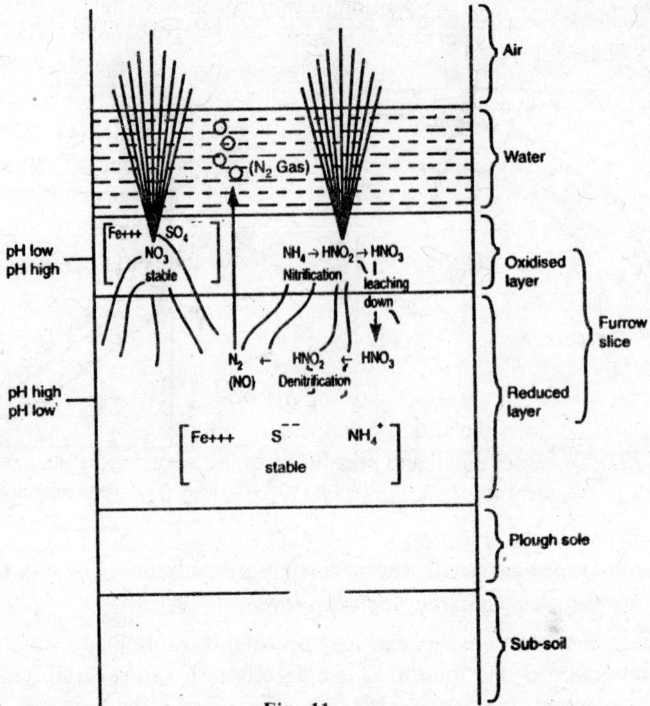

Fig. 11

Chemical changes in Flooded Conditions : The changes shown in the figure below take place in the soil projtect under flood conditions.

EFFECT OF DIFFERENT LIGHT WAVE-LENGTHS ON SOME PLANT METABOLIC REACTIONS

Metabolic reaction	*Red-yellow* **7800-5600 *A***	*Blue-violet* **4800-3800 *A***
longitudinal growth	accelerated	retarded
transversal growth	retarded	accelerated
leaf colour	dark-green	light-green
chlorophyll-A content	augmented	diminished
chlorophyll-B content	diminished	augmented
anthocyanin formation	augmented	diminished
formation of dry matter	diminished	augmented
cell wall	thin and weak	thick and strong
lignification	worsened	improved
carotin formation	diminished	augmented
nitrate reduction	retartded	accelerated
permeability`	worsened	improved
activity of dissimilating enzymes	accelerated	retarded
uptake of potassium	increased	decreased

* Venema, K. C. W. : "The influence of light and transpiration on the uptake of potassium by plants". Potash and Tropical Agriculture 1, pp. 10 (1958).

Water Potential : The system of description of water behaviour and movement in soils and plants is based on potential energy in aqueous system and it is expressed *vis-a-vis* potential energy of water. The water in soils and plants is not chemically pure and is physically constrained by forces *viz*., polar attractions, gravity and pressure and hence its potential energy is less than that of pure water. In the soil and plant potential energy of water is called *potential*. The unit of its measurement as y (psi; a Greek letter) and is expressed as force per unit area and is expressed as bar or pascal (Pa) ; 1 bar = 10^5 Pa = 10^6dynes/cm^2 = 0.99 atmosphere or 10^2 Joules/kg. Pure water has a potential equal to zero bar. The water potential in plants and soils is less than zero bar, *i.e*., it is negative, the more the negative value, the lower the water potential which in plants and soils is the sum total of ψ_m (matric potential), ψ_s (solute/osmotic potential), ψ_p (pressure / turgor potential) and ψ_z (gravitational potential) and is written as $\psi_w + \psi_m + \psi_p + \psi_z$.

Allometry : The relationship between the growth rates of individual parts of an organ or organism is called *Allometry* which may be expressed as $y = bx^K$, where x and y are physical parameters, while b and k are constants and k is allometric constant. K is equal to log b + k log x ; obtained by plotting y against x on log scale, which produces a straight line, the slope of which is K. It may be also determined by linear regression analyses of the data set y and x. If the length and breadth of an organ such as leaf, expand at the same rate, the slope of the regression line (Coefficient of allometry / K) is equal to 1.0; the growth rates of the two parameters are perfectly correlated.

Electromagnetic wave theory : It denotes that light travels through space as a wave and the number of waves passing a specified point in a certain interval of time is the frequency.

$$u = \frac{c}{\lambda}$$

where, u = frequency, that is, wavelength per second; c = speed of light, which is 3×10^{10} cm per second; λ = wavelength and speed of light divided by frequency is equal to wavelength.

Quantum Theory : According to this theory light travels in a stream of particles known as *photons* and the energy present in one photon is proportional to frequency, the photon can be expressed in terms of wavelength and the energy per photon is inversely proportional to wavelength. Here,

$$E = hv = \frac{c}{\lambda}$$

where, E = photon energy/quantum; h = Planck's constant (662×10^{-7} erg per second)

c = speed of light 3×10^{10} cm per second); l = wavelength

Net Assimilation Rate : The dry matter accumulation rate per unit of leaf area per unit of time is known as *Net Assimilation Rate* (NAR) and is usually expressed as grammes per metre (leaf area) per day and comprises a measure of photosynthetic efficiency. It excludes non-laminar photosynthesis.

Non-laminar photosynthesis : It is the photosynthesis carried out by plant parts other than leaves *viz*., petioles, stems, sheaths and inflorescence. It can contribute significantly to crop yield.

TABLES

CONSUMPTION OF MAJOR FERTILIZERS (IN LAKH TONNES)

Fertilizer	*2008-09*	*2009-10*	*2010-11*
N	150.9	155.8	165.6
P	65.06	72.74	80.5
K	33.13	23.35	35.1
N + P + K	249.09	264.86	281.2
Per ha Consumption (kg/ha)	127.2	135.8	144.14

INTERNATIONAL CLASSIFICATION OF SOILS (ACCORDING TO TEXTURE)

			Parts by Weight of the Fractions in %			
Kind of Soil	***Clay Slit*** **< 2 μ**	***Slit*** **2.20 μ**	***Clay & Silt*** **< 20 μ**	***Total Sand*** **20-2,000 μ**	***Fine Sand*** **20-200 μ**	***Coarse Sand*** **200-2,000 μ**
1. Loamy Coarse Sand	–	–	<15	> 85	–	> 45
2. Loamy Fine Sand	–	–	<15	> 85	> 40	–
3. Coarse Sandy Loam	<15	–	15-35	65-85	–	> 45
4. Fine Sandy Loam	–	–	15-35	65-85	> 40	–
5. Loam	–	< 45	> 35	< 65	–	–
6. Silty Loam	–	> 45	–	–	–	–
7. Sandy Clay Loam	–	< 20	< 45	>55	–	–
8. Clay Loam	15-25	< 20	< 45	> 55	–	–
9. Silty-clay Loam	> 45	> 60	< 40	–	–	–
10. Sandy Clay	–	< 20	< 45	> 55	–	–
11. Loamy Clay	25-45	<45	> 45	< 55	–	–
12. Silty Clay	–	> 45	> 70	< 30	–	–
13. Heavy Clay	> 45	–	–	–	–	–

FOOD GRAIN PRODUCTION

Crop	*2004-05*	*2005-06*	*2007-08*	*2008-09*	*2009-10*	*2011-12*	*2012-13*
Rice	83·13	91·7	96·43	99·15	89·1	104.3	–
Wheat	68·64	69·35	78·57	80·68	80·7	93.9	–
Coarse cereals	33·46	34·06	40·70	40·30	33·77	–	38.47
Pulses	13·2	13·39	14·80	14·60	14·10	–	17.58
Food grains							
Kharif	102·6	109·87	120·95	118·14	103·80	129.9	–
Rabi	103·5	98·73	109·83	116·13	117·0	127.5	–
Total food grain	206·4	208·60	230·78	234·27	220·80		

State first in food grain production U. P.

State first in rice production. West Bengal

State first in wheat production U.P.

COMMERICAL CROP PRODUCTION

Million tonnes

Crop	2004-05	2005-06	2007-08	2008-09	2009-10	2011-12	2012-13
Ground nut	6·5	5·9	9·18	7·3	5·51	6·9	–
Mustard	7·6	8·13	5·83	7·2	6·41	6·8	–
Soyabean	6·8	8·3	10·9	9·91	10·05	–	–
Total oil seeds	24·8	27·9	29·7	27·80	24·90	29·8	29·5
Cotton*	16·4	18·5	25·8	22·28	23·90	35·2	33·8
Jute and Mesta**	10·2	10·8	11·2	10·36	11·30	11·4	10·6
Sugar cane	237·0	281·12	348·2	285·03	277·75	361·0	334·0

* Million bales of 170 kgs eath

**Million bales of 188 kgs each

AREA AND PRODUCTION OF MAJOR HORTICULTURAL CROPS

Area -Million hectares, Production -million tonnes

Crops	2005-06		2009-10		2010-11		2011-12	
	Area	Production	Area	Production	Area	Production	Area	Production
Fruits	5·0	53·1	55·54	59·5	6·38	74·8	–	76·0
Vegetables	6·1	91·6	75·81	114·99	8·50	146·6	–	156·0
Spices	2·5	4·1	24·48	39·53	2·94	5·35	–	–
Coconut	—	—	—	—	—	—	—	—
Cashew	—	—	—	—	—	—	—	—
Arecanut	—	—	—	—	—	—	—	—
Others	—	—	—	—	—	—	—	—
Total	17·8	164·1	193·89	191·81				

Horticulture

In the world India's Position :

1st – Coconut, Arecanut, Cashew, Ginger, Turmeric, Black pepper

2nd – Fruits and vegetables.

Vegetables

Overall India ranks IInd

1st – Cauliflower 2nd – Onion 3rd – Cabbage.

TABLE PRODUCTION OF FISH, MILK, EGGS AND WOOL

Year	*Fish (Lakh t)*	*Milk (million t)*	*Eggs (million No.)*	*Wool (million kg)*	*Meat (million t)*
1985-86	28·76	44·0	16,128	39·1	N.A.
1990-91	38·36	53·9	21,100	41·2	N.A.
1995-96	49·49	66·2	27,200	42·4	N.A.
2000-01	56·56	80·6	36,632	48·4	1.9
2001-02	59·56	84·8	39,068	50·0	1.9
2002-03*	62·00	87·3	40,252	50·5	2.1
2003-04**	63.99	91·1	40,400	48·5	2.1
2004-05	63·05	92.5	45,200	44.6	2.2
2005-06	65.72	97.1	46,200	44.9	2.3
2006-07	68.69	102.6	50,663	45.1	2.3
2007-08	71.27	107.9	53,532	43.9	4.0
2008-09	76·16	112·2	55,638	42·8	4·3
2009-10	79·98	116·4	60,300	43·1	4·6
2010-11	N.A.	121·8	N.A.	43.0	4.9

Note : * Provisional, ** Anticipated.

Source: *Agricultural Statistics at a Glance*, 2004, Directorate of Economics and Statistics.

Milk production in 2009-10 (Provisional)— 112·5 million tonnes.

Fish production in 2009-10 (Provisional) —7850 thousand tonnes.

PROJECTED FOODGRAIN PRODUCTION & CONSUMPTION AND USE OF INPUTS BY THE END OF 11TH PLAN

Items	*Unit*	*2011-12*
Per capita consumption of foodgrains	kg	223.35
Foodgrains production	million t	337.30
Rice	million t	128.16
Wheat	million t	130.45
Coarse cereals	million t	48.93
Pulses	million t	29.76
Oilseeds	million t	58.56
Sugarcane	million t	679.64
Net area sown	million ha	142.00
Gross area sown	million ha	219.15
Gross irrigated area	million ha	105.50
Fertiliser consumption ($N+P_2O_5+K_2O$)		
Total	million t	45.48
Per hectare of gross cropped area	kg	207.53

Source : *Fertiliser Statistics, 2002-2003,* The Fertiliser Association of India, New Delhi.

TABLE AREA AND PRODUCTION OF HORTICULTURE CROPS IN INDIA

(Area in Lakh Hectare & Production in Lakh Mt)

Crops	*2007-08*		*2008-09*		*2009-10*		*2010-11*	
	Area	*Production*	*Area*	*Production*	*Area*	*Production*	*Area*	*Production*
Fruits								
Mango	2201	13997	2309	12750	2312	15027	2297	15188
Apple	264	2001	274	1985	283	1777	289	2891
Banana	658	23823	709	26217	770	26470	830	29780
Citrus	867	8015	924	8623	987	9638	846	7464
Guava	179	1981	204	2270	220	2572	205	2462
Grapes	68	1735	80	1878	106	881	111	1235
Litchi	69	418	72	423	74	483	78	497
Papaya	83	2909	98	3629	96	3913	106	4196
Pineapple	80	1245	84	1341	92	1387	89	1415
Pomegranate	124	884	109	807	125	820	107	743
Sapota	152	1258	156	1308	159	1347	160	1424
Others	1112	7321	1083	7234	1105	7201	1265	7583
Total	**5857**	**65587**	**6101**	**68466**	**6329**	**71516**	**9383**	**74878**
Vegetables								
Potato	1795	34658	1828	34391	1835	36577	1863	42339
Onion	821	13900	834	13565	756	12159	1064	15118
Tomato	566	10303	599	11149	634	12433	865	16526
Brinjal	561	9678	600	10378	612	10563	680	11896
Cabbage	266	5910	310	6870	331	7281	369	7949
Cauliflower	312	5777	349	6532	348	6569	369	6745
Okra	407	4179	432	4528	452	4803	498	5784
Peas	313	2491	348	2916	365	3029	370	3517
Tapioca	270	9056	280	9623	232	8060	221	8076
Sweet Potato	123	1094	124	1120	119	1095	113	1047
Others	2414	31402	2275	28006	2300	31168	2083	27557
Total	**7848**	**128449**	**7981**	**129077**	**7985**	**133738**	**8495**	**146554**

Aromatic	397	396	430	430	509	573	510	605
Almond/Walnut	132	177	136	173	142	193	(include fruits)	
Flowers Loose	166	868	167	987	183	1021	191	1031
Flowers Cut*		43644		47942		66671		69027
Plantation Crops	3190	11300	3217	11336	3265	11928	3306	12007
Mushroom		37		37		41		
Honey		65		65		65		
Spices	2617	4357	2629	4145	2464	4016	2940	5350
Total	**20207**	**211235**	**20662**	**214716**	**20876**	**223089**	**21825**	**240531**

TABLE PERCENTAGE GROWTH OF HORTICULTURAL CROPS

Crops	*07-08 over 06-07*		*08-09 over 07-08*		*09-10 over 08-09*		*10-11 over 09-10*	
	Area	*Production*	*Area*	*Production*	*Area*	*Production*	*Area*	*Production*
Horticulture	4.22	10.13	2.25	1.65	1.0	3.9	4.5	7.8
Fruit	5.46	10.11	4.16	4.39	3.7	4.5	0.8	4.7
Vegetables	3.53	11.70	1.69	0.49	0.1	3.6	6.4	9.6

Units of Area or Surface

1 are	=	100 square metres	=	1,076·39 sq. feet
1 square (building)	=	100 square feet	=	9·29 sq. metres
1 square chain	=	4,356 square feet	=	404·69 sq. metres
1 square link	=	62·73 square inches	=	404·69 sq. metres
1 square perch	=	272·25 square feet	=	25·29 sq. metres
1 square pole	=	272·25 square feet	=	25·29 sq. metres
1 township	=	36 square miles	=	93·24 sq. kms

Units of Volume

1 cubic inch	=	0·00058 cubic foot	=	16·39 cubic cms
1 cubic foot	=	1·728 cubic inches	=	28·32 cubic dms
1 cubic yard	=	27 cubic feet	=	0·76 cubic metre
1 cubic millimetre	=	0·001 cubic cm	=	0·000061 cubic in.
1 cubic centimetre	=	1,000 cubic mms	=	0·6 cubic inch
1 cubic decimetre	=	1,000 cubic cms	=	61·02 cubic inches
1 cubic metre	=	1,000 cubic dms	=	35·31 cubic feet
1 stere	=	1 cubic metre	=	35·31 cubic feet

Units of Capacity (Liquid)

1 barrel	=	31 to 42 gallons	=	117·34 to 158·98 litres
1 cubic foot	=	7·48 gallons	=	28·32 litres
1 cubic inch	=	0·55 fluid ounce	=	0·02 centilitre
1 decalitre	=	10 litres	=	2·64 gallons
1 gallon(British Imperial)	=	1·20 gallons (U.S.)	=	4·55 litres
1 gill	=	4 fluid ounces	=	0·12 centilitre
1 minim	=	0·002 fluid ounce	=	0·06 millilitre
1 quart (British)	=	1·20 quarts (U.S.)	=	1·14 litres
1 tablespoon	=	0·5 fluid ounce	=	1·45 centilitres
1 teaspoon	=	1·33 fluid drams	=	4·92 millilitres

Units of Capacity (Dry)

1 barrel (standard)	=	105 quarts	=	115·61 litres
1 barrel (cranberries)	=	86·70 quarts	=	95·46 litres
1bushel (U.S.).struck measure	=	32 quarts	=	35·24 litres
1 cubic inch	=	0·15 quart	=	0·16 litre
1 cord (firewood)	=	128 cubic feet	=	3·62 cubic metres
1 cubic decimetre	=	1 litre	=	0·91 quart
1 peck	=	8 quarts	=	8·81 litres
1 pint	=	0·5 quart	=	0·55 litre
1 quart (U.S.)	=	67·2 cubic inches	=	1·1 litres
1 quart (British)	=	1·032 quarts (U.S.)	=	1·036 litres

Temperature	
°C	°F
–5	22
0	32
5	41
15	59
20	68
30	86
40	104
50	122
60	140
70	167
80	167
90	194
100	212

Tyres Pressures	
lb/in^2	kg/cm^2
20	1·41
22	1·55
24	1·69
26	1·83
28	1·97
30	2·11
32	2·25
34	2·39

Wind speeds	
7 mph	light wind
11 mph	light breeze
16 mph	gentle breeze
20 mph	moderate breeze
25 mph	fresh breeze
30 mph	strong breeze
35 mph	moderate gale
45 mph	fresh gale
50 mph	strong gale
60 mph	whole gale
70 mph	storm
80 mph	hurricane

Maximum root zone depth of various crops

Crop	Root Zone depth (mm)
Wheat	500-750
Barley	600-750
Maize	400-600
Sorghum	1000-1500
Pearlmillet	300-450
Italian millet	300-450
Crowfoot millet	300-450
Jute	450-500
Sugarcane	500-750
Gourds	400-600
Cucumber	400-600
Groundnut	600-800
Cotton	900-2000
Tabacco	200-750
Mustard	500-1500
Toria	300-500
Sunflower	500-1500
Safflower	500-2500
Seasame	350-750
Castor	1000-4000
Cole crops	200-500
Berseem	500-3000